AF478058

British Watercolours

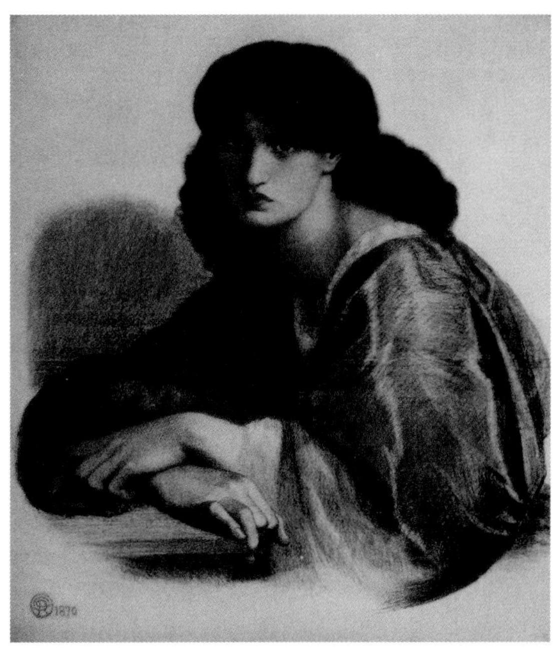

in

The Whitworth Art Gallery,
The University of Manchester

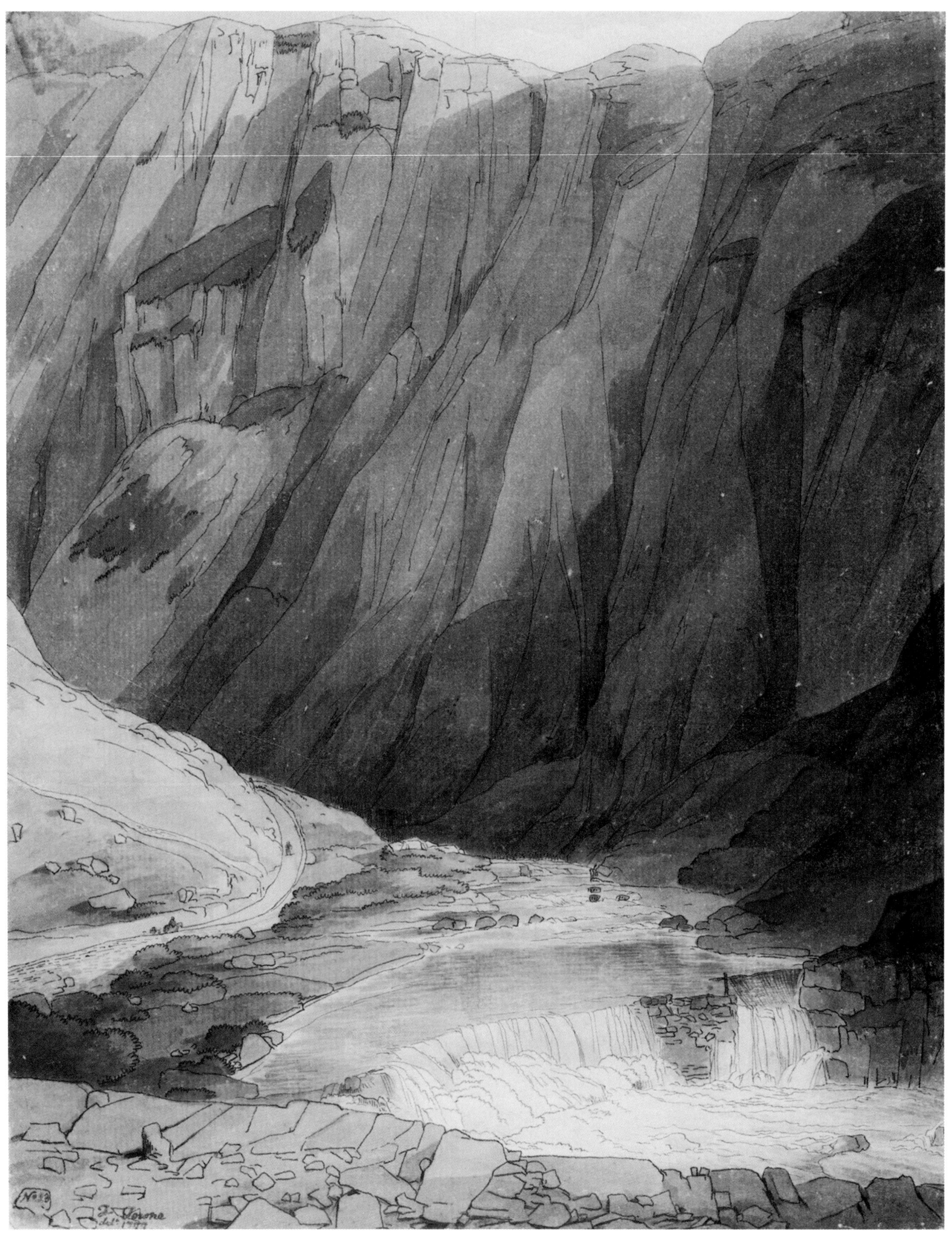

No 13
J. Florone
del. 1788

British Watercolours

in

THE WHITWORTH ART GALLERY, THE UNIVERSITY OF MANCHESTER

A Summary Catalogue of Drawings and Watercolours by Artists born before 1880

Charles Nugent

Philip Wilson Publishers

in association with The Whitworth Art Gallery, The University of Manchester

PUBLISHER'S NOTE
Owing to shortage of space within the catalogue
text, it was decided that in the cases of multiple
funding packages, the four funding bodies who
have helped the Whitworth with acquisitions
would be referred to in abbreviated form after
the accession details. Thus the Victoria & Albert
Museum Purchase Grant Fund, since 1985 the
Museums and Galleries Commission/Victoria &
Albert Museum Purchase Grant Fund and since
2000 the Re: Source/Victoria & Albert Museum
Purchase Grant Fund is referred to as V. & A., the
National Art Collections Fund is referred to as
N.A.C.F., the Pilgrim Trust is referred to as P.T. and
the Friends of the Whitworth as F.O.W.

First published in 2003 by
Philip Wilson Publishers
7 Deane House
27 Greenwood Place
London
NW5 1LB

Text and illustrations © 2002,
Whitworth Art Gallery

Designed by Caroline Hillier

Printed and bound in Hong Kong by
Colorprint Offset

ISBN 0 85667 547 4

HALF TITLE
Dante Gabriel Rossetti
La Donna della Finestra, 1870
D. 1921.35

FRONTISPIECE
Francis Towne
The Salmon Leap, Pont Aberglaslyn, 1777
D. 1999.22

Contents

Foreword

In 1958 the University of Manchester became the owner of the Whitworth Art Gallery, consequently accepting the responsibility of maintaining and developing its building, its adjacent park, and its collection of fine and decorative arts. One of these collections, the historic British Watercolours, had been recognised as being of particular importance even before the Whitworth's building was officially opened in 1908. Fifty years later this specific collection was to attract to the Whitworth Francis Hawcroft, a recognised watercolour specialist.

As one of the Gallery's first full-time members of staff to be trained in the History of Art, Hawcroft eagerly assumed responsibility for all aspects of management of the fine art collections. During his thirty years at the Whitworth (as Keeper and then Principal Keeper), he oversaw the unglamorous processes of security, storage, framing, conservation and much else besides.

While developing all parts of the collections, Hawcroft concentrated particularly on the rich holdings of historic British Watercolours, putting in hand a series of acquisitions which Charles Nugent describes as making the Whitworth 'the envy of galleries all over the world'. He also organised a number of exhibitions, now seen to be 'classics' of their time, which included monographic treatments of J. R. Cozens (1971) and Thomas Girtin (1975). Hawcroft's untimely death in 1988 precluded the completion of his introductory text on Thomas Jones, the discovery of whose previously unknown oil studies in 1954 has perhaps been one of the most exciting events in the field in the past fifty years. His planned exhibition *Travels in Italy*, based on Jones's diaries, was carried out by colleagues.

When he came to the Whitworth, Hawcroft inherited not only a collection of British watercolours but also a small library focusing on this area, including earlier catalogues of the collection, the most recent of which had been published in 1956. In addition, there existed the usual documentation attached to such a collection: an inventory, a series of index cards, letters from interested scholars and notes of all descriptions, many of which were handwritten and intriguingly illegible or otherwise obscure. Aided by a series of youthful Research Assistants, Hawcroft embarked on the process of imposing some rigour on the archive with a view to publishing a comprehensive catalogue. This task proved impossible due to his other commitments and his characteristic ambition to record every detail of process or provenance relating to a particular watercolour. In an effort to speed up the process, every summer Hawcroft would down his administrative tools and spend a month tussling with the records of the collection. He was described as being 'in purdah'. However, his gregarious nature guaranteed that purdah was not rigidly interpreted and memories of summer lunches in the Senior Common Room are vivid.

The archive amassed by Francis and his assistants, and by others beforehand, forms the basis of the work of Charles Nugent, compiler of this illustrated Summary Catalogue. I offer him my admiration, congratulation and gratitude for effecting an idea that was long in mind. The catalogue provides basic information about the Whitworth's collection of historic British Watercolours, and an illustration of almost all of them, thus adding to the information which is already available to those with access to our website.

Alistair Smith, Director, June 2002

Preface and Author's Acknowledgements

On my appointment as Curator of Drawings and Watercolours at the Whitworth Art Gallery in July 1991, I always considered it to be my remit to complete the earlier cataloguing work spearheaded by Francis Hawcroft. As in his case, however, work on individual exhibitions both from within the Gallery and from outside it, and on changing displays from the permanent collection, meant that the project was constantly delayed and interrupted. Also, consensus had still not been reached on the format and scope of the catalogue. After extensive meetings internally and discussions with publishers and with the Paul Mellon Centre for Studies in British Art in London, it was decided that the catalogue would contain summary entries only and would not be fully illustrated. Various models were discussed including *The British Council Collection* catalogue (1984), the *National Gallery Illustrated General Catalogue* (1980), the *British Watercolours in the Victoria & Albert Museum – an Illustrated Summary Catalogue of the National Collection* (1980) and the more recent *The Victorian Watercolours and Drawings in the Collection of Her Majesty the Queen* (1995). After consultation with the publishers, it was decided to opt for something between the Victoria & Albert and the Royal Collection catalogues, with short biographies of artists, summary entries and more illustrations than in either of the two models. It was also decided that the catalogue would not include unattributed works, no works painted by an artist born in 1880 or later, nor any works painted by artists born before 1880 who worked in a modern style. This soon precipitated an ongoing discussion as to what constituted 'modern'. A considerable number of artists born before 1880, such as Roger Fry and John Singer Sargent, were considered unsuitable for inclusion in the catalogue because they worked in a modern or modernist style. Others – and these were generally less well-known names such as Alfred Heaton Cooper, Percy Lancaster and Arthur Tucker – were included because they continued to work in a traditional manner. Decisions as to whom to include and not to include were made after much internal discussion on an artist-by-artist basis.

The organisation which has enabled the Whitworth's project to publish the catalogue after decades of research is the Paul Mellon Centre for Studies in British Art and in particular its Director of Studies, Brian Allen. After much correspondence and discussion, in March 1999 the Centre offered a grant of unprecedented size towards the publication of the catalogue. I am deeply grateful to Dr Allen for his encouragement throughout this long project. I am also grateful to Marcia Pointon who, in her capacity as Pilkington Professor of History of Art at the University of Manchester and as a member of the Advisory Council of the Paul Mellon Centre, was unfailingly supportive.

Within the Gallery my task has been facilitated by many willing colleagues. In particular, I would like to thank Jennifer Harris, without whose guidance and support the project would not have come to fruition. Other colleagues read part of the book in manuscript, including Mary Griffiths, David Morris, Alistair Smith and Christine Woods. The project required a great deal of new photography and I extend my thanks to those who facilitated this process: Penny Haworth, who typed out the lists and prepared the labels, Cliff Lomax, who carried out the necessary unframing, and Michael Pollard and Derek Trillo, the University photographers;

they all took on the extra work with unfailing calm and good humour. I would also like to thank the Gallery's Paper Conservator, Nicola Walker, who worked on many of the drawings in this catalogue and unearthed a number of previously undiscovered inscriptions and watermarks. This project would not have been accomplished without the work of Julian Tomlin, who saw that the task of creating a catalogue of the collection would be best accomplished using a computer cataloguing system, which was introduced in 1987. This system was replaced in 2000 by a more sophisticated collections information system, known as KE Emu, purchased from Australia with a grant from the Designation Challenge Fund. The Designation Scheme was launched in 1997 to identify, celebrate and support pre-eminent collections held in non-national museums. Julian was responsible for the export of data from KE Emu, which has provided the text for the catalogue entries. The Gallery's website www.whitworth.ac.uk now provides a link to KE Emu to allow searching of almost all the collection.

It is an important fact in the field of art connoisseurship that knowing who to ask is much more important than what one knows oneself, and with a project as large as this one many people have been prodigal with their knowledge and expertise. I am grateful to all those who helped me; I alone am responsible for any errors. Those who helped include artists, art historians, dealers, scholars and fellow museum curators, many of whom have over the many years of this project become friends. I hope they will forgive me if I include them in a list, whilst I offer my apologies to those I have inadvertently left out: John Abbott, Noël Annesley, Chris Beetles, Shelley Bennett, Peter Bower, Patsy Campbell, John Christian, Kerry Downes, Bill Drummond, Andrew Edmunds, Judy Egerton, David Fraser, John Harris, David Hill, Anne Lyles, Margaret Macdonald, Hamish Miles, Christopher Newall, Patrick Noon, Felicity Owen, Cecilia Powell, Christopher Powney, Anthony Reed, Jane Roberts, Kim Sloan, Sam Smiles, Greg Smith, the late Dudley Snelgrove, Richard Stephens, Bill Thomson, Katrina Thomson, Pieter van der Merwe, Jane Wallis, Ian Warrell, Stephen Wildman, the late Ian Fleming-Williams, Andrew Wilton, Andrew Wyld and Jeremy Yates. I would like to extend particular thanks to Andrew Wyld of Agnew's, who over the last ten years has looked at every British drawing in the Whitworth's collection, attributed and unattributed; it is fitting that the Whitworth's relationship with Agnew's, which began in 1889, continues to this day. This project would not have come to fruition had it not been for the Whitworth's association with Philip Wilson Publishers. I would especially like to thank the managing editor Cangy Venables, the production manager Norman Turpin and the catalogue designer Caroline Hillier.

Finally, I would like to thank my wife Lulu – who, unlike the author, studied History of Art at 'A' level – for her patience and understanding in the long gestation of this book.

Charles Nugent, Curator (Drawings & Watercolours), July 2002

An Historical Overview of the British Watercolour Collection at The Whitworth Art Gallery

The early history of the watercolour collection at the Whitworth is inextricably linked with the complicated story of the foundation of the Gallery itself. The Whitworth, originally the Whitworth Institute, received its Royal Charter in 1889. It came into existence as a result of two unrelated events that occurred in 1887, both of immense importance to Manchester. The first was the death in January of that year of Sir Joseph Whitworth, the Stockport-born engineer, who left a fortune of more than £1,000,000, to be administered by three residuary legatees. The second was the hugely successful Royal Jubilee Exhibition, which took place in Manchester from May to October 1887 in a specially designed building that covered more than fourteen acres (Fig. 1).

Sir Joseph Whitworth (Fig. 2) came from humble origins but made a fortune through his engineering skills. He was created a baronet in 1869 and perpetuated his name by establishing the first uniform and internationally recognised standard for screwthreads. In common with many self-made men in the North of England in the nineteenth century, he did own some paintings by Royal Academicians, although he does not seem to have been keenly interested in art, and the Whitworth Art Gallery and its collections, as they are today, were never envisaged

Fig. 1: The Manchester Royal Jubilee Exhibition, general view of the exhibition and grounds

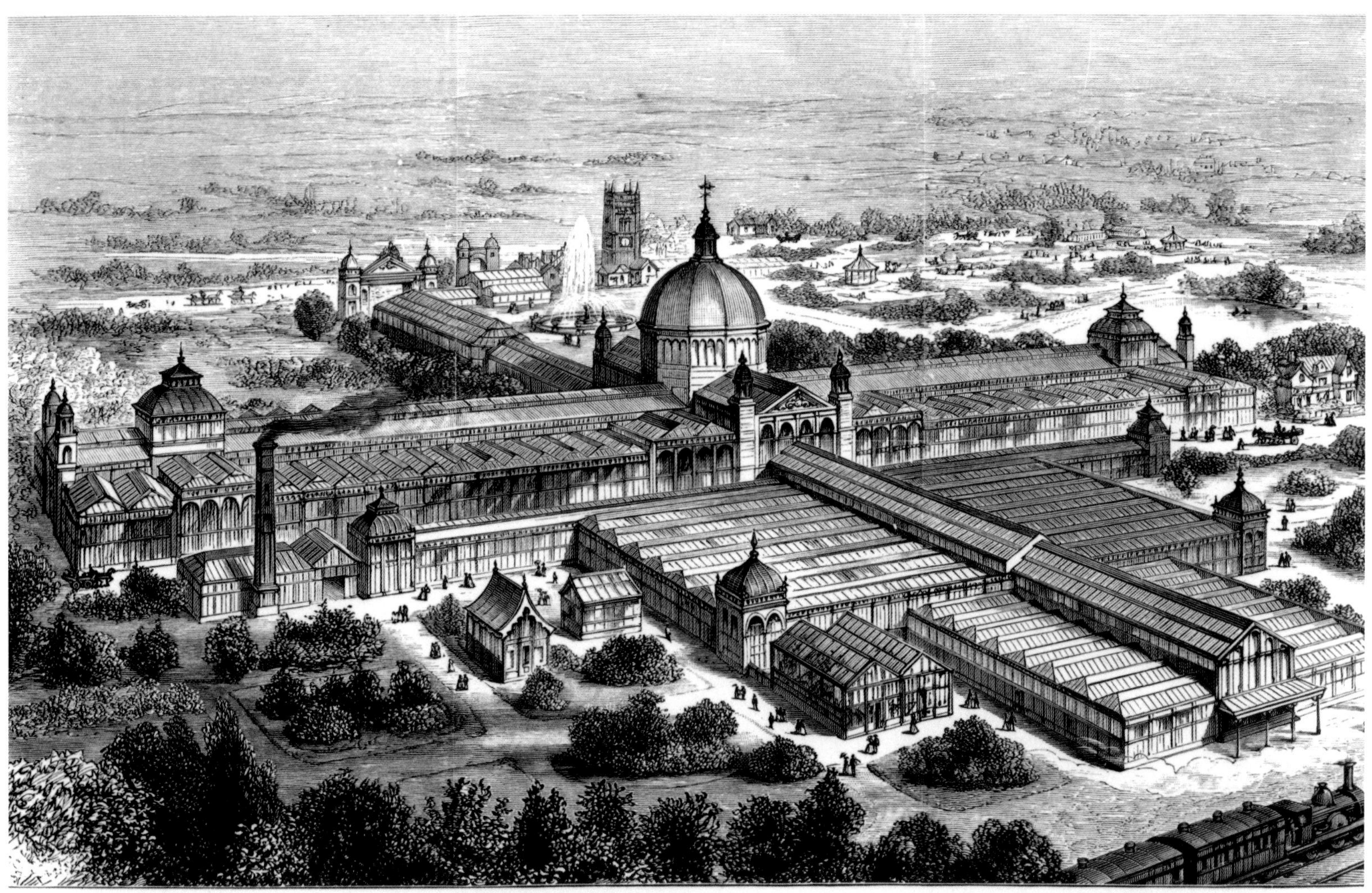

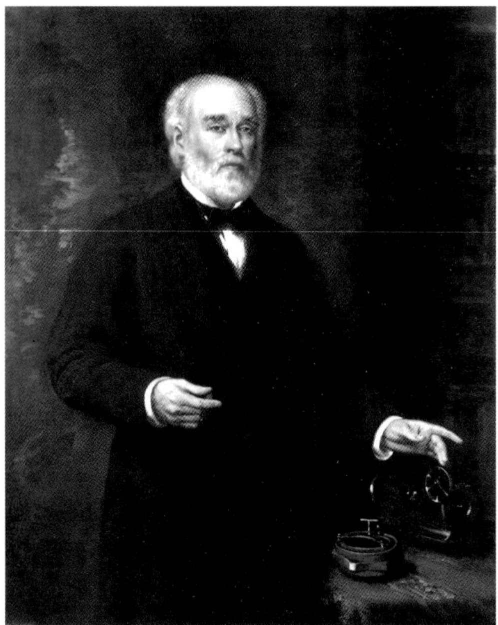

Fig. 2: Thomas Benjamin Kennington,
Portrait of Sir Joseph Whitworth

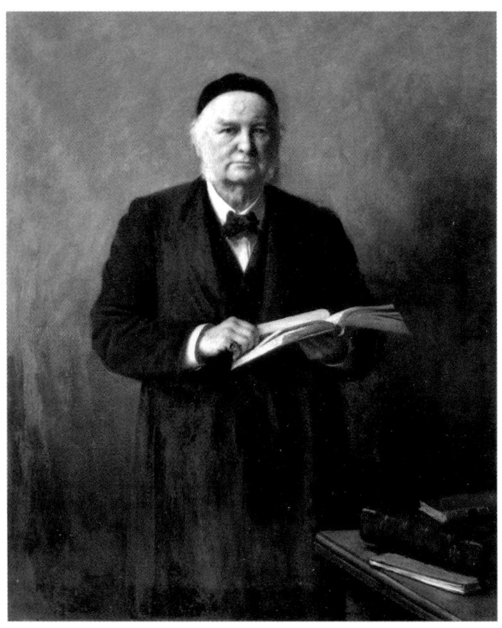

Fig. 3: Thomas Benjamin Kennington,
Portrait of Robert Dukinfield Darbishire

by Sir Joseph. Rather, it is to one of the legatees of Sir Joseph's will, Robert Dukinfield Darbishire (Fig. 3), that the Gallery more directly owes its existence.

The second person who prompted the foundation of the Gallery, and was responsible for the evolution of its policy during the early years, particularly with regard to the purchasing of watercolours, was Sir William Agnew. Agnew was chairman of the firm of art dealers, then based in Manchester, and the organiser of the Fine Arts section of the Royal Jubilee Exhibition. The main organiser of the exhibition was Sir Joseph Lee (1832–94), a partner in the textile manufacturers Tootal Broadhurst Lee and Co., who was Chairman of the Executive Committee, and it was he who proposed dividing the exhibition up into eleven sections, one of which was Fine Arts.

As early as 1881 Ellis Lever, a Manchester industrialist, had suggested in a pamphlet proposing 'a grand International Exhibition' that a 'permanent Institution might be purchased out of the profits of the Exhibition; and the nucleus of a collection could also be formed by a portion of its exhibits'. Since the Royal Jubilee Exhibition eventually attracted nearly 5,000,000 paying visitors and delivered a large profit, Lever's proposal became a real possibility. His proposals were given more concrete direction by a critic in the *City Light*, who, in reviewing the Fine Arts section of the Exhibition, and praising the extensive coverage it had given to watercolours, called for a permanent 'representative Exhibition of English Water-colour painting from its crude beginnings . . . up to the present time. This branch of art has long been looked on as peculiarly English.'

In view of the similarity of aims of the Royal Jubilee Exhibition and the proposed Whitworth Institute, after prolonged discussion between Darbishire and Sir Joseph Lee, a Whitworth Committee was formed in November 1887, and the Guarantors of the Exhibition transferred its surplus of over £40,000 to the Institute, £10,000 of which was to be used to found a School of Art, £20,000 for the purchase of works of art, and the remainder to set up a School of Technology. Sadly, aside from Sir Joseph's bequest, this was to be the only major gift of money that the Institute received, and, from the beginning, finances were on shaky foundations.

The original intention of Sir Joseph's legatees, who believed that they were carrying out his wishes, was to found a School of Technology and a School of Art. These were to be alongside an Art Gallery, which became Darbishire's main preoccupation. The intention was that exposure to good art would enable young engineers to produce better designs. The newly formed Whitworth Committee therefore bought a plot of land to the south of the University and renamed it Whitworth Park. On the site stood Grove House, which was hastily adapted for the purpose of showing exhibitions. The Whitworth Institute received its Royal Charter in 1889, but the wide-ranging and ambitious aims of the legatees were not realised, as the Manchester Corporation took over both the School of Technology and the School of Art, and the Institute was absolved of responsibility for the students and allowed to concentrate on the function of the Art Gallery.

The first purchases of watercolours were made in the summer of 1891, with Agnew's acting as the Gallery's agents at a series of high-profile sales in London. A number of Turner watercolours were acquired, which laid the foundations of what has become one of the most prestigious collections of Turner watercolours outside London. Later that year the Whitworth opened an exhibition of watercolours 'Illustrative of the Progress and Development of that Branch of the Fine Arts in Great Britain'. By this time the purchase fund granted by the Guarantors of the Royal Jubilee Exhibition, known as the Jubilee Fund, had been used to purchase thirty-eight works. In all, fifty-four watercolours were eventually purchased with this Fund, which was not exhausted until 1905. Watercolours purchased included eight by Turner, six by William Henry Hunt, four by David Roberts, four by David Cox, four by Samuel Prout, three by Peter de Wint and two by Clarkson Stanfield; this effectively laid the basis of the historic watercolour collection. Records of the early purchases by the Whitworth are unfortunately incomplete, as it was seldom recorded from whom the purchase was made, but it is certainly significant that from the 1890s to the 1920s the seller, when known, in the majority of cases, was Agnew's. There can be no doubt that Sir William Agnew, as Chairman of Agnew's, as well as President of the Council of the Gallery, used his dual role in order to sell to the Gallery, just as he had earlier used his position organising his section of the Royal Jubilee Exhibition to benefit his company. Although Agnew's initially bid at auction for the Whitworth without charge, by the later 1890s they were charging a commission for doing so. There were also abundant cases of Agnew's selling good-quality watercolours to the Whitworth which they had found difficult to sell elsewhere. The most extreme case involved a George Cattermole watercolour bought at auction in 1889 and not sold to the Whitworth until 1898. This is meant in no way to disparage Sir William, who was a man of immense altruism and public spirit, and to whom the Whitworth owes an immense debt of gratitude for many years of service and guidance.

The Whitworth was fortunate to be buying at this time, since in 1890 the watercolour collection of Dr John Percy was sold at Christie's in London. Percy was a successful metallurgist, and had amassed one of the largest and most complete collections of English watercolours ever assembled. His sale, which lasted seven days, was described as 'comprising upwards of 1,500 drawings by nearly 700 painters of the English water-colour school, and forming an almost complete history of water-colour art from the commencement of the 18th century to the present day'. Such a description would have struck a chord with the Whitworth Committee who, under the leadership of Sir William Agnew, had similar intentions with regard to the Whitworth's collection of watercolours. Although the Gallery did not begin making purchases until 1891 and therefore did not buy directly at the Percy sale, several works were acquired from that prestigious collection, either by purchase through Agnew's using the Jubilee Fund or by gifts or bequests from individual benefactors. In all, some forty watercolours with a Percy provenance are now in the Whitworth's collection.

Then, in 1892, came the Taylor Gift of watercolours and drawings, by far the largest and most important that the Gallery has ever received. It consisted of 154 works, and includes some of the drawings and watercolours for which the Gallery is best known today. John Edward Taylor was the owner of the *Manchester Guardian* newspaper and a keen art collector. He had lent nine works to the Royal Jubilee Exhibition and was a supporter of the Whitworth's first watercolour exhibition in 1891, lending about seventy items. Some time in 1892, Taylor, according to a report written by Sir William Agnew, 'allowed to be selected from his own collection' a group of watercolours of high quality and importance 'with a special regard to the aim of the Institute at developing the Exhibition of the History of the Art of Water-colour Painting in England'. Taylor had been a regular buyer at Agnew's and knew Sir William well. It was presumably Sir William who made the selection and, as the emphasis was intended to be on the development of watercolour painting – at this date considered by many to be a national art – he tended to choose representative examples of particular artists, and often ones which showed their stylistic development. Thus, eleven of the eighteen Turner watercolours given by Taylor date from before 1802. Other highlights include William Blake's *The Ancient of Days*, undoubtedly the Whitworth's most widely known and celebrated watercolour, as well as the same artist's six illustrations to Milton's *Hymn on the Morning of Christ's Nativity*. The gift also included two Italian watercolours by John Robert Cozens, two English views by Girtin, and important works by lesser artists such as Edward Dayes and Thomas Hearne. Interestingly, there is no replication between the Jubilee Fund purchases and the works in the Taylor Gift, indicating that there was a deliberate policy of selection. As well as the Taylor gift of 1892, Taylor also gave a series of more than 120 drawings by William Mulready as well as a watercolour of Bushey Churchyard by William Henry Hunt; these are now accessioned separately to the Taylor gift but seem to have been given at the same time. Taylor was elected a Governor of the Gallery in 1895 and died in 1905. After his widow's death in 1912, a sale was held of the contents of Taylor's

Fig. 4: The Whitworth Art Gallery from the south-east, showing Grove House and the newly-completed South Gallery to the left, ca. 1900

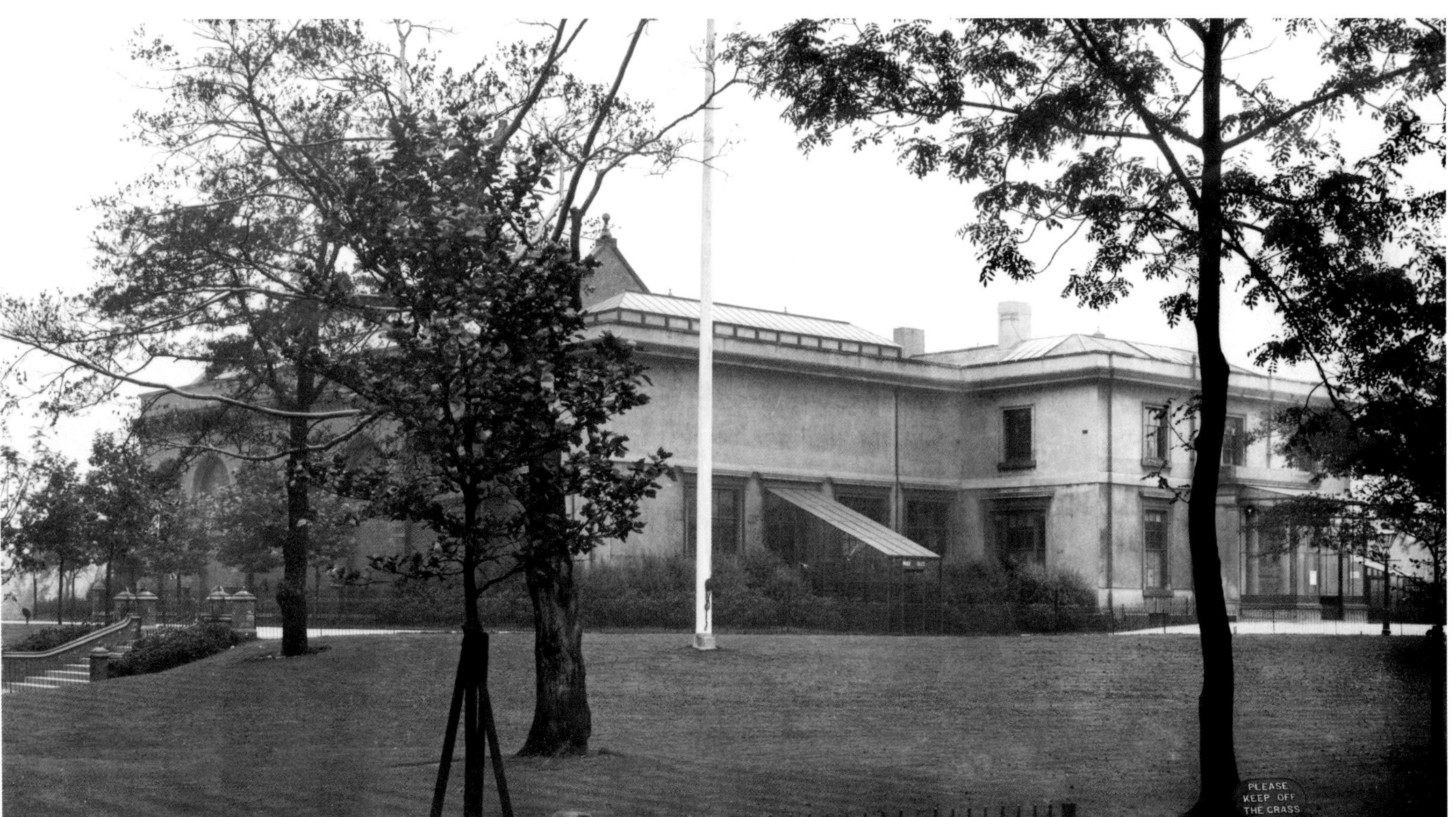

London house. There were over a hundred watercolours by Turner in the sale and Taylor's four nephews bought three of them and presented them to the Whitworth in his memory. Taylor's gift, together with the Jubilee Fund purchases thus formed, very early in the Gallery's history and before the current building was even completed, the nucleus of the watercolour collection.

In 1894 the Whitworth received a small bequest of watercolours from Charles Lees, one of the Gallery's original Governors. This includes an Edward Dayes, which had formerly been in the Percy Collection. Also in 1894 a major catalogue of the Whitworth's holdings was published, and, in the same year, the Institute approved plans for the building of new galleries, the first phase of which was completed between 1895 and 1897 (Fig. 4). The second phase was completed in 1908, by which time Grove House had been demolished, and the Gallery assumed the external appearance which has remained to this day (Fig. 5).

The core collection of British watercolours, assembled within only a few years of the Gallery's foundation, has been added to – inevitably in a piecemeal fashion – both by purchase and bequest, since the beginning of the last century. Early gifts and bequests include those from Mary Worthington, who gave a group of watercolours by Thomas Hearne, Edward Dayes, John Martin, John Webber, Michael 'Angelo' Rooker and others in 1900, and then left a further large collection of watercolours and drawings in her will of 1904. This included eight watercolours by Turner and others by Samuel Prout, David Cox and Copley Fielding, as well as a complete set of forty-two drawings by Daniel Maclise illustrating the story of the Norman Conquest, which had formerly been the property of Mrs Worthington's

Fig. 5: The Whitworth Art Gallery from the east, the new facade, after 1908

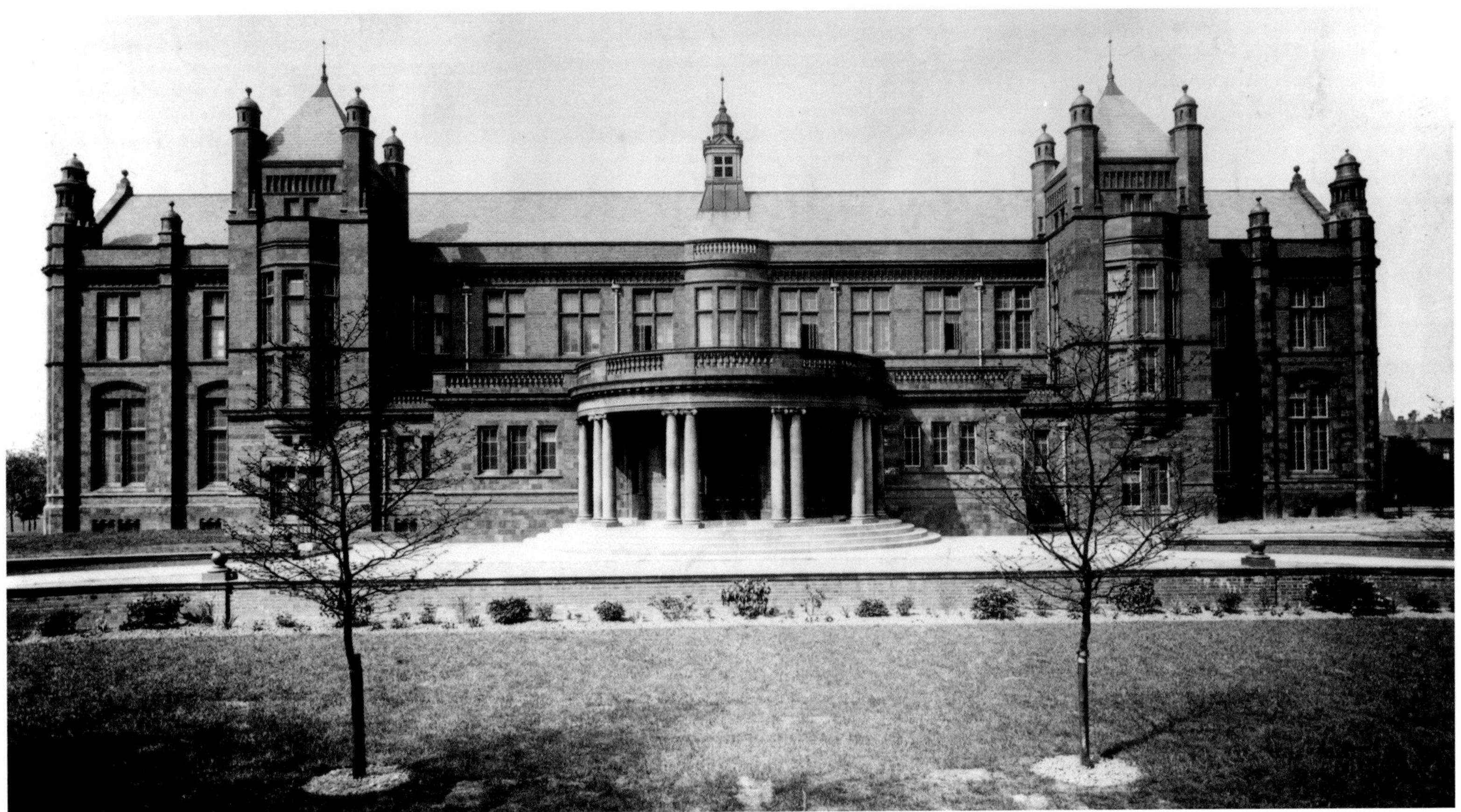

father Henry McConnell, a Manchester cotton maufacturer and himself a collector of note.

In 1906 the Whitworth began its long association with the generous benefactor Arthur Anderson. Anderson was a wealthy bachelor living in Surrey, whose practice it was to buy works of art at London galleries and present them directly to art galleries around the country (apart from the Whitworth, he also gave works to the Ashmolean and Nottingham, as well as being a generous donor to the Williamson Art Gallery in Birkenhead). A very shy man, Anderson never visited the Whitworth, although between 1906 and his death in 1938, he presented well over 300 drawings and watercolours to the Gallery. These included twenty-four drawings and watercolours by James Ward, four by Gainsborough, as well as many others by Richard Wilson, Thomas Rowlandson, Sir James Thornhill, Peter de Wint and John Sell Cotman.

The 1920s and 1930s were rich in acquisitions and bequests, one of which was the group of fifty-seven watercolours left to the Gallery in 1924 by Sir Edward and Lady Broadhurst. The Broadhursts were Manchester textile manufacturers and like many of their kind were clients of Agnew's. Their collection included groups of watercolours by John Varley, Samuel Prout and David Cox and other works by David Roberts, Paul Sandby and Michael 'Angelo' Rooker; they also owned two Turner watercolours, one of which was for the famous *England and Wales* series of engravings. In 1927, the Whitworth benefited from a change that J. R. Holliday made to his will very late in life. A Birmingham solicitor and collector of the Pre-Raphaelites and others, Holliday had intended to leave his entire collection to Birmingham Museum and Art Gallery. However, he seems to have been offended when Birmingham Corporation removed him from one of their art committees on grounds of age and made a will, giving his executor Sidney Cockerell the authority to divide his collection amongst public collections around the country. As a result, the Whitworth received more than a hundred drawings and watercolours, including large groups of works by David Cox and Burne-Jones, and the complete 1844 series of King Lear drawings by Ford Madox Brown.

However, the 1920s and 1930s were not easy times for the Whitworth, which found that its investments, chiefly of railway stock, yielded less income year by year, with the result that the Gallery was running on a deficit that increased each year. This steady decline was slowed partly by the decision to utilise the fund originally set aside for the purchase of works of art for repairs to the building, and partly by the regrettable decision to sell works from the collection. From its very early days, the Whitworth had also been collecting oil paintings and by the 1930s had a number of paintings by artists such as John Linnell, David Roberts, Clarkson Stanfield, Briton Riviere, Edward William Cooke and several other of their nineteenth-century contemporaries. All the paintings of any value were either sold privately (through Agnew's) or at auction at Christie's in 1935. The removal of the vast majority of the oil paintings gave the historic collection an imbalance that survives to this day and has served to give the watercolour collection a prominence that it might not otherwise have had.

The 1930s marked two events which were of radical significance for the future of the gallery and of the watercolour collection. The first was the foundation of the

Friends of the Whitworth in 1933. Their special brief was to help with the purchase of works of art, a role which they have fulfilled admirably. The second event was the appointment of Margaret Pilkington as Honorary Director of the Gallery in 1936. Pilkington (1891–1974), a member of the wealthy Cheshire industrial family, had served as a Governor of the Gallery since 1924, and, in order to save the expenditure of one salary, gave her services as Honorary Director of the Gallery free of charge for over twenty years. In the years after 1936 Pilkington – a former Slade School student and a proficient wood engraver – and her sister Dorothy, contributed to the gallery in many ways, generally unpublicised. It was not unusual for them to go to a London selling exhibition and to buy works using their own personal resources before presenting them directly to the Whitworth.

Another major bequest came in 1937 when works that had formerly belonged to the Manchester collector Jesse Haworth came to the Whitworth on the death of his widow. These included works by Helen Allingham, David Cox, Samuel Prout and Samuel Palmer, as well as two Holman Hunt watercolours painted in the Middle East, an *England and Wales* Turner watercolour, and a Turner watercolour of a Swiss subject, dating from 1845, that had belonged to Ruskin. However, in spite of such generous bequests, and some far-sighted purchasing by the Friends of the Whitworth, such as a Shoreham-period Palmer and a Richard Wilson drawing that had belonged to Lord Dartmouth, both acquired in 1954, the revenue problems of the Gallery remained. These were alleviated only in 1958 when, after years of negotiation, the Gallery relinquished its status as a privately funded body and became the property of the University of Manchester. Two years later the University agreed that the teaching collection formed by the History of Art Department should be transferred into the Whitworth's care. Although this collection contained mostly Old Master drawings, there were some British works, including an album of more than sixty Thomas Sunderland watercolours.

For a few years in the early 1960s, an attempt was made to form a small collection of oil paintings to take the place of those sold in the 1930s. A few paintings, such as the famous John Frederick Lewis *Indoor Gossip*, were acquired, but this policy, typical of the mood of optimism of those years, was soon discontinued as impracticable. In recent years, with the inexorable rise in the price of works of art, particularly watercolours, and the increasing availability of grants from the national grant-giving bodies, such as the Purchase Grant Fund, administered by the Victoria & Albert Museum, and the National Art Collections Fund, the Friends of the Whitworth have tended, except in some special cases, to make supplementary contributions towards purchase rather than give the full amount. The Friends of the Whitworth have been vital to the survival of the Whitworth and its continued role as an active collector of British watercolours. An outstanding example is their crucial contribution towards the acquisition of the Gallery's virtually unrivalled collection of John Robert Cozens's works. These include a rare English view, bought in 1972, the high-profile purchase of seven sketchbooks from his trip to Italy in 1782–83, bought in 1975, and the acquisition of six Grand Tour watercolours in 1984.

During his time as Keeper and Principal Keeper at the Whitworth (1959–88), Francis Hawcroft masterminded a number of adventurous purchases, both in the historic and modern field. Those that stand out in the former category, aside from the Cozens purchases already mentioned, include Thomas Girtin's only known book of sketches, purchased in 1977, after an export licence application for it had been deferred, and the Gallery's most famous John Martin watercolour, *Manfred and the Witch of the Alps*, bought in 1974. Since then, the gallery has continued to collect historic watercolours, filling gaps where applicable and buying complementary material. Significant purchases of recent years are the Thomas Hearne watercolour *Autumn*, bought in 1993, which joined its pair *Summer* that had been in the collection since 1892, and the two large West Indian Hearne watercolours, bought in 1994. There have also been attempts to complement the Gallery's already extensive collection of works associated with the Grand Tour, with the purchase of works by Thomas Manby, one of the earliest British artists to visit Rome, in 1992 and 1999, and a watercolour by Michel Vincent Brandoin in 1999. Works by artists not previously represented in the collection have been acquired, including a watercolour by the Leeds painter John William Inchbold, purchased from Agnew's in 1992 and a landscape with wild flowers by the Irish painter Andrew Nicholl, purchased at Christie's in 1995. The most recent high-profile purchase was of a John White Abbott watercolour of a Devon landscape bought at Sotheby's in 2001.

However, the two most important groups of watercolours and drawings acquired since Francis Hawcroft's time were not purchases. The first was the transfer in 1998 from the Department of Architecture in the University of Manchester of their collection of architectural drawings. This contained a number of important watercolours by Alfred Waterhouse and his office relating to Manchester Town Hall and Owens College. The second was the gift by Miss Aydua Scott-Elliot in 1999 of her collection of works by British and foreign artists. Miss Scott-Elliot became Keeper of Prints and Drawings in the Print Room of the Royal Library at Windsor Castle after the Second World War and served there until her retirement in 1969. During this time she came to know the great watercolour collector Paul Oppé (1878–1957), who was working at Windsor, cataloguing the English drawings in the collection there. As a result of their friendship, she acquired a number of watercolours from Oppé's collection; these include four drawings by Alexander Cozens and watercolours of international importance such as Francis Towne's *The Salmon Leap*, John Downman's *The Entrance of the Wood near Marino* and John Varley's *Sunrise from the Top of Cader Idris*. Miss Scott-Elliot's donation (the works from Oppé's collection were given in his memory) is easily the most important gift that the Gallery has received since before the Second World War.

The collection does not aspire to give a comprehensive survey of British watercolour painting and many gaps need to be filled. Generally, it is much stronger in works from the eighteenth than the nineteenth century, and the numerical bias is strongly towards landscape. However, there are some fine figure drawings from both centuries. In spite of its omissions, the historic British drawings and watercolours collection at the Whitworth remains one of the finest in the country outside the national collections in London and Edinburgh.

Charles Nugent, Curator (Drawings & Watercolours), July 2002

Colour Plates

MANBY, THOMAS
The Roman Forum
Boyd of Merton, Viscount (purchase, 1999)
(V. & A., N.A.C.F.) (D.1999.12)

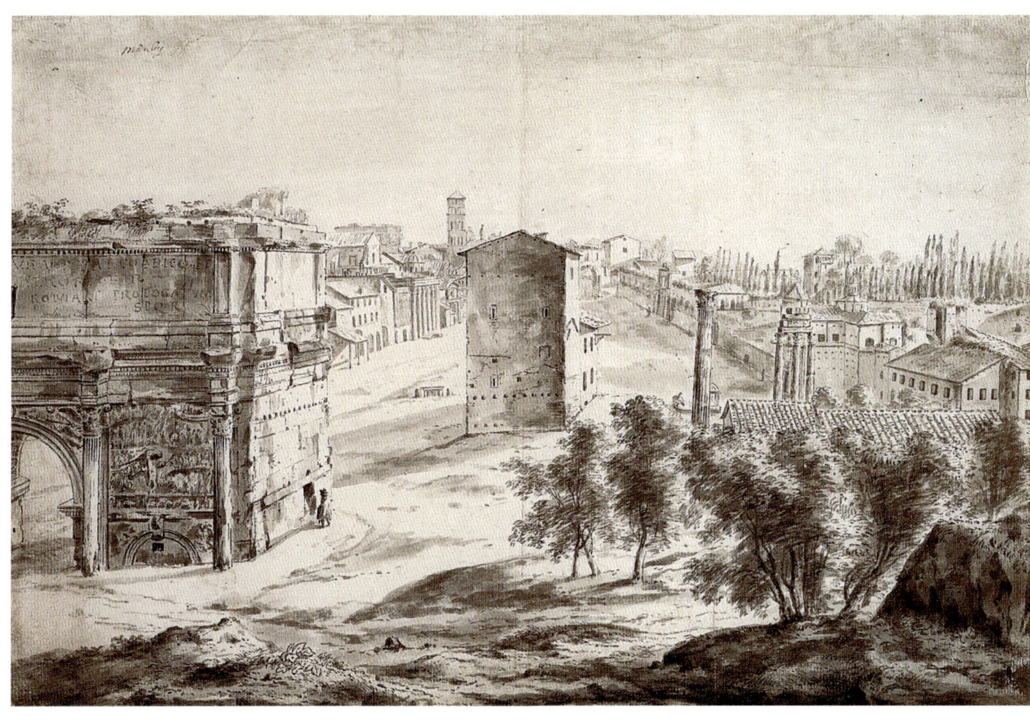

THORNHILL, SIR JAMES
View of Hampton Court Ferry from the Artist's Lodgings
7.1730
Anderson, A. E. (gift, 1935) (D.1935.5)

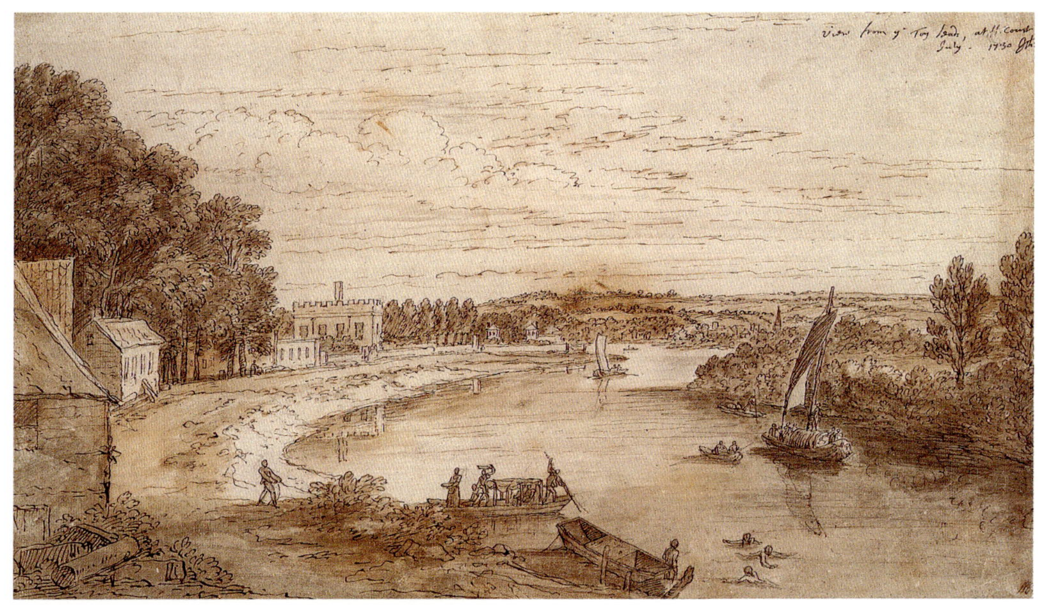

COZENS, ALEXANDER
A rocky Island
Anderson, A. E. (gift, 1929) (D.1929.26)

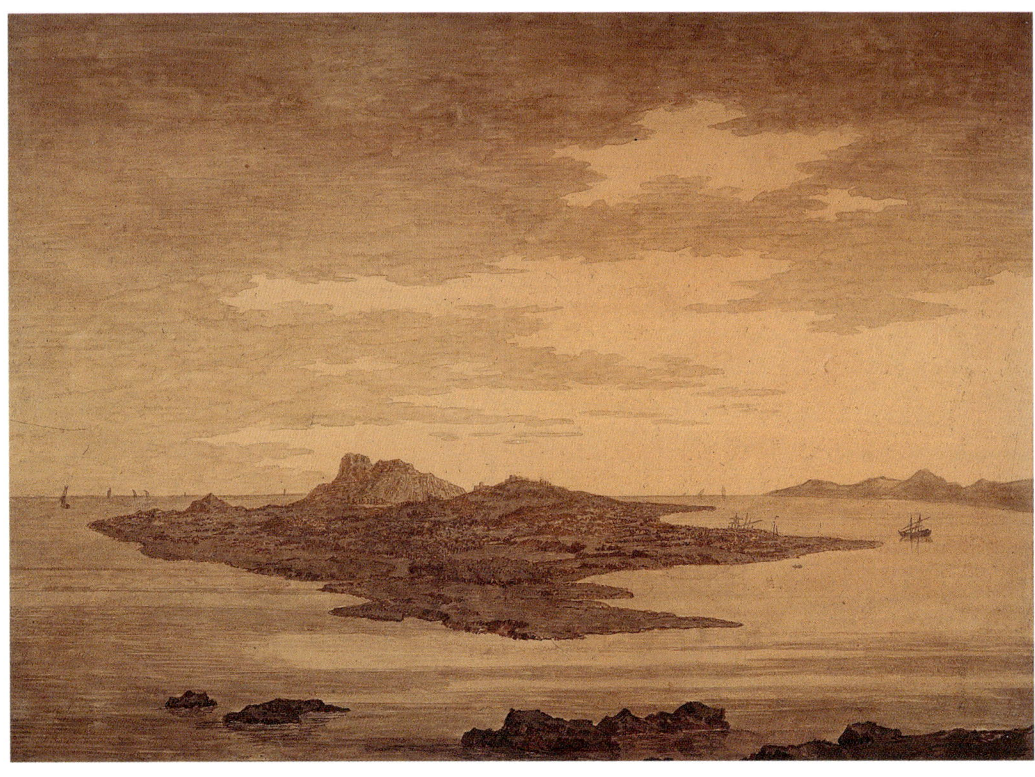

COZENS, JOHN ROBERT
**Cetara, a Fishing Town on
the Gulf of Salerno, Italy**
Keith, Mrs Cecil, Agnew's (via) (purchase,
1984) (V. & A., N.A.C.F., F.O.W.) (D.1984.10)

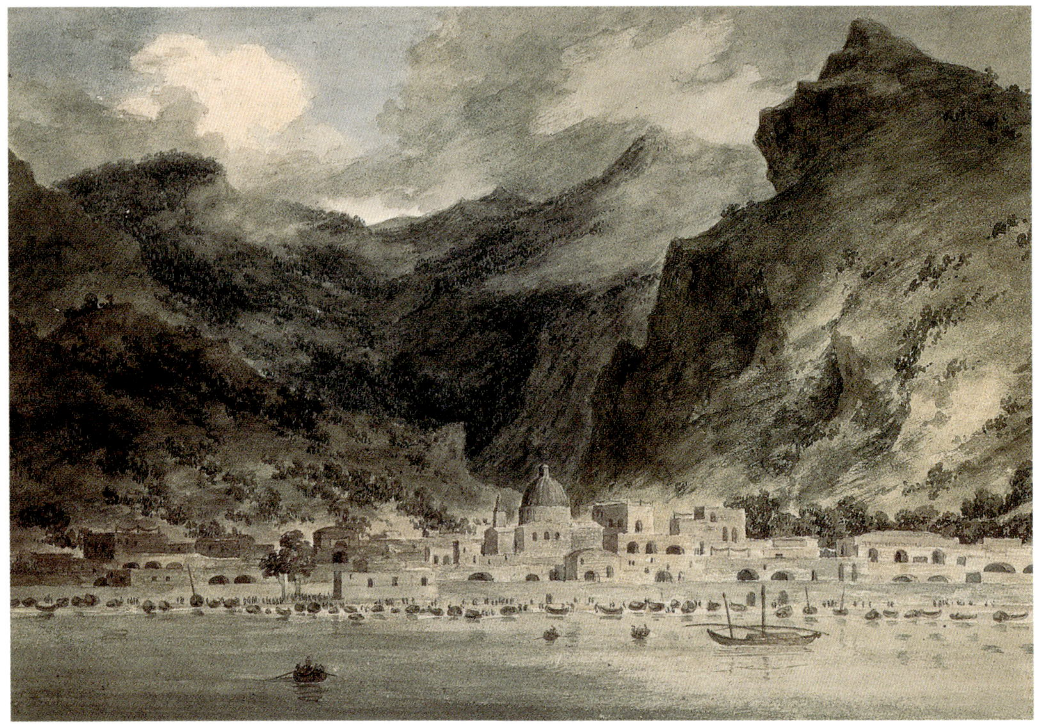

HEARNE, THOMAS
**Summertime: an Illustration to
Thomson's 'The Seasons', Book II**
1783
Taylor, John Edward (gift, 1892) (D.1892.17)

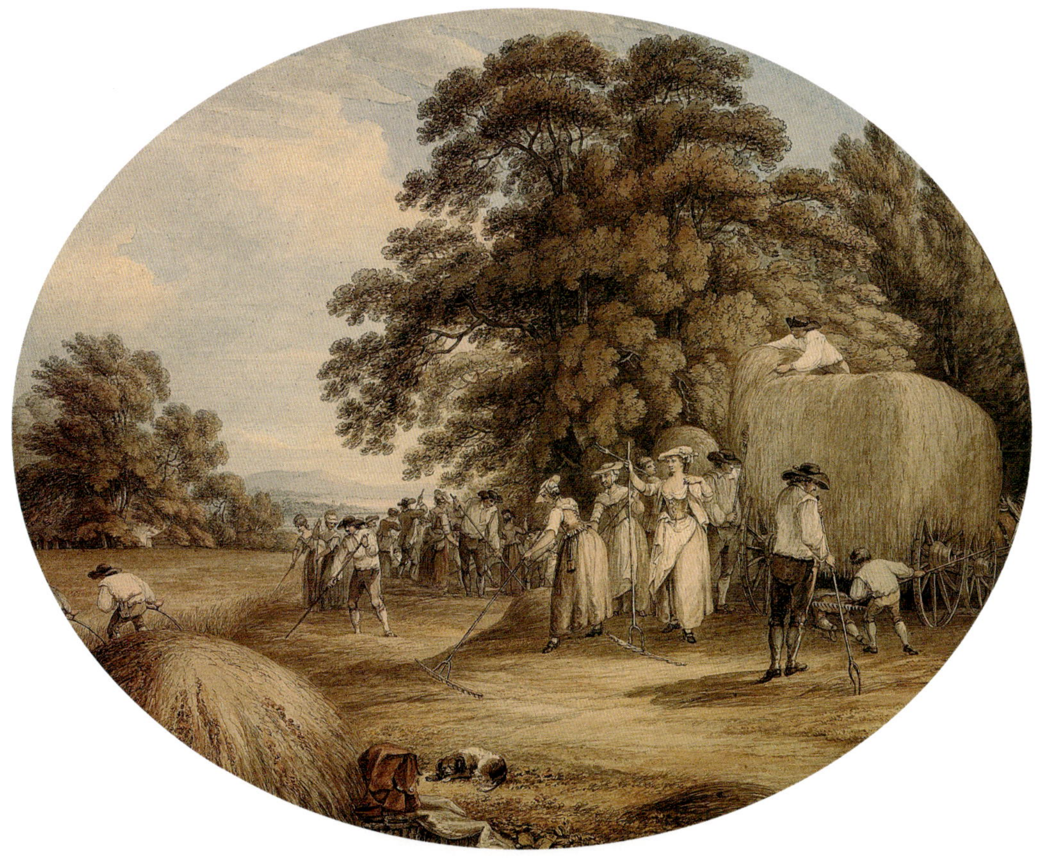

HEARNE, THOMAS
**Autumn (Palemon and Lavinia):
an Illustration to Thomson's
'The Seasons', Book III**
1783
Richmond Gallery, Agnew's (via)
(purchase, 1993) (V. & A., F.O.W.) (D.1993.9)

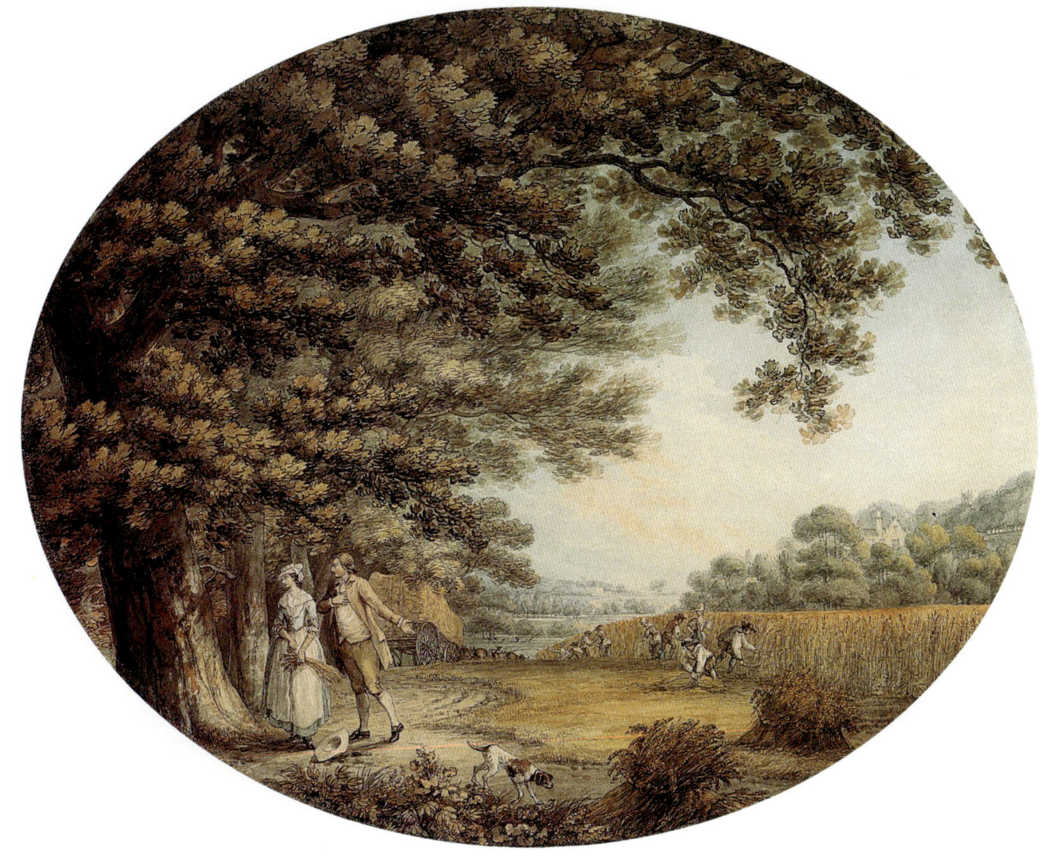

Blake, William
'Europe', Plate I,
Frontispiece,
'The Ancient of Days'
1827 (?)
Taylor, John Edward (gift, 1892)
(D.1892.32)

Blake, William
The Descent of
Peace: Milton's Hymn
'On the Morning of
Christ's Nativity'
1809
Taylor, John Edward (gift, 1892)
(D.1892.26)

Blake, William
The Descent of Typhon
and the Gods into
Hell: Milton's Hymn
'On the Morning of
Christ's Nativity'
1809
Taylor, John Edward (gift, 1892)
(D.1892.30)

Blake, William
The Angels appearing to
the Shepherds: Milton's
Hymn 'On the Morning of
Christ's Nativity'
1809
Taylor, John Edward (gift, 1892)
(D.1892.27)

Blake, William
Sullen Moloch: Milton's
Hymn 'On the Morning of
Christ's Nativity'
1809
Taylor, John Edward (gift, 1892)
(D.1892.29)

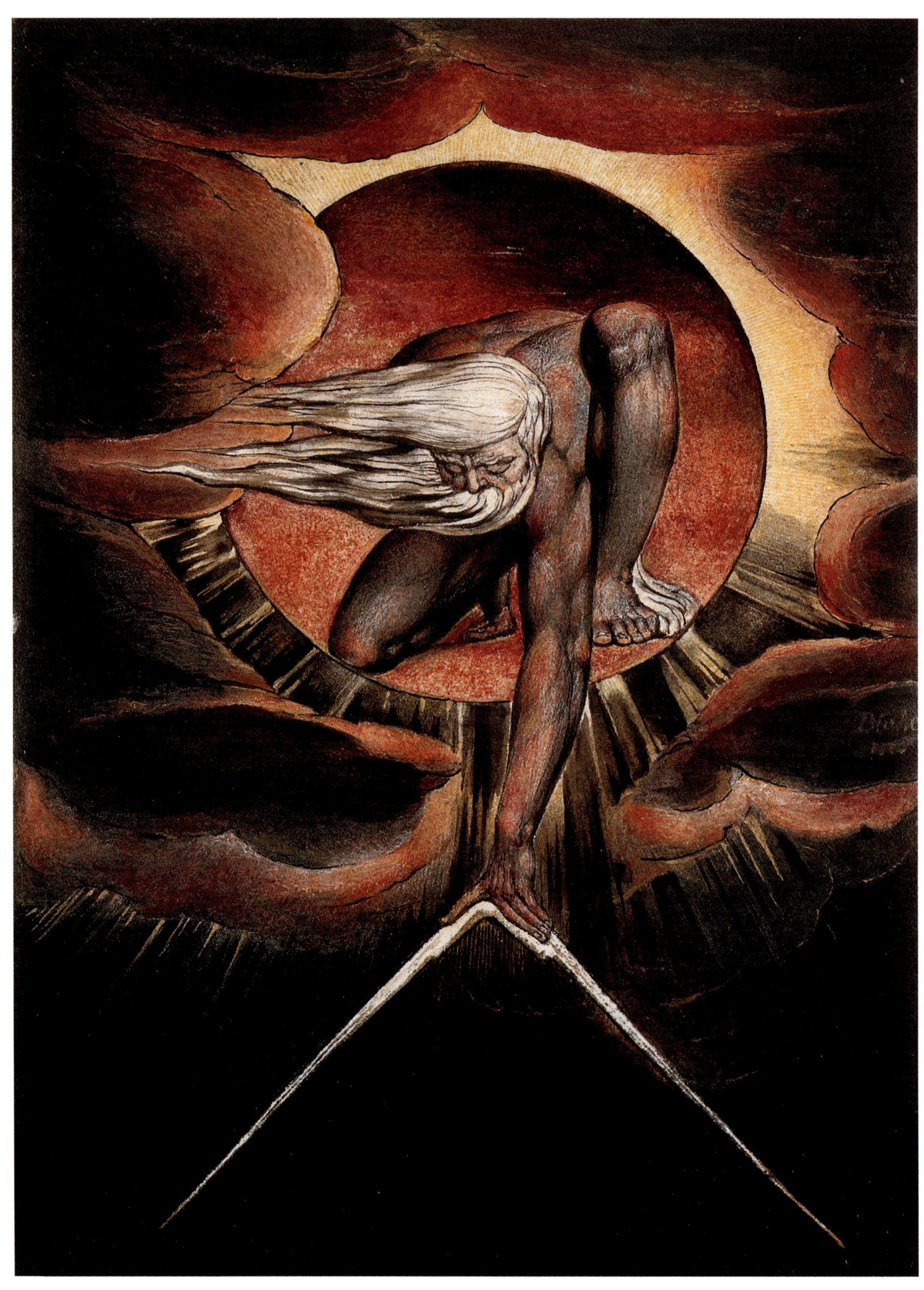

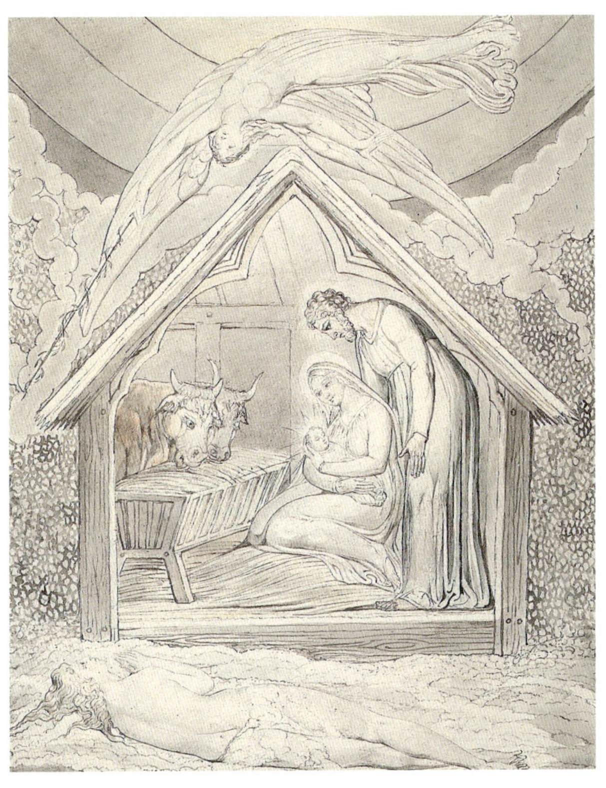

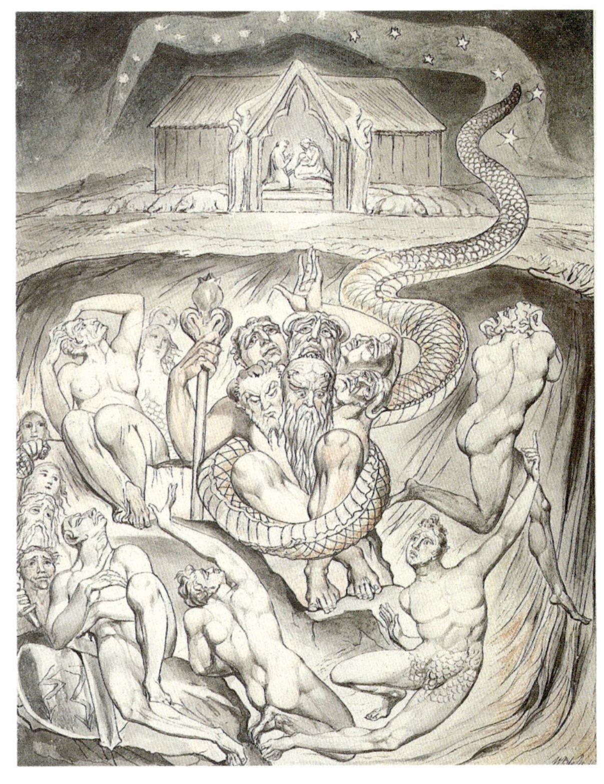

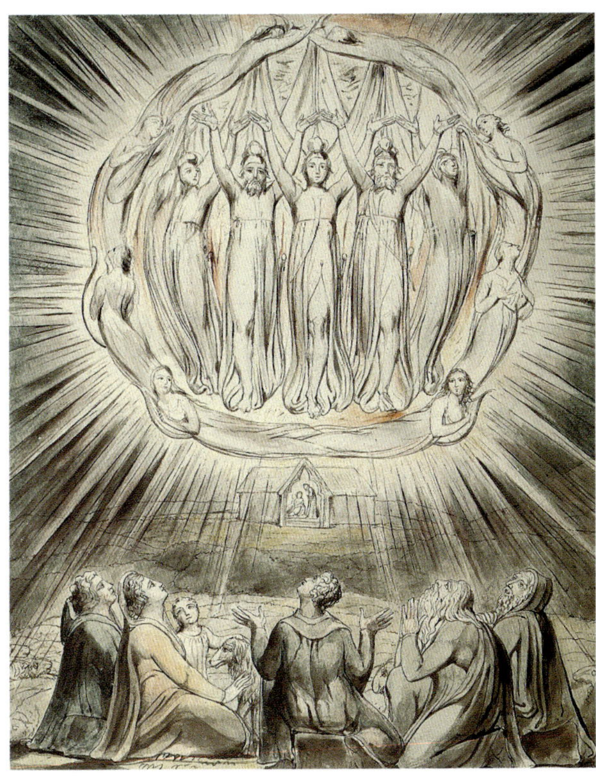

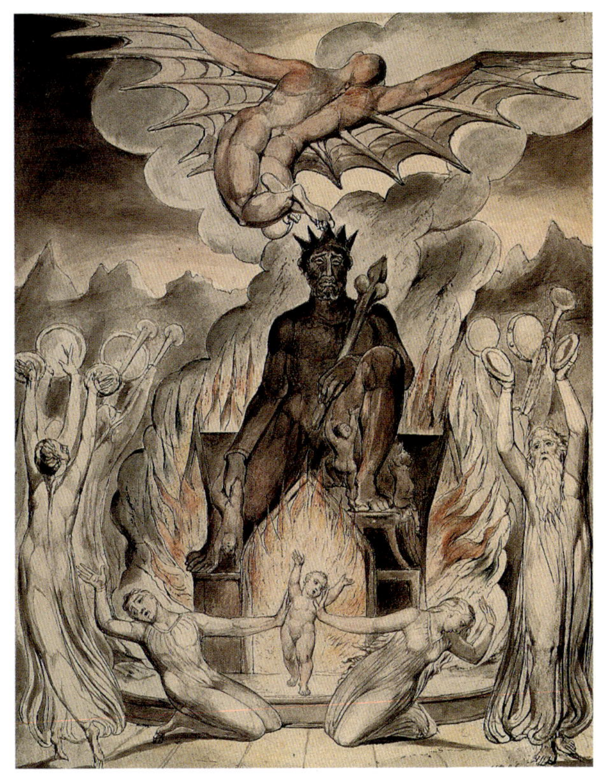

**TURNER, JOSEPH
MALLORD WILLIAM**
**Storm in the Pass of
St Gotthard, Switzerland**
1845
Haworth, Jesse (bequest, 1937) (D.1937.23)

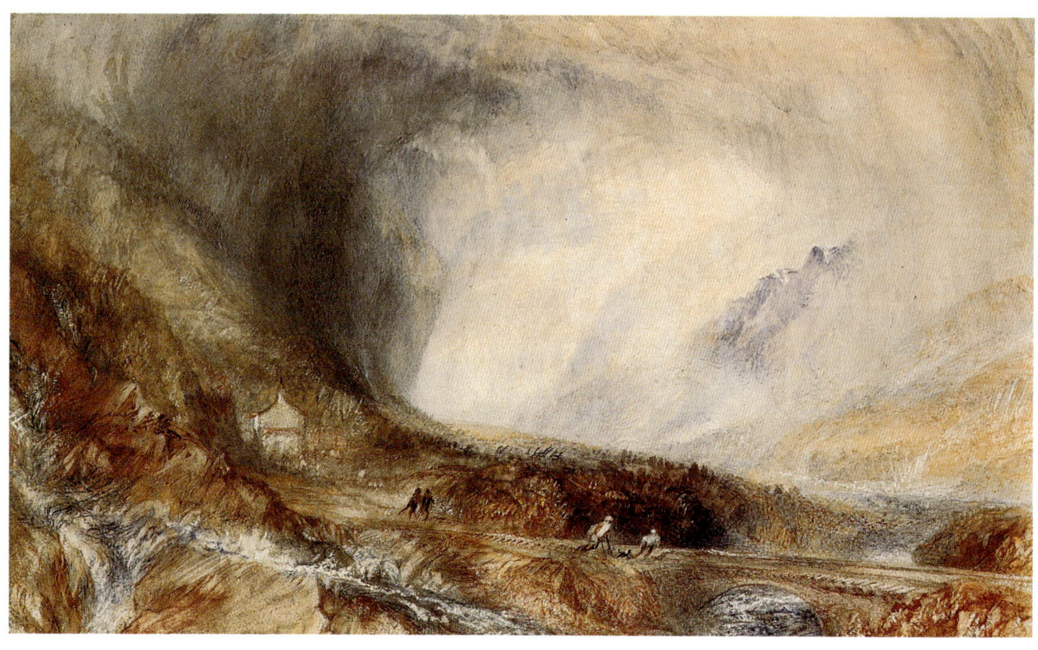

**TURNER, JOSEPH
MALLORD WILLIAM**
Warwick Castle, Warwickshire
1830–31
Haworth, Jesse (bequest, 1937) (D.1937.22)

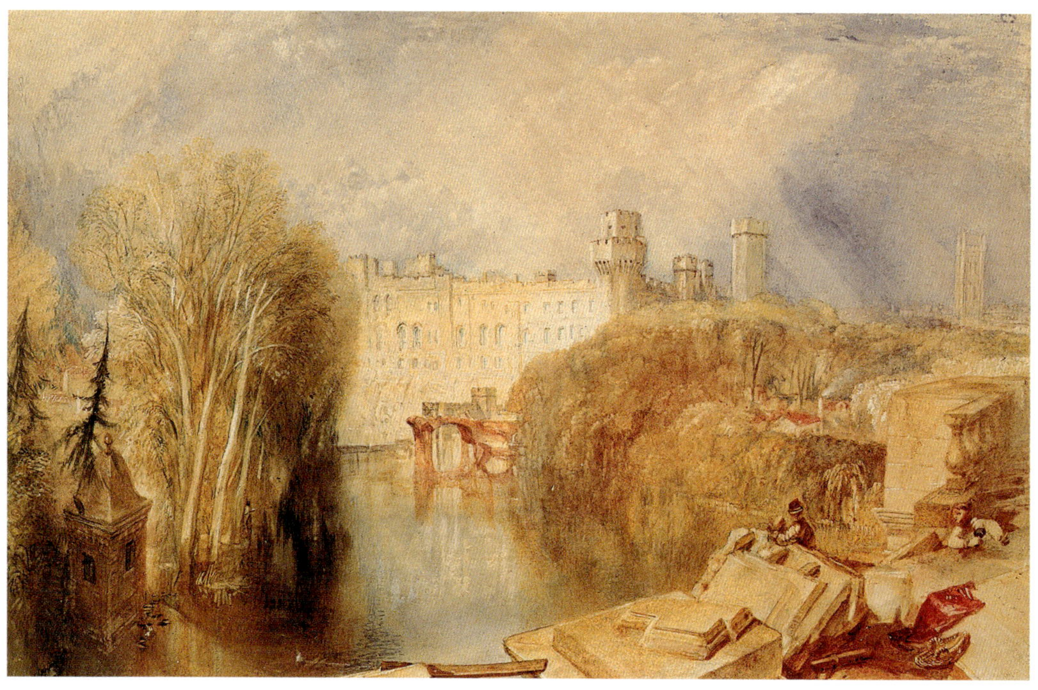

GIRTIN, THOMAS
**Durham Cathedral and Bridge,
from the River Wear**
1799
Taylor, John Edward (gift, 1892) (D.1892.110)

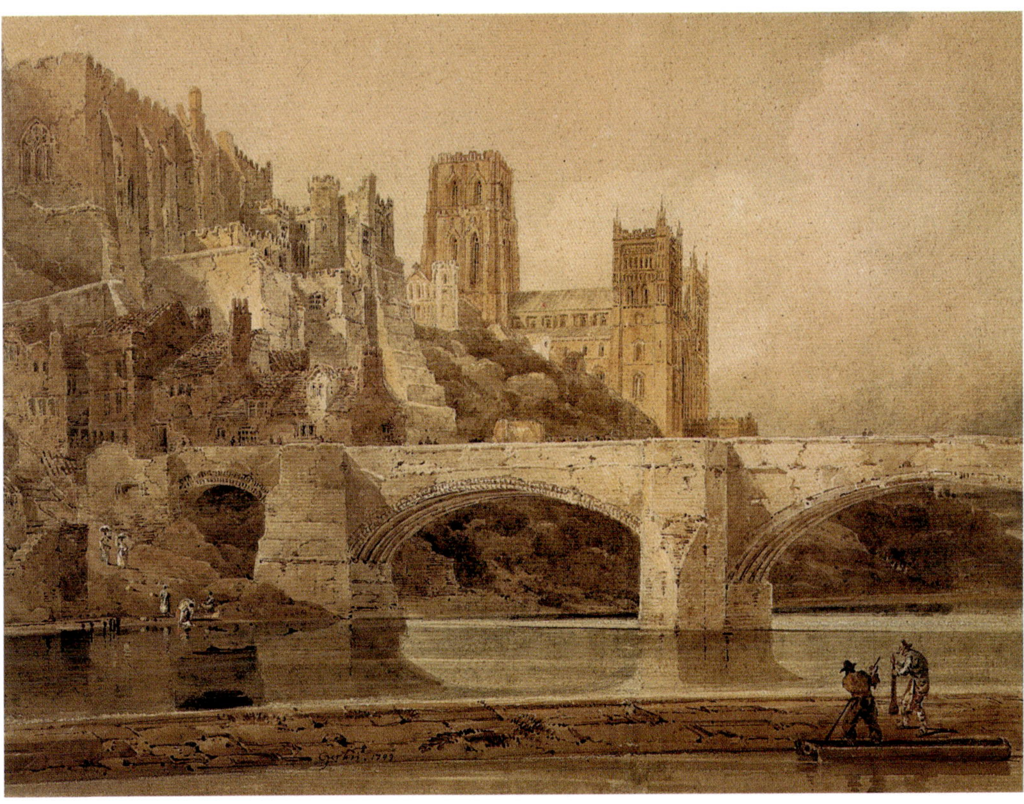

GAINSBOROUGH, THOMAS
**A wooded Landscape with a
Country Mansion, elegant Figures
and Peasants**
1780–81
Messrs E. Parsons and Co. (purchase, 1927)
(D.1927.20)

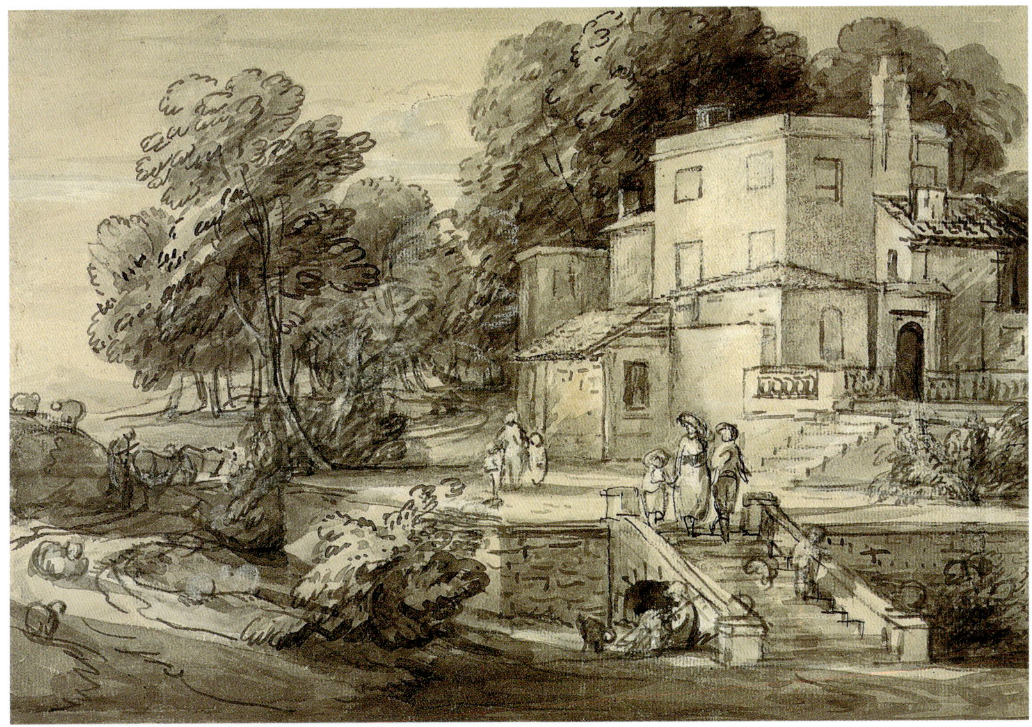

BONINGTON, RICHARD PARKES
Rouen with the Tower of Saint Ouen – Sunset
1825
Pilkington, Margaret, Friends of the Whitworth
(via) (gift, 1946) (D.1946.8)

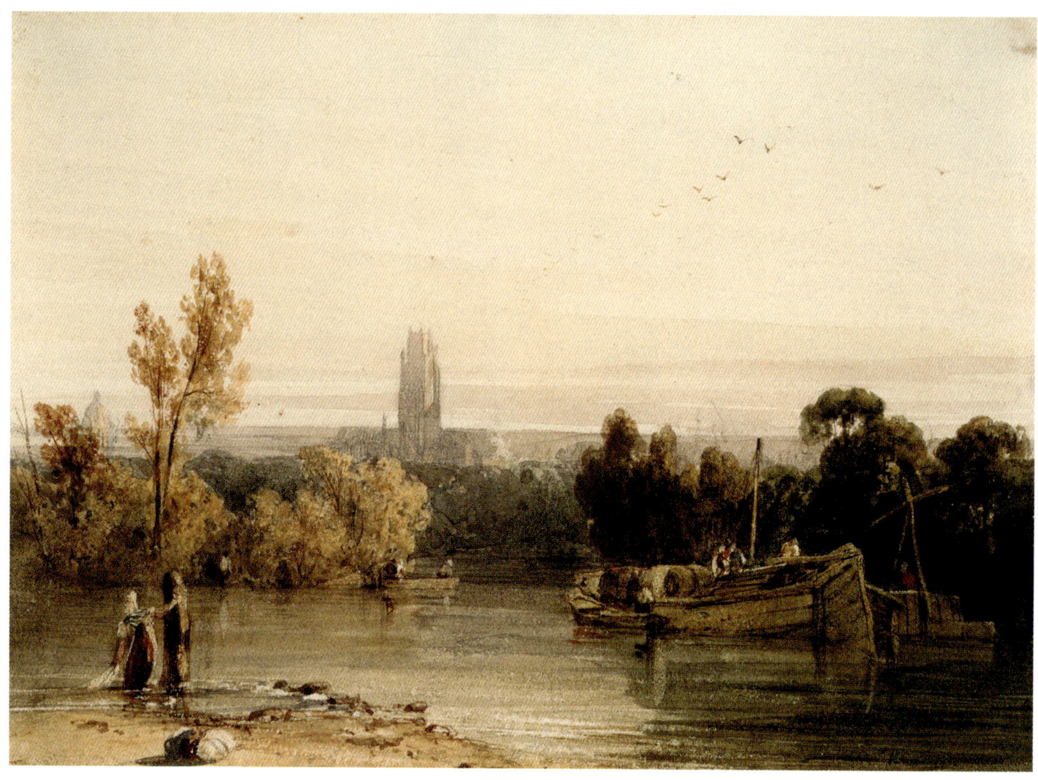

BOYS, THOMAS SHOTTER
Banks of the Seine, Rouen, France, with the Cathedral Towers
Agnew's (purchase, 29.11.1905) (D.1905.4)

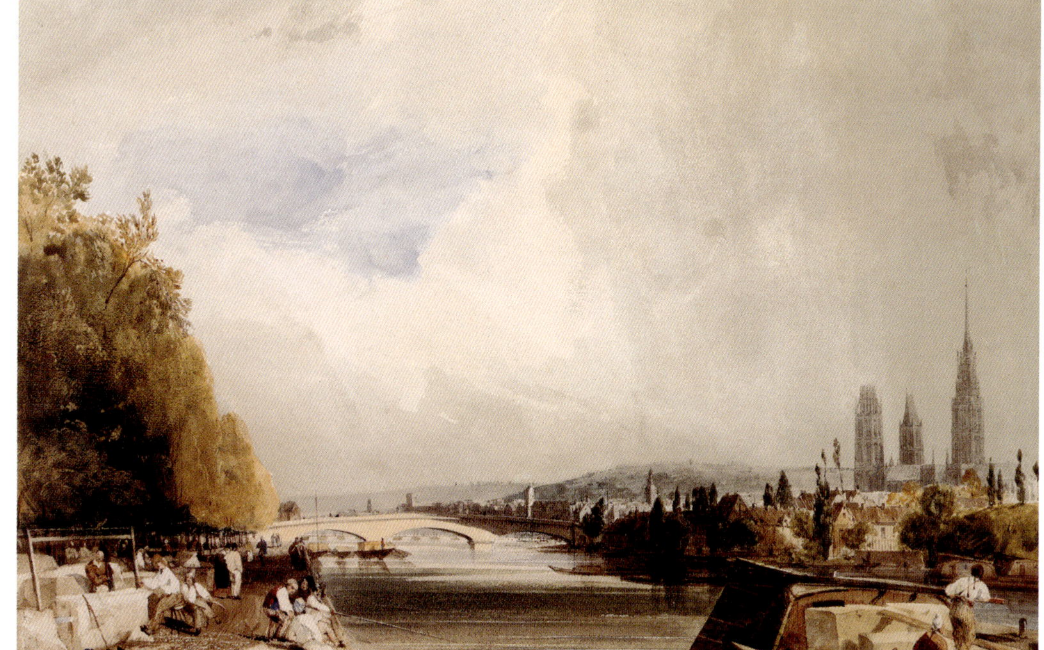

WEBBER, JOHN
Mont Blanc and Chamonix, France
1787
Scott-Elliot, Miss Aydua, in memory of Paul
Oppé (gift, 4.11.1999) (D.1999.24)

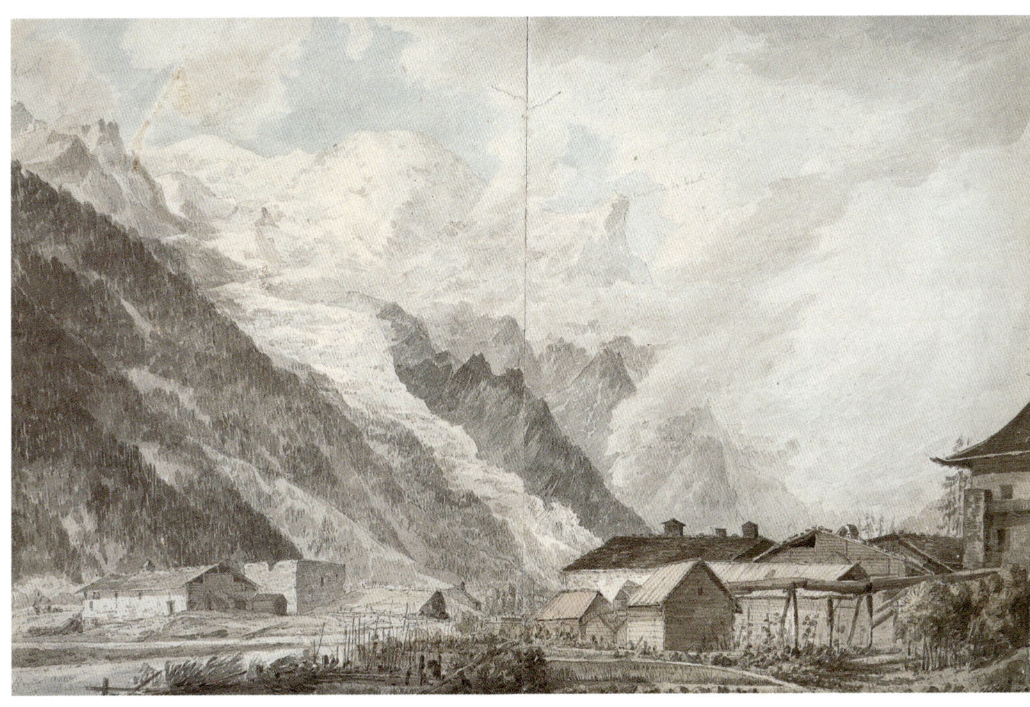

COX, DAVID
The Welsh Funeral, Bettws-y-Coed,
Caernarvonshire, Wales
1847–49
Agnew's (purchase, 1919) (D.1919.7)

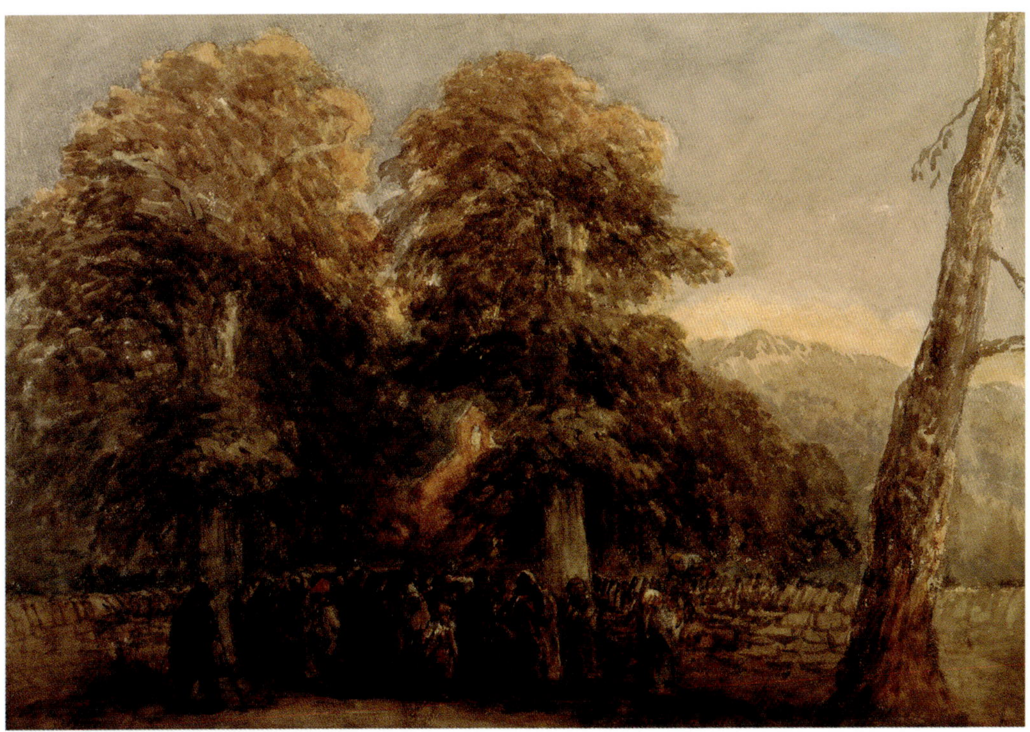

PALMER, SAMUEL
**Calypso's Island, Departure of
Ulysses, or Farewell to Calypso**
1848–49
Haworth, Jesse (bequest, 1937) (D.1937.17)

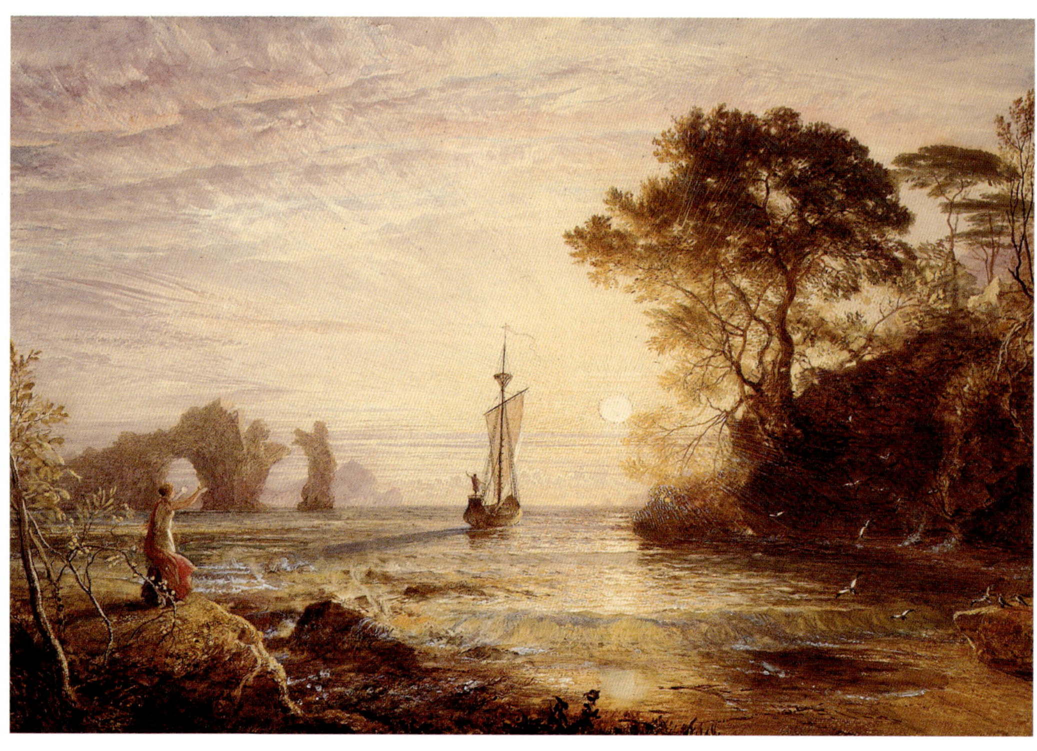

BODICHON, BARBARA
Ireland-1846
1846
Crabbe, John (purchase, 1994) (D.1994.1)

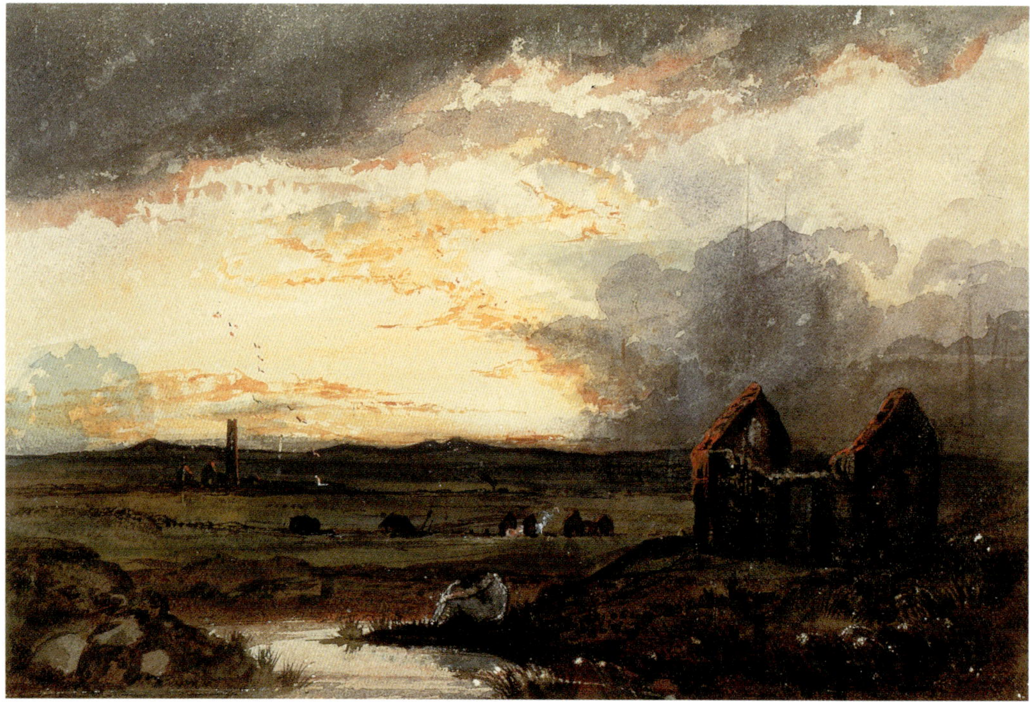

WALKER, FREDERICK
The Well Sinkers
1868
Agnew, Sir William (gift, 1906) (D.1906.2)

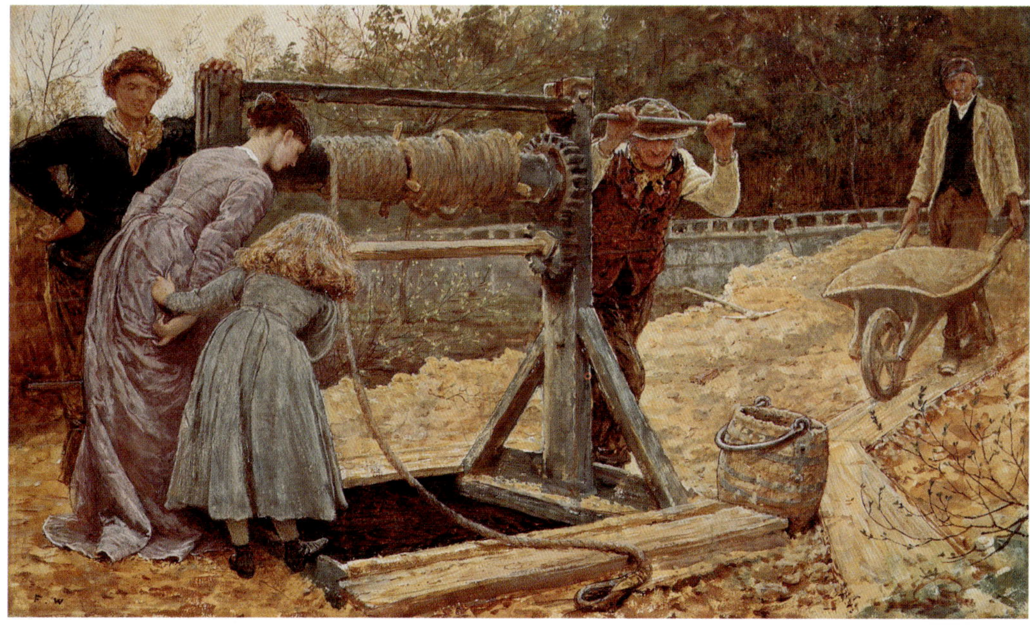

BOYCE, GEORGE PRICE
Yanwath Hall, Cumbria
1884
Anthony Reed Ltd (purchase, 1988) (D.1988.12)

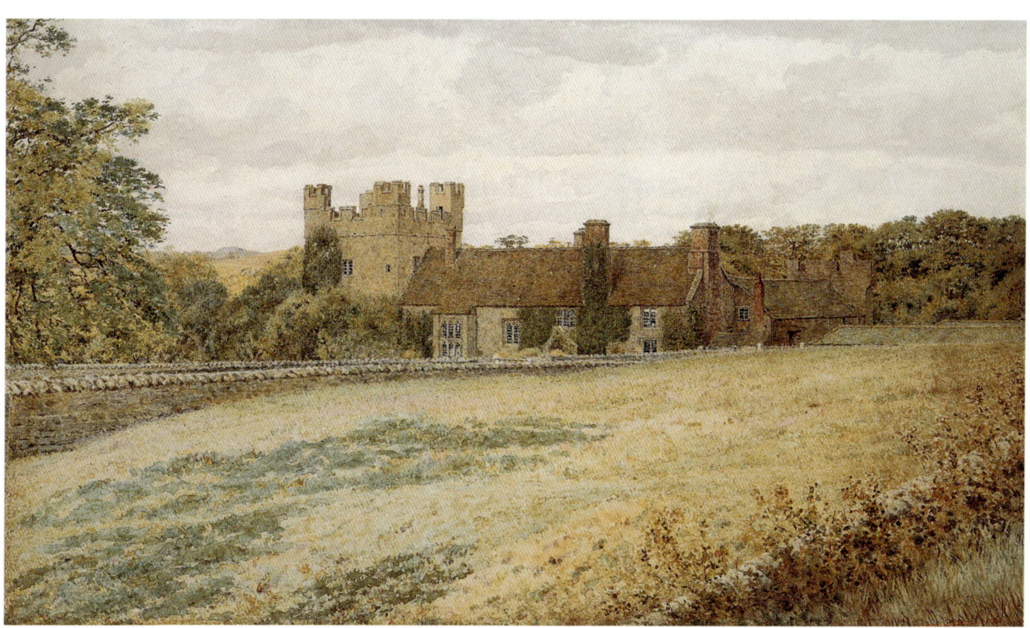

INCHBOLD, JOHN WILLIAM
**A Mediterranean Port,
possibly Algiers**
1877
Agnew's (purchase, 1992) (V. & A., F.O.W.)
(D.1992.3)

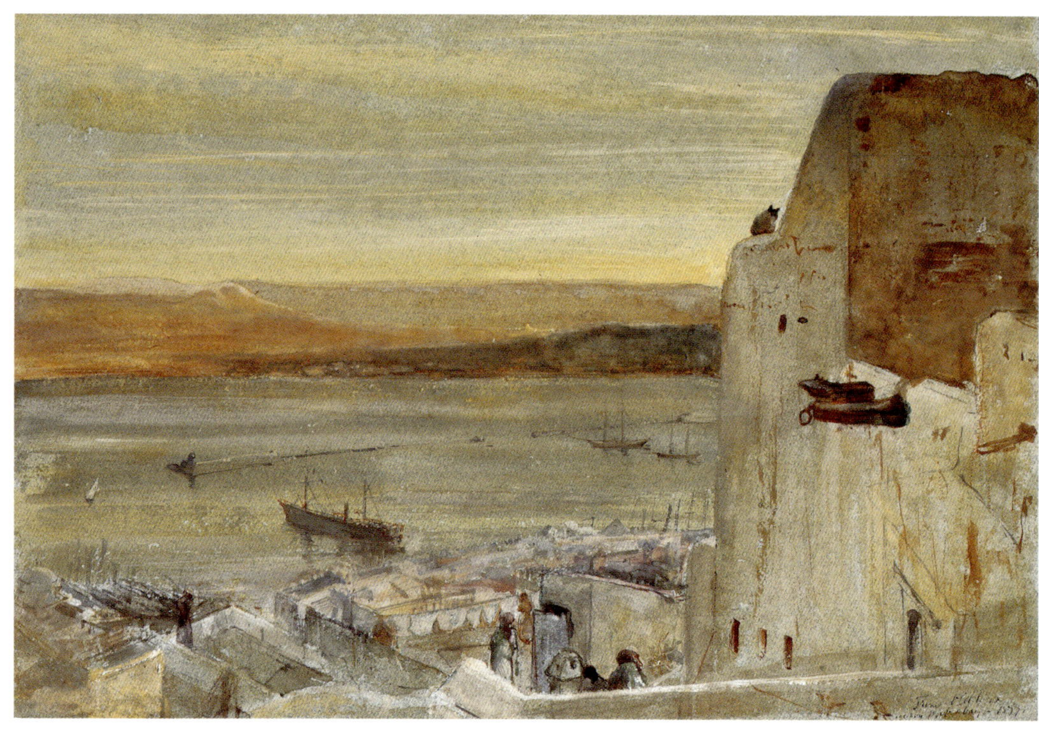

BRETT, JOHN EDWARD
**River Scene, near Goring-on-Thames,
Oxfordshire**
1865
Friends of the Whitworth (gift, 1965)
(D.1965.11)

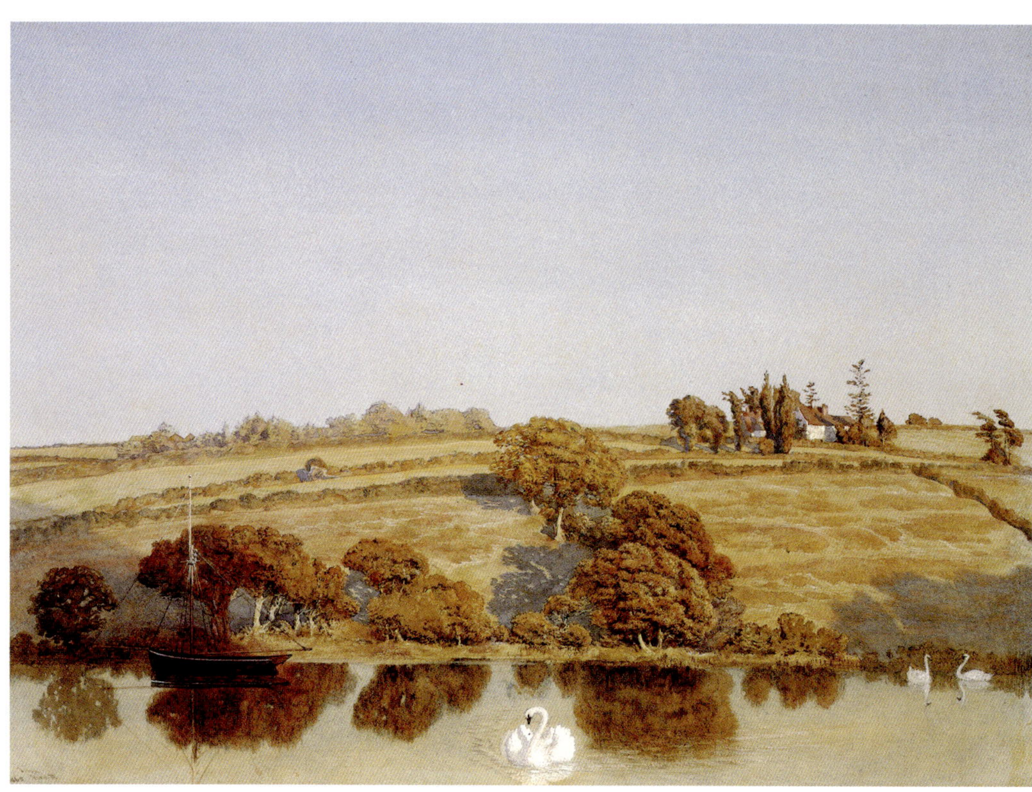

HUNT, WILLIAM HOLMAN
View of Nazareth
1855 and 1860–61
Haworth, J. G. (family of) (gift, 1961)
(D.1961.5)

BELOW
MILLAIS, SIR JOHN EVERETT
The Black Brunswicker
1867
Haworth, Jesse (bequest, 1937) (D.1937.16)

BELOW, RIGHT
ROSSETTI, DANTE GABRIEL
La Donna della Finestra
1870
Thomson, D. Croal (purchase, 1921)
(D.1921.35)

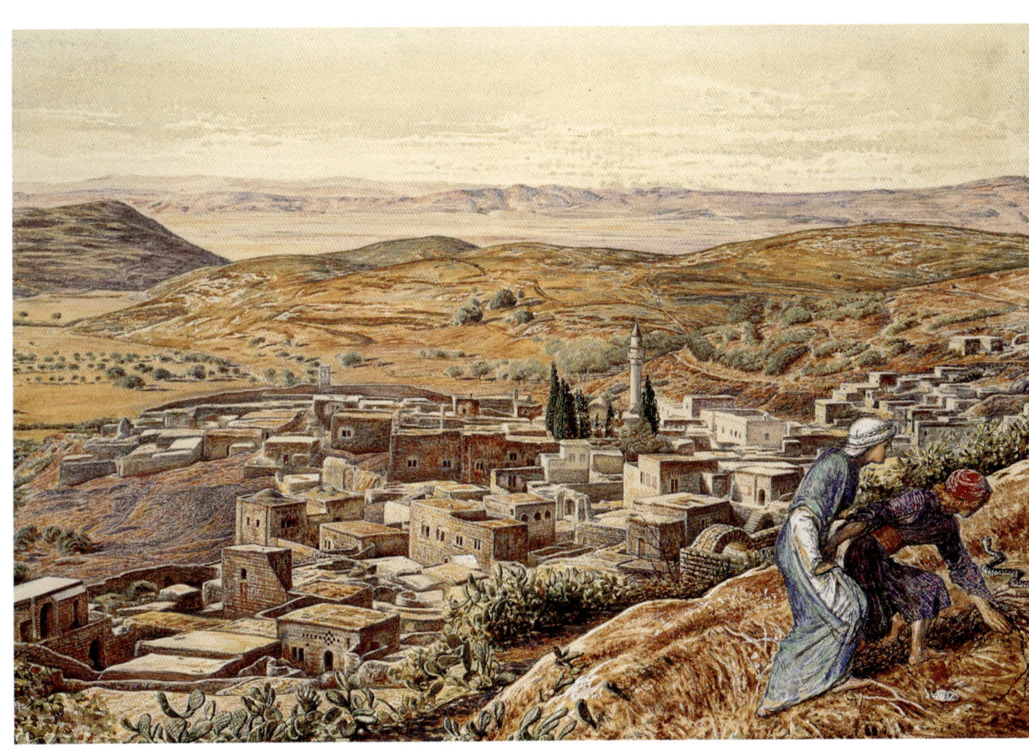

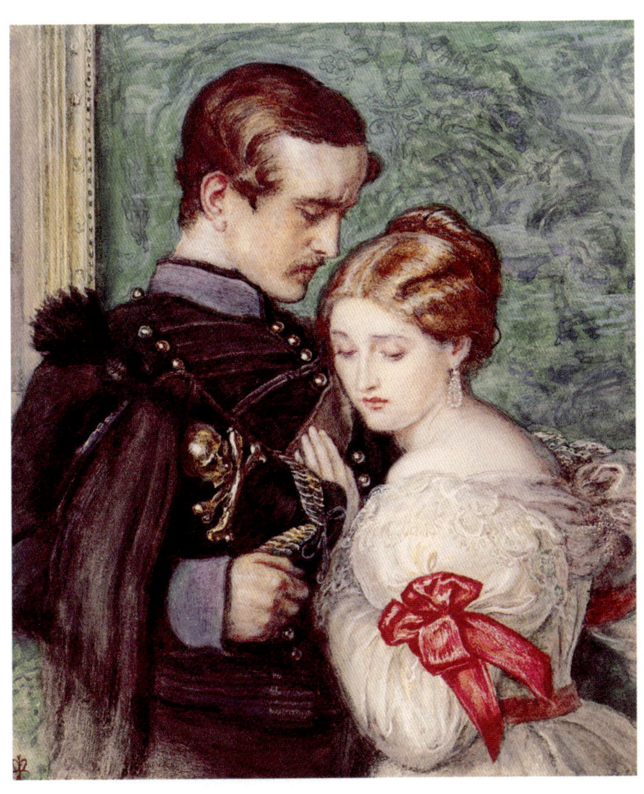

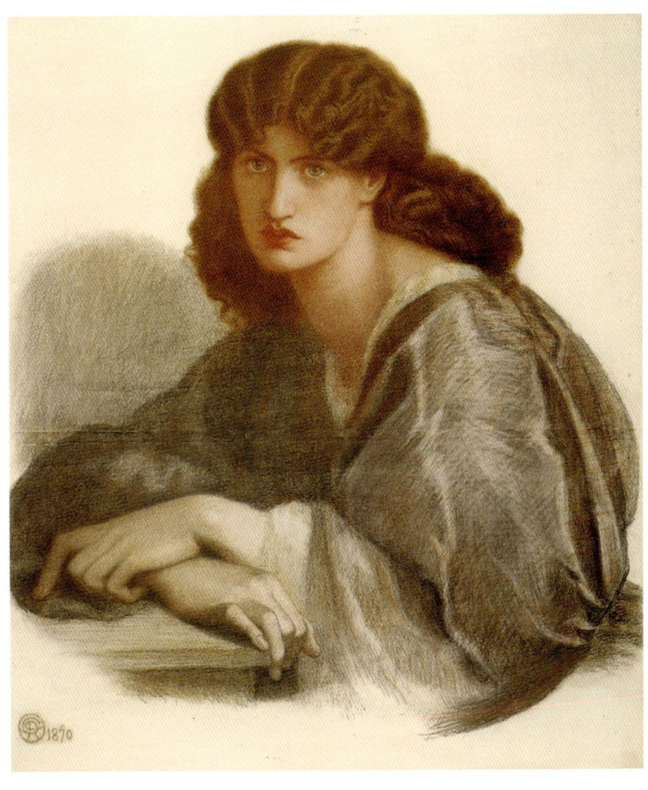

**BURNE-JONES, SIR
EDWARD COLEY**
**Venus Concordia, Study for the
Predella Panel of 'The Story of Troy'**
1871
Leicester Galleries, London (purchase, 1921)
(D.1921.32)

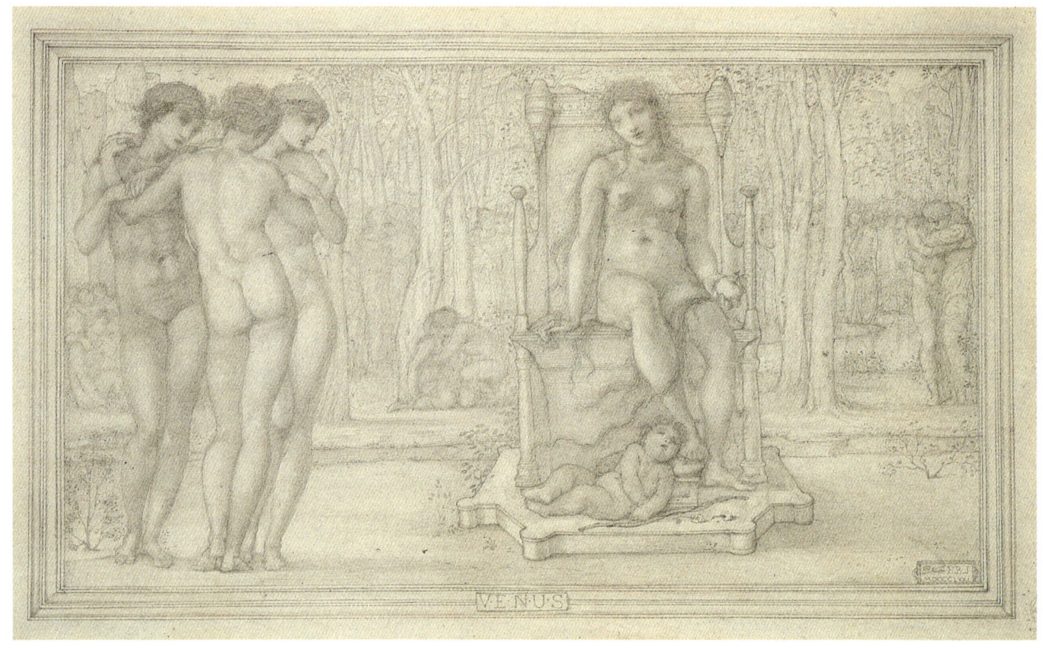

**BURNE-JONES, SIR
EDWARD COLEY**
**Venus Discordia, Study for the
Predella Panel of 'The Story of Troy'**
1871
Leicester Galleries, London (purchase, 1921)
(D.1921.34)

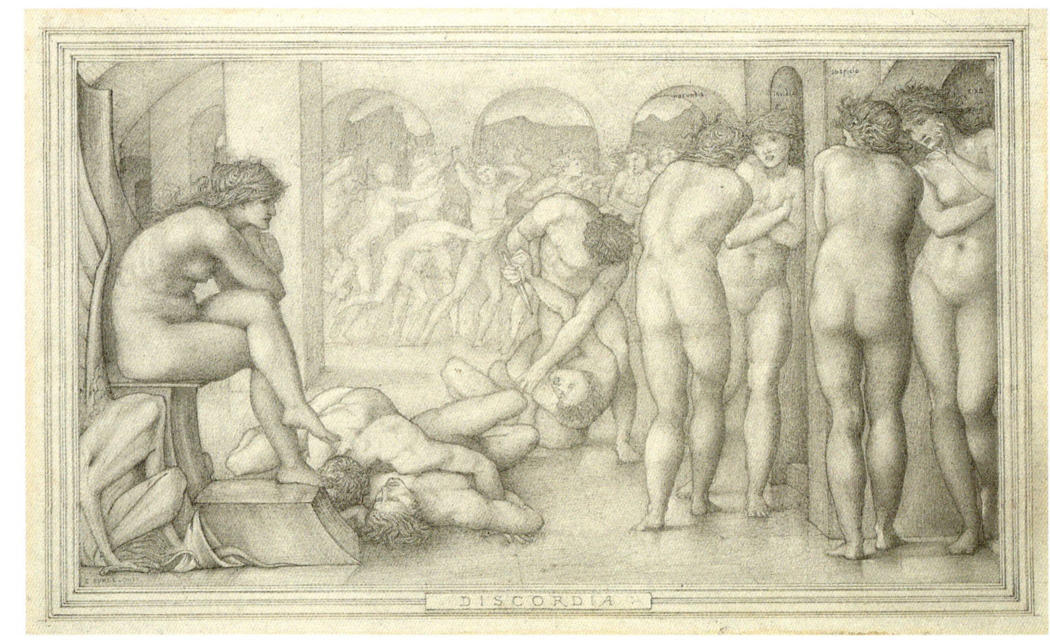

HUNT, CECIL ARTHUR
**Bunratty Castle,
Co. Limerick, Ireland**
1938
Hunt, Cecil Arthur (gift, 1939) (D.1939.14)

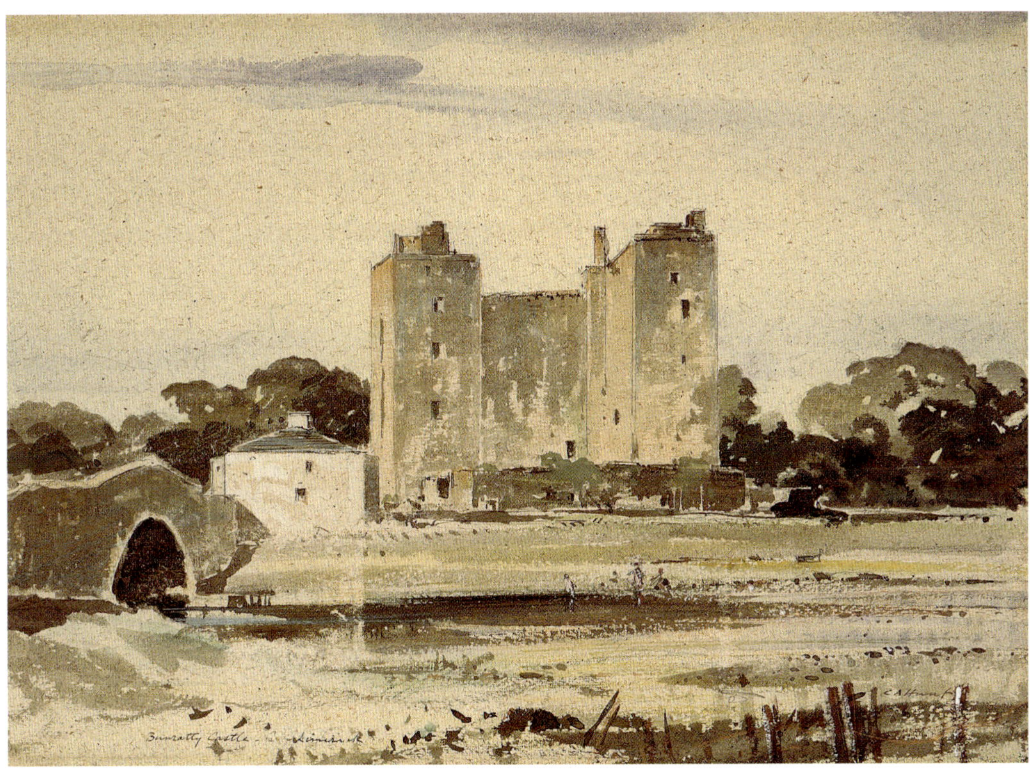

ALLAN, ROBERT WEIR
Middleton Church, Manchester
1892
untraced (purchase, 1892) (D.1892.154)

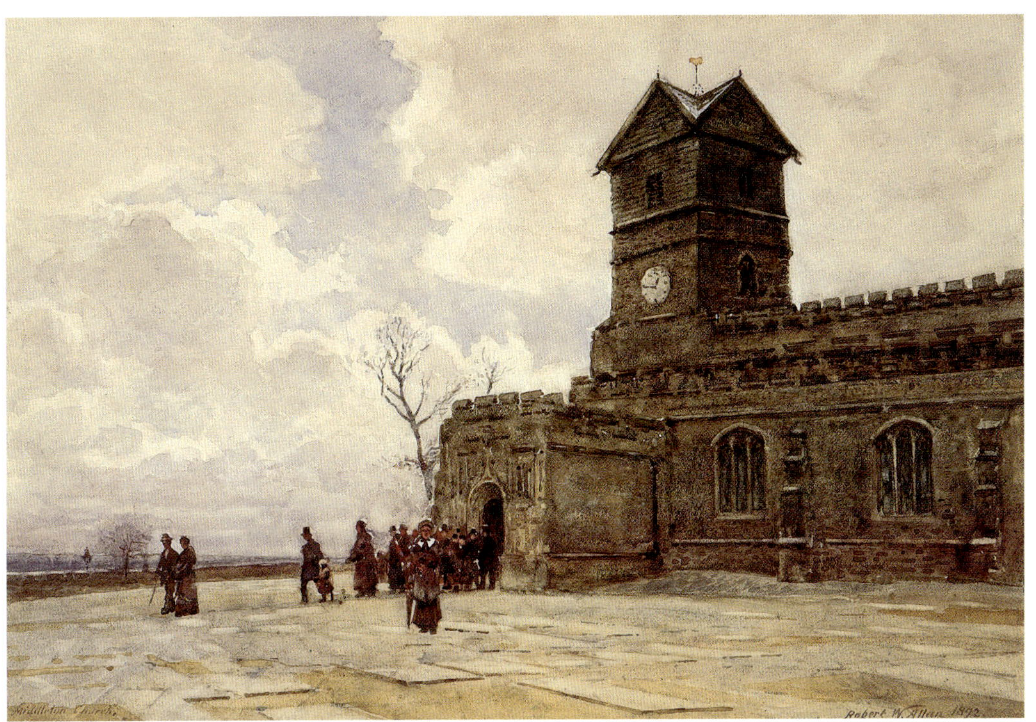

TUCKER, ARTHUR
Kentmere Hall, Westmorland
untraced (purchase, 1901) (D.1901.4)

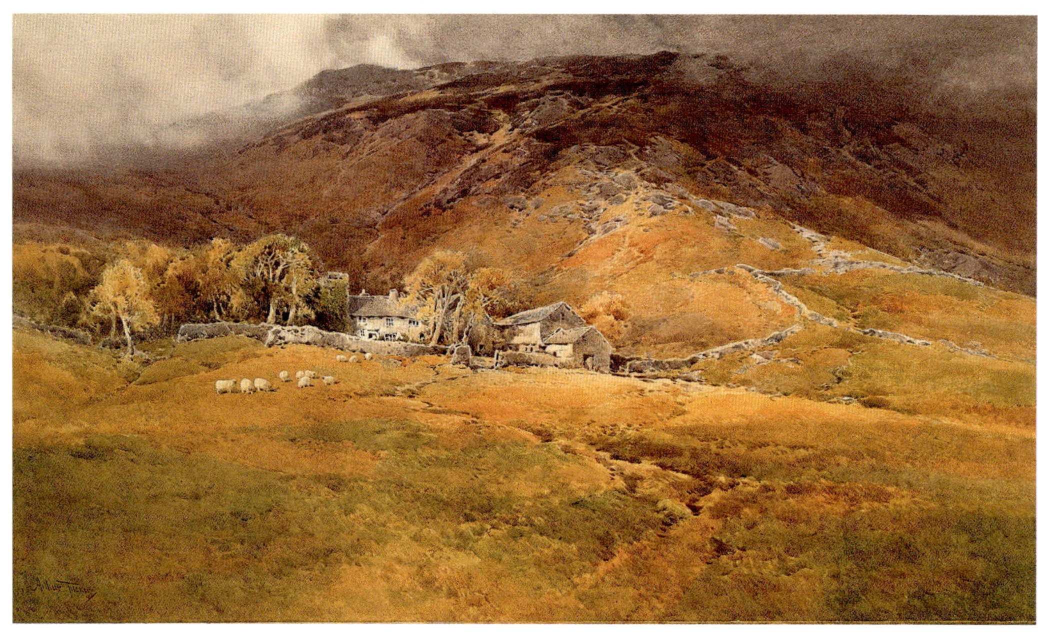

LANCASTER, PERCY
**Travellers Rest, at the Head of
Kirkstone Pass, Westmorland**
1943
Pilkington, Denis F. (gift, 1944) (D.1944.5)

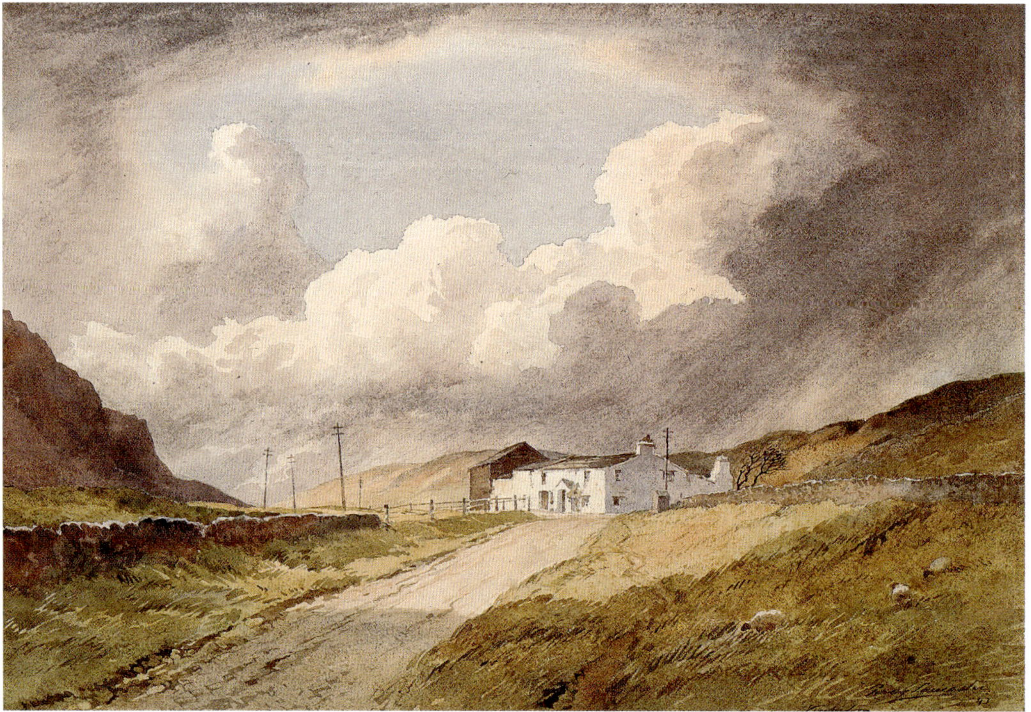

Catalogue

■ **ABBOTT, JOHN WHITE (1763–1851)**

Abbott is by far the most significant of the amateur pupils of Francis Towne. Based in Exeter, he showed regularly at the Royal Academy as an honorary exhibitor between 1793 and 1805 and again between 1810 and 1822. His landscapes are almost all views of Devonshire. He was also a prolific copyist.

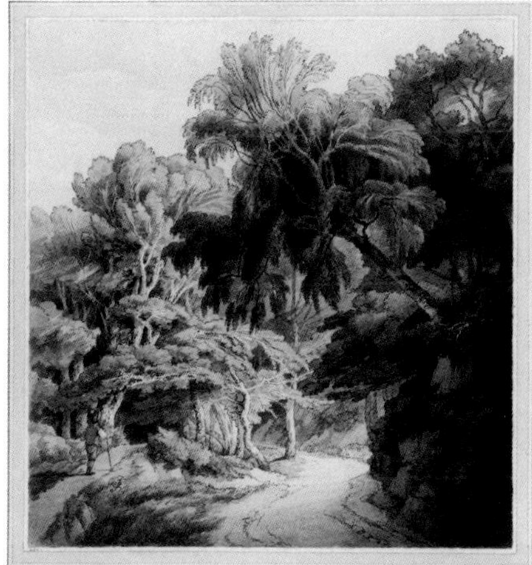

D.1938.12

Study of Trees at Timberscombe, Somerset
31.5.1800
pen and brown ink, watercolour
signed & dated on reverse of mount: *Timberscombe – Somerset / J W A. May 31.1800.*; numbered on lower left of mount: *XXVI*
252 × 230 mm
Pilkington, Margaret, Friends of the Whitworth (via) (gift, 1938) (D.1938.12)

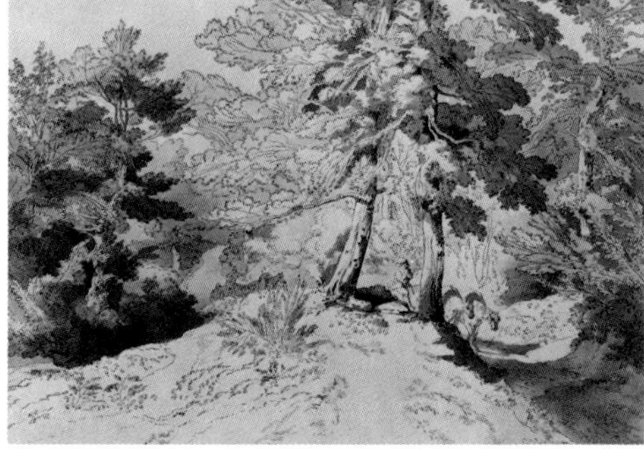

D.1952.2

Scene in a Wood near Canonteign, Devon
25.9.1805
pen and grey ink, grey watercolour
inscribed & dated upper left verso: *near* [virtually erased] *Canonteign. Sept.25 1805*
271 × 378 mm
Pilkington, Margaret (gift, 1952) (D.1952.2)

Hagar and the Angel
20.6.1828
pencil, pen and grey ink, grey watercolour
dated lower left: *June 20. 1828*
190 × 305 mm
Berwick Fine Art, Shrewsbury (Christopher Powney) (purchase, 1993) (D.1993.10)

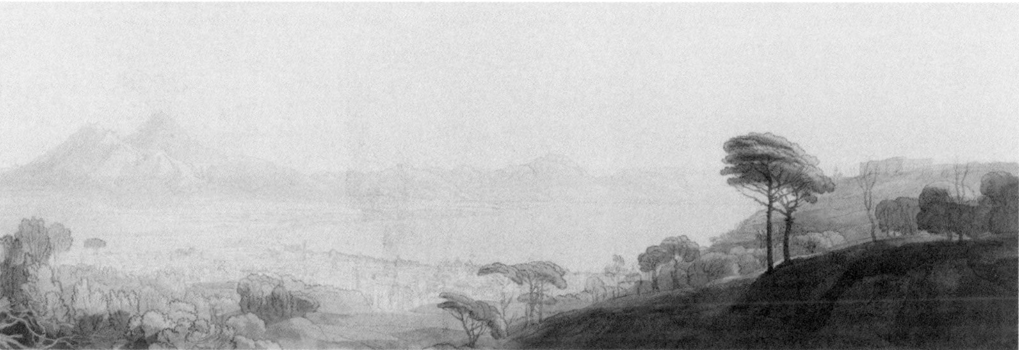

D.2001.6

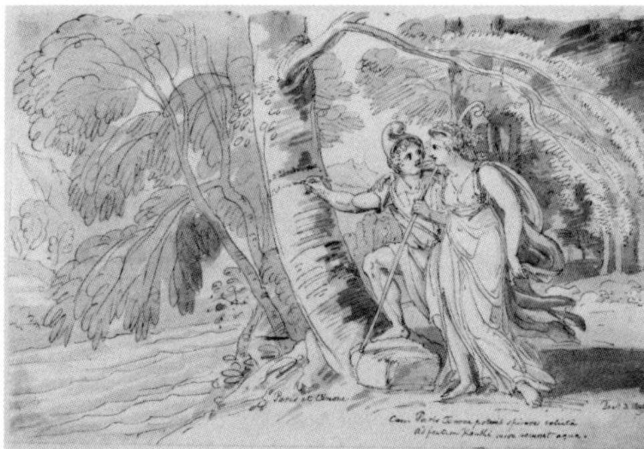

D.1993.10

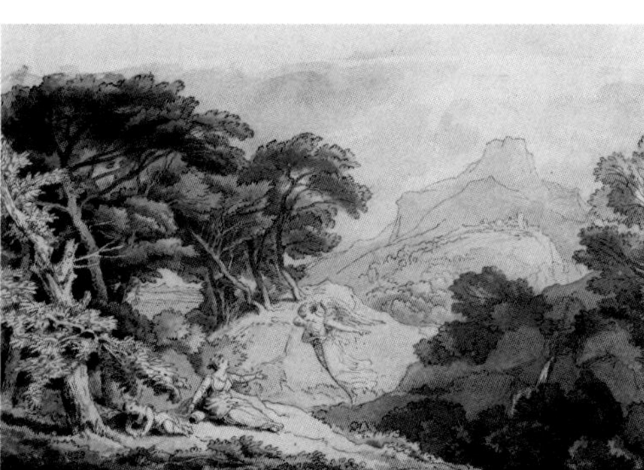

D.1993.11

Paris and Oenone
3.12.1809
pencil, pen and brown ink, brown watercolour
dated lower right: *Decr. 3.1809;* inscribed lower centre: *Paris et Oenone;* inscribed lower right: *Cum Paris Oenone poterit spirare relicta / Ad fontem Xanthi versa recurret aqua.*
187 × 276 mm
Berwick Fine Art, Shrewsbury (Christopher Powney) (purchase, 1993) (D.1993.11)

Study of Trees at Canonteign, Devon
14.6.1800
pen and brown ink, watercolour; two joined sheets
signed, inscribed & dated upper centre verso with intials: *Canonteign Devon June 14.1800 / JWA*
337 × 367 mm
Sotheby's, London (purchase, 2001) (V. & A., N.A.C.F., F.O.W.) (D.2001.5)

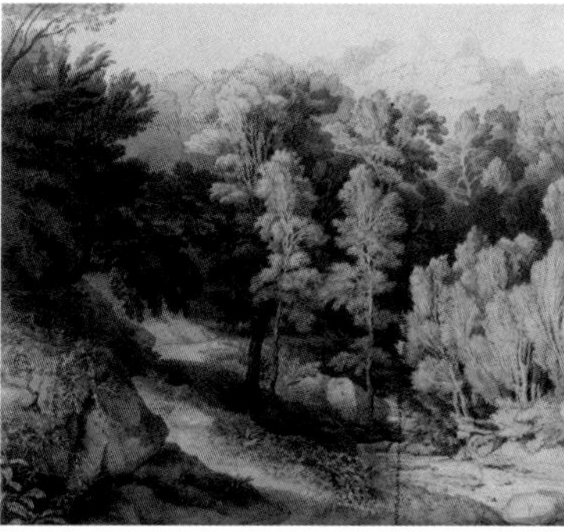

D.2001.5

The Bay of Naples, after Francis Towne
pen and brown ink, watercolour; two joined sheets; watermark JWHATMAN 1813
signed & inscribed verso with initials: *Naples. Vesuvius – Mount Lactarius – St. Martin & Castle St. Elmo. / F.T. JWA*
310 × 944 mm
Friends of the Whitworth (gift) (D.2001.6)

■ **ADAM, ROBERT (1728–92)**

Robert Adam is best known as a prolific and influential neo-classical architect. Having completed a lengthy Grand Tour in 1758, Adam was the most fashionable architect in England during the 1760s and '70s. His imaginative watercolours often show the influence of Paul Sandby, with whom he was acquainted.

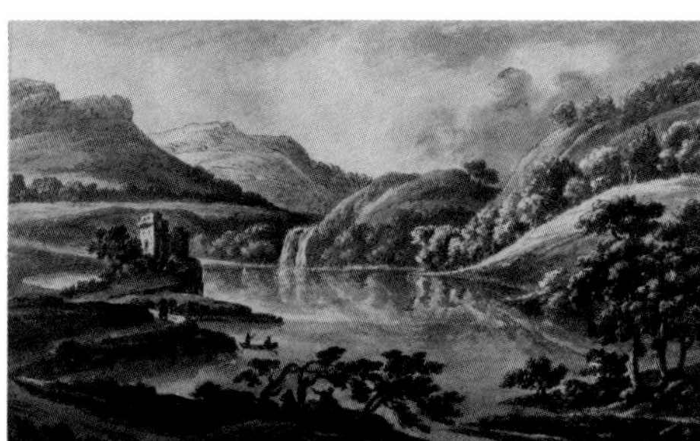

D.1938.11

An imaginary Landscape with a Castle above a Lake with a Waterfall
pen and brown ink, watercolour
308 × 507 mm
Pilkington, Margaret, Friends of the Whitworth (via) (gift, 1938) (D.1938.11)

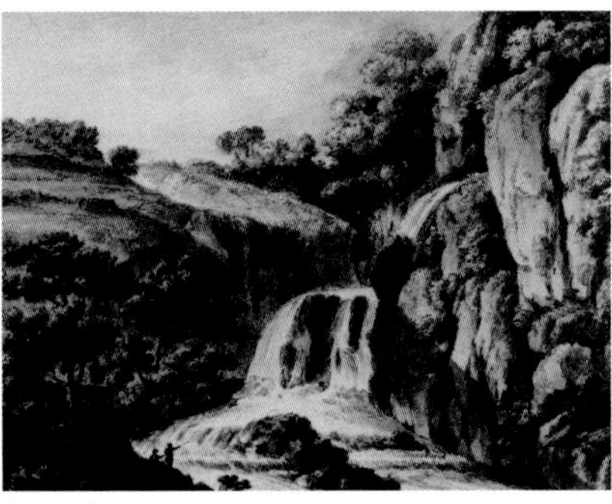

D.1970.6

Landscape with a Waterfall
1784
pen and brown ink, watercolour
signed & dated on mount lower left: *Robt Adam Invt delint.1784.*
254 × 309 mm
Towlson, Hector J. (bequest, 1969) (D.1970.6)

■ AGLIO, AGOSTINO (1777–1857)

Aglio was an Italian artist who settled in England in 1803. He worked as a scene painter, decorator and landscape painter. His drawings were influenced by – and are sometimes mistaken for – the work of John Constable.

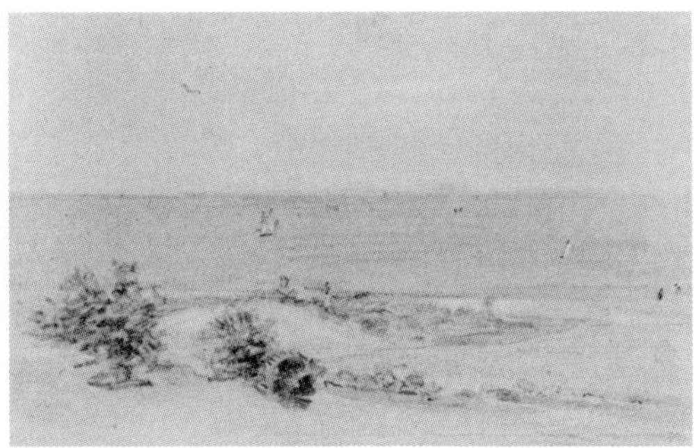

D.1996.4

Coast Scene near Brighton
pencil, black chalk, white chalk, blue watercolour, yellow watercolour; light blue paper
signed (?) lower right with monogram (?): *AA*
118 × 185 mm
University of Manchester, Picture Loan Scheme (transfer, 1996) (D.1996.4)

■ ALEXANDER, WILLIAM (1767–1816)

Alexander was one of the official draughtsmen to Lord Macartney's Embassy to China in 1792 and many of his watercolours derive from this famous trip. In 1802 he was appointed Professor of Drawing at the Royal Military College at Great Marlow and in 1808 he became Keeper of Prints and Drawings at the British Museum.

A Barge approaching a Glacis, near Ning-po, China
II.1793
pencil, watercolour
signed lower right: *W A*; dated on reverse of backing: *November 1793*
241 × 373 mm
Worthington, Mary (gift, 1899) (D.1899.4)

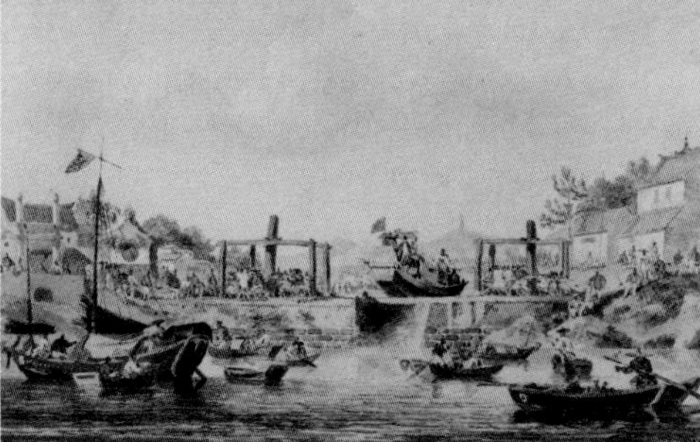

D.1899.4

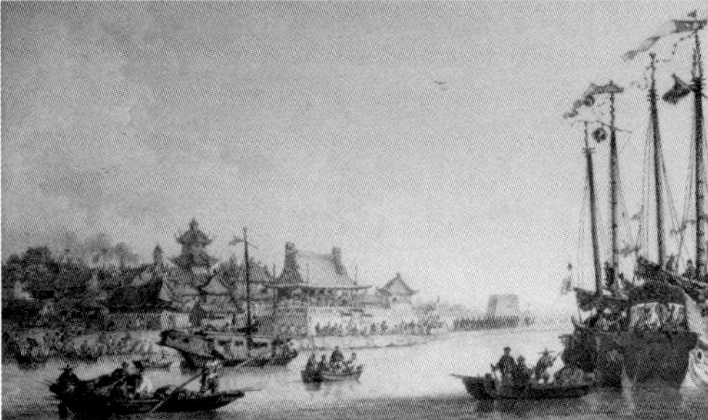

D.1955.4

River Scene, Tientsin, China, on the Occasion of Lord Macartney's Embassy to China
1796
pencil, watercolour
signed & dated lower right: *WAlexander 96*
286 × 457 mm
Lupton, Katharine C., Friends of the Whitworth (via) (gift, 1955) (D.1955.4)

■ ALKEN, HENRY THOMAS (1785–1851)

H. T. Alken is the best known of a large family of sporting artists which spanned several generations. He specialised in sporting – particularly hunting – scenes, and much of his work has been reproduced.

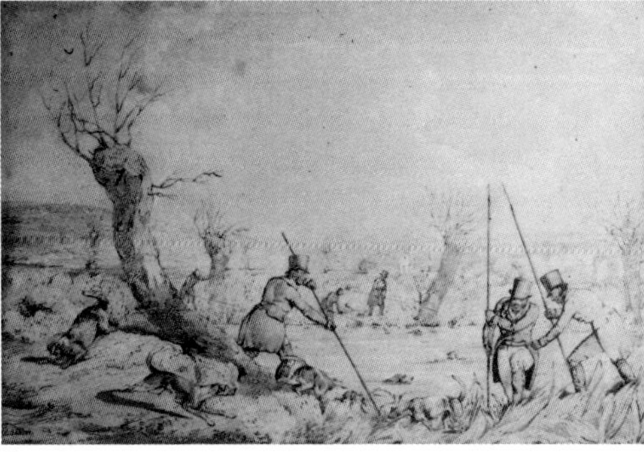

D.1892.72

Otter hunting
pencil, watercolour
signed lower left: *H.Alken*
235 × 338 mm
Taylor, John Edward (gift, 1892) (D.1892.72)

■ ALKEN, SAMUEL (1784–1825)

The brother of H. T. Alken, Samuel Alken concentrated on the same kind of subject matter. There is much confusion between the various members of the Alken family owing to the similarity of their styles and subjects.

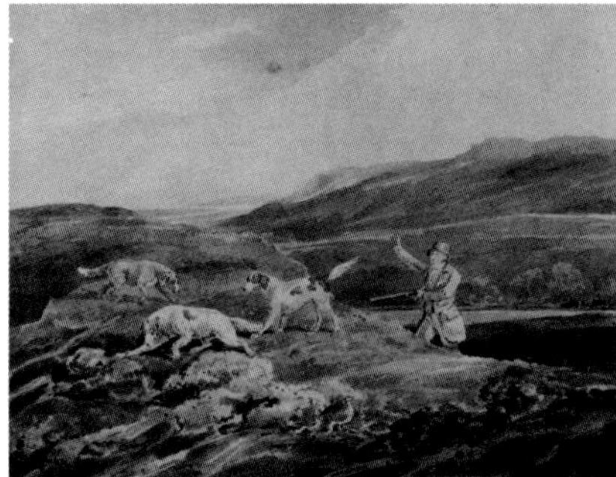

D.1892.22

Grouse Shooting
pencil, watercolour
310 × 392 mm
Taylor, John Edward (gift, 1892) (D.1892.22)

■ ALLAN, ROBERT WEIR (1851–1942)

Born in Glasgow, Allan studied in Paris before coming to London in 1881. Elected an associate of the Royal Watercolour Society in 1887 and a full member in 1896, he travelled extensively in Europe. He also visited India from 1890 to 1892 and Japan in 1907.

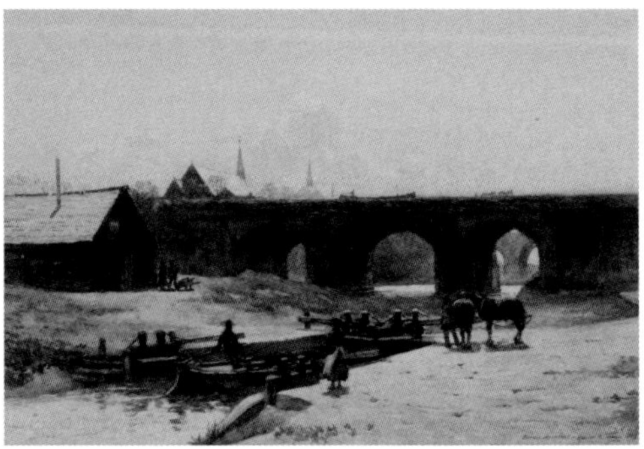

D.1892.153

Barton Aqueduct on the Worsley-Manchester Canal
1892
watercolour
signed, inscribed & dated lower right: *Barton Aqueduct – Robert W.Allan 1892*
531 × 762 mm
untraced (purchase, 1892) (D.1892.153)

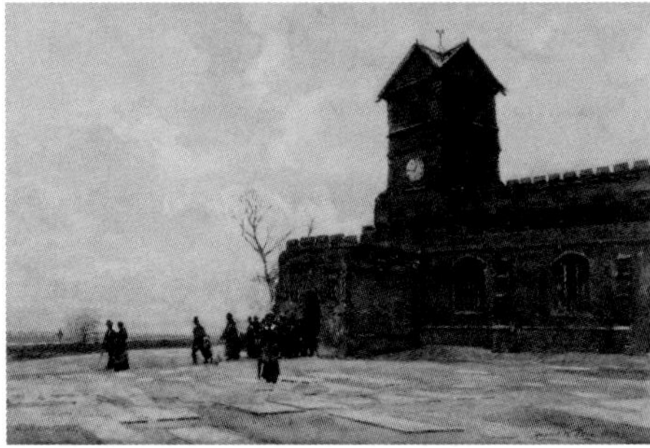

D.1892.154

Middleton Church, Manchester
1892
watercolour
signed & dated lower right: *Robert W.Allan 1892*; inscribed lower left: *Middleton Church*
367 × 526 mm
untraced (purchase, 1892) (D.1892.154)

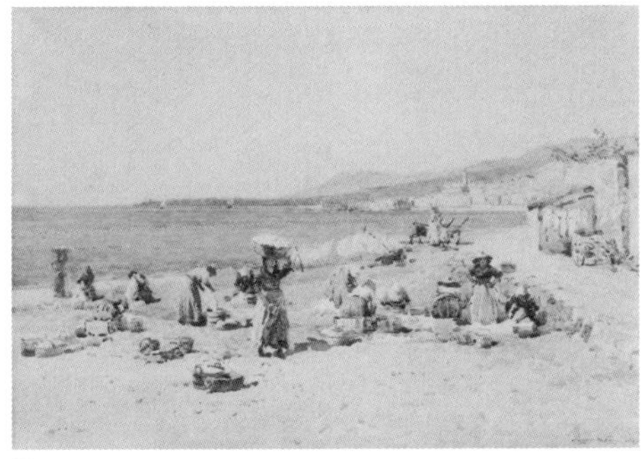

D.1902.10

Toil amidst Sunshine
1899
watercolour
signed & dated lower right: *Robert W.Allan.1899*
534 × 761 mm
untraced (purchase, 1902) (D.1902.10)

■ **ALLEN, JOSEPH WILLIAM** (1803–52)
Allen began his career as a theatrical scene painter in London before exhibiting at the New Watercolour Society and becoming the first drawing master at the City of London School.

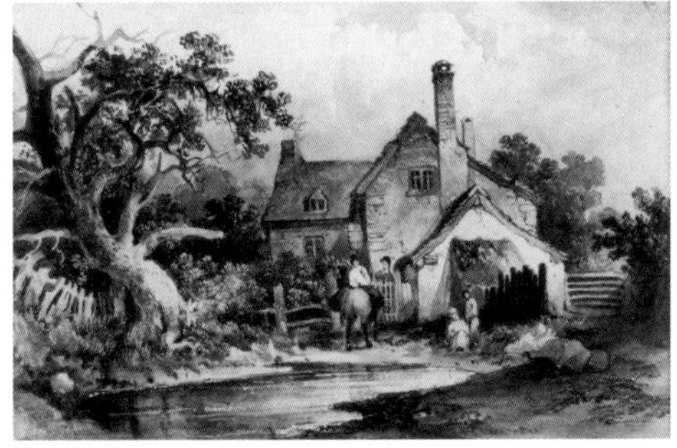

D.1948.9

Figures beside a House among Trees
watercolour
161 × 235 mm
Nettlefold, F. J. (gift, 1948) (D.1948.9)

■ **ALLINGHAM, HELEN** (1848–1926)
Allingham studied at Birmingham and the Royal Academy Schools and began her career working for the *Graphic*. She married the Irish poet William Allingham in 1874 and was elected an associate of the Royal Watercolour Society in 1875 and a full member in 1890. She specialised in Surrey and Berkshire cottages and gardens.

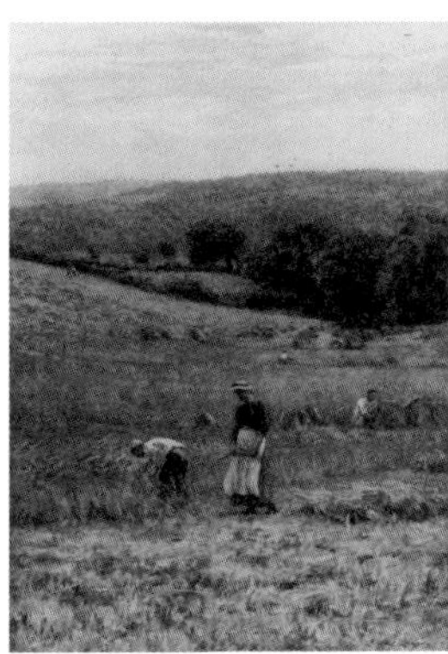

D.1937.9

Harvest Field, near Westerham, Kent
watercolour
signed lower right: *H.Allingham*
254 × 177 mm
Haworth, Jesse (bequest, 1937) (D.1937.9)

■ **ANDERSON, WILLIAM** (1757–1837)
Born in Scotland, Anderson came to London and became a marine painter in both oil and watercolour. He exhibited at the Royal Academy from 1787 to 1834, specialising in small river and sea views.

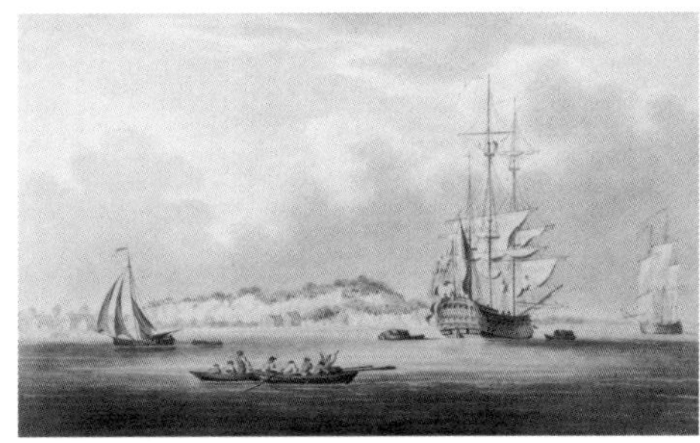

D.1970.7

Coast Scene with Shipping
pencil, watercolour, gum arabic
182 × 291 mm
Towlson, Hector J. (bequest, 1969) (D.1970.7)

■ **ANDREWS, GEORGE HENRY** (1816–98)
Andrews was both an engineer and a landscape and marine painter who worked for the *Illustrated London News* and the *Graphic*. He illustrated the Prince of Wales's tour of Canada and the United States in 1860 for the *Illustrated London News* and covered the Franco-Prussian war for the *Graphic*. He was elected an associate of the Old Watercolour Society in 1856 and a full member in 1878.

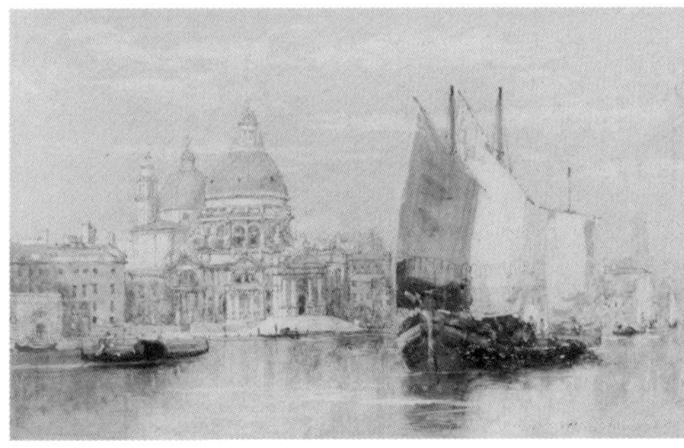

D.1970.8

The Church of Santa Maria della Salute, Venice
1875
pencil, watercolour, bodycolour
signed & dated lower right: *G.H.Andrews 75*
164 × 257 mm
Towlson, Hector J. (gift, 1969) (D.1970.8)

■ **ANGELL, HELEN CORDELIA** (1847–84)
Angell, sister of the artist W. S. Coleman, was a flower painter who began her career working for Minton's. In 1879 she became Flower Painter in Ordinary to the Queen.

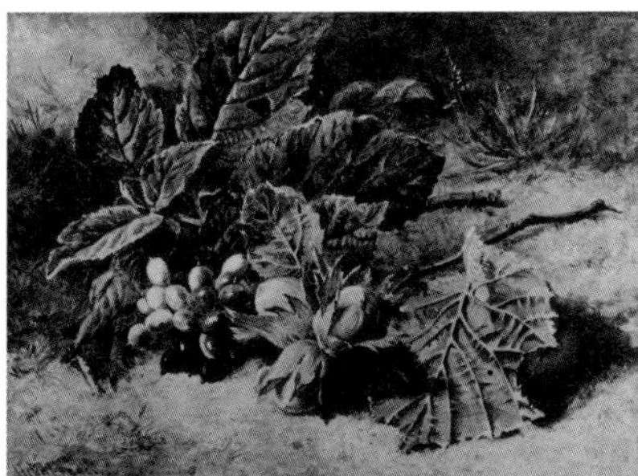

D.1970.9

Nuts and Berries
watercolour, bodycolour (heightened with white)
signed lower left: *Helen C.Angell*
151 × 210 mm
Towlson, Hector J. (bequest, 1969) (D.1970.9)

■ **ARCHER, G.** (dates unknown)
Unknown amateur artist.

An Oak Tree (recto); Landscape Sketch (verso)
1820
black chalk, white chalk (recto); blue paper
signed lower right: *G.Archer*; dated lower left: 1820
266 × 350 mm
Ogden, William Sharp (bequest, 1926) (D.1926.316)

■ **ARTAUD, WILLIAM** (1763–1823)
Artaud was the son of a Huguenot jeweller, and first exhibited at the Royal Academy in 1780. A portrait and history painter, he travelled through Italy from 1795 to 1799. His works were among those engraved in Macklin's illustrated Bible of 1800.

Study of a Child's Head; Copy of a Detail from Reynold's 'Heads of Angels Miss Frances Isabella Gordon'
black chalk, grey watercolour
watermark: 8-pointed star
356 × 296 mm
Ogden, William Sharp (bequest, 1926) (D.1926.184)

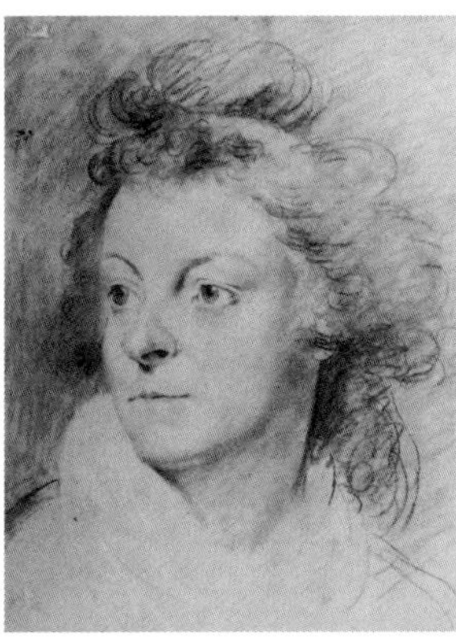

D.1972.17

Portrait Study of Susanna Tayler, the Artist's Sister
1794–96
black chalk, white chalk; buff paper
inscribed (later hand) lower centre verso:
Mrs. Wager TAYLER / nee Anna Susanna ARTAUD /
(the artist's sister) *c.1795*
366 × 276 mm
Tayler, Mrs E. M. (gift, 1972) (D.1972.17)

Portrait Study of a Man, perhaps Wager Tayler, the Artist's Brother-in-law (recto); Half-Length Study of a Man (verso)
black chalk, white chalk (recto); buff paper
inscribed lower centre verso in later hand: *perhaps Wager TAYLER*
459 × 295 mm
Tayler, Mrs E. M. (gift, 1972) (D.1972.18)

Portrait Study of a Man, a Member of the Wood Family, probably John Wood
pastel; brown paper
inscribed on lower right verso in later hand: *Member of the Wood family / probably John WOOD*
505 × 333 mm
Tayler, Mrs E. M. (gift, 1972) (D.1972.19)

Study of a Woman's Hand resting on a Book
black chalk, white chalk, red chalk; cream paper
208 × 241 mm
Tayler, Mrs E. M. (gift, 1972) (D.1972.20)

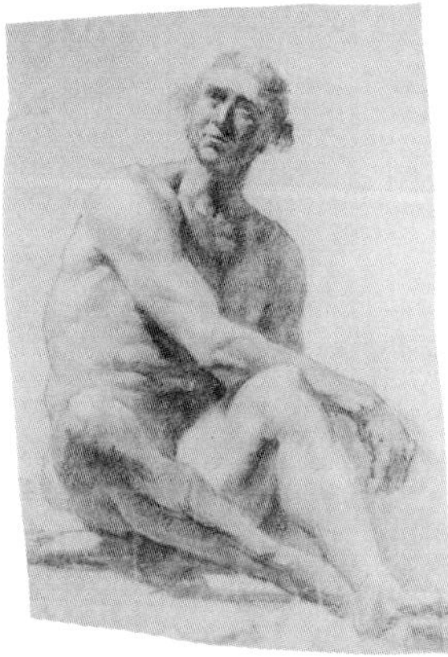

D.1972.21

Study of a seated male Nude
black chalk, white chalk; blue-grey paper
308 × 198 mm
Tayler, Mrs E. M. (gift, 1972) (D.1972.21)

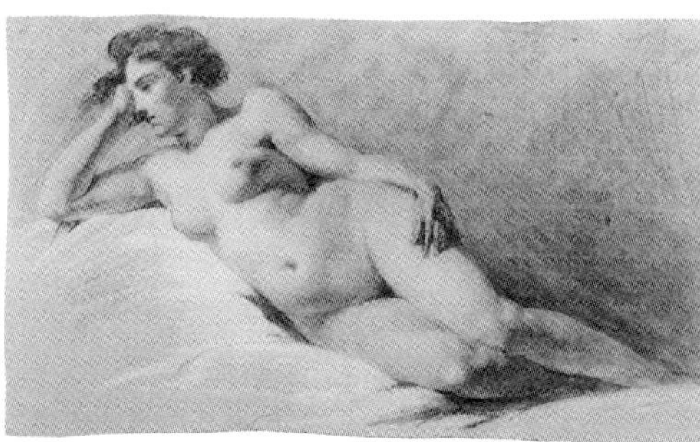

D.1972.22

Study of a reclining female Nude
black chalk, white chalk; blue-grey paper
244 × 401 mm
Tayler, Mrs E. M. (gift, 1972) (D.1972.22)

The Flight into Egypt
9.1813
pen and brown ink, brown watercolour
signed, inscribed & dated centre verso: *Flight into Egypt* [erased] / *Flight into Egypt / Wm Artaud / Pinxit / September 1813*
315 × 267 mm
Tayler, Mrs E. M. (gift, 1972) (D.1972.23)

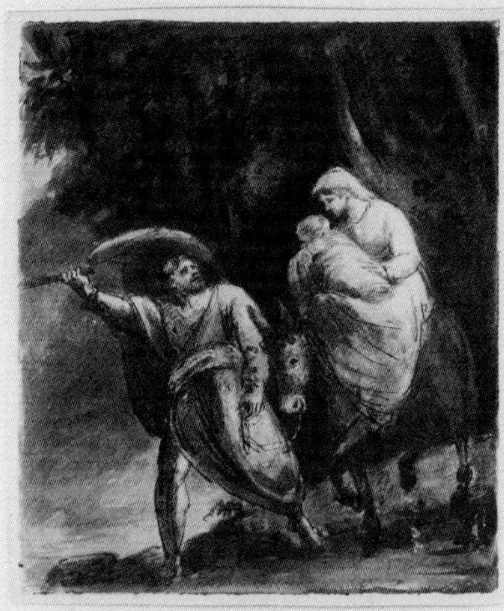

D.1972.23

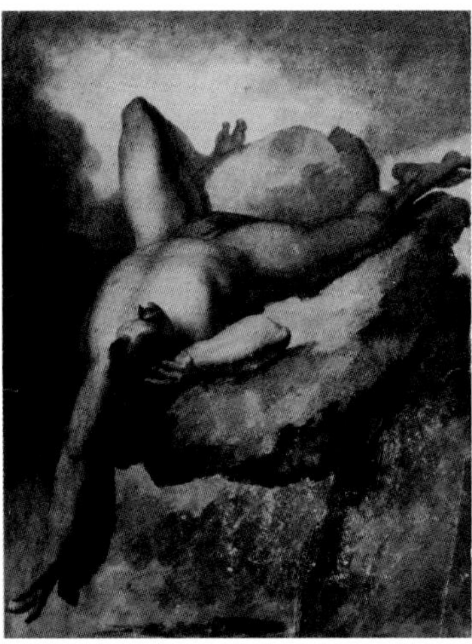

D.1972.24

'Danger', from Collins' 'Ode to Fear'
pencil, watercolour; buff paper
inscribed centre verso: *Danger. from Colins* (sic) *Ode to Fear*
412 × 303 mm
Tayler, Mrs E. M. (gift, 1972) (D.1972.24)

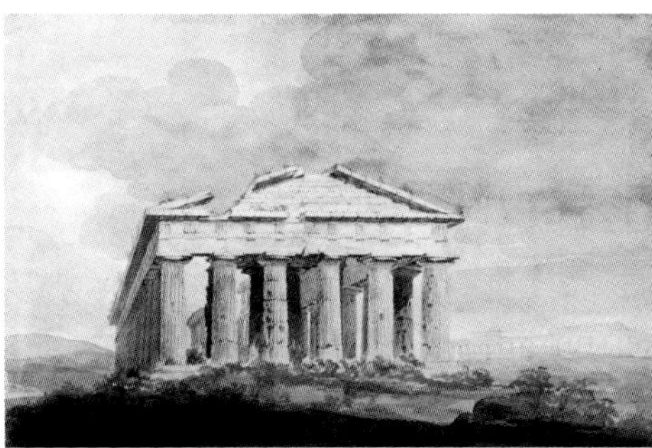

D.1972.25

The Temple of Hera II at Paestum
1797
pencil, watercolour
301 × 438 mm
Tayler, Mrs E. M. (gift, 1972) (D.1972.25)

Portrait of a Gentleman, bust length
black chalk, white chalk; buff paper
457 × 305 mm
Sewter, Albert Charles (bequest, 1983) (D.1983.5)

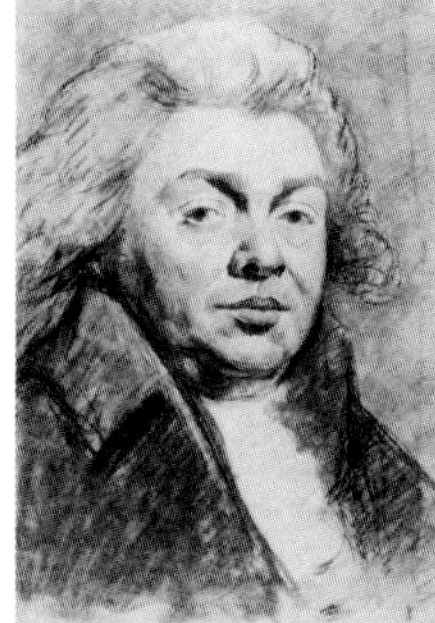

D.1983.5

■ ATKINS, SAMUEL (fl. 1787–1808)

Little is known of Atkins, a prolific marine watercolour painter who exhibited at the Royal Academy between 1787 and 1808. According to Martin Hardie, he lived in the East Indies from 1796 to 1804.

Dutch Vessels off a Harbour
pen and grey ink, watercolour
signed on a piece of wood lower left: *S Atkins*
238 × 343 mm
Taylor, John Edward (gift, 1892) (D.1892.47)

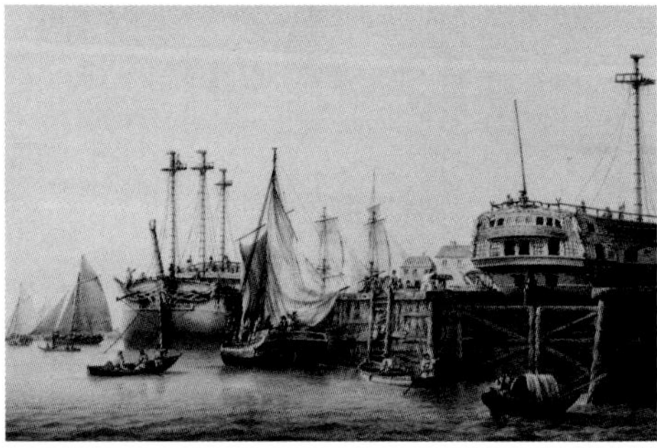

D.1892.143

Docks at Deptford, Kent
watercolour
signed on plank lower right: *Atkins*
367 × 542 mm
Taylor, John Edward (gift, 1892) (D.1892.143)

Leaving Port
pen and grey ink, watercolour; oval
signed lower right: *Atkins*
228 × 331 mm
Worthington, Mary (gift, 1899) (D.1899.2)

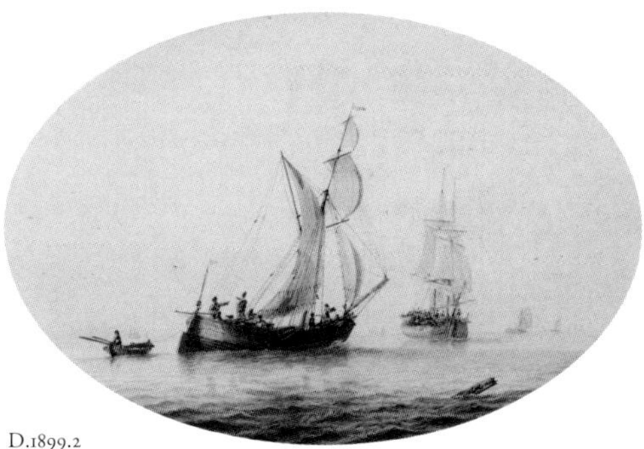

D.1899.2

Ships at Anchor off Dover
pen and grey ink, watercolour; oval
signed lower left: *Atkins*
229 × 333 mm
Worthington, Mary (gift, 1899) (D.1899.2)

■ ATKINSON, JOHN AUGUSTUS (1775–post 1833)

Atkinson was born in London and went to Russia in 1784, returning to London in 1801. He was elected a member of the Old Watercolour Society in 1808 but resigned in 1812. He exhibited at the Royal Academy from 1803 to 1818, specialising in battle scenes and spirited figure subjects.

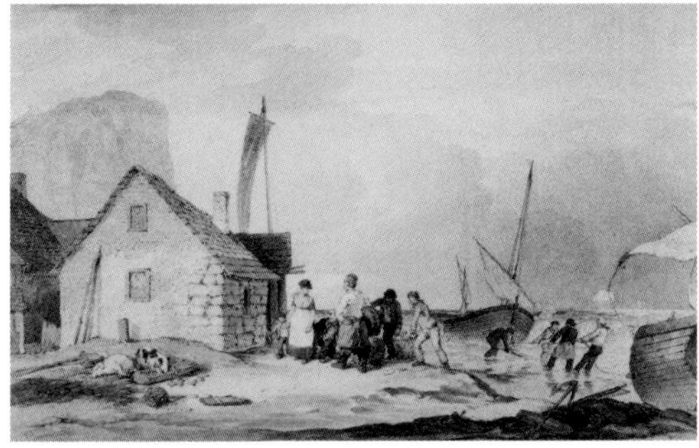

D.1892.64

Coast Scene with Fishermen bringing in the Catch
pen and brown ink, watercolour
318 × 493 mm
Taylor, John Edward (gift, 1892) (D.1892.64)

■ AUSTIN, SAMUEL (1796–1834)

Austin, a Liverpool artist, was taught by Peter de Wint. He exhibited at the Royal Academy in 1820 and was a founder member of the Society of British Artists in 1824. He travelled extensively in Europe but the bulk of his subjects are of Lancashire and North Wales. He was elected an associate of the Old Watercolour Society in 1827 and became a full member on his deathbed in 1834.

In the Channel
pencil, watercolour
signed lower centre: *S AUSTIN*
143 × 226 mm
Taylor, John Edward (gift, 1892) (D.1892.130)

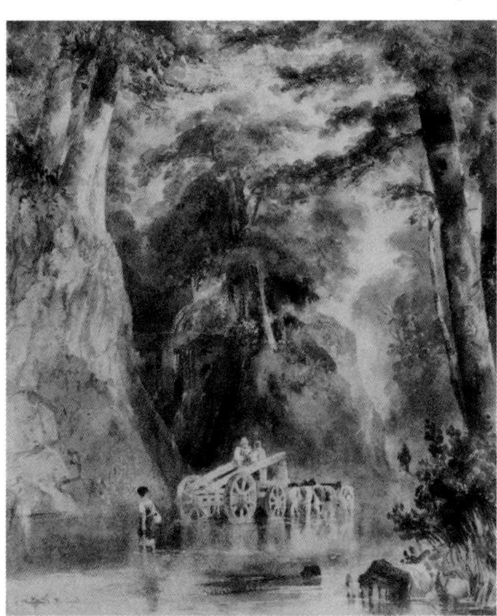

D.1892.131

A flooded Road in Wales
pencil, watercolour
395 × 325 mm
Taylor, John Edward (gift, 1892) (D.1892.131)

■ BAMFORD, ALFRED BENNETT (fl. 1880–93)

There is no information on Bamford, apart from the fact that he lived in the south east and specialised in church interiors and architectural details.

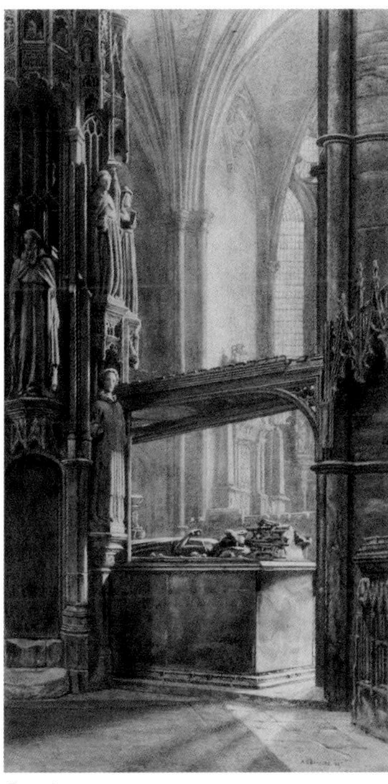

D.1926.290

Tomb of Philippa, Queen of Edward II, Westminster Abbey, London
1887
watercolour
signed & dated lower right: *ABBAMFORD.1887.*
465 × 241 mm
Ogden, William Sharp (bequest, 1926) (D.1926.290)

■ BAMPFYLDE, COPLESTONE WARRE (1720–91)

Bampfylde was a prolific amateur topographical draughtsman who exhibited at the Royal Academy, Society of Artists and the Free Society between 1763 and 1783. Many of his drawings depict views of his estate at Hestercombe in Somerset, as well as other estates in the county, such as Stourhead.

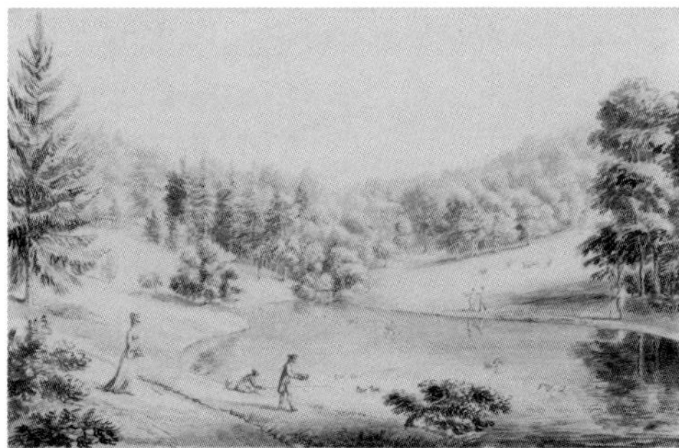

D.1965.8

Pear Pond, Hestercombe, Somerset
pencil, grey watercolour
inscribed on verso: *Hestercombe*
437 × 672 mm
Lockett, G. Derek (gift, 1965) (D.1965.8)

■ BANCROFT, ELIAS MOLLINEAUX (1846–1924)

Bancroft was a Manchester landscape painter who exhibited at the Royal Academy from 1874. He painted in Lancashire, Wales, Germany and Switzerland.

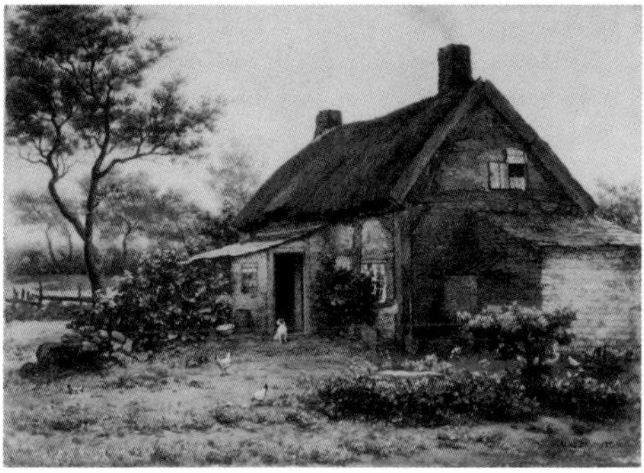

D.1892.152

Cottage at Carrington, near Flixton, Merseyside
1892
watercolour, bodycolour (heightened with white)
signed & dated lower right: *ELIAS BANCROFT. / –1892–*; signed, inscribed & dated on backboard: *No.1 / A CHESHIRE COTTAGE / Elias Bancroft.1892. / At Carrington. Nr. Flixton.*; inscribed on old label on backboard: *City Art Gallery Manchester / Spring Exhibition* [illegible] */ No1 / A Cheshire Cottage / (Carrington nr Flixton) / £42.0.0 / Elias Bancroft / 18 York Place / Oxford Rd. / Manchester*
563 × 766 mm
untraced (purchase, 1892) (D.1892.152)

■ BANKS, ROBERT (fl. 1816–22)

There is no information on this artist.

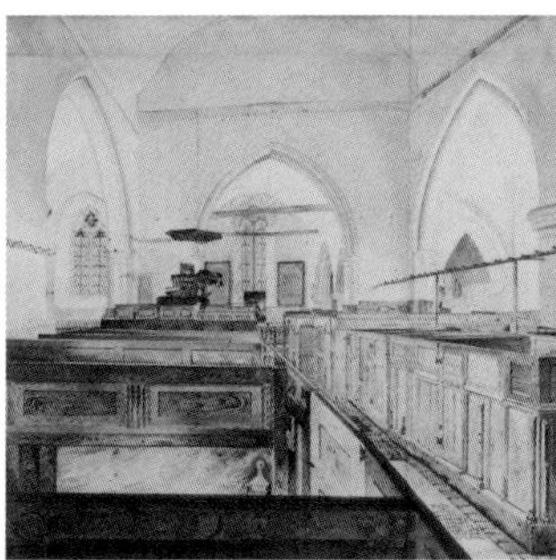

D.1926.186

Interior of St Mary's Church, Willesden, London
9.1821
pencil, watercolour; two joined sheets of paper
signed & inscribed lower left margin: *Accurately drawn on the Spot by Robert Banks by Permission of* [blank]; inscribed & dated lower right margin: [illegible] *September 1821 Ann Dom*
353 × 355 mm
Ogden, William Sharp (bequest, 1926) (D.1926.186)

Interior of the Savoy Chapel, London
8.9.1822
watercolour; buff paper
signed, inscribed & dated on painted label attached to upper centre verso: *THE ANTIQUITIES / of the Savoy Chapel Court. / Drawn on the Spot in Aug & Sept 1822 by Robt & Mary Banks*
329 × 329 mm
Ogden, William Sharp (bequest, 1926) (D.1926.185)

■ Barker, Benjamin (1776–1838)

Benjamin Barker, a member of a family of painters from Bath, exhibited in London from 1800 until his death.

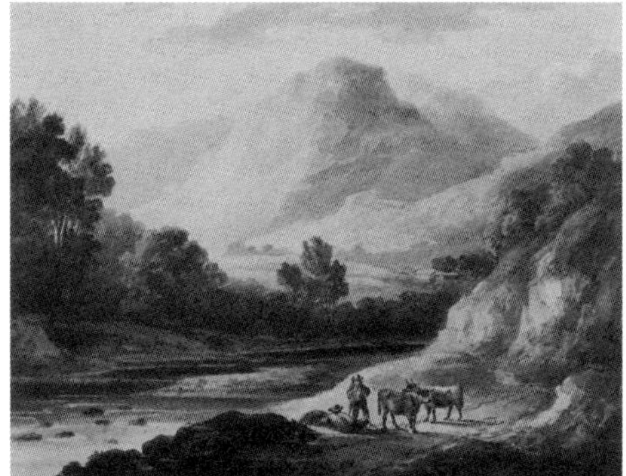

D.1908.3

Mountainous Landscape with Cattle and Figures
1807
watercolour
signed & dated lower right: *B.Barker / 1807*
487 × 624 mm
Palser, J. and Son, London (purchase, 1908) (D.1908.3)

View from Shotover Hill, Oxfordshire
watercolour
signed lower left: *Ben.Barker.fect.*
233 × 346 mm
anonymous, Friends of the Whitworth (via) (gift, 1947)
(D.1947.57)

■ Barker, Thomas (1769–1847)

Thomas Barker, elder brother of Benjamin, is the best-known member of the family of Bath painters. He exhibited at the Royal Academy from 1791 until 1847.

Portrait Study of the Artist's Son and Daughter
black chalk
watermark: *SIMMONS / 1820*
232 × 186 mm
Phillips, W. L. (gift, 1925) (D.1925.17)

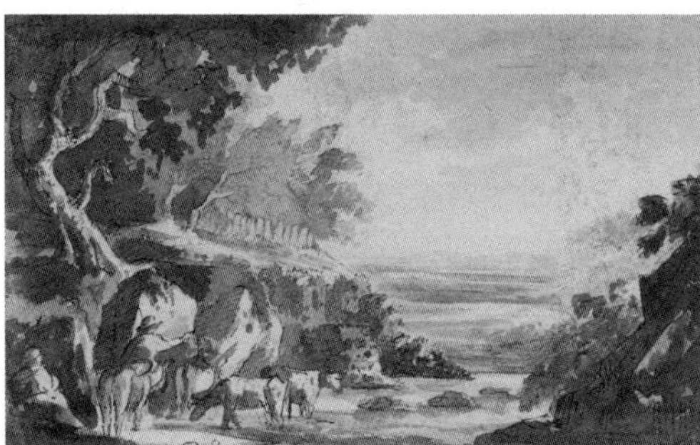

D.1926.187

Landscape with Cattle and a Figure on Horseback
pencil, pen and brown ink, brown watercolour
303 × 484 mm
Ogden, William Sharp (bequest, 1926) (D.1926.187)

Figures and Cattle among Trees
watercolour
208 × 296 mm
untraced (purchase, 1900) (D.1900.25)

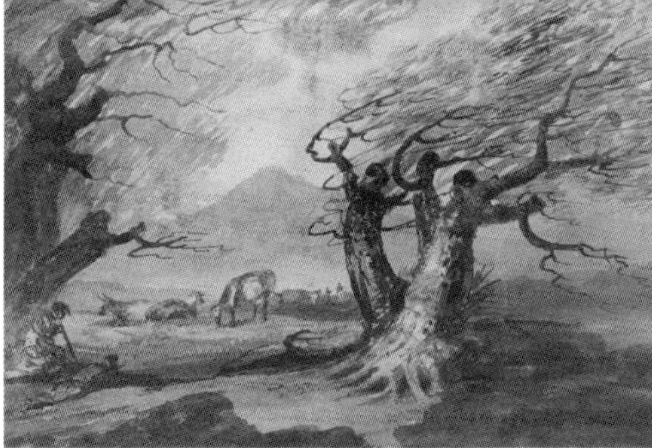

D.1900.25

■ Barratt, Reginald (1861–1917)

Barratt was an illustrator and painter of Oriental scenes, and studied architecture under Norman Shaw and painting under Bouguereau. He travelled widely in Europe and North Africa, and exhibited in London from 1885. He was elected a member of the Royal Watercolour Society in 1913.

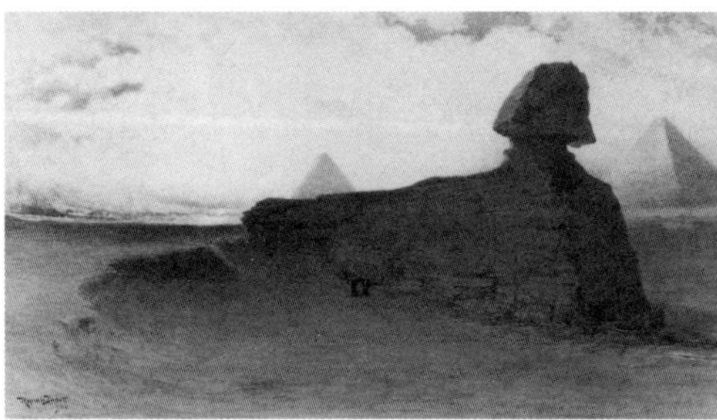

D.1942.9

The Sphinx at Sunset
1902
watercolour
signed & dated lower left: *Reginald Barratt. / 1902*
308 × 540 mm
Bragg, Sir W. Lawrence (in memory of his father) (gift, 1942)
(D.1942.9)

The Gold Mosque, Masemain, Baghdad, Iraq
1916
watercolour
signed & dated lower right: *R.Barratt. / 1916.*
308 × 227 mm
Bragg, Sir W. Lawrence (in memory of his father) (gift, 1942)
(D.1942.10)

■ Barret, Jun., George (1767/68–1842)

Barret was one of the sixteen founder members of the Old Watercolour Society. His earlier works were views in the home counties and a few in Wales but he increasingly turned to romantic compositions of a Claudian type showing poetic sunrises and sunsets without reference to locality.

Kingston Bridge on the Thames
pencil, watercolour
147 × 291 mm
Taylor, John Edward (gift, 1892) (D.1892.52)

A Sussex Landscape with a Timber Waggon
pencil, watercolour
208 × 459 mm
Taylor, John Edward (gift, 1892) (D.1892.53)

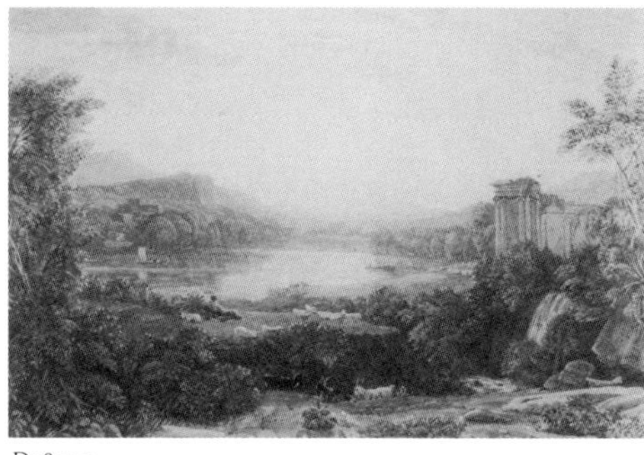

D.1892.54

Sunset with a ruined Temple and a Lake
pencil, watercolour
327 × 475 mm
Taylor, John Edward (gift, 1892) (D.1892.54)

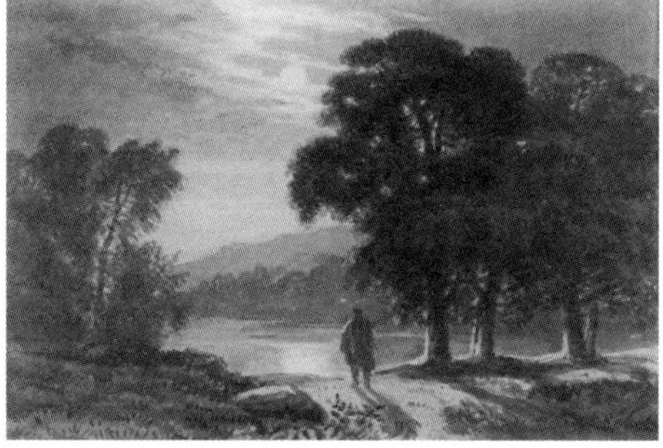

D.1917.10

Landscape with Lake by Moonlight
pencil, watercolour
213 × 308 mm
Anderson, A. E. (gift, 1917) (D.1917.10)

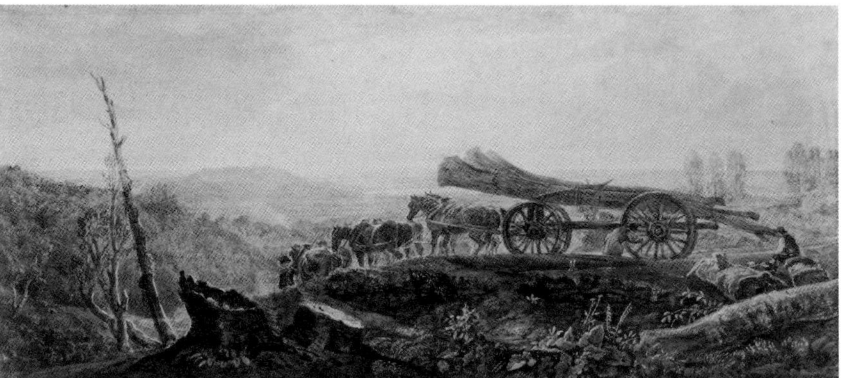

D.1892.53

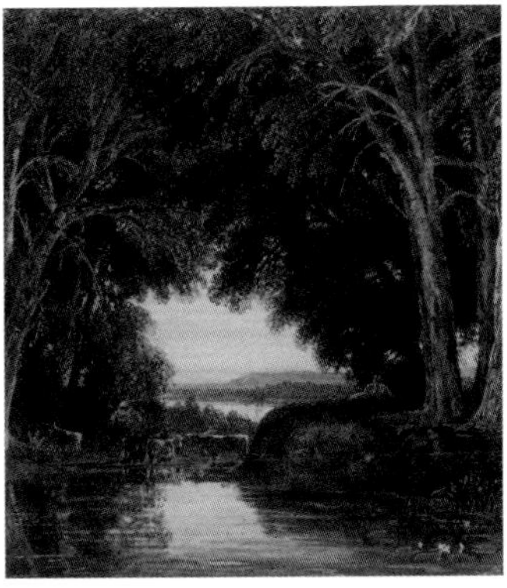

D.1917.11

Landscape at Sunset with Cattle

1828
watercolour; card
signed & dated lower right: *G.Barret / 1828*
303 × 264 mm
Anderson, A. E. (gift, 1917) (D.1917.11)

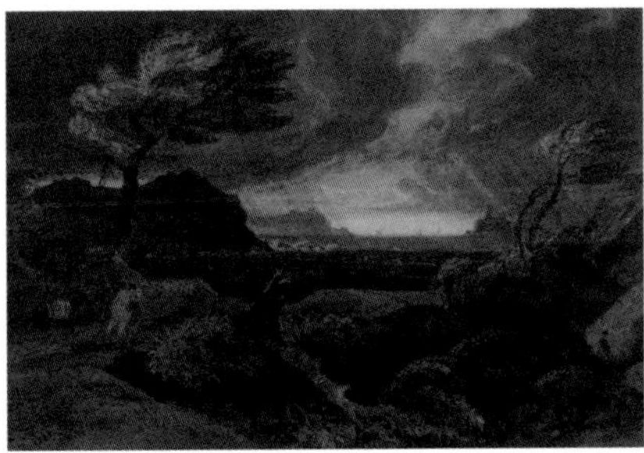

D.1919.18

Coast Scene with Storm

pencil, brown watercolour
278 × 400 mm
Anderson, A. E. (gift, 1919) (D.1919.18)

Landscape with River and Fishermen

pencil, brown watercolour
255 × 363 mm
Anderson, A. E. (gift, 1919) (D.1919.19)

A Capriccio Landscape with Lake and Ruins

1820
pencil, pen and brown ink, watercolour
signed & dated lower left: *George Barret / 1820*
320 × 432 mm
Broadhurst, Sir Edward Tootal, and Broadhurst, Lady
(bequest, 1924) (D.1924.74)

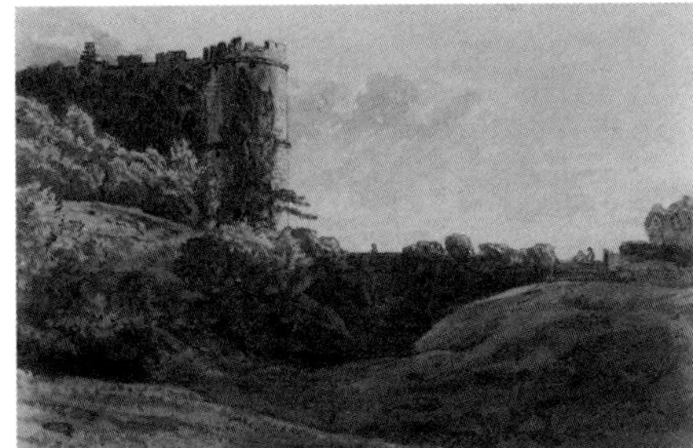

D.1947.15

Part of the Gatehouse, Carisbrooke Castle, Isle of Wight

pencil, pen and grey ink, watercolour
151 × 226 mm
Friends of the Whitworth (gift, 1947) (D.1947.15)

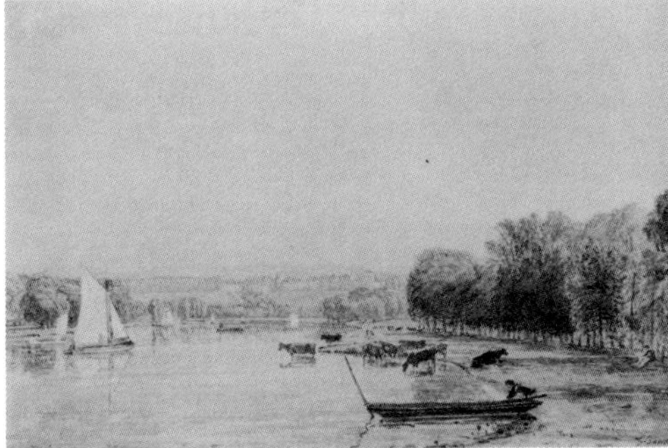

D.1951.7

View of the Thames opposite Eel-Pie Island, looking downstream to Richmond

1821
pencil, watercolour
signed & dated lower right: *G.Barret 1821*
155 × 229 mm
Dunkerley, F. B. (bequest, 1951) (D.1951.7)

Farm Scene with Cattle watering

watercolour
171 × 242 mm
Towlson, Hector J. (bequest, 1969) (D.1970.13)

■ BARRET, Sen., GEORGE (1728/32–84)

George Barret Sen. was born in Dublin and came
to London in 1762. He was a founder member
of the Royal Academy in 1768. Barret Sen. was a very
fashionable painter in the 1770s and collaborated
with the horse painter Sawrey Gilpin. He is best
known for his bodycolour landscapes.

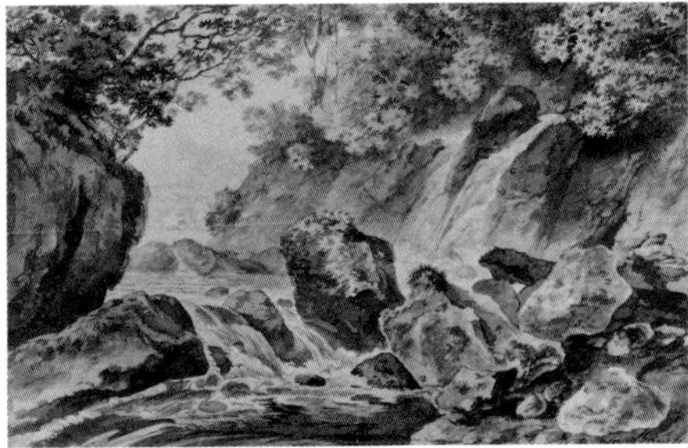

D.1951.11

The Waterfall

pencil, watercolour
signed lower right: *George Barrett*; numbered
lower left: *No1*
280 × 436 mm
Pilkington, Margaret (gift, 1951) (D.1951.11)

■ BARTHOLOMEW, VALENTINE (1799–1879)

Bartholomew was a largely self-taught London flower
painter who also painted landscapes. He was elected
an associate of the Old Watercolour Society in 1835,
and was appointed Flower Painter in Ordinary to
the Queen in 1837.

Windsor Castle from the River Thames

1836
pencil, watercolour
signed & dated lower left: *1836 V.Bartholomew*
216 × 282 mm
Towlson, Hector J. (bequest, 1969) (D.1970.14)

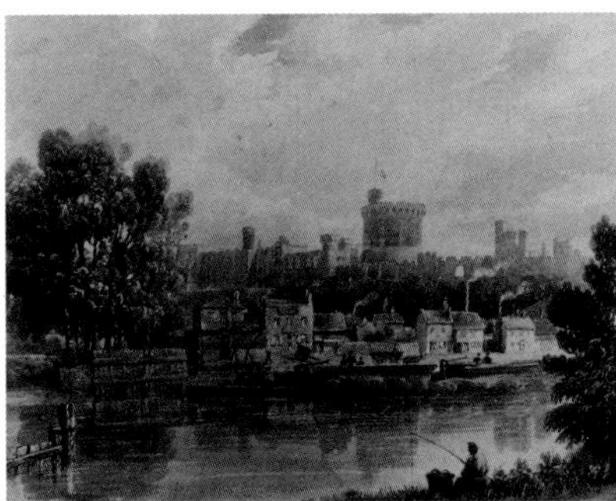

D.1970.14

■ BAYNES, JAMES (1766–1837)

Baynes studied under Romney and at the Royal
Academy Schools to become a fashionable drawing
master. He exhibited landscapes of England and Wales
at the Royal Academy from 1796 until his death.

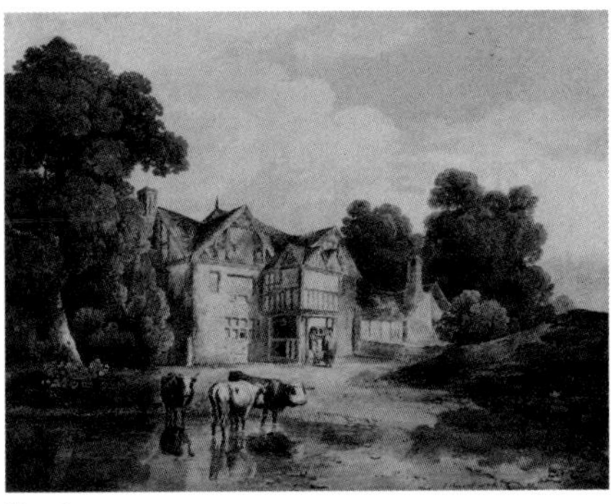

D.1928.41

Cattle watering outside a Building

1806
pencil, watercolour
signed & dated lower right: *J Baynes 1806*
396 × 502 mm
Anderson, A. E. (gift, 1928) (D.1928.41)

■ BEAUMONT, SIR GEORGE HOWLAND (1753–1827)

Beaumont was an important amateur and collector,
who studied under Alexander Cozens at Eton and
Malchair at Oxford. He was friend and patron of many
major British artists including Constable, and was one
of the principal founders and benefactors of the
National Gallery. He travelled extensively abroad.

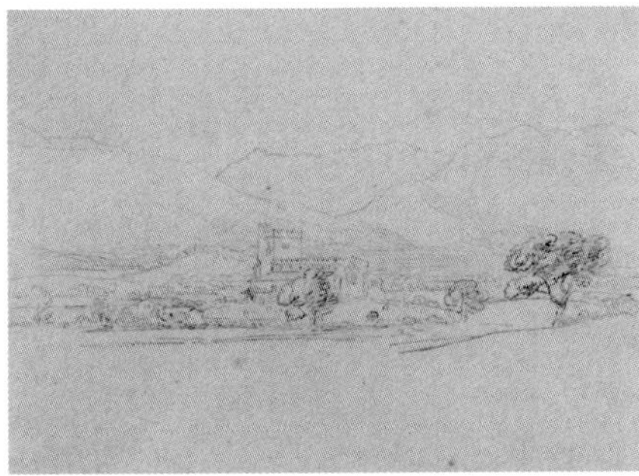

D.1974.11

St Kentigern's Church, Crosthwaite, Cumberland

pencil, black chalk; grey paper
inscribed lower centre margin: *Keswick Church*
238 × 306 mm
Bonham-Carter, Lady (gift, 1974) (D.1974.11)

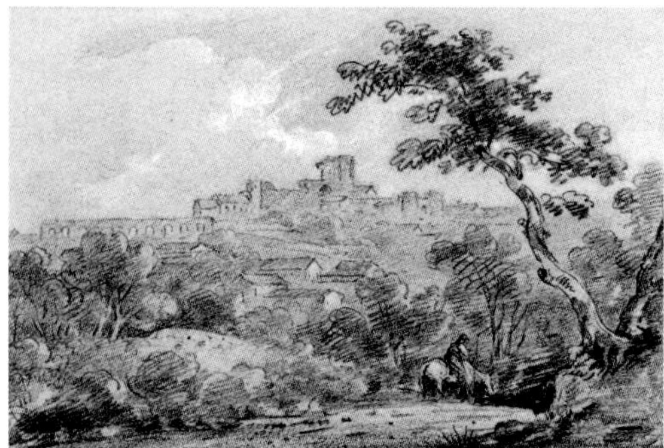

D.1974.12

Distant View of Denbigh, Denbighshire, Wales
8.1802
black chalk, white chalk; blue paper
inscribed lower centre margin: *Denbigh*; inscribed &
dated upper right margin: *Benarth Aug.1802*
166 × 246 mm
Bonham-Carter, Lady (gift, 1974) (D.1974.12)

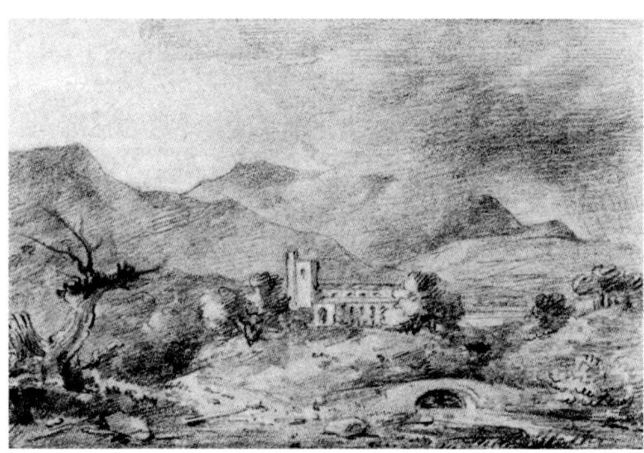

D.1974.13

**St Kentigern's, Crosthwaite, Cumberland,
from the River Greta**
8.1802
black chalk, white chalk; blue paper
inscribed lower centre margin: *Keswick*; inscribed &
dated upper right margin: *Benarth Aug.1802*
167 × 247 mm
Bonham-Carter, Lady (gift, 1974) (D.1974.13)

**View of The Rivals Mountain Range,
Caernarvonshire, North Wales**
8.1802
black chalk, white chalk; blue paper
inscribed lower centre margin: *The Rivals*; inscribed &
dated upper right margin: *Benarth Aug.1802.*
165 × 247 mm
Bonham-Carter, Lady (gift, 1974) (D.1974.14)

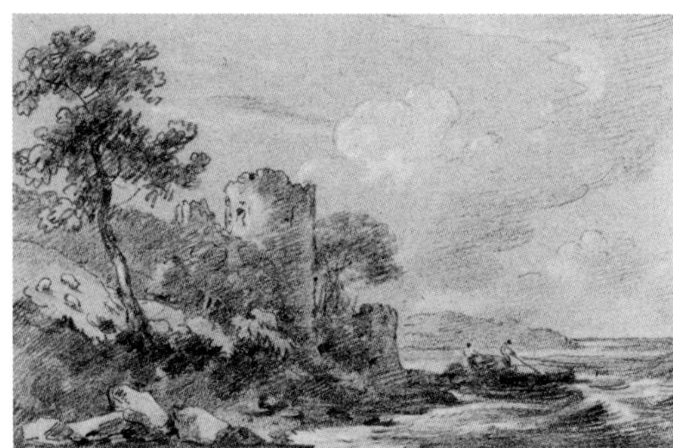

D.1974.15

Conway Castle, Caernarvonshire, North Wales
26.8.1802
black chalk, white chalk; blue paper
inscribed lower centre margin: *Conway Castle*; inscribed
& dated upper right margin: *Benarth Aug 26
1802./Thursday*
165 × 247 mm
Bonham-Carter, Lady (gift, 1974) (D.1974.15)

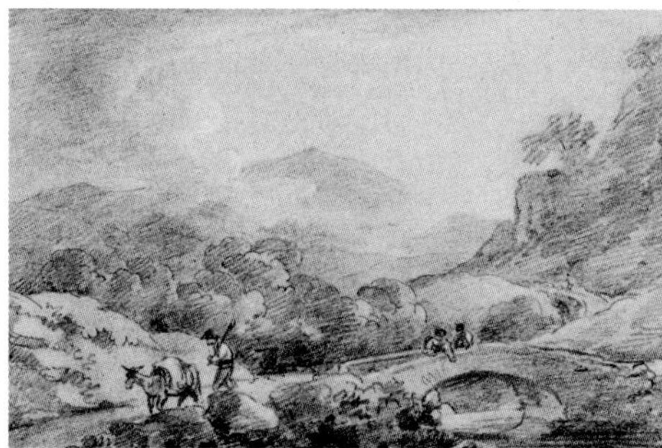

D.1974.16

Moel Siabod, Caernarvonshire, North Wales
27.8.1802
black chalk, white chalk; blue paper
inscribed lower centre margin: *Moel Siabod*; inscribed
& dated upper right margin: *friday Aug 27.1802.*
165 × 247 mm
Bonham-Carter, Lady (gift, 1974) (D.1974.16)

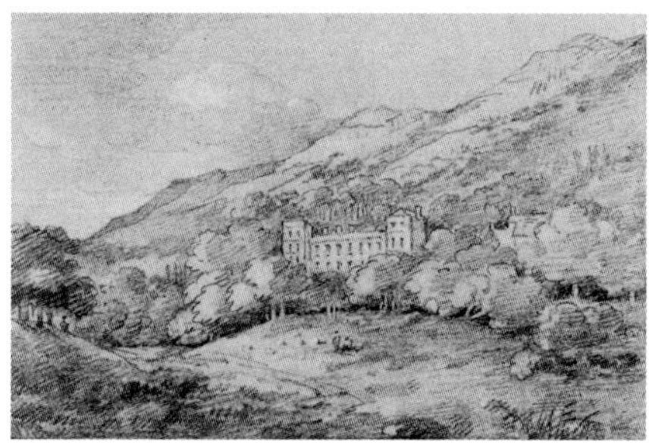

D.1974.17

**Marle, opposite Conway, Caernarvonshire,
North Wales**
28.8.1802
black chalk, white chalk; blue paper
inscribed lower centre margin: *Marle opposite Conway*:
inscribed & dated upper right margin: *Benarth
Saturday/Aug.28 1802.*
167 × 245 mm
Bonham-Carter, Lady (gift, 1974) (D.1974.17)

**View on the River near Conway,
Caernarvonshire, North Wales**
3.9.1802
black chalk, white chalk; blue paper
inscribed lower centre margin: *Near Conway*; inscribed
& dated upper right margin: *Benarth friday Sept.3.1802.*
165 × 245 mm
Bonham-Carter, Lady (gift, 1974) (D.1974.18)

**Cave near Great Orme's Head,
Caernarvonshire, Wales**
13.9.1802
black chalk, white chalk; blue paper
inscribed lower centre margin: *Cave near Orm's Head*;
inscribed & dated upper right margin: *Benarth Monday
Sept.13/1802.*
165 × 247 mm
Bonham-Carter, Lady (gift, 1974) (D.1974.19)

**Bridge over the River Conway, between Llanrwst
and Conway, Caernarvonshire, Wales**
13.9.1802
black chalk, white chalk; blue paper
inscribed lower centre margin: *Between Llanrwst &
Conway*; inscribed & dated upper right margin:
Benarth Monday Sept.13.1802.
165 × 246 mm
Bonham-Carter, Lady (gift, 1974) (D.1974.20)

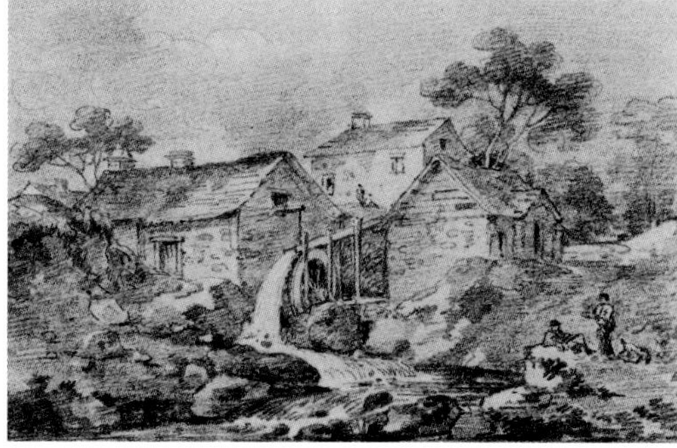

D.1974.21

**Houses and Watermill, Beddgelert,
Caernarvonshire, Wales**
14.9.1802
black chalk, white chalk; blue card
inscribed lower centre margin: *Bethgellert*; inscribed &
dated upper right margin: *Benarth Tuesday Sept.14/1802.*
163 × 245 mm
Bonham-Carter, Lady (gift, 1974) (D.1974.21)

**Mountain Scene with Waterfall, between
Llanrwst and Conway, Caernarvonshire, Wales**
15.9.1802
black chalk, white chalk; blue paper
inscribed lower centre margin: *Between Llanrwst &
Conway*; inscribed & dated upper right margin:
Benarth Wednesday Sept.15.1802
163 × 247 mm
Bonham-Carter, Lady (gift, 1974) (D.1974.22)

**Waterfall between Llanrwst and Conway,
Caernarvonshire, Wales**
16.9.1802
black chalk, white chalk; blue paper
inscribed lower centre margin: *Do.Do.*; inscribed &
dated upper right margin: *Benarth
Thursday.Sept.16.1802.*
165 × 245 mm
Bonham-Carter, Lady (gift, 1974) (D.1974.23)

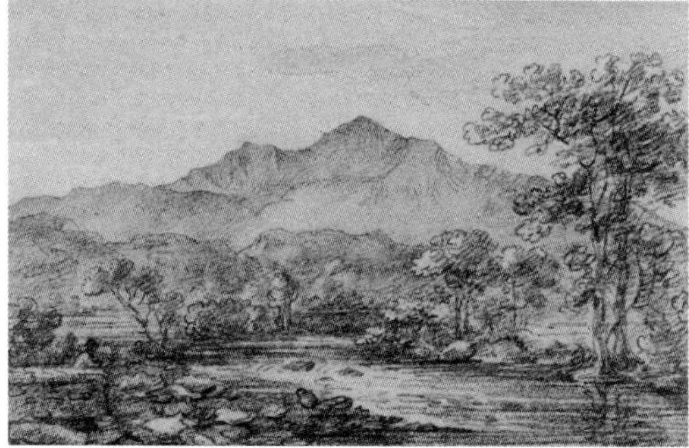

D.1974.24

View of Snowdon, Caernarvonshire, Wales

20.9.1802
black chalk, white chalk; blue paper
inscribed lower centre margin: *Snowdon*; inscribed &
dated upper right margin: *Benarth Monday
Sept.20./1802.*
164 × 245 mm
Bonham-Carter, Lady (gift, 1974) (D.1974.24)

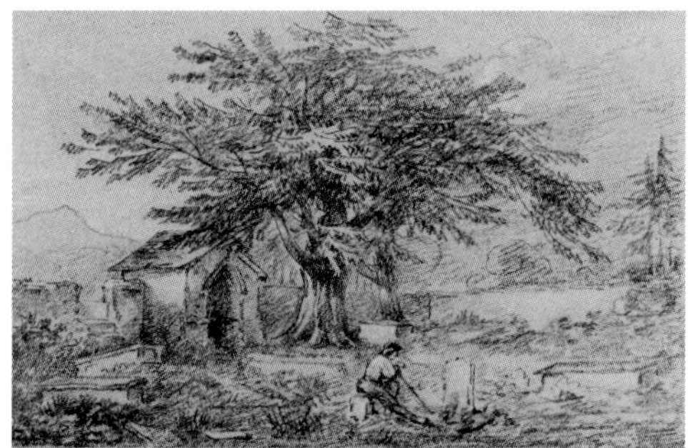

D.1974.25

Churchyard of St Grwst's, Llanrwst, Denbighshire, Wales

9.1802
black chalk, white chalk; blue paper
inscribed lower centre margin: *Llanrwst*; inscribed &
dated upper right margin: *Benarth Tuesday Sept./1802*
164 × 244 mm
Bonham-Carter, Lady (gift, 1974) (D.1974.25)

Lane in Surrey

22.9.1802
black chalk, white chalk; blue paper
inscribed lower centre margin: *Lane in Surry*; inscribed
& dated upper right margin: *Benarth Wednesday
Sept.22/1802.*
163 × 245 mm
Bonham-Carter, Lady (gift, 1974) (D.1974.26)

Cottage on the Banks of the Conway, Caernarvonshire, Wales

23.9.1802
black chalk, white chalk; blue paper
inscribed lower centre margin: *On the banks of the
Conway*; inscribed & dated upper right margin:
Benarth Thursday 23.1802
162 × 248 mm
Bonham-Carter, Lady (gift, 1974) (D.1974.27)

Travellers on the Banks of the Conway, Caernarvonshire, Wales

24.9.1802
black chalk, white chalk; blue paper
inscribed lower centre margin: *Do.*; inscribed & dated
upper right margin: *Benarth friday Sept.24.1802.*
162 × 248 mm
Bonham-Carter, Lady (gift, 1974) (D.1974.28)

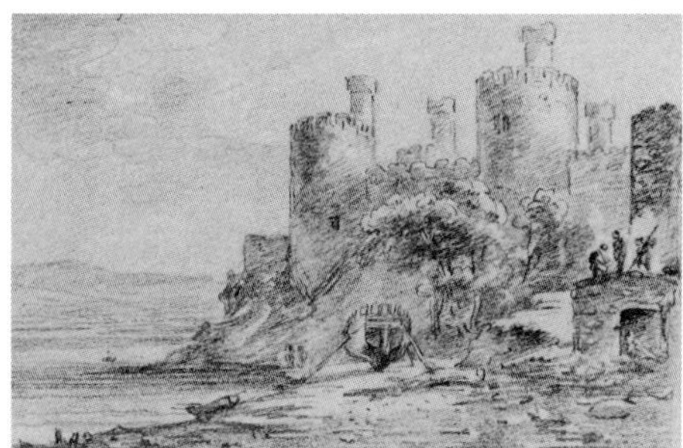

D.1974.29

View of Conway Castle, Caernarvonshire, Wales, from the North

27.9.1802
black chalk, white chalk; blue paper
inscribed lower centre margin: *Conway Castle*; inscribed
& dated upper right margin: *Benarth Monday
Sept.27.1802*
163 × 249 mm
Bonham-Carter, Lady (gift, 1974) (D.1974.29)

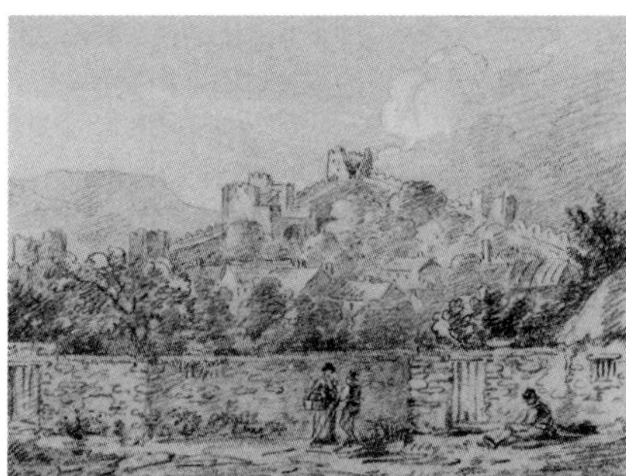

D.1974.30

View of Conway, Caernarvonshire, Wales

28.9.1802
black chalk, white chalk; blue paper
inscribed lower centre margin: *Town of Conway*;
inscribed & dated upper right margin: *Beenarth
Tuesday Sept.28.1802.*
185 × 249 mm
Bonham-Carter, Lady (gift, 1974) (D.1974.30)

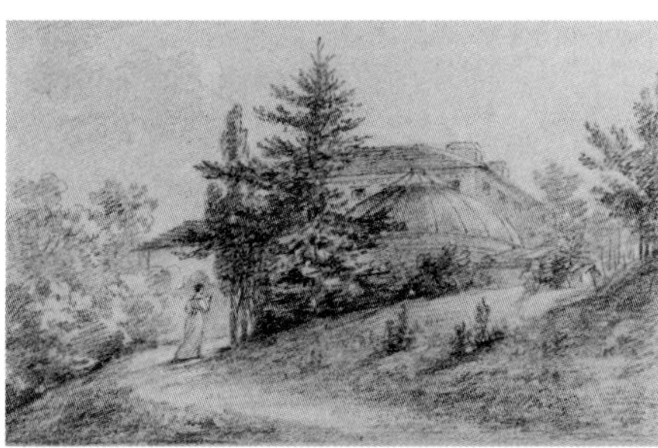

D.1974.31

Benarth Hall, Caernarvonshire, Wales

29.9.1802
black chalk, white chalk; blue card
inscribed lower centre margin: *Benarth*; inscribed &
dated upper right margin: *Benarth Wednesday Sept.29
1802.*
163 × 248 mm
Bonham-Carter, Lady (gift, 1974) (D.1974.31)

View from Benarth, Caernarvonshire, Wales

1.10.1802
black chalk, white chalk; blue paper
inscribed lower centre margin: *From Benarth*; inscribed
& dated upper right margin: *Benarth Friday Oct.1.1802*
187 × 249 mm
Bonham-Carter, Lady (gift, 1974) (D.1974.32)

Benarth Wood, Caernarvonshire, Wales on the Bank of the River Conway

2.10.1802
black chalk, white chalk; blue paper
inscribed lower centre margin: *Benarth Wood*; inscribed
& dated upper right margin: *Benarth Saturday
Oct.2.1802*
175 × 279 mm
Bonham-Carter, Lady (gift, 1974) (D.1974.33)

Waterfall at Dolmelynllyn, Caernarvonshire, Wales

18.10.1802
black chalk, white chalk; blue paper
inscribed lower centre margin: *Waterfall of
Dollymylinthlin*; inscribed & dated upper right margin:
Benarth Monday Oct.18.1802.
183 × 249 mm
Bonham-Carter, Lady (gift, 1974) (D.1974.34)

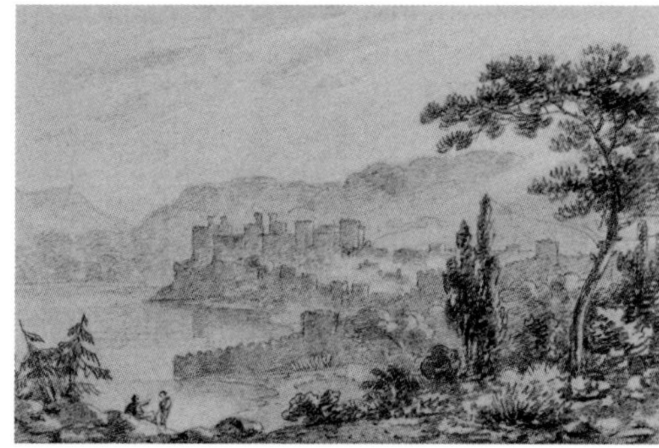

D.1974.35

View of Conway Castle and Town, Caernarvonshire, Wales, from the North

18.10.1802
black chalk, white chalk; blue paper
inscribed lower centre margin: *Conway Castle & Town*;
inscribed & dated upper right margin: *Cheltenham
Monday Oct.18.1802.*
166 × 248 mm
Bonham-Carter, Lady (gift, 1974) (D.1974.35)

Cottage in Essex

18.10.1802
black chalk, white chalk, grey watercolour; blue paper
inscribed lower centre margin: *Cottage in Essex*;
inscribed & dated upper right margin: *Cheltenham
Monday Oct.18 1802.*
170 × 250 mm
Bonham-Carter, Lady (gift, 1974) (D.1974.36)

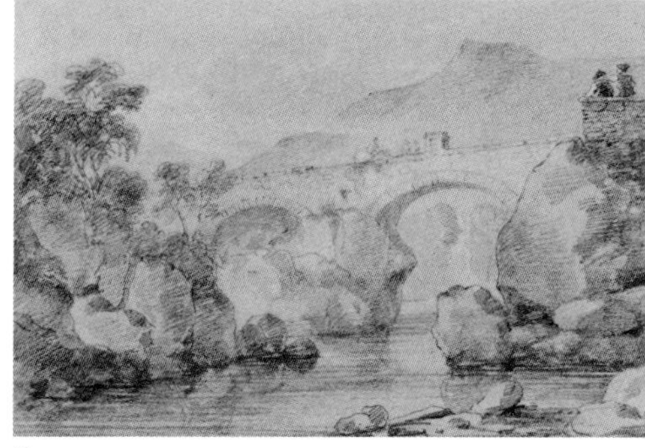

D.1974.37

Bridge near the Source of the Conway, Caernarvonshire, Wales

19.10.1802
black chalk, white chalk; blue paper
inscribed lower centre margin: *Near the source of the
Conway*; inscribed & dated upper right margin:
Cheltenham Tuesday Oct.19 1802
171 × 250 mm
Bonham-Carter, Lady (gift, 1974) (D.1974.37)

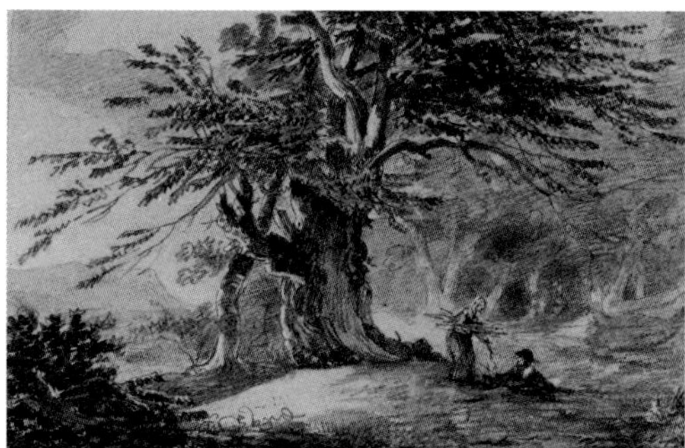

D.1974.38

Yew Tree at Foxley, Herefordshire
20.10.1802
black chalk, white chalk, grey watercolour; blue paper
inscribed lower centre margin: *Yew Tree at Foxley*;
inscribed & dated upper right margin: *Cheltenham Wednesday Oct.20.1802.*
162 × 254 mm
Bonham-Carter, Lady (gift, 1974) (D.1974.38)

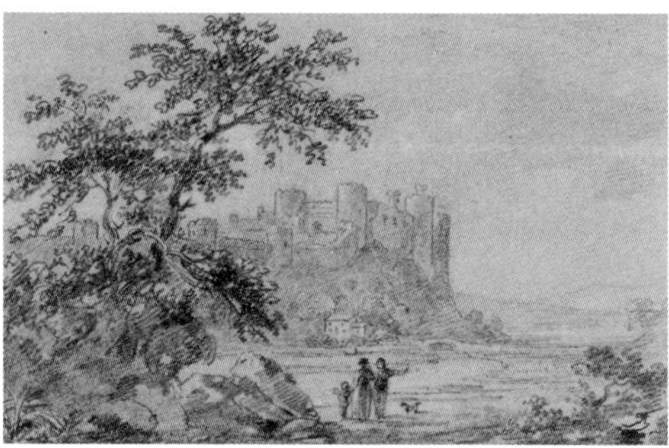

D.1974.39

Conway Castle, Caernarvonshire, Wales, from the West
20.10.1802
black chalk, white chalk; blue paper
inscribed lower centre margin: *Conway Castle;* inscribed & dated upper right margin: *Cheltenham Wednesday Oct.20.1802.*
160 × 249 mm
Bonham-Carter, Lady (gift, 1974) (D.1974.39)

Footbridge over a River, near Cheltenham, Gloucestershire
23.10.1802
black chalk, white chalk, grey watercolour; blue paper
inscribed lower centre margin: *Near Cheltenham;*
inscribed & dated upper right margin: *Cheltenham Saturday Oct.23.1802.*
161 × 248 mm
Bonham-Carter, Lady (gift, 1974) (D.1974.40)

Imaginary Landscape
1802
black chalk, white chalk, grey watercolour; blue paper
inscribed lower centre margin: *Fancy*
161 × 249 mm
Bonham-Carter, Lady (gift, 1974) (D.1974.41)

Footbridge across a Ravine, North Wales
4.12.1802
black chalk, white chalk, grey watercolour; blue paper
inscribed lower centre margin: *North Wales;* inscribed & dated upper right margin: *Dunmow Saturday Dec.4.1802.*
188 × 250 mm
Bonham-Carter, Lady (gift, 1974) (D.1974.42)

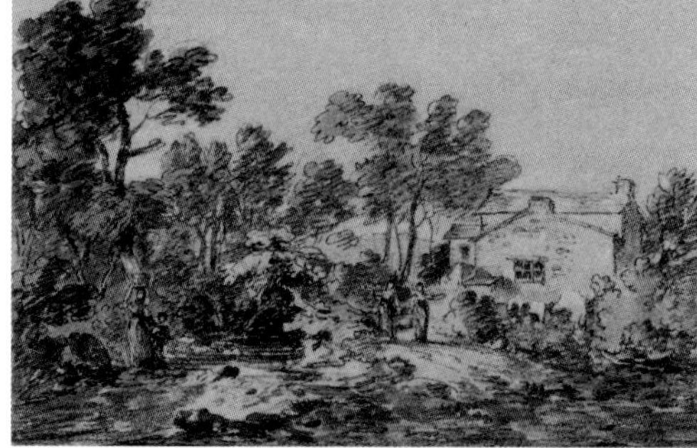

D.1974.43

House on the Banks of the River Greta, Cumberland
1803
black chalk, white chalk, grey watercolour; blue paper
dated upper right margin: *1803;* inscribed lower centre margin: *On the banks of the Greta*
160 × 249 mm
Bonham-Carter, Lady (gift, 1974) (D.1974.43)

Footbridge, Mulgrave, Yorkshire
1803
black chalk, white chalk, grey watercolour; blue paper
dated upper right margin: *1803;* inscribed lower centre margin: *Mulgrave*
161 × 250 mm
Bonham-Carter, Lady (gift, 1974) (D.1974.44)

Village Church in Essex
1803
black chalk, white chalk, grey watercolour; blue paper
dated upper right margin: *1803;* inscribed lower centre margin: *Essex*
162 × 248 mm
Bonham-Carter, Lady (gift, 1974) (D.1974.45)

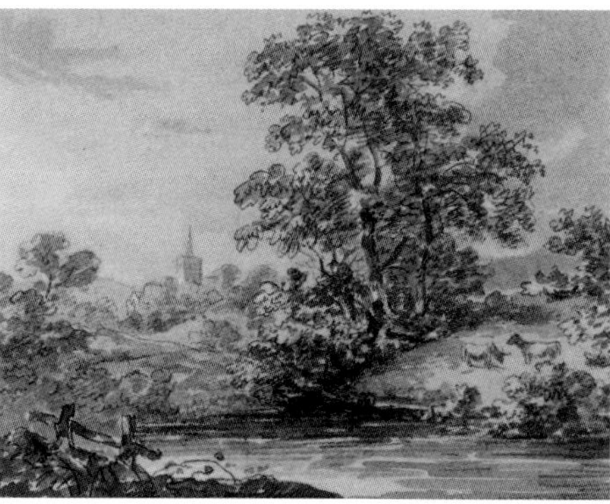

D.1974.46

View near Dunmow, Essex
14.6.1804
black chalk, white chalk, grey watercolour; blue paper
inscribed lower centre margin: *Near Dunmow;*
inscribed & dated upper right margin: *Coleorton Thursday/June 14.1804.*
196 × 250 mm
Bonham-Carter, Lady (gift, 1974) (D.1974.46)

View at Coleorton, Leicestershire
14.6.1804
black chalk, white chalk, grey watercolour; blue paper
inscribed lower centre margin: *Coleorton;* inscribed & dated upper right margin: *Coleorton Thursday/.June 14.1804*
163 × 252 mm
Bonham-Carter, Lady (gift, 1974) (D.1974.47)

Figures resting by a Road, Coleorton, Leicestershire
6.1804
black chalk, white chalk, grey watercolour; blue paper
inscribed lower centre margin: *Do.;* inscribed & dated upper right margin: *Coleorton June/1804*
161 × 250 mm
Bonham-Carter, Lady (gift, 1974) (D.1974.48)

Horse drinking by the Roadside, Coleorton, Leicestershire
21.6.1804
black chalk, white chalk, grey watercolour; blue paper
inscribed lower centre margin: *Do.;* inscribed & dated upper right margin: *Coleorton Wednesday June 21./1804.*
161 × 249 mm
Bonham-Carter, Lady (gift, 1974) (D.1974.49)

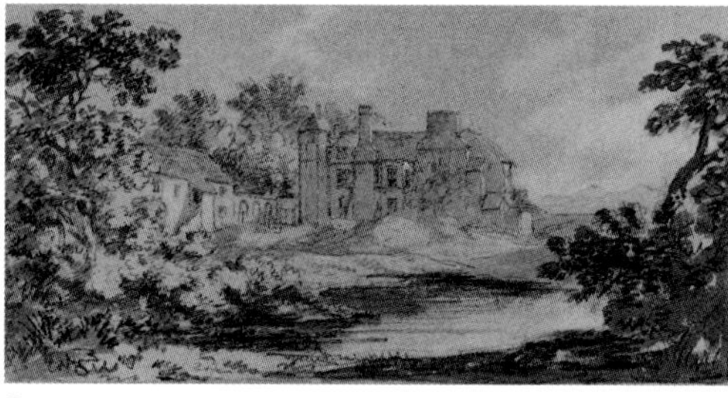

D.1974.50

The Old House, Coleorton, Leicestershire
22.6.1804
black chalk, white chalk, grey watercolour; blue paper
inscribed lower centre margin: *The old House at Coleorton;* inscribed & dated upper right margin: *Coleorton Thursday June 22.1804.*
200 × 387 mm
Bonham-Carter, Lady (gift, 1974) (D.1974.50)

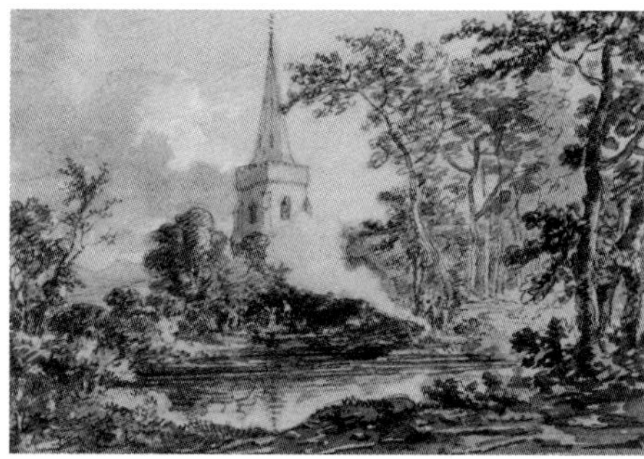

D.1974.51

The West Tower of St Mary's Church, Coleorton, Leicestershire
25.6.1804
black chalk, white chalk, grey watercolour; blue paper
inscribed lower centre margin: *Coleorton Church;* inscribed & dated upper right margin: *Coleorton Monday June 25/1804.*
174 × 249 mm
Bonham-Carter, Lady (gift, 1974) (D.1974.51)

Road through a Wood, Grace Dieu, Leicestershire
29.6.1804
black chalk, white chalk, grey watercolour; blue paper
inscribed lower centre margin: *Gracedieu;* inscribed & dated upper right margin: *Coleorton Friday June 29./1804.*
163 × 251 mm
Bonham-Carter, Lady (gift, 1974) (D.1974.52)

**Woodland Scene with Figures, near
Grace Dieu, Leicestershire**
2.7.1804
black chalk, white chalk, grey watercolour; blue paper
inscribed lower centre margin: *Do.*; inscribed & dated
upper right margin: *Colorton July 2.1804./Monday.*
164 × 250 mm
Bonham-Carter, Lady (gift, 1974) (D.1974.53)

**Figures by a Footbridge, Grace Dieu,
Leicestershire**
3.7.1804
black chalk, white chalk, grey watercolour; blue paper
inscribed lower centre margin: *Do.*; inscribed & dated
upper right margin: *Coleorton Tuesday July 3/1804.*
163 × 253 mm
Bonham-Carter, Lady (gift, 1974) (D.1974.54)

Imaginary Landscape with River and Castle
5.7.1804
black chalk, white chalk, grey watercolour; blue paper
inscribed lower centre margin: *Fancy*; inscribed &
dated upper right margin: *Coleorton Thursday July
5/1804.*
162 × 252 mm
Bonham-Carter, Lady (gift, 1974) (D.1974.55)

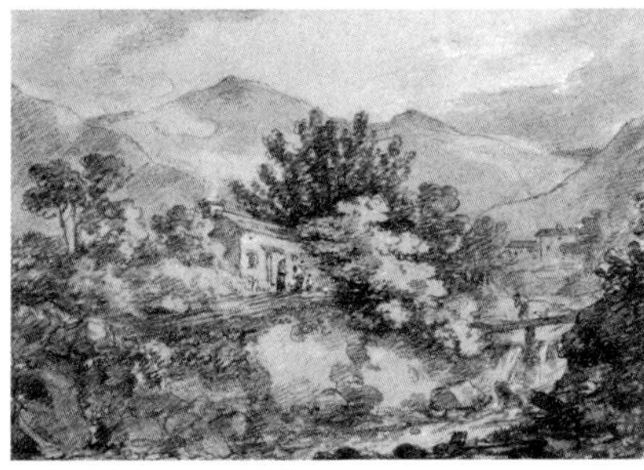

D.1974.56

**View of Applethwaite, Cumberland, with
Skiddaw in the Distance**
5.7.1804
black chalk, white chalk, grey watercolour; blue paper
inscribed lower centre margin: *Applethwaite &
Skiddaw*; inscribed & dated upper right margin:
Coleorton friday July 5/1804.
182 × 253 mm
Bonham-Carter, Lady (gift, 1974) (D.1974.56)

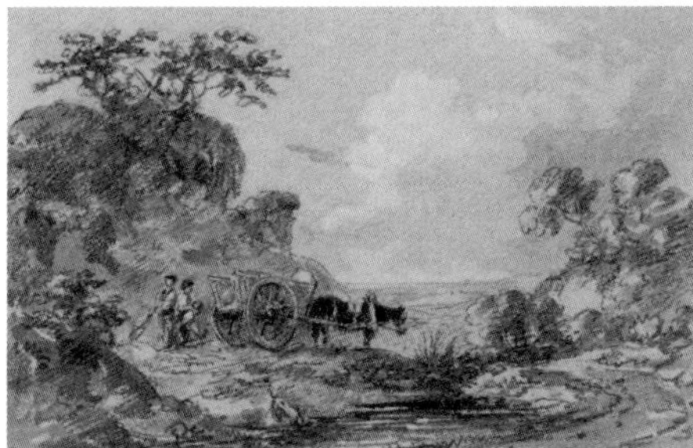

D.1974.57

**Woodcutter returning to his Cottage,
Coleorton, Leicestershire**
7.7.1804
black chalk, white chalk, grey watercolour; blue paper
inscribed lower centre margin: *Coleorton*; inscribed &
dated upper right margin: *Coleorton July
7.1804./Saturday.*
181 × 252 mm
Bonham-Carter, Lady (gift, 1974) (D.1974.57)

House by a Stream, Coleorton, Leicestershire
10.7.1804
black chalk, white chalk, grey watercolour; blue paper
inscribed lower centre margin: *Do.*; inscribed & dated
upper right margin: *Coleorton tuesday July 10/1804.*
186 × 252 mm
Bonham-Carter, Lady (gift, 1974) (D.1974.58)

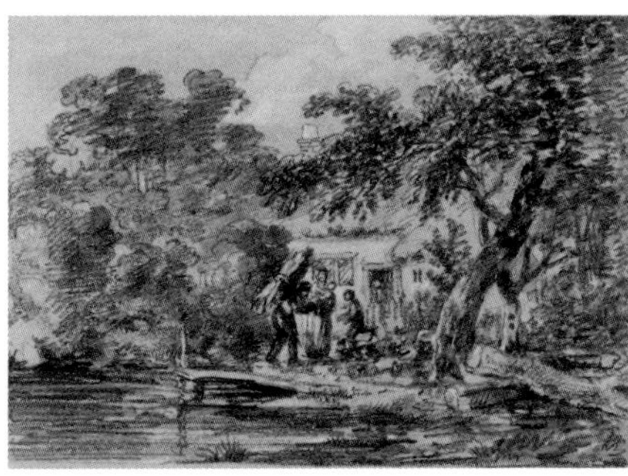

D.1974.59

**Horse and Cart with Men digging,
Coleorton, Leicestershire**
10.7.1804
black chalk, white chalk, grey watercolour; blue paper
inscribed lower centre margin: *Do.*; inscribed & dated
upper right margin: *Coleorton tuesday July 10/1804.*
164 × 253 mm
Bonham-Carter, Lady (gift, 1974) (D.1974.59)

**Landscape with distant View of Town and
Mountains in the North of England**
12.7.1804
black chalk, white chalk, grey watercolour; blue paper
inscribed lower centre margin: *North of England*;
inscribed & dated upper right margin: *Coleorton
Thursday July 12/1804*
163 × 251 mm
Bonham-Carter, Lady (gift, 1974) (D.1974.60)

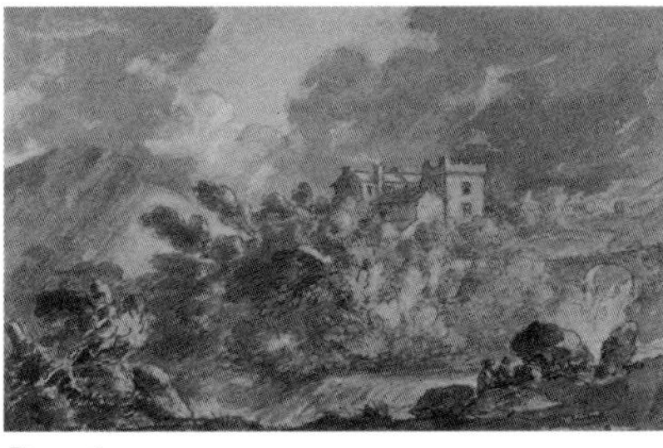

D.1974.61

**Greta Hall, near Keswick, Cumberland, the
Home of Robert Southey**
14.7.1804
pencil, black chalk, white chalk, grey watercolour
blue paper
inscribed lower centre margin: *Greta Hall Southey's
house*; inscribed & dated upper right margin: *Coleorton
Saturday July 14/1804*
162 × 252 mm
Bonham-Carter, Lady (gift, 1974) (D.1974.61)

Cottage in the Grove, Coleorton, Leicestershire
17.7.1804
black chalk, white chalk, grey watercolour; blue paper
inscribed lower centre margin: *In the grove Coleorton*;
inscribed & dated upper right margin: *Coleorton
tuesday July 17./1804.*
190 × 266 mm
Bonham-Carter, Lady (gift, 1974) (D.1974.62)

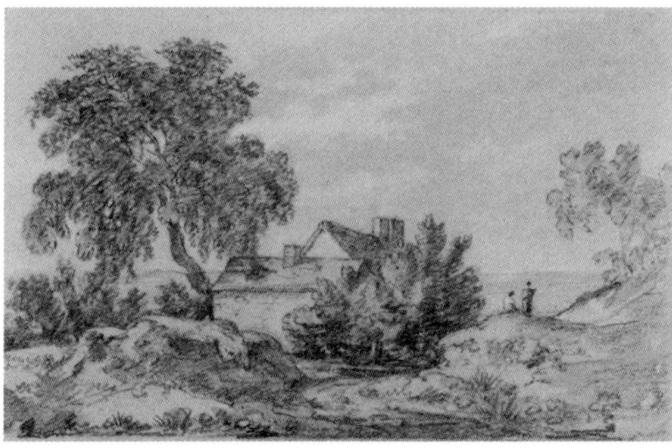

D.1974.63

Cottage, Coleorton, Leicestershire
19.7.1804
black chalk, white chalk, grey watercolour; blue paper
inscribed lower centre margin: *Cottage Coleorton*;
inscribed & dated upper right margin: *Coleorton
Thursday July 19/1804.*
175 × 273 mm
Bonham-Carter, Lady (gift, 1974) (D.1974.63)

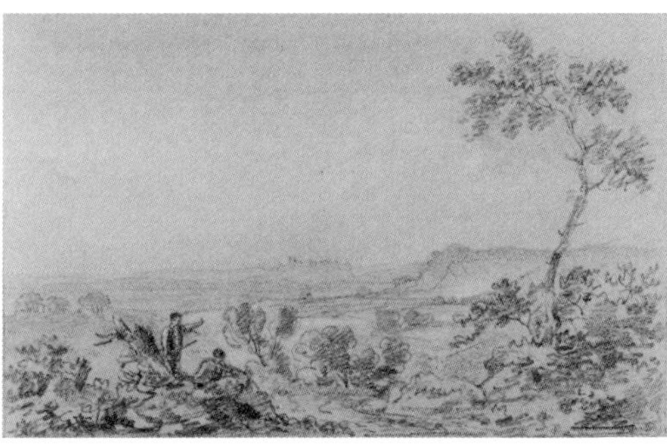

D.1974.64

**Distant View of St Mary's, Breedon-on-the-Hill,
from Coleorton, Leicestershire**
21.7.1804
black chalk, white chalk; blue paper
inscribed lower centre margin: *Bredon Church from
Coleorton*; inscribed & dated upper right margin:
Coleorton friday July 21/1804
176 × 273 mm
Bonham-Carter, Lady (gift, 1974) (D.1974.64)

**Lime Works near Breedon-on-the-Hill,
Leicestershire, with a distant View of the Village**
22.7.1804
pencil, black chalk, white chalk,
grey watercolour; blue card
inscribed lower centre margin: *Lime works near Bredon*;
inscribed & dated upper right margin: *Coleorton
Saturday July 22/1804*
181 × 272 mm
Bonham-Carter, Lady (gift, 1974) (D.1974.65)

**Imaginary Landscape with Timber Waggon
and Bridge**
23.7.1804
pencil, black chalk, white chalk,
grey watercolour; blue paper
inscribed lower centre margin: *Fancy*; inscribed &
dated upper right margin: *Coleorton Monday July
23/1804*
187 × 272 mm
Bonham-Carter, Lady (gift, 1974) (D.1974.66)

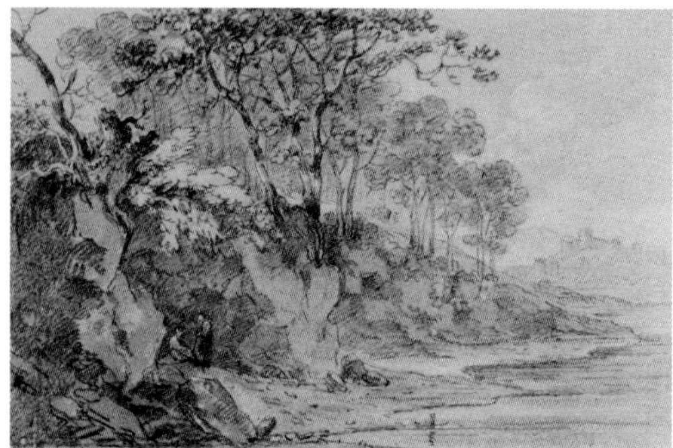

D.1974.67

Road through Benarth Wood, with a distant View of Conway, Caernarvonshire, Wales
25.7.1804
pencil, black chalk, white chalk,
grey watercolour; blue paper
inscribed lower centre margin: *Road through Benarth wood*; inscribed & dated upper right margin: *Coleorton Thursday July 25./1804.*
197 × 302 mm
Bonham-Carter, Lady (gift, 1974) (D.1974.67)

View near Coleorton, Leicestershire, with St Mary's Church in the Distance
25.7.1804
pencil, black chalk, white chalk,
grey watercolour; blue paper
inscribed lower centre margin: *Near Coleorton*; inscribed & dated upper right margin: *Coleorton Thursday July 25/1804.*
175 × 271 mm
Bonham-Carter, Lady (gift, 1974) (D.1974.68)

Conway Castle, Caernarvonshire, Wales, from the South
28.7.1804
pencil, black chalk, white chalk,
grey watercolour; blue paper
inscribed lower centre margin: *Conway Castle*; inscribed & dated upper right margin: *Coleorton Saturday July 28/1804.*
181 × 300 mm
Bonham-Carter, Lady (gift, 1974) (D.1974.69)

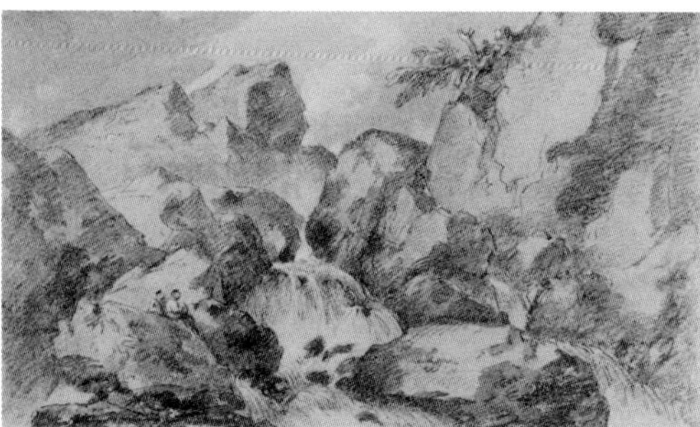

D.1974.70

Mountain Gorge between Llanrwst and Conway, Caernarvonshire, Wales
1.8.1804
pencil, black chalk, white chalk,
grey watercolour; blue paper
inscribed lower centre margin: *Between Llanwrust & Conway*; inscribed & dated upper right margin: *Coleorton Wednesday Aug.1./1804.*
182 × 300 mm
Bonham-Carter, Lady (gift, 1974) (D.1974.70)

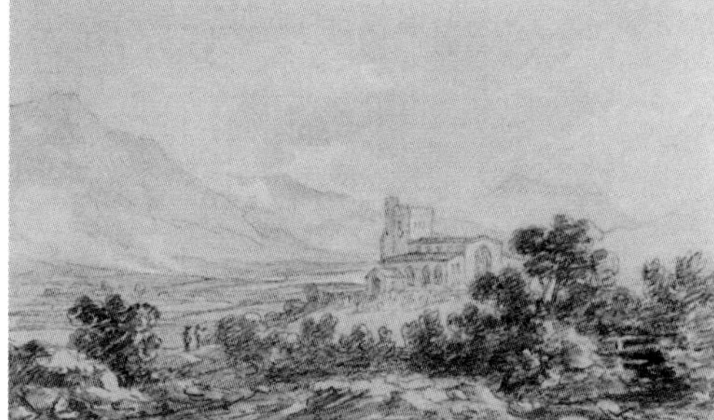

D.1974.71

St Kentigern's, Crosthwaite, Cumberland, from the North-East
3.8.1804
pencil, black chalk, white chalk,
grey watercolour; blue paper
inscribed lower centre margin: *Keswick*; inscribed & dated upper right margin: *Coleorton friday Aug.3.1804.*
181 × 299 mm
Bonham-Carter, Lady (gift, 1974) (D.1974.71)

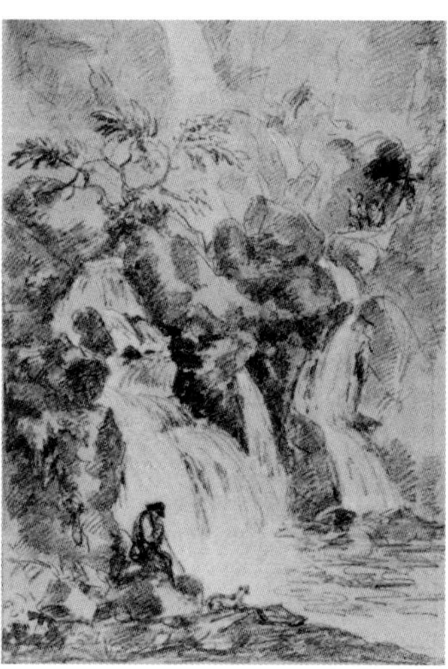

D.1974.72

Lower-Part of Lodore Falls, Cumberland
10.8.1804
black chalk, white chalk, grey watercolour; blue paper
inscribed lower centre margin: *Lower-Part of Lodore Waterfall*; inscribed & dated lower right margin: *Coleorton friday Aug.10/1804.*
285 × 199 mm
Bonham-Carter, Lady (gift, 1974) (D.1974.72)

A Horse and Cart beside a Bridge, near Coleorton, Leicestershire
11.8.1804
pencil, black chalk, white chalk,
grey watercolour; blue paper
inscribed lower centre margin: *near Coleorton*; inscribed & dated upper right margin: *Coleorton Saturday Aug.11/1804*
168 × 247 mm
Bonham-Carter, Lady (gift, 1974) (D.1974.73)

Study of a Tree, Coleorton, Leicestershire
1808
pencil, black chalk; blue paper
inscribed lower centre margin: *Coleorton*; inscribed & dated upper right margin: *Coleorton 1808*
167 × 247 mm
Bonham-Carter, Lady (gift, 1974) (D.1974.74)

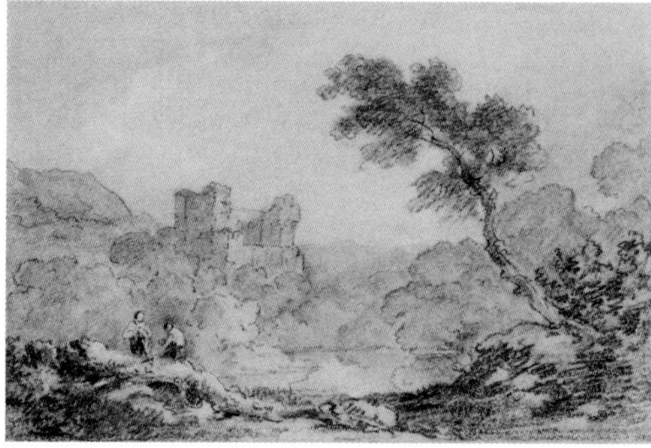

D.1974.75

Distant View of Denbigh Castle, Denbighshire, Wales
15.9.1809
black chalk, white chalk, grey watercolour; blue paper
inscribed lower centre margin: *Denbigh*; inscribed & dated upper right margin: *Coleorton Saturday/Sept.15 1809.*
167 × 248 mm
Bonham-Carter, Lady (gift, 1974) (D.1974.75)

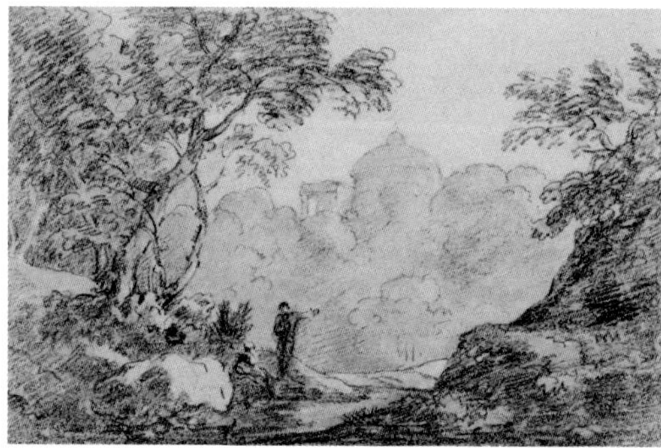

D.1974.76

Ariccia, near Lake Albano, Italy
10.1809
black chalk, white chalk, grey watercolour; blue paper
inscribed lower centre margin: *Larici*; inscribed & dated upper right margin: *Coleorton Oct.1809.*
168 × 248 mm
Bonham-Carter, Lady (gift, 1974) (D.1974.76)

Imaginary Landscape, with two Figures resting by a Stream
10.10.1809
pencil, black chalk, white chalk; blue paper
inscribed lower centre margin: *Fancy*; inscribed & dated upper right margin: *Coleorton Tuesday Oct.10/1809*
168 × 246 mm.
Bonham-Carter, Lady (gift, 1974) (D.1974.77)

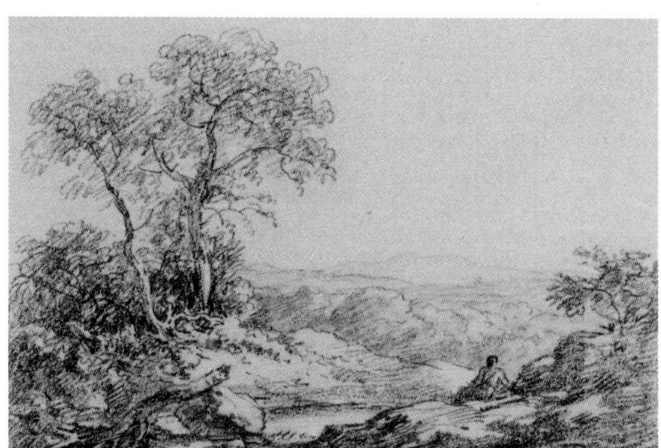

D.1974.78

Landscape View at Coleorton, Leicestershire

24.10.1809
black chalk, white chalk; blue paper
inscribed lower centre margin: *Coleorton*; inscribed &
dated upper right margin: *Coleorton Tuesday
Oct.24/1809.*
168 × 248 mm
Bonham-Carter, Lady (gift, 1974) (D.1974.78)

Figures resting by a Pool at Coleorton, Leicestershire

30.10.1809
pencil, black chalk, white chalk,
grey watercolour; blue paper
inscribed lower centre margin: *Coleorton*; inscribed &
dated upper right margin: *Coleorton
Oct.30.1809/Monday*
193 × 248 mm
Bonham-Carter, Lady (gift, 1974) (D.1974.79)

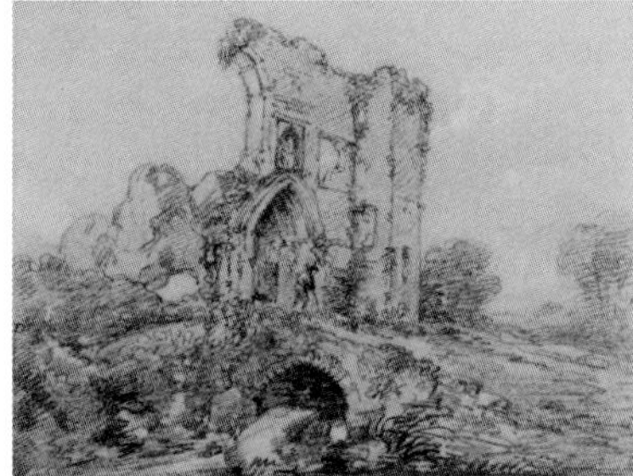

D.1974.80

The ruined Gatehouse, Denbigh Castle, Denbighshire, Wales

31.10.1809
pencil, black chalk, white chalk; blue paper
inscribed lower centre margin: *Denbigh*; inscribed &
dated upper right margin: *Coleorton Tuesday Oct.31.1809*
191 × 248 mm
Bonham-Carter, Lady (gift, 1974) (D.1974.80)

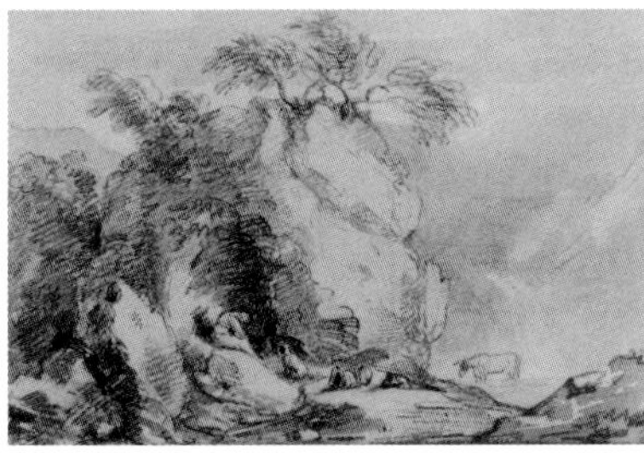

D.1974.81

Illustration to Wordsworth's Poem 'Peter Bell'

2.11.1809
pencil, black chalk, white chalk, grey watercolour
blue paper
inscribed lower centre margin: *Poem of Peter Bell
Wordsworth*; inscribed & dated upper right margin:
Coleorton Thursday Nov.2 1809
167 × 246 mm
Bonham-Carter, Lady (gift, 1974) (D.1974.81)

Imaginary Woodland Scene with a Shepherd

4.11.1809
pencil, black chalk, white chalk; blue paper
inscribed lower centre margin: *Fancy*; inscribed &
dated upper right margin: *Coleorton Saturday
Nov.4.1809*
167 × 246 mm
Bonham-Carter, Lady (gift, 1974) (D.1974.82)

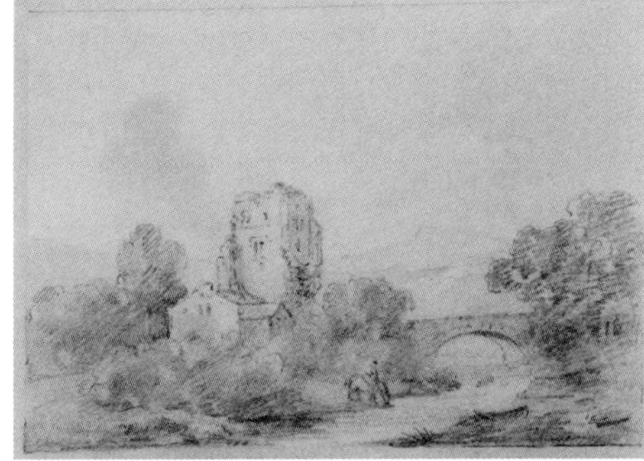

D.1974.83

Shap Abbey, Lowther, Westmorland

8.11.1809
pencil, black chalk, white chalk; blue paper
inscribed lower centre margin: *Shap Abbey near
Lowther*; inscribed & dated upper right margin:
Coleorton Wednesday Nov.8./1809
178 × 246 mm
Bonham-Carter, Lady (gift, 1974) (D.1974.83)

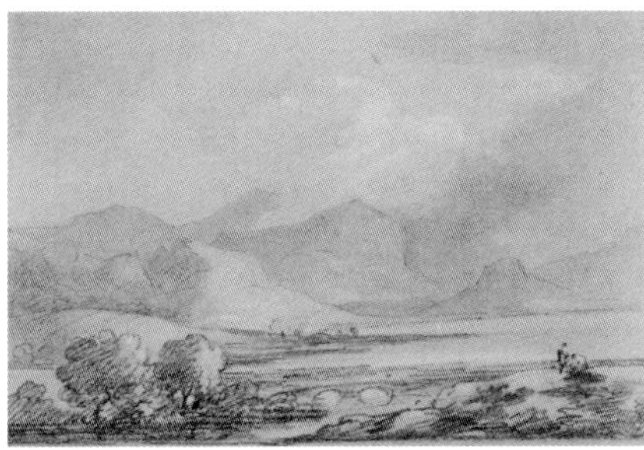

D.1974.84

Landscape with Mountains and Lake in the North of England

9.11.1809
pencil, black chalk, white chalk; blue paper
inscribed lower centre margin: *North of England*,
inscribed & dated upper right margin: *Coleorton
Thursday Nov.9/1809.*
166 × 246 mm
Bonham-Carter, Lady (gift, 1974) (D.1974.84)

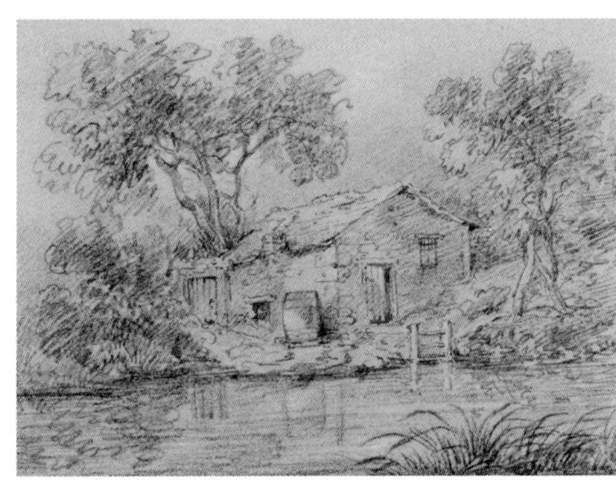

D.1974.85

Cottage on the Banks of the River Greta, Cumberland

12.11.1809
black chalk, white chalk; blue paper
inscribed lower centre margin: *Banks of the Greta*;
inscribed & dated upper right margin: *Coleorton
Saturday Nov.12 1809*
187 × 247 mm
Bonham-Carter, Lady (gift, 1974) (D.1974.85)

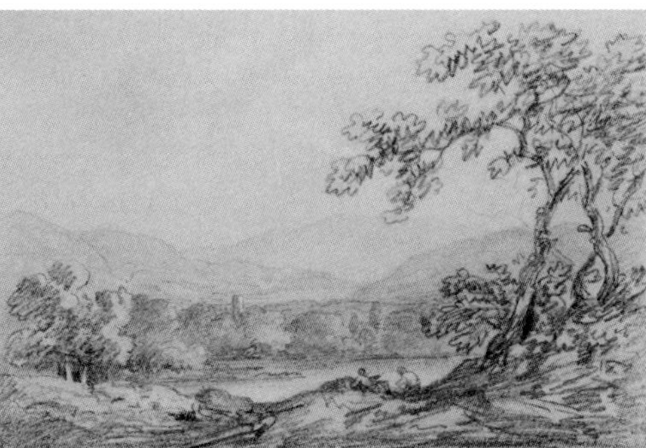

D.1974.86

Mountainous Landscape in the North of England

10.11.1809
black chalk, white chalk; blue paper
inscribed lower centre margin: *North of England*;
inscribed & dated upper right margin: *Coleorton friday
Nov.10.1809.*
167 × 247 mm
Bonham-Carter, Lady (gift, 1974) (D.1974.86)

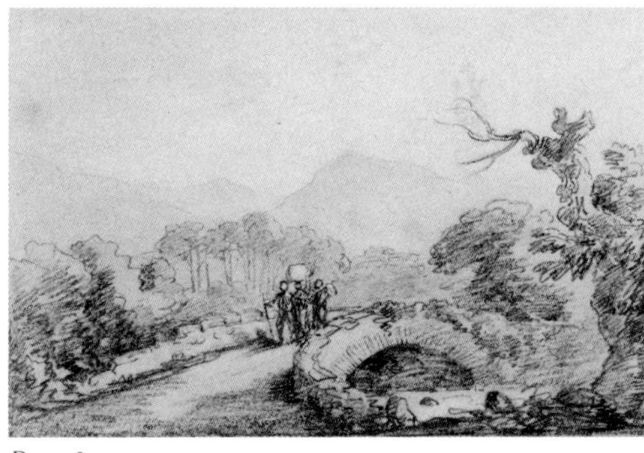

D.1974.87

Imaginary Landscape with Travellers crossing a Bridge

15.11.1809
black chalk, white chalk; blue paper
inscribed lower centre margin: *Fancy*; inscribed &
dated upper right margin: *Coleorton Wednesday
Nov.15./1809*
166 × 246 mm
Bonham-Carter, Lady (gift, 1974) (D.1974.87)

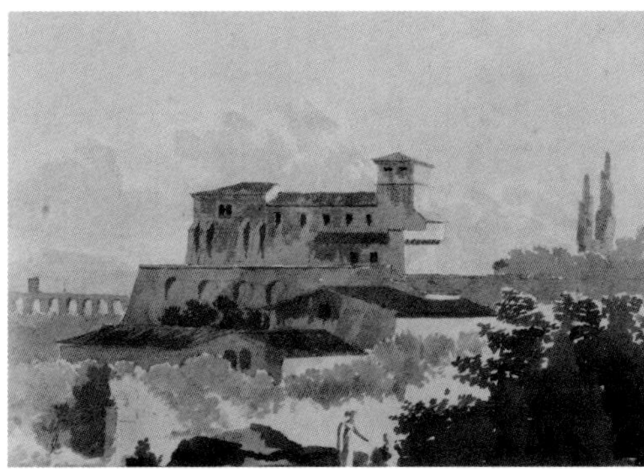

D.1979.5

The Villa of Maecenas, Tivoli

pencil, grey watercolour
inscribed (later hand) lower right verso: *The Villa of
Maecenas / Tivoli 62*
141 × 200 mm
Alexander, Jonathan J. G. (Dr) (gift, 1979) (D.1979.5)

■ SIR GEORGE BEAUMONT (circle of)

Landscape Study (recto); Oval Vignette, Landscape with Cottage (verso)
black chalk, grey watercolour (recto); blue paper
206 × 289 mm
Ogden, William Sharp (bequest, 1926) (D.1926.190)

■ BECKER, EDMUND (fl. 1780–1810)
Edmund Becker was probably an amateur pupil of Richard Cooper Jun. He is known for his monochrome landscapes.

Smith Lane, Windsor Park
pencil, pen and grey ink, grey watercolour
inscribed lower edge: *Windsor Park Smith Lane*
256 × 357 mm
Anderson, A. E., National Art Collections Fund (via) (gift, 1923) (D.1923.21)

Lake Scene with Cattle
pencil, pen and grey ink, grey watercolour
202 × 332 mm
Anderson, A. E., National Art Collections Fund (via) (gift, 1923) (D.1923.22)

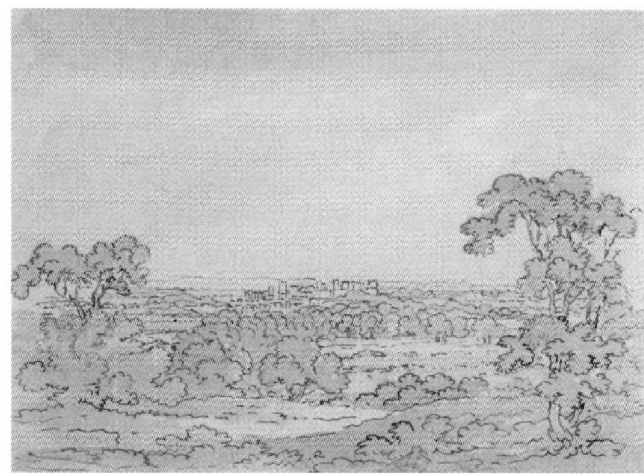
D.1954.17

Landscape with distant View of Windsor Castle
pencil, pen and brown ink, grey watercolour
191 × 258 mm
Sewter, Albert Charles (gift, 1954) (D.1954.17)

■ BECKER, FERDINAND (fl. 1793–1825)
Ferdinand Becker was a landscape painter.

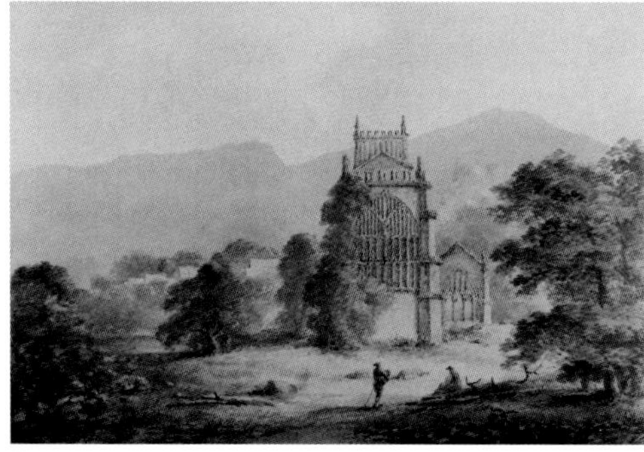
D.1904.26

Exterior of Malvern Priory Church, Worcestershire, from the East
pencil, watercolour
331 × 468 mm
Worthington, Mary (bequest, 1904) (D.1904.26)

■ BENGER, BERENGER ERNEST (1868–1935)
Benger was born in Gloucestershire and studied in Antwerp. He exhibited at the Royal Institute from 1884 and the Royal Academy from 1890, and was a member of the Royal Cambrian Academy. He lived first in Liverpool and latterly in Sussex. Benger illustrated the A. & C. Black colour plate book, *Highways and Hedges*, published in 1911.

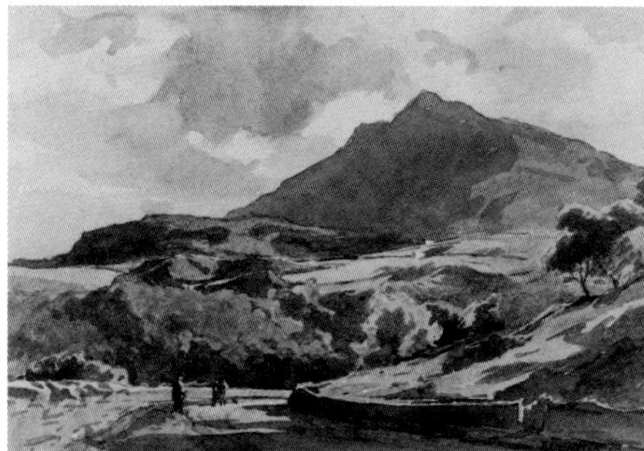
D.1936.4

Moel Siabod from the Road between Bettws-y-Coed and Capel Curig, Caernarvonshire, Wales
watercolour
signed lower right: *Berenger Benger*
276 × 399 mm
Benger, Berenger Ernest (bequest, 1936) (D.1936.4)

■ BENNETT, WILLIAM (1811–71)
Bennett, a landscape watercolourist, may have been a pupil of David Cox. He was elected an associate of the New Watercolour Society in 1848 and a full member in 1849.

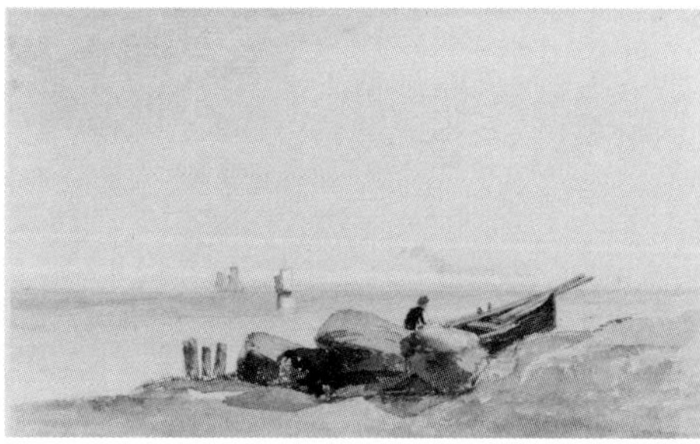
D.1933.1

Shore Scene
pencil, watercolour
206 × 331 mm
Thomson, G. Douglas (gift, 1933) (D.1933.1)

■ BENTLEY, CHARLES (1806–54)
Bentley was a marine artist who began his career working for the Fielding brothers as an engraver. He was elected an associate of the Old Watercolour Society in 1834 and a full member in 1843. He painted scenes from all round Britain and visited the Channel Islands and northern France.

Porthmadoc, Caernarvonshire, Wales, Low Tide
1844
pencil, watercolour, bodycolour
(heightened with white)
signed & dated lower right: *CBentley / 1844*
501 × 755 mm
Palser, J. and Son, London (purchase, 1912) (D.1912.9)

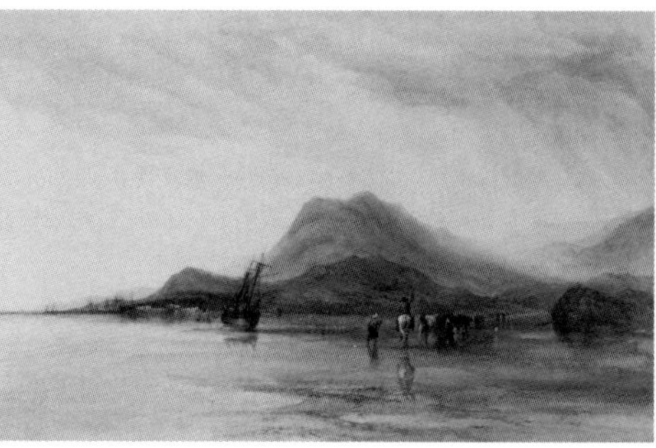
D.1912.9

Coast Scene with Shipping off Whitby, North Yorkshire
1845
pencil, watercolour, bodycolour
(heightened with white)
signed & dated lower right: *CBentley / 1845*
340 × 501 mm
Anderson, A. E. (gift, 1918) (D.1918.2)

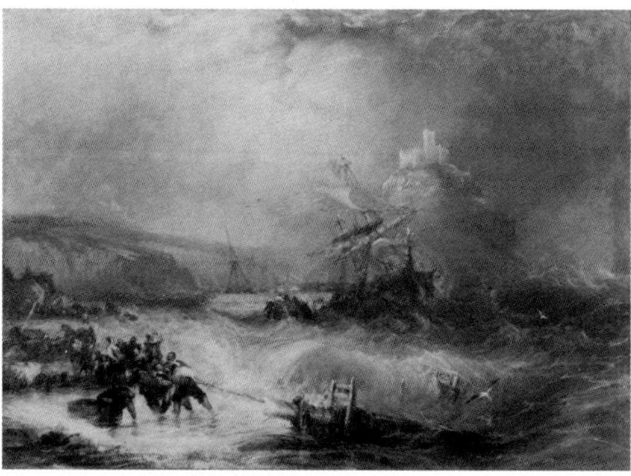
D.1930.15

Shipwreck off St Michael's Mount, Cornwall
1833
pencil, watercolour, bodycolour (heightened with white)
signed & dated lower left: *CBentley / 1833*
1086 × 1502 mm
Yates, John (gift, 1930) (D.1930.15)

■ BERESFORD, M. E. (fl. 1861)
Unknown amateur.

St Mary's Parish Church, Hornsey, London
1861
pencil, bodycolour (heightened with white); grey paper
signed, inscribed & dated lower left: *Hornsey Church / M.E.Beresford / 1861*
356 × 266 mm
Ogden, William Sharp (bequest, 1926) (D.1926.320)

■ BEVERLEY, WILLIAM ROXBY (1811–89)
Beverley was an actor, scene painter and theatre manager, and worked in Scotland, the North of England and Manchester before returning to London in about 1846. In addition to working at Drury Lane, he exhibited marine watercolours in the Bonington tradition at the Royal Academy between 1865 and 1880.

French Luggers
watercolour
303 × 448 mm
Anderson, A. E. (gift, 1915) (D.1915.7)

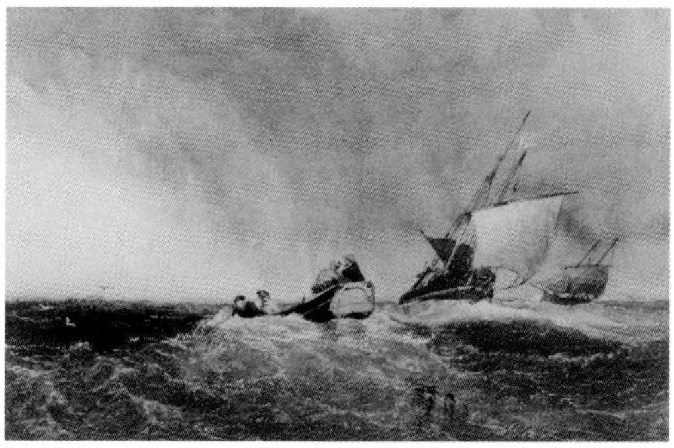

D.1915.7

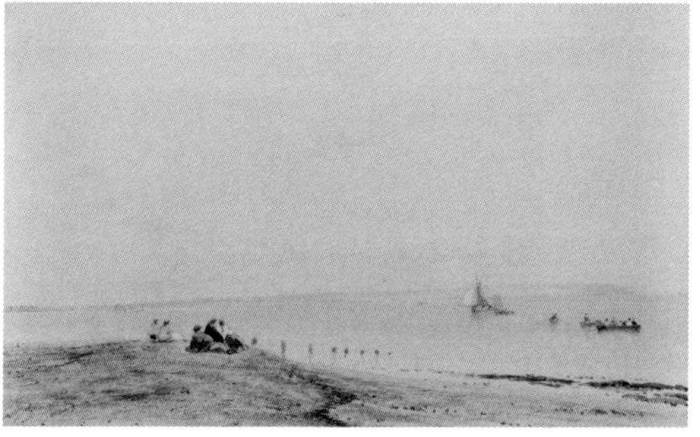

D.1933.8

Pevensey Bay, East Sussex
pencil, watercolour, bodycolour
(heightened with white)
signed lower left margin: *GR(?)/W R Beverly*
289 × 464 mm
Anderson, A. E. (gift, 1933) (D.1933.8)

■ **BILLINGS, ROBERT WILLIAM (1813–74)**
Billings, an architect as well as a landscape painter,
exhibited at the Royal Academy from 1845 to 1872.
He specialised in churches and architecture.

Shaw House, Berkshire
1831
pencil, pen and brown ink, watercolour
signed & inscribed centre on roof of house: *RWBillings
drew the house / and coloured it*; inscribed lower-left
verso: *In this House Charles I resided in / 1646 and one of
the Parliamentary / Army attempted & nearly assassinated
/ him.*; inscribed lower centre verso: *Shaw House –
Berkshire / Exterior in 1581.* [all underlined] / *Drawn
and restored by R. W. Billings, author of Baronial
Antiquities, 1831. Signed, see roof*; inscribed lower right
verso: *Shaw House / Exterior 1581*
471 × 667 mm
Ogden, William Sharp (bequest, 1926) (D.1926.191)

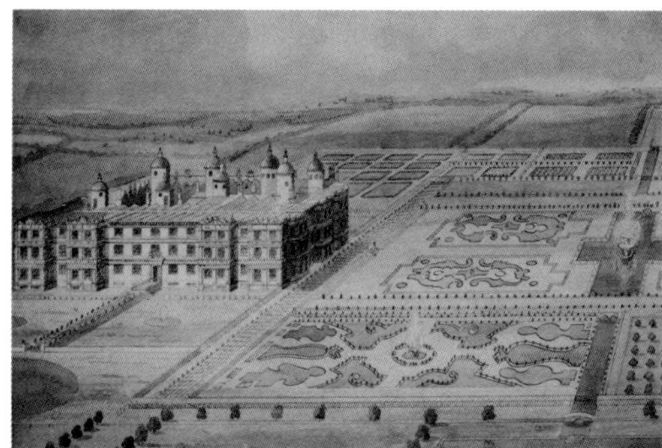

D.1926.192

Longleat House and Gardens, Wiltshire
pencil, pen and brown ink, watercolour
inscribed lower right verso: *Longleat House and Gardens
Wiltshire*; inscribed lower centre verso: *Longleat House
& Gardens Wiltshire / Seat of Marquis of Salisbury*
[erased] *Bath* [added] / *Erected 1567* [underlined]
470 × 689 mm
Ogden, William Sharp (bequest, 1926) (D.1926.192)

■ **BIRD, EDWARD (1772–1819)**
Bird was born in Wolverhampton, but moved to
Bristol and set up a drawing school there in 1797. He
exhibited at the Royal Academy from 1809 and was
elected a member in 1815.

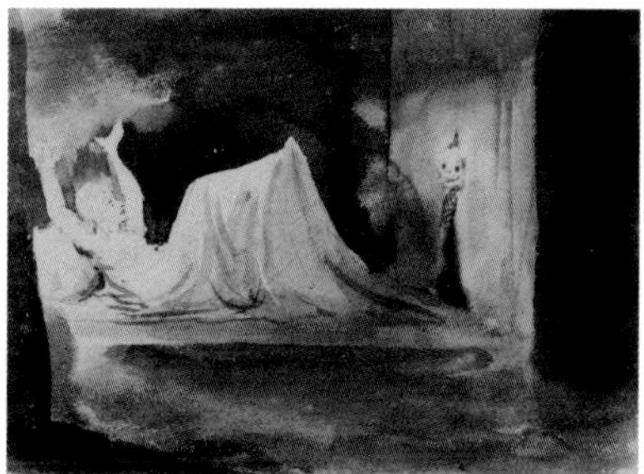

D.1926.15

The Apparition
pencil, grey watercolour
110 × 146 mm
Wallis, Miss J. K., Wallis, Miss R. (gift, 1926) (D.1926.15)

Landscape with Lake and Temple
21.1.1808
brown watercolour
signed & dated upper left with initials: *E.B.Jany.21 /
1808*
136 × 185 mm
Wallis, Miss J. K., Wallis, Miss R. (gift, 1926) (D.1926.16)

A Woman giving a Loaf of Bread to a seated Girl
pencil, pen and brown ink, brown watercolour
120 × 184 mm
Wallis, Miss J. K., Wallis, Miss R. (gift, 1926) (D.1926.17)

■ **BLAKE, WILLIAM (1757–1827)**
Blake – poet, painter, engraver and visionary thinker –
stands out among his contemporaries. He is hugely
admired today for his bright visionary watercolours and
for his illuminated books, which use relief etching to
combine text and illustration in a unique way. He was,
however, largely ignored or dismissed as an eccentric in
his own day.

**The Descent of Peace: Milton's Hymn
'On the Morning of Christ's Nativity'**
1809
pencil, pen and brown ink, watercolour
signed & dated lower centre: *WBlake 1809* [date cut]
255 × 195 mm
Taylor, John Edward (gift, 1892) (D.1892.26)

**The Angels appearing to the Shepherds: Milton's
Hymn 'On the Morning of Christ's Nativity'**
1809
pencil, pen and brown ink, watercolour
signed & dated lower left: *WBlake 1809*
255 × 193 mm
Taylor, John Edward (gift, 1892) (D.1892.27)

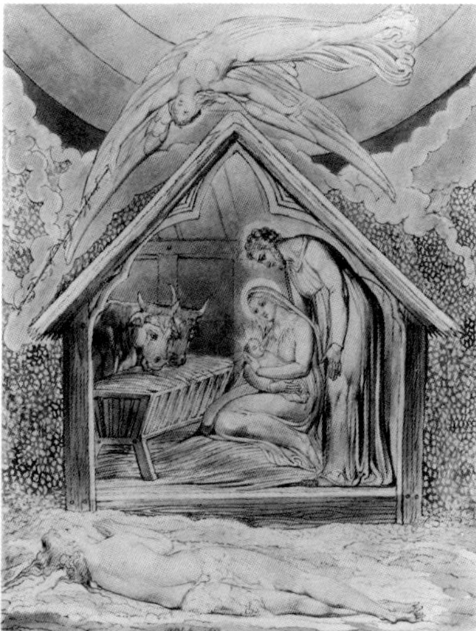

D.1892.26

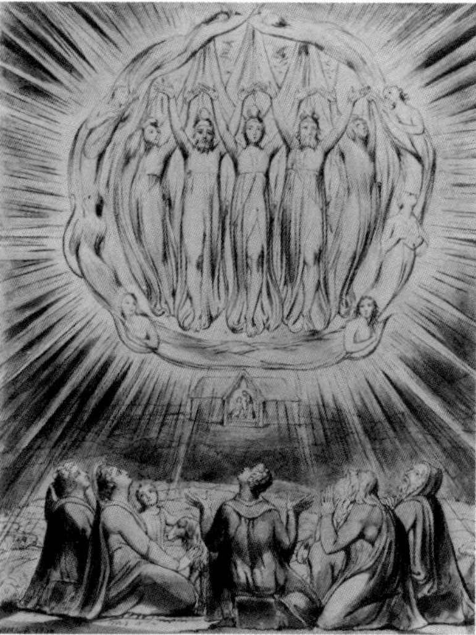

D.1892.27

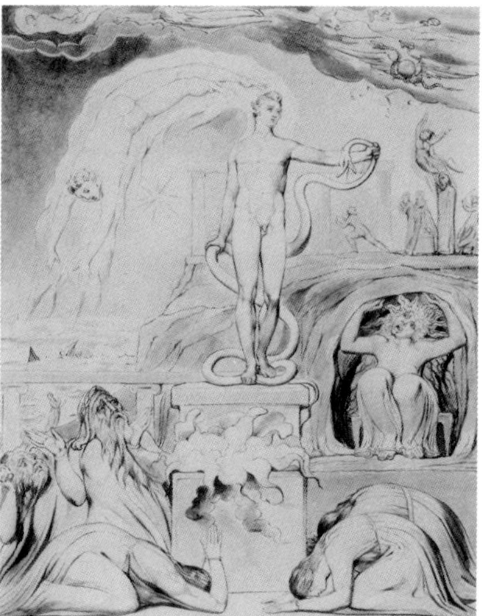

D.1892.28

**The Shrine of Apollo: Milton's Hymn
'On the Morning of Christ's Nativity'**
1809
pencil, pen and brown ink, watercolour
251 × 194 mm
Taylor, John Edward (gift, 1892) (D.1892.28)

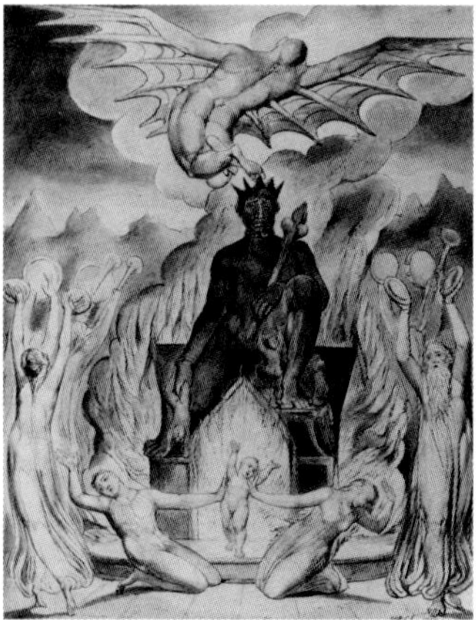

D.1892.29

Sullen Moloch: Milton's Hymn 'On the Morning of Christ's Nativity'
1809
pencil, pen and brown ink, watercolour
signed & dated lower right: *WBlake 1809*
[last digit trimmed]
258 × 197 mm
Taylor, John Edward (gift, 1892) (D.1892.29)

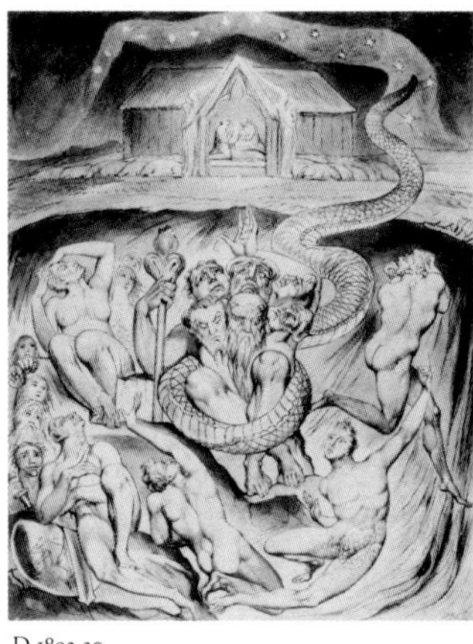

D.1892.30

The Descent of Typhon and the Gods into Hell: Milton's Hymn 'On the Morning of Christ's Nativity'
1809
pencil, pen and brown ink, watercolour
signed & dated lower right: *WBlake 18* [date cut]
252 × 193 mm
Taylor, John Edward (gift, 1892) (D.1892.30)

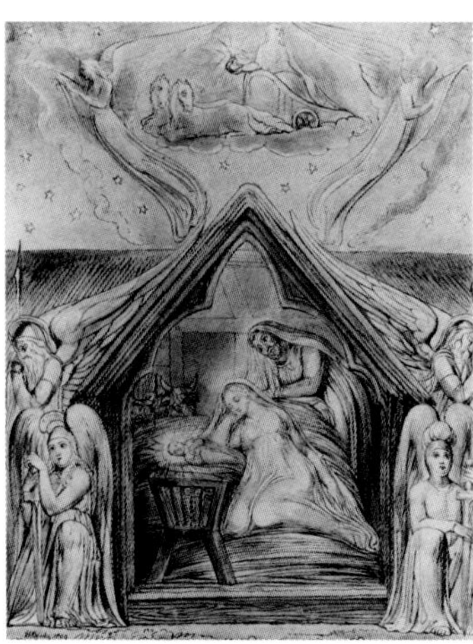

D.1892.31

The Night of Peace: Milton's Hymn 'On the Morning of Christ's Nativity'
1809
pencil, pen and brown ink, watercolour
signed & dated lower left: *WBlake 1809*
256 × 193 mm
Taylor, John Edward (gift, 1892) (D.1892.31)

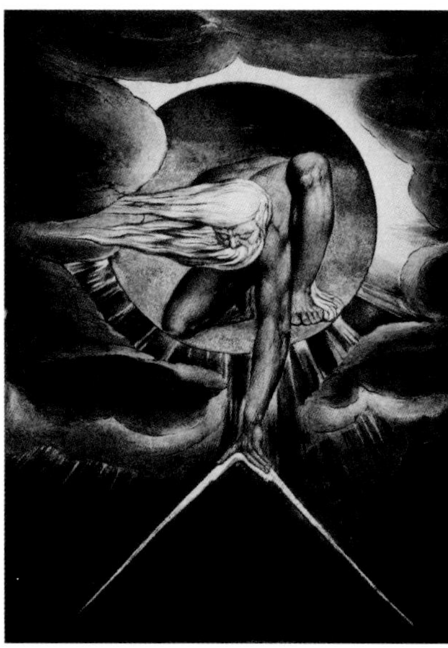

D.1892.32

'Europe', Plate I, Frontispiece, 'The Ancient of Days'
1827 (?)
etching, pen and brown ink, watercolour, gold bodycolour
signed & dated (?), date (?) centre right is hard to read and may be a smudged 'inv' *Blake / [?]*
232 × 170 mm
Taylor, John Edward (gift, 1892) (D.1892.32)

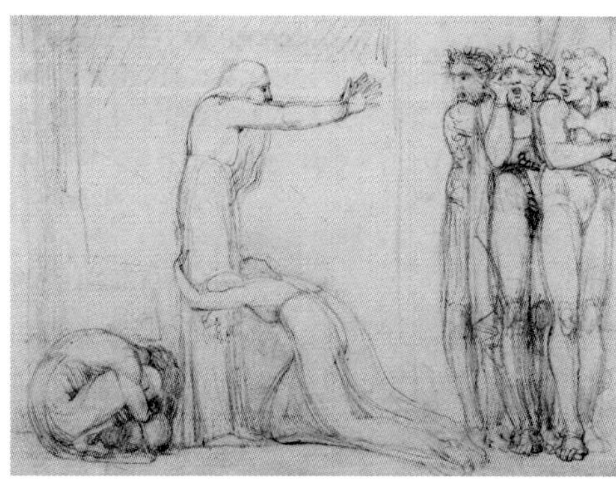

D.1914.29

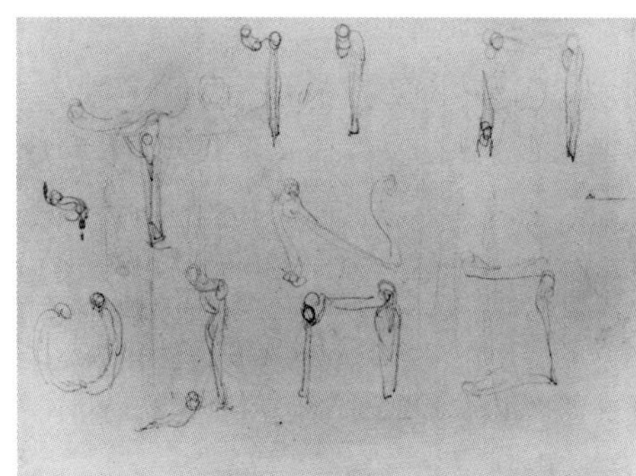

D.1914.29 (verso)

Study for 'Tiriel denouncing his Sons and Daughters' (recto); Studies of Hebrew Characters in human Form (verso)
1789
pencil
178 × 238 mm
Harvey, Francis (purchase, 1914) (D.1914.29)

■ BLIGH, JABEZ (fl. 1863–89)

Bligh, a painter of flowers, began his career in Worcester and moved to London in the 1860s. He exhibited in London and elsewhere from 1863 to 1889.

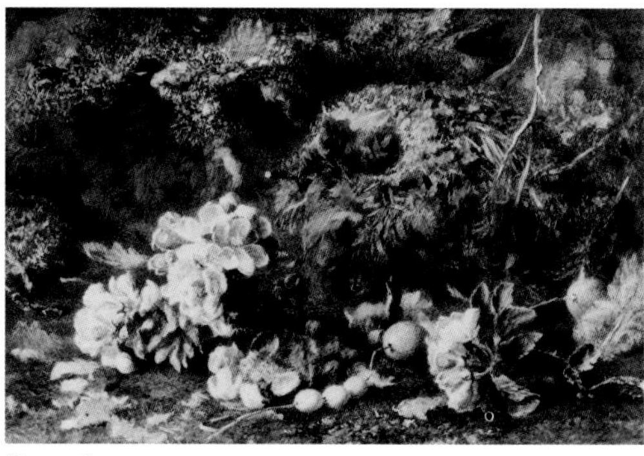

D.1970.16

Apple Blossom
watercolour, bodycolour
signed lower right: *J.BLIGH*
233 × 350 mm
Towlson, Hector J. (bequest, 1969) (D.1970.16)

■ BLUNDEN, ANNA ELIZABETH (1830–1915)

Inspired by Ruskin's *Modern Painters*, Blunden abandoned her career as a governess in order to become an artist. She exhibited from 1853 and was encouraged by Ruskin. She moved to Italy in 1867, returning to Britain in 1872 in order to marry her dead sister's husband. Blunden (or Mrs Martino as she became) settled in Birmingham and exhibited there until her death.

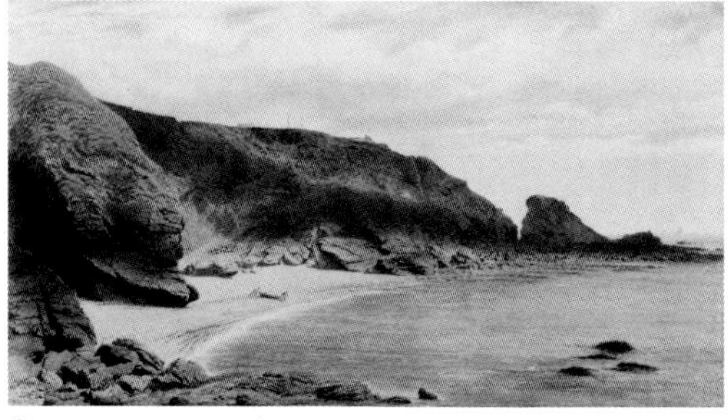

D.1993.3

The Lizard Point, Cornwall
1862
watercolour, bodycolour (heightened with white)
signed and dated lower left with initial in monogram:
ABlunden 1862
329 × 565 mm
Abbott and Holder, London (purchase, 24.6.1993) (D.1993.3)

■ BODDINGTON, HENRY (1849–1925)

Boddington retired from the chairmanship of the family's Manchester brewery in 1891 and devoted the rest of his life to collecting and painting. In 1908 he was made a founder member of the Allied Artists Association. Financially independent, he never sold his work, which remained with his family until 1987.

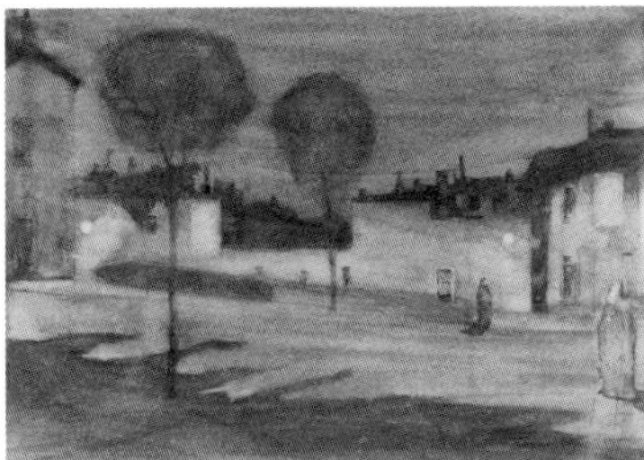

D.1987.4

African Nocturne
1911
pencil, watercolour
177 × 250 mm
Tib Lane Gallery, Manchester (purchase, 1987) (D.1987.4)

■ BODICHON, BARBARA (1827–91)

Bodichon, a pupil of William Henry Hunt and a friend of George Eliot, was a tireless campaigner for women's rights and a founder of Girton College, Cambridge. Her watercolours, which she frequently exhibited, reflected her political interests as well as her travels in Algeria and America.

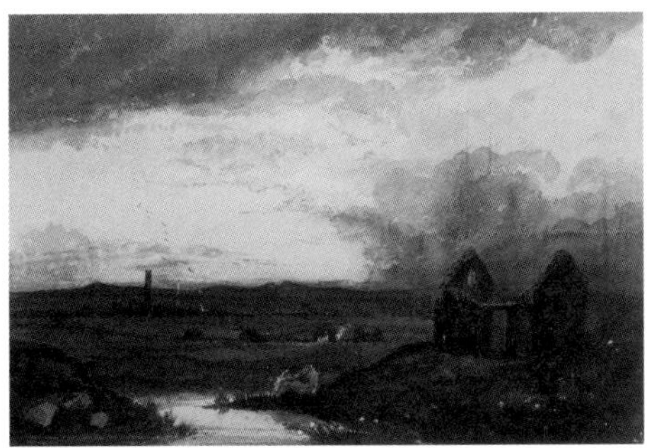

D.1994.1

Ireland-1846
1846
watercolour, bodycolour (heightened with white)
230 × 333 mm
Crabbe, John (purchase, 1994) (D.1994.1)

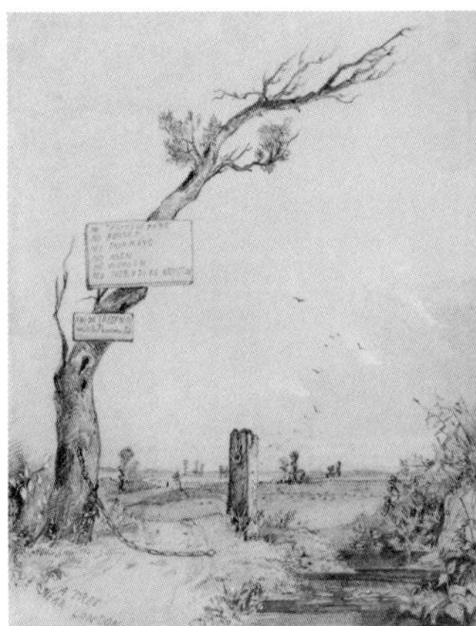

D.1994.2

A Tree near London
10.1849
pencil, white chalk; buff paper
dated lower right verso: *Oct 1849*; titled lower left:
A TREE NEAR LONDON
337 × 260 mm
Crabbe, John (purchase, 1994) (D.1994.2)

■ BONINGTON, RICHARD PARKES (1802–28)

Bonington was born in Nottingham, and studied in Calais with Francis Louis Thomas Francia and in Paris in the studio of Baron Gros. He returned briefly to England in 1825 before moving to Italy in 1826. Despite his short working life, Bonington had a huge influence on Continental painting and on a whole generation of English artists working in Paris in the 1820s and '30s.

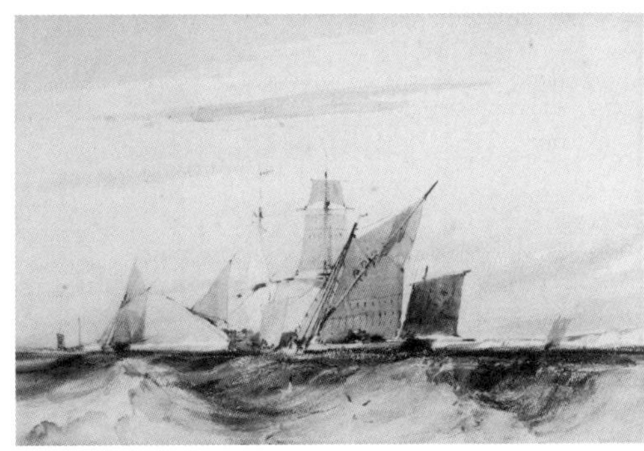

D.1892.135

Shipping off the French Coast
watercolour
signed on sail of central vessel with initials: *RPB*
165 × 237 mm
Taylor, John Edward (gift, 1892) (D.1892.135)

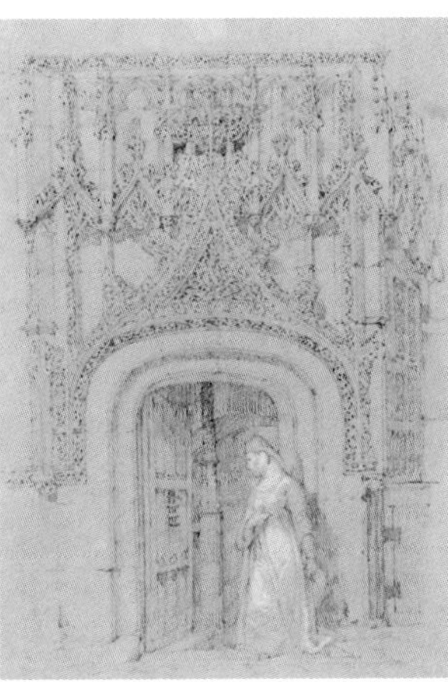

D.1918.8

Church Doorway in Normandy
1823–24
pencil, white chalk; buff paper
375 × 258 mm
Coleman, Sir Jeremiah, National Art Collections Fund (via)
(gift, 1918) (D.1918.8)

On the Staircase
1828
watercolour, bodycolour, surface scratching
signed & dated lower left with initials: *RPB / 1828*
198 × 143 mm
Agnew's (purchase, 1920) (D.1920.7)

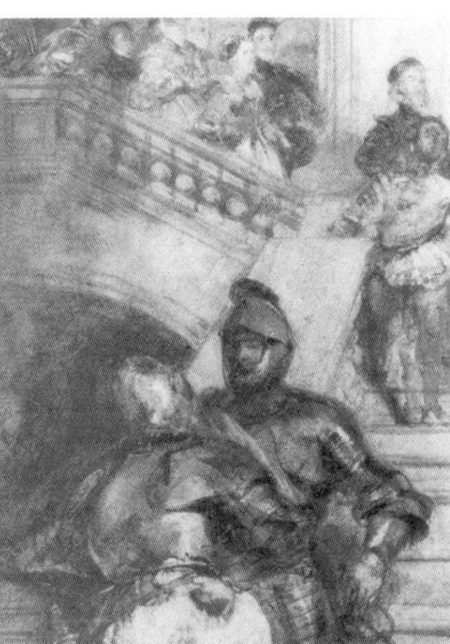

D.1920.7

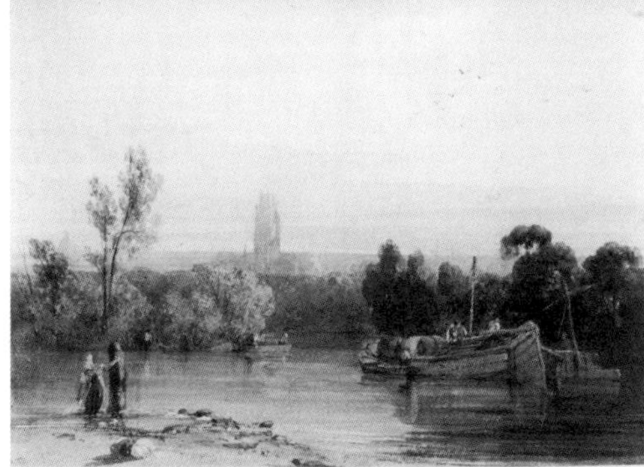

D.1946.8

Rouen with the Tower of Saint Ouen - Sunset
1825
pencil, watercolour
signed & dated lower left with initials: *RPB.1825*
174 × 235 mm
Pilkington, Margaret, Friends of the Whitworth (via)
(gift, 1946) (D.1946.8)

■ BOUGH, SAMUEL (1822–78)

Bough was born in Carlisle, and began his career as a scene painter in Manchester in 1845. He moved to Glasgow in 1848 and Edinburgh in 1849, still working as a scene painter, before turning to easel painting. He was elected an associate of the Royal Scottish Academy in 1856 and did not become a full member until 1875.

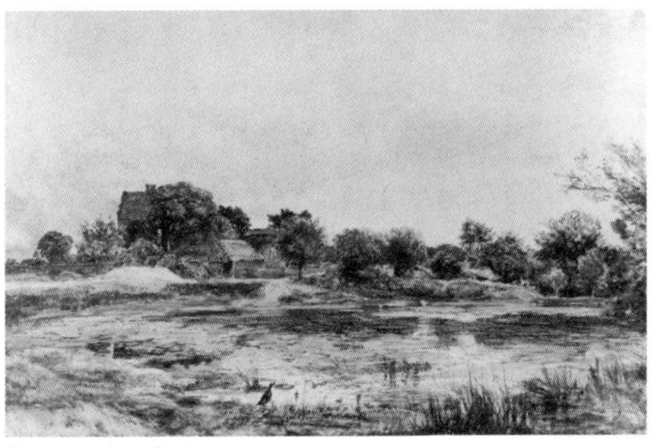

D.1904.27

The Drinking Place
1856
watercolour, bodycolour (heightened with white)
signed & dated lower left: *1856 / Sam Bough*
351 × 525 mm
Worthington, Mary (bequest, 1904) (D.1904.27)

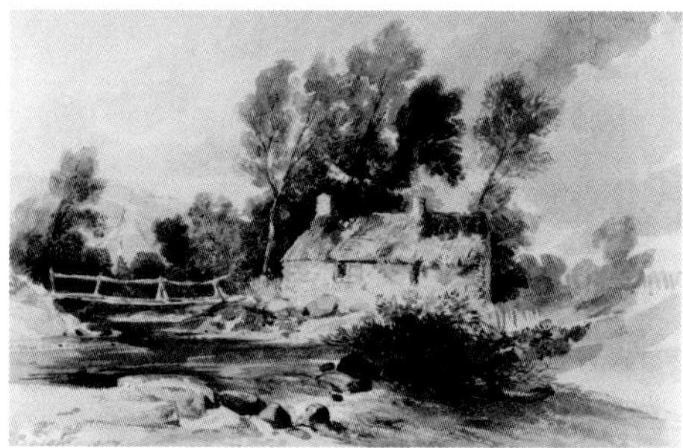

D.1924.83

Wooden Bridge on the Caldew, Cumberland
1857
pencil, watercolour, bodycolour
(heightened with white)
signed & dated lower left: *S Bough 1857*
293 × 453 mm
Broadhurst, Sir Edward Tootal, Broadhurst, Lady
(bequest, 1924) (D.1924.83)

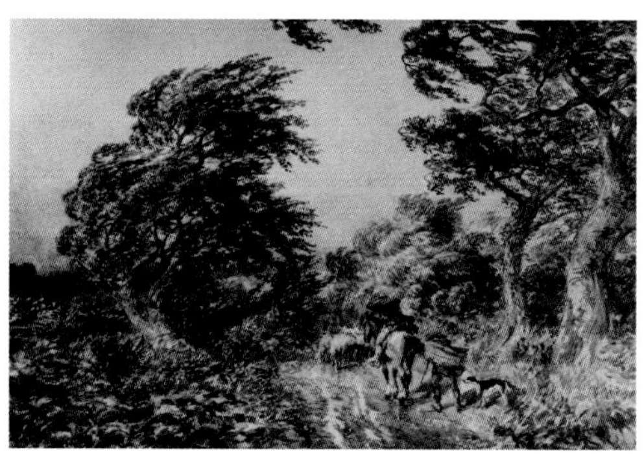

D.1930.61

A windy Day
watercolour, bodycolour (heightened with white)
signed lower centre: *Sam Bough*
355 × 510 mm
Falkner, Frank (bequest, 1930) (D.1930.61)

Border Landscape
1861
watercolour
signed & dated lower left: *Sam Bough 1861*;
numbered lower left: *56*
232 × 357 mm
Lancaster, Percy (gift, 1946) (D.1946.20)

■ **BOURNE, REV. JAMES (1773–1854)**
Bourne, a prolific drawing master who worked in
London from about 1796, toured Wales with Sir
George Beaumont in 1800. He usually worked in
monochrome. Bourne may have met Girtin and Turner
and his work is sometimes mistaken for theirs.

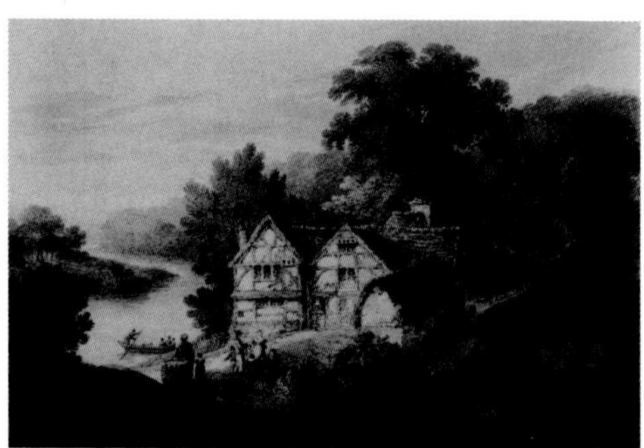

D.1892.105

**Bridge Sollers Ferry on the
River Wye, Herefordshire**
pencil, watercolour
292 × 428 mm
Taylor, John Edward (gift, 1892) (D.1892.105)

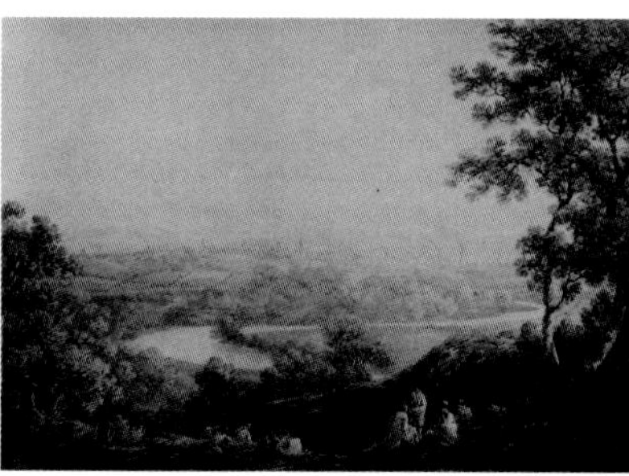

D.1917.26

View of Manchester from Kersal Moor
1806
pencil, watercolour
signed, inscribed & dated verso of mount:
*View of Manchester / from Kersal Moor / James Bourne /
London 1806*
308 × 436 mm
untraced (purchase, 1917) (D.1917.26)

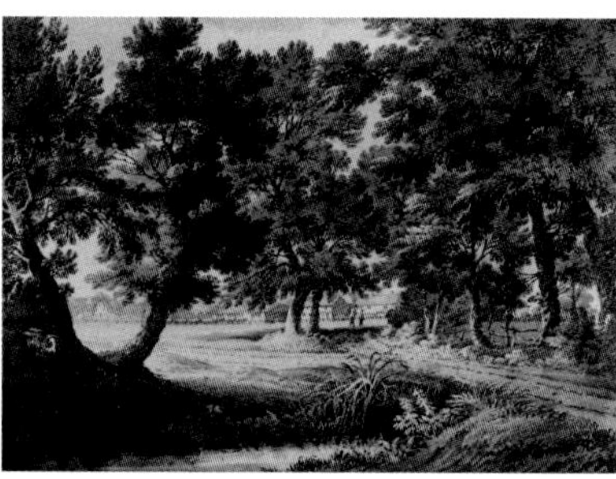

D.1922.14

**Scene on the River Wandle, near
Croydon, Surrey**
pencil, grey watercolour
signed & inscribed on mount centre verso: *A Scene on
the River Wandle / near Croyden – Surrey / Mr Bourne
No 7 Somerset Street / Portman Sqr*
332 × 452 mm
Meatyard (purchase, 1922) (D.1922.14)

River Scene, North Wales
pencil, grey watercolour
inscribed (not artist's hand) upper right verso:
In North Wales; inscribed (different hand) centre verso:
In North Wales / Merioneth
259 × 342 mm
Ogden, William Sharp (bequest, 1926) (D.1926.329)

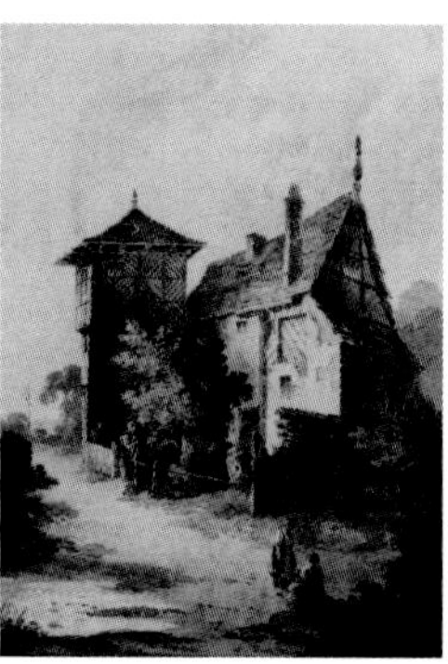

D.1936.15

Hulme Hall, Lancashire
pencil, watercolour
signed & inscribed centre verso: *Hulme Hall /
Lancashire / J.Bourne / Princes St. Cavendish*
[remainder cut]
329 × 234 mm
Powell, Dr Herbert A., National Art Collections Fund (via)
(gift, 1936) (D.1936.15)

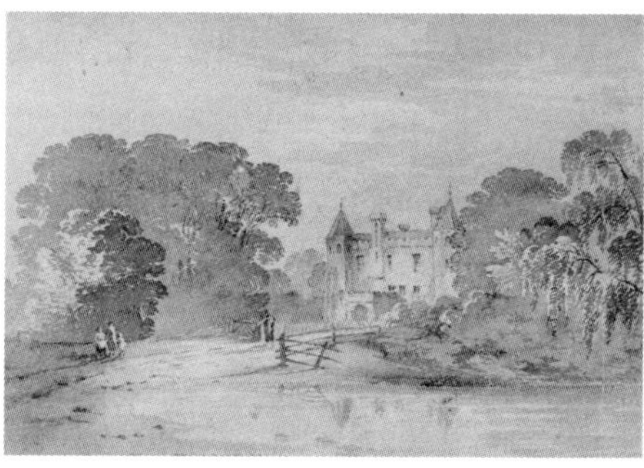

D.1944.13

Wickham Court, Wickhambreaux, Kent
pencil, blue watercolour, grey watercolour
signed & inscribed centre verso: *MrBourne / No7
Somerset St.Portman Sqr*; inscribed centre verso:
Wickham Court
211 × 297 mm
National Art Collections Fund (gift, 1944) (D.1944.13)

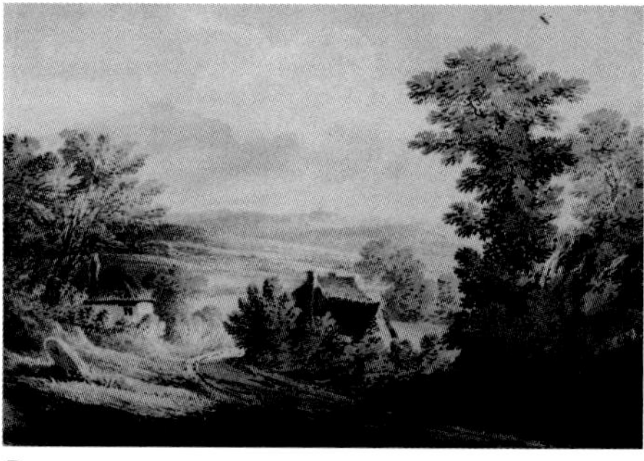

D.1944.14

Distant View of Harrow, London
blue watercolour, grey watercolour
signed & inscribed centre verso: *Distant view of
Harrow / JBourne 7 Somerset St. Portman Sqr*
258 × 365 mm
National Art Collections Fund (gift, 1944) (D.1944.14)

Hampstead from Primrose Hill, London
pencil
signed & inscribed centre verso: *A Scene from Primrose
Hill / JBourne 7 Somerset St. Portman Sqr*; inscribed
lower left: *Hampstead / from Primrose hill*
276 × 376 mm
National Art Collections Fund (gift, 1944) (D.1944.15)

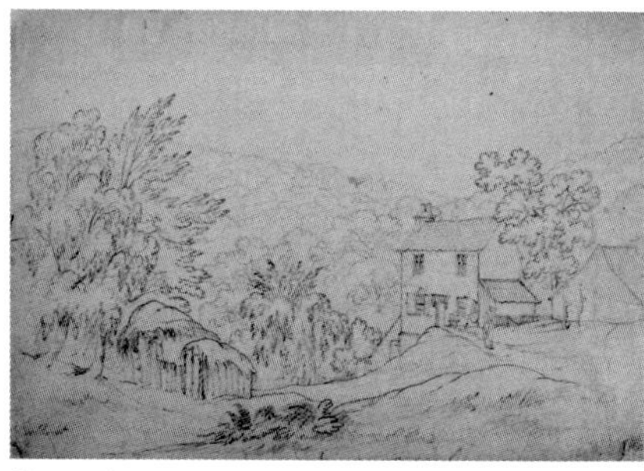

D.1944.16

Cottage and Woods at Chiselhurst, Kent
pencil
signed & inscribed centre verso: *MrBourne / No7
Somerset St. Portman Sqr*; inscribed lower left:
Chiselhurst
265 × 373 mm
National Art Collections Fund (gift, 1944) (D.1944.16)

Lane at Chiselhurst, Kent
pencil
inscribed lower left: *Chiselhurst*; inscribed centre verso:
7 Somerset St. Portman Sqr
263 × 373 mm
National Art Collections Fund (gift, 1944) (D.1944.17)

Cottage at Brockham, Surrey
pencil; corners of paper cut
numbered upper left: *10*; inscribed lower left: *Brockham
Surry*; inscribed centre verso: *No7 Somerset Street /
Portman Sqr*
119 × 175 mm
National Art Collections Fund (gift, 1944) (D.1944.18)

The Bridge at Whalley Abbey, Lancashire
watercolour
signed & inscribed upper centre verso: *MrBourne /
[erased mostly illegible address]*; inscribed lower left:
Bridge at Whalley / Abbey; inscribed centre verso: *Bridge
at Whalley Abbey*
195 × 260 mm
National Art Collections Fund (gift, 1944) (D.1944.19)

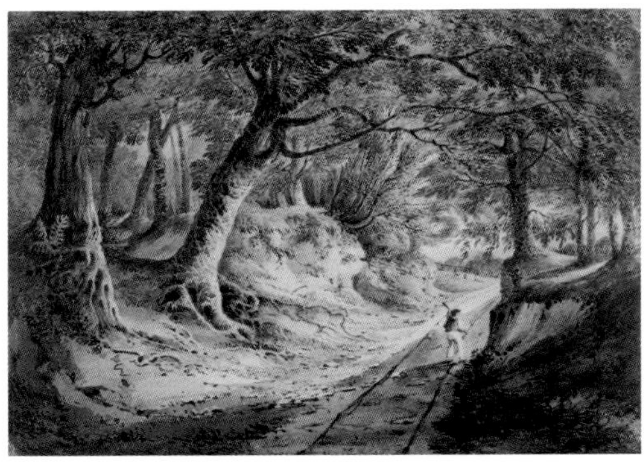
D.1944.20

A sunken Road, Somerhill, near Tonbridge, Kent
watercolour
signed & inscribed centre verso: *Somer Hill / nr
Tunbridge / Kent / JBourne / 7Somerset St. / Portman
Sqr*; inscribed lower centre: *Somer Hill, near Tunbridge*
265 × 369 mm
National Art-Collections Fund (gift, 1944) (D.1944.20)

View near Waddon, Surrey
pencil
signed & inscribed centre verso: *Croydon / MrBourne /
No7 Somerset Street / Portman Sqr*; inscribed lower left:
near Waddon
260 × 367 mm
National Art Collections Fund (gift, 1944) (D.1944.21)

Lane at East Sheen, Surrey
blue watercolour, grey watercolour
signed & inscribed centre verso: *East Sheen / JBourne
No7 Somerset St. Portman Sqr*; inscribed lower left:
East Sheen
356 × 264 mm
National Art Collections Fund (gift, 1944) (D.1944.22)

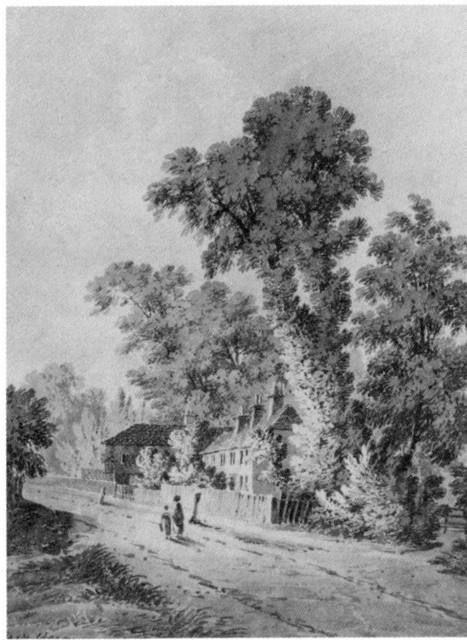
D.1944.22

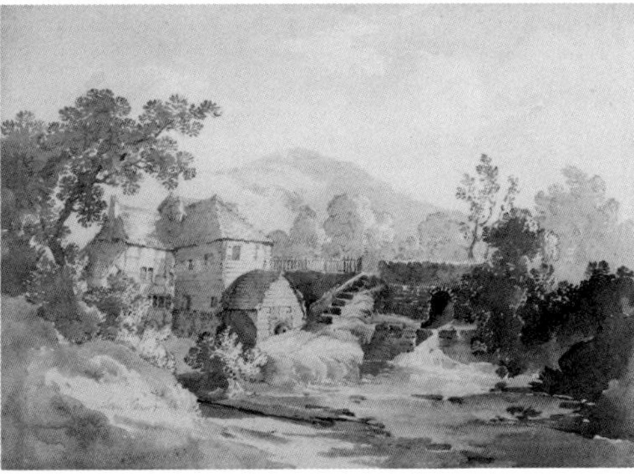
D.1944.23

Mill at Milton Court, Surrey
pencil, blue watercolour, grey watercolour
signed & inscribed centre verso: *MrBourne / No7
Somerset St Portman Sqr*; inscribed lower left: *Mill at
Milton Court*
274 × 364 mm
National Art Collections Fund (gift, 1944) (D.1944.23)

Cottage at Beddington, Surrey
pencil
signed & inscribed centre verso: *MrBourne / No7
Somerset St. / Portman Sqr*; inscribed lower left:
Beddington; inscribed lower left: *Beddington*
122 × 172 mm
National Art Collections Fund (gift, 1944) (D.1944.24)

Thatched Cottage by a Lane in Worcestershire
pencil
signed & inscribed centre verso: *JBourne / 20Princes
St.Cavendish Sqr*; inscribed lower left: *[illegible]
Worcestershire*
120 × 179 mm
National Art Collections Fund (gift, 1944) (D.1944.25)

**On the River Wye at Tintern,
Monmouthshire, Wales**
1800
grey watercolour
signed, inscribed & dated centre verso: *on the River
Wye / at Tintern / JBourne 1800.*; inscribed lower left:
On the river Wye / at Tintern
228 × 283 mm
National Art Collections Fund (gift, 1944) (D.1944.26)

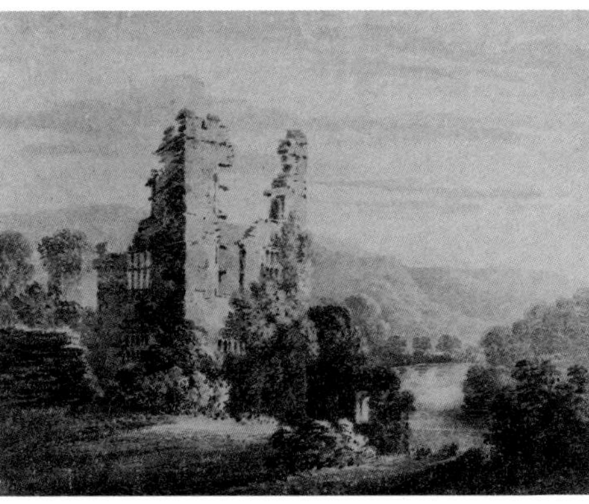
D.1944.26

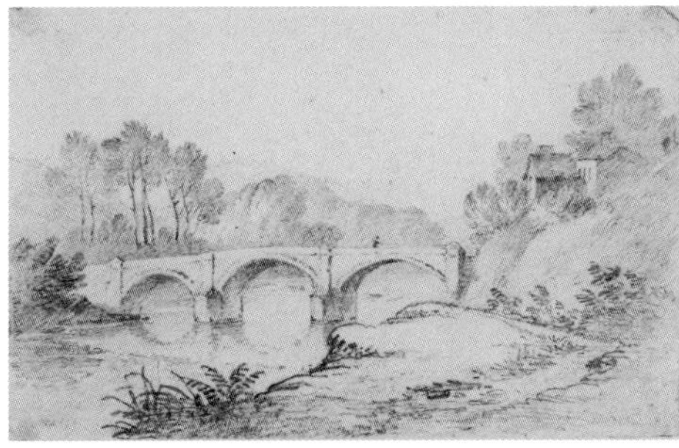
D.1944.28

Whaley Bridge, Lancashire
pencil
signed & inscribed centre verso: *Whaley Bridge /
Lancashire / JBourne 7 Somerset St. Portman Sqr*;
inscribed on page of album lower centre: *Whaley Bridge
– Lancashire*
115 × 179 mm
Benson, Dr Annette, National Art Collections Fund (via)
(gift, 1944) (D.1944.28)

Cottage near Altrincham, Cheshire
pencil
signed & inscribed centre verso: *Cottage near
Altrincham / Cheshire / JBourne / 7 Somerset St. Portman
Sqr*; inscribed on page of album lower centre: *nr
Altrincham Cheshire*
110 × 174 mm
Benson, Dr Annette, National Art Collections Fund (via)
(gift, 1944) (D.1944.29)

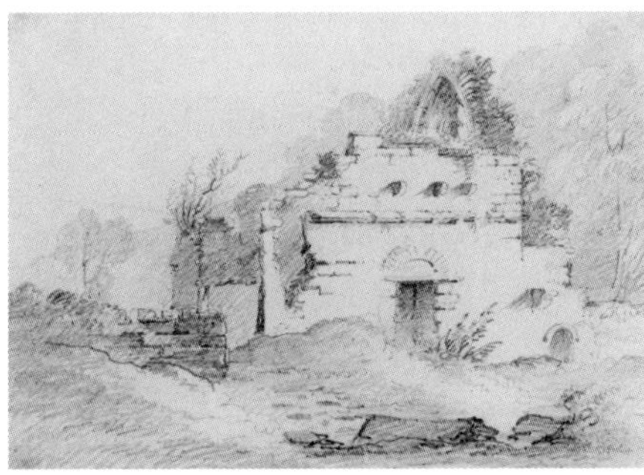
D.1944.30

Easby Abbey, Yorkshire
pencil
signed & inscribed centre verso: *Easby Abbey / Yorkshire
/ JBourne / No7 Somerset St. Portman Sqr*; inscribed on
page of album lower centre: *Easby Abbey Yorkshire*
118 × 170 mm
Benson, Dr Annette, National Art Collections Fund (via)
(gift, 1944) (D.1944.30)

Cottage at Sandown, Lancashire
pencil
signed & inscribed centre verso: *At Sandown nr Garstang / Lancashire / JBourne / No.7 Somerset St. Portman Sqr*; inscribed lower right: *Cottage at Sandown Lancashire*; inscribed on page of album lower centre: *Sandown – Lancashire*
119 × 172 mm
Benson, Dr Annette, National Art Collections Fund (via) (gift, 1944) (D.1944.31)

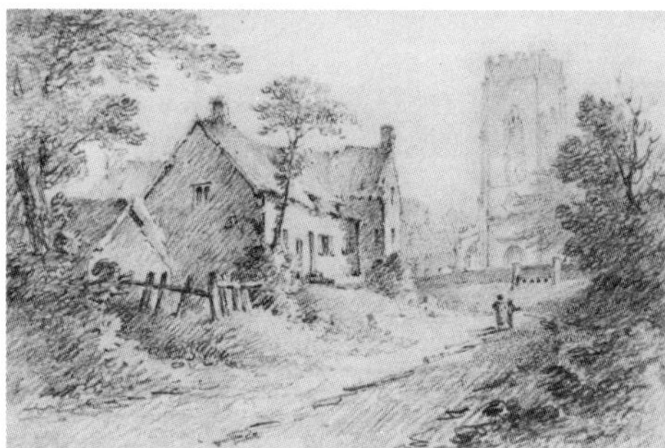
D.1944.32

Church and Cottage, Bowdon, Cheshire
pencil
signed & inscribed centre verso: *Bowden* (sic) / *Cheshire / JBourne / No.7 Somerset St. Portman Sqr*; inscribed on page of album lower centre: *Bowden* (sic) *Cheshire – Earl of Stamfords*
118 × 177 mm
Benson, Dr Annette, National Art Collections Fund (via) (gift, 1944) (D.1944.32)

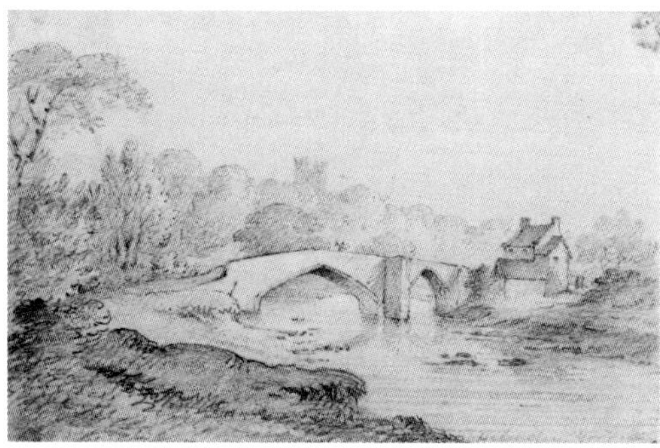
D.1944.33

Rye Bridge, Helmsley, Yorkshire, with Helmsley Castle Tower among distant Trees
pencil
signed & inscribed centre verso: *Helmsley Bridge & Castle / Yorkshire / Jas.Bourne 7 Somerset St. Portman Sqr*; inscribed lower right: *Helmsley Yorkshire*; inscribed on page of album lower centre: *Helmsley – Yorkshire –*
118 × 177 mm
Benson, Dr Annette, National Art Collections Fund (via) (gift, 1944) (D.1944.33)

Cottage with Bolton Castle, Yorkshire, in the Distance
pencil
signed & inscribed centre verso: *Cottage near Bolton Castle / Yorkshire / JBourne / No 7 Somerset St. Portman Sqr*; inscribed lower right: *Bolton Castle*; inscribed on page of album lower centre: *near Bolton Castle – Yorkshire*
117 × 171 mm
Benson, Dr Annette, National Art Collections Fund (via) (gift, 1944) (D.1944.34)

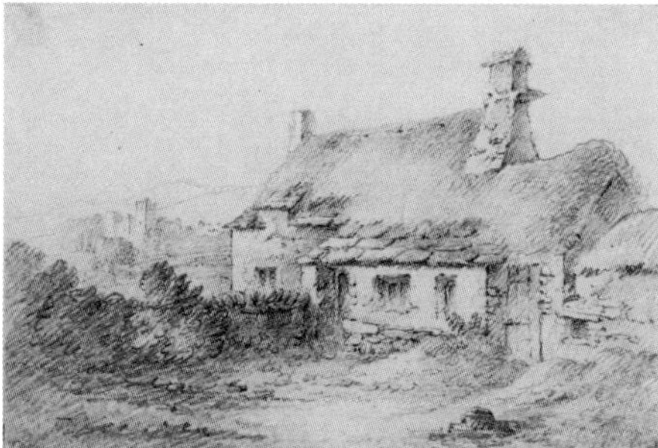
D.1944.34

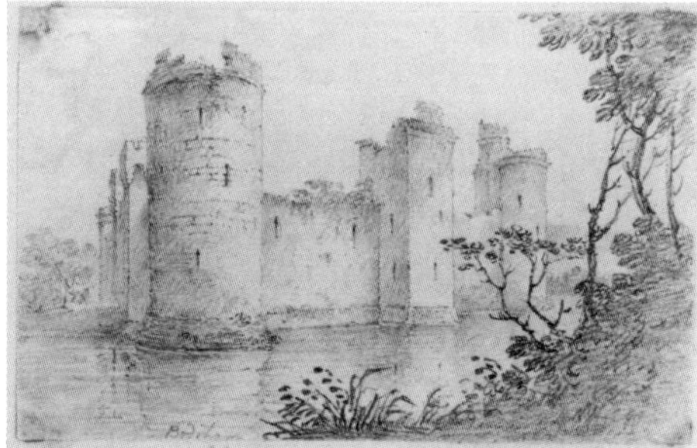
D.1944.35

Bodiam Castle, Sussex, from the North West
pencil
signed & inscribed centre verso: *Bodiham* (sic) *Castle / Sussex / Jas.Bourne / 7 Somerset St. Portman Sqr*; inscribed lower left: *Bodiham* (sic); inscribed on page of album lower centre: *Bodiham* (sic) *Castle, Sussex*
110 × 173 mm
Benson, Dr Annette, National Art Collections Fund (via) (gift, 1944) (D.1944.35)

Half-timbered House at Heaton, Manchester, with Heaton Park Temple in the Distance
pencil
signed & inscribed centre verso: *Scene near Heaton – / Earl of Wiltons / JBourne / No7 Somerset St. Portman Sqr*; inscribed on page of album lower centre: *Earl of Wiltons, Heaton Lancashire*
116 × 170 mm
Benson, Dr Annette, National Art Collections Fund (via) (gift, 1944) (D.1944.36)

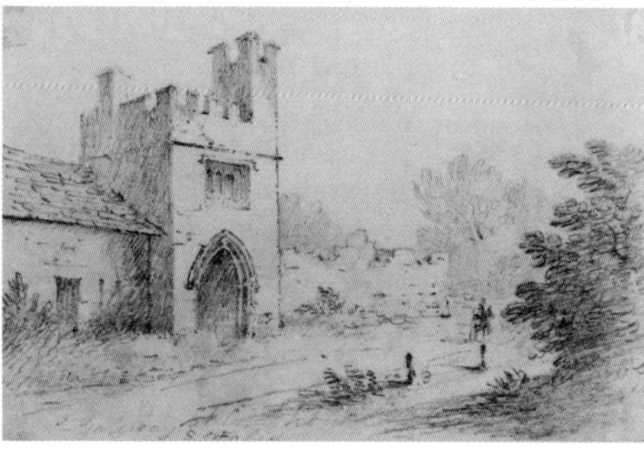
D.1944.37

Gateway at Crickhowell, Breconshire, Wales
pencil
signed & inscribed centre verso: *MrBourne / 7 Somerset St.Portman Sqr / Gateway at Crickhowel* (sic) *S Wales*; inscribed lower left: *Gateway at Crickhowel* (sic). / *S.Wales*; inscribed on page of album lower centre: *Crickhowel* (sic). *S.Wales*
118 × 177 mm
Benson, Dr Annette, National Art Collections Fund (via) (gift, 1944) (D.1944.37)

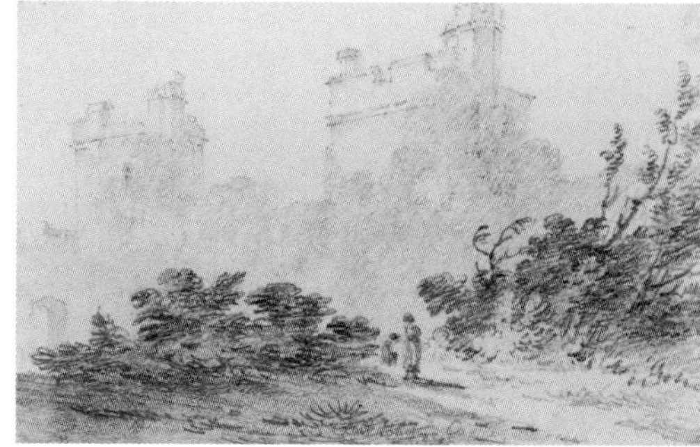
D.1944.38

Interior of Bodiam Castle, Sussex
pencil
signed & inscribed centre verso: *Bodiham* (sic) *Castle Sussex / JBourne 7 Somerset St. Portman Sqr*; inscribed on page of album lower centre: *Bodiham* (sic) *Castle*
115 × 175 mm
Benson, Dr Annette, National Art Collections Fund (via) (gift, 1944) (D.1944.38)

Cottage at Malham, Yorkshire, with a Pond in the Foreground
pencil
signed & inscribed centre verso: *Cottage at Malham / Yorkshire / JBourne / 20 Princes St. Cavendish Sqr*; inscribed on page of album lower centre: *At Malham – Yorkshire –*
117 × 171 mm
Benson, Dr Annette, National Art Collections Fund (via) (gift, 1944) (D.1944.39)

Half-timbered Cottage, near Altrincham, Cheshire
pencil
signed & inscribed centre verso: *Cottage at Altrincham / Cheshire / JBourne 7Somerset St. Portman Sqr.*; inscribed on page of album lower centre: *nr Altrincham Cheshire*
117 × 166 mm
Benson, Dr Annette, National Art Collections Fund (via) (gift, 1944) (D.1944.40)

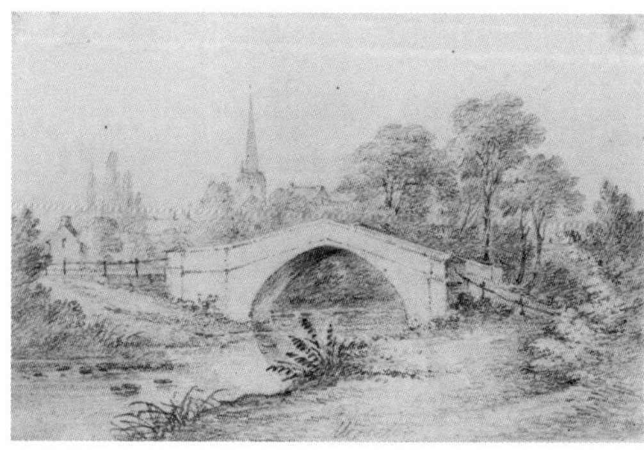
D.1944.41

Bridge at Uttoxeter, Staffordshire, with St Mary's Church Spire in the Distance
pencil
signed & inscribed centre verso: *JBourne / 7Somerset St. / Portman Sqr*
inscribed lower centre: *Utoxeter* (sic); inscribed on page of album lower centre: *Utoxeter* (sic) – *Staffordshire*
117 × 172 mm
Benson, Dr Annette, National Art Collections Fund (via) (gift, 1944) (D.1944.41)

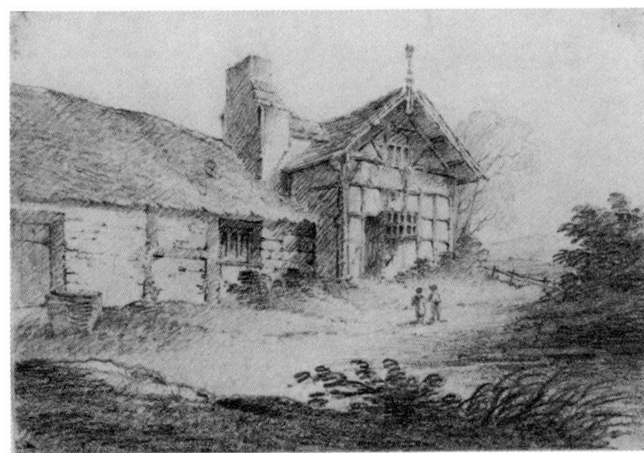

D.1944.42

Farmhouse at Bowdon, Cheshire

pencil

signed & inscribed centre verso: *Bowden* (sic) *Cheshire / JBourne / 7Somerset St.Portman Sqr*; inscribed on page of album lower centre: *Bowden* (sic) *Cheshire*

117 × 168 mm

Benson, Dr Annette, National Art Collections Fund (via) (gift, 1944) (D.1944.42)

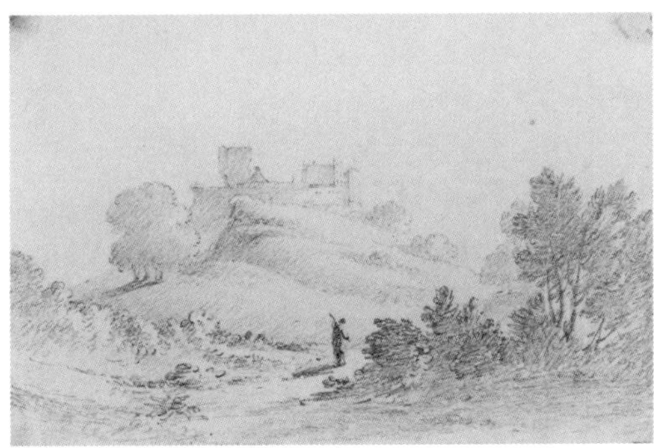

D.1944.43

Distant View of Clitheroe Castle, Lancashire

pencil

signed & inscribed centre verso: *Clitheroe Castle / Lancashire / JBourne / 7Somerset St.Portman Sqr*; inscribed page of album lower centre: *Clitheroe Castle, Lancashire —*

118 × 178 mm

Benson, Dr Annette, National Art Collections Fund (via) (gift, 1944) (D.1944.43)

Cottage near Hubberholme, Yorkshire

pencil

signed & inscribed centre verso: *Hubberholme / Yorkshire / JBourne / 7Somerset St.Portman Sqr*; inscribed on page of album lower centre: *Hubberholme Yorkshire*

118 × 171 mm

Benson, Dr Annette, National Art Collections Fund (via) (gift, 1944) (D.1944.44)

Cottages near Askrigg, Yorkshire, with Hills in the Distance

pencil

signed & inscribed centre verso: *A Cottage nr Askrigg / with Cam* [underlined] *in the distance / JBourne / 7Somerset St.Portman Sqr*; inscribed on page of album lower centre: *Cam* [underlined] *near Hawes Yorkshire*

113 × 172 mm

Benson, Dr Annette, National Art Collections Fund (via) (gift, 1944) (D.1944.45)

Cottage, near Settle, Yorkshire

pencil

signed & inscribed centre verso: *JBourne / 7 Somerset St.Portman Sqr*; inscribed lower right: *Cottage nr Settle*; inscribed on page of album lower centre: *near Settle — Yorkshire —*

118 × 172 mm

Benson, Dr Annette, National Art Collections Fund (via) (gift, 1944) (D.1944.46)

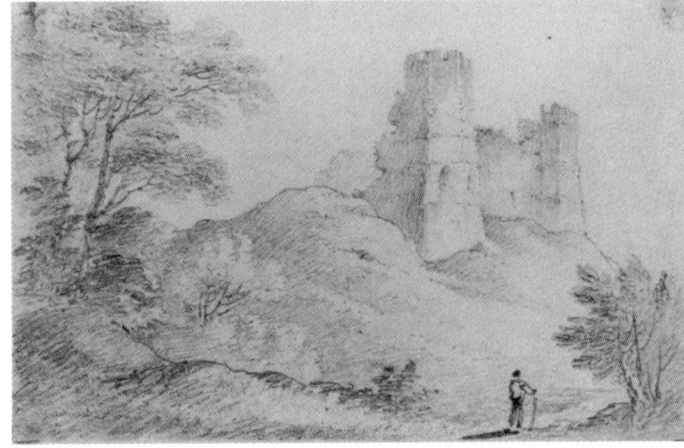

D.1944.47

Ruins of Lewes Castle, Sussex

pencil

signed & inscribed centre verso: *Lewis* (sic) *Castle Sussex / JBourne / 7 Somerset Street Portman Square*; inscribed on page of album lower centre: *Lewis* (sic)*, Sussex*

112 × 173 mm

Benson, Dr Annette, National Art Collections Fund (via) (gift, 1944) (D.1944.47)

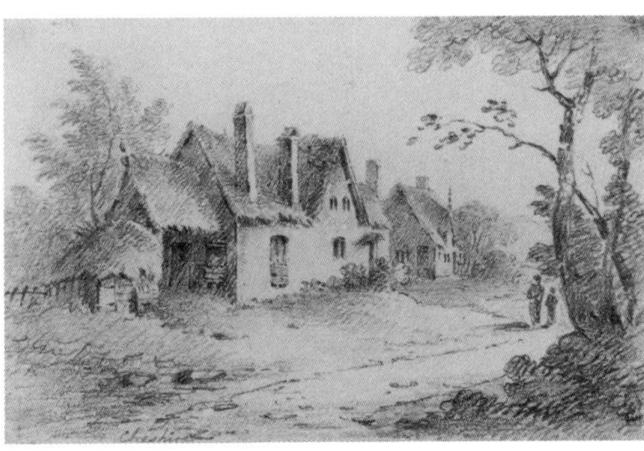

D.1944.48

Cottage near Dunham Massey, Cheshire

pencil

signed & inscribed centre verso: *JBourne / 7Somerset St.Portman Sqr*; inscribed lower left: *Cheshire*; inscribed on page of album lower centre: *nr Dunham Massey, Earl of Stamfords*

118 × 177 mm

Benson, Dr Annette, National Art Collections Fund (via) (gift, 1944) (D.1944.48)

Cottages at Knaresborough, Yorkshire, with Rocks behind

pencil

signed & inscribed centre verso: *Knaresborough / JBourne / 7 Somerset St.Portman Sqr*; inscribed lower centre: *Knaresborough*; inscribed on page of album lower centre: *Knaresborough, Yorkshire*

117 × 172 mm

Benson, Dr Annette, National Art Collections Fund (via) (gift, 1944) (D.1944.49)

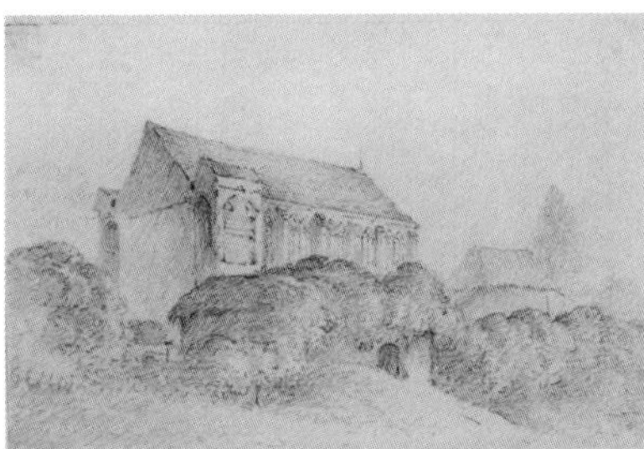

D.1944.50

The Great Hall, Eltham Palace, London

pencil

signed & inscribed centre verso: *King Johns Palace / Eltham / Kent / JBourne / 20 Princes St.Cavendish Sqr*; inscribed on page of album lower centre: *King John's Palace, Eltham — Kent —*

119 × 177 mm

Benson, Dr Annette, National Art Collections Fund (via) (gift, 1944) (D.1944.50)

Cottage at Bowdon, Cheshire, with St Mary's Church on a distant Hill

pencil

signed & inscribed centre verso: *Bowden* (sic) *Cheshire / JBourne / No.7Somerset St.Portman / Sqr*; inscribed on page of album lower centre: *Bowden* (sic)*, Cheshire*

117 × 172 mm

Benson, Dr Annette, National Art Collections Fund (via) (gift, 1944) (D.1944.51)

Barn at Buckland, Yorkshire

pencil

signed & inscribed centre verso: *Buckland / Yorkshire / JBourne / 7 Somerset St.Portman Sqr*; inscribed on page of album lower centre: *Buckland, Yorkshire*

118 × 171 mm

Benson, Dr Annette, National Art Collections Fund (via) (gift, 1944) (D.1944.52)

Severndroog Castle, Shooter's Hill, London

pencil

signed & inscribed centre verso: *Lady James's Tower / Shooter hill — Kent / JBourne 7 Somerset St.Portman Sqr*; inscribed on page of album lower centre: *Lady James's Tower, Kent —*

118 × 178 mm

Benson, Dr Annette, National Art Collections Fund (via) (gift, 1944) (D.1944.53)

Distant View of Penyghent, Yorkshire, with Farm Buildings in the Foreground

pencil

signed & inscribed centre verso: *Penygent hill / at a distance / JBourne 7 Somerset St.Portman Sqr*; inscribed lower right: *Distant view of Penygent*; inscribed on page of album lower centre: *Distant View of Penygent — Yorkshire —*

118 × 171 mm

Benson, Dr Annette, National Art Collections Fund (via) (gift, 1944) (D.1944.54)

Thatched Cottage, near Altrincham, Cheshire

pencil

signed & inscribed centre verso: *JBourne / 7Somerset St.Portman Sqr*; inscribed lower left: *Cottage* [remainder illegible]; inscribed on page of album lower centre: *near Altrincham — York* [erased] *Ches* [added above] *hire*

118 × 172 mm

Benson, Dr Annette, National Art Collections Fund (via) (gift, 1944) (D.1944.55)

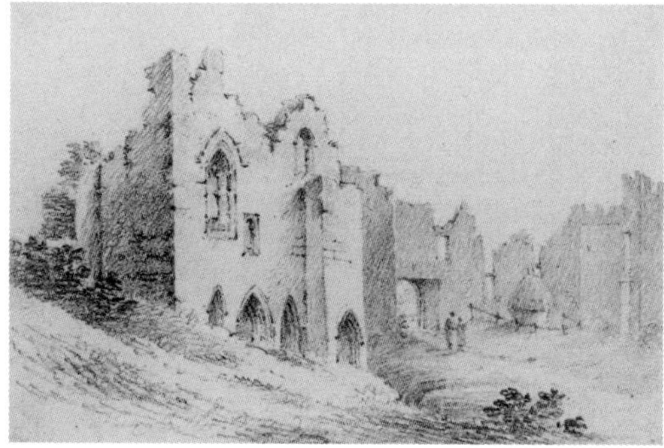

D.1944.56

Inside the Ruins of Tutbury Castle, Staffordshire
pencil
signed & inscribed centre verso: *Tutbury Castle / Staffordshire / JBourne / No7 Somerset St.Portman Sqr*; inscribed lower left: *Tutbury Castle Staffordshire*; inscribed on page of album, lower centre: *Tutbury Castle – Staffordshire*
117 × 172 mm
Benson, Dr Annette, National Art Collections Fund (via) (gift, 1944) (D.1944.56)

The Hut, near Liverpool, with a Cottage by a Stream
pencil
inscribed on page of album lower centre: *The Hut near Liverpool*
116 × 171 mm
Benson, Dr Annette, National Art Collections Fund (via) (gift, 1944) (D.1944.57)

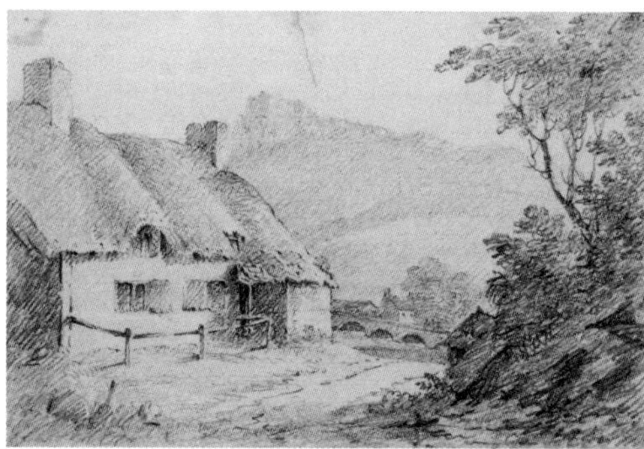

D.1944.58

Thatched Cottage at Alton, Staffordshire, with Bridge
pencil
signed & inscribed centre verso: *Alton / Staffordshire / JBourne / 7 Somerset St. Portman Sqr*; inscribed on page of album lower centre: *Alvedon* (sic) – *Staffordshire*
117 × 172 mm
Benson, Dr Annette, National Art Collections Fund (via) (gift, 1944) (D.1944.58)

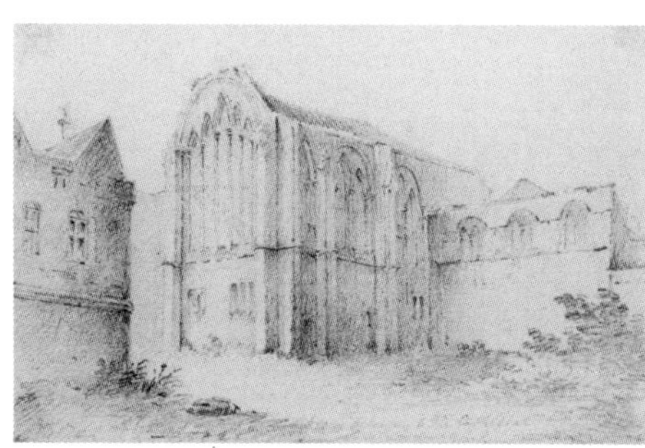

D.1944.59

The Library of York Minster
pencil
signed & inscribed centre verso: *JBourne / No.7 Somerset St. / Portman Sqr*; inscribed lower right: *Library belonging to the Cathedral / York*; inscribed on page of album lower centre: *Library at York Cathedral*
117 × 178 mm
Benson, Dr Annette, National Art Collections Fund (via) (gift, 1944) (D.1944.59)

Ingleborough, Yorkshire, with Farmhouse in Foreground
pencil
signed & inscribed centre verso: *Ingleborough / JBourne / 7 Somerset St. Portman Sqr*; inscribed lower right: *at the* [illegible] / *Ingleborough*; inscribed on page of album lower centre: – *Ingleborough* –
118 × 171 mm
Benson, Dr Annette, National Art Collections Fund (via) (gift, 1944) (D.1944.60)

Thatched Cottage at Mountsorrel, Leicestershire
pencil
signed & inscribed centre verso: *JBourne / 20 Princes St.Cavedish Sqr*; inscribed lower left: *Cottage at Mount Sorrel* (sic)*, Leicestershire*; inscribed on page of album lower centre: *Mount Sorrell* (sic) – *Leicestershire*
118 × 178 mm
Benson, Dr Annette, National Art Collections Fund (via) (gift, 1944) (D.1944.61)

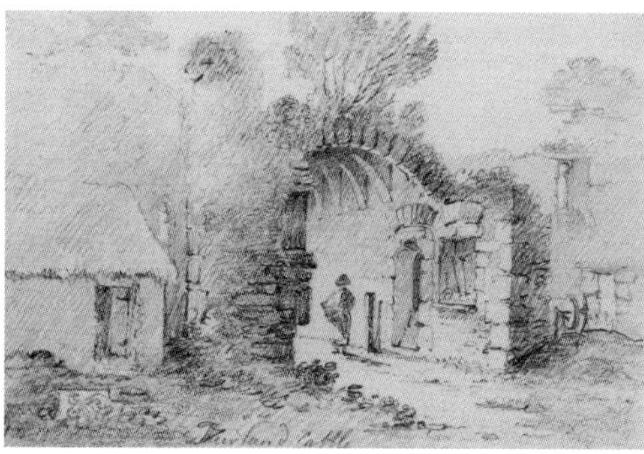

D.1944.62

Ruined Gateway, Thurland Castle, Lancashire
pencil
inscribed centre verso: *Thurland Castle / Lancashire*; inscribed lower left: *Thurland Castle*; inscribed on page of album lower centre: *Thurland Castle, Lancashire*
118 × 173 mm
Benson, Dr Annette, National Art Collections Fund (via) (gift, 1944) (D.1944.62)

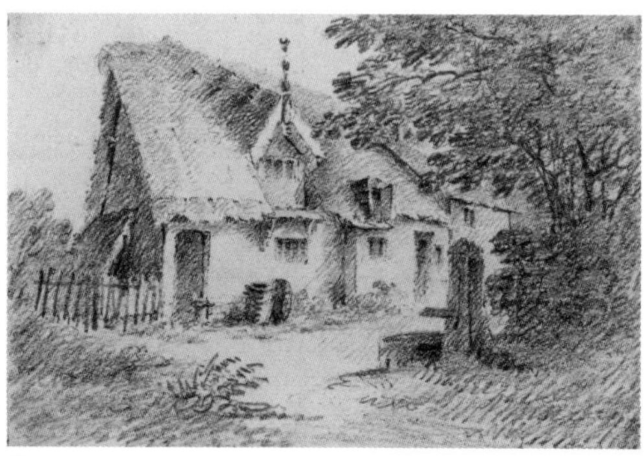

D.1944.63

Cottage by a Path at Altrincham, Cheshire, with Pump and Trees
pencil
signed & inscribed centre verso: *at Altrincham / Cheshire / JBourne / 7 Somerset St. Portman Sqr*; inscribed on page of album lower centre: *Near Altrincham – Cheshire*
117 × 172 mm
Benson, Dr Annette, National Art Collections Fund (via) (gift, 1944) (D.1944.63)

View of Wigan from Haigh, Lancashire, with Cottages by a Pond
pencil
signed & inscribed centre verso: *Wigan from Haigh Hall / Earl of Balcarras* (sic) / *JBourne / 7 Somerset St. Portman Sqr*; inscribed lower right: *Haigh / near / Wigan*: inscribed on page of album lower centre: *Distant View of Wigan*
117 × 173 mm
Benson, Dr Annette, National Art Collections Fund (via) (gift, 1944) (D.1944.64)

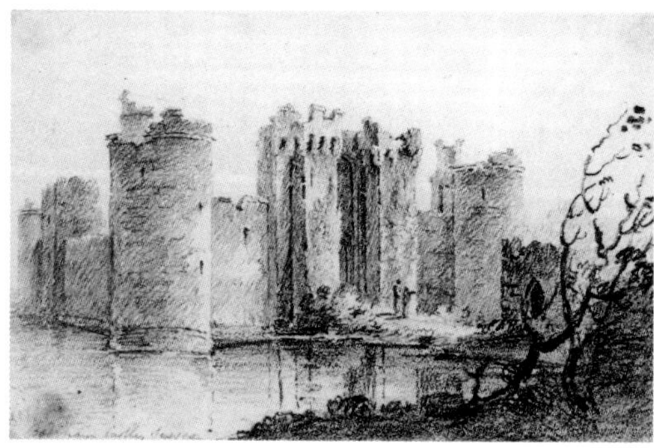

D.1944.65

Bodiam Castle, Sussex, from the North East
pencil
inscribed lower left: *Bodiham* (sic) *Castle, Sussex*; inscribed on page of album lower centre: *Bodiham* (sic) *Castle, Sussex* –
116 × 176 mm
Benson, Dr Annette, National Art Collections Fund (via) (gift, 1944) (D.1944.65)

Cottage by a Stream, Malham, Yorkshire
pencil
signed & inscribed centre verso: *JBourne / 7 Somerset St.Portman Sqr*; inscribed lower right: *Cottage at Malham Yorkshire*; inscribed on page of album lower centre: *Malham Yorkshire*
118 × 172 mm
Benson, Dr Annette, National Art Collections Fund (via) (gift, 1944) (D.1944.66)

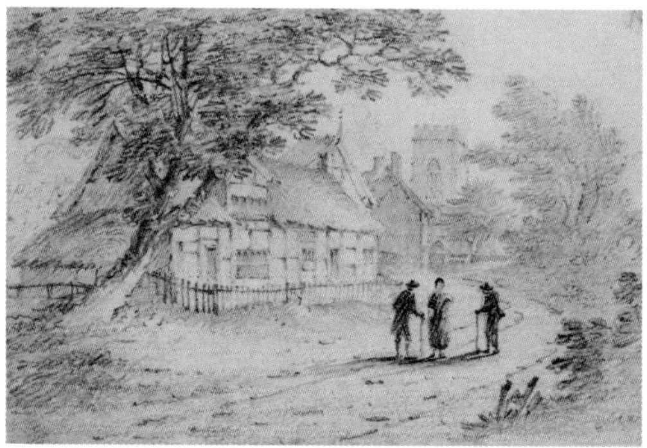

D.1944.67

St Mary's Church and Cottages, Bowdon, Cheshire
pencil
signed & inscribed centre verso: *Bowden (sic) Cheshire / JBourne / 7 Somerset St. Portman Sqr*; inscribed on page of album lower centre: *Bowden (sic – Cheshire –*
118 × 172 mm
Benson, Dr Annette, National Art Collections Fund (via) (gift, 1944) (D.1944.67)

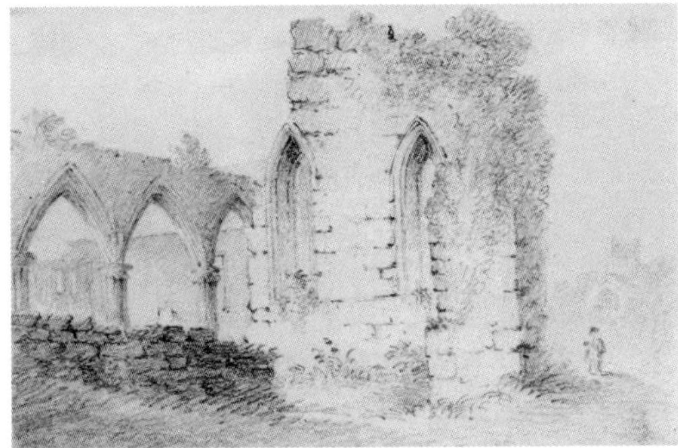
D.1944.68

The Ruins of Coverham Abbey, Yorkshire, with Holy Trinity Church in the Distance
pencil
signed & inscribed centre verso: *Coverham Abbey / nr Middleham / Yorkshire / JBourne / 7Somerset St.Portman Sqr*; inscribed on page of album lower centre: *Coverham Abbey – Yorkshire*
119 × 178 mm
Benson, Dr Annette, National Art Collections Fund (via) (gift, 1944) (D.1944.68)

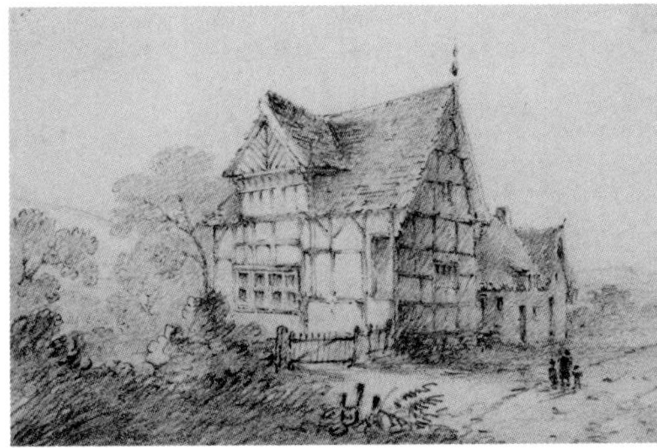
D.1944.69

Half-timbered House at Bowdon, Cheshire
pencil
signed & inscribed centre verso: *Bowden (sic) / Cheshire / JBourne 7 Somerset St. Portman Square*; inscribed on page of album lower centre: *Bowden (sic) – Cheshire*
117 × 173 mm
Benson, Dr Annette, National Art Collections Fund (via) (gift, 1944) (D.1944.69)

Lane, near Hawes, Yorkshire
pencil
signed & inscribed centre verso: *Lane near Hawes / Yorkshire / JBourne / 7Somerset St.Portman Sqr*; inscribed on page of album lower centre: *near Hawes – Yorkshire*
118 × 172 mm
Benson, Dr Annette, National Art Collections Fund (via) (gift, 1944) (D.1944.70)

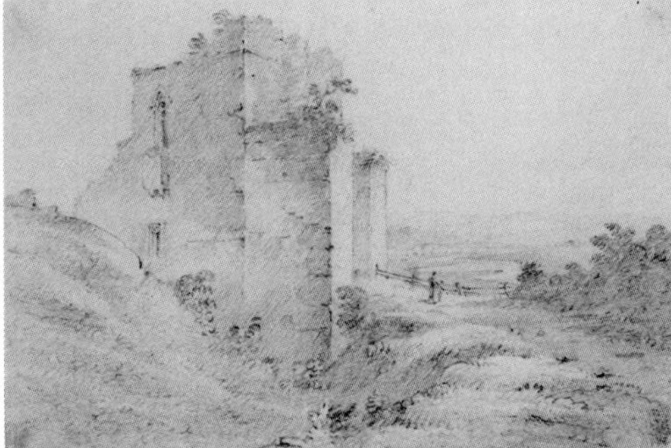
D.1944.71

Ruins of Tutbury Castle, Staffordshire, with distant View of the River Dove
pencil
signed & inscribed centre verso: *Tutbury Castle / Staffordshire / JBourne / 7 Somerset St.Portman Sqr*; inscribed on page of album lower centre: *Tutbury Castle – Staffordshire*
118 × 172 mm
Benson, Dr Annette, National Art Collections Fund (via) (gift, 1944) (D.1944.71)

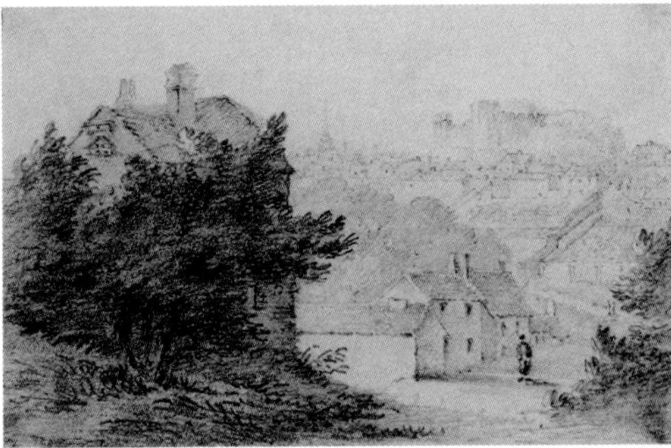
D.1944.72

The Town of Lewes, Sussex, with the Castle in Distance
pencil
signed & inscribed centre verso: *Lewis (sic) / Sussex / JBourne No 7 Somerset St. Portman Sqr*; inscribed on page of album lower centre: *Lewes – Sussex*
112 × 172 mm
Benson, Dr Annette, National Art Collections Fund (via) (gift, 1944) (D.1944.72)

Cottage, near Altrincham, Cheshire, with Hills in the Distance
pencil
signed & inscribed centre verso: *At Altrincham / Cheshire / JBourne /7 Somerset St. Portman Sqr*; inscribed on page of album lower centre: *near Altrincham – Cheshire*
117 × 173 mm
Benson, Dr Annette, National Art Collections Fund (via) (gift, 1944) (D.1944.73)

Ruins of Battle Abbey, Sussex
pencil
signed lower right: *JBourne*; inscribed lower right: *Battle Abbey*; inscribed on page of album lower centre: *Battle Abbey – Sussex*
112 × 175 mm
Benson, Dr Annette, National Art Collections Fund (via) (gift, 1944) (D.1944.74)

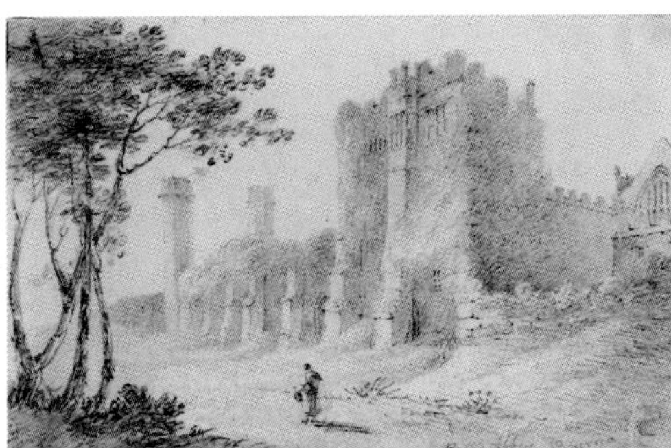
D.1944.74

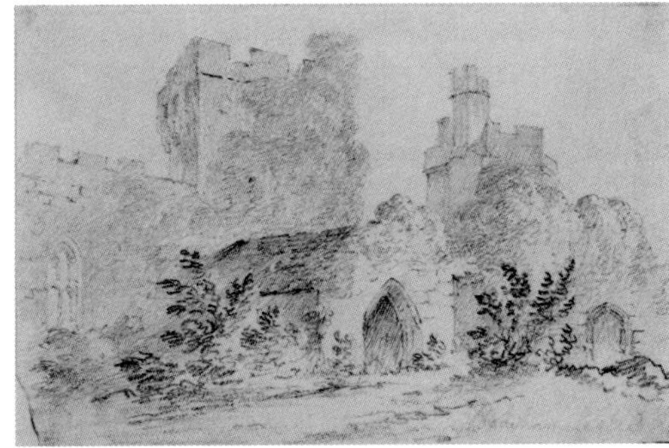
D.1944.75

Inside the Walls of Bodiam Castle, Sussex
pencil
signed & inscribed centre verso: *Bodiham (sic) Castle / Sussex – / JBourne / 7 Somerset St. Portman Sqr*; inscribed lower right: *Bodiham (sic) Castle*; inscribed on page of album lower centre: *Bodiham (sic) Castle – Sussex*
117 × 176 mm
Benson, Dr Annette, National Art Collections Fund (via) (gift, 1944) (D.1944.75)

Cottages by a Stream, Malham, Yorkshire
pencil
signed & inscribed centre verso: *Cottage at Malham / Yorkshire / JBourne / 7 Somerset St. Portman Sqr*; inscribed lower right: *Malham Yorkshire Malham*; inscribed on page of album lower centre: *Malham Yorkshire*
117 × 172 mm
Benson, Dr Annette, National Art Collections Fund (via) (gift, 1944) (D.1944.76)

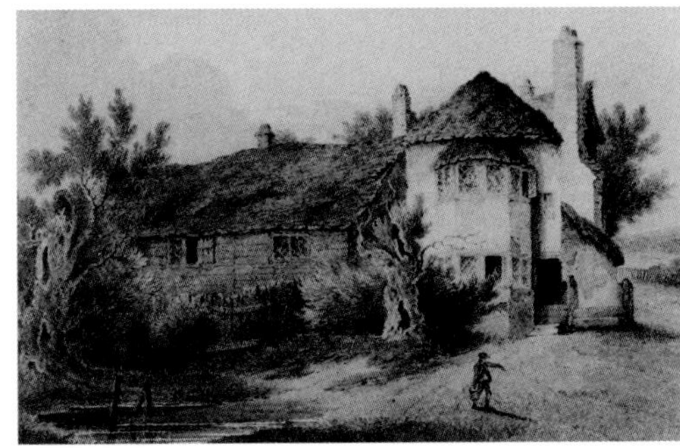
D.1970.17

Old Farmhouse with Willows
watercolour
317 × 453 mm
Towlson, Hector J. (bequest, 1969) (D.1970.17)

■ BOYCE, GEORGE PRICE (1826–97)

Boyce trained as an architect but turned to painting after meeting David Cox in 1849. He was an associate of the Pre-Raphaelites and a close friend of Rossetti. He exhibited at the Royal Academy between 1853 and 1861 and was elected an associate of the Old Watercolour Society in 1864 and a full member in 1877.

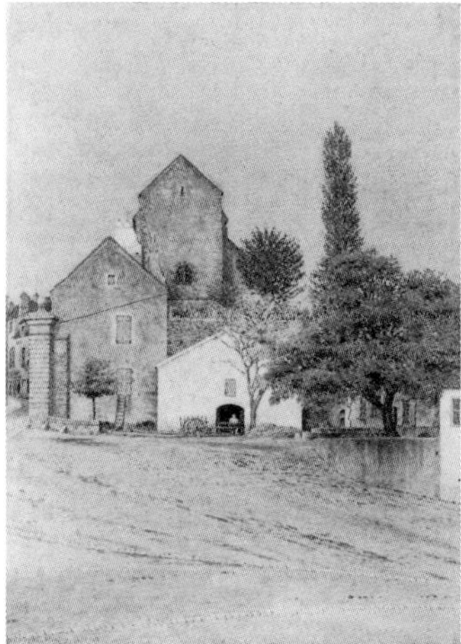
D.1944.4

Place du Barle, Vezelay, France
1878–85
watercolour
signed, inscribed & dated lower left:
G.P.Boyce.Vezelay.1878–85
435 × 305 mm
Barlow, Sir Thomas, Friends of the Whitworth (gift, 1944)
(D.1944.4)

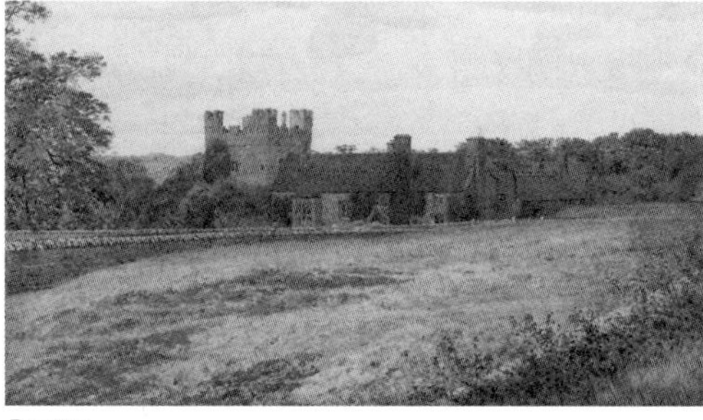
D.1988.12

Yanwath Hall, Westmorland
1884
watercolour
signed & dated lower centre: *G.P.Boyce 1884.*
307 × 522 mm
Anthony Reed Ltd (purchase, 1988) (D.1988.12)

■ BOYS, THOMAS SHOTTER (1803–74)

Boys was born in London and initially trained as an engraver. He moved to Paris in 1823 and worked as a lithographer and watercolourist. He was in regular contact with Bonington, becoming his closest English follower. He returned to London in 1837 and in 1841 produced his famous book of chromolithographs of London views.

Banks of the Seine, Rouen, France, with the Cathedral Towers
watercolour
334 × 475 mm
Agnew's (purchase, 29.11.1905) (D.1905.4)

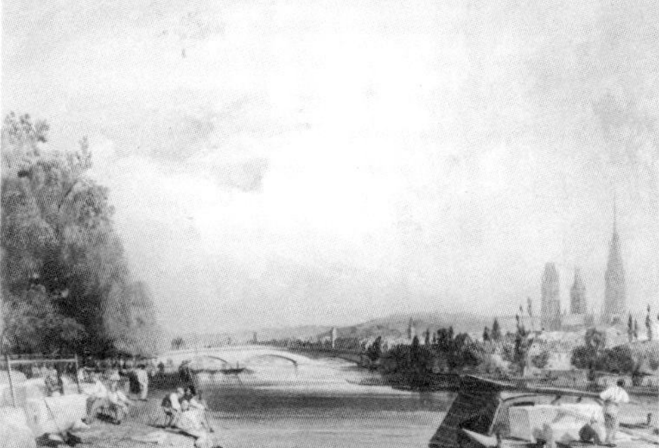
D.1905.4

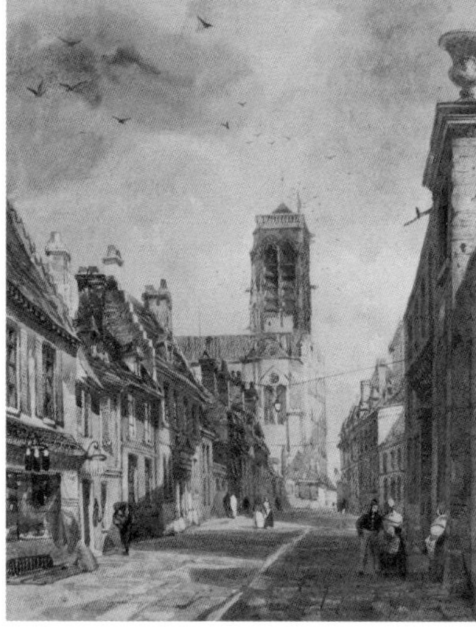
D.1920.8

Street Scene, Soissons, France, with a View of the Cathedral from the North
1835
watercolour
signed & dated lower left: *T.Boys 1835.*
282 × 211 mm
Palser, J. and Son, London (purchase, 1920) (D.1920.8)

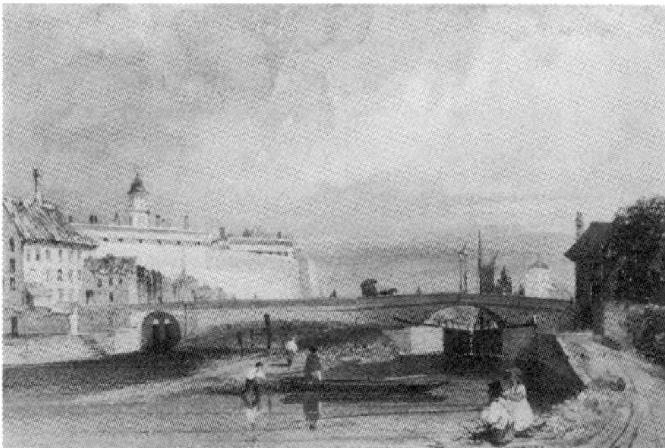
D.1933.23

View of the Castle Mills and Bridge over the Foss, York
1830
watercolour
signed & dated lower right: *T.Boys / 1830*
182 × 270 mm
Dalton, Mrs W. B., Plummer, Miss E. M. (gift, 1933)
(D.1933.23)

■ BRABAZON, HERCULES BRABAZON (1821–1906)

Brabazon, who was educated at Harrow and Cambridge, was financially independent. He travelled extensively in Europe, North Africa and India before he was persuaded by Sargent to agree to the first exhibition of his work in 1891. Brabazon was influenced by Turner, Cox, Muller and de Wint and produced many 'tributes' or copies of the work of other artists.

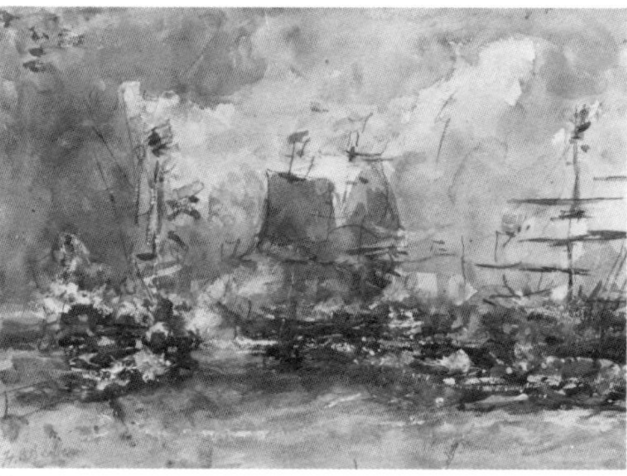
D.1920.15

The Embarkation of Admirals De Ruyter and De Witt (recto); Study of a Man's Head and Arm (verso)
black chalk, watercolour, bodycolour (recto)
signed lower left recto: *HBBrabazon*
263 × 361 mm
Combes, Mrs Brabazon (purchase, 1920) (D.1920.15)

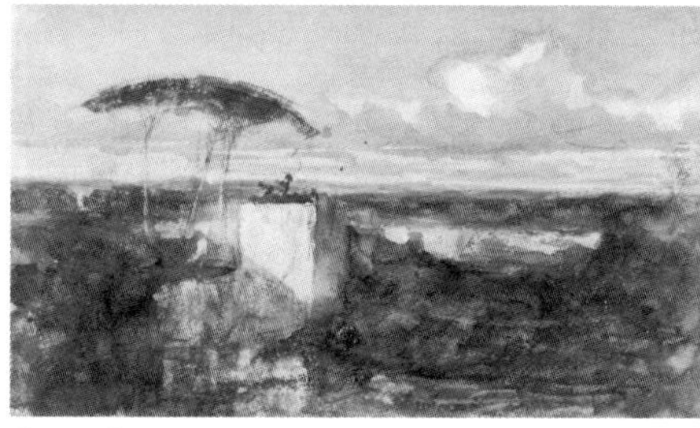
D.1920.16

A Well in the East, after Decamps
pencil, watercolour, bodycolour (heightened with white)
188 × 305 mm
Combes, Mrs Brabazon (purchase, 1920) (D.1920.16)

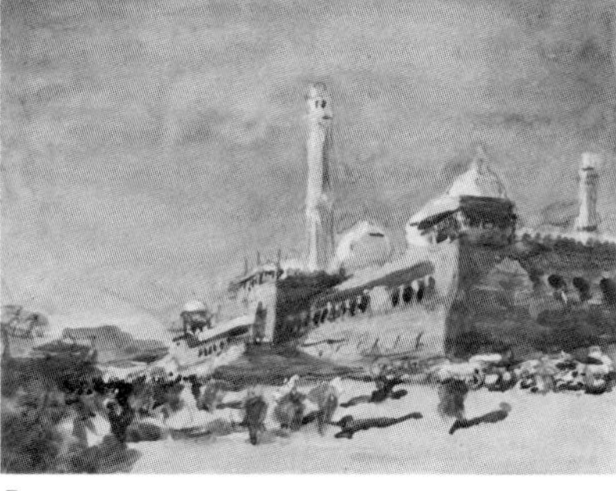
D.1920.17

The Jami Masjid, Delhi, India, from the South-East
black chalk, watercolour, bodycolour; grey paper
signed lower right with initials: *HBB*
224 × 284 mm
Combes, Mrs Brabazon (purchase, 1920) (D.1920.17)

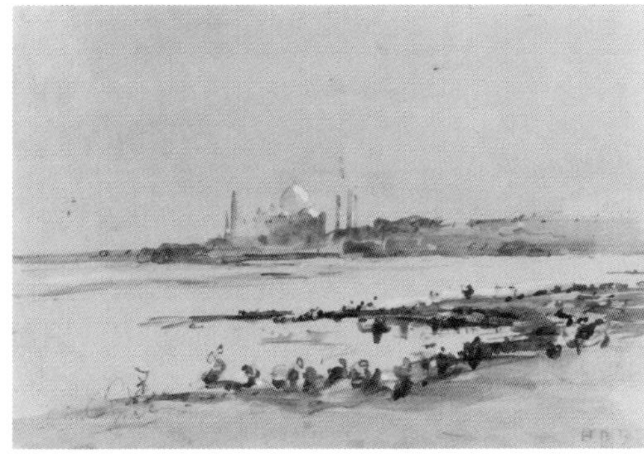

D.1920.18

The River Jumna, India, with the Taj Mahal in the Distance
black chalk, watercolour, bodycolour (heightened with white); blue-grey paper
signed lower right with initials: *HBB*
185 × 263 mm
Combes, Mrs Brabazon (purchase, 1920) (D.1920.18)

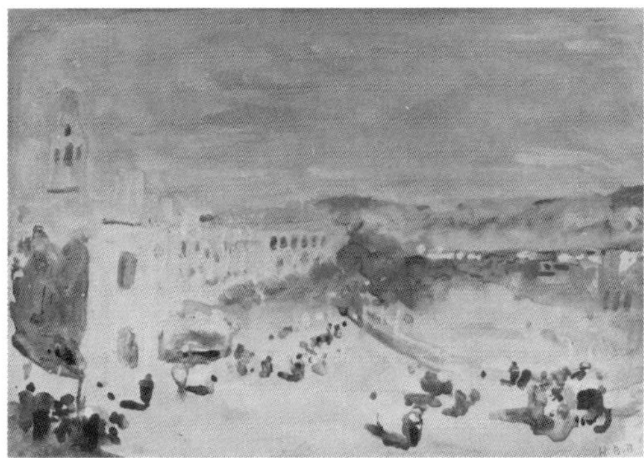

D.1920.19

View of Aosta, Italy
black chalk, watercolour, bodycolour
signed lower left: *H B Brabazon*
253 × 353 mm
Combes, Mrs Brabazon (purchase, 1920) (D.1920.19)

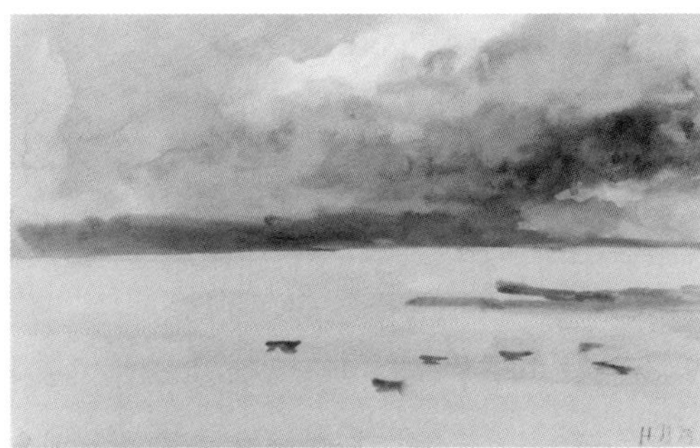

D.1920.20

Lake Geneva, Switzerland
watercolour, bodycolour; buff paper
signed lower right with initials: *HBB*
137 × 217 mm
Combes, Mrs Brabazon (purchase, 1920) (D.1920.20)

Pot of Flowers
watercolour, bodycolour
inscribed; not artist's hand: *Presented by / Mrs Brabazon Combe to / the Whitworth Gallery / Manchester* (sic)
188 × 121 mm
Combes, Brabazon (Mrs) (in memory of F. W. Jackson) (gift, 1920) (D.1920.28)

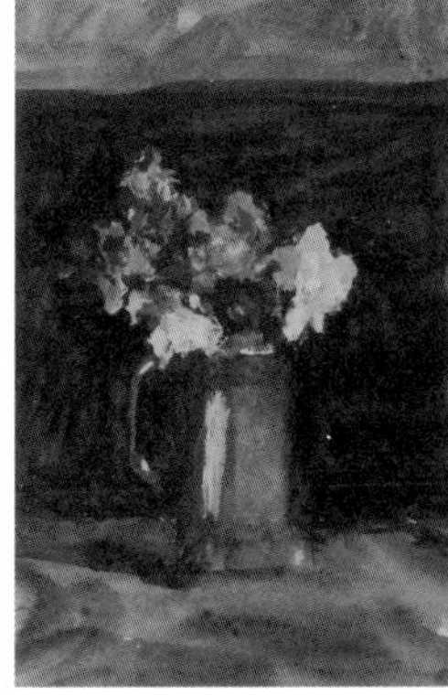

D.1920.28

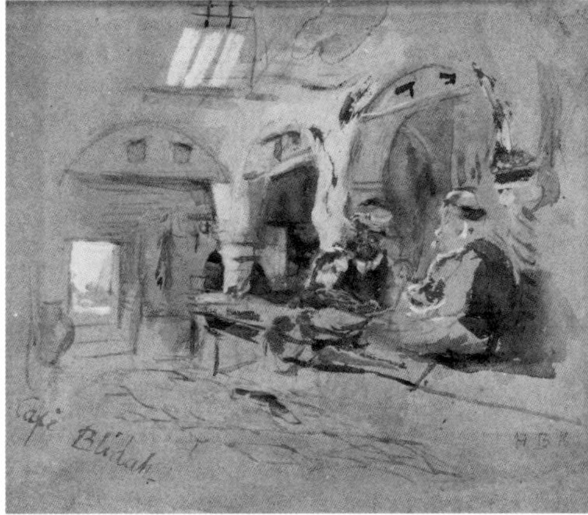

D.1920.29

Cafe Blidah, Cairo
pencil, black chalk, watercolour, bodycolour (heightened with white); grey paper
signed in lower right with initials: *HBB*; inscribed lower left: *Cafe Blidah*
308 × 353 mm
Combes, Brabazon (Mrs) (in memory of F. W. Jackson) (gift, 1920) (D.1920.29)

Lake and Mountains
pastel
signed lower left: *HBBrabazon*
187 × 300 mm
Fine Art Society, London (purchase, 1924) (D.1924.6)

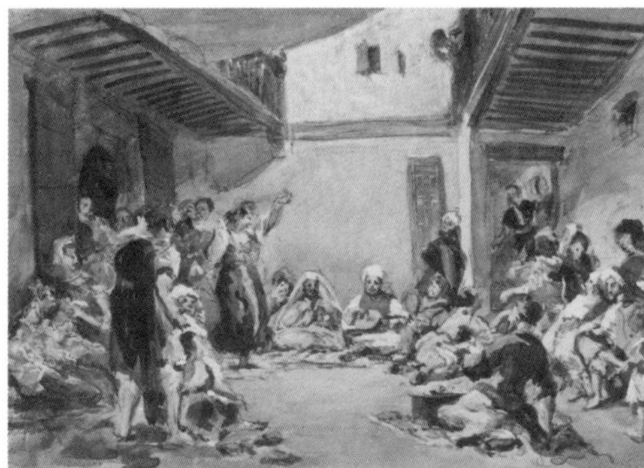

D.1927.29

A Jewish Marriage in Morocco, after Delacroix
pencil, black chalk, watercolour, bodycolour
grey paper
signed lower left with initials: *HBB*
250 × 353 mm
Agnew's (purchase, 1927) (D.1927.29)

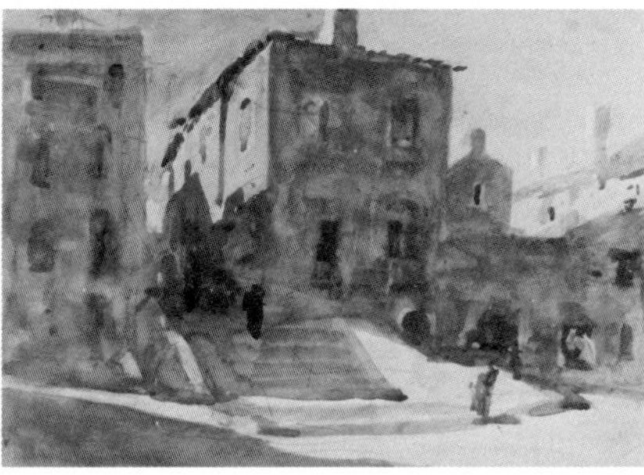

D.1928.42

Corner of Venice
pencil, watercolour, bodycolour (touches of); grey paper
signed lower left with initials: *HBB*
254 × 355 mm
Anderson, A. E., National Art Collections Fund (via) (gift, 1928) (D.1928.42)

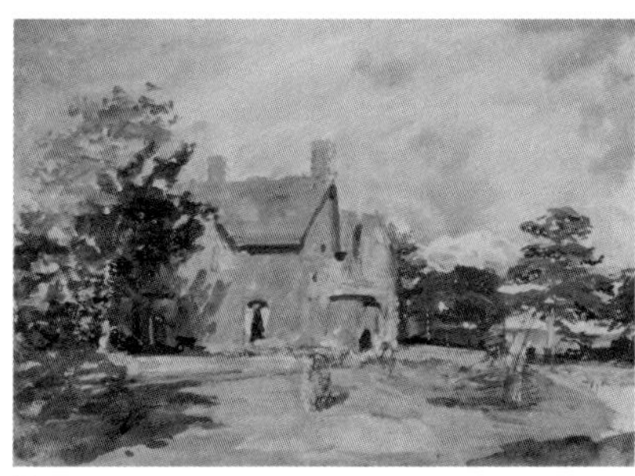

D.1931.1

The Red House, Westfield Place, London
black chalk, watercolour, bodycolour
signed lower left with initials: *HBB*
258 × 357 mm
Anderson, A. E. (gift, 1931) (D.1931.1)

Landscape at Nice
pastel; grey paper faded to brown
signed lower right with initials: *HBB*
144 × 218 mm
Blakeley, R. W. (gift, 1941) (D.1941.3)

Coast Scene, Mentone, South of France
watercolour, bodycolour; beige paper
signed lower right with initials: *HBB*; signed lower right over initials: *HBBrabazon*; inscribed lower right, partly covered by signatures: *Mentone*
251 × 354 mm
Coleman, H. C. (bequest, 1949) (D.1949.14)

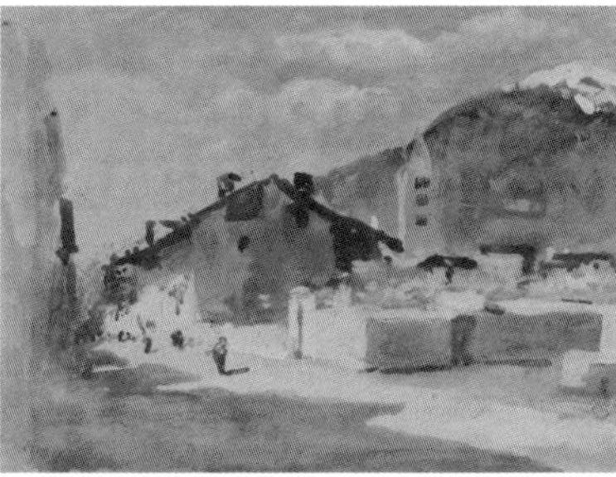

D.1949.16

A North African Town
watercolour, bodycolour
signed lower right with initials: *HBB*
252 × 350 mm
Coleman, H. C. (bequest, 1949) (D.1949.16)

Mediterranean Coast
watercolour, bodycolour; buff paper
signed lower left: *H.B.Brabazon*
228 × 287 mm
Coleman, H. C. (bequest, 1949) (D.1949.16)

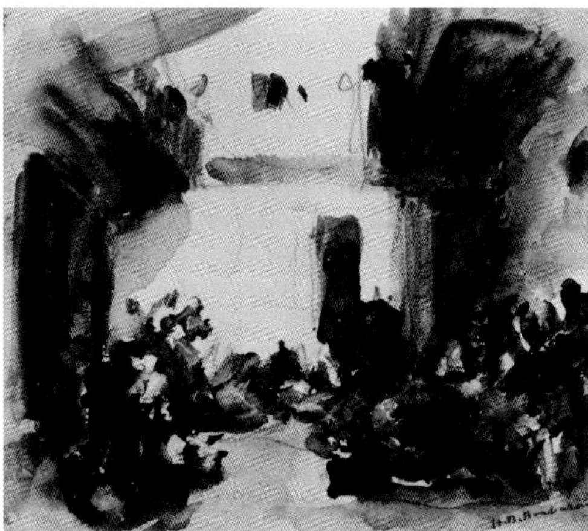

D.1949.17

Study for 'A Jewish Marriage in Morocco, after Delacroix'
pencil, black chalk, watercolour, bodycolour
signed lower right: *H.B.Brabazon*
240 × 266 mm
Coleman, H C (bequest, 1949) (D.1949.17)

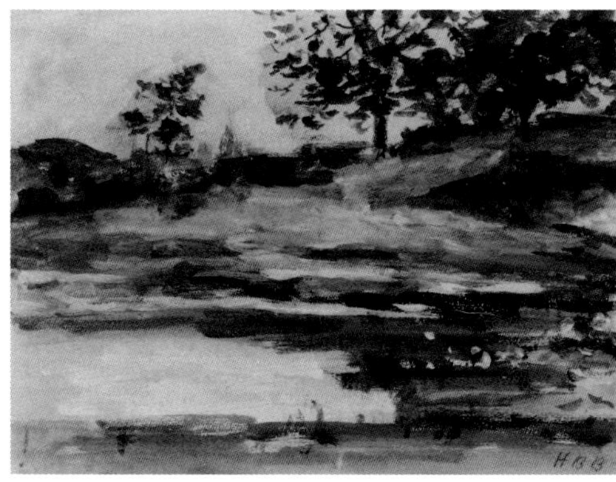

D.1949.18

Landscape with Pond (recto); Scene in a Wood (verso)
pencil, watercolour, bodycolour (recto); grey paper
signed lower right recto with initials: *HBB*; numbered
(in a square box) lower centre verso: *183*
208 × 270 mm
Coleman, H. C. (bequest, 1949) (D.1949.18)

Coast Scene, Mentone, South of France
pencil, coloured chalk, pastel; grey paper
signed lower left with initials: *HBB*; inscribed lower
right: *Mentone*
176 × 230 mm
University of Manchester, History of Art Department
(transfer, 1960) (D.1960.66)

Greville Church, France, after J. F. Millet
black chalk, watercolour, bodycolour
(heightened with white)
signed lower right with initials: *HBB*
164 × 231 mm
Watson, A (gift, 1965) (D.1965.4)

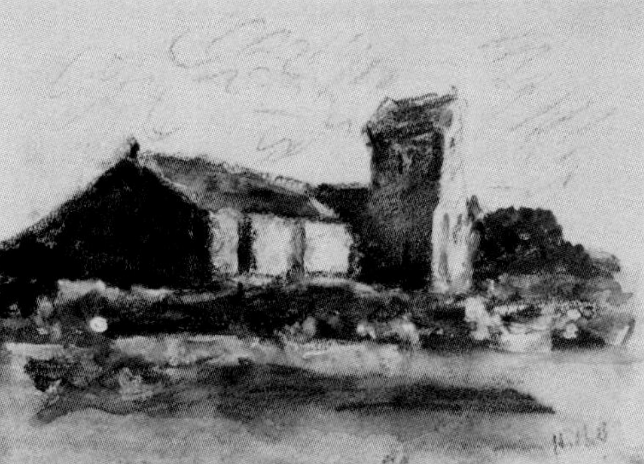

D.1965.4

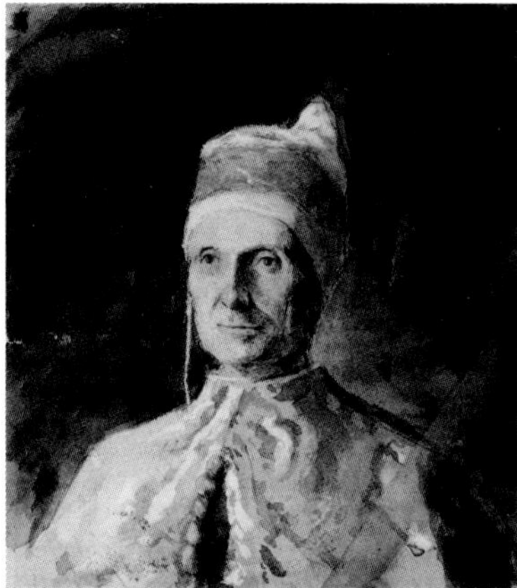

D.1970.18

Portrait of the Doge Leonardo Loredan, after Giovanni Bellini (recto); Study of a Woman's Head (verso)
pencil, watercolour, bodycolour (heightened with
white) (recto); grey paper
signed lower left with initials: *HBB*
190 × 168 mm
Towlson, Hector J. (bequest, 1969) (D.1970.18)

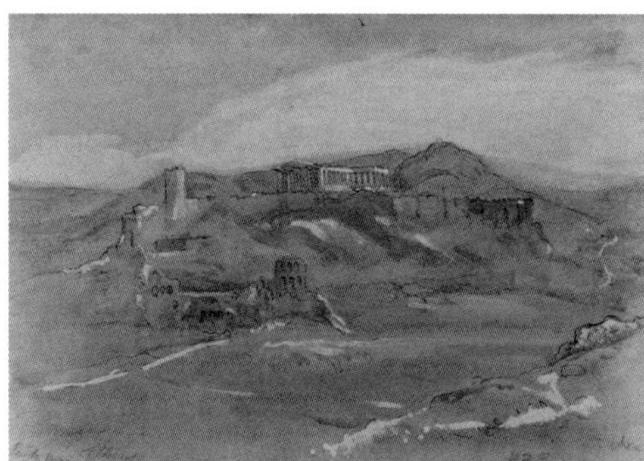

D.1987.1

The Acropolis, Athens, early Morning
pencil, watercolour, bodycolour (heightened with
white); grey paper
signed lower right with initials: *HBB*; inscribed lower
right: *Athens*; inscribed lower left: *Acropolis / Athens /
Early Morning*
175 × 252 mm
Wynne, Mrs Margaret (gift, 1987) (D.1987.1)

Canal Scene, Venice
pencil, white chalk; grey paper faded to brown
signed lower left with initials: *HBB*
172 × 274 mm
Wynne, Mrs Margaret (gift, 1987) (D.1987.2)

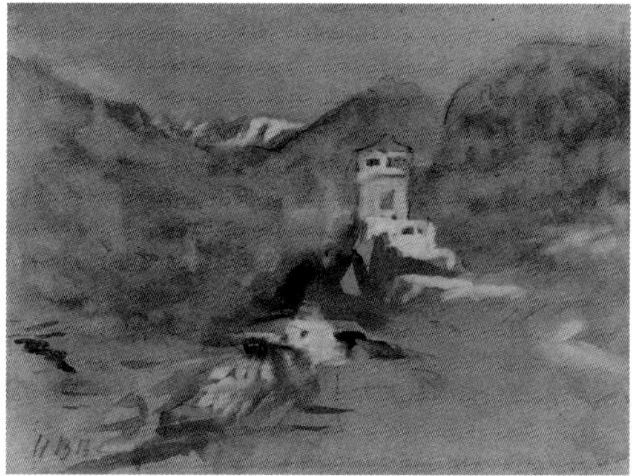

D.1987.3

Mountain Scene with Castle
pencil, watercolour, bodycolour; grey paper
signed lower left with initials: *HBB*
186 × 241 mm
Wynne, Mrs Margaret (gift, 1987) (D.1987.3)

■ **BRADSHAW, S. (fl. 1831–65)**
Unknown artist.

The Departure of Briseis from the Tent of Achilles
12.9.1831
pencil
dated lower centre: *Sep.12.1831*; watermark:
JWHAT[MAN] / TURKEY [MILL] / 1825
131 × 132 mm
untraced, 1966 (D.1966.3)

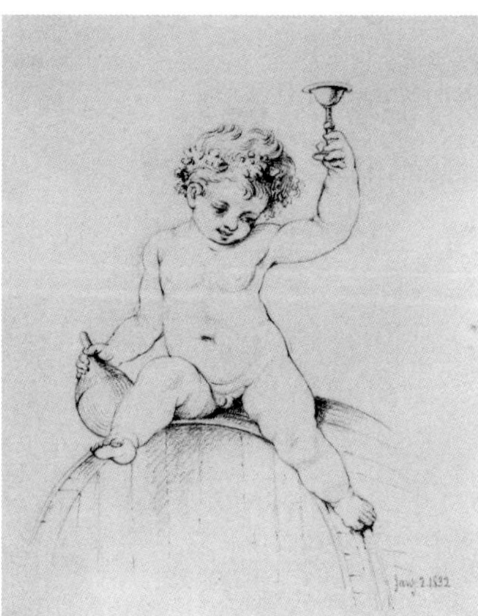

D.1966.4

Study of the Infant Bacchus astride a Cask
2.1.1832
pencil
dated lower right: *Jany.2.1832*
135 × 106 mm
untraced, 1966 (D.1966.4)

Study of Putti
4.1.1832
pencil
dated lower right: *Jany.4.1832*
94 × 102 mm
untraced, 1966 (D.1966.5)

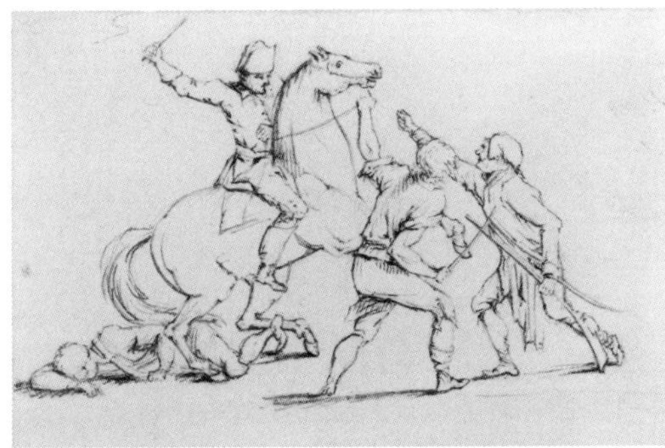

D.1966.6

Man on Horseback attacked by Brigands
pencil
73 × 106 mm
untraced, 1966 (D.1966.6)

Study of a Horse
pencil
139 × 139 mm
untraced, 1966 (D.1966.7)

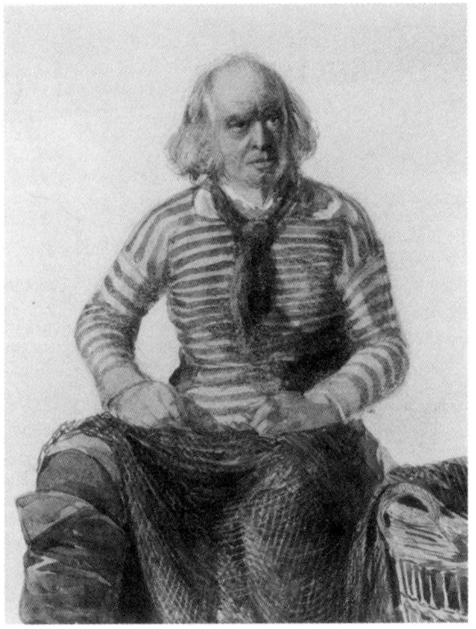

D.1966.8

Seated Fisherman with Net
pencil, watercolour
229 × 173 mm
untraced , 1966 (D.1966.8)

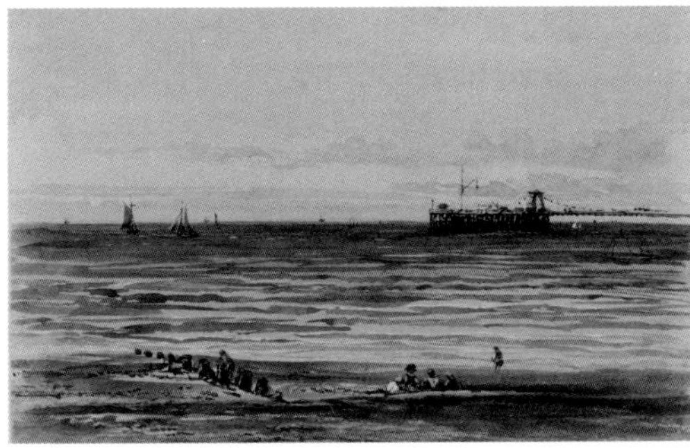

D.1966.9

The Old Chain Pier, Brighton, from the Shore
pencil, watercolour, bodycolour (heightened
with white)
163 × 249 mm
untraced, 1966 (D.1966.9)

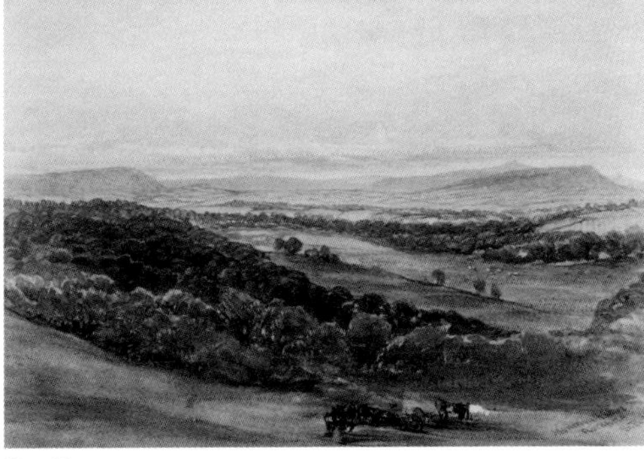

D.1966.10

**View across a wooded Landscape at Rockfield,
Monmouthshire, Wales**
pencil, watercolour, bodycolour (heightened
with white)
signed, inscribed & dated lower right: *Monmouthshire /
Rockfield / S.B.1865*; inscribed lower right verso:
Gy.Monmouthshire drystamped [cut] *–ECHERTIER
BAR–* [cut]
184 × 261 mm
untraced, 1966 (D.1966.10)

View across Fields
pencil
118 × 174 mm
untraced, 1966 (D.1966.11)

**Woman with an Umbrella (recto); Study of a
Woman seen from behind (verso)**
pencil
133 × 71 mm
untraced, 1966 (D.1966.12)

Medallion of Pope Innocent XII
pencil
watermark: *[JWHA]TMAN [18]18*
121 × 143 mm
untraced, 1966 (D.1966.13)

■ BRANDARD, ROBERT (1805–62)
Born in Birmingham, Brandard studied engraving
under Edward Goodall in 1824–25. Although Brandard
was mainly an engraver (he worked on several plates
for Turner's *Picturesque Views in England and Wales*), he
was also a watercolourist and exhibited at the Royal
Academy between 1831 and 1838.

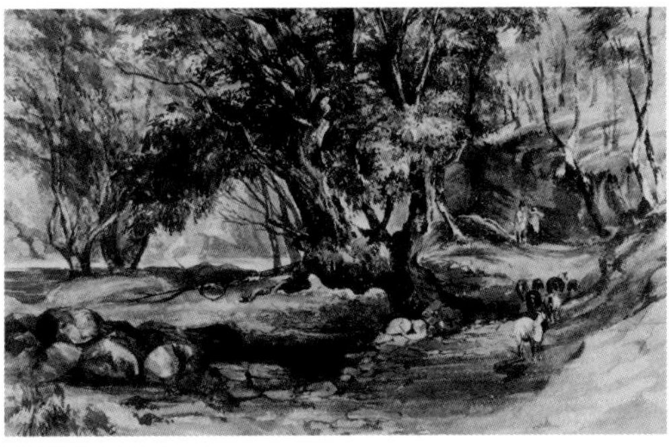

D.1900.23

Figures and Sheep
watercolour
323 × 496 mm
untraced (purchase, 1900) (D.1900.23)

Dover from the East
pencil, watercolour
signed (?) lower right with monogram (?): *RB* (?)
214 × 302 mm
Reekie, W. Maxwell (gift, 1942) (D.1942.3)

Sunny Day
1833
watercolour
signed & dated lower right: *R.Brandard.1833*
215 × 307 mm
Towlson, Hector J. (bequest, 1969) (D.1970.19)

■ BRANDOIN, MICHEL VINCENT CHARLES (1733–90)
Brandoin was a Swiss artist who worked in
London ca. 1770 and later retired to Vevay on
Lac Leman, Switzerland.

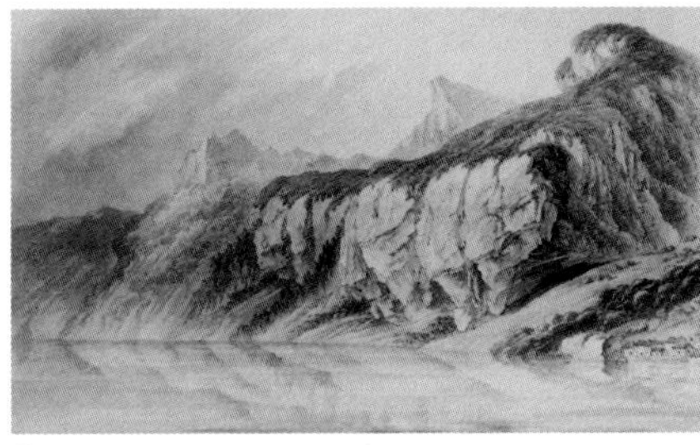

D.1999.10

The Rocks of Meillerie, Lac Leman, Switzerland
pencil, pen and grey ink, watercolour
inscribed lower centre verso in artist's hand: *Rochers de
Meillerie.*[erased word]; inscribed verso along lower
edge above French inscription in later hand (the
owner's?): *The Rocks of Meillerie =*
270 × 435 mm
Sotheby's, Hazlitt, Gooden and Fox Ltd (via)
(purchase, 15.7.1999) (V. & A.) (D.1999.10)

■ BRANWHITE, CHARLES (1817–80)
Branwhite, who was born in Bristol, was a pupil of
his father (also an artist) and William James Muller.
Branwhite was elected an associate of the Old
Watercolour Society in 1849, and was a regular
exhibitor in London for the rest of his life. He was
an important member of the Bristol School.

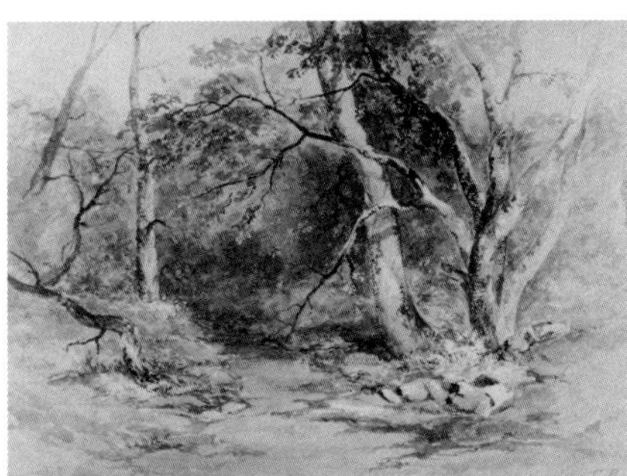

D.1970.21

**At the Head of Nightingale Valley, Leigh Woods,
near Bristol**
pencil, watercolour, bodycolour (heightened with
white); grey paper
signed lower right with initials: *C.B.*
254 × 351 mm
Towlson, Hector J. (bequest, 1969) (D.1970.21)

■ BRETT, JOHN EDWARD (1831–1902)

Brett was a landscape painter who was much influenced by Ruskin and the Pre-Raphaelites in the 1850s, although his later work is looser in style. He was elected an associate of the Royal Academy in 1881.

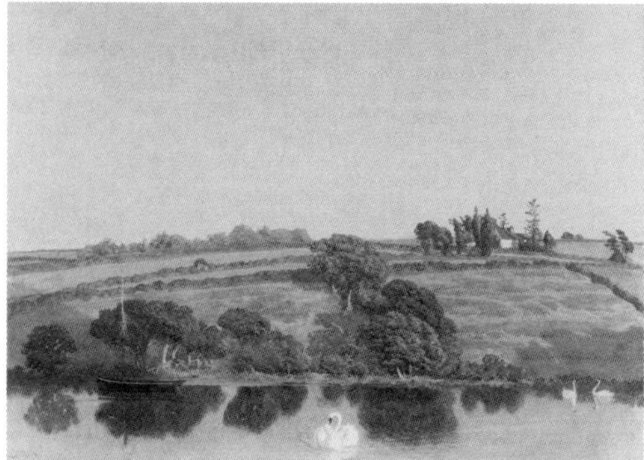

D.1965.11

River Scene, near Goring-on-Thames, Oxfordshire

1865
pencil, pen and brown ink, watercolour, bodycolour (heightened with white)
signed & dated lower left: *John / 1865 / Brett*
inscribed lower right margin with colour note: *hint of violet / over hill*
327 × 460 mm
Friends of the Whitworth (gift, 1965) (D.1965.11)

■ BRIGHT, HENRY (1814–73)

Bright, a landscape and marine painter, was a member of the Norwich School. He moved to London in 1836 and became a successful drawing master. Bright was a member of the New Watercolour Society from 1839 to 1845 and exhibited in Norwich from 1848.

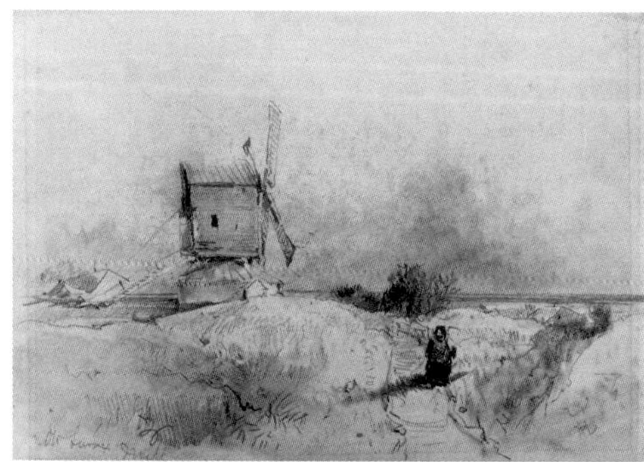

D.1912.2

Old Sussex Windmill (recto); Old Sussex Windmill (verso)

pencil, black chalk; grey paper
signed lower right recto with monogram: *HB*; signed lower right verso with monogram: *HB*; inscribed lower left recto: *Old Sussex Mill*; inscribed lower left verso: *Old / Sussex / Mill*
253 × 353 mm
Anderson, A. E. (gift, 1912) (D.1912.2)

A Farmyard with ruined Buildings

pencil, black chalk, red chalk, watercolour, bodycolour (heightened with white); grey paper
261 × 408 mm
Anderson, A. E. (gift, 1912) (D.1912.3)

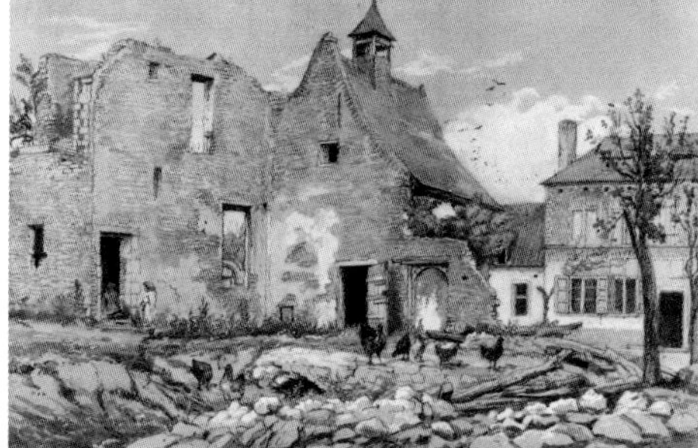

D.1912.3

Dutch River Scene

pastel; grey paper
signed (?) lower left; illegible: *HBright* (?)
264 × 368 mm
Buckley, C. R. (gift, 1912) (D.1912.12)

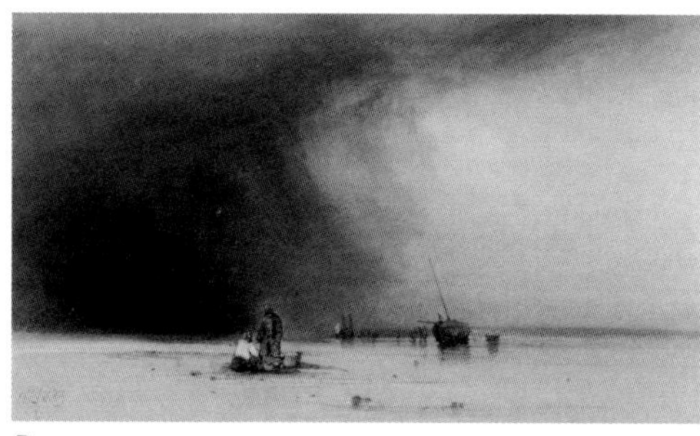

D.1914.1

The coming Storm, Yarmouth Beach, Norfolk

1833
pastel; brown paper
signed & dated lower left with initials: *HB/1833*
261 × 408 mm
Anderson, A. E. (gift, 1914) (D.1914.1)

Landscape with a Clump of Trees

coloured chalk; brown paper
228 × 430 mm
Nockolds, Dr Robert, Nockolds, Mrs Tilly (gift, 1978) (D.1978.3)

■ BRITTEN, WILLIAM EDWARD FRANK (1848–1916)

Britten, a painter of mythological subjects, exhibited at the Royal Academy from 1884 to 1888 and then at the Grosvenor Gallery and the New Gallery.

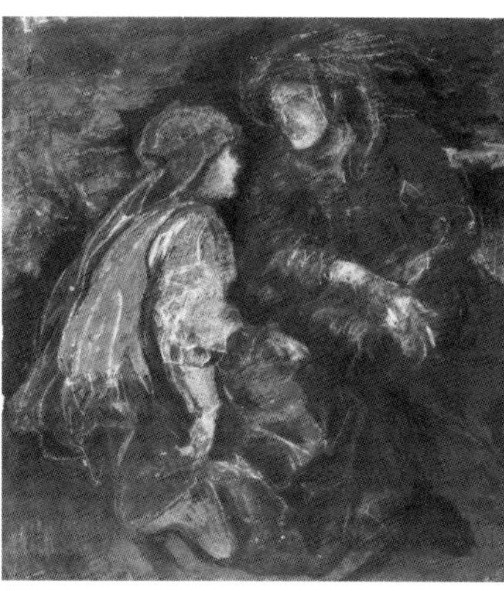

D.1928.24

Paolo and Francesca

pastel, bodycolour; card
522 × 478 mm
Anderson, A. E., National Art Collections Fund (via) (gift, 1928) (D.1928.24)

■ BRITTON, JOHN (1771–1857)

Britten was a topographer and architectural watercolourist, and was responsible for a number of antiquarian publications including *Architectural Antiquities of Great Britain* (1805–14) and *Cathedral Antiquities of England* (1814–35).

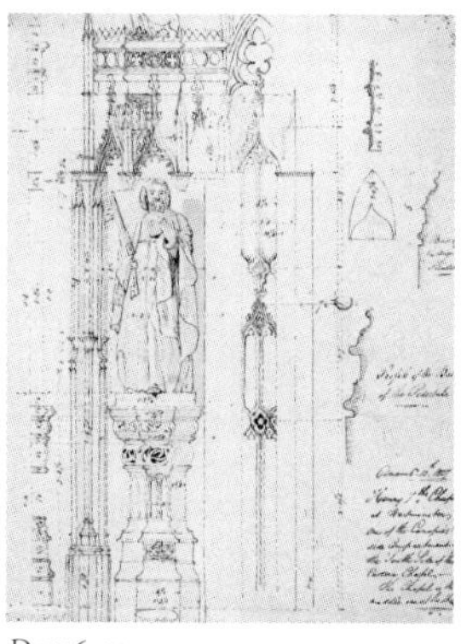

D.1926.193

Statue of St Peter and surrounding Canopy in Henry VII's Chapel, Westminster Abbey

10.12.1807
pen and brown ink, brown watercolour
signed lower right: *JBritton*; inscribed upper right: *Base of / the Angers / Pilasters*; inscribed centre right: *Profile of the Base / of the Pedestals*; inscribed & dated lower right: *Decembr.10th 1807 / Henry 7th. Chapel / at Westminster / one of the Canopies & a / side Compartment of / the South Side of the / Eastern Chapel - / The Chapel is the middle one of three*
290 × 213 mm
Ogden, William Sharp (bequest, 1926) (D.1926.193)

■ BROOKE, WILLIAM HENRY (1772–1860)

Brooke, a member of a family of Irish artists, was a portrait painter, illustrator and landscape watercolourist. He was elected an associate of the Royal Hibernian Academy in 1828.

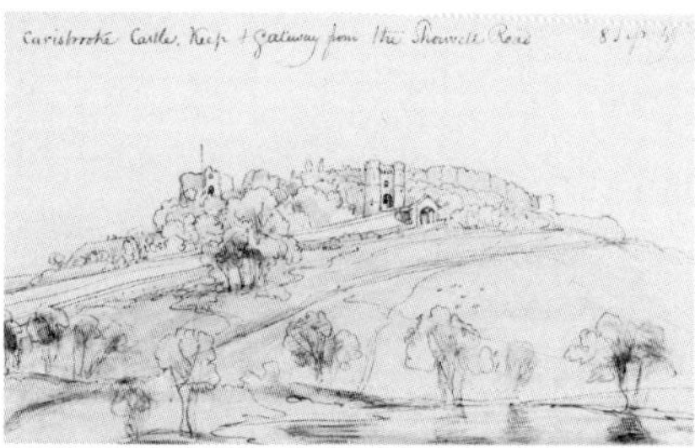

D.1947.1

Carisbrooke Castle, Isle of Wight, Keep and Gateway from the Shorwell Road

8.9.1849
pencil, pen and brown ink, watercolour
inscribed & dated along top edge: *Carisbrooke Castle. Keep & Gateway from the Shorwell Road 8 Sep.49*
103 × 165 mm
Pilkington, Margaret, Friends of the Whitworth (via) (gift, 1947) (D.1947.1)

■ Brown, Ford Madox (1821–93)

Brown was an important Pre-Raphaelite artist although, being older than the founder members, he was never part of the Brotherhood. He was a designer for Morris & Co. between 1861 and 1874, and executed a famous series of murals for Manchester Town Hall, which occupied him from 1878 until his death.

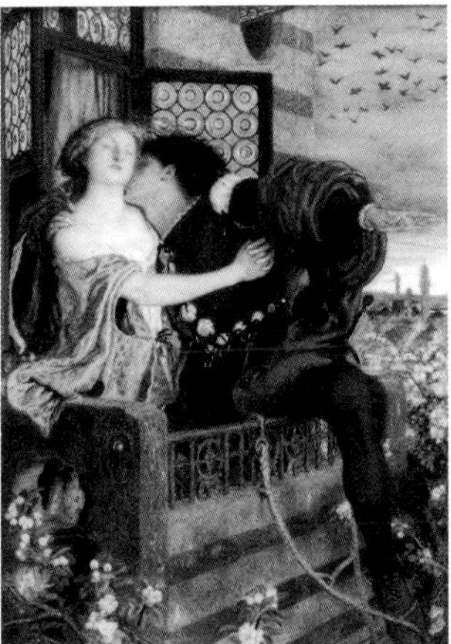

D.1917.20

Romeo and Juliet
1867
watercolour, bodycolour
signed & dated lower right: *MADOX BROWN–67*
480 × 330 mm
Gresham, James (purchase, 1917) (D.1917.20)

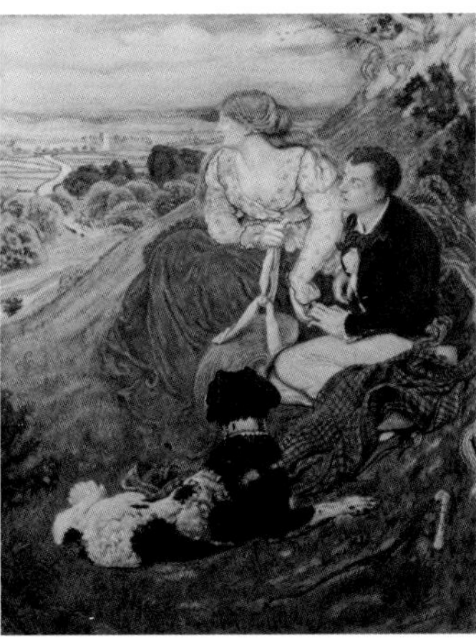

D.1920.12

Byron's Dream
1889
pencil, watercolour
signed & dated lower right with monogram: *FMB–89*
713 × 549 mm
Jackson, C. A. (purchase, 1920) (D.1920.12)

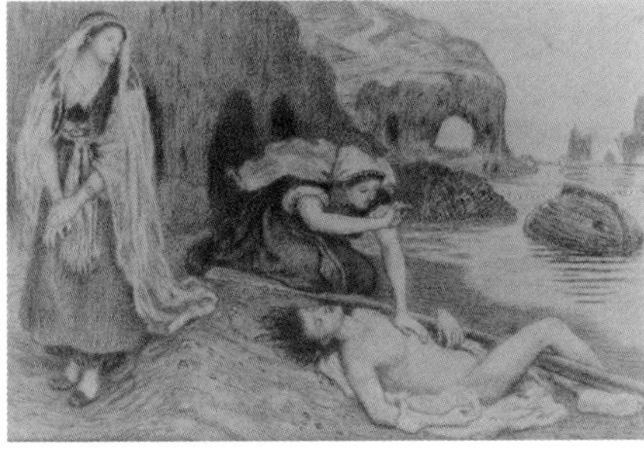

D.1921.26

Study of Don Juan for 'The Finding of Don Juan by Haidee'
1869
pencil, black chalk
254 × 275 mm
Brown and Phillips Ltd, London (purchase, 1921) (D.1921.26)

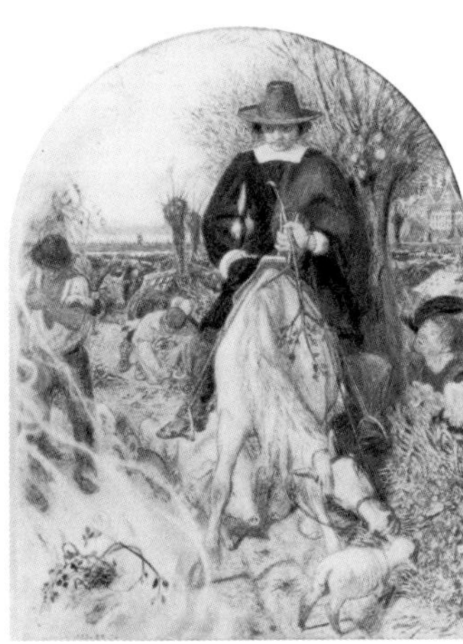

D.1925.30

Cromwell on his Farm at St Ives, 1636
1853 & 1856 & 1874
pencil, pen and brown ink, pastel, watercolour, bodycolour (heightened with white); arched paper
signed & dated lower left: *F.Madox Brown. 1853–56–74*
345 × 249 mm
Boddington, Henry (executors of) (purchase, 1925) (D.1925.30)

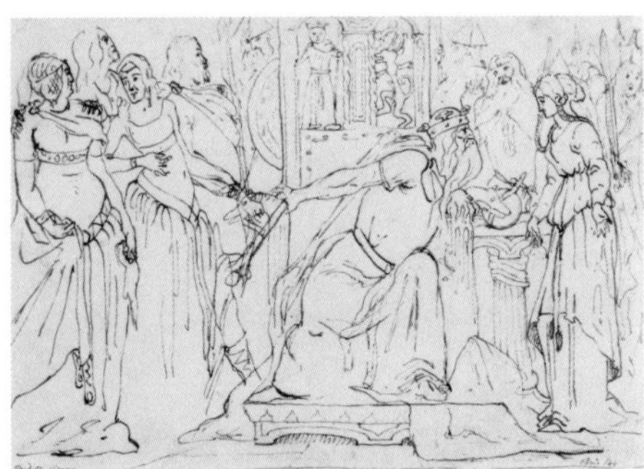

D.1927.51

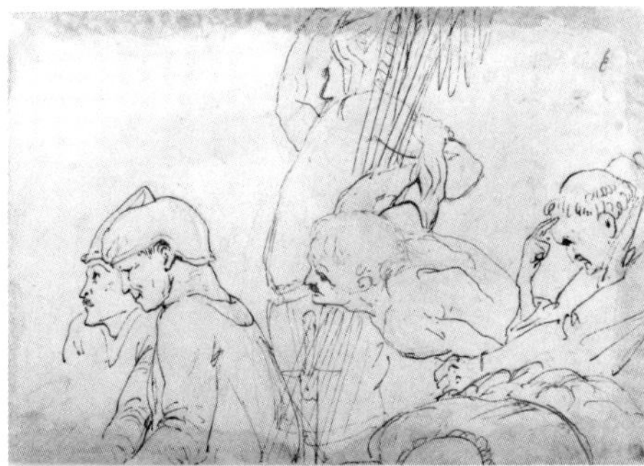

D.1927.51 (verso)

Study for King Lear, Lear questions Cordelia (recto); Study for The Body of Harold brought before William the Conqueror (verso)
1844
pencil, pen and brown ink
signed lower left: *Ford M.Brown*; inscribed & dated lower right: *Paris/44*
210 × 288 mm
Holliday, J. R. (bequest, 1927) (D.1927.51)

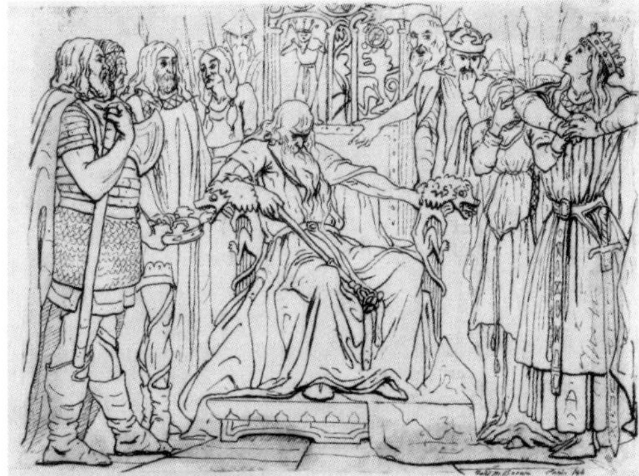

D.1927.52

France claims the dispossessed Cordelia
1844
pencil, pen and brown ink
signed, inscribed & dated lower right: *FordMBrown Paris/44*
216 × 280 mm
Holliday, J. R. (bequest, 1927) (D.1927.52)

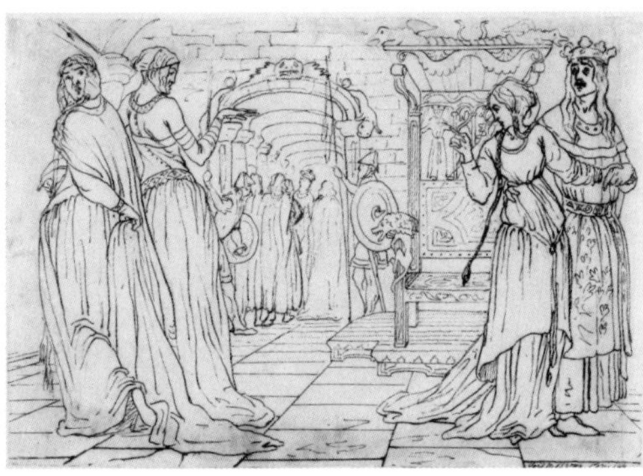

D.1927.53

Cordelia parting from her Sisters
1844
pencil, pen and brown ink
signed, inscribed & dated lower right: *FordM Brown Paris/44*
205 × 292 mm
Holliday, J. R. (bequest, 1927) (D.1927.53)

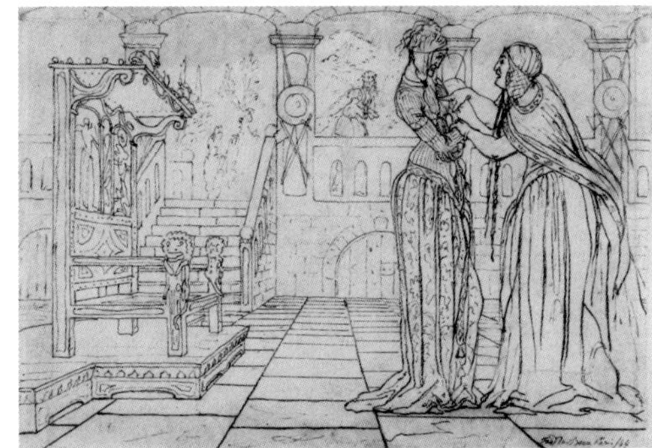

D.1927.54

Goneril and Regan together
1844
pencil, pen and brown ink
signed, inscribed & dated lower right: *FordM Brown Paris/44*
202 × 289 mm
Holliday, J. R. (bequest, 1927) (D.1927.54)

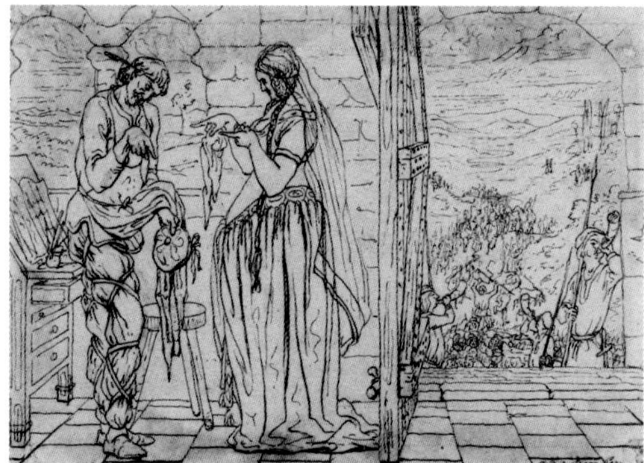

D.1927.55

Goneril tells Oswald how to treat Lear
1844
pencil, pen and brown ink
signed, inscribed & dated lower right; paper loss
affecting inscription and date: *FordM Brown Pari[s/4]4*
206 × 282 mm
Holliday, J. R. (bequest, 1927) (D.1927.55)

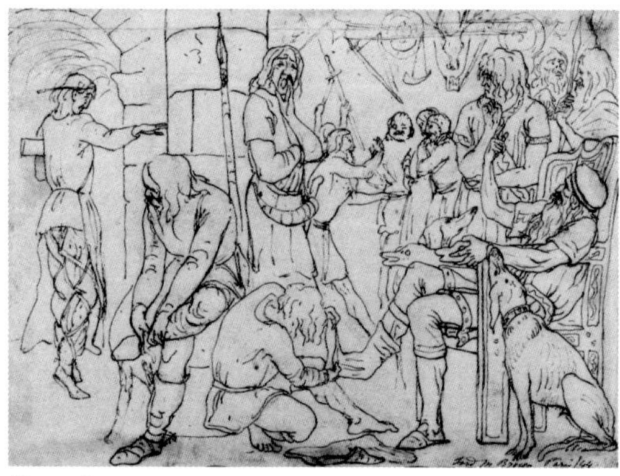

D.1927.56

Oswald's Insolence to Lear
1844
pencil, pen and brown ink
signed, inscribed & dated lower right: *FordM Brown
Paris/44*
207 × 274 mm
Holliday, J. R. (bequest, 1927) (D.1927.56)

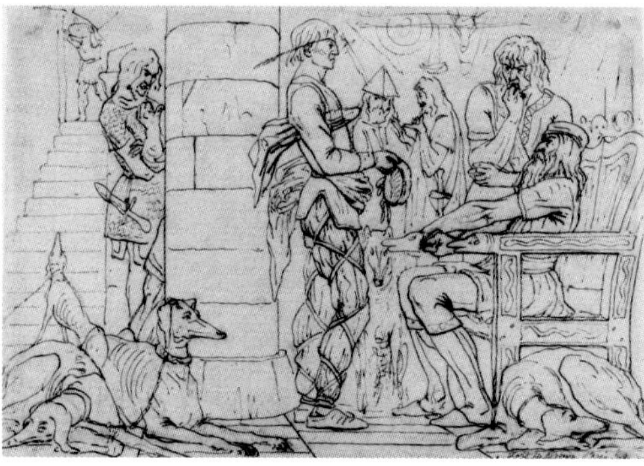

D.1927.57

Lear rebukes Oswald
1844
pencil, pen and brown ink
signed, inscribed & dated lower right: *FordM Brown
Paris/44*
200 × 282 mm
Holliday, J. R. (bequest, 1927) (D.1927.57)

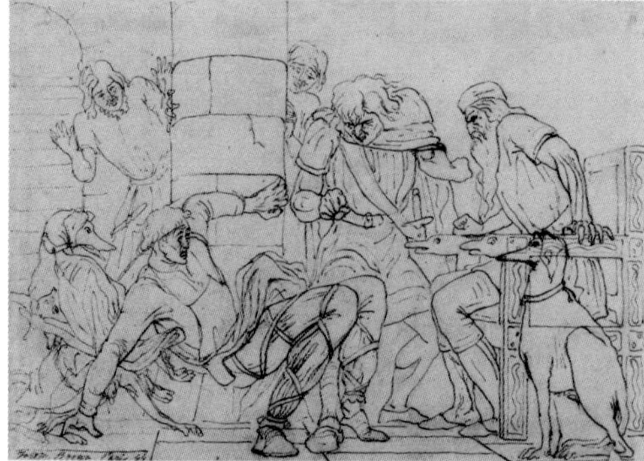

D.1927.58

Kent trips Oswald
1844
pencil, pen and brown ink
signed, inscribed & dated lower left: *FordM.Brown
Paris 44*
200 × 278 mm
Holliday, J. R. (bequest, 1927) (D.1927.58)

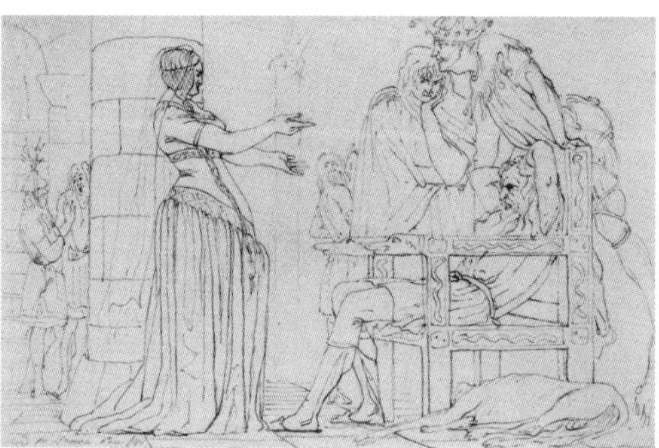

D.1927.59

Goneril's Complaint to Lear
1844
pencil, pen and brown ink
signed, inscribed & dated lower left: *Ford M.Brown
Paris/44*
184 × 280 mm
Holliday, J. R. (bequest, 1927) (D.1927.59)

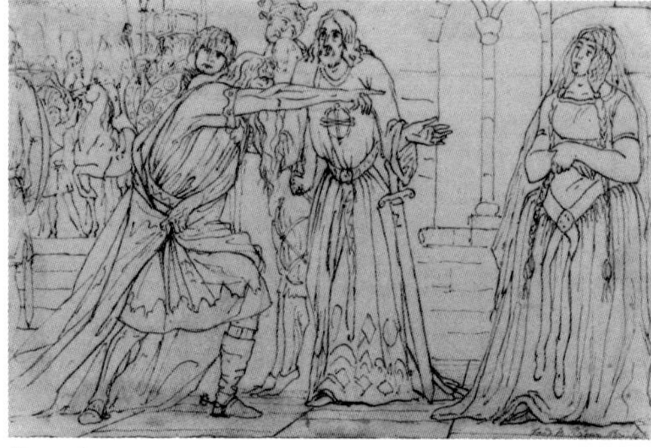

D.1927.60

Lear curses Goneril's Infidelity
1844
pencil, pen and brown ink
signed, inscribed & dated lower right: *FordM Brown
Paris/44*
187 × 277 mm
Holliday, J. R. (bequest, 1927) (D.1927.60)

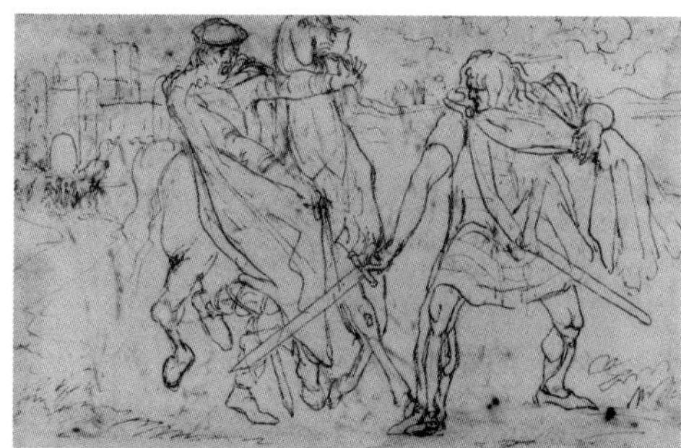

D.1927.61

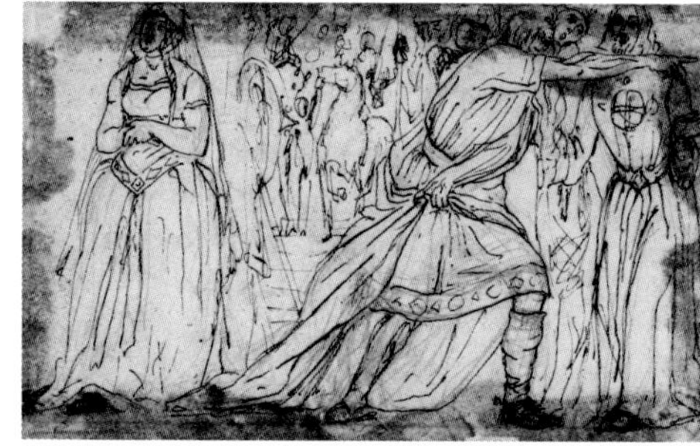

D.1927.61 (verso)

**Kent challenges Oswald (recto); Lear curses
Goneril's Infidelity (verso)**
1844
pen and brown ink (recto)
signed, inscribed & dated lower right recto; illegible as
sheet has been cut and only the tops of the capital
letters are visible: *Ford M Brown Paris/44* [presumably]
149 × 236 mm
Holliday, J. R. (bequest, 1927) (D.1927.61)

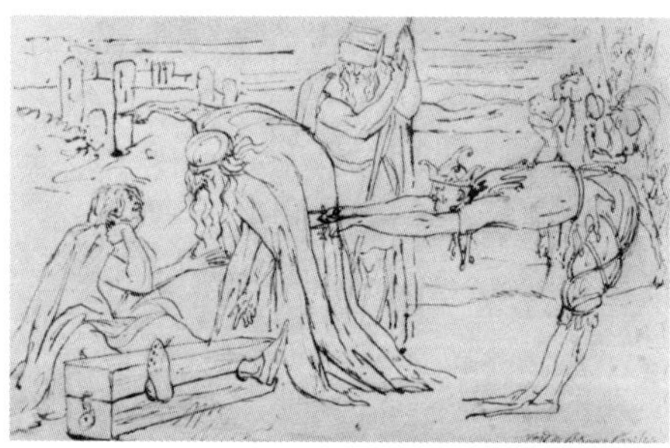

D.1927.62

**Kent in the Stocks (recto); In the Farmhouse
adjoining the Castle (verso)**
1844
pencil, pen and brown ink (recto)
signed, inscribed & dated lower right: *FordM Brown
Paris/44*
155 × 235 mm
Holliday, J. R. (bequest, 1927) (D.1927.62)

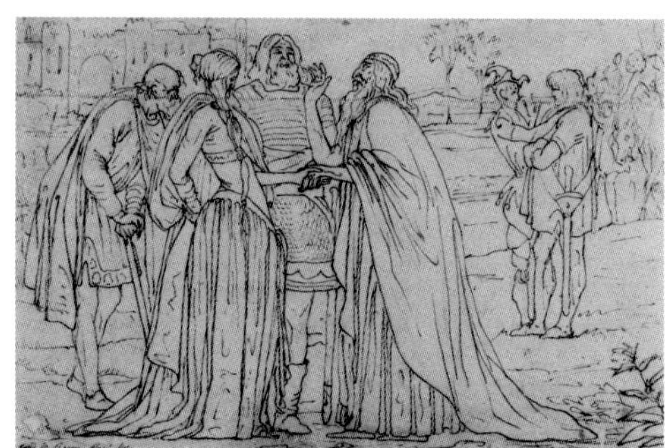

D.1927.63

Lear recounts his Wrongs to Regan
1844
pencil, pen and brown ink
signed, inscribed & dated lower left: *Ford M.Brown Paris/44*
189 × 280 mm
Holliday, J. R. (bequest, 1927) (D.1927.63)

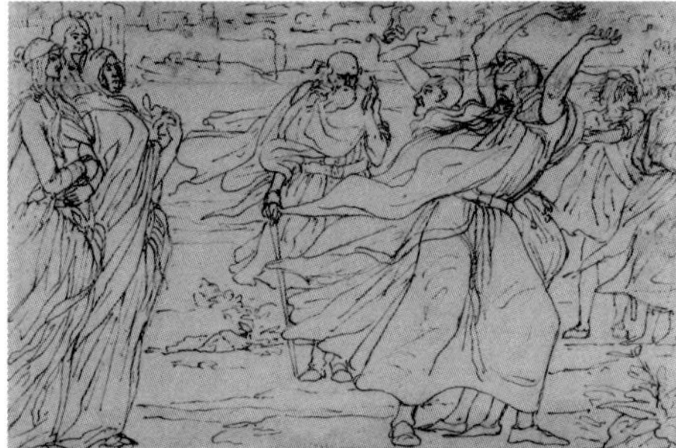
D.1927.64

Lear parts from Regan and Goneril cursing
1844
pencil, pen and brown ink
signed, inscribed & dated lower right: *Ford M Brown Paris/44*
195 × 279 mm
Holliday, J. R. (bequest, 1927) (D.1927.64)

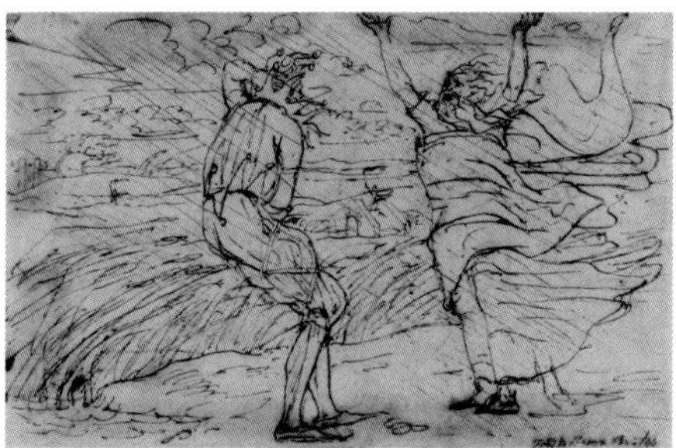
D.1927.65

Lear and the Fool in the Storm (recto); Alternative Study for Lear (verso)
1844
pencil, pen and brown ink
signed, inscribed & dated lower right recto: *FordM Brown Paris/44*
156 × 236 mm
Holliday, J. R. (bequest, 1927) (D.1927.65)

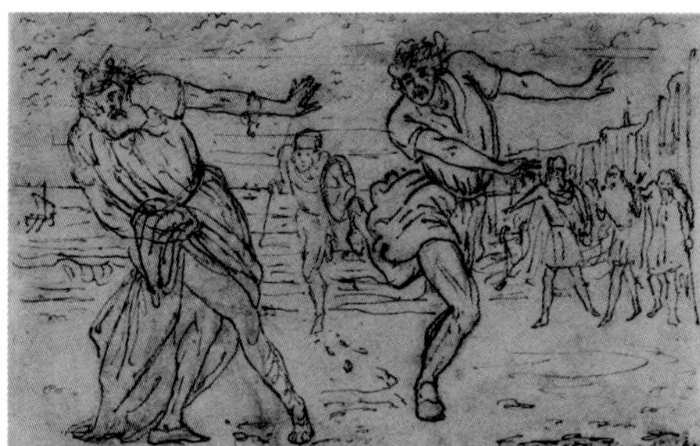
D.1927.66

Lear mad on the Beach at Dover
1844
pencil, pen and brown ink
signed, inscribed & dated lower right: *FordM Brown Paris/44*
152 × 236 mm
Holliday, J. R. (bequest, 1927) (D.1927.66)

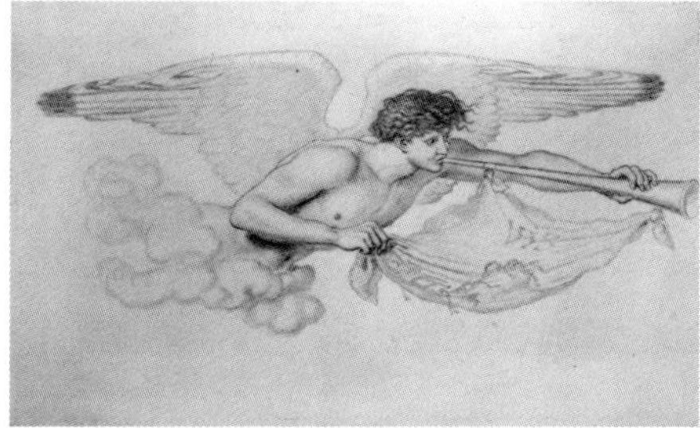
D.1930.6

Design for a decorative Panel for the Manchester Royal Jubilee Exhibition, 1887: Angel blowing Trumpet
1887
red chalk, black chalk; buff paper
424 × 647 mm
Clegg, Mrs Neville (gift, 1930) (D.1930.6)

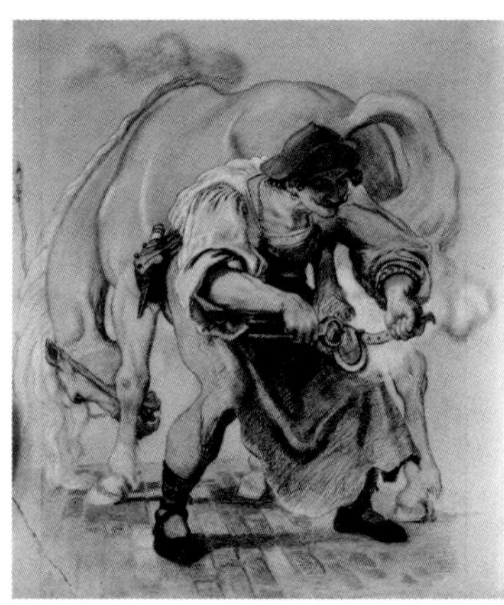
D.1930.7

Design for a decorative Panel for the Manchester Royal Jubilee Exhibition, 1887: The Farrier
1887
pen, coloured chalk; buff paper
signed & dated lower left, with initials in monogram: *FMB – 87*
763 × 652 mm
Clegg, Mrs Neville (gift, 1930) (D.1930.7)

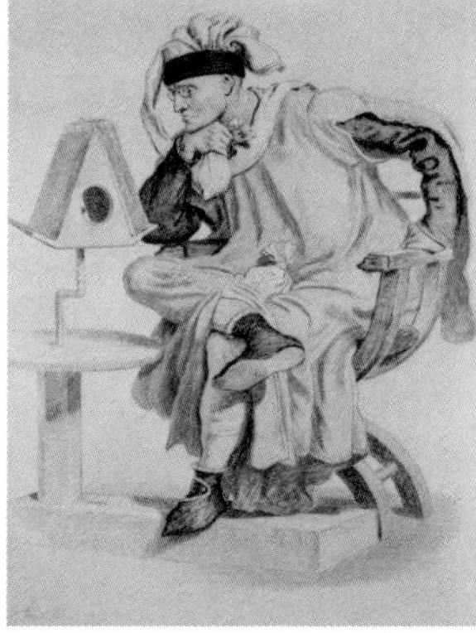
D.1930.8

Design for a decorative Panel for the Manchester Royal Jubilee Exhibition, 1887: The Merchant
1887
pencil, coloured chalk; buff paper
signed & dated lower left, with initials in monogram: *FMB – 87*
762 × 551 mm
Clegg, Mrs Neville (gift, 1930) (D.1930.8)

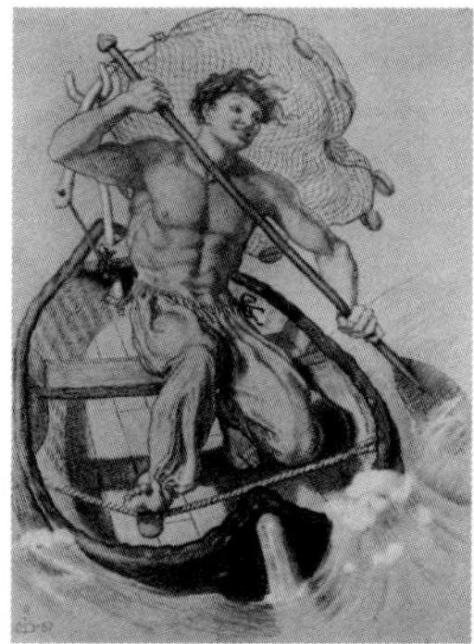
D.1930.9

Design for a decorative Panel for the Manchester Royal Jubilee Exhibition, 1887: The Fisherman
1887
pencil, coloured chalk; buff paper
signed & dated lower left, with initials in monogram: *FMB – 87*
763 × 552 mm
Clegg, Mrs Neville (gift, 1930) (D.1930.9)

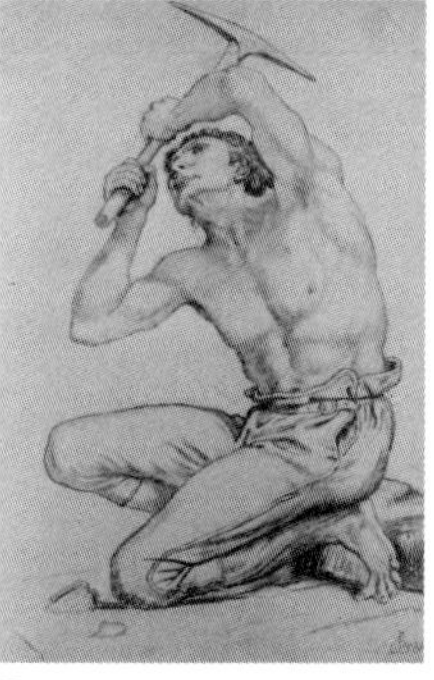
D.1930.10

Design for a decorative Panel for the Manchester Royal Jubilee Exhibition, 1887: The Collier
1886
red chalk; buff paper
signed & dated lower right, with initials in monogram: *FMB – 86*
831 × 548 mm
Clegg, Mrs Neville (gift, 1930) (D.1930.10)

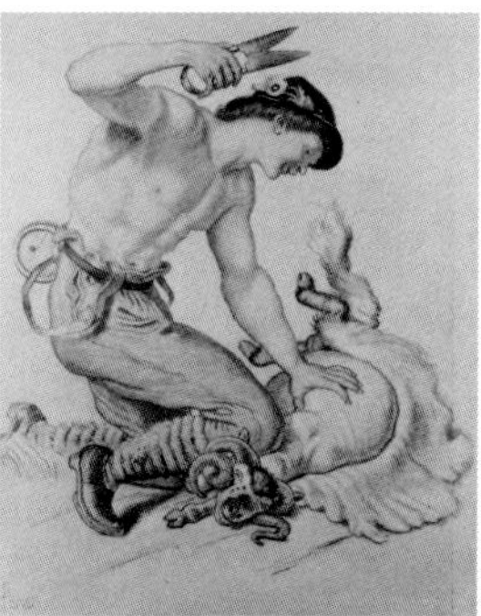
D.1930.11

Design for a decorative Panel for the Manchester Royal Jubilee Exhibition, 1887: Shearing the Sheep
1887
black chalk, red chalk; buff paper
signed & dated lower left, with initials in monogram: *FMB – 87*
763 × 592 mm
Clegg, Mrs Neville (gift, 1930) (D.1930.11)

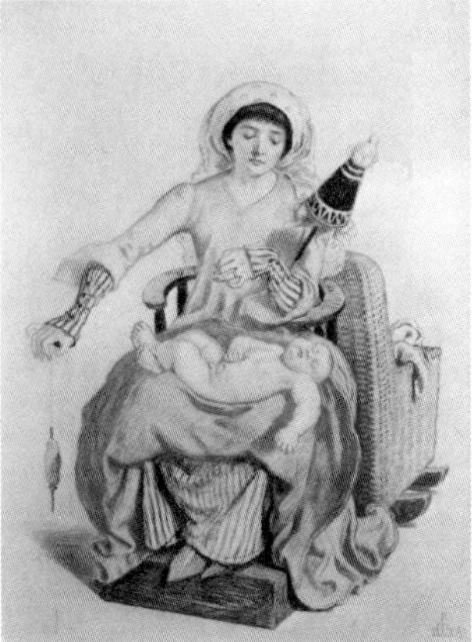

D.1930.12

Design for a decorative Panel for the Manchester Royal Jubilee Exhibition, 1887: Spinning
1887
pencil, red chalk, black chalk
signed & dated lower right, with initials in monogram:
FMB – 87
751 × 546 mm
Clegg, Mrs Neville (gift, 1930) (D.1930.12)

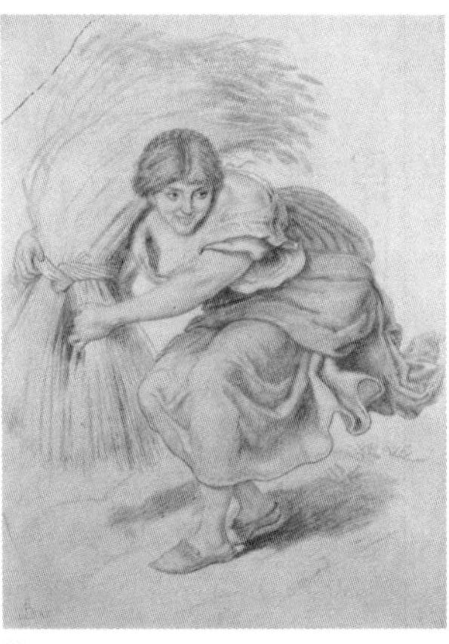

D.1930.13

Design for a decorative Panel for the Manchester Royal Jubilee Exhibition, 1887: Harvesting the Wheat
1887
pencil, brown chalk, black chalk, red chalk
signed & dated lower left, with initials in monogram:
FMB – 87
762 × 547 mm
Clegg, Mrs Neville (gift, 1930) (D.1930.13)

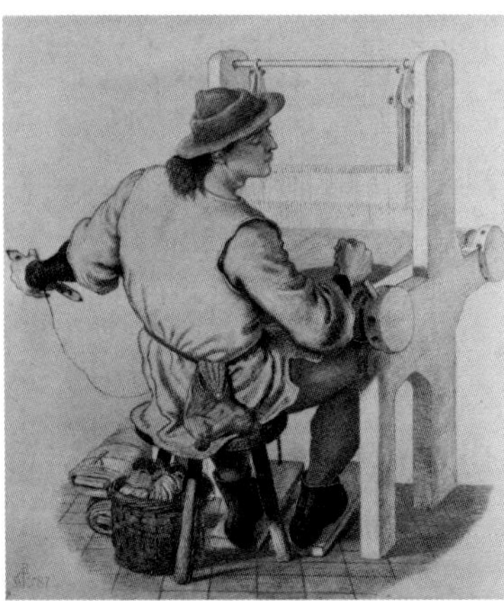

D.1930.14

Design for a decorative Panel for the Manchester Royal Jubilee Exhibition, 1887: The Weaver
1887
pencil, black chalk, red chalk
signed & dated lower left, with initials in monogram:
FMB – 87
754 × 645 mm
Clegg, Mrs Neville (gift, 1930) (D.1930.14)

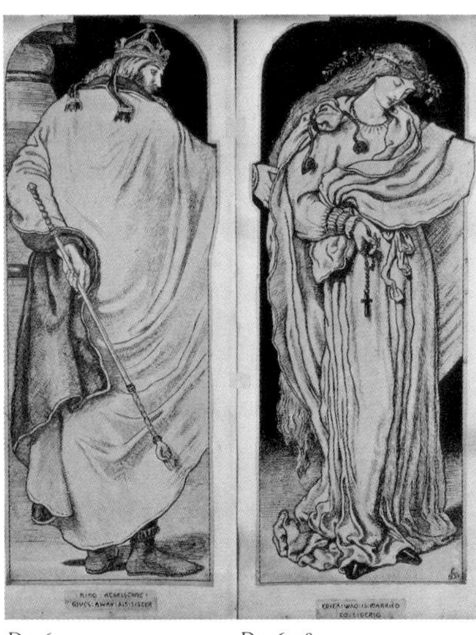

D.1963.27   D.1963.28

Athelstan, King of the West Saxons and Mercians, giving away his Sister, St Editha: Cartoon for the first Window of the south Side of the Chancel Clerestory, St Edith's, Tamworth, Staffordshire
1873
pen and black ink, black watercolour, bodycolour
(heightened with white); brown paper
1048 × 401 mm
Axon, Mrs D. (purchase, 1963) (D.1963.27)

St Editha: Cartoon for the first Window of the south Side of the Chancel Clerestory, St Edith's, Tamworth, Staffordshire
1873
pen and black ink, black watercolour, bodycolour
(heightened with white); brown paper
signed & dated lower right, with monogram: *FMB73*
1035 × 419 mm
Axon, Mrs D. (purchase, 1963) (D.1963.28)

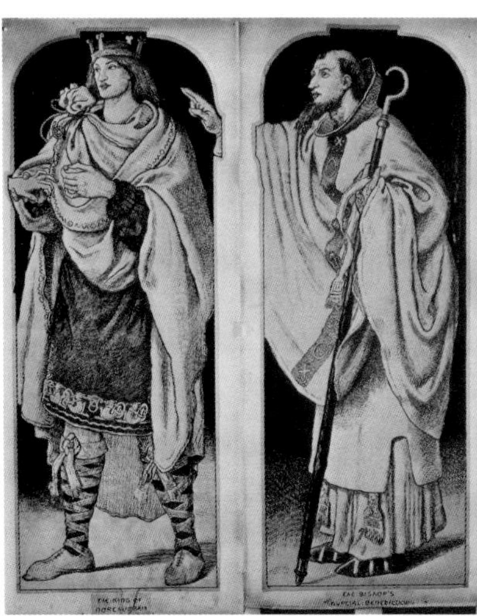

D.1963.29   D.1963.30

Sigtrig, King of Northumbria, placing a Ring on Editha's Finger: Cartoon for the first Window of the south Side of the Chancel Clerestory, St Edith's, Tamworth, Staffordshire
1873
pen and black ink, black watercolour, bodycolour
(heightened with white)
1046 × 413 mm
Axon, Mrs D. (purchase, 1963) (D.1963.29)

Aella, Bishop of Lichfield, giving his Blessing: Cartoon for the first Window of the south Side of the Chancel Clerestory, St Edith's, Tamworth, Staffordshire
1873
pen and black ink, black watercolour, bodycolour
(heightened with white)
1045 × 406 mm
Axon, Mrs D. (purchase, 1963) (D.1963.30)

■ **BROWNE, HABLOT KNIGHT ('PHIZ')
(1815–82)**
Browne, best known as the illustrator – under the name 'Phiz' – of all the major novels of Dickens from *Pickwick Papers* to *A Tale of Two Cities*, also illustrated the work of the Irish novelist Charles Lever, as well as exhibiting in both oil and watercolour.

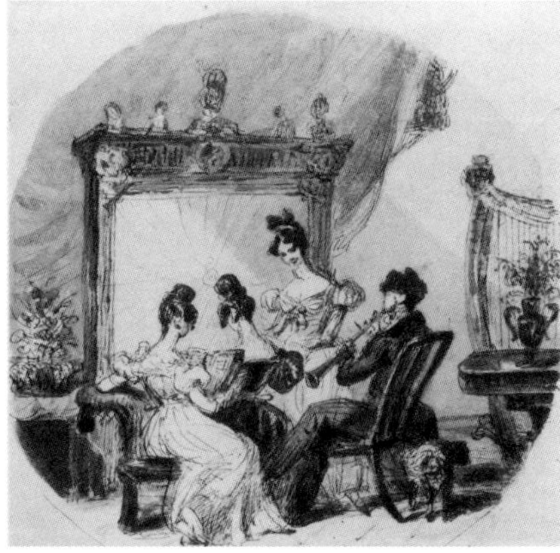

D.1926.198

Musical Party
pen and brown ink, brown watercolour,
grey watercolour
179 × 175 mm
Ogden, William Sharp (bequest, 1926) (D.1926.198)

■ **BUCK, SAMUEL (1696–1779) and BUCK, NATHANIEL (ca. 1700–ca. 1770)**
The Buck brothers together produced more than 500 views of abbeys castles and houses as well as more extensive views of towns and cities, which were published as engravings. These often have a marked horizontal format.

Restormel Castle, Cornwall
1734
pen and grey ink, grey watercolour; paper
with watermark VI
inscribed along top edge *THE WEST VIEW OF LESTORMEL CASTLE, IN THE COUNTY OF CORNWALL*; inscribed in lower right margin:
1.Lestwithiel Town. 2 River Foy
171 × 364 mm
Drummond, William (purchase, 29.1.1996) (D.1996.1)

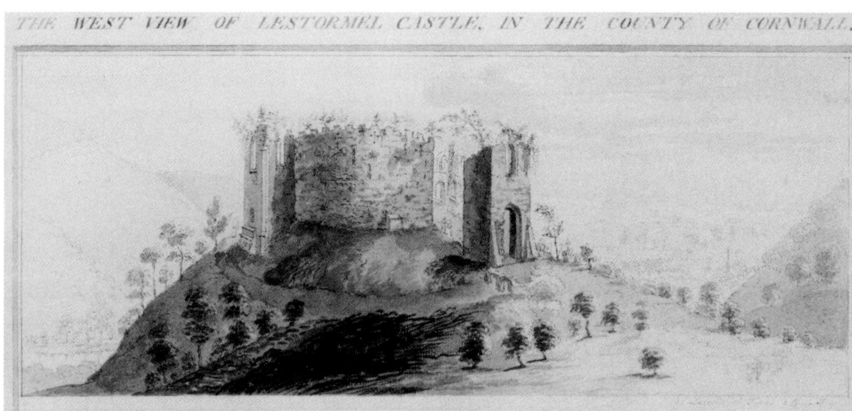

D.1996.1

■ BUCKLER, JOHN CHESSELL (1793–1894)

John Chessell Buckler, the eldest son of John, took on his architectural practice in 1826. He was a tireless recorder of old Gothic buildings as well as a designer in the Gothic style. Buckler was runner-up in the competition to rebuild the Houses of Parliament in 1835.

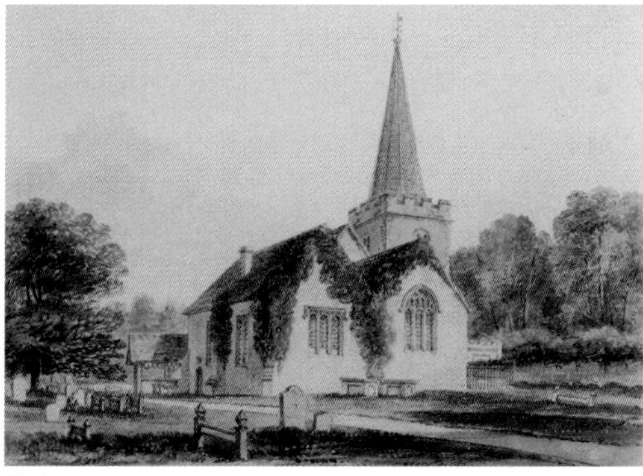

D.1893.5

St Giles' Church, Stoke Poges, Buckinghamshire, from the Churchyard
1829
pencil, pen and brown ink, watercolour
268 × 371 mm
Agnew's (purchase, 18.12.1893) (D.1893.5)

■ BUCKLEY, C. F. (fl. 1840–69)

C. F. Buckley was a landscape painter who probably came from Cork. He exhibited views all over Britain, including the Royal Academy, from 1841 to 1869.

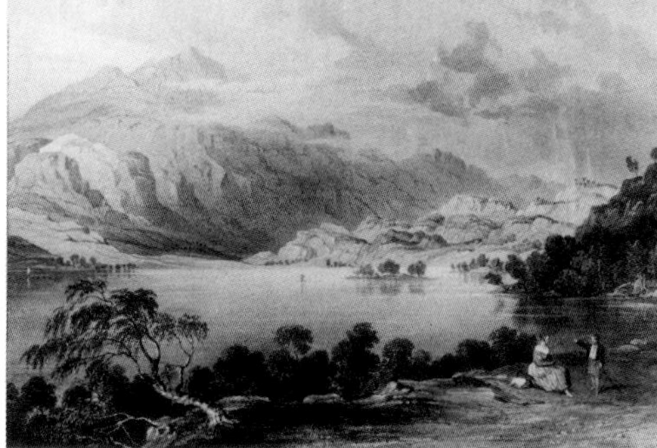

D.1970.22

Loch Achray and Ben Venue, Perthshire
watercolour
signed lower right: *CFBuckley.*
262 × 376 mm
Towlson, Hector J. (bequest, 1969) (D.1970.22)

■ BULMAN, JOB (fl. 1740–after 1779)

Bulman was an amateur who is said to have been a friend of Paul Sandby. He painted extensively all over Britain but little is known of his life aside from dated drawings.

Middleham Castle, Yorkshire
watercolour
331 × 611 mm
Pearson, Norman G. (gift, 1954) (D.1954.25)

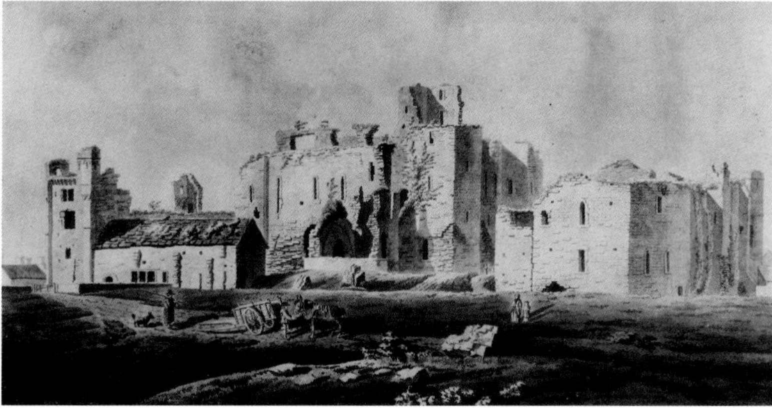

D.1954.25

■ BUNBURY, HENRY WILLIAM (1750–1811)

Bunbury was an amateur caricaturist, whose works were often etched by professionals. His caricatures were social rather than political. Bunbury exhibited at the Royal Academy as an honorary exhibitor between 1780 and 1808.

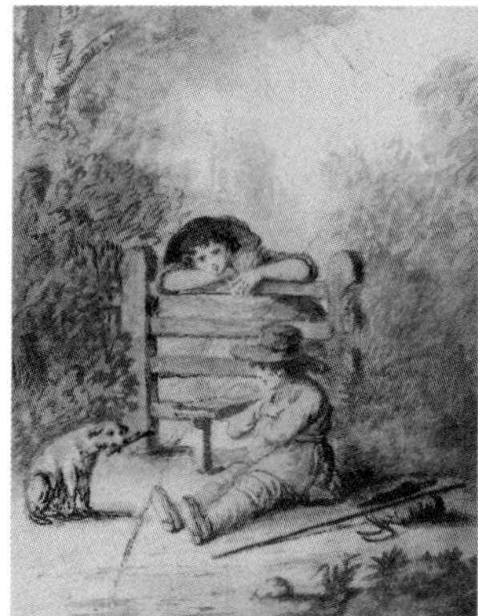

D.1916.5

Children and a Dog at a Stile
pencil, pen and brown ink, watercolour;
light brown paper
309 × 234 mm
Anderson, A. E. (gift, 1916) (D.1916.5)

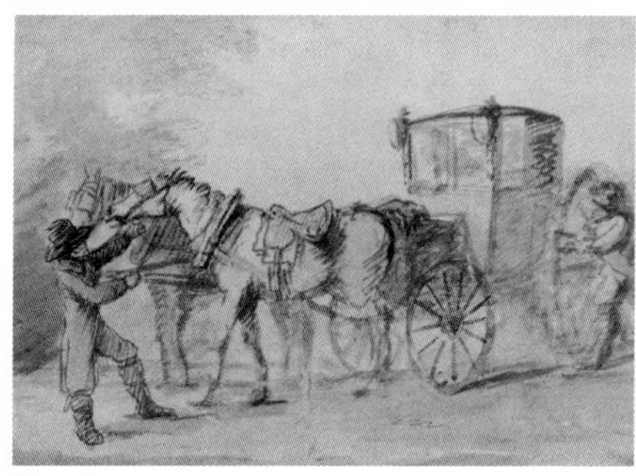

D.1917.6

A Coach and Horses
pencil, watercolour
220 × 295 mm
Anderson, A. E. (gift, 1917) (D.1917.6)

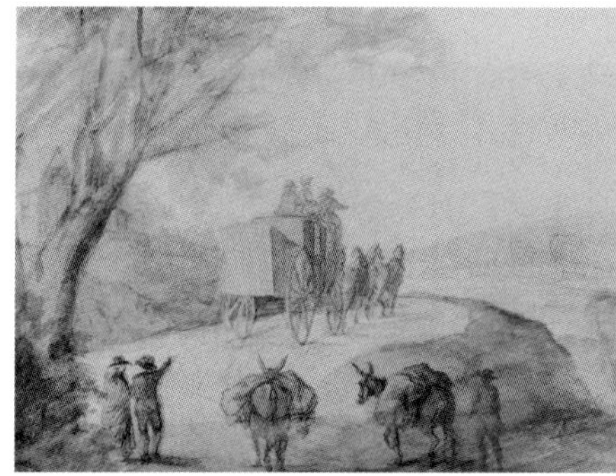

D.1917.7

Stage Coach travelling (recto); Studies of Girls (verso)
1787–89
pencil, watercolour
inscribed & dated in upper left verso; not a signature:
Stage Coach. / HWB. about 1788.
292 × 390 mm
Anderson, A. E. (gift, 1917) (D.1917.7)

Return from Work, a Youth on Horseback
brown watercolour; light brown paper
signed lower right with initials: *HWB*; signed on
mount lower left: *Henry William Bunbury delint.*
239 × 295 mm
Anderson, A. E. (gift, 1917) (D.1917.12)

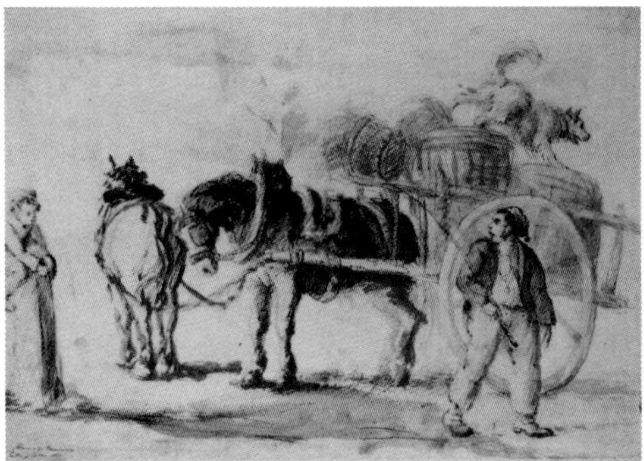

D.1917.13

The Market Cart
1800
pencil, black chalk, brown watercolour
inscribed & dated lower left; not a signature:
Henry W.Bunbury / Sir Henry's Father 1800
485 × 675 mm
Anderson, A. E. (gift, 1917) (D.1917.13)

■ BURGESS, HENRY WILLIAM
(fl. 1809–44)
Henry William Burgess, a member of a family of
artists, exhibited landscapes from 1809 to 1844. He was
a drawing master at Charterhouse, and published *Views
of the General Character and Appearance of Trees* in 1827.

Study of Trees
pencil
228 × 267 mm
Ogden, William Sharp (bequest, 1926) (D.1926.195)

Study of a Tree
pencil, black chalk
signed lower left: *HWBurgess*
228 × 269 mm
Ogden, William Sharp (bequest, 1926) (D.1926.196)

■ BURGESS, JOHN (attributed to)
(1814–74)
John Burgess, another member of the Burgess
artistic family, visited Italy between 1833 and 1837.
He became a drawing master at Leamington in
1840 and was elected an associate of the Old
Watercolour Society in 1851.

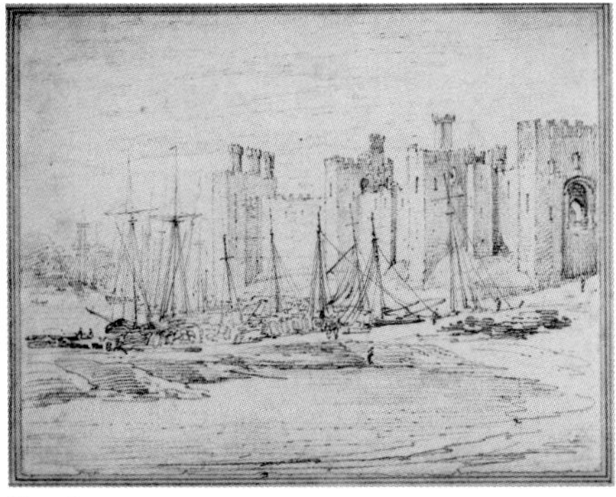

D.1926.197

View of Caernarvon Castle, Caernarvonshire, Wales, from the South
pencil
inscribed on mount lower centre: *Caernarvon Castle*
283 × 230 mm
Ogden, William Sharp (bequest, 1926) (D.1926.197)

■ BURGESS, WILLIAM (1749–1812)
William Burgess, a topographical draughtsman, was
one of the founders of the Burgess artistic dynasty. He
visited South Wales and the Wye valley in 1785.

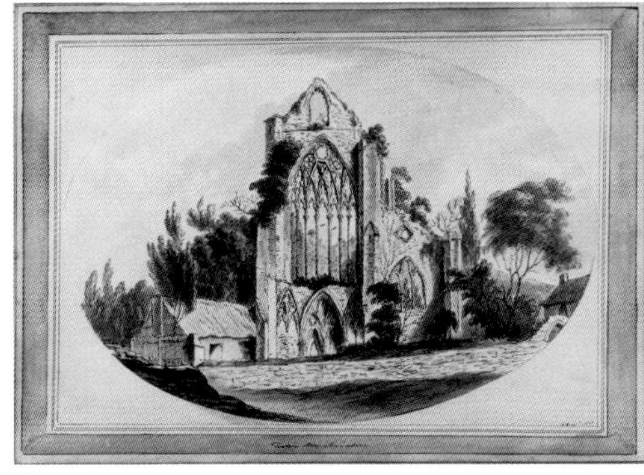

D.1907.2

View of the West Front, Tintern Abbey, Monmouthshire, Wales
1785
pen and brown ink, watercolour
signed & dated on mount lower right: *WBurgess 1785*
inscribed on mount lower centre: *Tintern Abbey.
Monmouthshire*
259 × 365 mm
untraced (purchase, 1907) (D.1907.2)

■ BURNE-JONES, SIR EDWARD COLEY
(1833–98)
Burne-Jones was born in Birmingham, and went to
Exeter College, Oxford. There he met his lifelong
friend and collaborator William Morris, with whom
he founded Morris & Co. in 1861. A prolific stained-
glass designer, Burne-Jones was a member of the
Old Watercolour Society between 1864 and 1870.
He was one of the most important artists of the
nineteenth century, and took his subjects from
medieval legend and classical myth as well as the
Bible and his own imagination. He was created a
baronet by Gladstone in 1894.

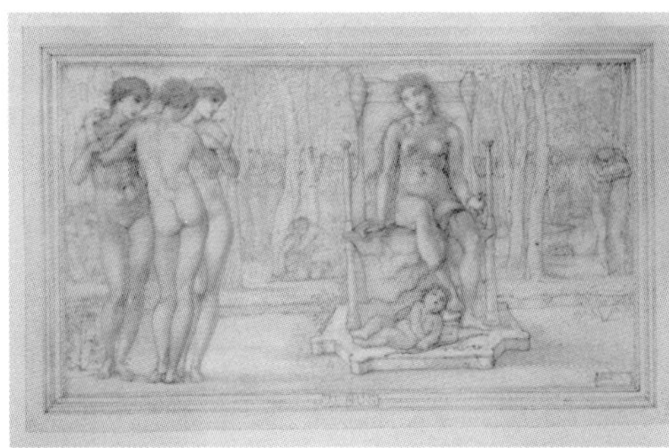

D.1921.32

Venus Concordia, Study for the Predella Panel of 'The Story of Troy'
1871
pencil
signed & dated on cartouche lower right: *E.B.J /
MDCCCLXXI*; inscribed on cartouche lower centre:
V.E.N.U.S
303 × 484 mm
Leicester Galleries, London (purchase, 1921) (D.1921.32)

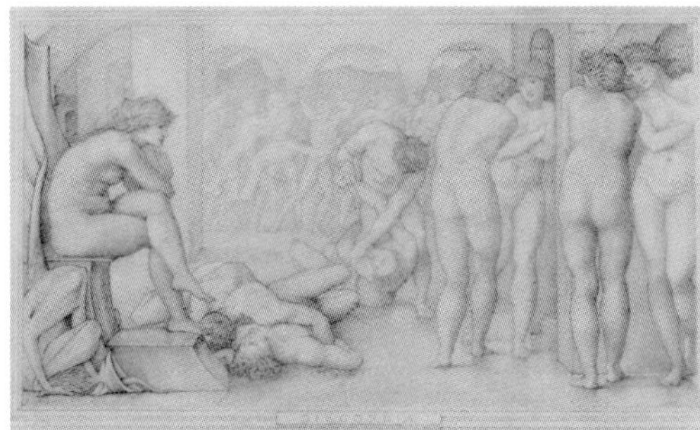

D.1921.34

Venus Discordia, Study for the Predella Panel of 'The Story of Troy'
1871
pencil
signed lower left: *E.BURNE JONES*; inscribed on
cartouche lower centre: *DISCORDIA*; inscribed upper
right above each of the four figures the names of the
figures: *iracundia invidia suspicio rixa*
298 × 481 mm
Leicester Galleries, London (purchase, 1921) (D.1921.34)

Two Studies of the Heads and Hands of two Figures in 'The Eve of the Deluge'
1863
pencil
inscribed lower left, in Charles Fairfax Murray's hand:
Noah entering the Ark; inscribed lower right, in Charles
Fairfax Murray's hand: *E.B.J.*; watermark:
[JWH]ATMAN / [18]62
180 × 160 mm
Holliday, J. R. (bequest, 1927) (D.1927.69)

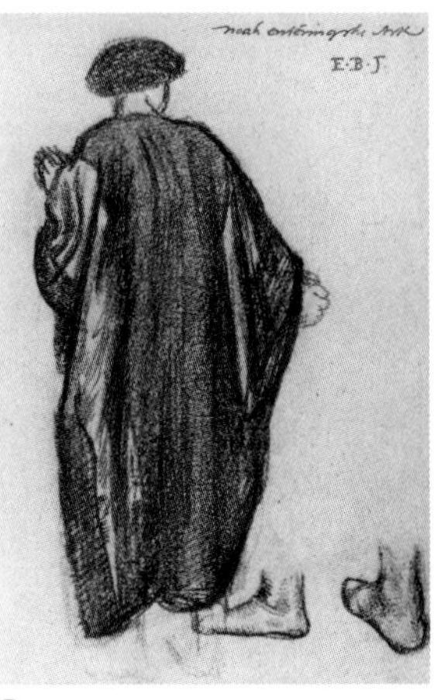

D.1927.70

Study for Noah in 'The Eve of the Deluge'
1863
pencil, black chalk
inscribed upper right, in Charles Fairfax Murray's
hand: *Noah entering the Ark / E.B.J.*
154 × 101 mm
Holliday, J. R. (bequest, 1927) (D.1927.70)

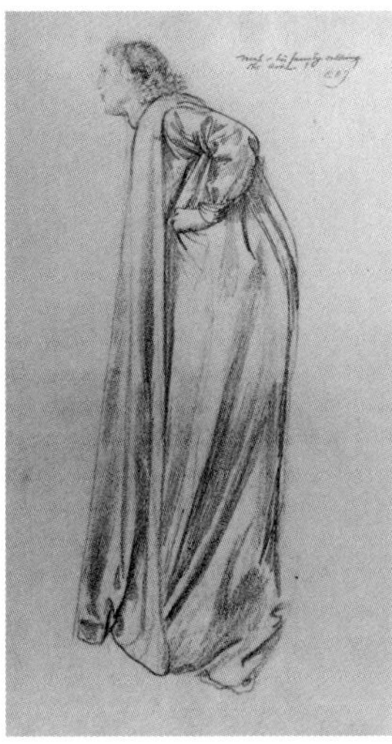

D.1927.71

Study for the Figure on the extreme right in 'The Eve of the Deluge'
1863
pencil
inscribed upper right, in Charles Fairfax Murray's hand: *Noah – his family entering the Ark ? / E.B.J.*
318 × 174 mm
Holliday, J. R. (bequest, 1927) (D.1927.71)

Study of a standing male Figure
pencil, black chalk
inscribed upper right, in Charles Fairfax Murray's hand: *E.B.J.*
352 × 142 mm
Holliday, J. R. (bequest, 1927) (D.1927.72)

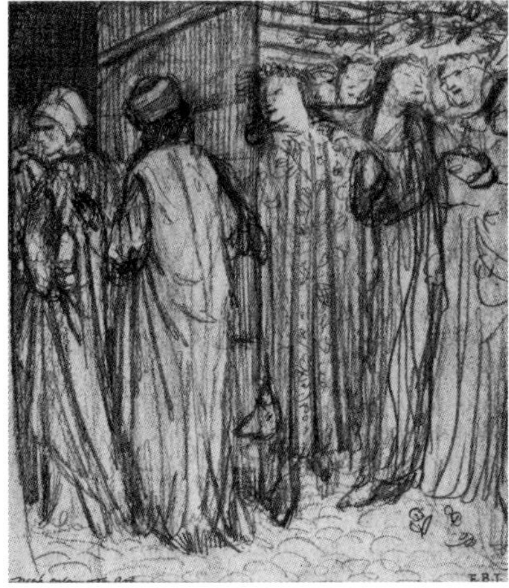

D.1927.73

Study for the Composition of 'The Eve of the Deluge' (recto); Studies for an Embroidery illustrating Characters from the 'Morte d'Arthur' (verso)
1863
pencil
inscribed lower left recto, in Charles Fairfax Murray's hand: *Noah entering the Ark*; inscribed lower right recto, in Charles Fairfax Murray's hand: *E.B.J.*; inscribed lower left verso, in Charles Fairfax Murray's hand: *Sketches for Tapestry*, and upper edge verso with the names of Arthurian characters, in Burne-Jones's hand
178 × 154 mm
Holliday, J. R. (bequest, 1927) (D.1927.73)

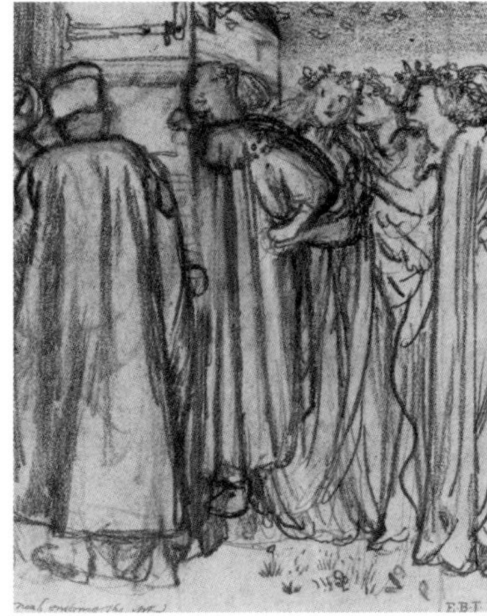

D.1927.74

Study for the Composition of 'The Eve of the Deluge'
1863
pencil, black chalk
inscribed lower left, in Charles Fairfax Murray's hand: *Noah entering the Ark*; inscribed lower right, in Charles Fairfax Murray's hand: *E.B.J.*
180 × 138 mm
Holliday, J. R. (bequest, 1927) (D.1927.74)

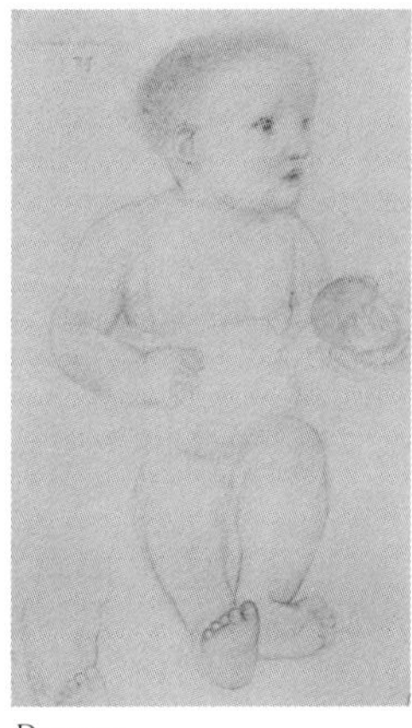

D.1927.75

Study for the Infant Christ in 'The Adoration of the Kings'
pencil
inscribed upper left, in Charles Fairfax Murray's hand: *Adoration of the Kings / E.B.J.*
225 × 129 mm
Holliday, J. R. (bequest, 1927) (D.1927.75)

Figure Study, possibly for a King in 'The Adoration of the Kings'
pencil
inscribed upper right, in Charles Fairfax Murray's hand: *Adoration of the Kings* ?; inscribed centre right in Charles Fairfax Murray's hand: *E.B.J.*
311 × 135 mm
Holliday, J. R. (bequest, 1927) (D.1927.76)

Study of a King for 'The Adoration of the Kings'
pencil
inscribed upper right, in Charles Fairfax Murray's hand: *Adoration of the Kings*; inscribed centre right in Charles Fairfax Murray's hand: *E.B.J.*
277 × 161 mm
Holliday, J. R. (bequest, 1927) (D.1927.77)

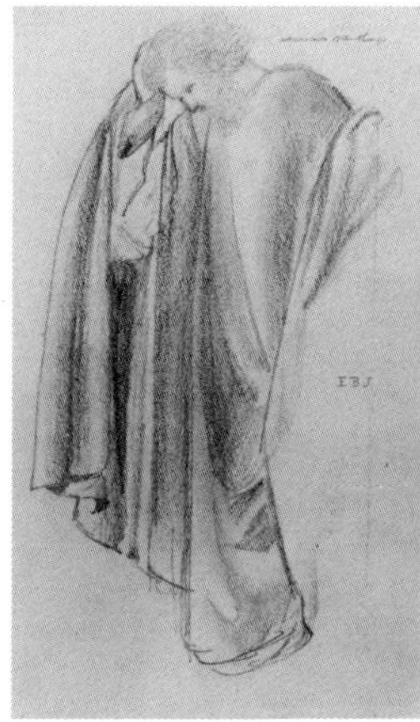

D.1927.77

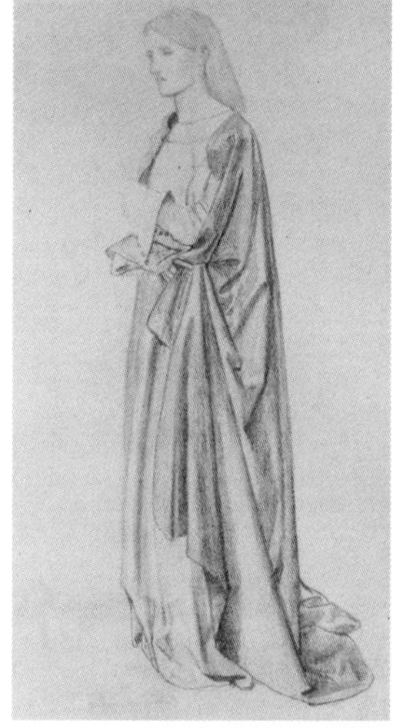

D.1927.78

Woman in Medieval Dress
pencil
watermark: *JWHATMAN / 1859*
331 × 178 mm
Holliday, J. R. (bequest, 1927) (D.1927.78)

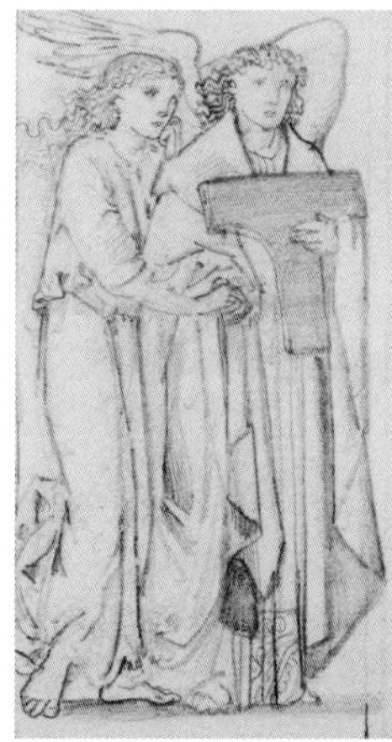

D.1927.79

Study of an Angel and a Woman, for the East Window of the Chancel of St John the Evangelist, Torquay, Devon
1865
pencil
190 × 104 mm
Holliday, J. R. (bequest, 1927) (D.1927.79)

**Study of two Angels clasping the
Foot of the Cross, for the East Window of
All Saints Church, Catton, Yorkshire**
1865
pencil
inscribed lower centre, partially cut: [illegible] *two
angels*; inscribed upper right: *Feet of Christ on Cross /
come down to here*
196 × 119 mm
Holliday, J. R. (bequest, 1927) (D.1927.80)

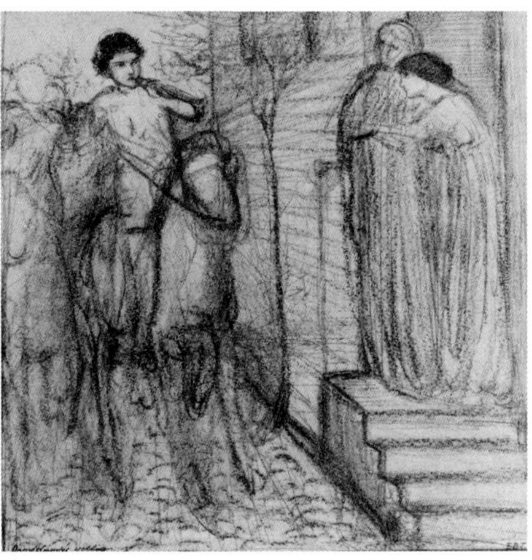

D.1927.81

**Study for the 'Meeting of Buondelmonte
and Ciulla, the Origin of the Guelph and
Ghibelline Quarrel in Florence'**
1860–61
pencil, black chalk
inscribed lower left, in Charles Fairfax Murray's hand:
Buondelmonte's wedding; inscribed lower right in
Charles Fairfax Murray's hand: *E.B.J.*
256 × 249 mm
Holliday, J. R. (bequest, 1927) (D.1927.81)

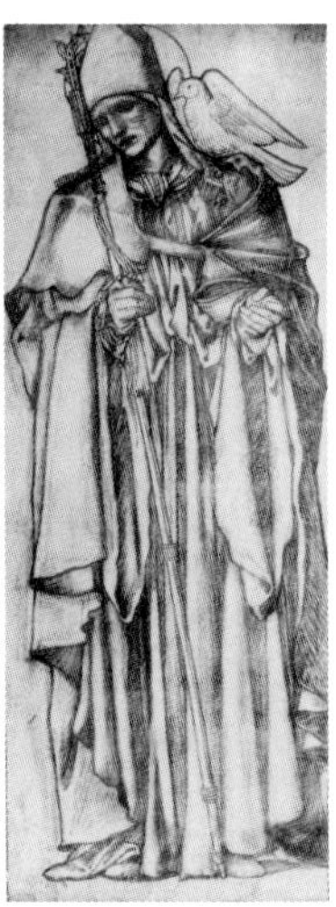

D.1927.82

**St David with a Dove on his Shoulder: Cartoon
for a Window in the Church of St Mary the
Virgin Mother, Margam, West Glamorgan**
1873
black chalk
inscribed upper right: *Morris and Company*; serial
number *L.P.65*; inscribed upper right: *FIXED*
1819 × 661 mm
Holliday, J. R. (bequest, 1927) (D.1927.82)

**St Bernard holding a Book and a Pen: Cartoon
for a Window in the Church of St Mary the
Virgin Mother, Margam, West Glamorgan**
1873
black chalk
inscribed upper right Morris and Company serial
number: *L.P.64*; inscribed upper right: *FIXED*;
inscribed upper left: *St Barnard*
1816 × 661 mm
Holliday, J. R. (bequest, 1927) (D.1927.83)

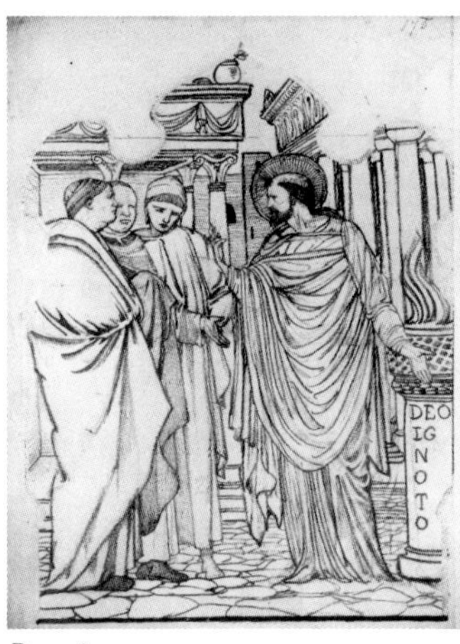

D.1927.84

**St Paul at Athens: Study for a Window in Coats
Parish Church, Coatbridge, Lanarkshire**
1876
pencil, black chalk
711 × 526 mm
Holliday, J. R. (bequest, 1927) (D.1927.84)

**Christ calling St Peter and St Andrew on the Sea
Shore: Study for a Window in Coats Parish
Church, Coatbridge, Lanarkshire**
1876
black chalk
711 × 526 mm
Holliday, J. R. (bequest, 1927) (D.1927.85)

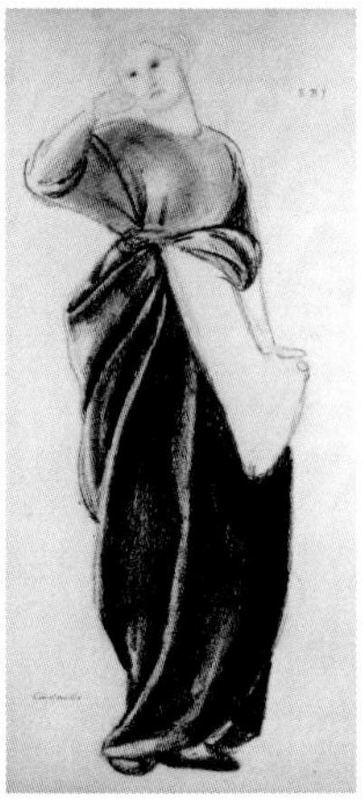

D.1927.86

Study for 'Cinderella'
1862–63
pencil, black chalk
inscribed lower left in Charles Fairfax Murray's hand:
Cinderella; inscribed upper right in Charles Fairfax
Murray's hand: *E.B.J.*
360 × 182 mm
Holliday, J. R. (bequest, 1927) (D.1927.86)

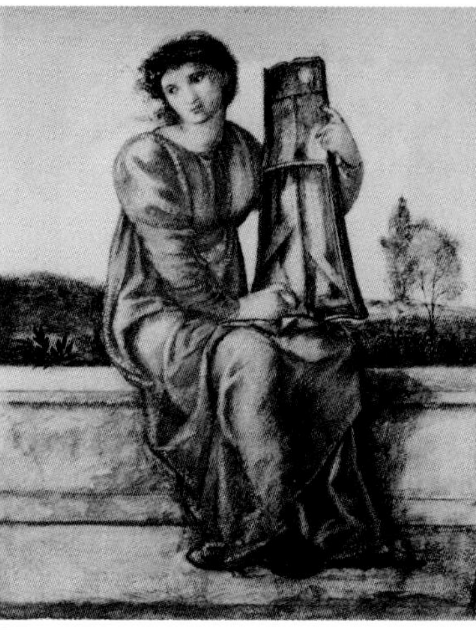

D.1927.87

**A seated female Musician, Study for
'The Lament'**
1866
pencil, watercolour, bodycolour
342 × 268 mm
Holliday, J. R. (bequest, 1927) (D.1927.87)

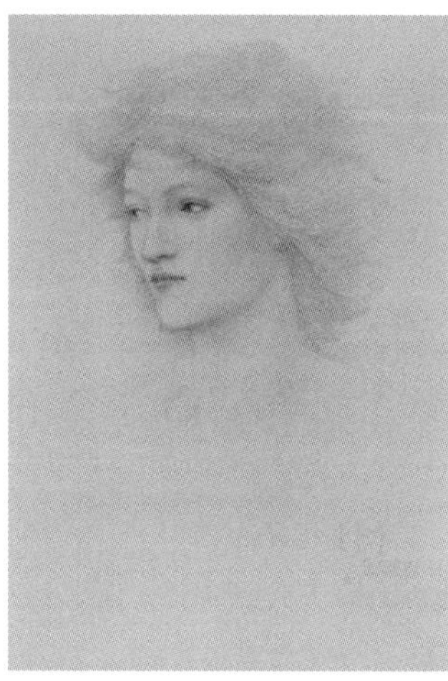

D.1939.3

**Study for a Nereid's Head for
'Perseus and the Nereids'**
1895
pencil
signed, inscribed & dated lower right with initials:
EB–J / for PERSEUS & / the NEREIDS / 1895
510 × 337 mm
Holliday, Mrs J. R. (bequest, 1939) (D.1939.3)

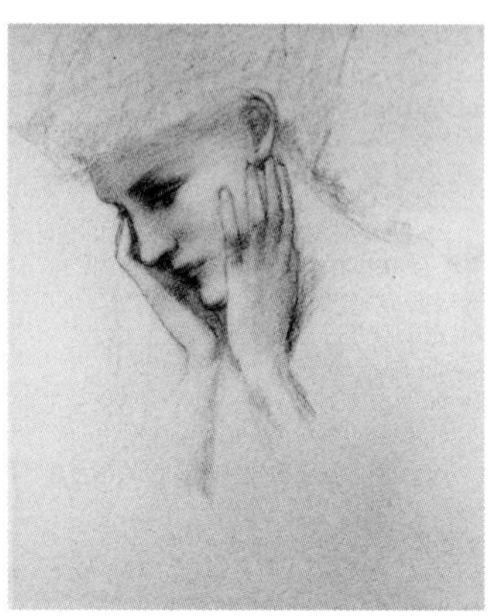

D.1939.4

Study of a female Head for 'The Sleep of King Arthur in Avalon'
red chalk, black chalk; pink paper
381 × 305 mm
Holliday, Mrs J. R. (bequest, 1939) (D.1939.4)

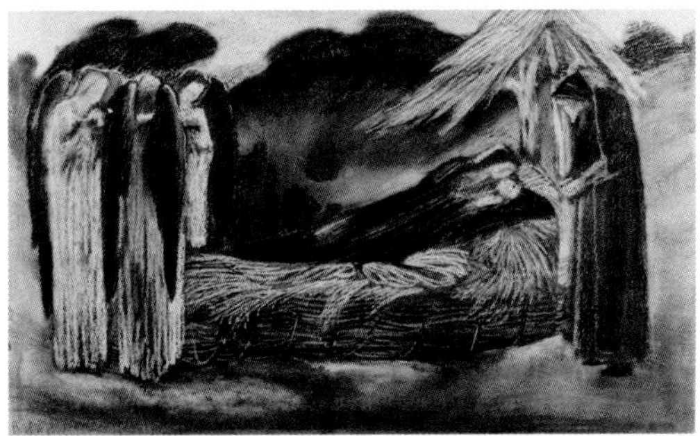

D.1960.27

Study for the Composition of 'The Nativity', St John's Church, Torquay, Devon
1888
pastel
398 × 609 mm
Friends of the Whitworth (gift, 1960) (D.1960.27)

Study of an Angel bearing a Chalice for 'The Nativity'
1888
black chalk
inscribed upper right: *Angel bearing cup*
332 × 240 mm
Sewter, Albert Charles (gift, 1960) (D.1960.44)

Study of an Angel bearing a Chalice for 'The Nativity'
1888
black chalk
332 × 233 mm
Sewter, Albert Charles (gift, 1960) (D.1960.45)

Study of the Hands of the Angel bearing a Chalice for 'The Nativity'
1888
black chalk
inscribed upper right: *Cup 1. / light to come from / other side*
332 × 251 mm
Sewter, Albert Charles (gift, 1960) (D.1960.46)

Study of an Angel bearing a Spikenard for 'The Nativity'
1888
black chalk
inscribed upper right: *Angel bearing* / [illegible word erased] *spikenard*
334 × 249 mm
Sewter, Albert Charles (gift, 1960) (D.1960.47)

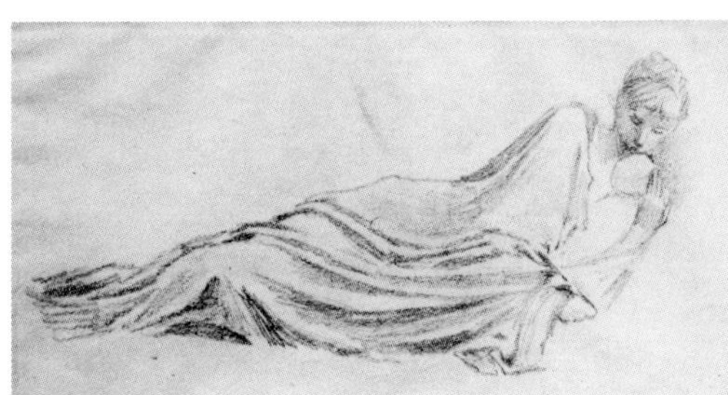

D.1960.48

Study of the Virgin and Child for 'The Nativity'
1888
black chalk
234 × 332 mm
Sewter, Albert Charles (gift, 1960) (D.1960.48)

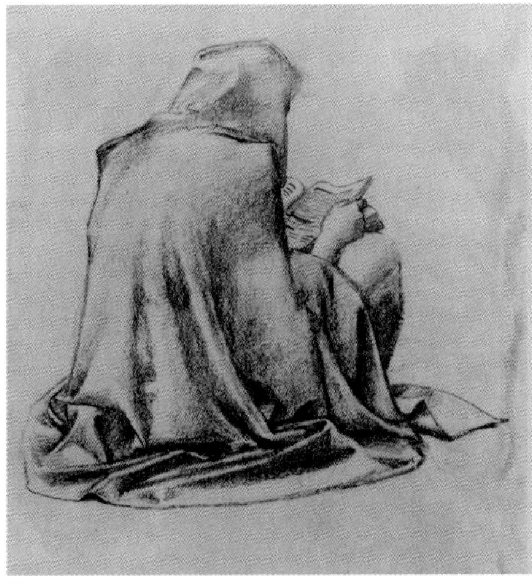

D.1960.49

Study of St Joseph for 'The Nativity'
1888
black chalk
267 × 224 mm
Sewter, Albert Charles (gift, 1960) (D.1960.49)

Tracing of the Composition for 'The Nativity'
1888
black chalk, purple chalk; tracing paper
238 × 364 mm
Sewter, Albert Charles (gift, 1960) (D.1960.50)

Tracing of the Three Angels for 'The Nativity'
1888
pencil, red chalk; tracing paper
374 × 253 mm
Sewter, Albert Charles (gift, 1960) (D.1960.51)

Tracing of the Figure of St Joseph for 'The Nativity'
1888
pencil, black chalk, red chalk; tracing paper
351 × 256 mm
Sewter, Albert Charles (gift, 1960) (D.1960.52)

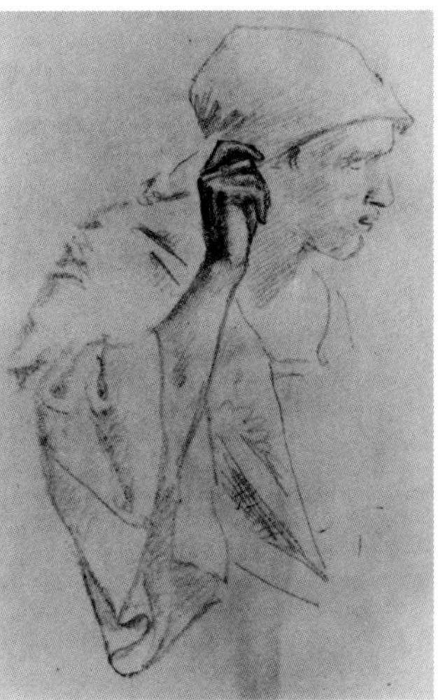

D.1960.53

Study of the Head, right Arm and Shoulder of the Shepherd for the 'King and Shepherd with Angels', St John's Church, Torquay, Devon (recto); Study of the Legs of the Shepherd for the 'King and Shepherd with Angels', St John's Church, Torquay, Devon (verso)
1888
black chalk
332 × 240 mm
Sewter, Albert Charles (gift, 1960) (D.1960.53)

Study of the King's Head and his right Hand holding an inlaid Casket for 'King and Shepherd with Angels'
1888
black chalk
inscribed upper right: *Mage*
332 × 233 mm
Sewter, Albert Charles (gift, 1960) (D.1960.54)

Study of the clasped Hands of the King and the Angel for 'King and Shepherd with Angels'
1888
black chalk
332 × 232 mm
Sewter, Albert Charles (gift, 1960) (D.1960.55)

Tracing of the Composition for 'King and Shepherd with Angels'
black chalk, purple chalk; tracing paper
250 × 369 mm
Sewter, Albert Charles (gift, 1960) (D.1960.56)

Three Music-making Angels for the north Transept Window, Albion Congregational Church, Ashton-under-Lyne, Manchester, top right Section
1895–96
pencil, coloured chalk
1213 × 832 mm
Friends of the Whitworth (gift, 1960) (D.1960.57)

Five Music-making Angels for the north Transept Window, Albion Congregational Church, Ashton-under-Lyne, Manchester, lower left Section
1895–96
pencil, coloured chalk; brown paper
1391 × 1149 mm
Friends of the Whitworth (gift, 1960) (D.1960.58)

Five Music-making Angels for the north Transept Window, Albion Congregational Church, Ashton-under-Lyne, Manchester, lower right Section
1895–96
pencil, coloured chalk; brown paper
1391 × 1153 mm
Friends of the Whitworth (gift, 1960) (D.1960.59)

Ten Music-making Angels for the south Transept Window, Albion Congregational Church, Ashton-under-Lyne, Manchester, top centre Section
1895–96
pencil, coloured chalk; brown paper
1505 × 1568 mm
Friends of the Whitworth (gift, 1960) (D.1960.60)

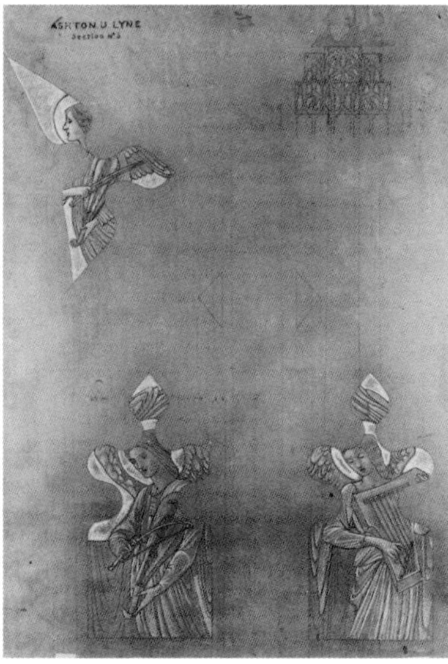

D.1960.61

Three Music-making Angels for the south Transept Window, Albion Congregational Church, Ashton-under-Lyne, Manchester, top right Section
1895–96
pencil, black chalk, white chalk; brown paper
1206 × 838 mm
Friends of the Whitworth (gift, 1960) (D.1960.61)

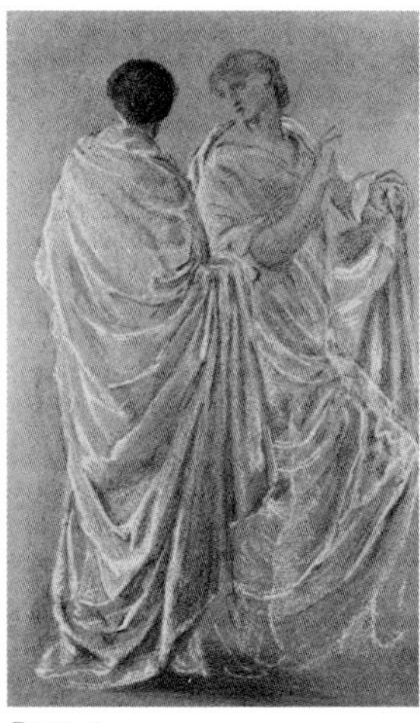

D.1960.69

Study of two standing female Figures
1864–66
black chalk, white chalk; brown paper
336 × 200 mm
University of Manchester, History of Art Department
(transfer, 1960) (D.1960.69)

Study of the Head and Torso of a nude female Figure for 'The Car of Love'
black chalk, white chalk; brown paper
353 × 218 mm
University of Manchester, History of Art Department
(transfer, 1960) (D.1960.70)

Study of a full-length nude female Figure for 'The Car of Love'
black chalk; brown paper
380 × 226 mm
University of Manchester, History of Art Department
(transfer, 1960) (D.1960.71)

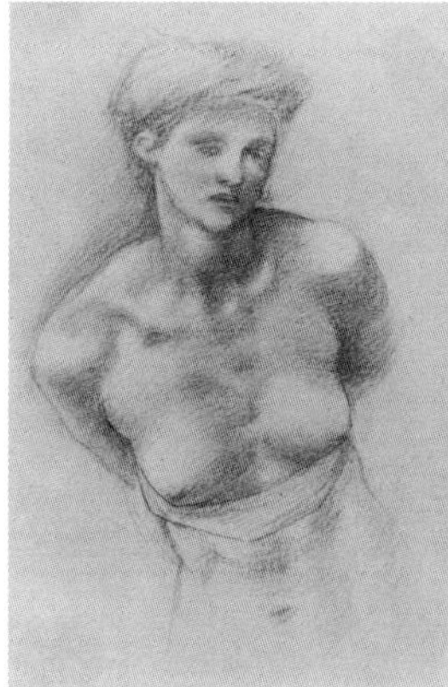

D.1960.70

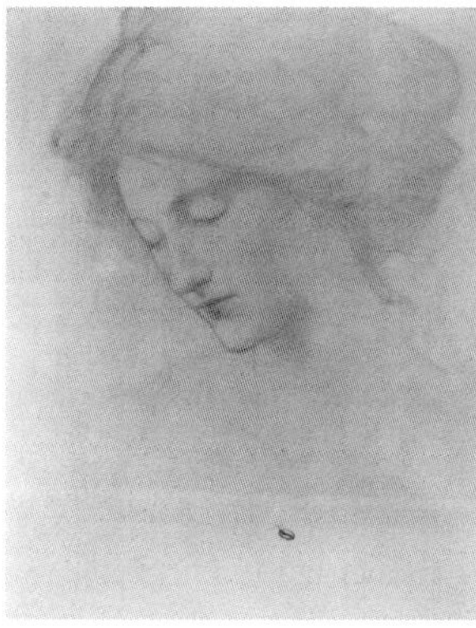

D.1960.72

Study of a young Woman's Head
1895
pencil
462 × 257 mm
University of Manchester, History of Art Department
(transfer, 1960) (D.1960.72)

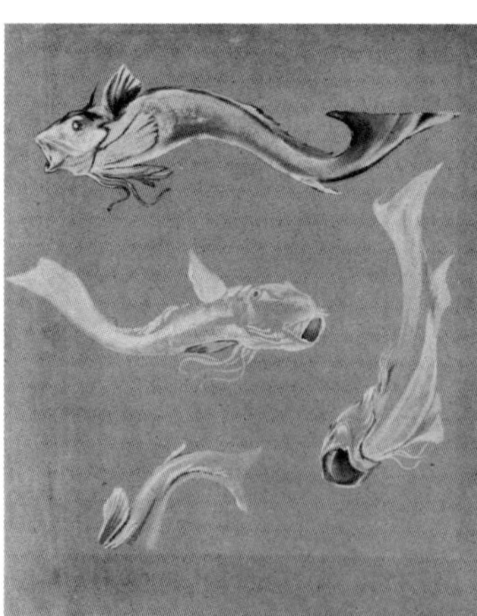

D.1974.2

Studies of Fish for 'The Sea Nymph'
1880
watercolour, bodycolour; brown paper
492 × 401 mm
David Carritt Ltd (purchase, 1974) (D.1974.2)

Study of Enoch for the north Aisle Window, St John the Divine, Frankby, Cheshire
1873
pencil
252 × 178 mm
Sewter, Albert Charles (bequest, 1983) (D.1983.4)

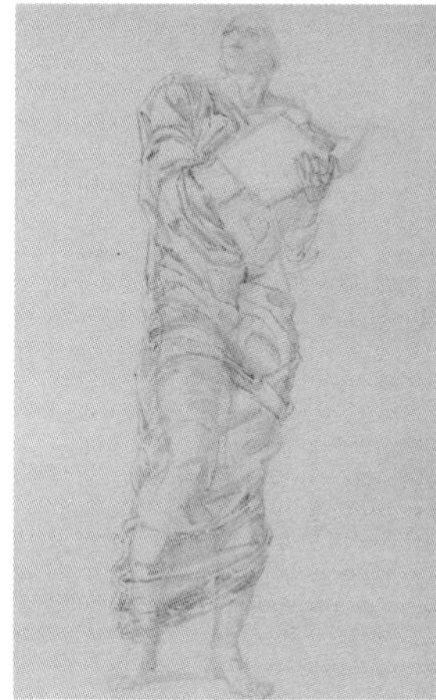

D.1983.4

■ **BYRNE, JOHN (1786–1847)**
John Bryne, son of the well-known landscape engraver William Byrne, trained under his father and was elected an associate of the Old Watercolour Society in 1827. He exhibited there until 1846.

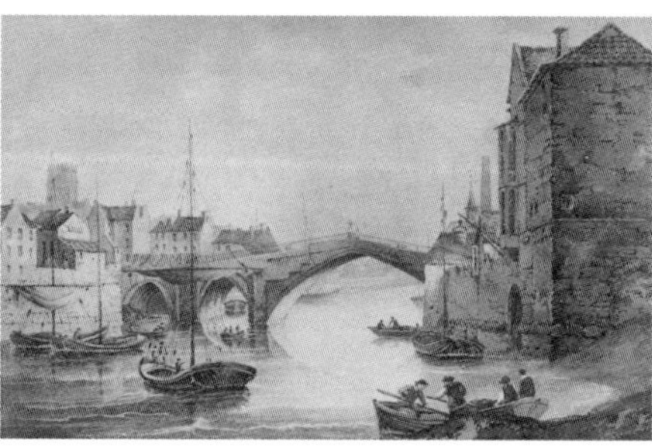

D.1900.24

The Old Ouse Bridge, York
pencil, watercolour
293 × 429 mm
untraced (purchase, 1900) (D.1900.24)

■ **CAFE, THOMAS (1817–68)**
Cafe, one of a family of artists, exhibited topographical and landscape subjects at the Royal Academy and elsewhere between 1844 and 1868.

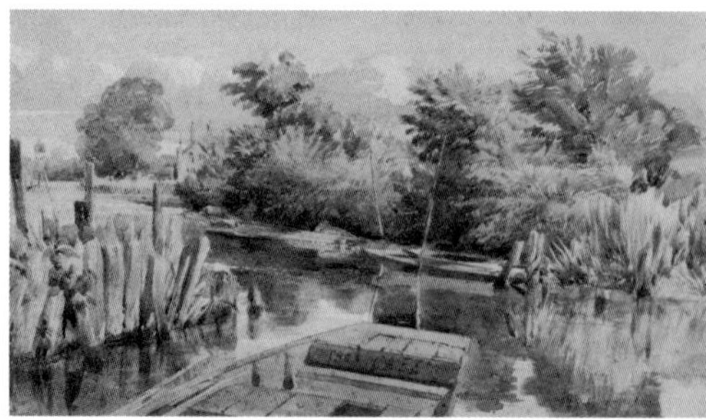

D.1947.60

View along the River Bank, Molesey, Surrey
9.1847
pencil, watercolour
signed lower centre: *Thos Cafe*; inscribed & dated on label attached to centre of reverse of backing:
MOULSEY, SEPT, '47 / ORIGINAL WATER–COLOUR / BY / THOS CAFE
195 × 329 mm
Friends of the Whitworth (gift, 1947) (D.1947.60)

■ CALDECOTT, RANDOLPH (1846–86)

Born in Chester, Caldecott was a caricaturist who moved to London in 1872 and worked for the *Graphic* and *Punch*. A brilliant and prolific children's book illustrator, Caldecott exhibited watercolours at the Royal Academy and the New Watercolour Society between 1872 and 1885.

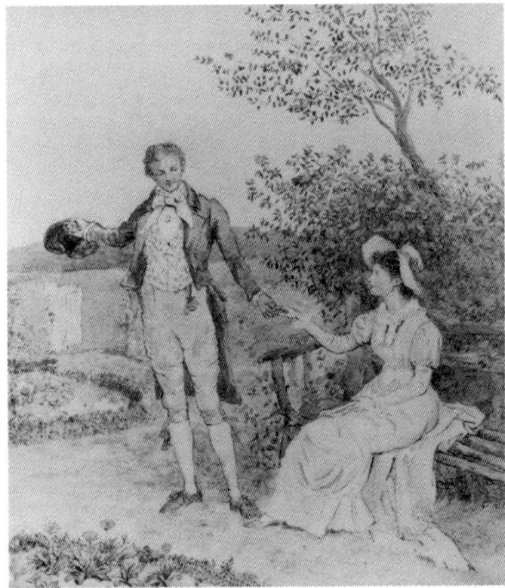

D.1902.4

The Farmer's Boy
1881
pen and brown ink, watercolour
signed lower right with initials: *R C*
203 × 174 mm
Agnew, Sir William (gift, 1902) (D.1902.4)

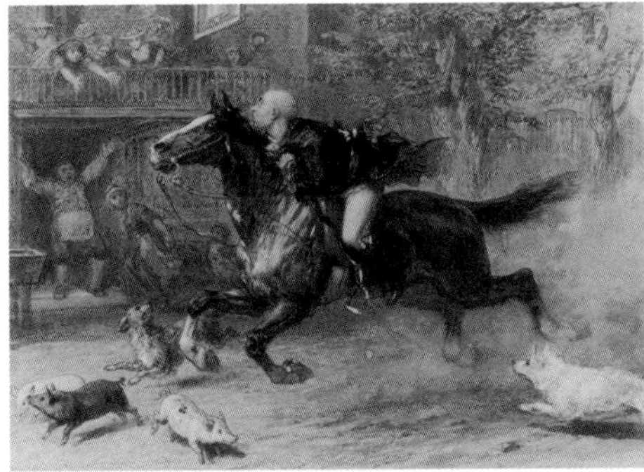

D.1912.11

John Gilpin's Ride
watercolour, bodycolour
255 × 342 mm
Messrs J. Bowland (purchase, 1912) (D.1912.11)

The three jovial Huntsmen
1879–81
pencil, pen and brown ink, watercolour
signed lower right with initials: *R C*
118 × 197 mm
University of Manchester, History of Art Department
(transfer, 1960) (D.1960.73)

■ CALDERON, PHILIP HERMOGENES (1833–98)

Calderon was a painter of domestic, religious and historical scenes and leader of the St John's Wood Clique. He was elected a member of the Royal Academy in 1867, and after 1870 he turned increasingly to portraiture. Calderon was elected Keeper of the Royal Academy in 1887 and managed the Royal Academy Schools.

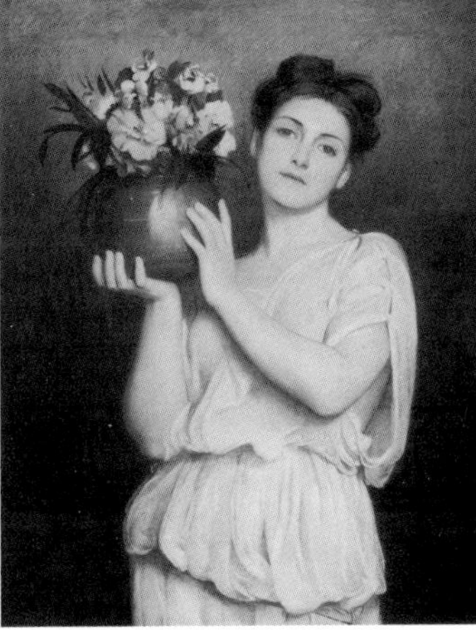

D.1901.5

An Offering. A young Woman holding a Pot of Flowers
1868
bodycolour; canvas
signed & dated lower left with initials in monogram:
PHCALDERON.–1868
915 × 708 mm
Agnew, Sir William (gift, 1901) (D.1901.5)

■ CALLCOTT, SIR AUGUSTUS WALL (1779–1844)

Callcott, a painter of landscapes and seascapes, was elected a member of the Royal Academy in 1810. Knighted in 1837, he was classed in the same league as his friend Turner, whose rival he was considered to be. His romantic classical landscapes earned him the title 'the English Claude'. Callcott's watercolours were among those engraved in the Finden publication *Landscape Illustrations of the Bible* in 1836.

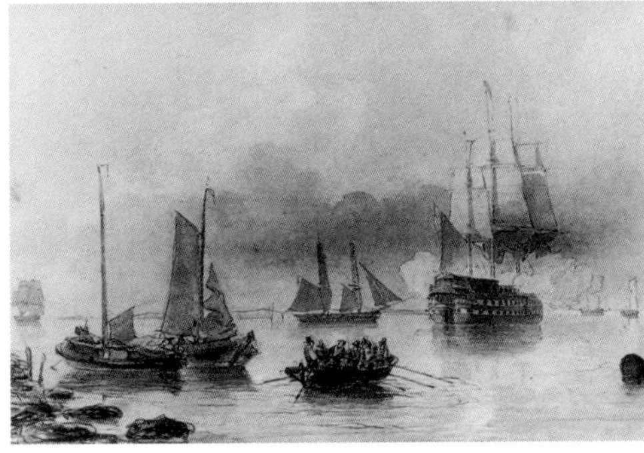

D.1892.69

Firing a Salute
pencil, watercolour
242 × 376 mm
Taylor, John Edward (gift, 1892) (D.1892.69)

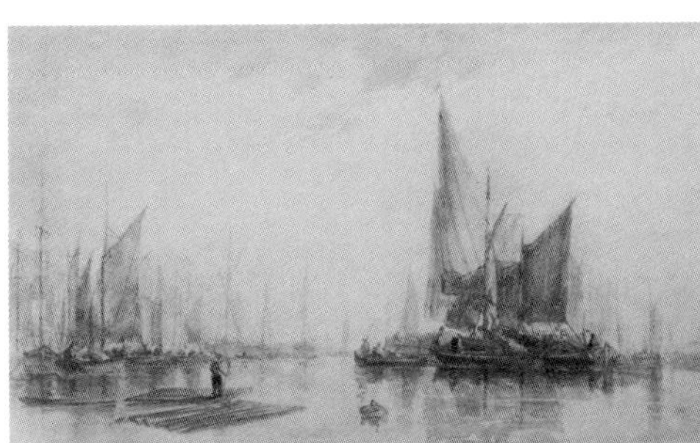

D.1892.70

The Pool below London Bridge
1815–17
pencil, watercolour
147 × 244 mm
Taylor, John Edward (gift, 1892) (D.1892.70)

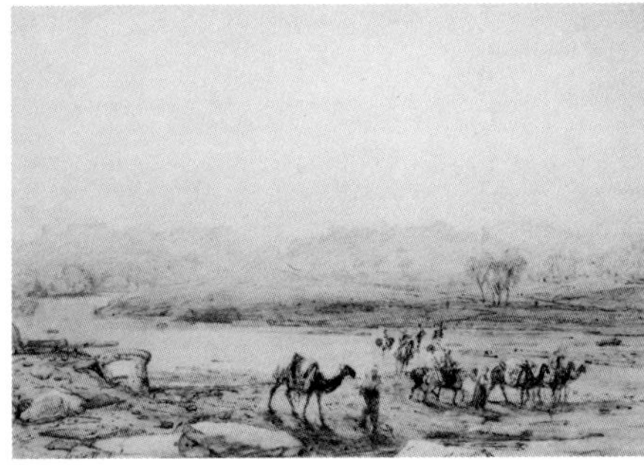

D.1924.82

A Caravan, Ascalon, on the Coast of Israel
1835 (?)
pencil, pen and brown ink, watercolour
signed & dated lower left: *A W Callcott / 1835*(?) [last digit illegible]
164 × 230 mm
Broadhurst, Sir Edward Tootal, Broadhurst, Lady (bequest, 1924) (D.1924.82)

■ CALLCOTT, SIR AUGUSTUS WALL (attributed to) (1779–1844)

The Thames near London Bridge
pencil, pen and brown ink; watermark RUSE / 1804
224 × 395 mm
Holliday, J. R. (bequest, 1927) (D.1927.147)

■ CALLOW, WILLIAM (1812–1908)

Callow was born in Greenwich and began his career working for the Fielding family in London and Paris. In 1831 he moved to France, sharing a studio in Paris with Thomas Shotter Boys. Callow was a tireless traveller, visiting Italy and Germany regularly, and sending Continental views annually to the Old Watercolour Society, of which he was elected a member in 1848. He had a number of aristocratic pupils, both in France and England. His later work is markedly inferior to that of the 1830s.

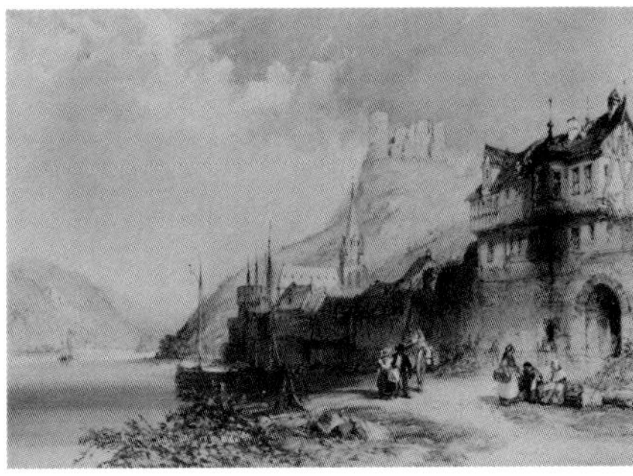

D.1898.6

Oberwesel on the Rhine and the Castle of Schonburg, Germany
1841
watercolour, bodycolour
signed & dated: *W.Callow 1841*
485 × 655 mm
Agnew's (purchase, 20.12.1898) (D.1898.6)

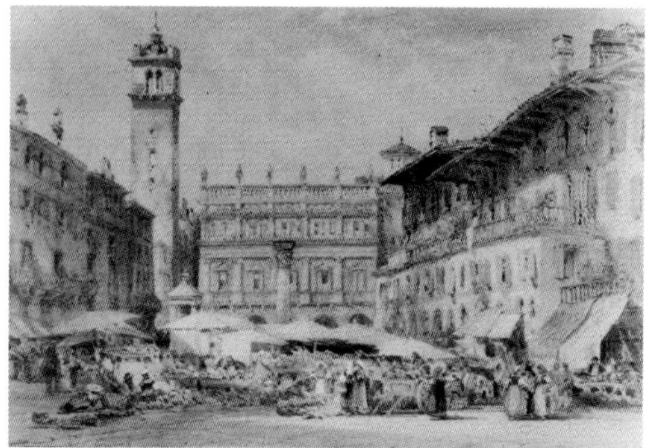

D.1904.2

Piazza Erbe, Verona, with the Palazzo Maffei
1903
pencil, watercolour, bodycolour
(heightened with white)
signed & dated lower right: *William Callow. / 1903*
394 × 570 mm
Callow (?), William (purchase, 1904) (D.1904.2)

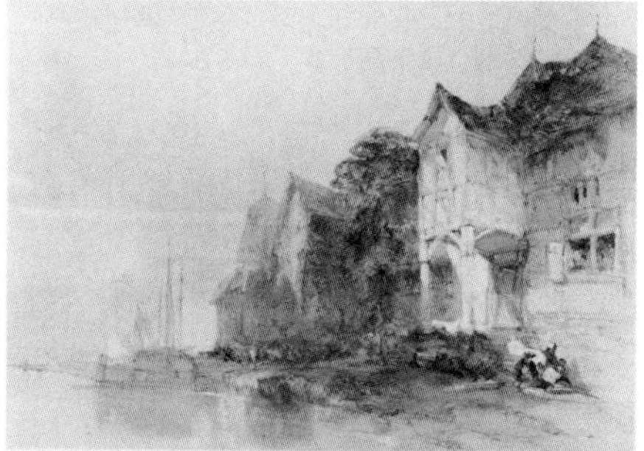

D.1951.6

Bacharach on the Rhine, Germany
pencil, watercolour, bodycolour
(heightened with white)
271 × 373 mm
Dunkerley, F. B. (bequest, 1951) (D.1951.6)

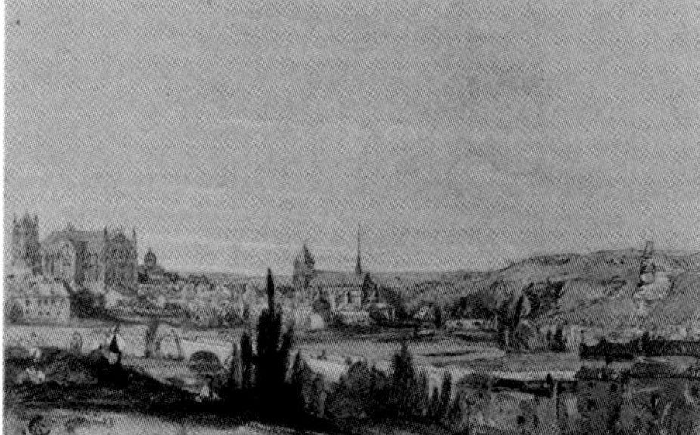

D.1952.5

View of Poitiers, France, from across the River
24.6.1836
pencil, watercolour, bodycolour; blue-grey paper
signed lower left with monogram: *WC*
inscribed & dated lower left: *Cath et Eglise de
Montiereneuf a Poitier* (sic). *Juin 24.36.*
178 × 271 mm
Pilkington, Margaret (gift, 1952) (D.1952.5)

On the Rhine
1860
pencil, watercolour
signed & dated lower right: *W Callow / 1860*
171 × 248 mm
Towlson, Hector J. (bequest, 1969) (D.1970.23)

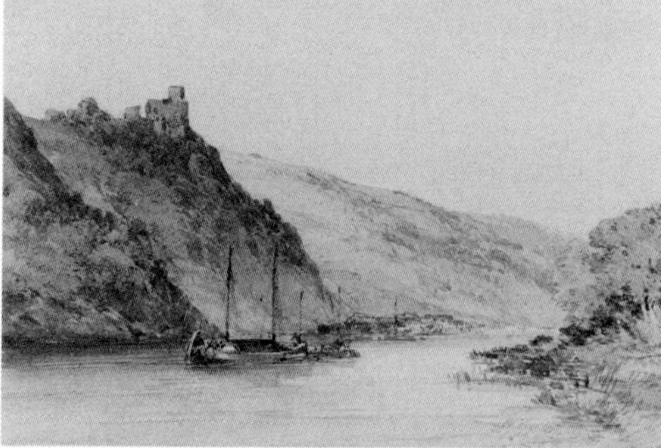

D.1970.23

■ CALVERT, EDWARD (1799–1883)

Calvert, friend and disciple of William Blake and
Samuel Palmer, was one of the 'Ancients' and paid
regular visits to Shoreham in the late 1820s. Later
he came to specialise in classical and mythological
subject matter.

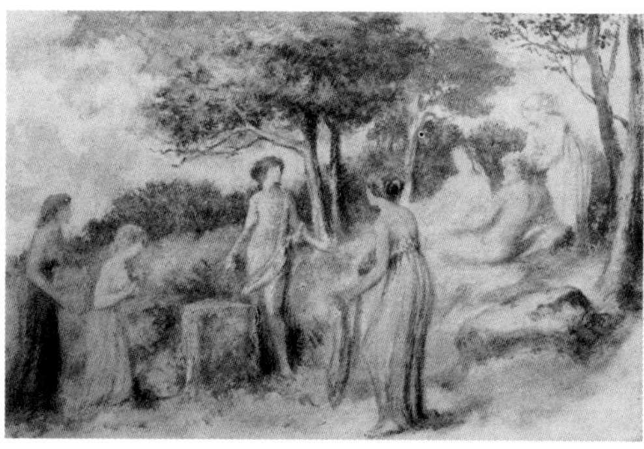

D.1928.5

Classical Composition: Olympus
oil paint
stamped with signature (twice): *ECalvert*; inscribed
upper left verso: *votive / Olympus*
250 × 375 mm
Leicester Galleries, London (purchase, 1928) (D.1928.5)

A Suggestion by Lessore
oil paint
346 × 258 mm
Barlow, Sir Thomas, Friends of the Whitworth (via)
(gift, 1939) (D.1939.21)

■ CAMPION, GEORGE BRYANT (1796–1870)

Campion was a prolific landscape painter who taught
at the Royal Military Academy at Woolwich. He was
elected a member of the New Watercolour Society in
1834 and in later life lived in Munich.

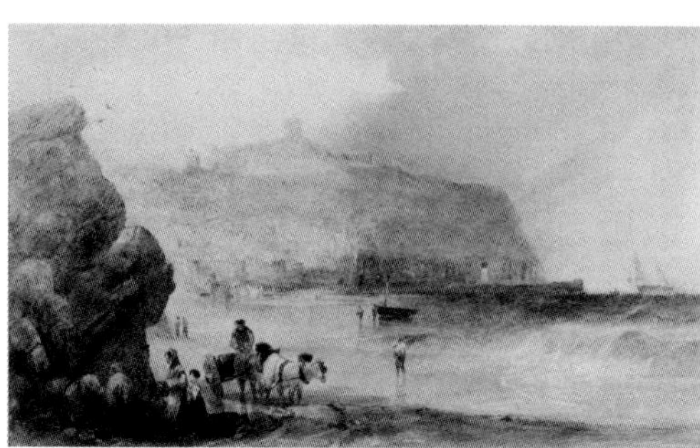

D.1970.10

**Scarborough, the Town and Castle
from the Beach**
watercolour, bodycolour (heightened with white)
271 × 446 mm
Towlson, Hector J. (bequest, 1969) (D.1970.10)

■ CAPON, WILLIAM (1757–1827)

Capon began his career as a scene painter and worked
with John Kemble at Drury Lane. Later he produced
topographical views of London. Capon exhibited at the
Royal Academy and elsewhere from 1788 to 1827.

Isaack Walton's House, Chancery Lane, London
1798
pencil
signed, inscribed & dated along lower edge: *corner of
Chancery Lane as in 1798 – Sketched by W.Capon –
[drawing of a hand with a long pointing finger] House
of Isaack Walton.*
138 × 146 mm
Ogden, William Sharp (bequest, 1926) (D.1926.199)

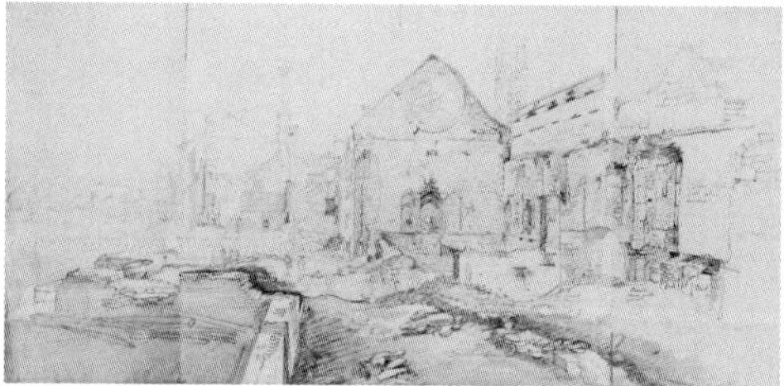

D.1926.200

**North West View of the Ruins of Winchester
Palace, Southwark, London**
pencil, black chalk, watercolour
inscribed in pencil over drawing many identificatory
notes; inscribed centre verso in W. S. Ogden's hand:
*This is a sketch of the / ruins of Winchester Palace –
Bankside / adjoining St Saviours Southwark – / the palace
was destroyed by fire in 1814 - / Drawn by / W Capon –
this sketch was engraved on a reduced / scale in 1828 /
W.S. Ogden*
390 × 787 mm
Ogden, William Sharp (bequest, 1926) (D.1926.200)

■ CARTER, HENRY BARLOW (1803–67)

A marine and landscape painter, Carter was one of the
few professional pupils of Peter de Wint. Having
served in the Navy, he settled in Scarborough in the
1830s where he taught drawing. His watercolours are
often mistaken for the work of more important artists;
several of his sons painted in a similar style.

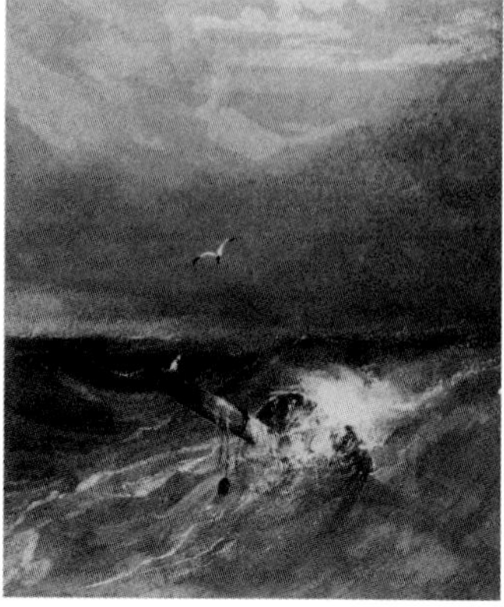

D.1892.80

Wreckage in a rough Sea
watercolour, bodycolour (heightened with white)
207 × 170 mm
Taylor, John Edward (gift, 1892) (D.1892.80)

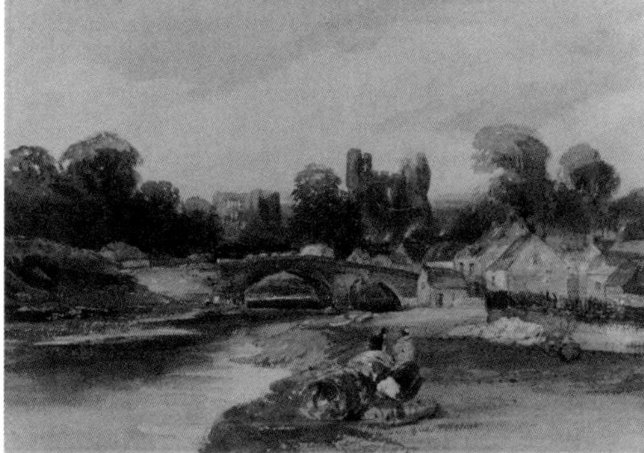

D.1948.10

View of Helmsley, Yorkshire
watercolour
275 × 382 mm
Nettlefold, F. J. (gift, 1948) (D.1948.10)

■ CARTER, JOHN (1748–1817)

Carter, an architectural draughtsman and writer, was elected a fellow of the Society of Antiquaries in 1795. Between 1798 and 1817 he published a series of papers in the *Gentleman's Magazine* entitled 'Pursuits of Architectural Innovation', which were an attack on misguided architectural restoration as carried out by James Wyatt and his imitators. Described as 'Antiquity's most resolute friend', Carter saved the Gothic altar screens at Durham Cathedral from destruction in 1796. He had a small architectural practice.

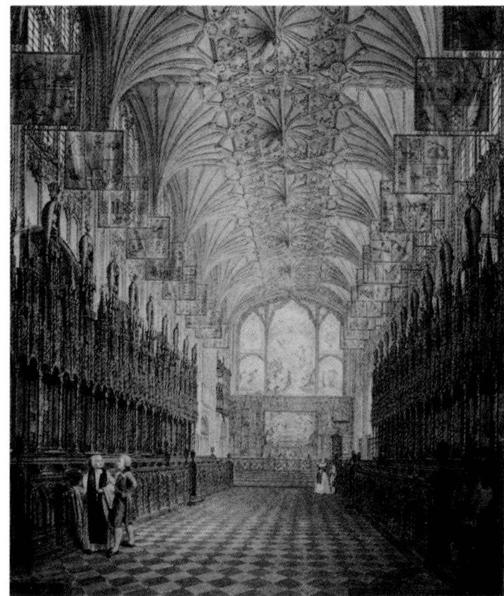

D.1895.124

**St George's Chapel, Windsor,
View in the Choir looking east**
1785
pencil, pen and brown ink, watercolour
signed, inscribed & dated lower right: *View of the Choir of St Georges Chapel. Windsor. / John Carter delt 1785.*
603 × 498 mm
Agnew's (purchase, 7.6.1895) (D.1895.124)

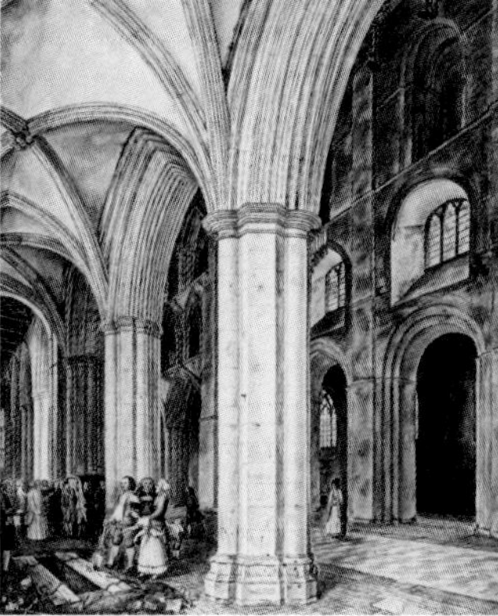

D.1939.11

The Nave, St Albans Abbey, Hertfordshire
1780
pen and grey ink, watercolour
signed & dated lower right: *J Carter delt. June 1780*
355 × 290 mm
Barlow, Sir Thomas, Friends of the Whitworth (gift, 1939) (D.1939.11)

Detail of the Arcading, East Wall of the Lady Chapel, St Albans Abbey, Hertfordshire
pen and grey ink, grey watercolour
169 × 148 mm
Barlow, Sir Thomas, Friends of the Whitworth (gift, 1939) (D.1939.12)

■ CASTLE, HORACE FAULKNER (early 20th century)

An architect who exhibited at the Royal Academy in 1910 and 1914.

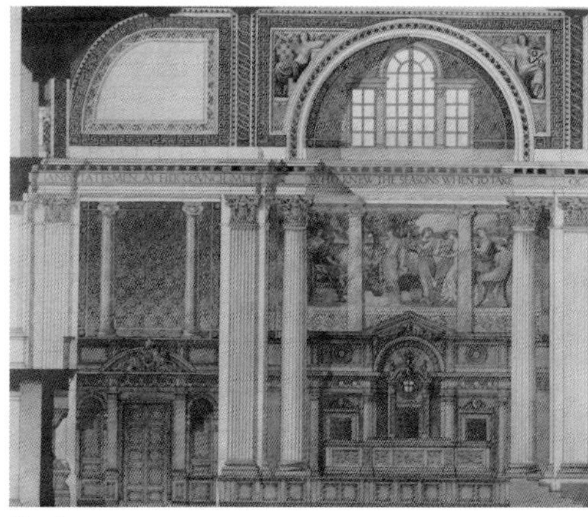

D.1998.31

Scheme for the Colour Decoration of a Council Chamber
pencil, pen and black ink, bodycolour (heightened with white)
inscribed on top left on linen backing (Exh 09); inscribed centre right: *Horace Faulkner Castle/Woodside/Coalbrookdale/Shropshire*; inscribed lower right: *1910 Royal Academy*
567 × 663 mm
University of Manchester, Architecture Department (transfer, 1998) (D.1998.31)

■ CATTERMOLE, GEORGE (1800–1868)

Cattermole came from a family of artists, and was elected a member of the Old Watercolour Society in 1833. His earlier drawings, which are very much in the manner of David Cox, are generally of buildings. His later drawings are of historical figure subjects, often in interiors.

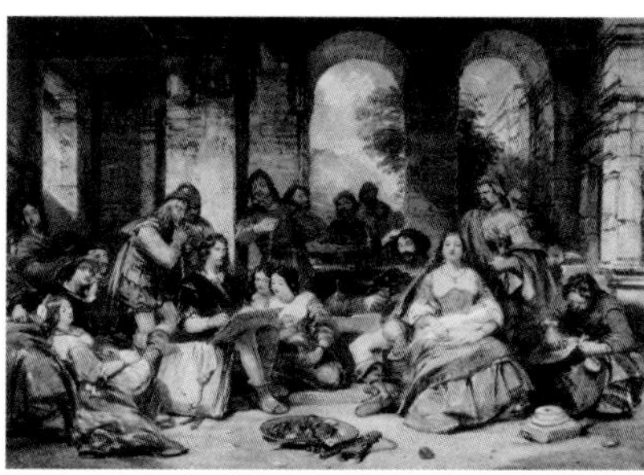

D.1898.4

Salvator Rosa sketching amongst the Banditti of the Abruzzi
1838
watercolour, bodycolour (heightened with white)
signed lower centre with monogram: *GC*
545 × 762 mm
Agnew's (purchase, 21.6.1898) (D.1898.4)

The Mill Stream
black chalk, watercolour, bodycolour (heightened with white); oatmeal paper
signed centre left edge, with monogram: *GC*
264 × 514 mm
Broadhurst, Sir Edward Tootal, Broadhurst, Lady (bequest, 1924) (D.1924.38)

An unidentified historical Scene
pencil, watercolour
signed under mount lower left with monogram: *GC*
226 × 501 mm
Langley, Mrs E. P. (gift, 1965) (D.1965.12)

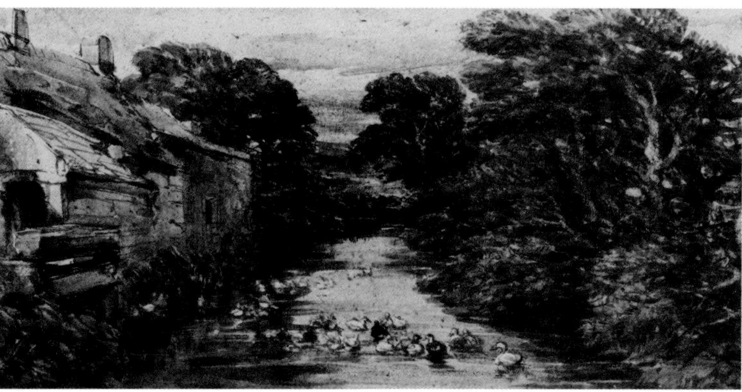

D.1924.38

■ CHALON, ALFRED EDWARD (1780–1860)

Alfred Edward Chalon, son of a Huguenot refugee from Geneva, entered the Royal Academy schools in 1797. In 1808, with his brother and F. Stevens, he founded the Sketching Society. He was elected a member of the Royal Academy in 1816 and later specialised in small watercolour portraits.

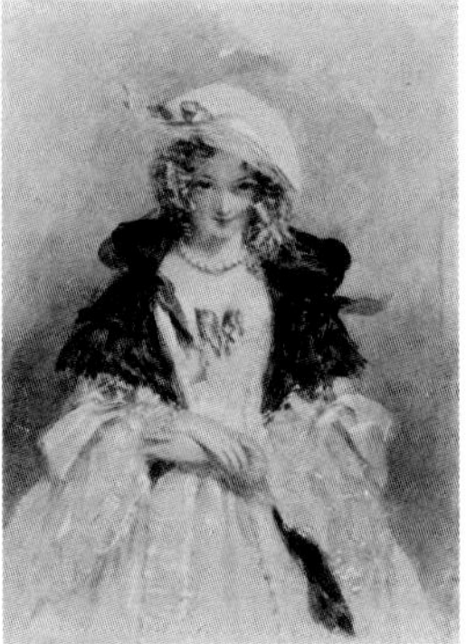

D.1894.3

Phoebe, Portrait of Miss Manners Sutton
1832
watercolour
signed & dated lower right: *A E Chalon RA 1832*
266 × 191 mm
Lees, Charles E. (gift, 1894) (D.1894.3)

■ CHALON, JOHN JAMES (1778–1854)

John James Chalon, elder brother of Alfred Edward, became a member of the Old Watercolour Society in 1807. He worked as a drawing master and was elected a member of the Royal Academy in 1841.

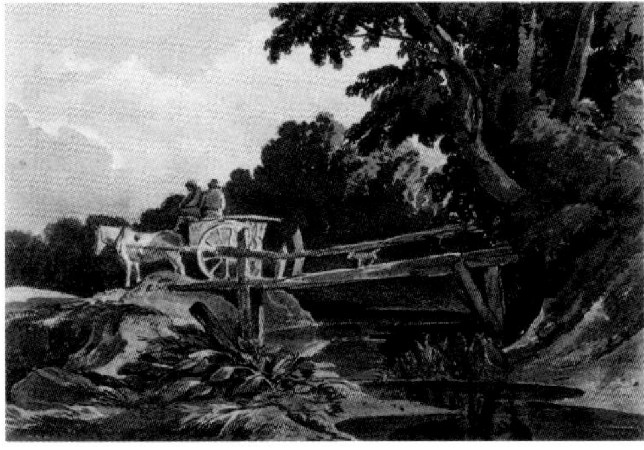

D.1947.23

A Landscape with a Horse and Cart crossing a wooden Bridge
pencil, watercolour
222 × 322 mm
Friends of the Whitworth (gift, 1947) (D.1947.23)

■ CHAMBERS, GEORGE (1803–40)

Chambers went to sea at the age of ten, and later became a scene painter, before specialising in river and coastal scenery. He was elected a member of the Old Watercolour Society in 1835.

Dutch Shipping Scene
1837
watercolour, bodycolour (heightened with white)
signed & dated lower right: *GChambers / 1837*
175 × 229 mm
Agnew's (purchase, 3.6.1891) (D.1887.46)

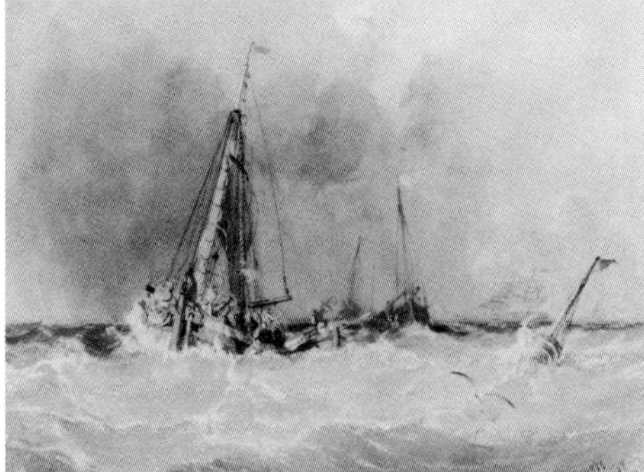

D.1887.46

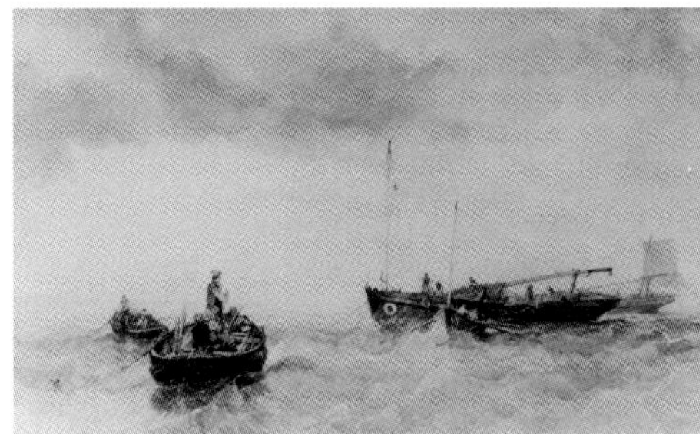

D.1887.47

Herring Fishing
1833
pencil, watercolour
signed & dated on the stern of one of the fishing boats with initials: *G.C. / 1833*
236 × 385 mm
Agnew's (purchase, 3.6.1891) (D.1887.47)

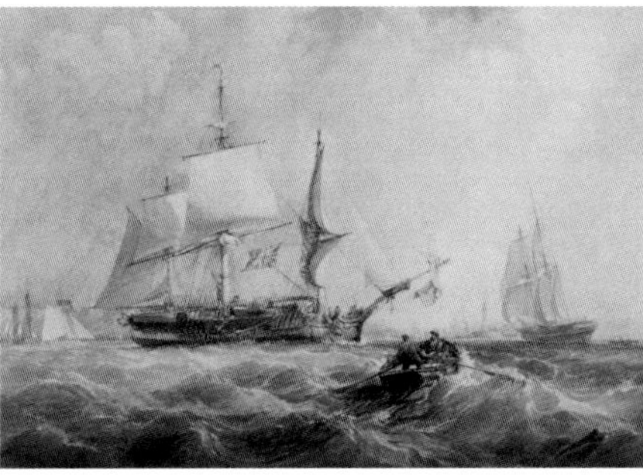

D.1893.9

Taking a Pilot on Board, off the Port of Whitby, North Yorkshire
1835
pencil, watercolour
signed & dated lower left: *GChambers / 1835*
588 × 823 mm
Agnew's (purchase, 18.12.1893) (D.1893.9)

■ CHATELAIN, JEAN-BAPTISTE-CLAUDE (1710–71)

Chatelain was an artist and engraver of French descent who was born in London. He produced topographical and imaginary drawings and was employed as an engraver by the print publisher John Boydell.

Figures in a Landscape with a Town in the Distance and Mountains beyond
pencil
215 × 301 mm
Anderson, A. E. (gift, 1933) (D.1933.17)

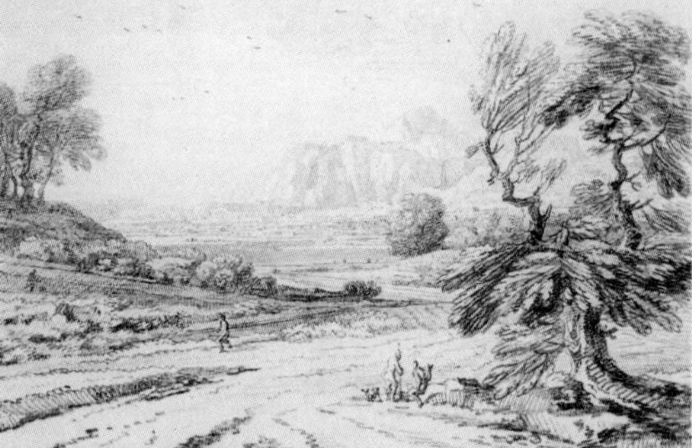

D.1933.17

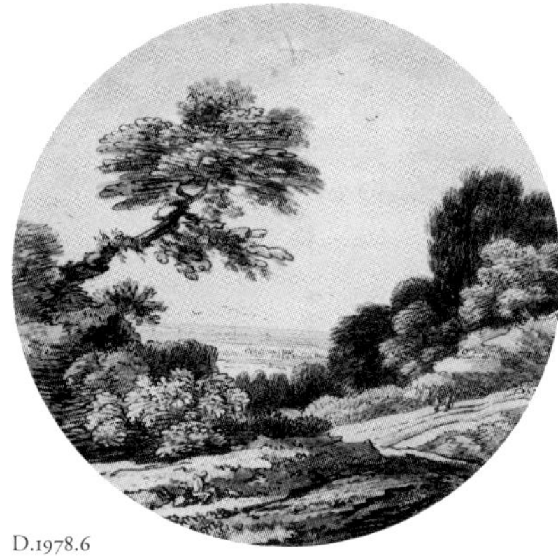

D.1978.6

A Landscape with Travellers by a Roadside
pencil, pen and brown ink, brown watercolour, grey watercolour; circular
195 (H) mm
Nockolds, Dr Robert, Nockolds, Mrs Tilly (gift, 1978) (D.1978.6)

■ CHINNERY, GEORGE (1774–1852)

Chinnery was a landscape and portrait painter who began his career in Ireland. In 1802 he sailed to Madras and remained in India, settling in Calcutta and Dacca until 1825, when he moved to Macao, where he died. Chinnery is known for his portraits and also for his innumerable studies of Indian and Chinese figures, often inscribed in his own shorthand. He had many pupils both in India and Macao.

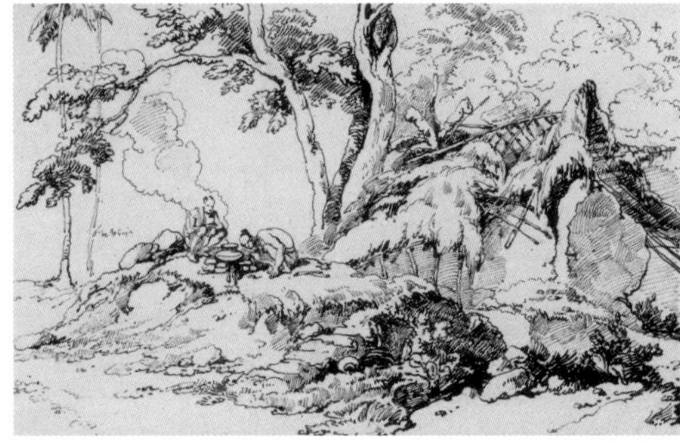

D.1947.22

An Indian camping Scene
29.10.1821
pen and brown ink
dated upper right in artist's shorthand: *October 29, / 1821.*; inscribed centre left in artist's shorthand [last word illegible]: *very dark blue green* [?]
109 × 133 mm
Friends of the Whitworth (gift, 1947) (D.1947.22)

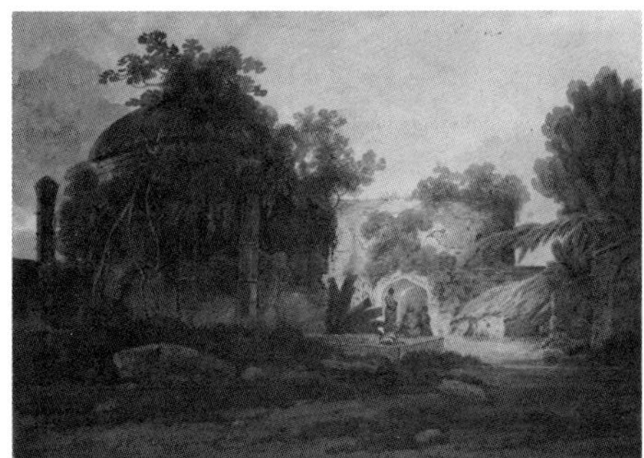

D.1962.2

An Indian Temple with Figures
pencil, watercolour
265 × 362 mm
Friends of the Whitworth (gift, 1962) (D.1962.2)

■ CLENNELL, LUKE (1781–1840)

Clennell, a native of Northumberland, was initially
apprenticed to Thomas Bewick. In 1804 he moved to
London and continued to work as an engraver until
1810. In 1812 he was elected an associate of the Old
Watercolour Society. However, due to pressure of work
Clennell had a mental breakdown in 1817, and he died
in a lunatic asylum.

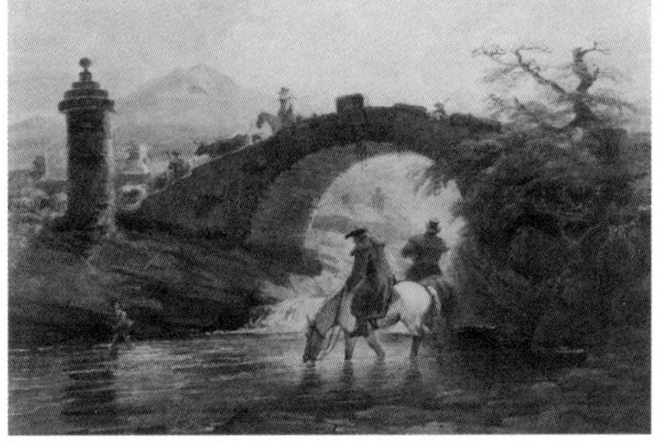

D.1892.102

A Bridge over a Stream, Scotland
pencil, watercolour
414 × 596 mm
Taylor, John Edward (gift, 1892) (D.1892.102)

River Scene: Boat unloading
pencil, watercolour
signed on the gunwale of the boat: *L.Clennell*
246 × 401 mm
Worthington, Mary (bequest, 1904) (D.1904.17)

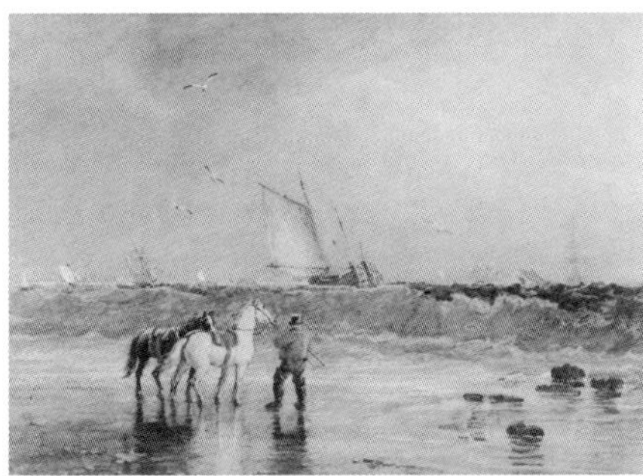

D.1915.6

A Boat offshore in stormy Weather
pencil, watercolour, surface scratching
541 × 598 mm
Anderson, A. E. (gift, 1945) (D.1915.6)

■ CLEVELEY, ROBERT (attributed to) (1747–1809)

Cleveley was the twin brother of John Cleveley Jun.,
and was influenced by the work of Paul Sandby.
Cleveley exhibited marine subjects at the Royal
Academy between 1780 and 1803 and was Marine
Painter to the Prince of Wales.

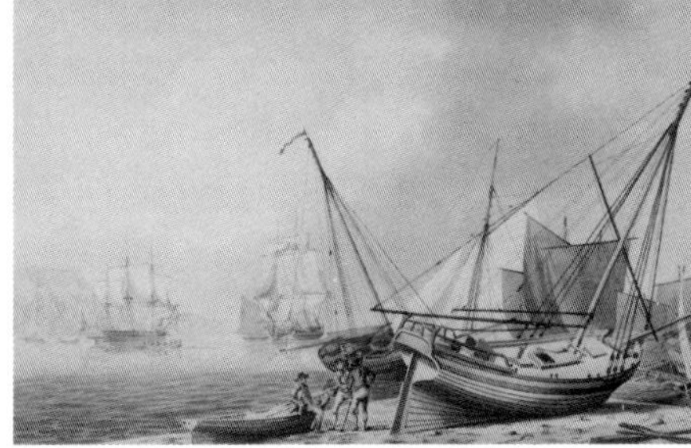

D.1892.11

Ships off the Coast of Kent
pencil, watercolour
278 × 423 mm
Taylor, John Edward (gift, 1892) (D.1892.11)

■ CLEVELEY, JUN., JOHN (attributed to) (1747–86)

A marine draughtsman who accompanied Sir Joseph
Banks on his expedition to the Orkneys and Iceland in
1772. In 1773 he was draughtsman to Commodore
Phipp's abortive expedition to the North Pole.

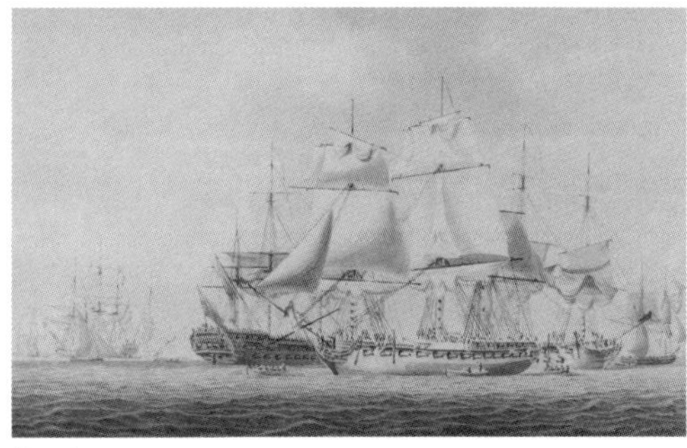

D.1926.205

Shipping Scene, Men of War
watercolour
289 × 449 mm
Ogden, William Sharp (bequest, 1926) (D.1926.205)

■ COCKRAM, GEORGE (1861–1950)

Cockram was born in Birkenhead and studied in
Liverpool and Paris. He was elected a member of the
Royal Cambrian Academy in 1886. For many years he
lived at Rhosneigr on Anglesey and specialised in
scenes from North Wales and Anglesey.

**Landscape with Ploughman and Field of
yellow Iris**
watercolour
signed lower right: *george Cockram*
499 × 731 mm
Turner, Frederick Bancroft (bequest, 1966) (D.1966.17)

Storm Clouds over Fields
watercolour
229 × 431 mm
Turner, Frederick Bancroft (bequest, 1966) (D.1966.18)

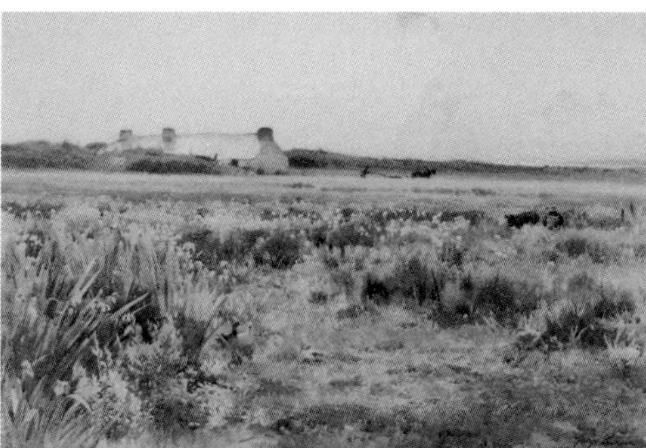

D.1966.17

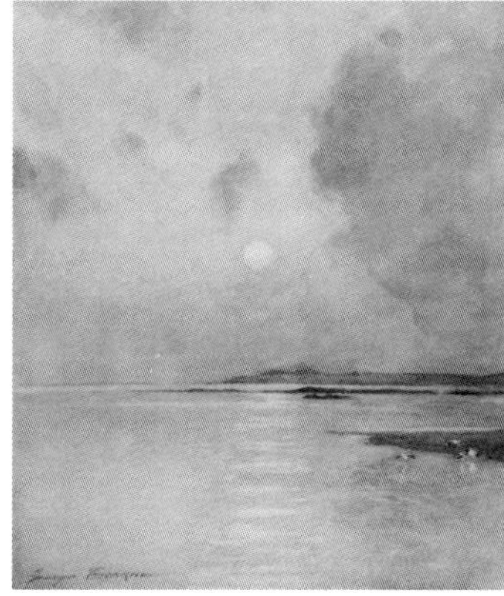

D.1966.19

Sunset, Cymmeran Bay, Anglesey, Wales
watercolour, bodycolour (heightened with white)
signed lower left: *George Cockram*
396 × 333 mm
Turner, Frederick Bancroft (bequest, 1966) (D.1966.19)

■ COLE, EDWARD S. (fl. 1837–68)

Cole is an artist of whom little is known beyond the
fact that he specialised in architecture and church
interiors. He exhibited intermittently at the Royal
Academy between 1837 and 1868. He published *Outline
Sketches of Old Buildings in Bruges* in 1851.

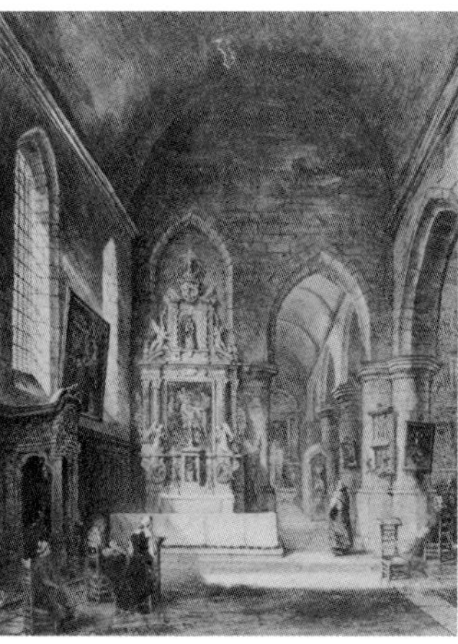

D.1919.6

**Interior of the Church of Saint-Michel,
Roulers, Belgium**
watercolour, bodycolour (heightened with white)
signed & inscribed lower left with initials: *Roulers /
Belgium / ESC*
259 × 192 mm
Philips, Mrs Herbert (bequest, 1919) (D.1919.6)

■ **COLEMAN, WILLIAM STEPHEN
(1829–1904)**
Coleman exhibited between 1865 and 1879. His early
work is of rustic cottages rather in the style of Birket
Foster and he later turned to depicting naked nubile
girls in a classical or Egyptian setting. In 1871 he
became Director of Minton's Art Pottery Studio.

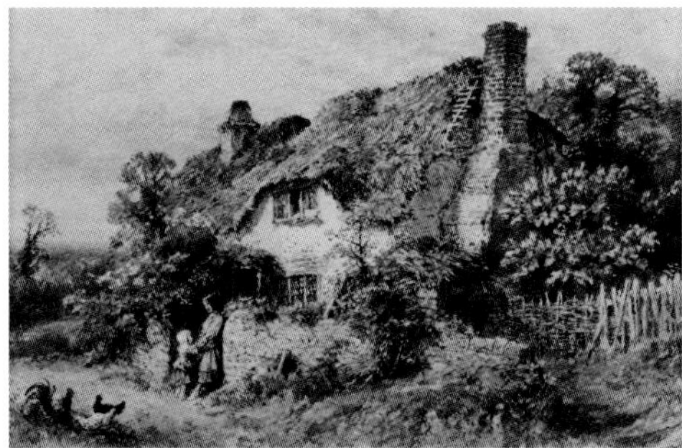
D.1987.54

A Surrey Cottage
watercolour, bodycolour
signed lower left with initials: *WSC*
127 × 198 mm
Hitchon, Brian (Dr) (in appreciation of his student years at
Manchester University, 1949–55) (gift, 1987) (D.1987.54)

■ **COLLIER, THOMAS (1840–91)**
Collier, a landscape painter who studied at Manchester
School of Art, carried on the traditions of Cox and de
Wint late into the nineteenth century. He was elected a
member of the New Watercolour Society in 1872. He
painted in North Wales, East Anglia and Sussex.

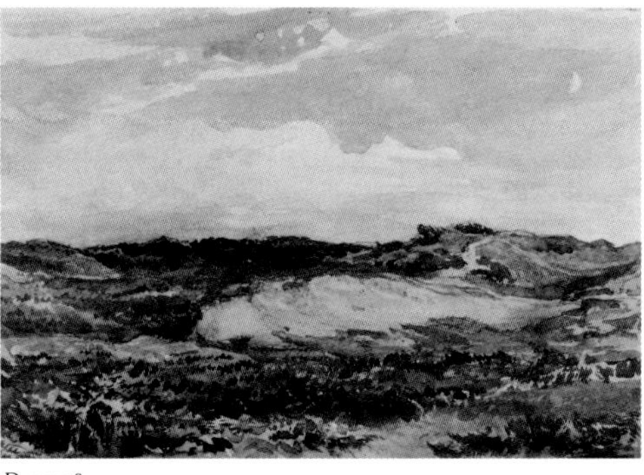
D.1921.38

Hampstead Heath, London
7.1874
watercolour
stamped with signature lower right: *Thos.Collier*
254 × 360 mm
Collectors' Gallery, Manchester (purchase, 1921) (D.1921.38)

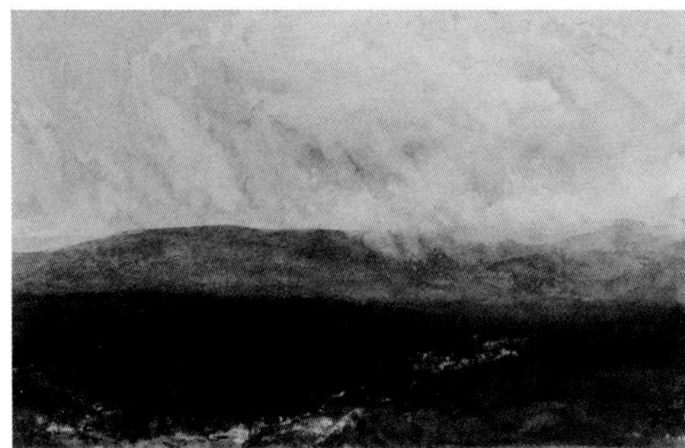
D.1921.39

Moorland in stormy Weather
watercolour
signed lower right: *Thos Collier*
166 × 251 mm
Collectors' Gallery, Manchester (purchase, 1921) (D.1921.39)

Moorland Scene
watercolour
stamped with signature lower left: *Thos.Collier*
155 × 249 mm
Collectors' Gallery, Manchester (purchase, 1921) (D.1921.40)

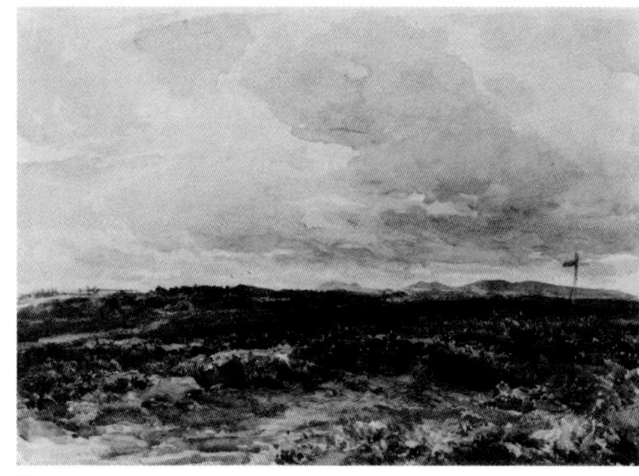
D.1921.41

Picket Post, New Forest, Hampshire
watercolour
stamped with signature lower right: *Thos.Collier*
234 × 323 mm
Collectors' Gallery, Manchester (purchase, 1921) (D.1921.41)

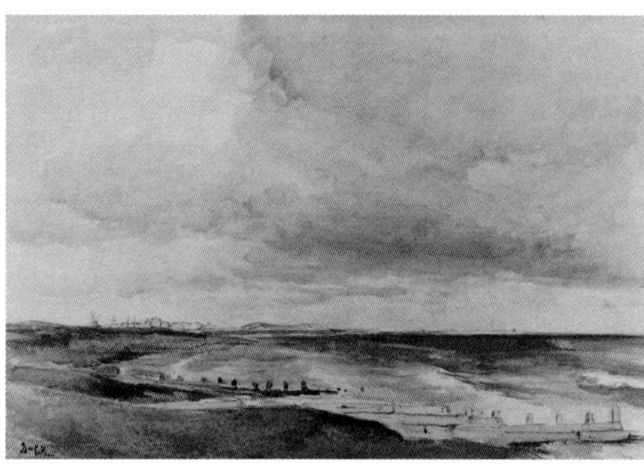
D.1930.34

The Bay, Newhaven, Sussex
pencil, watercolour
stamped with signature lower left: *Thos.Collier*
273 × 385 mm
Anderson, A. E. (gift, 1930) (D.1930.34)

Moel Siabod, Caernarvonshire, Wales
pencil, watercolour
signed lower left: *T.Collier*
177 × 254 mm
Nettlefold, F. J. (gift, 1948) (D.1948.11)

■ **CONEY, JOHN (1786–1833)**
Coney was an architectural and topographical
draughtsman and engraver who exhibited
intermittently at the Royal Academy between 1805 and
1821. He specialised in exterior and interior views of
medieval ecclesiastical buildings.

Trinity Chapel, Canterbury Cathedral
1814
pencil, watercolour
signed & dated lower right: *J.Coney.1814.*
457 × 598 mm
Taylor, John Edward (gift, 1892) (D.1892.127)

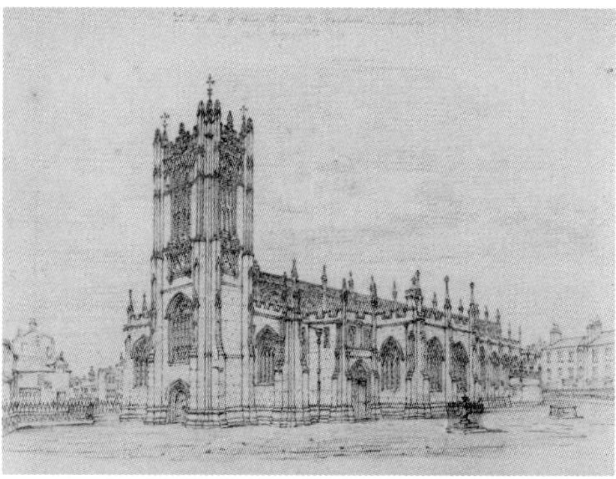
D.1904.1

Manchester Cathedral from the South West
1822
pencil
signed, inscribed & dated upper centre: *S.W. View of
Christ Ch.Coll.Ch. Manchester – Lancashire – / Jn Coney
– 1822 –*
386 × 498 mm
untraced (purchase, 1904) (D.1904.1)

■ **CONSTABLE, JOHN (1776–1837)**
Constable was born into a Suffolk mill-owning family
and developed late as a draughtsman. He entered the
Royal Academy Schools in 1799 but was not elected a
member of the Royal Academy until 1829. His primary
work was in oil but he produced a significant amount
of work on paper. Constable, who never went abroad,
is now regarded as the quintessentially English
landscape painter and his work has received much
attention in recent years.

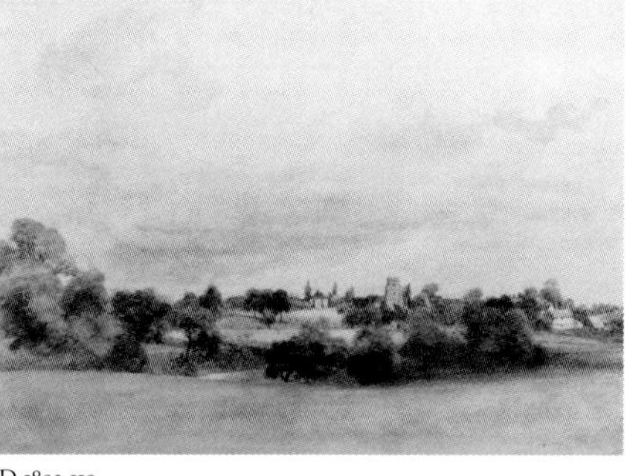
D.1892.119

**All Saint's Church and Parsonage, Feering,
near Kelvedon, Essex**
1814
pencil, watercolour
267 × 362 mm
Taylor, John Edward (gift, 1892) (D.1892.119)

**Bristol House Terrace, Putney Heath,
London (recto); Profile Study of a young
Man's Head (verso)**
1818
pen and brown ink, watercolour
122 × 270 mm
Anderson, A. E. (gift, 1930) (D.1930.22)

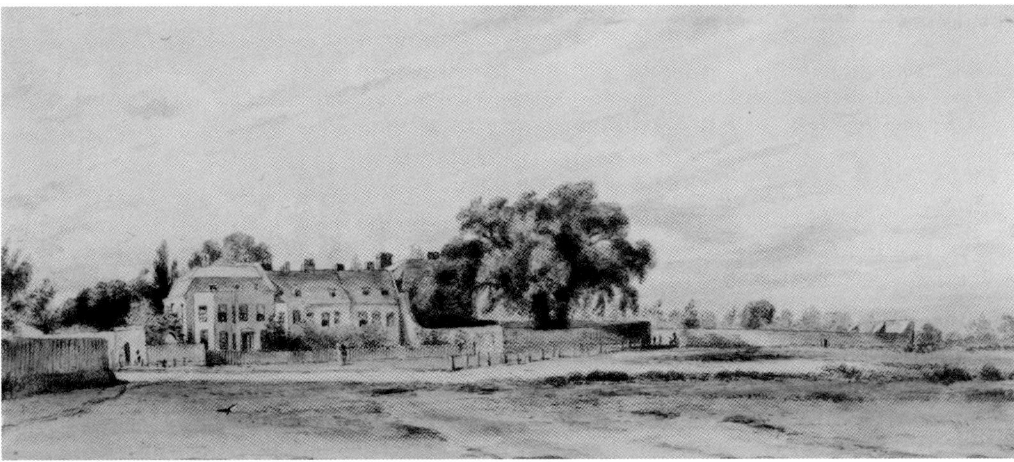

D.1930.22

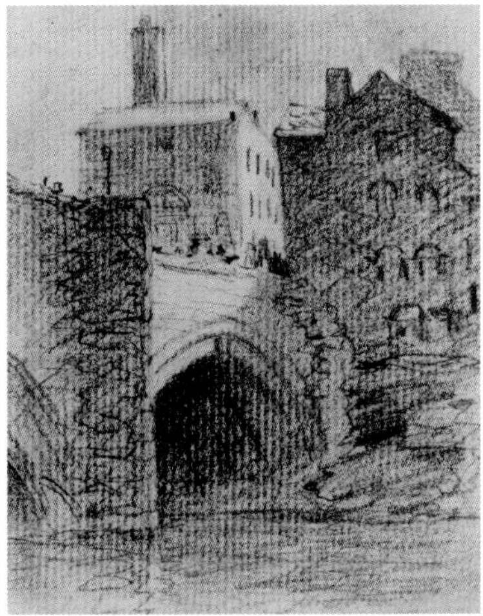

D.1936.13

Old Salford Bridge
27.8.1806
pencil
inscribed & dated along right edge of verso reading
vertically from the top of the sheet: *Manchester*
27 Aug 1806
104 × 80 mm
Dalton, Mrs W. B., Plummer, Miss E. M. (gift, 1936)
(D.1936.13)

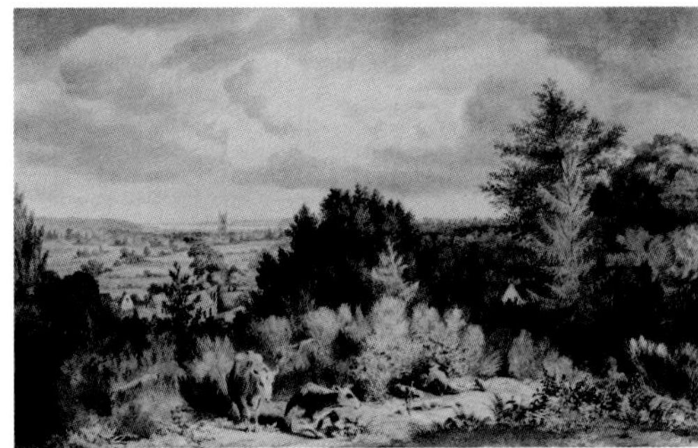

D.1943.7·

Dedham Church and Vale, Suffolk
1800
pen and grey ink, watercolour
346 × 527 mm
Friends of the Whitworth (gift, 1943) (D.1943.7)

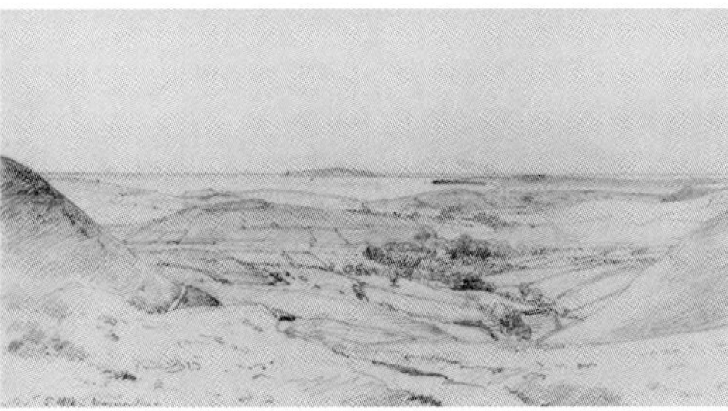

D.1949.9

**Weymouth Bay from the Downs, with Portland
Island in the Distance, Dorset**
5.11.1816
pencil; watermark Brittania
inscribed & dated lower left: *Novr.5.1816.Weymouth*
173 × 313 mm
Agnew's (purchase, 1949) (D.1949.9)

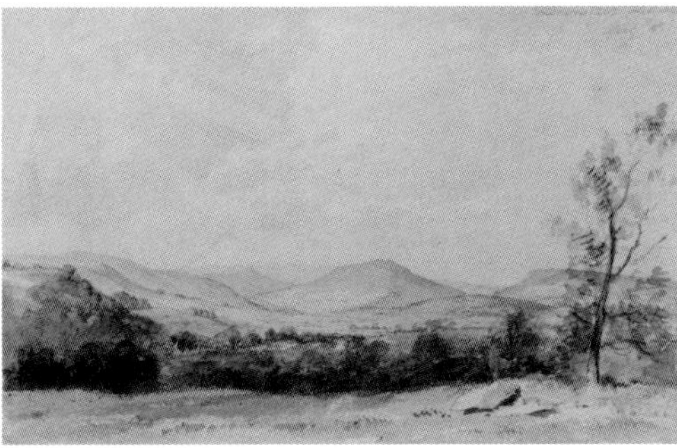

D.1949.10

View of Derwent Dale, Derbyshire
8.8.1801
pencil, grey watercolour
inscribed & dated upper right: *Derwent Dale / Aug 8*
170 × 263 mm
Agnew's (purchase, 1949) (D.1949.10)

■ **CONSTABLE, LIONEL BICKNELL
(1828–87)**
Lionel Bicknell Constable, the youngest son of
John Constable, exhibited at the Royal Academy
intermittently between 1849 and 1855. It has
proved difficult to differentiate his work from
that of his father.

Study of a Lake
pencil, watercolour
259 × 363 mm
Anderson, A. E. (gift, 1930) (D.1930.23)

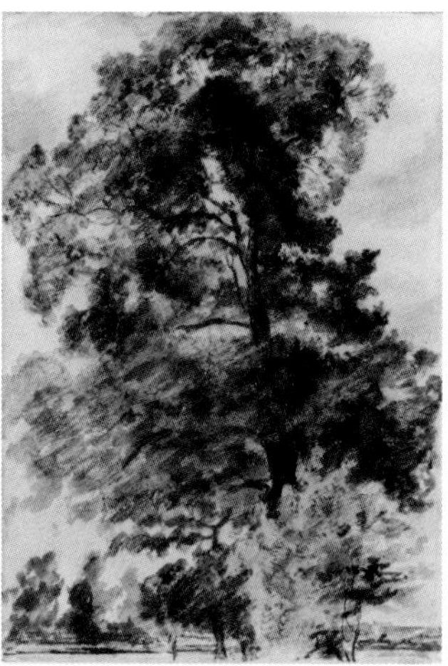

D.1949.11

Study of Trees in Spring
pencil, watercolour
256 × 175 mm
Agnew's (purchase, 1949) (D.1949.11)

■ **CONSTABLE, LIONEL BICKNELL
(attributed to)**

Cloudy Sky over Tree-tops
pencil
176 × 246 mm
Agnew's (purchase, 1949) (D.1949.8)

■ **COOKE, HENRY (1642–1700)**
Henry Cooke was a decorative painter who visited Italy
and may have been a pupil of Salvator Rosa. Much of
his decorative work is now destroyed and drawings by
him are extremely rare.

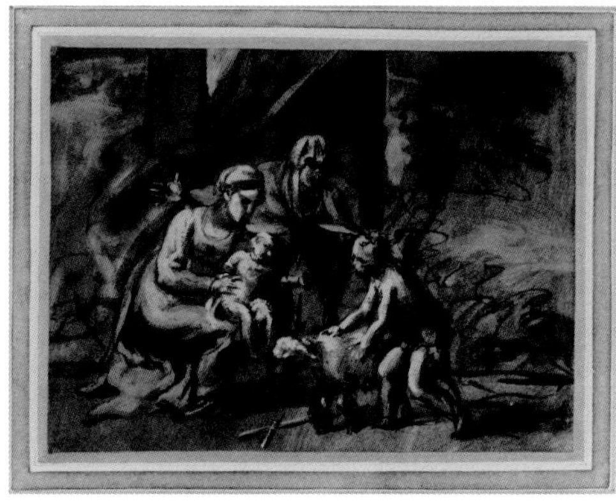

D.1947.58

**The Virgin and Child with St Anne and the
Infant St John the Baptist**
pen and brown ink, brown watercolour,
bodycolour; paper (prepared brown)
inscribed on collector's mount lower centre in the hand
of an 18th-century collector: *Old Cook*
194 × 250 mm
anonymous, Friends of the Whitworth (via) (gift, 1947)
(D.1947.58)

■ COOK, HERBERT MOXON (1844–1929)

Herbert Moxon Cook was a landscape painter who exhibited at the Royal Academy and elsewhere from 1868. In later life he lived at Prestatyn in North Wales.

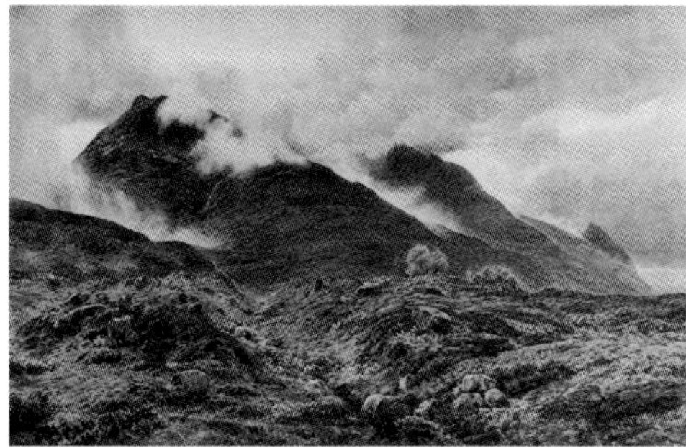

D.1903.1

Late Autumn in the Isle of Arran
11.1880
watercolour
signed & dated lower right: *H Moxon Cook / Nov 1880*
596 × 924 mm
Fry (Mrs) (in memory of Joseph Fry) (gift, 1903) (D.1903.1)

■ COOPER, ALFRED HEATON (1864–1929)

Alfred Heaton Cooper was a landscape painter who trained at Westminster School of Art and exhibited in London from 1885. He moved to the Lake District and latterly lived in Ambleside, where he died. Cooper worked extensively for A. & C. Black, providing illustrations for a number of their publications including the colour plate book *The English Lakes* in 1905.

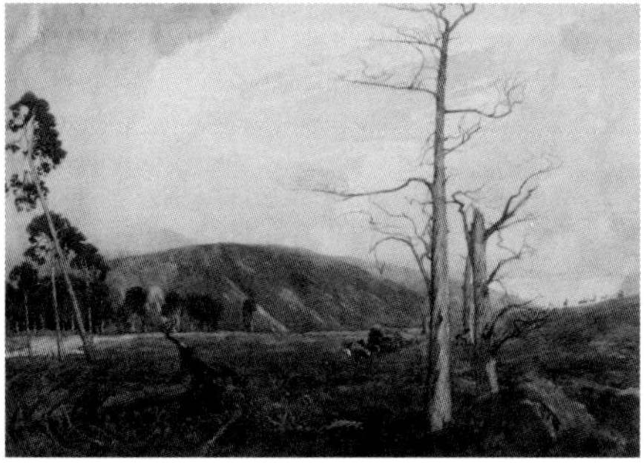

D.1987.55

The Ancient Forest of Mar, Aberdeenshire
watercolour
signed lower left: *A.Heaton.Cooper*
558 × 770 mm
Hitchon, Brian (Dr) (in appreciation of his student years at Manchester University, 1949–55) (gift, 1987) (D.1987.55)

■ COOPER, ALFRED W. (C. 1830–C. 1900)

Unknown artist.

A Woman seated above the Sea at Whitley, Northumberland
6.1871
pencil, watercolour, bodycolour (heightened with white); buff paper
signed lower right: *AWCooper*
inscribed and dated lower left: *Whitley Rocks / June 1871*
137 × 220 mm
Danos, Dr Edith (gift, 1996) (D.1996.43)

■ COOPER, GEORGE GORDON BYRON (1850–1933)

George Gordon Byron Cooper studied at the Manchester Academy of Fine Arts. He lived at Bowdon in Cheshire and exhibited Lancashire landscapes in London and elsewhere.

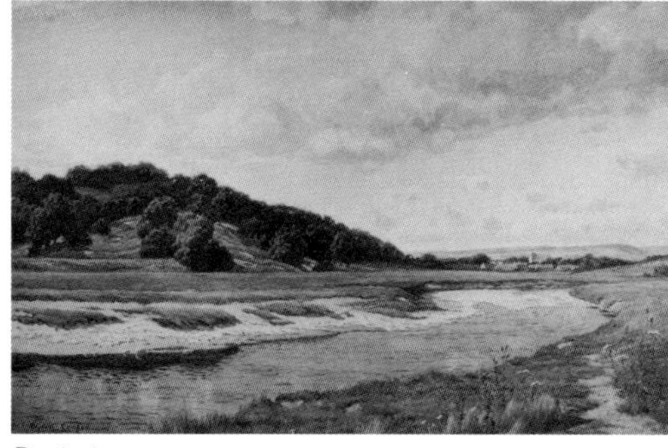

D.1960.38

Whalley Nab, Lancashire
watercolour
signed lower left: *Byron Cooper*
609 × 914 mm
Cooper, Enid (bequest, 1960) (D.1960.38)

■ COOPER, Jun., RICHARD (1740–1814)

Richard Cooper Jun. studied under his father – an engraver and occasional watercolourist – and later in Paris. It appears that he went to Italy in about 1770 and may have remained there until 1776; Italian or Italianate views predominate in his work. During the 1780s he was Drawing Master at Eton.

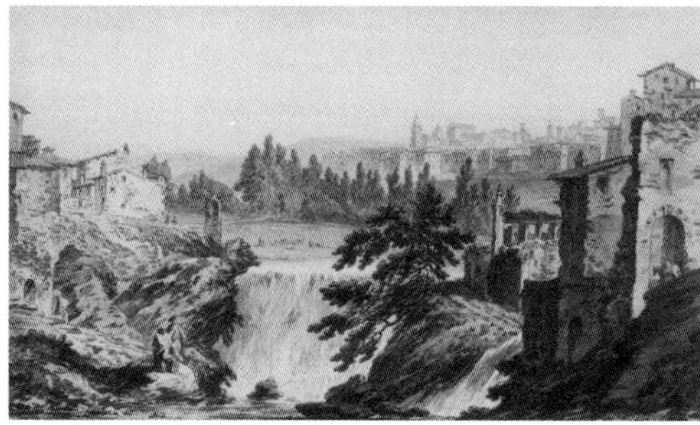

D.1933.42

The Falls of Tivoli, Italy
1770–76
pen and brown ink, watercolour
signed: *R.Cooper delt.*
357 × 640 mm
Anderson, A. E. (bequest, 1933) (D.1933.42)

Italian Landscape
pencil, pen and brown ink, watercolour
245 × 322 mm
Pilkington, Margaret (gift, 1951) (D.1951.2)

■ COOPER, THOMAS SIDNEY (1803–1902)

Cooper was an animal painter of remarkable longevity. He specialised in pictures of cows and sheep in a landscape setting, and was elected a member of the Royal Academy in 1867. He founded the Sidney Cooper Gallery of Art in Canterbury in 1868, and gave it to the city in 1882.

Cattle, early Morning
1851
watercolour
signed & dated lower right: *TSCooper ARA / 1851*
395 × 518 mm
Agnew, Sir William (gift, 1906) (D.1906.3)

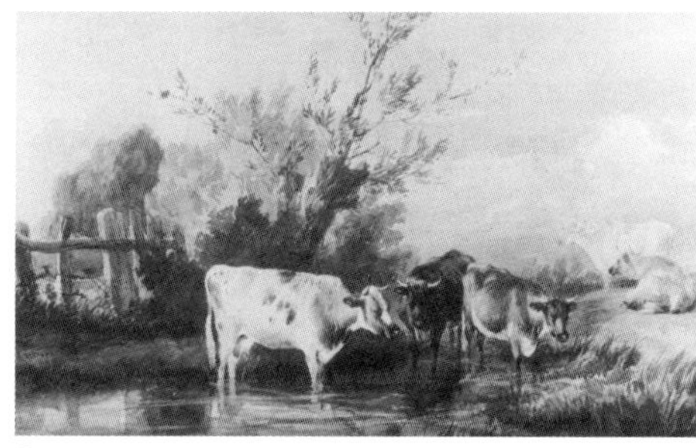

D.1910.11

Landscape with Cattle
1859
watercolour
signed & dated lower left: *TSCooper 1859*
217 × 350 mm
Cox, G. F. (bequest, 1910) (D.1910.11)

■ COSWAY, MARIA LOUISA CATHERINE CECILIA (1759–1838)

Maria Cosway was the wife of the miniaturist and portrait painter Richard Cosway, from whom she was for many years estranged. She founded a college and convent at Lodi in North Italy for girl's education.

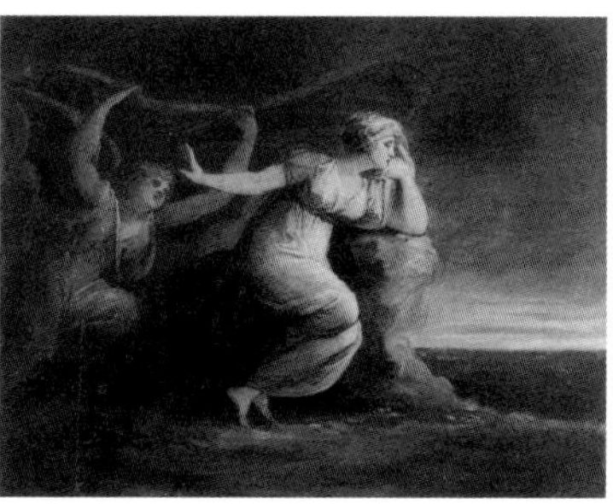

D.1946.2

A Girl by the Sea repelling the Spirit of Melancholy
pen and brown ink, watercolour, bodycolour, oil paint
191 × 234 mm
Barlow, Sir Thomas (gift, 1946) (D.1946.2)

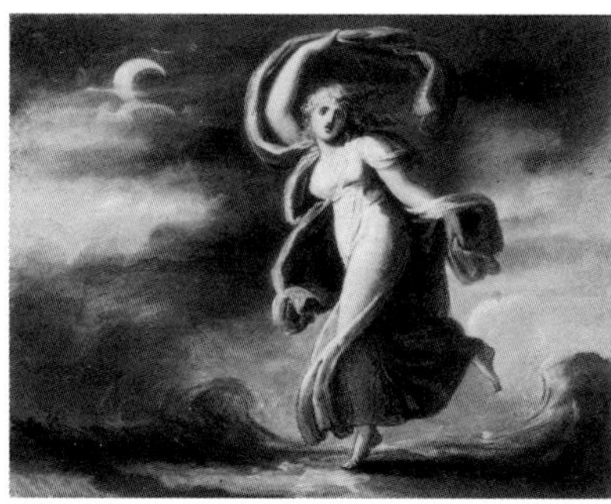

D.1946.3

A Girl dancing by the Sea by Moonlight
pen and brown ink, watercolour, bodycolour, oil paint
188 × 232 mm
Barlow, Sir Thomas (gift, 1946) (D.1946.3)

■ COTMAN, JOHN JOSEPH (1814–78)

John Joseph Cotman was the second and most gifted son of John Sell. In 1834 he accompanied his father to London to assist him with his drawing classes at King's College but returned to Norwich, his place of birth, the following year. Like his father, he suffered from mental depression.

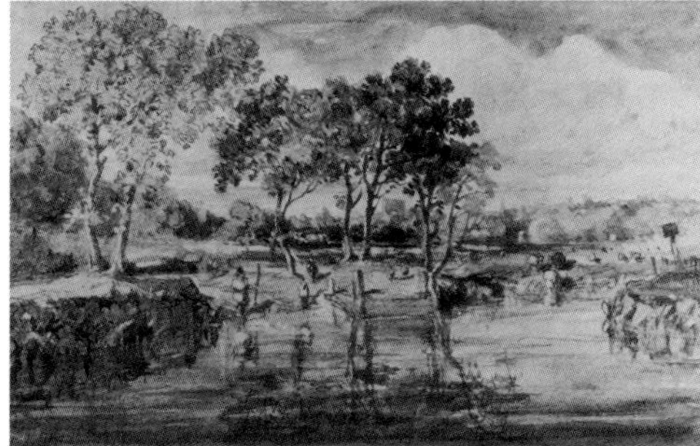

D.1934.11

Norwich from the River Yare
1873
pencil, watercolour
signed & dated lower left: *J.J.Cotman 1873*
225 × 349 mm
Anderson, A. E. (gift, 1934) (D.1934.11)

■ COTMAN, JOHN JOSEPH (attributed to)

Irmingland Hall, near Aylsham, Norfolk
pencil, watercolour, bodycolour
(heightened with white)
333 × 482 mm
Anderson, A. E. (gift, 1924) (D.1924.34)

■ COTMAN, JOHN SELL (1782–1842)

John Sell Cotman was born in Norwich, and came to London in 1798 where he studied at the house of Dr Monro while exhibiting at the Royal Academy. After failing to establish himself in London, he returned to Norwich in 1806 and set himself up as a drawing master. For financial reasons, Cotman was reliant on the whims of antiquarian patrons such as Dawson Turner, who sent him to Normandy in 1817, 1818 and 1820. In 1834, he was appointed drawing master at King's College, London.

River Scene with Cattle
watercolour
174 × 368 mm
untraced (purchase, 1914) (D.1914.3)

Water Tower, York
1804
pencil, grey watercolour, brown watercolour
signed & dated lower right: *J S Cotman / 1804*
224 × 432 mm
untraced (purchase, 1914) (D.1914.4)

Low Tide
1840–42
black chalk, white chalk; brown paper
225 × 345 mm
Anderson, A. E. (gift, 1916) (D.1916.2)

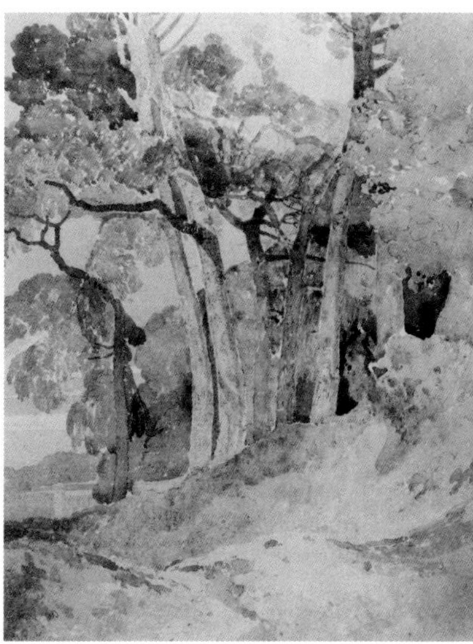

D.1916.3

Study of Trees, Harrow
1.7.1805
pencil, watercolour
dated lower right: *July 1st.1805*; inscribed lower left:
Harrow Midilex
359 × 279 mm
Anderson, A. E. (gift, 1916) (D.1916.3)

The Abbey Gate of St Martin d'Auchy, Aumale, Normandy
1830
pencil, white bodycolour; brown paper
signed & dated lower right: *JSCotman 1830.*; inscribed
lower left: *Abbey Gate of St Martin at Aumale*
408 × 298 mm
Anderson, A. E. (gift, 1917) (D.1917.1)

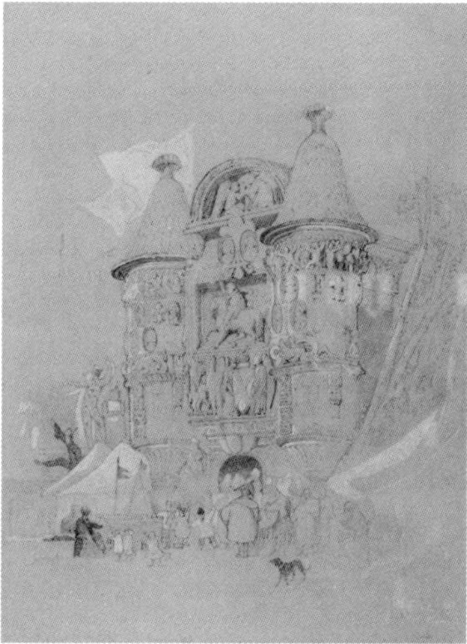

D.1917.1

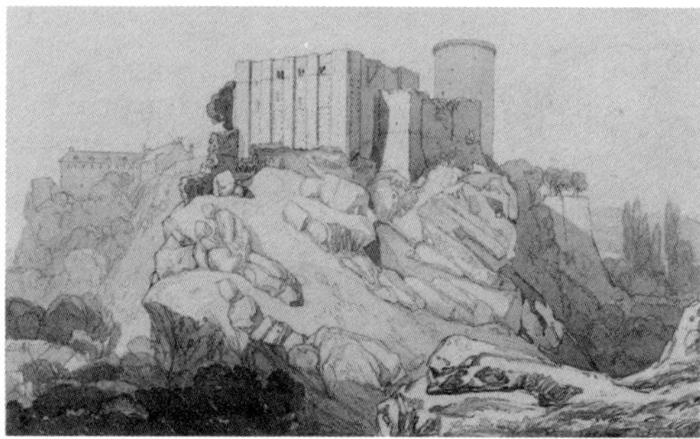

D.1918.7

Castle of Falaise, Normandy, the North West View
16.9.1818
pencil, brown watercolour
signed & dated lower right in full and with initials:
J.S.Cotman Sept 16.1818.J S; inscribed lower left in
margin: *Castle at Falaise.*; numbered upper left margin:
16.
243 × 376 mm
Coleman, Sir Jeremiah, National Art Collections Fund (via)
(gift, 1918) (D.1918.7)

Four Sides of a Capital, Castle of Falaise, Normandy
1818
pencil, brown watercolour
inscribed lower left: *Four sides of a capital in the Castle
at Falaise*
188 × 251 mm
Coleman, Sir Jeremiah, National Art Collections Fund (via)
(gift, 1918) (D.1918.9)

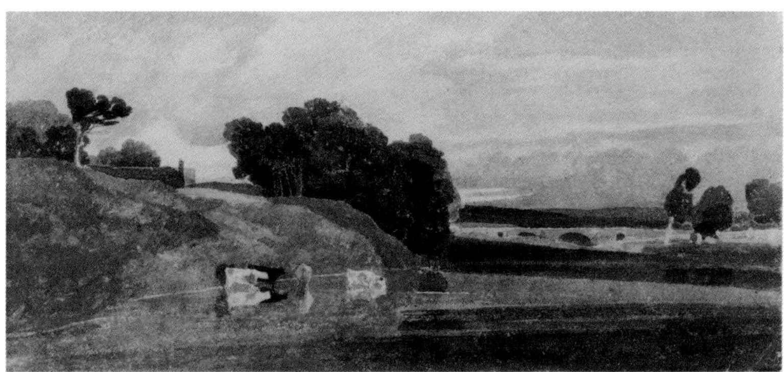

D.1914.3

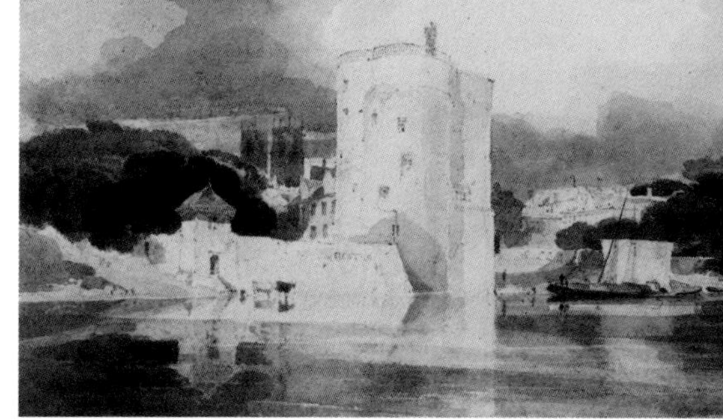

D.1914.4

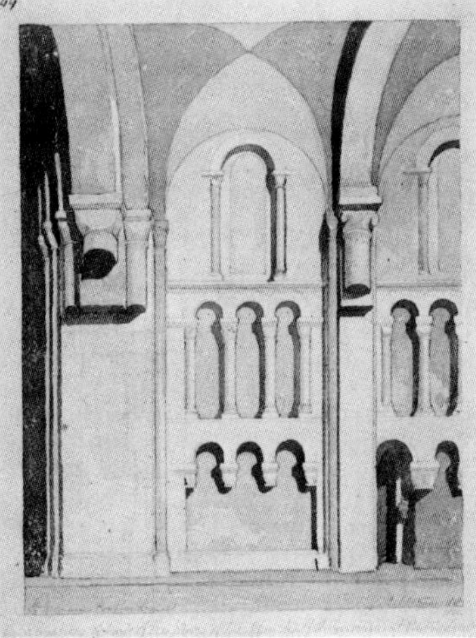

D.1918.11

**Elevation of Part of the Nave of the Church
of St Germain, Pont-Audemer, Normandy**
1818–20
pencil, brown watercolour
signed & dated lower right of image: *JSCotman 1818*;
dated lower right margin below other date: *1820.*;
inscribed lower left of image: *St Germain. Pontaudemer*;
inscribed lower edge margin: *Elevation of Part of the
Nave of the Church of St Germain at Pontaudemer*;
numbered lower left margin: *8*; numbered upper left
margin: *49*
288 × 216 mm
Coleman, Sir Jeremiah, National Art Collections Fund (via)
(gift, 1918) (D.1918.11)

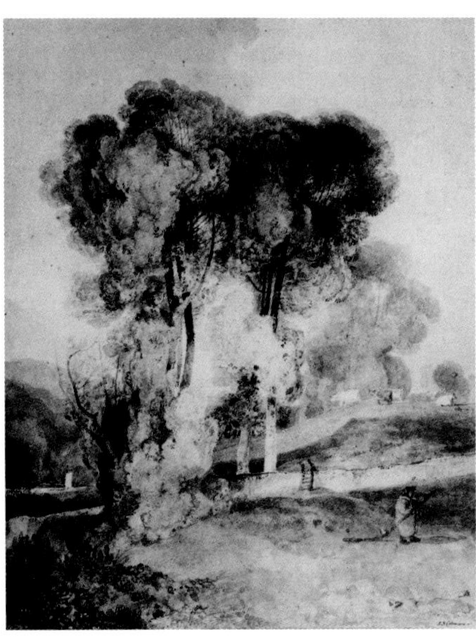

D.1920.6

Landscape with Trees
1805
pencil, watercolour
signed lower right: *JSCotman*
416 × 320 mm
Palser, J. and Son, London (purchase, 1920) (D.1920.6)

The Devil's Bridge, Cardiganshire
1829–31
pencil, bodycolour (heightened with white)
brown paper
184 × 254 mm
Walker's Galleries, London (purchase, 1925) (D.1925.36)

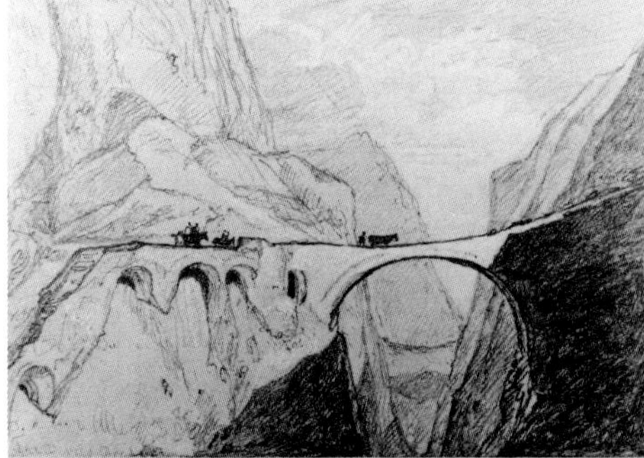

D.1925.36

Font at St Gregory's, Heckingham, Norfolk
1817
pencil, brown watercolour
signed & dated lower right: *J S. Cotman 1817*
inscribed lower left: *Heckingham Font*; numbered lower
right: *1722*
228 × 173 mm
Sidebotham, Dr E. J. (gift, 1926) (D.1926.19)

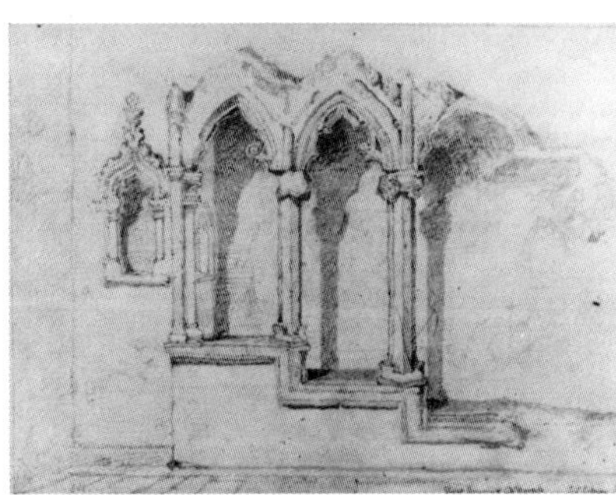

D.1933.12

**The Sedilia and Piscina, St Mary's,
Great Snoring, Norfolk**
1815
pencil
signed, inscribed & dated lower right: *Great Snoring
Ch.Norfolk – J.S.Cotman.1815*; numbered lower left:
2434; inscribed vertically up right edge of verso:
[M]iss Turner
188 × 247 mm
Anderson, A. E. (gift, 1933) (D.1933.12)

**Monuments of Dame Agatha of Narborough,
and Sir John and Lady Spelman, All Saints
Church, Narborough, Norfolk**
1814–16
pencil
inscribed on mount lower right in later hand: *About
1815*; inscribed centre verso in later hand (different):
*Monuments of Lady Agatha Narborough 12 / and Sir
John and Lady Sherman 18* [remainder cut]
193 × 165 mm
University of Manchester, History of Art Department
(transfer, 1960) (D.1960.74)

**Interior of the Great Hall, Little Moreton
Hall, Cheshire (recto); Two Studies of
Greyhounds (verso)**
pencil
inscribed lower right: *Old Morton Hall*; inscribed left
edge with colour notes: *All above / Wht washd / Sky seen
/ tho boards / 3 Wht / 4 Brown Pannel*(?) */ H. Red / 5
Grey*
360 × 265 mm
Colnaghi's (purchase, 1972) (D.1972.14)

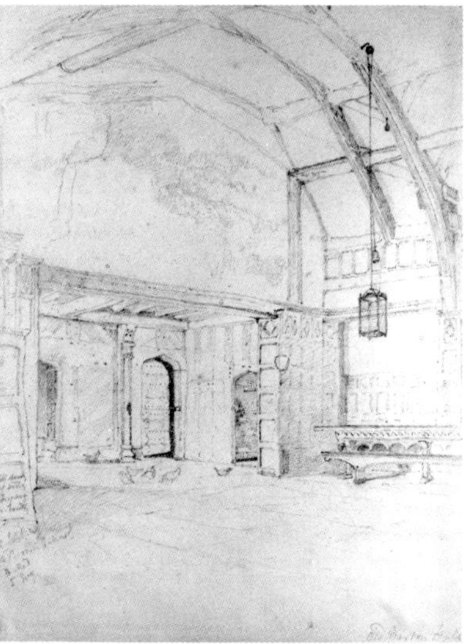

D.1972.14

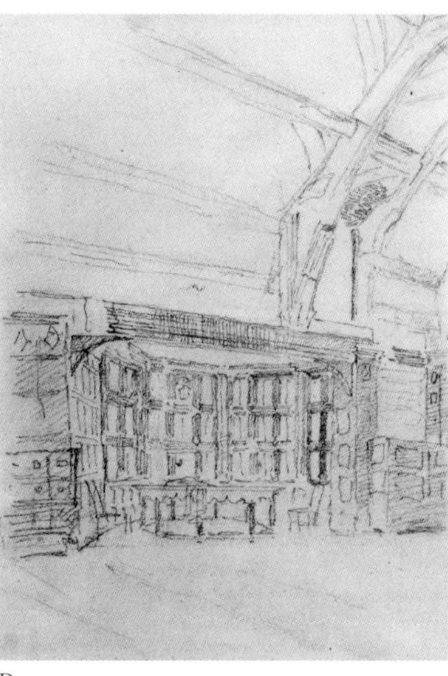

D.1979.3

**Interior of the Great Hall, Little Moreton
Hall, Cheshire**
pencil
368 × 256 mm
Judges, Mrs Kathleen (in memory of her father Francis
Voltaire Mitchell) (purchase, 1979) (D.1979.3)

■ **Cotman, Miles Edmund (1810–58)**
Miles Edmund Cotman, the eldest son of John Sell,
took over his father's teaching practice in Norwich in
1834. He followed his father to London and in 1834
became Drawing Master at King's College, London.
His style is very close to that of his father and the two
are frequently mistaken for each other.

Ships off Yarmouth, Norfolk
watercolour
inscribed lower left verso; not artist's hand:
M.E Cotman
163 × 238 mm
Taylor, John Edward (gift, 1892) (D.1892.79)

Dutch Vessels off the Isle of Wight
watercolour
254 × 343 mm
Taylor, John Edward (gift, 1892) (D.1892.116)

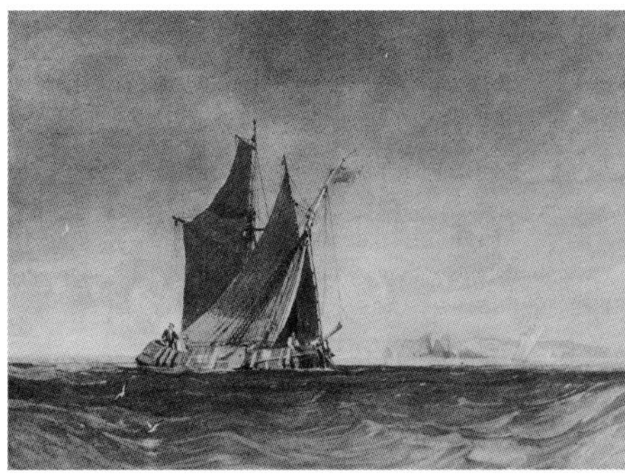
D.1892.116

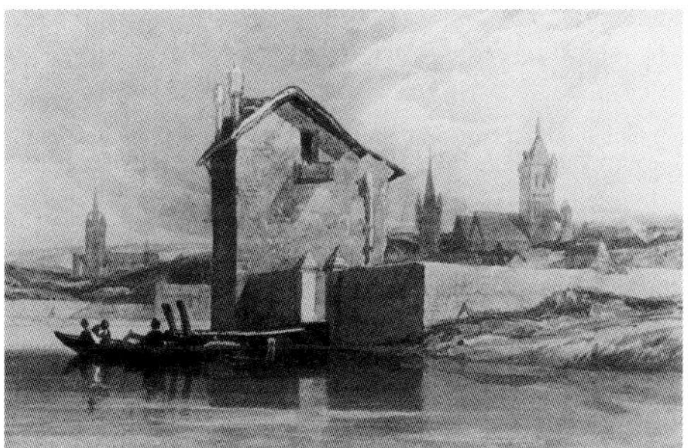
D.1892.117

On the River Sarthe, Normandy, with Alençon in the Distance
1823–25
pencil, watercolour
169 × 257 mm
Taylor, John Edward (gift, 1892) (D.1892.117)

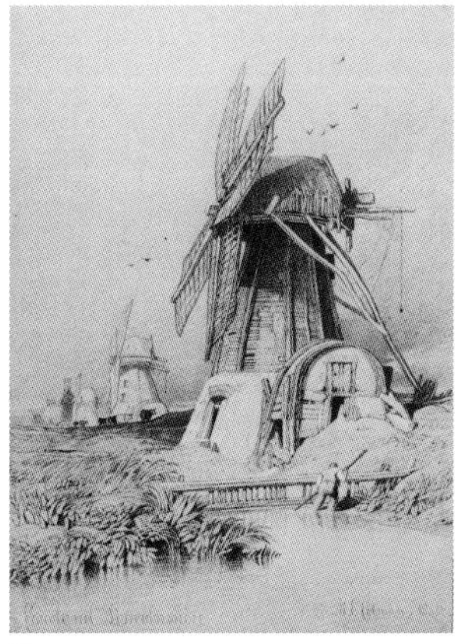
D.1970.27

Draining Mills, Crowland, Lincolnshire
1846
black chalk, white chalk; grey paper
signed & dated lower right: *M.E.Cotman, 1846.*;
inscribed lower left: *Crowland Lincolnshire*
452 × 309 mm
Towlson, Hector J. (bequest, 1969) (D.1970.27)

■ Cox, David (1783–1859)

Cox was born in Birmingham and moved to London in 1804, initially working as a scene painter. He began a career as a drawing master and joined the Old Watercolour Society in 1812. From 1814 to 1827 he taught drawing in Hereford, then he moved back to London before returning to Birmingham in 1841. Cox published a number of teaching manuals and is one of the most influential of English watercolourists, known in particular for his ability to depict wind and rain.

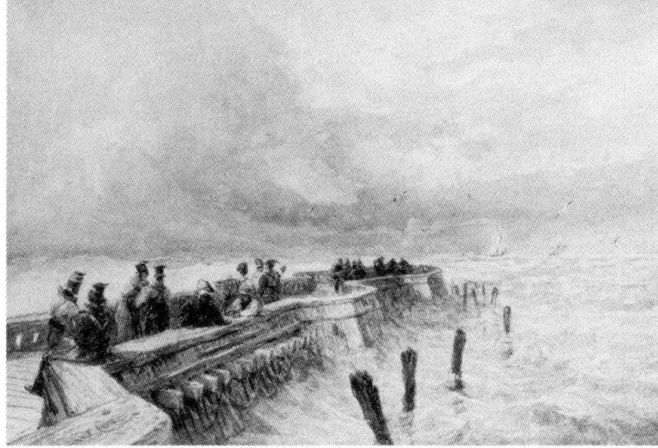
D.1887.18

Calais Pier, France
watercolour, bodycolour (heightened with white)
signed lower left: *David Cox*
247 × 350 mm
Agnew's (purchase, 2.5.1892) (D.1887.18)

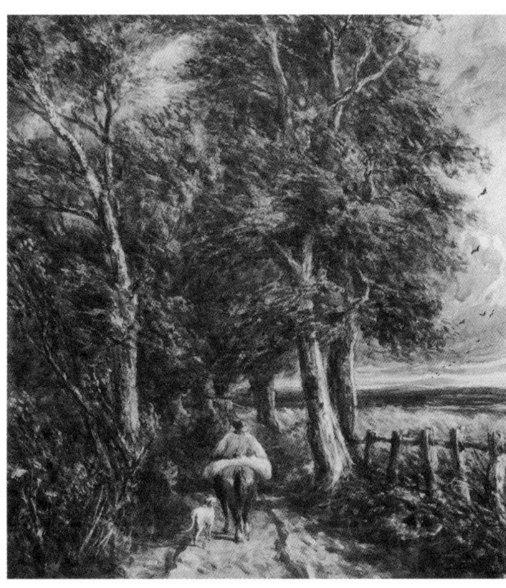
D.1887.19

Lane at Harborne, Warwickshire
1849
watercolour
signed & dated lower left: *David Cox / 1849*
510 × 455 mm
Agnew's (purchase, 2.5.1892) (D.1887.19)

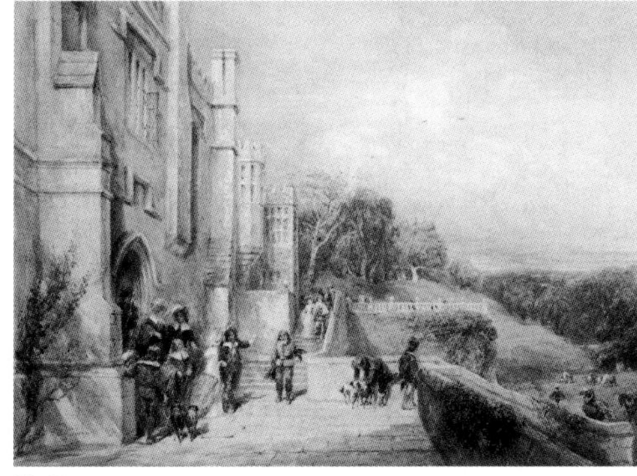
D.1887.27

Going out Hawking
1838
watercolour, bodycolour
signed & dated lower left: *David Cox / 1838*
460 × 618 mm
Wright, T. W. (purchase, 1892) (D.1887.27)

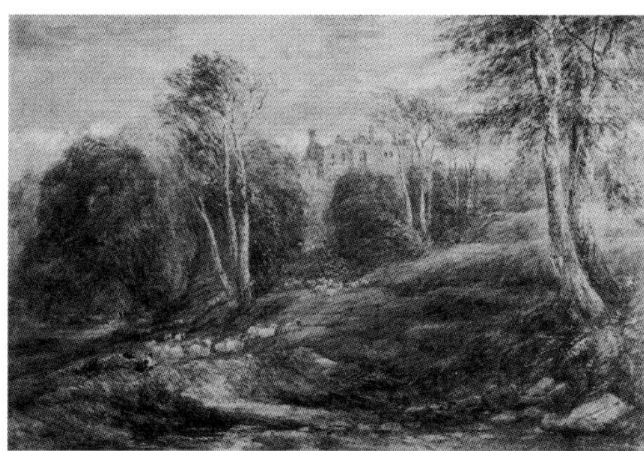
D.1887.28

Barden Tower, Yorkshire
1849
watercolour, bodycolour (heightened with white)
signed & dated lower left: *David Cox / 1849*
606 × 861 mm
Agnew's (purchase, 2.5.1892) (D.1887.28)

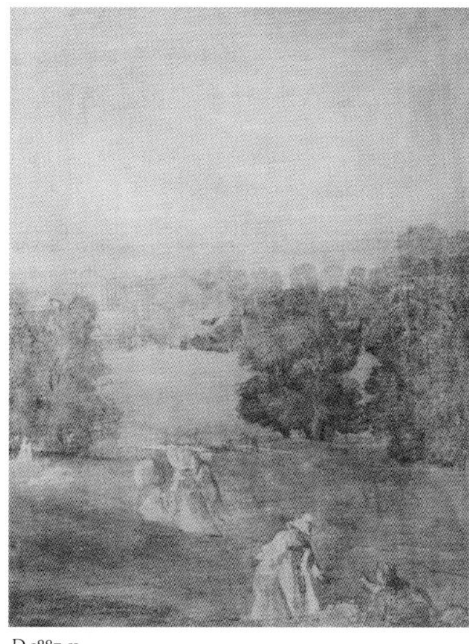
D.1887.51

Figures in Greenwich Park
1838
watercolour
618 × 460 mm
Wright, T. W. (purchase, 1892) (D.1887.51)

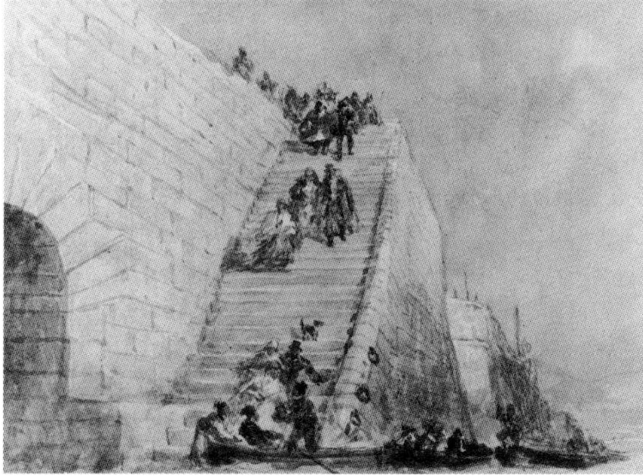
D.1893.8

The Old Pierhead, Liverpool
1839–41
pencil, watercolour
185 × 257 mm
Agnew's (purchase, 18.12.1893) (D.1893.8)

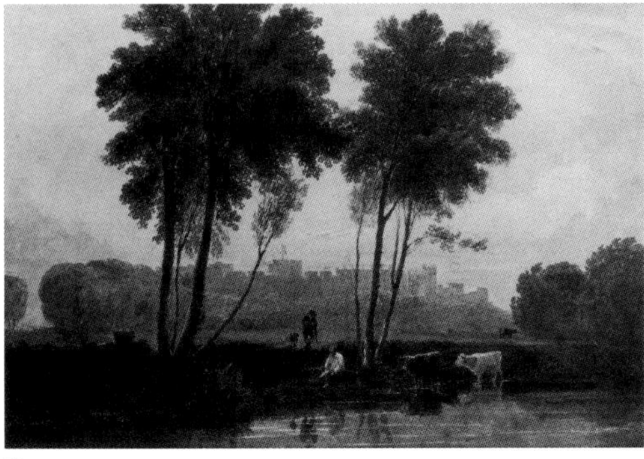

D.1904.24

Windsor Castle from the Thames
pencil, watercolour
292 × 429 mm
Worthington, Mary (bequest, 1904) (D.1904.24)

Market Street and the Old Exchange, Manchester
1835
pencil, watercolour; three joined sheets; inscribed; not
artist's hand: *D Cox*; inscribed left edge of verso:
(naming the shops in the street): *Billiards / Farmer,
Tailor / Pennyhough / Stock / and / Share Broker / Burk /
Engraver / & Printer*; inscribed lower right of verso:
(inscription cut): *to the Queen / Street, Manchester / 4
Exchange Street Manchester*
187 × 443 mm
Agnew's (purchase, 27.6.1905) (D.1905.7)

Study of Trees in Windsor Great Park
black chalk; grey paper
196 × 274 mm
Anderson, A. E. (gift, 1910) (D.1910.3)

**Study of Trees and River at Bettws-y-Coed,
Caernarvonshire, Wales**
black chalk
188 × 271 mm
Anderson, A. E. (gift, 1910) (D.1910.4)

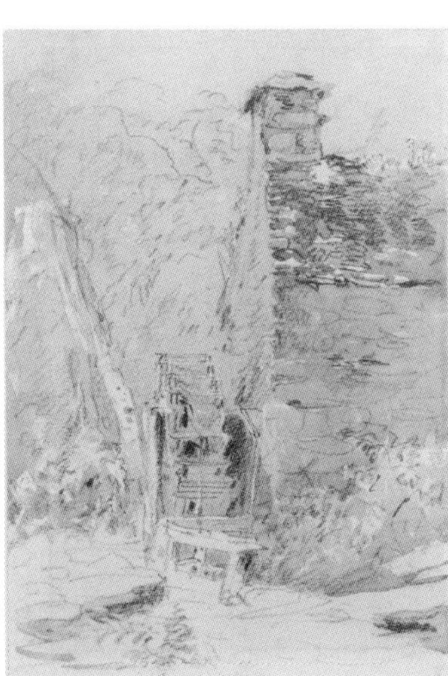

D.1910.5

**Water Mill at Bettws-y-Coed,
Caernarvonshire, Wales**
black chalk, watercolour
277 × 189 mm
Anderson, A. E. (gift, 1910) (D.1910.5)

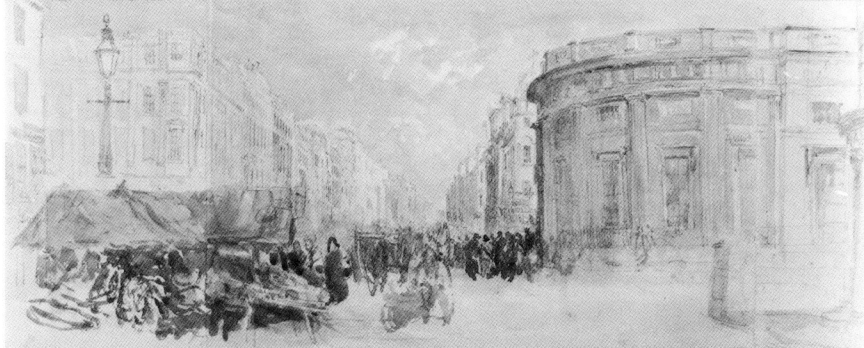

D.1905.7

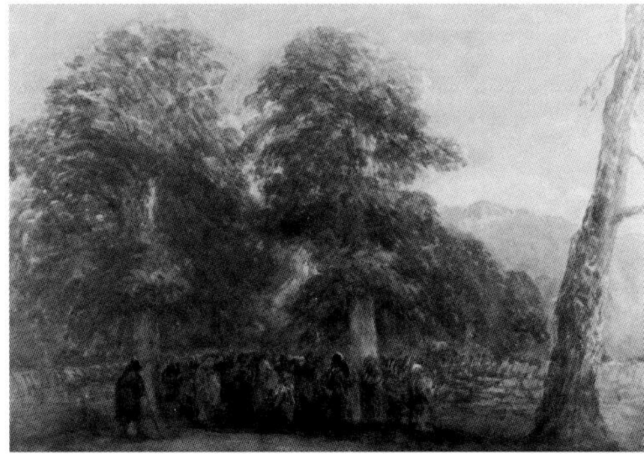

D.1919.7

**The Welsh Funeral, Bettws-y-Coed,
Caernarvonshire, Wales**
1847–49
black chalk, watercolour
600 × 855 mm
Agnew's (purchase, 1919) (D.1919.7)

Changing Pastures
pen and brown ink, watercolour
128 × 185 mm
Broadhurst, Sir Edward Tootal, Broadhurst, Lady
(bequest, 1924) (D.1924.48)

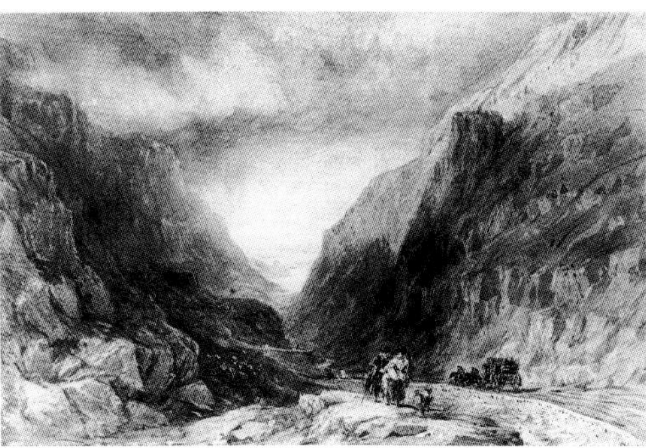

D.1924.54

Pass of Llanberis, Caernarvonshire, Wales
1835–36
pencil, watercolour
195 × 287 mm
Broadhurst, Sir Edward Tootal, Broadhurst, Lady
(bequest, 1924) (D.1924.54)

Coast Scene in squally Weather
black chalk, watercolour
187 × 278 mm
Broadhurst, Sir Edward Tootal, Broadhurst, Lady
(bequest, 1924) (D.1924.55)

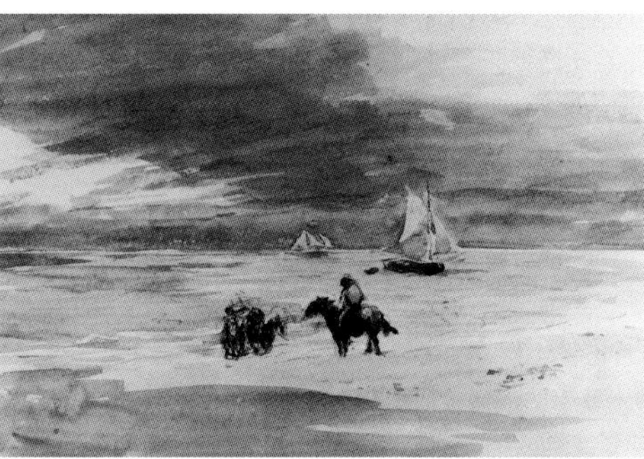

D.1924.55

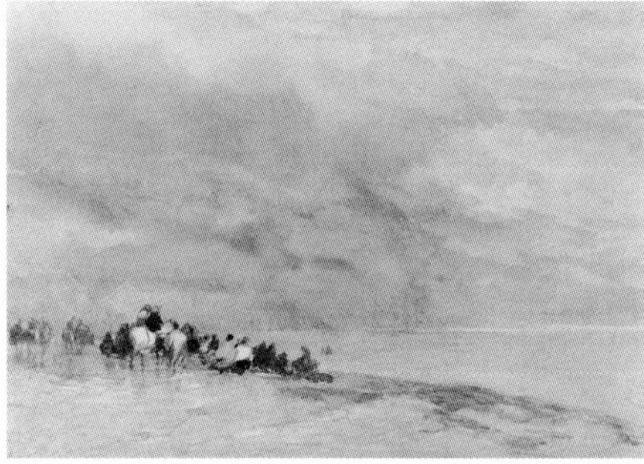

D.1924.56

Ulverston Sands, Lancashire
1834–35
watercolour
153 × 211 mm
Broadhurst, Sir Edward Tootal, Broadhurst, Lady
(bequest, 1924) (D.1924.56)

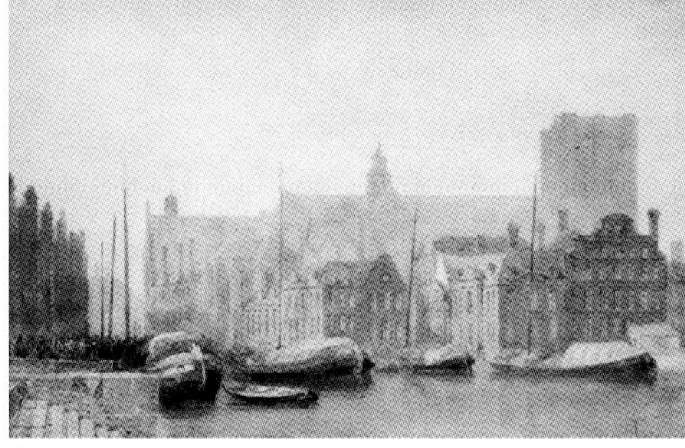

D.1924.57

**The Church of St Michel from the Quai aux
Herbes, Ghent, Belgium**
1826
pencil, watercolour
223 × 338 mm
Broadhurst, Sir Edward Tootal, Broadhurst, Lady
(bequest, 1924) (D.1924.57)

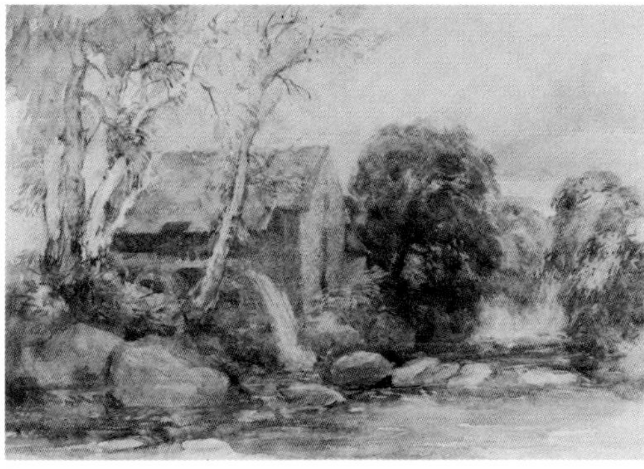

D.1924.58

Balder Mill, Cotherstone, Yorkshire
pencil, watercolour
266 × 368 mm
Broadhurst, Sir Edward Tootal, Broadhurst, Lady
(bequest, 1924) (D.1924.58)

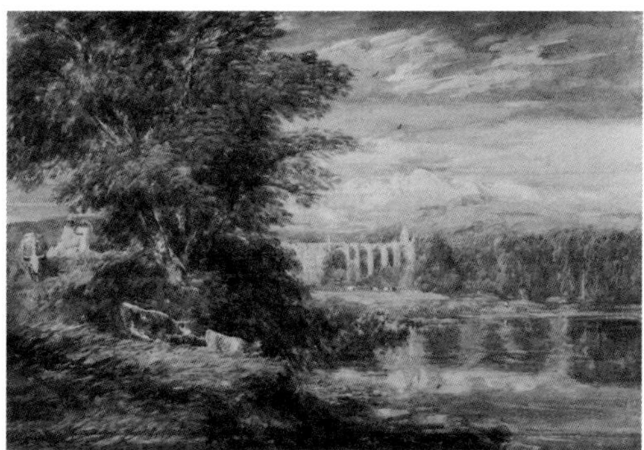

D.1924.64

Bolton Abbey, Yorkshire
1847
pencil, watercolour; two joined sheets
signed & dated lower left: *David Cox / 1847*
611 × 863 mm
Broadhurst, Sir Edward Tootal, Broadhurst, Lady
(bequest, 1924) (D.1924.64)

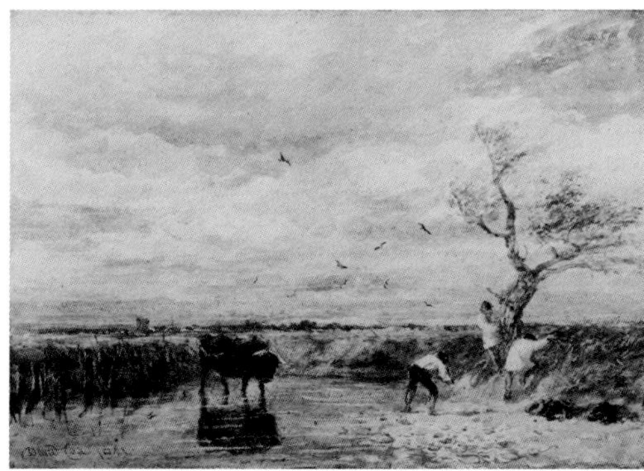

D.1924.65

Bathers disturbed by a Bull
1853
black chalk, watercolour
signed & dated lower left: *David Cox 1853*
273 × 377 mm
Broadhurst, Sir Edward Tootal, Broadhurst, Lady
(bequest, 1924) (D.1924.65)

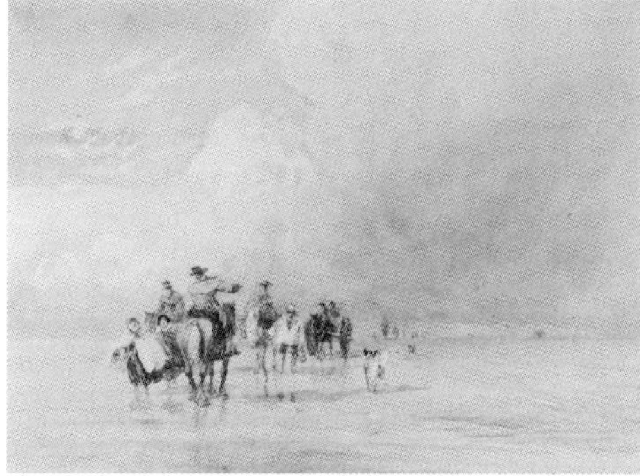

D.1924.66

Crossing Lancaster Sands
watercolour
signed lower left: *David Cox*
259 × 353 mm
Broadhurst, Sir Edward Tootal, Broadhurst, Lady
(bequest, 1924) (D.1924.66)

Country Lane
pencil, watercolour
274 × 376 mm
Broadhurst, Sir Edward Tootal, Broadhurst, Lady
(bequest, 1924) (D.1924.67)

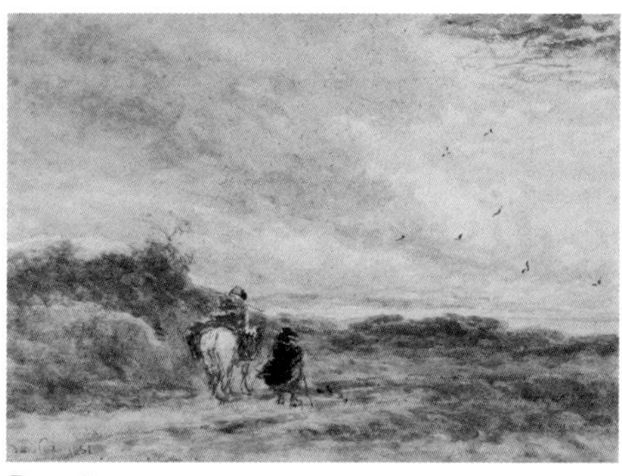

D.1924.68

Crossing the Moor
1851
pencil, black chalk, watercolour; oatmeal paper
signed & dated lower left: *David Cox / 1851*
274 × 376 mm
Broadhurst, Sir Edward Tootal, Broadhurst, Lady
(bequest, 1924) (D.1924.68)

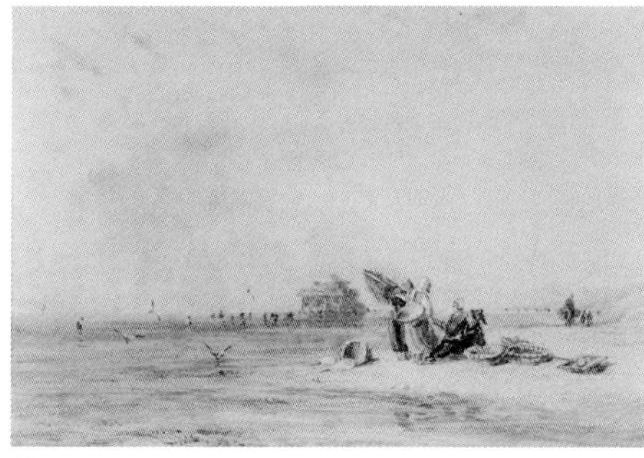

D.1924.69

Fort Rouge, Calais, France
1832
pencil, pen and brown ink, watercolour
signed & dated lower left: *D.Cox.1832*
181 × 261 mm
Broadhurst, Sir Edward Tootal, Broadhurst, Lady
(bequest, 1924) (D.1924.69)

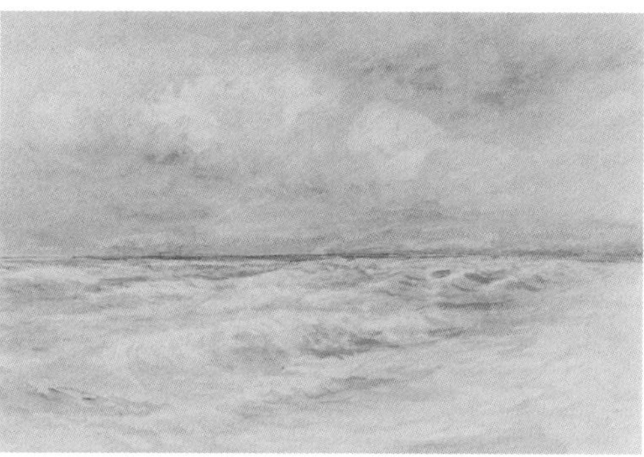

D.1924.70

Sea after a Storm
pencil, watercolour
307 × 447 mm
Broadhurst, Sir Edward Tootal, Broadhurst, Lady
(bequest, 1924) (D.1924.70)

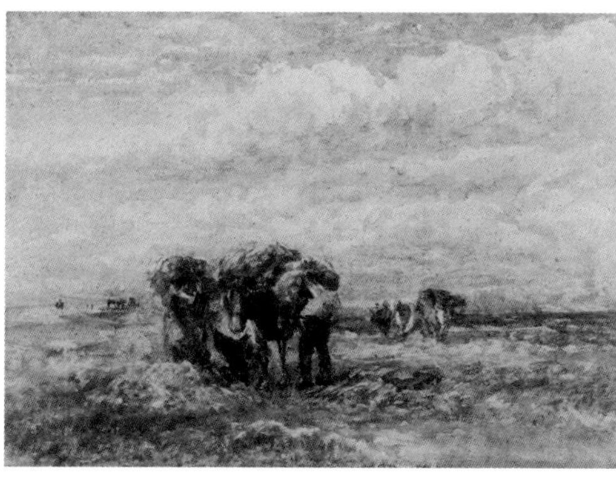

D.1924.71

Carrying the Hay
black chalk, watercolour
270 × 367 mm
Broadhurst, Sir Edward Tootal, Broadhurst, Lady
(bequest, 1924) (D.1924.71)

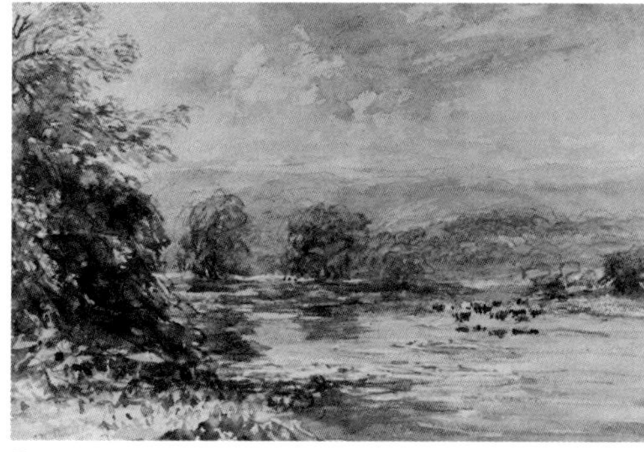

D.1924.72

On the River Wharfe, Yorkshire
black chalk, watercolour
inscribed lower left: *On the Wharf*; inscribed upper
centre verso: *On the Wharve / No 3*
186 × 272 mm
Broadhurst, Sir Edward Tootal, Broadhurst, Lady
(bequest, 1924) (D.1924.72)

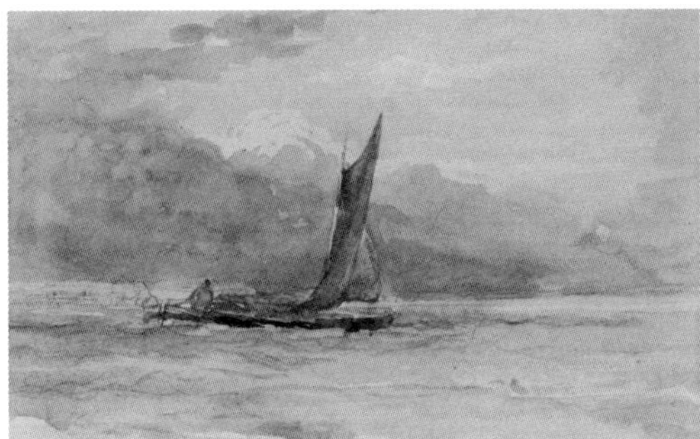

D.1924.79

Thames Barge, London
pencil, black chalk, watercolour
inscribed lower centre verso: *Thames*
142 × 125 mm
Broadhurst, Sir Edward Tootal, Broadhurst, Lady
(bequest, 1924) (D.1924.79)

Autumn Landscape
pencil, watercolour
362 × 509 mm
Holliday, J. R. (bequest, 1927) (D.1927.88)

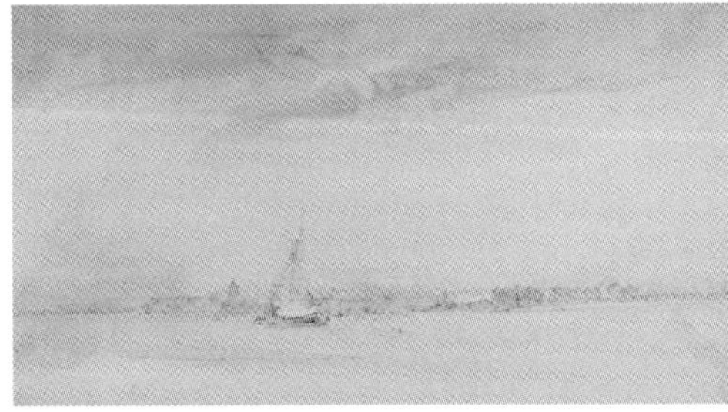

D.1927.90

Liverpool from the Mersey
1834–36
pencil, watercolour; watermark JWHATMAN / 1832
inscribed verso vertically along left hand edge: *Liverpool like Ulverston Sand in effect*
289 × 525 mm
Holliday, J. R. (bequest, 1927) (D.1927.90)

Moorland Scene with Sheep
black chalk
296 × 420 mm
Holliday, J. R. (bequest, 1927) (D.1927.91)

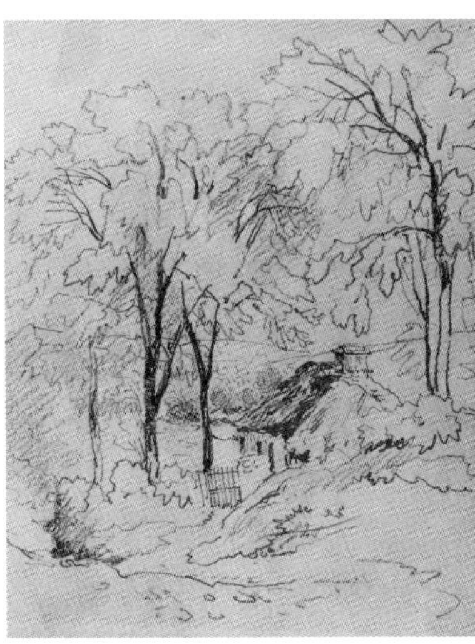

D.1927.92

Landscape with Cottage (recto); Study of Trees and a Man (verso)
pencil
numbered right: *19*
260 × 197 mm
Holliday, J. R. (bequest, 1927) (D.1927.92)

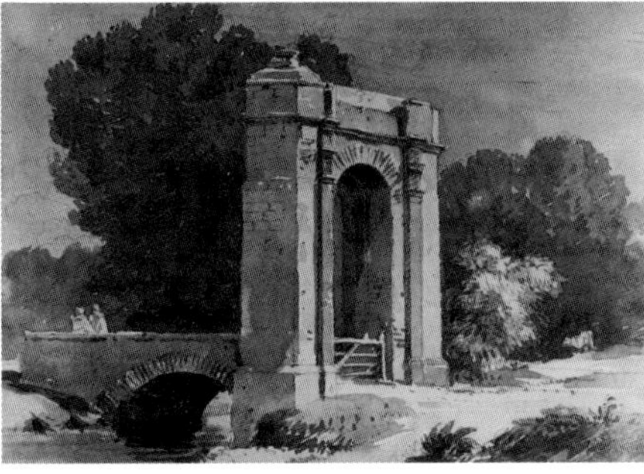

D.1927.94

Gateway and Bridge near Hereford
pencil, brown watercolour
inscribed upper edge of verso: *Near Hereford*
165 × 239 mm
Holliday, J. R. (bequest, 1927) (D.1927.94)

Harvest Scene, Metchley, Birmingham (recto); Study of Foliage (verso)
black chalk
inscribed lower left: *Metchley Harbourne*
198 × 275 mm
Holliday, J. R. (bequest, 1927) (D.1927.95)

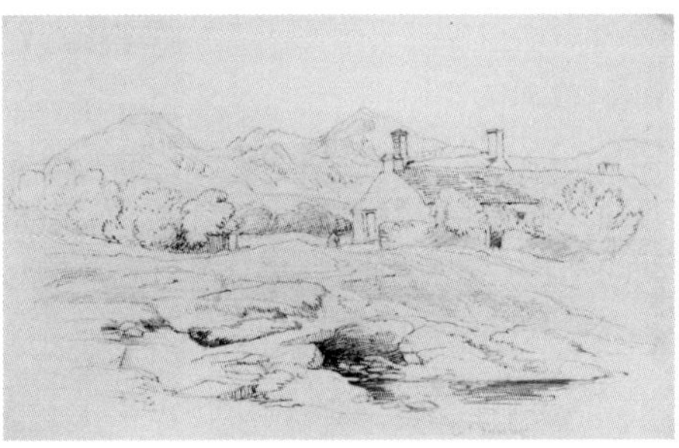

D.1927.96

Farm near Ffestiniog, Merioneth, Wales, with Moelwyn Mawr and Cnicht in the Distance
pencil, pen and brown ink
inscribed lower right: *Nr Festiniog*
182 × 288 mm
Holliday, J. R. (bequest, 1927) (D.1927.96)

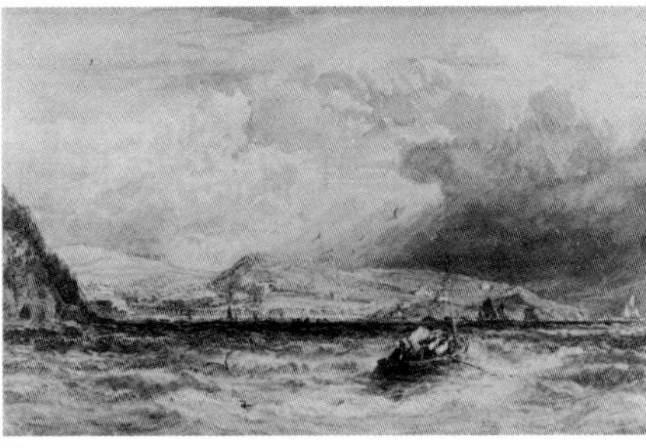

D.1927.97

Torquay, Devon, from the Bay
1831
pencil, pen and red ink, watercolour
117 × 179 mm
Holliday, J. R. (bequest, 1927) (D.1927.97)

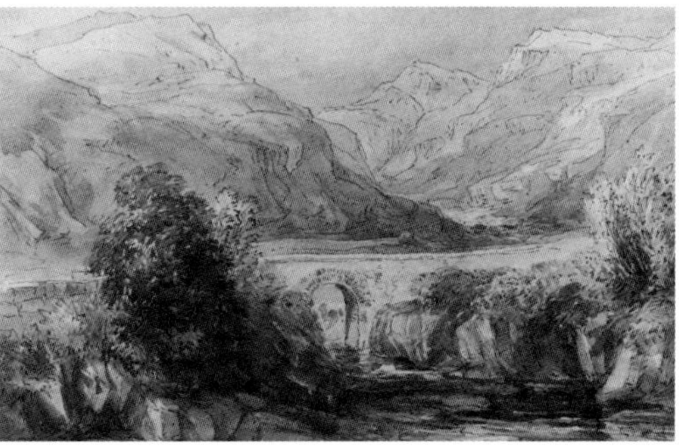

D.1927.98

Pont Aberglaslyn, Merioneth/ Caernarvonshire, Wales
pen and brown ink, brown watercolour
inscribed lower right verso; not artist's hand: *In the Lledr Valley*
154 × 236 mm
Holliday, J. R. (bequest, 1927) (D.1927.98)

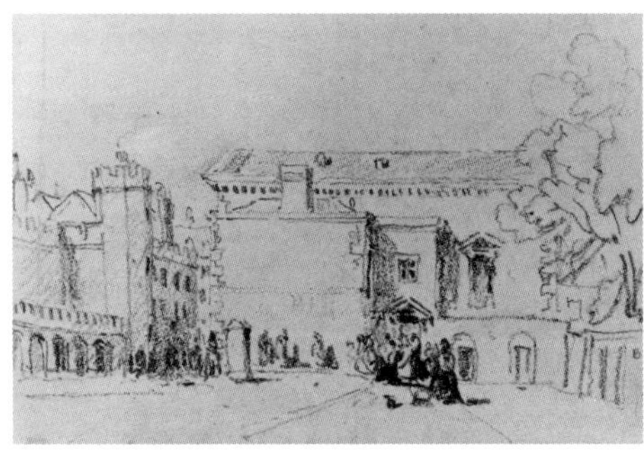

D.1927.99

The Queen's Chapel and Part of St James's Palace, London
black chalk
123 × 180 mm
Holliday, J. R. (bequest, 1927) (D.1927.99)

At the Gates of Chelsea Hospital, London (recto); Study of a Building (verso)
pencil
135 × 204 mm
Holliday, J. R. (bequest, 1927) (D.1927.100)

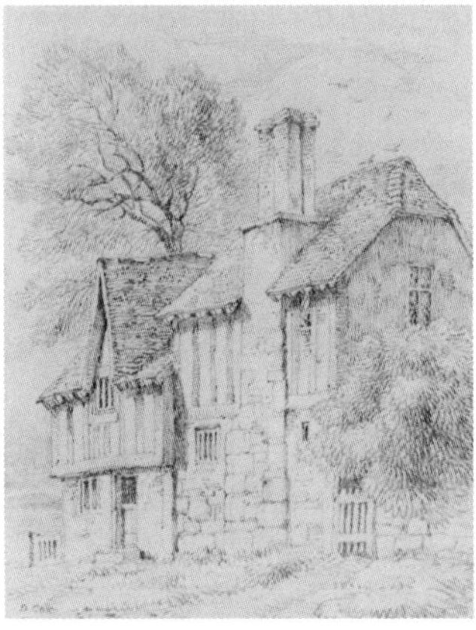

D.1927.108

The Manor House
black chalk (recto)
signed lower left: *D.COX*; signed lower right verso in reverse: *D.COX*
168 × 128 mm
Holliday, J. R. (bequest, 1927) (D.1927.108)

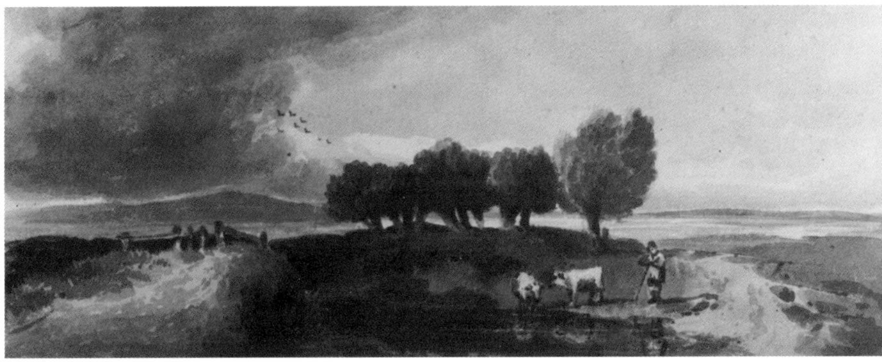

D.1927.109

Landscape Study with Cattle at a Stream
grey watercolour
105 × 260 mm
Holliday, J. R. (bequest, 1927) (D.1927.109)

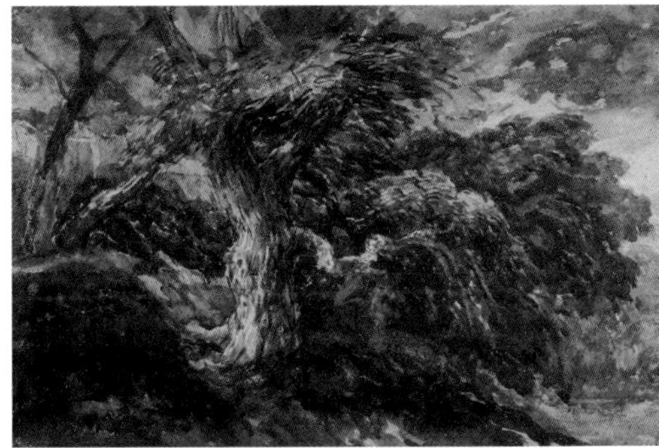

D.1931.33

Study of Trees
black chalk, watercolour
signed lower right: *David Cox*
364 × 542 mm
Richardson, Edward H. (gift, 1931) (D.1931.33)

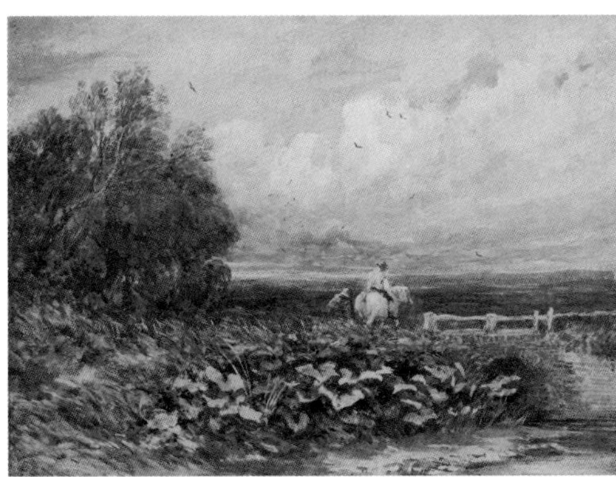

D.1937.10

Returning Home
1845
black chalk, watercolour
signed & dated lower centre: *David Cox 1845*
464 × 608 mm
Haworth, Jesse (bequest, 1937) (D.1937.10)

House and Lane with Mountains in the Distance
pencil, watercolour
190 × 264 mm
Nettlefold, F. J. (gift, 1948) (D.1948.12)

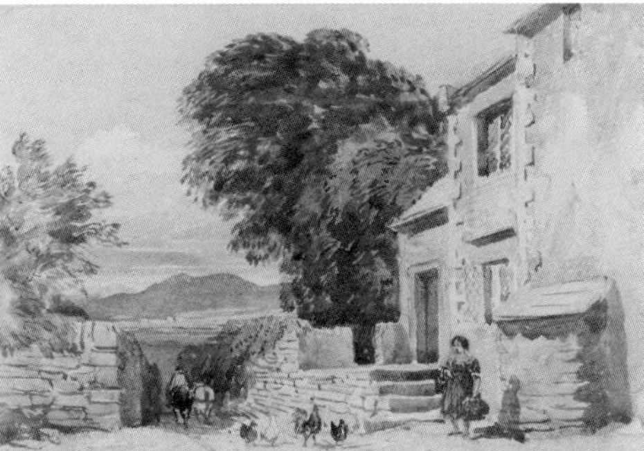

D.1948.12

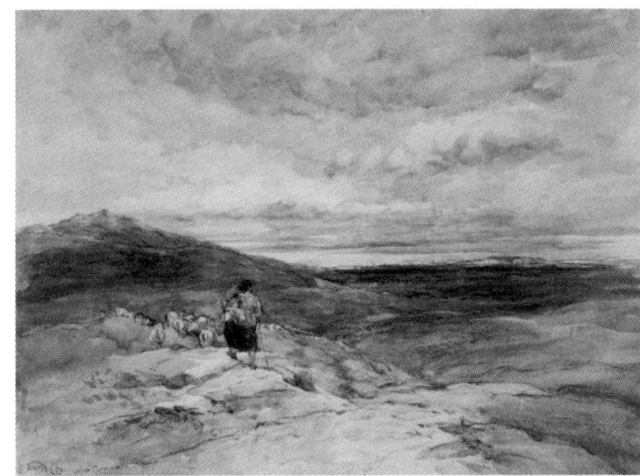

D.1960.4

Landscape with Shepherdess, near Caernarvon, Caernarvonshire, Wales
black chalk, watercolour
signed & inscribed lower left: *David Cox. Near Carnarvon N. Wales*
463 × 625 mm
Allen, C. C. A., Macilwane, C., Schnadhorst, T., Speckley, J., Wells-Cole, F. (gift, 1960) (D.1960.4)

Study of a Pack Horse
black chalk, watercolour; oatmeal paper
235 × 301 mm
University of Manchester, History of Art Department (transfer, 1960) (D.1960.75)

A Farmyard
black chalk, white chalk; blue paper
112 × 180 mm
Danos, Dr Edith (gift, 1996) (D.1996.40)

A wooded Landscape with a Church
pen and brown ink, watercolour
inscribed lower right; not artist's hand (?): *D.COX*
167 × 250 mm
Danos, Dr Edith (gift, 1996) (D.1996.41)

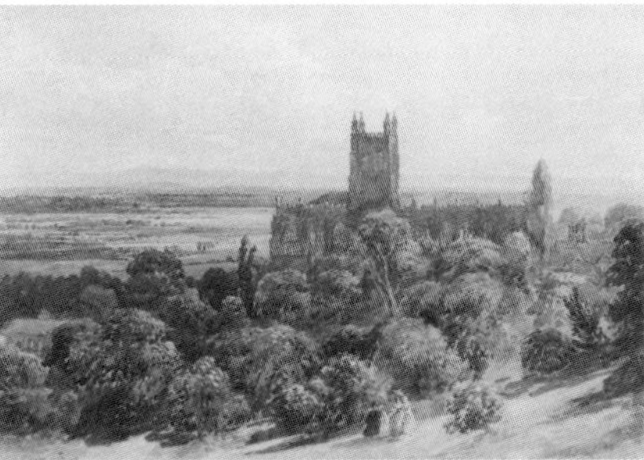

D.1999.1

Great Malvern Priory, Worcestershire
watercolour
signed & dated lower left; last two digits of date illegible: *D.COX 18*[—]
258 × 366 mm
Whitehead, Mrs Clare (in memory of her mother Frances Jackson) (gift, 14.5.1999) (D.1999.1)

■ **Cox, Jun., David** (1809–85)
David Cox Jun., son of David Cox, never really escaped from his father's shadow, and took over his teaching practice in 1841. He was a member of the New Watercolour Society from 1841 to 1845 before becoming an associate of the Old Watercolour Society, of which his father was a stalwart member, in 1848. His work is very similar to, and frequently mistaken for, that of his father.

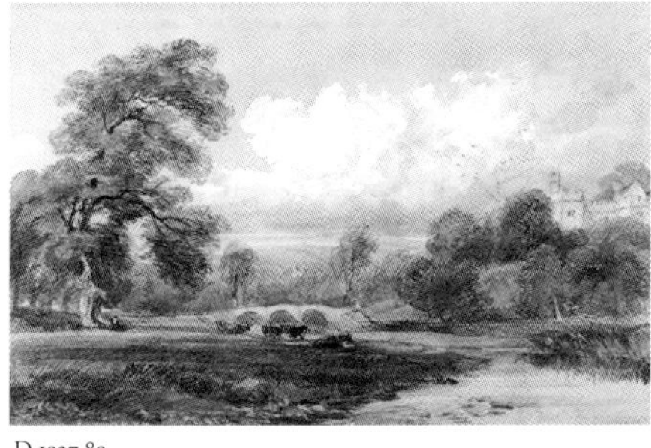

D.1927.89

Haddon Hall, Derbyshire, from the River
pencil, watercolour
stamped lower left: *D.Cox Junior*, numbered upper left verso: *105*; numbered lower left verso: *438*; inscribed lower right verso: *Haddon*
255 × 381 mm
Holliday, J. R. (bequest, 1927) (D.1927.89)

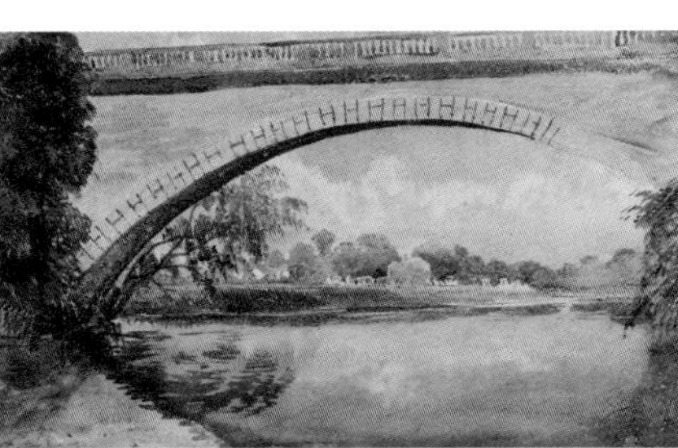

D.1942.5

View through a Bridge
pencil, watercolour
stamped lower left: *D.Cox Junior*; stamped lower right verso: *D.Cox Junior*; inscribed & numbered lower left verso: *412 Sketch through / a Bridge*
267 × 426 mm
Hills, The Reverend Henry (gift, 1942) (D.1942.5)

■ COZENS, ALEXANDER (1717–86)

Alexander Cozens was born in Russia but educated in England and visited Italy in 1746–47. He was Drawing Master at Christ's Hospital from 1749 to 1754 and at Eton from 1763 to 1768. Cozens was a successful and influential teacher, publishing a number of books and teaching manuals. Almost all of his work in oil is now lost but most of his monochrome work in watercolour still exists.

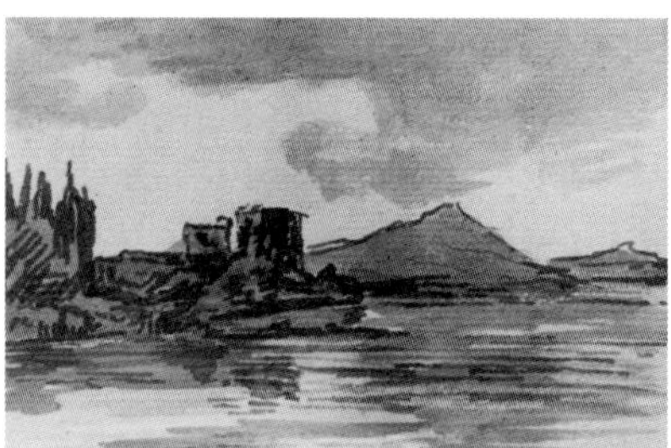
D.1912.14

Castle by a Lake and Mountains
6.7.1755
pencil, brown watercolour
signed & dated lower left margin: *6 July 1755 A Cozens*
90 × 136 mm
untraced (gift, 1912) (D.1912.14)

Landscape with a wooded Hill
pencil, brown watercolour
signed on mount lower left: *Alexr. Cozens.*
233 × 314 mm
Sadler, Sir Michael E. (gift, 1921) (D.1921.24)

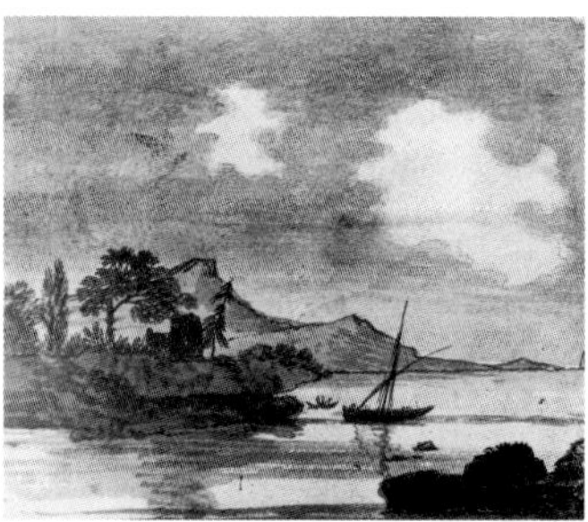
D.1921.25

Boats beside the Shore with Mountains beyond
pencil, pen and brown ink, brown watercolour
signed on mount lower left: *Alexr. Cozens.*
157 × 183 mm
Sadler, Sir Michael E. (gift, 1921) (D.1921.25)

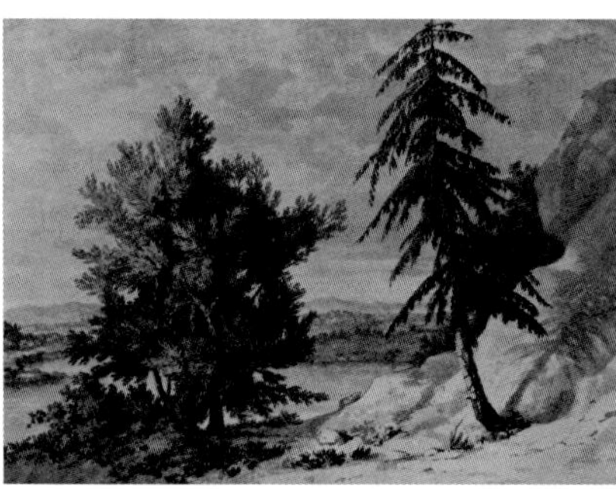
D.1922.7

Study of two Trees
brown watercolour; paper (prepared brown)
367 × 487 mm
Agnew, Gerald (gift, 1922) (D.1922.7)

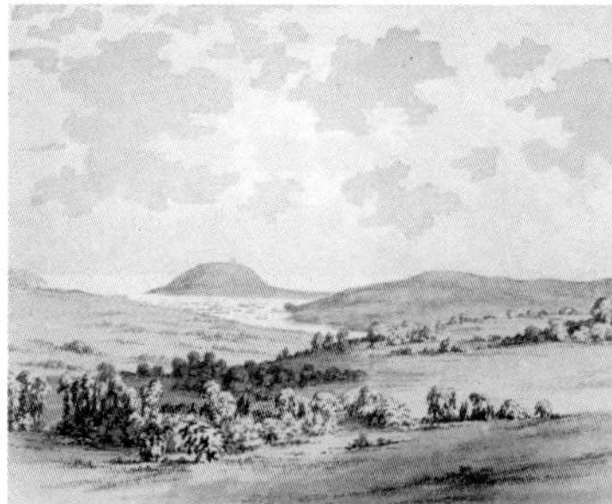
D.1925.26

Weymouth Harbour, Dorset, with Portland Bill in the Distance
pencil, watercolour
178 × 261 mm
Cotswold Gallery, London (purchase, 1925) (D.1925.26)

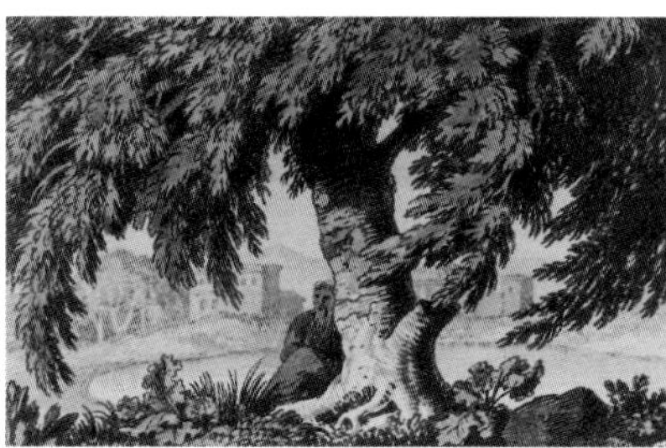
D.1927.110

Classical Landscape: A bearded Man seated under a Tree
1764
brown watercolour
signed, inscribed & dated verso: *A Singleton Invt.1764 A Cozens delt.*
127 × 195 mm
Holliday, J. R. (bequest, 1927) (D.1927.110)

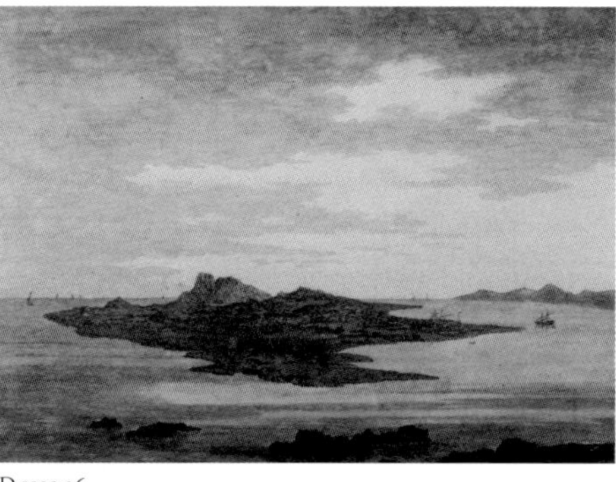
D.1929.26

A rocky Island
pen, brown ink, brown watercolour
signed on mount lower left: *Alexr.Cozens.*
463 × 625 mm
Anderson, A. E. (gift, 1929) (D.1929.26)

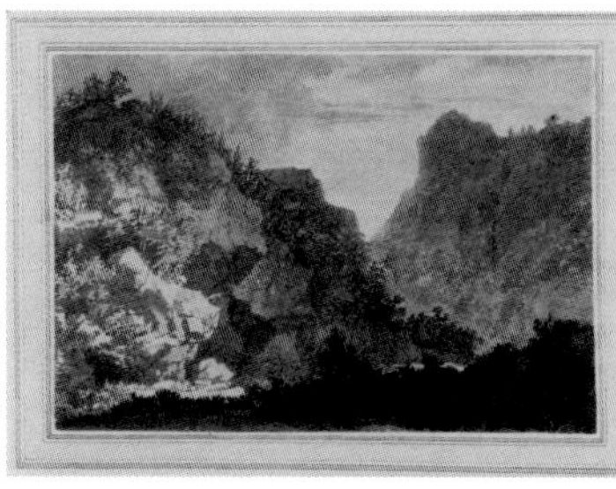
D.1931.18

A Mountain Gorge
brown watercolour
212 × 304 mm
Sadler, Sir Michael E., National Art Collections Fund (via) (gift, 1931) (D.1931.18)

Study of a Tree
grey watercolour
378 × 441 mm
Sadler, Sir Michael E., National Art Collections Fund (via) (gift, 1931) (D.1931.19)

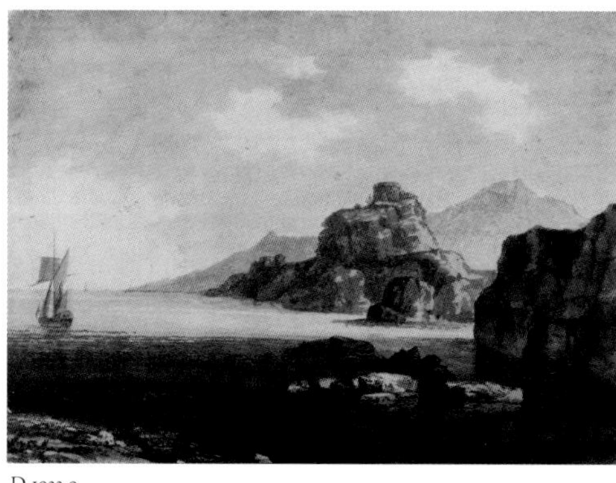
D.1933.9

A rocky Seascape
pen and brown ink, brown watercolour
493 × 659 mm
Sadler, Sir Michael E., National Art Collections Fund (via) (gift, 1933) (D.1933.9)

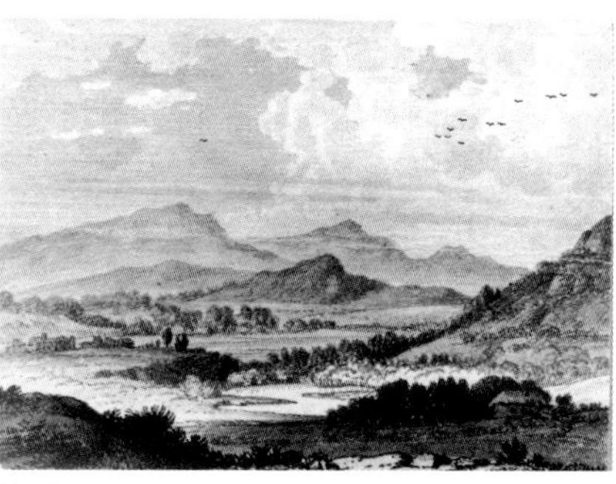
D.1933.10

Landscape with Mountains and Lake
pen and brown ink, brown watercolour
100 × 136 mm
Anderson, A. E. (gift, 1933) (D.1933.10)

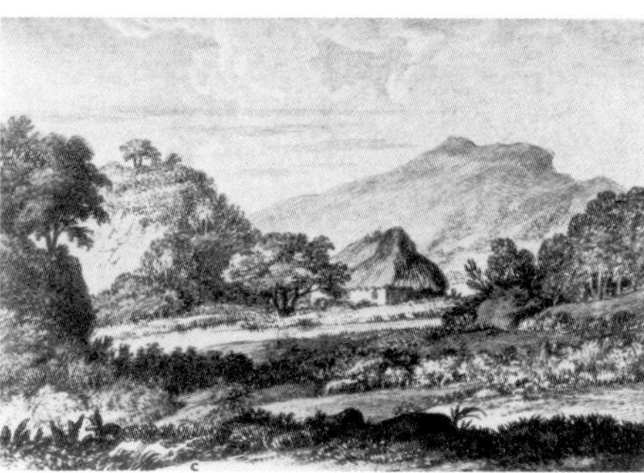
D.1933.11

Mountainous Landscape with Cottage
pen and brown ink, brown watercolour
signed (?) lower left: *C*
98 × 139 mm
Anderson, A. E. (gift, 1933) (D.1933.11)

Classical Landscape Study
black chalk; paper (prepared brown)
signed on mount lower left: *Alexr. Cozens.*
257 × 401 mm
Friends of the Whitworth (gift, 1934) (D.1934.5)

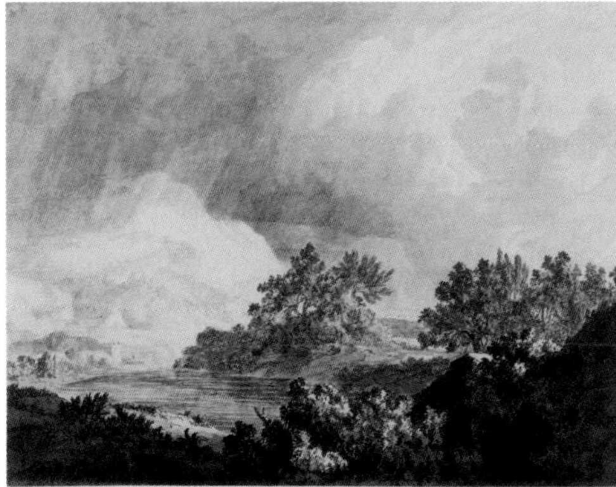
D.1934.8

Rainstorm over Mountains
pencil, brown watercolour
432 × 542 mm
Friends of the Whitworth (gift, 1934) (D.1934.8)

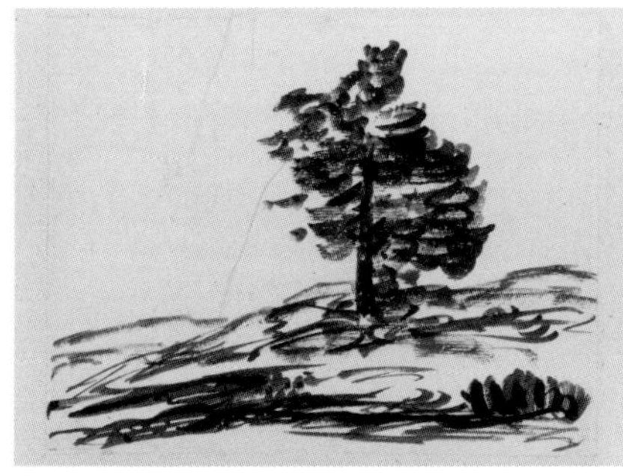
D.1936.7

Study of a Tree (blot drawing)
brown watercolour
159 × 197 mm
Friends of the Whitworth (gift, 1936) (D.1936.7)

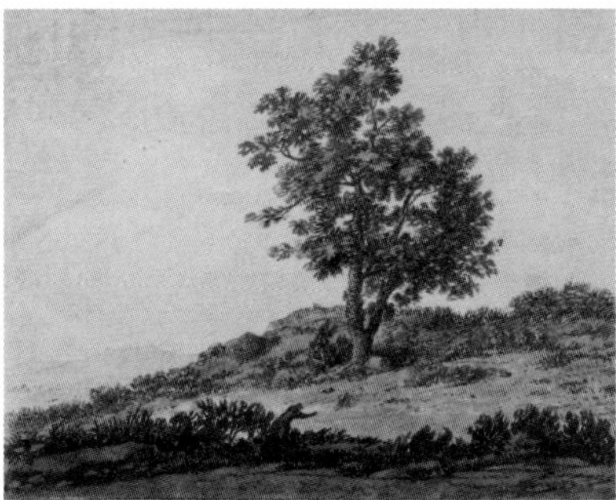
D.1936.8

Study of a Tree (finished drawing)
brown watercolour
161 × 198 mm
Friends of the Whitworth (gift, 1936) (D.1936.8)

Blot Landscape: A Hill, Lake and Trees
brown watercolour
signed on mount lower left: *Alexr. Cozens.*
129 × 176 mm
Scott-Elliot, Miss Aydua, in memory of Paul Oppé
(gift, 4.11.1999) (D.1999.14)

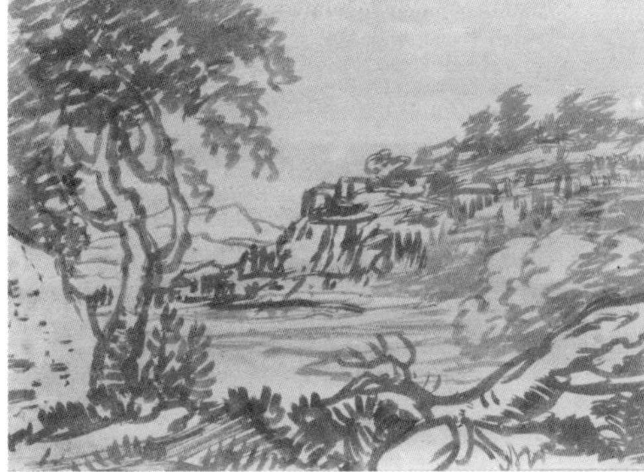
D.1999.14

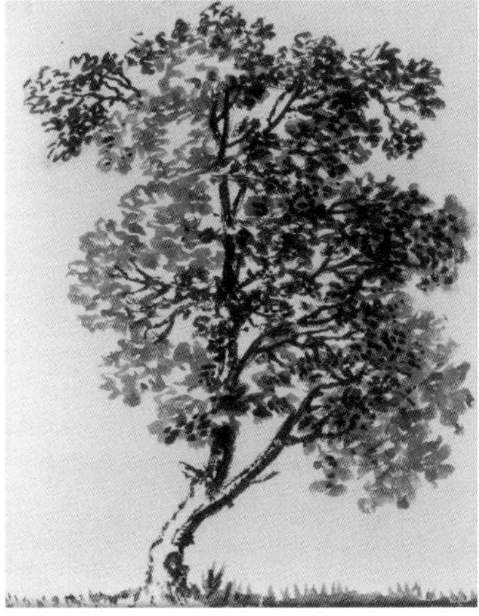
D.1999.15

Study of a Birch Tree
brown watercolour
99 × 75 mm
Scott-Elliot, Miss Aydua, in memory of Paul Oppé
(gift, 4.11.1999) (D.1999.15)

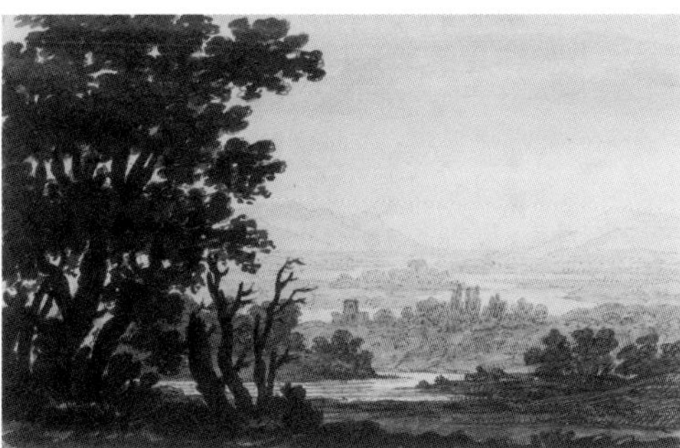
D.1999.16

Classical Landscape : A wide Valley
pen and brown ink, grey watercolour
numbered upper right: *23*
127 × 193 mm
Scott-Elliot, Miss Aydua, in memory of Paul Oppé
(gift, 4.11.1999) (D.1999.16)

Blot Landscape: Trees by a Lake
brown watercolour
157 × 201 mm
Scott-Elliot, Miss Aydua, in memory of Paul Oppé
(gift, 4.11.1999) (D.1999.17)

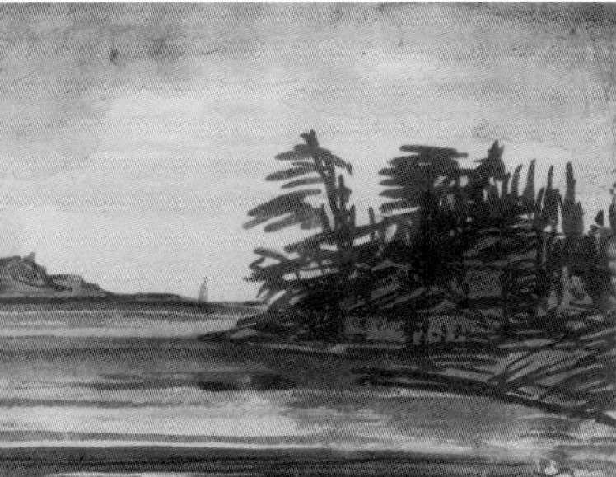
D.1999.17

■ Cozens, John Robert (1752–97)

John Robert Cozens, perhaps one of the most famous
of English watercolourists, was his father Alexander's
pupil. He visited Italy from 1776 to 1779 with Richard
Payne Knight and again in 1782–83 with William
Beckford. On his return to England, he was chiefly
occupied in producing finished watercolours of his
sketches made in Europe, some of which exist in many
versions. His ability to record atmosphere with a very
limited range of colours remains unsurpassed: John
Constable described him as 'the greatest genius that
ever touched landscape'.

**View from Mirabella looking towards the Villa
Luvigliano in the Euganean Hills, Italy**
pencil, watercolour
263 × 372 mm
Agnew's (purchase, 22.6.1891) (D.1887.1)

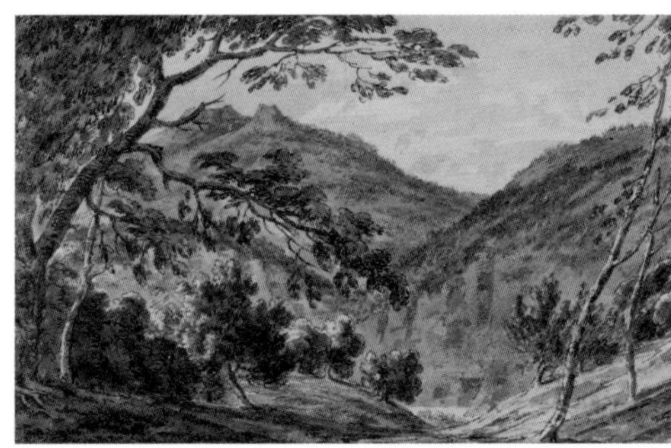
D.1892.4

Near Sallanches, Savoy, France
pencil, pen and brown ink, watercolour
237 × 362 mm
Taylor, John Edward (gift, 1892) (D.1892.4)

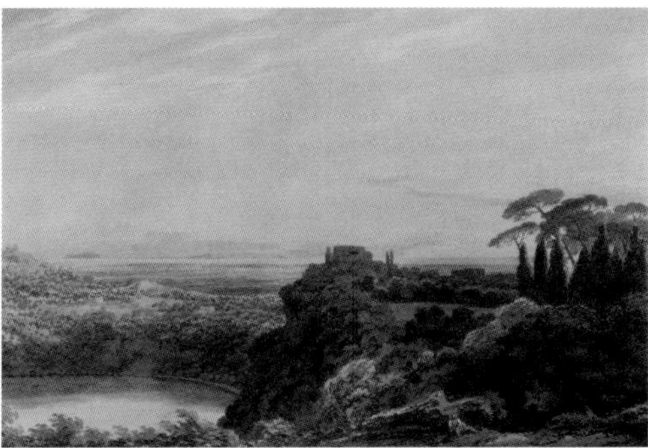
D.1892.24

**The Lake of Nemi looking towards
Genzano, Italy**
watercolour
360 × 528 mm
Taylor, John Edward (gift, 1892) (D.1892.24)

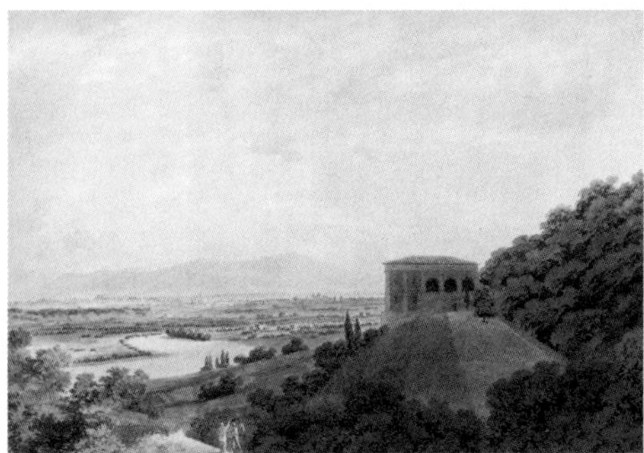

D.1892.25

Rome from the Villa Madama
1791
pencil, watercolour
signed & dated on mount lower left; signature and
date now trimmed: *J.Cozens 1791*
369 × 533 mm
Taylor, John Edward (gift, 1892) (D.1892.25)

**The Lake of Nemi looking towards
Genzano, Italy**
pencil, watercolour
259 × 376 mm
Taylor, John Edward (gift, 1892) (D.1892.121)

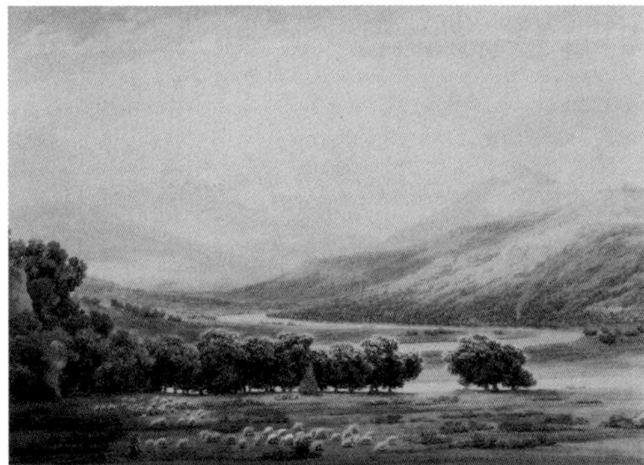

D.1904.72

The Valley of Isarco, near Brixen, Italy
pencil, watercolour
signed lower left: *John Cozens*
492 × 680 mm
Worthington, Mary (bequest, 1904) (D.1904.72)

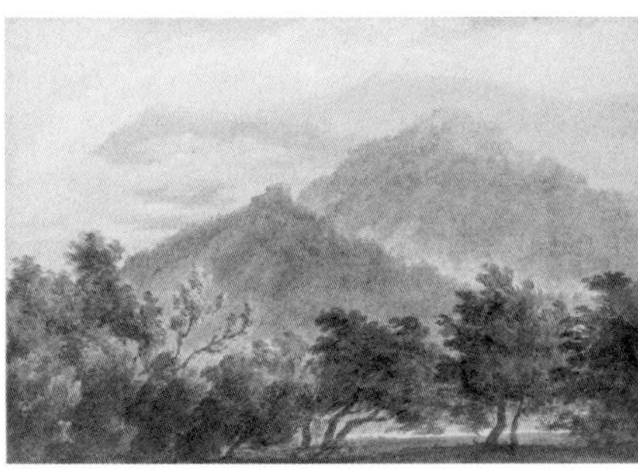

D.1933.31

Between Bolzano and Trent, Italy
pencil, watercolour
258 × 371 mm
Anderson, A. E. (gift, 1933) (D.1933.31)

On the Gulf of Salerno, near Vietri, Italy
pencil, watercolour
257 × 375 mm
Barlow, Sir Thomas (gift, 1950) (D.1950.17)

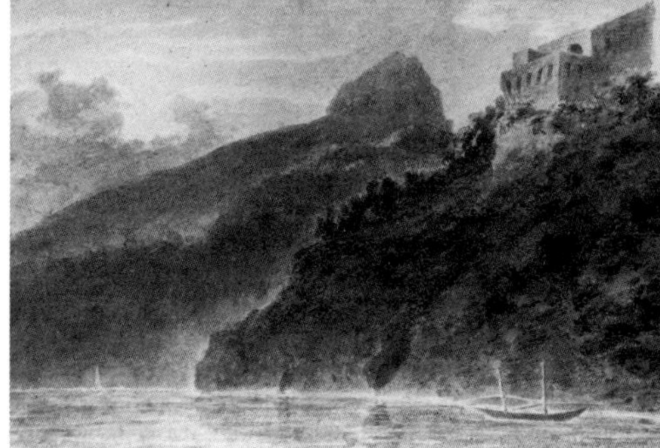

D.1950.17

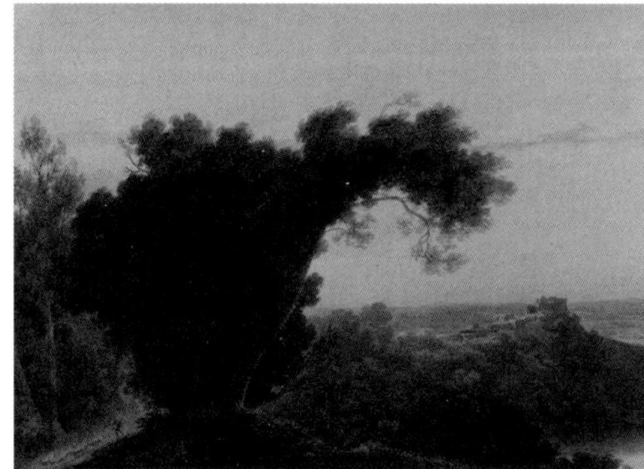

D.1950.18

The Lake of Albano and Castel Gandolfo, Italy
pencil, watercolour
signed lower centre: *J.Cozens*
485 × 668 mm
Barlow, Sir Thomas (gift, 1950) (D.1950.18)

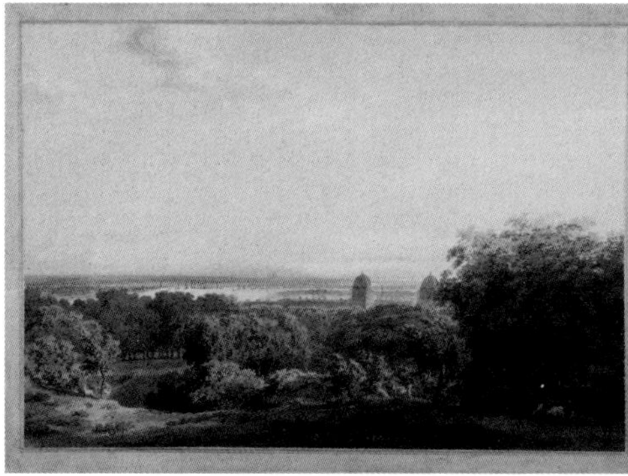

D.1972.16

**A View of the Thames from Greenwich
Park looking over Greenwich Hospital
towards St Paul's**
pencil, watercolour
signed lower centre: *John Cozens*
495 × 704 mm
Agnew's, London (purchase, 1972) (D.1972.16)

The Villa d'Este, Tivoli, Italy
watercolour
378 × 261 mm
Pilkington, Margaret (bequest, 1974) (D.1974.10)

Sketchbook, Volume I
1782
pencil, grey watercolour
185 × 244 mm
Leger Galleries, London (purchase, 1975) (V. & A., N.A.C.F.,
F.O.W., P.T.) (D.1975.4)

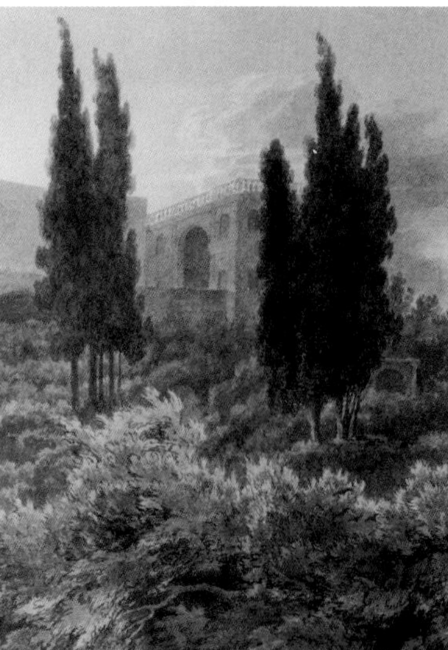

D.1974.10

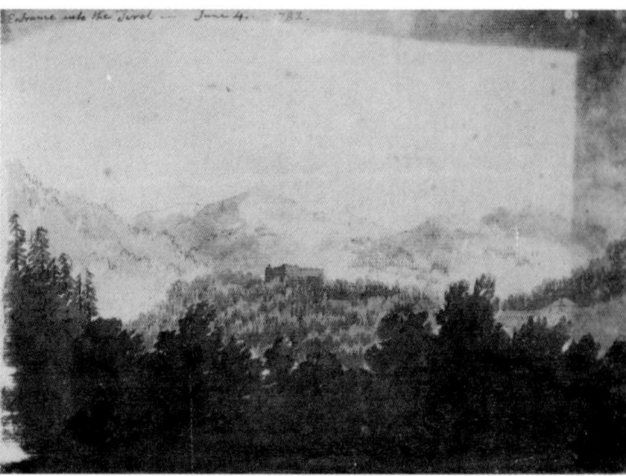

D.1975.4.1

**View of a Castle among Trees at the Entrance
to the Tyrol**
4.6.1782
pencil, grey watercolour
inscribed & dated upper left: *Entrance into the Tirol –
June 4.1782.*
185 × 244 mm
Leger Galleries, London (purchase, 1975) (D.1975.4.1)

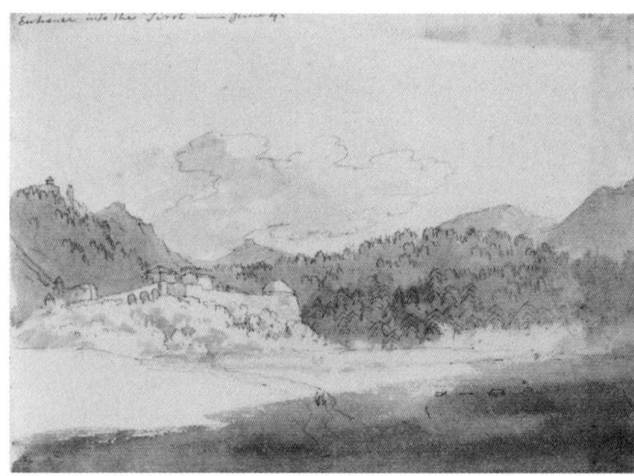

D.1975.4.2

**View of a Castle among Trees at the Entrance
to the Tyrol**
4.6.1782
pencil, grey watercolour
inscribed & dated upper left: *Entrance into the Tirol –
June 4.*
185 × 244 mm
Leger Galleries, London (purchase, 1975) (D.1975.4.2)

Timber Chalets among Fir Trees in the Tyrol
5.6.1782
pencil, grey watercolour
inscribed & dated upper left: *In the Tirol – June 5.*
185 × 244 mm
Leger Galleries, London (purchase, 1975) (D.1975.4.3)

View along the River Inn in the Tyrol
5.6.1782
pencil, grey watercolour
inscribed & dated upper left: *Upon the River Inn in the Tirol – June 5*
185 × 244 mm
Leger Galleries, London (purchase, 1975) (D.1975.4.4)

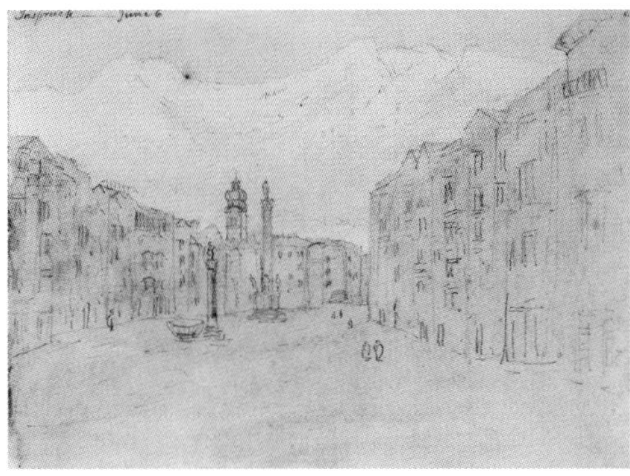
D.1975.4.5

View of Maria-Theresien-Strasse and Anna Saule, Innsbruck
6.6.1782
pencil, grey watercolour
inscribed & dated upper left: *Inspruck* (sic) *– June 6*
185 × 244 mm
Leger Galleries, London (purchase, 1975) (D.1975.4.5)

View of Tree-covered Hills near Innsbruck
6.6.1782
pencil, grey watercolour
inscribed & dated upper left:
Near Inspruck (sic) *– June 6*
185 × 244 mm
Leger Galleries, London (purchase, 1975) (D.1975.4.6)

Chalets on a wooded Hillside between Innsbruck and Schonberg
6.6.1782
pencil, grey watercolour
inscribed & dated upper left: *Between Inspruck* (sic) *& Schonberg – June 6.*
185 × 244 mm
Leger Galleries, London (purchase, 1975) (D.1975.4.7)

View of wooded Mountain Slopes near Schonberg
6.6.1782
pencil
inscribed & dated upper left: *near Schonberg – June 6.*
185 × 244 mm
Leger Galleries, London (purchase, 1975) (D.1975.4.8)

View of a Church among Trees near Sterzing in the Tyrol
7.6.1782
pencil, grey watercolour
inscribed & dated upper left: *Near Stirzengen – Tirol – June 7*
244 × 185 mm
Leger Galleries, London (purchase, 1975) (D.1975.4.9)

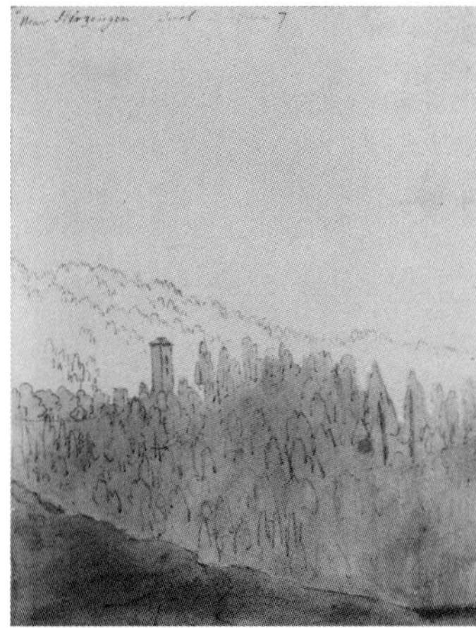
D.1975.4.9

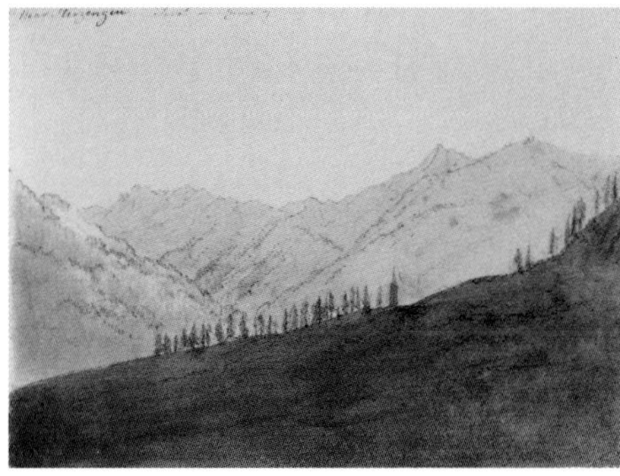
D.1975.4.10

View of a Church Spire among Fir Trees on a Slope near Sterzing in the Tyrol
7.6.1782
pencil, grey watercolour
inscribed & dated upper left: *Near Stirzengen Tirol – June 7*
185 × 244 mm
Leger Galleries, London (purchase, 1975) (D.1975.4.10)

View of Chalets beside a River with Mountains behind, near Brixen in the Tyrol
7.6.1782
pencil
inscribed & dated upper left: *Near Brixen. – June 7*
185 × 244 mm
Leger Galleries, London (purchase, 1975) (D.1975.4.11)

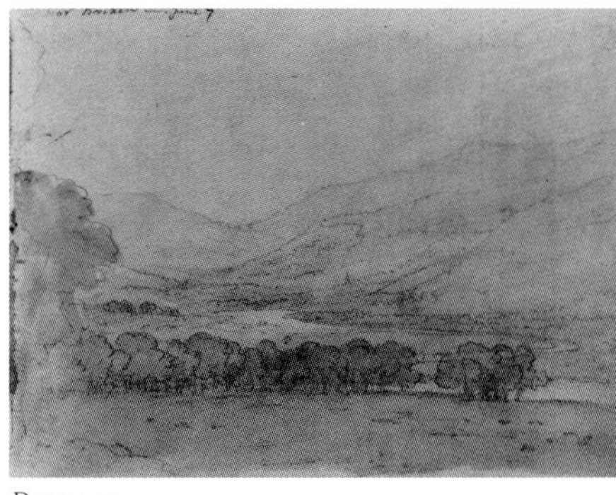
D.1975.4.12

View of the Valley of the Isarco, near Brixen
7.6.1782
pencil, grey watercolour
inscribed & dated upper left: *near Brixen – June 7*
185 × 244 mm
Leger Galleries, London (purchase, 1975) (D.1975.4.12)

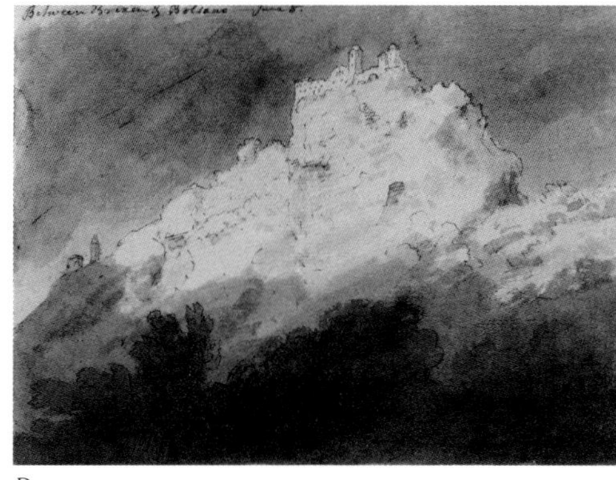
D.1975.4.13

Castle on a wooded Hillside between Brixen and Bolzano
8.6.1782
pencil, grey watercolour
inscribed & dated upper left: *Between Brixen & Bolsano – June 8.*
185 × 244 mm
Leger Galleries, London (purchase, 1975) (D.1975.4.13)

View between Bolzano and Trent in the Tyrol, with the River Adige in the Foreground
8.6.1782
pencil, grey watercolour
inscribed & dated upper left: *Between Bolsano & Trent – June 8*
185 × 244 mm
Leger Galleries, London (purchase, 1975) (D.1975.4.14)

Schloss Hadernburg on a rocky Spur between Bolzano and Trent in the Tyrol
8.6.1782
pencil
inscribed & dated upper right: *Between Bolsano & Trent / June 8.*
244 × 185 mm
Leger Galleries, London (purchase, 1975) (D.1975.4.15)

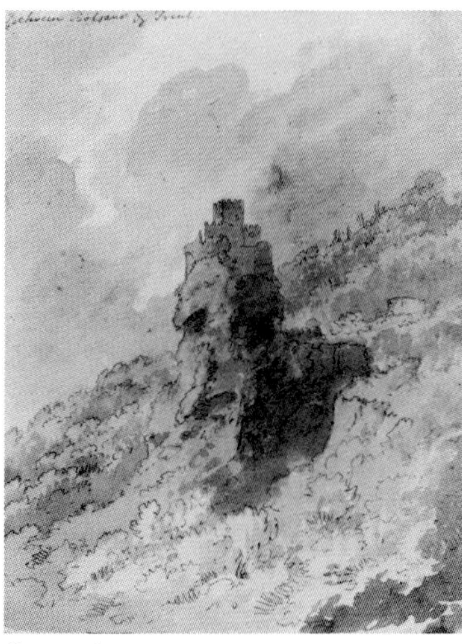
D.1975.4.16

Schloss Hadernburg silhouetted against the Sky
6.1782
pencil, grey watercolour
inscribed upper left: *Between Bolsano & Trent*
244 × 185 mm
Leger Galleries, London (purchase, 1975) (D.1975.4.16)

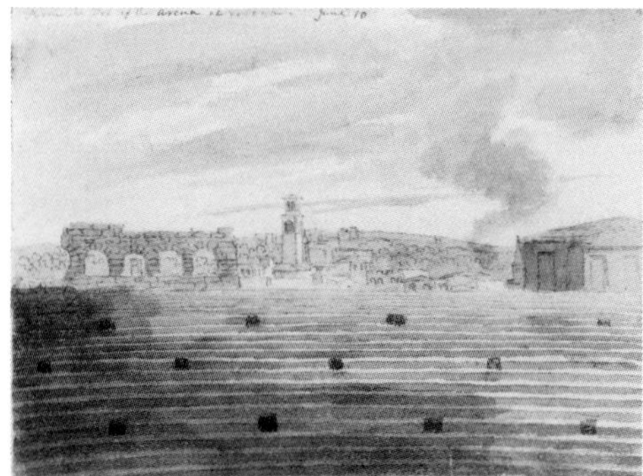

D.1975.4.17

View of the Town from the Arena, Verona
10.6.1782
pencil, grey watercolour
inscribed & dated upper left: *From the Top of the Arena at Verona – June 10*
185 × 244 mm
Leger Galleries, London (purchase, 1975) (D.1975.4.17)

View of the Island of San Giorgio in Alga across the Lagoon, Venice
15.6.1782
pencil
inscribed & dated upper left: *Sant Giorgio in Alga – Venice / June 15*; inscribed upper right: *the light seen thro' the window of / the tower*; inscribed centre right: *Euganian hills*
185 × 244 mm
Leger Galleries, London (purchase, 1975) (D.1975.4.18)

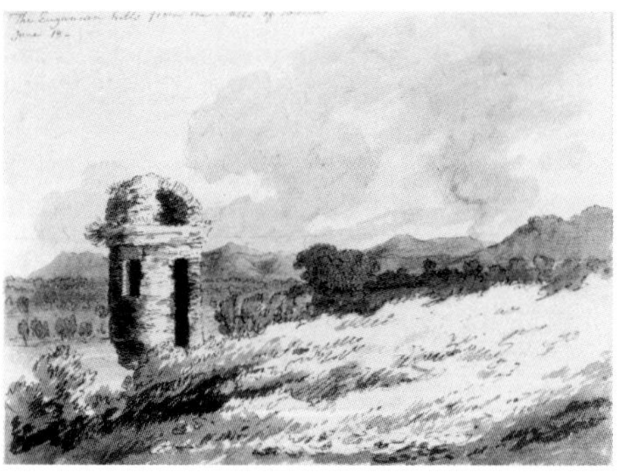

D.1975.4.19

A ruined Well-house in the Euganean Hills, seen from the Walls of Padua
18.6.1782
pencil, grey watercolour
inscribed & dated upper left: *The Euganian hills from the walls of Padua / June 18 –*
185 × 244 mm
Leger Galleries, London (purchase, 1975) (D.1975.4.19)

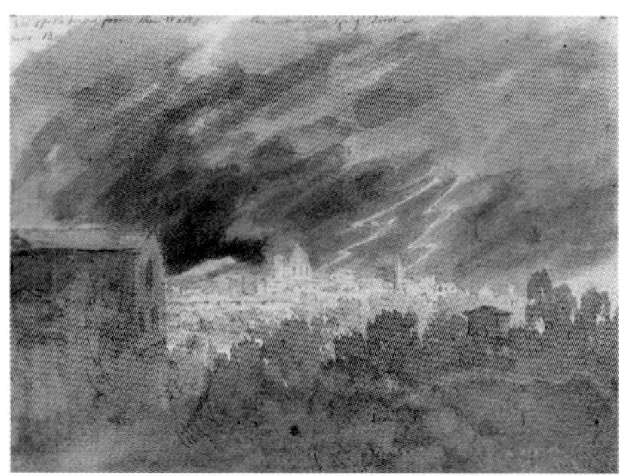

D.1975.4.20

Part of Padua seen from the Walls, Lightning striking the Town
18.6.1782
pencil, grey watercolour
inscribed & dated upper left: *Part of Padua from the Walls – the mountains of ye Tirol – / June 18.*
185 × 244 mm
Leger Galleries, London (purchase, 1975) (D.1975.4.20)

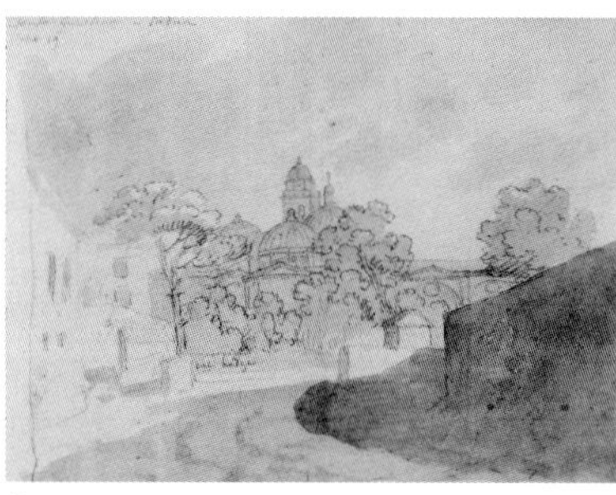

D.1975.4.21

A Tree-lined Road leading to the Church of Santa Giustina, Padua
19.6.1782
pencil, grey watercolour
inscribed & dated upper left: *Santa Giustina – Padua / June 19*
185 × 244 mm
Leger Galleries, London (purchase, 1975) (D.1975.4.21)

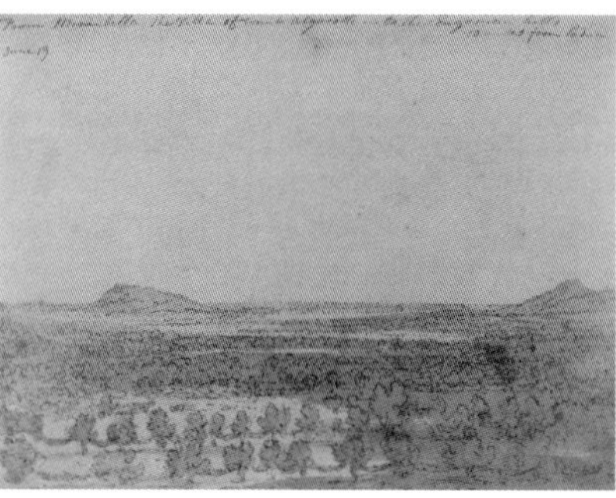

D.1975.4.22

View from the Villa of Count Algarotti, Mirabella, in the Euganean Hills
19.6.1782
pencil, grey watercolour
inscribed & dated top edge: *From Mirabella the Villa of Count Algarotti – On the Euganian hills / 10 miles from Padua / June 19*
185 × 244 mm
Leger Galleries, London (purchase, 1975) (D.1975.4.22)

View of a Convent on a wooded Hillside from Mirabella
6.1782
pencil, grey watercolour
inscribed upper left: *Convent of* [blank] *from Mira – bella –*
185 × 244 mm
Leger Galleries, London (purchase, 1975) (D.1975.4.23)

From Mirabella looking towards the Villa Luvigliano
19.6.1782
pencil, grey watercolour
inscribed & dated upper left: *From Mira – bella – / June 19.*
185 × 244 mm
Leger Galleries, London (purchase, 1975) (D.1975.4.24)

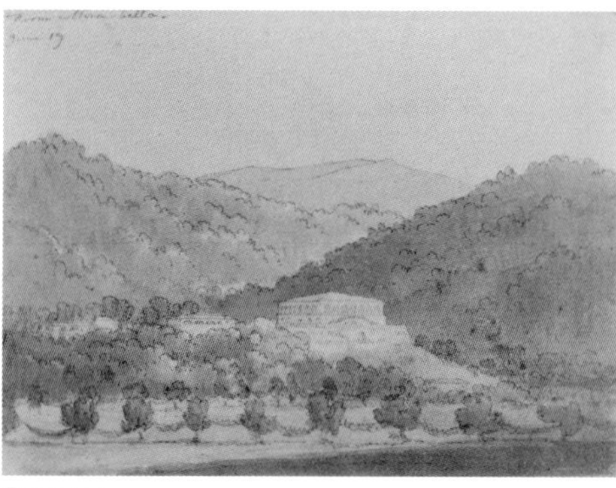

D.1975.4.24

View of Monte della Madonna, the Residence of Petrarch, in the Euganean Hills
19.6.1782
pencil, grey watercolour
inscribed & dated top edge: *Monte della Madona near Arqua the residence of Petrarch – Euganian hills / June 19.*
185 × 244 mm
Leger Galleries, London (purchase, 1975) (D.1975.4.25)

A Castle on a wooded Hillside between Padua and Ferrara
23.6.1782
pencil, grey watercolour
inscribed & dated upper left: *Between Padua & Farara (sic) / June 23.*
185 × 244 mm
Leger Galleries, London (purchase, 1975) (D.1975.4.26)

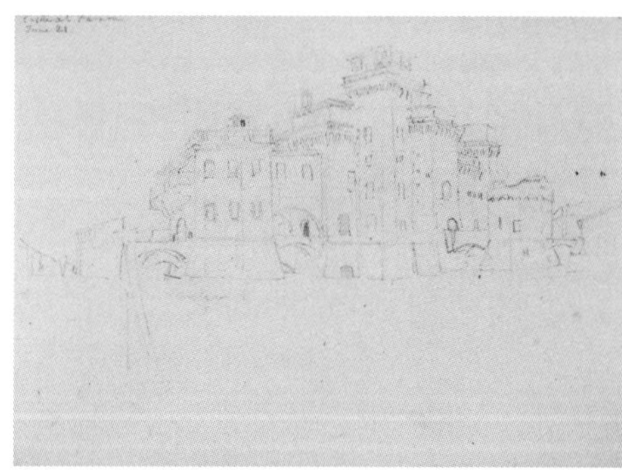

D.1975.4.27

The Castle at Ferrara
21.6.1782
pencil
inscribed & dated upper left: *Castle at Farara. (sic) / June 21.*
185 × 244 mm
Leger Galleries, London (purchase, 1975) (D.1975.4.27)

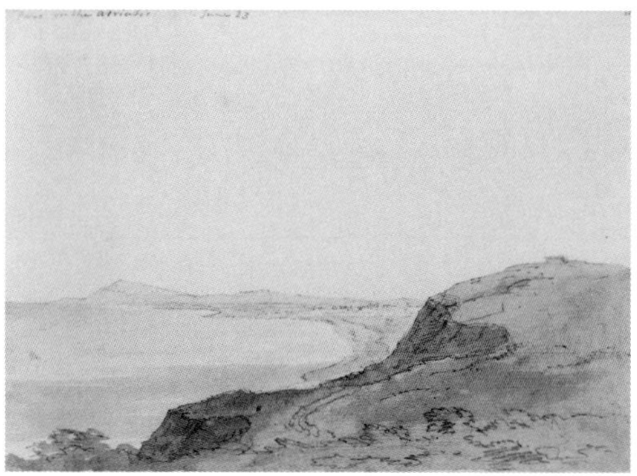

D.1975.4.28

View of the Bay of Fano on the Adriatic Coast
23.6.1782
pencil, grey watercolour
inscribed & dated upper left: *Fano on the Adriatic.*
June 23
185 × 244 mm
Leger Galleries, London (purchase, 1975) (D.1975.4.28)

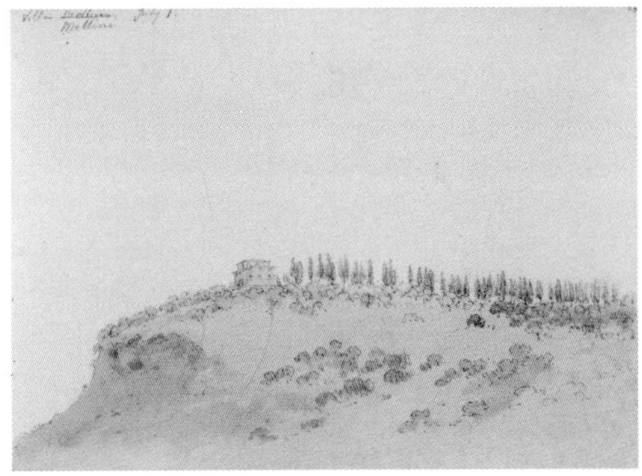
D.1975.4.29

A distant View of the Villa Mellini, near Rome
1.7.1782
pencil, grey watercolour
inscribed & dated upper left: *Villa Mellini* [erased]
Mellini [written below] *July 1.*
185 × 244 mm
Leger Galleries, London (purchase, 1975) (D.1975.4.29)

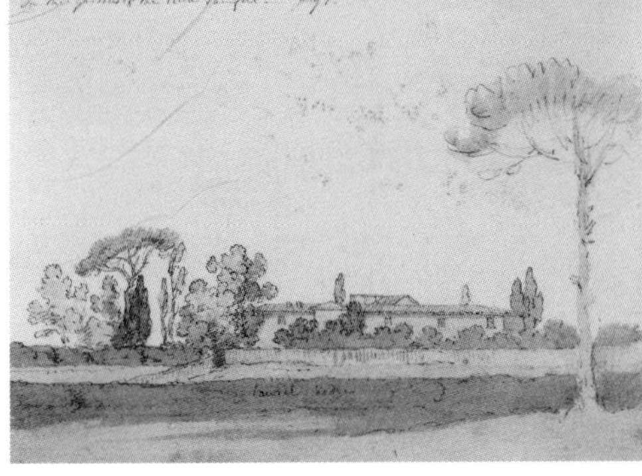
D.1975.4.30

A View of Buildings and Trees in the Gardens of the Villa Pamphili
1.7.1782
pencil, grey watercolour
inscribed & dated upper left: *In the Gardens of the Villa Pamfili – July 1.*; inscribed lower centre: *laurel hedge*
185 × 244 mm
Leger Galleries, London (purchase, 1975) (D.1975.4.30)

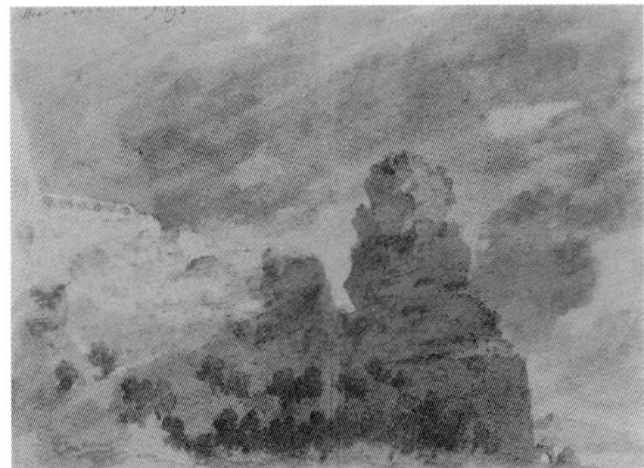
D.1975.4.31

View near Terracina, the Pesco Montano
5.7.1782
pencil, grey watercolour
inscribed & dated upper left: *Near Terracina. July 5.*
185 × 244 mm
Leger Galleries, London (purchase, 1975) (D.1975.4.31)

Part of Terracina, on a Hillside, against a stormy Sky (recto); View of Monte Circeo from Terracina (verso)
5.7.1782
pencil, grey watercolour
inscribed & dated upper left: *Part of Terracina – July 5.*;
inscribed & dated upper left verso: *Monte Circeo from Terracina – July 5.*
185 × 244 mm
Leger Galleries, London (purchase, 1975) (D.1975.4.32)

Sketchbook, Volume II
1782
pencil, grey watercolour
179 × 240 mm
Leger Galleries, London (purchase, 1975) (V. & A., N.A.C.F., F.O.W., P.T.) (D.1975.5)

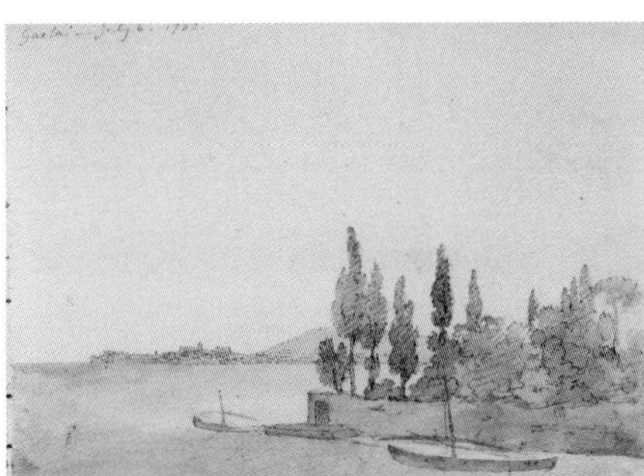
D.1975.5.2

View of Gaeta from across the Bay, near Formia
6.7.1782
pencil, grey watercolour
inscribed & dated upper left: *Gaeta – July 6.1782*
179 × 240 mm
Leger Galleries, London (purchase, 1975) (D.1975.5.2)

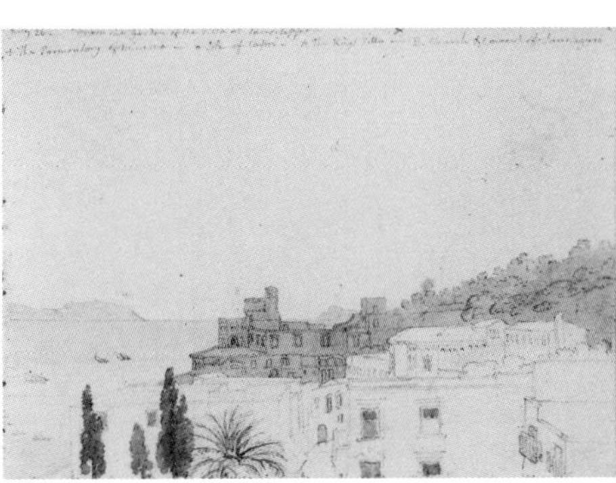
D.1975.5.3

View from the Garden at Posillipo
26.7.1782
pencil, grey watercolour
inscribed & dated upper left: *July 26 – From the Garden of the Villa at Pausilippo –* ; inscribed upper edge; below inscription and date the key identifying the symbols on the drawing: + *The Promontory of Minerva – o Isle of Capri- A. The King's Villa- B. Church & Convent of Lanazzaro*
179 × 240 mm
Leger Galleries, London (purchase, 1975) (D.1975.5.3)

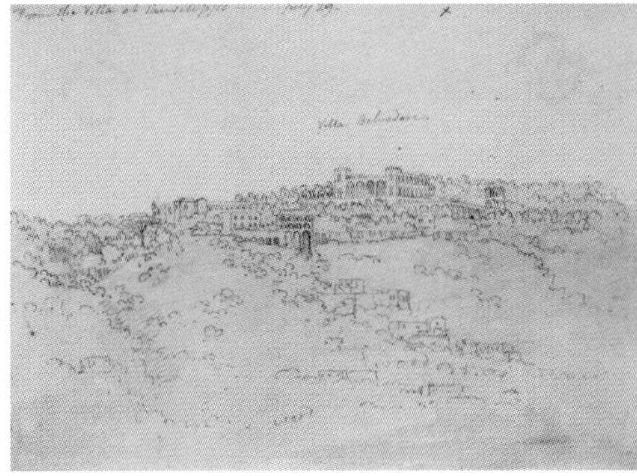
D.1975.5.4

View of the Villa Belvedere from the Villa at Posillipo
29.7.1782
pencil, grey watercolour
inscribed & dated upper left: *From the Villa at Pausilippo – July 29.*; inscribed upper centre identifying the building: *Villa Belvedere*
179 × 240 mm
Leger Galleries, London (purchase, 1975) (D.1975.5.4)

Virgil's Tomb
1.8.1782
pencil, grey watercolour
inscribed & dated: *Virgil's Tomb. August.1.*
179 × 240 mm
Leger Galleries, London (purchase, 1975) (D.1975.5.5)

Sunset at Portici
9.8.1782
pencil
inscribed & dated upper left: *at Portici – August 9 – evening.*
179 × 240 mm
Leger Galleries, London (purchase, 1975) (D.1975.5.6)

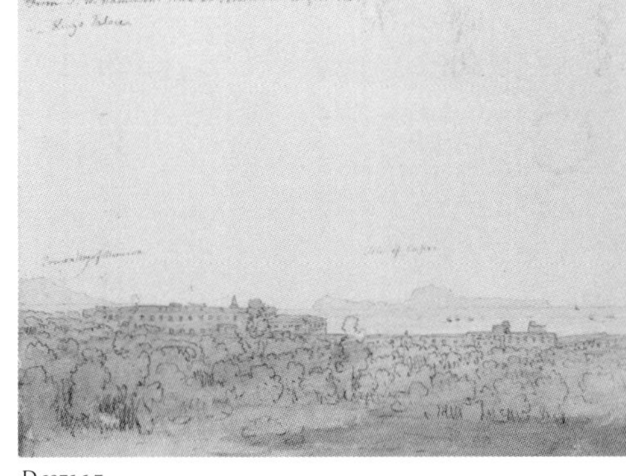
D.1975.5.7

View from Sir William Hamilton's Villa at Portici
12.8.1782
pencil, grey watercolour
inscribed & dated upper left: *From Sr.W Hamilton's Villa at Portici. – August 12.*; inscribed upper left; below inscription and date the key identifying a symbol on the drawing: *x – King's Palace*; inscribed left centre: *Promontory of Minerva*; inscribed lower centre: *Isle of Capri*
179 × 240 mm
Leger Galleries, London (purchase, 1975) (D.1975.5.7)

View from Sir William Hamilton's Villa at Portici

12.8.1782

pencil, grey watercolour

inscribed & dated upper left: *From Sr.W Hamilton's Villa at Portici – August 12.*; inscribed upper left; below inscription and date the key identifying symbols on the drawing: *x Isle of Ischia – A.Part of Portici – B Procida*

179 × 240 mm

Leger Galleries, London (purchase, 1975) (D.1975.5.8)

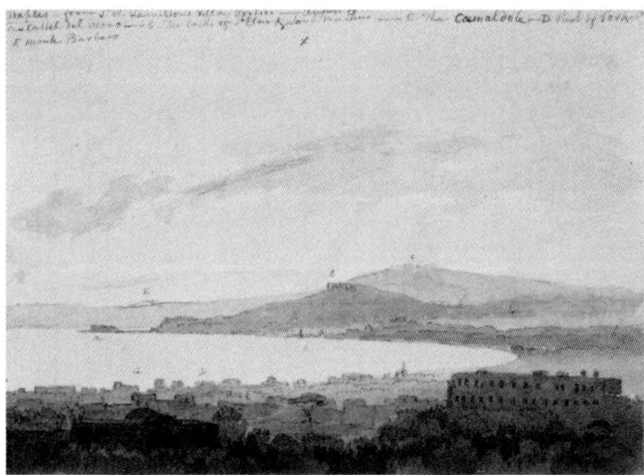

D.1975.5.9

View of Naples from Sir William Hamilton's Villa at Portici

19.8.1782

pencil, grey watercolour

inscribed & dated upper left: *Naples – from Sr W.Hamilton's Villa.Portici – August 19*; inscribed upper edge; below inscripton and date the key identifying symbols on the drawing: *a – Castel del Novo – b – The Castle of St. Elmo & San Martini (?) – C. The Camaldole – D. Part of Portici / E. Monte Barbaro*

179 × 240 mm

Leger Galleries, London (purchase, 1975) (D.1975.5.9)

A panoramic View from the Myrtle Plantation at Sir William Hamilton's Villa at Portici

18.8.1782

pencil, grey watercolour

inscribed & dated upper left of left hand page: *From the Myrtle Plantation at Sr.W.Hamilton's Villa – Portici – August 18*

179 × 480 mm

Leger Galleries, London (purchase, 1975) (D.1975.5.9/10)

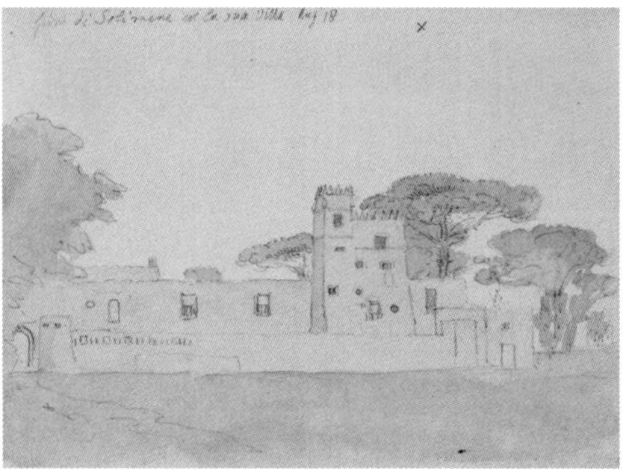

D.1975.5.11

Solimena's Villa and Pines

18.8.1782

pencil, grey watercolour

inscribed & dated upper left in Italian: *pini di Solimene col la sua Villa Aug 18*

179 × 240 mm

Leger Galleries, London (purchase, 1975) (D.1975.5.11)

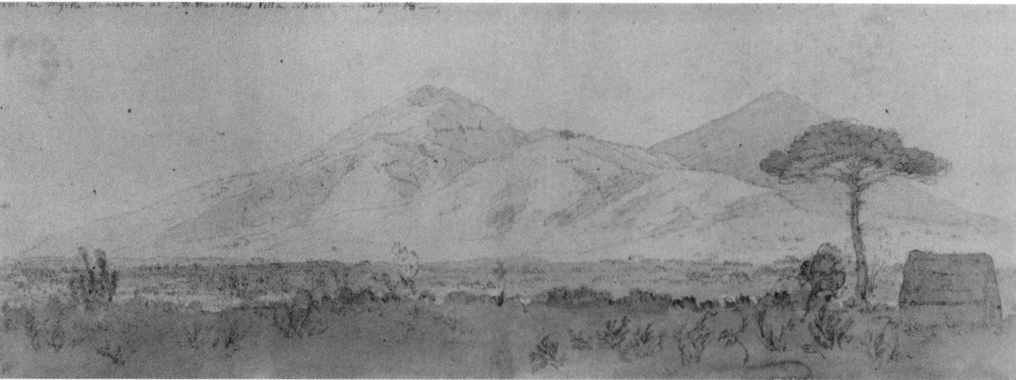

D.1975.5.9/10

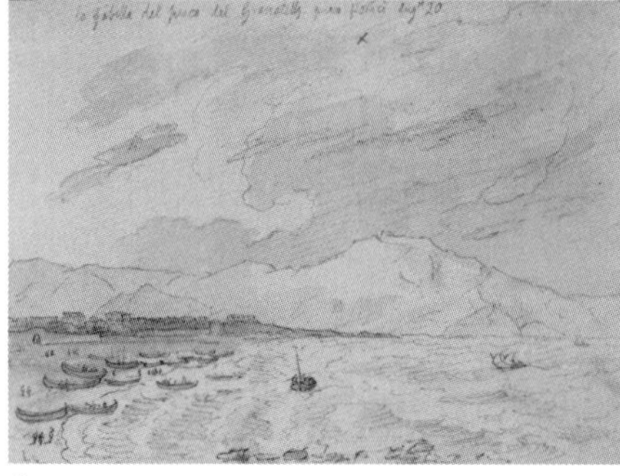

D.1975.5.12

The Fish Tax at the Granatello, near Portici

20.8.1782

pencil, grey watercolour

inscribed & dated upper edge in Italian: *la Gabella del pesce del Granatello presso Portici Augst 20*

179 × 240 mm

Leger Galleries, London (purchase, 1975) (D.1975.5.12)

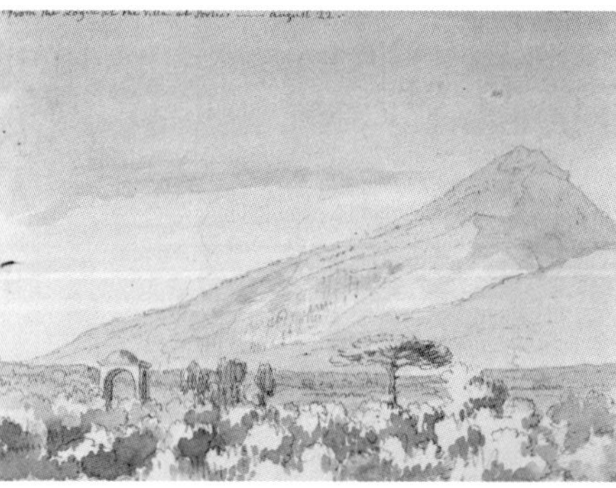

D.1975.5.13

View of Mount Somma from the Loggia at the Villa at Portici

22.8.1782

pencil, grey watercolour

inscribed & dated upper left: *From the Logia* (sic) *at the Villa at Portici – August 22.*

179 × 240 mm

Leger Galleries, London (purchase, 1975) (D.1975.5.13)

An Avenue in the Boschetto at Portici, with Vesuvius in the Distance

23.8.1782

pencil, grey watercolour

inscribed & dated upper left: *In the Boschetto at Portici – August 23*; inscribed left centre, identifying the mountain in the distance: *Vesuve*

240 × 179 mm

Leger Galleries, London (purchase, 1975) (D.1975.5.14)

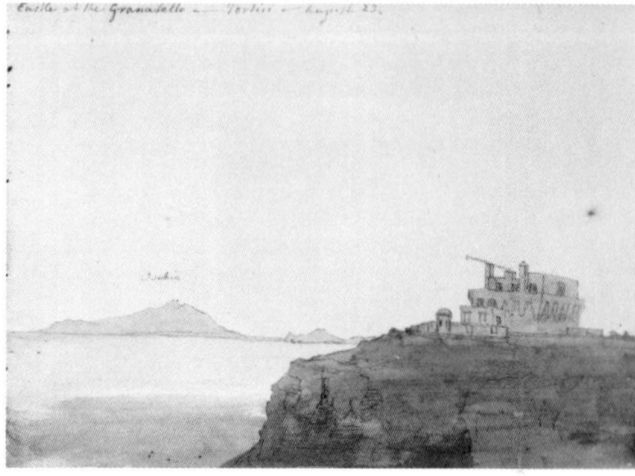

D.1975.5.15

Castle at the Granatello, Portici, with Ischia in the Distance

23.8.1782

pencil, grey watercolour

inscribed & dated upper left: *Castle at the Granatello – Portici – August 23.*; inscribed left centre, identifying the island on the horizon: *Ischia*

179 × 240 mm

Leger Galleries, London (purchase, 1975) (D.1975.5.15)

The Fortress in the Boschetto at Portici

26.8.1782

pencil, grey watercolour

inscribed & dated upper left: *The Fortress in the Boschetto – Portici – August 26.*

179 × 240 mm

Leger Galleries, London (purchase, 1975) (D.1975.5.16)

The King's Pallone Court in the Boschetto at Portici

26.8.1782

pencil, grey watercolour

inscribed & dated upper left: *In the Boschetto – the place where the king plays at Palloni* (sic) *– August 26 –*

179 × 240 mm

Leger Galleries, London (purchase, 1975) (D.1975.5.17)

View of the King's Palace at Portici, with Vesuvius in the Distance

28.8.1782

pencil, grey watercolour

inscribed & dated upper left: *King's Palace at Portici – August 28 –*

179 × 240 mm

Leger Galleries, London (purchase, 1975) (D.1975.5.18)

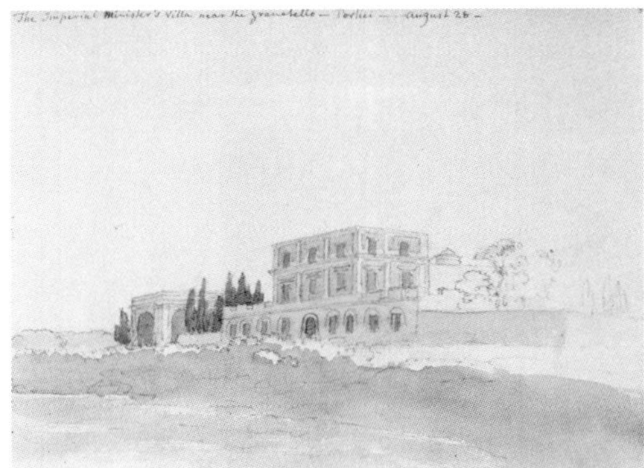

D.1975.5.19

The Imperial Minister's Villa near the Granatello, Portici (recto); An Opening in a Wall (verso)
28.8.1782
pencil, grey watercolour
inscribed & dated upper left: *The Imperial Minister's Villa near the Granatello – Portici – August 28 –* ;
inscribed upper centre verso: *Form of the / opening in the / wall*
179 × 240 mm
Leger Galleries, London (purchase, 1975) (D.1975.5.19)

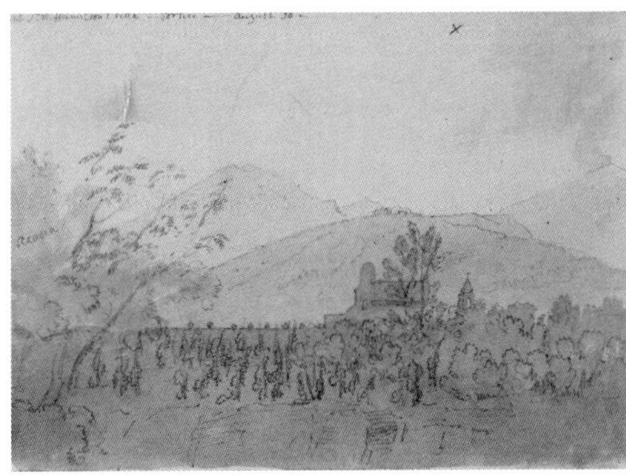

D.1975.5.20

View at Sir William Hamilton's Villa at Portici, with a Convent and Vesuvius in the Distance
30.8.1782
pencil, grey watercolour
inscribed & dated upper left: *At Sr. W. Hamilton's Villa – Portici – August 30 –*
179 × 240 mm
Leger Galleries, London (purchase, 1975) (D.1975.5.20)

An Aloe in Flower, cut down from a Wall of Lava, near Portici
30.8.1782
pencil
inscribed & dated upper left of right hand page: *An Aloe in flower-cut down from a wall of lava near Portici – August 30*
179 × 480 mm
Leger Galleries, London (purchase, 1975) (D.1975.5.20/21)

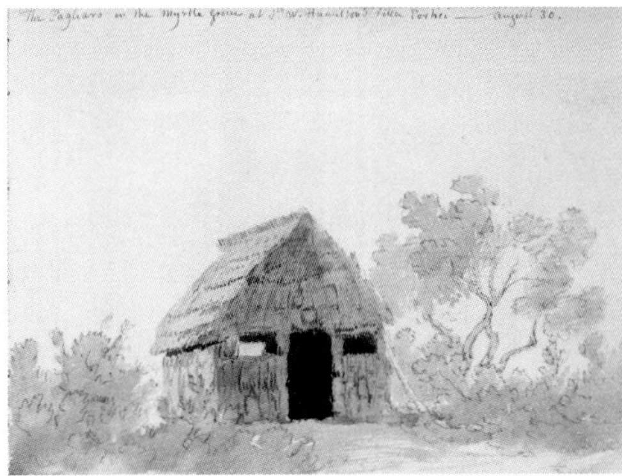

D.1975.5.22

The Straw Hut in the Myrtle Grove at Sir William Hamilton's Villa at Portici
30.8.1782
pencil, grey watercolour
inscribed & dated upper left: *The Pagliaro in the Myrtle Grove at Sr. W. Hamilton's Villa Portici – August 30.*
179 × 240 mm
Leger Galleries, London (purchase, 1975) (D.1975.5.22)

The Mole at Portici with Fishermen and their Boats
31.8.1782
pencil, grey watercolour
inscribed & dated upper left: *The Mole at Portici – August 31.*
179 × 240 mm
Leger Galleries, London (purchase, 1975) (D.1975.5.23)

View of Portici from the Sea with Vesuvius and Somma in the Distance
1.9.1782
pencil, grey watercolour
inscribed & dated upper left: *Portici – September 1*
179 × 240 mm
Leger Galleries, London (purchase, 1975) (D.1975.5.24)

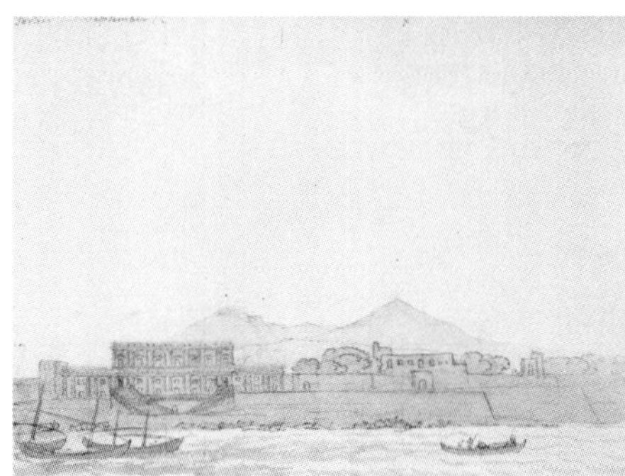

D.1975.5.24

View of the King's Palace at Portici from the Boschetto, with Capri in the Distance
2.9.1782
pencil, grey watercolour
inscribed & dated upper left of right hand page: *King's Palace at Portici – from the Boschetto – Sepr. – 2.*; inscribed left centre of right hand page identifying the island on the horizon: *Capri*
179 × 480 mm
Leger Galleries, London (purchase, 1975) (D.1975.5.24/25)

View from the Russian Minister's House at Portici
3.9.1782
pencil, grey watercolour
inscribed & dated upper left of right hand page: *From the Russian Minister's house – Portici – Septr.3.*
179 × 480 mm
Leger Galleries, London (purchase, 1975) (D.1975.5.25/26)

View by the Sea at Portici, the Villa D'Elbeuf in the Foreground, the Granatello and the Mole in the middle Distance
6.9.1782
pencil, grey watercolour
inscribed & dated upper left: *On the Sea side at Portici – Septr.6*
179 × 240 mm
Leger Galleries, London (purchase, 1975) (D.1975.5.27)

View from the Palace at Portici, with Capri on the Horizon
7.9.1782
pencil, grey watercolour
inscribed & dated upper left: *From the Palace at Portici – Septr.7.*; inscribed centre right identifying the island on the horizon: *capri*
179 × 240 mm
Leger Galleries, London (purchase, 1975) (D.1975.5.28)

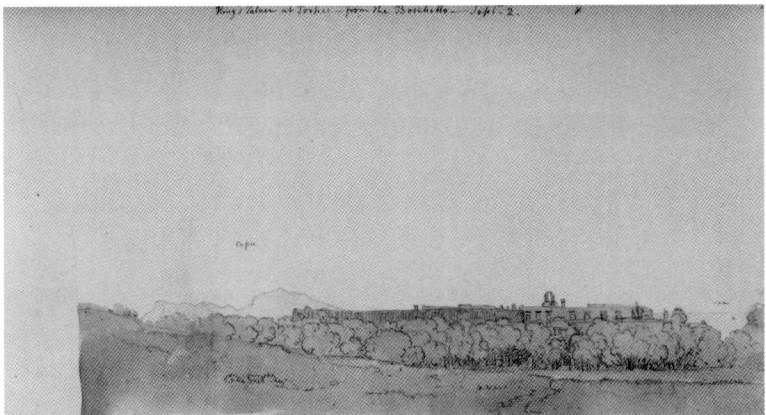
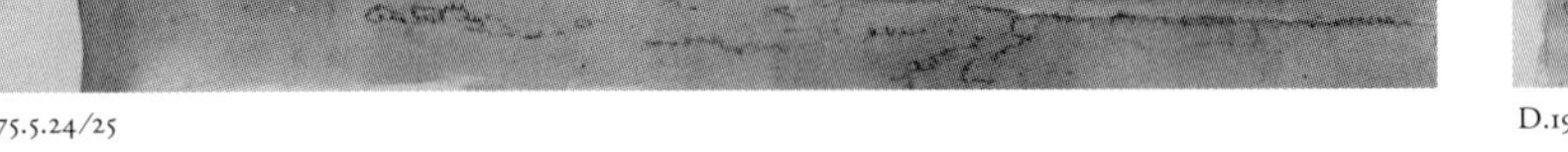

D.1975.5.24/25

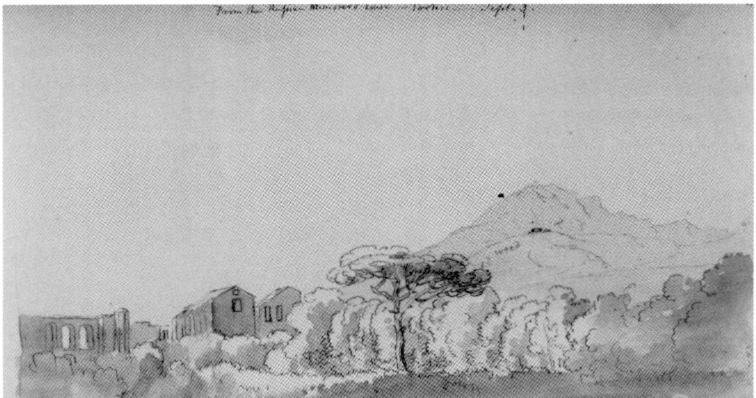

D.1975.5.25/26

View of the Sea Shore at Portici, with the Villa D'Elbeuf in the Foreground
7.9.1782
pencil, grey watercolour
inscribed & dated upper left: *Sea Shore at Portici – Septr.7*
179 × 240 mm
Leger Galleries, London (purchase, 1975) (D.1975.5.29)

Sketchbook, Volume III
1782
pencil, grey watercolour
178 × 241 mm
Leger Galleries, London (purchase, 1975) (V. & A., N.A.C.F., F.O.W., P.T.) (D.1975.6)

View of Salerno
18.9.1782
pencil, grey watercolour
inscribed & dated upper left: *Salerno – Septr.18 – 1782*; inscribed upper left verso: *See Dryden's Sig* [erased] *Tancred & Sygismunda*
241 × 178 mm
Leger Galleries, London (purchase, 1975) (D.1975.6.1)

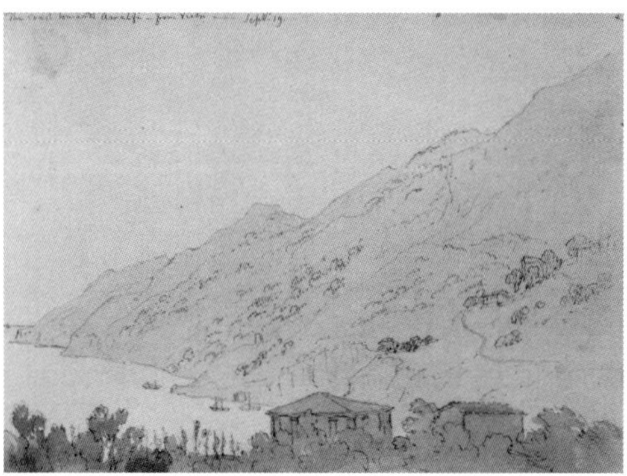

D.1975.6.2

View of the Coast towards Amalfi looking from Vietri
19.9.1782
pencil, grey watercolour
inscribed & dated upper left: *The Coast towards Amalfi – from Vietri – Septr.19.*
178 × 241 mm
Leger Galleries, London (purchase, 1975) (D.1975.6.2)

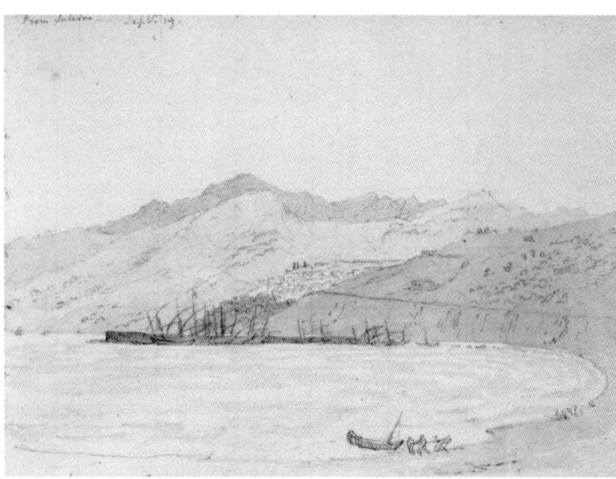

D.1975.6.3

View from Salerno looking towards Vietri
19.9.1782
pencil, grey watercolour
inscribed & dated upper left: *From Salerno – Septr.19.*
178 × 241 mm
Leger Galleries, London (purchase, 1975) (D.1975.6.3)

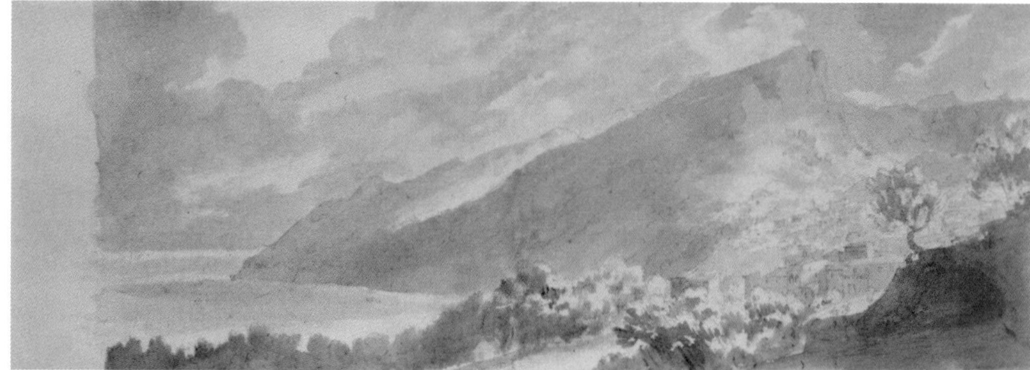

D.1975.6.3/4

View of Vietri and Raito on the Bay of Salerno, with Monte Pertuso
20.9.1782
pencil, grey watercolour
inscribed & dated upper left of right hand page: *Vietri & Raito – Septr.20.*
178 × 482 mm
Leger Galleries, London (purchase, 1975) (D.1975.6.3/4)

Villa on a Cliff in the Valley, near Vietri
20.9.1782
pencil, grey watercolour
inscribed & dated upper left: *In the Valley near Vietri – Septr.20*
178 × 241 mm
Leger Galleries, London (purchase, 1975) (D.1975.6.5)

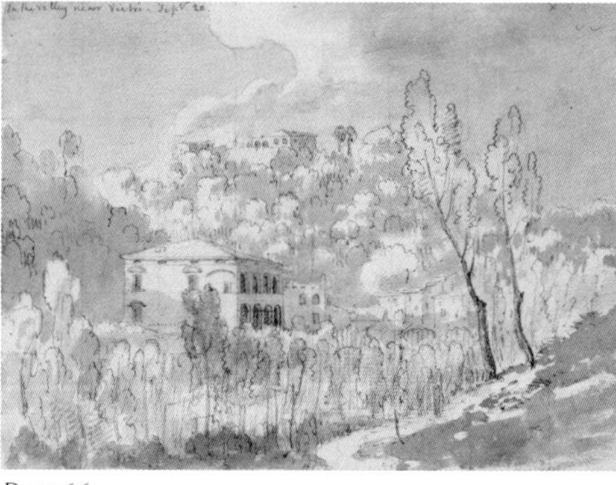

D.1975.6.6

Villas among Trees in the Valley, near Vietri
20.9.1782
pencil, grey watercolour
inscribed & dated upper left: *In the Valley near Vietri Sept.20*
178 × 241 mm
Leger Galleries, London (purchase, 1975) (D.1975.6.6)

View of the Sea near Raito on the Gulf of Salerno
20.9.1782
pencil, grey watercolour
inscribed & dated upper left: *Near Raito on the Gulf / of Salerno – Septr.20*; inscribed upper right the key to a symbol on the drawing: *A. The place near which Pestum (sic) stands*
178 × 241 mm
Leger Galleries, London (purchase, 1975) (D.1975.6.7)

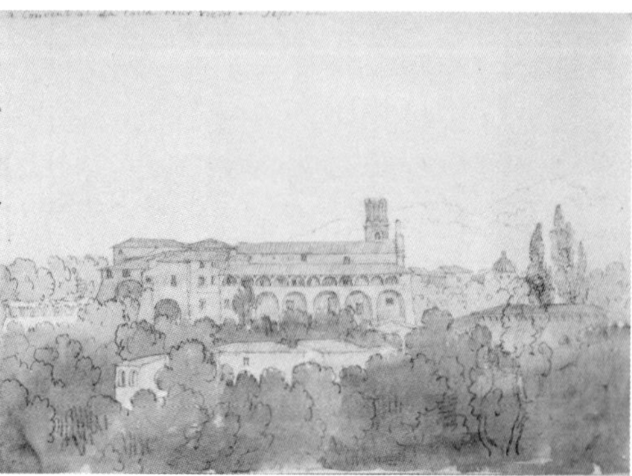

D.1975.6.8

View of a Convent at La Cava near Vietri
22.9.1782
pencil, grey watercolour
inscribed & dated upper left: *A Convent at La Cava near Vietri – Septr.22*
178 × 241 mm
Leger Galleries, London (purchase, 1975) (D.1975.6.8)

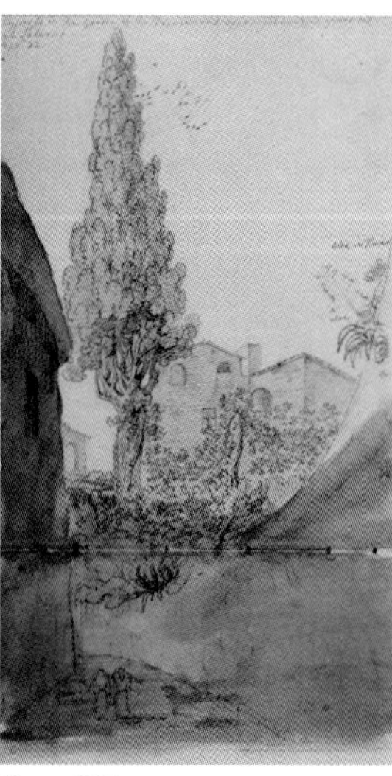

D.1975.6.8/9

The eight hundred year old Cypress in the Garden of the Franciscans at Salerno
22.9.1782
pencil, grey watercolour
inscribed & dated top edge: *Cypress in the Garden of the Franciscans near eight hundred years old / at Salerno – / Septr.22*; inscribed centre right: *Aloe in flower*
482 × 178 mm
Leger Galleries, London (purchase, 1975) (D.1975.6.8/9)

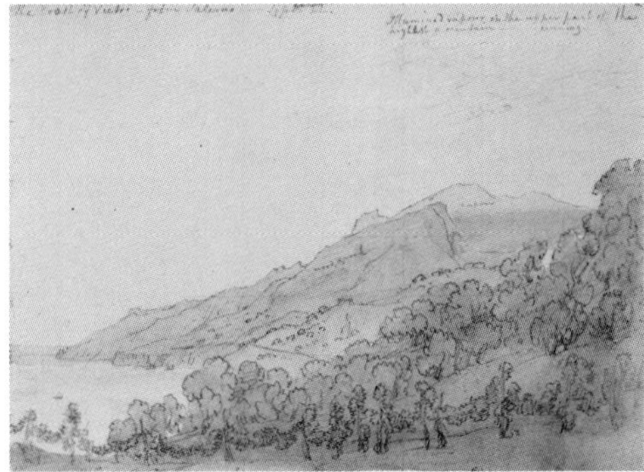

D.1975.6.10

View of the Coast of Vietri from Salerno, with a Vineyard in the Foreground
22.9.1782
pencil, grey watercolour
inscribed & dated upper left: *The Coast of Vietri – from Salerno – Septr.22.*; inscribed upper right: *Illumined vapour on the upperpart of the / highest mountain – evening –*
178 × 241 mm
Leger Galleries, London (purchase, 1975) (D.1975.6.10)

View from Vietri to Raito
23.9.1782
pencil, grey watercolour
inscribed & dated upper left: *From Vietri – Septr.23.*; inscribed upper right the key to symbols on the drawing *a Raito b.Marina di Vietri*; inscribed upper half of verso: *In the place where Marina de* (sic) *Vietri stands was anciently a city of the name of Marcinna / one of the three great cities on the Gulf of* [erased] *now called Salerno – The others were Vicensa / & Pestum – several statues & other remains were found in the subterraneous places & / a Temple of Diana – Marcinna extended a considerable way up the valley and was / destroyd above 2000 years ago by an innundation of the river Livone – on the hill where Vietri stands was a castle / an appendage to the city it was called Castel Vetero from which the name of Vietri is derived / Vicensa stood 4 or 5 miles to the east of Salerno / - The arch on the left hand, built by Carlo Quinto*
178 × 241 mm
Leger Galleries, London (purchase, 1975) (D.1975.6.11)

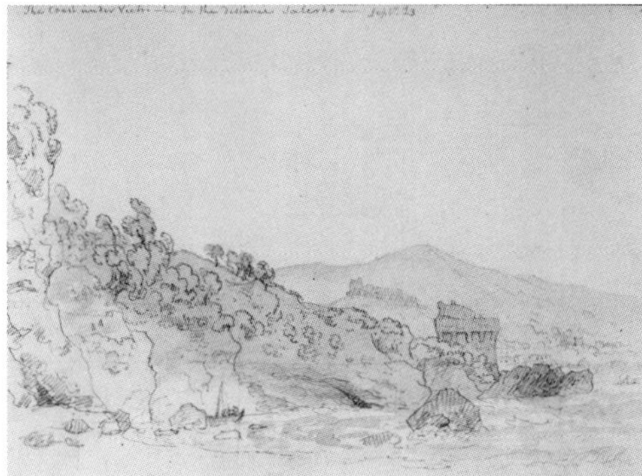

D.1975.6.12

View of the Coast under Vietri with a Castle, the Torre Crestarella and Salerno in the Distance
23.9.1782
pencil, grey watercolour
inscribed & dated upper left: *The Coast under Vietri – In the distance Salerno – Septr.23*
178 × 241 mm
Leger Galleries, London (purchase, 1975) (D.1975.6.12)

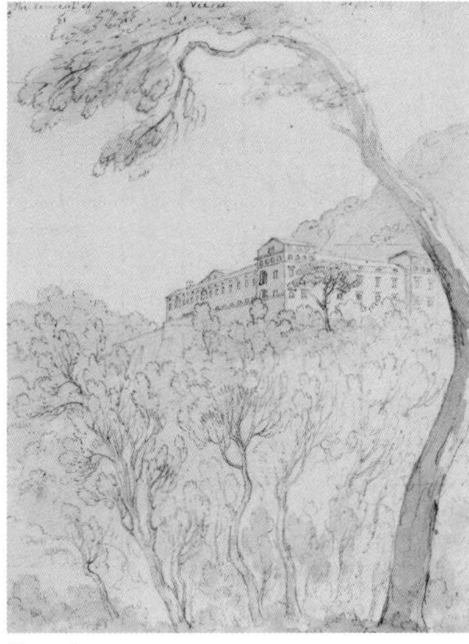

D.1975.6.13

View of a Convent at Vietri
24.9.1782
pencil, grey watercolour
dated upper right: *Septr.24*; inscribed upper left: *The Convent of* [blank] *at Vietri*
241 × 178 mm
Leger Galleries, London (purchase, 1975) (D.1975.6.13)

View of a Convent at Vietri
26.9.1782
pencil, grey watercolour
inscribed & dated upper left: *The Convent of* [blank] *at Vietri – Septr.26*
178 × 241 mm
Leger Galleries, London (purchase, 1975) (D.1975.6.14)

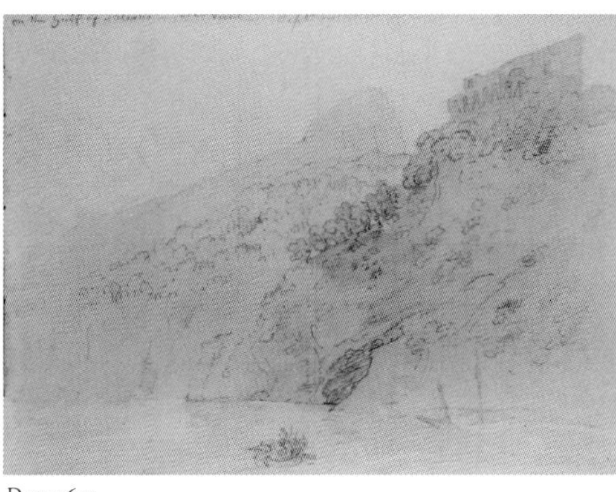

D.1975.6.15

View on the Gulf of Salerno, near Vietri, with a Castle and Monte Pertuso
27.9.1782
pencil, grey watercolour
inscribed & dated upper left: *on the Gulf of Salerno – near Vietri – Septr.27.*
178 × 241 mm
Leger Galleries, London (purchase, 1975) (D.1975.6.15)

View near Vietri, showing the Torre di Mano d'Albore
27.9.1782
pencil, grey watercolour
inscribed & dated upper left: *Near Vietri – Septr.27*
178 × 241 mm
Leger Galleries, London (purchase, 1975) (D.1975.6.16)

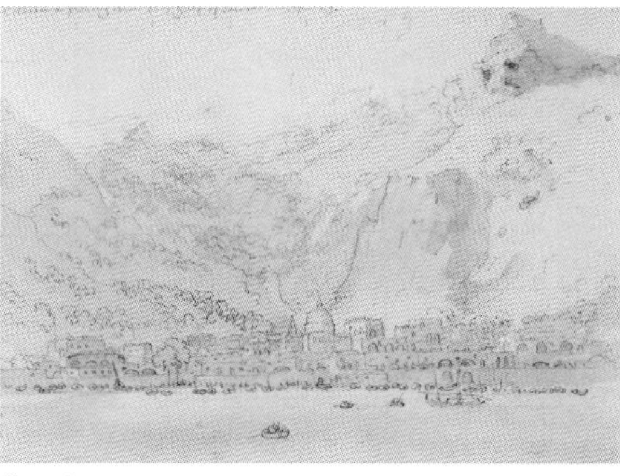

D.1975.6.17

View of Cetara, a Fishing Town on the Gulf of Salerno
29.9.1782
pencil, grey watercolour
inscribed & dated upper left: *Citaria* (sic) *a fishing town on ye Gulf of Salerno – Septr.29.*
178 × 241 mm
Leger Galleries, London (purchase, 1975) (D.1975.6.17)

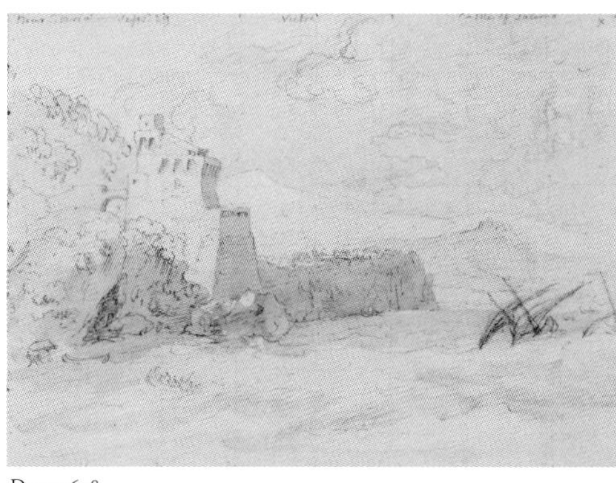

D.1975.6.18

View of the Coast, near Cetara, with Vietri and the Castle of Salerno in the Distance
29.9.1782
pencil, grey watercolour
inscribed upper left: *Near Citaria* (sic) *– Septr.29.*; inscribed upper centre, identifying the town in the distance: *Vietri*; inscribed upper right identifying the castle in the distance: *Castle of Salerno*
178 × 241 mm
Leger Galleries, London (purchase, 1975) (D.1975.6.18)

The Convent of Santa Francesca at La Cava
20.9.1782
pencil, grey watercolour
inscribed & dated upper left: *Convent of Santa Francesca at La Cava – Septr.20*
178 × 241 mm
Leger Galleries, London (purchase, 1975) (D.1975.6.19)

View of La Marina, near Vietri
1.10.1782
pencil, grey watercolour
inscribed & dated upper left: *La Marina near Vietri – October.1.*
178 × 241 mm
Leger Galleries, London (purchase, 1975) (D.1975.6.20)

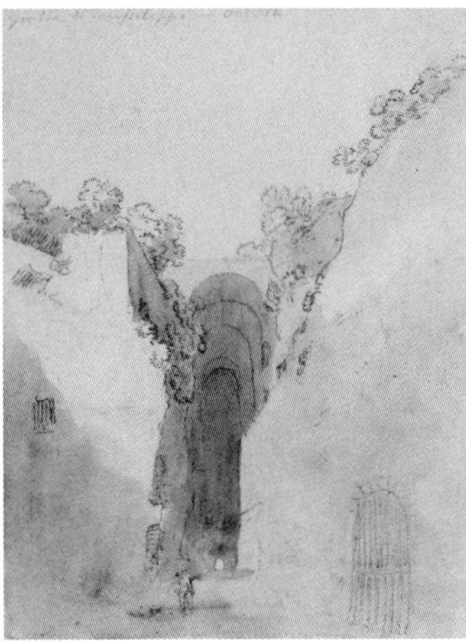

D.1975.6.21

The Grotto at Posillipo
12.10.1782
pencil, grey watercolour
inscribed & dated upper left in Italian: *Grotta di Paussilippo* (sic) – *Octr.12*
241 × 178 mm
Leger Galleries, London (purchase, 1975) (D.1975.6.21)

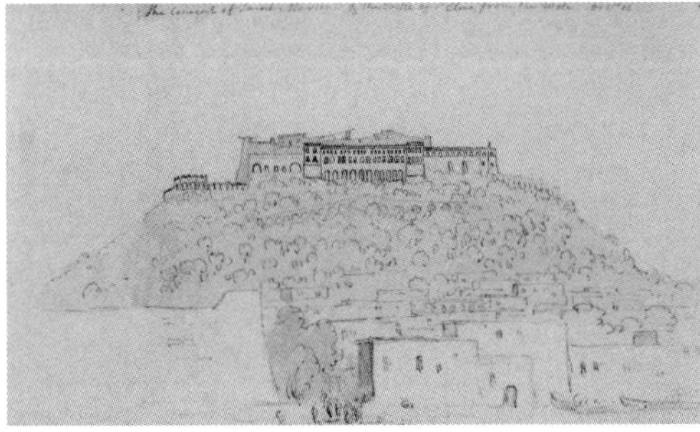

D.1975.6.22

View of the Convent of San Marino and the Castle of St Elmo from the Mole at Naples
16.10.1782
pencil, grey watercolour
inscribed & dated upper left of right hand page:
The Convent of Saint Martini & the Castle of St Elmo, from the Mole. Octr.16.
178 × 480 mm
Leger Galleries, London (purchase, 1975) (D.1975.6.22)

View of the Casino Sannazzaro at Posillipo
16.10.1782
pencil, grey watercolour
inscribed & dated upper left: *Casino Sannazzaro at Pausilippo* (sic) – *Octr.16*
178 × 241 mm
Leger Galleries, London (purchase, 1975) (D.1975.6.23)

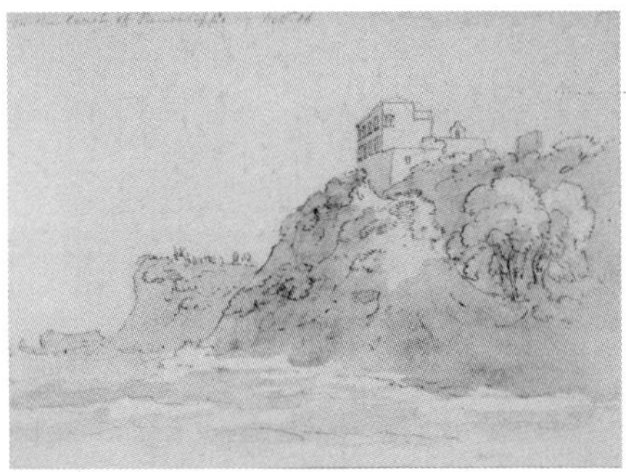

D.1975.6.24

View of Buildings on a Promontory on the Coast of Posillipo
16.10.1782
pencil, grey watercolour
inscribed & dated upper left: *On the Coast of Pausilippo* (sic) – *Octr.16*
178 × 241 mm
Leger Galleries, London (purchase, 1975) (D.1975.6.24)

View of Part of the Walls of Naples near Ponte Nuovo, showing the Convent of San Giovanni a Carbonara
17.10.1782
pencil, grey watercolour
inscribed & dated upper left: *Part of the Walls of Naples near Ponte nuovo – Octr.17.*
178 × 241 mm
Leger Galleries, London (purchase, 1975) (D.1975.6.25)

D.1975.6.26

View of a Convent on the Walls of Naples near Ponte Nuovo, San Giovanni a Carbonara rising beyond
16.10.1782
pencil, grey watercolour
inscribed & dated top edge: *The Convent of* [blank] *on the walls of Naples near Ponte Nuovo – Octr.16*
178 × 241 mm
Leger Galleries, London (purchase, 1975) (D.1975.6.26)

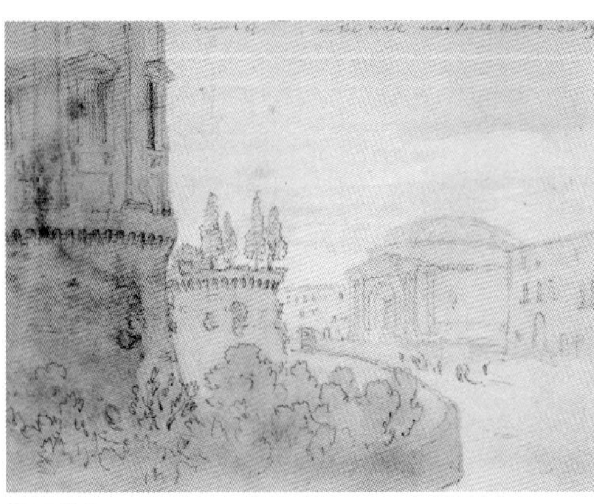

D.1975.6.27

View of a Convent on the Walls of Naples near Ponte Nuovo, with San Giovanni a Carbonara on the left and the Church of San Carlo all'Arena on the right
19.10.1782
pencil, grey watercolour
inscribed & dated upper right: *Convent of* [blank] *on the wall near Ponte Nuovo – Octr.19*
178 × 241 mm
Leger Galleries, London (purchase, 1975) (D.1975.6.27)

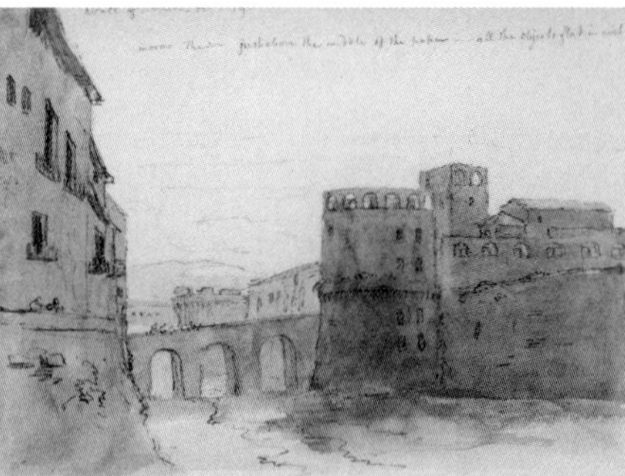

D.1975.6.28

View of the Wall of Naples, showing the Moat spanned by the Ponte Nuovo
19.10.1782
pencil, grey watercolour
inscribed & dated upper left: *Wall of Naples – Octr.19.*;
inscribed top edge below inscription and date: *morn = The sun just above the middle of the paper – all the objects flat in mist*
178 × 241 mm
Leger Galleries, London (purchase, 1975) (D.1975.6.28)

View of the Walls of Naples near Ponte Nuovo
19.10.1782
pencil, grey watercolour
inscribed & dated upper left: *The Wall of Naples near Ponte Nuovo – Octr.19.*
178 × 241 mm
Leger Galleries, London (purchase, 1975) (D.1975.6.29)

Sketchbook, Volume IV
1782
pencil, grey watercolour
178 × 241 mm
Leger Galleries, London (purchase, 1975) (V. & A., N.A.C.F., F.O.W., P.T.) (D.1975.7)

View of Arches with a Background of Trees
1782
pencil
178 × 241 mm
Leger Galleries, London (purchase, 1975) (D.1975.7.1)

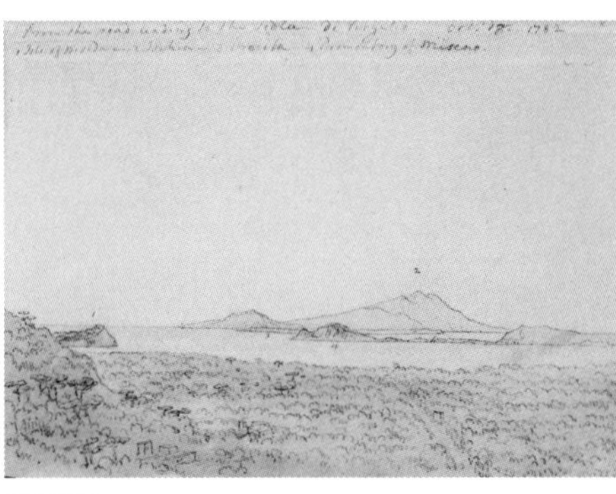

D.1975.7.2

View of the Islands of Nisida, Ischia and Procida, and the Promontory of Miseno from the Road leading to the Scuola di Virgilio
18.10.1782
pencil, grey watercolour
inscribed & dated top edge: *From the road leading to the Schola di Virgilio – Oct.17* [8 overwritten] – *1782 / 1 Isle of Nisida – 2 Ischia – 3 Procita* (sic) – *4 Promontory of Miseno* [identifying the numbers on the drawing]
178 × 241 mm
Leger Galleries, London (purchase, 1975) (D.1975.7.2)

View of the Scuola di Virgilio
18.10.1782
pencil
inscribed & dated upper left: *Scola di Virgilio – Octr.18*;
inscribed top edge of verso: *The Sea has encroached so
far on the shore as to reach the Ruin / called the Scola di
Virgilio which was in the times of the Ancients / at a
considerable distance from the sea -*
178 × 241 mm
Leger Galleries, London (purchase, 1975) (D.1975.7.3)

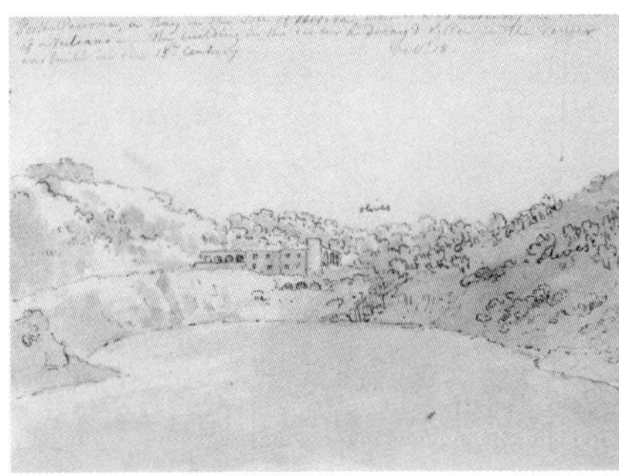

D.1975.7.4

View of Porto Pavon
18.10.1782
pencil, grey watercolour
inscribed & dated top edge: *Porta Pavone, a Bay in the
Isle of Nisida, which was evidently the Crater / of a
Vulcano – the building in the center a decay'd Villa – The
Tower / was built in the 15th.century – Octr.18.*; inscribed
lower centre: *olives*
178 × 241 mm
Leger Galleries, London (purchase, 1975) (D.1975.7.4)

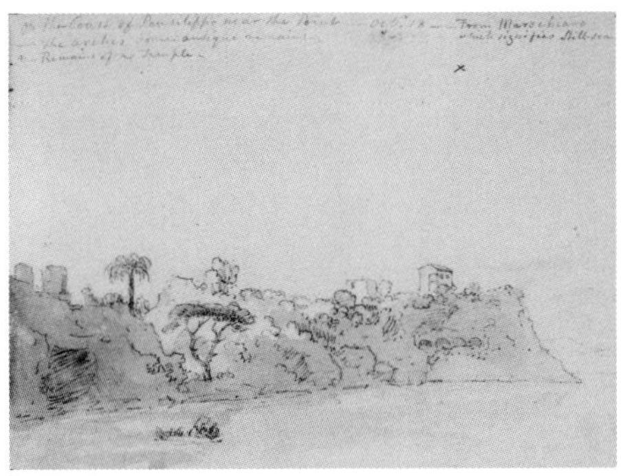

D.1975.7.5

View on the Coast of Posillipo, near the Point
18.10.1782
pencil, grey watercolour
inscribed & dated top edge: *On the Coast of Pausilippo
near the Point – Octr.18 – From Marechiano / which
signifies Still–sea.*; inscribed upper left the key
identifying symbols on the drawing: *— The arches,
some antique remains - / x – Remains of a Temple -*
178 × 241 mm
Leger Galleries, London (purchase, 1975) (D.1975.7.5)

View on the Road on the Top of Posillipo with
the Castle of St Elmo in the Distance
18.10.1782
pencil, grey watercolour
inscribed & dated top edge: *In the Road on the Top of
Pausilippo (sic) – Octr.18. / Castle of St.Elmo*; inscribed
near centre of image identifying parts of the drawing:
cloud / mountain / St.Elmo
241 × 178 mm
Leger Galleries, London (purchase, 1975) (D.1975.7.6)

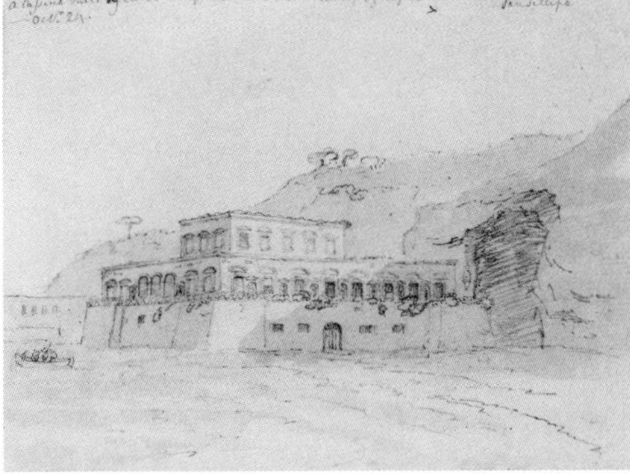

D.1975.7.7

View of the Casino built by Cardinal Spinelli
at Posillipo
24.10.1782
pencil, grey watercolour
inscribed & dated top edge: *A Cassino (sic) built by
Cardinal Spinelli when Arch Bishop of Naples –
Pausilippo (sic) / – Octr.24.*
178 × 241 mm
Leger Galleries, London (purchase, 1975) (D.1975.7.7)

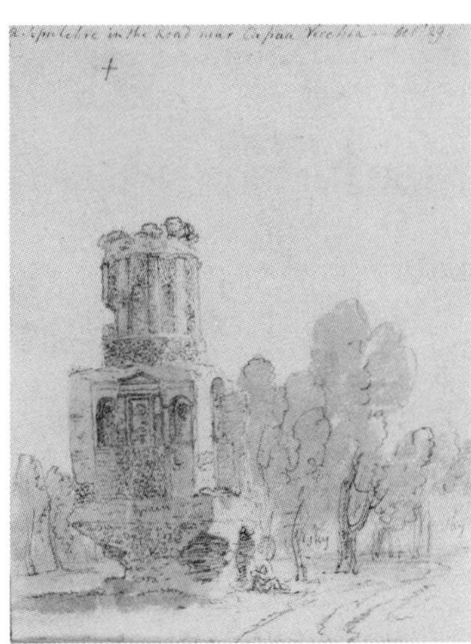

D.1975.7.8

The Tomb of Scipio Africanus by the
Road near Capua Vecchia
29.10.1782
pencil, grey watercolour
inscribed & dated top edge: *A Sepulchre near Capua
Vecchia – Octr.29.*
241 × 178 mm
Leger Galleries, London (purchase, 1975) (D.1975.7.8)

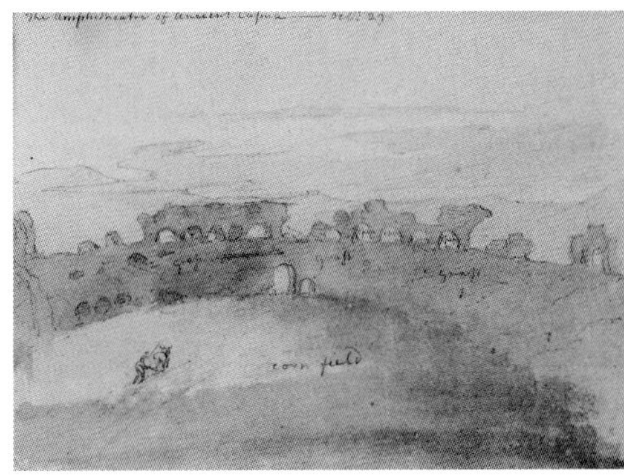

D.1975.7.9

Men ploughing in the Arena of the Amphitheatre
of ancient Capua
29.10.1782
pencil, grey watercolour
inscribed & dated upper left: *The Amphitheatre of
Ancient Capua – Octr 29.*; inscribed centre of image
identificatory notes: *grass / grass / grass / corn field*
178 × 241 mm
Leger Galleries, London (purchase, 1975) (D.1975.7.9)

The Ferry Between Eboli and Paestum
7.11.1782
pencil, grey watercolour
inscribed & dated top edge: *La Schaffa – The Ferry that
crosses the Carizzi between Evoli (sic) & Pestum (sic) –
Novr.7*
178 × 241 mm
Leger Galleries, London (purchase, 1975) (D.1975.7.10)

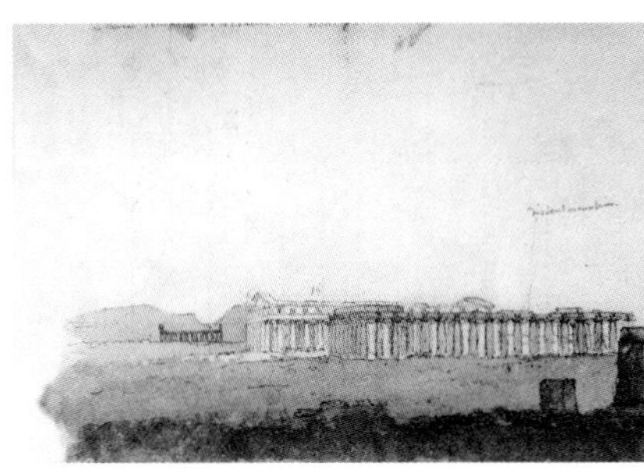

D.1975.7.11

The three Temples at Paestum
7.11.1782
pencil, grey watercolour
inscribed & dated upper left: *The three Temples at
Pestum (sic) – Novr.7*; inscribed centre right identifying
part of the landscape: *distant mountain*
178 × 241 mm
Leger Galleries, London (purchase, 1975) (D.1975.7.11)

The Temple of Neptune and the
Basilica at Paestum
7.11.1782
pencil, grey watercolour
inscribed & dated upper left: *The two great Temples –
Novr.7.*; inscribed lower left identifying part of the
landscape: *sea*; inscribed lower centre identifying part
of the landscape: *loose stones*
178 × 241 mm
Leger Galleries, London (purchase, 1975) (D.1975.7.12)

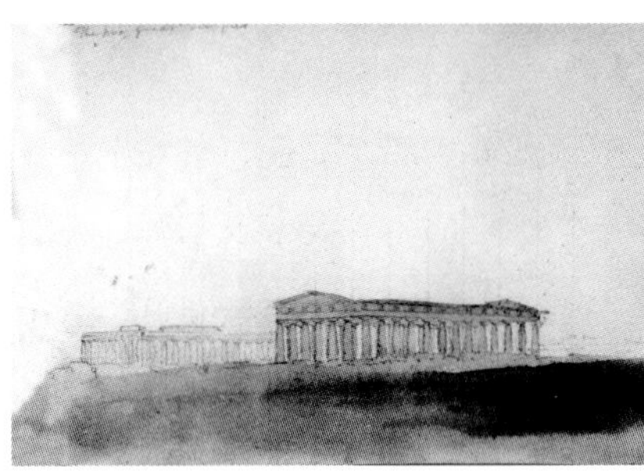

D.1975.7.13

View of the Temple of Neptune and the
Basilica at Paestum
1782
pencil, grey watercolour
inscribed upper left: *The two great Temples*
178 × 241 mm
Leger Galleries, London (purchase, 1975) (D.1975.7.13)

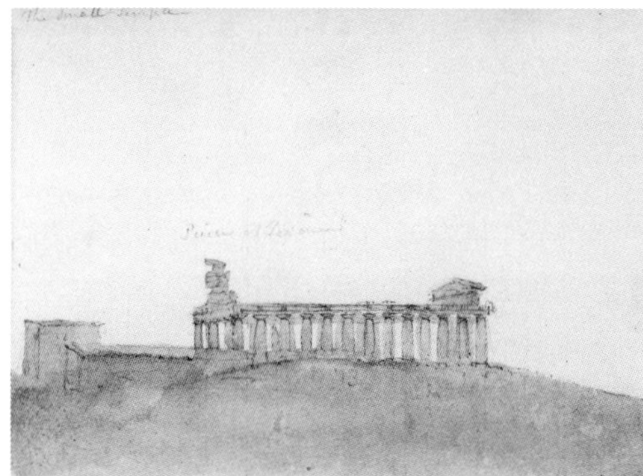

D.1975.7.14

The small Temple at Paestum
1782
pencil, grey watercolour
inscribed upper left: *The small Temple*; inscribed in centre of image identifying part of the temple: *Piece of Pediment*
178 × 241 mm
Leger Galleries, London (purchase, 1975) (D.1975.7.14)

View on the Road between Salerno and Eboli, looking towards Salerno
8.11.1782
pencil, grey watercolour
inscribed & dated top edge: *on the Road between Salerno & Evoli* (sic) *looking towards Salerno – Novr.7* [8 overwritten]; inscribed lower left identifying parts of the landscape: *sea / white houses*; inscribed lower right: *Raito*
178 × 241 mm
Leger Galleries, London (purchase, 1975) (D.1975.7.15)

View of a Hill-top Town between Salerno and Eboli
8.11.1782
pencil, grey watercolour
inscribed & dated upper left: *Between Salerno & Evoli* (sic) *– Novr.7* [8 overwritten]
178 × 241 mm
Leger Galleries, London (purchase, 1975) (D.1975.7.16)

View of a Castle on a Cliff, near Salerno
8.11.1782
pencil, grey watercolour
inscribed & dated upper left: *Near Salerno – Novr.7* [8 overwritten]
178 × 241 mm
Leger Galleries, London (purchase, 1975) (D.1975.7.17)

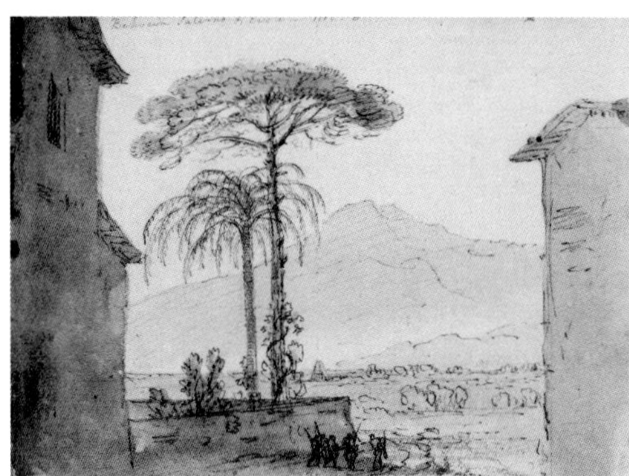

D.1975.7.18

View of a Plain and Mountains between Salerno and Eboli, seen through Buildings
8.11.1782
pencil, grey watercolour
inscribed & dated upper centre: *Between Salerno & Evoli* (sic) *– Novr.8*
178 × 241 mm
Leger Galleries, London (purchase, 1975) (D.1975.7.18)

View of a Group of Buildings, with Monte Pertuso in the Distance
8.11.1782
pencil, grey watercolour
inscribed & dated upper left: *La Cava – Novr.8.*
178 × 241 mm
Leger Galleries, London (purchase, 1975) (D.1975.7.19)

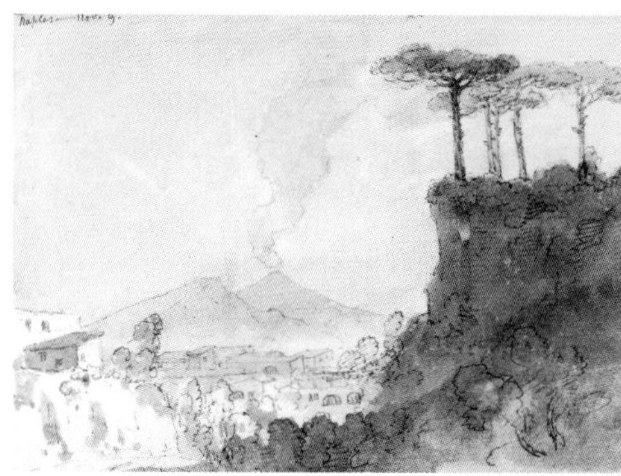

D.1975.7.20

View of Naples, with Somma and Vesuvius smoking in the Distance
9.11.1782
pencil, grey watercolour
inscribed & dated upper left: *Naples – Novr.9.*
178 × 241 mm
Leger Galleries, London (purchase, 1975) (D.1975.7.20)

The Castle of St Elmo, Naples
10.11.1782
pencil
dated upper right: *Novr.10 –*
178 × 241 mm
Leger Galleries, London (purchase, 1975) (D.1975.7.21)

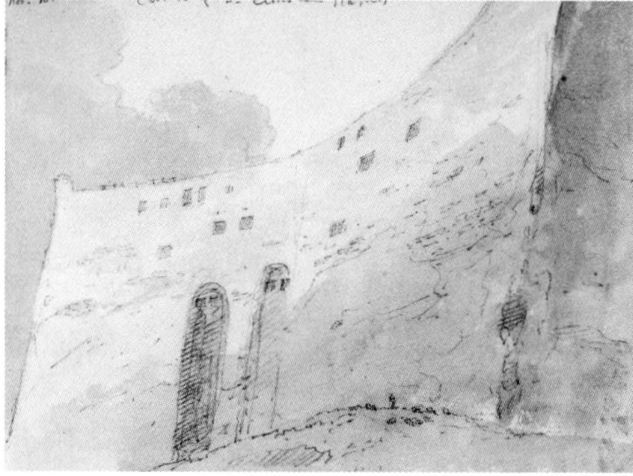

D.1975.7.22

The Castle of St Elmo, Naples
10.11.1782
pencil, grey watercolour
dated upper left: *Novr.10.*
inscribed upper centre: *Castle of St.Elmo – Naples*
178 × 241 mm
Leger Galleries, London (purchase, 1975) (D.1975.7.22)

View of a Shepherd's Hut and an Olive Press on the Shore between Naples and Portici
8.11.1782
pencil, grey watercolour
inscribed & dated upper left: *Between Naples & Portici – Novr.8.*
178 × 241 mm
Leger Galleries, London (purchase, 1975) (D.1975.7.23)

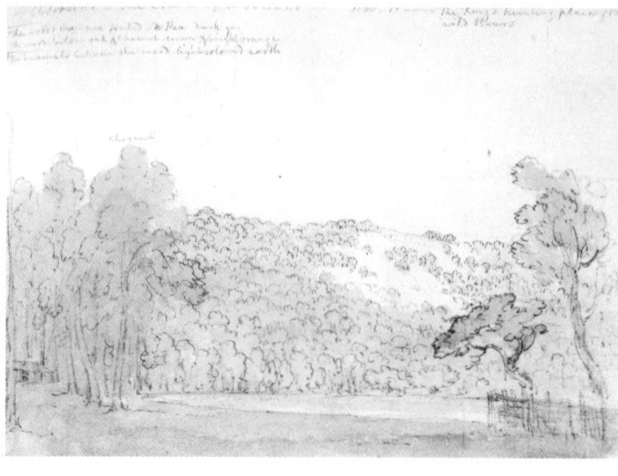

D.1975.7.24

View of the Crater of a Volcano at Astroni
11.11.1782
pencil, grey watercolour
inscribed & dated upper edge: *Astruni – The Crater of a Volcano – Novr.11 – The king's hunting place for / wild Boars*; inscribed upper left below inscription and date: *The woods that are tinted – Ilax. dark gr= / The woods below oak & chestnut-brown & bright orange / The intervals between the wood light coloured earth*
178 × 241 mm
Leger Galleries, London (purchase, 1975) (D.1975.7.24)

Astroni, the Bed of the Crater and the wooded Slopes on the further Side
11.11.1782
pencil, grey watercolour
inscribed & dated upper left: *Astruni – Novr.–11*; inscribed upper centre identifying the tree in the foreground: *oak*; inscribed upper right: *The tinted part. Ilax – the / rest brown and orange.*; inscribed lower centre: *chestnuts*
178 × 241 mm
Leger Galleries, London (purchase, 1975) (D.1975.7.25)

Astroni, the Bed of the Crater with Trees beyond
11.11.1782
pencil, grey watercolour
inscribed & dated upper left: *Astruni – Novr.11*; inscribed upper centre identifying the trees in the left foreground: *chesnut* (sic); inscribed upper centre: identifying the trees on the rim of the crater in the distance: *Ila*; inscribed upper right: *all bare earth / light colour*; inscribed lower centre: *Light earth – no verdure -*
178 × 241 mm
Leger Galleries, London (purchase, 1975) (D.1975.7.26)

Astroni, Panorama looking across the Crater
11.11.1782
pencil, grey watercolour
inscribed & dated upper left of left hand sheet: *Astruni – Novr.11. / The upperwoods Ilax – dark green / The lower-oak & chesnut* (sic) *– brown & orange.*
178 × 482 mm
Leger Galleries, London (purchase, 1975) (D.1975.7.27/28)

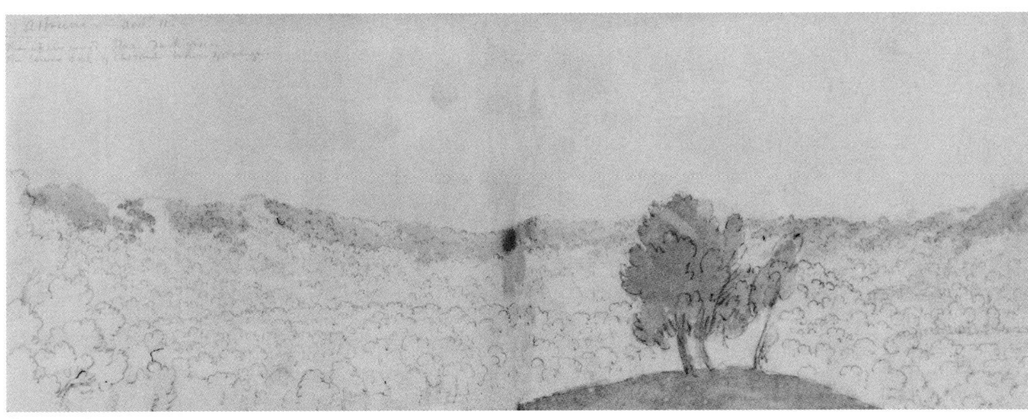

D.1975.7.27/28

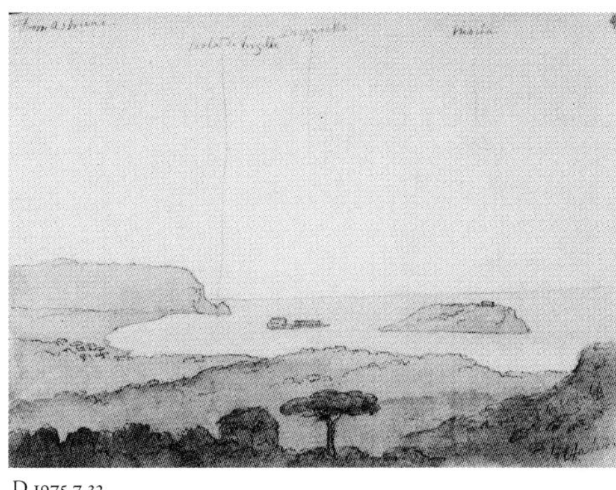

D.1975.7.32

Lake Agnano, seen from Astroni
11.11.1782
pencil, grey watercolour
inscribed & dated top edge: *Lago – d'Agnano – seen from Astruni – Novr.11.*; inscribed within image notes identifying parts of the landscape: *wood / sheep / wood*
178 × 241 mm
Leger Galleries, London (purchase, 1975) (D.1975.7.29)

The Gulf of Pozzuoli and the Isle of Nisida, seen from Astroni
1782
pencil, grey watercolour
inscribed upper left: *From Astruni.*; inscribed top edge, lines linking each word to parts of the landscape: *Scola di Virgilio / Lazzaretto / Nisita* (sic)
178 × 241 mm
Leger Galleries, London (purchase, 1975) (D.1975.7.32)

Sketchbook, Volume V
1782
pencil, grey watercolour
178 × 241 mm
Leger Galleries, London (purchase, 1975) (V. & A., N.A.C.F., F.O.W., P.T.) (D.1975.8)

Convent at Naples, with Vesuvius in the Distance
17.11.1782
pencil, grey watercolour
inscribed upper left of left hand page: *Convent at Naples – Novr.17.1782.*
178 × 482 mm
Leger Galleries, London (purchase, 1975) (D.1975.8.2/3)

A Range of Convents near Capodimonte with the Chinese Convent
24.11.1782
pencil, grey watercolour
inscribed & dated top edge of left hand page: *A Range of Convents near Capo di Monti* (sic) – *Novr.24*; inscribed upper right of right hand page: *The Chinese Convent*
178 × 482 mm
Leger Galleries, London (purchase, 1975) (D.1975.8.3/4)

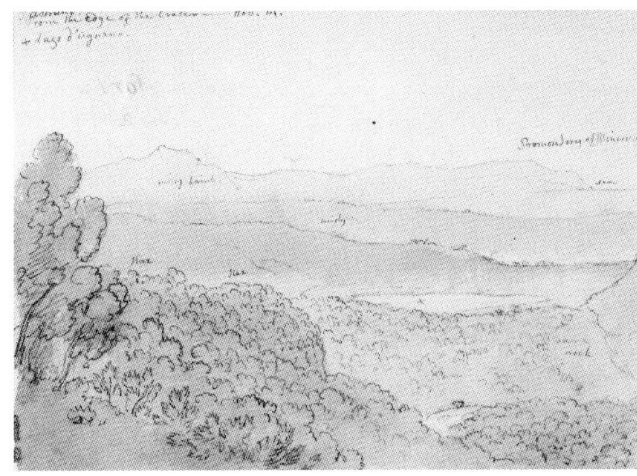

D.1975.7.30

Astroni, from the Edge of the Crater, with Lake Agnano and the Promontory of Miseno beyond
14.11.1782
pencil, grey watercolour
inscribed & dated upper left: *Astruni. / From the edge of the Crater – Novr.14. / x* [identifying a symbol on the drawing] *Lago d'Agnano*; inscribed in various places within the image: identifying colouring and parts of the Landscape: *misty faint / Ilax / Ilax / misty / Promontory of Minerva sea / rock*
178 × 241 mm
Leger Galleries, London (purchase, 1975) (D.1975.7.30)

Astroni, looking across the Crater from a Tree-covered Bank in the Foreground
14.11.1782
pencil, grey watercolour
inscribed & dated upper left: *Astruni – Novr.14. / The upperwoods Ilax dark gr / The lower— brown & orange*; inscribed lower right identifying colour of the foreground: *bare earth*
178 × 241 mm
Leger Galleries, London (purchase, 1975) (D.1975.7.31)

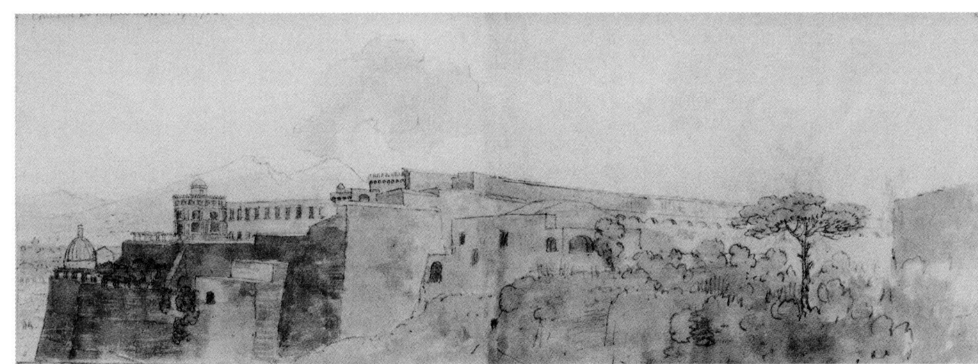

D.1975.8.2/3

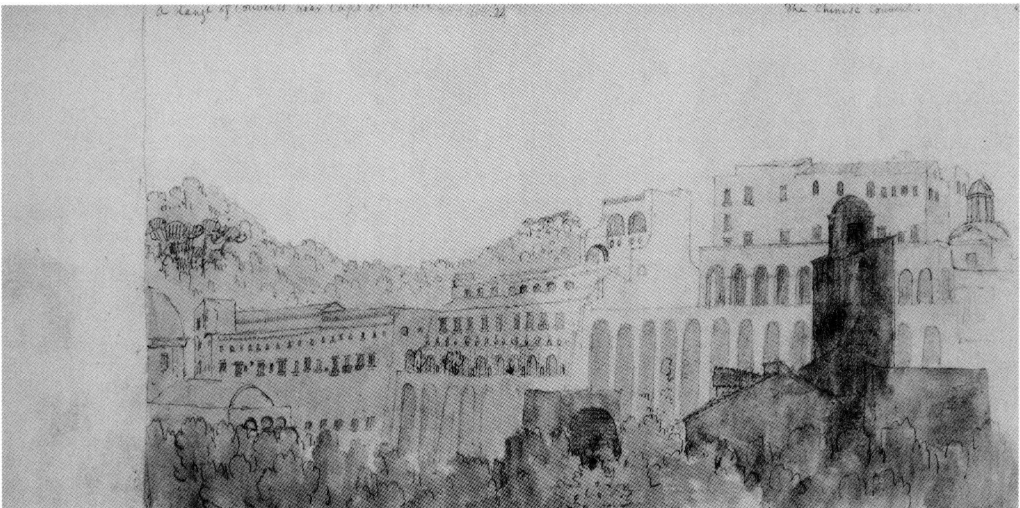

D.1975.8.3/4

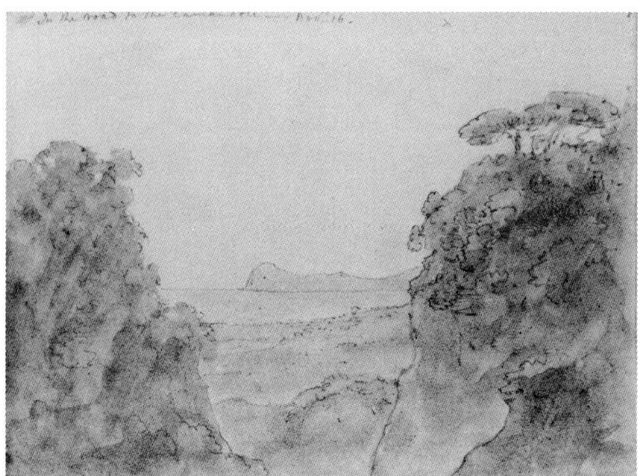

D.1975.8.5

On the Road to Camaldoli
16.11.1782
pencil, grey watercolour
inscribed & dated upper left: *In the road to Camaldoli – Novr.16.*
178 × 241 mm
Leger Galleries, London (purchase, 1975) (D.1975.8.5)

The Aqueduct, five Miles beyond Caserta, near Maddaloni
26.11.1782
pencil, grey watercolour
inscribed & dated upper left: *Aqueduct 5 miles beyond Caserta – Novr.26.*
178 × 241 mm
Leger Galleries, London (purchase, 1975) (D.1975.8.6)

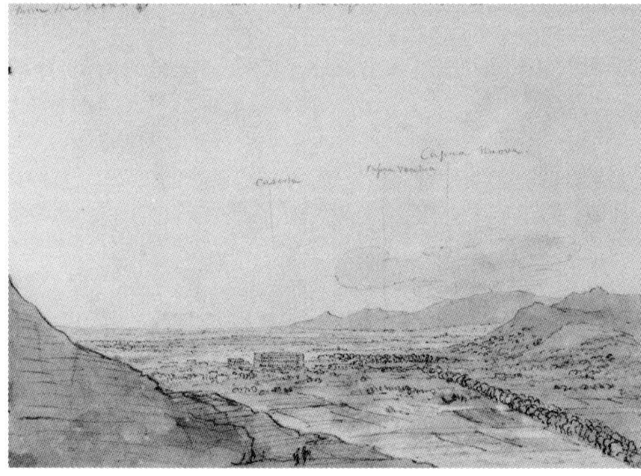

D.1975.8.7

View from the Road between Caserta and the Aqueduct
26.11.1782
pencil, grey watercolour
inscribed & dated upper left: *From the Road between Caserta & the Aqueduct – Novr.26*; inscribed in centre of image, lines linking each word to parts of the landscape; *Caserta / Capua Vecchia / Capua Nuova*; inscribed along upper edge verso: *27 windows in* [erased] *the side of the Palace in sight. Pillasters between of stone / - the colour of the Palace reddish.*
178 × 241 mm
Leger Galleries, London (purchase, 1975) (D.1975.8.7)

The Convent of Santa Lucia, beyond Caserta
26.11.1782
pencil, grey watercolour
inscribed & dated upper left: *Santa Lucia a Convent beyond Caserta – Novr.26*
178 × 241 mm
Leger Galleries, London (purchase, 1975) (D.1975.8.8)

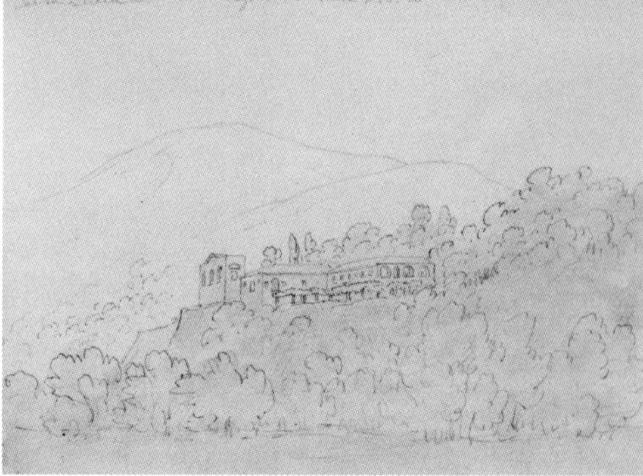

D.1975.8.8

The Palace of Monte Mileto
11.1782
pencil, grey watercolour
inscribed & dated upper left: *Pallazzo Mileto – Novr.–*; inscribed top edge of verso: *In the inside of the arches grotesque painting –*
178 × 241 mm
Leger Galleries, London (purchase, 1975) (D.1975.8.9)

View of the Promontory of Miseno, from the North East, with Ischia to the right
2.12.1782
pencil, grey watercolour
inscribed & dated upper left: *Promontory of Miseno – Decr.2.*; inscribed in various places on the image identifying colours and part of the landscape: *green / green / Ischia*
178 × 241 mm
Leger Galleries, London (purchase, 1975) (D.1975.8.10)

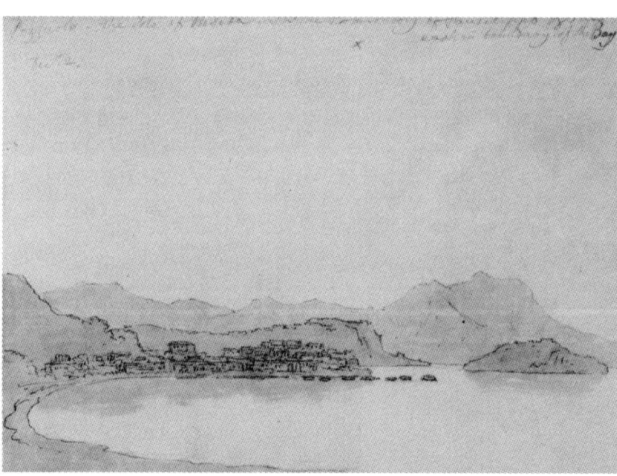

D.1975.8.11

Pozzuoli, the Isle of Nisida with the Promontory of Posillipo, and the Eastern Boundary of the Bay
2.12.1782
pencil, grey watercolour
inscribed & dated top edge: *Pozzuolo. The Isle of Nisita* (sic) *with the Promontory of Pausilippo* (sic) *& the / eastern boundary of the Bay / Decr.2.*
178 × 241 mm
Leger Galleries, London (purchase, 1975) (D.1975.8.11)

The Temple of Diana on the Bay of Baia
2.12.1782
pencil, grey watercolour
inscribed upper left: *Temple of Diana on the Bay of Baia*; inscribed upper right: *red brick – grey within*; inscribed upper left verso: *a few paces from the shore*
178 × 241 mm
Leger Galleries, London (purchase, 1975) (D.1975.8.12)

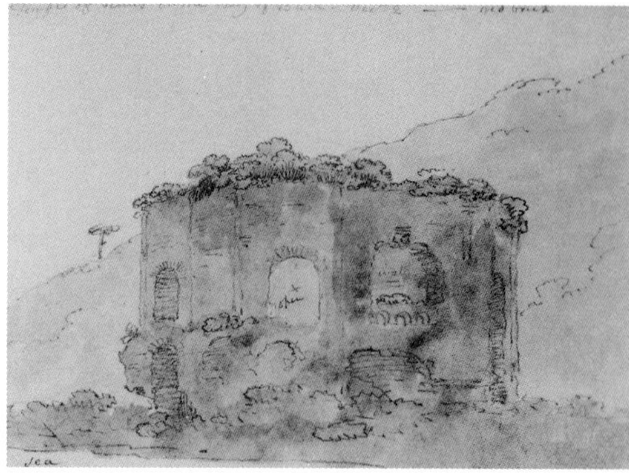

D.1975.8.13

The Temple of Venus on the Bay of Baia
2.12.1782
pencil, grey watercolour
inscribed & dated top edge: *Temple of Venus on the Bay of Baia. Decr.2 – red brick*; inscribed lower left: *sea*
178 × 241 mm
Leger Galleries, London (purchase, 1975) (D.1975.8.13)

Ruins of the Temple of Hercules on the Bay of Baia
2.12.1782
pencil, grey watercolour
inscribed & dated top edge: *Vestige of the Temple of Hercules in the Bay of Baia – in which / Agrippina the Mother of Nero was put to Death. / Decr.2.*
178 × 241 mm
Leger Galleries, London (purchase, 1975) (D.1975.8.14)

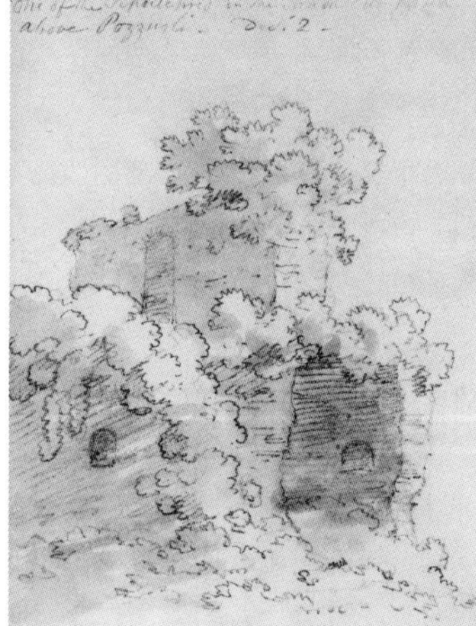

D.1975.8.15

One of the Sepulchres in the Strada Campana above Pozzuoli
2.12.1782
pencil, grey watercolour
inscribed & dated top edge: *One of the Sepulchres in the Strada Campana / Above Pozzuoli. Decr.2 –*
241 × 178 mm
Leger Galleries, London (purchase, 1975) (D.1975.8.15)

Mausoleum in the Strada Campana above Pozzuoli
2.12.1782
pencil
inscribed & dated top edge: *Mosoleum* (sic) *in the Strada Campana above Pozzuoli – the Via Appia /* [below erasure] *Decr.2.*
178 × 241 mm
Leger Galleries, London (purchase, 1975) (D.1975.8.16)

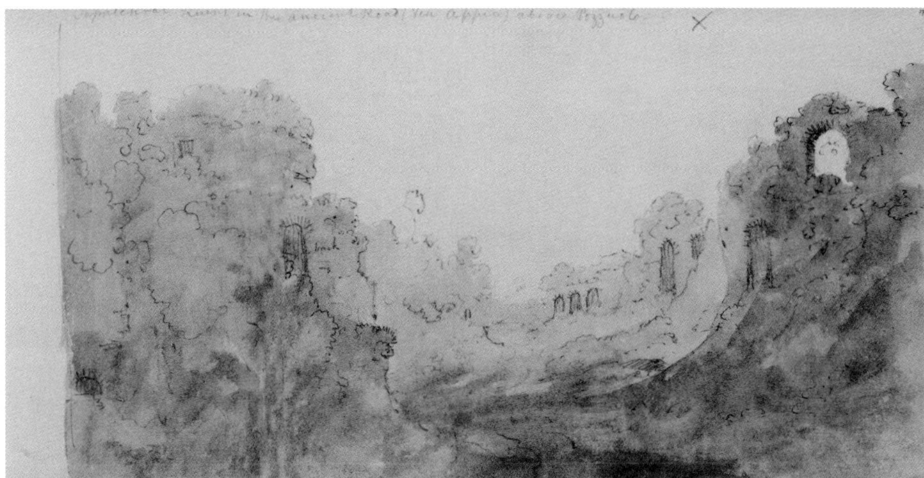

D.1975.8.16/17

Sepulchral Ruins on the Via Appia above Pozzuoli

12.1782
pencil, grey watercolour
inscribed upper right of left hand sheet and continuing onto upper left of right hand sheet: *Sepulchral Ruins in the Ancient Road (Via Appia) above Pozzuolo.*
178 × 482 mm
Leger Galleries, London (purchase, 1975) (D.1975.8.16/17)

Cliffs and Pines, near the Grotto of Posillipo

4.12.1782
pencil, grey watercolour
inscribed & dated top edge: *Near the Grotto of Pausillipo* (sic) – *Decr.4.*
241 × 178 mm
Leger Galleries, London (purchase, 1975) (D.1975.8.18)

View of Huts on the Plain, near the Mola di Gaeta

8.12.1782
pencil, grey watercolour
inscribed & dated upper left: *Near Mola di Gaeta – Decr.8.*
178 × 241 mm
Leger Galleries, London (purchase, 1975) (D.1975.8.19)

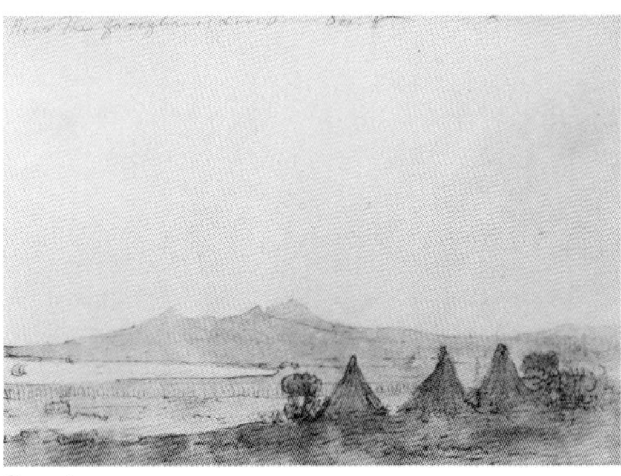

D.1975.8.20

View near the Garigliano, with conical Huts in the Foreground and the Bay of Gaeta beyond

8.12.1782
pencil, grey watercolour
inscribed & dated upper left: Near the Garigliano (Liris) – Decr.8
178 × 241 mm
Leger Galleries, London (purchase, 1975) (D.1975.8.20)

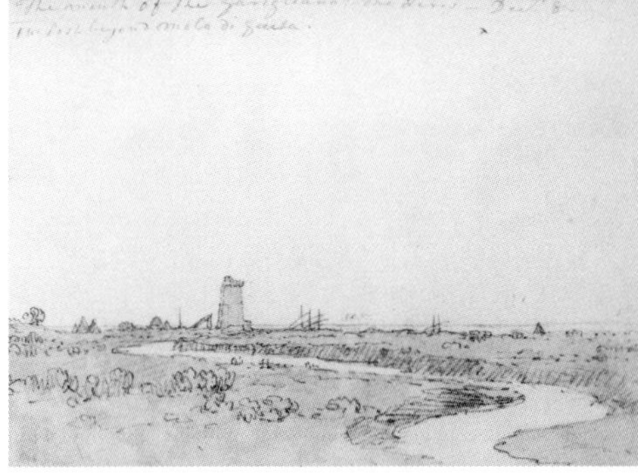

D.1975.8.21

View at the Mouth of the Garigliano

8.12.1782
pencil, grey watercolour
inscribed & dated top edge: *The mouth of the Garigliano (The Liris – Decr.8. / One Post beyond Molo di Gaeta.*; inscribed lower centre identifying a distant part of the landscape: *sea*
178 × 241 mm
Leger Galleries, London (purchase, 1975) (D.1975.8.21)

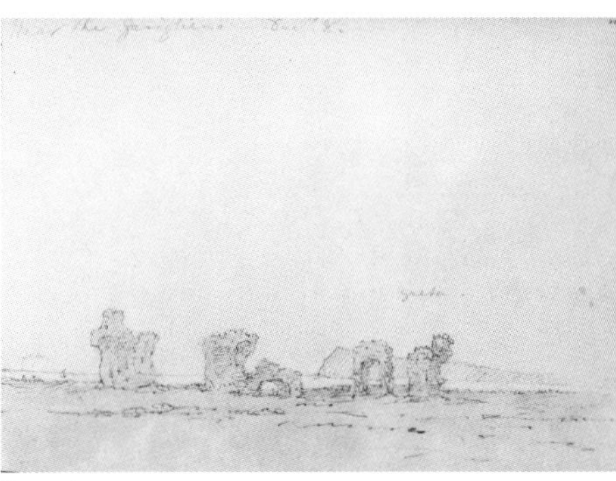

D.1975.8.22

View with Ruins, near the River Garigliano, Gaeta in the Distance

8.12.1782
pencil, grey watercolour
inscribed & dated upper left: *Near the Garigliano – Decr.8.*; inscribed lower left identifying a distant part of the landscape: *sea*; inscribed centre right: identifying a distant feature of the landscape and with a line linking the word to the feature: *Gaeta*
178 × 241 mm
Leger Galleries, London (purchase, 1975) (D.1975.8.22)

View of a Round Tower and Buildings

12.1782
pencil
178 × 241 mm
Leger Galleries, London (purchase, 1975) (D.1975.8.23)

View of Monte Circello from the Road between Terracina and Velletri

9.12.1782
pencil, grey watercolour
inscribed top edge: *Monte Circello, from the road between Terracina & Veletri – Decr.9.*
178 × 241 mm
Leger Galleries, London (purchase, 1975) (D.1975.8.24)

Sketchbook, Volume VI

1783
pencil, grey watercolour
174 × 238 mm
Leger Galleries, London (purchase, 1975) (V. & A., N.A.C.F., F.O.W., P.T.) (D.1975.9)

Falls of the Velino, near Terni

15.9.1783
pencil, grey watercolour
inscribed & dated upper left: *Velino – near Terni / Septr.15.1783*
238 × 174 mm
Leger Galleries, London (purchase, 1975) (D.1975.9.1)

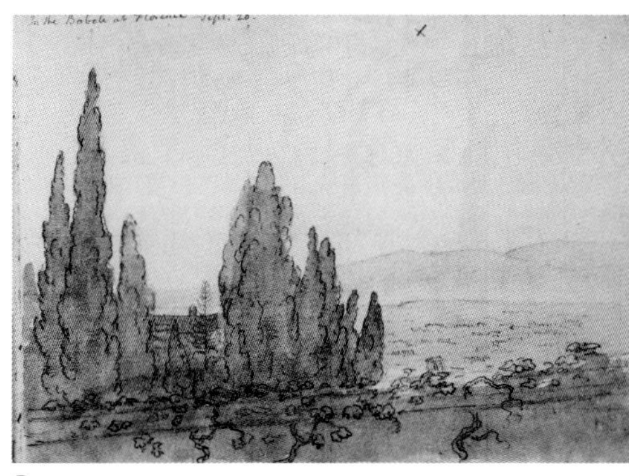

D.1975.9.2

View from the Boboli Gardens across the Val d'Arno

20.9.1783
pencil, grey watercolour
inscribed & dated upper left: *In the Boboli at Florence – Septr.20.*
174 × 238 mm
Leger Galleries, London (purchase, 1975) (D.1975.9.2)

View from near the Cascine

21.9.1783
pencil, grey watercolour
inscribed & dated upper right: *Near the Cascines* (sic) / *Septr.21.*
174 × 238 mm
Leger Galleries, London (purchase, 1975) (D.1975.9.3)

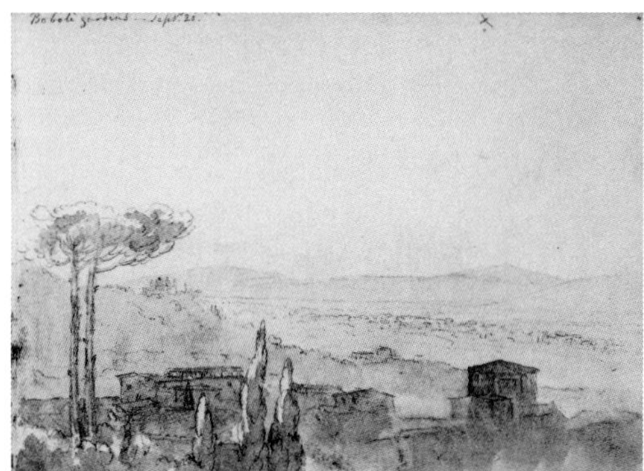

D.1975.9.4

View from the Boboli Gardens to the Val d'Arno
20.9.1783
pencil, grey watercolour
inscribed & dated upper left: *Boboli Gardens – Septr.20.*
174 × 238 mm
Leger Galleries, London (purchase, 1975) (D.1975.9.4)

**The Convent of Monte Oliveto, from the Banks
of the Arno**
21.9.1783
pencil, grey watercolour
inscribed & dated top edge: *Banks of ye Arno near
Florence Septr.21. – from the Cascines* (sic).
174 × 238 mm
Leger Galleries, London (purchase, 1975) (D.1975.9.5)

Study of Fir Trees at Vallombrosa
24.9.1783
pencil
inscribed & dated upper left: *Valombrosa* (sic) –
Septr 24.
174 × 238 mm
Leger Galleries, London (purchase, 1975) (D.1975.9.6)

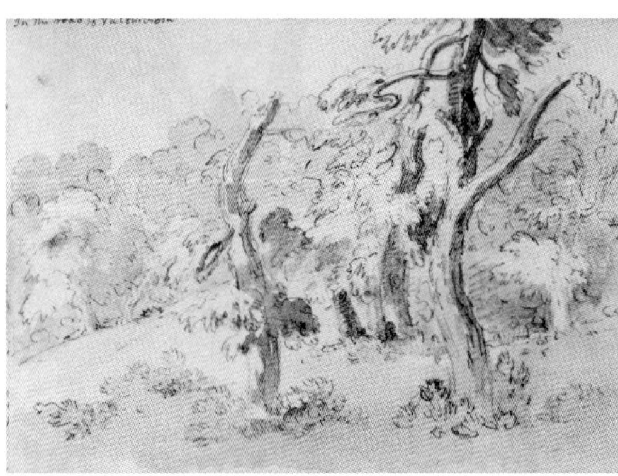

D.1975.9.7

On the Road to Vallombrosa
24.9.1783
pencil, grey watercolour
inscribed upper left: *In the road to valombrosa* (sic)
174 × 238 mm
Leger Galleries, London (purchase, 1975) (D.1975.9.7)

Study of Trees at Vallombrosa
24.9.1783
pencil, grey watercolour
inscribed & dated upper right: *Valombrosa* (sic).*Septr24*
238 × 174 mm
Leger Galleries, London (purchase, 1975) (D.1975.9.8)

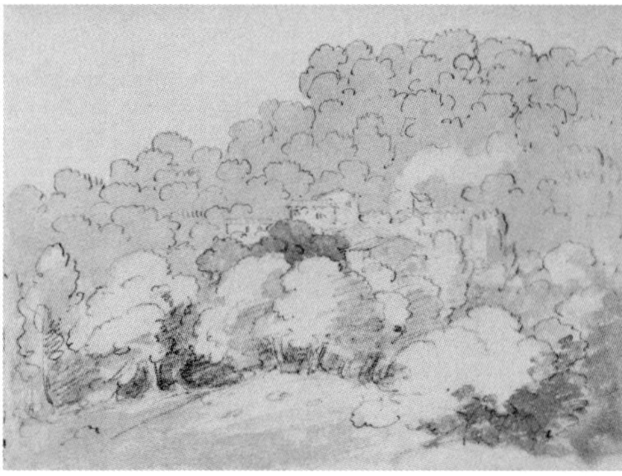

D.1975.9.9

View of Vallombrosa
24.9.1783
pencil, grey watercolour
174 × 238 mm
Leger Galleries, London (purchase, 1975) (D.1975.9.9)

The Edge of a Valley in the Forest at Vallombrosa
24.9.1783
pencil, grey watercolour
174 × 238 mm
Leger Galleries, London (purchase, 1975) (D.1975.9.10)

**Study of Trees on the Edge of a wooded
Valley at Vallombrosa**
24.9.1783
pencil, grey watercolour
174 × 238 mm
Leger Galleries, London (purchase, 1975) (D.1975.9.11)

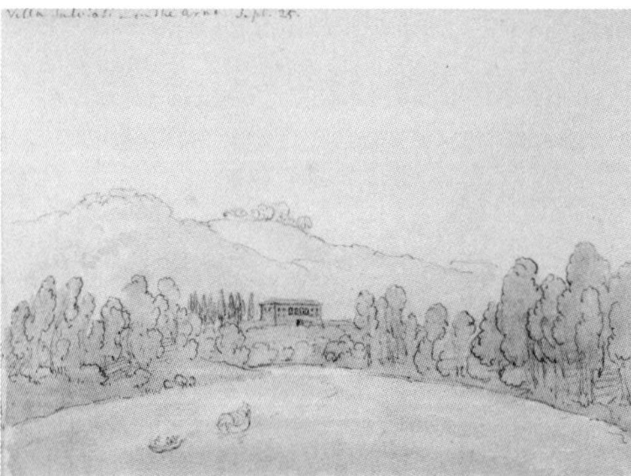

D.1975.9.12

Villa Salviati on the Arno
25.9.1783
pencil, grey watercolour
inscribed & dated upper left: *Villa Salviati – on the
Arno. Septr.25.*
174 × 238 mm
Leger Galleries, London (purchase, 1975) (D.1975.9.12)

View on the Arno
25.9.1783
pencil, grey watercolour
inscribed & dated upper left: *On the Arno – Septr.25.*
174 × 238 mm
Leger Galleries, London (purchase, 1975) (D.1975.9.13)

A Villa among Trees on the Arno
25.9.1783
pencil, grey watercolour
inscribed & dated upper left: *Arno – Septr.25*
174 × 238 mm
Leger Galleries, London (purchase, 1975) (D.1975.9.14)

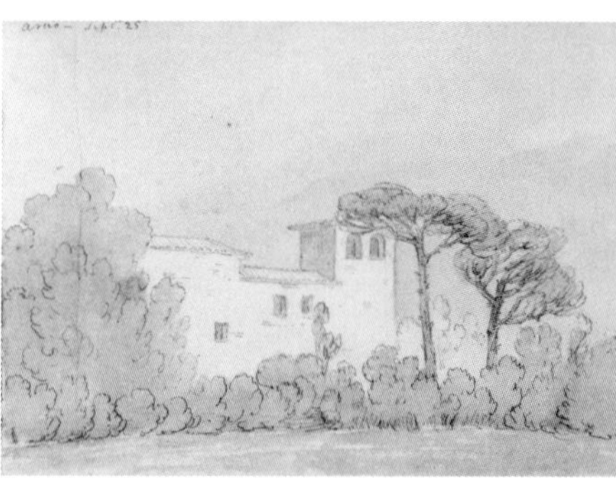

D.1975.9.14

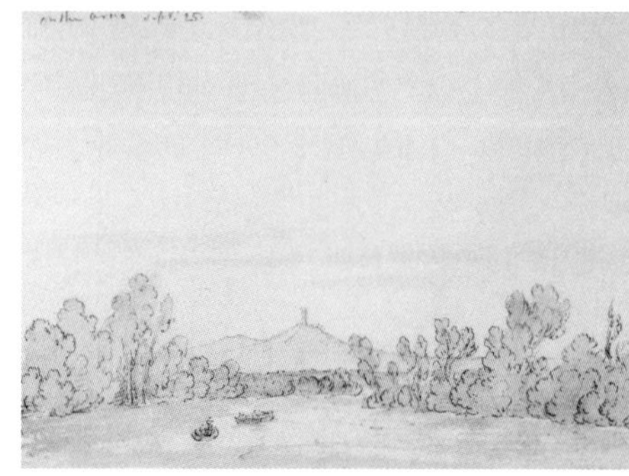

D.1975.9.15

View on the Arno with a Tower on a Hill
25.9.1783
pencil, grey watercolour
inscribed & dated upper left: *On the Arno Septr.25.*
174 × 238 mm
Leger Galleries, London (purchase, 1975) (D.1975.9.15)

View along the Arno
25.9.1783
pencil, grey watercolour
inscribed & dated upper left: *Arno. Septr.25.*
174 × 238 mm
Leger Galleries, London (purchase, 1975) (D.1975.9.16)

View of the Grand Duke's Palace from the Arno
25.9.1783
pencil
inscribed & dated upper left: *Arno. Septr.25. Grand
Duke's Palace*
174 × 238 mm
Leger Galleries, London (purchase, 1975) (D.1975.9.17)

Landscape View from the Arno
25.9.1783
pencil, grey watercolour
inscribed & dated upper left: *Arno. Septr.25.*
174 × 238 mm
Leger Galleries, London (purchase, 1975) (D.1975.9.18)

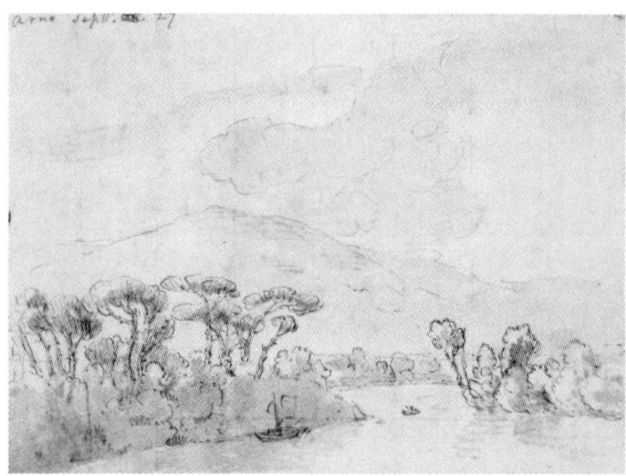

D.1975.9.19

View along the Arno
27.9.1783
pencil, grey watercolour
inscribed & dated upper left: *Arno Septr.* [erasure] *27*
174 × 238 mm
Leger Galleries, London (purchase, 1975) (D.1975.9.19)

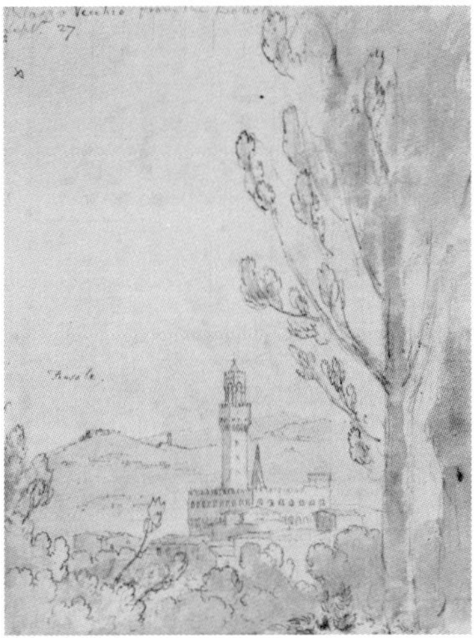

D.1975.9.20

View of the Palazzo Vecchio, with Fiesole in the Background, from the Boboli Gardens
27.9.1783
pencil, grey watercolour
inscribed & dated upper left: *Palazzo Vecchio from the Boboli / Sept.27.*; inscribed lower left identifying the town in the distance: *Fiesole*
238 × 174 mm
Leger Galleries, London (purchase, 1975) (D.1975.9.20)

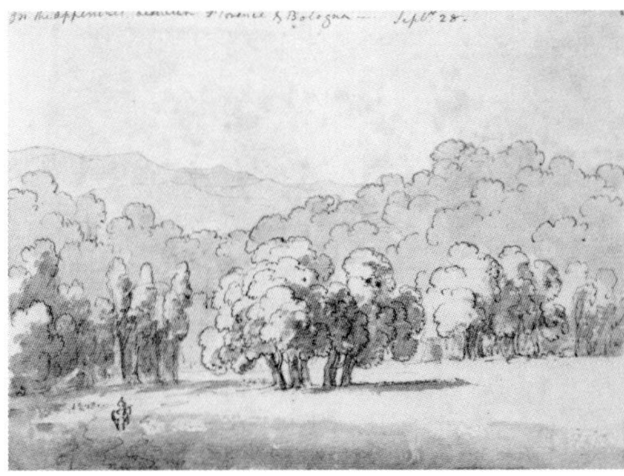

D.1975.9.21

View in the Apennines between Florence and Bologna
28.9.1783
pencil, grey watercolour
inscribed & dated upper edge: *On the Appenines* (sic) *between Florence & Bologna – Septr.28.*
174 × 238 mm
Leger Galleries, London (purchase, 1975) (D.1975.9.21)

A Villa on a Hillside among Trees between Florence and Bologna
28.9.1783
pencil, grey watercolour
inscribed & dated upper left: *Between Florence & Bologna – Septr.28 / A Villa –*
174 × 238 mm
Leger Galleries, London (purchase, 1975) (D.1975.9.22)

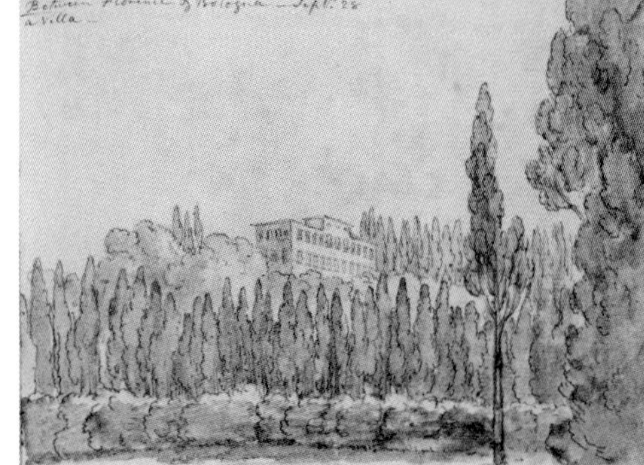

D.1975.9.22

Wooded Hills in the Apennines
28.9.1783
pencil, grey watercolour
inscribed & dated upper left: *Appenines – Septr.28.*
174 × 238 mm
Leger Galleries, London (purchase, 1975) (D.1975.9.23)

View of Lake Maggiore
10.10.1783
pencil, grey watercolour
inscribed & dated upper left: *On the Lago Magiore* (sic) *– Octr.10*; inscribed lower left with colour note: *dark blue*; inscribed in centre of drawing identifying colour of the mountain in the distance: *snow*
174 × 238 mm
Leger Galleries, London (purchase, 1975) (D.1975.9.24)

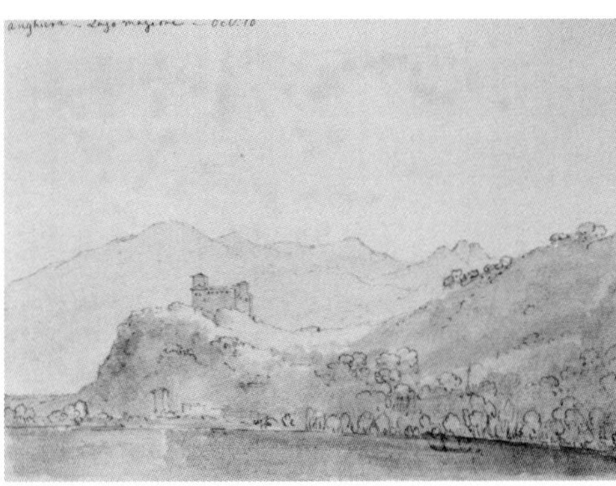

D.1975.9.25

Angera, View of a Castle on a Hill from Lake Maggiore
10.10.1783
pencil, grey watercolour
inscribed & dated upper left: *Anghiera – Lago Maggiore* (sic) *– Octr.10*
174 × 238 mm
Leger Galleries, London (purchase, 1975) (D.1975.9.25)

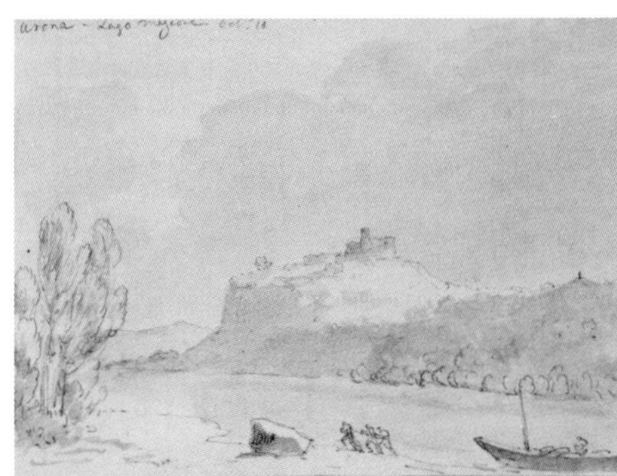

D.1975.9.26

Arona, View of a Castle on a Hill from Lake Maggiore, with Figures hauling a Boat ashore
10.10.1783
pencil, grey watercolour
inscribed & dated upper left: *Arona – Lago Magiore* (sic) *– Octr.10*
174 × 238 mm
Leger Galleries, London (purchase, 1975) (D.1975.9.26)

View on Lake Maggiore
10.10.1783
pencil
inscribed upper left: *Lago Magiore* (sic) *–*
174 × 238 mm
Leger Galleries, London (purchase, 1975) (D.1975.9.27)

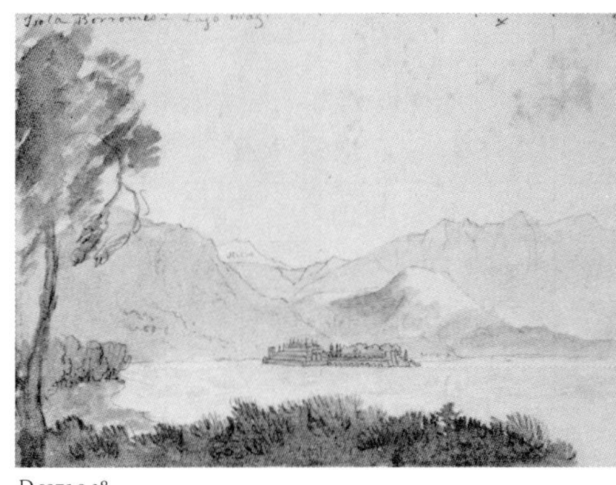

D.1975.9.28

View of Isola Borromea, Lake Maggiore
10.10.1783
pencil, grey watercolour
inscribed upper left: *Isola Borromeo – Lago Mag*
174 × 238 mm
Leger Galleries, London (purchase, 1975) (D.1975.9.28)

View of Isola Bella
10.10.1783
pencil
inscribed upper left: *Isola* [erased] *Isola.*
174 × 238 mm
Leger Galleries, London (purchase, 1975) (D.1975.9.29)

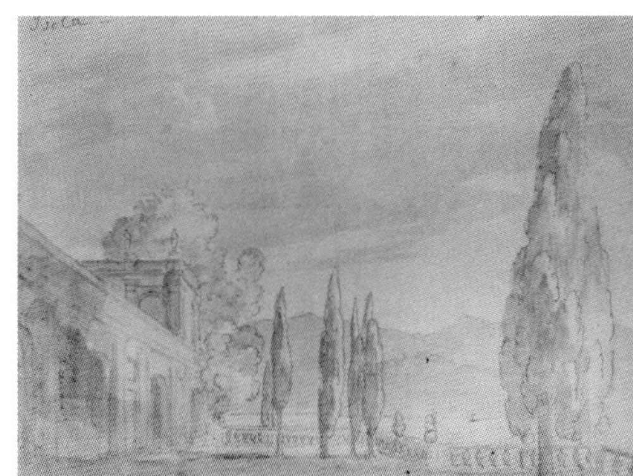

D.1975.9.30

View of a Terrace with Cypresses on Isola Bella
10.10.1783
pencil, grey watercolour
inscribed upper left: *Isola –*
174 × 238 mm
Leger Galleries, London (purchase, 1975) (D.1975.9.30)

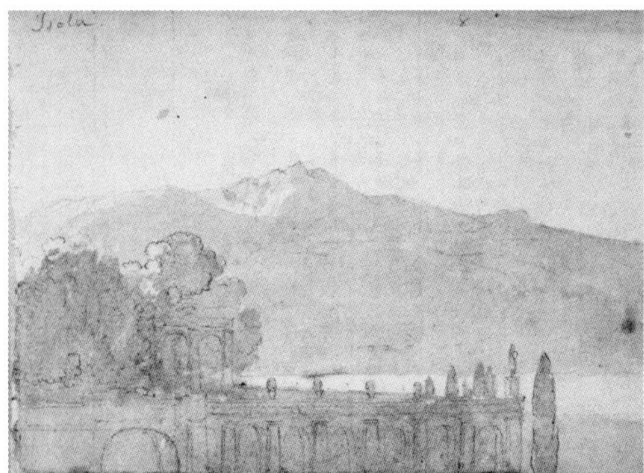

D.1975.9.31

View of a Terrace on Isola Bella
10.10.1783
pencil, grey watercolour
inscribed upper left: *Isola.*
174 × 238 mm
Leger Galleries, London (purchase, 1975) (D.1975.9.31)

Sketchbook, Volume VII
1783
pencil, grey watercolour
175 × 239 mm
Leger Galleries, London (purchase, 1975) (V. & A., N.A.C.F.,
F.O.W., P.T.) (D.1975.10)

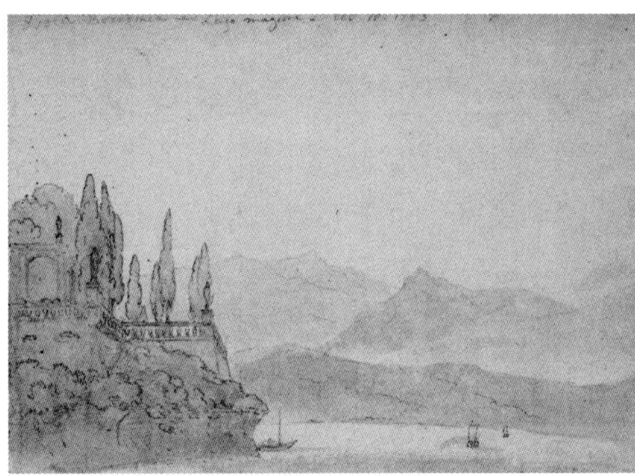

D.1975.10.1

Isola Borromea, Lake Maggiore
10.10.1783
pencil, grey watercolour
inscribed & dated upper edge: *Isola Borromea – Lago
Magiore* (sic) *– Octr.10.1783*
175 × 239 mm
Leger Galleries, London (purchase, 1975) (D.1975.10.1)

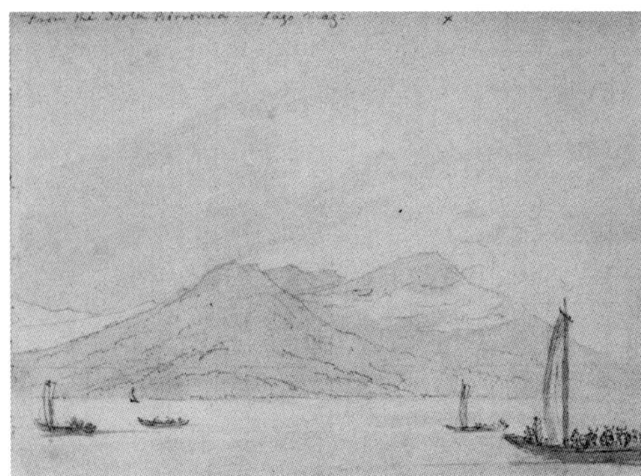

D.1975.10.2

View of Lake Maggiore from Isola Borromea
10.1783
pencil, grey watercolour
inscribed upper left: *From the Isola Borromea –
Lago Mag*
175 × 239 mm
Leger Galleries, London (purchase, 1975) (D.1975.10.2)

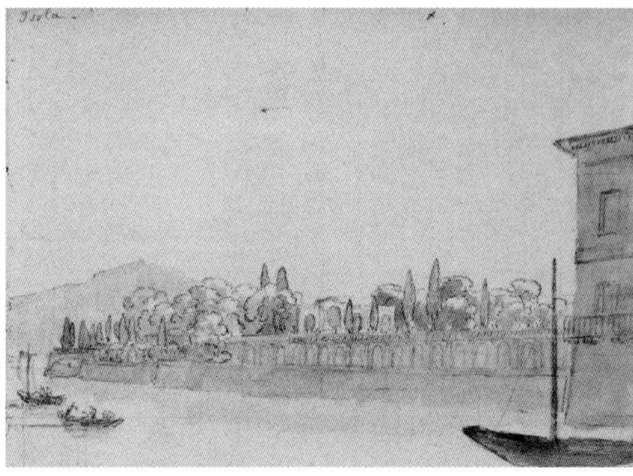

D.1975.10.3

View of an arcaded Terrace on Isola Bella
10.1783
pencil, grey watercolour
inscribed upper left: *Isola.*
175 × 239 mm
Leger Galleries, London (purchase, 1975) (D.1975.10.3)

View of San Michele, Piedmont
10.1783
pencil, grey watercolour
inscribed upper left: *S – Michele – Piedmont – Octr.18.*
175 × 239 mm
Leger Galleries, London (purchase, 1975) (D.1975.10.4)

View on Mont Cenis
20.10.1783
pencil, grey watercolour
inscribed & dated upper left: *On M.Cenis – Octr.20.*;
inscribed upper centre, identifying colour of mountain
in the distance: *snow*
175 × 239 mm
Leger Galleries, London (purchase, 1975) (D.1975.10.5)

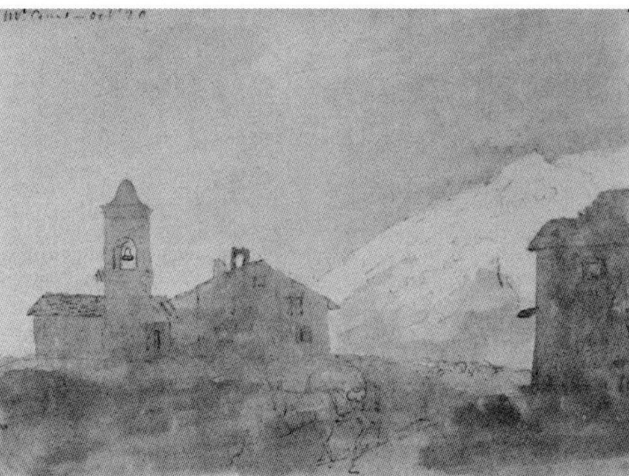

D.1975.10.6

View of the Hospice on Mont Cenis
20.10.1783
pencil, grey watercolour
inscribed & dated upper left: *Mt.Cenis – Octr.20*;
inscribed on mountain in distance identifying colour:
snow / snow
175 × 239 mm
Leger Galleries, London (purchase, 1975) (D.1975.10.6)

View of Peaks under a stormy Sky, Mont Cenis
10.1783
pencil, grey watercolour
inscribed upper left: *Mt.Cenis*; inscribed on mountains
in distance identifying colour: *snow / snow*; inscribed
lower left identifying part of the landscape: *Plain*
175 × 239 mm
Leger Galleries, London (purchase, 1975) (D.1975.10.7)

View of Mont Cenis, with rocky Boulders in the Foreground
10.1783
pencil, grey watercolour
inscribed upper left: *Mt.Cenis*
175 × 239 mm
Leger Galleries, London (purchase, 1975) (D.1975.10.8)

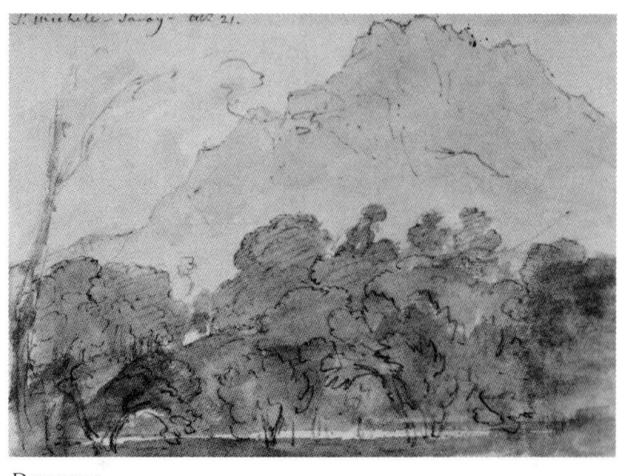

D.1975.10.9

View of St Michel, Savoy
21.10.1783
pencil, grey watercolour
inscribed & dated upper left: *St.Michele – Savoy –
Octr.21.*
175 × 239 mm
Leger Galleries, London (purchase, 1975) (D.1975.10.9)

View of a Pass and Mountain Peaks, near Aiguebelle
22.10.1783
pencil, grey watercolour
inscribed & dated upper left: *Near Aguebelle – Octr.22.*
175 × 239 mm
Leger Galleries, London (purchase, 1975) (D.1975.10.10)

View of a narrow Gorge between rocky Cliffs leading to the Grande Chartreuse
24.10.1783
pencil, grey watercolour
inscribed & dated upper edge: *Leading to the Grand
Chartreuse – Octr.24*
239 × 175 mm
Leger Galleries, London (purchase, 1975) (D.1975.10.11)

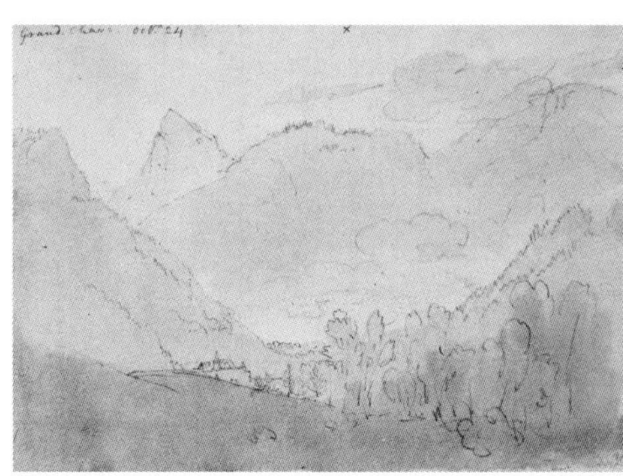

D.1975.10.12

The Convent of the Grande Chartreuse, surrounded by Trees and Mountains
24.10.1783
pencil, grey watercolour
inscribed & dated upper left: *Grand Char. Octr.24*
175 × 239 mm
Leger Galleries, London (purchase, 1975) (D.1975.10.12)

View of Tree-lined Precipices, near the Grande Chartreuse
1783
pencil, grey watercolour
inscribed upper left: *Grand – Char.*
175 × 239 mm
Leger Galleries, London (purchase, 1975) (D.1975.10.13)

Fir Trees near the Grande Chartreuse
1783
pencil
inscribed lower left going up page: *Grand Char –*
239 × 175 mm
Leger Galleries, London (purchase, 1975) (D.1975.10.14)

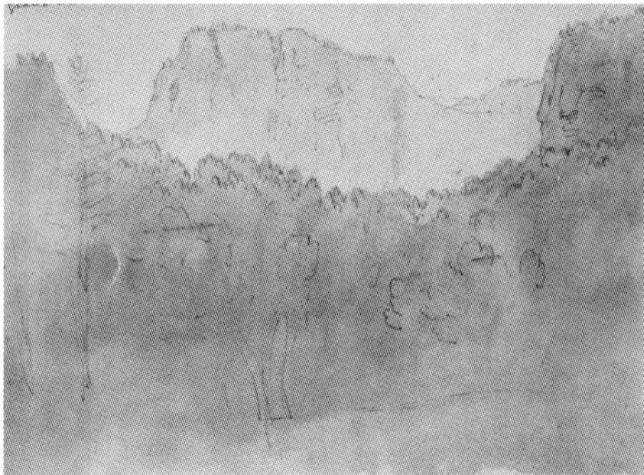
D.1975.10.15

View of wooded Heights at the Grande Chartreuse
1783
pencil, grey watercolour
inscribed upper left: *Grand Char*
175 × 239 mm
Leger Galleries, London (purchase, 1975) (D.1975.10.15)

D.1975.10.16

View of Mountain Peaks rising beyond the Forest at the Grande Chartreuse
1783
pencil, grey watercolour
inscribed upper left: *Grand Char*
239 × 175 mm
Leger Galleries, London (purchase, 1975) (D.1975.10.16)

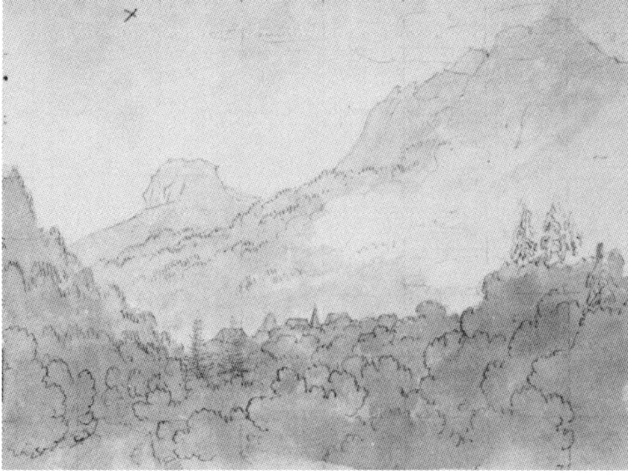
D.1975.10.17

The Convent Roof of the Grande Chartreuse seen above the Tree-tops, with Mountains in the Background
1783
pencil, grey watercolour
175 × 239 mm
Leger Galleries, London (purchase, 1975) (D.1975.10.17)

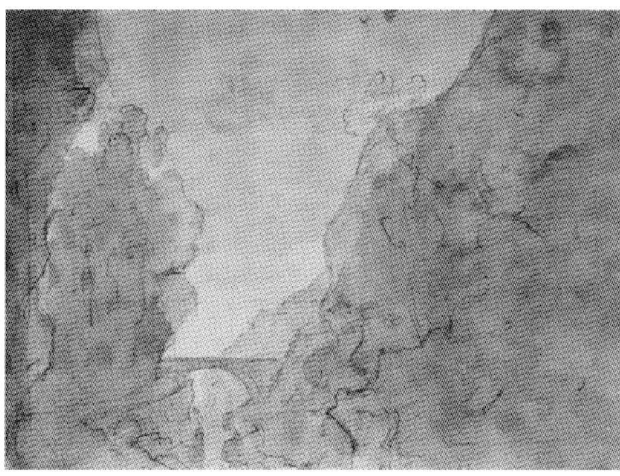
D.1975.10.18

The Pont St Bruno spanning a rocky Gorge, near the Grande Chartreuse
1783
pencil, grey watercolour
175 × 239 mm
Leger Galleries, London (purchase, 1975) (D.1975.10.18)

View of wooded Precipices and a Gorge, near the Grande Chartreuse
1783
pencil, grey watercolour
175 × 239 mm
Leger Galleries, London (purchase, 1975) (D.1975.10.19)

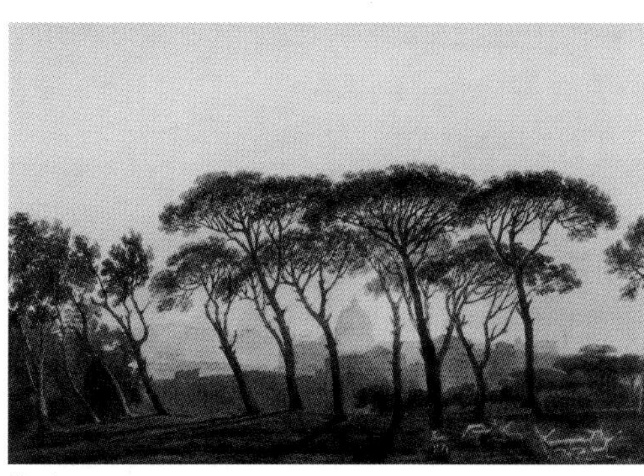
D.1984.5

St Peter's from the Villa Borghese, Rome
pencil, watercolour
257 × 371 mm
Agnew, Peter G. (purchase, 1984) (V. & A., N.A.C.F., F.O.W.)
(D.1984.5)

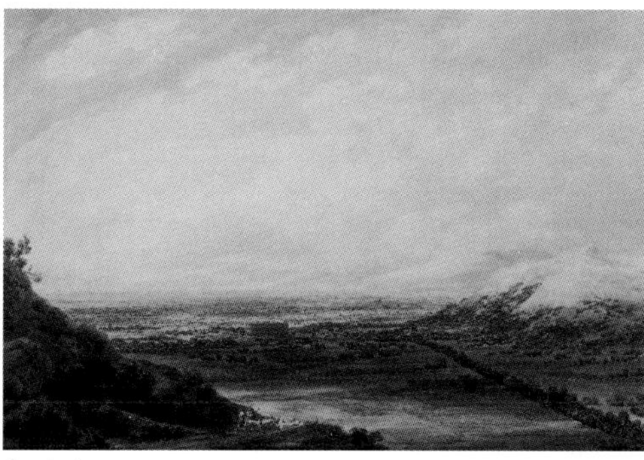
D.1984.6

From the Road between Caserta and the Aqueduct, Italy
pencil, watercolour
370 × 534 mm
Agnew, Peter G. (purchase, 1984) (V. & A., N.A.C.F., F.O.W.)
(D.1984.6)

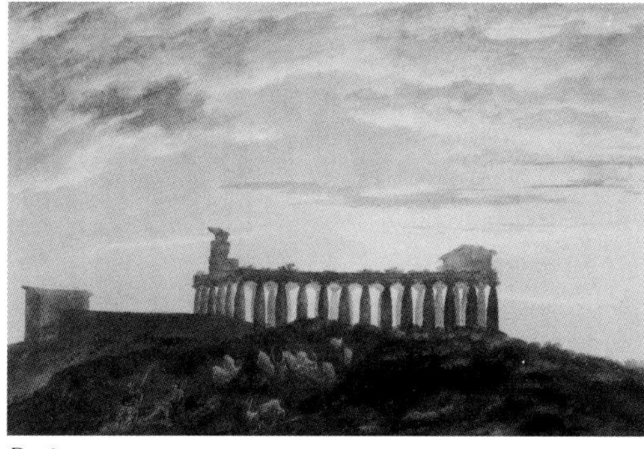
D.1984.7

The small Temple at Paestum, Italy
pencil, watercolour
253 × 370 mm
Agnew, Peter G. (purchase, 1984) (V. & A., N.A.C.F., F.O.W.)
(D.1984.7)

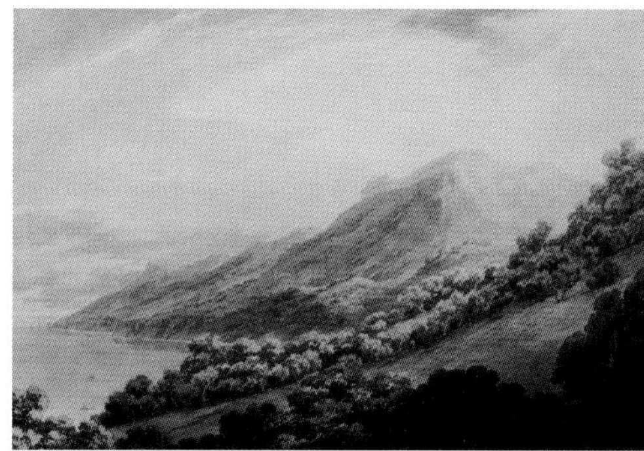
D.1984.8

The Coast of Vietri from Salerno, Italy
1789
pencil, watercolour
signed & dated on mount lower left: *J.Cozens 1789*
368 × 534 mm
Agnew, Peter G. (purchase, 1984) (V. & A., N.A.C.F., F.O.W.)
(D.1984.8)

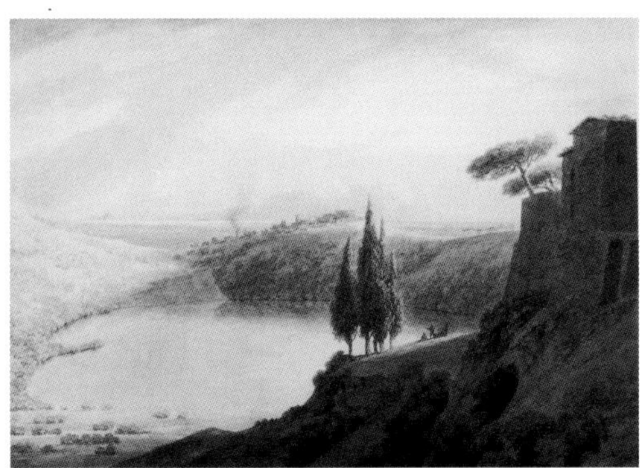

D.1984.9

Lake Nemi, Italy
pencil, watercolour
483 × 667 mm
Agnew, Peter G. (purchase, 1984) (V. & A., N.A.C.F., F.O.W.)
(D.1984.9)

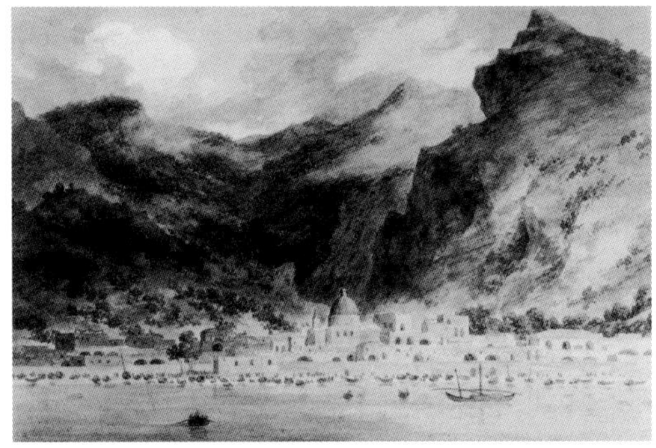

D.1984.10

Cetara, a Fishing Town on the Gulf of Salerno, Italy
pencil, watercolour
numbered: *34*; inscribed verso: *Citario a Fishing Town in the Bay of Salerno*; inscribed verso: *Citaria a Fishing Town in the gulph of Salerno*
261 × 374 mm
Keith, Mrs Cecil, Agnew's (via) (purchase, 1984) (V. & A., N.A.C.F., F.O.W.) (D.1984.10)

■ CRANE, WALTER (1845–1915)

Crane, born in Liverpool, is best known as a prolific designer and book illustrator. He spent two years in Italy from 1871–73. He was a member of the Royal Institute from 1882 to 1886 but resigned in 1889 in order to become a member of the Royal Watercolour Society. In later life Crane was a committed Socialist and follower of William Morris.

Night and Day, Design for a painted Ceiling at Wortley Hall, Yorkshire
1876
watercolour, white bodycolour, gold bodycolour
brown paper
556 × 342 mm
Lees, Charles E. (gift, 1894) (D.1894.6)

Europa and the Bull, Study for 'Europa'
1881
watercolour, bodycolour
244 × 534 mm
Lees, Charles E. (gift, 1894) (D.1894.7)

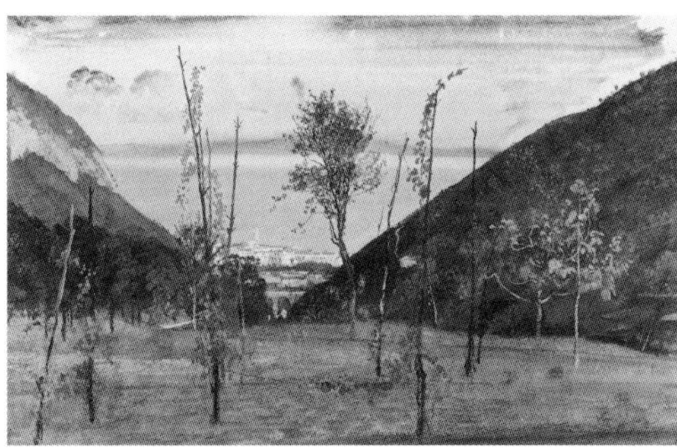

D.1894.6

Design for a Christmas Card
1877–79
pen and brown ink, brown watercolour, bodycolour (heightened with white); card (reddish brown)
signed centre left with monogram of crane within capital C; inscribed lower edge within a cartouche:
THIS XMASTIDE, BENEATH THE BERRY, / FEAST YOU HAPPY, & REST YOU MERRY.
214 × 141 mm
Barlow, Sir Thomas (gift, 1942) (D.1942.6)

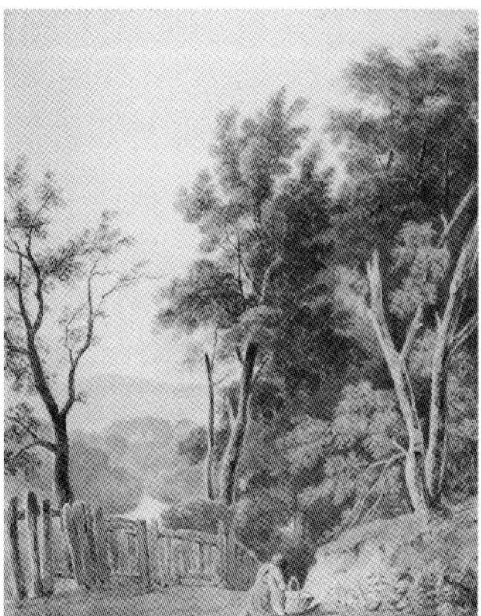

D.1954.5

Vietri on the Gulf of Salerno, from Cava dei Terreni, Italy
1872
watercolour, bodycolour
201 × 311 mm
untraced (gift, 1954) (D.1954.5)

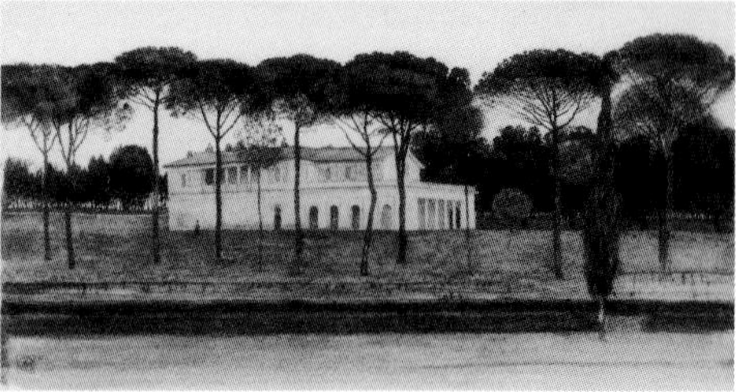

D.1973.11

An Italian Villa
1872
watercolour
signed & dated lower left with monogram in the form of a crane within a circle within a square: *1872*
189 × 352 mm
Friends of the Whitworth (gift, 1973) (D.1973.11)

■ CRANMER, Jun., CHARLES (1780–1841)

There is little information on this artist. Grant describes Charles Cranmer's pictures as being 'not of high class, being green transcriptions of roadside and meadow . . . done in a commonplace, even common, manner which often brings them down to "furniture" level'.

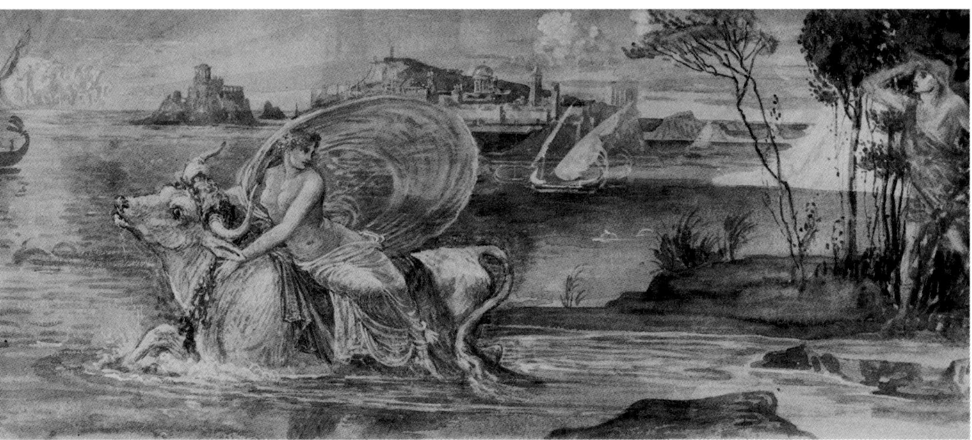

D.1934.2

A wooded Path above a River
1810
watercolour
signed & dated lower left with initials in monogram: *CC 1810*
347 × 270 mm
Friends of the Whitworth (gift, 1934) (D.1934.2)

D.1894.7

■ CRISTALL, JOSHUA (1767–1847)

Cristall entered the Royal Academy Schools in 1792. He was a founder member of the Old Watercolour Society in 1804 and its President in 1816, 1819 and from 1821 to 1831. In 1822 he moved to Goodrich on the River Wye, Herefordshire. His watercolours with large female figures are often a reckless combination of the real and the classical.

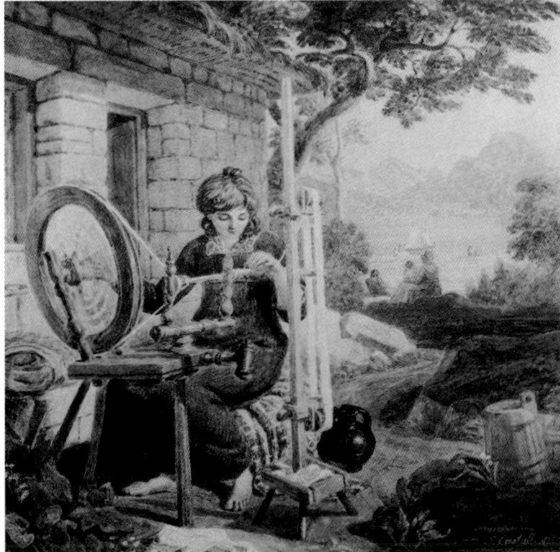

D.1892.46

A Girl spinning at a Cottage Door

1822
pencil, watercolour
signed & dated lower right: *J.Cristall 1822*
387 × 391 mm
Taylor, John Edward (gift, 1892) (D.1892.46)

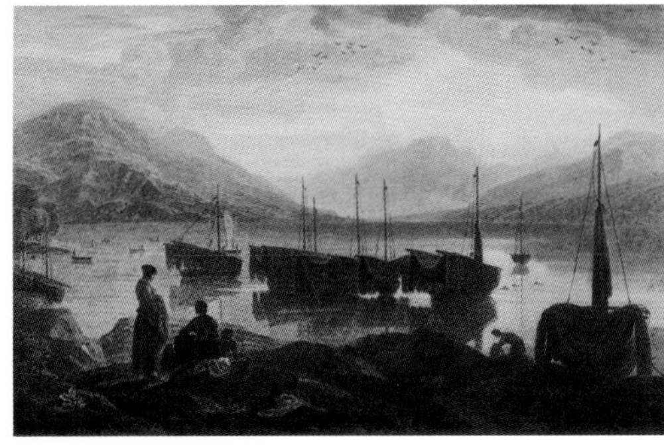

D.1892.146

Fishing Boats with Nets drying, Loch Fyne, Argyllshire

1833
pencil, watercolour
signed & dated lower left: *J.Cristall 1833*
317 × 471 mm
Taylor, John Edward (gift, 1892) (D.1892.146)

Study of Trees on the Thames near Culham Court, Berkshire

1816
pencil, brown watercolour, blue watercolour; three joined sheets of paper
signed & dated lower right with initials: *J.C. / 1816*;
inscribed lower right: *near Cullum* (sic) *Court Bucks*
137 × 344 mm
Pilkington, Margaret (gift, 1947) (D.1947.3)

A Group of Figures in a Wood: Study for a Classical Subject

pen and brown ink, brown watercolour
154 × 193 mm
Pilkington, Margaret (gift, 1947) (D.1947.4)

Study of Hermia and Lysander, from 'A Midsummer Night's Dream', Act III, Scene II (recto); Study of a male Nude (verso)

pen and brown ink, grey watercolour (recto); two joined sheets of paper
164 × 151 mm
Pilkington, Margaret (gift, 1947) (D.1947.5)

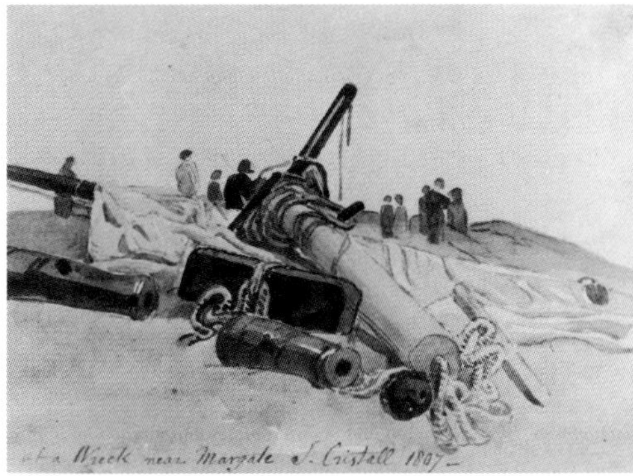

D.1950.4

Wreck near Margate, Kent

1807
pencil, watercolour; grey paper
signed, inscribed & dated lower edge: *at a Wreck near Margate J.Cristall 1807–*
145 × 194 mm
Pilkington, Margaret (gift, 1950) (D.1950.4)

Study of Mary Rogers gathering Sticks, Harley, Berkshire

7.9.1816
pencil, watercolour
signed & dated lower left: *J.Cristall 1816– Berkshire*;
signed, inscribed & dated centre upper edge of verso:
Mary Rogers / Harley Berks / 7.Sepr.–1816.–J.Cristall
342 × 187 mm
University of Manchester, History of Art Department (transfer, 1960) (D.1960.76)

Study of Figures on Copped Wood Hill, Herefordshire

pen and brown ink, black chalk, white chalk, brown watercolour; brown paper with top corners cut
inscribed lower right: *Coppet Hill*
102 × 137 mm
University of Manchester, History of Art Department (transfer, 1960) (D.1960.77)

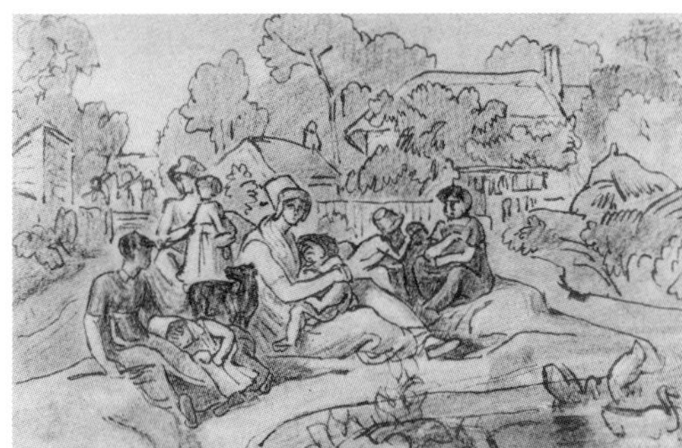

D.1960.78

Study of Women and Children by a Village Pond (recto); Study of a standing Woman with a Dog (verso)

pen and brown ink, black chalk, white chalk (recto) blue paper
133 × 204 mm
University of Manchester, History of Art Department (transfer, 1960) (D.1960.78)

Study of Figures by a Mountain Lake

pen and brown ink, black chalk, white chalk brown paper
121 × 194 mm
University of Manchester, History of Art Department (transfer, 1960) (D.1960.79)

■ CROME, JOHN (1768–1821)

Crome, sometimes known as 'the father of the Norwich school', was based in Norwich for the whole of his artistic career. He was one of the founders of the society that later became known as the Norwich Society of Artists and in 1808 was elected President. Crome was primarily an oil painter and his watercolours are rare. His son was also an artist, and he is sometimes referred to as 'Old Crome'.

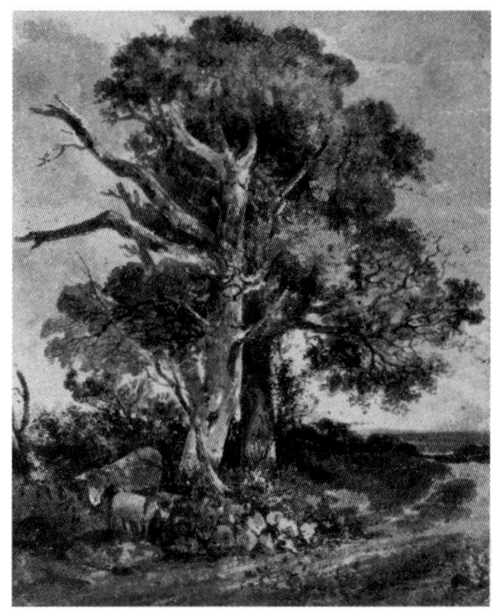

D.1905.1

By the Roadside

watercolour
260 × 210 mm
Agnew's (purchase, 21.6.1905) (D.1905.1)

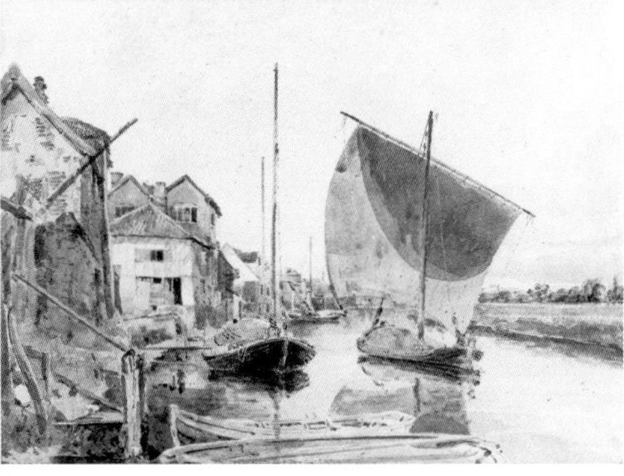

D.1945.7

Houses and Wherries on the River Wensum, Norwich

pencil, watercolour
301 × 398 mm
Colnaghi's (purchase, 1945) (D.1945.7)

■ CROME, JOHN (attributed to)

View on the Thames at Battersea, London
(1768–1821)
pencil, watercolour
216 × 307 mm
Barlow, Sir Thomas (gift, 1956) (D.1956.3)

■ CROMEK, THOMAS HARTLEY (1809–73)
The son of the engraver Robert Cromek, Thomas Cromek lived in Italy – mainly based in Rome – between 1831 and 1849. He travelled widely in both Italy and Greece and painted European views. In later life he settled in Wakefield.

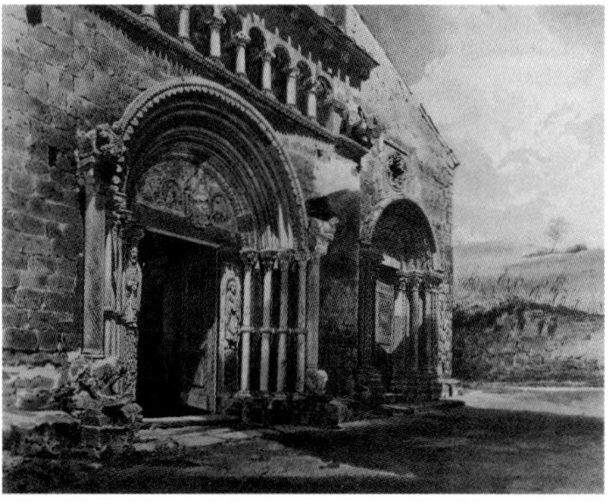
D.1946.1

The Central Portal of Santa Maria Maggiore, Toscanella, Italy
pen and brown ink, watercolour
383 × 472 mm
Barlow, Sir Thomas (gift, 1946) (D.1946.1)

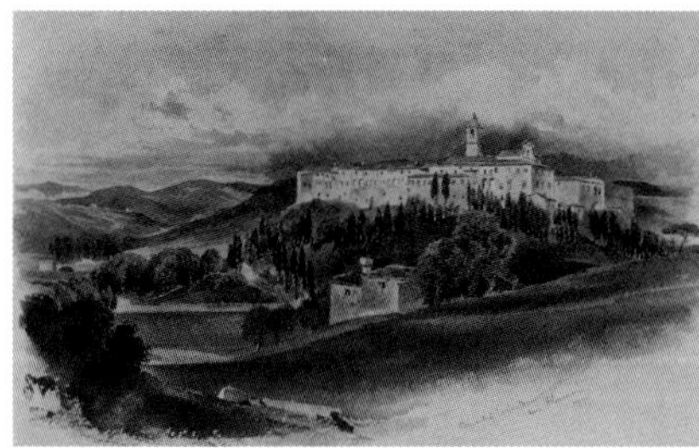
D.1972.7

The Carthusian Monastery of Certosa di Val d'Ema, Galluzzo, near Florence
1837
watercolour
inscribed & dated lower right: *Convent of La Certosa / near Florence / 1837*
245 × 382 mm
Colnaghi's (purchase, 1972) (D.1972.7)

■ CROTCH, WILLIAM (1775–1847)
Crotch was composer and organist at Christ Church, Oxford. An amateur pupil of Malchair, his drawings exercised an influence on the young Constable, with whom he is sometimes confused. Crotch's drawings are markedly left handed.

A distant View of Lancaster from the North East
pencil, pen and brown ink, grey watercolour
blue-grey paper
257 × 359 mm
Lockett, G. Derek (gift, 1966) (D.1966.2)

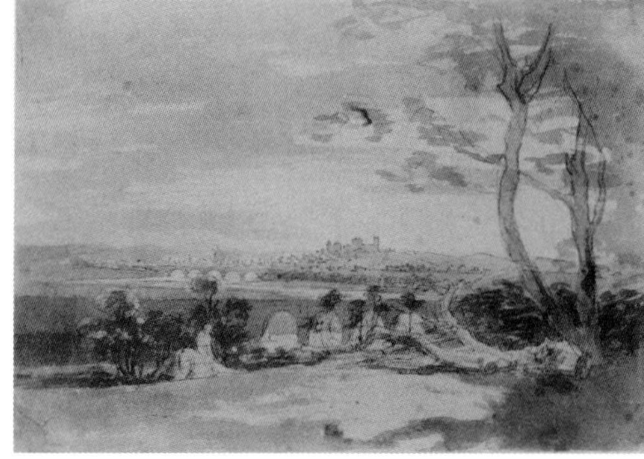
D.1966.2

■ CROWTHER, JOSEPH STRETCH (1820–93) (and office)
Crowther was a Manchester-based architect who had a practice with James Bowman and co-wrote with him *Churches of the Middle Ages* (1845–53); together they built a number of Gothic churches. Pevsner described Crowther as 'a learned architect and a man of considerable talent'.

Design for St Benedict's, Ardwick: Foundation Plan
1877
pencil, pen and black ink, pink watercolour
inscribed lower left: *Cordingley & Stopford*; inscribed upper left: *St. Benedict's Church / Ardwick No 2*; inscribed lower centre: *Foundation Plan*
371 × 537 mm
Martin, Sir Leslie (gift, 1996) (D.1996.31)

Design for St Benedict's, Ardwick: West Elevation
17.12.1877
pencil, pen and black ink
inscribed and dated lower right: *M J Crowther, Architect / Manchester Decr. 17th.1877*; inscribed lower left: *Orlando Cordingley / pro Cordingley & Stopford*; inscribed upper left: *St Benedict's Church / Ardwick / No 6*; inscribed lower centre: *West Elevation*
521 × 372 mm
Martin, Sir Leslie (gift, 1996) (D.1996.32)

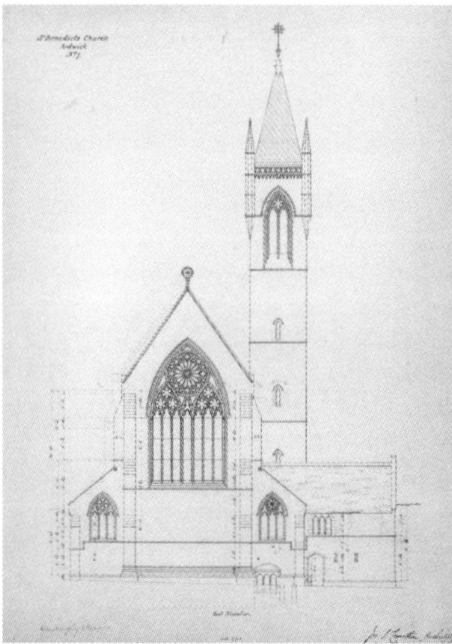
D.1996.33

Design for St Benedict's, Ardwick: East Elevation
17.12.1877
pencil, pen and black ink
inscribed and dated lower right: *M J Crowther, Architect / Manchester Decr. 17th*; inscribed lower left: *Cordingley & Stopford*; inscribed upper left: *St Benedict's Church / Ardwick / No 7*; inscribed lower centre: *East Elevation*
521 × 372 mm
Martin, Sir Leslie (gift, 1996) (D.1996.33)

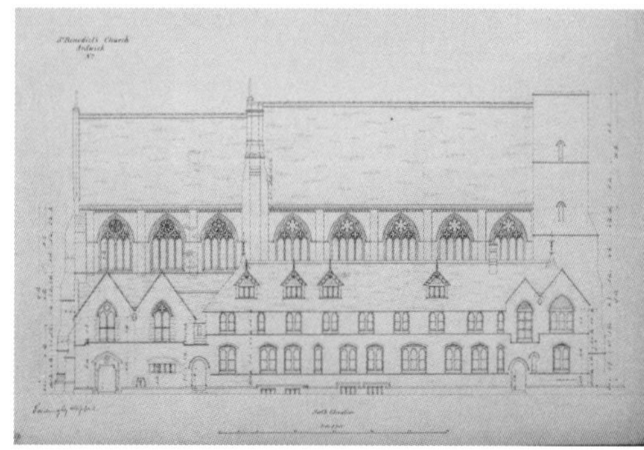
D.1996.34

Design for St Benedict's, Ardwick: North Elevation
1877
pen and black ink
inscribed lower left: *Cordingley & Stopford*; inscribed upper left: *St. Benedict's Church / Ardwick / No* [blank]; inscribed lower centre: *North Elevation*
374 × 534 mm
Martin, Sir Leslie (gift, 1996) (D.1996.34)

Design for St Benedict's, Ardwick: Sections
1877
pencil, pen and black ink, watercolour
inscribed lower left: *Cordingley & Stopford*; inscribed lower left: *Vertical Section through Campanile / looking South*; inscribed lower centre: *Transverse Section through Nave*; inscribed upper centre: *St.Benedict's Church / Ardwick /No 9*
524 × 379 mm
Martin, Sir Leslie (gift, 1996) (D.1996.35)

■ CRUIKSHANK, ISAAC (1756–1810)
Cruikshank, born in Edinburgh, moved to London and became a political and social caricaturist. He exhibited at the Royal Academy between 1789 and 1792.

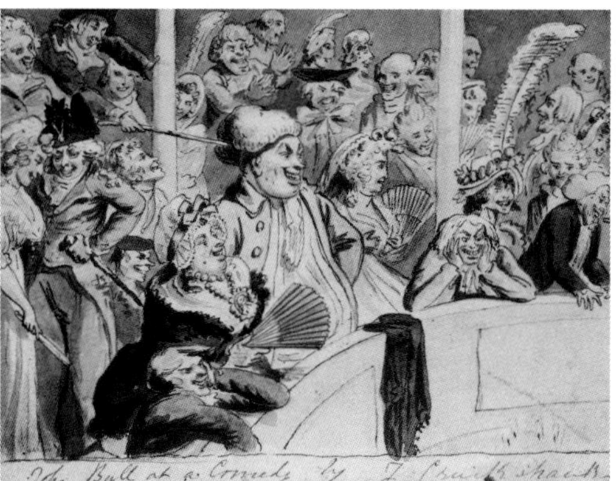
D.1972.1

John Bull at a Comedy
pen and brown ink, red chalk, watercolour
inscribed lower edge in later hand: *John Bull at a Comedy by I Cruikshank–*
186 × 236 mm
Leger Galleries, London (purchase, 1972) (D.1972.1)

■ CRUIKSHANK, ROBERT (1789–1856)

In common with his father Isaac and brother George, Robert Cruikshank was a caricaturist and illustrator. He sometimes collaborated with his better known brother.

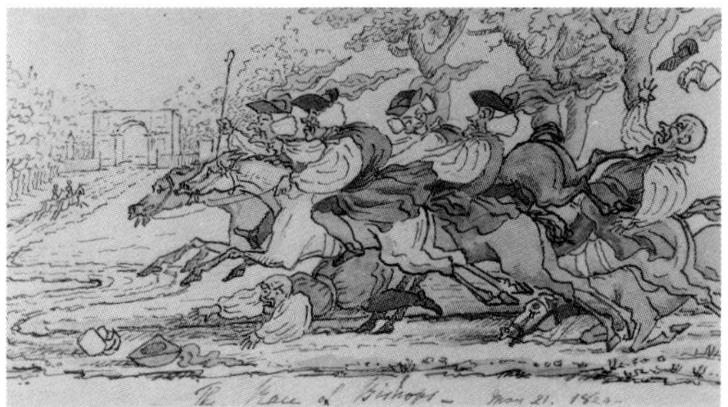
D.1950.5

The Race of Bishops, 21st May, 1829
pencil, pen and brown ink, watercolour
inscribed & dated lower centre: *The Race of Bishops– May 21.1829–*
111 × 188 mm
Friends of the Whitworth (gift, 1950) (D.1950.5)

■ DADD, RICHARD (1819–87)

Dadd entered the Royal Academy Schools in 1837 and went on a tour of Europe and the Middle East with Sir Thomas Phillips in 1842–43. He murdered his father in August 1843 and spent the rest of his life in a lunatic asylum, firstly at Bethlem Hospital and then in Broadmoor. Dadd continued to paint while in prison and produced highly detailed fairy paintings and imaginative watercolours.

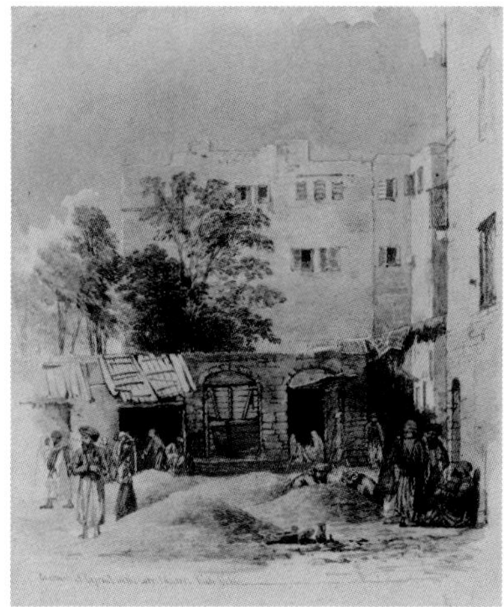
D.1947.8

The Corn Market, Beirut
1842
pencil, watercolour
signed & inscribed lower left: *Sketched at Beyrout in the Corn Market Rich Dadd*
238 × 196 mm
Barlow, Sir Thomas (gift, 1947) (D.1947.8)

■ DAHL, MICHAEL (1658/60–1743)

Dahl was born in Stockholm, and visited England in 1678 before studying in France and Italy. He returned to England in 1788 where he set himself up as a fashionable portrait painter numbering Queen Anne among his sitters.

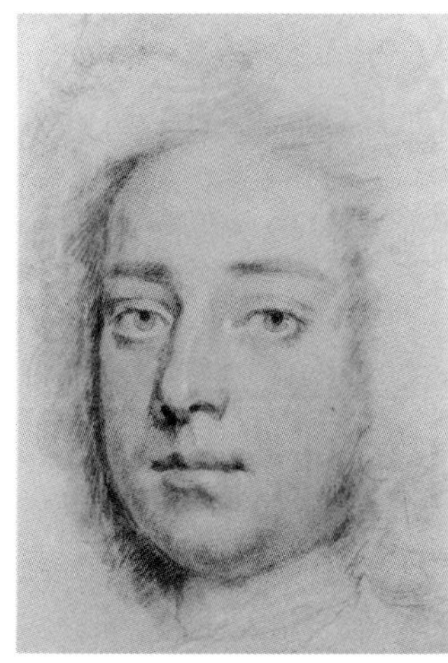
D.1960.92

Head of a Man
black chalk, white chalk; blue paper
315 × 216 mm
University of Manchester, History of Art Department (transfer, 1960) (D.1960.92)

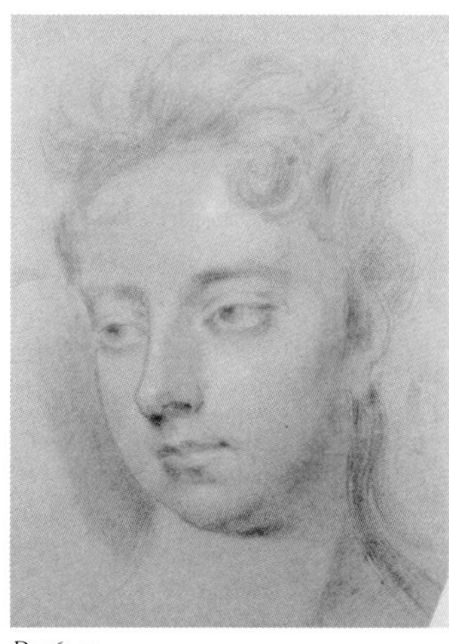
D.1960.93

Head of a Woman
black chalk, white chalk; blue paper
298 × 218 mm
University of Manchester, History of Art Department (transfer, 1960) (D.1960.93)

■ DANCE, GEORGE (1741–1825)

Dance, founder member of the Royal Academy and its Professor of Architecture from 1798 to 1805, produced portraits in pencil and chalk, as well as pen and ink or watercolour caricatures.

Portrait of a Man
13.5.1796
pencil, black chalk, blue chalk
signed & dated lower left: *Geo Dance / May 13th.1796*
254 × 193 mm
Friends of the Whitworth (gift, 1947) (D.1947.25)

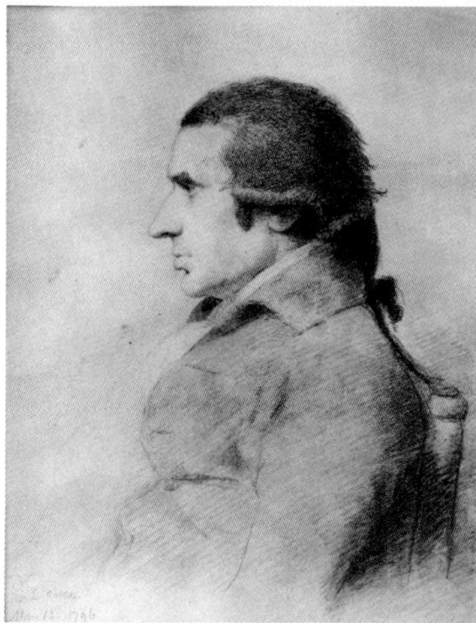
D.1947.25

■ DANCE, GEORGE (attributed to)

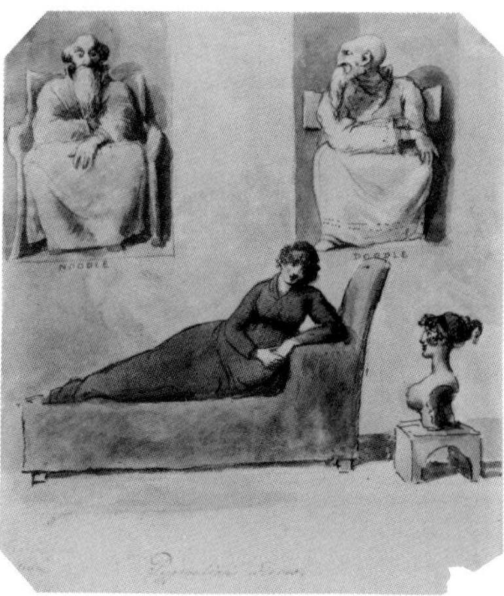
D.1926.330

Pygmalion's Widow
pencil, pen and brown ink, watercolour; corners cut
signed lower left: *Cianciafera* [i.e. Italian for the joker] / *Fecit*
217 × 186 mm
Ogden, William Sharp (bequest, 1926) (D.1926.330)

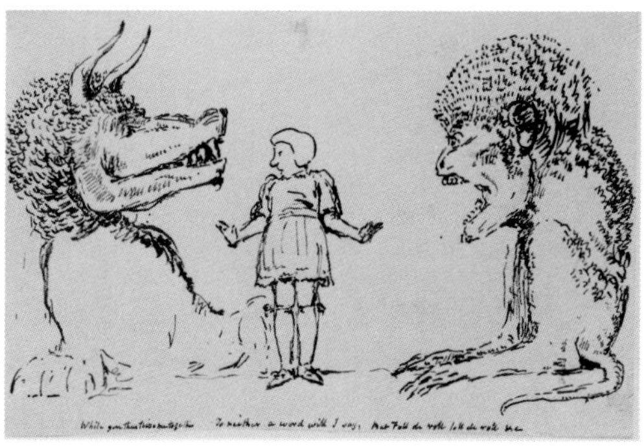
D.1926.332

Caricature of a boy standing between a Monkey and a horned Wolf
pen and brown ink
inscribed along lower edge: *While you thus teize* [difficult to read] *me togethery To neither a word will I say But Foll de roll loll de roll &c*
153 × 226 mm
Ogden, William Sharp (bequest, 1926) (D.1926.332)

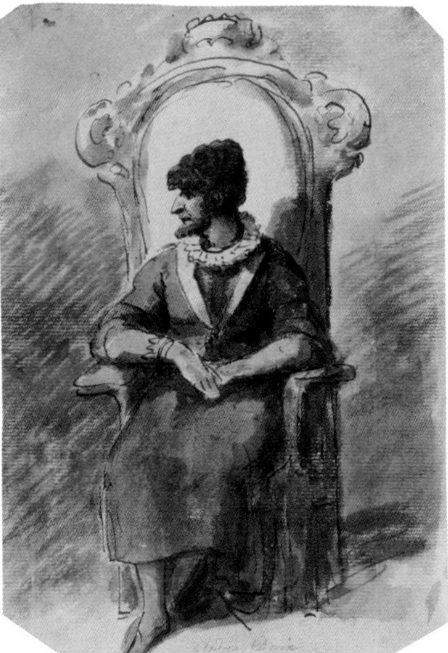

D.1926.333

Andrea Doria
pencil, pen and brown ink, brown watercolour
corners cut
inscribed lower centre: *Andrea Doria*; inscribed upper
edge verso: *Mr.James.Mountague*
247 × 167 mm
Ogden, William Sharp (bequest, 1926) (D.1926.333)

**Caricature of Major Cartwright as
Major Dungcart**
pencil, pen and brown ink; corners cut
inscribed lower left: *Major Dungcart*; inscribed centre
left in a speech bubble: *Hunt! Cobbett! / Cochrane! /
Burdett for ever!*
187 × 138 mm
Ogden, William Sharp (bequest, 1926) (D.1926.334)

**Caricature of a political Reformer
wearing a Mask**
pencil, pen and brown ink; corners cut
inscribed upper left vertically in a speech bubble:
Reform for ever! Universal Suffrag[e] */ Cobbett, Hunt,
and perfect felicity / under Burdettism & Cochranism*
190 × 145 mm
Ogden, William Sharp (bequest, 1926) (D.1926.335)

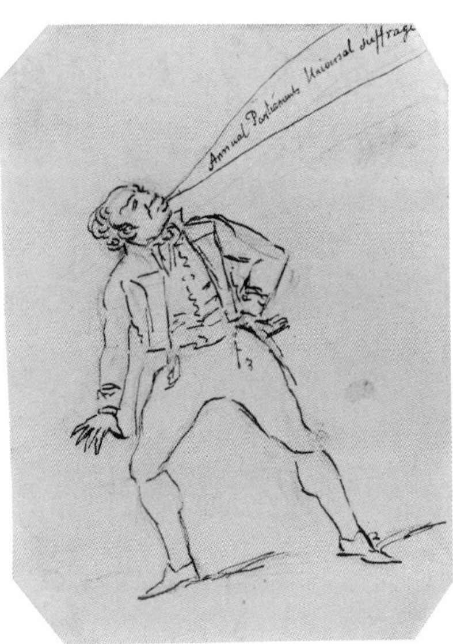

D.1926.336

Caricature of a Man protesting
pencil, pen and brown ink; corners cut
inscribed upper right in a speech bubble: *Annual
Parliaments Universal suffrage*
185 × 134 mm
Ogden, William Sharp (bequest, 1926) (D.1926.336)

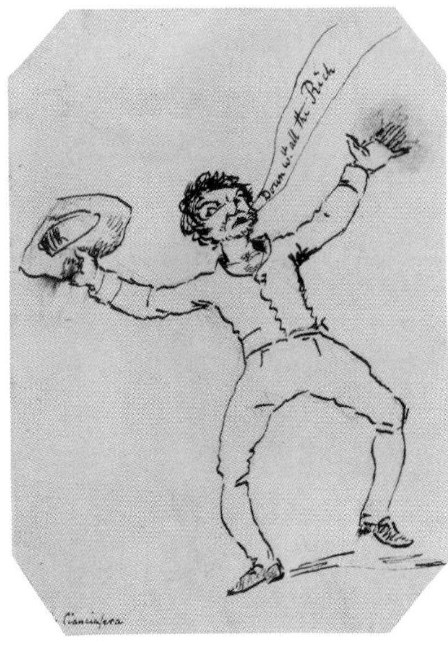

D.1926.337

Caricature of a Labourer protesting
pencil, pen and brown ink; corners cut
inscribed lower left partly cut: *Cinciafera*
[i.e. Italian for the joker]; inscribed upper right,
in a speech bubble: *Down wth. all the Rich*
191 × 135 mm
Ogden, William Sharp (bequest, 1926) (D.1926.337)

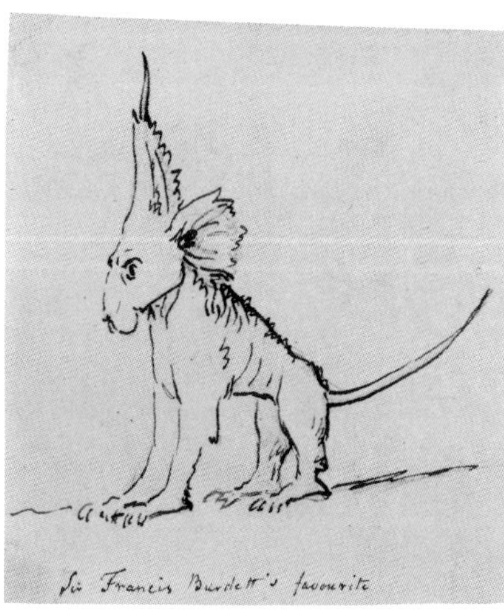

D.1926.338

Sir Francis Burdett's Favourite
pencil, pen and brown ink
inscribed lower edge: *Sir Francis Burdet's favourite*
133 × 115 mm
Ogden, William Sharp (bequest, 1926) (D.1926.338)

Caricature after a celebrated Master
pencil; corners cut
inscribed lower left; not a signature: *N.Dance*
inscribed lower right: *after a celebrated Master*
186 × 222 mm
Ogden, William Sharp (bequest, 1926) (D.1926.339)

A Donkey Ride
pencil, pen and brown ink, brown watercolour
corners cut
157 × 101 mm
Ogden, William Sharp (bequest, 1926) (D.1926.340)

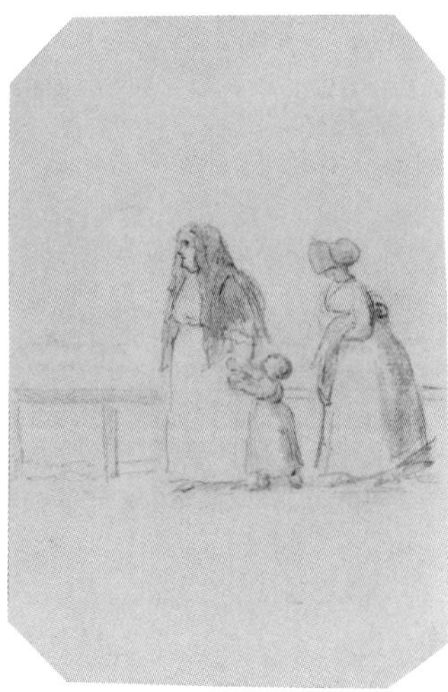

D.1926.341

Two Women with a Child
pencil, pen and brown ink, brown watercolour
corners cut
156 × 101 mm
Ogden, William Sharp (bequest, 1926) (D.1926.341)

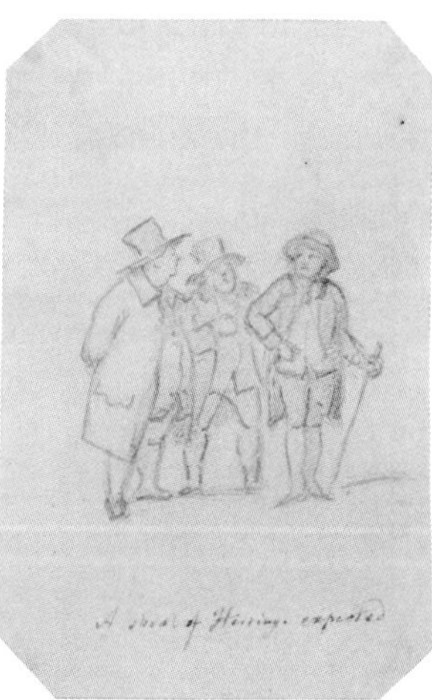

D.1926.342

Three Men in Conversation
pencil, pen and brown ink; corners cut
inscribed lower centre: *A shoal of Herrings expected*
158 × 100 mm
Ogden, William Sharp (bequest, 1926) (D.1926.342)

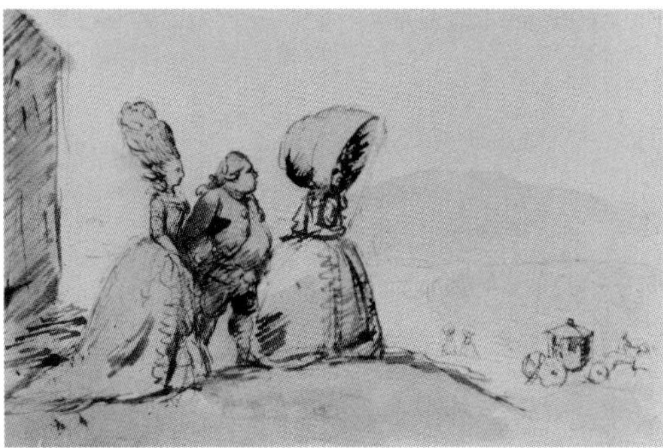

D.1987.22

A Man and two Women on a Hill above a Beach
pencil, pen and brown ink, watercolour
154 × 228 mm
Burton, Hal (bequest, 1987) (D.1987.22)

■ Dance, George (circle of)

Portrait of Thomas Girtin, bust length, in profile, facing to the left
1797–99
pencil, red chalk
inscribed lower centre in Girtin's hand: *T.Girtin*
246 × 191 mm
Girtin, Tom (bequest, 1995) (D.1995.11)

■ Dance-Holland, Sir Nathaniel (1735–1811)

Dance-Holland was the elder brother of George Dance and also a founder member of the Royal Academy. In 1790 he gave up painting professionally and entered politics; he was created a baronet in 1800. Like his brother he produced pen and ink or watercolour caricatures, and the two artists are frequently confused.

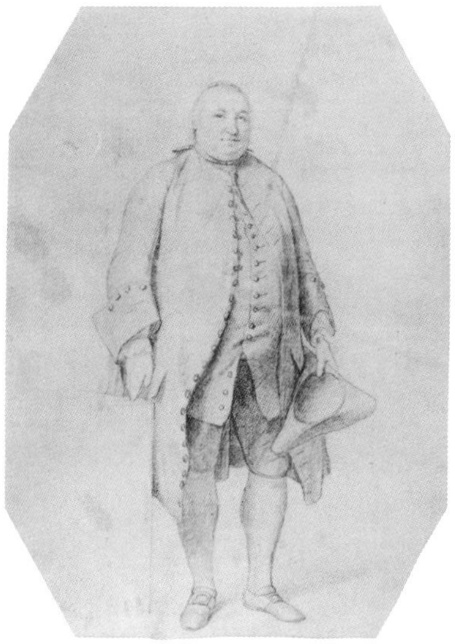

D.1926.49

Portrait of Francis Grose, the Antiquarian
pencil; corners cut
signed lower left: [name cut] *del.*
224 × 159 mm
Ogden, William Sharp (bequest, 1926) (D.1926.49)

■ Daniell, Samuel (1775–1811)

Samuel Daniell, the younger brother of William, exhibited at the Royal Academy for the first time in 1792. In 1799, he sailed for the Cape and in 1801 joined as secretary and draughtsman on an expedition to Bechuanaland, which had never been visited by Europeans. His drawings of African tribesmen that he produced at this time are refreshingly unconventional.

Korah Man with a Spear in a Landscape
12.1.1802
pencil, black chalk, brown watercolour
inscribed & dated lower right: *Jany.12 1802.Korah.Orange River*
263 × 187 mm
Spink and Son Ltd, London (purchase, 1973) (D.1973.6)

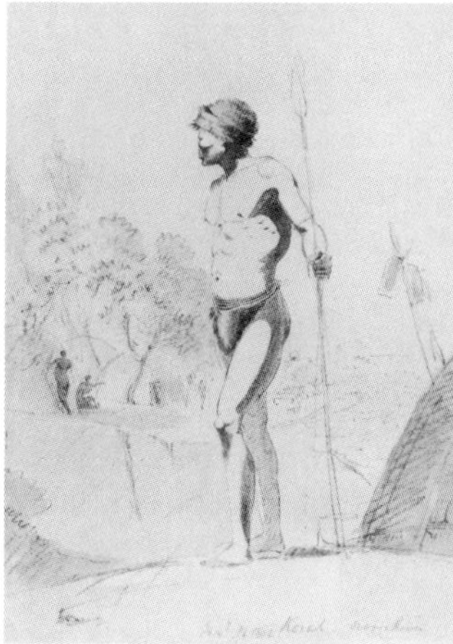

D.1973.6

■ Daniell, Thomas (1749–1840)

Thomas Daniell started off his career as a coach painter before exhibiting at the Royal Academy for the first time in 1772. He toured India from 1785–94 with his young nephew William, producing many prints that were published as aquatints in *Oriental Scenery*. Elected a member of the Royal Academy in 1797, he exhibited for the last time in 1830.

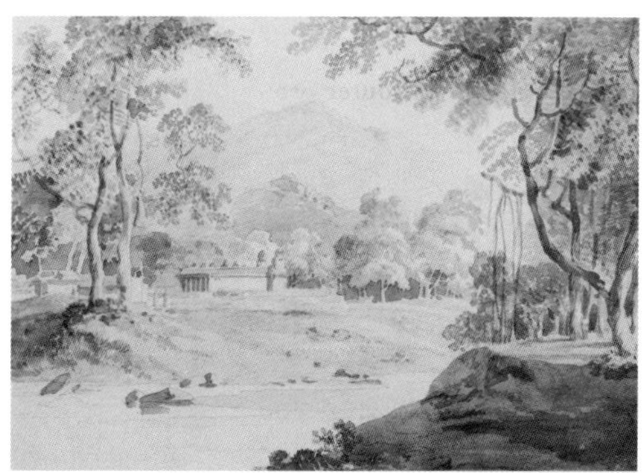

D.1951.3

Bottom of Toppur Pass, in the Salem Region of Madras, India
1791–93
pencil, watercolour
270 × 378 mm
Pilkington, Margaret (gift, 1951) (D.1951.3)

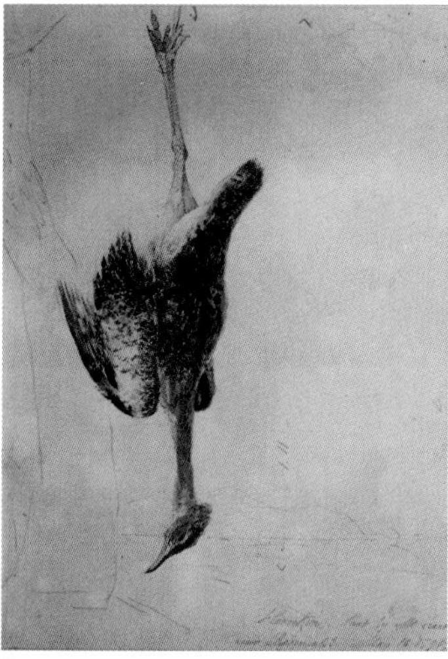

D.1963.9

A Floriken shot by Mr Grant, the British Resident, near Rajmahal, India
10.5.1790
pencil, watercolour
inscribed & dated lower right: *Florikin Shot by Mr.Grant / near Rajemahl May 10.1790*
327 × 223 mm
Friends of the Whitworth (gift, 1963) (D.1963.9)

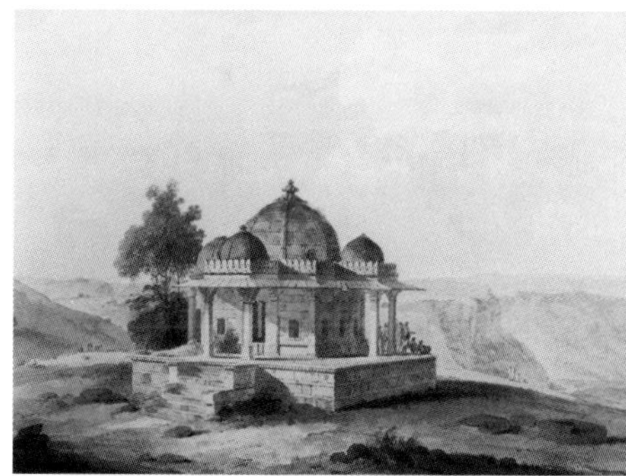

D.1975.2

Small Hindu Temple, with a distant View of the Escarpment, Rohtasgarh, Bihar, India
1790
pencil, watercolour
375 × 483 mm
Spink and Son Ltd, London (purchase, 1975) (F.O.W.) (D.1975.2)

■ Daniell, William (1769–1837)

William Daniell accompanied his uncle Thomas on tour through India from 1785 to 1794, and then collaborated with him on *Oriental Scenery*. He made his name as an aquatint engraver, publishing six views of London in 1805 and the mammoth *Voyage round Great Britain*, which contained 308 plates and was published in eight volumes between 1814 and 1825. Daniell was elected a member of the Royal Academy in 1822.

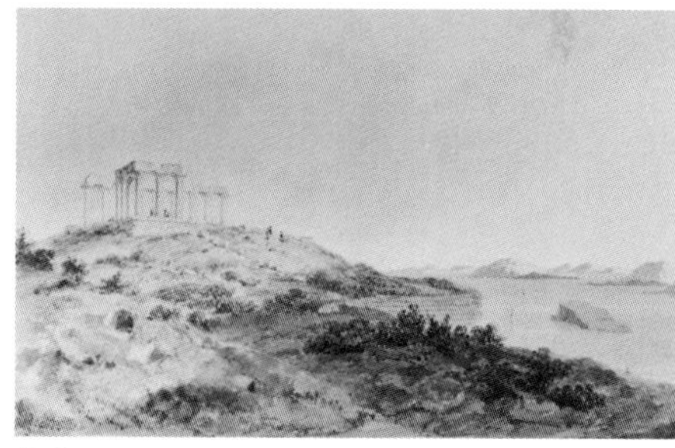

D.1892.59

Temple of Poseidon, Sounion, Greece
pencil, watercolour
inscribed lower centre margin: *THE TEMPLE OF MINERVA AT SUNIUM*
283 × 433 mm
Taylor, John Edward (gift, 1892) (D.1892.59)

■ Davis, John Scarlett (1804–45)

Born in Leominster in Herefordshire, Davis entered the Royal Academy Schools in 1820, exhibiting there sporadically until 1841. Details of his life are scanty, but he spent much of his career abroad working for private patrons. He specialised in domestic and church interiors and is one of the more accomplished followers of Bonington.

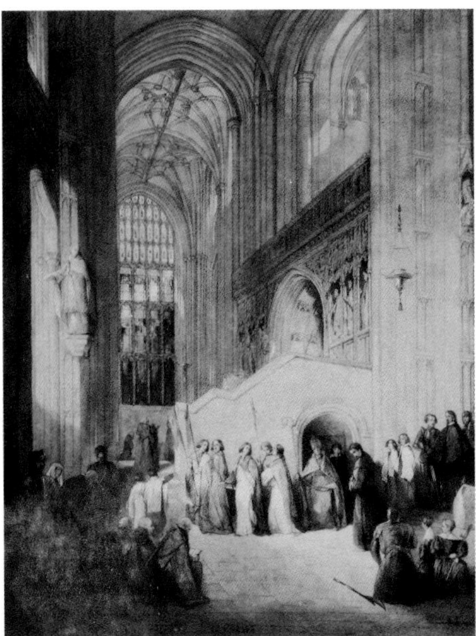

D.1933.24

The North Transept and Crossing, Canterbury Cathedral, the Scene of the Martyrdom of St Thomas Becket
1836
pencil, watercolour
signed & dated lower right on stone above figure holding sword with initials: *J S D / 1836*
389 × 292 mm
Dalton, Mrs W. B., Plummer, Miss E. M. (gift, 1933) (D.1933.24)

■ DAY, WILLIAM (1764–1807)

Day exhibited at the Royal Academy as an Honorary Exhibitor from 1782 to 1801. He accompanied his friend John Webber on tours of Derbyshire in 1789 and Wales in 1790; occasionally they are known to have sketched the same subject. Day was very interested in geology and his watercolours show his preoccupation with the texture of stone.

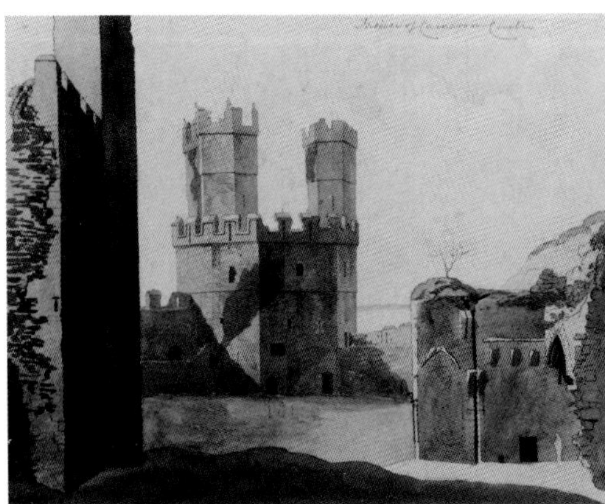

D.1954.19

Interior of Caernarvon Castle, Wales, looking towards the Eagle Tower
1790
pencil, pen and grey ink, watercolour
inscribed upper right: *Interior of Carnarvon Castle*; numbered on reverse twice: *53*
195 × 239 mm
Barlow, Sir Thomas (gift, 1954) (D.1954.19)

The South Transept, Netley Abbey, Hampshire
pencil, grey watercolour, brown watercolour
inscribed below mount lower left: *South Transept of Netley Abbey*; inscribed on stone in left foreground colour notes: *Chalky Stone & Morter* (sic) / *Strong white in Sunshine*; inscribed on stone in centre foreground: *Covered with moss Grass / & weeds very rich in colour*
547 × 377 mm
Pilkington, Margaret (gift, 1954) (D.1954.26)

■ DAYES, EDWARD (1763–1804)

Now chiefly known as the teacher of Thomas Girtin, Dayes exhibited topographical drawings, landscapes and literary subjects at the Royal Academy from 1786 to 1804. His tinted drawings with their elegantly drawn figures exercised a strong influence on the young Turner. Dayes committed suicide in 1804 and his posthumously published *The Works of the late Edward Dayes* sheds interesting light on his working methods.

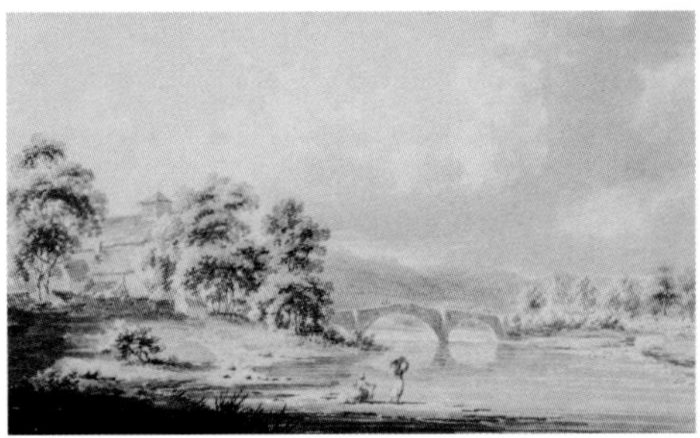

D.1887.7

Bridge at Llanrwst, Denbighshire, Wales
pencil, watercolour
238 × 381 mm
Agnew's (purchase, 1891) (D.1887.7)

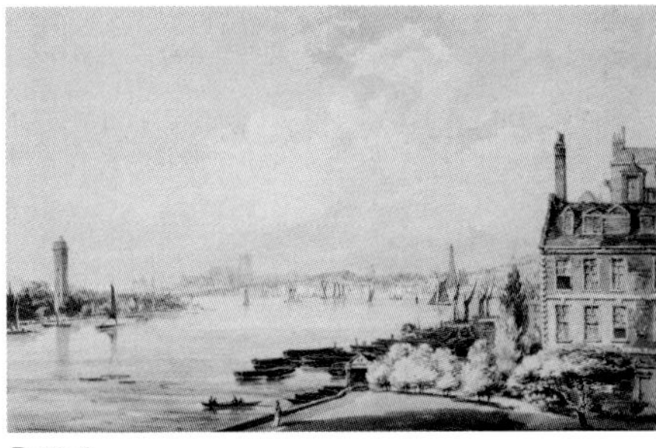

D.1887.8

The Thames looking from the Inner Temple Gardens towards Westminster
pencil, watercolour
264 × 411 mm
Agnew's (purchase, 6.6.1891) (D.1887.8)

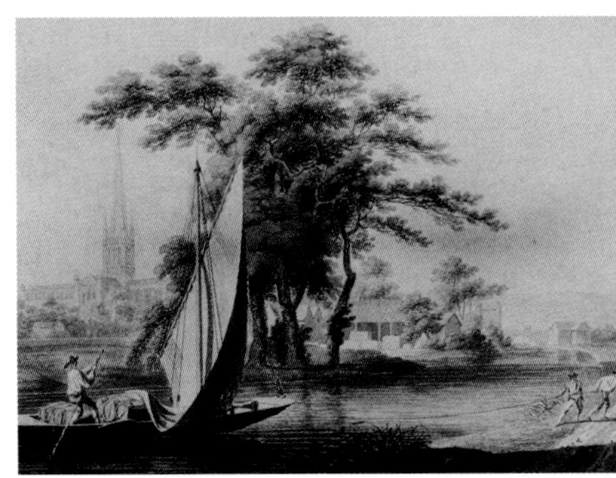

D.1892.45

Norwich Cathedral, from the River Wensum
1788
pencil, pen and grey ink, watercolour
signed & dated lower left: *Edwd. Dayes 1788*
321 × 416 mm
Taylor, John Edward (gift, 1892) (D.1892.45)

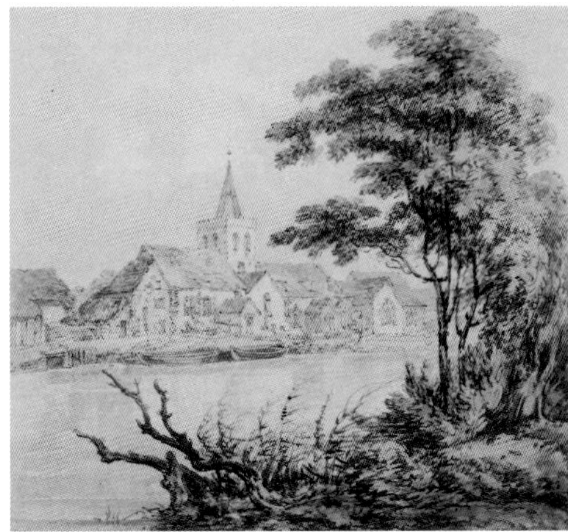

D.1892.82

All Saints Church, Great Marlow, Buckinghamshire
pencil, watercolour
180 × 192 mm
Taylor, John Edward (gift, 1892) (D.1892.82)

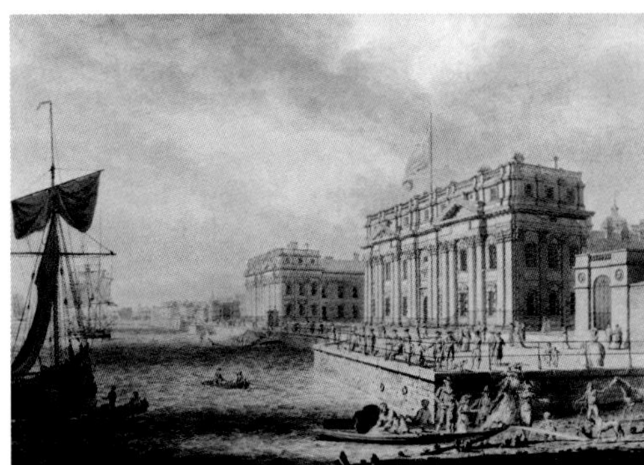

D.1892.147

Greenwich Hospital, London, View along the River Front
1789
pen and grey ink, watercolour
signed & inscribed on stern of ship lower left: *EDWD. DAYES LONDON*; dated lower left: *1789*
433 × 596 mm
Taylor, John Edward (gift, 1892) (D.1892.147)

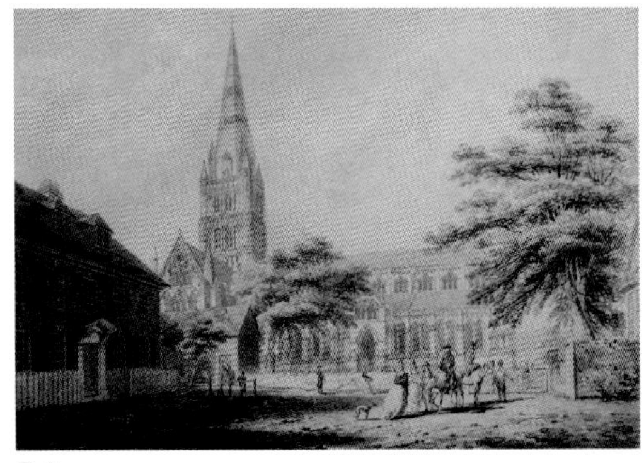

D.1899.7

Salisbury Cathedral, Wiltshire, from the North
pencil, pen and grey ink, watercolour
337 × 477 mm
Lees, Charles E. (gift, 1899) (D.1899.7)

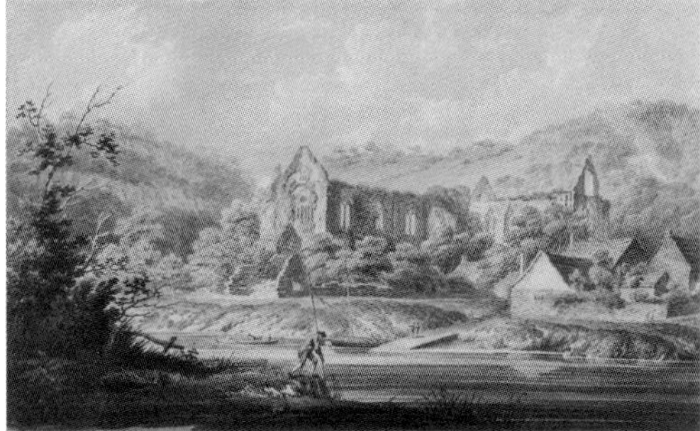

D.1899.8

Tintern Abbey, Monmouthshire, and the River Wye
1794
pencil, watercolour
signed & dated lower left: *Edw.Dayes 1794*
248 × 394 mm
Worthington, Mary (gift, 1899) (D.1899.8)

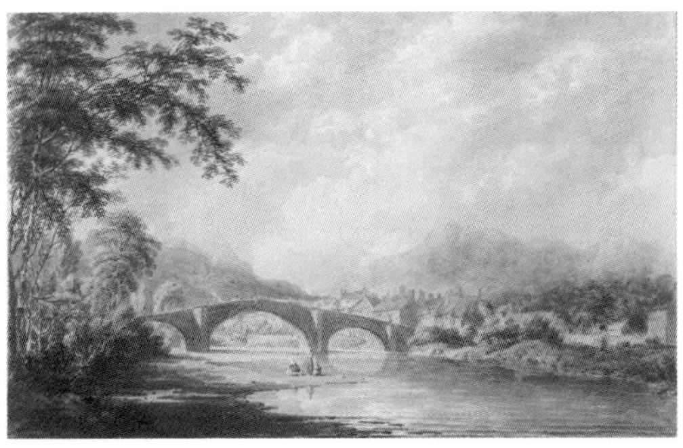

D.1924.40

Bridge at Llanrwst, Denbighshire, Wales
1793
pencil, watercolour
signed & dated lower left: *EDayes 1793*
240 × 373 mm
Broadhurst, Sir Edward Tootal, Broadhurst, Lady
(bequest, 1924) (D.1924.40)

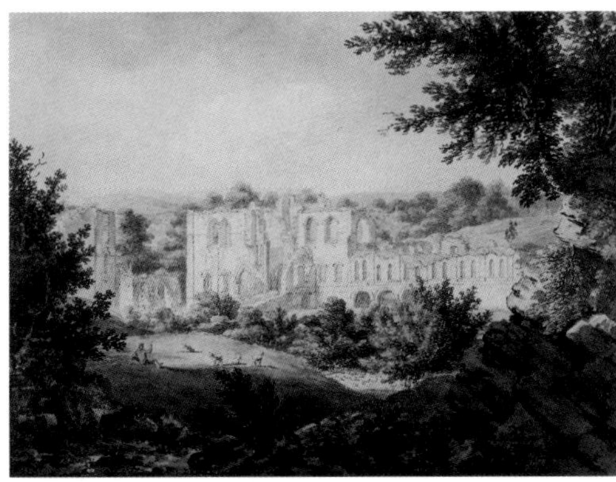

D.1924.84

Furness Abbey, Lancashire, from the North East
pencil, pen and grey ink, watercolour
381 × 504 mm
Broadhurst, Sir Edward Tootal, Broadhurst, Lady (bequest, 1924) (D.1924.84)

The Thames from Richmond Hill, Surrey
pencil, watercolour
203 × 288 mm
Cotswold Gallery, London (purchase, 1930) (D.1930.54)

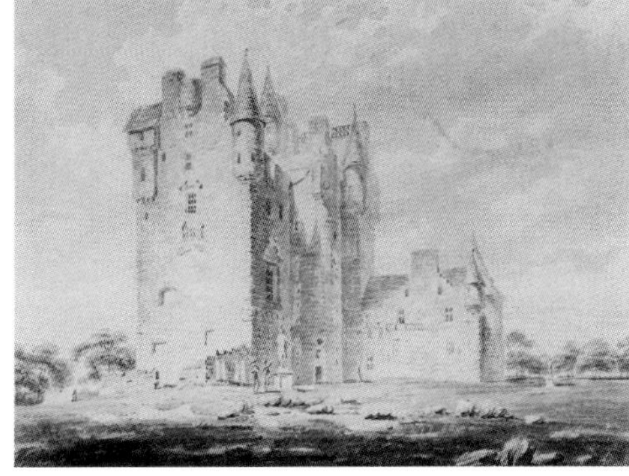

D.1955.7

Glamis Castle, Angus
pencil, watercolour
170 × 221 mm
Morley, Mrs John (gift, 1955) (D.1955.7)

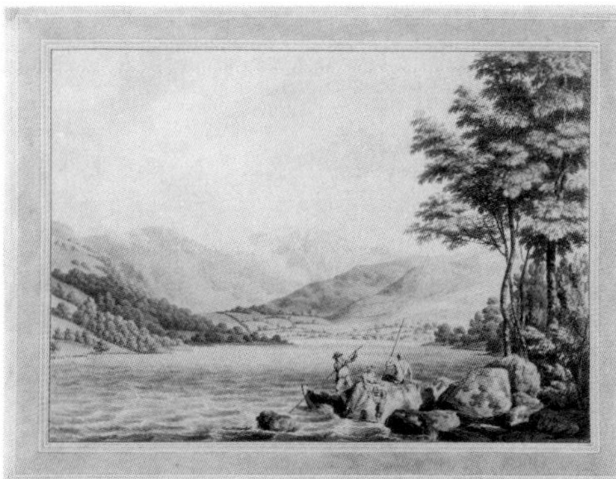

D.1967.8

View on Hawes Water, Westmorland
1795
pencil, pen and brown ink, watercolour
signed & dated lower right: *E Dayes / 1795*
358 × 493 mm
Tillotson, John (gift, 1967) (D.1967.8)

■ DE CORT, HENDRIK (1742–1810)

De Cort studied in Antwerp and Paris before coming to England in 1789. He travelled widely and specialised in brown wash topographical landscapes and view paintings in oil. He exhibited at the Royal Academy from 1790 to 1803.

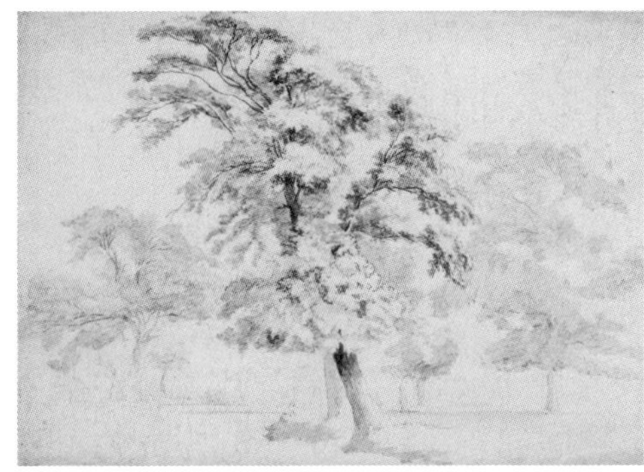

D.1926.215

Landscape, Hyde Park
pencil, brown watercolour; watermark VI
inscribed upper left verso: *en Hyde Park*
324 × 446 mm
Ogden, William Sharp (bequest, 1926) (D.1926.215)

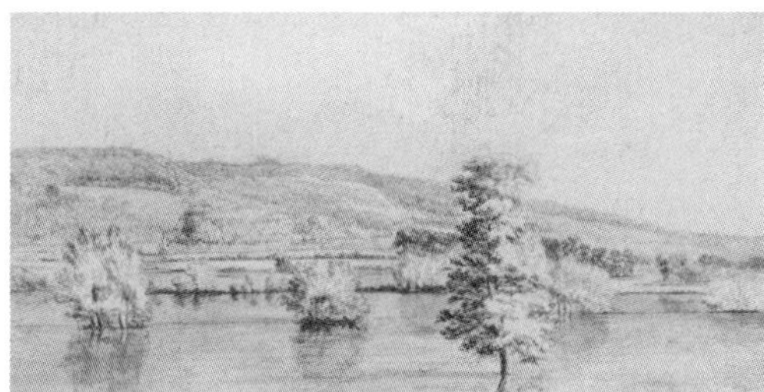

D.1926.216

The Thames at Great Marlow
1797
pencil, brown watercolour
inscribed & dated upper right verso: *the opposite shore – from the window / towards the river / overflown 1797 / at Court Garden / Rob Davenport Esq / Great Marlow / Buckse*
242 × 462 mm
Ogden, William Sharp (bequest, 1926) (D.1926.216)

Hyde Park near the Ring by the Serpentine River
1794
pencil, brown watercolour; watermark Strasbourg lily
signed, inscribed & dated upper left verso: [illegible word, partly cut] *near the Ring by the Serpentyn River / H DeCort 1794*; inscribed upper right verso: *Hyde Park, London*; inscribed upper centre verso in later hand: *The Old Conduit to the left*
325 × 432 mm
Ogden, William Sharp (bequest, 1926) (D.1926.227)

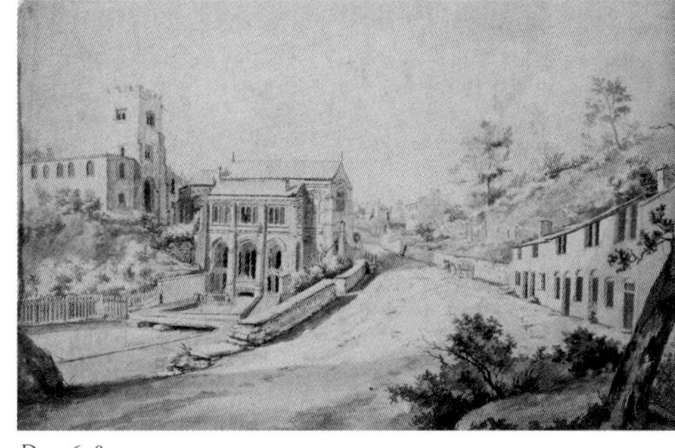

D.1926.385

St Winifred's Church, Holywell, Flintshire, Wales
pencil, grey watercolour; watermark JWHATMAN
411 × 634 mm
Ogden, William Sharp (bequest, 1926) (D.1926.385)

■ DE FLEURY, J. (fl. 1799–1822)

Described by Iolo Williams as 'a minor general utility watercolourist', little is known of de Fleury, who exhibited in London – mainly at the Royal Academy – from 1799 to 1822. His earlier work comprised sentimental subject pictures and he later turned to topographical subjects.

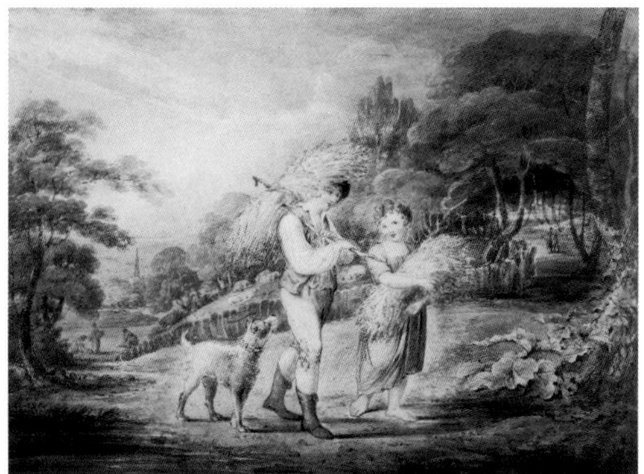

D.1900.11

The Gleaners
pencil, pen and grey ink, watercolour
signed lower right: *J De Fleury del*
378 × 500 mm
Worthington, Mary (gift, 1900) (D.1900.11)

■ DE LOUTHERBOURG, PHILIPPE JACQUES (1740–1812)
Born in Strasbourg, de Loutherbourg studied there and in Paris before coming to England in 1771. His dramatic subject matter, featuring shipwrecks and natural disasters, earned him membership of the Royal Academy in 1781. He was the painter and owner of the Eidophusikon, a theatrical panorama with dramatic lighting effects, which was much admired in the later eighteenth century.

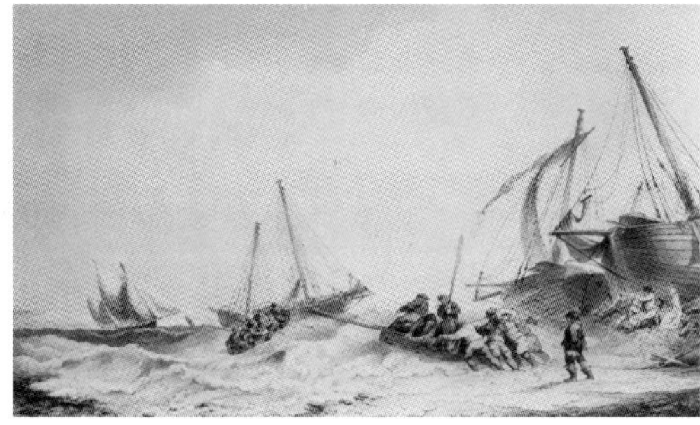

D.1900.1

Off the South Coast
pen and brown ink, watercolour
signed lower centre: *P J de Loutherbourg R A*
291 × 480 mm
Worthington, Mary (gift, 1900) (D.1900.1)

Ferry Scene
pen and brown ink, brown watercolour, white chalk
brown paper
signed lower left: *Lutherburgh*
280 × 447 mm
Towlson, Hector J. (bequest, 1969) (D.1970.55)

■ DE WILDE, SAMUEL (1747–1832)
De Wilde was born in Holland and began to exhibit at the Society of Artists in 1776 and the Royal Academy in 1782. In his later career he worked on a long series of theatrical portraits.

Henry Angelo, the Fencing Master
pencil, black chalk; watermark JWHATMAN
inscribed lower right: *Angelo*; inscribed right centre verso: *resided at Carlisle House / Carlisle Street Soho Square / where he kept a Riding school*; inscribed lower right verso in later hand: *Angelo the Fencing Master / by De Wilde*
282 × 223 mm
Ogden, William Sharp (bequest, 1926) (D.1926.203)

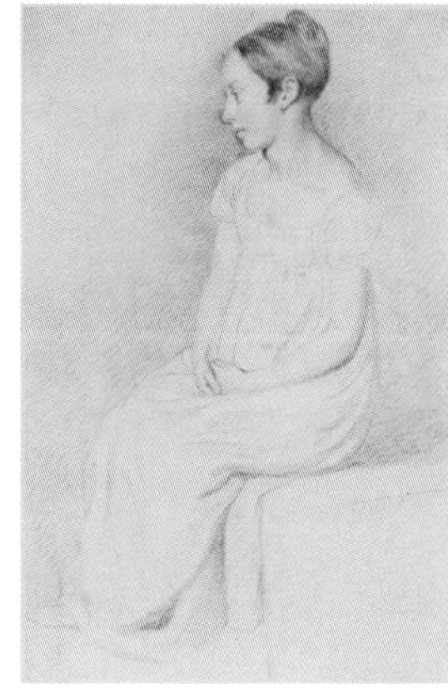

D.1947.10

Study of a seated Girl
pencil, black chalk, red chalk, brown chalk
signed lower right: *SDWilde*
311 × 202 mm
Barlow, Sir Thomas (gift, 1947) (D.1947.10)

■ DE WINT, PETER (1784–1849)
Born in Staffordshire of Anglo-Dutch descent, de Wint was apprenticed to the mezzotint engraver John Raphael Smith. In about 1805–06, de Wint became acquainted with John Varley and began to attend the Monro Academy. He exhibited at the Associated Artists in 1808 and 1809, and at the British Institution intermittently between 1808 and 1824. The vast majority of his exhibits, however, were at the Old Watercolour Society, to which he sent over 400 drawings between 1810 and 1849. He worked as a drawing master in Lincoln and had numerous pupils whose work is frequently confused with his own.

Newark Castle and Bridge, Nottinghamshire
pencil, watercolour
512 × 768 mm
Orrock, James (purchase, 19.5.1891) (D.1887.29)

The River at Kingston-upon-Thames, Surrey
pencil, watercolour; two joined sheets
236 × 646 mm
untraced (purchase, 1891) (D.1887.30)

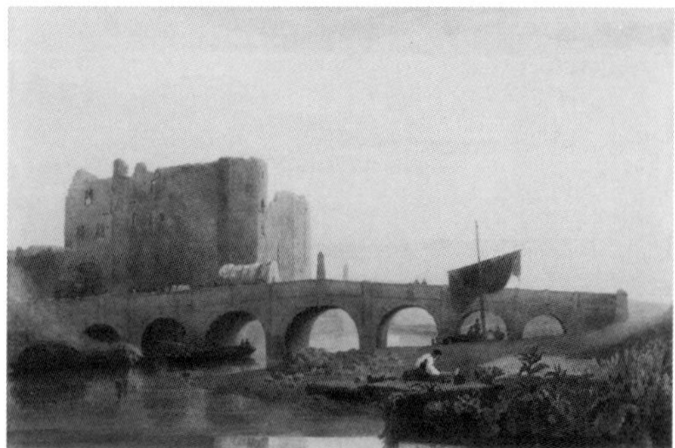

D.1887.29

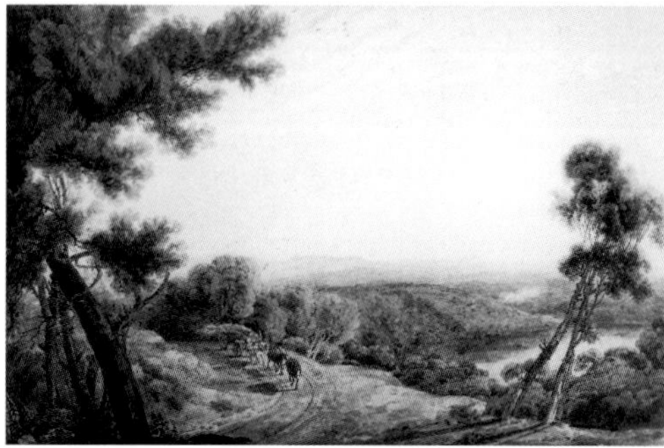

D.1892.75

A Landscape with Horses drawing Timber on a Cart
pencil, watercolour
404 × 613 mm
Taylor, John Edward (gift, 1892) (D.1892.75)

Landscape with a Church Tower
watercolour
240 × 476 mm
Anderson, A. E. (gift, 1917) (D.1917.2)

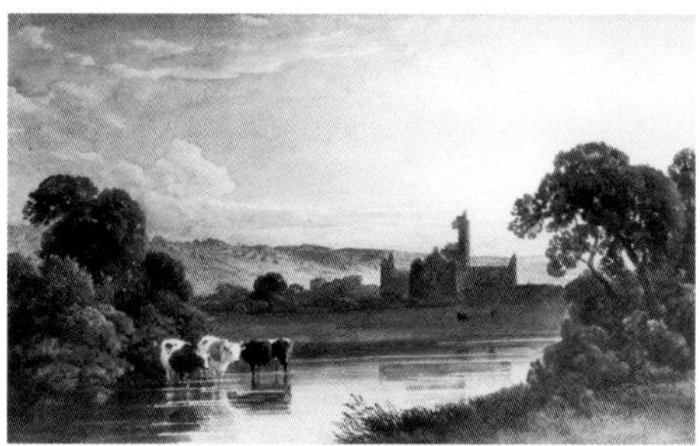

D.1924.35

Kirkstall Abbey, Yorkshire, from the River Aire
pencil, watercolour
327 × 515 mm
Broadhurst, Sir Edward Tootal, Broadhurst, Lady (bequest, 1924) (D.1924.35)

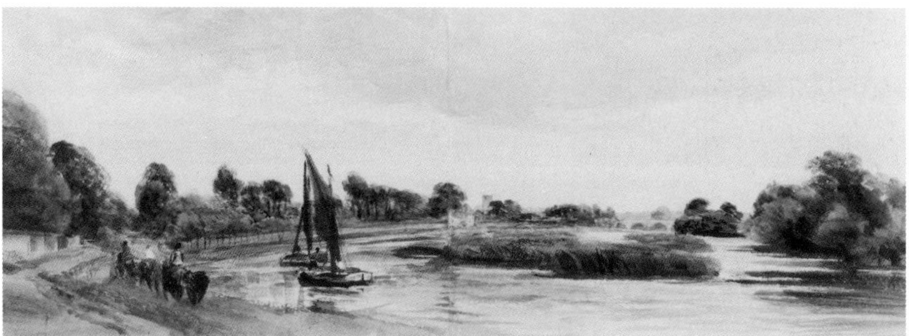

D.1887.30

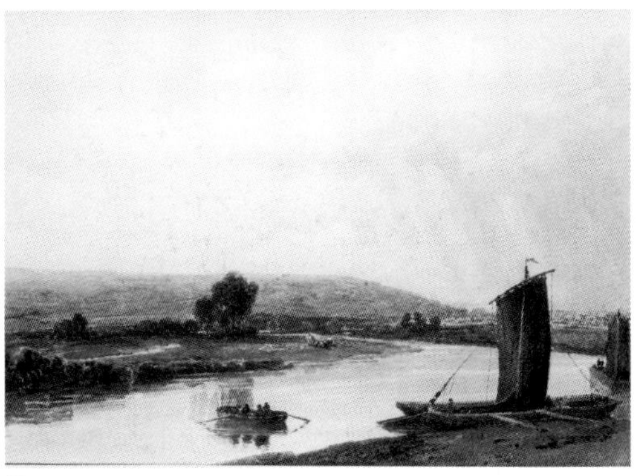

D.1924.37

On the Trent
pencil, watercolour
317 × 444 mm
Broadhurst, Sir Edward Tootal, Broadhurst, Lady
(bequest, 1924) (D.1924.37)

A Lancashire Cornfield
watercolour
295 × 464 mm
Barlow, Helen (gift, 1967) (D.1924.39)

Gathering the Corn
watercolour
294 × 657 mm
Broadhurst, Sir Edward Tootal, Broadhurst, Lady
(bequest, 1924) (D.1924.59)

The Cumberland Hills from Matterdale
pencil, watercolour; two joined sheets
153 × 647 mm
Broadhurst, Sir Edward Tootal, Broadhurst, Lady
(bequest, 1924) (D.1924.63)

Landscape with a Windmill
pencil, watercolour
185 × 293 mm
Rienaecker, Victor, National Art Collections Fund (via)
(gift, 1925) (D.1925.38)

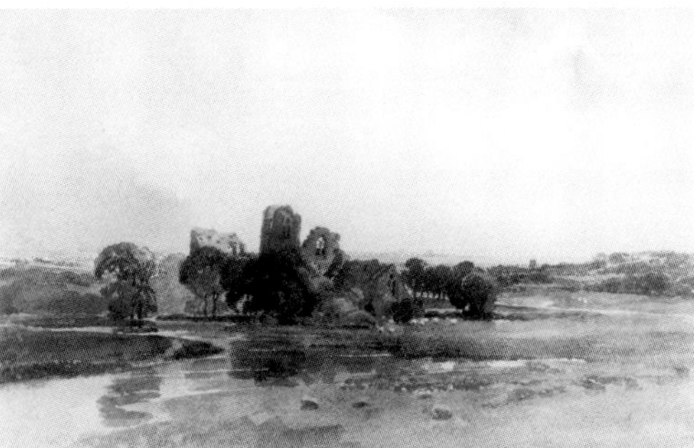

D.1945.9

A ruined Abbey on a River
pencil, watercolour
281 × 425 mm
National Art-Collections Fund (gift, 1945) (D.1945.9)

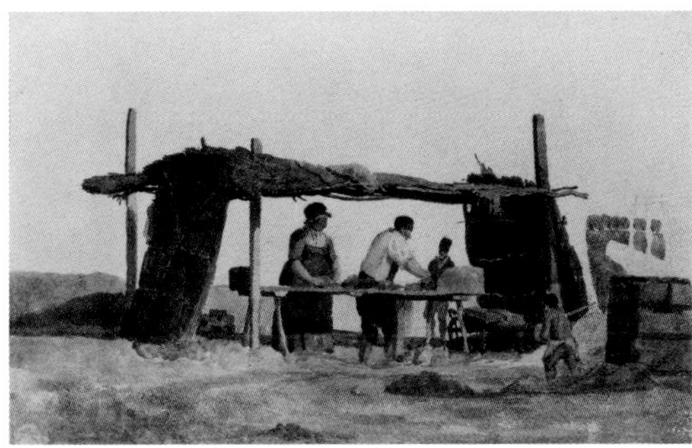

D.1950.19

Study of Figures brickmaking
pencil, watercolour
227 × 355 mm
Barlow, Sir Thomas (gift, 1950) (D.1950.19)

Harvesting
pencil, watercolour
360 × 532 mm
Maitland, Bertha Elizabeth May (bequest, 1969) (D.1969.13)

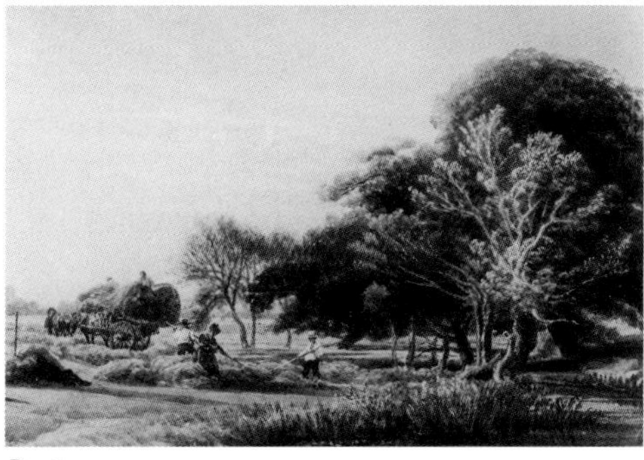

D.1969.13

View of London from Greenwich Hill
watercolour
222 × 338 mm
Brocklehurst, Lt Col C. P. (bequest, 1977) (D.1977.14)

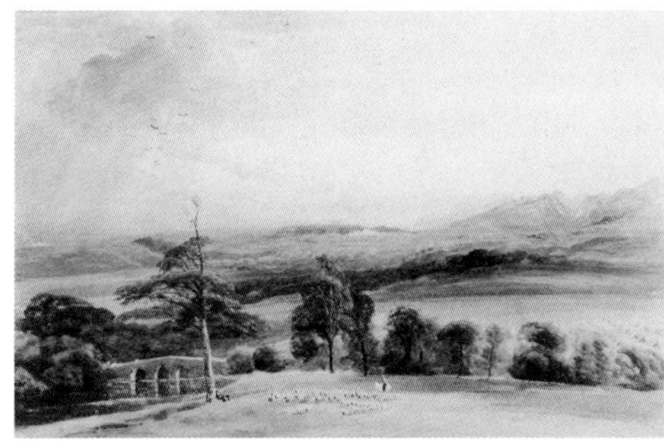

D.1984.11

Distant View of Lowther Castle, Westmorland
watercolour, bodycolour (heightened with white)
524 × 778 mm
Lupton, Katharine C. (bequest, 1984) (D.1984.11)

■ **DELAMOTTE, WILLIAM (1775–1863)**
Delamotte was a landscape watercolourist who
was appointed drawing master to the Royal Military
Academy at Great Marlow in 1803. Delamotte's
work is uninspired and shows little development
through his long career.

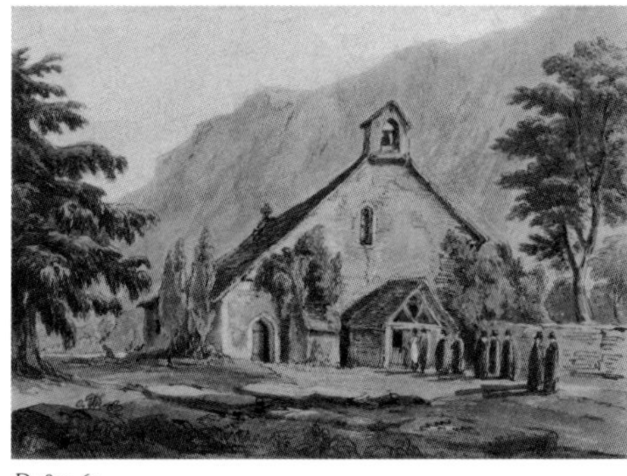

D.1892.62

Beddgellert Church, Caernarvonshire, Wales
1810
pen and brown ink, white chalk, watercolour
grey paper
signed & dated lower centre: *Wm Delamotte / 1810*;
inscribed lower left: *Beddkellert. N Wales*; inscribed
lower right verso in later hand (?): *Bedkellert Church
North Wales / WDelamotte*
222 × 304 mm
Taylor, John Edward (gift, 1892) (D.1892.62)

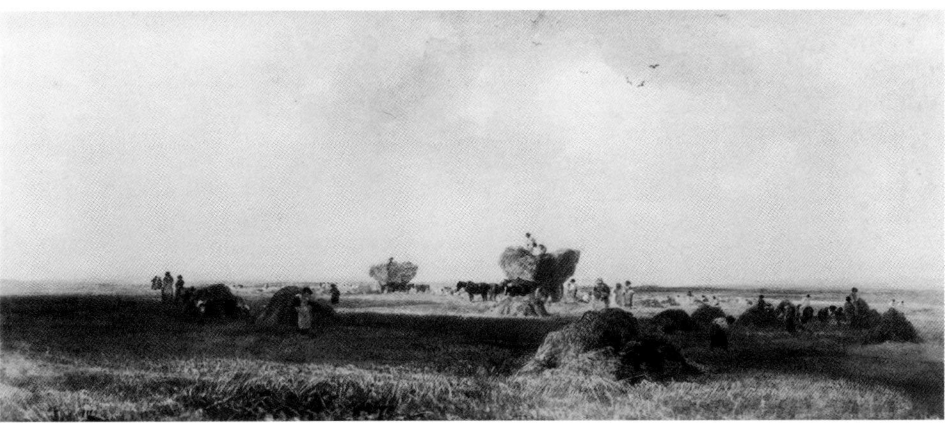

D.1924.59

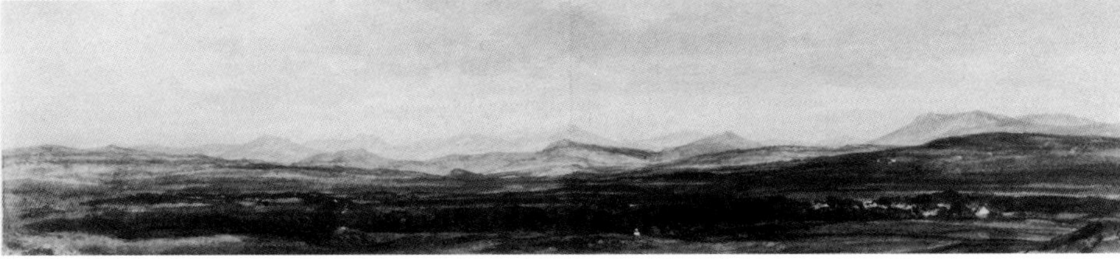

D.1924.63

■ DEVIS, ANTHONY (1729–1817)

Devis, born into a family of painters from Preston in Lancashire, moved to London in the 1740s. Between 1761 and 1781 he exhibited at the Free Society and the Royal Academy. He travelled extensively through Britain and normally worked in a combination of pen and ink and blue or grey wash.

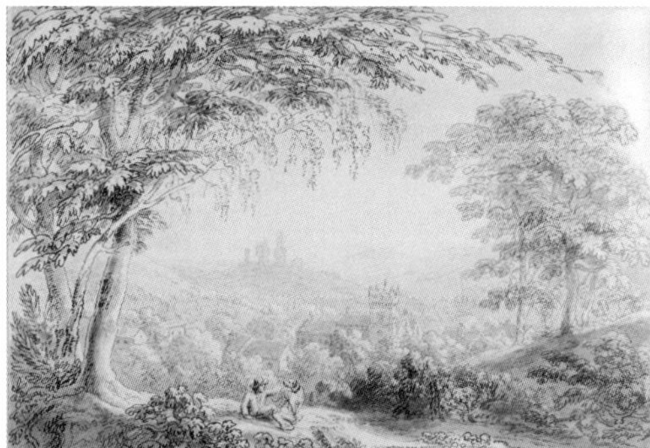

D.1923.8

View of a coastal Village with a Church and a ruined Castle

pencil, pen and grey ink, pen and brown ink, watercolour
signed lower left with monogram: *AD*
304 × 431 mm
Anderson, A. E., National Art Collections Fund (via) (gift, 1923) (D.1923.8)

Landscape with Sheep, near Netley, Hampshire

pencil, pen and grey ink, watercolour
signed lower right initial in monogram: *ADevis*
350 × 479 mm
Anderson, A. E., National Art Collections Fund (via) (gift, 1923) (D.1923.9)

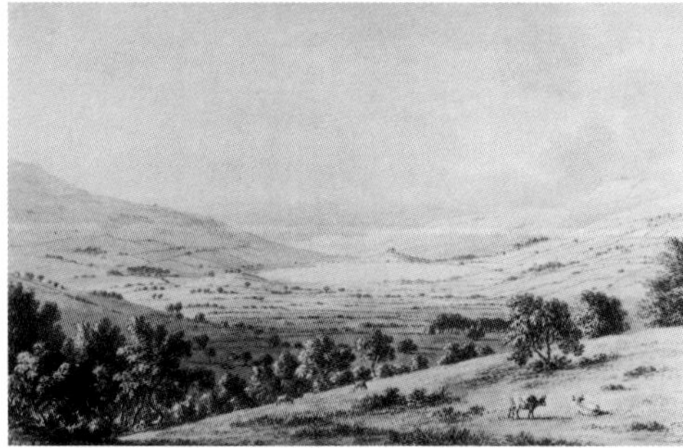

D.1970.28

Landscape with a Lake

pencil, chalk, pen and brown ink, watercolour
signed lower left: *A Devis*
257 × 385 mm
Towlson, Hector J. (bequest, 1969) (D.1970.28)

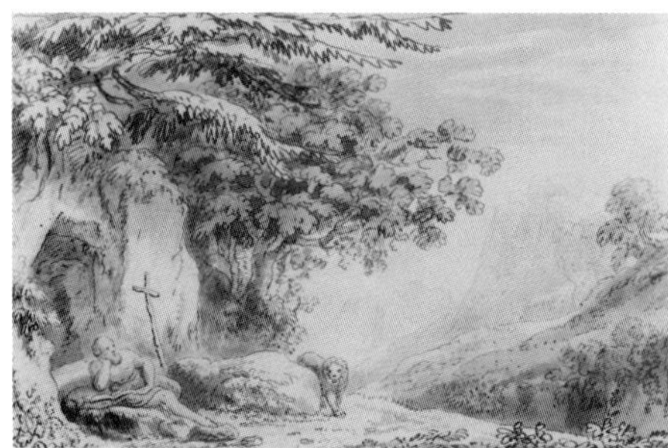

D.1978.4

St Jerome in a mountainous Landscape

pencil, pen and grey ink, watercolour
signed lower right with monogram: *AD*
157 × 223 mm
Nockolds, Dr Robert, Nockolds, Mrs Tilly (gift, 1978) (D.1978.4)

■ DIBDIN, CHARLES ISAAC MUNGO (1745–1814)

Dibdin, an amateur artist, was a pupil of William Payne.

Figures on a wooded Shoreline with a Port beyond

pencil, grey watercolour
inscribed lower left in border in later hand:
Chas Dibdin 1745–1814
170 × 235 mm
Ogden, William Sharp (bequest, 1926) (D.1926.201)

■ DIGHTON, ROBERT (1752–1814)

Dighton, a member of a family of painters and caricaturists, exhibited at the Royal Academy between 1775 and 1799. His typical works are full-length social satires of a slightly unsubtle nature.

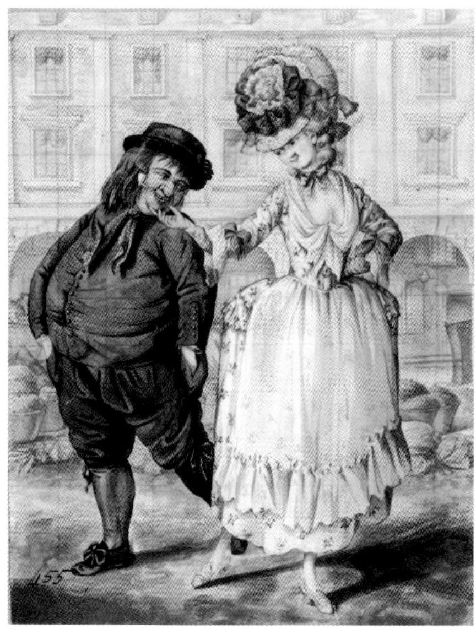

D.1978.1

An English Sloop engaging a Dutch Man-of-War

pencil, watercolour, bodycolour (heightened with white)
numbered lower left: *455*
304 × 233 mm
Sotheby's, London (purchase, 1978) (D.1978.1)

■ DIXON, ROBERT (1780–1815)

Dixon, a scene painter at the Norwich Theatre, was also a drawing master. His works vary greatly in quality and are often mistakenly attributed to more important artists.

Landscape with Bridge

watercolour
439 × 685 mm
Independent Gallery, London (purchase, 1928) (D.1928.6)

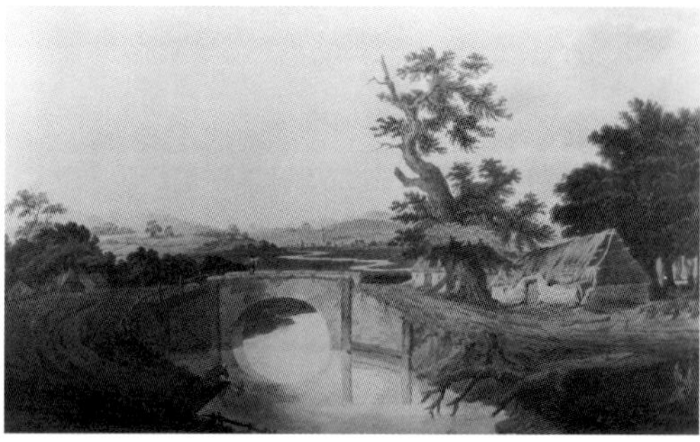

D.1928.6

■ DIXON, ROBERT (attributed to)

A waterside Cottage with Figures

grey watercolour
167 × 227 mm
Holliday, J. R. (bequest, 1927) (D.1927.93)

■ DODGSON, GEORGE HAYDOCK (1811–80)

Dodgson began his career as an engineer apprenticed to George Stephenson but turned to landscape painting. He became a member of the Old Watercolour Society in 1848 and worked in Wales, Cumbria and Yorkshire.

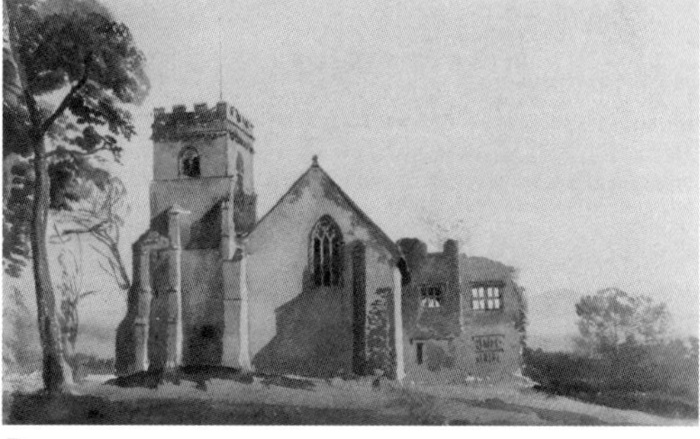

D.1924.1

Exterior View of St Mary's Church, Bromfield, Shropshire

pencil, watercolour
294 × 463 mm
Smith, Frank Hindley (gift, 1924) (D.1924.1)

■ DORRELL, EDMUND (1778–1857)

Dorrell was born in Warwick and began to exhibit at the Royal Academy in 1807, and at the Old Watercolour Society from 1809 to 1819. He was not a prolific artist, and many of his works are probably misattributed to others.

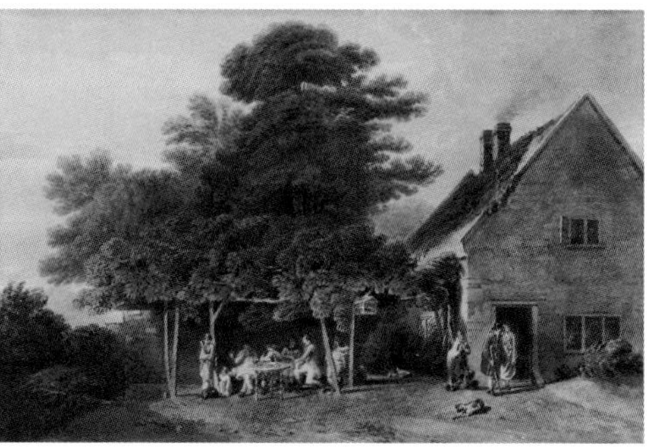

D.1904.16

Figures outside a roadside Inn
1814
pencil, watercolour
signed & dated lower left: *EDorrell.1814.*
307 × 455 mm
Worthington, Mary (bequest, 1904) (D.1904.16)

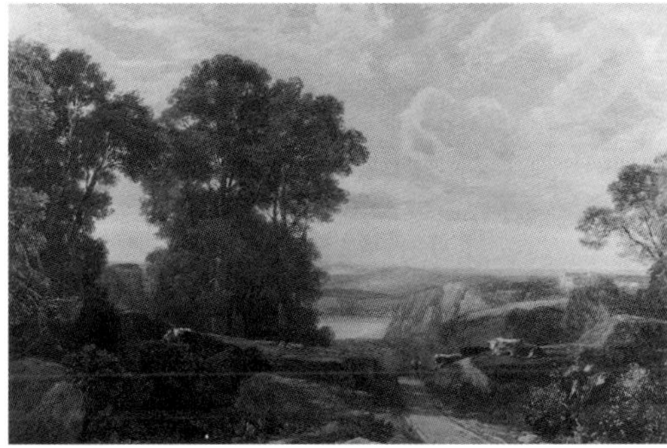

D.1970.29

St Donat's Castle, Glamorgan
watercolour
504 × 747 mm
Towlson, Hector J. (bequest, 1969) (D.1970.29)

■ **DORRELL, EDMUND (circle of)**

A Cottage at the Edge of a Wood in a hilly Landscape
pencil, watercolour
231 × 317 mm
Towlson, Hector J. (bequest, 1969) (D.1970.57)

■ **DOWNMAN, JOHN (1750–1824)**
Downman, the most important watercolour portrait painter of the late eighteenth century, exhibited at the Royal Academy from 1770 to 1819. He also painted imaginary and literary subjects. The majority of his portraits are small half-length ovals. He visited Italy with Joseph Wright of Derby in 1773–74. Downman's only known landscapes derive from his visit to Italy and a tour of the Lake District in 1812.

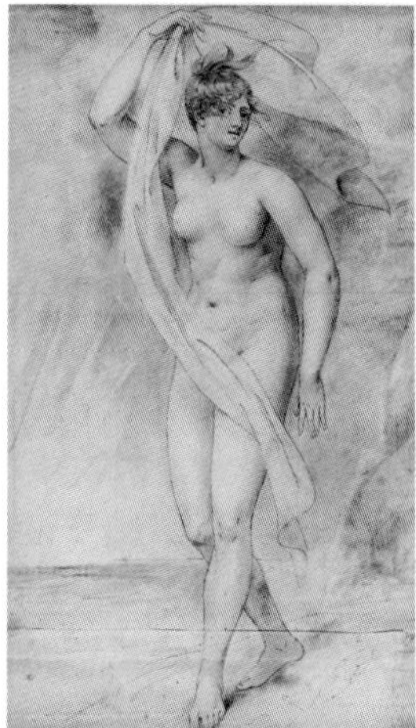

D.1926.315

A standing female Nude
pen and brown ink, black stump, red stump
signed with initials lower left: *JoD*
703 × 400 mm
Ogden, William Sharp (bequest, 1926) (D.1926.315)

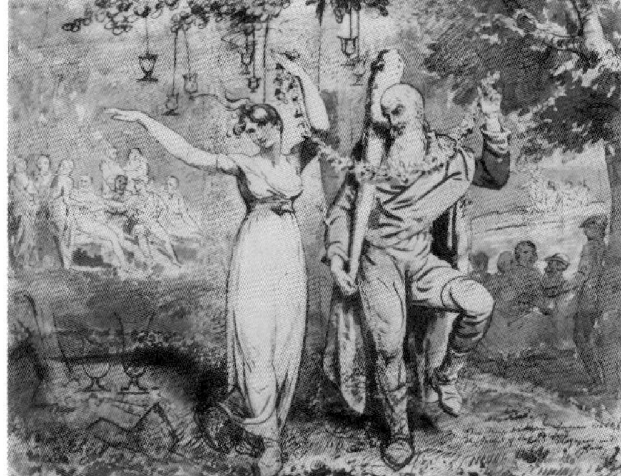

D.1948.4

Diogenes and Lais on the Island of the Blessed, from Lucian's 'The True History'
pencil, pen and brown ink, brown watercolour
signed with initials & inscribed lower right: *The True History Lucian Vol.2d B2 / The Island of the Blessed / Diogenes and / Lais / JoD*
333 × 415 mm
Pilkington, Margaret (gift, 1947) (D.1948.4)

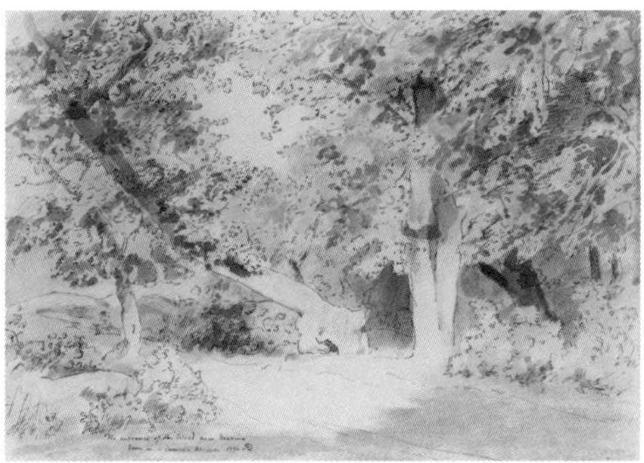

D.1999.18

The Entrance to a Wood near Marino
1774
pencil, pen and brown ink, watercolour
signed with initials, inscribed & dated lower left:
The entrance of the wood near Marino / done in a camera obscura 1774 JoD
262 × 360 mm
Scott-Elliot, Miss Aydua, in memory of Paul Oppé
(gift, 4.11.1999) (D.1999.18)

■ **DU BOIS, EDWARD (1619–96)**
Du Bois, the son of a portrait painter, was born in Antwerp. He spent some eight years in Italy before moving to England where he spent the rest of his life. He painted portraits and studies after the Old Masters. Drawings by du Bois are extremely rare.

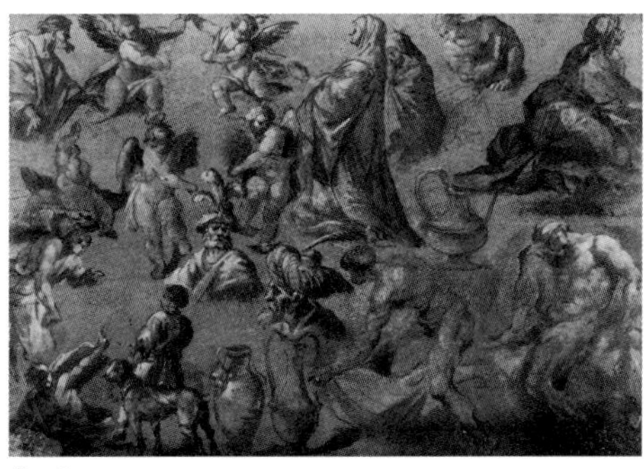

D.1960.229

Sheet of Studies after various Old Masters
oil paint; reddish brown paper
215 × 304 mm
University of Manchester, History of Art Department
(transfer, 1960) (D.1960.229)

■ **DU MAURIER, GEORGE LOUIS PALMELLA BUSSON (1834–96)**
Du Maurier, a pen-and-ink illustrator (grandfather of Daphne du Maurier), was the chief cartoonist for *Punch* from 1864. He studied in Paris between 1856 and 1860, where he was a friend of Poynter. Du Maurier published three novels at the end of his life, of which the most famous is *Trilby*.

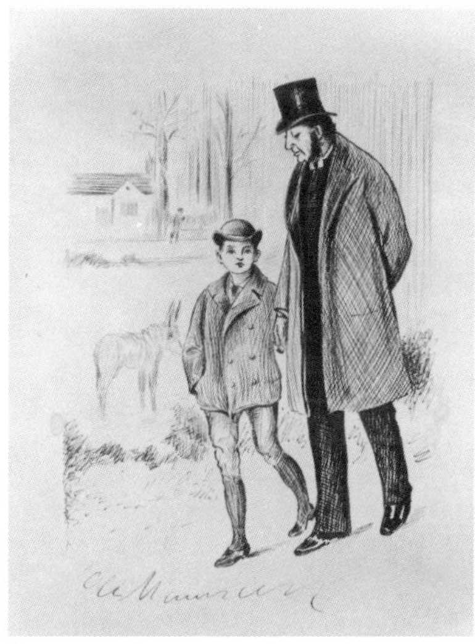

D.1930.64

Man and Boy walking
pencil, pen and brown ink
signed lower edge: *du Maurier*
260 × 205 mm
Barlow, Sir Thomas (gift, 1930) (D.1930.64)

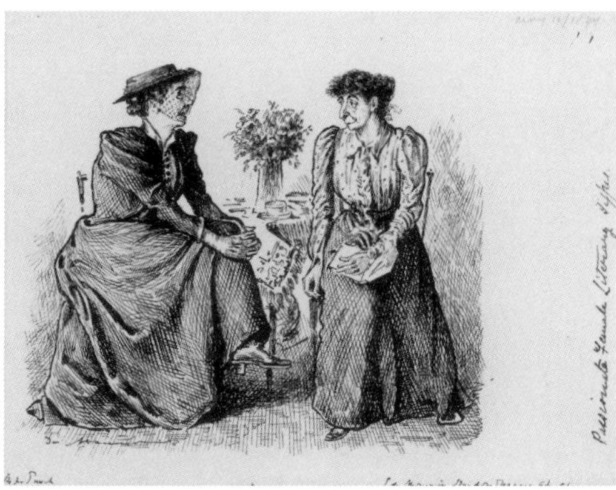

D.1935.9

Passionate Female Literary Types: an Illustration to *Punch*
4.1894
pen and brown ink
signed lower left: *du Maurier*; signed, inscribed & dated lower right: *G du Maurier Stanhope Terrace Ap.94*; dated upper right with date of publication: *May 12/1894*; inscribed right edge written vertically: *Passionate Female Literary Types*
180 × 231 mm
National Art Collections Fund (gift, 1935) (D.1935.9)

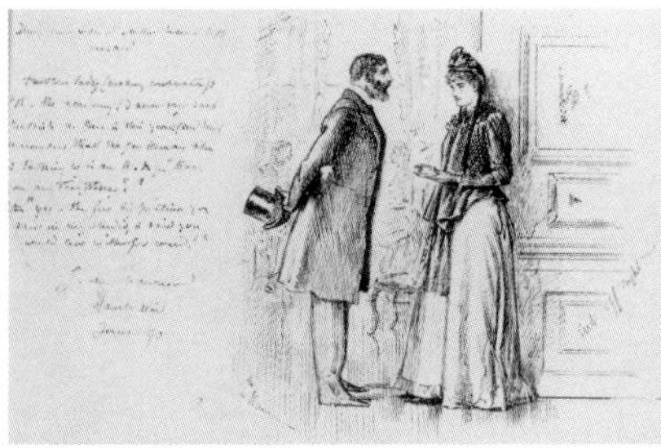

D.1935.10

Things one would rather have left unsaid: an Illustration to *Punch*
6.1890
pen and brown ink
signed lower centre: *du Maurier*; dated lower right with date of publication: *July 12/1890*; signed, extensively inscribed & dated June 90 on left hand side
163 × 254 mm
National Art Collections Fund (gift, 1935) (D.1935.10)

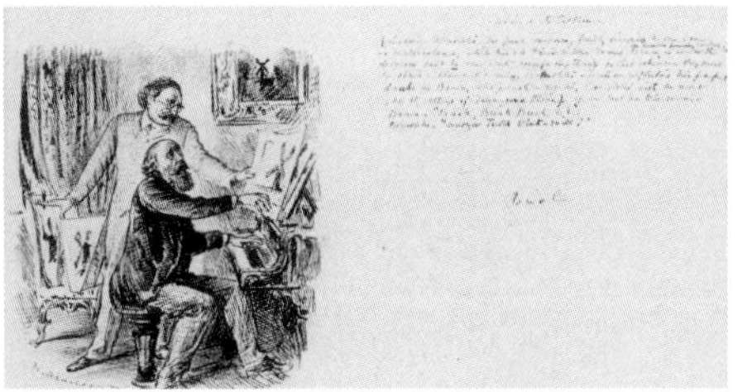

D.1935.11

Genius and its Hobbies: an Illustration to *Punch*
11.1879
pencil, pen and brown ink
signed lower left: *du Maurier*; dated lower right with date of publication: *Nov 15 / 79*; extensively inscribed upper right
253 × 344 mm
National Art Collections Fund (gift, 1935) (D.1935.11)

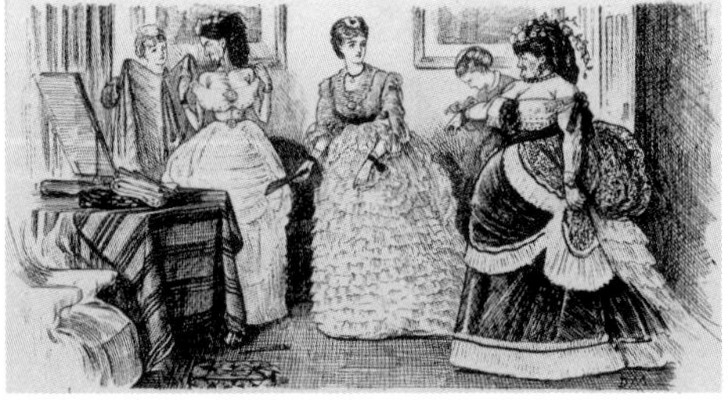

D.1935.12

Young Heads upon old Shoulders: an Illustration to *Punch*
7.1872
pencil, pen and brown ink
signed lower right with initials: *DM*; dated lower right with date of publication: *July 27/72*
257 × 362 mm
National Art Collections Fund (gift, 1935) (D.1935.12)

An Illustration to *The Mystery of Mirbridge* for the *Graphic*
pencil, pen and brown ink, grey watercolour; card
inscribed lower left: *The Mystery of Mirbridge / Graphic / – "If I do marry you, it will be in / Steerbridge church, & with the full consent / of your mother. / Part XV.CH.XXVII*; extensively inscribed upper left
267 × 361 mm
National Art Collections Fund (gift, 1935) (D.1935.13)

■ DUNCAN, EDWARD (1803–82)

Duncan, son-in-law of the Liverpool painter William Huggins, joined the New Watercolour Society in 1834. He resigned in 1847 in order to join the Old Watercolour Society, of which he became a member in 1849. He specialised in coastal scenes with boats and river landscapes.

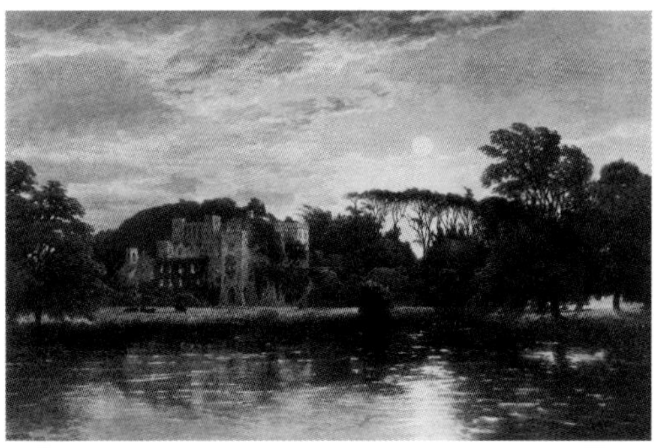

D.1897.6

Guy's Cliffe House, Warwick
1862
pencil, watercolour
signed & dated lower left: *E.Duncan / 1862*
408 × 610 mm
anonymous (in memory of Sir Joseph Whitworth) (gift, 1897) (D.1897.6)

The Thames near Blackwall, London
pencil, watercolour
stamped with signature lower right studio stamp: *ED*
200 × 295 mm
Friends of the Whitworth (gift, 1947) (D.1947.14)

■ DURELL, AMY CLARA (dates unknown)

An amateur portrait painter.

Portrait of Benjamin Disraeli
20.6.1881
black chalk, white chalk
signed & dated lower right: *Amy C.Durell / June 20th.1881*
363 × 291 mm
Ogden, William Sharp (bequest, 1926) (D.1926.312)

■ DYCE, WILLIAM (1806–64)

Dyce was born in Aberdeen, and visited Rome in 1825–26 and again in 1827–28, where he came in contact with the Nazarenes and developed a style which later became known as Pre-Raphaelite. Famous as a writer, scientist and administrator, he advocated the revival of fresco painting to decorate the newly built Houses of Parliament. He painted biblical, mythological and literary subjects.

Courtesy: Sir Tristram harping to La Belle Iseult; Cartoon for a Fresco in Queen's Robing Chamber, House of Lords, Palace of Westminster, London
1851–53
charcoal, brown chalk; brown paper laid on canvas
3391 × 1765 mm
University of Manchester, History of Art Department (transfer, 1959) (D.1959.10)

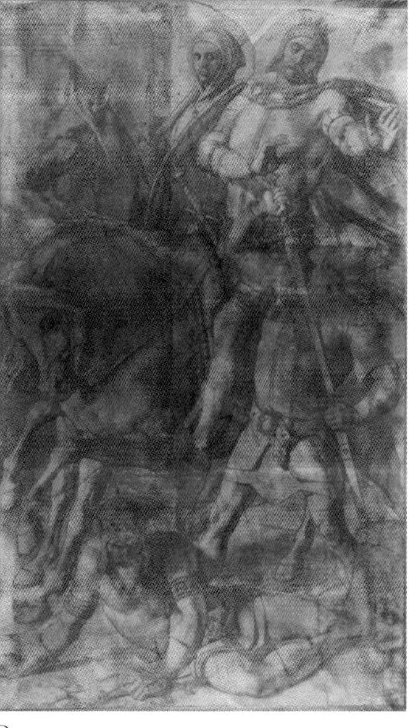

D.1959.11

Generosity: Sir Lancelot sparing King Arthur unhorsed; Cartoon for a Fresco in the Queen's Robing Chamber, House of Lords, Palace of Westminster, London
1851–53
charcoal; brown paper laid on canvas
3061 × 1778 mm
University of Manchester, History of Art Department (transfer, 1959) (D.1959.11)

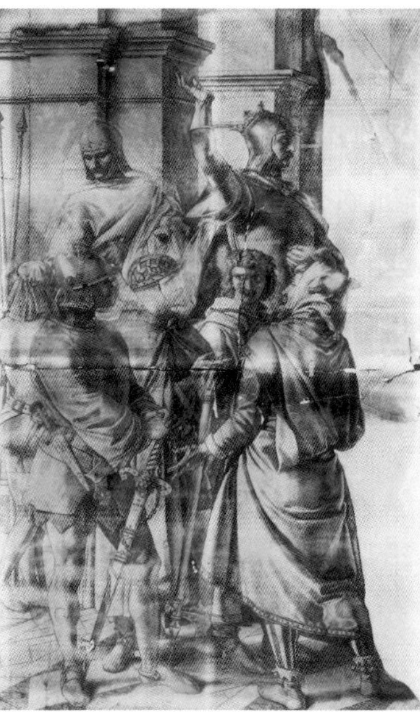

D.1959.12

Hospitality: Sir Tristram admitted to the Fellowship of the Round Table; Cartoon for the left-hand Section of the Fresco in the Queen's Robing Chamber, House of Lords, Palace of Westminster, London
1852
charcoal, brown chalk; brown paper laid on canvas
3404 × 2086 mm
University of Manchester, History of Art Department (transfer, 1959) (D.1959.12)

Hospitality: Sir Tristram admitted to the Fellowship of the Round Table; Cartoon for the central Section of the Fresco in the Queen's Robing Chamber, House of Lords, Palace of Westminster, London
1852
charcoal, brown chalk; brown paper laid on canvas
3404 × 2686 mm
University of Manchester, History of Art Department
(transfer, 1959) (D.1959.13)

Hospitality: Sir Tristram admitted to the Fellowship of the Round Table; Cartoon for the right-hand Section of the Fresco in the Queen's Robing Chamber, House of Lords, Palace of Westminster, London
1852
charcoal, brown chalk; brown paper laid on canvas
3379 × 2553 mm
University of Manchester, History of Art Department
(transfer, 1959) (D.1959.14)

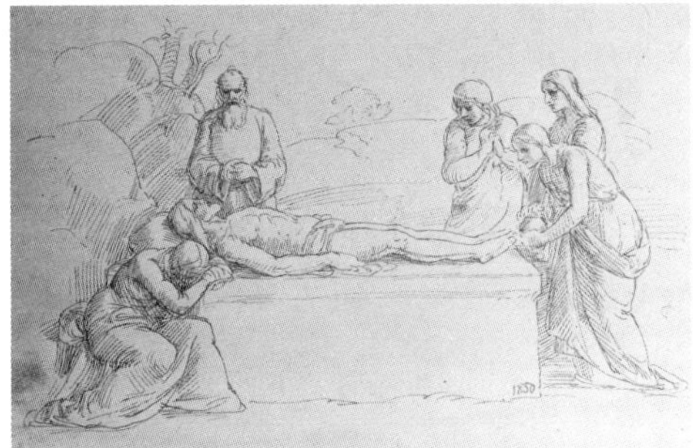
D.1960.32

The Entombment
1850
pen and brown ink
dated lower right: *1850*
212 × 328 mm
Friends of the Whitworth (gift, 1960) (D.1960.32)

■ EAGLES, REV. JOHN (1783–1855)
Eagles, an amateur painter, was a member of Danby's Sketching Club in Bristol. His drawings are almost always monochrome and of imaginary subjects. Eagles was an art critic and wrote for *Blackwood's Magazine*, and it was his attack on a Turner painting in 1836 that first inspired the young John Ruskin to write in defence of the artist.

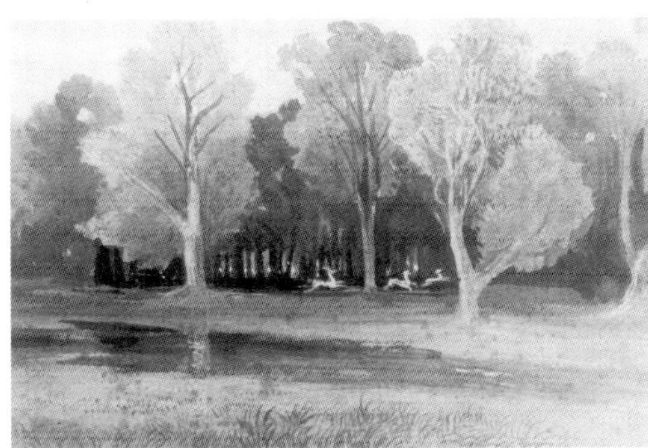
D.1930.32

The enchanted Forest
white chalk, watercolour; blue paper
305 × 447 mm
Anderson, A. E. (gift, 1930) (D.1930.32)

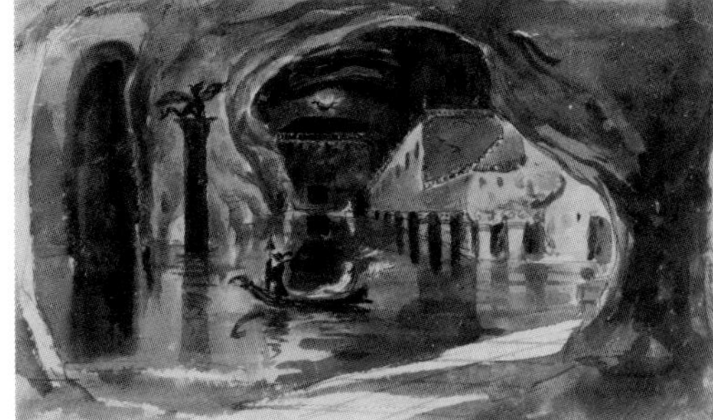
D.1996.47

A Fantasy with a subterranean Lagoon
grey watercolour, brown watercolour, bodycolour (heightened with white); buff paper
266 × 426 mm
Powney, Christopher (purchase, 1996) (D.1996.47)

■ EAST, SIR ALFRED (1849–1913)
East, after studying at Glasgow School of Art and in Paris, settled in London. He was a prolific painter and travelled widely, visiting Japan in 1889 as well as North Africa, Spain, France and Italy. He was knighted in 1910 and elected a member of the Royal Academy in the year of his death.

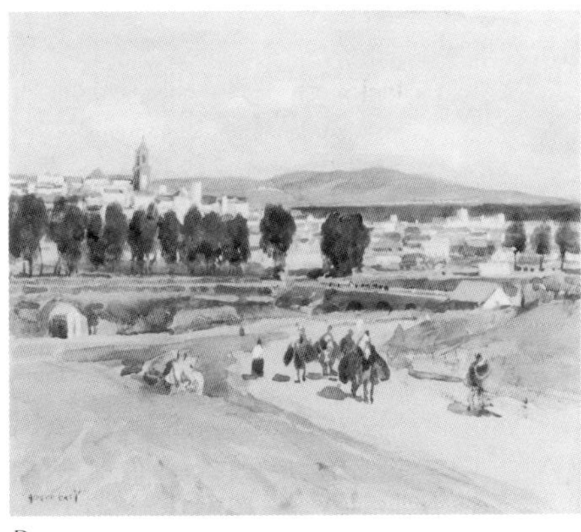
D.1929.9

View of a coastal Town, Morocco
pencil, watercolour, bodycolour (heightened with white)
signed lower left: *ALFRED EAST*
229 × 330 mm
Anderson, A. E. (gift, 1929) (D.1929.9)

■ EDE, MABEL B. (fl. 1894–1924)
Ede was probably an amateur artist. She exhibited a few works in Manchester, Liverpool and at the Royal Cambrian Academy between 1902 and 1923.

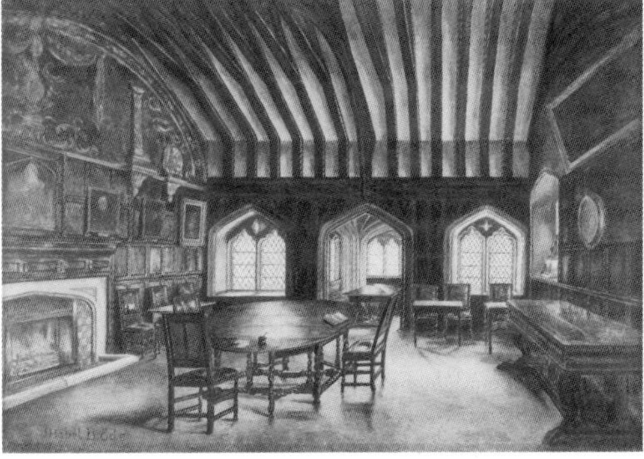
D.1902.9

The Reading Room in the Library of Sir Humphrey Chetham's Hospital School, Manchester
pencil, watercolour, bodycolour (heightened with white)
signed lower left: *Mabel B. Ede*
515 × 719 mm
anonymous (in memory of Sir Joseph Whitworth) (gift, 1902) (D.1902.9)

■ EDRIDGE, HENRY (1769–1821)
Edridge attended the Royal Academy Schools in 1784 and became friendly with Thomas Hearne and Joseph Farington. He was a very prolific watercolour portrait painter who specialised in small full or three-quarter length works. Edridge is more significant, however, as a landscape draughtsman; his work is reminiscent of a number of artists in the Monro circle, including Girtin. Edridge visited Northern France in 1817 and 1819, and was elected an associate member of the Royal Academy, where he had exhibited continuously since 1786.

Hastings Beach, Sussex
pencil, watercolour, bodycolour (heightened with white)
230 × 445 mm
Agnew's (purchase, 22.6.1891) (D.1887.49)

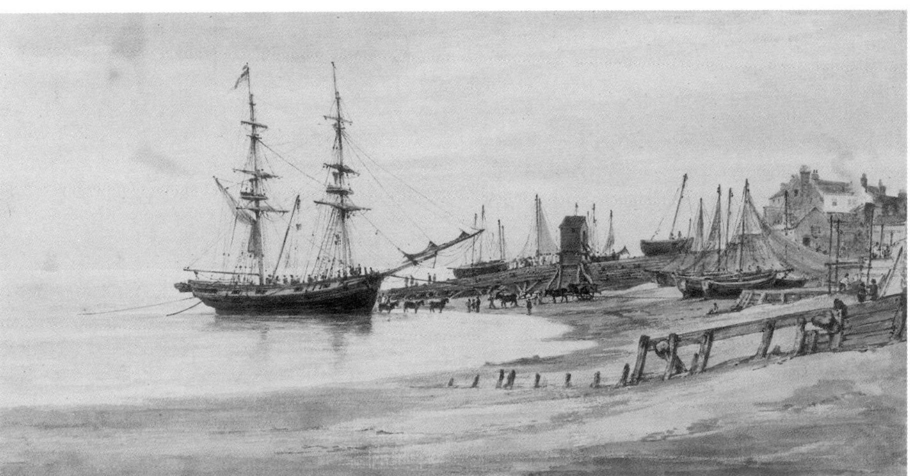
D.1887.49

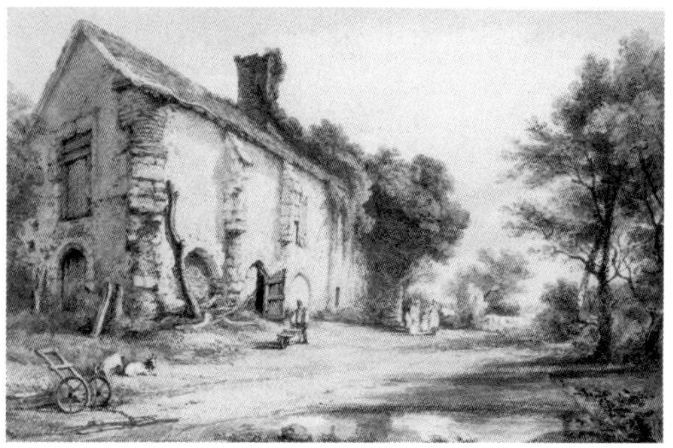

D.1892.57

Remains of the Dominican Friary, Kings Langley, Hertfordshire
pencil, watercolour
294 × 450 mm
Taylor, John Edward (gift, 1892) (D.1892.57)

Landscape with Cowherd, near Harrow
pencil, watercolour
signed lower right: *H.Edridge.delt.*
263 × 368 mm
Lees, Charles E. (gift, 1894) (D.1894.8)

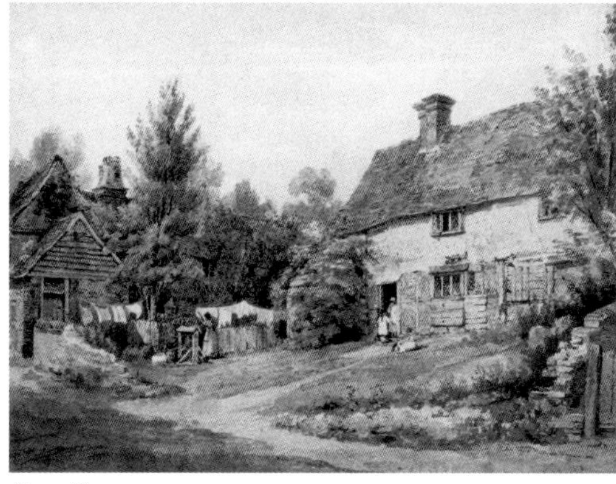

D.1924.88

Hertfordshire Cottage
pencil, watercolour
inscribed lower right in later hand: *H Edridge A R A*
325 × 470 mm
Broadhurst, Sir Edward Tootal, Broadhurst, Lady
(bequest, 1924) (D.1924.88)

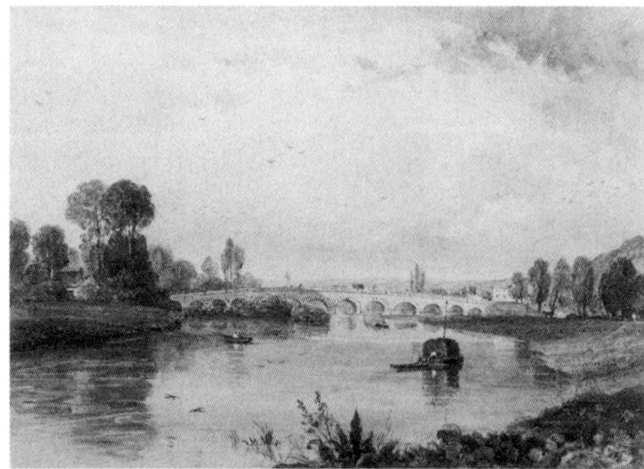

D.1924.89

Walton Bridge on the Thames, Middlesex
pencil, watercolour
256 × 358 mm
Broadhurst, Sir Edward Tootal, Broadhurst, Lady
(bequest, 1924) (D.1924.89)

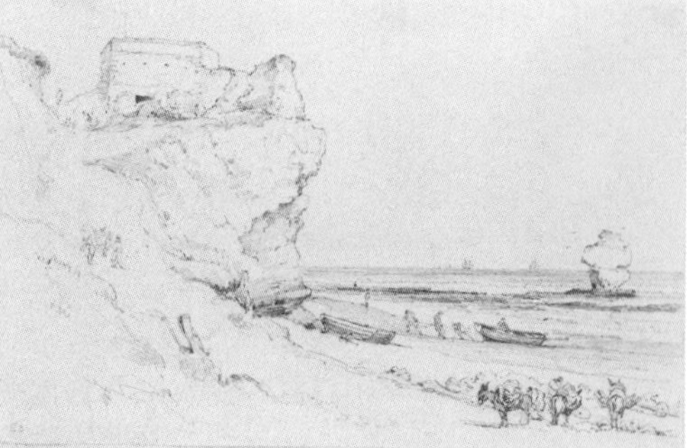

D.1927.111

Coast Scene, Dawlish, Devon
pencil; two joined sheets
215 × 327 mm
Holliday, J. R. (bequest, 1927) (D.1927.111)

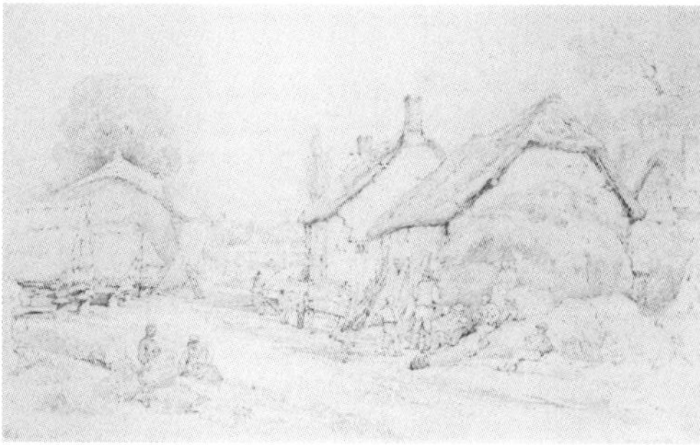

D.1927.112

Cottages and Hayricks
1.8.1818
pencil
signed lower left: *H.Edridge.delt.*; dated lower right:
Aug 1.1818
238 × 386 mm
Holliday, J. R. (bequest, 1927) (D.1927.112)

Old Shops in Chester
pencil
signed lower left: *Edridge*; inscribed in pencil
lower right: *Chester.*
296 × 216 mm
University of Manchester, History of Art Department
(transfer, 1960) (D.1960.80)

■ EMES, JOHN (fl. 1786–1810)
Emes was an obscure artist who exhibited Cumberland
views at the Royal Academy in 1791. He may have been
a pupil of the engraver William Woollett, and his
drawing style was certainly influenced by that of
Thomas Hearne.

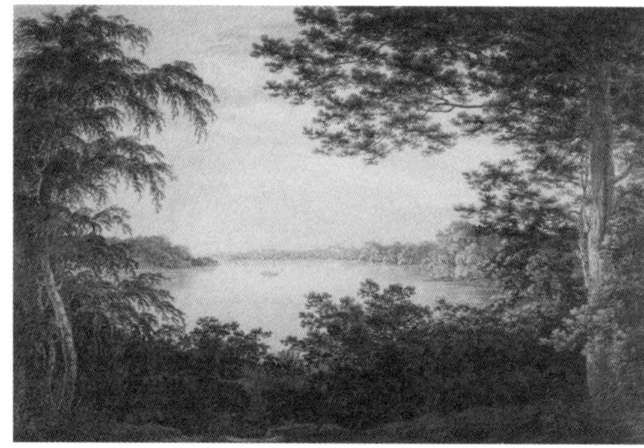

D.1900.10

The Lake at Combermere, Cheshire
1790
pen and brown ink, watercolour, gum arabic
signed & dated: *J Emes 1790*; signed & dated on
mount: *J.Emes delt 1790*
421 × 605 mm
Worthington, Mary (gift, 1900) (D.1900.10)

■ ESTALL, WILLIAM (1857–97)
Estall, a painter of landscapes, was brought up in
Manchester and studied in London, France and
Germany. He specialised in cattle and sheep scenes,
in mist, at dusk or in moonlight. He exhibited
intermittently at the Royal Academy between 1878
and 1896.

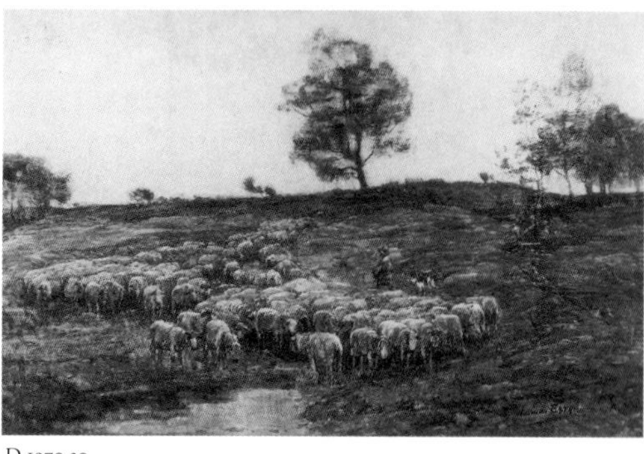

D.1970.30

A Shepherd with a Flock of Sheep
watercolour
signed lower right: *William Estall*
419 × 619 mm
Towlson, Hector J. (bequest, 1969) (D.1970.30)

■ EVANS, WILLIAM (OF BRISTOL) (1809–58)
Evans, born in Bristol and known as 'of Bristol' to
distinguish him from the Eton drawing master of the
same name, was elected an associate member of the
Old Watercolour Society in 1845 and exhibited there
until his death. He painted in North Wales, and visited
Italy and Germany in the 1850s.

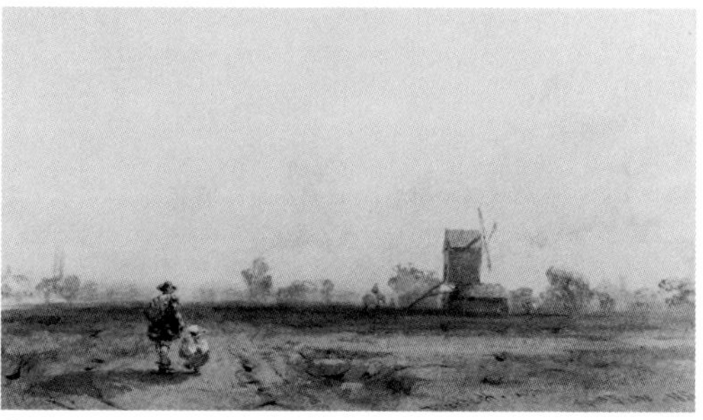

D.1970.31

Landscape with Windmill, Blackheath, London
1850
watercolour
signed & dated lower right: *Wm Evans.1850.*; inscribed
lower right: *Blackheath*
190 × 317 mm
Towlson, Hector J. (bequest, 1969) (D.1970.31)

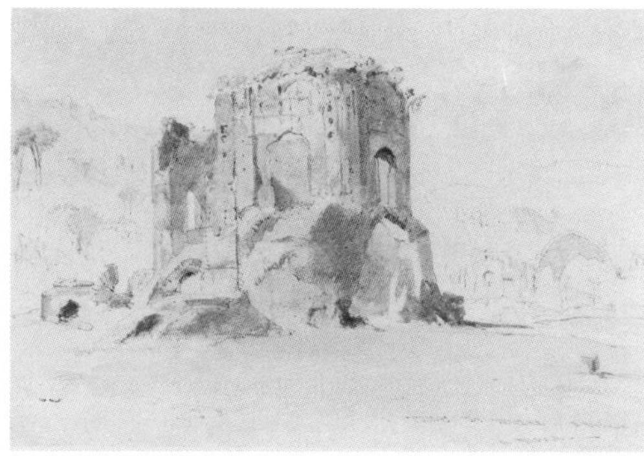

D.1988.1

The Temple of Venus, Baiae, near Naples
1852–54
pencil, watercolour
inscribed lower right: *TEMPI DI VENERE EDIANA /
A BAIA*
257 × 384 mm
Martyn Gregory Gallery, London (purchase, 1988) (F.O.W.)
(D.1988.1)

■ **FAIRBAIRN, THOMAS (1820–84)**
Fairbairn, a Scottish artist who was a pupil of Andrew
Donaldson in Glasgow, lived in Hamilton and exhibited
in London from 1865 to 1877. He was an unsuccessful
candidate for the New Watercolour Society in 1867.

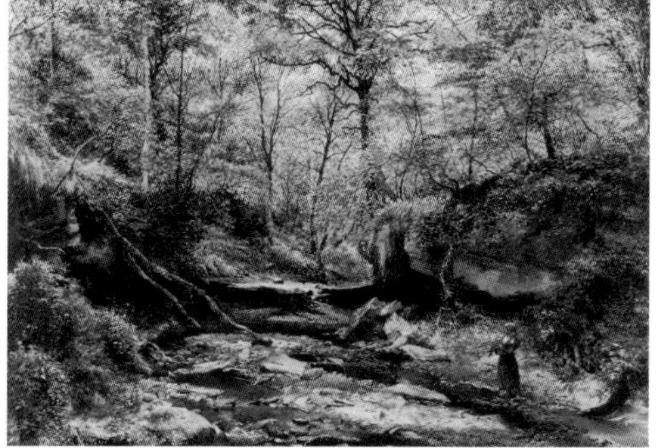

D.1910.13

The Woodland Brook
1861
watercolour, bodycolour (heightened with white)
signed & dated lower left: *Thomas Fairbairn / 1861*
553 × 763 mm
Cox, G. F. (bequest, 1910) (D.1910.13)

■ **FALKLAND, M. (dates unknown)**
Unknown amateur artist.

Landscape with Men fishing
pencil
signed lower left: *M.Falkland*
237 × 284 mm
Ogden, William Sharp (bequest, 1926) (D.1926.347)

■ **FARINGTON, JOSEPH (1747–1821)**
Farington was one of the first pupils at the Royal
Academy Schools in 1769. Between 1776 and 1781 he
spent each summer at the Lake District before settling
in London where he remained, apart from annual
sketching tours, until the end of his life. Elected a
member of the Royal Academy in 1785, Farington
became closely involved in its affairs and in artistic

politics. Famous today for his *Diary*, which is one of
the chief sources of knowledge of the arts during this
period, Farington was a prolific draughtsman,
producing views of Scotland, the Lake District and the
Thames Valley, many of which were made into prints.

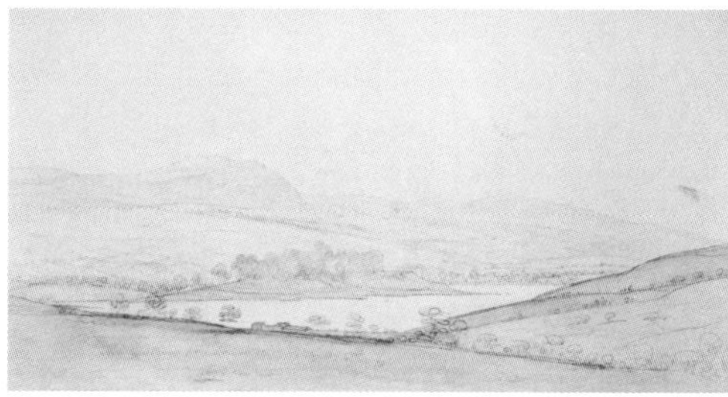

D.1922.4

**Linlithgow Palace, West Lothian, Scotland,
from across the Loch**
1.9.1788
pencil, watercolour
dated lower centre: *Septr.1st. – 88*; inscribed lower left:
Linlithgow Palace from Bonside / North east view
257 × 495 mm
Walker's Galleries, London (purchase, 1922) (D.1922.4)

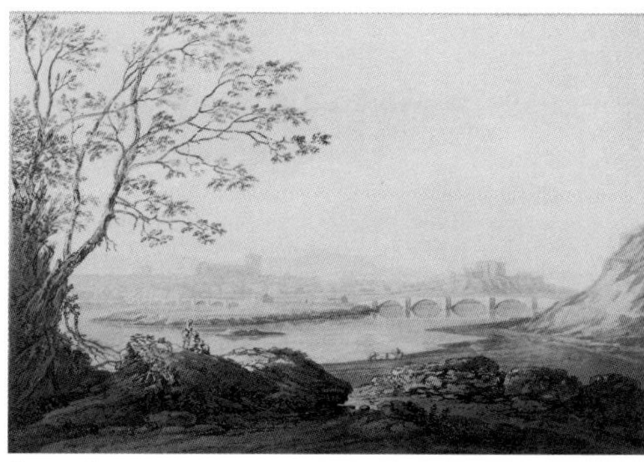

D.1922.36

**View of Carlisle, Cumberland, from across the
River Eden**
pencil, pen and ink, blue watercolour, grey watercolour
319 × 462 mm
Anderson, A. E. (gift, 1922) (D.1922.36)

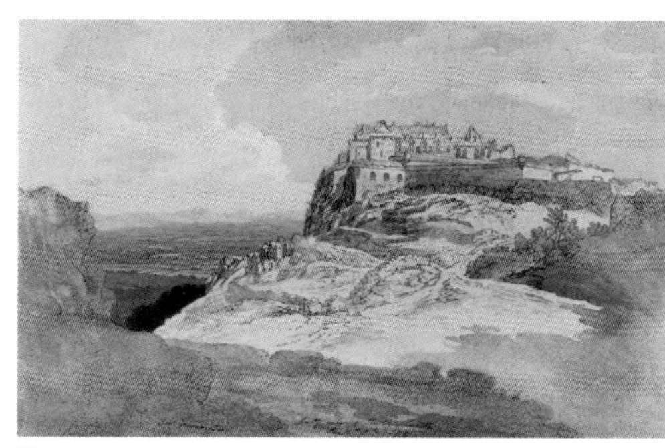

D.1922.37

Stirling Castle, Stirlingshire, from the South
5.9.1788
pencil, pen and brown ink, brown watercolour,
oil paint
signed lower left: *Jos Farington*; inscribed & dated
lower centre: *South View of Sritling Castle / Sepr.5th.1788*
272 × 425 mm
Anderson, A. E. (gift, 1922) (D.1922.37)

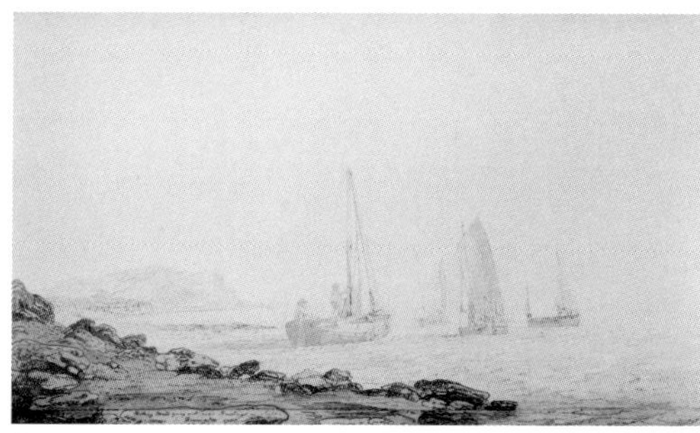

D.1924.47

Fishing Boats, near Hastings, Sussex
1785
pencil, pen and brown ink, watercolour
signed, inscribed & dated lower left: *Fishing Boats going
out near Hastings in Sussex. / Jos Farington 1785.–*
439 × 730 mm
Broadhurst, Sir Edward Tootal, Broadhurst, Lady
(bequest, 1924) (D.1924.47)

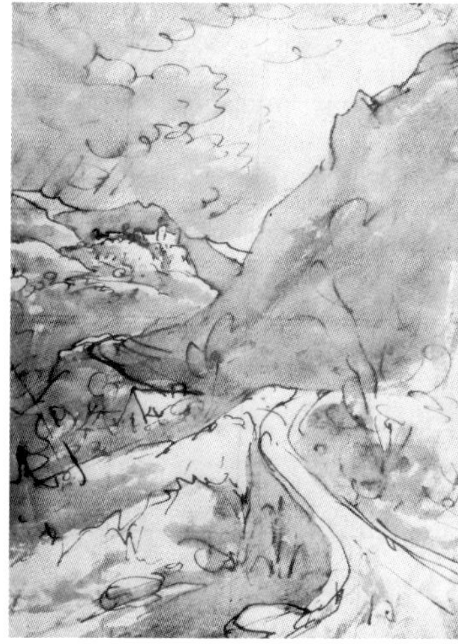

D.1925.52

A mountainous Landscape with a distant Castle
pen and brown ink, brown watercolour
224 × 170 mm
Witt, Sir Robert, Witt, Lady, National Art Collections Fund
(via) (gift, 1925) (D.1925.52)

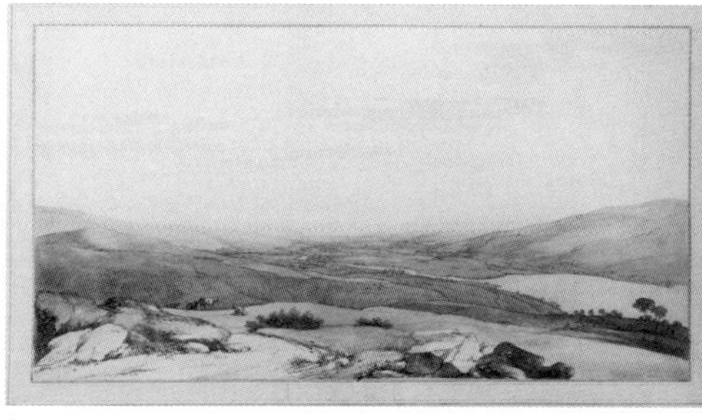

D.1925.54

**View towards Dumbarton with Dumbarton Rock
in the Distance, Dumbartonshire**
7.10.1788
pencil, watercolour
signed & dated lower left: *Jos Farington / Octr.7th 1788*;
inscribed on mount lower centre: *View looking towards
Dumbarton / including the end of Loch Lomond / & the
course of the River Kelvin*
415 × 777 mm
Agnew's (purchase, 1925) (D.1925.54)

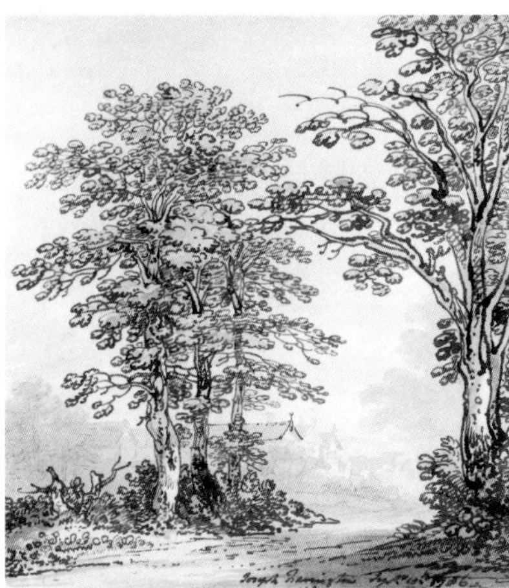

D.1927.113

Study of a Manor House among Trees
10.9.1786
pencil, pen and brown ink, grey watercolour
signed & dated lower right: *Joseph Farington
Septr.10th.1786.*
247 × 213 mm
Holliday, J. R. (bequest, 1927) (D.1927.113)

**Keswick Vale from Braithwaite
Brows, Cumberland**
17.8.1778
pencil, pen and brown ink
dated lower left: *August 17 – 78*; inscribed & dated
centre verso: *A General view of Keswick Vale, (looking /
towards Keswick) from Braithwaite Brows. / August 17th.
– 1778.*; watermark: Strasburg lily over GR:
275 × 482 mm
University of Manchester, History of Art Department
(transfer, 1960) (D.1960.81)

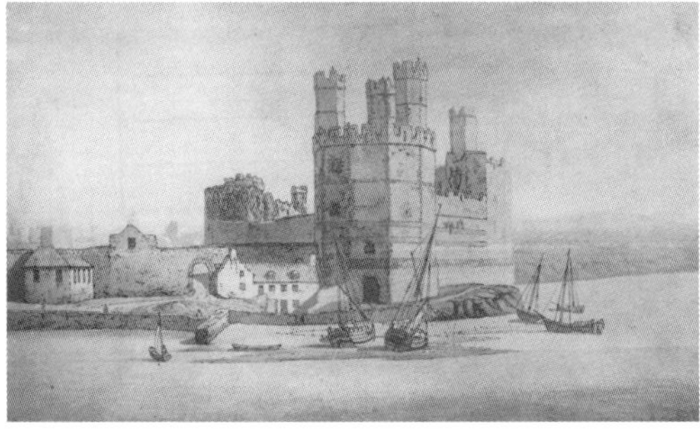

D.1966.21

**The Eagle Tower, Caernarvon Castle, seen from
across the River**
16.8.1791
pencil, pen and brown ink, watercolour
signed & dated lower right: *Jos Farington August 16.
1791*
217 × 359 mm
Lockett, G. Derek (gift, 1966) (D.1966.21)

■ **FARINGTON, JOSEPH & SMIRKE,
ROBERT (1752–1845)**
Smirke was an architect and occasional draughtsman.
He was elected a member of the Royal Academy in 1791.

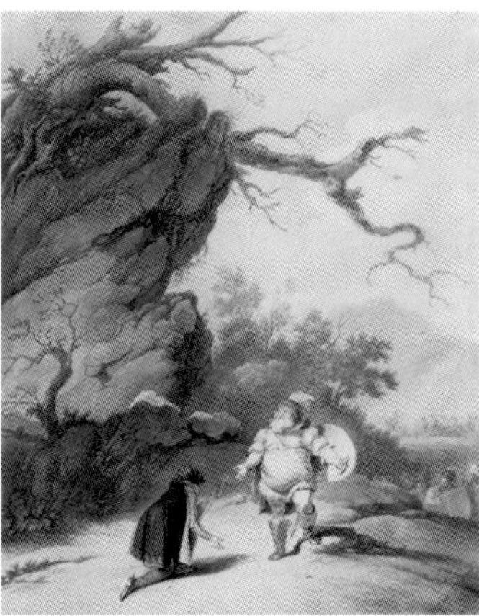

D.1996.49

**An Illustration to Shakespeare's 'Henry IV Part
II', Act IV, Scene III: Sir John Coleville
surrenders to Falstaff**
1796
pen and brown ink, grey watercolour,
brown watercolour
signed & dated lower left in Farington's hand: *Jos
Farington / Robt.Smirke* [these two names bracketed] /
1796
409 × 331 mm
Agnew's (purchase, 22.11.1996) (D.1996.49)

■ **FARMER, EMILY (1826–1905)**
Farmer exhibited at the Royal Academy and the New
Watercolour Society from 1847. She initially produced
miniatures but then turned to genre scenes, particularly
incorporating children. Farmer was elected a member
of the New Watercolour Society in 1854.

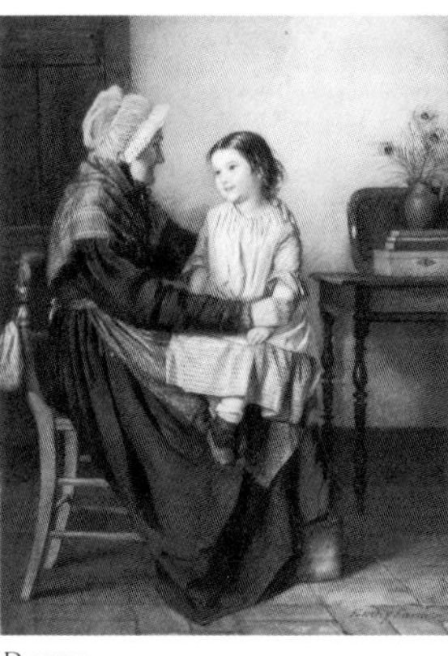

D.1919.1

An old Woman with a Girl on her Knee
watercolour, bodycolour
signed lower right: *Emily Farmer*
375 × 274 mm
Philips, Mrs Herbert (bequest, 1919) (D.1919.1)

■ **FAULKNER, JOHN (ca. 1825–ca. 1890)**
Faulkner, an Irish landscape and marine painter
who exhibited at the Royal Hibernian Academy
from 1852, was elected a member in 1861. Apparently
expelled from the Academy in 1870, he visited
America before going to London. Faulkner sent
watercolours to the Royal Academy in 1884, 1885
and 1888; his last exhibited watercolour was in 1890.
Although his later life was described as 'irregular',
virtually nothing is known of it.

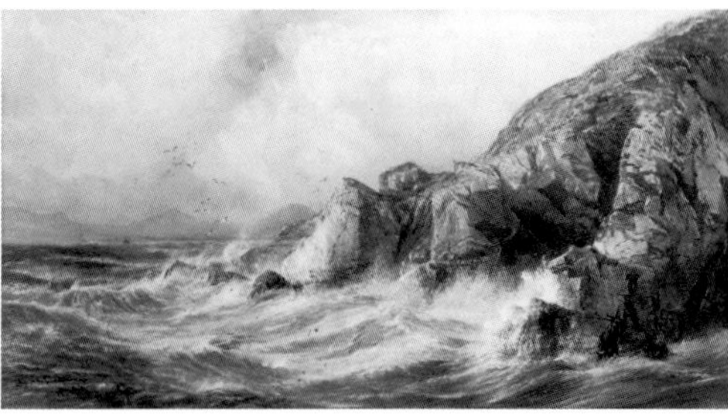

D.1899.6

**Cliffs at the Base of Slievemore, Achill Island,
Co. Mayo, Ireland**
1879
watercolour, bodycolour (heightened with white)
signed, inscribed & dated lower left: *Cliffs at the base
of Slievemore / Achill Island / John Faulkner 1879*
690 × 1203 mm
anonymous (in memory of Sir Joseph Whitworth) (gift, 1899)
(D.1899.6)

■ **FIELDING, ANTHONY VANDYKE COPLEY
(1787–1855)**
One of four artist sons of a Yorkshire portrait painter,
Anthony Vandyke Copley Fielding was a pupil of John
Varley. He became a member of the Old Watercolour
Society in 1812; his annual exhibition average there was
over 40 works for 43 years. Fielding was President of
the Society from 1831 until his death. He had a
successful teaching practice and was hugely prolific and
repetitive; his works were described by Roget as having
'the air more of models of art than guides to nature'.

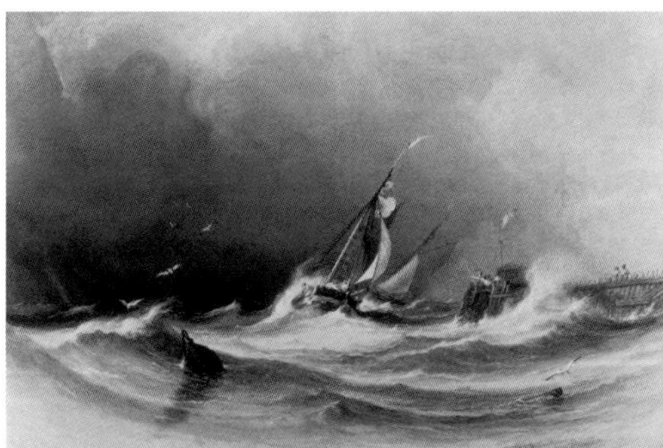

D.1887.36

Boats entering Dover Harbour
watercolour
signed lower right: *Copley Fielding* and with an erased
signature lower right
617 × 905 mm
Wright, Thomas W. (purchase, 1891) (D.1887.36)

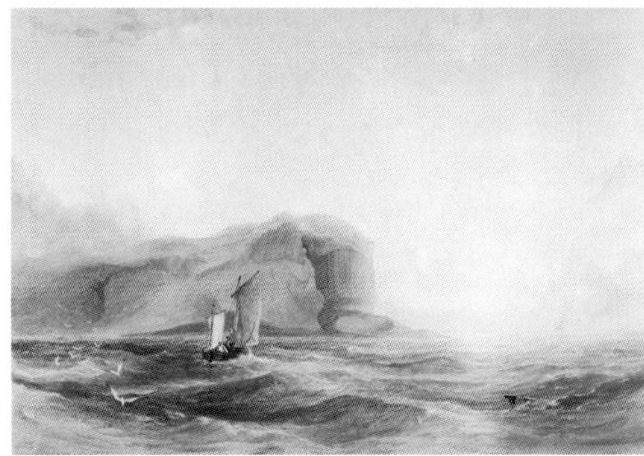

D.1898.3

Fingal's Cave, Staffa, Inner Hebrides, Argyllshire
watercolour
434 × 604 mm
anonymous (in memory of Sir Joseph Whitworth) (gift, 1898)
(D.1898.3)

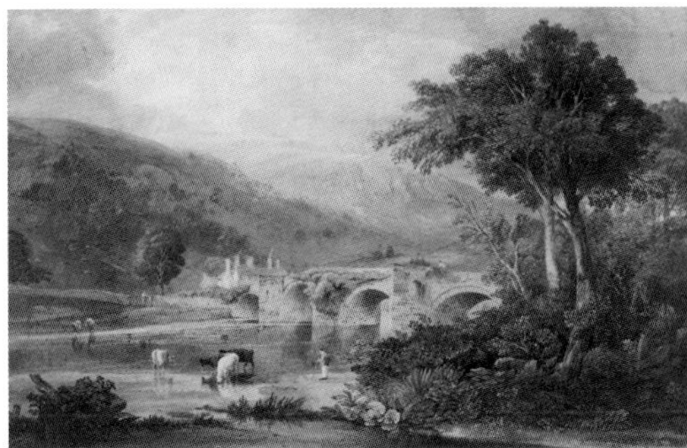

D.1904.25

Old Newby Bridge, Lancashire
1818
pencil, watercolour
signed & dated lower left with initials: *C.V.F.1818*
515 × 784 mm
Worthington, Mary (bequest, 1904) (D.1904.25)

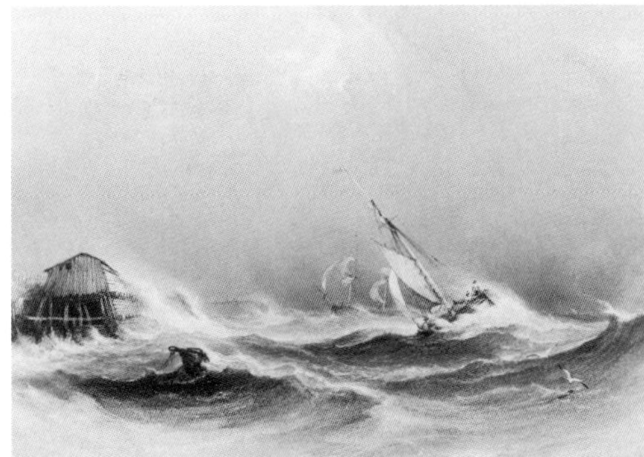

D.1910.10

Boats in a Storm, Bridlington Harbour, Yorkshire
watercolour
460 × 624 mm
Cox, G. F. (bequest, 1910) (D.1910.10)

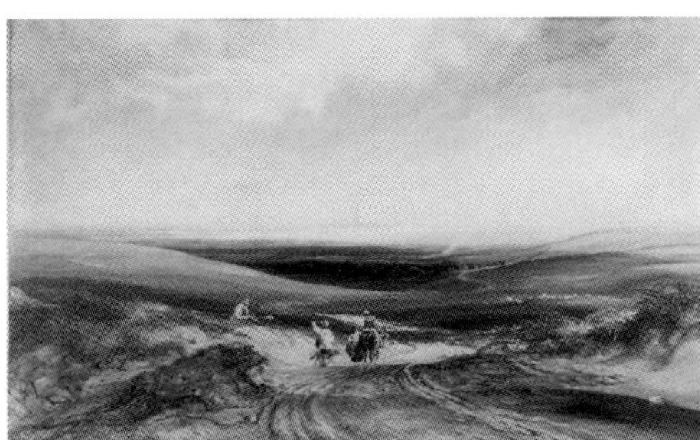

D.1922.32

The Foreland from Fairlight Downs, Sussex
1853
watercolour
signed & dated lower left: *Copley Fielding 1853*
719 × 1165 mm
Broadhurst, Sir Edward Tootal (bequest) (D.1922.32)

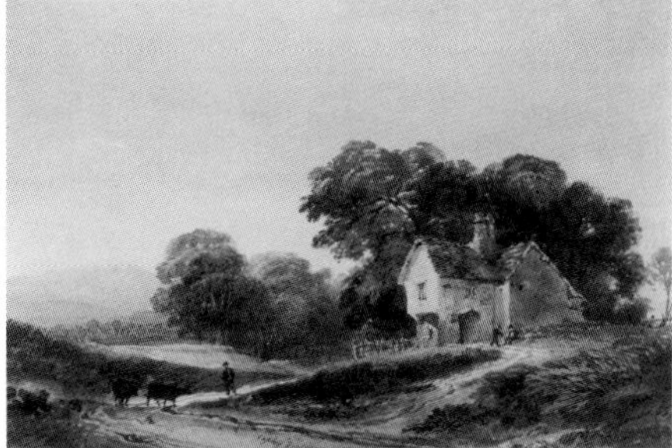

D.1924.36

Cottage near Cuckfield, East Sussex
1849
pencil, watercolour
signed & dated lower centre: *Copley Fielding 1849*
175 × 257 mm
Broadhurst, Sir Edward Tootal, Broadhurst, Lady
(bequest, 1924) (D.1924.36)

Landscape at Sunset
watercolour
signed lower right: *Copley Fielding*
166 × 250 mm
Broadhurst, Sir Edward Tootal, Broadhurst, Lady
(bequest, 1924) (D.1924.50)

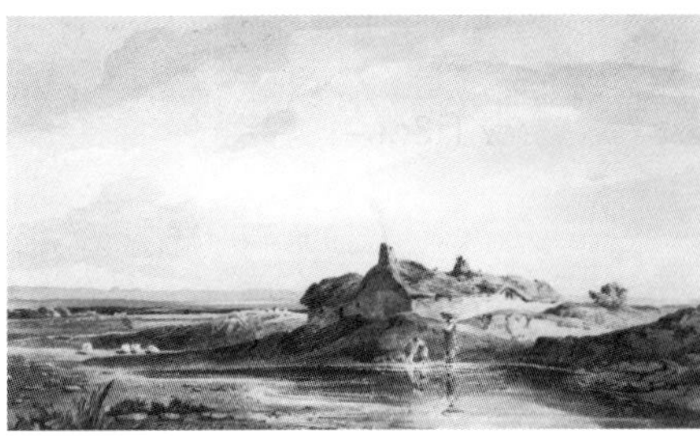

D.1924.51

Cottage and Pool
1809
pencil, watercolour
signed & dated lower left: *C.V.Fielding 1809*
258 × 418 mm
Broadhurst, Sir Edward Tootal, Broadhurst, Lady
(bequest, 1924) (D.1924.51)

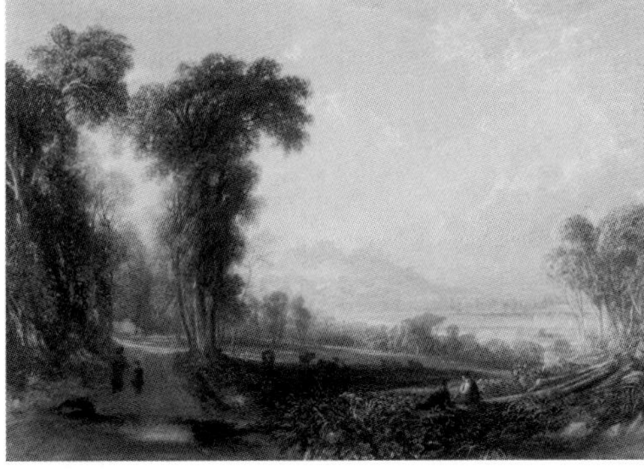

D.1961.18

View of Lancaster, from the North East, with the River Lune
1845
watercolour
signed & dated lower left: *Copley Fielding 1845*
564 × 771 mm
Haworth, C., Haworth, S., Haworth, M. (in memory of Frank
A. Haworth) (gift, 1961) (D.1961.18)

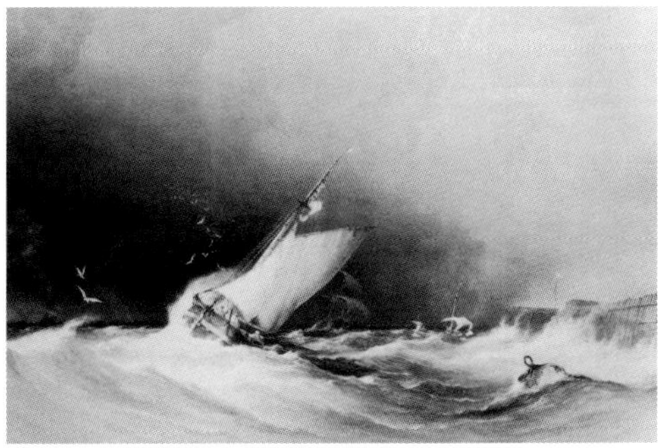

D.1977.11

Storm, Fishing Boats approaching Harbour
watercolour
643 × 913 mm
Whitehead, James Edward (bequest, 1977) (D.1977.11)

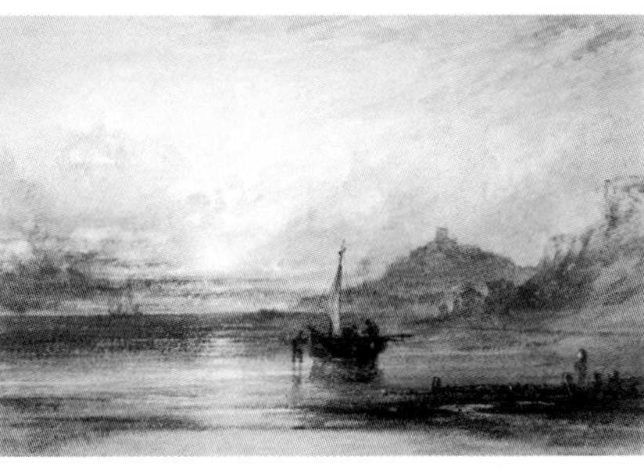

D.1977.12

Coast Scene at Sunset
1853
watercolour
signed & dated lower left: *Copley Fielding 1853*
182 × 266 mm
Whitehead, James Edward (bequest, 1977) (D.1977.12)

■ FIELDING, THALES (1793–1837)

Thales Fielding, younger brother of Copley, exhibited
at the Old Watercolour Society from 1816 to 1820,
when he went to Paris to run the French end of the
Fielding family business. Here he met Delacroix and
came across the watercolours of Bonington, which had
a strong and lasting effect on his work. On his return
from Paris in 1827 Fielding became a drawing master at
the Royal Military Academy at Woolwich and an
associate member of the Old Watercolour Society in
1829, exhibiting there annually until his death.

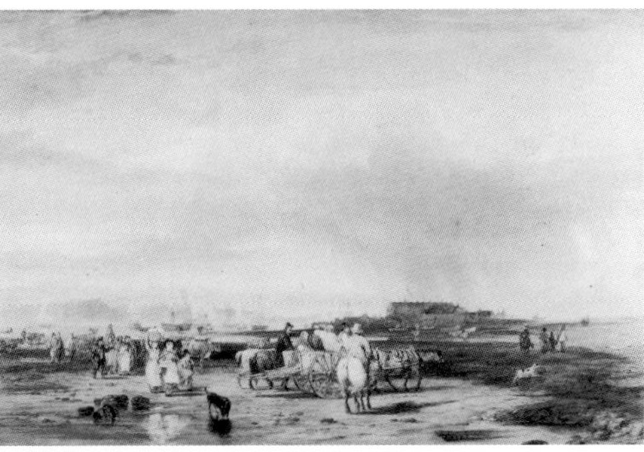

D.1912.13

Crossing Solway Sands
pencil, watercolour
signed lower left: *T Fielding*
642 × 957 mm
Blair, J. T. (gift, 1912) (D.1912.13)

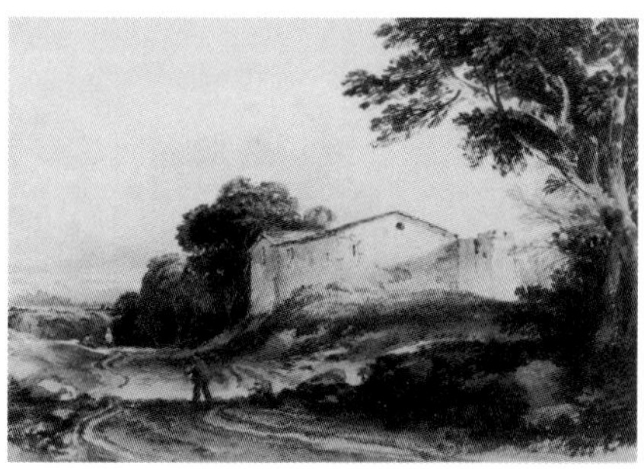

D.1949.35

Landscape with Barn
pencil, watercolour
180 × 255 mm
Pilkington, Denis F. (gift, 1949) (D.1949.35)

■ Finch, Francis Oliver (1802–62)

Finch was born in London and studied under John
Varley. He started exhibiting at the Royal Academy in
1817 and was elected a member of the Old Watercolour
Society in 1827. Finch was a friend of Samuel Palmer
and one of the artists in William Blake's circle in the
1820s. He produced few topographical landscapes and
his preference was for imaginary romantic landscapes
showing the influence of Claude and Poussin.

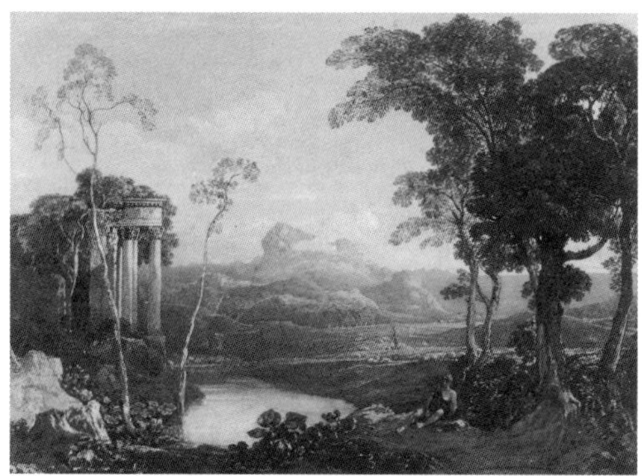

D.1927.2

Classical Landscape
pencil, watercolour
signed: *F.O.FINCH*
339 × 457 mm
Blair, G. B. (gift, 1927) (D.1927.2)

■ Fisher, Sir George Bulteel (1764–1834)

Sir George Bulteel Fisher was a proficient amateur
landscape painter who was an officer in the Royal
Artillery and served in many parts of the world. He
later became Commandant at the Royal Military
Academy at Woolwich.

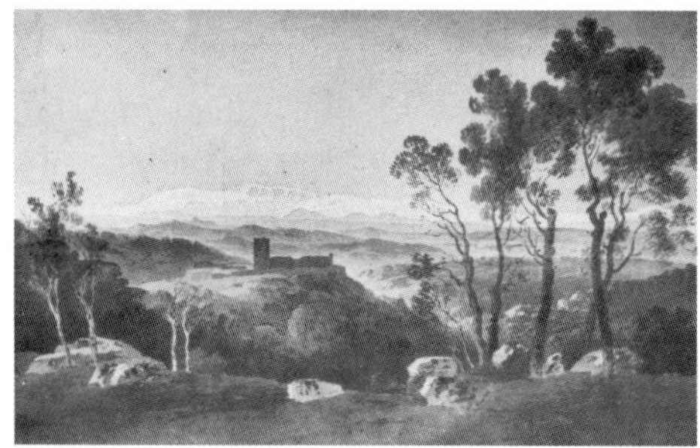

D.1938.13

Villa Nova, near Covilas, Portugal
pencil, watercolour
262 × 418 mm
Pilkington, Margaret, Friends of the Whitworth (via)
(gift, 1938) (D.1938.13)

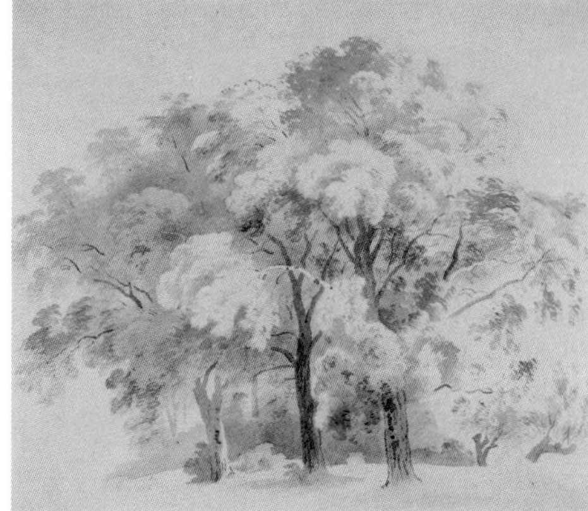

D.1963.23

Study of Trees
pencil, watercolour
361 × 388 mm
Lockett, G. Derek (gift, 1963) (D.1963.23)

■ Fisher, John (1748–1825)

John Fisher was the eldest brother of Sir George
and also an amateur of consequence. He was in Italy
from 1785 to 1786. In 1803, he became Bishop of Exeter
and in 1807 he was appointed Bishop of Salisbury. As
well as being an accomplished amateur artist, he was
also a connoisseur and patron, numbering Constable
among his protégés. He should not be confused with
his nephew and namesake, the Archdeacon, who
acted as his chaplain in Salisbury and was Constable's
closest friend.

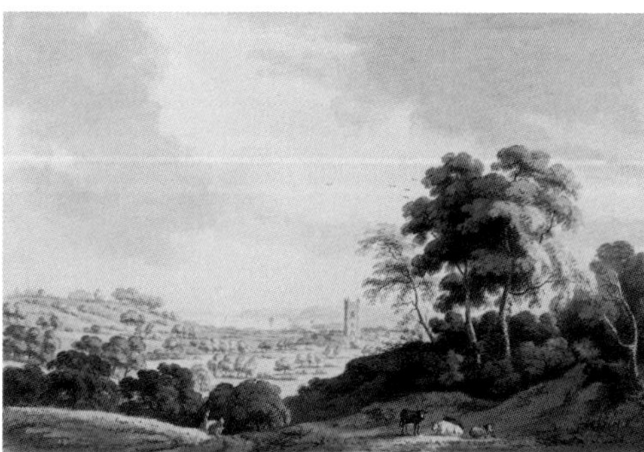

D.1934.22

A distant View of Dedham, Suffolk
pencil, watercolour
344 × 512 mm
Anderson, A. E. (gift, 1934) (D.1934.22)

■ Fisher, William Mark (1841–1923)

William Mark Fisher, a painter of landscapes and
cattle, was born in Boston, Massachusetts. He studied
there and in Gleyre's studio in Paris, where he was
influenced by the work of Corot. Fisher moved to
England in 1872 and was elected a member of the
Royal Institute in 1881. He exhibited at the Royal
Academy from 1872 and was elected a member in 1919.

In the Meadows
pencil, watercolour, bodycolour
(heightened with white)
signed lower left: *M. Fisher*
219 × 318 mm
Darbishire, Robert Dukinfield (gift, 1908) (D.1908.24)

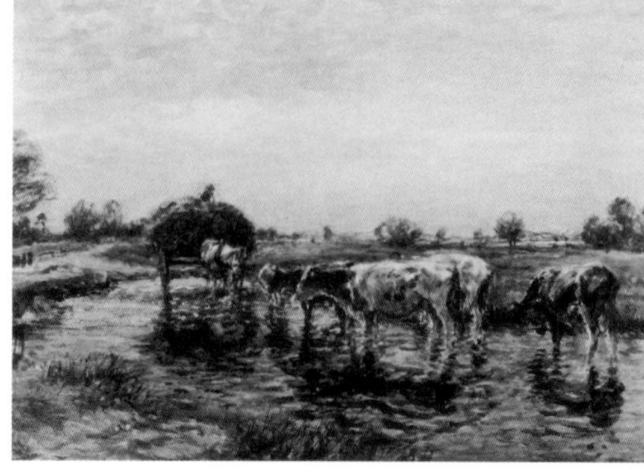

D.1921.45

The Ford
black chalk, watercolour, bodycolour
(heightened with white)
signed lower right: *Mark Fisher*
453 × 605 mm
Jackson, C. A. (purchase, 1921) (D.1921.45)

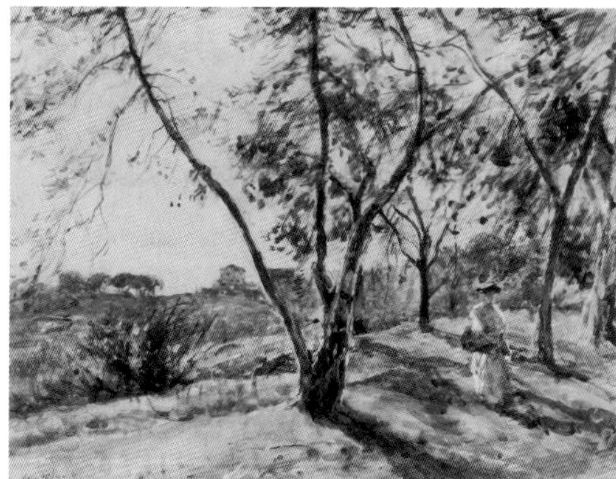

D.1924.8

Evening Sunlight
pencil, watercolour, bodycolour
(heightened with white)
signed lower left: *Mark Fisher*
274 × 375 mm
Wood, W. H. (gift, 1924) (D.1924.8)

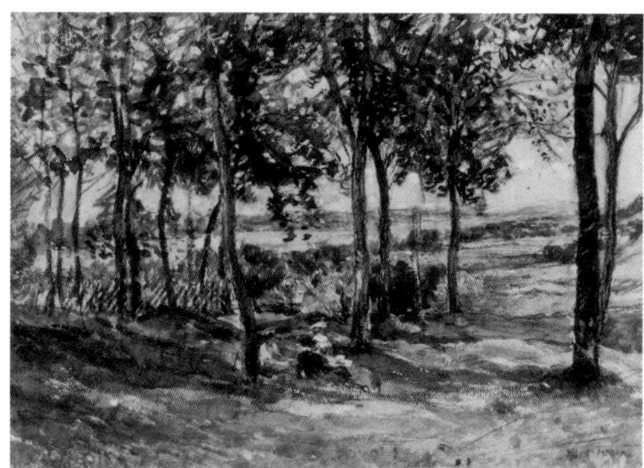

D.1924.9

Landscape, near Bordeaux, France
black chalk, watercolour, bodycolour
(heightened with white)
signed lower right: *Mark* [illegible] *Fisher*
279 × 352 mm
Wood, W. H. (gift, 1924) (D.1924.9)

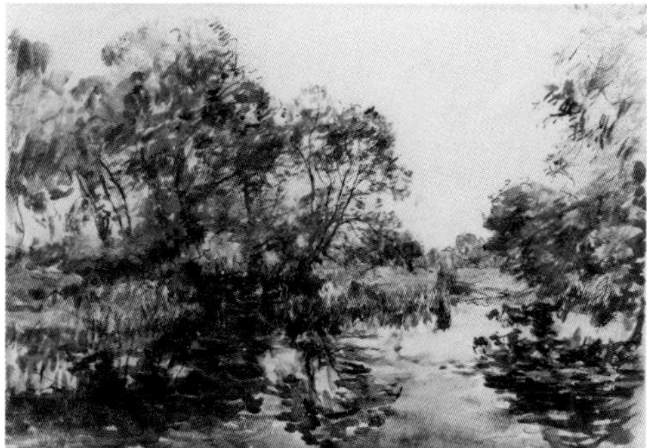

D.1998.30

The Lakeside
pen and brown ink, watercolour
254 × 356 mm
University of Manchester, Picture Loan Scheme (transfer, 1998)
(D.1998.30)

■ **FLAXMAN, JOHN (1755–1826)**
Flaxman, one of the most influential exponents of the
neo-classical style, was in Rome from 1787 to 1794,
where he consolidated his reputation with his
illustrations to Homer, Aeschylus and Dante. On
returning to England he was elected a member of the
Royal Academy in 1800, eventually becoming Professor
of Sculpture. Flaxman's flowing neo-classical style as
seen on Wedgwood porcelain and in his sculpture and
drawings had a huge impact on his contemporaries.

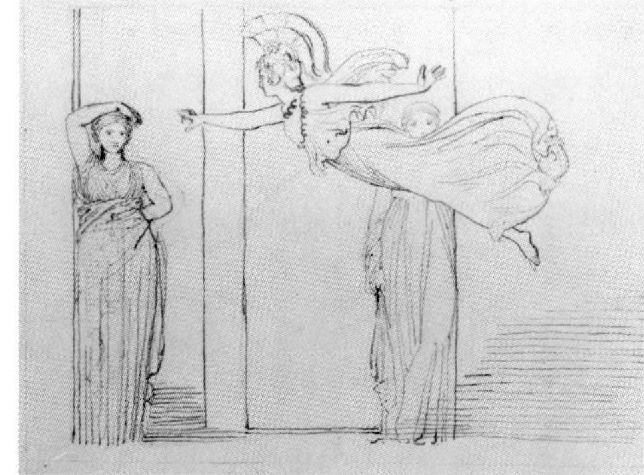

D.1889.1

**Descent of Minerva to Ithaca, Study for
'The Odyssey of Homer' (recto); Study of
Figures (verso)**
pencil, pen and grey ink
inscribed lower right below mount: *Od 6–20*
210 × 241 mm
Agnew, Sir William (gift, 1889) (D.1889.1)

**Penelope unwinding her Web, Study for
'The Odyssey of Homer' (recto); Alternative
Composition Study (verso)**
pencil, pen and grey ink
inscribed on upper left verso: *Odyssey Bk 2 Page 19 /
Penelope undoing her web*
167 × 240 mm
Agnew, Sir William (gift, 1889) (D.1889.2)

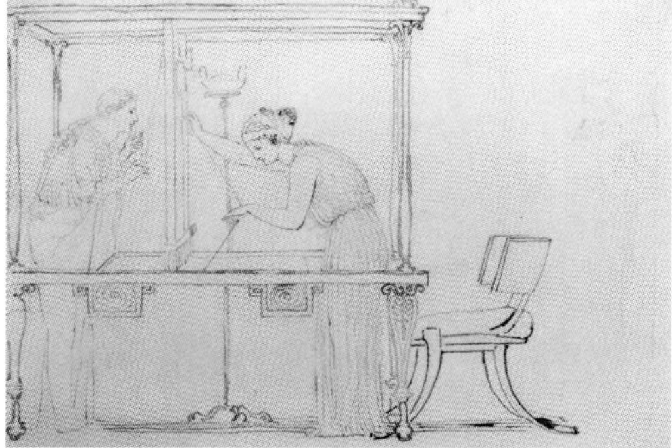

D.1889.2

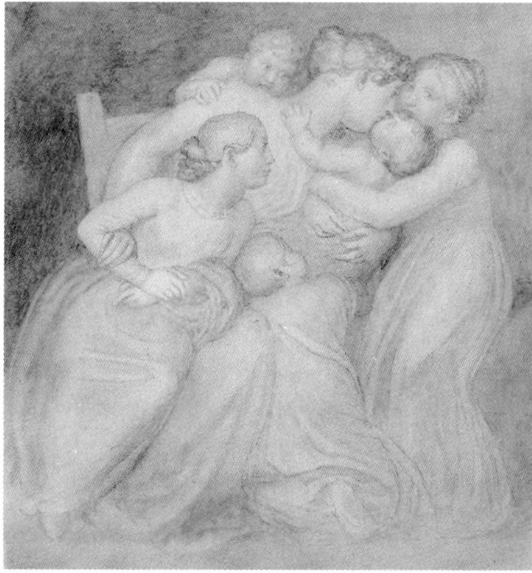

D.1892.20

Maternal Love
pencil, pen and grey ink, brown watercolour
inscribed lower centre: *Maternal Love*
239 × 207 mm
Taylor, John Edward (gift, 1892) (D.1892.20)

Study for a Monument to William Collins
pencil, pen and grey ink, grey watercolour
signed & inscribed lower right: *Thought for a
Monument for Colins* (sic) *the Poet. / J.Flaxman.*
264 × 190 mm
Agnew's (purchase, 1920) (D.1920.26)

**Comfort the Afflicted, Study for
'The Acts of Mercy'**
pen and grey ink, grey watercolour
inscribed lower centre: *Comfort the Afflicted*
198 × 315 mm
Agnew's (purchase, 1920) (D.1920.27)

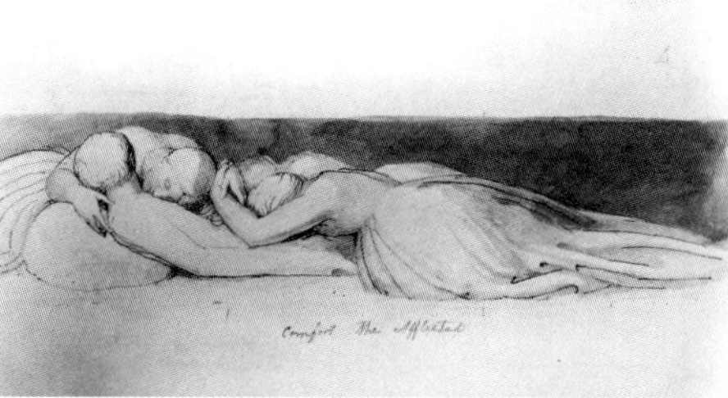

D.1920.27

**Study of a Classical Relief in the Palazzo
Giustiniani, Rome**
1787–94
pen and grey ink, grey watercolour
inscribed along lower edge; the words 'part of' are a
superscript: *Euridice killed by the serpent, Orpheus in
despair for her death & afterward torn in pieces by the
Ciconian women, part of the front of a marble
sarcophagus in the wall of the cortile of the Palace
Gustiniani, Rome / the figures about 22 inches high, of
very ordinary workmanship 'tho of a Noble composition,
some of the heads are broken off as well as the most
projecting arms & the original workmanship is competent
where / the drawing appears so*
247 × 651 mm
Friends of the Whitworth (gift, 1960) (D.1960.42)

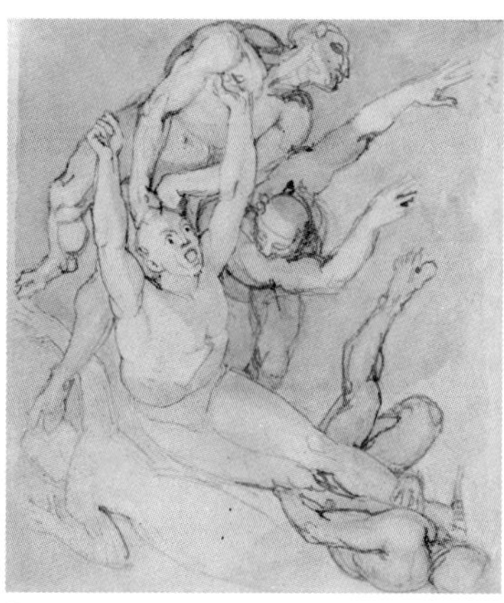

D.1976.1

**'To whom ye yield yourselves Slaves to obey, his
Slaves ye are': Bible Illustration, Romans 6, 16**
pencil, pen and brown ink, brown watercolour
inscribed lower right: *St.Paul*
180 × 207 mm
Heim Gallery, London (purchase, 1976) (F.O.W.) (D.1976.1)

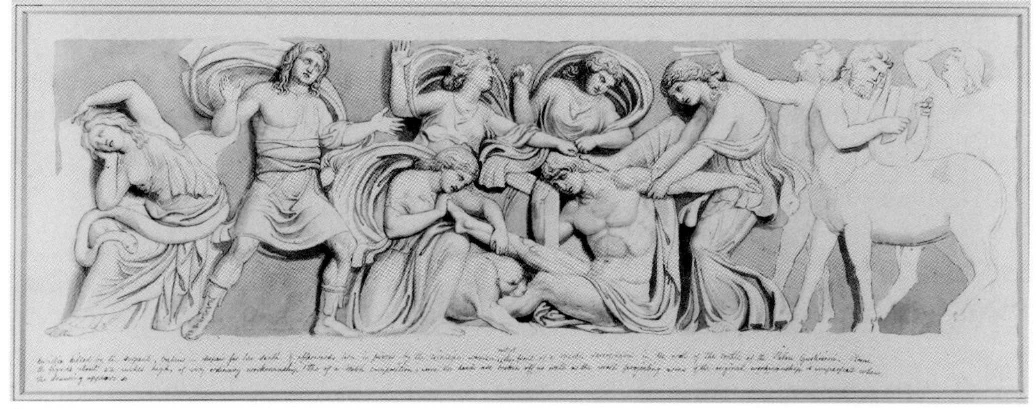

D.1960.42

■ FLAXMAN, JOHN (attributed to)

**David rescued from many Waters (recto);
A Lady leaving the Bedside of a dying
young Man (verso)**
pencil, pen and grey ink, grey watercolour
301 × 406 mm
University of Manchester, History of Art Department
(transfer, 1960) (D.1960.82)

■ FOSTER, MYLES BIRKET (1825–99)

Foster began his career as an engraver and black-and-white illustrator but turned to watercolour after 1859. He was elected a member of the Old Watercolour Society in 1862 and thereafter exhibited there frequently. He was a regular traveller to the Continent. His highly finished landscapes with figures, employing much white bodycolour, were hugely admired in their time, resulting in many forgeries of his work.

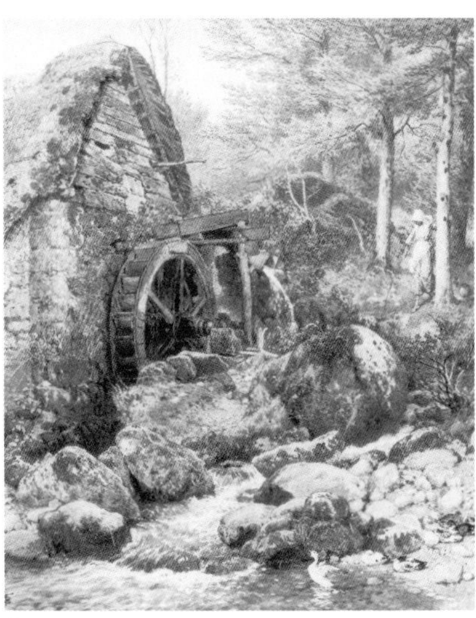

D.1910.14

The Old Mill
pencil, watercolour, bodycolour
(heightened with white)
signed lower left with monogram: *BF*
345 × 284 mm
Cox, G. F. (bequest, 1910) (D.1910.14)

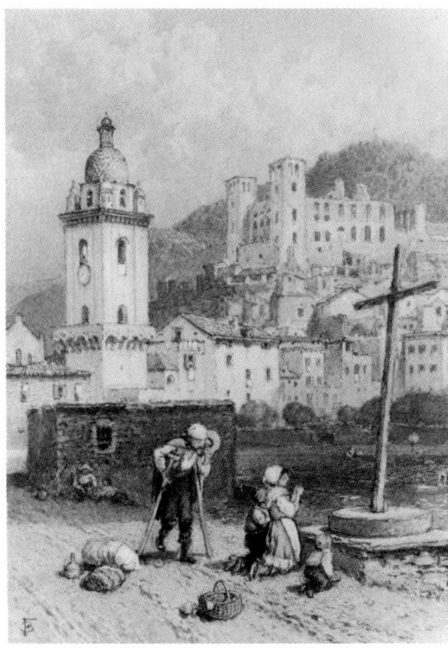

D.1910.16

View of Dolceaqua, Italy
pencil, watercolour, bodycolour
(heightened with white)
signed lower left with monogram: *BF*
142 × 100 mm
Cox, G. F. (bequest, 1910) (D.1910.16)

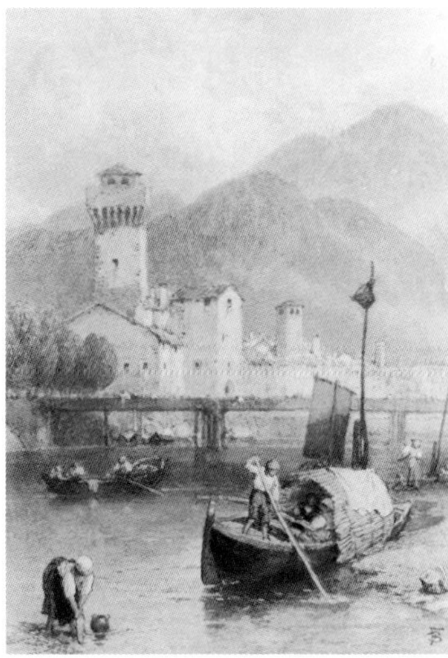

D.1910.17

View of the Citadella, Pisa
watercolour, bodycolour (heightened with white)
signed lower right with monogram: *BF*
142 × 100 mm
Cox, G. F. (bequest, 1910) (D.1910.17)

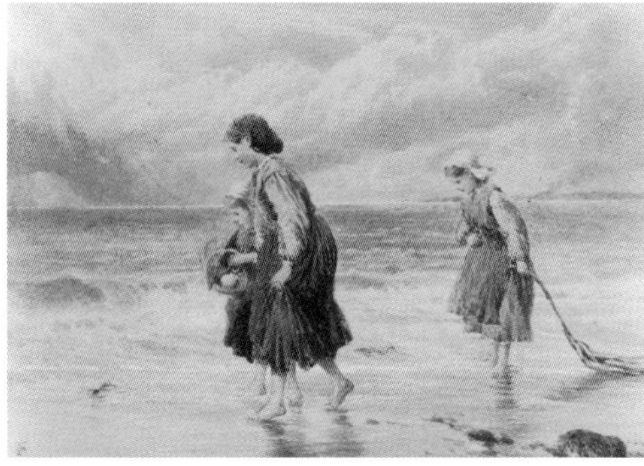

D.1937.12

Children by the Sea Shore
pencil, watercolour, bodycolour
(heightened with white)
signed lower left with monogram: *BF*
198 × 276 mm
Haworth, Jesse (bequest, 1937) (D.1937.12)

■ FRANCIA, ALEXANDRE (1815/20–84)

Alexandre Francia was born in Calais, the son and pupil of François Louis Thomas, and exhibited at the Salon in Paris from 1841 to 1866. His earlier works are frequently confused with those of his father.

French Boats
1834
pencil, watercolour
signed & dated lower left: *Francia 1834*
238 × 377 mm
Taylor, John Edward (gift, 1892) (D.1892.66)

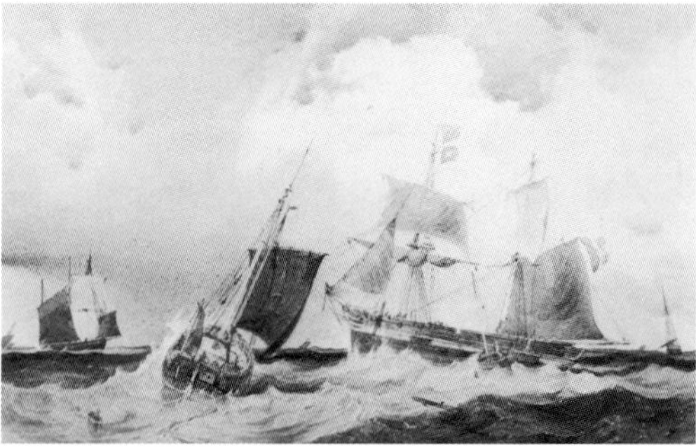

D.1892.66

■ FRANCIA, FRANÇOIS LOUIS THOMAS (1772–1839)

François Louis Thomas Francia was born in Calais and came to England in 1795. He was a fellow student at the Monro Academy with Thomas Girtin. In 1799, he was Secretary and co-founder of Girtin's Sketching Club 'The Brothers'. From 1805 Francia was working as a drawing master in London. In 1817, he returned to Calais where he set up as a drawing master and gave lessons to William Wyld and his most famous pupil, Richard Parkes Bonington.

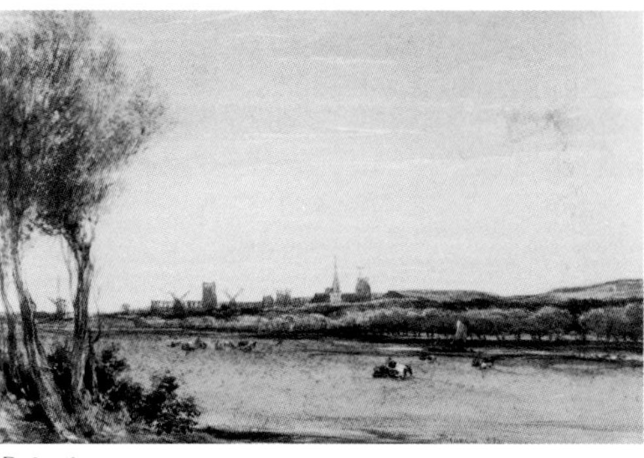

D.1892.67

Saint-Omer, France, from the Meadows
1832
pen and brown ink, watercolour
signed & dated lower right: *Francia 1832*
164 × 236 mm
Taylor, John Edward (gift, 1892) (D.1892.67)

■ FRIPP, ALFRED DOWNING (1822–95)

Alfred Downing Fripp, brother of George and grandson of Nicholas Pocock, was born in Bristol, coming to London in 1840. In 1843 he made the first of three visits to the west of Ireland and Irish peasant subjects feature prominently in his early work. Fripp was elected a member of the Old Watercolour Society in 1846 and from 1850 to 1858 lived in Italy, painting Neapolitan, Roman and Venetian subjects.

The Spring at Lulworth, Dorset
1885
watercolour
signed & dated lower left: *Alfred D.Fripp 1885*
533 × 423 mm
anonymous (in memory of Sir Joseph Whitworth) (gift, 1897)
(D.1897.5)

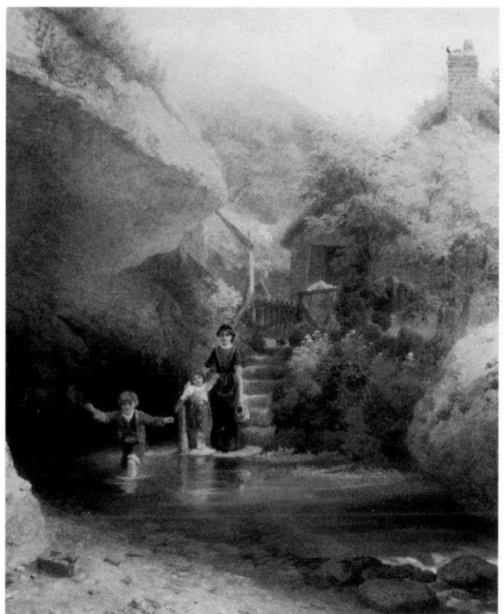

D.1897.5

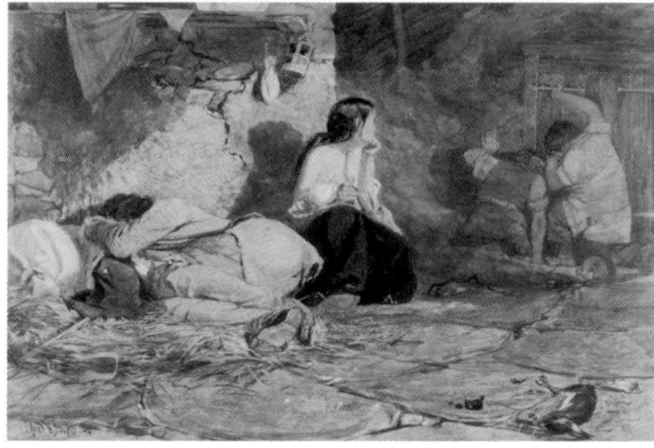

D.1923.11

The Poachers alarmed
1844
pencil, watercolour, bodycolour (heightened
with white)
signed & dated lower left: *Alfred DFripp 44*
369 × 537 mm
Anderson, A. E., National Art Collections Fund (via)
(gift, 1923) (D.1923.11)

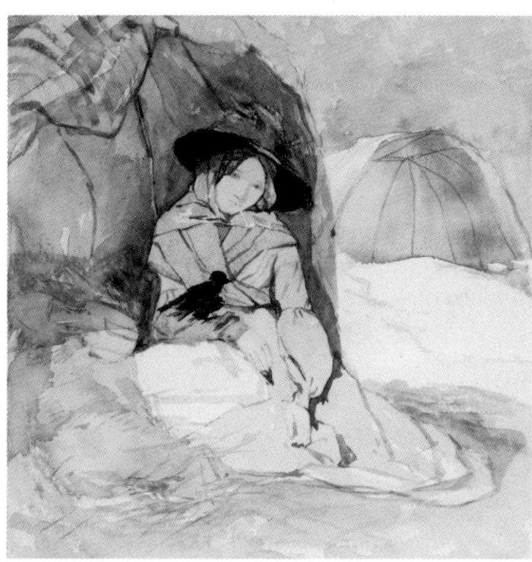

D.1948.19

Gipsy Girl
pencil, watercolour
298 × 280 mm
Friends of the Whitworth (gift, 1948) (D.1948.19)

■ Fripp, George Arthur (1813–96)

George Arthur Fripp was the brother of Alfred and
friend of William James Muller, with whom he
travelled down the Rhine and in Italy in 1833–34.
Elected a member of the Old Watercolour Society in
1845, Fripp was invited to Balmoral by Queen Victoria
in 1860 and commissioned to paint a dozen views of
Balmoral and the surrounding area. He was Secretary
of the Old Watercolour Society from 1848 to 1854.

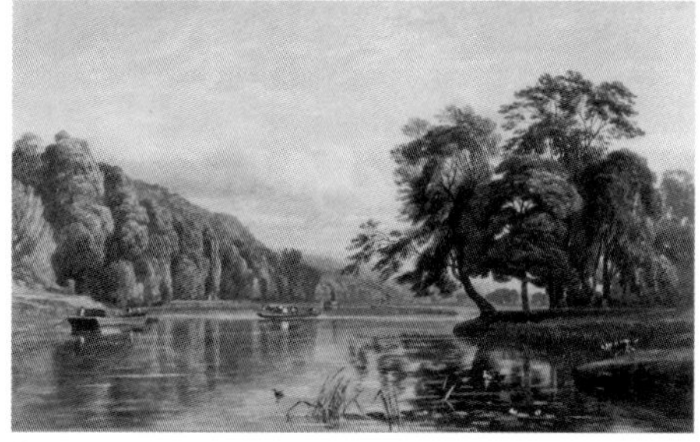

D.1897.4

On the Thames
pencil, watercolour, bodycolour (heightened
with white)
signed lower right: *G.A Fripp*
317 × 502 mm
anonymous (in memory of Sir Joseph Whitworth) (gift, 1897)
(D.1897.4)

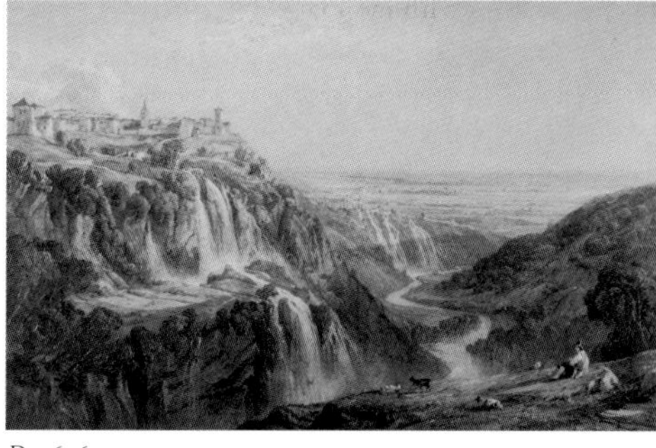

D.1963.6

The Cascades, Tivoli, Italy
1841
pencil, watercolour
signed & dated lower right: *G A Fripp / 1841*
471 × 702 mm
Langton, Miss F. M., National Art Collections Fund (via)
(bequest, 1963) (D.1963.6)

■ Frost, George (1734–1821)

Frost, a Suffolk amateur artist, was an admirer of
Gainsborough and a friend of Constable. His subjects
are taken from Ipswich and neighbouring areas and are
mostly chalk drawings. These are sometimes mistaken
for the work of Gainsborough or Constable, and the
latter was briefly influenced by Frost.

**A wooded Landscape with Figures,
Cattle and Sheep**
black chalk
242 × 198 mm
Meatyard, F. R. (purchase, 1922) (D.1922.17)

A Path in a Wood
black chalk
608 × 444 mm
Christie's, London (purchase, 1930) (D.1930.18)

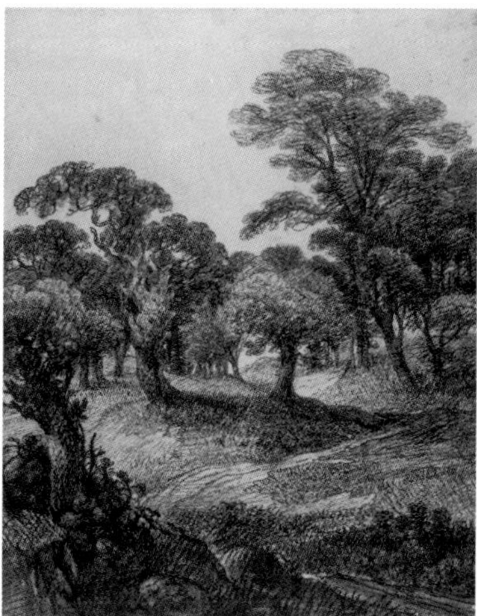

D.1930.18

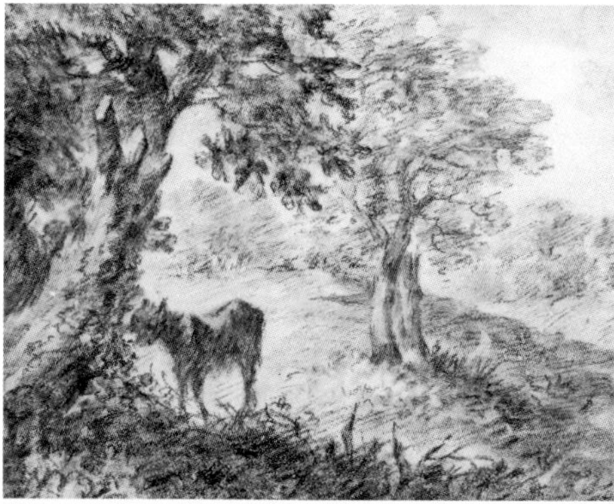

D.1931.3

A Donkey in a Wood
black chalk, grey watercolour
200 × 242 mm
Anderson, A. E. (gift, 1931) (D.1931.3)

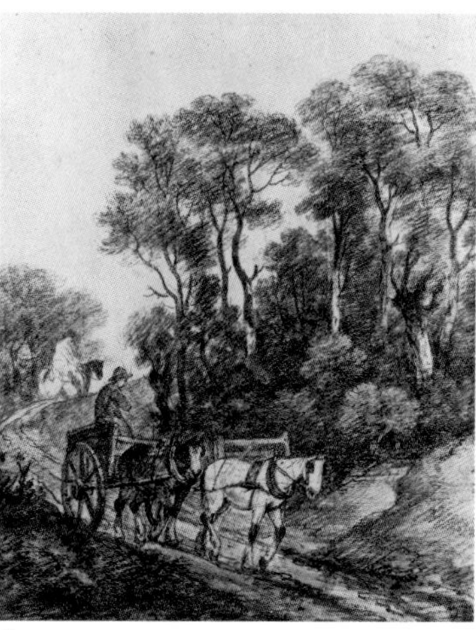

D.1935.17

The Farm Waggon
black chalk
403 × 314 mm
Friends of the Whitworth (gift, 1935) (D.1935.17)

■ Furnell, J. (dates unknown)

If the inscription on the reverse of this drawing is
to be believed, Furnell was a watchmaker as well
as an amateur artist.

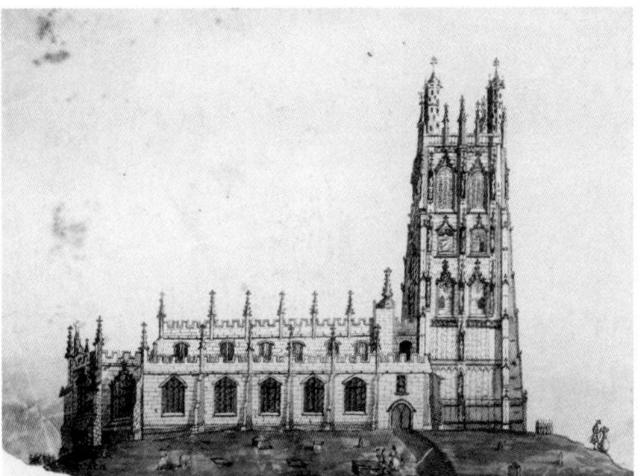

D.1926.281

North Elevation, St Giles Church, Wrexham, Denbighshire, Wales
pen and brown ink, watercolour
inscribed lower left: *WREXHAM / CHURCH*;
inscribed lower right verso: *Drawn by JFurnell Watch–maker* [superscript] *who also etched this view half this size*
237 × 316 mm
Ogden, William Sharp (bequest, 1926) (D.1926.281)

■ **FUSELI, JOHANN HEINRICH (1741–1825)**
Born in Zurich as Johann Heinrich Füssli, Fuseli began his career as a Zwinglian minister in 1761 but left Zurich two years later. He came to England in 1764 and in 1769 travelled to Rome, where he remained until 1778 at the centre of a group of artists of different nationalities. Fuseli then returned to England and was elected a member of the Royal Academy in 1790, and in the same year was also appointed Professor of Painting. His lectures strongly influenced the younger generation of artists. Fuseli's subjects are taken from literature or mythology and are often quite dramatic.

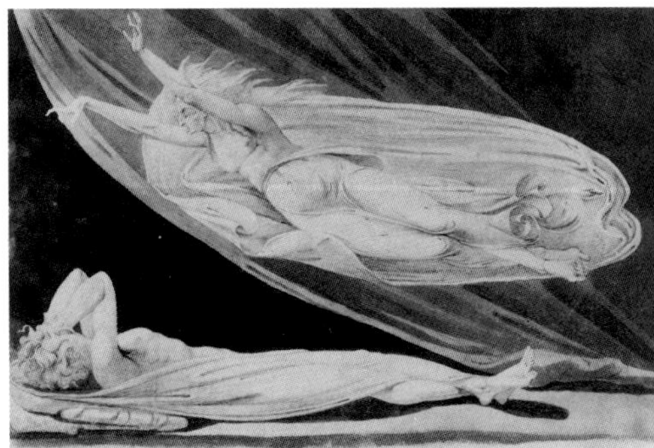

D.1960.15

Julia appearing to Pompey in a Dream
pencil, grey watercolour
264 × 384 mm
Angus-Butterworth, L. M. (in memory of his father Walter Butterworth), National Art Collections Fund (via) (gift, 1960) (D.1960.15)

■ **FUSELI, JOHANN HEINRICH (circle of)**

Scene in the Underworld
pen and brown ink, watercolour
231 × 384 mm
Pilkington, Margaret (gift, 1946) (D.1946.15)

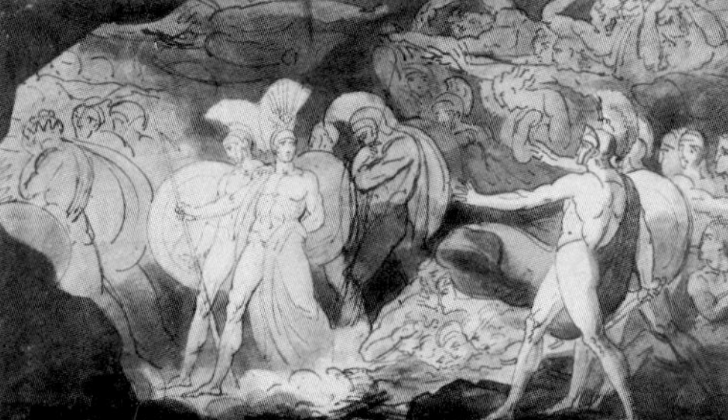

D.1946.15

■ **GAINSBOROUGH, THOMAS (1727–88)**
Born in Sudbury, Gainsborough is one of the most important figures in the development of eighteenth-century landscape. He was a pupil of Francis Hayman from 1742–45. After working in Ipswich, he moved to Bath in 1760, where he quickly established a reputation as a portrait painter. Although a founder member of the Royal Academy in 1768, he did not move permanently to London until 1774. Gainsborough was one of the great pioneers of imaginative draughtsmanship. His style was much imitated and many pastiches and forgeries are often mistaken for originals.

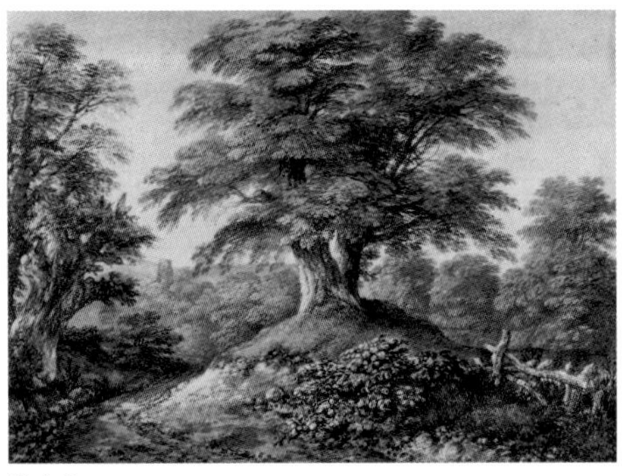

D.1896.1

Beech Trees at Foxley, Herefordshire, with Yazor Church in the Distance
1760
pencil, watercolour
signed & dated on a piece of paper formerly attached to the backboard: *Tho Gainsborough / del 1760*
301 × 401 mm
Agnew's (purchase, 20.4.1896) (D.1896.1)

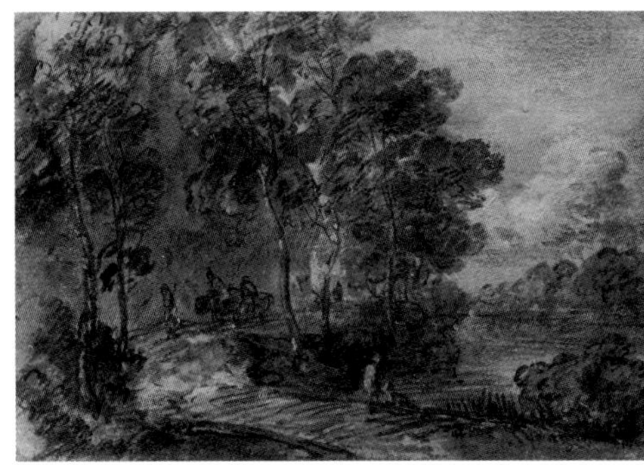

D.1917.17

Wooded Landscape with Riders
black chalk, watercolour, bodycolour, varnish
inscribed lower centre in later hand: *Gainsborough*
216 × 314 mm
Colnaghi's (purchase, 1917) (D.1917.17)

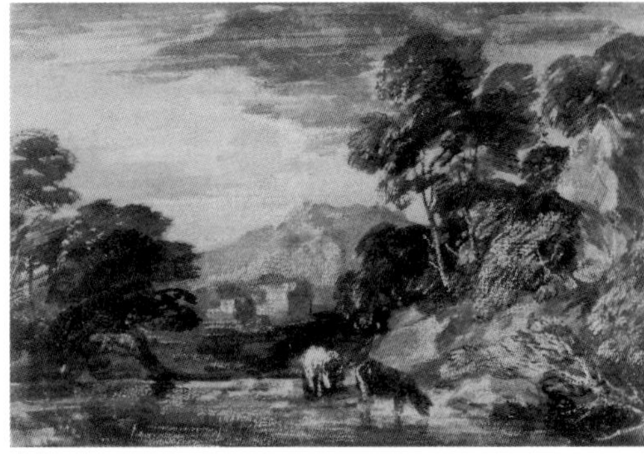

D.1925.24

Classical Landscape with Buildings and Cattle at a Pool
1765–70
black chalk, watercolour, white lead, varnish
217 × 304 mm
Anderson, A. E., National Art Collections Fund (via) (gift, 1925) (D.1925.24)

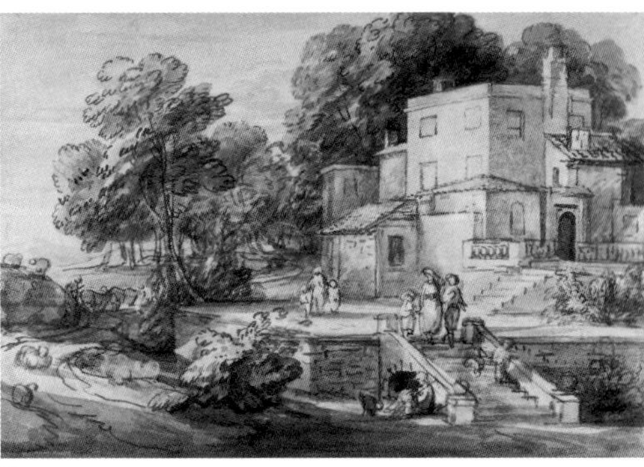

D.1927.20

A wooded Landscape with a Country Mansion, elegant Figures and Peasants
1780–81
white chalk, black chalk, pen and brown ink, grey watercolour
261 × 370 mm
Messrs E. Parsons and Co (purchase, 1927) (D.1927.20)

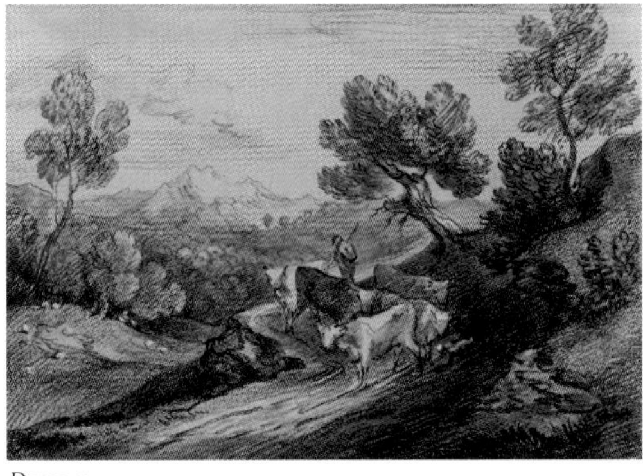

D.1927.50

A wooded Mountain Landscape with a Herdsman driving Cattle along a Road
1780–85
black chalk, stump, watercolour, bodycolour (heightened with white); buff paper
279 × 378 mm
Anderson, A. E., National Art Collections Fund (via) (gift, 1927) (D.1927.50)

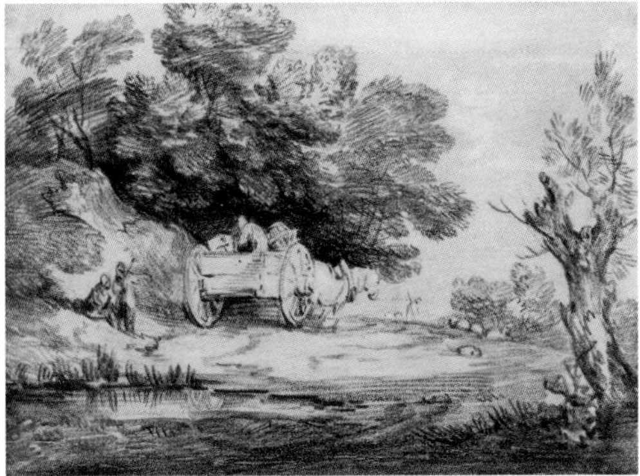

D.1931.4

A wooded Landscape with a Country Cart and Figures
1778-1779
black chalk, white chalk, bodycolour; grey paper
249 × 333 mm
Anderson, A. E. (gift, 1931) (D.1931.4)

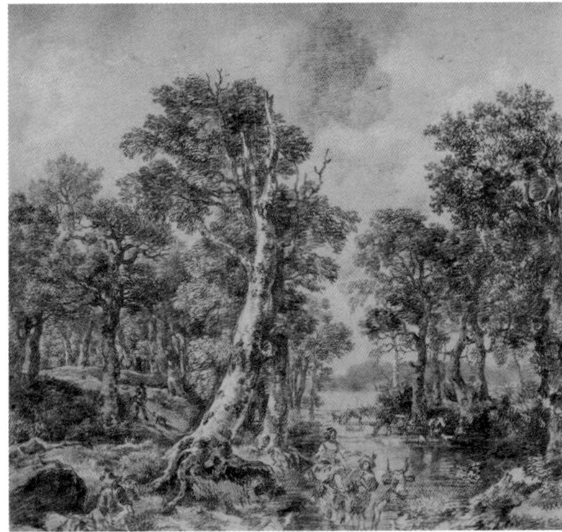

D.1935.2

A wooded Landscape with a River, Cattle and Figures, after Jacob van Ruisdael
1746-47
black chalk, white chalk; buff paper
409 × 423 mm
Anderson, A. E. (gift, 1935) (D.1935.2)

■ GARDNOR, REV. JOHN (1729–1808) and WHEATLEY, FRANCIS (1747–1801)

Gardnor was a drawing master before entering the Church when he became vicar of Battersea in 1778, officiating at William Blake's wedding in 1782. Gardnor exhibited lansdcapes at the Royal Academy as an Honorary Exhibitor from 1778 to 1796. He is known to have collaborated with Francis Wheatley, who provided the figures in his landscapes.

Cilgerran Castle, Pembrokeshire, Wales
pen and grey ink, watercolour
inscribed centre verso: *Kilgarren / Castle, South Wales / by the Revnd.J Gardnor*
355 × 454 mm
Towlson, Hector J. (bequest, 1970) (D.1970.32)

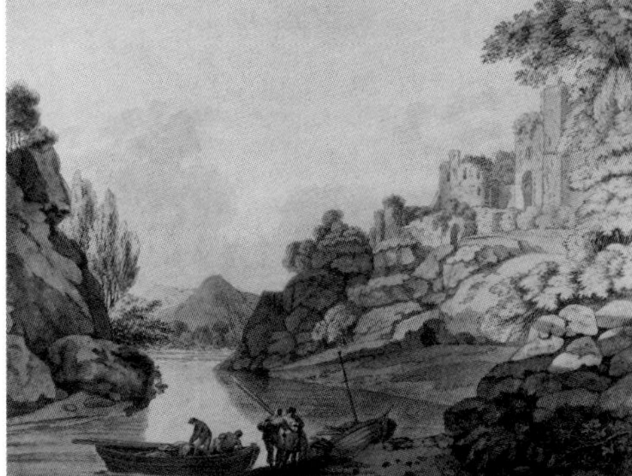

D.1970.32

■ GASTINEAU, HENRY (1791–1876)

Of French extraction, Gastineau exhibited at the Royal Academy between 1812 and 1830. He was elected a member of the Old Watercolour Society in 1823 and was a very prolific exhibitor there, showing more than 1,300 watercolours. Gastineau travelled extensively through Great Britain and Ireland, and also visited Switzerland and Italy. He had a large practice as a drawing master.

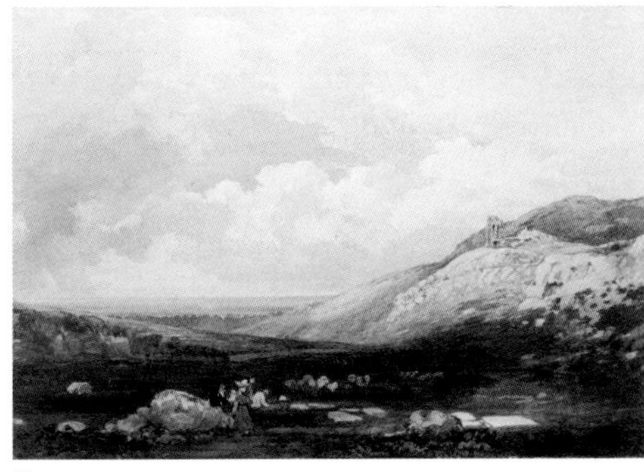

D.1933.37

A moorland Landscape
pencil, watercolour
333 × 464 mm
Anderson, A. E. (gift, 1933) (D.1933.37)

■ GASTINEAU, MARIA (ca. 1830–90)

Maria Gastineau, daughter of Henry, exhibited between 1855 and 1889, and was a member of the Society of Women Artists.

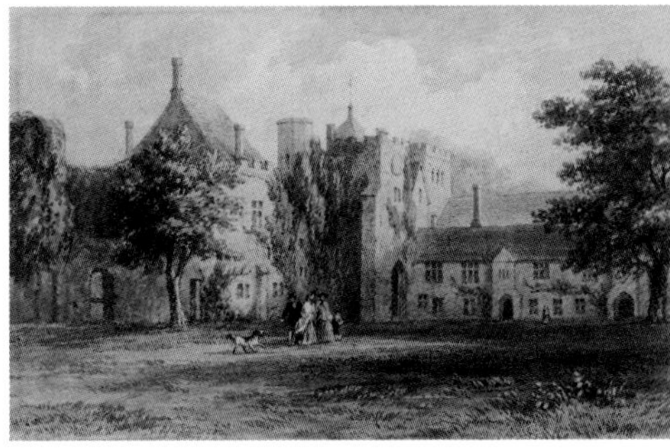

D.1919.2

Dartington Hall, near Totnes, Devon
pencil, watercolour, bodycolour
(heightened with white)
194 × 296 mm
Philips, Mrs Herbert (bequest, 1919) (D.1919.2)

■ GEDDES, ANDREW (1783–1844)

Geddes, born in Edinburgh, studied at the Royal Academy Schools from 1806 and in 1810 set himself up as a portrait painter in Edinburgh. He later settled in London and was elected an associate member of the Royal Academy in 1832.

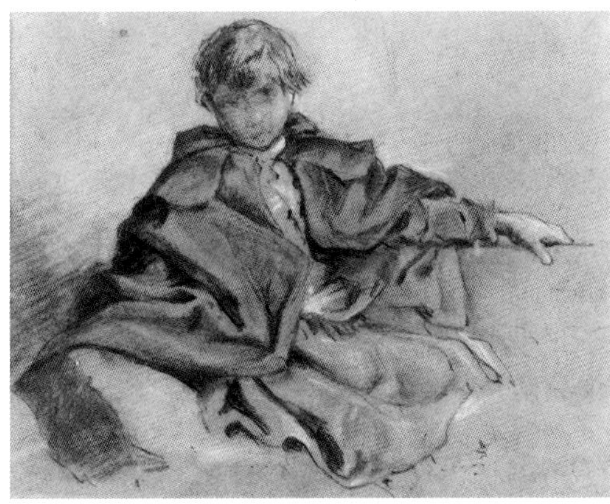

D.1948.20

Study of a Boy in a Cloak
black chalk, white chalk; brown paper
156 × 196 mm
Friends of the Whitworth (gift, 1948) (D.1948.20)

■ GELDART, JOSEPH (attributed to) (1808–82)

Joseph Geldart, friend, sketching companion and imitator of John Joseph Cotman, the son of John Sell, is frequently mistaken for more important Norwich School artists.

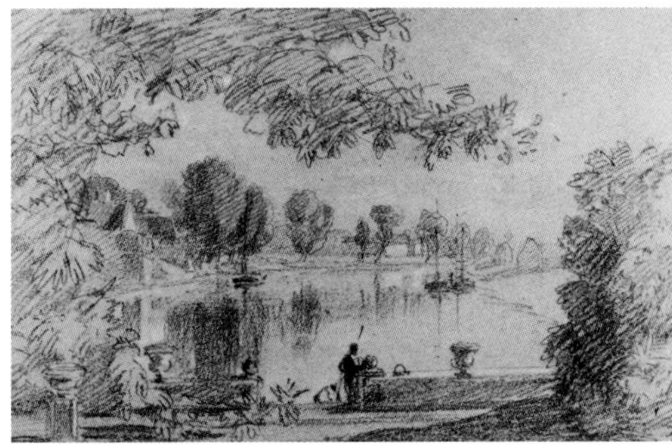

D.1933.13

The River Yare at Thorpe, near Norwich
black chalk, white chalk; grey paper
168 × 262 mm
Anderson, A. E. (gift, 1933) (D.1933.13)

■ GEORGE, SIR ERNEST (1839–1922)

George entered the Royal Academy Schools in 1858. He had an architectural practice from 1861 and was elected President of the Royal Institute of British Architects in 1908. He is responsible for the style known as Pont Street Dutch. He was elected a member of the Royal Academy in 1917. George's watercolours are mostly the results of summer holiday tours abroad.

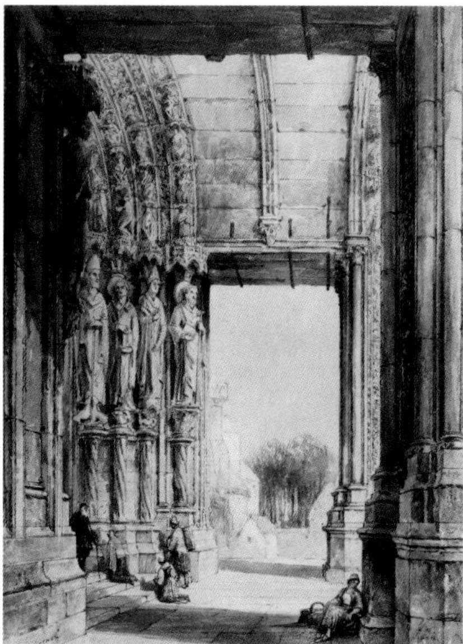

D.1927.39

The South Porch, Chartres Cathedral, France
1868
pencil, watercolour
signed & dated lower right with initials: *E.G. / 1868*
inscribed lower left: *CHARTRES*
343 × 248 mm
Anderson, A. E. (in memory of his brother Frank Anderson)
(gift, 1927) (D.1927.39)

■ **GETHIN, PERCY FRANCIS (1874–1916)**
Gethin was born in Ireland and studied at the Royal
College of Art, the Westminster School of Art and in
Paris. He taught life drawing at the Central School of
Arts and Crafts and exhibited at the New English Arts
Club. He was killed at the Battle of the Somme.

Two Portrait Studies
pencil, pen and brown ink, black chalk, red chalk,
brown watercolour
signed centre right margin with initials: *P.F.G.–*
366 × 266 mm
Anderson, A. E. (gift, 1917) (D.1917.8)

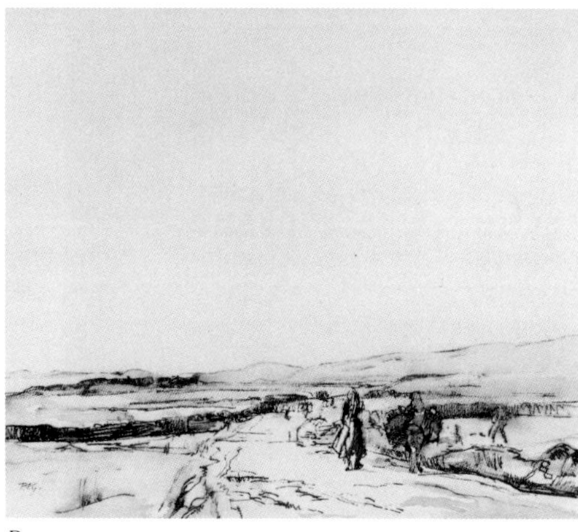

D.1917.9

Bog Road in Co. Mayo, Ireland
pen and black ink, grey watercolour; buff paper
signed lower left: *P.F.G.*
183 × 206 mm
Anderson, A. E. (gift, 1917) (D.1917.9)

■ **GIBSON, PATRICK (1782–1829)**
Gibson was born in Edinburgh and studied under
Alexander Nasmyth before moving on to the Trustees'
Academy, then under the direction of John Graham.
He settled briefly in London before returning to
Edinburgh to become a watercolour painter of some
success and also a writer on art. In 1817 he published
*Selected Views of Edinburgh with Historical and
Explanatory Notes* and in 1826 he was a founder
member of the Royal Scottish Academy. Gibson's style
has been described as 'pleasing if slightly frozen'.

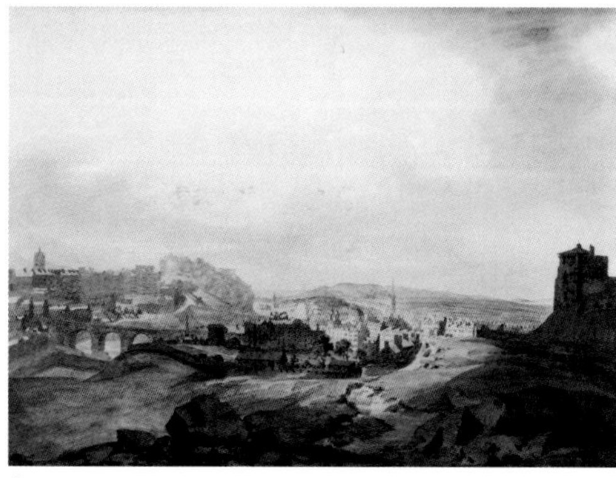

D.1927.12

**Edinburgh from Calton Hill, looking towards
the Castle**
ink (etched outline), watercolour
446 × 594 mm
Walker's Galleries, London (purchase, 1927) (D.1927.12)

■ **GILL, EDWYN W. (fl. 1812)**
Unknown amateur sporting artist.

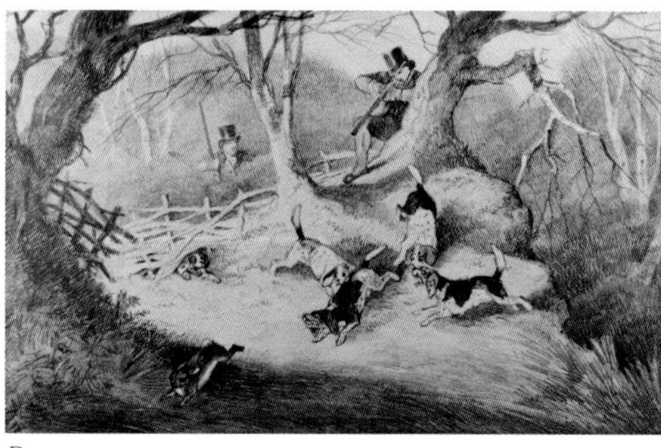

D.1970.33

Rabbit Shooting
pencil, watercolour
226 × 355 mm
Towlson, Hector J. (bequest, 1969) (D.1970.33)

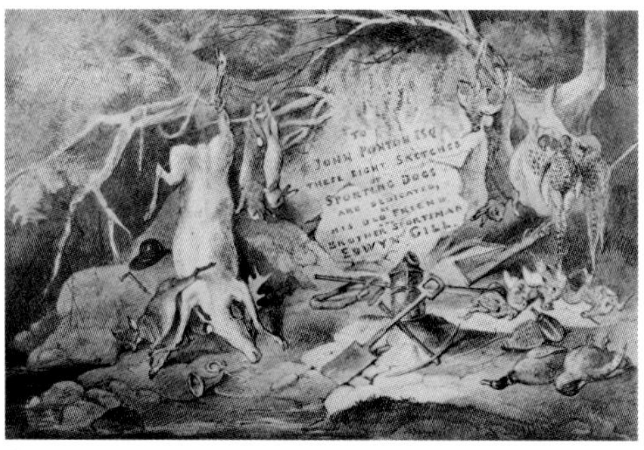

D.1970.34

Dead Game
pencil, watercolour
signed & inscribed centre right (dedication): *TO /
JOHN PONTON ESQ / THESE EIGHT SKETCHES /
OF / SPORTING DOGS / ARE DEDICATED, / BY /
HIS OLD FRIEND / AND / BROTHER SPORTSMAN
/ EDWYN GILL.*
222 × 327 mm
Towlson, Hector J. (bequest, 1969) (D.1970.34)

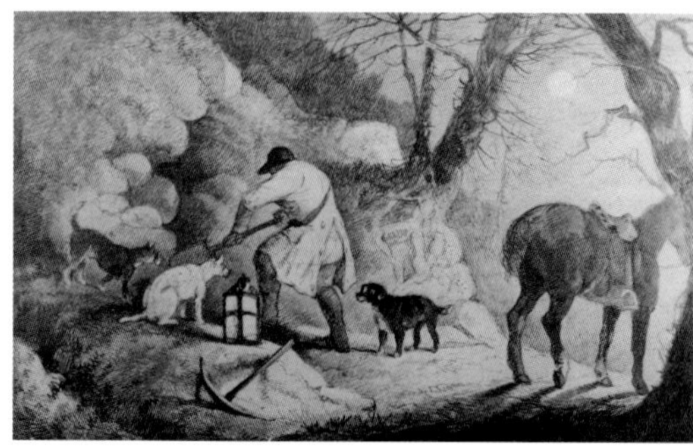

D.1970.35

Earth stopping
pencil, watercolour
225 × 354 mm
Towlson, Hector J. (bequest, 1969) (D.1970.35)

■ **GILPIN, SAWREY (1733–1807)**
The younger brother of the Rev. William, Sawrey
Gilpin trained under the marine painter Samuel Scott.
He turned to animal painting, after being employed by
the Duke of Cumberland at Windsor and Newmarket.
His drawings and paintings of animals, particularly
horses, are of a very high quality. He frequently
painted the horses in the landscapes of George
Barret Sen. Gilpin was elected a member of the
Royal Academy in 1797.

Study of a Cow
pencil
signed lower left: *S Gilpin*
139 × 201 mm
University of Manchester, History of Art Department
(transfer, 1960) (D.1960.83)

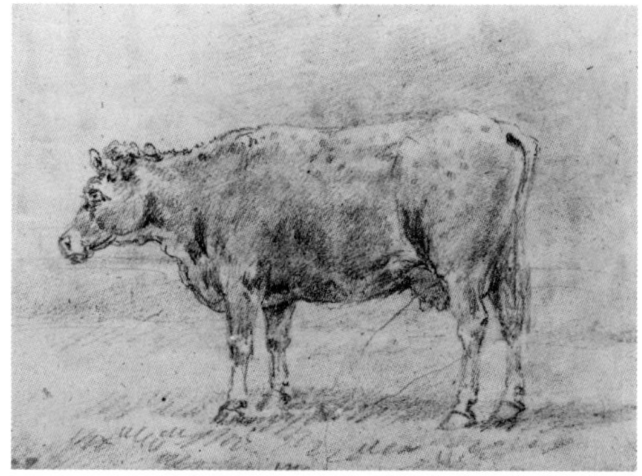

D.1960.84

Study of a Cow
pencil
152 × 203 mm
University of Manchester, History of Art Department
(transfer, 1960) (D.1960.84)

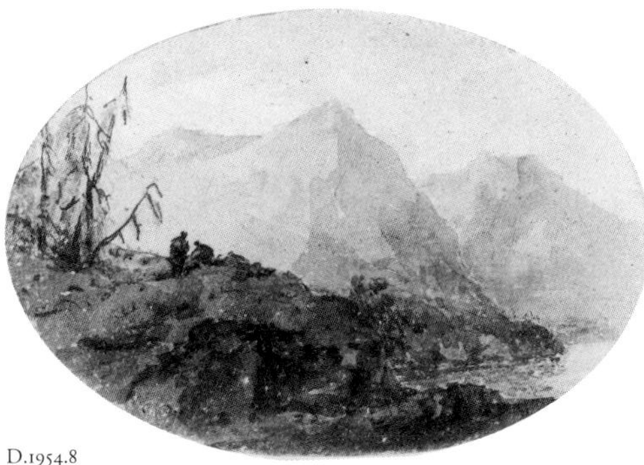

D.1954.8

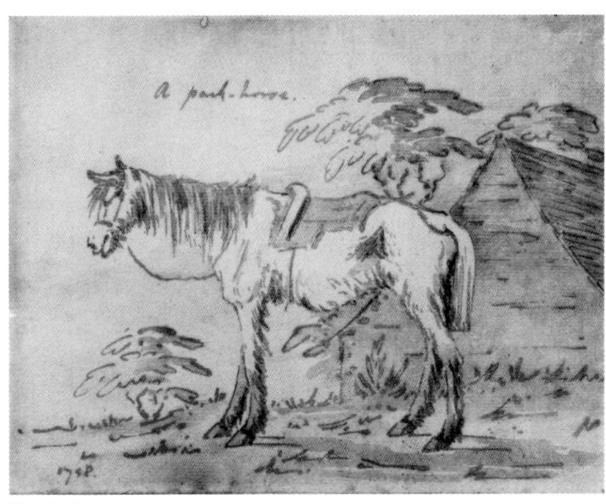

D.1960.85

A Pack-horse
1798
pen and brown ink, brown watercolour
dated lower left: *1798*; inscribed upper left: *A pack-horse*
166 × 205 mm
University of Manchester, History of Art Department
(transfer, 1960) (D.1960.85)

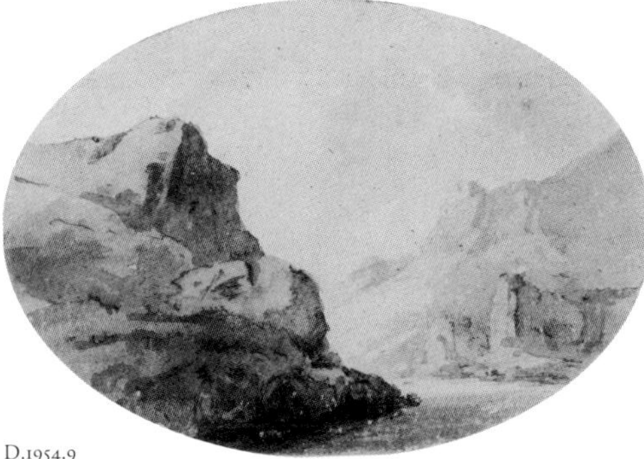

D.1954.9

A rocky Gorge
pencil, pen and brown ink, watercolour
164 × 236 mm
Sewter, Albert Charles (gift, 1954) (D.1954.9)

■ **GILPIN, WILLIAM SAWREY (1762–1843)**
The son of Sawrey Gilpin and the nephew of
William Gilpin, W. S. Gilpin was elected the first
President of the Old Watercolour Society in 1805.
He later taught at the Royal Military College at Great
Marlow and at Sandhurst; he then became a landscape
gardener, publishing *Practical Hints upon Landscape
Gardening. . .* in 1832.

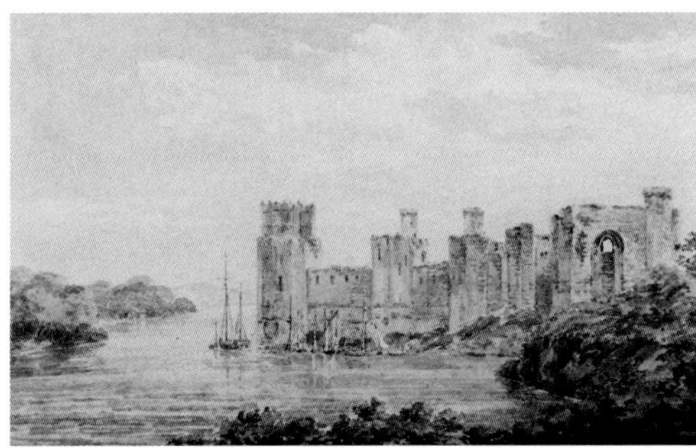

D.1893.13

**Caernarvon Castle, Caernarvonshire, Wales,
from the South**
pencil, watercolour
188 × 299 mm
Agnew's (purchase, 18.12.1893) (D.1893.13)

Cliffs near Folkestone, Kent
pencil, watercolour
259 × 378 mm
Friends of the Whitworth (gift, 1953) (D.1953.1)

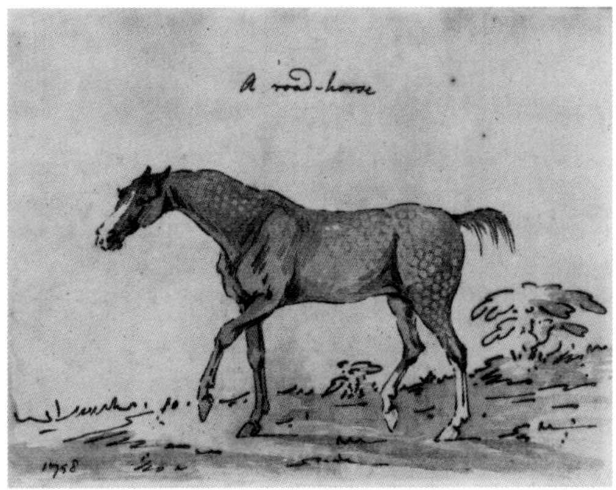

D.1960.86

A Road-horse
1798
pen and brown ink, brown watercolour
dated lower left: *1798*; inscribed upper centre:
A road-horse
166 × 208 mm
University of Manchester, History of Art Department
(transfer, 1960) (D.1960.86)

■ **GILPIN, REV. WILLIAM (1724–1804)**
Gilpin, known as the 'High Priest of the Picturesque',
was ordained in 1746 and then took over the running
of a school at Cheam in Surrey, where he remained for
the next 30 years. From 1780 he published a series of
books describing tours in various different parts of
Britain in search of the Picturesque, a term which he
invented. Each of these books was illustrated with
aquatints after his own drawings. These supposedly real
views were embellished to conform with the writer's
theories and exercised a huge influence on a whole
generation of tourists and amateur sketchers.

Mountain Landscape with Pines
pencil, pen and brown ink, watercolour
166 × 235 mm
Sewter, Albert Charles (gift, 1954) (D.1954.8)

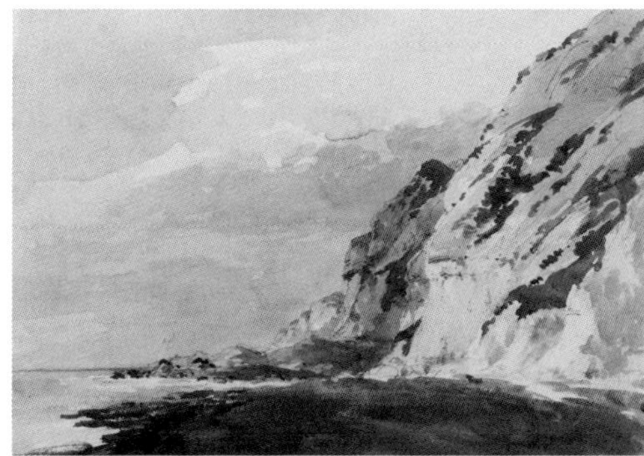

D.1953.1

■ **GIRTIN, THOMAS (1775–1802)**
Girtin was apprenticed to Edward Dayes and was well
grounded in the eighteenth-century topographical
tradition. From 1794–97 he worked alongside Turner,
his exact contemporary, at the Monro Academy. He
toured the north of England in 1796 and 1798, making
sketches. In 1801, he painted and exhibited a huge
panorama of London. He was planning to execute a
similar panorama of Paris but died before this could be
achieved. Girtin remains the archetypal case of the
artistic genius cut short in youth.

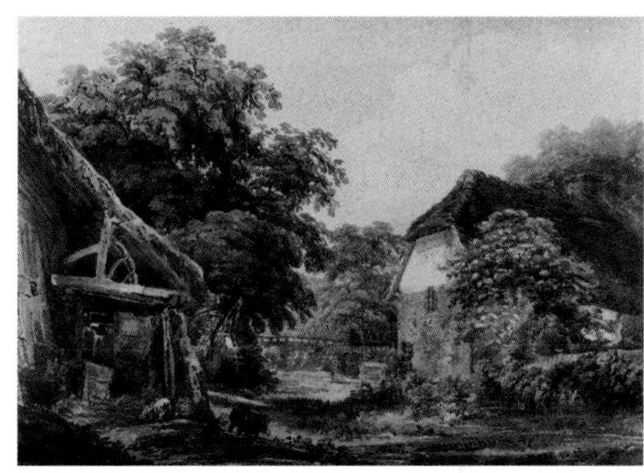

D.1887.3

Surrey Farm Buildings
pencil, watercolour
333 × 460 mm
Agnew's (purchase, 22.6.1891) (D.1887.3)

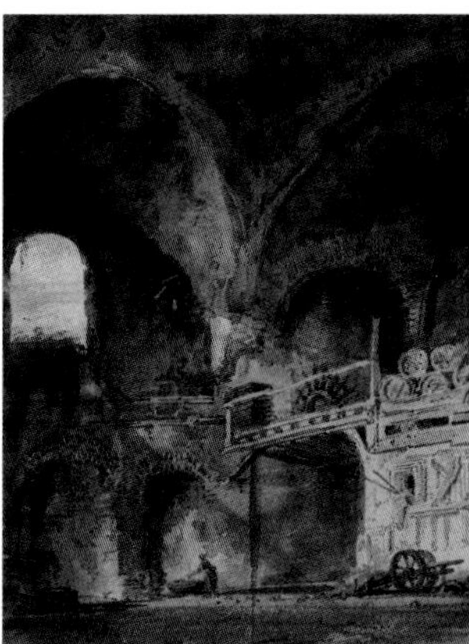

D.1892.73

The Roman Baths, Hotel de Cluny, Paris
1801–02
watercolour
315 × 241 mm
Taylor, John Edward (gift, 1892) (D.1892.73)

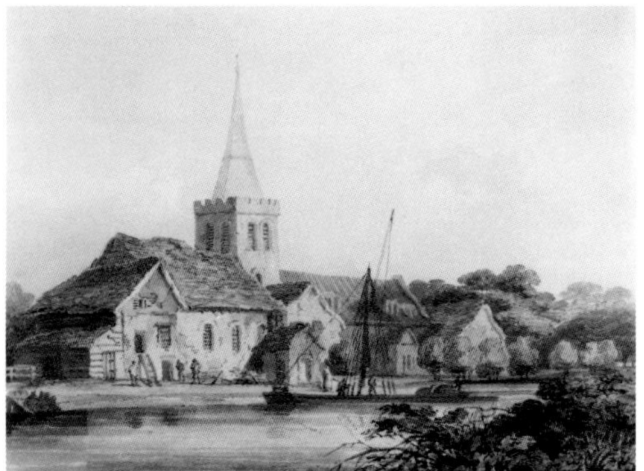

D.1892.74

**All Saints Church, Great Marlow,
Buckinghamshire**
1795–96
pencil, watercolour
signed lower centre: *T Girtin*
208 × 276 mm
Taylor, John Edward (gift, 1892) (D.1892.74)

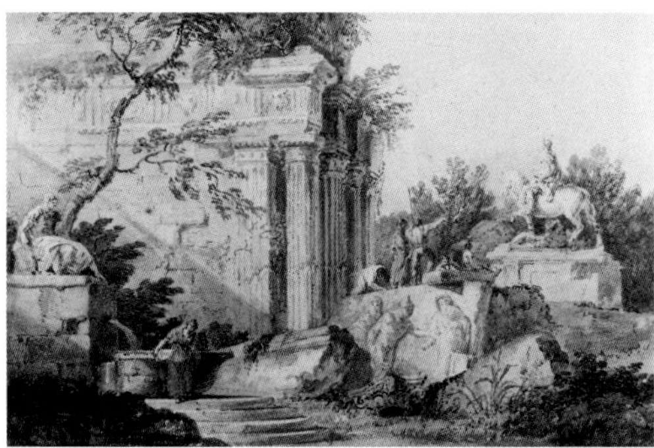

D.1892.76

Classical Composition, after Marco Ricci
1798–99
pencil, watercolour
319 × 470 mm
Taylor, John Edward (gift, 1892) (D.1892.76)

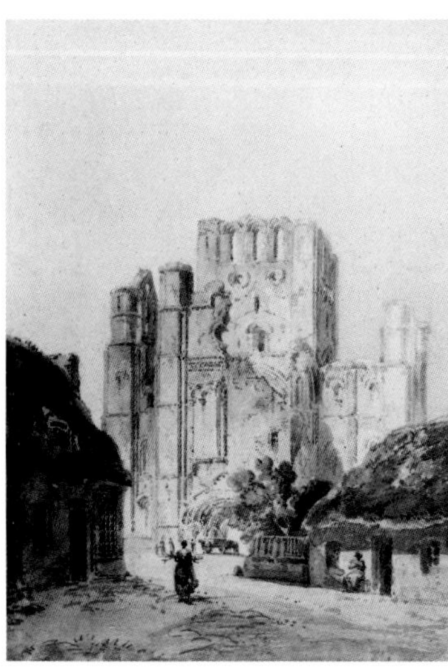

D.1892.77

Kelso Abbey, Roxburghshire, Scotland
1796–97
pencil, watercolour
398 × 278 mm
Taylor, John Edward (gift, 1892) (D.1892.77)

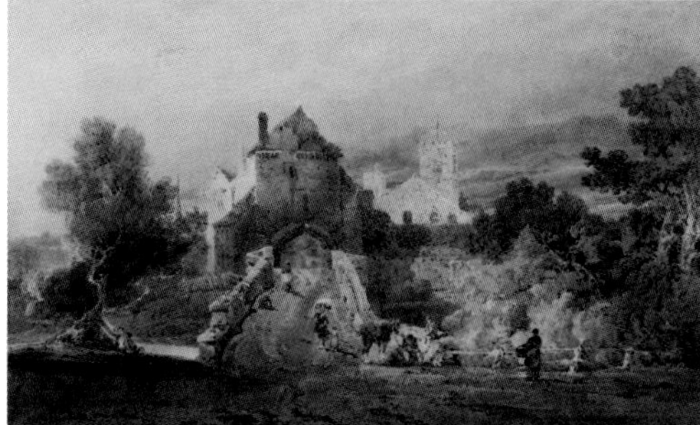

D.1892.107

The Layerthorpe Bridge and Postern, York
1802
pencil, watercolour
323 × 518 mm
Taylor, John Edward (gift, 1892) (D.1892.107)

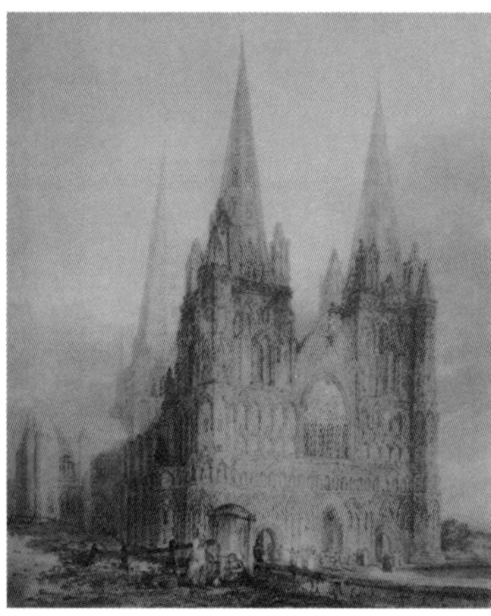

D.1892.108

West Front of Lichfield Cathedral, Staffordshire
1795
watercolour
466 × 380 mm
Taylor, John Edward (gift, 1892) (D.1892.108)

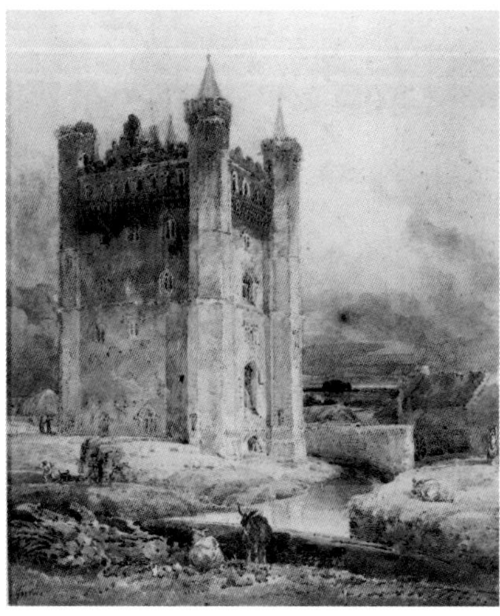

D.1892.109

Tattershall Castle, Lincolnshire
1798
pencil, watercolour
signed lower left: *Girtin*
322 × 265 mm
Taylor, John Edward (gift, 1892) (D.1892.109)

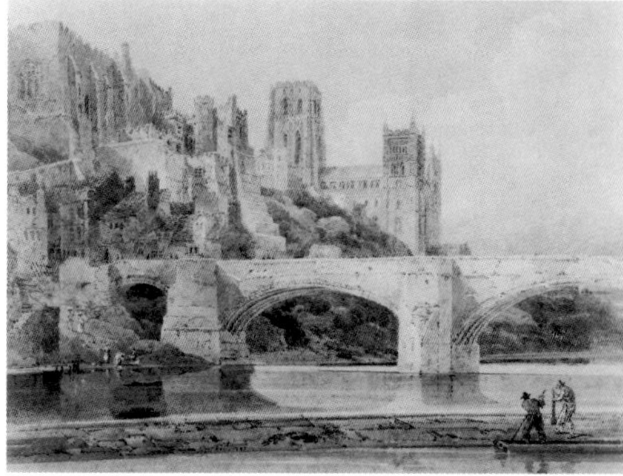

D.1892.110

**Durham Cathedral and Bridge, from the
River Wear**
1799
pencil, watercolour
signed and dated lower left: *Girtin. 1799*
416 × 537 mm
Taylor, John Edward (gift, 1892) (D.1892.110)

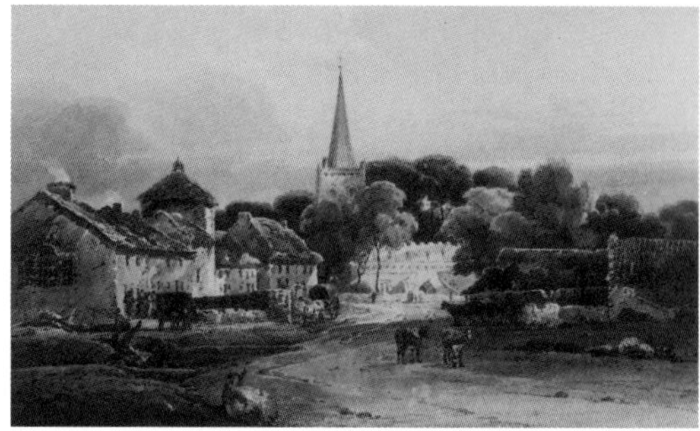

D.1892.111

Kirk Deighton Church, Yorkshire
1800
pencil, watercolour
signed & dated lower left: *Girtin 1800*
321 × 522 mm
Taylor, John Edward (gift, 1892) (D.1892.111)

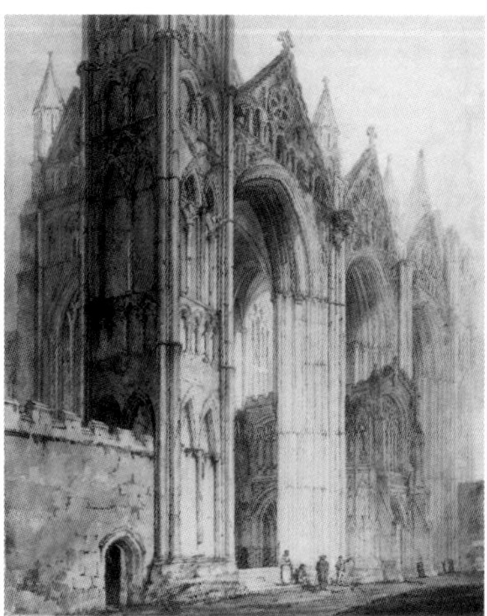

D.1892.112

**West Front of Peterborough Cathedral,
Northamptonshire**
1796–97
pencil, watercolour
446 × 352 mm
Taylor, John Edward (gift, 1892) (D.1892.112)

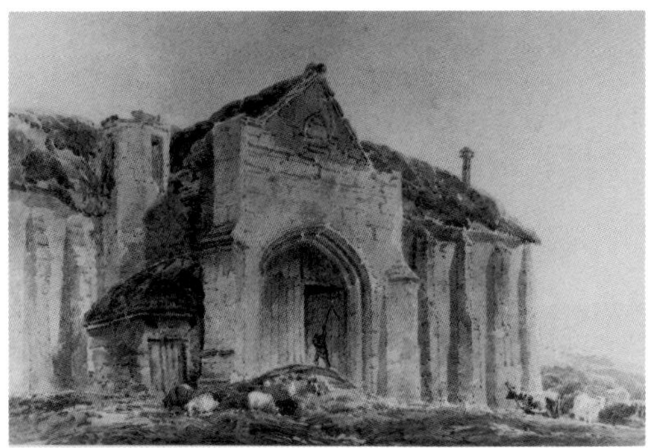

D.1921.11

The Abbot's Tythe Barn, Abbotsbury, Dorset
1798
pencil, watercolour
310 × 462 mm
Anderson, A. E. (gift, 1921) (D.1921.11)

The Chancel, Netley Abbey, Hampshire
1797
pencil, watercolour
198 × 270 mm
Broadhurst, Sir Edward Tootal, Broadhurst, Lady
(bequest, 1924) (D.1924.75)

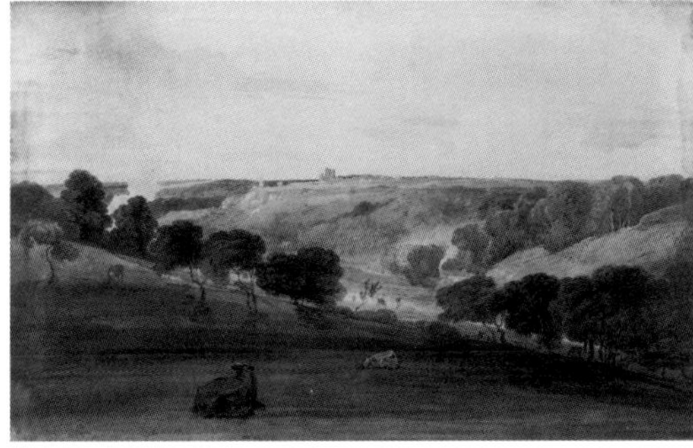

D.1928.7

**A distant View of Knaresborough, Yorkshire,
from the South East**
1801
pencil, watercolour
signed & dated lower left: *Girtin 1801*
660 × 990 mm
Independent Gallery, London (purchase, 1928) (D.1928.7)

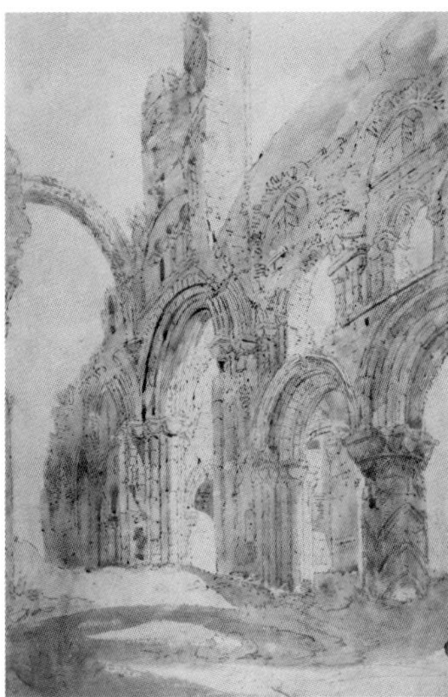

D.1937.36

**Interior of the Priory Church, Holy Island,
Northumberland**
pencil, pen and brown ink, grey watercolour,
brown watercolour
inscribed lower centre: *Holy Island*; inscribed lower
centre verso: *Holy Island*
382 × 250 mm
Pilkington, Margaret (gift, 1937) (D. 1937.36)

Sketchbook
pencil, pen and ink, watercolour
146 × 217 mm
Baskett and Day (purchase, 1977) (V. & A., N.A.C.F.,
F.O.W., P.T.) (D.1977.15)

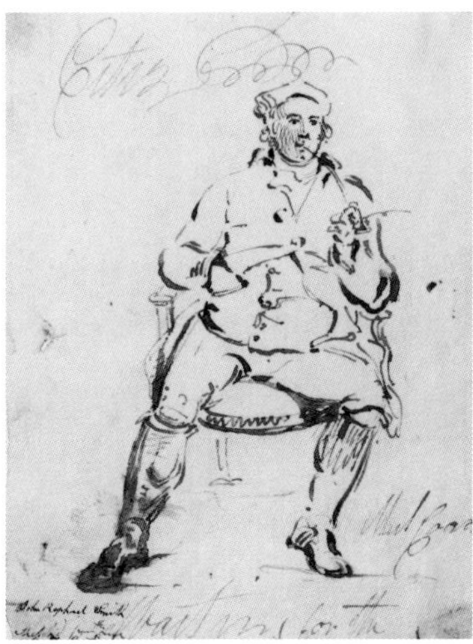

D.1977.15.1

Portrait of John Raphael Smith
pencil, pen and brown ink
inscribed lower left: *John Raphael Smith / Sketch'd from
the Life / by T.Girtin*; inscribed lower edge: *Waiting for
the / Mail Coach*
187 × 140 mm
Baskett and Day (purchase, 1977) (D.1977.15.1)

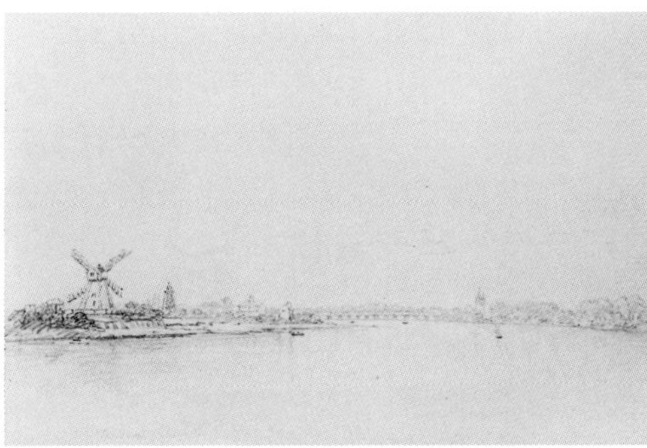

D.1977.15.11

View of Battersea Reach, London
pencil
inscribed lower left: *Battersea Reach*; watermark:
WELGAR / 1801
146 × 217 mm
Baskett and Day (purchase, 1977) (D.1977.15.11)

**Mountain Scenery at Beddgellert,
Caernarvonshire, North Wales**
pencil
inscribed lower right verso: *Bedgellert*
146 × 217 mm
Baskett and Day (purchase, 1977) (D.1977.15.14)

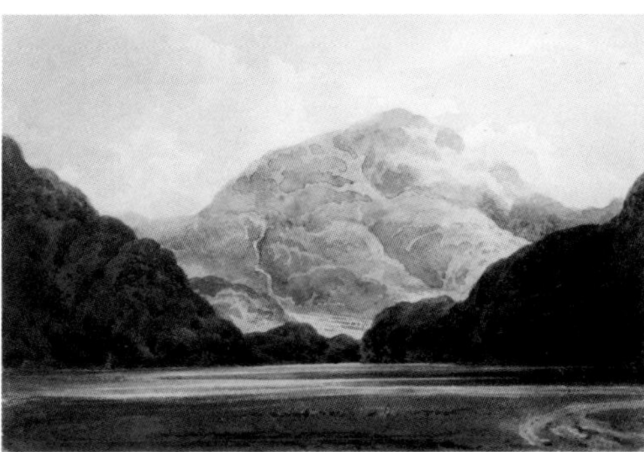

D.1977.15.15

Beddgellert, Caernarvonshire, North Wales
watercolour
inscribed lower left verso: *Bedgellert*
146 × 217 mm
Baskett and Day (purchase, 1977) (D.1977.15.15)

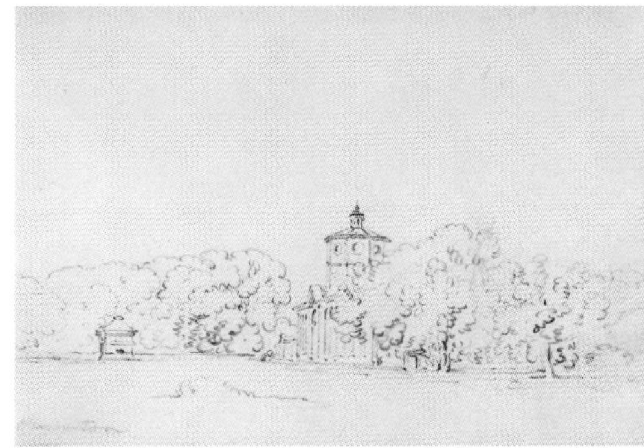

D.1977.15.17

**The Hall Stables, Plompton Park,
North Yorkshire**
pencil
inscribed lower left: *Plumton*; inscribed up right hand
edge of verso referring to a sketch no longer in the
book: *Sketch of Harewood House in Pencil sold to Mr
Hargreaves / #1.1.0*
146 × 217 mm
Baskett and Day (purchase, 1977) (D.1977.15.17)

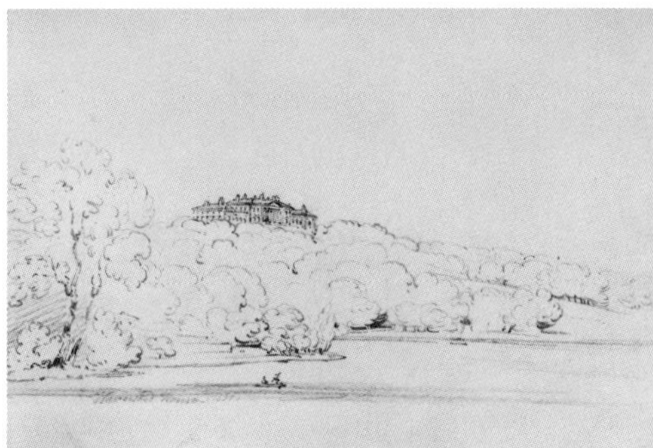

D.1977.15.18

**Harewood House, Yorkshire, from the
South West**
1800
pencil
inscribed & dated lower left: *Harewood House.1800.*
146 × 217 mm
Baskett and Day (purchase, 1977) (D.1977.15.18)

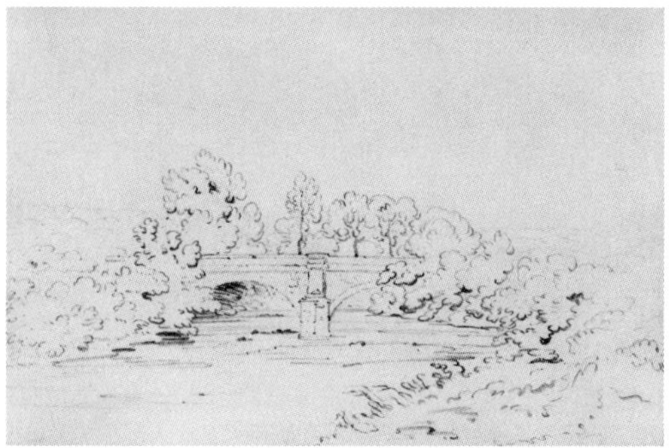

D.1977.15.20

**Grimbald Bridge, near Knaresborough,
North Yorkshire**
pencil
146 × 217 mm
Baskett and Day (purchase, 1977) (D.1977.15.20)

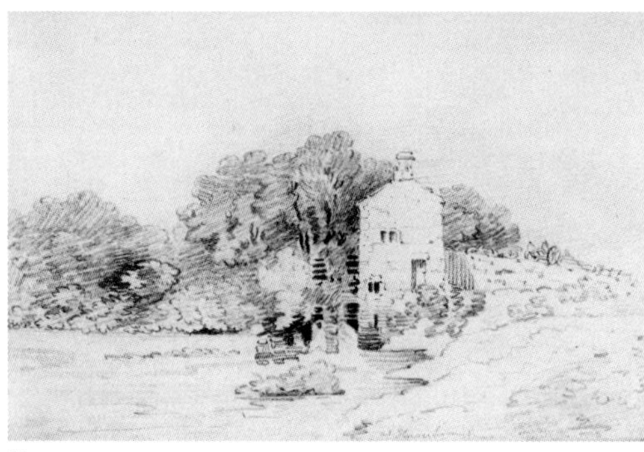

D.1977.15.24

**The Abbey Mill, Knaresborough,
North Yorkshire**
pencil
inscribed lower right: *at Knaresborough*; inscribed upper
left verso: *at Knaresborough*; watermark: *179* [cut]
146 × 217 mm
Baskett and Day (purchase, 1977) (D.1977.15.24)

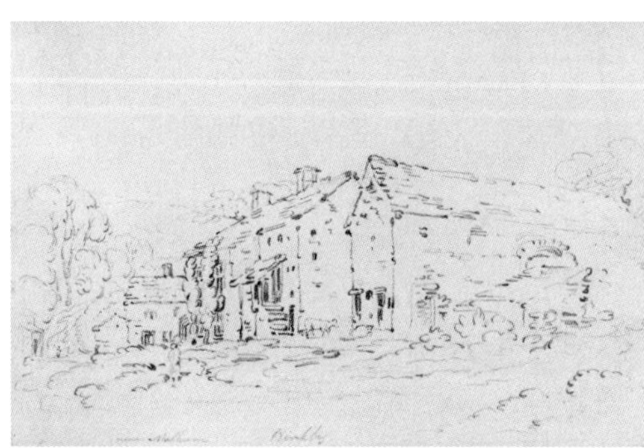

D.1977.15.25

Kirkby Priory, near Malham, North Yorkshire
pencil
inscribed lower edge: *near Malham Kirkby*; inscribed
right hand edge on verso referring to a drawing no
longer in the book: *Kirby Church*
146 × 217 mm
Baskett and Day (purchase, 1977) (D.1977.15.25)

View of Sandsend, near Whitby, North Yorkshire
pencil
146 × 217 mm
Baskett and Day (purchase, 1977) (D.1977.15.28)

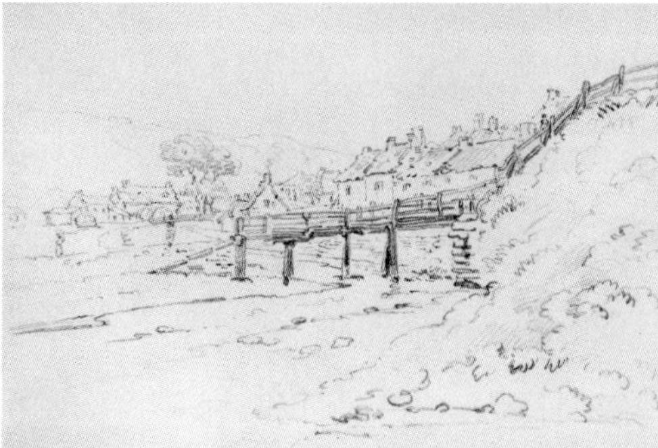

D.1977.15.28

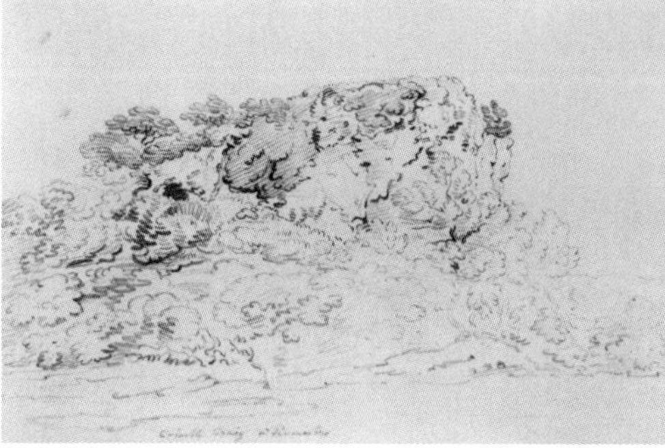

D.1977.15.29

**Grimbald Crag, near Knaresborough,
North Yorkshire**
pencil
inscribed lower left: *Grimble Crag nr Knaresbro*
146 × 217 mm
Baskett and Day (purchase, 1977) (D.1977.15.29)

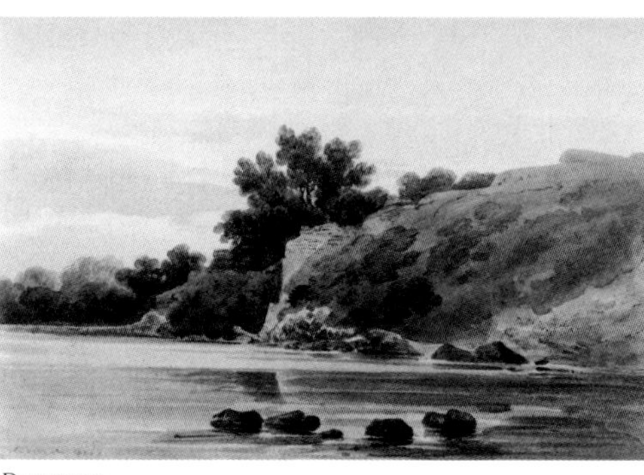

D.1977.15.30

**Grimbald Crag, with the River Nid in
the Foreground**
pencil, watercolour
inscribed lower left: *River Nid*
146 × 217 mm
Baskett and Day (purchase, 1977) (D.1977.15.30)

Guisborough Priory, North Yorkshire
pencil
inscribed lower left: *Gisbro*
217 × 146 mm
Baskett and Day (purchase, 1977) (D.1977.15.32)

**View of Bolton Abbey on the River Wharfe,
North Yorkshire**
pencil
inscribed lower left: *Bolton*
146 × 217 mm
Baskett and Day (purchase, 1977) (D.1977.15.36)

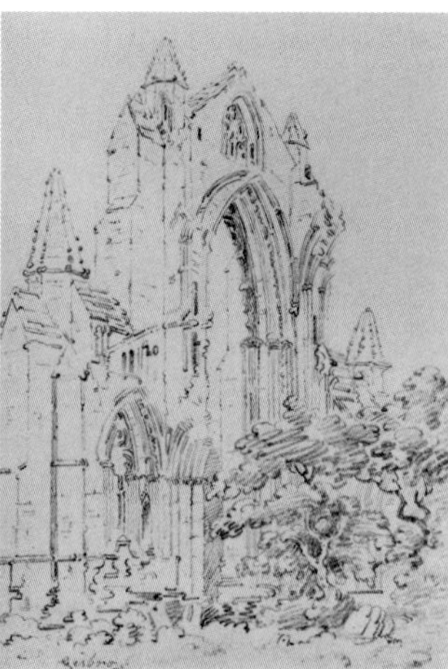

D.1977.15.32

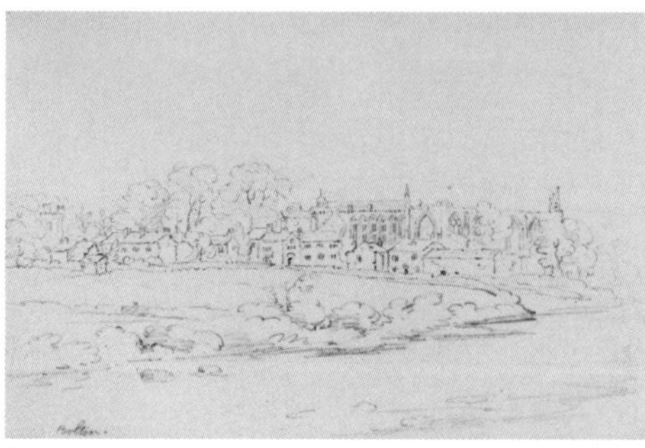

D.1977.15.36

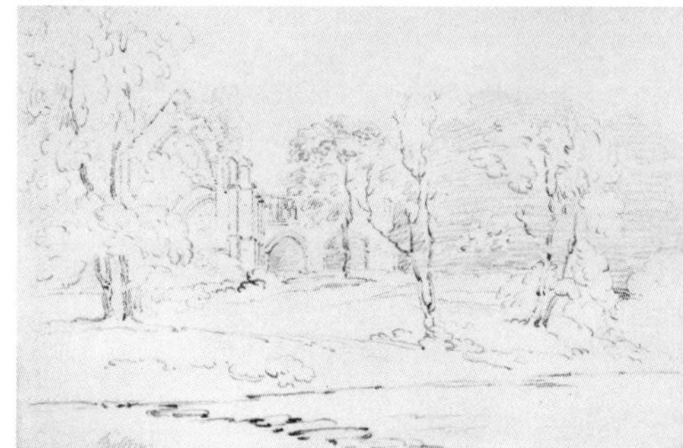

D.1977.15.37

**View of the East End of Bolton Abbey,
North Yorkshire**
pencil
inscribed lower left: *Bolton*
146 × 217 mm
Baskett and Day (purchase, 1977) (D.1977.15.37)

**View of the East End of Bolton Abbey,
North Yorkshire**
pencil
inscribed lower left of right hand sheet: *Bolton*;
inscribed right hand edge verso referring to a drawing
no longer in the book: *Sketch / Rippon* (sic) *Minster
Cold. on the Spot / sold to* [blank] *8.8 o*
146 × 434 mm
Baskett and Day (purchase, 1977) (D.1977.15.38)

**Distant View of Middleham Castle, North
Yorkshire, with the River Nid in the Foreground**
pencil
inscribed lower left: *Middleham Castle*
146 × 217 mm
Baskett and Day (purchase, 1977) (D.1977.15.40)

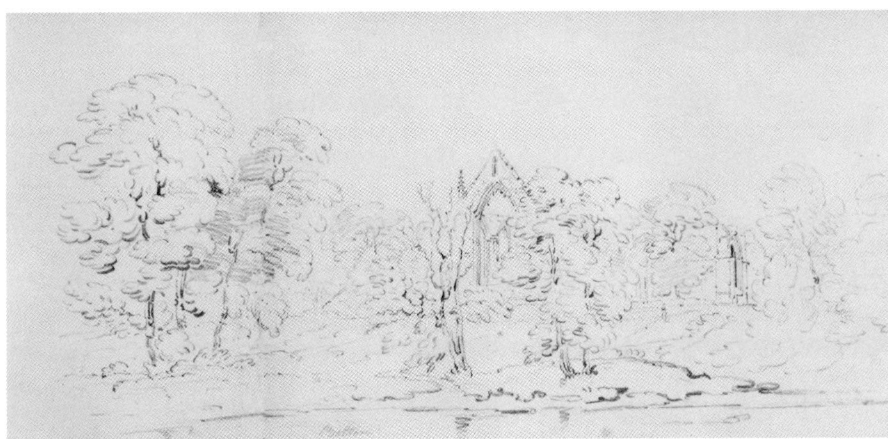

D.1977.15.38

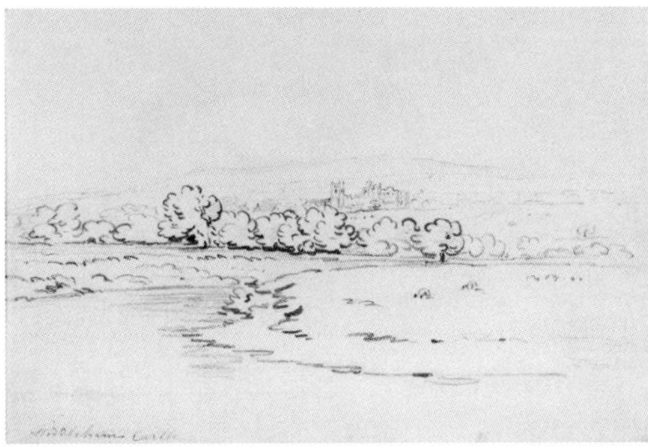

D.1977.15.40

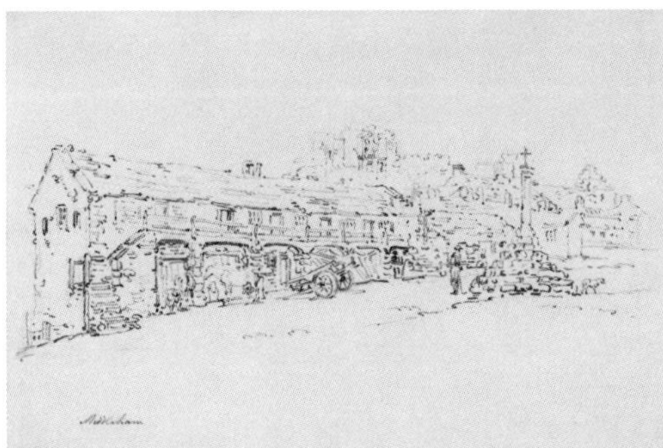

D.1977.15.41

View of Middleham, North Yorkshire, with the Castle in the Background
pencil
inscribed lower left: *Middleham*; watermark:
E & P / 1801
146 × 217 mm
Baskett and Day (purchase, 1977) (D.1977.15.41)

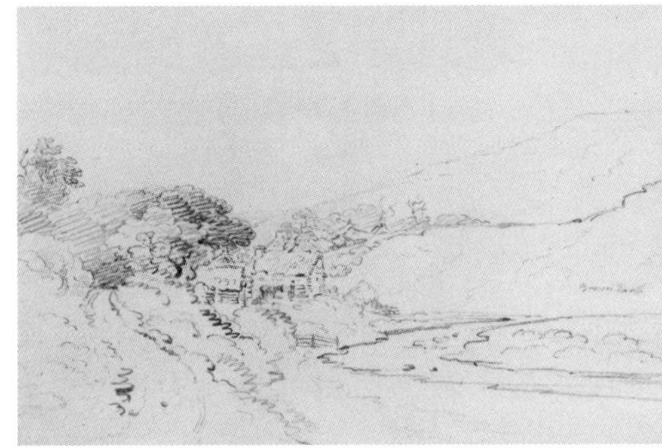

D.1977.15.43

View of a Village
pencil
inscribed centre right colour note: *Brown earth*
146 × 217 mm
Baskett and Day (purchase, 1977) (D.1977.15.43)

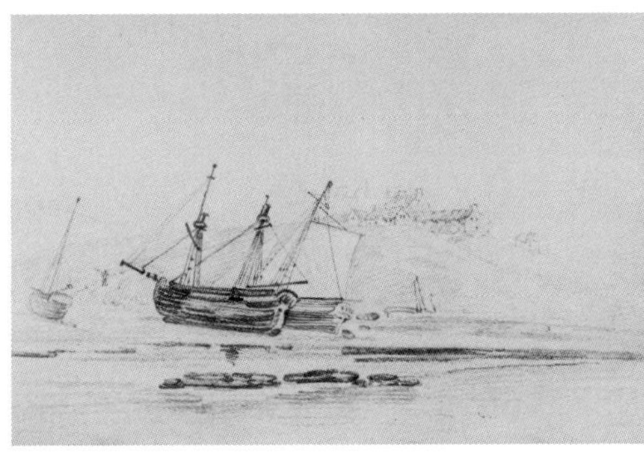

D.1977.15.45

Fishing Boats
pencil
146 × 217 mm
Baskett and Day (purchase, 1977) (D.1977.15.45)

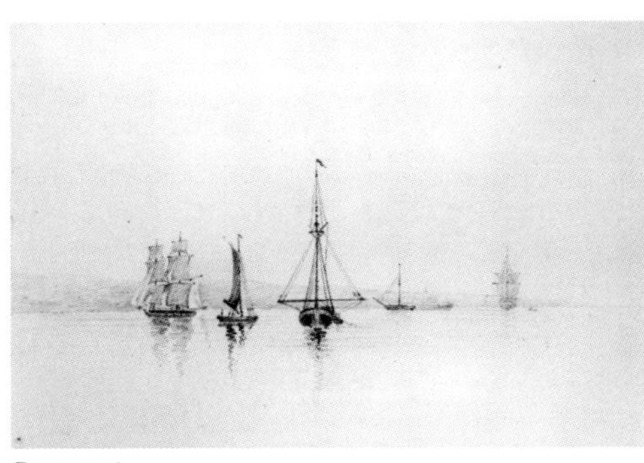

D.1977.15.46

Shipping off the Coast in a calm Sea
pencil
146 × 217 mm
Baskett and Day (purchase, 1977) (D.1977.15.46)

Shipping off the Coast in a calm Sea at Mount Edgcumbe, Cornwall
pencil, watercolour
inscribed upper right verso: *Mount Edgcumbe*
146 × 217 mm
Baskett and Day (purchase, 1977) (D.1977.15.47)

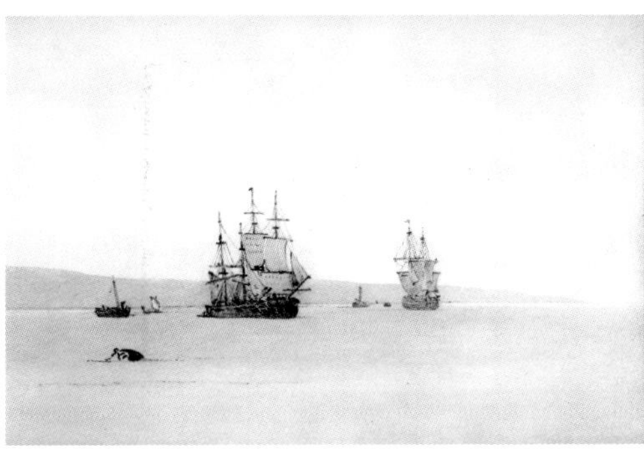

D.1977.15.47

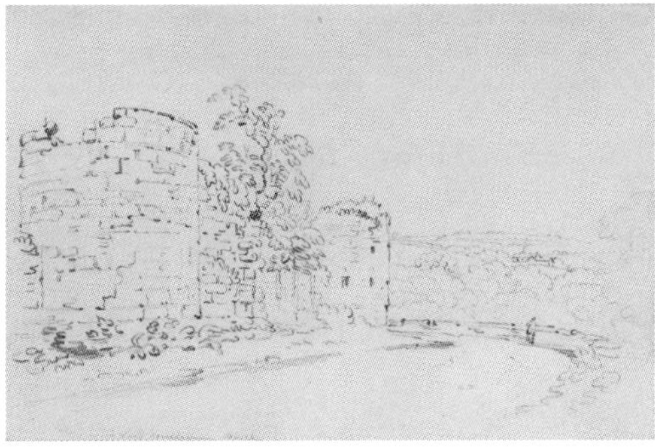

D.1977.15.48

Ruins of Old Mulgrave Castle, North Yorkshire
pencil
inscribed lower left: *Ruins in Lord Mulgrave's Park*
146 × 217 mm
Baskett and Day (purchase, 1977) (D.1977.15.48)

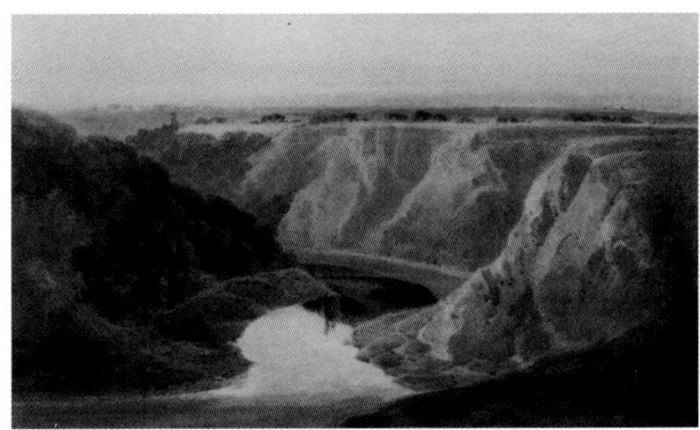

D.1997.4

St Vincent's Rocks, Clifton
1802
watercolour
321 × 528 mm
H. M. Treasury (Acceptance in Lieu Scheme) (gift, 1997)
(D.1997.4)

■ GIRTIN, THOMAS (attributed to)

Study of a Donkey
pencil, grey watercolour
83 × 124 mm
Girtin, Tom (bequest, 1995) (D.1995.9)

Sketch of a Bridge
pencil
inscribed lower left verso in later hand: *Roughing out
for picture / ? Unidentified "The Bridge" Coll Pilkington*;
inscribed lower left verso in different hand: *no*
325 × 323 mm
Girtin, Tom (bequest, 1995) (D.1995.10)

■ GLOVER, JOHN (1767–1849)

Glover was born in Leicestershire and began his career as a provincial drawing master and started to exhibit at the Royal Academy in 1795. He was a founder member of the Old Watercolour Society in 1804 and exhibited there until 1817. He failed to become a member of the Royal Academy but became a founder member of the Society of British Artists in 1824. Glover had an extensive teaching practice, passing on his 'split-brush' technique to his pupils, and emigrated to Tasmania in 1831.

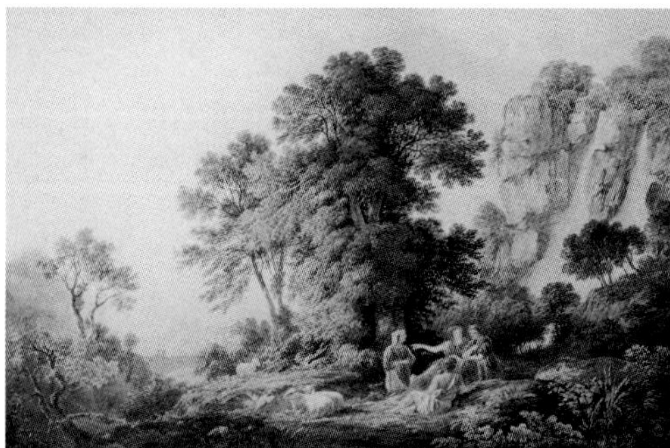

D.1892.49

Arcadian Landscape with Waterfall
pencil, watercolour
406 × 595 mm
Taylor, John Edward (gift, 1892) (D.1892.49)

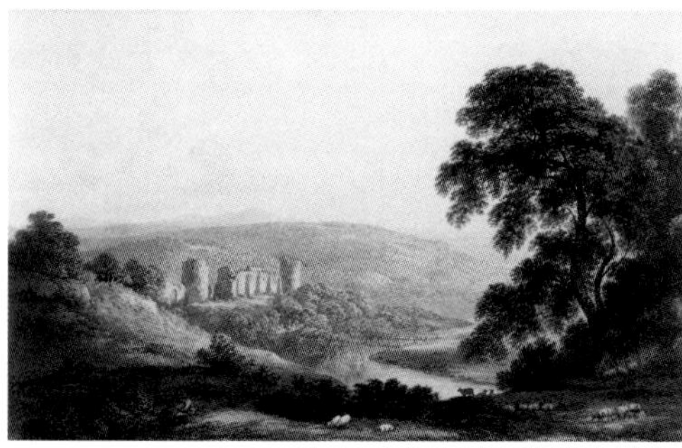

D.1894.9

Castle above the River Tweed
watercolour
inscribed on backing in centre in later hand:
J. Glover, 1801
270 × 416 mm
Lees, Charles E. (gift, 1894) (D.1894.9)

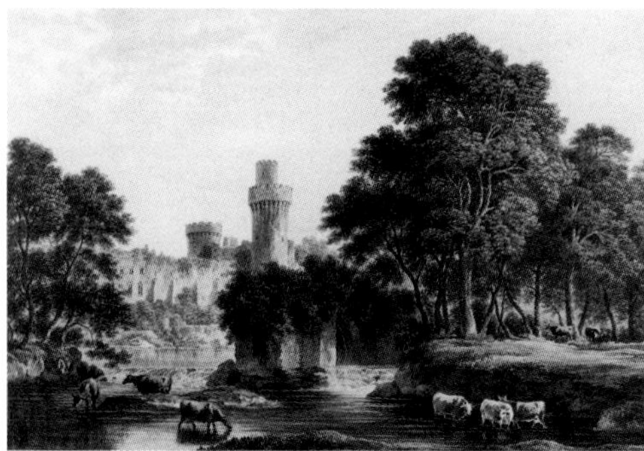

D.1970.36

Warwick Castle from the River Avon
watercolour
328 × 472 mm
Towlson, Hector J. (bequest, 1969) (D.1970.36)

■ GOLDIE, CHARLES (fl. 1858–79)

A little-known artist.

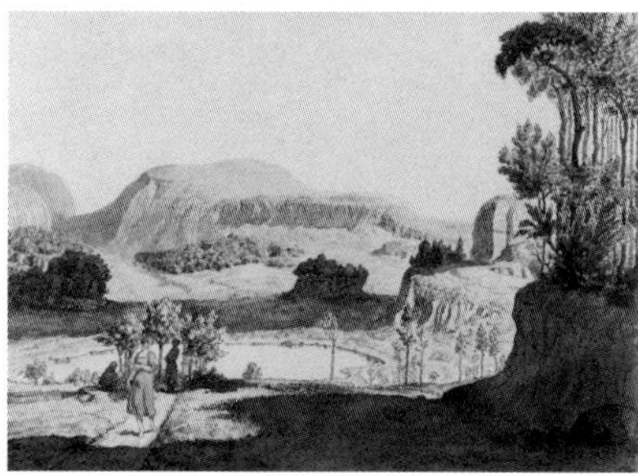

D.1930.49

The Pool
pencil, pen and brown ink, watercolour
signed lower right with initials: *CG*
212 × 291 mm
Anderson, A. E. (gift, 1930) (D.1930.49)

■ GOODALL, W. (fl. early 19th century)

Unknown amateur artist.

Flower Study, Fritillaria Pyrenaica
pen and brown ink, watercolour
signed & inscribed lower centre: *Fritillaria, Pyrenaica. / Fritillaria, nigra, Salisb / foliis sparsis complanatis subcoriaceis glaucis, infimis latioribus; corolla / coriaceo incrassata campanulata superne recurvato patula. /*; inscribed upper centre: *Flexandria, / Monogynia*; inscribed upper right: *Gen 5 5*; inscribed lower right: *Bot.M 664*; inscribed lower left: *Pyrennees*
324 × 198 mm
Ward, Roy (gift, 1986) (D.1986.4)

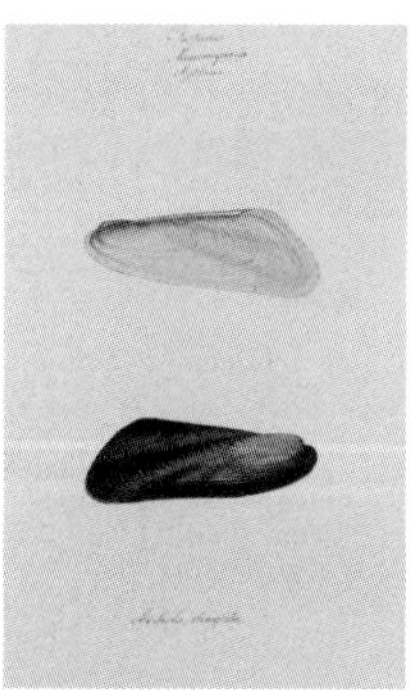

D.1986.5

Two Shells
pen and brown ink, watercolour
watermark KENT/1821
signed lower centre: *W Goodall*; inscribed upper centre: *Testacea / Monomyaria / Mytilacea*; inscribed lower centre: *Modiola, elongata*; inscribed lower right: *Swainson*
318 × 194 mm
Ward, Roy (gift, 1986) (D.1986.5)

White-eyed Cowry
pen and brown ink, watercolour
signed & inscribed lower centre: *Cypraea, Exantherna, var Gray. / Cypraea, Leucopis, Shaw. / subferruginea, ocellis albis pupilla fusea / White–eyed Cowry / W Goodall*; inscribed lower left: *West Indies*; inscribed lower right: *Shaw*
152 × 195 mm
Ward, Roy (gift, 1986) (D.1986.6)

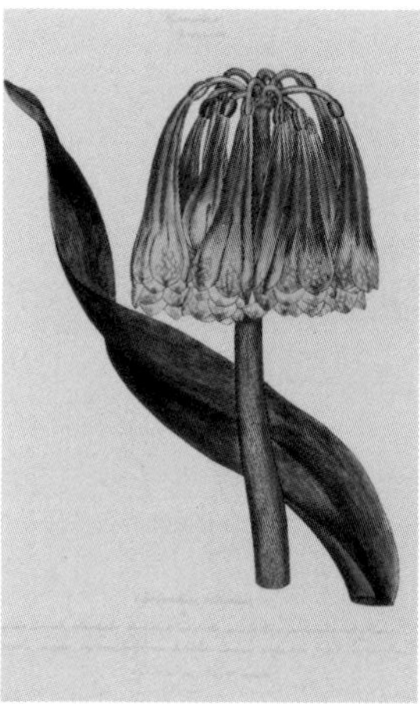

D.1986.7

Flower Study, Cyrtanthus Obliquus
pen and brown ink, watercolour; watermark 1802
signed & inscribed lower centre: *Cyrtanthus, obliquus, / foliis loratis, obliquatis distichis; umbellae multiflorae pedicellis retroflexis; / corolla cernua, infundibuliformi tubulosa; laciniis rectis, tubo triplo brevioribus. / Cyrtanthus, oblique-leaved. W. Goodall*; inscribed upper centre: *Flexandria / Monogynia* inscribed lower left: *C.S.H.*; inscribed lower right: *Bot.M:1133*
316 × 193 mm
Ward, Roy (gift, 1986) (D.1986.7)

■ GOODWIN, ALBERT (1845–1932)

Albert Goodwin was a pupil of Arthur Hughes and Ford Madox Brown. In 1872, he accompanied John Ruskin to Italy, who encouraged him to study the work of Turner. Goodwin later became a tireless traveller, visiting Europe, America, India and the Caribbean. He was elected a member of the Royal Watercolour Society in 1881 and exhibited at the Royal Academy from 1860.

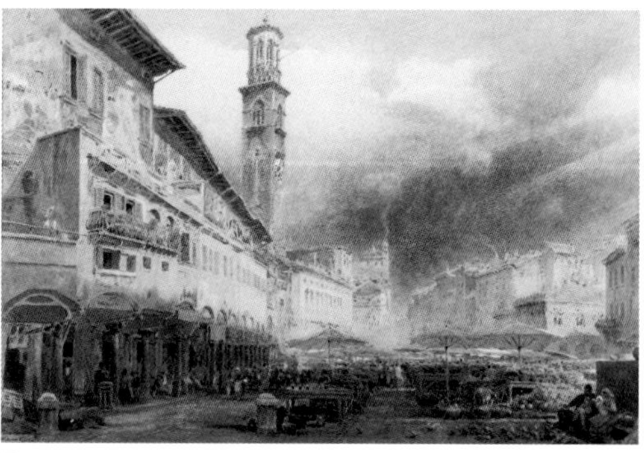

D.1905.9

Piazza Erbe, Verona, Italy
1873
watercolour
signed & dated lower left: *Albert Goodwin./73*
481 × 711 mm
Salomons, Edward (purchase, 1905) (D.1905.9)

Lichfield Cathedral, Staffordshire, by Moonlight
watercolour, bodycolour; grey paper
signed lower right: *Albert Goodwin*; inscribed lower left: *Litchfield*
212 × 282 mm
Milne, J. D. (gift, 1907) (D.1907.1)

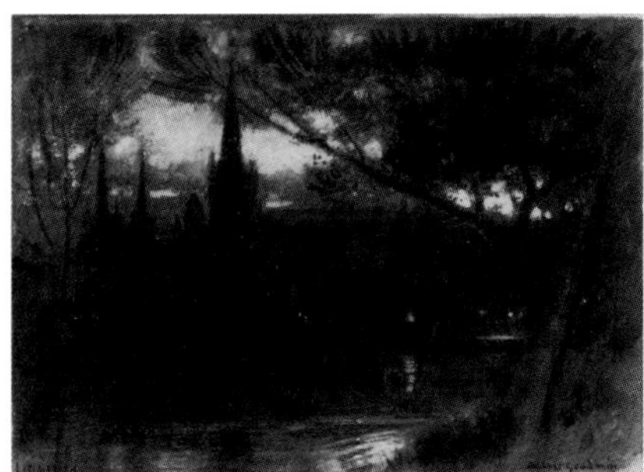

D.1907.1

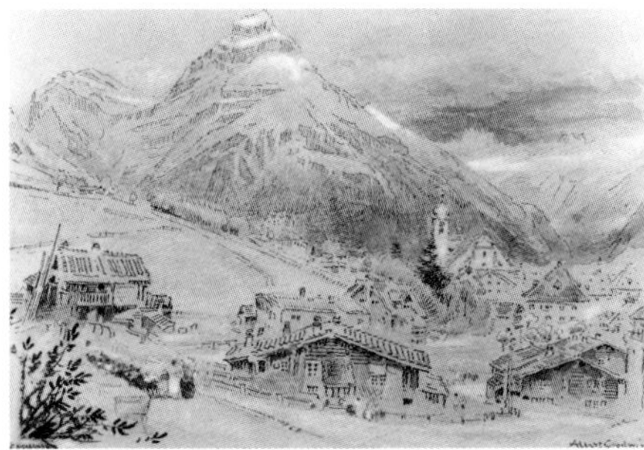

D.1929.10

View of Engelberg, Switzerland
pen and black ink, watercolour; beige paper
signed lower right: *Albert Goodwin*; inscribed lower
left: *Engelberg*
224 × 312 mm
Anderson, A. E. (gift, 1929) (D.1929.10)

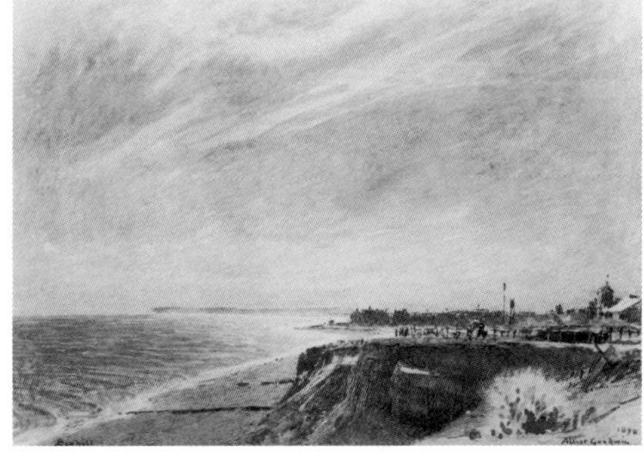

D.1930.33

The Seafront, Bexhill, Sussex
1898
watercolour
signed & dated lower right: *1898 / Albert Goodwin*;
inscribed lower left: *Bexhill*
264 × 366 mm
Anderson, A. E. (gift, 1930) (D.1930.33)

■ **GOODWIN, EDWARD (fl. 1801–15)**
Edward Goodwin lived in Manchester and Liverpool.
He exhibited at the Royal Academy and the Old
Watercolour Society between 1801 and 1815.

**View from Liverpool Lighthouse into
North Wales**
pencil, watercolour
signed lower right: *E Goodwin*; signed & inscribed
centre reverse of mount: *View from Liverpool Light
house / looking into North Wales – Flintshire / E Goodwin*
422 × 689 mm
anonymous (in memory of Sir Joseph Whitworth) (gift, 1897)
(D.1897.2)

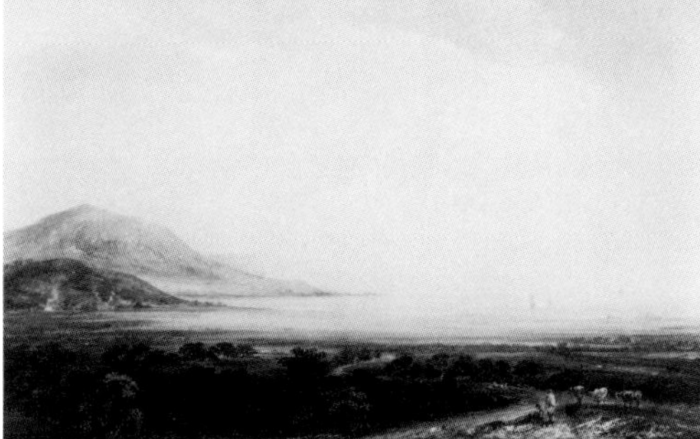

D.1897.2

■ **GOODWIN, HARRY (1842–1926)**
Harry Goodwin, elder brother of Albert, and with a
similar style, accompanied him to the Italian Lakes in
1887. He exhibited at the Royal Academy from 1868.

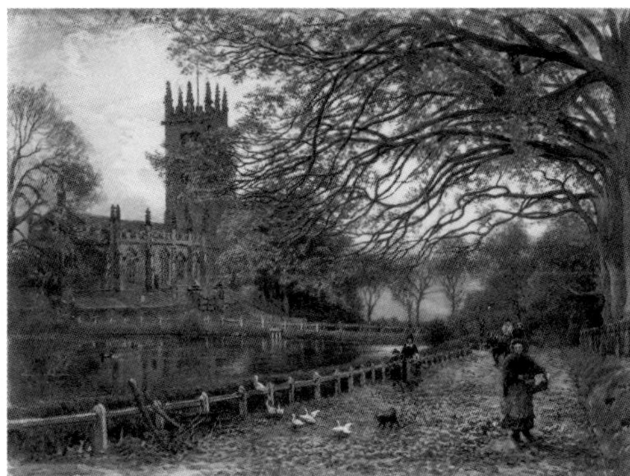

D.1892.155

An Autumn Sunset, Gawsworth, Cheshire
1891
pen and brown ink, watercolour, bodycolour
(heightened with white)
signed & dated lower right with monogram: *HG 1891*
265 × 361 mm
untraced (purchase, 1892) (D.1892.155)

■ **GOODWIN, KATE (fl. 1873–1900)**
Kate Goodwin, landscape painter and wife of Harry,
exhibited at the Royal Academy between 1873 and 1893.

**Copy of the 'Dream of St Ursula' by
Vittore Carpaccio**
1886–87
watercolour
855 × 830 mm
Horsfall, Thomas Coghlan (gift, 1908) (D.1908.25)

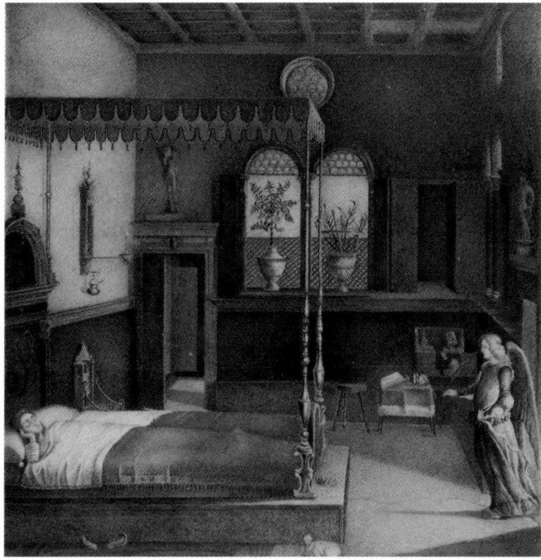

D.1908.25

■ **GORE, CHARLES (1729–1807)**
Gore was an amateur artist whose speciality was
marine draughtsmanship. He visited Lisbon, then
Italy; he also toured Sicily with Richard Payne Knight
and Philipp Hackert. In 1791 Gore settled in Weimar
and became a friend of Goethe.

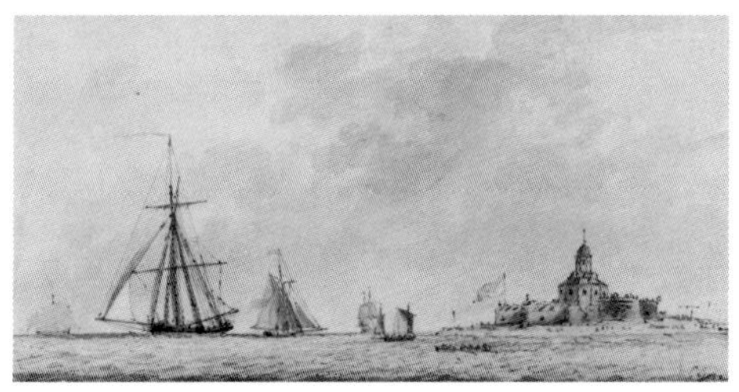

D.1926.97

Hurst Castle, Hampshire, from the Sea
1772
pencil, pen and brown ink, watercolour
signed lower right: *CGore*; inscribed & dated centre
verso in later hand: *Hurst Castle / 1772*
107 × 203 mm
Ogden, William Sharp (bequest, 1926) (D.1926.97)

■ **GORTIN, JOHN (fl. early 19th century)**
An amateur artist who was presumably a pupil of
George Chinnery in India.

**Figures on a Road beside a classical Building
overlooking an Estuary**
pencil
signed lower right verso: *John Gortin*
119 × 357 mm
Ogden, William Sharp (bequest, 1926) (D.1926.280)

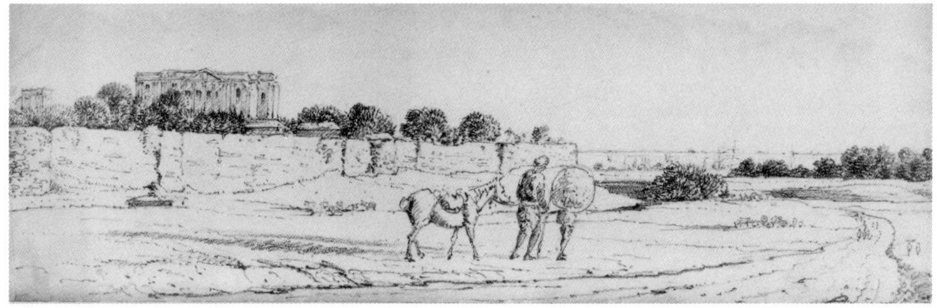

D.1926.280

■ GRAY, RONALD (1868–1951)

Gray studied at the Westminster School of Art and at the Academie Julien in Paris. He exhibited at the New English Art Club and became a member in 1923. A friend of Philip Wilson Steer, he was elected a member of the Royal Watercolour Society in 1942.

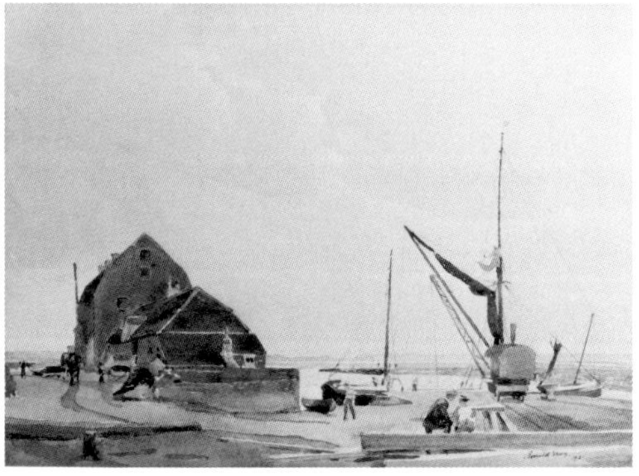

D.1925.6

Fawley Mill, Southampton Water, Hampshire
1921
pencil, watercolour
signed & dated lower right: *Ronald Gray. / 1921*
253 × 344 mm
Anderson, A. E., National Art Collections Fund (via)
(gift, 1925) (D.1925.6)

Hythe Dockyard, Kent
1921
pencil, watercolour
signed & dated lower left: *Ronald Gray 1921*
222 × 295 mm
Anderson, A. E., National Art Collections Fund (via)
(gift, 1925) (D.1925.7)

■ GREAVES, HENRY (1850–1900) and GREAVES, WALTER (1846–1930)

Henry Greaves, an unpaid pupil and studio assistant of Whistler, sometimes collaborated with his brother Walter, who was also taught by, and assisted, Whistler in his studio.

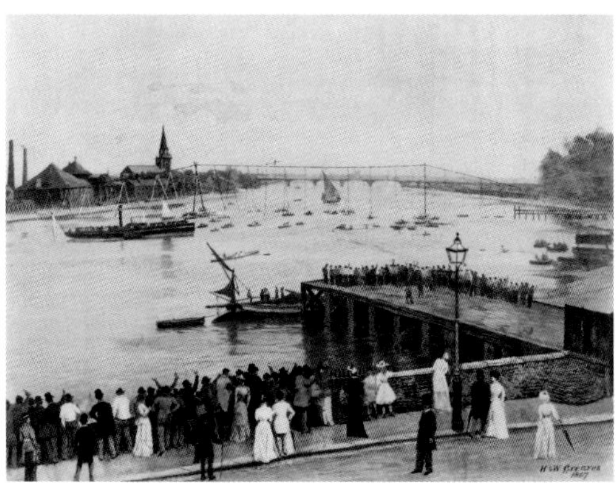

D.1929.4

The Female Blondin crossing the Thames on a Tightrope from Battersea to Cremorne, 19 August 1861
1867
watercolour
signed & dated lower right: *H & W Greaves / 1867*
481 × 620 mm
Jackson, C. and Son, Manchester (purchase, 1929) (D.1929.4)

■ GREEN, AMOS (1735–1807)

Amos Green, one of a family of artists from Halesowen near Birmingham, was a professional painter in oil and watercolour. Based in Bath for many years, Green gave drawing lessons there and made tours of the Lake District, Wales, Scotland and elsewhere, often in company with his wife, Harriet, who was already an accomplished artist and whom he married in 1796. Green overpainted the landscape backgrounds of Stubbs's *Labourers* and *Gamekeepers* in order to engrave them in 1790.

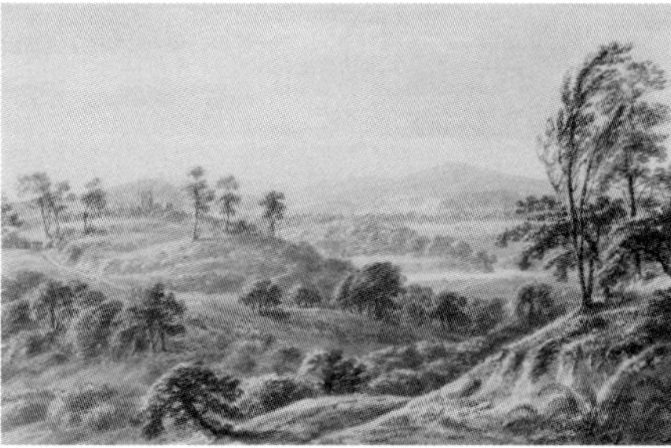

D.1950.13

Landscape, near Gresford, Denbighshire, Wales
1801
pencil, pen and brown ink, watercolour
243 × 371 mm
Pilkington, Margaret (gift, 1950) (D.1950.13)

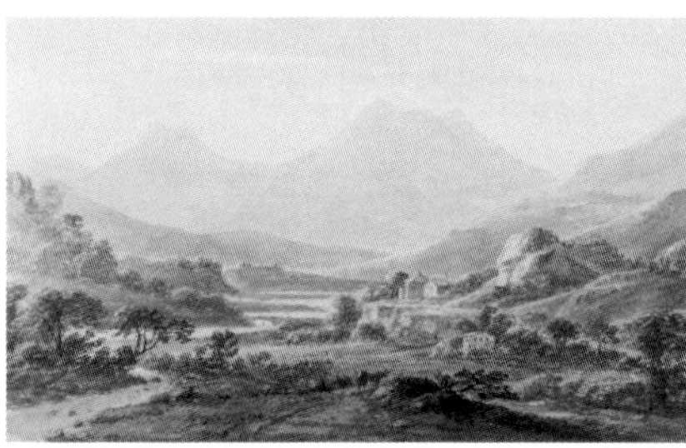

D.1963.31

Snowdon from Capel Curig, Caernarvonshire, Wales
1801
pencil, pen and grey ink, watercolour
245 × 393 mm
Lockett, G Derek (gift, 1963) (D.1963.31)

■ GREEN, BENJAMIN (1738–98)

Benjamin Green, brother of Amos and a mezzotint engraver, was the drawing master at Christ's Hospital from 1766 until 1796. He exhibited at the Society of Artists and supplemented his income with printmaking, publishing *Drawing and Painting in Watercolour* (1755) and *A Drawing Book of Landscape* (1786).

East End of St Albans Abbey, Hertfordshire
9.4.1779
etching, watercolour
signed lower left on edge of decorative border:
BENn.GREEN Deln. & fecit; inscribed & dated lower centre within cartouche in the decorative border: *ABBY CHURCH of / St. ALBANS Aprl. 9 1779*; inscribed & dated lower edge beneath decorative border: *Pubd. & Sold by BENJn. GREEN: Drawing Master to Xts HOSPITAL. LONDON. Sepr.9.1782 No 23*
157 × 131 mm
Ogden, William Sharp (bequest, 1926) (D.1926.51)

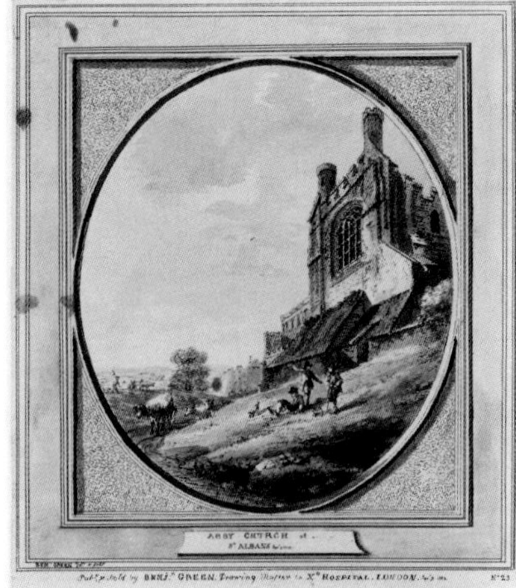

D.1926.51

■ GREEN, CHARLES (1840–98)

Charles Green was an illustrator who also painted genre scenes in watercolour. He worked for the *Graphic* and *Once a Week*, as well as producing book illustrations. Green was elected a member of the New Watercolour Society in 1867.

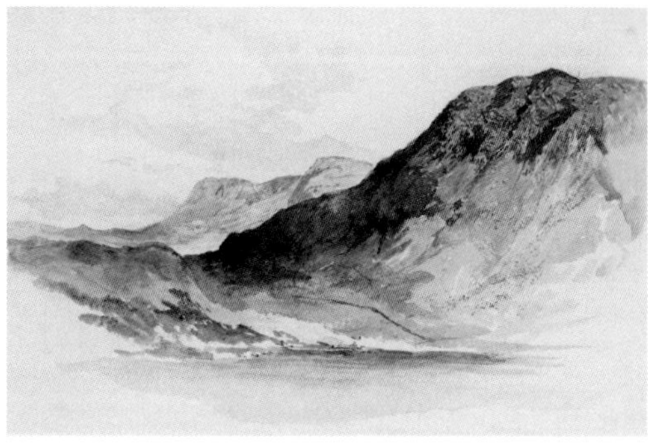

D.1926.50

Landscape with Mountains and a Lake
watercolour
194 × 289 mm
Ogden, William Sharp (bequest, 1926) (D.1926.50)

■ GREEN, HARRIET LISTER (fl. 1784–1823)

Harriet Lister Green is said to have been a pupil of her husband Amos, but there is no proof of this and she was already an accomplished landscape watercolourist when they met in Bath in 1793. She accompanied Amos on sketching tours all over England, Scotland and Wales, and her drawings are often virtually indistinguishable from those of her husband.

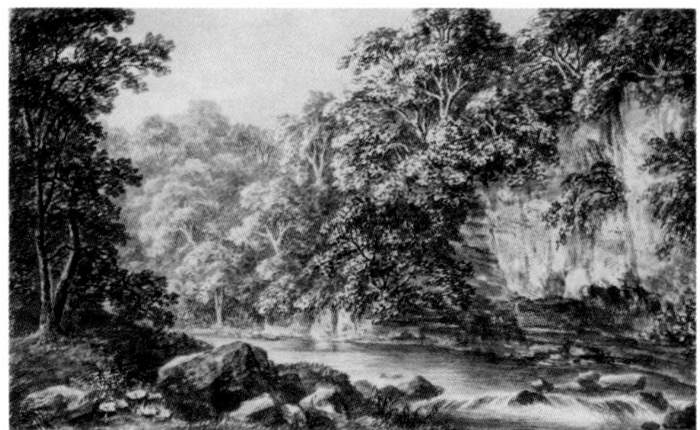

D.1963.24

Below East Wood, near Greta Bridge, Yorkshire
pencil, watercolour
inscribed on mount lower centre: *Below East Wood*;
inscribed on mount lower centre (added below ink
inscription): *above* [two illegible words]; inscribed on
reverse lower centre of mount: referring to a drawing
removed from the album page: *Scargill is on the right, /
Brignal Banks on the left, where concealed beneath the
Fern / is Guy Denzil's Cave, as described / in Scott's Poem
of Rokeby.*
240 × 382 mm
Lockett, G. Derek (gift, 1963) (D.1963.24)

■ GREEN, WILLIAM (1761–1823)
William Green was born in Manchester and began
his career as a surveyor before moving to London to
study engraving. In 1801, he moved to the Lake
District, settling in Ambleside, where he produced
prints and watercolours of Lake District subjects in
very large quantities. In 1819 he published *The Tourist's
Guide to the Lakes* illustrated with his own etchings
and aquatints.

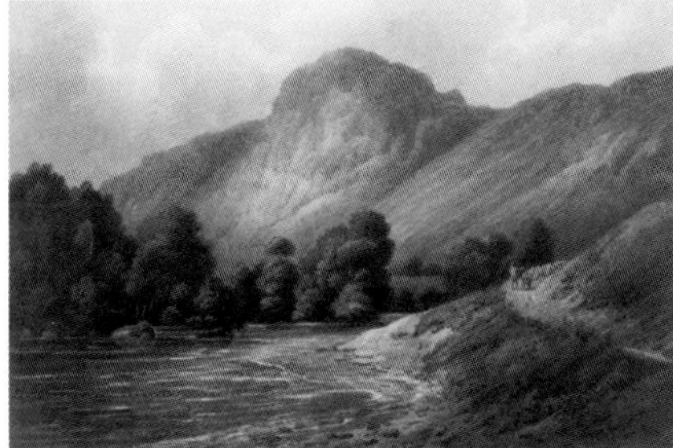

D.1917.27

Raven Crag, Thirlmere, Cumberland
watercolour
209 × 302 mm
Hudson, The Reverend W. A. (gift, 1917) (D.1917.27)

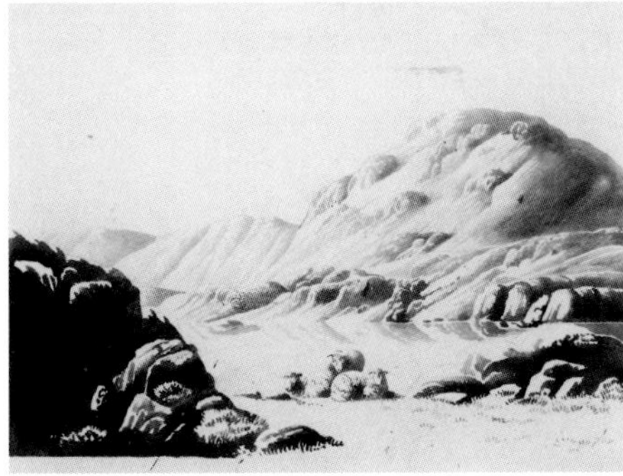

D.1917.29

**Great Gable and Sprinkling Tarn, Cumberland;
Stage 2 in the Completion of a Landscape
Watercolour Drawing**
pencil, watercolour
inscribed lower left margin: *No 2*
208 × 305 mm
Hudson, The Reverend W. A. (gift, 1917) (D.1917.29)

**Great Gable and Sprinkling Tarn, Cumberland;
Stage 3 in the Completion of a Landscape
Watercolour Drawing**
pencil, watercolour
inscribed lower left margin: *No 3*
210 × 305 mm
Hudson, The Reverend W. A. (gift, 1917) (D.1917.30)

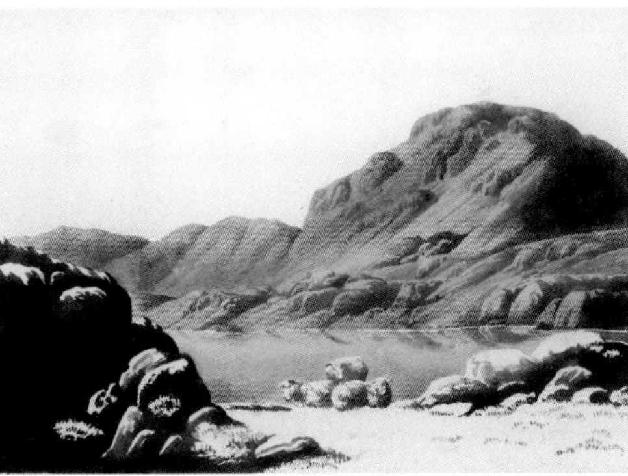

D.1917.30

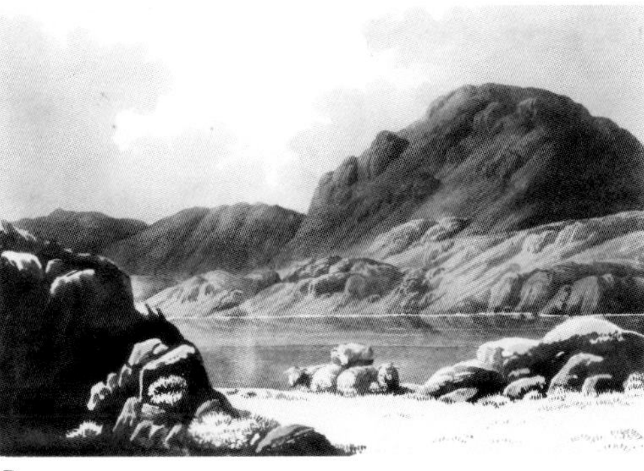

D.1917.31

**Great Gable and Sprinkling Tarn, Cumberland;
Stage 4 in the Completion of a Landscape
Watercolour Drawing**
pencil, watercolour
inscribed lower left margin: *No 4*
208 × 303 mm
Hudson, The Reverend W. A. (gift, 1917) (D.1917.31)

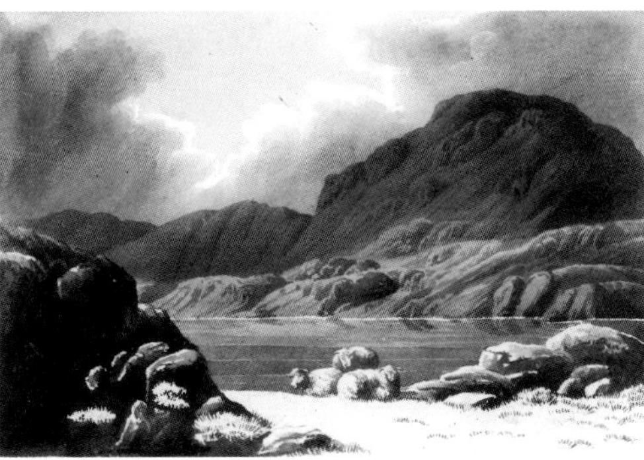

D.1917.32

**Great Gable and Sprinkling Tarn, Cumberland;
Stage 5 in the Completion of a Landscape
Watercolour Drawing**
pencil, watercolour
inscribed lower left margin: *No 5*
208 × 302 mm
Hudson, The Reverend W. A. (gift, 1917) (D.1917.32)

**Great Gable and Sprinkling Tarn, Cumberland;
Stage 6 in the Completion of a Landscape
Watercolour Drawing**
pencil, watercolour
inscribed lower left margin: *No 6*
208 × 302 mm
Hudson, The Reverend W. A. (gift, 1917) (D.1917.33)

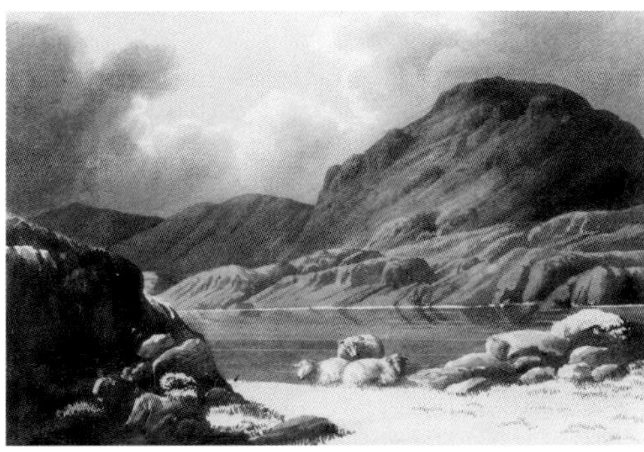

D.1917.33

■ GREENAWAY, KATE (1846–1901)
Greenaway began to exhibit in 1868 and worked as an
illustrator for *Illustrated London News*, *Little Folks* and
other papers. She was elected a member of the Royal
Institute in 1889. In 1877 she began to work for the
engraver and publisher Edmund Evans, producing a
long series of childrens' books and from 1883 to 1895 a
yearly almanac. Greenaway's elegant childlike figures
were immensely popular with the Victorians; John
Ruskin was a huge admirer.

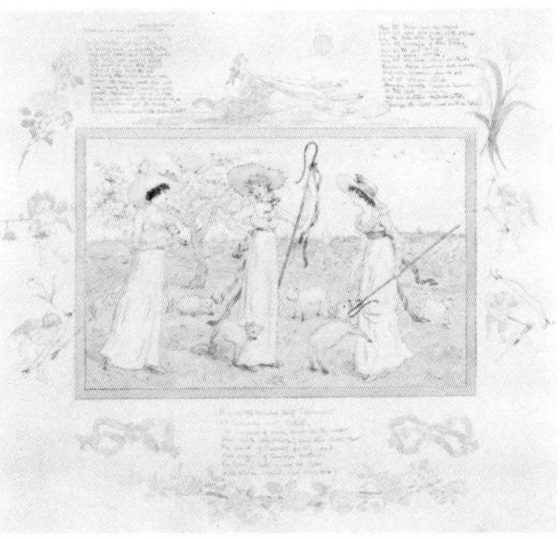

D.1902.7

Page Design for the Calendar Month of May
1882–84
pencil, watercolour
inscribed upper left, upper right and lower centre
with three verses of a lengthy poem
255 × 268 mm
untraced (purchase, 1902) (D.1902.7)

Portrait of a Child
pencil, watercolour; circular
52 × 52 mm
Hilton, Arthur (gift, 1944) (D.1944.89)

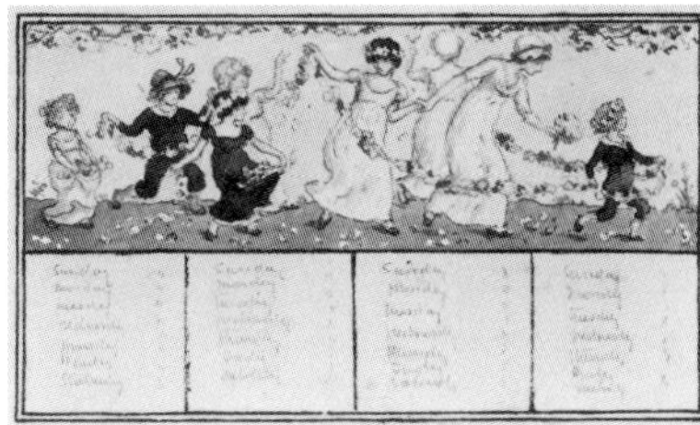

D.1944.90

Calendar for the Month of May
pencil, pen and brown ink, watercolour
69 × 103 mm
Hilton, Arthur (gift, 1944) (D.1944.90)

■ GRIFFITH, MOSES (1747–1819)

Griffith was born in Caernarvonshire, and spent his entire career working for the antiquarians Thomas Pennant and his son David Pennant, as a manservant. Apparently self-taught, Griffith's watercolours consist of antiquarian details, natural history illustrations, views of ruins and stately homes, small portraits and general landscapes.

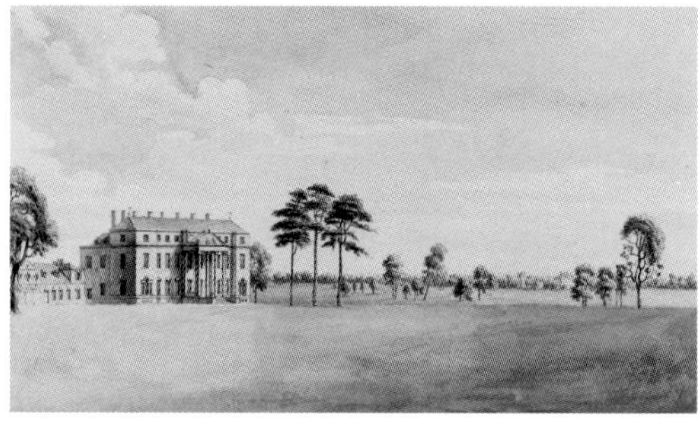

D.1963.25

Fisherwick Park, Staffordshire, the Seat of Lord Donegal

4.1778
pen and grey ink, watercolour; paper (watermark Strasbourg lily)
numbered: *72*; inscribed & dated: *The portico is now placed / in front of the inn at Walsall / Fisherwick the seat of Lord Donegal / April 1778 / Taken down in* [blank]; *the Portico removed / to the front of the inn at Walsall*
252 × 414 mm
Lockett, G. Derek (gift, 1963) (D.1963.25)

■ GRIMM, SAMUEL HIERONYMUS (1733–94)

Grimm, born in Switzerland, was a pupil of Johann Ludwig Aberli in Berne. He was in Paris from 1765 to 1768, when he came to England where he remained for the rest of his life. In 1776 he provided the illustrations for Gilbert White's *The Natural History of Selborne*. Grimm spent much of his career working for antiquarians but he also produced caricatures, political satires and lively figure groups.

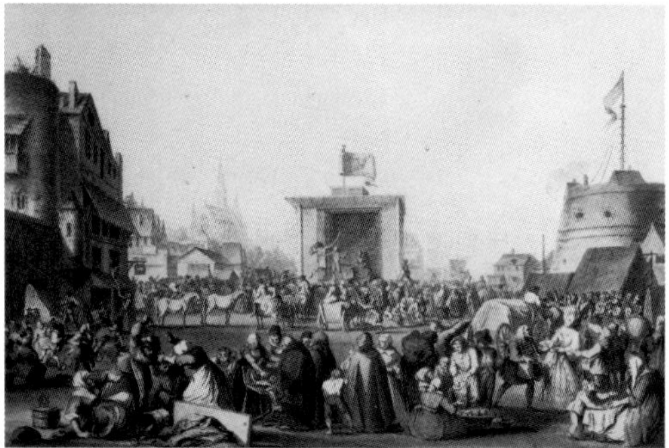

D.1916.12

Mountebanks at a Fair

1770
pen and brown ink, watercolour
signed & dated lower right: *S.H.Grimm fecit 1770.*
372 × 539 mm
untraced (purchase, 1916) (D.1916.12)

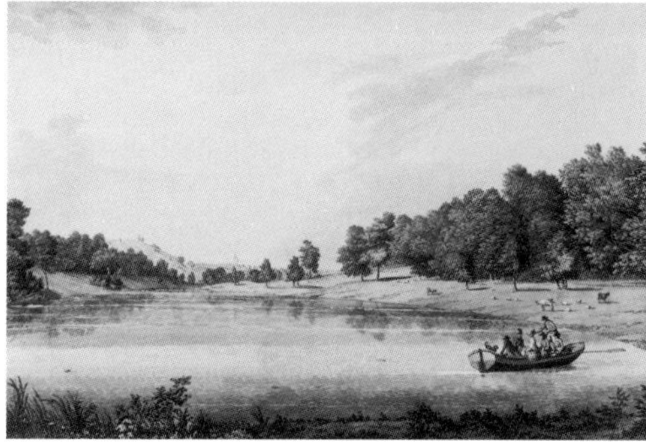

D.1933.41

A fishing Party on Roche Abbey Lake with Laughton-en-le-Morthen Church in the Distance, Yorkshire

1781
pen and grey ink, watercolour, bodycolour (heightened with white)
signed & dated lower right: *S.H.Grimm fecit / 1781*
numbered: *14*
373 × 546 mm
Anderson, A. E. (gift, 1933) (D.1933.41)

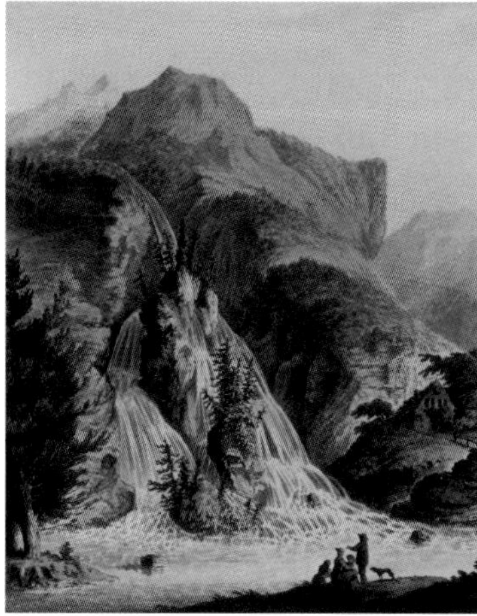

D.1987.51

Cascade of Oltshibach, Berne, Switzerland

1770
pencil, pen and brown ink, watercolour
signed & dated on rock in river lower left: *S.H.Grimm fecit 1770*
355 × 283 mm
Leger Galleries, London (purchase, 1987) (D.1987.51)

■ GROSE, FRANCIS (attributed to) (1731–91)

Grose, a prolific antiquarian and topographical draughtsman, exhibited as an Honorary Exhibitor at the Royal Academy between 1769 and 1777. He made numerous sketching tours all over the British Isles, often with other amateurs and draughtsmen such as Thomas Pennant and Moses Griffith. Grose published *The Antiquities of England and Wales* (1773–87), *The Antiquities of Scotland* (1789–91) and *The Antiquities of Ireland* (1791–95).

Arnoll Puplett's Coal Wharf and the Corn Mill at Wandsworth, Surrey

watercolour
300 × 478 mm
Anderson, A. E. (gift, 1933) (D.1933.7)

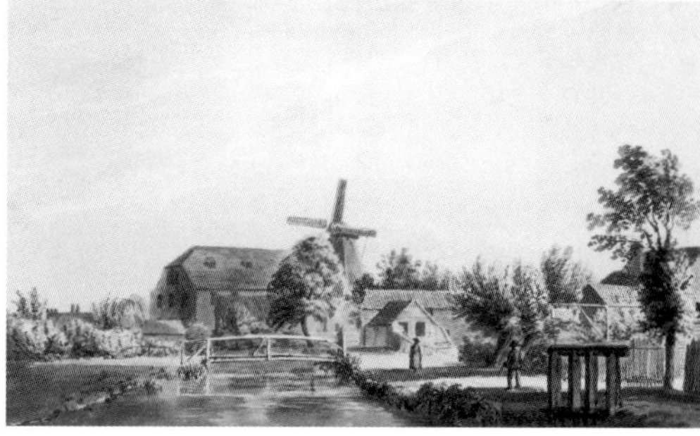

D.1933.7

■ HAAG, CARL (1820–1915)

Haag was born in Bavaria and studied in Nuremberg and Munich. He came to England in 1847 to study at the Royal Academy schools, and became a member of the Old Watercolour Society in 1853. He attracted the attention of Queen Victoria and was invited to stay at Balmoral in 1853, 1854, and 1855. Haag travelled widely in Europe and the Middle East, recording the scenery there. He became Court Painter to Ernest II, Duke of Saxe-Coburg and elder brother to Prince Albert, and died at Oberwesel.

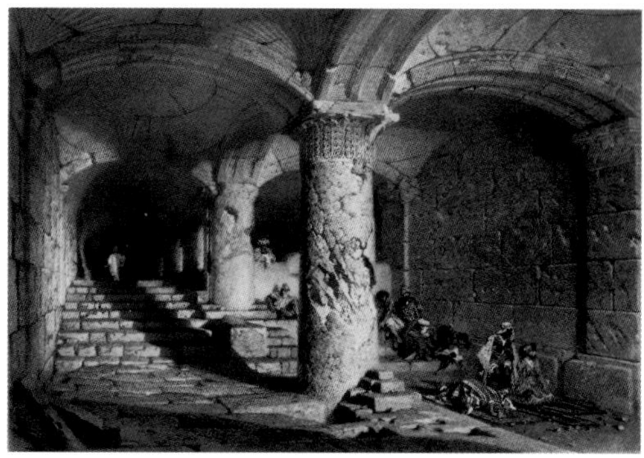

D.1904.3

The Ancient Vestibule to the Southern Entrance beneath the Temple Area, Jerusalem

watercolour
510 × 714 mm
untraced (purchase, 1904) (D.1904.3)

■ HADFIELD, THOMAS RALEIGH (1835–1918)

A Manchester-based amateur artist.

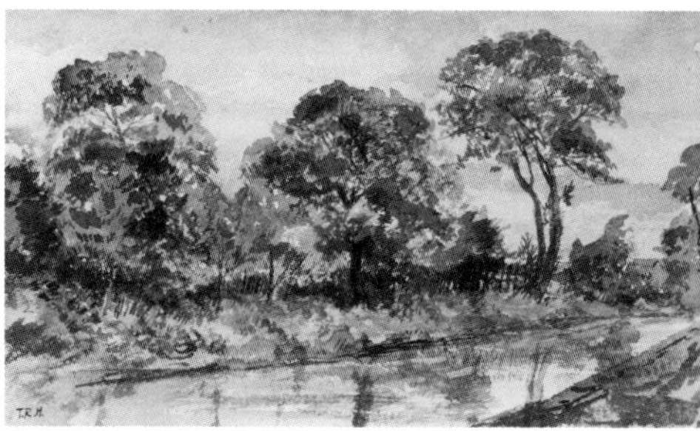

D.1941.5

The Canal, Old Trafford, Manchester

watercolour
signed lower left with initials: *T.R.H.*
138 × 229 mm
Hadfield, Amy (gift, 1941) (D.1941.5)

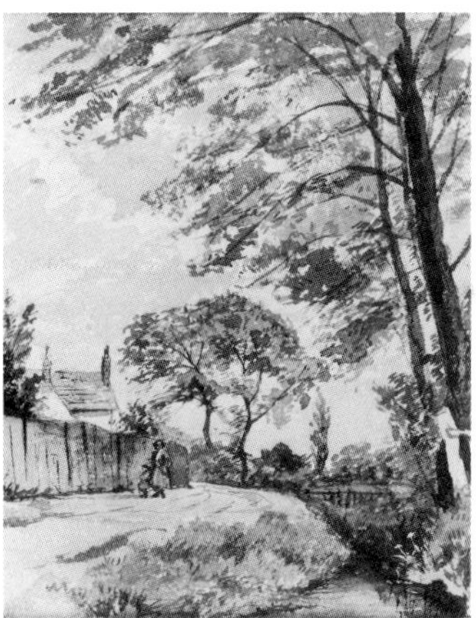
D.1941.6

Hullard Hall Lane, Stretford, Manchester
1864
watercolour
signed, inscribed & dated upper edge of verso with
initials in monogram: *Hullard Hall Lane / Stretford
McR / TRH / 1864*
173 × 138 mm
Hadfield, Amy (gift, 1941) (D.1941.6)

Study of a Schoolboy
black chalk, white chalk; blue paper
signed lower left: *TRHadfield*
219 × 128 mm
Hadfield, Amy (gift, 1941) (D.1941.7)

Study of a Schoolboy
black chalk, white chalk; blue paper
219 × 128 mm
Hadfield, Amy (gift, 1941) (D.1941.8)

■ **HAITE, GEORGE CHARLES (1855–1924)**
Haite exhibited in London from 1883 and was
elected a member of the Royal Institute in 1901.
As well as producing English landscapes, he also
worked in Spain and Morocco.

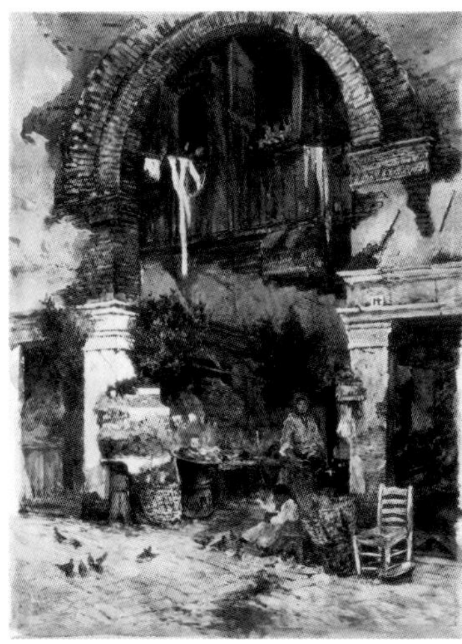
D.1904.5

Fruit Stalls under an Archway, Venice
1903
watercolour, bodycolour (heightened with white)
signed & dated lower left: *Geo.C.Haite / 1903*
710 × 552 mm
untraced (purchase, 1904) (D.1904.5)

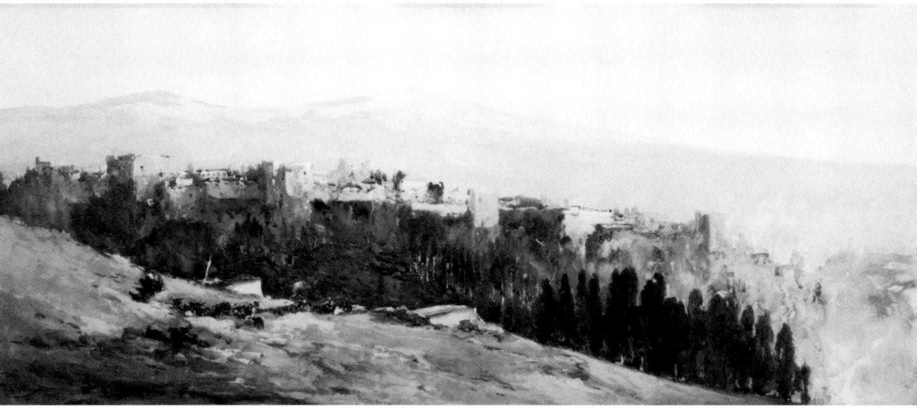
D.1904.6

Over the Hills, Granada, Spain
1900
watercolour, bodycolour
signed & dated lower left: *Geo.C.Haite / 1900*
322 × 746 mm
untraced (purchase, 1904) (D.1904.6)

■ **HALL, OLIVER (1869–1957)**
Hall studied at the Royal College of Art from 1887 to
1890. He painted widely in the north of England,
particularly Yorkshire and Cumbria. He also travelled
extensively in Europe. Hall was elected a member of
the Royal Academy in 1927.

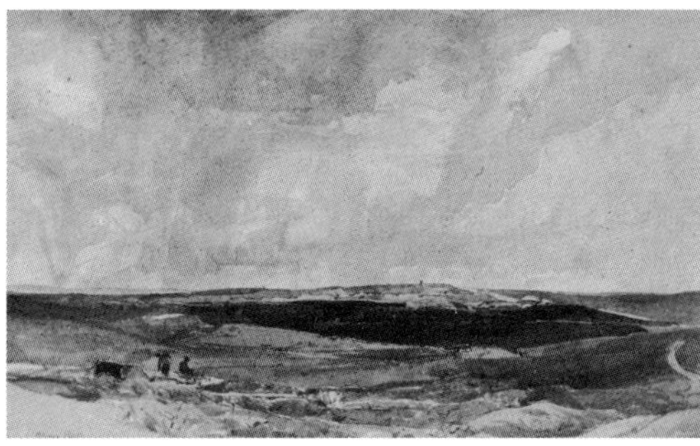
D.1919.17

On the Moors, Shap, Westmorland
pencil, pen and brown ink, watercolour; grey paper
signed lower left: *Oliver Hall*
377 × 560 mm
Brown and Phillips Ltd, London (purchase, 1919) (D.1919.17)

■ **HAMER, JOHN JAMES (1867–1944)**
Born at Darwen in Lancashire, Hamer studied at
the Royal College of Art. He taught at Londonderry
School of Art and was head of Huddersfield School
of Art for 25 years.

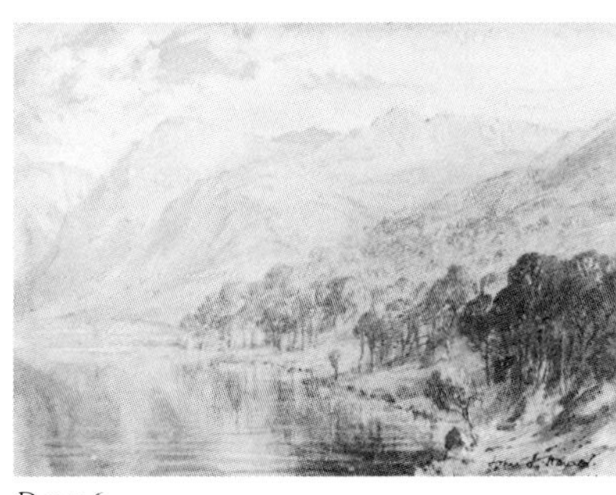
D.1945.6

View of Ennerdale, Cumberland
1927
pencil, watercolour
signed lower right: *John J.Hamer*
142 × 192 mm
Hamer, Mary (in memory of J. J. Hamer) (gift, 1945)
(D.1945.6)

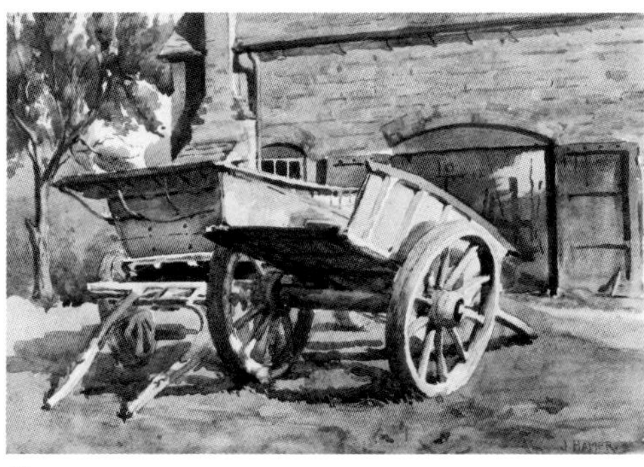
D.1975.19

Farm Carts, near Dunchurch, Warwickshire
pencil, watercolour
signed lower right: *J.HAMER*
195 × 277 mm
Hamer, Mary (bequest, 1975) (D.1975.19)

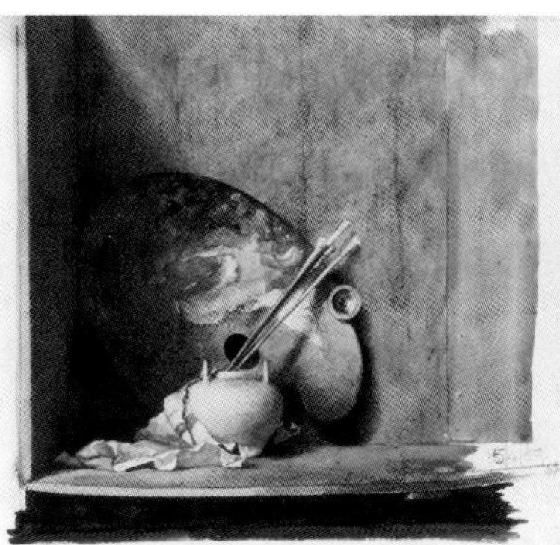
D.1975.20

Still Life with Palette, Jar and Brushes
15.4.1889
pencil, watercolour, bodycolour
(heightened with white)
signed lower right: *J.Hamer*; dated lower right: *15/4/89*;
inscribed lower right indicating the time the artist took
to complete this student exercise: *4h.*
247 × 255 mm
Hamer, Mary (bequest, 1975) (D.1975.20)

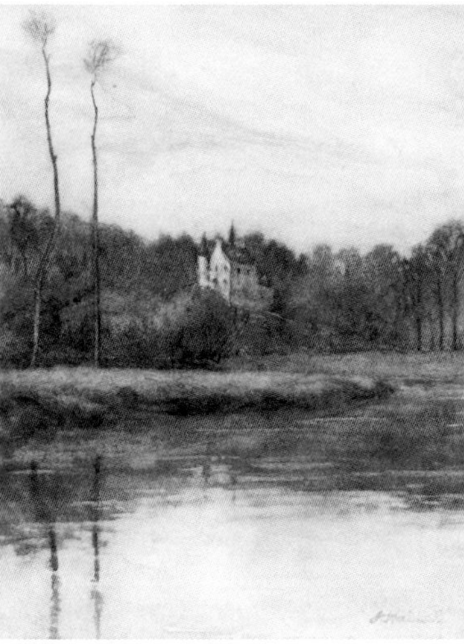

D.1975.21

Chateau, near St Lo, Normandy
watercolour
signed lower right: *J.Hamer*; inscribed upper centre
verso of mount: *Chateau / near St.Lo. / Normandy.* [last
line underlined]; inscribed verso upper centre of mount
partially written over other inscription: *Chateau / near
St. Lo, Norm*
196 × 145 mm
Hamer, Mary (bequest, 1975) (D.1975.21)

Field of Cabbages
watercolour
signed lower right: *John J.Hamer.*
242 × 159 mm
Hamer, Mary (bequest, 1975) (D.1975.22)

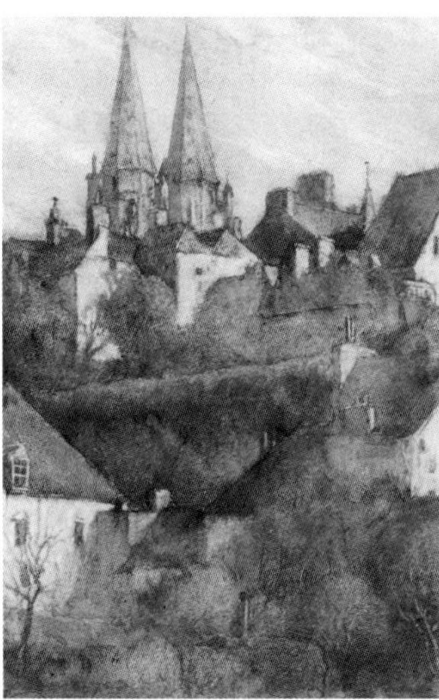

D.1975.23

Houses with the Cathedral, St Lo, Normandy
4.1911
watercolour
signed lower right: *J.Hamer–*
243 × 158 mm
Hamer, Mary (bequest, 1975) (D.1975.23)

Sheep in a Country Lane
1911
watercolour
signed & dated lower right: *J.Hamer.1911.* [underlined]
313 × 236 mm
Hamer, Mary (bequest, 1975) (D.1975.24)

■ **HAMILTON, WILLIAM (1751–1801)**
Hamilton trained in Rome under Zucchi,
returning to England in 1769. Elected a member
of the Royal Academy in 1789, Hamilton specialised
in literary, mythological and historical subjects, often
containing many figures.

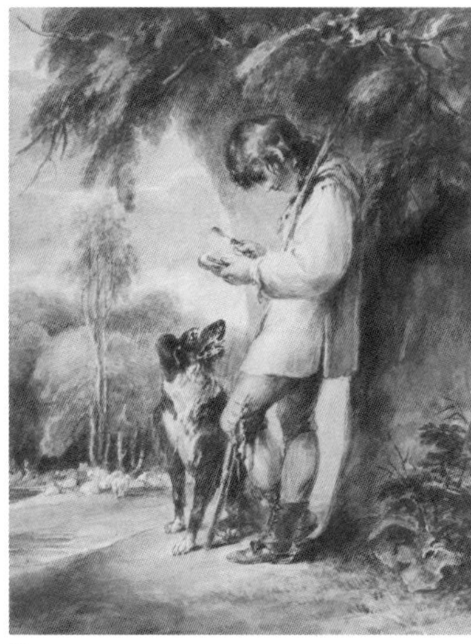

D.1900.3

A Shepherd Boy and his Dog
1795
pencil, watercolour
signed & dated lower right: *Wm Hamilton RA 1795*
299 × 227 mm
Worthington, Mary (gift, 1900) (D.1900.3)

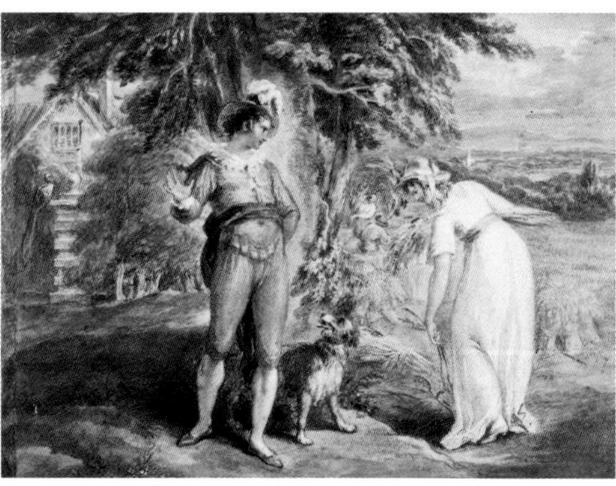

D.1944.2

**Palemon's first Sight of Lavinia, from Thomson's
'The Seasons'**
1794
pencil, watercolour, bodycolour
(heightened with white)
221 × 281 mm
Friends of the Whitworth (gift, 1944) (D.1944.2)

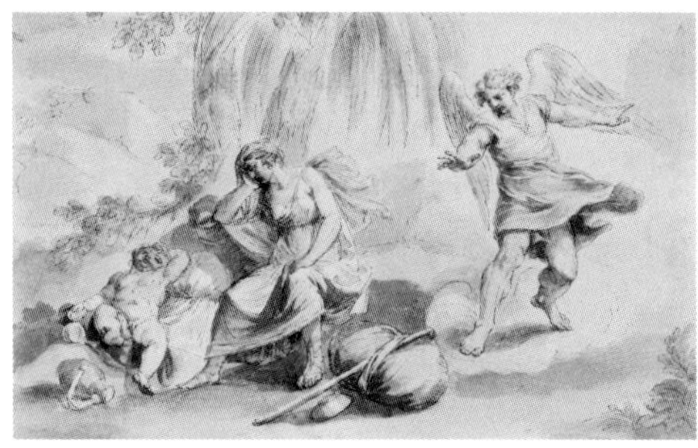

D.1960.88

Hagar and Ishmael
pen and brown ink, watercolour
182 × 286 mm
University of Manchester, History of Art Department
(transfer, 1960) (D.1960.88)

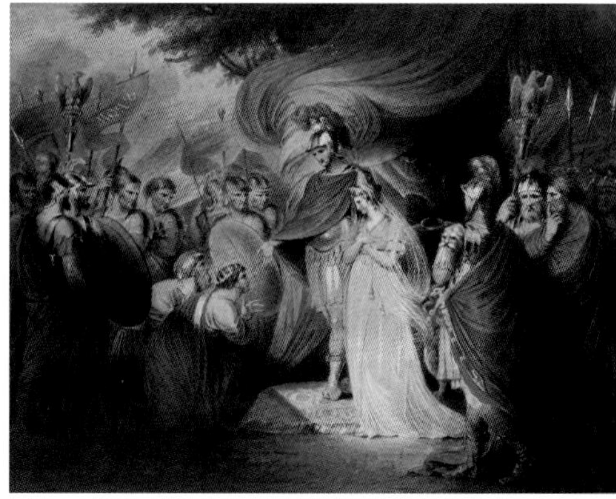

D.1962.21

The Continence of Scipio
pencil, pen and grey ink, watercolour, bodycolour
(heightened with white)
inscribed within a cartouche on lower centre of
decorative mount: *The Continence of Scipio*
393 × 492 mm
Mathews, Alister (purchase, 1962) (D.1962.21)

■ **HARDIE, MARTIN (1875–1952)**
Hardie studied etching under Sir Frank Short and
exhibited at the Royal Academy from 1908. He joined
the Victoria & Albert Museum in 1898 and from 1921
to 1935 was Keeper in charge of the departments of
painting and engraving, illustration and design. He was
elected an honorary member of the Royal Watercolour
Society in 1942. He is now chiefly famous for his
writings, in particular *Water-Colour Painting in Britain*,
a three-volume book that remains one of the standard
books on the subject.

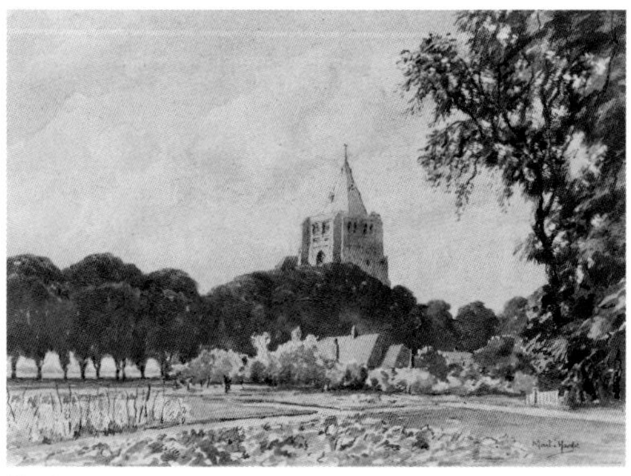

D.1965.5

Crowland Abbey, Lincolnshire
7.1933
pencil, pen and brown ink, watercolour
signed lower right: *Martin Hardie*; signed, inscribed &
dated centre verso: *Croyland* (sic) *Abbey / Martin
Hardie / –July,1933.*
288 × 389 mm
Watson, A. (gift, 1965) (D.1965.5)

■ HARDING, JAMES DUFFIELD (1797–1863)

Harding was a teacher and popular drawing master, numbering John Ruskin among his pupils in the 1840s. He was elected a member of the Old Watercolour Society in 1821. A prolific lithographer, Harding made prints after Lewis, Stanfield, Bonington and Roberts, as well as from his own works.

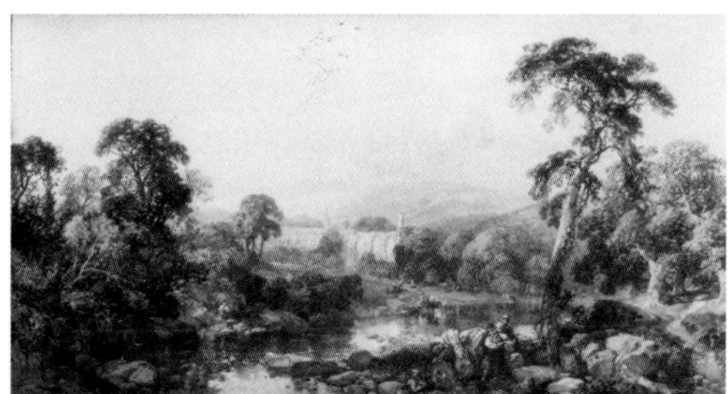
D.1898.5

Bolton Abbey, Yorkshire, Summer Evening
watercolour, bodycolour (heightened with white)
590 × 1062 mm
Agnew's (purchase, 20.12.1898) (D.1898.5)

Landscape with Mountains
pencil, brown watercolour
signed lower right with initials: *J.D.H.*
241 × 186 mm
Ogden, William Sharp (bequest, 1926) (D.1926.208)

On the Rhine
pencil, black chalk, watercolour, bodycolour (heightened with white); buff paper
273 × 390 mm
Towlson, Hector J. (bequest, 1970) (D.1970.38)

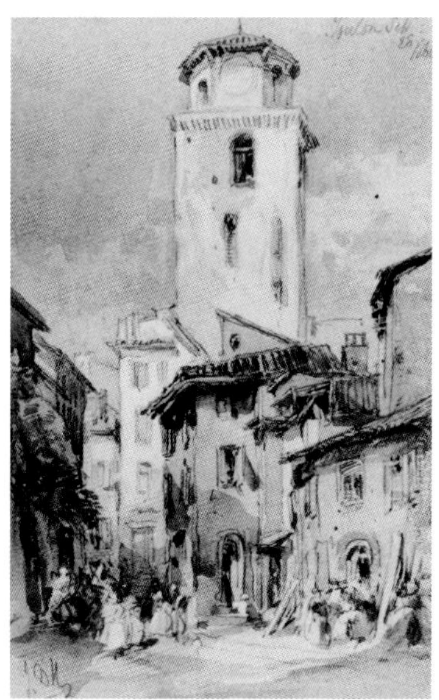
D.1970.39

Street Scene in Toulon, France
28.9.1860
pencil, watercolour, bodycolour (heightened with white); grey paper
signed lower left with initials: *J.DH*; inscribed & dated upper right: *Toulon Sepr / 28 / 1860*
204 × 127 mm
Towlson, Hector J. (bequest, 1970) (D.1970.39)

■ HARDY, THOMAS BUSH (1842–97)

Hardy was a marine painter who visited France, Holland and Italy. He was fond of using the pallette knife to scratch out the paper in order to depict rough water. In later life Hardy suffered from alcoholism.

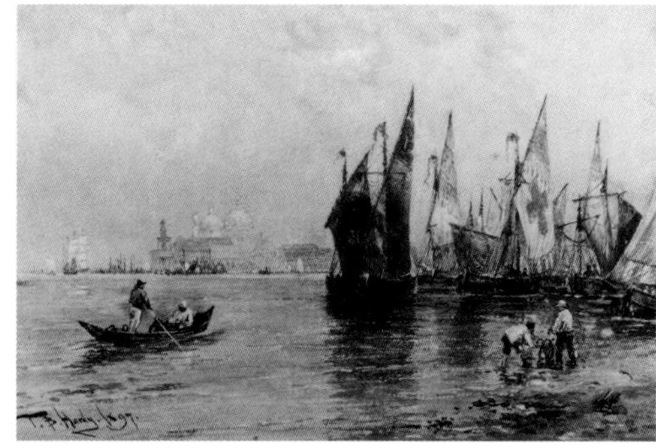
D.1970.40

Fishing Boats with the Dogana and Church of Sta Maria della Salute beyond, Venice
1897
watercolour, bodycolour (heightened with white)
signed & dated lower left: *T.B.Hardy.1897.*
178 × 258 mm
Towlson, Hector J. (bequest, 1970) (D.1970.40)

■ HARE, AUGUSTUS JOHN CUTHBERT (1836–1903)

Hare, author of numerous guide and travel books, as well as biographies, was a competent amateur watercolourist who was widely travelled, particularly in Italy.

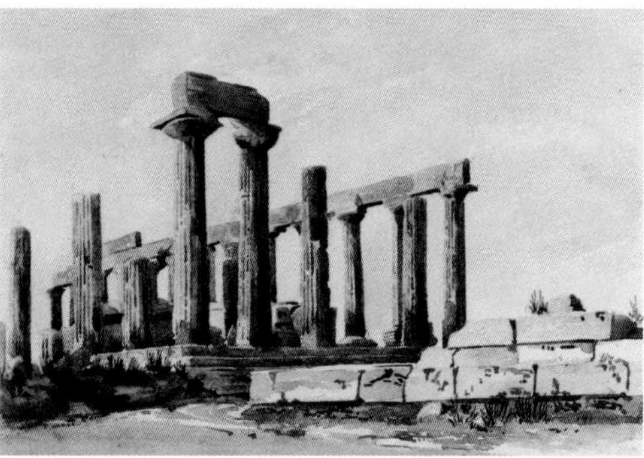
D.1971.1

Temple of Juno or Hera Lacinia, Agrigento, Sicily
pencil, watercolour
276 × 409 mm
Albany Gallery, London (purchase, 1971) (D.1971.1)

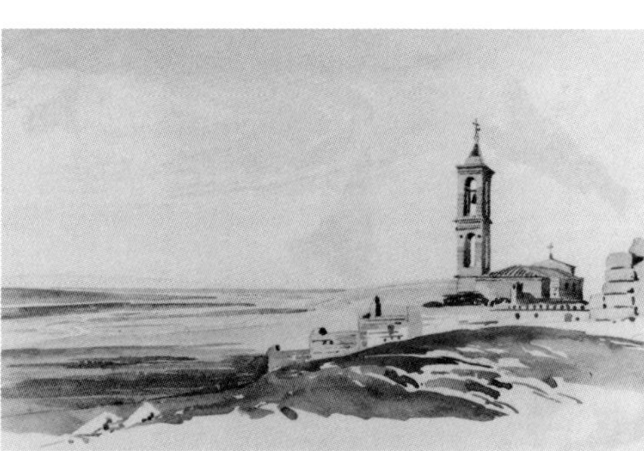
D.1971.2

Battlefield of Cannae from Canossa, Italy
pencil, watercolour
241 × 359 mm
Albany Gallery, London (purchase, 1971) (D.1971.2)

■ HARPER, JOHN (1809–42)

Harper was an architect who studied under Benjamin and Philip Wyatt, and practised in York. He died while travelling to Italy to study art.

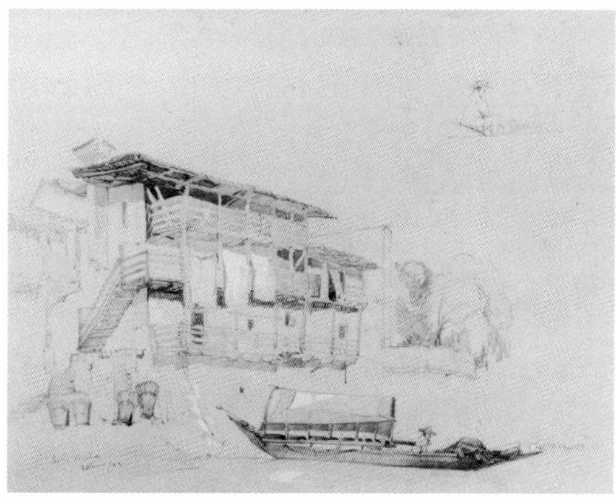
D.1960.24

Study of a lakeside House, Isola Bella, Italy
20.6.1842
pencil, watercolour, bodycolour (heightened with white); buff paper
inscribed & dated lower left: *Isola Bella / 20 June/42*
237 × 301 mm
Laws, Grace M., Victoria and Albert Museum (via) (gift, 1960) (D.1960.24)

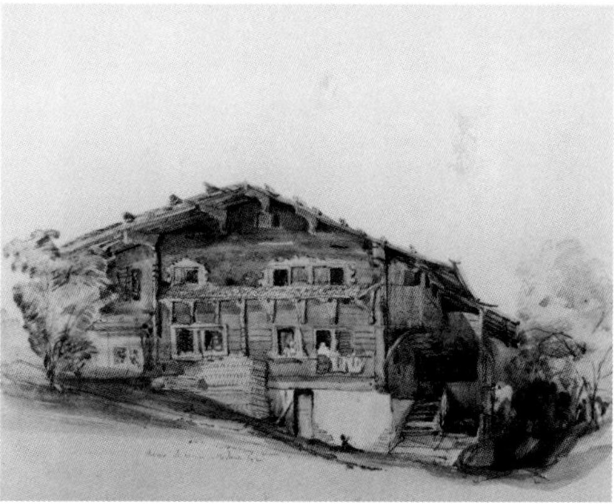
D.1960.25

Chalet, near Lucerne, Switzerland
16.6.1842
pencil, watercolour; buff paper
inscribed & dated lower left: *near Lucerne–16 June/42*
237 × 294 mm
Laws, Grace M., Victoria and Albert Museum (via) (gift, 1960) (D.1960.25)

■ HARRADEN, RICHARD BANKES (1778–1862)

Harraden was an engraver and topographical artist who worked with his father Richard on a series of prints of Cambridge colleges. Father and son also made prints after Girtin's Parisian views.

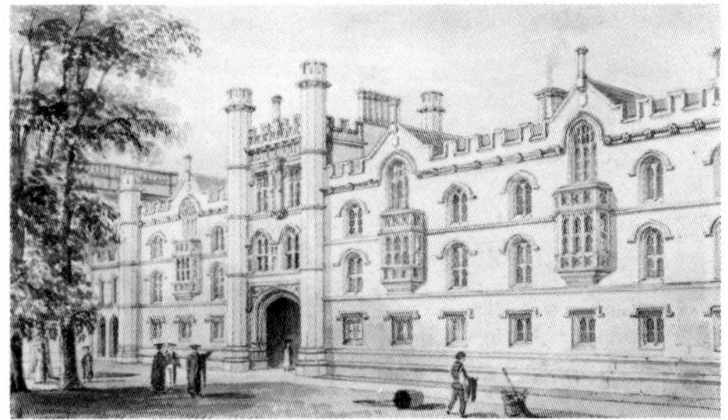

D.1926.207

The Gatehouse, New Court, Corpus Christi College, Cambridge
pencil, brown watercolour
inscribed upper centre in border above image: *Corpus Christi or / Bennet*; inscribed lower edge in border next to the corresponding object reading from left to right: *Path between Trees Grass plot Grass Roller Gardener. Basket & broom Grass Gravel Wal*[k]
128 × 216 mm
Ogden, William Sharp (bequest, 1926) (D.1926.207)

New Court, Trinity College, Cambridge
pencil, brown watercolour
signed in border lower left: *R.B.Harraden delt.*; inscribed in border lower centre: *(King's Court.)* [underlined] / *TRINITY COLLEGE.* [ruled above and underlined] / *Published by R.B.Harraden Cambridge.* [underlined]
126 × 218 mm
Ogden, William Sharp (bequest, 1926) (D.1965.3)

■ **HARRINGTON, CHARLES (1865–1943)**
Harrington was a Sussex artist who exhibited intermittently at the Royal Academy from 1913. He was killed during a German air raid.

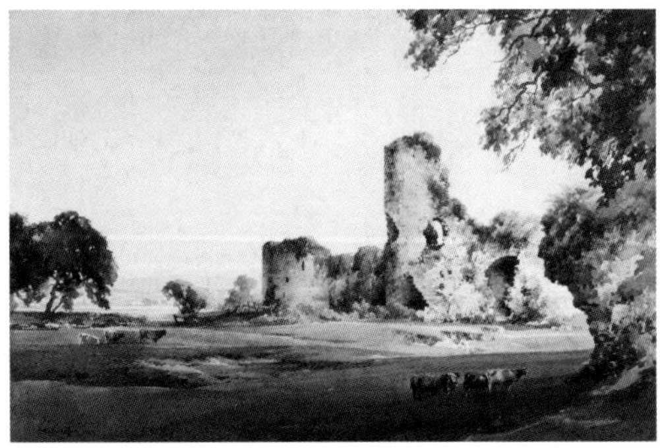

D.1925.23

Pevensey Castle, Sussex
1923
pencil, watercolour
signed & dated lower left: *C Harrington/23*
380 × 560 mm
Burke, C. J. (gift, 1925) (D.1925.23)

■ **HASTINGS, EDMUND (fl. 1804–61)**
Hastings was a landscape and portrait painter who exhibited at the Royal Academy from 1804.

On the Tweed, near Kelso, Roxburghshire, Scotland
pencil, watercolour
signed lower right: *EHastings*
133 × 206 mm
Towlson, Hector J. (bequest, 1970) (D.1970.41)

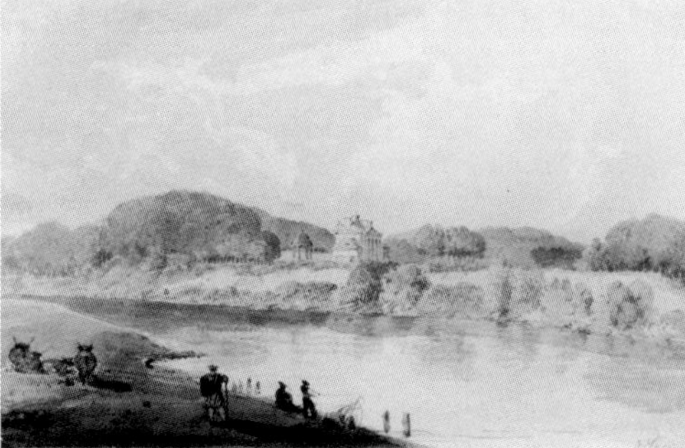

D.1970.41

■ **HAVELL, FREDERICK JAMES (1801–40)**
Frederick James Havell was a member of the Reading family of artists and engravers.

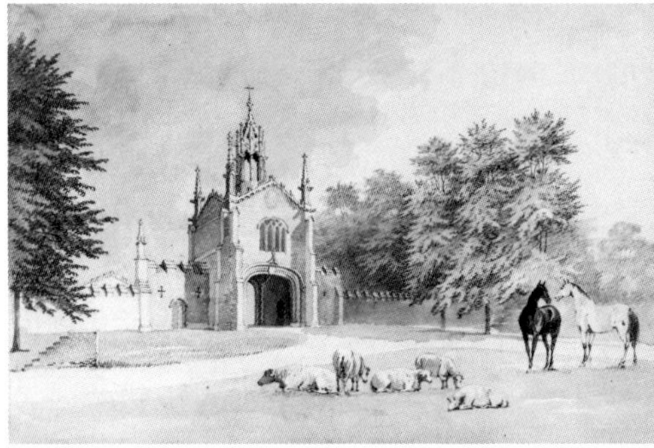

D.1926.314

The Entrance to Highgate Cemetery, London
pencil, grey watercolour
249 × 361 mm
Ogden, William Sharp (bequest, 1926) (D.1926.314)

■ **HAVELL, WILLIAM (1782–1857)**
Williamn Havell, the most talented of a large family of artists and engravers, exhibited at the first exhibition of the Old Watercolour Society in 1805. He resigned his membership in 1816 and accompanied Lord Amherst's expedition to China. Havell visited South America and India, where he lived between 1817 and 1825, and toured Italy in 1828–29.

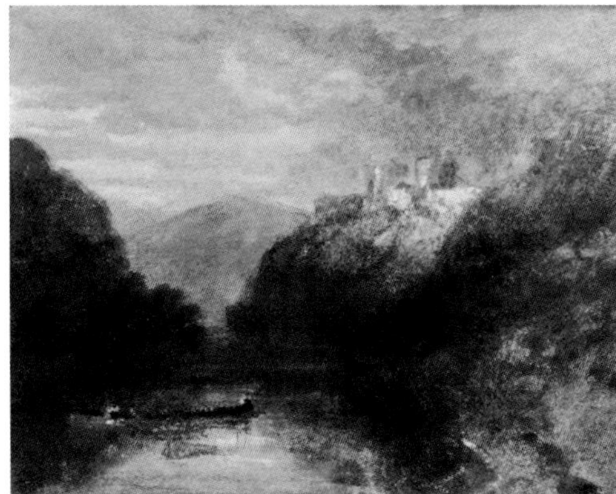

D.1892.124

Cilgerran Castle, Sunset, Pembrokeshire, Wales
pencil, watercolour, bodycolour (heightened with white)
129 × 158 mm
Taylor, John Edward (gift, 1892) (D.1892.124)

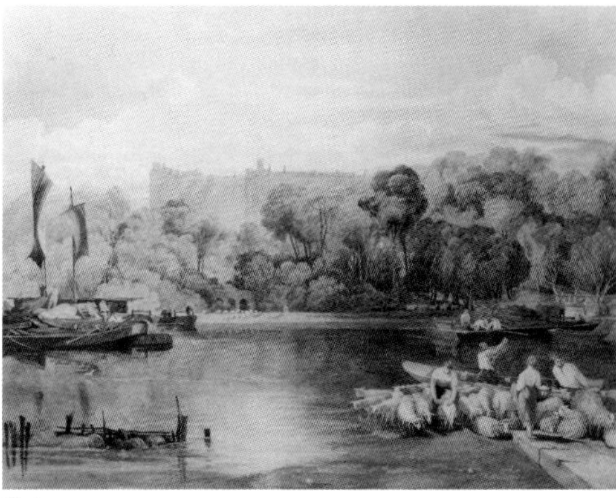

D.1892.125

Windsor Castle from the Thames
pencil, watercolour
382 × 500 mm
Taylor, John Edward (gift, 1892) (D.1892.125)

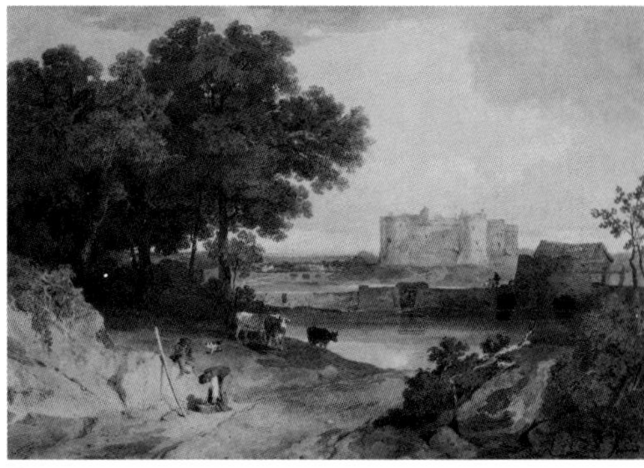

D.1898.2

Carew Castle, Pembrokeshire, Wales, from the Millpond
1805
pencil, watercolour
signed & dated lower left: *W.HAVELL / 1805*
527 × 722 mm
Agnew's (purchase, 20.12.1898) (D.1898.2)

■ **HAWARD, FRANCIS (1759–97)**
Haward engraved a number of paintings by Reynolds and Angelica Kauffmann. He started exhibiting at the Royal Academy in 1783.

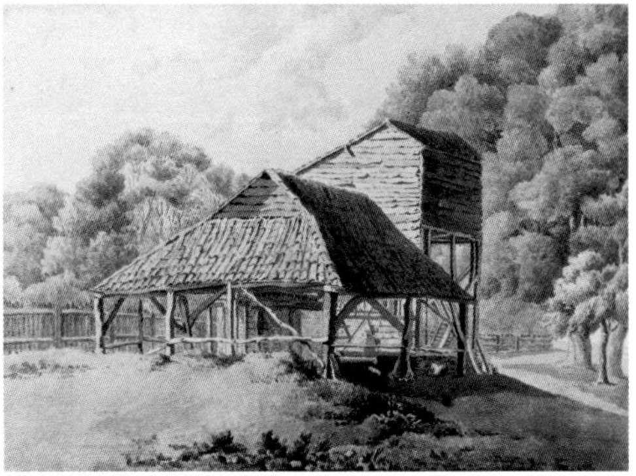

D.1941.1

Old Farm Buildings
pencil, blue watercolour, grey watercolour
231 × 341 mm
Wilson, R. E. A. (purchase, 1941) (D.1941.1)

■ HAYDON, BENJAMIN ROBERT (1786–1846)

Haydon is now best known as a failed history painter. Although he had many pupils, Haydon was perpetually short of money and it was his debts as much as his lack of recognition that led him to commit suicide.

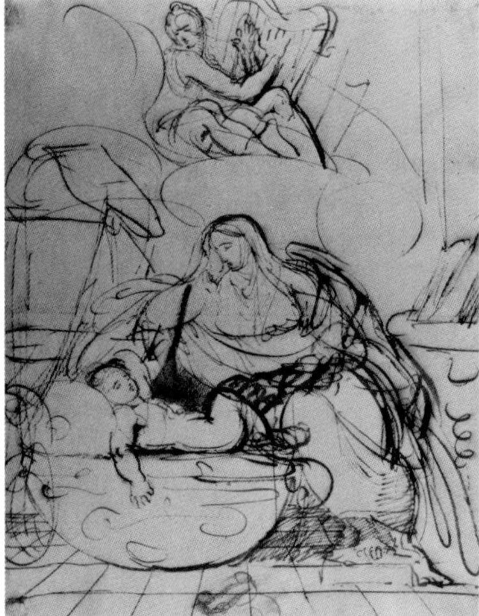

D.1959.7

The Virgin watching the sleeping Christ
pen and brown ink, brown watercolour
404 × 316 mm
Friends of the Whitworth (gift, 1959) (D.1959.7)

Study of Figures for 'Macbeth' (recto); Sketches for the Composition of 'Macbeth' (verso)
1808–11
pen and brown ink
inscribed lower right in later hand: *For Picture of Macbeth / by / Haydon*; inscribed verso vertically along upper right edge: *(1810 for Sir Geo Beaumont)*
180 × 110 mm
University of Manchester, History of Art Department (transfer, 1960) (D.1960.89)

■ HAYES, CLAUDE (1852–1922)

Claude Hayes, son of the artist Edwin, was a painter of country scenes in watercolour which are very much in the Cox-Collier tradition. He was elected a member of the Royal Institute in 1881.

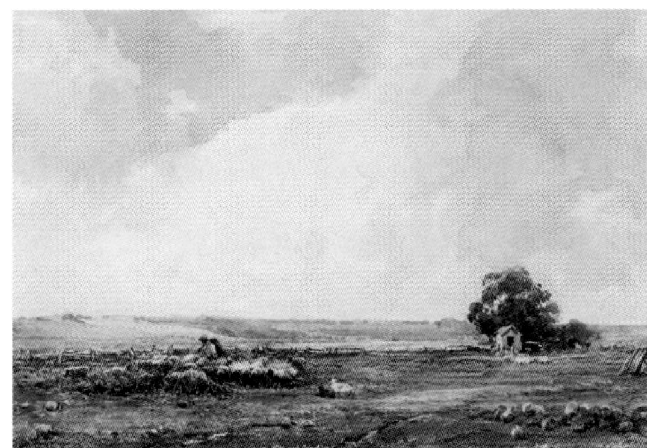

D.1922.5

By the Sheep Pens
watercolour
signed lower left: *Claude Hayes*
383 × 535 mm
Walker's Galleries, London (purchase, 1922) (D.1922.5)

■ HAYMAN, FRANCIS (1708–76)

Hayman was a portrait, genre and history painter, whose works became generally known through his decorations of the supper boxes at Vauxhall Gardens, executed for the owner Jonathan Tyers between 1741 and 1761. Hayman produced conversation pieces, literary subjects and scenes from rural folklore. He was involved in the formation of the Society of Artists in 1760 and was a Founder Member of the Royal Academy.

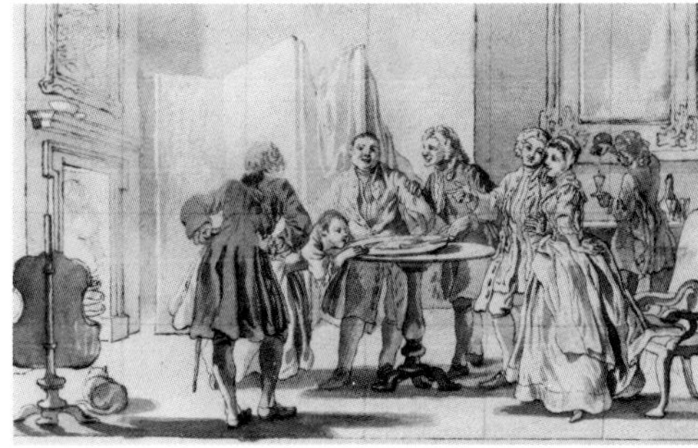

D.1957.13

'The Cutting of Flour', Study for a Supper Box Decoration, Vauxhall Gardens, London
1740–43
pen and brown ink, grey watercolour
141 × 227 mm
Friends of the Whitworth (gift, 1957) (D.1957.13)

■ HAYWARD, JOHN SAMUEL (1778–1822)

Hayward, amateur artist and friend of Joshua Cristall, exhibited figures and landscapes at the Royal Academy between 1798 and 1816. He travelled in Europe and throughout the British Isles. A member of the Sketching Society and an acquaintance of Thomas Girtin, Hayward was also involved in panorama painting.

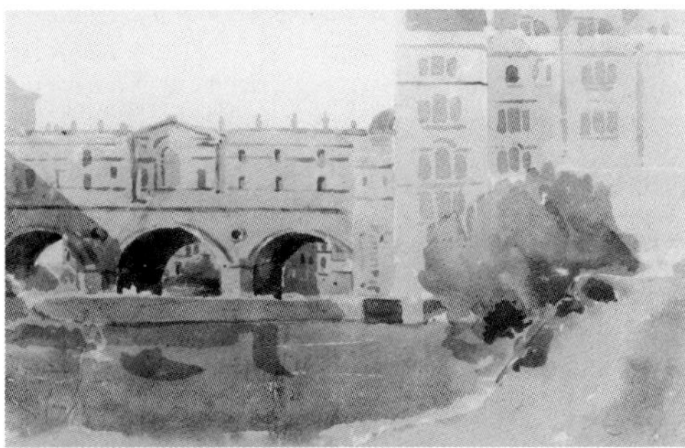

D.1974.9

Pulteney Bridge, Bath
1807
watercolour
171 × 257 mm
Manning Galleries Ltd (purchase, 1974) (D.1974.9)

■ HEARNE, THOMAS (1744–1817)

Hearne was apprenticed to the engraver William Woollett between 1765 and 1771, and was the principal topographical artist of the generation preceding Turner. He was in the West Indies from 1771 to 1774 and is now best known for the watercolours he contributed for engravings in *The Antiquities of Great Britain*, published from 1778. Hugely admired in his day, Hearne was a strong influence on the young Turner.

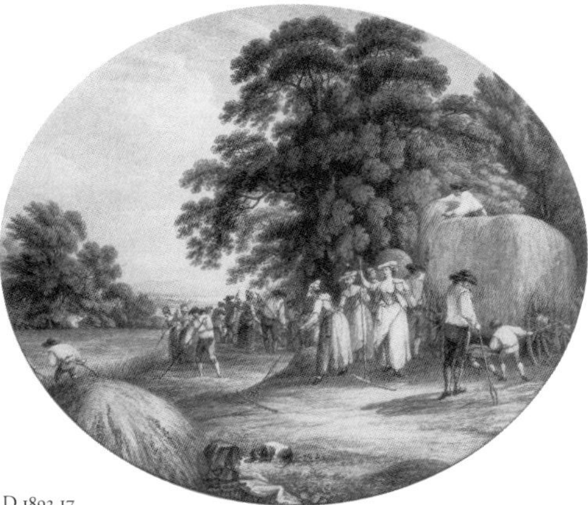

D.1892.17

Summertime: an Illustration to Thomson's 'The Seasons', Book II
1783
pencil, pen and brown ink, watercolour; oval
signed & dated lower centre margin: *Hearne 1783*
283 × 334 mm
Taylor, John Edward (gift, 1892) (D.1892.17)

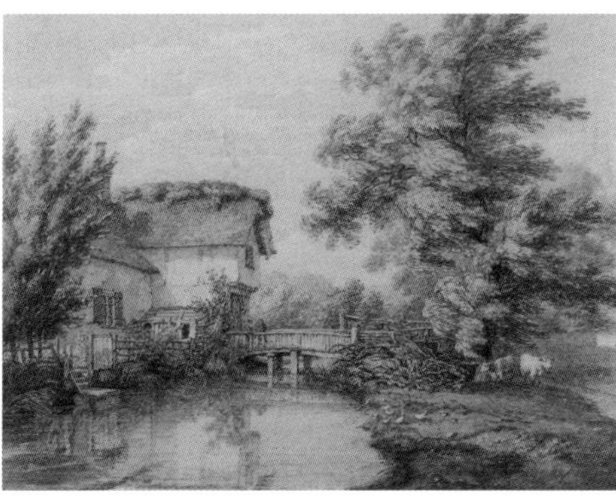

D.1892.18

The Cake House, Hyde Park, London
1798
pencil, watercolour
signed lower left: *Hearne*
233 × 304 mm
Taylor, John Edward (gift, 1892) (D.1892.18)

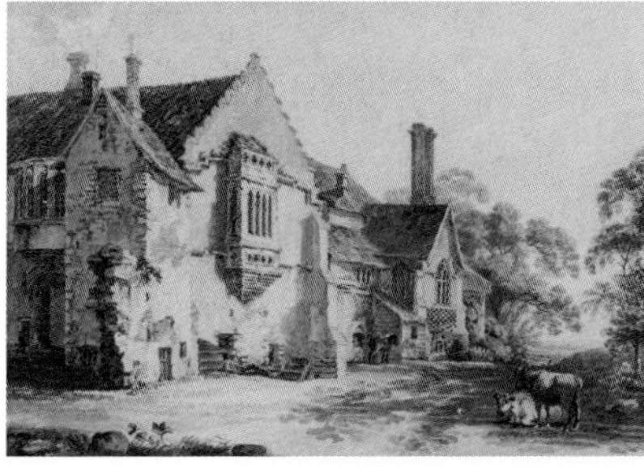

D.1892.19

Castle Acre Priory, Norfolk
1771
pencil, watercolour
signed lower right: *Hearne*
inscribed lower half of verso in later hand: *Castle Acre Priory / Norfolk* [underlined] – / *Drawing made in / 1771* [underlined] / *by THearne* [surname underlined] / *May 1843 – / Engraved in / Hearnes & Byrnes Antiquities / of Great Britain* [cut]
151 × 222 mm
Taylor, John Edward (gift, 1892) (D.1892.19)

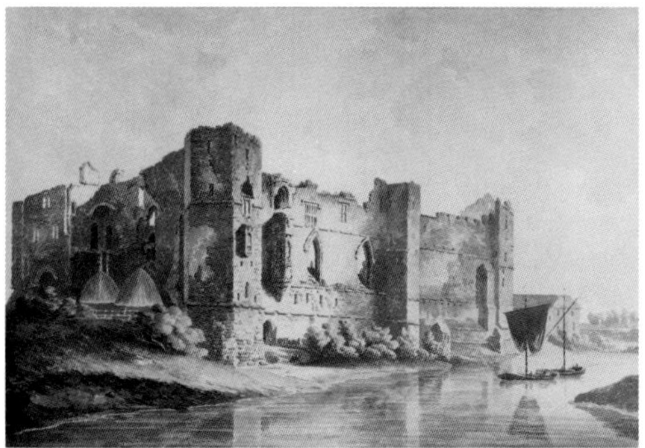

D.1894.10

Newark Castle, Nottinghamshire, from the North West
pencil, watercolour
inscribed lower centre verso with name of
previous owner: *Henderson*
362 × 518 mm
Lees, Charles E. (gift, 1894) (D.1894.10)

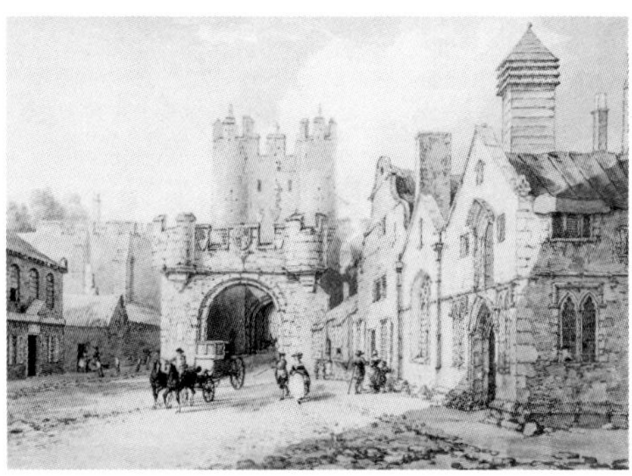

D.1900.2

Micklegate Bar and the Hospital of St Thomas, York
1777
pencil, pen and grey ink, watercolour
184 × 257 mm
Worthington, Mary (gift, 1900) (D.1900.2)

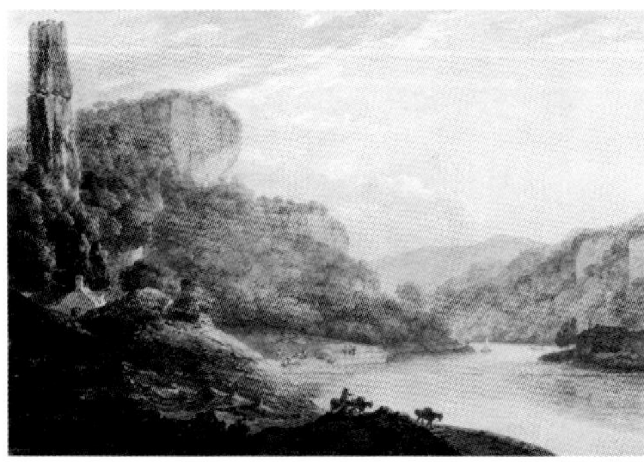

D.1924.81

Symonds Yat on the River Wye, Herefordshire
pencil, watercolour
signed lower left: *Hearne*
242 × 346 mm
Broadhurst, Sir Edward Tootal, Broadhurst, Lady
(bequest, 1924) (D.1924.81)

The Watermill
pencil, watercolour
signed lower left: *Hearne*
146 × 214 mm
Towlson, Hector J. (bequest, 1969) (D.1970.43)

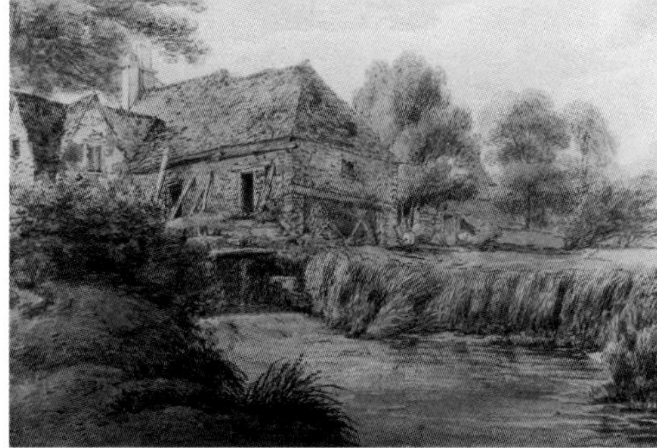

D.1970.43

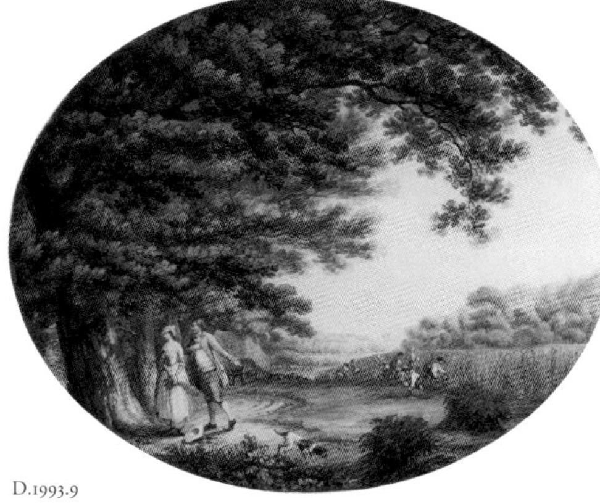

D.1993.9

Autumn (Palemon and Lavinia): an Illustration to Thomson's 'The Seasons', Book III
1783
pencil, pen and brown ink, watercolour; oval
270 × 326 mm
Richmond Gallery, Agnew's (via) (purchase, 1993)
(V. & A., F.O.W.) (D.1993.9)

The Island of Montserrat from the Road before the Town
1775–76
pen and brown ink, watercolour, bodycolour
(heightened with white); two joined sheets of paper
signed (?) lower left, not artist's hand (?): *THearn* (sic)
527 × 1512 mm
Christie's, London (purchase, 15.7.1994) (V. & A., N.A.C.F.,
F.O.W.) (D.1994.10)

St. Christopher's: The Salt Pond, Part of St. Christopher's and Nevis from the Shore at Basseterre
1775–76
pen and brown ink, watercolour, bodycolour
(heightened with white); two joined sheets of paper
527 × 1505 mm
Christie's, London (purchase, 15.7.1994) (V. & A., N.A.C.F.,
F.O.W.) (D.1994.11)

■ HEATON, BUTLER AND BAYNE (workshop of)

Design for a stained Glass Window: Christ blessing the Children
pencil, pen and brown ink, watercolour
455 × 283 mm
University of Manchester, History of Art Department
(transfer, 1960) (D.1960.68)

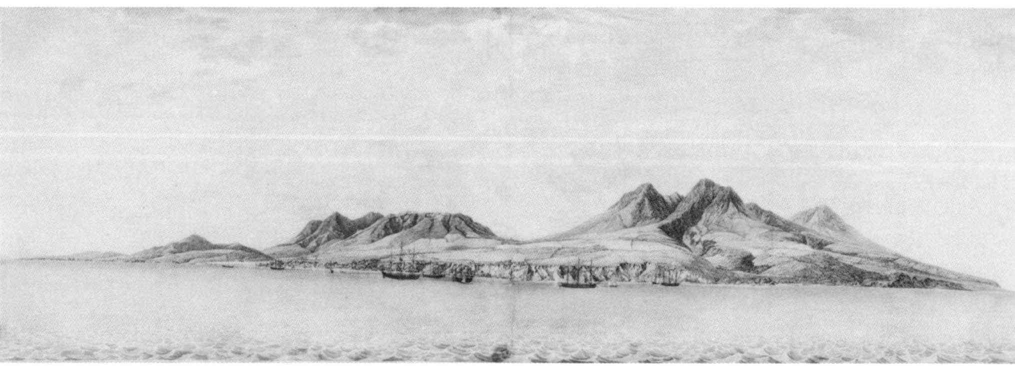

D.1994.10

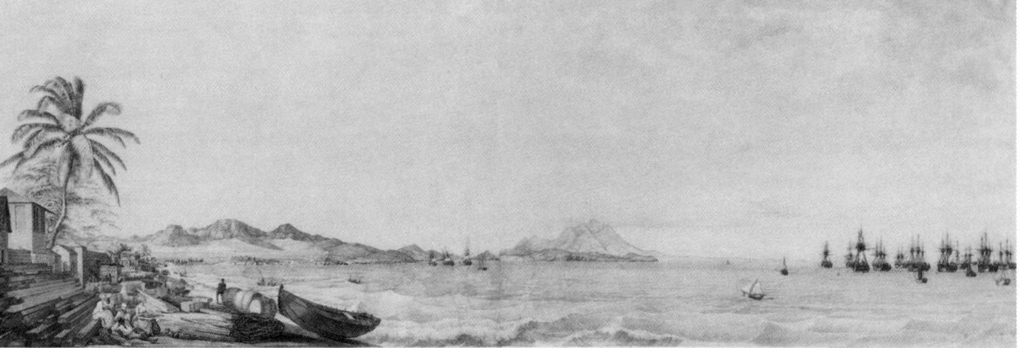

D.1994.11

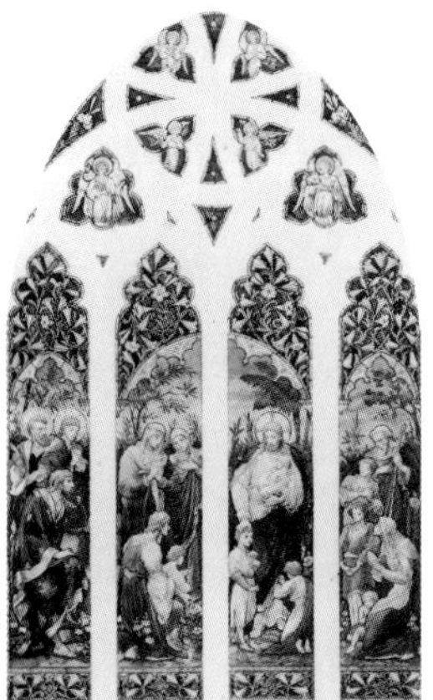

D.1960.68

■ HENDERSON, CHARLES COOPER (1803–77)

Charles Cooper Henderson, son of the amateur artist and collector John, was a prolific painter of sporting, particularly coaching, subjects.

The Start
pencil, pen and brown ink, watercolour
brown paper signed lower left with monogram:
CHC [last letter reversed]
146 × 209 mm
Towlson, Hector J. (bequest, 1969) (D.1970.44)

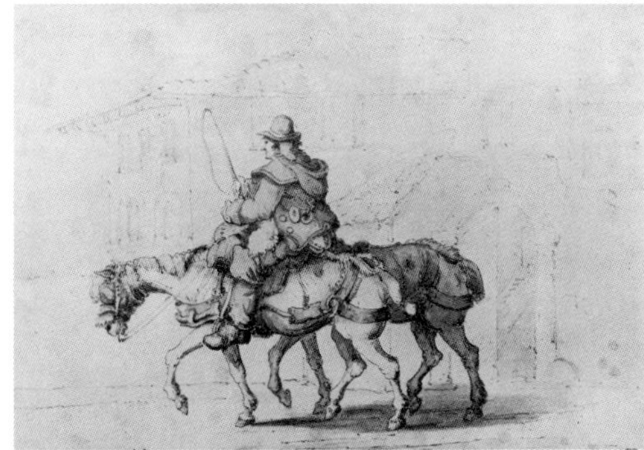

D.1970.45

The Return
pencil, pen and brown ink, watercolour; brown paper
signed lower right: *monogram CHC* [last letter reversed]
146 × 208 mm
Towlson, Hector J. (bequest, 1969) (D.1970.45)

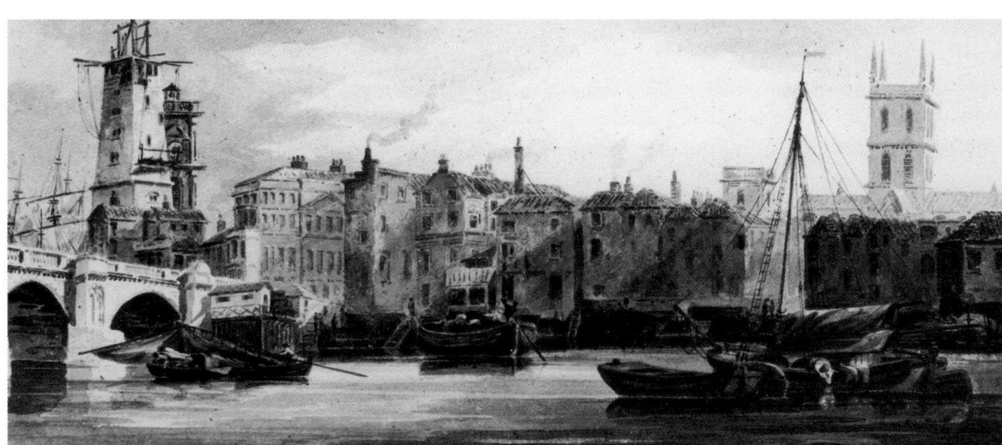

D.1892.78

■ HENDERSON, JOHN (1764–1843)

Henderson, an amateur artist, was a neighbour of Dr Monro in the 1790s and therefore came into contact with the young Girtin and Turner at Monro's house. He provided some of the prototypes for the copyists to work from. Henderson's drawings are sometimes mistaken for those of more important artists.

Old London Bridge, Southwark
pencil, watercolour
191 × 429 mm
Taylor, John Edward (gift, 1892) (D.1892.78)

Shipbuilder's Yard
pencil
443 × 562 mm
Ogden, William Sharp (bequest, 1926) (D.1926.206)

■ HENRY, GEORGE (1858–1943)

Henry studied at the Glasgow School of Art and was one of the founders of the Glasgow School. Elected a member of the Royal Scottish Academy in 1902 and the Royal Academy in 1920, he shared a studio with his friend Edward Atkinson Hornel, with whom he visited Japan in 1893–94. Henry worked mainly in Glasgow until 1901 when he moved to London.

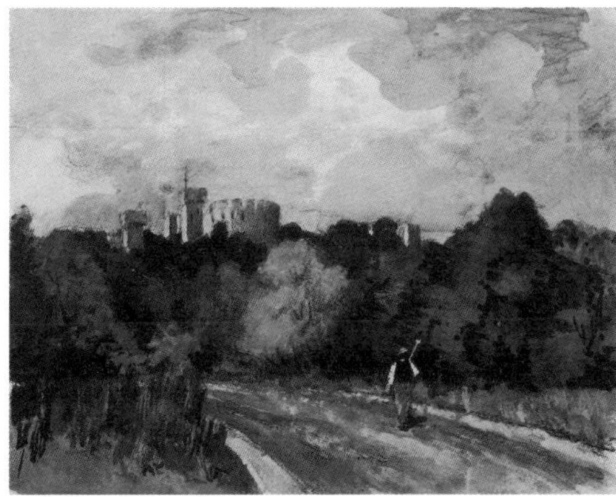

D.1945.3

Arundel Castle, Sussex
pencil, watercolour, bodycolour (heightened with white); grey paper
inscribed with colour notes in left and right margins
200 × 251 mm
Henry, George (Trustees of) (gift, 1945) (D.1945.3)

■ HENSHAW, FREDERICK HENRY (1807–91)

Henshaw was based in Birmingham but visited the Continent in 1837 and remained there for three years touring France, Germany, Italy and Switzerland. He painted landscapes, portraits and genre scenes in oil and watercolour.

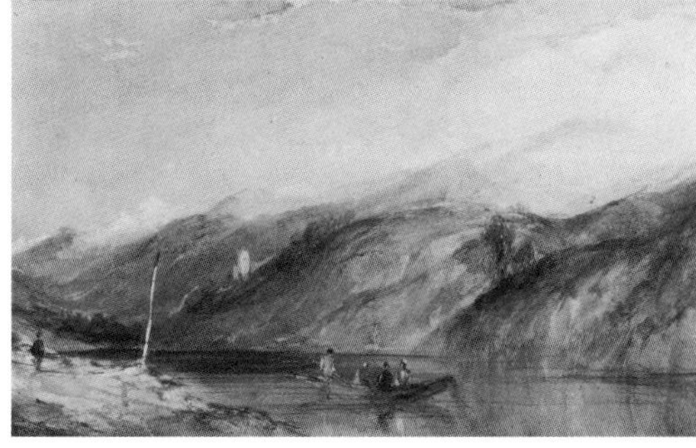

D.1970.46

Swiss Lake Scene
watercolour, bodycolour (heightened with white)
131 × 206 mm
Towlson, Hector J. (bequest, 1969) (D.1970.46)

■ HERALD, JAMES WATTERSON (1859–1914)

Herald was born in Forfar and studied at Dundee and Edinburgh before moving south to Herkomer's School of Art at Bushey; he then returned north and settled in Arbroath. Herald was a prolific painter of coastal and harbour scenes.

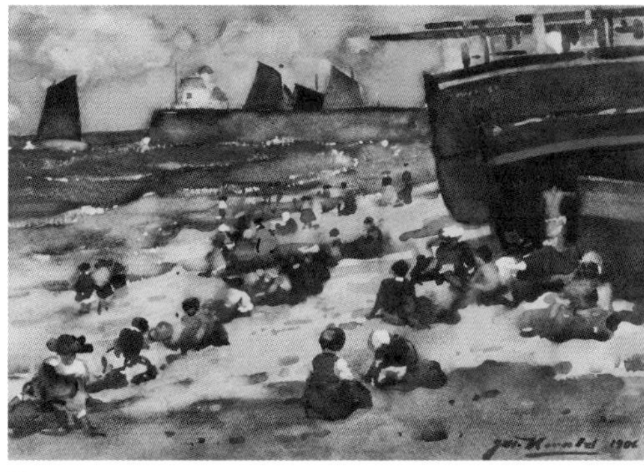

D.1912.4

Children on the Beach
1904
watercolour, bodycolour (heightened with white)
signed & dated lower right: *J W.Herald 1904*
259 × 361 mm
Anderson, A. E. (gift, 1912) (D.1912.4)

On the Sea Shore
watercolour
180 × 241 mm
Anderson, A. E. (gift, 1912) (D.1912.5)

The White Horse
watercolour
183 × 263 mm
Anderson, A. E. (gift, 1915) (D.1915.8)

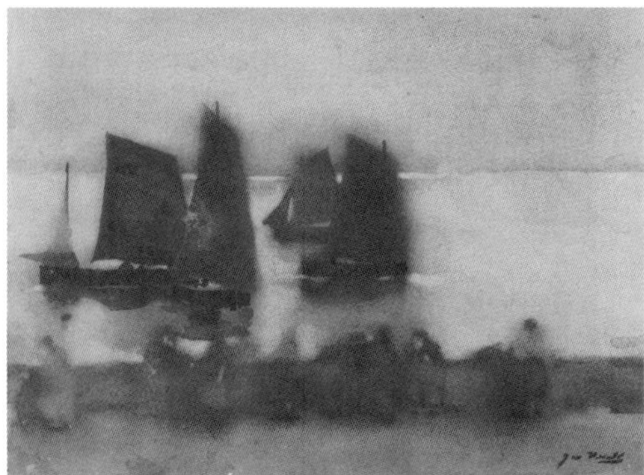

D.1915.9

Fishing Boats
watercolour
signed lower right: *J W Herald*
268 × 359 mm
Anderson, A. E. (gift, 1915) (D.1915.9)

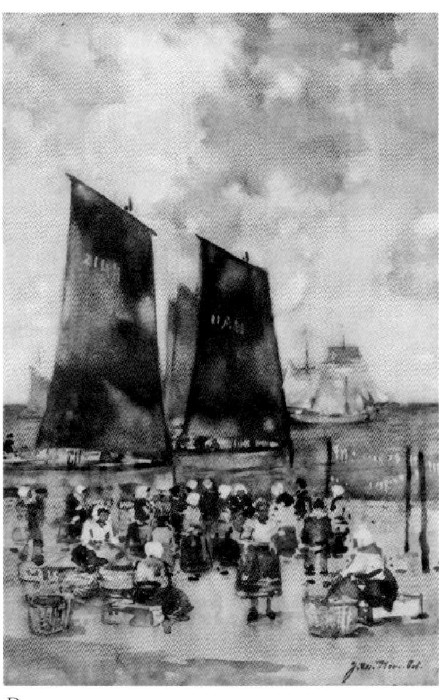

D.1921.12

The Herring Fishers
watercolour, bodycolour (heightened with white)
signed lower right: *J. W. Herald*
490 × 316 mm
Anderson, A. E. (gift, 1921) (D.1921.12)

■ HERBERT, ALFRED (attributed to)
(1819/21–61)
A marine and coastal painter who exhibited at the
Royal Academy and elsewhere from 1844 to 1860.

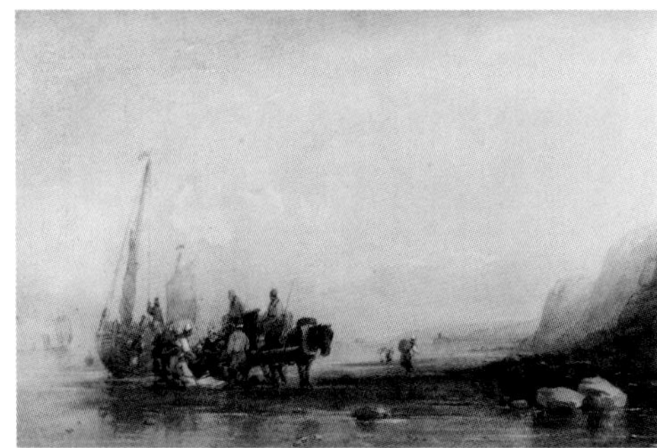

D.1970.15

**A Scene on the French Coast with Fishermen
unloading their Catch**
pencil, watercolour
214 × 313 mm
Towlson, Hector J. (bequest, 1969) (D.1970.15)

■ HERDMAN, WILLIAM GAVIN (1805–82)
Herdman was an art master from Liverpool who
exhibited a few paintings at the Royal Academy
between 1834 and 1861. He was a regular exhibitor at
the Liverpool Academy until resigning in protest at
Pre-Raphaelitism. He specialised in Liverpool, Cheshire
and North Wales topography.

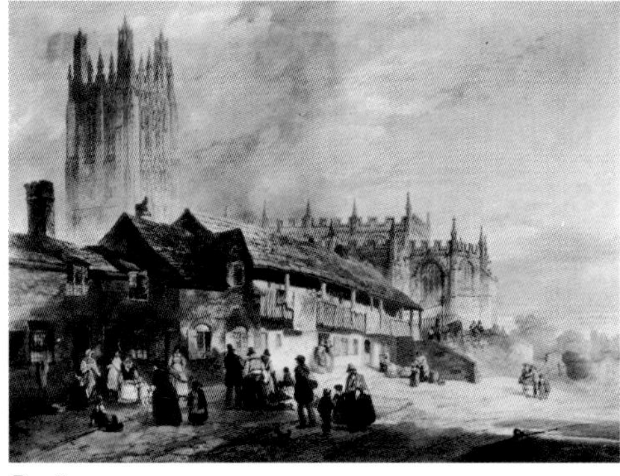

D.1918.4

St Giles Church, Wrexham, Denbighshire, Wales
1850
pencil, watercolour
signed & dated lower right: *W.G.Herdman.1850*
561 × 761 mm
Grantham, William (bequest, 1918) (D.1918.4)

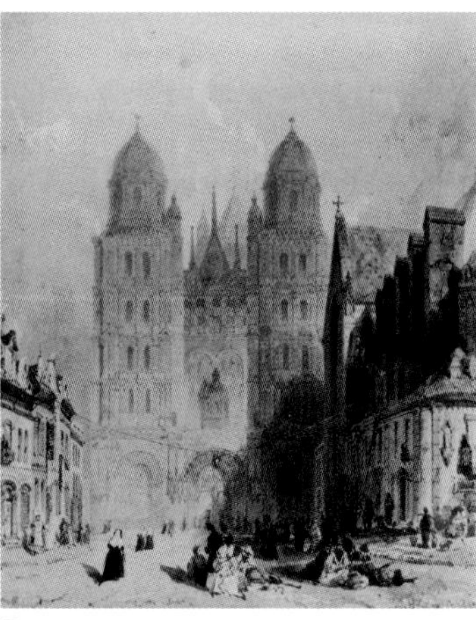

D.1970.47

West Front, Church of St Michael, Dijon, France
brown watercolour, bodycolour (heightened with
white); buff paper
signed & inscribed lower right: *Dijon / W.G.Herdman.*
340 × 270 mm
Towlson, Hector J. (bequest, 1969) (D.1970.47)

■ HERIOT, GEORGE (1766–1844)
Heriot, an amateur artist, was a pupil of Paul Sandby
at Woolwich. From 1799 to 1816 he was Deputy
Postmaster General of Canada, after which time he
travelled extensively on the Continent. He exhibited
Canadian views in London and published *Travels
through Canada* in 1807.

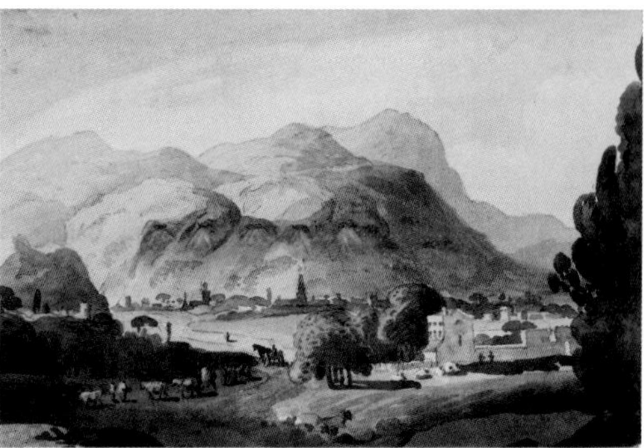

D.1950.3

Vents of the airy Caverns, Italy
pencil, watercolour
inscribed below image on mount: *View in Italy. Vents of
the airy Caverns*
171 × 248 mm
Pilkington, Margaret (gift, 1950) (D.1950.3)

■ HERRING, JOHN FREDERICK
(1795–1865)
Herring began his career as an animal and coach
painter and later turned to horse portraiture. He was a
member of the Society of British Artists from 1841. The
work of his son and namesake is remarkably similar.

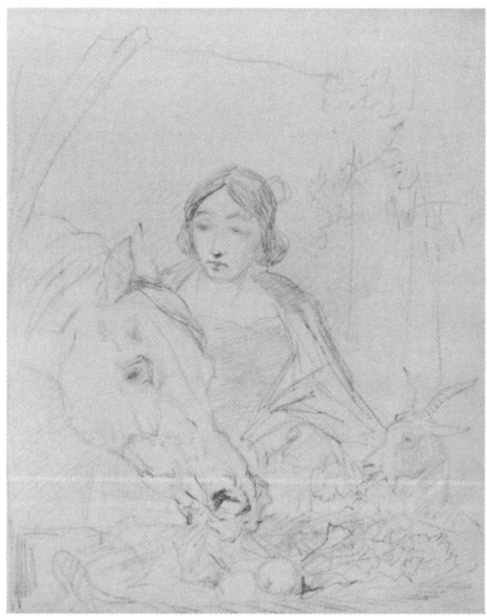

D.1926.209

A Woman with a Horse and a Goat
1851
pencil
signed & dated upper right with monogram: *JH / 1851*
280 × 225 mm
Ogden, William Sharp (bequest, 1926) (D.1926.209)

■ HERVE, FRANCIS (fl. 1818–40)
Herve was a miniature painter of whom little is known.

Portrait of Samuel Hesse
watercolour, bodycolour
98 × 81 mm
Langdon, Margaret (gift, 1977) (D.1977.6)

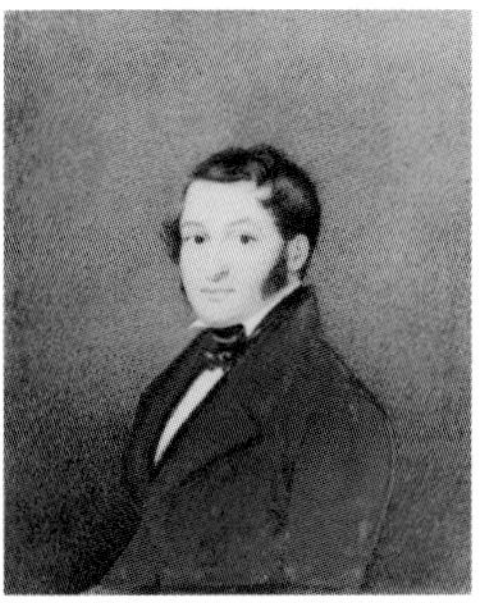

D.1977.6

■ HIBBERT, WILLIAM (fl. 1760–1800)

Unknown amateur artist.

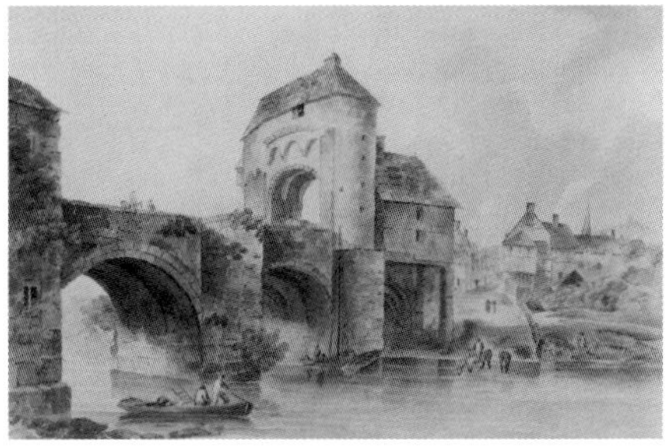

D.1892.144

**Monnow Bridge, Monmouth,
Monmouthshire, Wales**
pencil, watercolour
283 × 477 mm
Taylor, John Edward (gift, 1892) (D.1892.144)

■ HILLS, ROBERT (1769–1844)

Hills, a founder member of the Old Watercolour
Society, was a prolific painter of animals. He
made only one journey abroad – in 1815 – when
he toured Belgium, Holland and Flanders. His
drawings are often inscribed in shorthand. Hills
sometimes collaborated with George Fennel
Robson, painting animals in his landscapes.

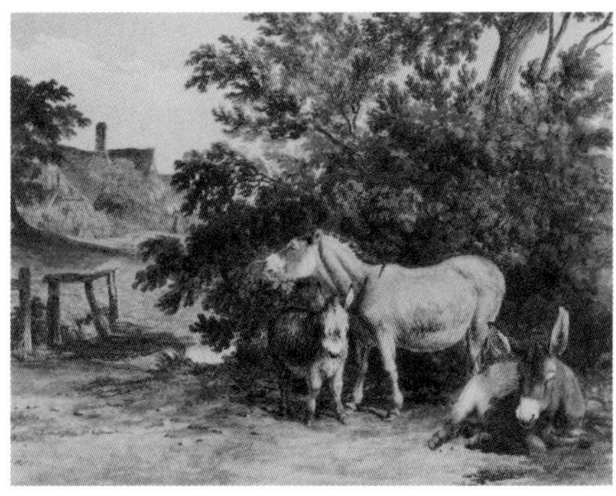

D.1887.4

Landscape with Donkeys
1814
pencil, watercolour
signed & dated lower left: *Robt. Hills. 1814.*
410 × 508 mm
Agnew's (purchase, 22.6.1891) (D.1887.4)

Study of Cows
pencil, watercolour
83 × 121 mm
Holliday, J. R. (bequest, 1927) (D.1927.117)

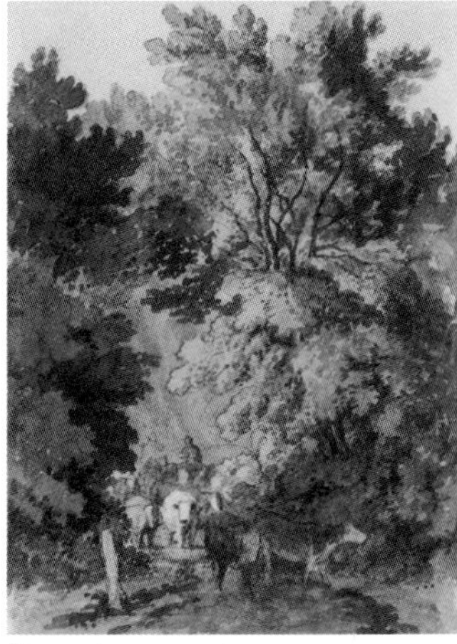

D.1927.118

Cows in a Lane followed by Oxen
pencil, watercolour
118 × 84 mm
Holliday, J. R. (bequest, 1927) (D.1927.118)

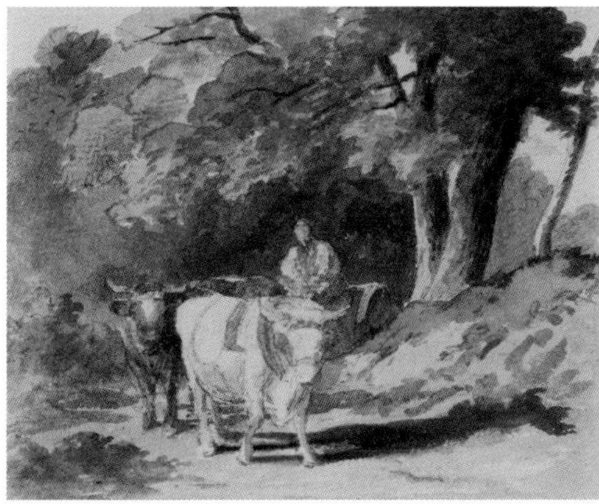

D.1927.119

Landscape with a Wagon pulled by Oxen
pencil, watercolour
129 × 154 mm
Holliday, J. R. (bequest, 1927) (D.1927.119)

Farmyard with Donkeys
pencil, watercolour
132 × 119 mm
Holliday, J. R. (bequest, 1927) (D.1927.120)

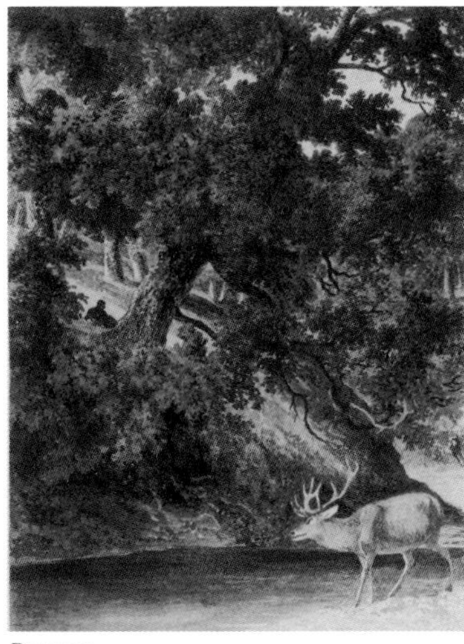

D.1927.121

Jaques and the wounded Stag
pencil, watercolour
197 × 143 mm
Holliday, J. R. (bequest, 1927) (D.1927.121)

Study of Cows
pencil, watercolour
94 × 148 mm
Holliday, J. R. (bequest, 1927) (D.1927.122)

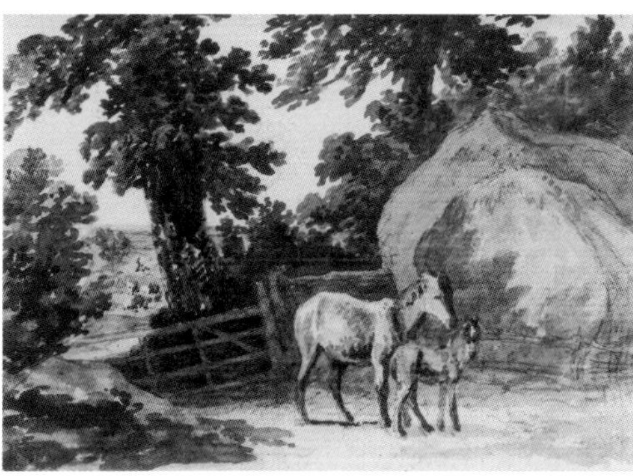

D.1927.123

A Horse and Foal by a Hayrick
pencil, watercolour
115 × 158 mm
Holliday, J. R. (bequest, 1927) (D.1927.123)

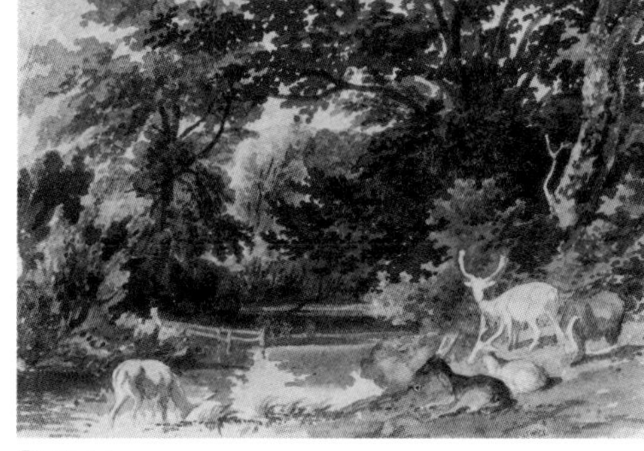

D.1927.124

River Scene with Deer
pencil, watercolour
118 × 165 mm
Holliday, J. R. (bequest, 1927) (D.1927.124)

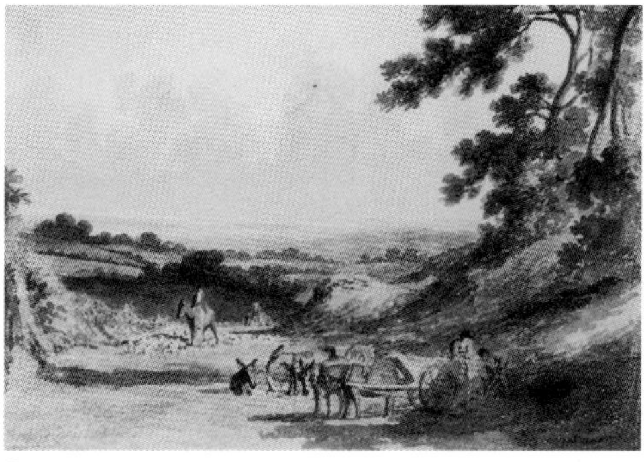

D.1927.125

Landscape with Donkeys and a Hunt
pencil, watercolour
inscribed lower centre verso name of patron (?):
Mr. Waite
128 × 180 mm
Holliday, J. R. (bequest, 1927) (D.1927.125)

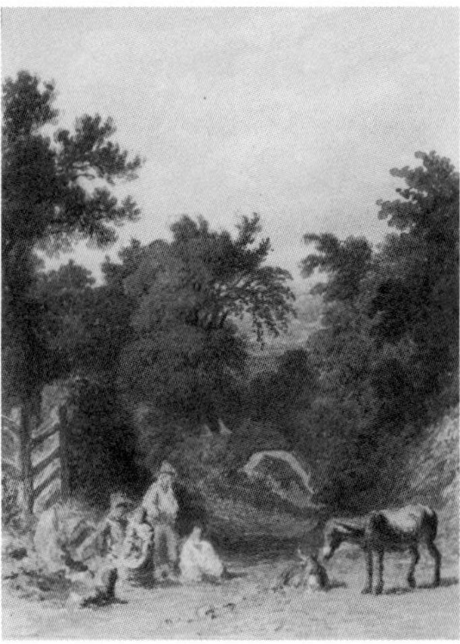

D.1927.126

Children in a Lane with a Donkey
pencil, watercolour
149 × 110 mm
Holliday, J. R. (bequest, 1927) (D.1927.126)

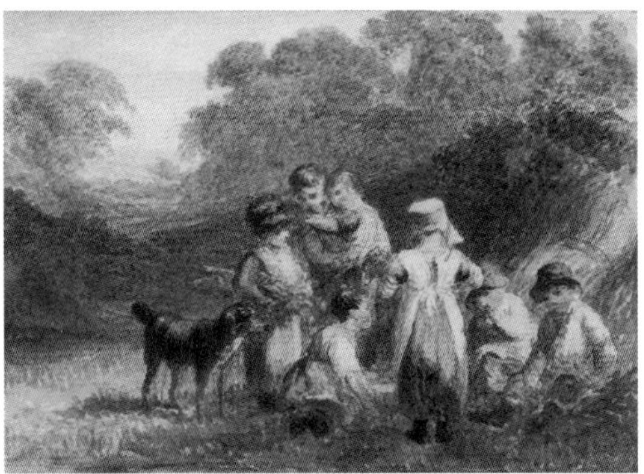

D.1927.127

Children in a Cornfield
pencil, watercolour
94 × 127 mm
Holliday, J. R. (bequest, 1927) (D.1927.127)

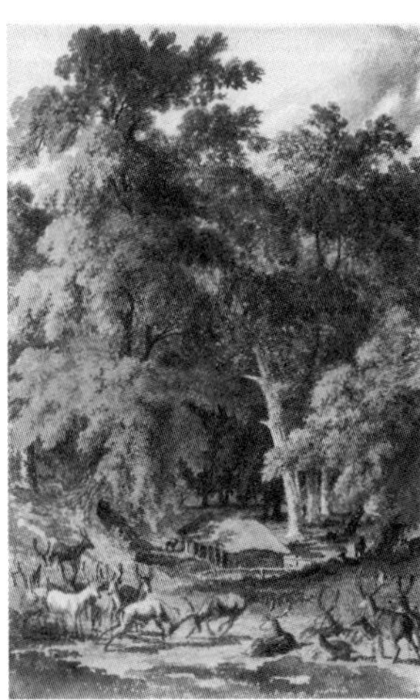

D.1927.128

Stags fighting in Knole Park
pencil, watercolour
inscribed lower centre verso name of patron (?):
Mr. J Garle [name hard to read]
226 × 143 mm
Holliday, J. R. (bequest, 1927) (D.1927.128)

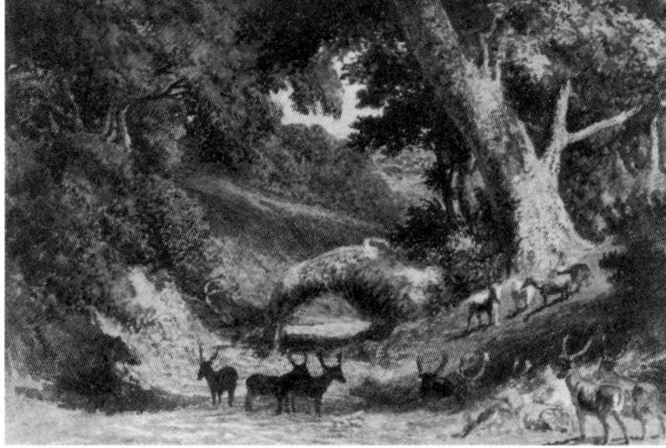

D.1927.129

Landscape with Deer by a Stream among Trees
pencil, watercolour
114 × 167 mm
Holliday, J. R. (bequest, 1927) (D.1927.129)

Study of a Cow
pencil, watercolour
inscribed lower left in the artist's shorthand
193 × 160 mm
Holliday, J. R. (bequest, 1927) (D.1927.130)

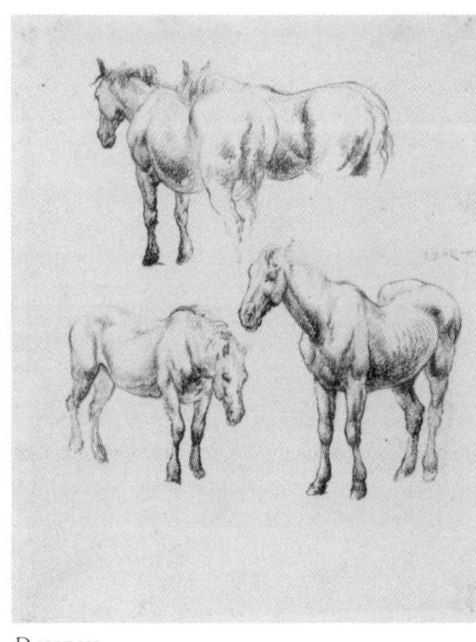

D.1927.131

Studies of Horses
pencil
inscribed centre right in the artist's shorthand
242 × 191 mm
Holliday, J. R. (bequest, 1927) (D.1927.131)

Study of a Cow
pencil
140 × 201 mm
Holliday, J. R. (bequest, 1927) (D.1927.132)

Study of a Bull (recto); Study of a Calf (verso)
pencil, watercolour (recto)
inscribed upper right (recto) in artist's shorthand
152 × 189 mm
Holliday, J. R. (bequest, 1927) (D.1927.133)

Studies of Cattle, a Wagon and a Gate
pencil
238 × 187 mm
Holliday, J. R. (bequest, 1927) (D.1927.134)

Studies of a Bull and Cattle
pencil
235 × 220 mm
Holliday, J. R. (bequest, 1927) (D.1927.135)

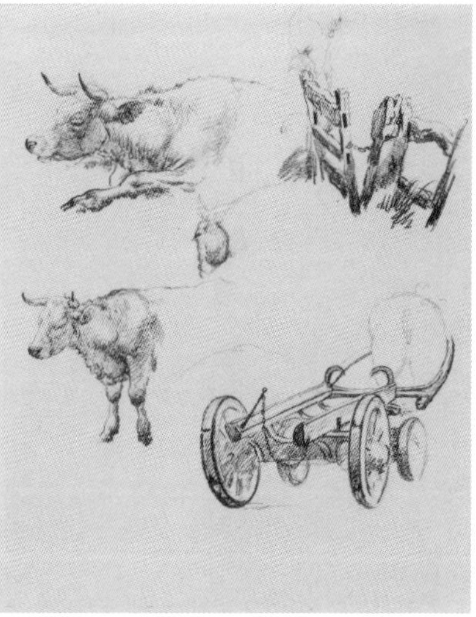

D.1927.134

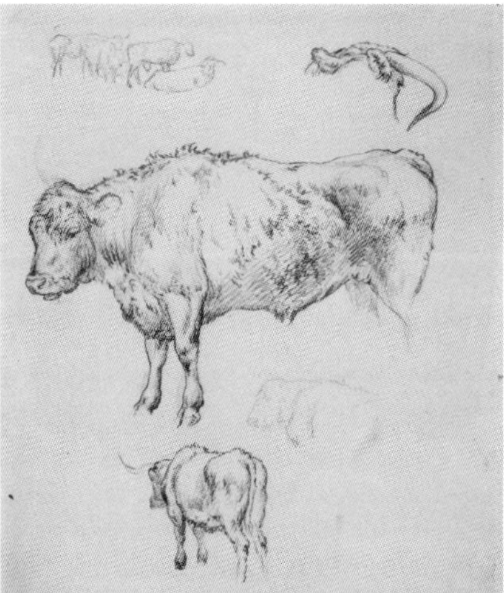

D.1927.135

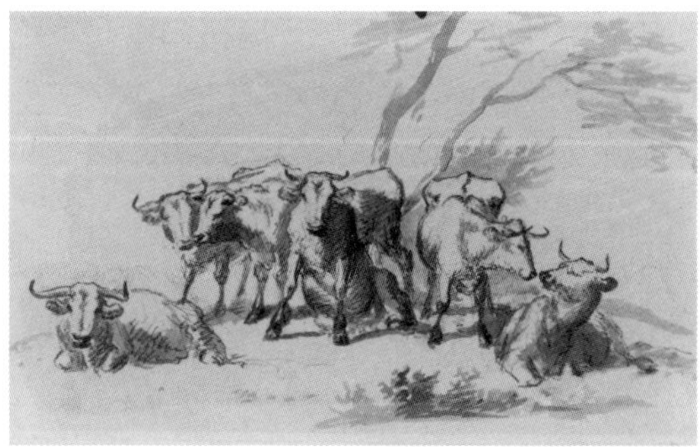

D.1927.136

Studies of Cattle (recto); Studies of Cattle and Sheep (verso)
pencil, grey watercolour (recto)
112 × 179 mm
Holliday, J. R. (bequest, 1927) (D.1927.136)

Studies of Cattle
pencil, grey watercolour
113 × 182 mm
Holliday, J. R. (bequest, 1927) (D.1927.137)

Study of Trees and Water
pencil, grey watercolour
335 × 239 mm
Holliday, J. R. (bequest, 1927) (D.1927.138)

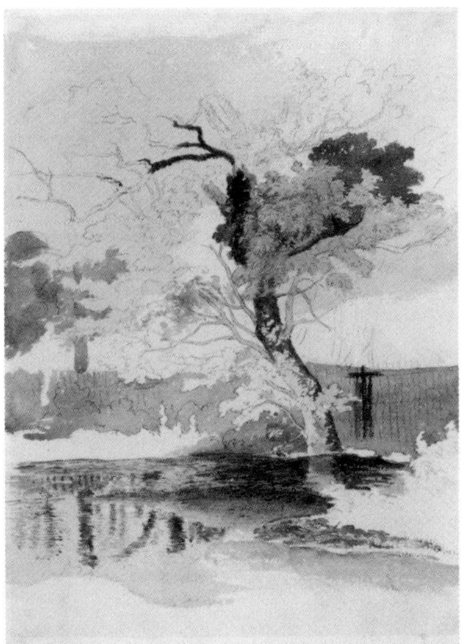

D.1927.138

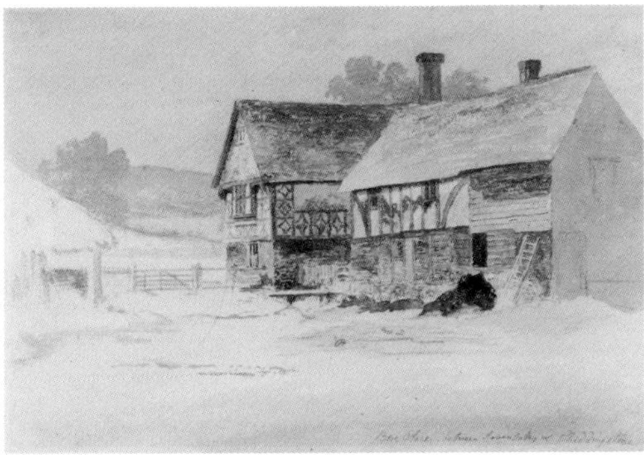

D.1927.139

**Bore Place, between Sevenoaks and
Chiddingstone, Kent**
pencil, grey watercolour; buff paper
inscribed lower right: *Bore Place between
Seven Oaks & Chiddingstone*
166 × 236 mm
Holliday, J. R. (bequest, 1927) (D.1927.139)

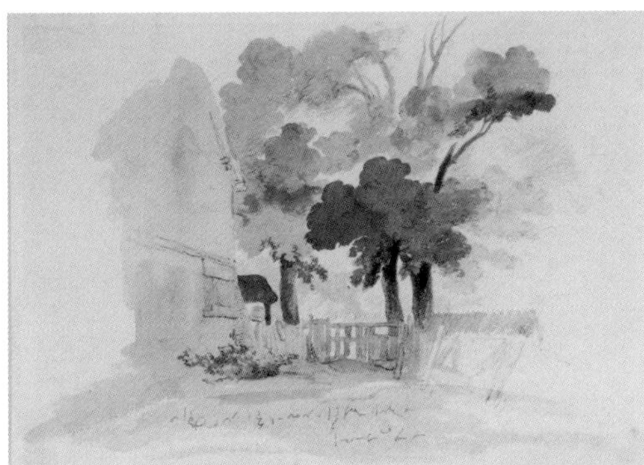

D.1927.140

Farm Buildings with Trees
pencil, grey watercolour, brown watercolour
inscribed lower centre in artist's shorthand
192 × 266 mm
Holliday, J. R. (bequest, 1927) (D.1927.140)

Study of a House
pencil, grey watercolour; buff paper
172 × 231 mm
Holliday, J. R. (bequest, 1927) (D.1927.141)

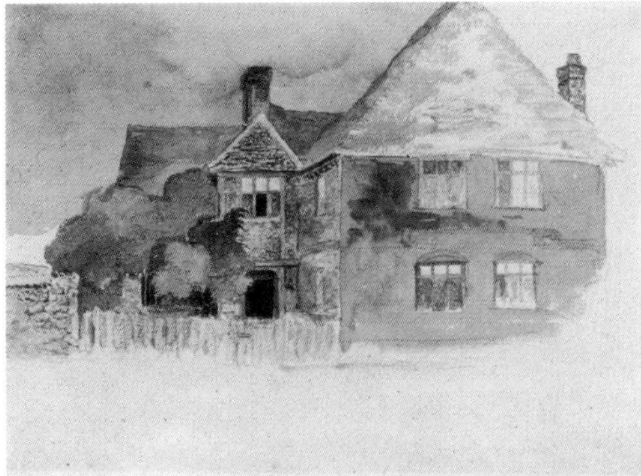

D.1927.141

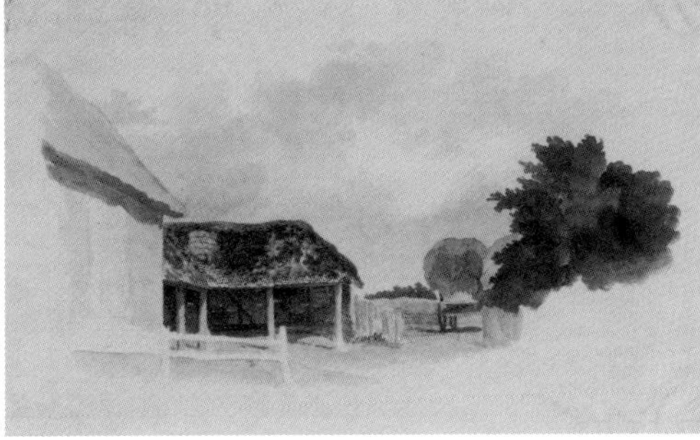

D.1927.142

Ivy House Farm
pencil, grey watercolour
inscribed lower right in the artist's shorthand; inscribed
lower right below shorthand: *Ivy House Farm* [followed
by two illegible words the second beginning 'Bo–']
184 × 290 mm
Holliday, J. R. (bequest, 1927) (D.1927.142)

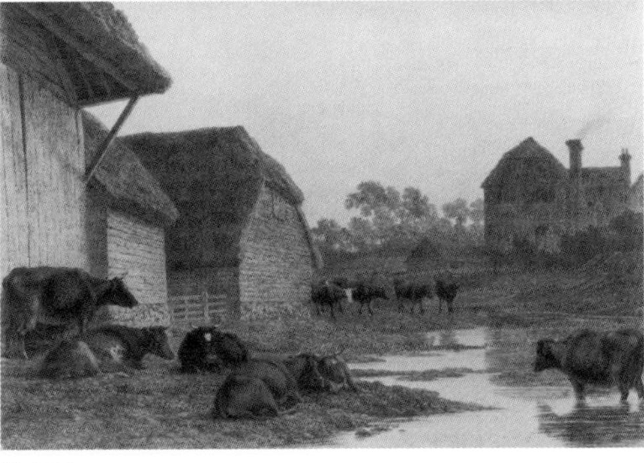

D.1939.2

Farmyard with Cattle
1821
watercolour
signed & dated lower left: *RHills 1821*
inscribed & numbered lower left verso: *12 Geo Smith /
62 Hamilton Terrace / St John's Wood*
297 × 422 mm
Holliday, Mrs J. R. (bequest, 1939) (D.1939.2)

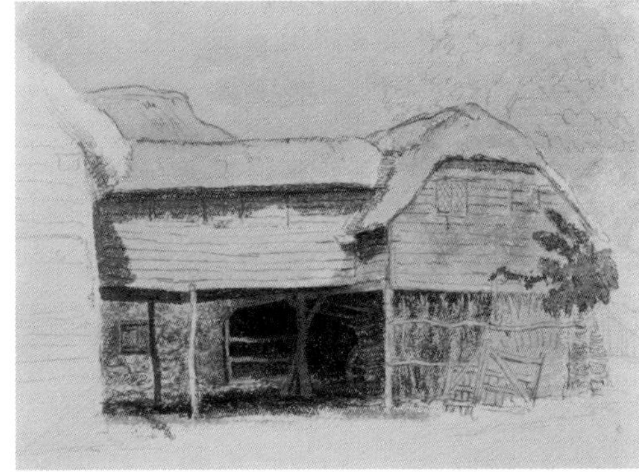

D.1950.22

Farm Buildings
pencil, watercolour
155 × 210 mm
Barlow, Sir Thomas (gift, 1950) (D.1950.22)

■ **HILLS, ROBERT** (follower of)

A Bull and Cow in a Landscape
pen and brown ink, watercolour
434 × 408 mm
Anderson, A. E. (gift, 1916) (D.1916.1)

■ **HINE, HENRY GEORGE** (1811–95)

Hine, a prolific painter of mainly Sussex landscapes,
drew for *Punch* and the *Illustrated London News* from
1841 to 1844. He was elected a member of the New
Watercolour Society in 1864.

Off the Isle of Wight
1865
watercolour
signed & dated lower left: *H.G.HINE 1865*
194 × 467 mm
Anderson, A. E. (gift, 1931) (D.1931.6)

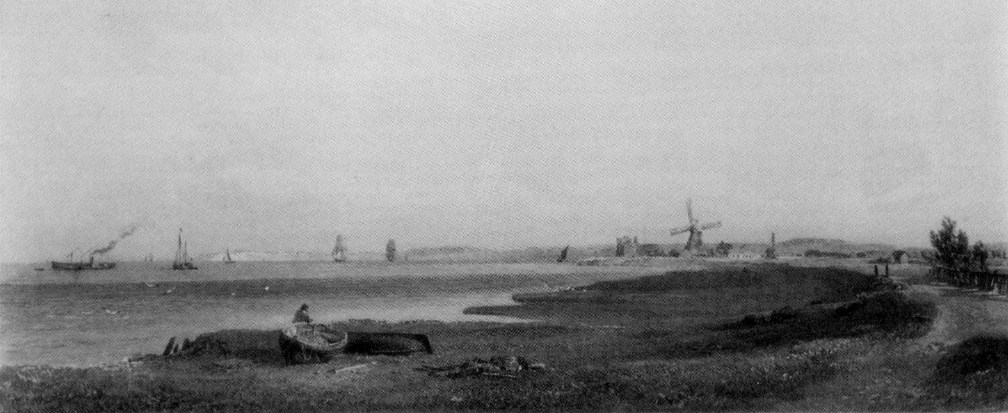

D.1931.6

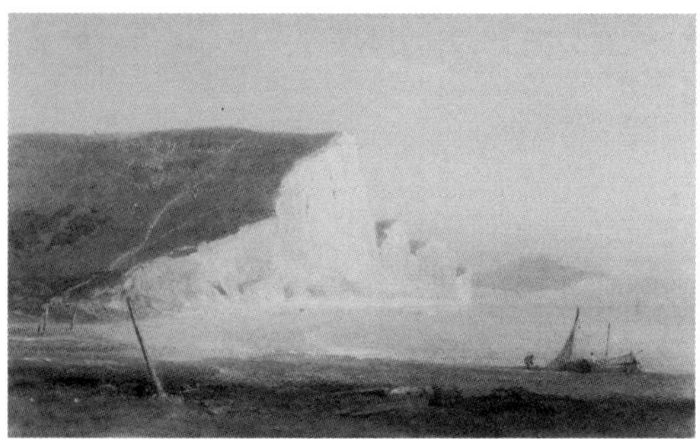

D.1955.10

Cuckmere Haven, Sussex
1876
watercolour
signed & dated lower left: *H G HINE 1876*
266 × 428 mm
Norris, Christopher (gift, 1955) (D.1955.10)

Swanage Bay, Dorset
1871
watercolour
signed & dated lower right: *H.G.HINE 1871*
286 × 584 mm
Norris, Christopher (gift, 1955) (D.1955.11)

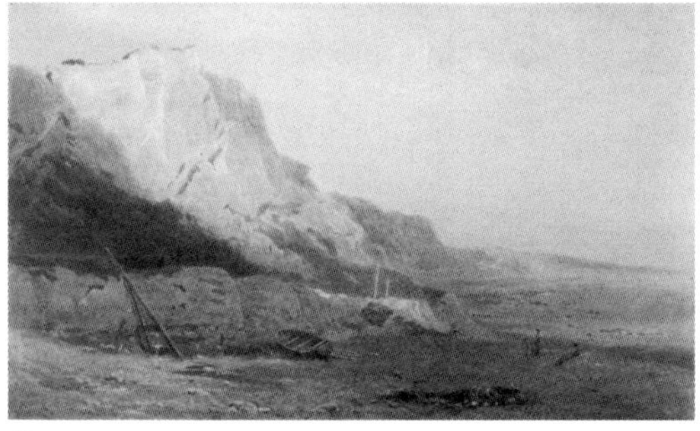

D.1955.12

Holywell, near Eastbourne, Sussex
1888
pencil, watercolour
signed & dated lower left: *H G Hine.1888*
322 × 531 mm
Norris, Christopher (gift, 1955) (D.1955.12)

■ HOLDING, EDGAR THOMAS (1870–1952)

After an early career in business, Edgar Thomas
Holding took up painting, producing landscapes in oil
and watercolour, particularly Sussex subjects. He was
elected a member of the Royal Watercolour Society in
1929 and was Secretary from 1931 to 1948.

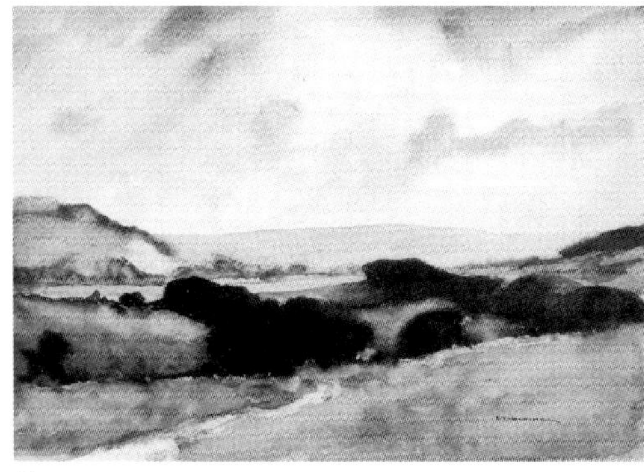

D.1924.30

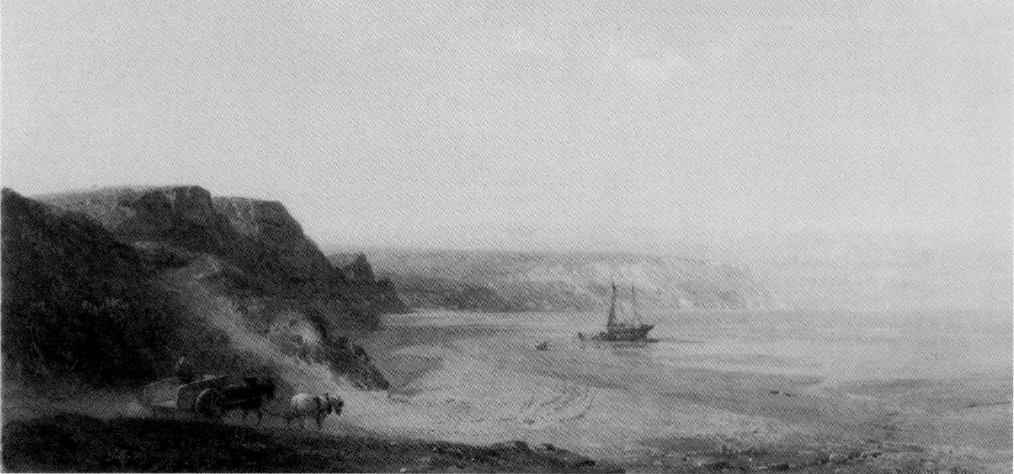

D.1955.11

Landscape, near Waterfield, Sussex
watercolour; grey paper
signed lower right: *E.T.HOLDING.*
250 × 355 mm
Anderson, A. E., National Art Collections Fund (via)
(gift, 1924) (D.1924.30)

■ HOLDING, FREDERICK (1817–74)

Frederick Holding was a Manchester artist who
specialised in Shakespearean subjects.

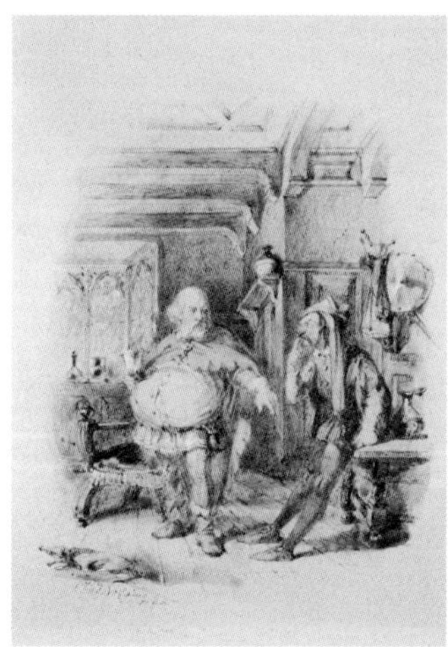

D.1915.12

Vignette of Falstaff and Bardolph
1866
pen and brown ink, watercolour, bodycolour
(heightened with white)
signed & dated lower left: *FredHolding/66*
283 × 204 mm
Reynolds, J. H. (gift, 1915) (D.1915.12)

■ HOLDING, HENRY JAMES (ca. 1833–72)

Henry James Holding, brother of Frederick, specialised
in Tudor scenes and landscapes in oil and watercolour.

**The Steps down to the Garden Terrace, Haddon
Hall, Derbyshire**
pencil, watercolour, bodycolour
(heightened with white)
339 × 510 mm
Cox, G. F. (bequest, 1910) (D.1910.6)

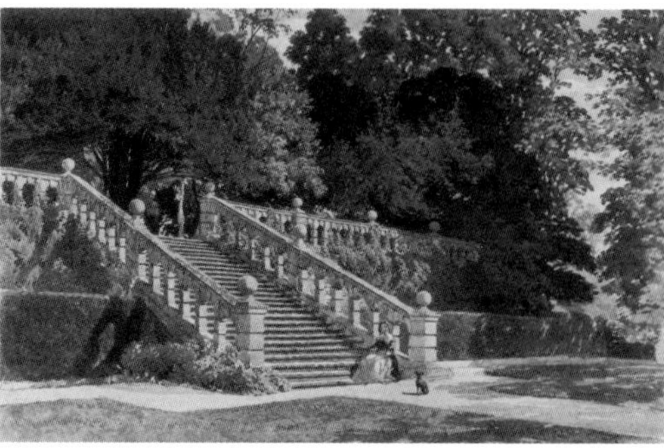

D.1910.6

■ HOLDING, JOHN (1815–99)

John Holding was an amateur artist.

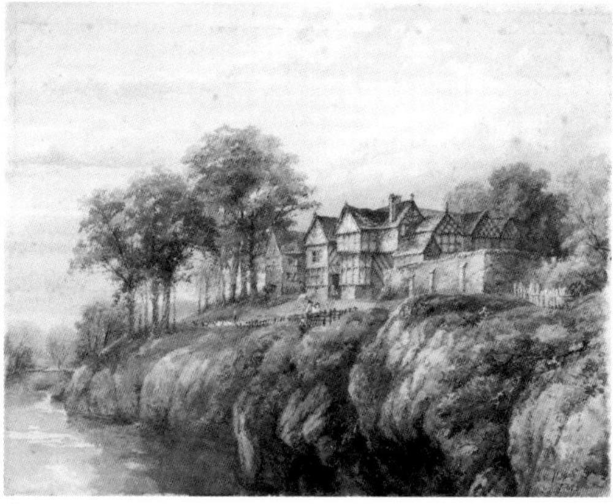

D.1996.16

Hulme Hall in 1835
1872
pencil, watercolour, bodycolour
(heightened with white)
signed and dated lower right: *John Holding / 1872*;
inscribed on label on back of frame: *Hulme Hall in 1835
/ by John Holding*
557 × 698 mm
Bishop, John (gift, 1996) (D.1996.16)

■ HOLLAND, JAMES (1800–1870)

Holland was born in Staffordshire, and began his
career as a flower painter and pottery designer. He
came to London in 1819 and set himself up as a

drawing master. He travelled extensively on the Continent, in particular Portugal and Italy, painting many Venetian and Portuguese subjects. Holland was elected a member of the Old Watercolour Society in 1857, having previously failed to gain membership of the Royal Academy.

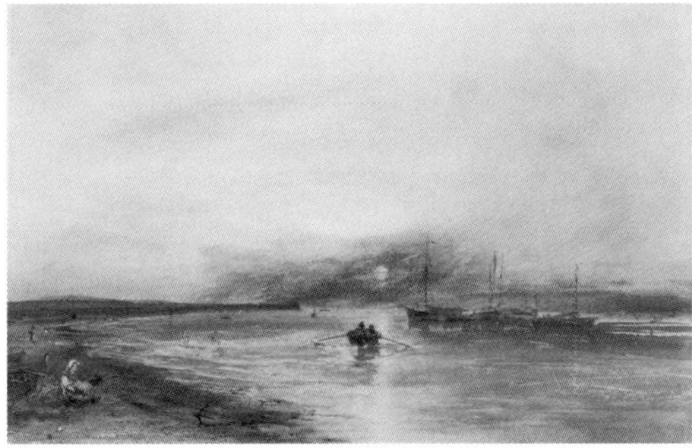

D.1887.45

Sunset on the Italian Coast
1853
watercolour
signed & dated lower left with initial: *H 53*
266 × 410 mm
Agnew's (purchase, 13.11.1893) (D.1887.45)

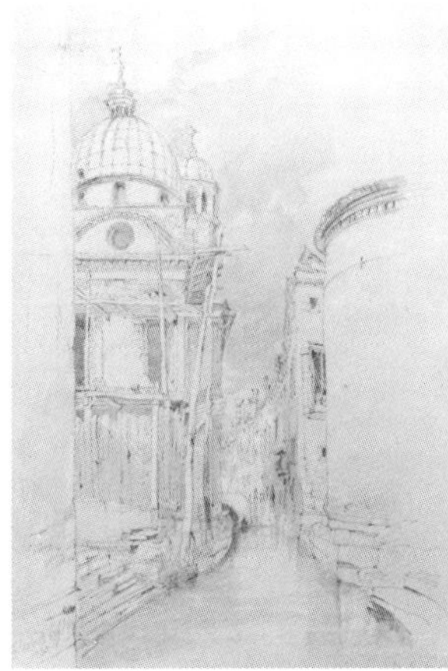

D.1918.3

The Church of Santa Maria dei Miracoli, Venice
30.9.1835
pencil, watercolour, bodycolour (heightened with white)
signed, inscribed & dated lower left with initials in monogram: *IH Venice Sept 30 / 1835*; inscribed lower right: *Delta di Miracoli*
357 × 239 mm
Anderson, A. E. (gift, 1918) (D.1918.3)

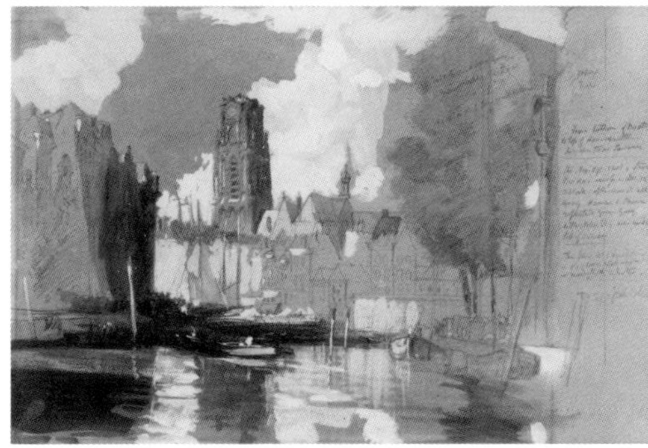

D.1952.3

The Tower of the Church of St Lawrence, Rotterdam
pencil, watercolour, bodycolour; buff paper
inscribed in centre and on left and right hand side with extensive colour notes
292 × 362 mm
Pilkington, Margaret (gift, 1952) (D.1952.3)

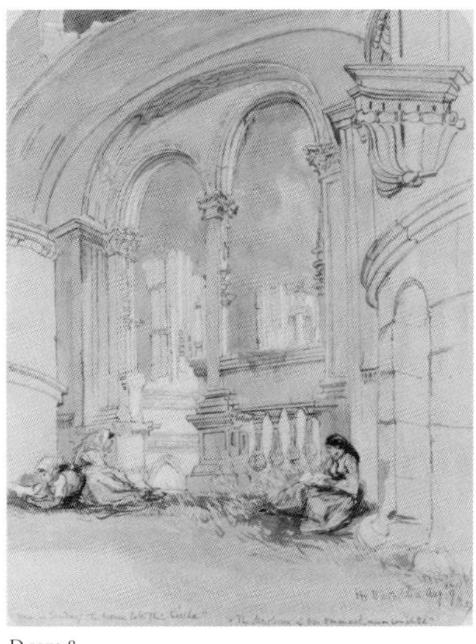

D.1972.8

Women taking their Siesta: The Mausoleum of Don Emanuel, Batalha Monastery, Portugal
9.8.1837
pencil, watercolour, bodycolour; grey paper with corners cut
signed, inscribed & dated lower right with initials in monogram: *IH Batalha.Aug. 9 1837*; inscribed lower left: *"Here on Sunday The Women Take Their Siesta"*; inscribed lower right: *"The Mosoleum* (sic) *of Don Emanuel, never completed"*
392 × 299 mm
Fine Art Society, London (purchase, 1972) (D.1972.8)

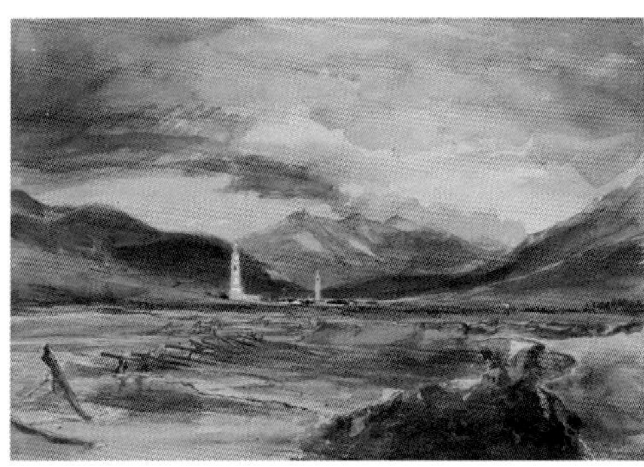

D.1999.13

A View of Ampezzo
1857
pencil, watercolour
signed, inscribed & dated lower right with initials in monogram: *IH. di Ampezzo / Tyrol / 1857*; inscribed lower left verso in Paul Oppé's hand: *bought at Puttick's Decr.1916. / A copy of this drawing by H.B.Brabazon / was in lot 348 of his sale at Christie's / March 18 & 19 1926. This drawing may have / been his property because it was bought / with a drawing which certainly belonged / to him & in the next lot were drawings / by him.*
368 × 522 mm
Scott-Elliot, Miss Aydua, in memory of Paul Oppé (gift, 4.11.199) (D.1999.13)

■ **HOLLOWAY, CHARLES EDWARD (1838–97)**
After studying at Leigh's Academy together with Fred Walker and Charles Green, Holloway began to exhibit landscapes and marine subjects at the Royal Academy and elsewhere from 1867. He was elected a member of the New Watercolour Society in 1879. He produced views of the Fens, the Thames and Venice.

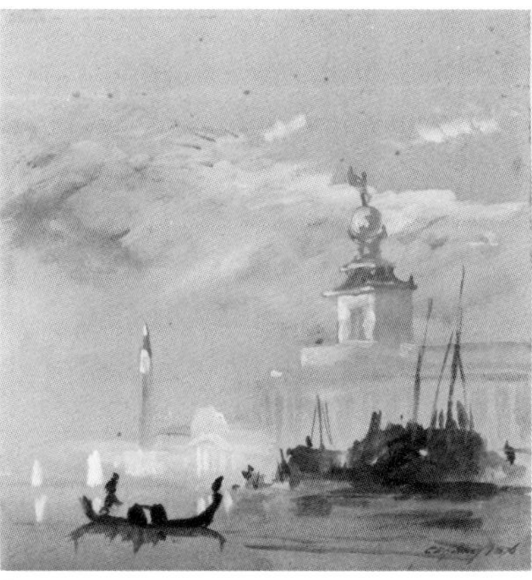

D.1922.35

Venice, the Dogana and S. Giorgio Maggiore
1876
watercolour, bodycolour; blue paper
signed & dated lower right: *CEHolloway 1876*
206 × 192 mm
Anderson, A. E. (gift, 1922) (D.1922.35)

■ **HOLMES, SIR CHARLES JOHN (1868–1936)**
Educated at Eton and Brasenose, Oxford, Holmes was Slade Professor of Art at Oxford from 1904 to 1910. Having served as Director of the National Portrait Gallery from 1909 to 1916, he was appointed Director of the National Gallery in the latter year. He wrote extensively on art, publishing on subjects and artists as widely diverse as Hokusai, Constable and Leonardo da Vinci. Holmes published the first catalogue of the Iveagh Bequest in 1928 and his autobiography *Self and Partners (Mostly Self)*, published in 1936, is a mine of information on the artistic matters of the day.

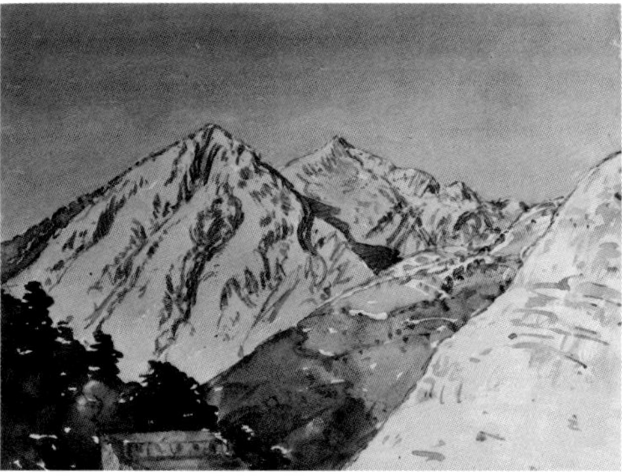

D.1923.7

Mountain behind Mentone, South of France
1921
black chalk, watercolour
signed, inscribed & dated lower left: *Behind Mentone / CJHolmes 1921*
260 × 342 mm
Anderson, A. E. (gift, 1923) (D.1923.7)

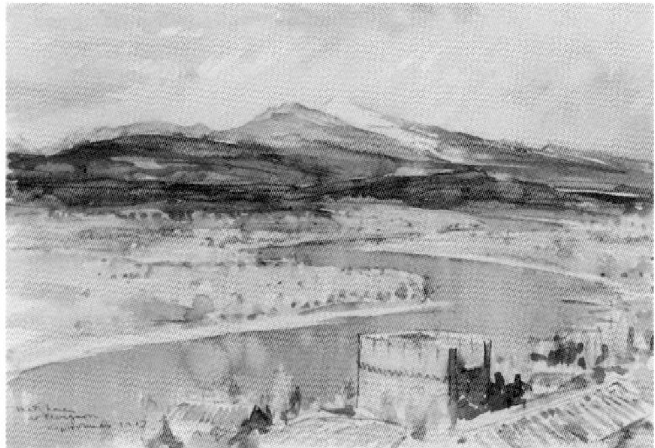

D.1924.3

The Rhone at Avignon, South of France
1922
pencil, watercolour
signed, inscribed & dated lower left: *The Rhone / at Avignon / C.J.Holmes 1922*; inscribed centre verso: *C.J.Holmes / No.1.*
239 × 346 mm
Colnaghi's (purchase, 1924) (D.1924.3)

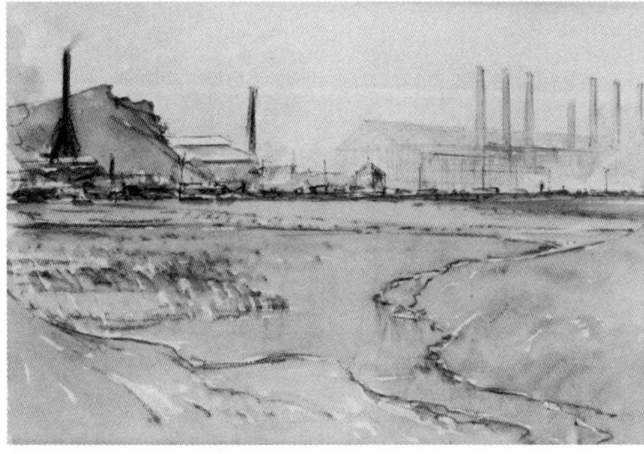

D.1937.34

Industrial Landscape
pencil, black chalk, watercolour
238 × 346 mm
Holmes, Lady (in memory of her husband) (gift, 1937) (D.1937.34)

■ **HOPPNER, JOHN (1758–1810)**
Primarily a portrait painter in oil, Hoppner also produced portrait drawings as well as chalk drawings which are influenced by and sometimes mistaken for Gainsborough.

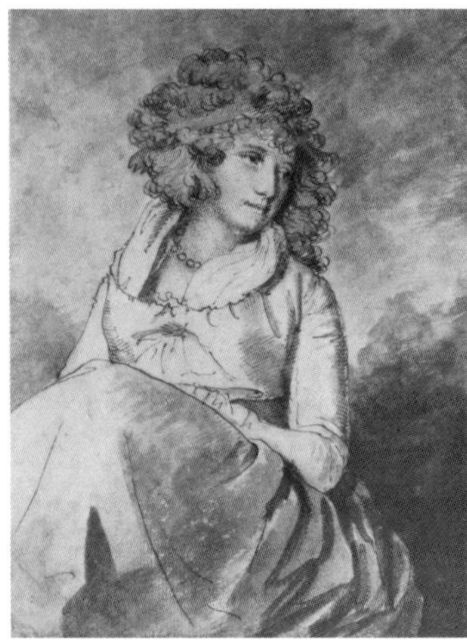

D.1925.51

Portrait of Mrs Crouch
pen and brown ink, watercolour
304 × 215 mm
Blair, G. B. (gift, 1925) (D.1925.51)

■ **HOWARD, GEORGE JAMES, EARL OF CARLISLE (1843–1911)**
Howard, educated at Eton and Cambridge, was a talented amateur painter who succeeded to the Earldom of Carlisle in 1889. A friend of Burne-Jones, Howard's chief artistic influence was Giovanni Costa. Howard was a founder member of the Etruscan School in 1883–84 and a regular exhibitor at the Dudley, Grosvenor and New Galleries. He was an honorary member of the Royal Watercolour Society.

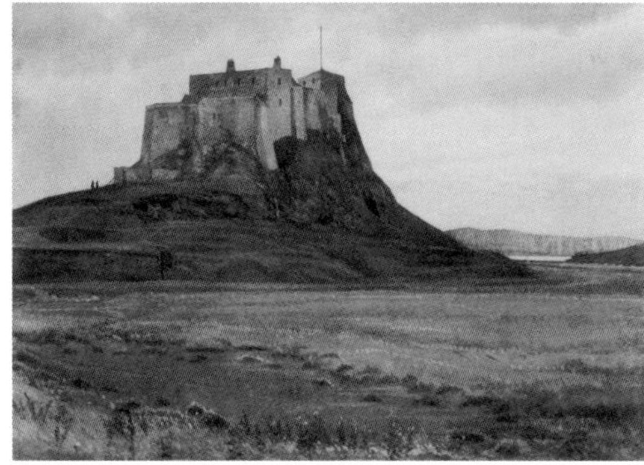

D.1994.12

Holy Island Castle, Northumberland
watercolour
260 × 360 mm
Spink (purchase, 10.1994) (F.O.W.) (D.1994.12)

■ **HOWARD, SQUIRE (1846–1924)**
Howard was a Manchester-based artist.

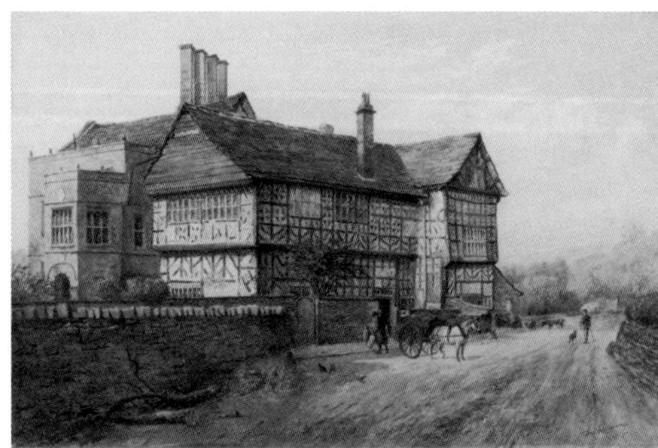

D.1892.156

Hall I' Th' Wood, Bolton, Lancashire
1892
pencil, watercolour, bodycolour
signed & dated lower right: *Sq. Howard/1892.*
497 × 751 mm
untraced (purchase, 1892) (D.1892.156)

■ **HOWITT, SAMUEL (1756–1822)**
Howitt was a country gentleman who became a sporting and animal painter. His style is influenced by his brother-in-law Thomas Rowlandson, and the two artists are occasionally confused. Howitt exhibited from 1783 at the Royal Academy and elsewhere.

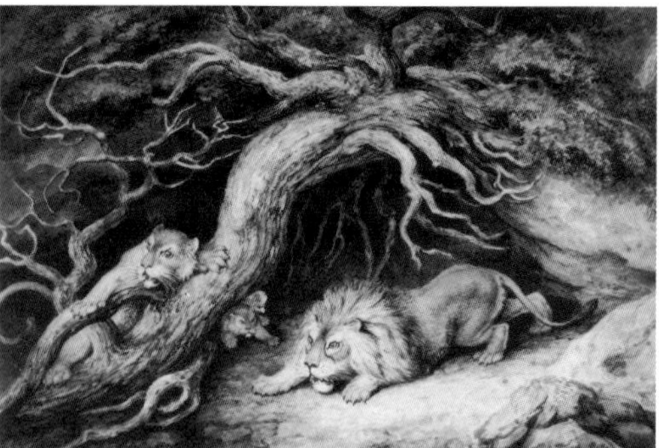

D.1892.48

The Lions disturbed
watercolour
326 × 477 mm
Taylor, John Edward (gift, 1892) (D.1892.48)

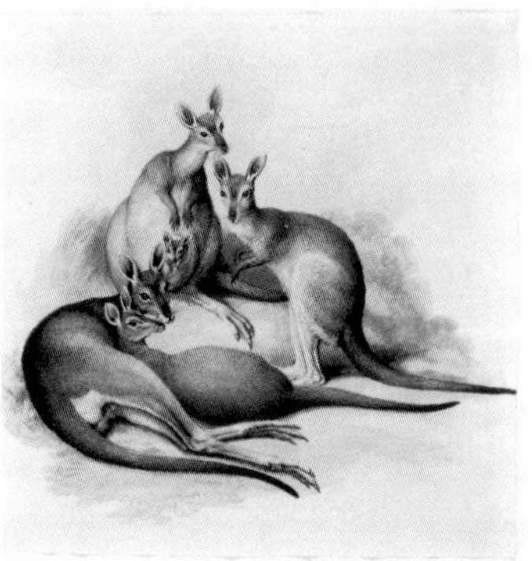

D.1917.25

Study of Wallabies
watercolour
signed lower centre: *Howitt*
237 × 224 mm
untraced (gift, 1917) (D.1917.25)

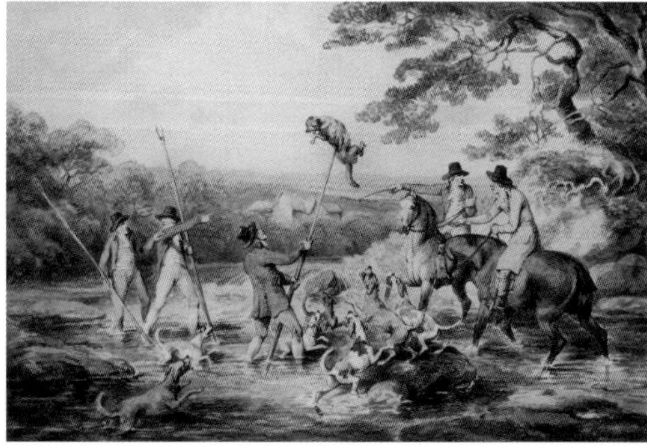

D.1955.5

Hunting the Otter
1792
pen and ink, watercolour
signed & dated lower right: *Howitt. 1792*
225 × 330 mm
Friends of the Whitworth (gift, 1955) (D.1955.5)

The Horse Fair
pen and grey ink, grey watercolour
103 × 152 mm
Towlson, Hector J. (bequest, 1969) (D.1970.48)

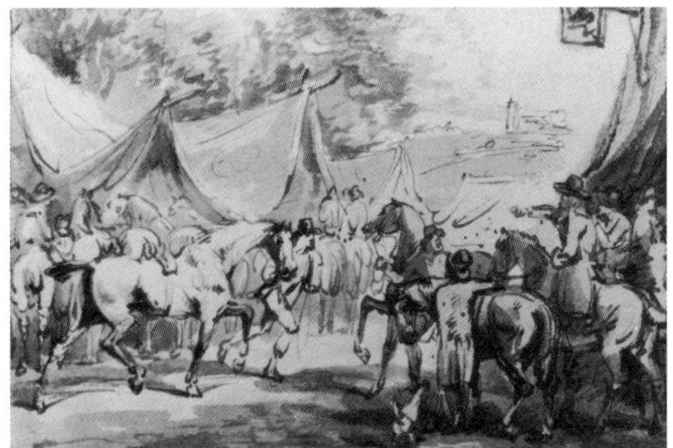

D.1970.48

■ HUGHES, ARTHUR (1832–1915)

Hughes, Pre-Raphaelite painter and illustrator, entered the Royal Academy Schools in 1847 and first exhibited at the Royal Academy in 1849. Inspired by Millais, Hughes produced a number of works in the 1850s that rank among the most memorable of all Pre-Raphaelite pictures, such as *April Love*, *The Long Engagement* and *Home from Sea*. He also illustrated a number of books from 1855, and was associated with writers such as Thomas Hughes, George Macdonald and Christina Rossetti.

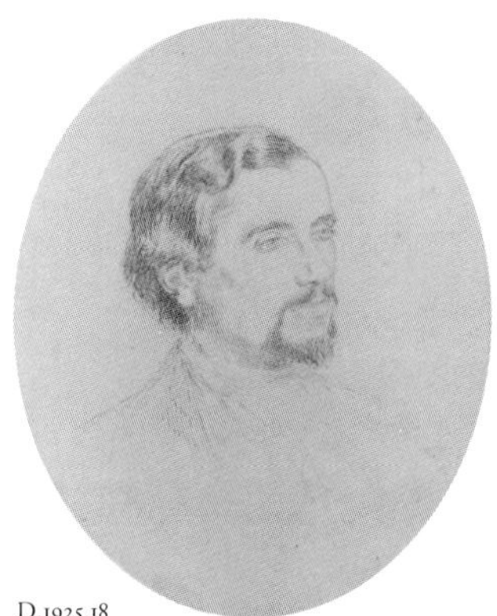

D.1925.18

Portrait of William Allingham
pencil, pen and brown ink, brown watercolour; oval
inscribed lower centre: *Sketch of W.A. by A.H. = Given by the latter to G.P.B.*; inscribed & dated on a separate sheet of paper attached to mount: *In the event of my death / this drawing to be handed over to Mrs. Wm. Allingham,*
158 × 126 mm
Allingham, E. G. (purchase, 1925) (D.1925.18)

■ HULK, ABRAHAM (1813–97)

Hulk, a Dutch-born marine and landscape painter, settled in London in 1870.

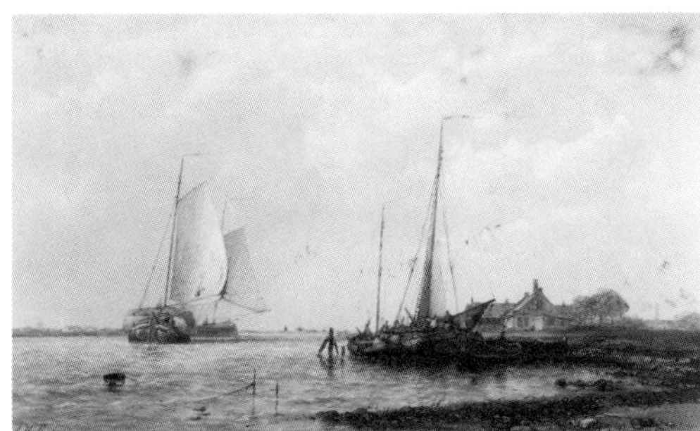

D.1987.57

Dutch Fishing Boats
watercolour, bodycolour (heightened with white)
signed lower left: *A.Hulk.f.* [underlined]
256 × 421 mm
Hitchon, Brian (Dr) (in appreciation of his student years at Manchester University, 1949–55) (gift, 1987) (D.1987.57)

■ HULL, WILLIAM (1820–80)

Hull worked as a printer's clerk in Manchester while studying at the School of Design and travelled on the Continent as a tutor from 1841 to 1844.

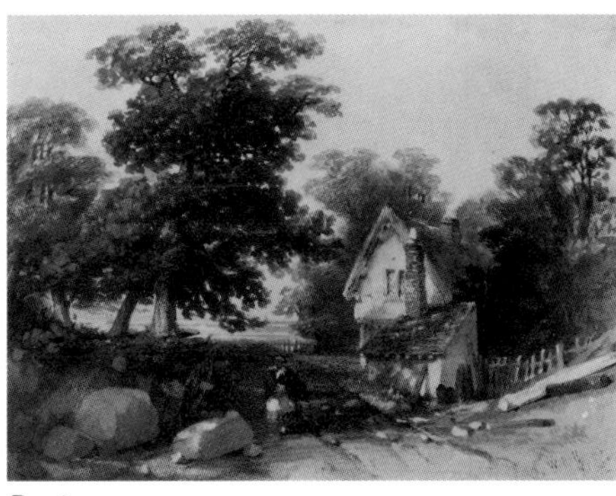

D.1918.5

Country Cottage and Trees
watercolour
signed lower right: *W.Hull*
247 × 323 mm
Grantham, William (bequest, 1918) (D.1918.5)

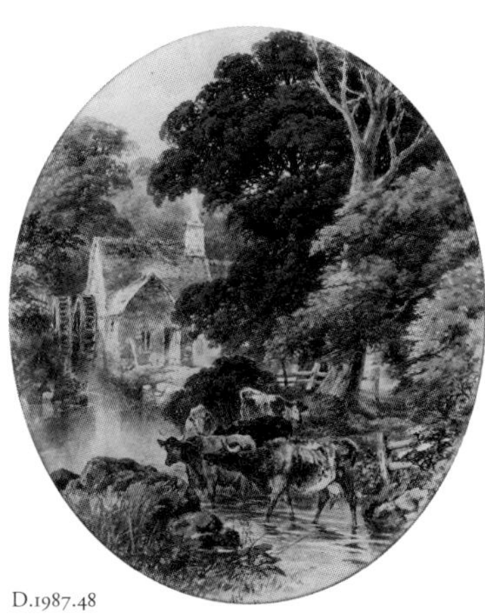

D.1987.48

Landscape with Mill and Cattle
1854
pencil, watercolour; oval
signed & dated lower centre: *W Hull / 1854*
412 × 335 mm
Brockbank, J. E. (bequest, 1987) (D.1987.48)

Landscape with Reapers
1853
pencil, watercolour; oval
signed & dated lower centre: *W Hull 1853*
418 × 344 mm
Brockbank, J. E. (bequest, 1987) (D.1987.49)

Cemetery with House and Figures
1854
watercolour; circular
signed & dated lower centre: *W Hull 1854*
341 (diam) mm
Brockbank, J. E. (bequest, 1987) (D.1987.50)

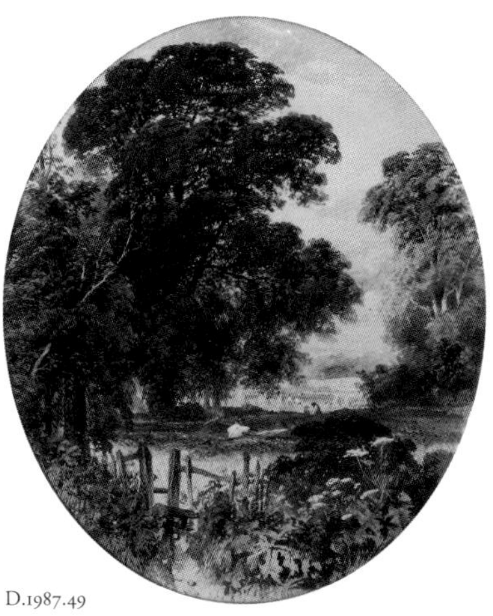

D.1987.49

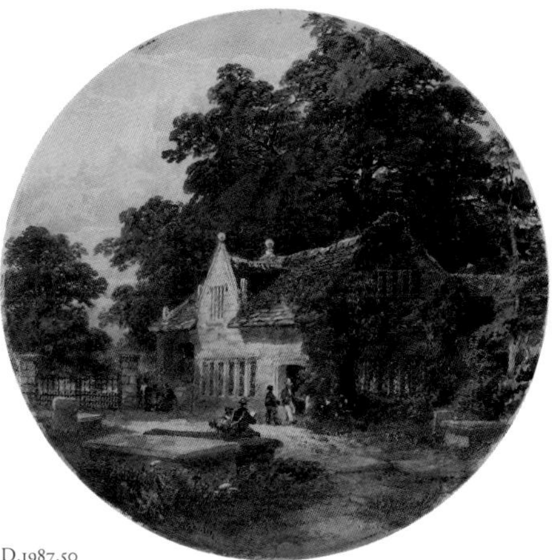

D.1987.50

■ HULME, FREDERICK WILLIAM (1816–84)

Hulme first exhibited in Birmingham in 1841 and later at the British Institution, the Royal Manchester Institution and the Royal Academy. He came to London in 1844 and worked for the *Art Journal*. He was also a drawing master.

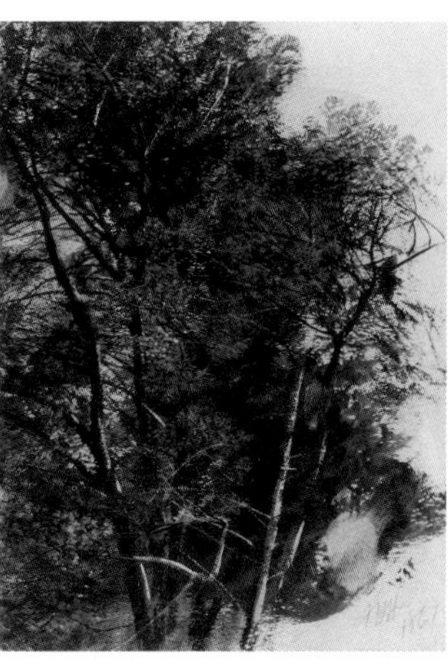

D.1926.47

Study of Trees
1861
watercolour, bodycolour (heightened with white)
signed & dated lower right with initials: *FWH / 1861*
188 × 136 mm
Ogden, William Sharp (bequest, 1926) (D.1926.47)

■ Humphrey, Ozias (1742–1810)

Humphrey, a portrait painter in miniature, oil and chalk, visited Italy with Romney in 1773 and remained until 1777. He exhibited at the Royal Academy between 1779 and 1783 and again between 1788 and 1797. In the mid-1780s Humphrey visited India. He was elected a member of the Royal Academy in 1791.

D.1954.23

Portrait of an Elderly Man
pencil, red chalk
231 × 188 mm
National Art Collections Fund (gift, 1954) (D.1954.23)

■ Hunt, Cecil Arthur (1873–1965)

Cecil Arthur Hunt was educated at Winchester and Trinity College, Cambridge, and worked as a barrister until 1919 when he turned to full-time watercolour painting. He was elected a member of the Royal Watercolour Society in 1925 and was Vice-President from 1930 to 1933. Widely travelled in the British Isles, Europe and the United States, Hunt also painted industrial subjects.

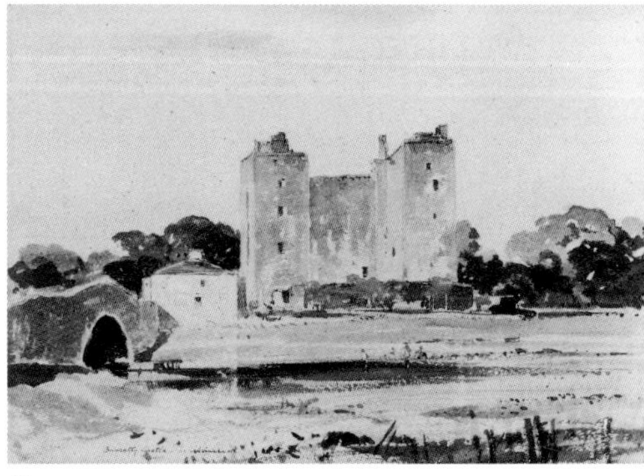

D.1939.14

Bunratty Castle, Co. Limerick, Ireland
1938
pencil, pen and brown ink, watercolour, bodycolour (heightened with white); oatmeal paper
signed lower right: *CAHunt*; inscribed lower left: *Bunratty Castle-Limerick*
287 × 388 mm
Hunt, Cecil Arthur (gift, 1939) (D.1939.14)

■ Hunt, William Henry (1790–1864)

Apprenticed to John Varley, William Henry Hunt studied at the Royal Academy Schools and with Dr Monro. His earlier work is pure landscape but he later turned to detailed still lives and studies of single figures, particularly children. His still lives were much admired by Ruskin and earned him the nickname 'Bird's Nest Hunt'. He was elected a member of the Old Watercolour Society in 1826 and exhibited nearly 800 works there during his career.

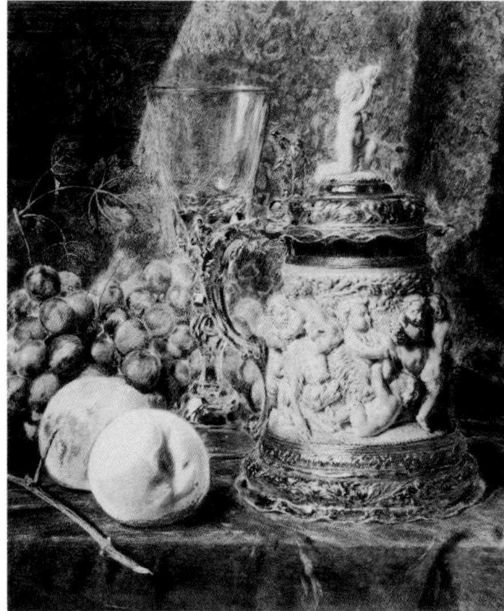

D.1887.24

Fruit and Tankard
1851
watercolour, bodycolour (heightened with white)
signed lower right: *W HUNT*
362 × 304 mm
Wright, Thomas W. (purchase, 1891) (D.1887.24)

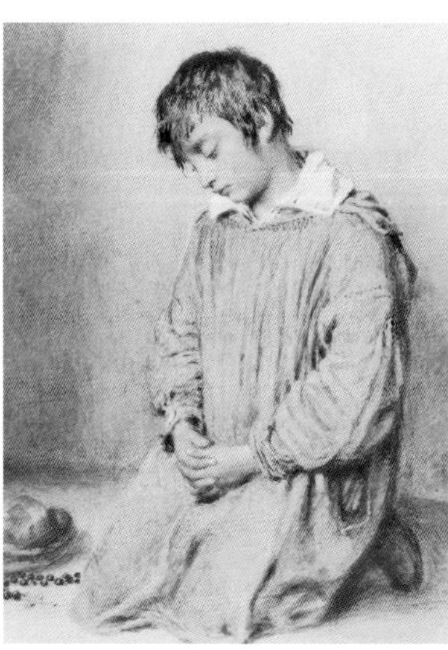

D.1887.25

Devotion
1833–36
watercolour
signed lower left: *W HUNT*
365 × 269 mm
Wright, Thomas W. (purchase, 1891) (D.1887.25)

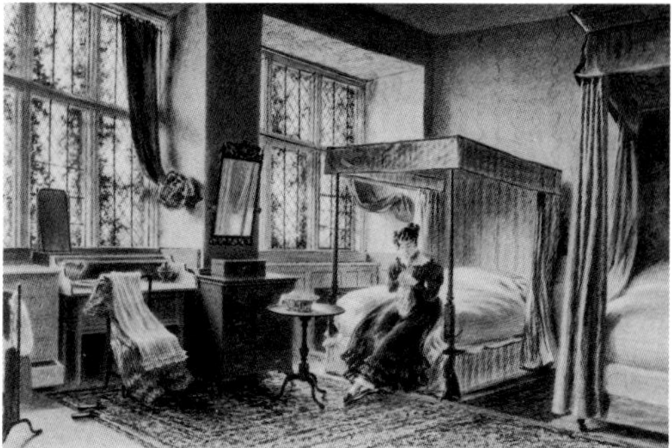

D.1887.32

A Woman sewing in a Bed Chamber
1839
watercolour
signed & dated lower left: *W.HUNT.1839*
304 × 445 mm
Agnew's (purchase, 22.6.1891) (D.1887.32)

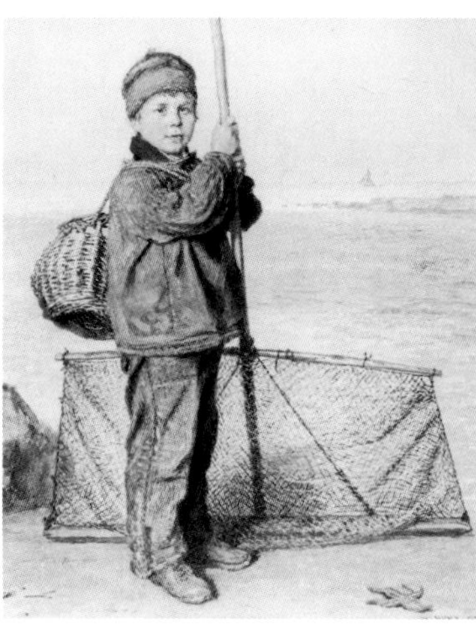

D.1887.33

The Shrimper
1835
pencil, watercolour
signed & dated lower right: *W.HUNT.1835*
387 × 318 mm
Agnew's (purchase, 23.5.1891) (D.1887.33)

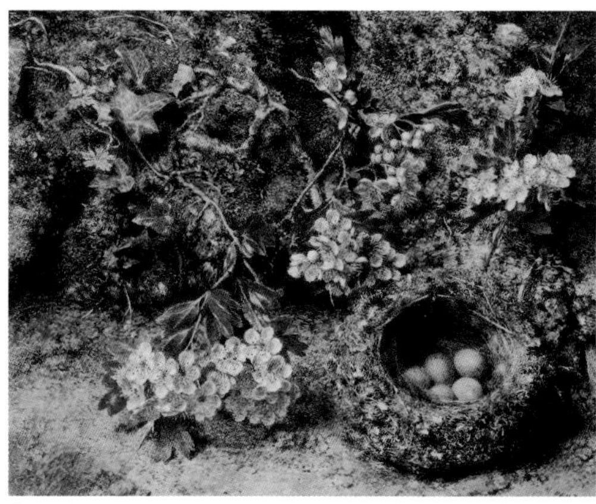

D.1887.34

White Hawthorn and Bird's Nest
watercolour, bodycolour (heightened with white)
signed lower right: *W.HUNT*
229 × 277 mm
Agnew's (purchase, 13.11.1893) (D.1887.34)

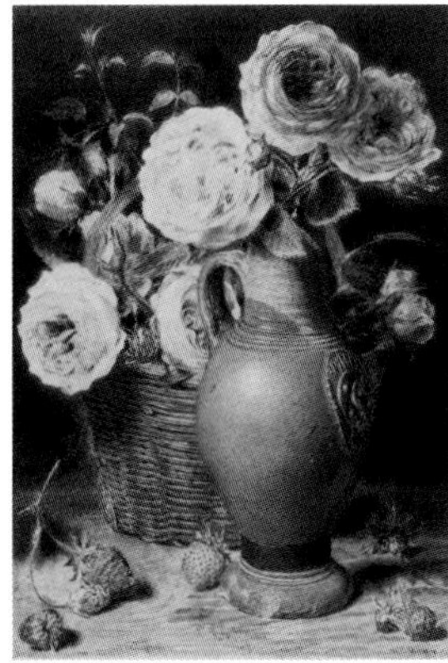

D.1887.35

Vase of Roses
1839–41
watercolour, bodycolour (heightened with white)
signed lower right: *W.HUNT*
293 × 202 mm
Agnew's (purchase, 5.5.1891) (D.1887.35)

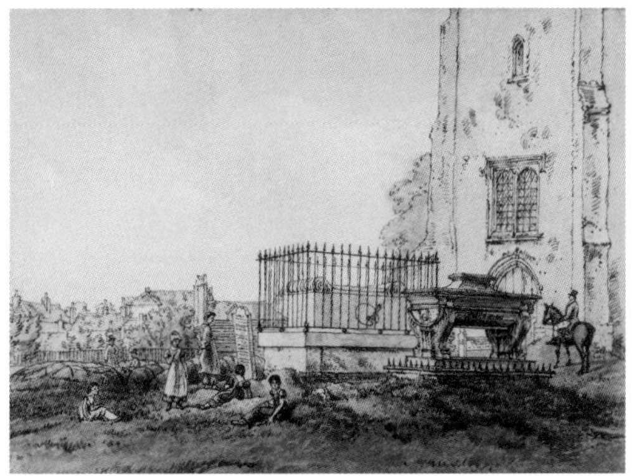

D.1895.29

Bushey Churchyard, Hertfordshire
1821–23
pencil, pen and brown ink, watercolour
signed lower right: *W.HUNT*
340 × 435 mm
Taylor, John Edward (gift, 1895) (D.1895.29)

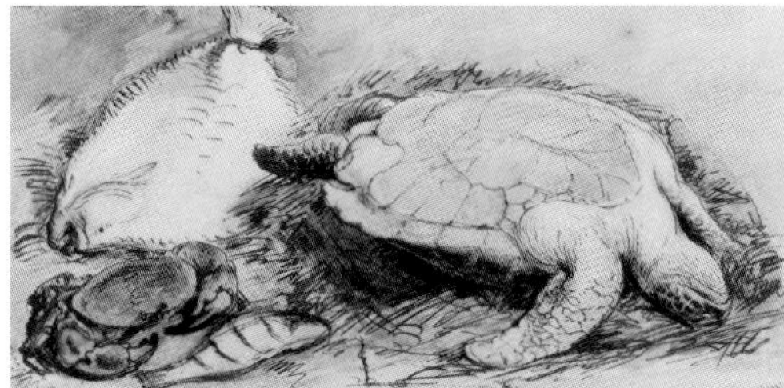

D.1900.19

Still-Life, Turtle, Crab and Fish
1826–28
pen and brown ink, watercolour
signed lower right: *W HUNT*
180 × 356 mm
Agnew, George W. (gift, 1900) (D.1900.19)

Bird's Nest and Apple Blossom
watercolour, bodycolour (heightened with white)
oval signed lower right: *W.HUNT*
224 × 296 mm
Agnew, Sir William (gift, 1902) (D.1902.1)

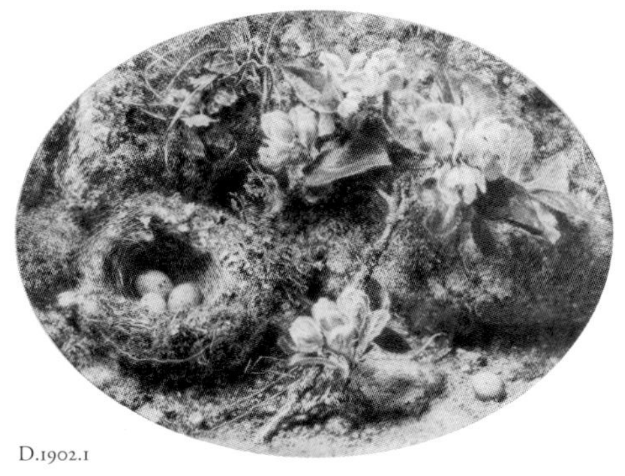

D.1902.1

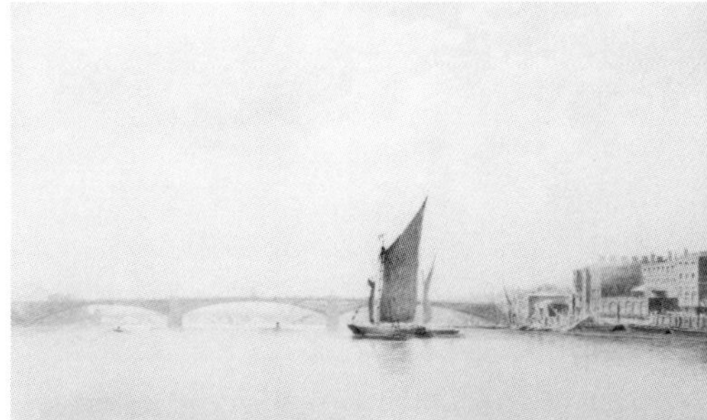

D.1902.2

The Thames, London, looking towards Southwark Bridge
1805–09
pencil, watercolour
signed lower right: *W.Hunt*
337 × 538 mm
Agnew, Sir William (gift, 1902) (D.1902.2)

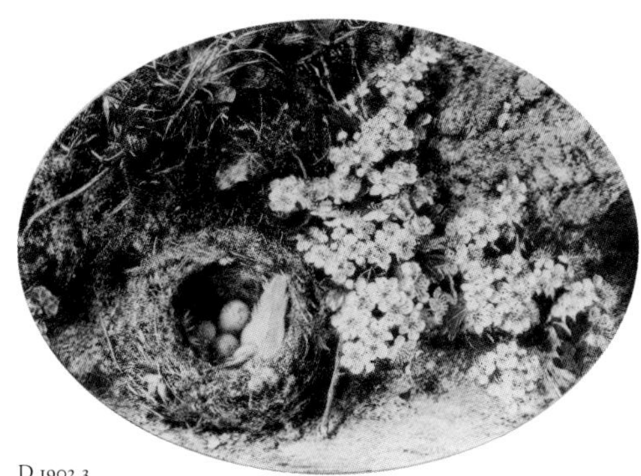

D.1902.3

Bird's Nest and Hawthorn
watercolour, bodycolour; oval
signed lower right: *WHUNT*
204 × 282 mm
Agnew, Sir William (gift, 1902) (D.1902.3)

The Valentine
1836
watercolour
signed & dated lower left: *W HUNT 1836*
235 × 178 mm
Broadhurst, Sir Edward Tootal, Broadhurst, Lady
(bequest, 1924) (D.1924.73)

What Shall I Sing?
1848
watercolour, bodycolour (heightened with white)
signed lower right: *W HUNT*
288 × 174 mm
Knight, Joseph (gift, 1944) (D.1944.12)

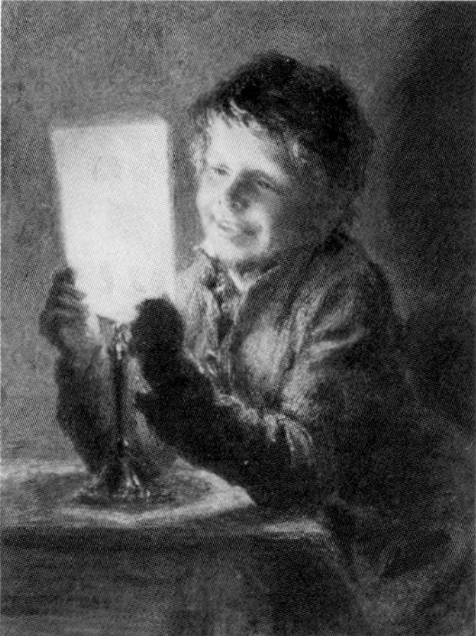

D.1924.73

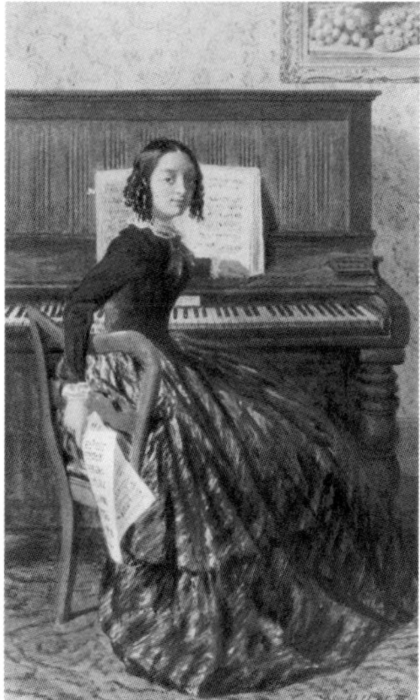

D.1944.12

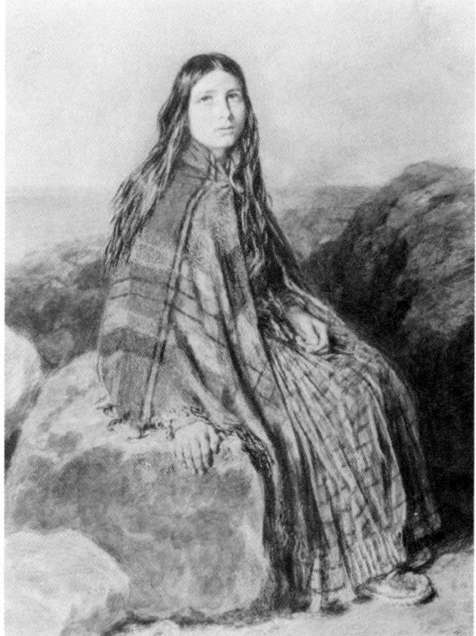

D.1977.10

A Peasant Girl seated on a Rock
1841–43
watercolour, bodycolour (heightened with white)
signed lower right: *W HUNT*
424 × 320 mm
Whitehead, James Edward (bequest, 1977) (D.1977.10)

■ HUNT, WILLIAM HOLMAN (1827–1910)

William Holman Hunt was one of the founder members of the Pre-Raphaelite Brotherhood and one of the most important painters of the nineteenth century. He visited Egypt and the Holy Land in 1854–55 and again from 1869 to 1872. Some of his paintings, such as *The Light of the World*, *The Hireling Shepherd*, *The Awakening Conscience* and *The Triumph of the Innocents*, have become icons of the Victorian era. Hunt was awarded the Order of Merit in 1905.

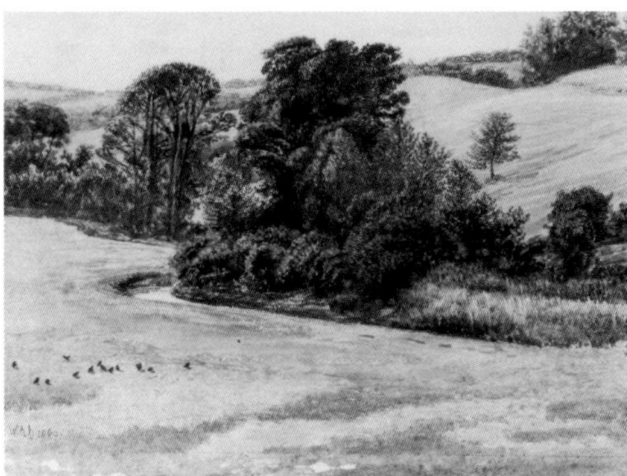

D.1925.11

Helston, Cornwall
1860
watercolour
signed & dated lower left with initials: *W. h h 1860*
193 × 257 mm
Whitworth Institute Committee, Members of (gift, 1925)
(D.1925.11)

Cairo, Sunset on the Gebel Mokattum
1854 and 1860–61
watercolour
signed & inscribed & dated lower right with monogram: *Whh Cairo 1854*
165 × 356 mm
Haworth, Jesse (bequest, 1937) (D.1937.13)

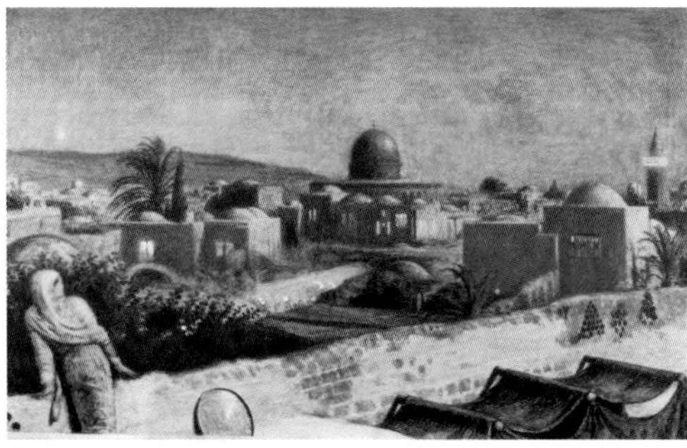

D.1937.14

The Mosque as Sakrah, Jerusalem, during Ramazan
1854–55 and 1860–61
watercolour, bodycolour (heightened with white)
223 × 356 mm
Haworth, Jesse (bequest, 1937) (D.1937.14)

The Plain of Rephaim from Zion, Jerusalem
1855 and 1860–61
watercolour, bodycolour (heightened with white)
signed & dated lower left with monogram: *Whh 55*
355 × 508 mm
Haworth, J. G. (family of) (gift, 1961) (D.1961.4)

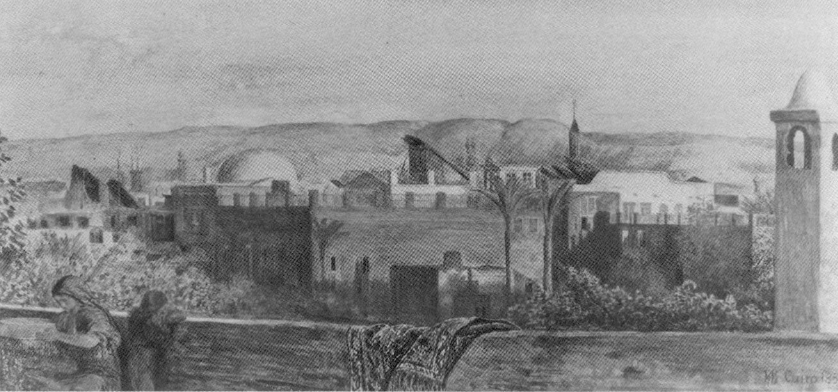

D.1937.13

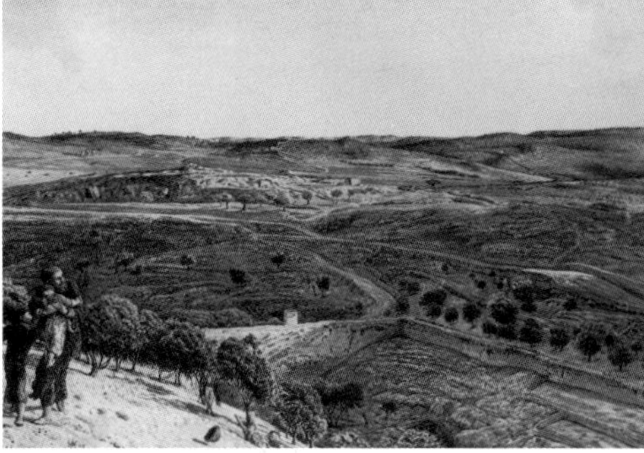

D.1961.4

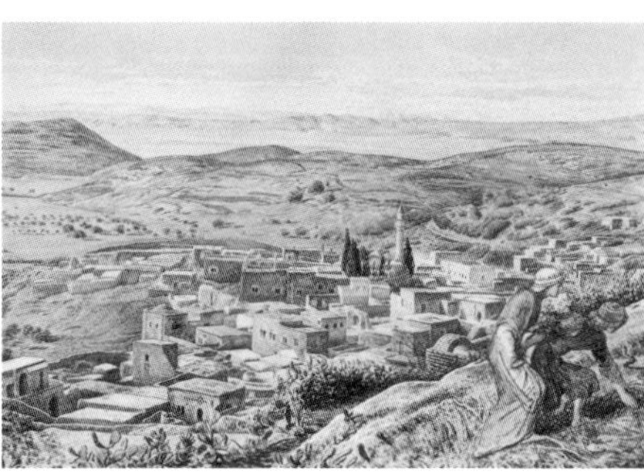

D.1961.5

View of Nazareth
1855 and 1860–61
watercolour, bodycolour
353 × 498 mm
Haworth, J. G. (family of) (gift, 1961) (D.1961.5)

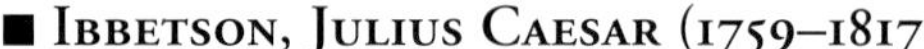

■ IBBETSON, JULIUS CAESAR (1759–1817)

Ibbetson was apprenticed to a ship's painter in Hull. He went to London in 1777 and began to exhibit at the Royal Academy in 1785. In 1788 Ibbetson was appointed draughtsman to Colonel Cathcart's Mission to China but Cathcart died on Java while on the way to China and Ibbetson returned to England. Ibbetson moved to Liverpool in 1798 and on to the Lake District around 1800, finally settling in North Yorkshire in 1805. He painted landscapes and portraits in oil and watercolour.

Merthyr Tydfil, Glamorgan, Wales, from Plymouth Furnace
pencil, pen and brown ink, watercolour
inscribed on mount lower centre within cartouche:
Merthir Tidville from Plymouth / Furnace
318 × 496 mm
Ogden, William Sharp (bequest, 1926) (D.1926.44)

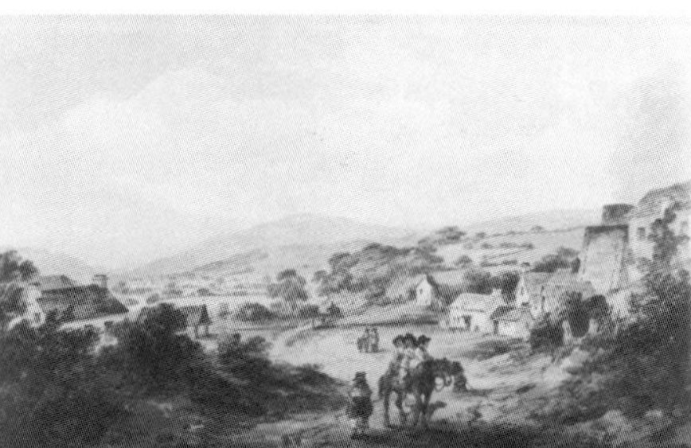

D.1926.44

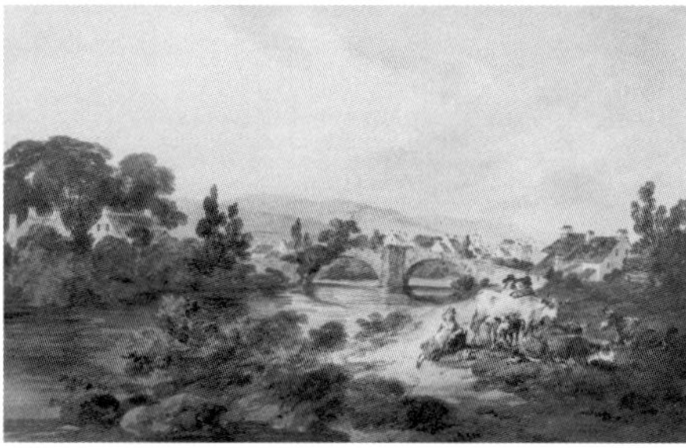

D.1926.45

Bridge at Merthyr Tydfil, Glamorgan, Wales
pencil, watercolour
inscribed on mount lower centre within cartouche:
Bridge at Merthir Tidville
325 × 498 mm
Ogden, William Sharp (bequest, 1926) (D.1926.45)

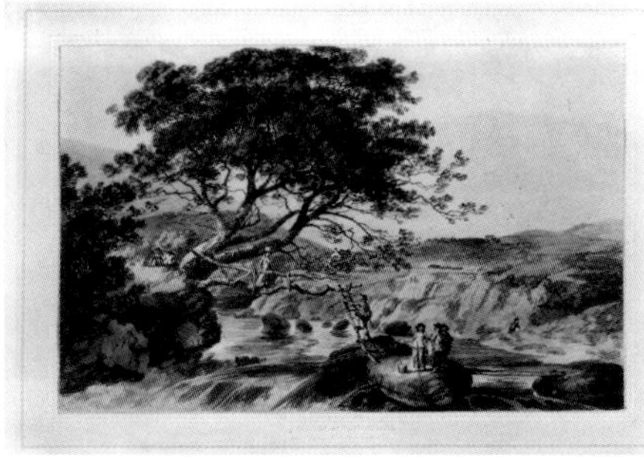

D.1926.211

Bridge at Cyfarthfa Iron Works, Merthyr Tydfil, Glamorgan, Wales
pen and brown ink, watercolour
inscribed on mount lower centre within cartouche: *A BRIDGE AT CYTHARTHFA / Iron Works Merthir Tidville*
326 × 499 mm
Ogden, William Sharp (bequest, 1926) (D.1926.211)

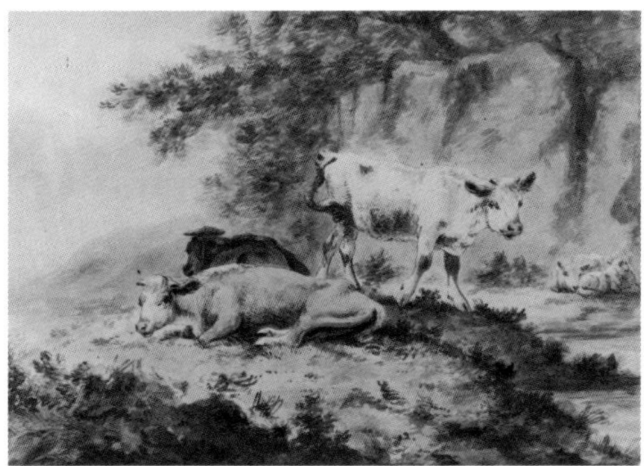

D.1970.50

Calves and Sheep
ink (etched outline), watercolour
140 × 202 mm
Towlson, Hector J. (bequest, 1969) (D.1970.50)

■ INCE, JOSEPH MURRAY (1806–59)

Born in Radnorshire, from 1823 to 1826 Ince was a pupil of David Cox in Hereford. He then moved to London and exhibited at the Royal Academy between 1826 and 1847. Later he travelled in Wales, Herefordshire, Shropshire and Devon, as well as in Europe.

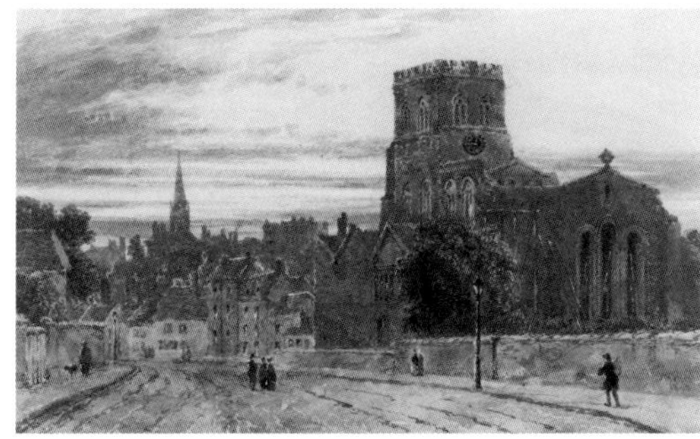

D.1900.9

Abbey Church, Shrewsbury, Shropshire
1850
watercolour
signed & dated lower right: *JMInce / 1850*
208 × 333 mm
Worthington, Mary (gift, 1900) (D.1900.9)

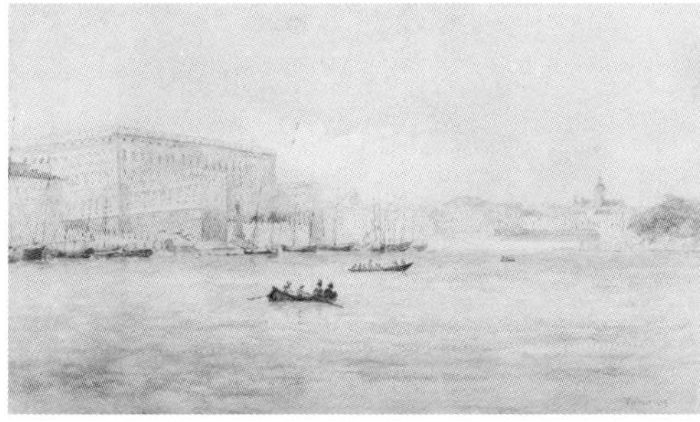

D.1947.12

The King's Palace, Stockholm, Sweden
1828
pencil, watercolour
signed & dated lower right: *JMInce 1828*
197 × 332 mm
Friends of the Whitworth (gift, 1947) (D.1947.12)

■ INCHBOLD, JOHN WILLIAM (1830–88)

Born in Leeds, the son of a newspaper owner, Inchbold became a student at the Royal Academy Schools in about 1847. He first exhibited at the Royal Academy in 1852 when he came in contact with the Pre-Raphaelites. Inchbold's landscapes of 1852–57 show the influence of the Pre-Raphaelites and of Ruskin, with whom he travelled to the Alps in 1856 and 1858. In later years, Inchbold moved away from Ruskin's influence and travelled abroad frequently, visiting Switzerland and North Africa.

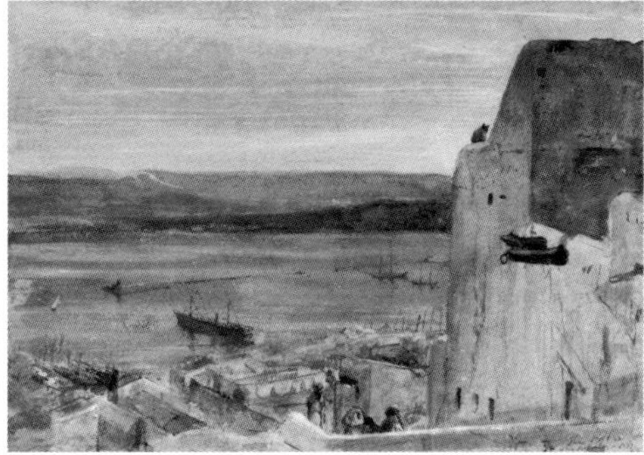

D.1992.3

A Mediterranean Port, possibly Algiers
1877
watercolour, bodycolour
dated & inscribed lower right: *From Old Town / across port & bay – 1877*
178 × 254 mm
Agnew's (purchase, 1992) (V. & A., F.O.W.) (D.1992.3)

■ IRELAND, ELIZABETH MARY (fl. mid-19th century)

Unknown amateur artist.

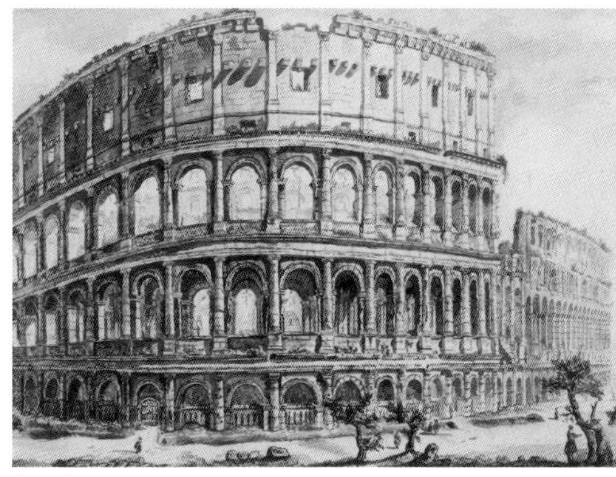

D.1926.309

The Colosseum, Rome
4.1.1851
pencil, brown watercolour
signed, inscribed & dated upper left verso: *The Colosseum / Jany.4th.1851. / [El]izabeth Mary Ireland*
405 × 540 mm
Ogden, William Sharp (bequest, 1926) (D.1926.309)

■ JACKSON, FREDERICK WILLIAM (1859–1918)

Jackson, a marine and landscape painter in oil and watercolour, studied at Oldham School of Art, the Manchester Academy and in Paris. He lived in Yorkshire and exhibited at the Royal Academy between 1880 and 1916, dividing his time between Hinderwell in North Yorkshire and Middleton in Lancashire. He travelled widely on the Continent and in North Africa.

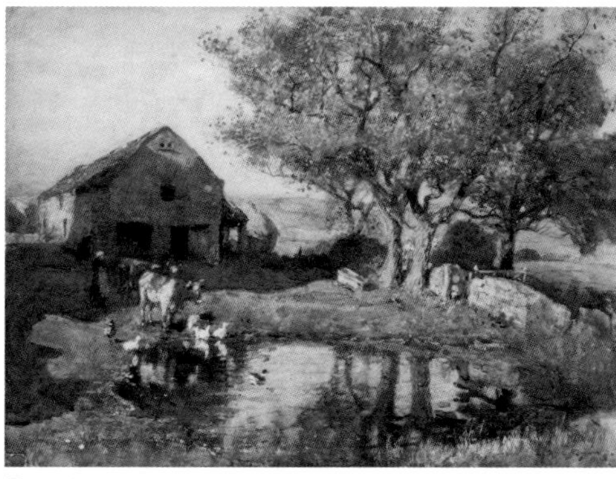

D.1902.8

The Farm Pond, Newton, Hinderwell, Yorkshire
1902
black chalk, watercolour
signed & dated lower right: *FWJackson / 1902*
530 × 712 mm
untraced (purchase, 1902) (D.1902.8)

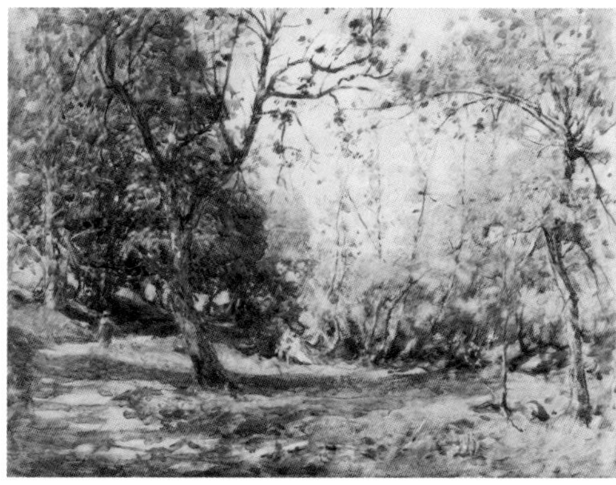

D.1917.22

Pathway under the Trees
watercolour, bodycolour (heightened with white)
signed lower left: *Fred WJackson*
430 × 560 mm
Sutton, E. F. M. (gift, 1917) (D.1917.22)

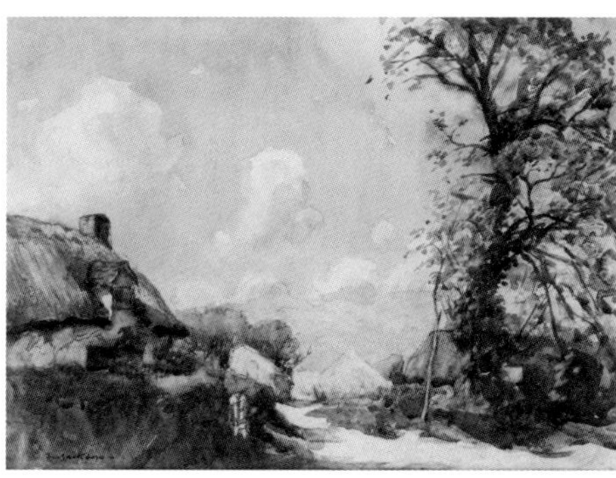

D.1919.9

The Lane, Blewbury, Wiltshire
black chalk, watercolour
signed lower left: *FWJackson–*
280 × 380 mm
Jackson, Frederick William (Memorial Committee) (gift, 1919) (D.1919.9)

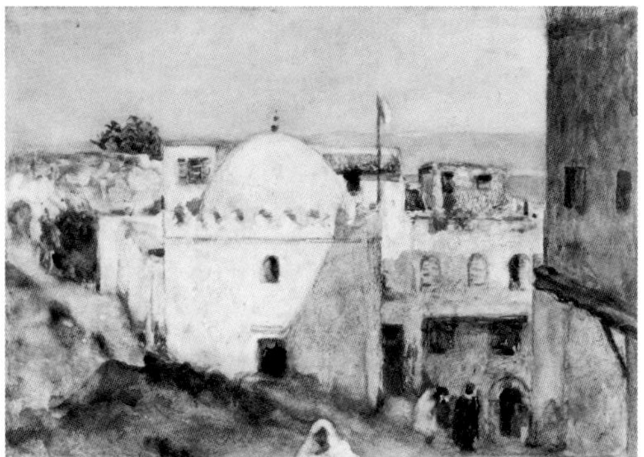

D.1919.10

Saint's Tomb, Tangier, Morocco
pencil, watercolour
signed lower right: *FredWJackson.*
268 × 364 mm
Jackson, Frederick William (Memorial Committee) (gift, 1919)
(D.1919.10)

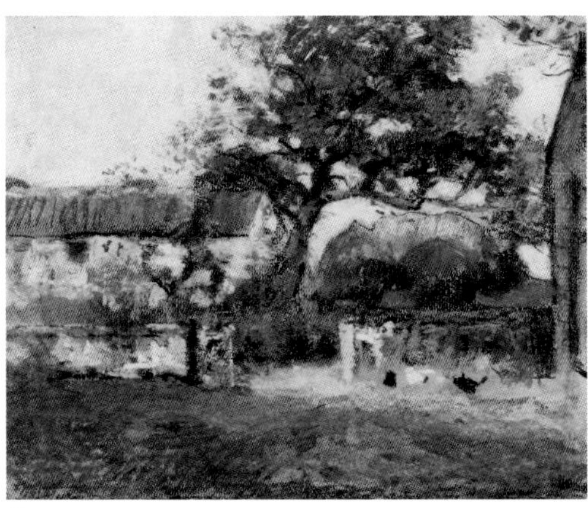

D.1919.11

The Farm
pastel; brown paper
signed (twice) lower left: *FWJackson*
237 × 291 mm
Jackson, Frederick William (Memorial Committee) (gift, 1919)
(D.1919.11)

Clouds and Field
black chalk, watercolour, bodycolour
(heightened with white)
signed lower right with initials: *F W J*
280 × 317 mm
Jackson, Frederick William (Memorial Committee) (gift, 1919)
(D.1919.12)

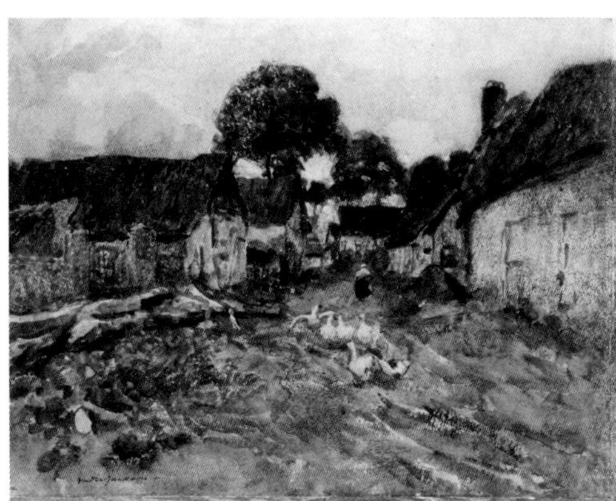

D.1919.13

Geese in a Lane, near Montreuil-sur-Mer
1896
black chalk, watercolour, bodycolour
(heightened with white)
signed lower left: *FredWJackson–*
301 × 382 mm
Jackson, Frederick William (Memorial Committee) (gift, 1919)
(D.1919.13)

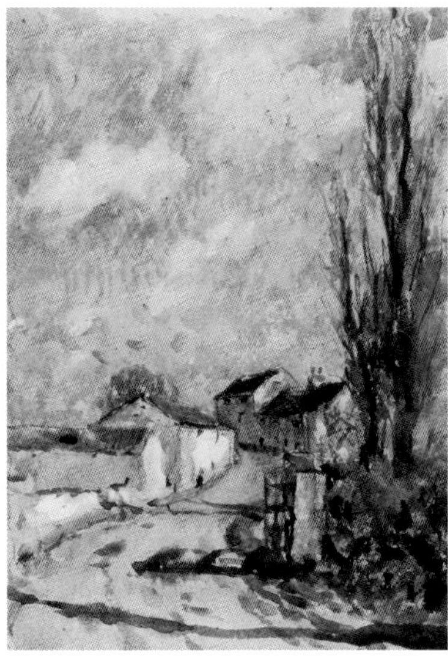

D.1921.46

**The Village Road (recto); Houses and
Barges on a Canal (verso)**
watercolour, bodycolour (heightened with white)
buff paper
348 × 248 mm
anonymous (in memory of the artist) (gift, 1921) (D.1921.46)

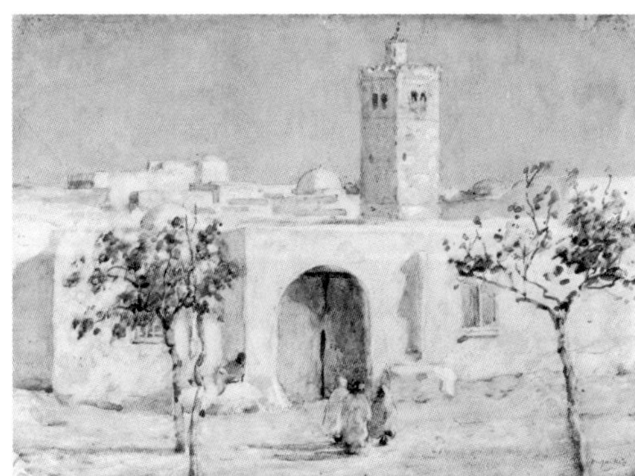

D.1939.19

A Mosque in Tunis
pencil, watercolour, bodycolour
(heightened with white)
signed lower right: *FWJackson*; signed, inscribed &
numbered verso of backing upper left: *No 1 / At Tunis /
FWJackson*
280 × 378 mm
Smith, Frank Hindley (bequest, 1939) (D.1939.19)

On the Outskirts of a Village
black chalk, watercolour, bodycolour
(heightened with white)
signed lower left: *FWJackson*
339 × 441 mm
Coleman, H. C. (bequest, 1949) (D.1949.21)

■ **JAMES, FRANCIS EDWARD (1849–1920)**
James, a painter of landscapes and flowers, was a
member of the New English Art Club and a friend of
Hercules Brabazon Brabazon. He was elected a
member of the Royal Watercolour Society in 1920.

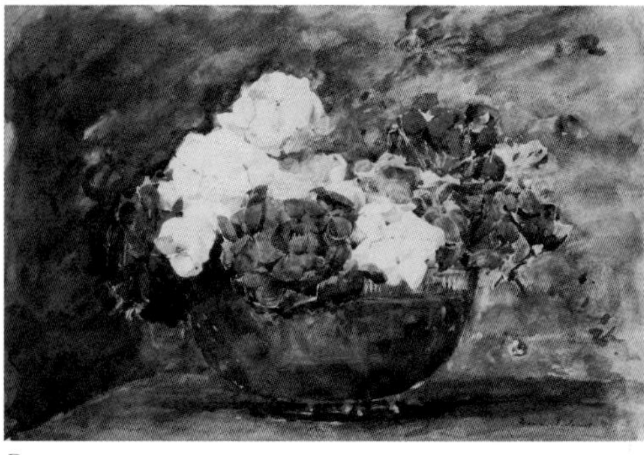

D.1920.13

Geraniums in a Glass Bowl
watercolour, bodycolour (heightened with white)
signed lower right: *Francis E.James.*
345 × 505 mm
anonymous (in memory of Frederick William Jackson)
(gift, 1920) (D.1920.13)

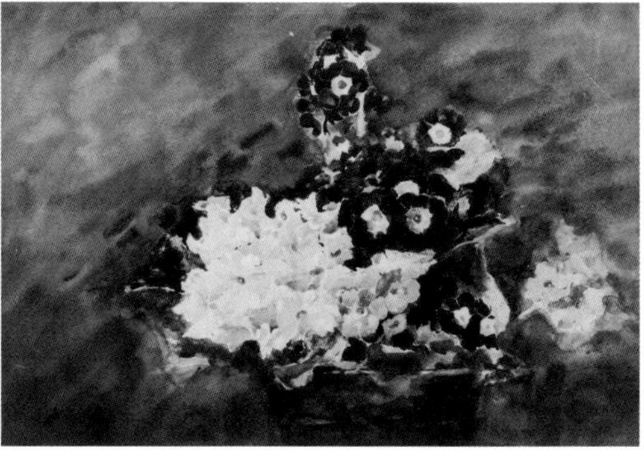

D.1920.14

Primulas in a Bowl
pencil, watercolour
signed lower left: *Francis E James*
348 × 496 mm
anonymous (in memory of Frederick William Jackson)
(gift, 1920) (D.1920.14)

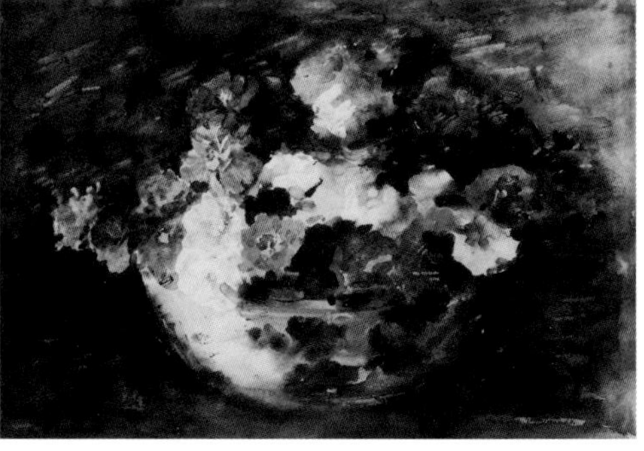

D.1927.38

Pelargoniums and Zinnias
watercolour, bodycolour (heightened with white)
signed lower right: *Francis E.James.*
329 × 464 mm
Anderson, A. E. (in memory of his brother Frank Anderson)
(gift, 1927) (D.1927.38)

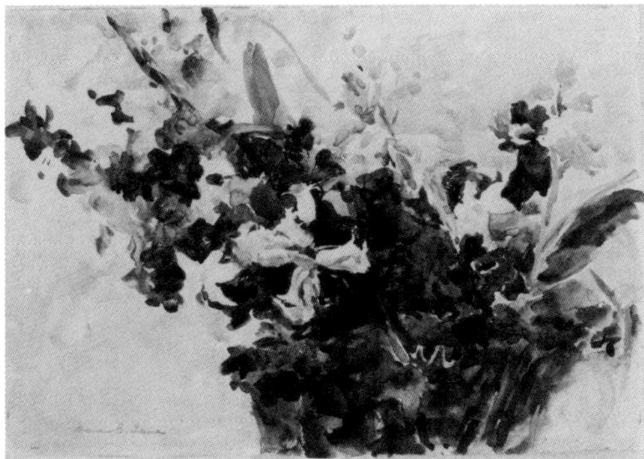

D.1930.66

Hyacinths
pencil, watercolour, bodycolour
(heightened with white)
signed lower left: *Francis E. James*
260 × 364 mm
Dawson, J. Greg (gift, 1930) (D.1930.66)

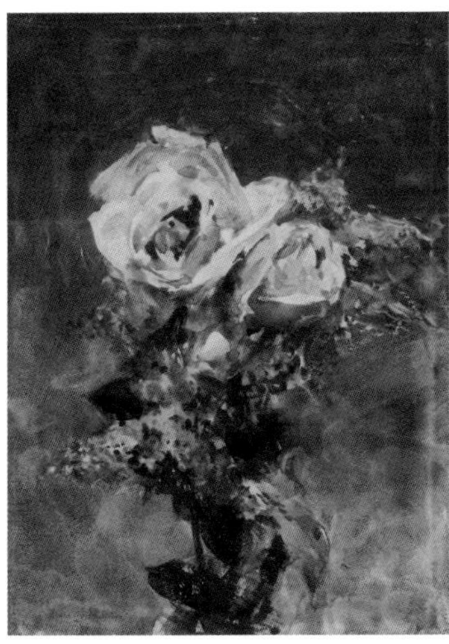

D.1931.7

Roses
watercolour; watermark T H S
signed lower left: *Francis E James*
370 × 267 mm
Anderson, A. E. (gift, 1931) (D.1931.7)

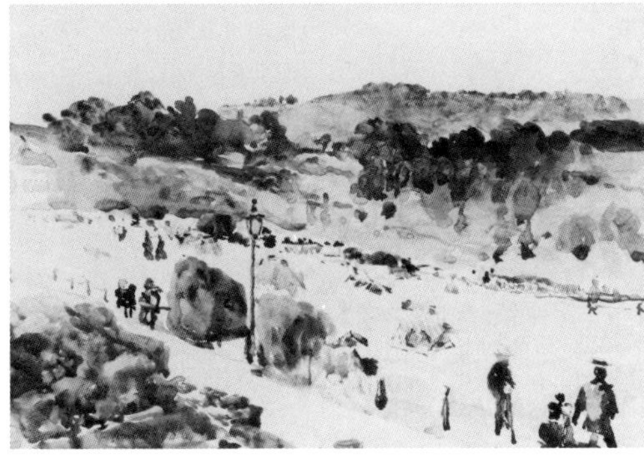

D.1933.35

The Beach, Babbacombe, Devon
watercolour, bodycolour (heightened with white)
signed lower left: *Francis E James*
267 × 376 mm
Dalton, Mrs W. B., Plummer, Miss E. M. (gift, 1933)
(D.1933.35)

■ JEWITT, THOMAS ORLANDO SKELTON (1799–1869)

Thomas Orlando Skelton Jewitt, son of the
topographer Arthur, was brought up in Derbyshire and
Yorkshire. He taught himself wood engraving and
contributed an account of a walking tour, illustrated by
himself, to the first number of *The Northern Star, or
Yorkshire Magazine*, published by his father in 1817.
Jewitt lived for a time in Oxford but then moved to
London, where he worked as a wood engraver.

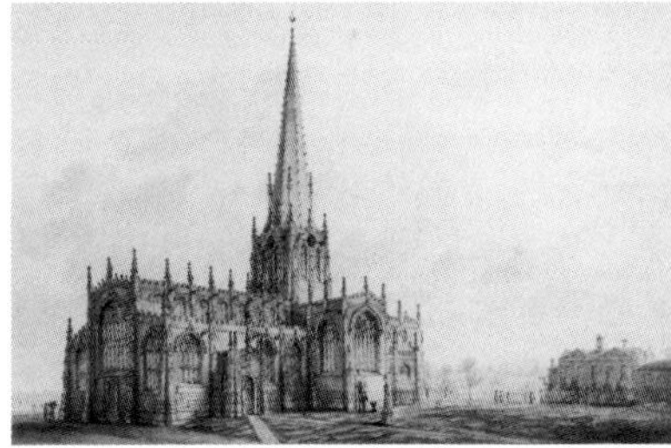

D.1893.10

Church of All Saints, Rotherham, Yorkshire
pencil, watercolour
inscribed centre verso (old attribution): *F.Nicholson*
[followed by illegible word]
174 × 262 mm
Agnew's (purchase, 18.12.1893) (D.1893.10)

■ JONES, THOMAS (1742–1803)

Jones, the second son of a Welsh landowner, studied
under Richard Wilson from 1763 to 1765. From 1776 to
1783 he visited Italy, during which time he kept a
journal that he later used to write his *Memoirs*; these
are an invaluable record of artistic life in Italy. Jones
found it difficult to sell his pictures and, on the death
of his elder brother in 1789, he inherited the family
estate, at which point his career as a professional artist
ended. He is now known for his innovative practice of
sketching in oil on paper.

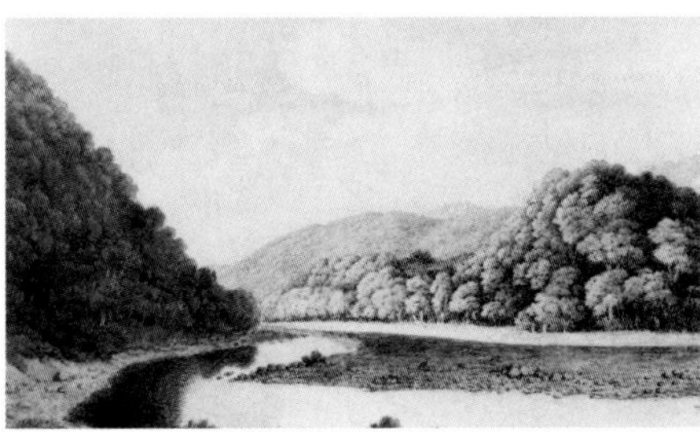

D.1956.2

The River Wye
pencil, watercolour
218 × 375 mm
Friends of the Whitworth (gift, 1956) (D.1956.2)

Lake Nemi looking towards Genzano, Italy
8.5.1777
pencil, watercolour
signed, inscribed & dated upper centre with initials:
*Looking over Gensano towards the promontory of Monte
Felice / from the Capuchin Convent 8 May 1777 Prince
Cesarini's Palace TJ*; inscribed on different parts of the
drawing identifying features of the landscape: *M Felice
/ Cesarini Palace / Capachini*
274 × 413 mm
Chorley, Lady, Friends of the Whitworth (via) (gift, 1961)
(D.1961.15)

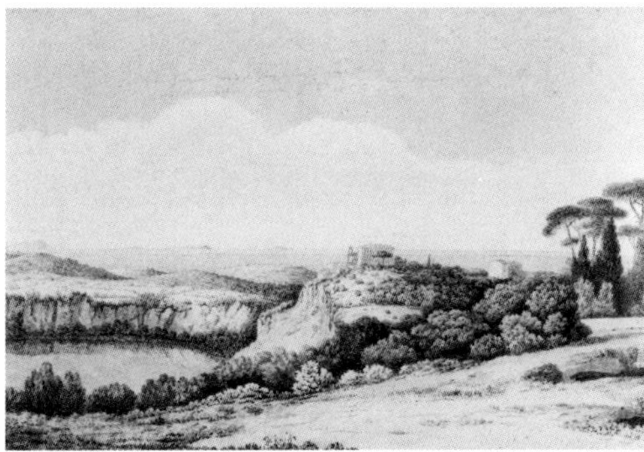

D.1961.15

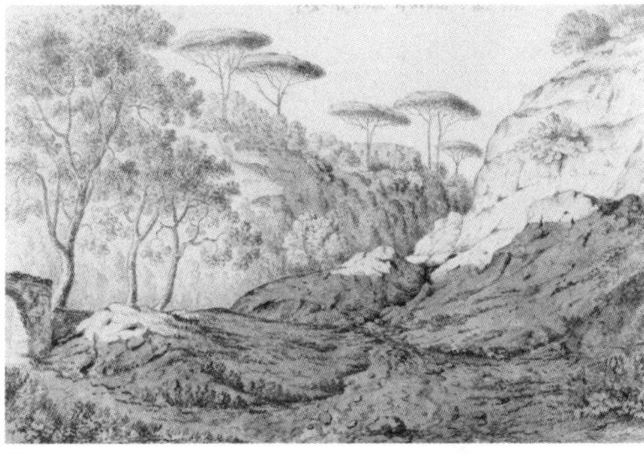

D.1962.3

**View of Santa Maria dei' Monti, near Naples
(recto); Study of the Church of St Efremo, near
Naples (verso)**
6.5.1781
pencil, watercolour
inscribed & dated upper centre: *Sa Ma de'Monti by
Naples 6 Oct* [month altered from May] *1781*
193 × 272 mm
Chorley, Lady, Friends of the Whitworth (via) (gift, 1962)
(D.1962.3)

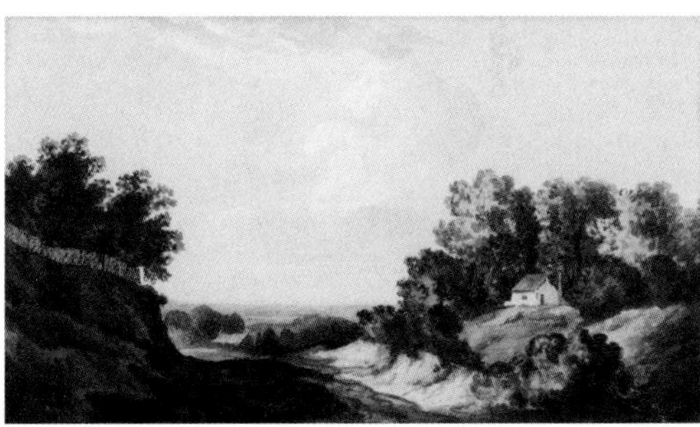

D.1989.2

A View in the Chilterns
24.8.1771
watercolour; watermark crown over HONI SOIT QUI
MAL Y PENSE
dated lower left: *24 August 1771–*
355 × 294 mm
Oliver, R. C. B. (gift, 1989) (D.1989.2)

A View in the Chilterns
20.8.1771
watercolour; watermark crown over HONI SOIT QUI
MAL Y PENSE
dated lower left: *August.20.1771*
355 × 294 mm
Evan-Thomas, Jane (bequest, 2000) (D.2000.5)

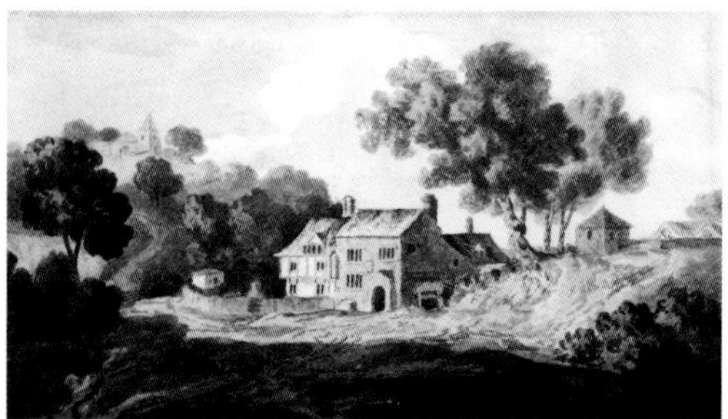

D.2000.6

A View in the Chilterns
26.8.1771
pen and brown ink, watercolour; watermark crown
over HONI SOIT QUI MAL Y PENSE
dated lower left: *August 26 1771*
355 × 294 mm
Evan-Thomas, Jane (bequest, 2000) (D.2000.6)

■ JOY, WILLIAM (1803–67)

Born in Yarmouth, Joy was a marine painter who
frequently collaborated with his brother John Cantiloe
Joy. The brothers later moved to Portsmouth where
they worked as government draughtsmen.

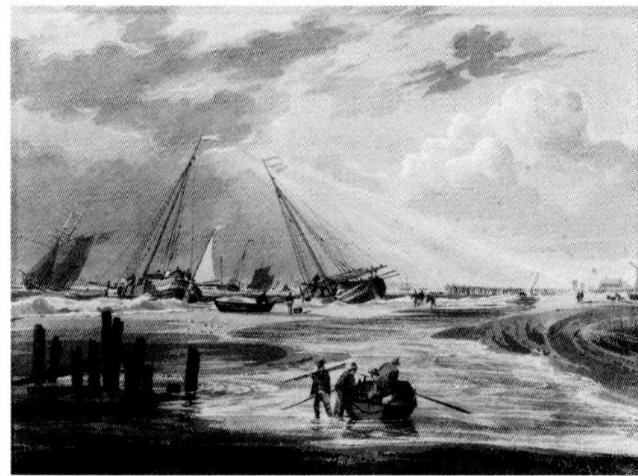

D.1982.9

Yarmouth Sands, Norfolk
watercolour
signed lower right: *W Joy*
inscribed upper left verso: [illegible word] *from Nature*
£1–1
250 × 337 mm
Hemmings, Lionel A. (gift, 1982) (D.1982.9)

■ KEENE, CHARLES SAMUEL (1823–91)

The greatest cartoonist of the Victorian period,
Keene began to draw for *Punch* in 1852 and worked for
the magazine for the rest of his life. His subjects are
urban and social rather than political. He was also a
book illustrator.

**'In the Park': Drawing for *Punch* Magazine
(recto); 'In the Pub': Drawing for *Punch*
Magazine (verso)**
pencil, watercolour, bodycolour
(heightened with white)
253 × 324 mm
Butterworth, W. (gift, 1913) (D.1913.8)

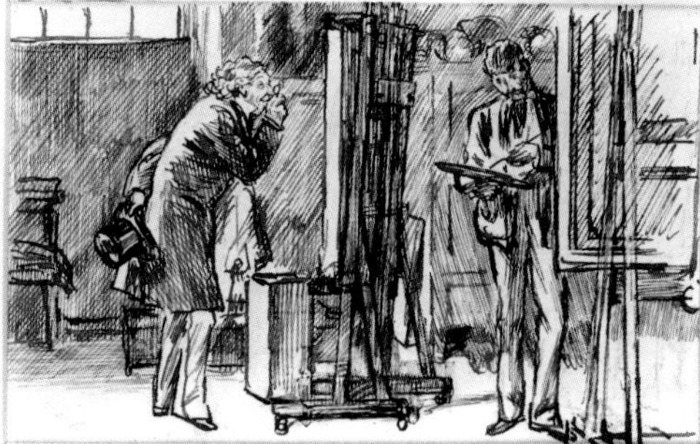

D.1958.4

**Prave 'Ords': "Dear Boy, How exquisitely you've
introduced your cool tertiaries": Drawing for
Punch Magazine**
1875
pen and brown ink, bodycolour
(heightened with white)
113 × 178 mm
Friends of the Whitworth (gift, 1958) (D.1958.4)

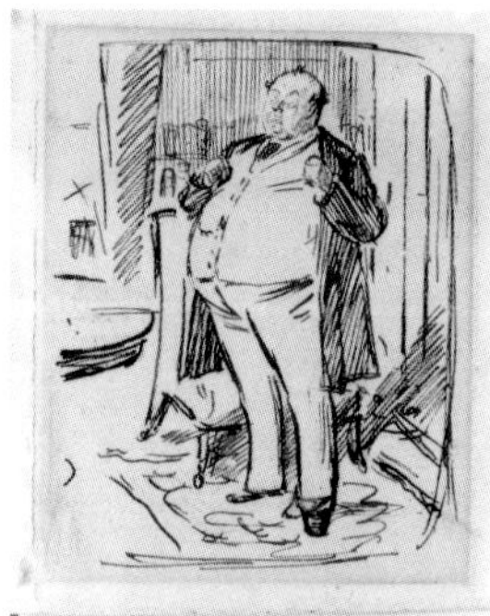

D.1960.90

'Matter': Drawing for *Punch* Magazine
1874
pen and brown ink; card
inscribed on separate sheet of paper attached to the
secondary support (accompanying caption): *"'Matter' /
Portly Old Swell (on reading Professor Tyndall's Speech) /
Dear me! Is it possible! Most 'xtr'ord'nary! – (throws /
down the Review) – That I should have been origin- / -
ally a 'Primordial Atomic Globule'!!'*
sheet 145 × 120 mm
University of Manchester, History of Art Department
(transfer, 1960) (D.1960.90)

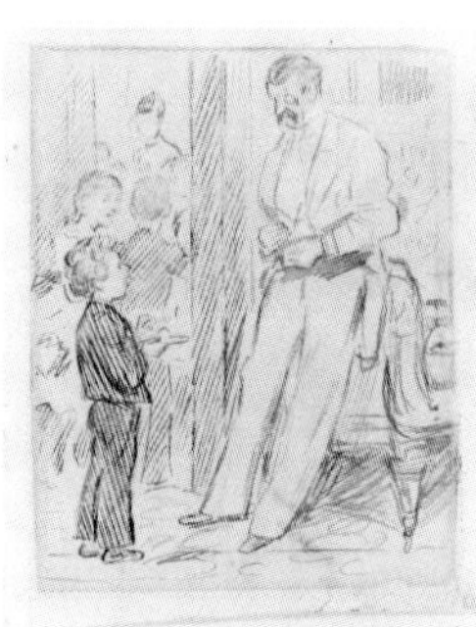

D.1960.91

'Natural Inference': Drawing for *Punch* Magazine
1878
pen and brown ink; card
inscribed on separate sheet of paper attached to the
secondary support (accompanying caption): *"'Natural
Inference' / Juvenile (to old Pawkins, who isn't "at home"
with / children). 'Ain't you going to dance?' / Pawkins
(doing his best) "Well, my boy – ah – / -yaas – eh – no – I
think –" / Juvenile "I s'ppose you're come for a regular /
"Stodge" at the supper!!".'*
sheet 161 × 118 mm
University of Manchester, History of Art Department
(transfer, 1960) (D.1960.91)

■ KENNION, EDWARD (attributed to) (1744–1809)

After an early career as a merchant in the West Indies,
Kennion became a drawing master and exhibited at the
Royal Academy between 1795 and 1807. His works are
influenced by George Barret Sen.

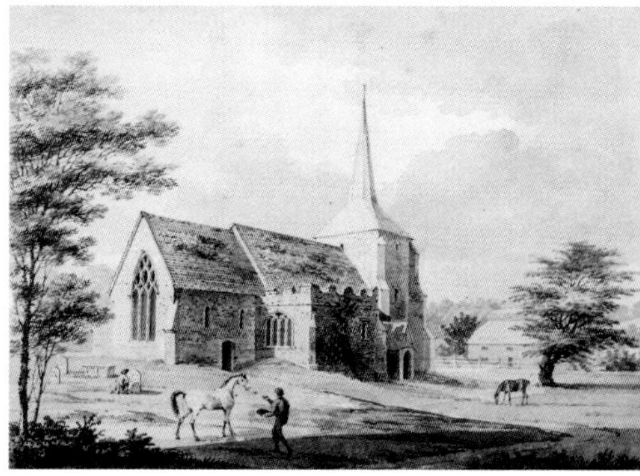

D.1926.325

A Country Church
pen and grey ink, grey watercolour
signed lower right: *Kenyon*
216 × 288 mm
Ogden, William Sharp (bequest, 1926) (D.1926.325)

■ KENT, WILLIAM (1684–1748)

Architect, designer and painter, Kent lived in Italy
from 1709 to 1719. On his return to Britain he was
employed on a number of projects by the Earl of
Burlington. Kent's most famous buildings are the
Horse Guards and the Treasury Building, both in
Whitehall. His architectural and decorative style was
hugely influential.

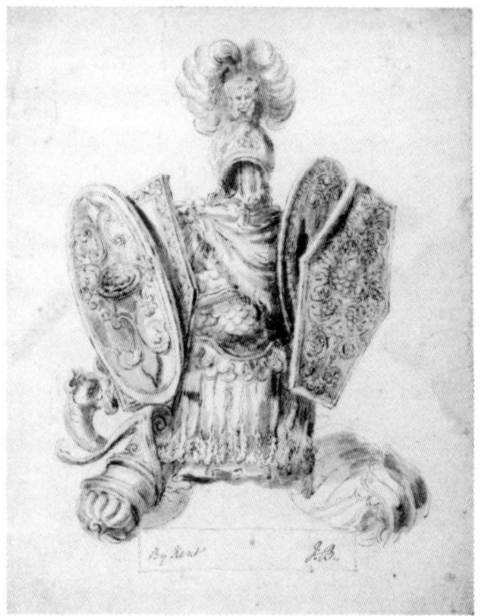

D.1965.2

Armorial Decoration
pen and brown ink, brown watercolour,
grey watercolour
inscribed lower left within cartouche in collector's
hand: *By Kent*; inscribed lower right within cartouche
with initials of the collector John Barnard (Lugt 1419):
J B–
213 × 163 mm
Sewter, Albert Charles (gift, 1965) (D.1965.2)

■ KERRICH, REV. THOMAS (1748–1828)

Kerrich graduated from Magdalene College,
Cambridge, in 1771, and travelled on the Continent
for the following four years. On his return he was
elected a fellow of Magdalene and in 1797 was
appointed principal librarian to the university.
A skilled draughtsman and printmaker, Kerrich
was interested in antiquarian subjects and painted
landscapes and portraits of his family and Cambridge
academic colleagues.

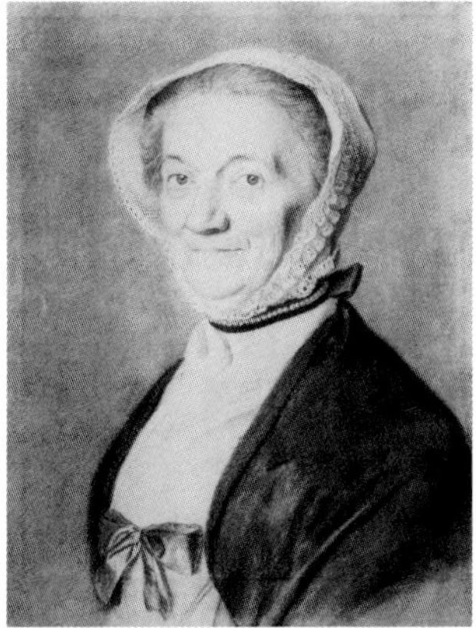
D.1991.9

Portrait of Elizabeth Postlethwayt
1.1777
black chalk, red chalk
signed, inscribed & dated lower left verso: *Elizabeth
Postlethwayt / aged 69 / Daughter of Matt.Postlethwayt
MA / Rector of Denton in / Norfolk. / T Kerrich delin /
Jan 1777 at Burnham / in Norfolk.*
465 × 339 mm
Berwick Fine Art, Shrewsbury (Christopher Powney)
(purchase, 10.1991) (F.O.W.) (D.1991.9)

■ KING, T. (dates unknown)

Unknown amateur artist.

Islington Light Horse
pen and brown ink, watercolour, bodycolour
(heightened with white)
signed lower right: *T.King fecit*
inscribed lower centre in border: *Islington Light Horse
1799*
321 × 263 mm
Ogden, William Sharp (bequest, 1926) (D.1926.291)

■ KNIGHT, JOHN BAVERSTOCK (1785–1859)

Born near Blandford in Dorset, Knight practised as a
land surveyor and made many tours of the British Isles
and the Continent. He was a competent amateur,
painting in oil and watercolour. He also produced
some prints.

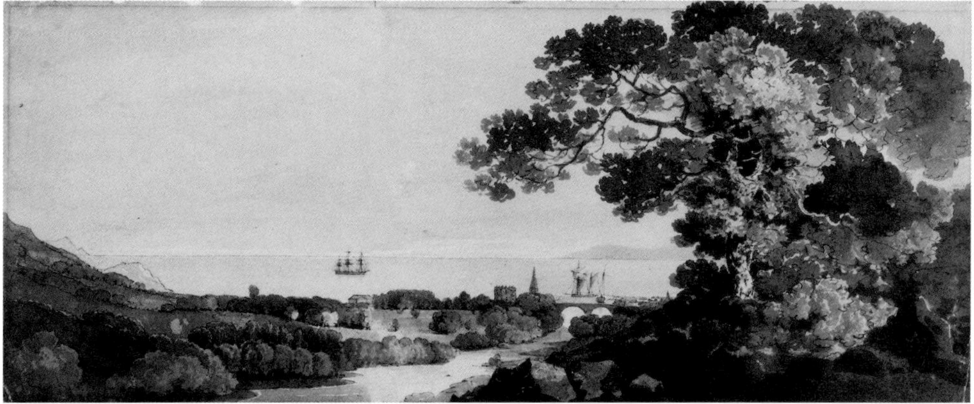
D.1932.1

**The Coast of Glenarm, Co Antrim,
Northern Ireland**
pen and brown ink, watercolour; two joined
sketchbook sheets
155 × 372 mm
Anderson, A. E. (gift, 1932) (D.1932.1)

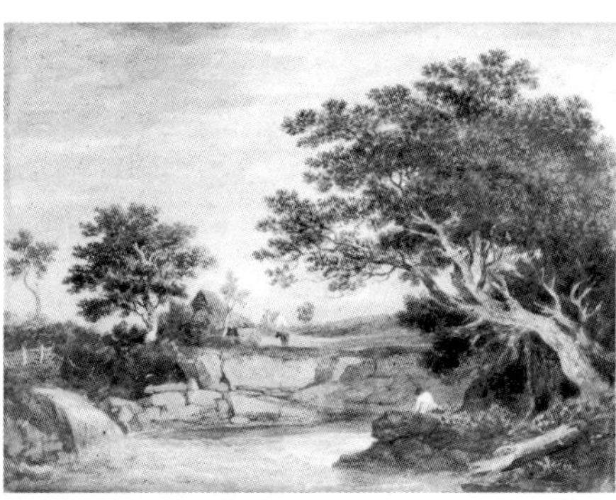
D.1932.2

Landscape with River
pencil, watercolour
221 × 287 mm
Anderson, A. E. (gift, 1932) (D.1932.2)

■ KNIGHT, JOHN WILLIAM BUXTON (1842–1908)

Born in Sevenoaks, Knight entered the Royal
Academy Schools in 1860 and exhibited at the
Royal Academy from 1861.

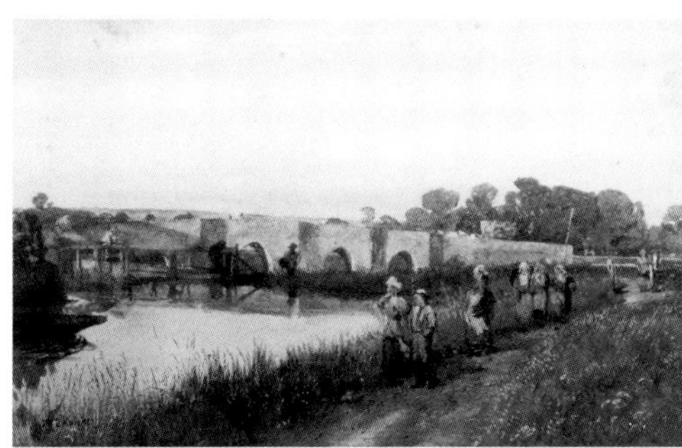
D.1912.10

The Bridge at Twyford, Evening
1876
watercolour, bodycolour (heightened with white)
signed & dated lower left: *JWBKnight / 76*
343 × 503 mm
Messrs Gooden and Fox (purchase, 1912) (D.1912.10)

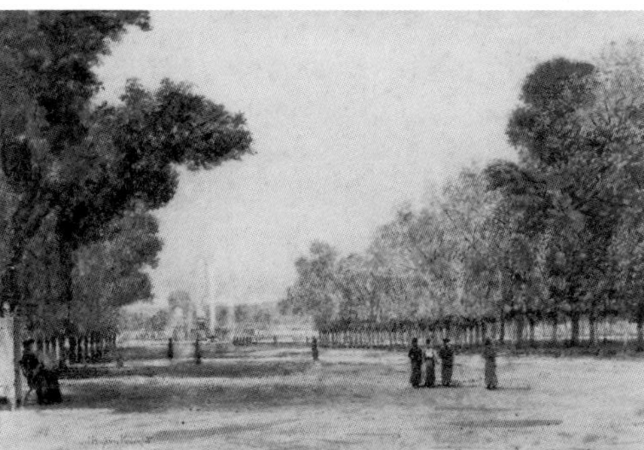
D.1939.20

The Tuileries Gardens, Paris
1904
watercolour, pen and brown ink, bodycolour
signed & dated lower left: *J Buxton Knight / 1904*
474 × 698 mm
Smith, Frank Hindley (bequest, 1939) (D.1939.20)

■ KNIGHT, JOSEPH (1837–1909)

Knight was born in Manchester and moved to London
in 1871. He settled in North Wales at Bettws-y-Coed in
1875. Knight was elected a member of the Institute of
Painters in Watercolours in 1881.

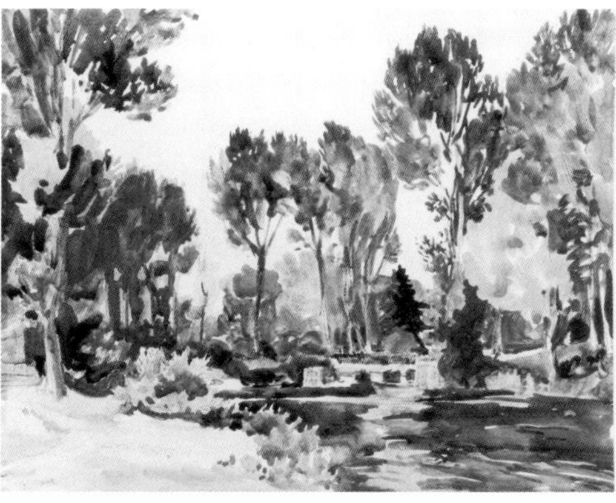
D.1934.9

**Stream through a Wood, near Chartres, France
(recto); Study of a House (verso)**
pencil, pen and red ink, watercolour (recto)
signed lower left: *J.KNIGHT.*
240 × 302 mm
Duxbury, Percival (gift, 1934) (D.1934.9)

■ LA CAVE, PETER (fl. 1789–1816)

La Cave was a prolific artist of whom little is known. Probably of French descent, he lived in London from around 1789 to 1816 and exhibited at the Royal Academy in 1801. Early in his career he produced topographical views, and later turned to watercolour groups of cattle, horses and peasants. La Cave had professional connections with Julius Caesar Ibbetson and George Morland.

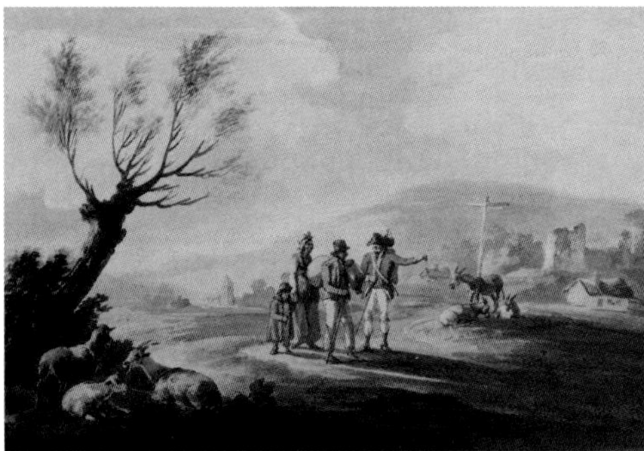

D.1924.4

A Soldier directing a Family along a Country Road

1797
pen and brown ink
signed & dated lower right: *La Cave / 1797*
240 × 347 mm
Dalmeny Gallery, London (purchase, 1924) (D.1924.4)

A Kennelman showing Greyhounds to two Gentlemen (recto); Study of Greyhounds (verso)

pencil
signed (?) lower left: *Le Cave*
248 × 345 mm
University of Manchester, History of Art Department (transfer, 1960) (D.1960.95)

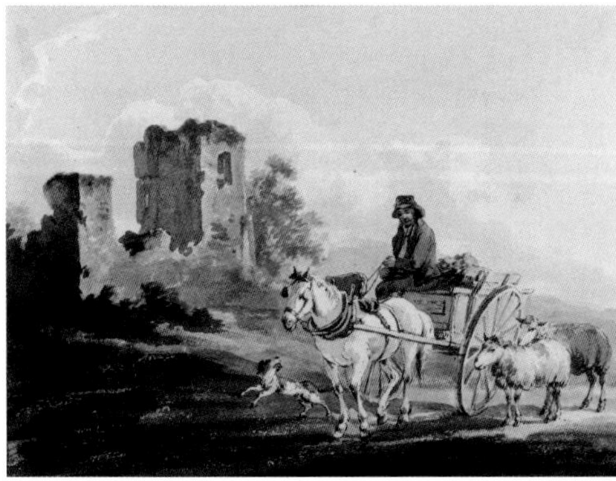

D.1970.51

A Horse and Cart by a Ruin

1800
pencil, pen and brown ink, watercolour
signed & dated lower right: *La Cave 1800*
198 × 258 mm
Towlson, Hector J. (bequest, 1969) (D.1970.51)

■ LANCASTER, PERCY (1878–1950)

Lancaster, a landscape painter in oil and watercolour, studied at the Manchester School of Art and worked in the Cox tradition. Living for many years in Southport in Lancashire, he was elected a member of the Royal Institute of Painters in Watercolours in 1921.

Yorkshire Moors

1924
pencil, watercolour
signed & dated lower right: *P.LANCASTER / 1924*
235 × 340 mm
Watson, A (gift, 1924) (D.1924.7)

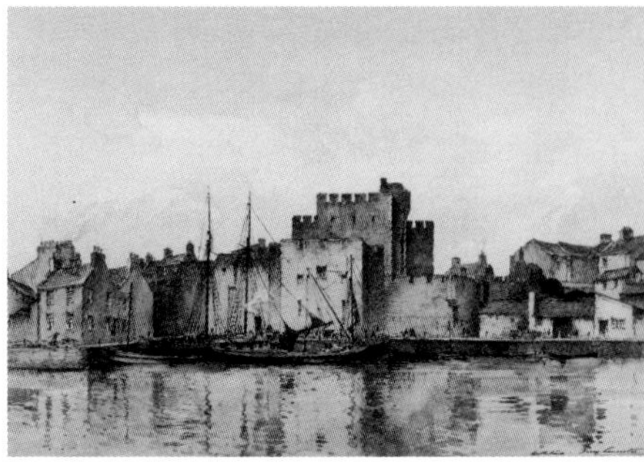

D.1937.7

Castletown, Isle of Man

pencil, black chalk, pen and black ink, watercolour
signed and inscribed lower right [surname underlined]:
Castletown. Percy. Lancaster.
354 × 506 mm
Lancaster, Percy (gift, 1937) (D.1937.7)

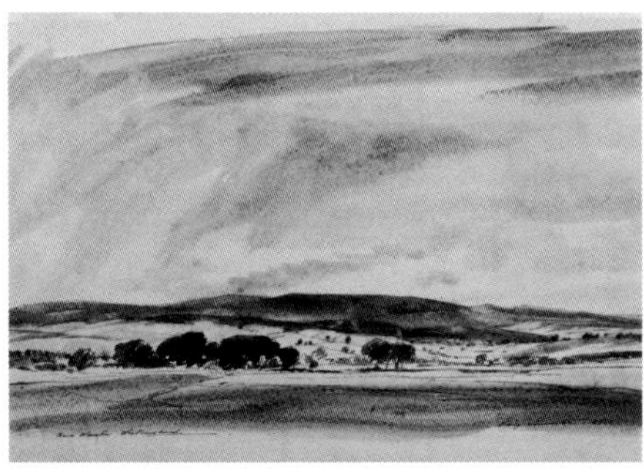

D.1937.8

Near Winster, Westmorland

1935
pen and brown ink, brown watercolour; beige paper
signed & dated lower right: *Percy Lancaster.35.*
inscribed lower left: *Near Winster. Westmorland.*
296 × 415 mm
Lancaster, Percy (gift, 1937) (D.1937.8)

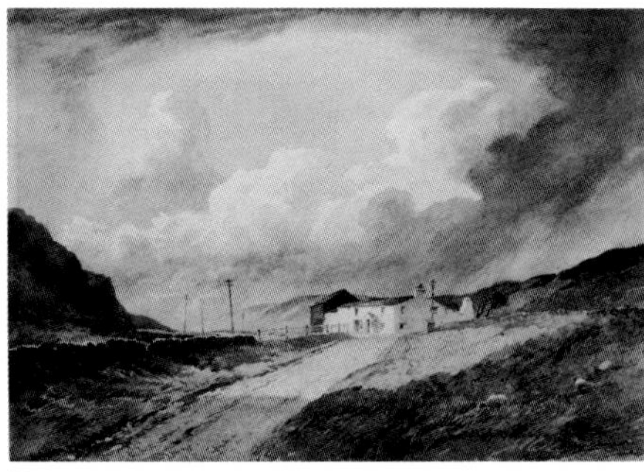

D.1944.5

Travellers Rest, at the Head of Kirkstone Pass, Westmorland

1943
pencil, watercolour
signed, inscribed & dated lower right:
Percy Lancaster / 43 / Kirkstone
351 × 507 mm
Pilkington, Denis F. (gift, 1944) (D.1944.5)

■ LANGTON, WILLIAM (1803–81)

Langton, an antiquary, financier and draughtsman, was the Managing Director of the Manchester and Salford Bank from 1854 to 1876. In 1846, Langton was Secretary of the Committee to obtain a university for Manchester, resulting in 1851 in the founding of Owens College, now called The University of Manchester.

Scarthwaite Church, Lancashire

pencil, brown watercolour
92 × 139 mm
Philips, Mrs Herbert (gift, 1913) (D.1913.18)

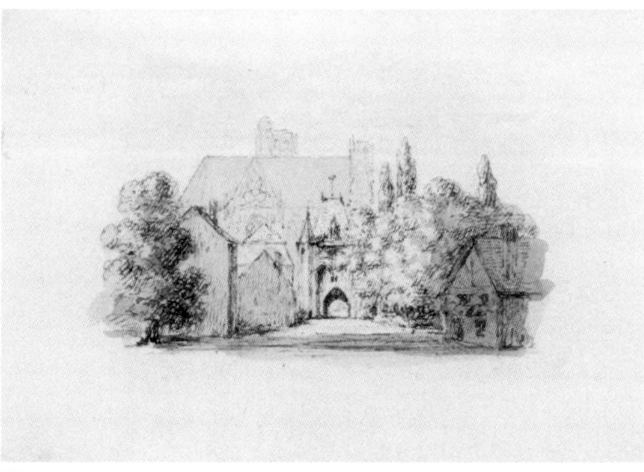

D.1913.31

A medieval Gateway in France, with a Church beyond

pencil, pen and brown ink, watercolour
113 × 155 mm
Philips, Mrs Herbert (gift, 1913) (D.1913.31)

■ LAPORTE, JOHN (1761–1839)

Laporte, a drawing master who exhibited at the Royal Academy from 1779, numbered Dr Thomas Monro among his pupils. He published a number of manuals on landscape watercolour painting, of which the most famous is *The Progress of a Water-Coloured Drawing* (ca. 1802), which went into several editions and showed fourteen stages in the outline and colouring of a watercolour.

Meeting of the Wye and Severn, Monmouthshire, Wales

watercolour, bodycolour (heightened with white)
249 × 299 mm
Watson, A. (gift, 1924) (D.1924.5)

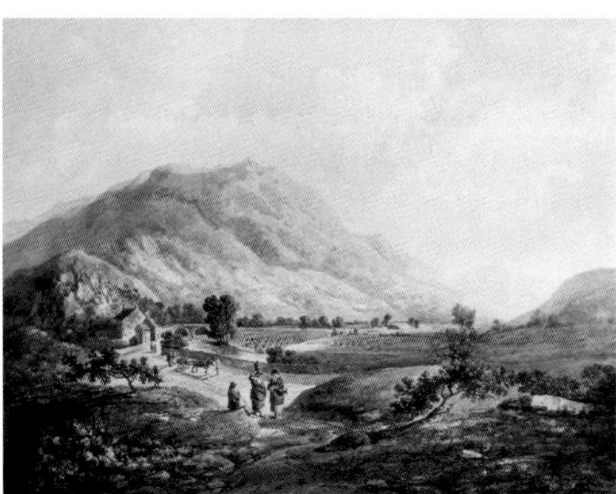

D.1931.37

View of Snowdon, Caernarvonshire, Wales
pencil, watercolour
490 × 627 mm
Goldschmidt, R. F. (gift, 1931) (D.1931.37)

■ LAROON, MARCELLUS (1679–1774)
Laroon, a painter of rococo conversations, fancy
pictures, stage scenes and occasional portraits, was
more of an amateur than a professional artist, but
consorted much with artists and with the stage and
musical worlds. He was a lively draughtsman of
Hogarthian figures.

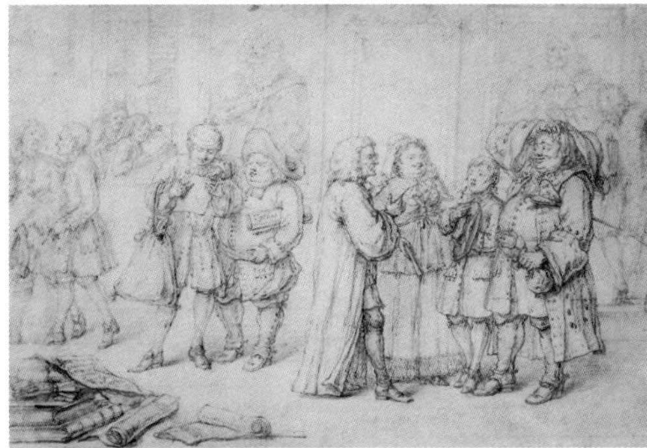

D.1920.1

**A Farmer putting his Son Apprentice
to an Attorney**
1731
pencil
signed & dated lower right margin: *Mar Laroon Fecit
1731*; inscribed lower left margin: *a Farmer putting his
son apprentice to an Attorney*
312 × 451 mm
untraced (purchase, 1920) (D.1920.1)

■ LASTON, ANNA (dates unknown)
Unknown artist.

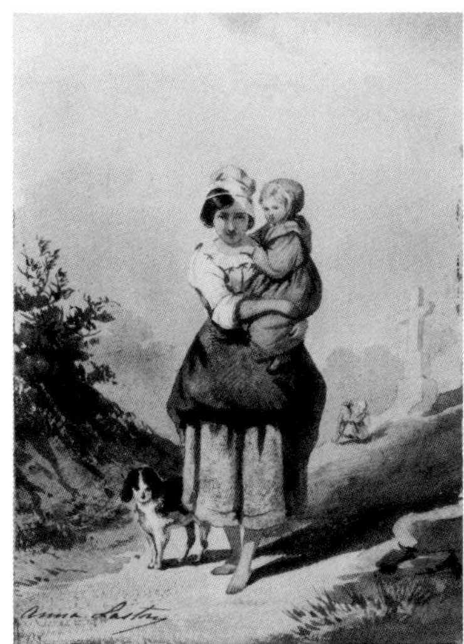

D.1987.58

A Peasant Woman holding a Baby on a Path
pencil, watercolour, bodycolour (heightened
with white)
signed lower left: *Anna Laston*
167 × 117 mm
Hitchon, Dr Brian (gift, 1987) (D.1987.58)

■ LAWSON, CECIL GORDON (1851–82)
Born in Shropshire and the son of a portrait painter,
Lawson came to London in 1861. He exhibited at the
Royal Academy from 1870 until his death.

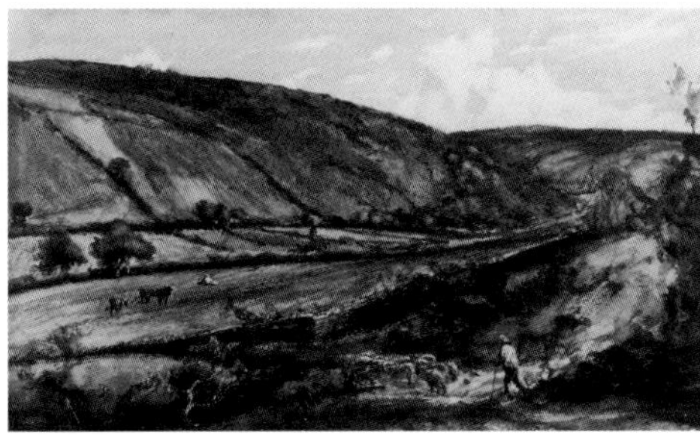

D.1927.30

The Brendon Valley, Devon
pencil, watercolour
245 × 410 mm
Agnew's (purchase, 1927) (D.1927.30)

■ LAWSON, FRANCIS WILFRID (1842–1935)
Francis Wilfrid Lawson, painter and illustrator and the
elder brother of Cecil Gordon, contributed illustrations
to the *Cornhill Magazine*, *The Graphic*, *Once a Week*
and other periodicals during the 1860s and 1870s.

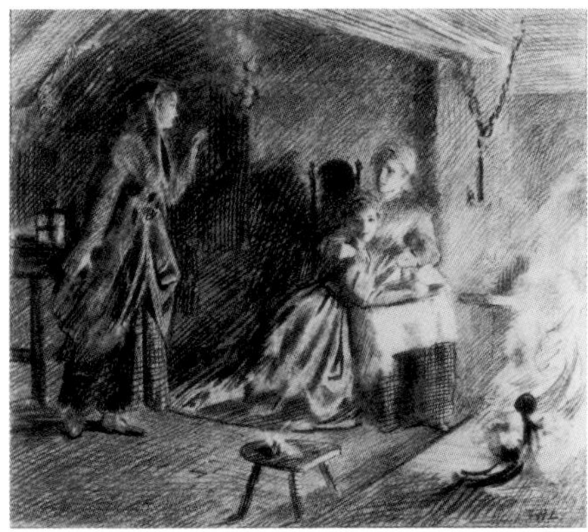

D.1914.5

**The Pastorate of John Barnett:
A Magazine Illustration**
1869
black chalk
signed lower left with initials: *F W L*; signed, inscribed
& dated in pencil on sheet of paper attached to verso:
*1868 Jan 1869 / Pastorate of John Barnett / No 1 /
F.Wilfrid Lawson*
189 × 216 mm
untraced (purchase, 1914) (D.1914.5)

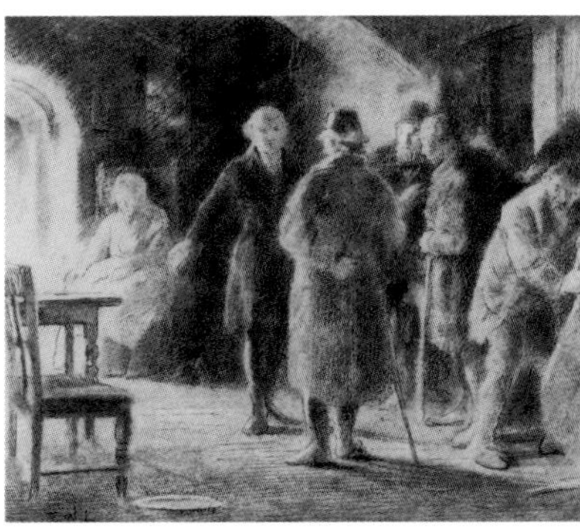

D.1914.6

**The Pastorate of John Barnett:
A Magazine Illustration**
8.1.1869
black chalk
signed lower right with initials: *F W L*; signed,
inscribed & dated in black chalk in margin below
image: *Gorway Engr / The Pastorate of John Barnett / No
2 / F.Wilfrid Lawson 8/1/69*
134 × 151 mm
untraced (purchase, 1914) (D.1914.6)

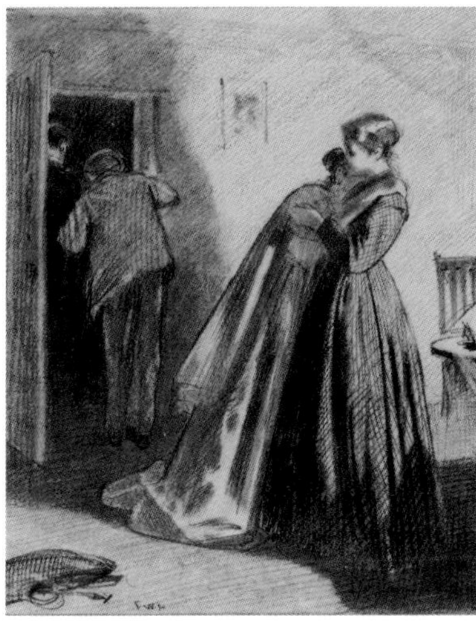

D.1914.8

**'What had I to do with the gaieties of the
world?': An Illustration to *Esther West* for
The Quiver Magazine**
10.11.1868
pencil
signed lower left with initials: *F W L*; signed, inscribed
& dated in margin below image:– *Phillips hurt /
F.Wilfrid Lawson 10th/11/68*
224 × 174 mm
untraced (purchase, 1914) (D.1914.8)

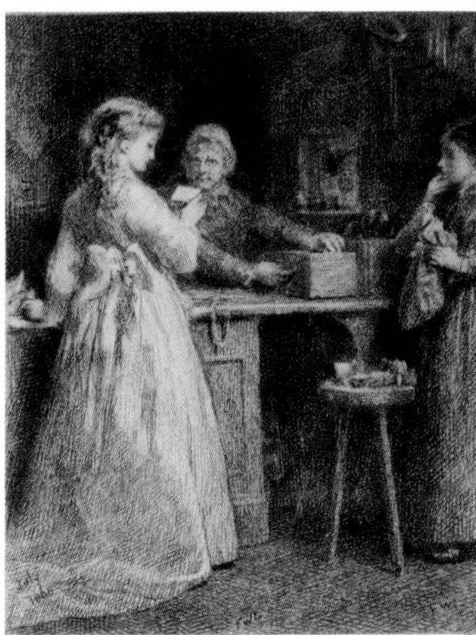

D.1914.9

**'"Yes, I will take it", she said': An Illustration to
Esther West for *The Quiver* Magazine**
1868
black chalk
signed lower centre with initials: *F W L*; dated lower
left: *July / 1868*; signed, inscribed & dated on a small
label attached to verso: *The Village Post – / F.W.L 1868*
152 × 120 mm
untraced (purchase, 1914) (D.1914.9)

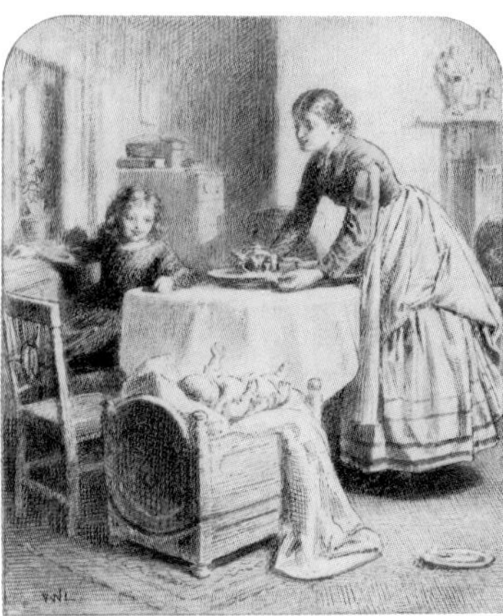

D.1914.10

A Woman and her Children in an Interior: An unused Illustration to Bishop Heber's *Hymns*
1865
pencil, pen and brown ink, grey watercolour
signed lower left with initials: *F W L*; signed, inscribed & dated in margin below image: *1865.66. / Heber's Hymns / F.Wilfrid Lawson / Engd by Cooper*
148 × 126 mm
untraced (purchase, 1914) (D.1914.10)

Study for 'Take care, darlint': An Illustration to *Esther West* **for** *The Quiver* **Magazine**
12.9.1868
black chalk
signed & dated in margin below image lower right with initials: *F.W.L. / Septr.12th.68.*
226 × 176 mm
untraced (purchase, 1914) (D.1914.11)

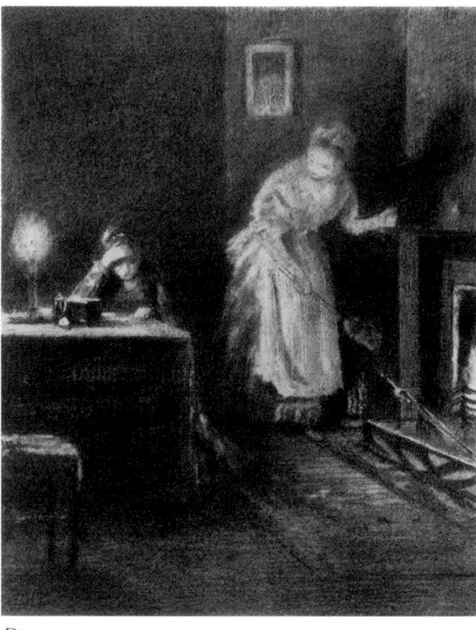

D.1914.12

'The old servant lingered to brush up the hearth': An Illustration to *Under Foot* **for** *The Quiver* **Magazine**
1869
black chalk, bodycolour (heightened with white)
signed lower left with initials: *F W L*; signed, inscribed & dated in margin below image with initials: *F.W.L. 11/2nd 69 / No 2 / The Old Nurse* [underlined] */ Quiver* [underlined] *drawing / (No 1 / The two friends* [underlined] *) / [illegible] Payne / Exted International Ex 1871*
225 × 174 mm
untraced (purchase, 1914) (D.1914.12)

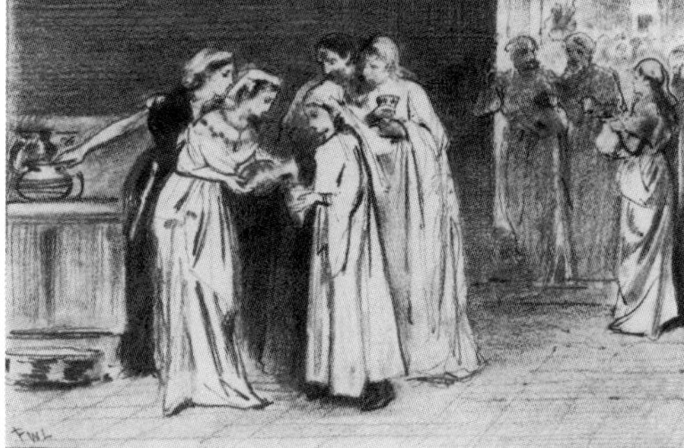

D.1914.13

The Wedding Feast
27.4.1869
black chalk
signed lower left with initials: *F W L*; signed & dated in margin below image lower right: *FWilfrid Lawson.27/4/69*; inscribed in margin below image lower centre: *The Wedding Feast*
101 × 151 mm
untraced (purchase, 1914) (D.1914.13)

Christ walking on the Water
23.4.1869
black chalk
signed & dated in margin below image lower right with initials: *23 Apl 69 – FWL*
103 × 149 mm
untraced (purchase, 1914) (D.1914.14)

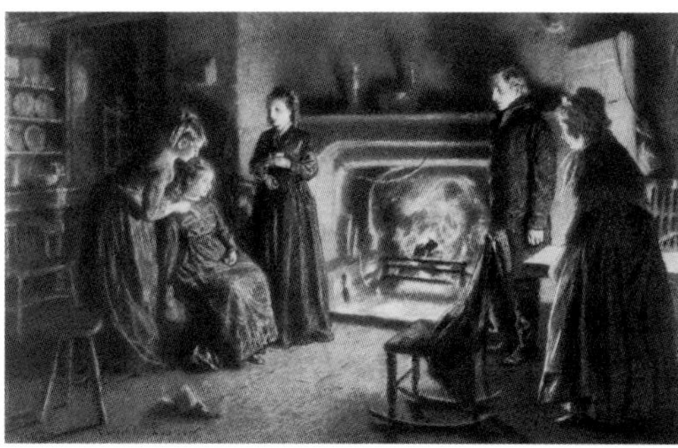

D.1914.15

An Interior with Figures by a Fireplace: A Magazine Illustration
black chalk, pen and brown ink, bodycolour (heightened with white)
signed lower left: *F Wilfid* [sic] *LAWSON*
263 × 404 mm
untraced (purchase, 1914) (D.1914.15)

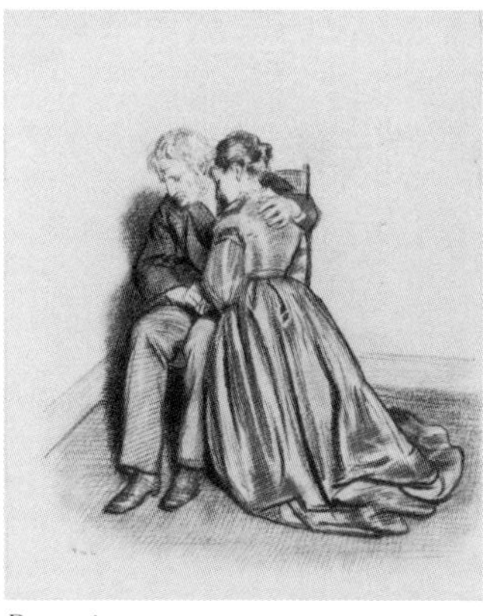

D.1914.16

'I shall leave you to one who will love you': An Illustration to *His By Right* **for** *The Quiver* **Magazine**
18.11.1871
black chalk, bodycolour (heightened with white)
signed lower left with initials: *F W L*; signed in margin below image lower left: *F W Lawson*; dated in margin below image lower right: *18 Nov 1871*
150 × 123 mm
untraced (purchase, 1914) (D.1914.16)

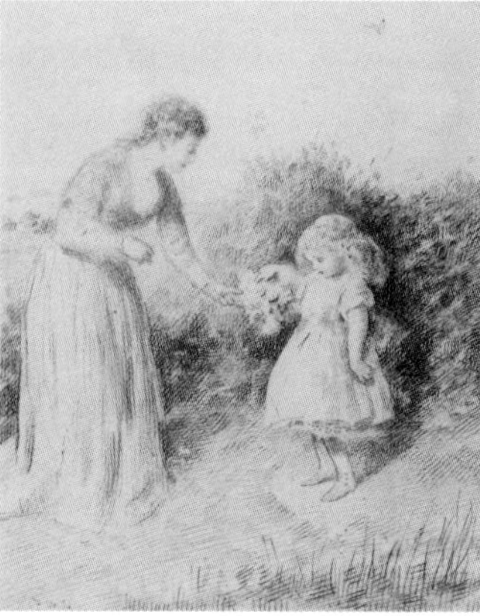

D.1914.17

'The child pointed to the newly-gathered white rose': An Illustration to *Esther West* **for** *The Quiver* **Magazine**
17.8.1868
pencil
signed lower left with initials: *F W L*; signed & dated in margin below image lower right: *F.Wilfrid Lawson Aug 17/68*; inscribed in margin below image lower centre: *Choosing*
115 × 172 mm
untraced (purchase, 1914) (D.1914.17)

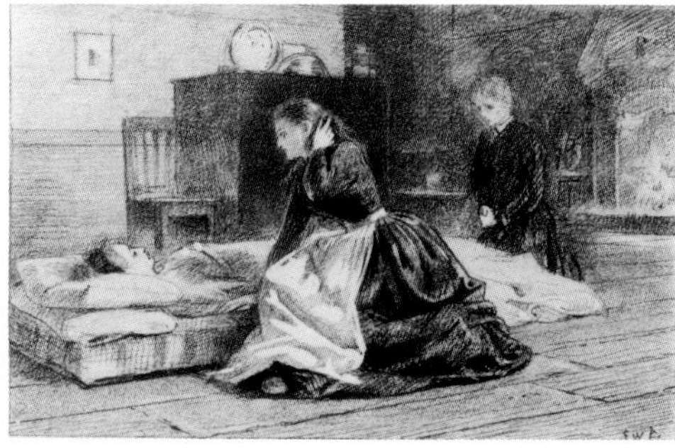

D.1914.18

'I shall go to him': An Illustration to *Avonhoe* **for** *The Cornhill Magazine*
black chalk, bodycolour (heightened with white)
signed lower right with initials: *F W L,* signed in margin below image lower right with initials: *F.W.L*
179 × 228 mm
untraced (purchase, 1914) (D.1914.18)

Lettice's Lovers: An Illustration to *Lettice Lisle* **for** *The Cornhill Magazine*
12.1868
black chalk, bodycolour (heightened with white)
signed, inscribed & dated in margin below image: *F.Wilfrid Lawson – / Lettice Lisle / Dec/68 / – Cornhill for Jan 7/69 –*
174 × 228 mm
untraced (purchase, 1914) (D.1914.19)

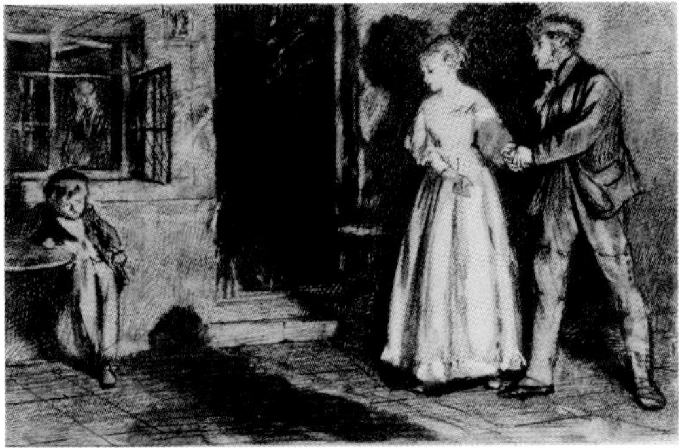

D.1914.19

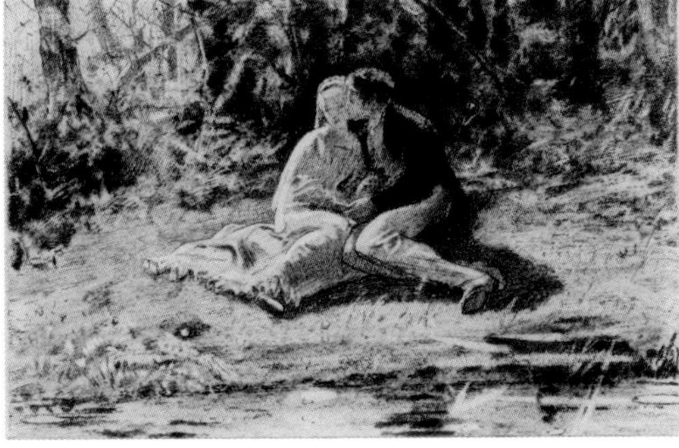

D.1914.20

Springtide: An Illustration to *Lettice Lisle* for *The Cornhill Magazine*
9.4.1869
black chalk, bodycolour (heightened with white)
signed, inscribed & dated in margin below image:
Cornhill Mag for May 69 / SPRINGTIDE / F.Wilfrid Lawson 9.4.69
158 × 228 mm
untraced (purchase, 1914) (D.1914.20)

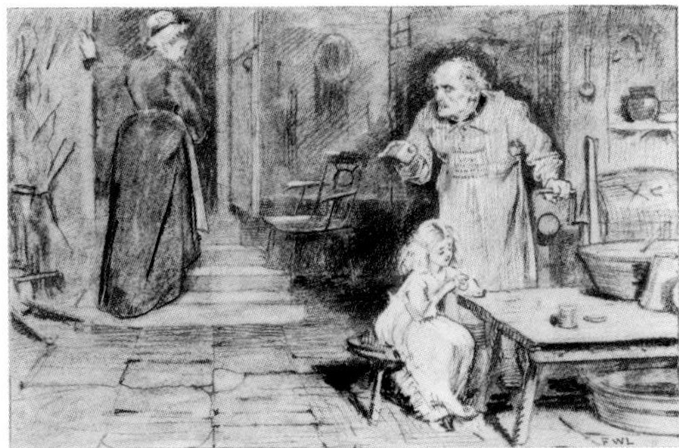

D.1914.21

Lettice sewing up the Amulet: An Illustration to *Lettice Lisle* for *The Cornhill Magazine*
1869
pencil, pen and brown ink, bodycolour
(heightened with white)
signed lower right with initials: *F W L*; signed,
inscribed & dated in margin below image: *Cornhill Mag/69 / Eyes to the Blind / F.W.Lawson*
105 × 157 mm
untraced (purchase, 1914) (D.1914.21)

Portrait of Cecil Lawson (recto); Study of a Boat (verso)
watercolour, bodycolour (heightened with white)
signed lower right: *FWLAWSON*
159 × 192 mm
untraced (purchase, 1914) (D.1914.22)

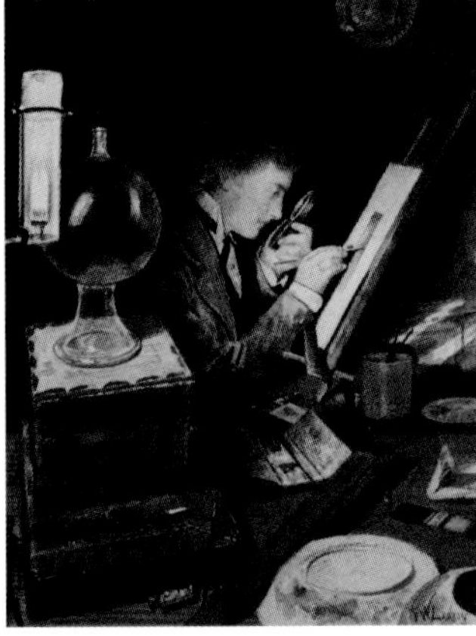

D.1914.22

■ LEAR, EDWARD (1812–88)

Painter, illustrator and author, Lear has become
one of the best-known Victorian artist travellers.
After an initial career as a bird illustrator, he
turned to landscape and spent most of the rest of
his life out of England, firstly in Italy, then in Corfu
and finally at San Remo in north Italy where he died.
Although now widely admired for his nonsense rhymes
and limericks, Lear was a hugely prolific and versatile
draughtsman. He published lithographs after his
drawings and also painted in oils.

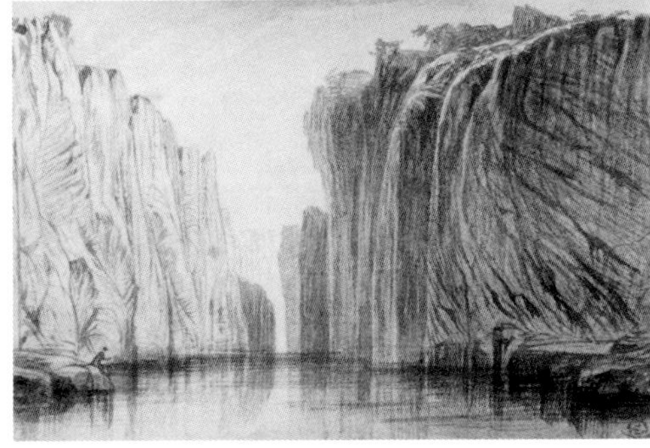

D.1926.39

Jubbulpore Rocks, India
watercolour, bodycolour (heightened with white)
signed lower right with monogram: *EL*; inscribed lower
centre on mount below image: *JUBBULPORE ROCKS*
120 × 184 mm
Zimmerman, Agnes (bequest, 1926) (D.1926.39)

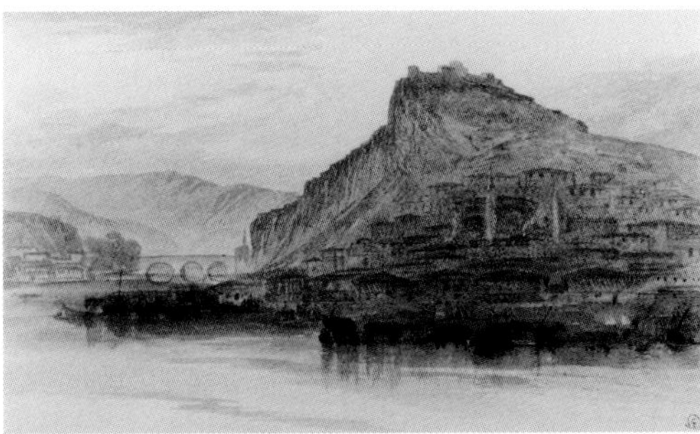

D.1926.40

Berat, Albania
watercolour, bodycolour (heightened with white)
signed lower right with monogram: *EL*
165 × 262 mm
Zimmerman, Agnes (bequest, 1926) (D.1926.40)

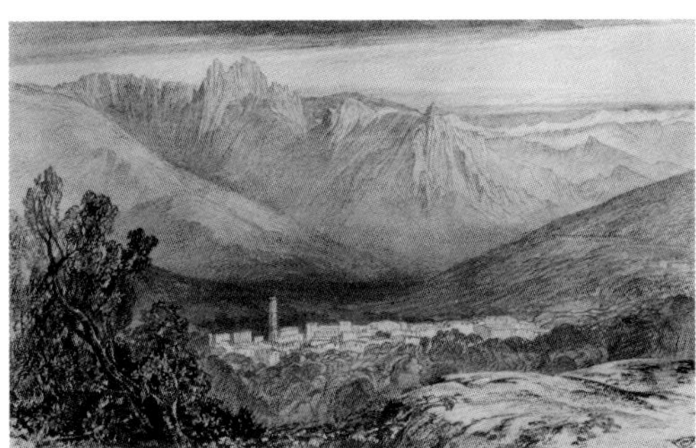

D.1926.41

Vico, Corsica, France
1868
pencil, pen and brown ink, watercolour, bodycolour
(heightened with white)
signed lower right with monogram: *EL*
122 × 194 mm
Zimmerman, Agnes (bequest, 1926) (D.1926.41)

View from Delphi across the Gulf of Corinth, Greece
pen and brown ink, watercolour, bodycolour
(heightened with white); blue paper
signed lower left with monogram: *EL*
177 × 377 mm
Zimmerman, Agnes (bequest, 1926) (D.1926.42)

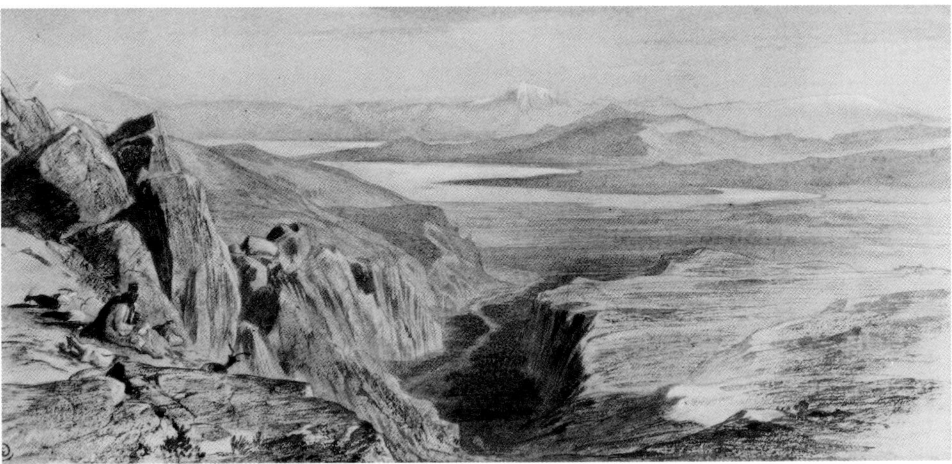

D.1926.42

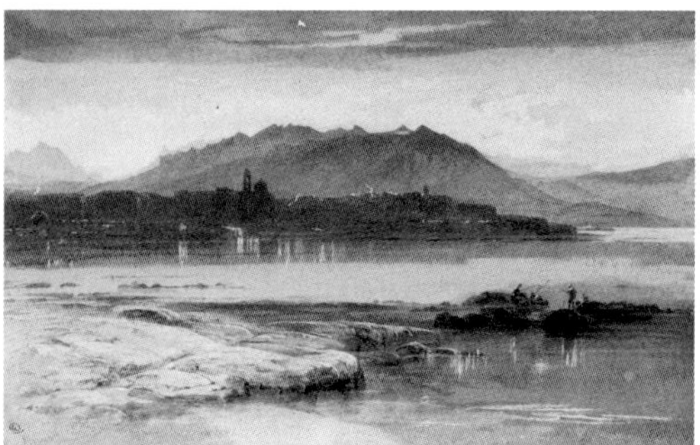

D.1926.43

Ajaccio, Corsica, France
pen and brown ink, watercolour, bodycolour
(heightened with white)
signed (twice) & inscribed lower left with monograms:
EL / Ajaccio / EL
296 × 463 mm
Zimmerman, Agnes (bequest, 1926) (D.1926.43)

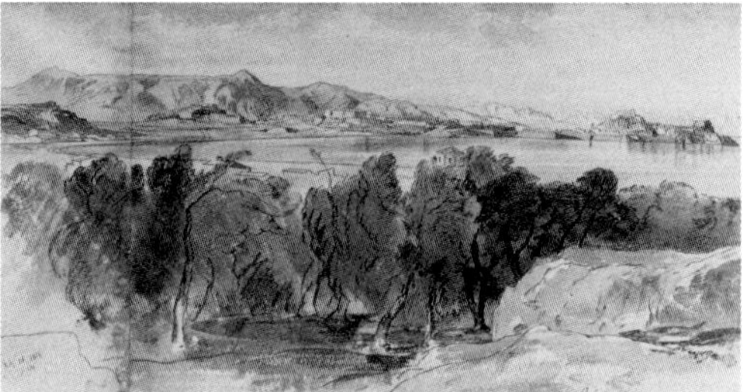

D.1930.69

The Bay at Corfu
26.2.1856
pencil, pen and brown ink, watercolour
dated lower left: *Feby.26.1856. / 5.P.M.*
350 × 657 mm
Craddock and Barnard, Messrs (gift, 1930) (D.1930.69)

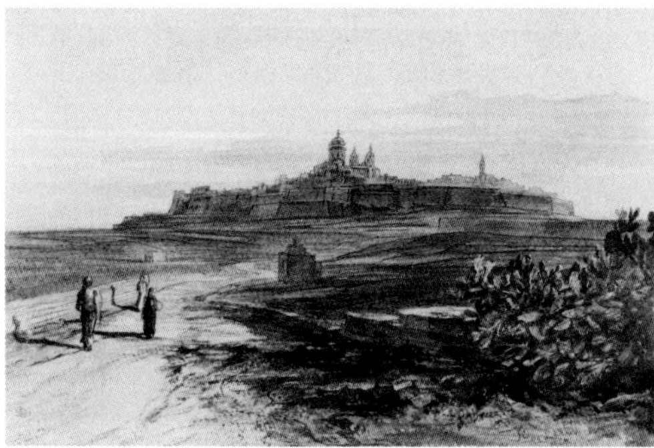

D.1963.3

View of Mdina, Malta
1866
pen and brown ink, watercolour, bodycolour
(heightened with white)
signed & dated lower right with initial in monogram:
ELear 1866; signed lower left with monogram: *EL*
181 × 271 mm
Langton, Miss F. M., National Art Collections Fund (via)
(bequest, 1963) (D.1963.3)

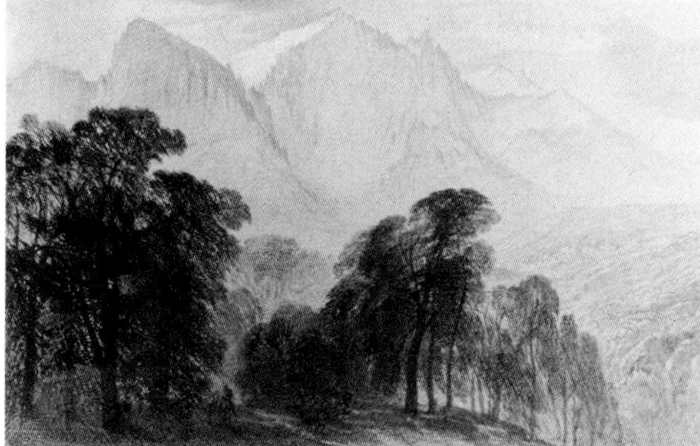

D.1963.4

Monte d'Oro, Corsica, France
1868
pencil, pen and brown ink, watercolour, bodycolour
(heightened with white)
126 × 198 mm
Langton, Miss F. M., National Art Collections Fund (via)
(bequest, 1963) (D.1963.4)

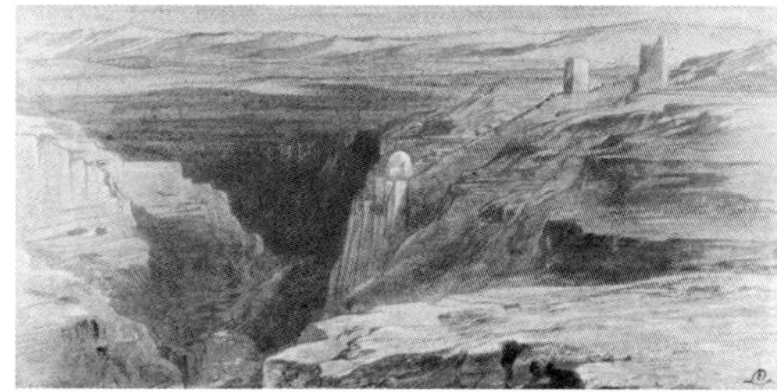

D.1963.5

The Monastery of Mar Saba, Jordan
watercolour, bodycolour (heightened with white)
blue paper
signed lower right with monogram: *EL*
102 × 203 mm
Langton, Miss F. M., National Art Collections Fund (via)
(bequest, 1963) (D.1963.5)

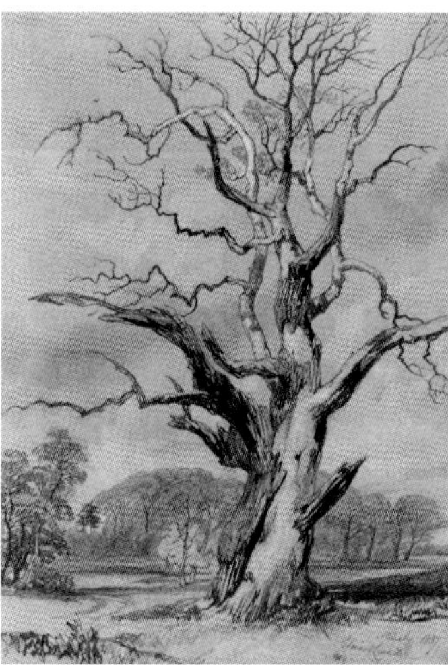

D.1981.1

Study of Trees in Alderley Park, Cheshire
1837
pencil, black chalk, bodycolour (heightened with
white); blue-grey paper
signed, inscribed & dated lower right: *Alderley.1837. /
Edward Lear.del.*
349 × 244 mm
John Baskett Ltd, London (purchase, 1981) (V. & A.,
N.A.C.F., F.O.W.) (D.1981.1)

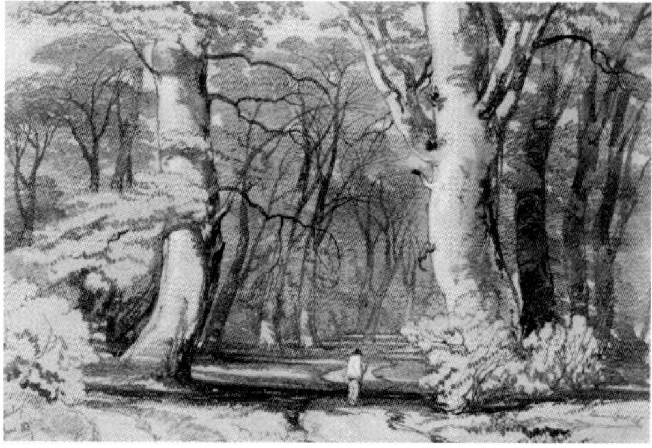

D.1981.2

Study of Trees in Alderley Park, Cheshire
6.1837
pencil, black chalk, bodycolour (heightened with
white); blue-grey paper
signed lower right: *Edward Lear. del.*; inscribed &
dated lower left: *Alderley.June.1837.*
247 × 355 mm
John Baskett Ltd, London (purchase, 1981) (V. & A.,
N.A.C.F., F.O.W.) (D.1981.2)

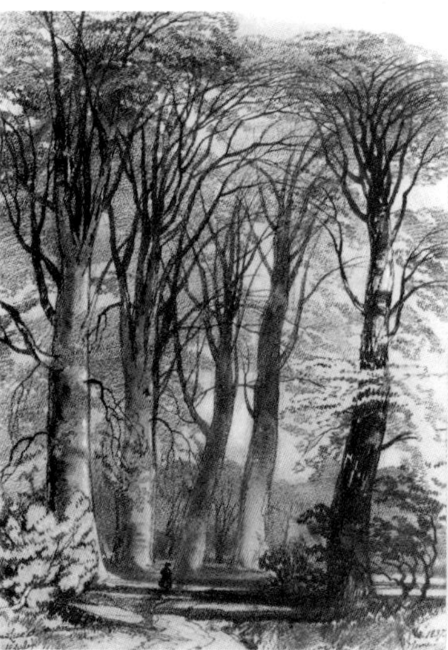

D.1981.3

Study of Trees in Alderley Park, Cheshire
6.1837
pencil, black chalk, bodycolour (heightened with
white); blue-grey paper
signed & inscribed lower left: *Edward Lear. del /
Alderley.*; dated lower right: *1837. / June.* [underlined]
355 × 247 mm
John Baskett Ltd, London (purchase, 1981)
(V. & A., N.A.C.F., F.O.W.) (D.1981.3)

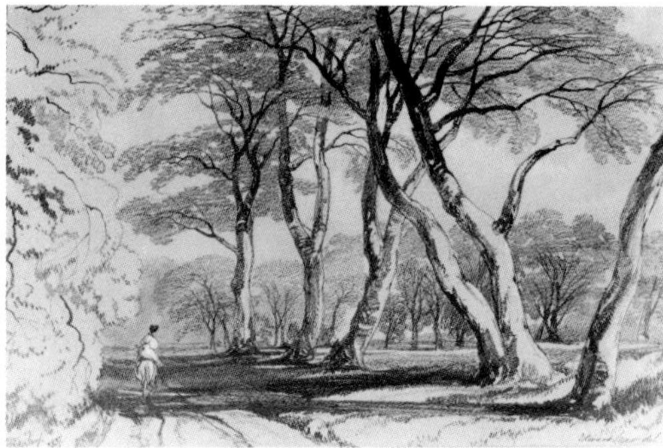

D.1981.4

Study of Trees in Alderley Park, Cheshire
6.1837
pencil, black chalk, bodycolour (heightened with
white); blue-grey paper
signed lower right: *Edward Lear.del.*; inscribed & dated
lower left: *Alderley. / June (cut). 1837.*
247 × 355 mm
John Baskett Ltd, London (purchase, 1981) (V. & A.,
N.A.C.F., F.O.W.) (D.1981.4)

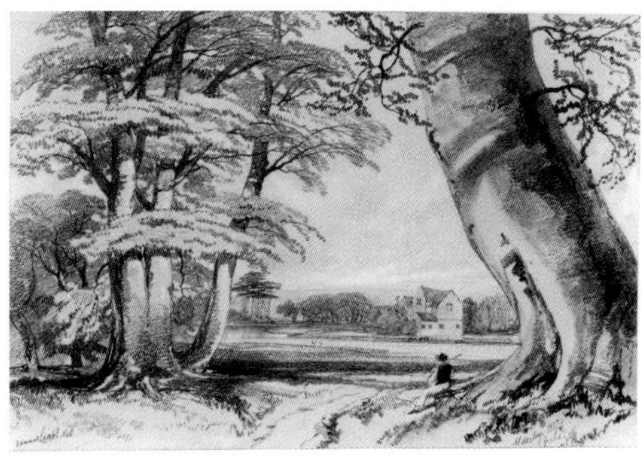

D.1981.5

Study of Trees in Alderley Park, Cheshire
6.1837
pencil, black chalk, bodycolour (heightened with
white); blue-grey paper
signed lower left: *Edward Lear. del.*; inscribed & dated
lower right: *Alderley. 1837. / June.*
252 × 355 mm
John Baskett Ltd, London (purchase, 1981) (V. & A.,
N.A.C.F., F.O.W.) (D.1981.5)

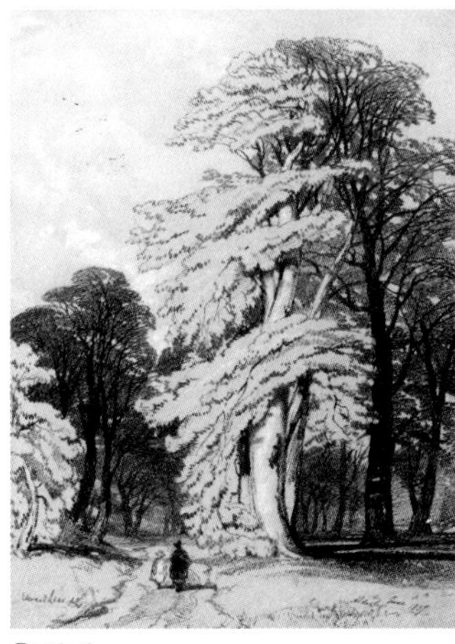

D.1981.6

Study of Trees in Alderley Park, Cheshire
6.1837
pencil, black chalk, bodycolour (heightened with
white); blue-grey paper
signed lower left: *Edward Lear. Del*; inscribed & dated
lower right: *Alderley.June.1837.*
349 × 252 mm
John Baskett Ltd, London (purchase, 1981) (V. & A.,
N.A.C.F., F.O.W.) (D.1981.6)

Festive Amazon Parrot
1836
watercolour
signed centre right on end of branch: *Lear.del.*;
inscribed lower left: *Plate.9.*; inscribed lower right:
Psittacus festivus
110 × 178 mm
Moore, Captain R. N. Hugh (bequest, 1985) (D.1985.6)

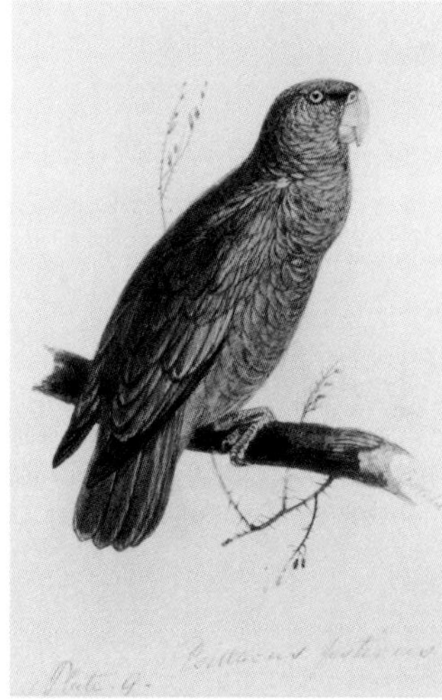

D.1985.6

■ LEECH, JOHN (1817–64)
Leech trained as a surgeon but in 1841 he began to
draw for the newly established magazine *Punch*,
continuing to do so for the rest of his life. His satirical
views of fashionable London life and his humorous
hunting scenes epitomise the Victorian age.

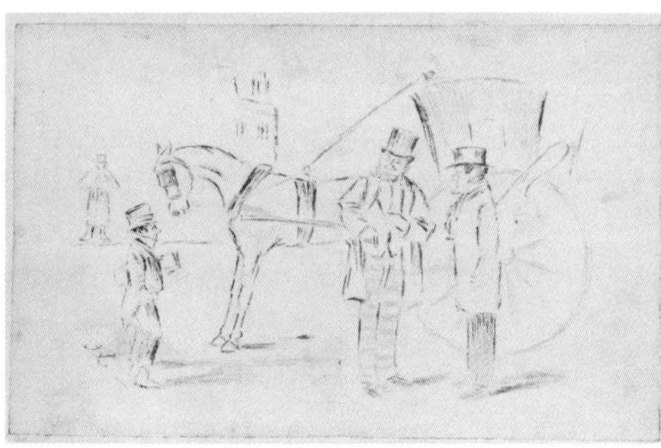

D.1930.65

Street Scene, Figures near a Hansom Cab
pencil, pen and brown ink
156 × 244 mm
Barlow, Sir Thomas (gift, 1930) (D.1930.65)

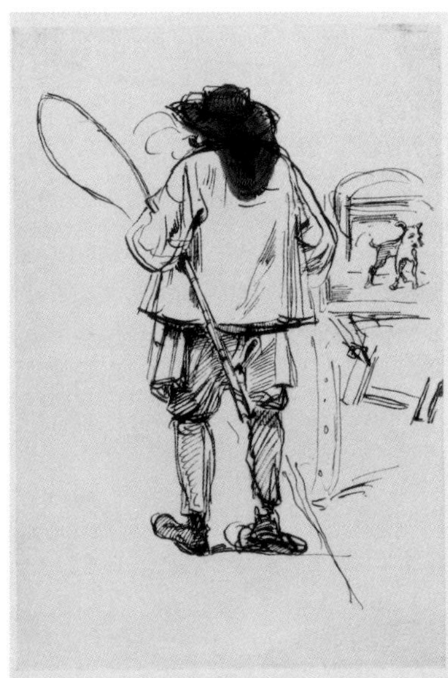

D.1960.96

Cart Driver
pen and ink; blue paper
201 × 134 mm
University of Manchester, History of Art Department
(transfer, 1960) (D.1960.96)

■ LEE-HANKEY, WILLIAM (1869–1952)
Lee-Hankey studied at Chester School of Art,
the Royal College of Art and in Paris. He exhibited
in London from 1893. Lee-Hankey lived in France
for some time and travelled widely in Europe. He
was elected a member of the Royal Watercolour
Society in 1936.

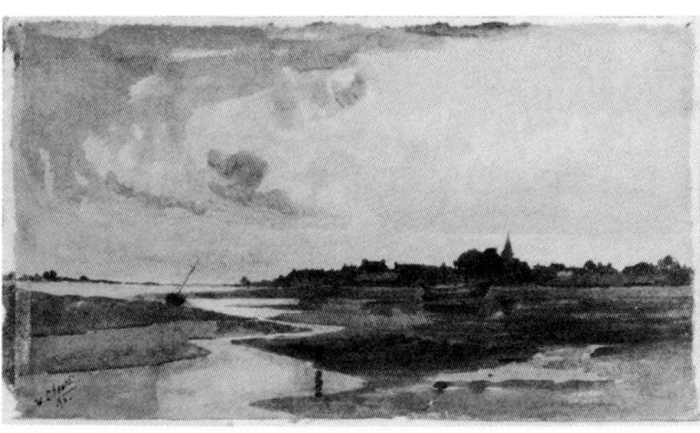

D.1951.8

Bosham, Sussex, from the Estuary
1895
watercolour
signed & dated lower left: *W.L.HANKEY. / .95.*
212 × 367 mm
Dunkerley, F. B. (executors of) (gift, 1951) (D.1951.8)

■ LEGÉ, F. A. (1779–1837)
Legé began his career as a sculptor in Liverpool, then
moved to London where he was employed by Sir
Francis Chantrey. He exhibited at the Royal Academy
between 1814 and 1825.

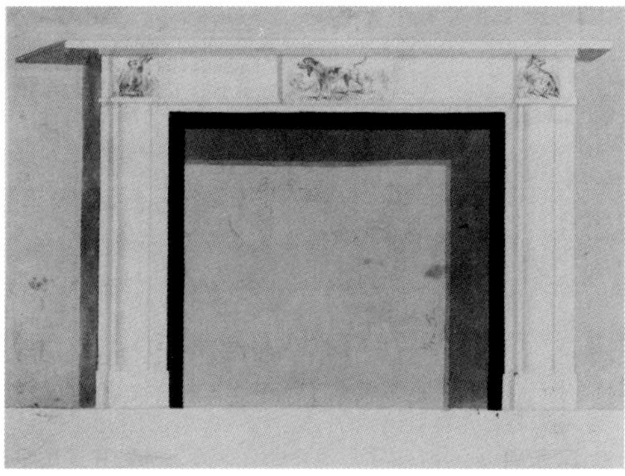

D.1960.97

**Design for a Chimneypiece (recto); Further
Study of the Design (verso)**
pencil, watercolour (recto)
signed lower left: *Lege*; inscribed centre twice
3" 5 – – –: inscribed centre verso referring to the
sculpted panels on the top left, upper centre and top
right of the mantelpiece which are numbered 1–3 on
the design: *These designs (1.2.3.) to be executed on a
handsome / statuary chimney piece – say to 35 Guineas - /
I have just sent them thinking them more original*
218 × 290 mm
University of Manchester, History of Art Department
(transfer, 1960) (D.1960.97)

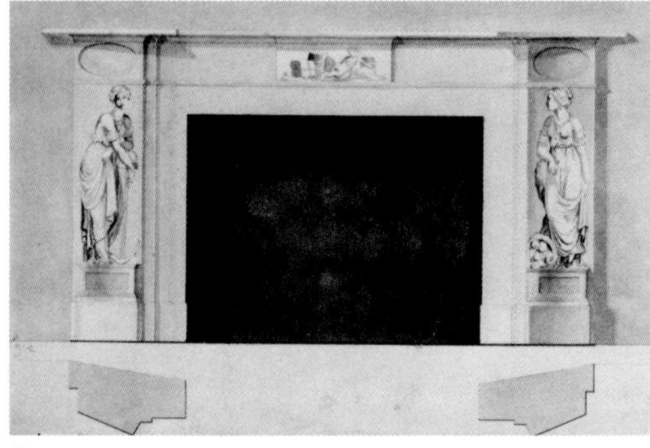

D.1960.98

Design for a Chimneypiece with large allegorical Figures (recto); Sketch for an alternative Design for a Chimneypiece (verso)

pen and brown ink, watercolour (recto); card
signed lower left: *Lege*
222 × 331 mm
University of Manchester, History of Art Department
(transfer, 1960) (D.1960.98)

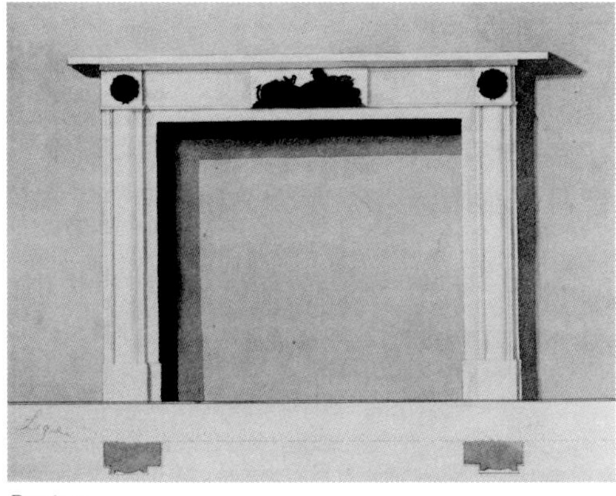

D.1960.99

Design for a Chimneypiece with a bronze Relief of Britannia

pencil, pen and brown ink, watercolour
signed lower left: *Lege*
222 × 281 mm
University of Manchester, History of Art Department
(transfer, 1960) (D.1960.99)

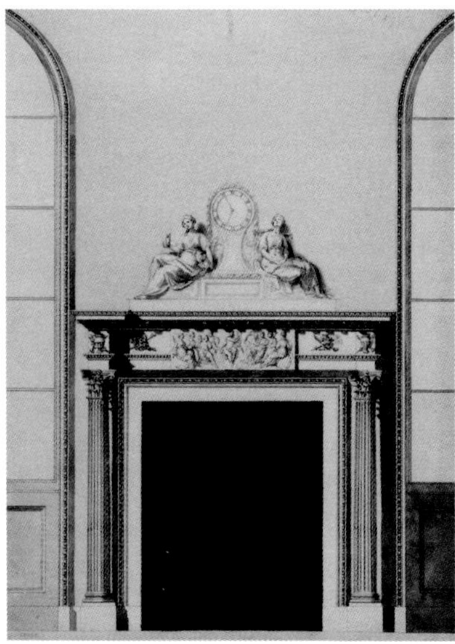

D.1960.100

Design for a Chimneypiece with a Relief of Apollo and the Muses

pen and brown ink, watercolour; watermark
JWHATMAN
signed lower left: *LEGEE*; inscribed lower right verso:
designed by / Legee / whilst working at Frances (sic) *in
Liverpool / at the time John Gibson was apprentice*
365 × 262 mm
University of Manchester, History of Art Department
(transfer, 1960) (D.1960.100)

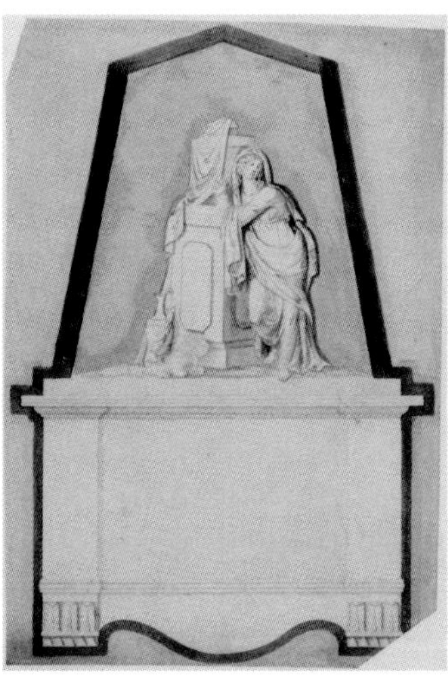

D.1960.101

Design for a Memorial, with a Relief of an Urn and mourning female Figure (recto); Sketch of an alternative Pose for the Figure (verso)

pencil, pen and brown ink, watercolour (recto)
signed lower left: *Lege*
367 × 251 mm
University of Manchester, History of Art Department
(transfer, 1960) (D.1960.101)

Design for a Sundial with a Putto

pencil, black chalk
signed lower left: *Lege*
289 × 215 mm
University of Manchester, History of Art Department
(transfer, 1960) (D.1960.102)

■ Leighton, Frederic, Lord (1830–96)

A highly important Victorian classical and figure painter, Leighton trained on the Continent. He then returned to London and was elected a member of the Royal Academy in 1868 and President in 1878. He produced hundreds of figure studies for his large oil paintings. Leighton is the only English artist to have received a peerage.

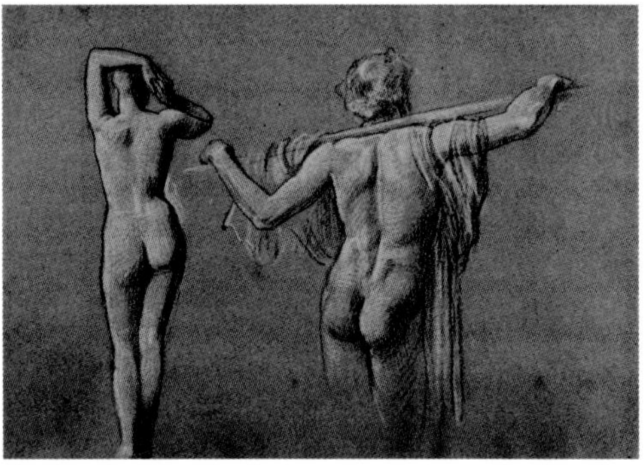

D.1915.16

Studies of Figures for 'Captive Andromache'

1886–87
black chalk, white chalk; blue paper
240 × 324 mm
Knight, E. A. (gift, 1915) (D.1915.16)

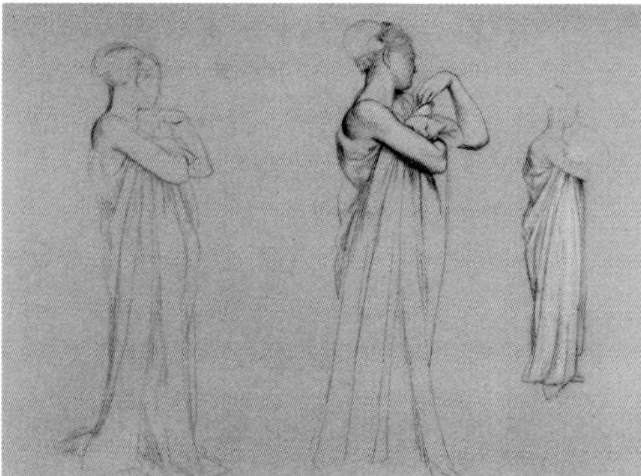

D.1954.7

Three Studies of draped female Figures

black chalk, white chalk; blue paper
367 × 493 mm
untraced (gift, 1954) (D.1954.7)

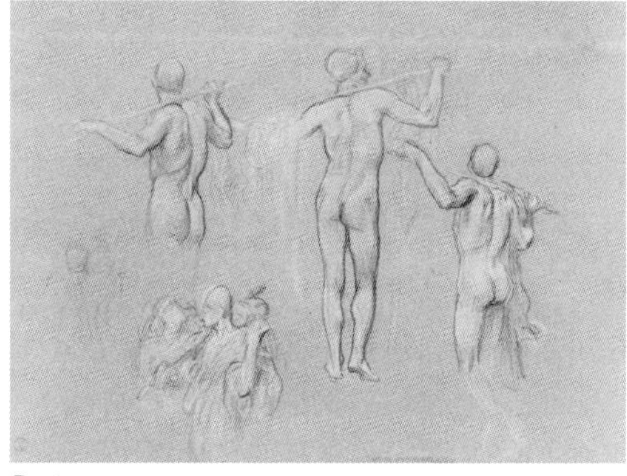

D.1960.103

Studies of Figures for 'Captive Andromache'

1886–87
black chalk, white chalk; blue paper
stamped lower left with the studio stamp (L.1741a)
(initials in monogram within a circle: *LL*)
241 × 327 mm
University of Manchester, History of Art Department
(transfer, 1960) (D.1960.103)

■ Leitch, William Leighton (1804–83)

Born in Glasgow, Leitch began his career as a scene painter and then moved to London. He painted scenery in London before visiting Italy between 1833 and 1837. On his return Leitch built up a very successful practice as a drawing master, numbering Queen Victoria among his pupils. Leitch exhibited at the Royal Academy between 1833 and 1861 and was elected a member of the New Watercolour Society in 1862.

Landscape with Ruins

watercolour, bodycolour (heightened with white)
grey paper
300 × 412 mm
Anderson, A. E., National Art Collections Fund (via)
(gift, 1923) (D.1923.12)

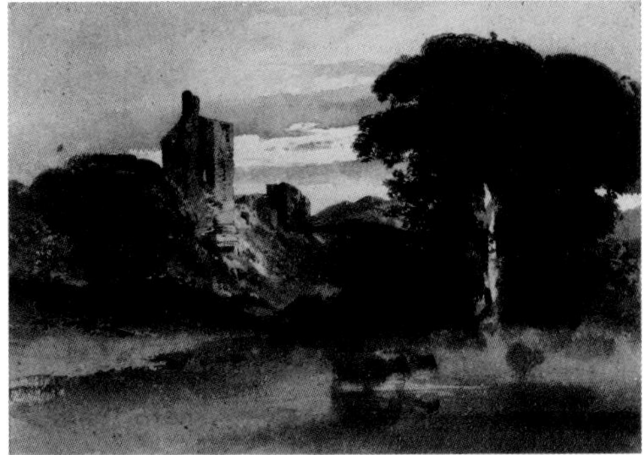

D.1923.12

■ LENON, D. (fl. mid-19th century)

Unknown amateur artist.

Windmill near Sandown Castle, Kent
pencil, pen and brown ink, brown watercolour
inscribed centre right verso: *Windmill near Sandown /
Castle Kent*
150 × 226 mm
Ogden, William Sharp (bequest, 1926) (D.1926.357)

■ LENS, BERNARD (1682–1740)

A miniaturist and topographical draughtsman, Lens
was a member of a large family of drawing masters. His
father, grandfather and son were also called Bernard
and their works are frequently confused. Lens was
Limner to George I and George II and taught at
Christ's Hospital as well as taking private pupils.

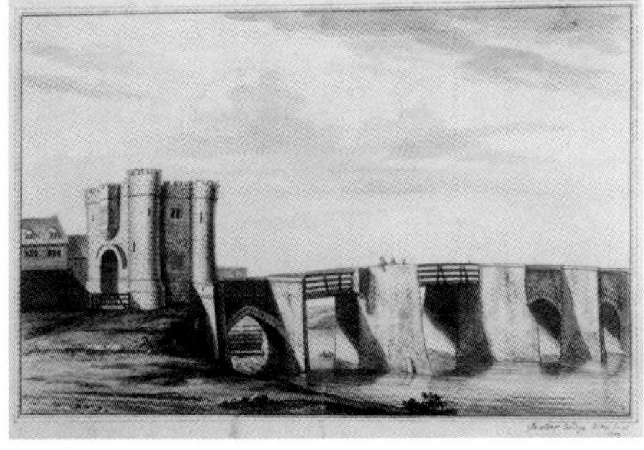

D.1926.140

Gloucester Bridge
1719
pen and brown ink, brown watercolour
signed, inscribed & dated lower right margin:
Glocester (sic) *Bridge BLens fecit / 1719*
172 × 243 mm
Ogden, William Sharp (bequest, 1926) (D.1926.140)

Landscape with a Church by a River
pen and grey ink, grey watercolour
104 × 237 mm
Friends of the Whitworth (gift, 1947) (D.1947.17)

■ LESLIE, CHARLES ROBERT (1794–1859)

Leslie was a literary and historical painter whose family
emigrated to America in 1800. He returned to England
in 1811 and studied under Benjamin West. Leslie
specialised in costume figure subjects based on
literature and was elected a member of the Royal
Academy in 1826. He was a close friend of John
Constable, of whom he wrote an important biography
entitled *Life and Letters of John Constable R.A.*

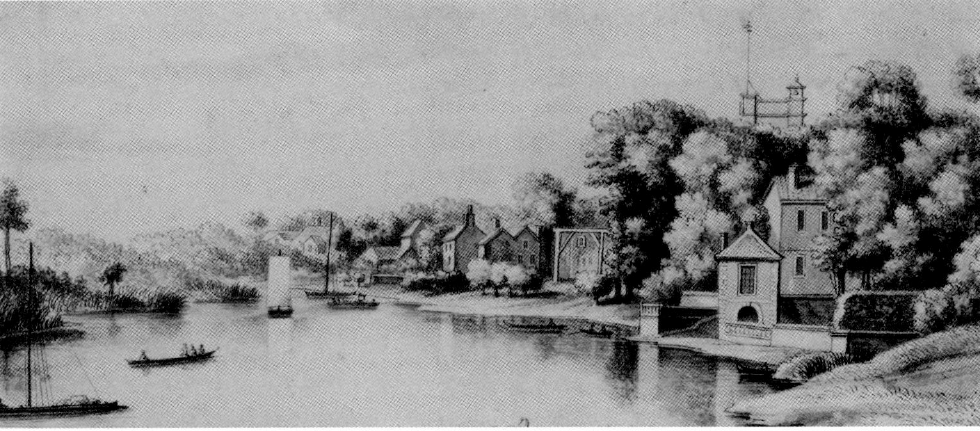

D.1947.17

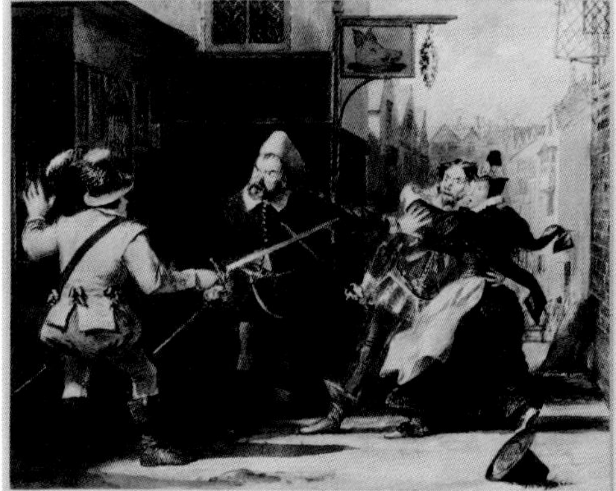

D.1896.3

**Illustration to Shakespeare's 'Henry V', Act II,
Scene I - Bardolph intercedes in the
Confrontation between Nym and Pistol**
watercolour
246 × 305 mm
Agnew, Sir William (gift, 1896) (D.1896.3)

■ LETHABY, WILLIAM RICHARD (1857–1931)

Born in Barnstaple, Lethaby was chief assistant to
Richard Norman Shaw from 1879 to 1889, before
setting up his own architectural practice. Although
Lethaby designed a number of buildings well ahead of
their time, it was as a teacher, writer and theorist that
his influence was greatest. He was a founder member
of the Art Workers' Guild in 1884 and helped to found
the Central School of Arts and Crafts. In 1900, he was
the first Professor of Design at the South Kensington
Royal College of Art, a post he held until 1918.

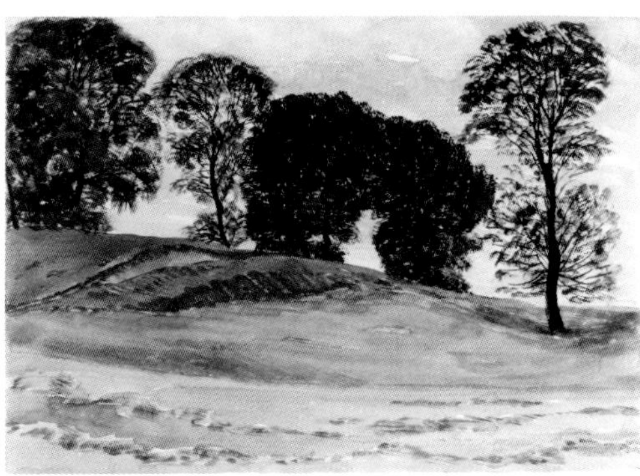

D.1933.44

Trees on a grassy Bank
pencil, watercolour; buff paper
255 × 355 mm
Lethaby, William Richard (bequest, 1933) (D.1933.44)

■ LEWIS, GEORGE ROBERT (1782–1871)

The brother of Frederick Christian and the uncle of
John Frederick, George Robert Lewis studied under
Fuseli at the Royal Academy Schools. He exhibited
portraits and landscapes at the Royal Academy between
1820 and 1859.

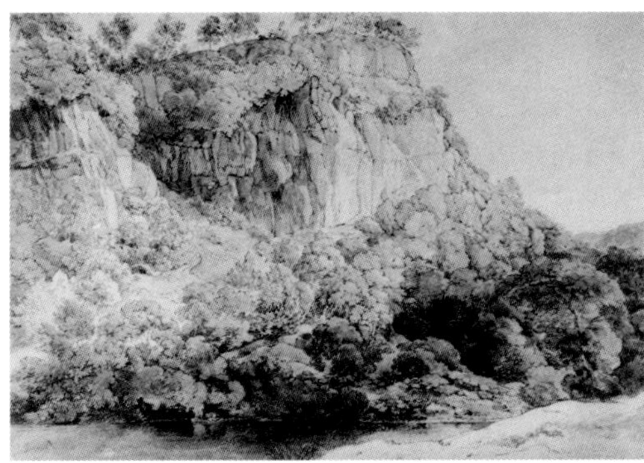

D.1970.52

Rocky Outcrop, near Matlock Bath, Derbyshire
pencil, watercolour
inscribed lower right: *Derbyshire*
333 × 470 mm
Towlson, Hector J. (bequest, 1969) (D.1970.52)

■ LEWIS, JOHN FREDERICK (1805–76)

Born into a family of artists and engravers, John
Frederick Lewis began his career as an animal and
sporting painter. He was elected a member of the Old
Watercolour Society in 1829 and visited Spain in
1833–34, publishing the lithographs in *Sketches of Spain
and Spanish Character* in 1836. Lewis travelled to Italy
in 1837, remaining there for two years. He left for the
East in 1840, travelling via Greece and Turkey to Cairo
where he remained for ten years. He returned home in
1851 and was elected a member of the Royal Academy
in 1865. Lewis is the most accomplished of the
Victorian Orientalists.

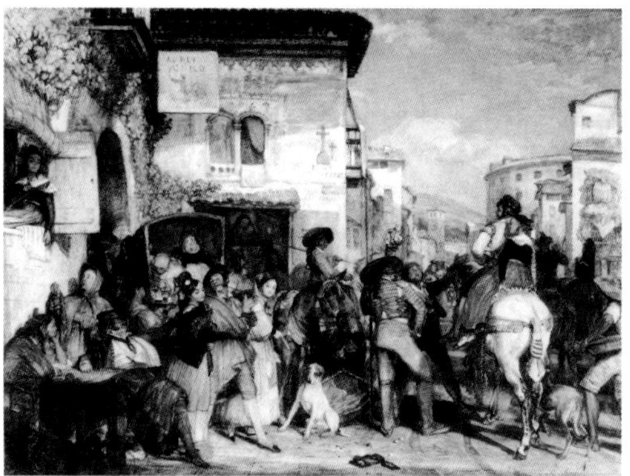

D.1887.44

The Suburbs of a Spanish City (Granada) on the Day of a Bull-fight
1836
watercolour, bodycolour
signed & dated: *J.F. Lewis / 1836*
661 × 864 mm
Wright, Thomas W. (purchase, 1891) (D.1887.44)

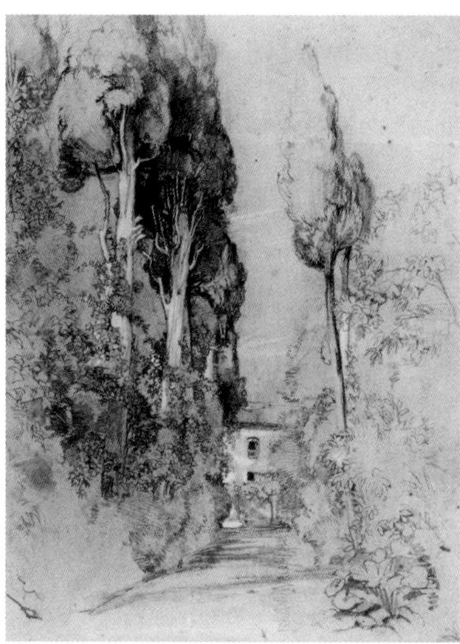

D.1970.53

Generalife Gardens, Granada, Spain
1833
pencil, brown watercolour, bodycolour (heightened with white); buff paper
inscribed lower right: *Generalife*
290 × 216 mm
Towlson, Hector J. (bequest, 1969) (D.1970.53)

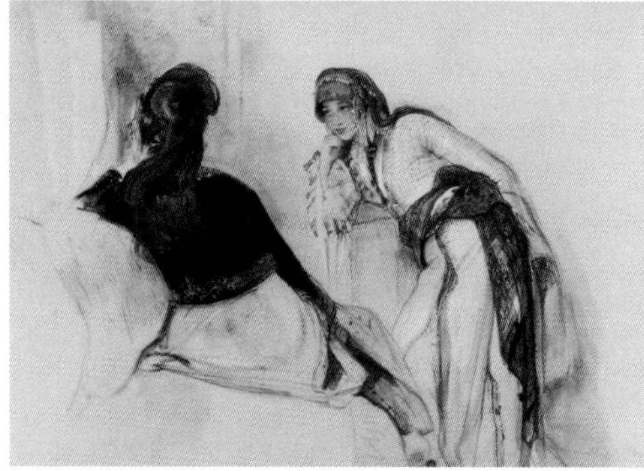

D.1984.4

Study of two Women, Brussa, Turkey
1841
pencil, black chalk, white chalk, watercolour, bodycolour (heightened with white); buff paper
signed, dated & inscribed lower right: *J.F. Lewis Brussa / 1841*
348 × 485 mm
Winter, Theodora (in memory of her father, Sir Thomas Barlow) (gift, 1984) (D.1984.4)

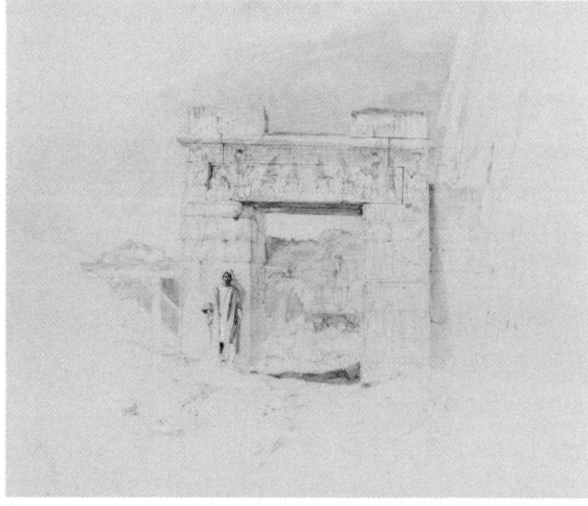

D.1985.2

Arch at Philae on the Nile, Egypt
pencil, watercolour, bodycolour (heightened with white); buff paper
signed & inscribed lower left: *Phila / Jany 4 / JFLewis*
403 × 343 mm
Bonham-Carter, Lady (gift, 1985) (D.1985.2)

■ LINNELL, JOHN (1792–1882)

Linnell, a landscape and portrait painter in oil and watercolour, entered the Royal Academy Schools in 1805 and was a pupil of John Varley. Linnell was also a member of the Monro circle and a friend of William Blake, to whom he introduced Varley. He painted portraits and built up a teaching practice before turning to landscape in 1847. Linnell was the father-in-law of Samuel Palmer.

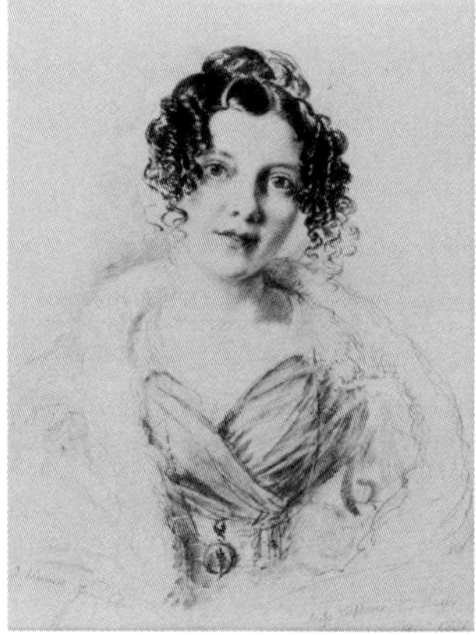

D.1929.20

Portrait of Catherine Stephens
1831
pencil, watercolour
signed & inscribed lower left: *J.Linnell From life*; inscribed lower right: *Miss Stephens The Singer / 1831*
274 × 220 mm
Anderson, A. E. (gift, 1929) (D.1929.20)

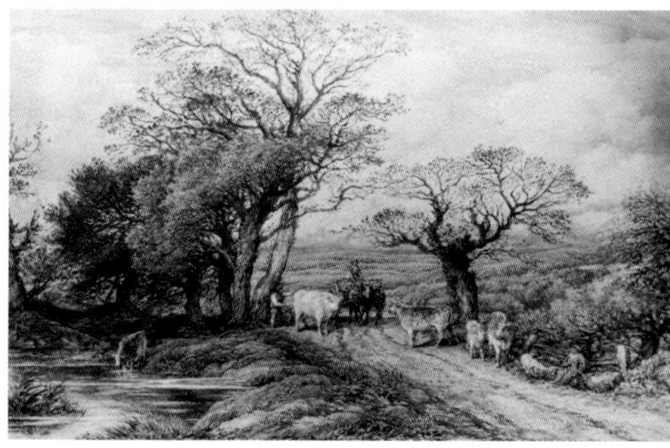

D.1937.15

Morning: Landscape with Cattle and Cart
1871
watercolour, bodycolour (heightened with white)
signed & dated lower right: *John Linnell 1871*
305 × 454 mm
Haworth, Jesse (bequest, 1937) (D.1937.15)

Two Studies of a Workman (recto); Study of a Workman (verso)
black chalk, white chalk; brown paper
278 × 235 mm
untraced (gift, 1954) (D.1954.10)

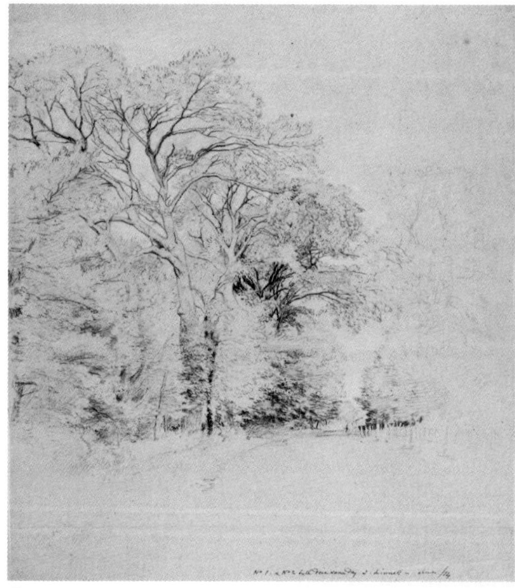

D.1954.27

A wooded Lane
1813–15
black chalk, white chalk; blue paper
signed, inscribed & dated lower right: *No1.& No2 both done same day J. Linnell – about /14*
461 × 397 mm
Abbot, R. E. (purchase, 1954) (D.1954.27)

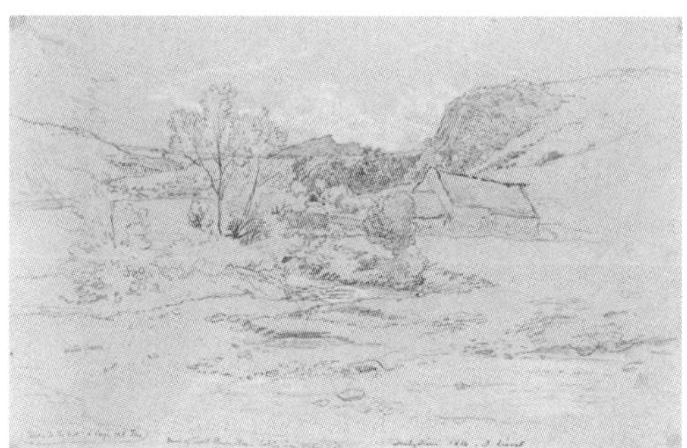

D.1960.106

View from Wetton Mill, Derbyshire
1814
pencil, white chalk; grey paper
signed & dated lower right: *Derbyshire 1814. J.Linnell*;
inscribed lower left within a circle: *More to the Left a large oak Tree*; inscribed lower centre: *View of Thirst House Star. looking from Wetton Mill*
206 × 317 mm
University of Manchester, History of Art Department (transfer, 1960) (D.1960.106)

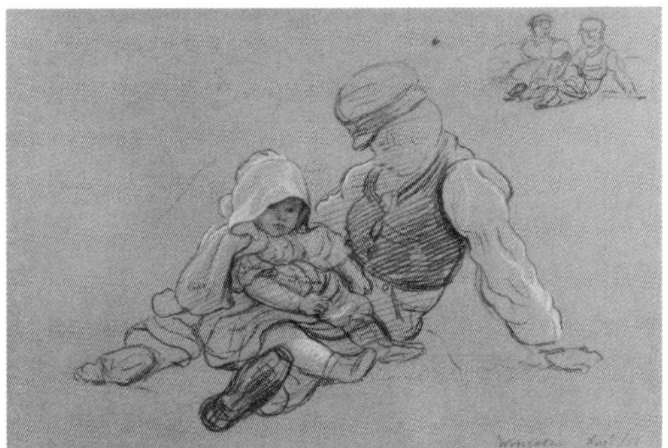

D.1960.107

Two Studies of a Boy nursing a Baby
8.1858
black chalk, white chalk; brown paper
inscribed & dated lower right: *Worsfolds Augt./58*
195 × 286 mm
University of Manchester, History of Art Department (transfer, 1960) (D.1960.107)

Portrait Study of a seated Man
pencil, red chalk, brown chalk, white chalk; buff paper
610 × 452 mm
University of Manchester, History of Art Department (transfer, 1960) (D.1960.168)

■ **LIVERSEEGE, HENRY (1803–32)**
Liverseege was born in Manchester, and went to study in London in 1827, returning to Manchester the following year. He specialised in historical and literary costume figure groups.

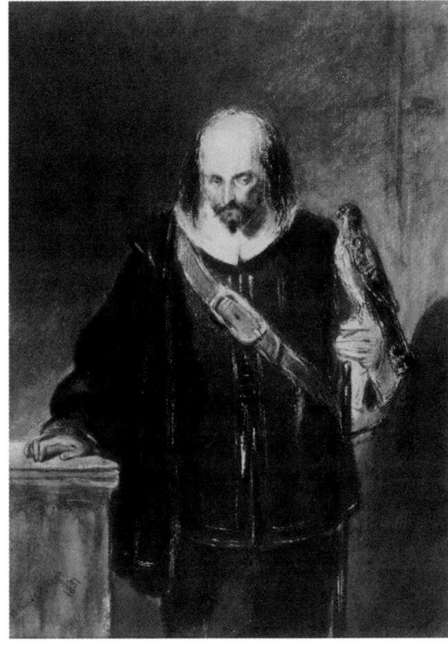

D.1892.133

Study for 'The Falconer'
1831
watercolour
signed & dated lower left: *H.Liverseege / 1831.*
302 × 210 mm
Taylor, John Edward (gift, 1892) (D.1892.133)

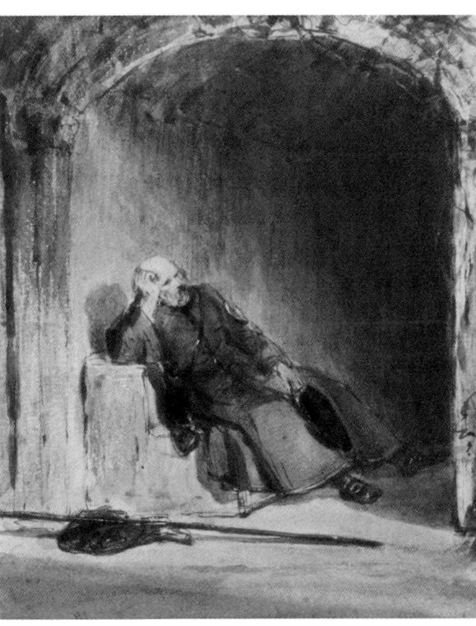

D.1892.134

Edie Ochiltree, from Sir Walter Scott's 'The Antiquary'
watercolour
signed lower left with initials: *H.L.*
232 × 184 mm
Taylor, John Edward (gift, 1892) (D.1892.134)

Study of Two Men's Heads, possibly Don Quixote and Sancho Panza
pencil
154 × 162 mm
Buckley, C. R., Oldham, R. (gift, 1911) (D.1911.6)

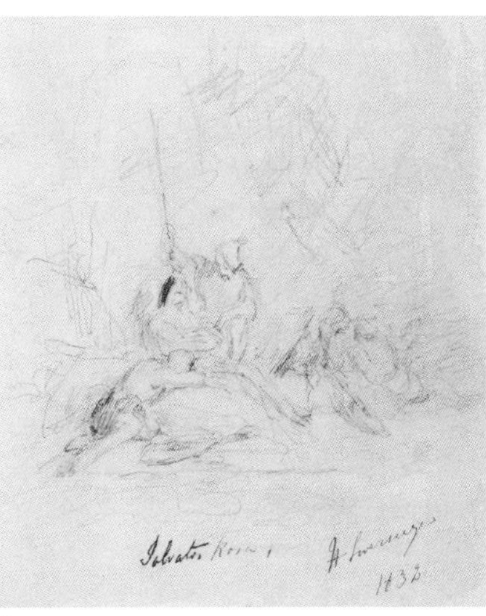

D.1911.7

Study for 'Salvator Rosa sketching'
1832
pencil
signed & dated lower right: *H Liverseege / 1832*;
inscribed lower centre: *Salvator Rosa.*
180 × 147 mm
Buckley, C. R., Oldham, R. (gift, 1911) (D.1911.7)

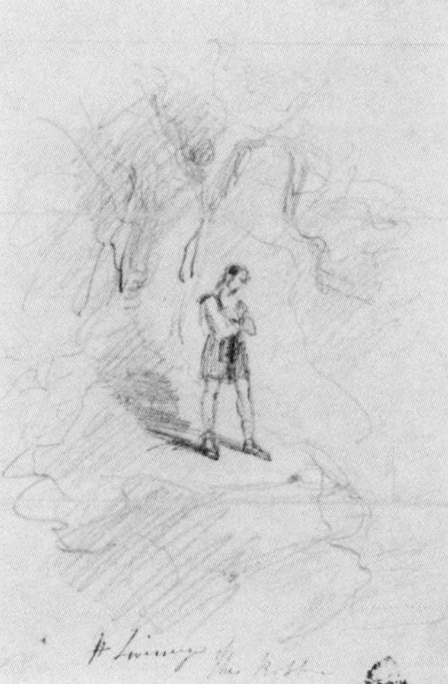

D.1911.8

Study for 'A Robber on the Outlook'
pencil
signed lower centre: *H Liverseege / The Robber*;
inscribed on verso a letter: *Dear Sir / I expect Mr. Bury / and another friend or two / to tea to morrow* (sic), *and / I shall be happy to / see you, Should you / feel disposed to dine / with Mr. Swain, I / presume it will not / prevent your taking / tea in Oldham* [illegible] */ I remain sincerely /* [illegible signature] */ Oldham / May 2nd/29*
163 × 111 mm
Buckley, C. R., Oldham, R. (gift, 1911) (D.1911.8)

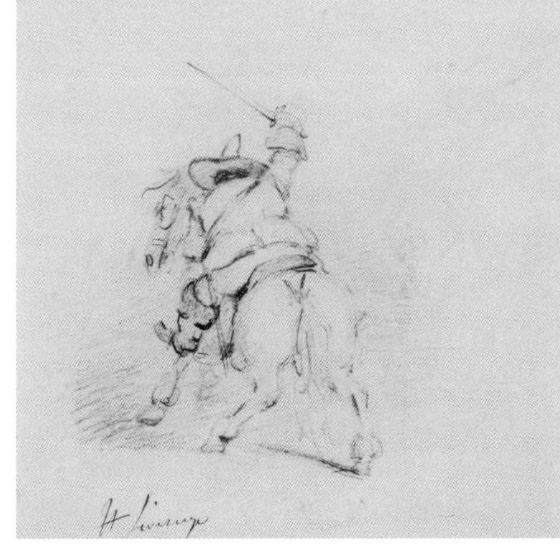

D.1911.9

Hudibras
pencil
signed lower left: *H Liverseege*; inscribed lower right: *Hudibras*
136 × 130 mm
Buckley, C. R., Oldham, R. (gift, 1911) (D.1911.9)

Study of a Man's Head
pencil
128 × 95 mm
Buckley, C. R., Oldham, R. (gift, 1911) (D.1911.10)

Study of the Head and Shoulders of a Man
1825
pencil
signed & dated lower left: *H.Liverseege. / 1825*
191 × 133 mm
Buckley, C. R. Oldham, R. (gift, 1911) (D.1911.11)

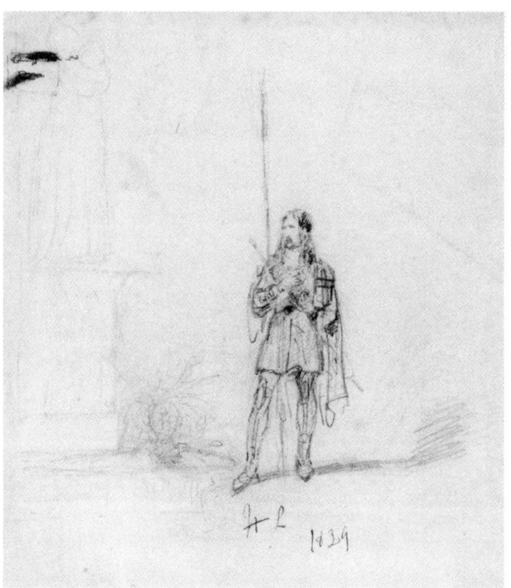

D.1911.12

Study of a Soldier standing near a Monument
1829
pencil
signed & dated lower centre with initials: *H L / 1829*
191 × 170 mm
Buckley, C. R., Oldham, R. (gift, 1911) (D.1911.12)

Study of Soldiers fighting, one in Armour
pencil
signed lower right: *H Liverseege*
162 × 202 mm
Buckley, C. R., Oldham, R. (gift, 1911) (D.1911.13)

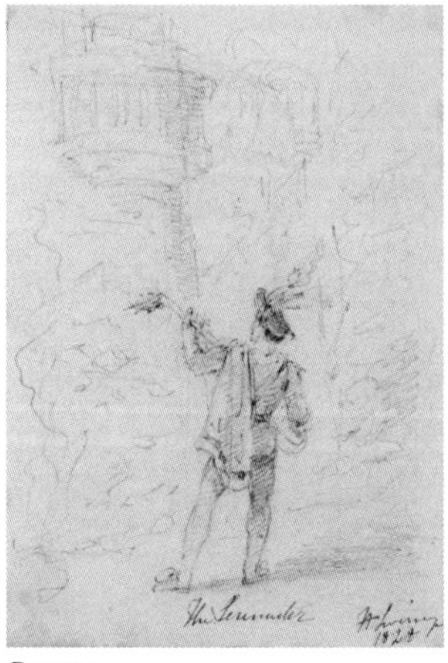

D.1911.14

The Serenader
1828
pencil
signed & dated lower right: *H Liverseege / 1828*;
inscribed lower centre: *The Serenader*
169 × 114 mm
Buckley, C. R., Oldham, R. (gift, 1911) (D.1911.14)

A Man on Rocks in a Storm
1827
pencil
signed & dated lower right: *H Liverseege / 1827 –*;
inscribed lower left; partly illegible: *mid the
lightning's glare and thunders peal / climb the
survivor up the craggy cliff / meanwhile the foaming
waves / are(?) battling with the storm.*
190 × 161 mm
Buckley, C. R., Oldham, R. (gift, 1911) (D.1911.15)

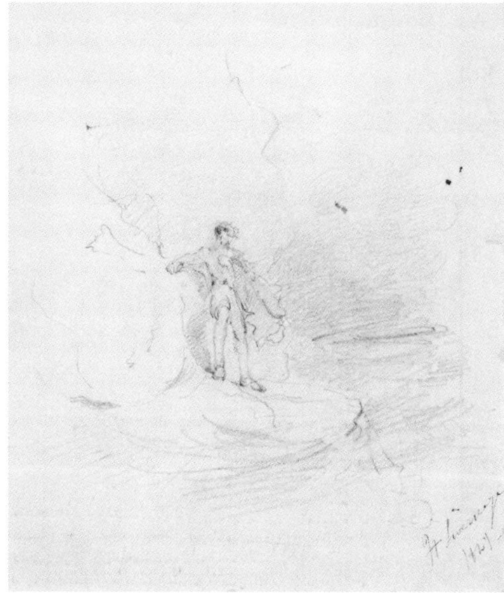

D.1911.15

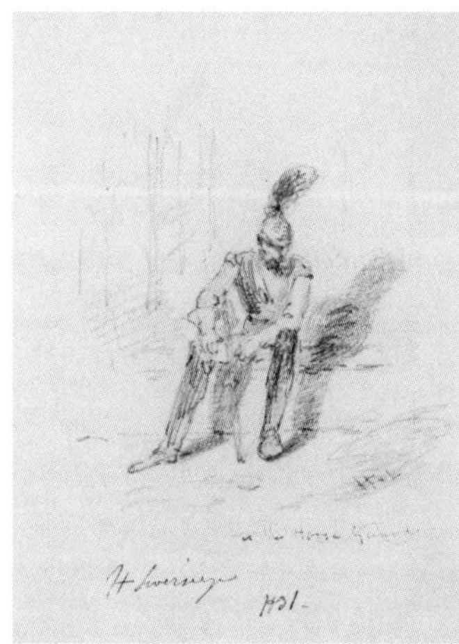

D.1911.16

At the Horseguards
1831
pencil
signed & dated lower left: *H Liverseege / 1831 –*;
inscribed lower right: *at the Horse Guards*
168 × 115 mm
Buckley, C. R., Oldham, R. (gift, 1911) (D.1911.16)

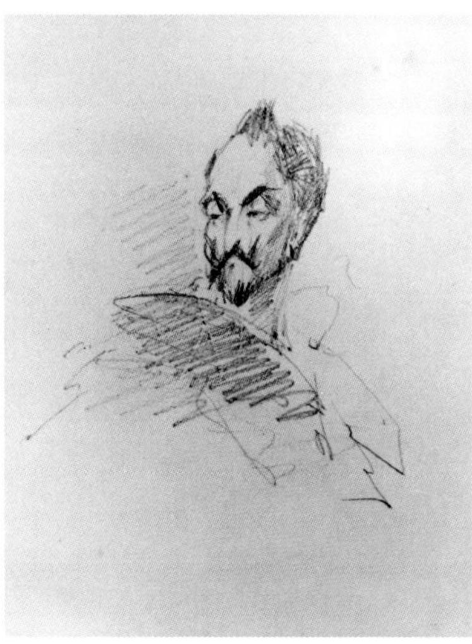

D.1911.17

Study for 'Don Quixote in his Study'
pencil; watermark JWHAT[MAN] 1829
165 × 133 mm
Buckley, C. R., Oldham, R. (gift, 1911) (D.1911.17)

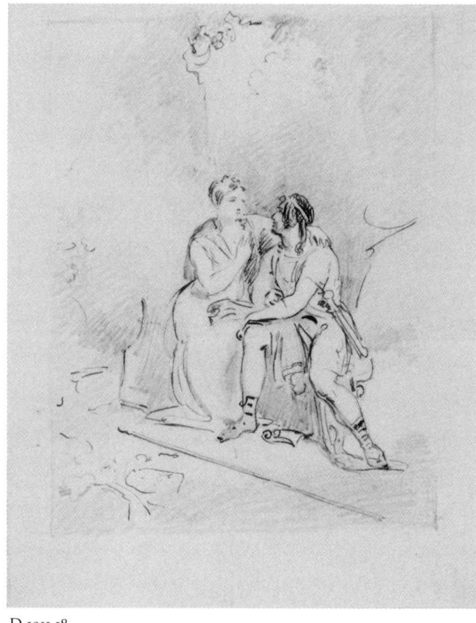

D.1911.18

Two seated Lovers in classical Dress
pencil, pen and brown ink
227 × 178 mm
Buckley, C. R., Oldham, R. (gift, 1911) (D.1911.18)

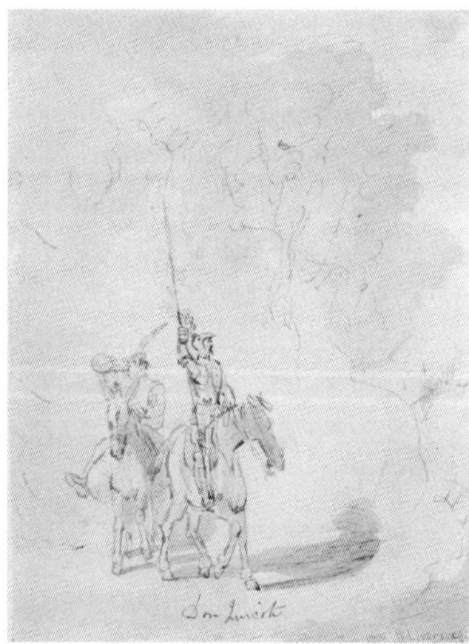

D.1911.19

**Don Quixote and Sancho Panza riding
through a Wood**
1828
pencil, pen and brown ink, brown watercolour
signed & dated lower right: *1828 H.Liverseege*
inscribed lower centre: *Don Quixote*
202 × 146 mm
Buckley, C. R., Oldham, R. (gift, 1911) (D.1911.19)

The Attack
black chalk; grey paper
signed & inscribed lower centre with initials:
The Attack H L
216 × 178 mm
Buckley, C. R., Oldham, R. (gift, 1911) (D.1911.20)

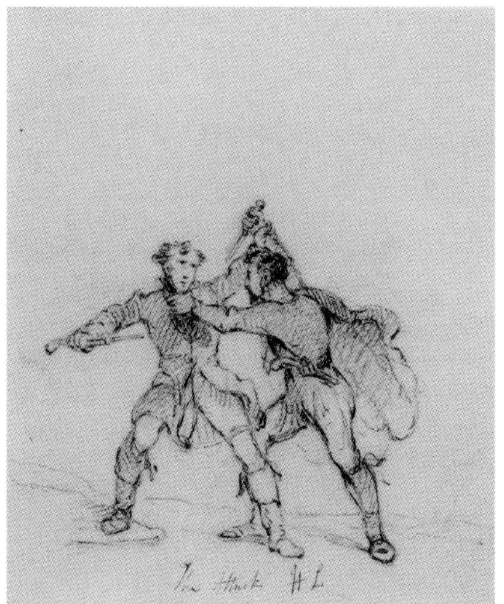

D.1911.20

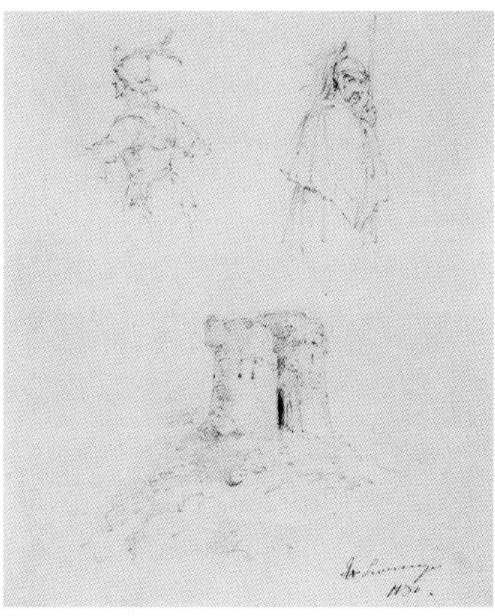

D.1911.21

Studies of two Warriors and a Castle
1830
pencil
signed & dated lower right: *H Liverseege / 1830.*
212 × 176 mm
Buckley, C. R., Oldham, R. (gift, 1911) (D.1911.21)

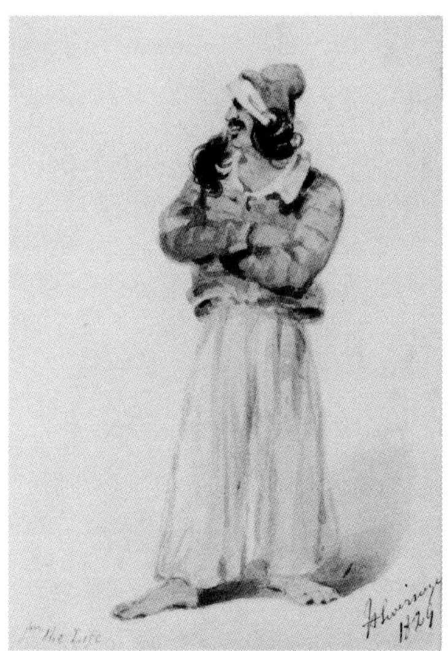

D.1911.22

Study of a Man
1829
watercolour
signed & dated lower right: *HLiverseege / 1829*;
inscribed lower left: *fm the Life*
212 × 176 mm
Buckley, C. R., Oldham, R. (gift, 1911) (D.1911.22)

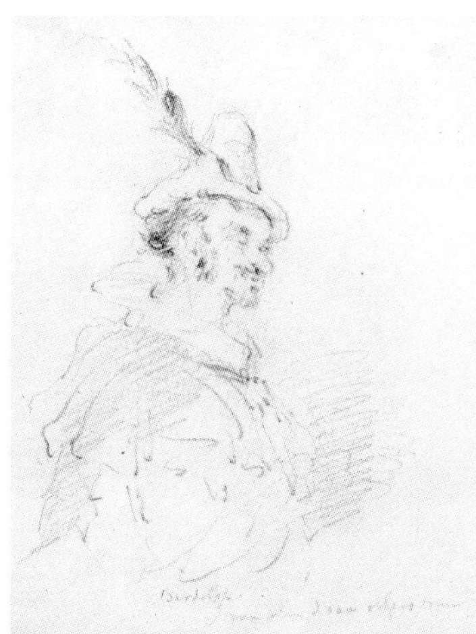

D.1911.23

**Bardolph, from Shakespeare's
'Henry IV, Part 1', Act II, Scene 4**
pencil
inscribed ilower centre: *Bardolph / I ran
when I saw others run*
141 × 108 mm
Buckley, C. R., Oldham, R. (gift, 1911) (D.1911.23)

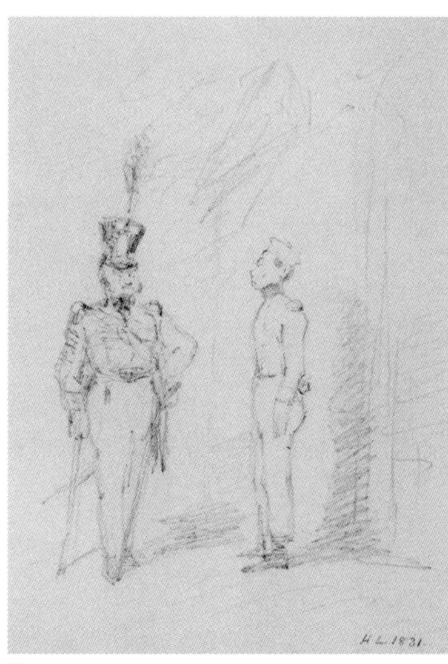

D.1911.24

Officer and Recruit
1831
pencil
signed & dated lower right with initials: *HL.1831.*
200 × 141 mm
Buckley, C. R., Oldham, R. (gift, 1911) (D.1911.24)

The Valentine
1832
watercolour
signed & dated lower centre: *H Liverseege / 1832*;
inscribed lower right: *The Valentine*
255 × 245 mm
Buckley, C. R., Oldham, R. (gift, 1911) (D.1911.25)

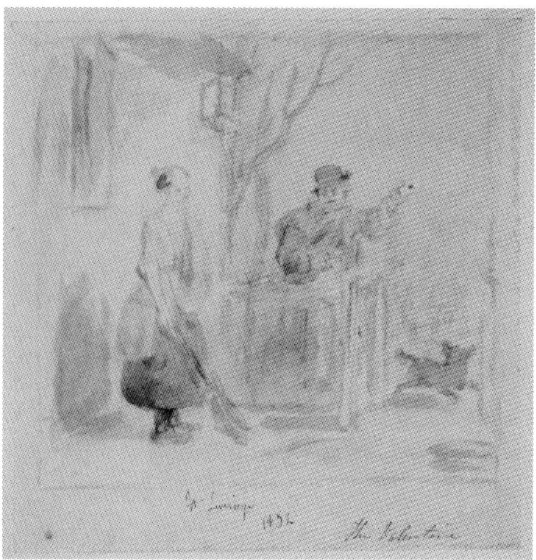

D.1911.25

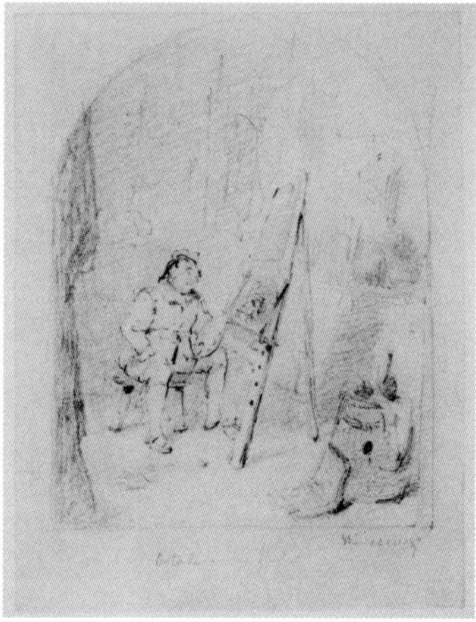

D.1911.26

Ostade in his Studio
pencil
signed lower right: *HLiverseege*; inscribed
lower centre: *Ostade in his Studio*
264 × 194 mm
Buckley, C. R., Oldham, R. (gift, 1911) (D.1911.26)

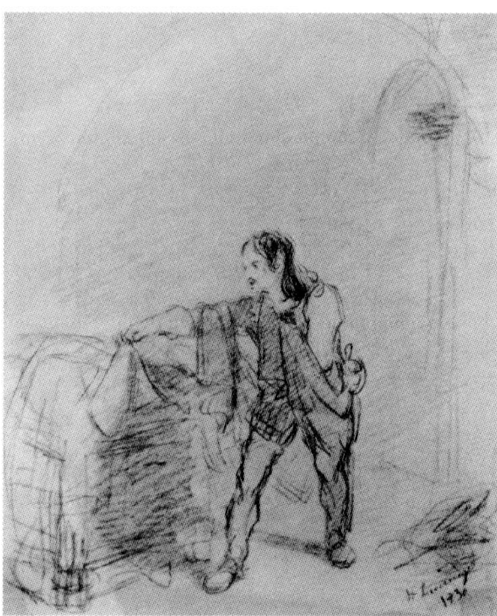

D.1911.27

The Tragedian, Study for 'Hamlet'
1830
black chalk, white chalk; buff paper
signed & dated lower right: *H Liverseege / 1830*
291 × 235 mm
Buckley, C. R., Oldham, R. (gift, 1911) (D.1911.27)

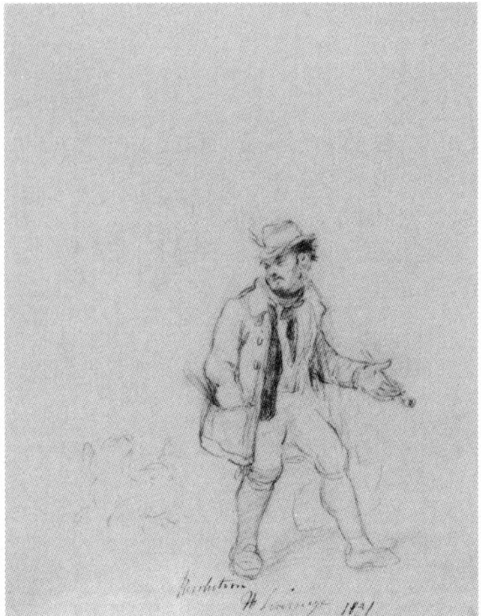

D.1911.29

Study for 'Good Resolution'
1831
black chalk; buff paper
signed, inscribed & dated lower centre:
Resolution / H Liverseege / 1831
277 × 216 mm
Buckley, C. R., Oldham, R. (gift, 1911) (D.1911.29)

A Man and a Woman seated near a spinning Wheel
pencil
330 × 243 mm
Buckley, C. R., Oldham, R. (gift, 1911) (D.1911.30)

■ LONG, AMELIA, LADY FARNBOROUGH (1762–1837)

Amelia Long was an amateur artist who was apparently Girtin's favourite pupil. She produced copies after Girtin and landscapes near her home at Bromley Hill in Kent. She was an honorary exhibitor at the Royal Academy from 1807.

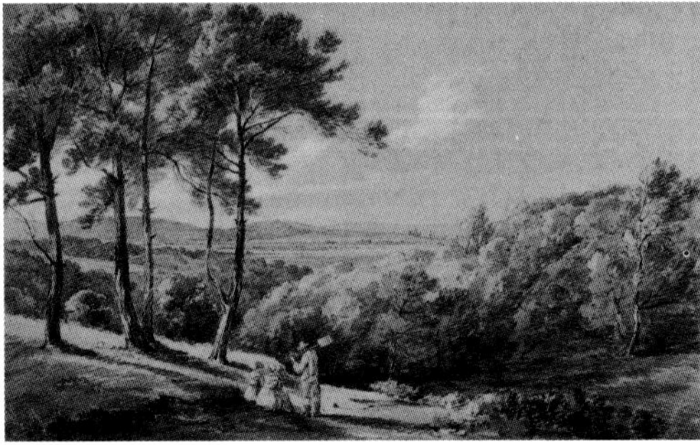

D.1934.1

Bromley Hill, Kent
1814
black chalk, white chalk, watercolour; blue paper
signed, inscribed & dated lower left: *Bromley Hill ALong 1814*
281 × 466 mm
Friends of the Whitworth (gift, 1934) (D.1934.1)

■ LONGSTAFF, WILLIAM FRANCIS (fl. early 20th century)

Unknown artist.

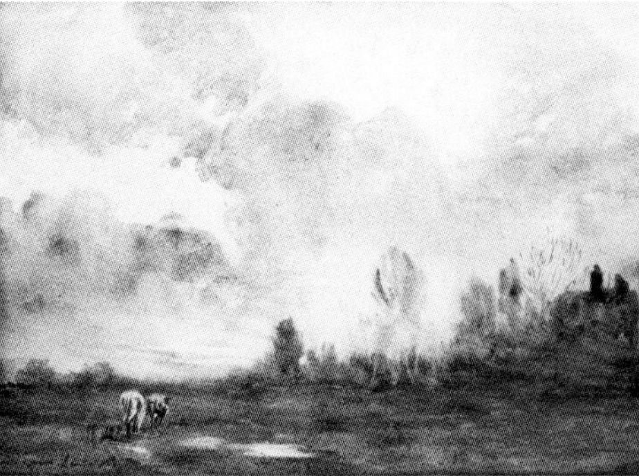

D.1923.4

An open Landscape on a rainy Day
watercolour
signed lower left: *Wm Longstaff*
265 × 367 mm
Anderson, A. E., National Art Collections Fund (via) (gift, 1923) (D.1923.4)

■ LOWE, MAURITIUS (1746–93)

The illegitimate son of Baron Southwell, Lowe studied under Cipriani and entered the Royal Academy Schools in 1769, winning the Academy's first gold medal for history painting. He left for Italy in 1771 on a Royal Academy travelling scholarship. He was back in London by 1777 and exhibited at the Royal Academy until 1786. Lowe had a reputation for idleness and died in penury.

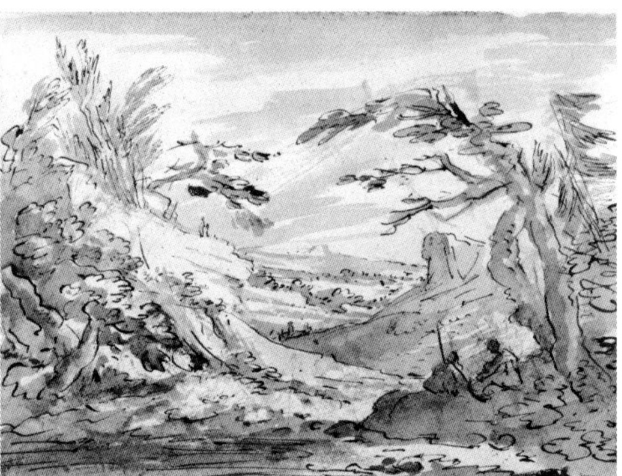

D.1954.13

Landscape with Rocks and Trees
pen and brown ink, grey watercolour
212 × 275 mm
Sewter, Albert Charles (gift, 1954) (D.1954.13)

■ LOWTHIAN, LOUIS (dates unknown)

Unknown artist.

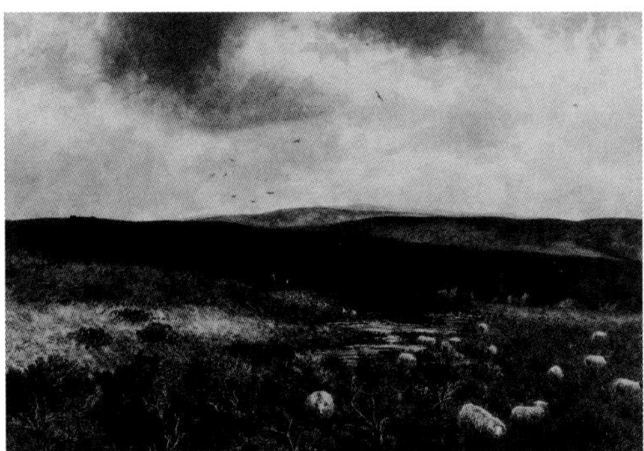

D.1887.50

Moorland, near Pooley Bridge, Westmorland
pen and brown ink, watercolour
signed (?) lower right; illegible
352 × 505 mm
untraced (untraced) (D.1887.50)

■ LUCAS, SAMUEL (1805–70)

Born at Hitchin and educated at a Quaker school in Bristol, Lucas returned to Hitchin in 1838 after an apprenticeship to a ship owner in Shoreham. His religion only permitted him to paint as an amateur. He produced landscapes in the Hitchin area.

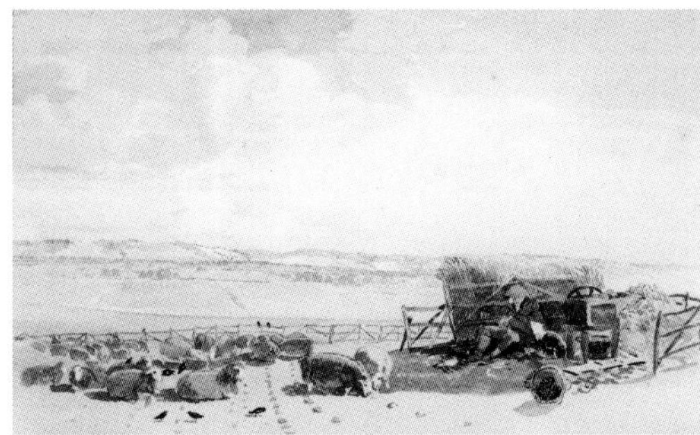

D.1929.22

An old Shepherd in melting Snow, near Offley Holes, Hertfordshire
pencil, watercolour
inscribed on mount under drawing lower right; not in artist's hand (?): *Offley Holes in the Distance*; inscribed & numbered on mount below top mount lower right; not in artist's hand (?): *30 Old shepherd in melting snow*
287 × 453 mm
Anderson, A. E. (gift, 1929) (D.1929.22)

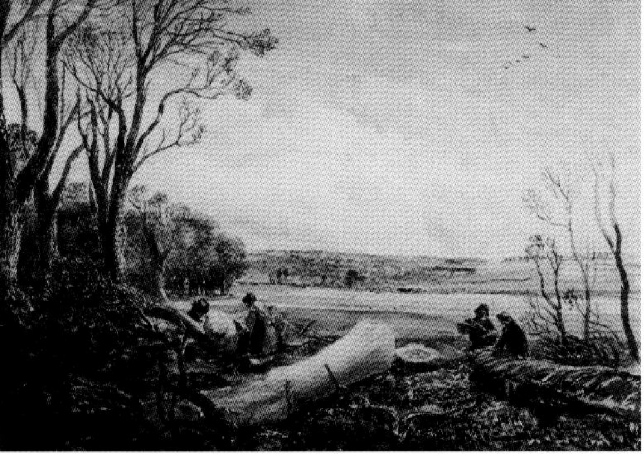

D.1929.23

Bark peeling, Westbury Wood
pencil, watercolour
245 × 342 mm
Anderson, A. E. (gift, 1929) (D.1929.23)

■ MACKENZIE, FREDERICK (1787–1854)

Mackenzie, an architectural and topographical draughtsman, worked for many of the leading publishers and engravers of the day. He became a member of the Old Watercolour Society in 1823 and was Treasurer from 1831 until his death. Mackenzie specialised in Gothic church interiors.

York Minster, the Nave looking east
watercolour
244 × 171 mm
Worthington, Mary (gift, 1900) (D.1900.8)

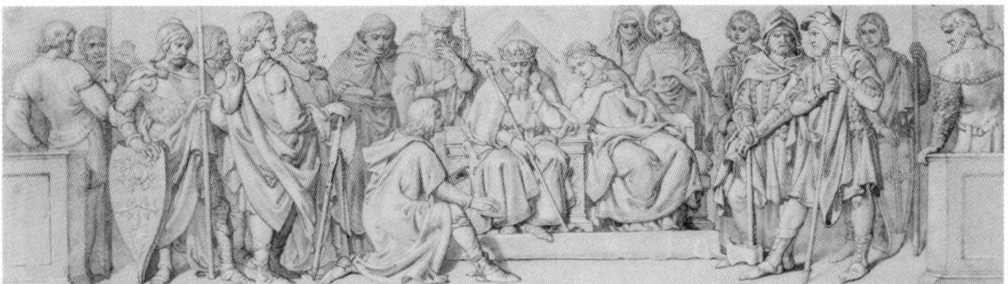

D.1904.30

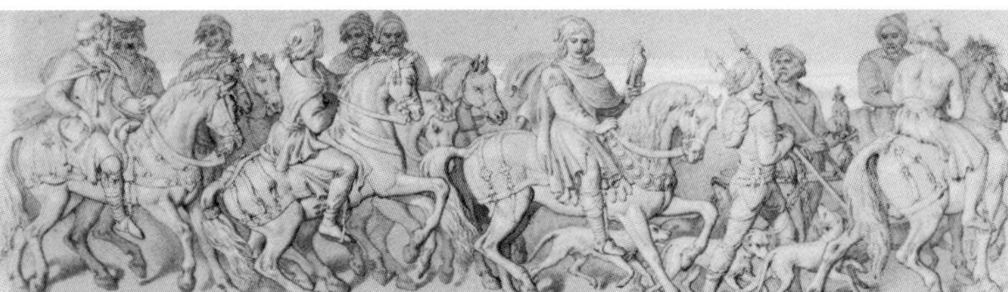

D.1904.31

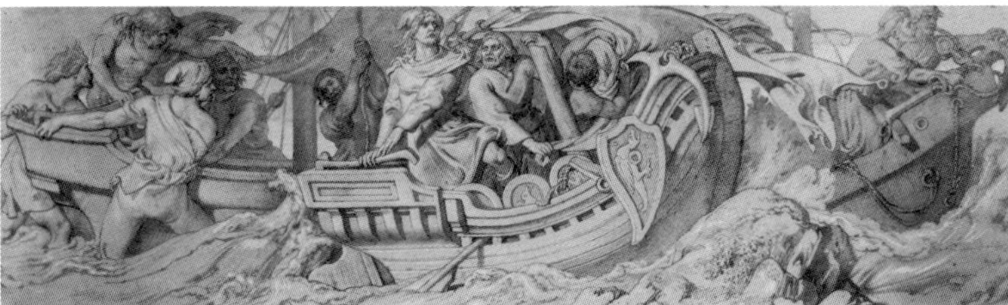

D.1904.32

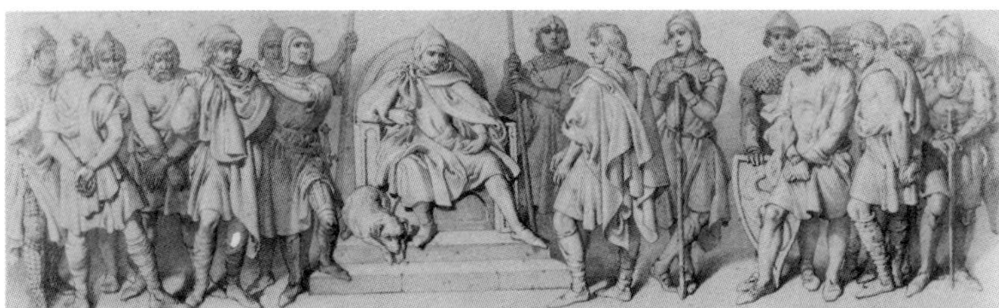

D.1904.33

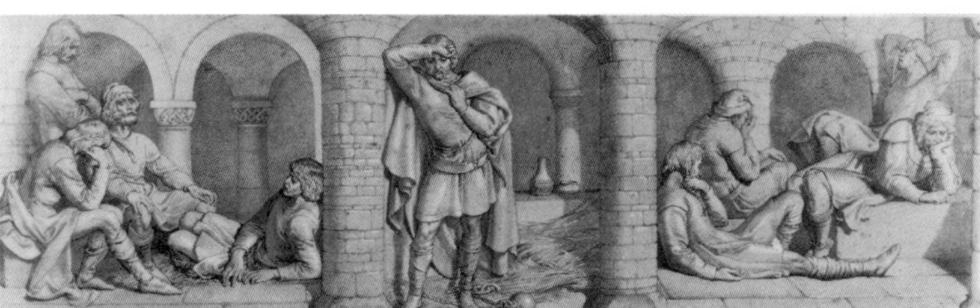

D.1904.34

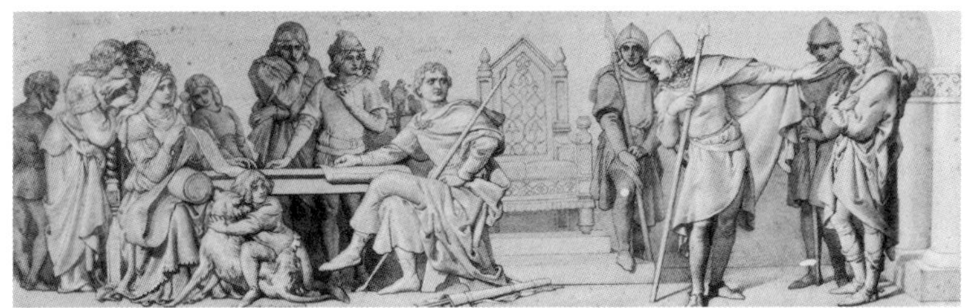

D.1904.35

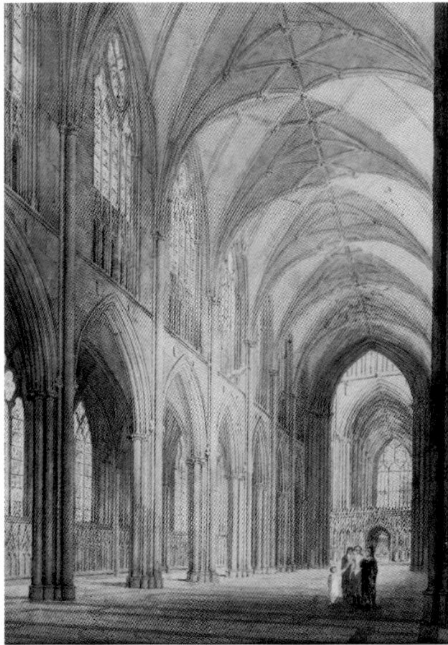

D.1900.8

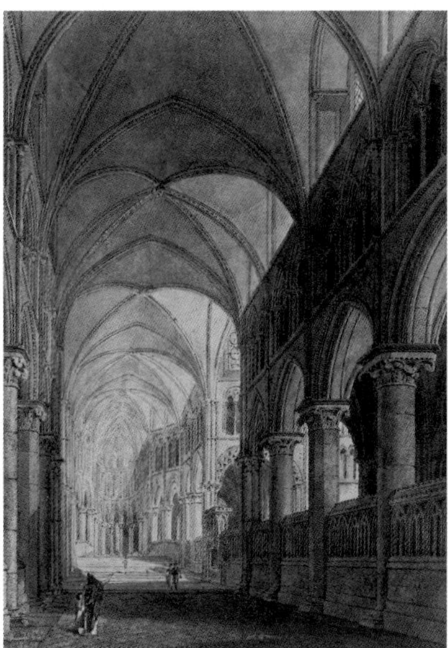

D.1900.27

Canterbury Cathedral, the side Aisle looking east
pen and brown ink, watercolour
246 × 170 mm
Worthington, Mary (gift, 1900) (D.1900.27)

Canterbury Cathedral, the south west Porch
pencil, black chalk, white chalk, bodycolour
(heightened with white); grey paper
inscribed lower right in later hand: *Canterbury
Cathedral-by Mackenzie*
459 × 381 mm
Ogden, William Sharp (bequest, 1926) (D.1926.139)

■ MACLISE, DANIEL (1811–70)

Born in Cork, Maclise came to London in 1827 and
entered the Royal Academy Schools the following year.
He is famous for his large romantic oil paintings and
for his work in the Houses of Parliament, for which he
painted *The Death of Nelson* and *Wellington and
Blücher*. He also contributed portraits to *Fraser's
Magazine* as well as producing illustrations to books
and periodicals. Maclise was elected a member of the
Royal Academy in 1840.

Harold takes leave of Edward the Confessor
pencil, bodycolour (heightened with white); buff paper
162 × 570 mm
Worthington, Mary (bequest, 1904) (D.1904.30)

Harold and his Knights ride to Bosham
pencil, bodycolour (heightened with white); buff paper
162 × 570 mm
Worthington, Mary (bequest, 1904) (D.1904.31)

Harold's Ship stranded on the Norman Coast
pencil, bodycolour (heightened with white); buff paper
178 × 581 mm
Worthington, Mary (bequest, 1904) (D.1904.32)

**Harold and his Companions brought as
Prisoners before Guy of Ponthieu**
pencil, bodycolour (heightened with white); buff paper
178 × 579 mm
Worthington, Mary (bequest, 1904) (D.1904.33)

**Harold and the Saxons confined in the
Castle of Beaurain**
pencil, bodycolour (heightened with white); buff paper
180 × 579 mm
Worthington, Mary (bequest, 1904) (D.1904.34)

**Harold's Captivity announced to William
of Normandy**
pencil, bodycolour (heightened with white); buff paper
182 × 578 mm
Worthington, Mary (bequest, 1904) (D.1904.35)

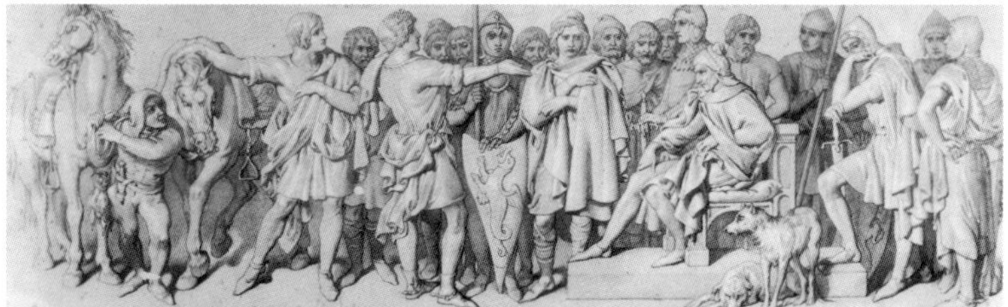

D.1904.36

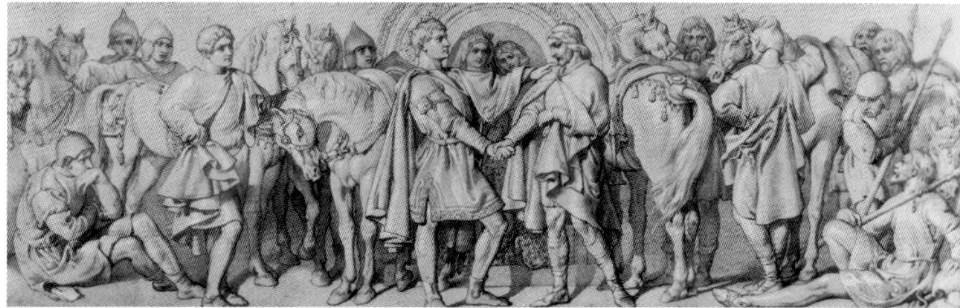

D.1904.37

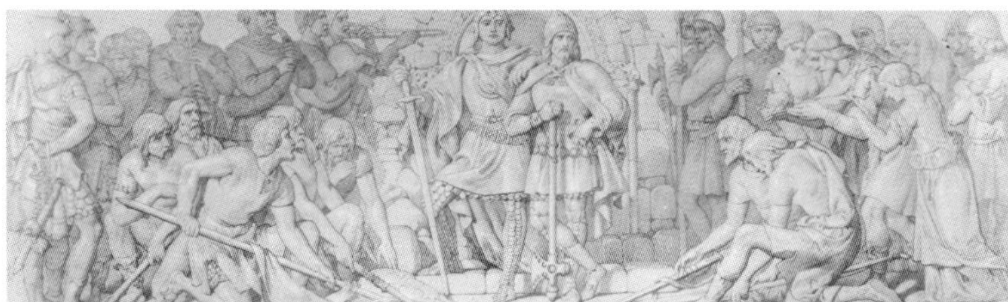

D.1904.38

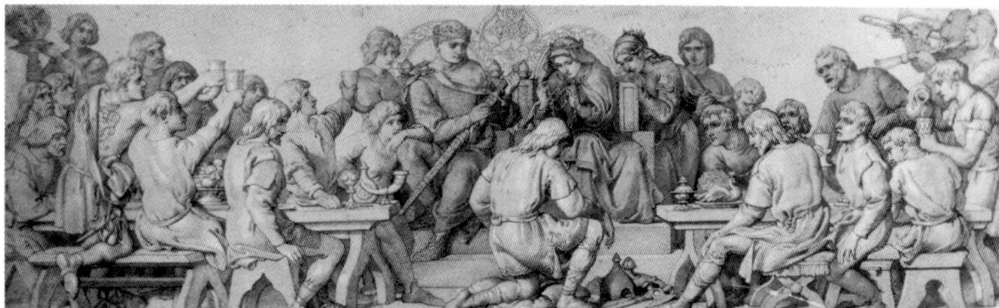

D.1904.39

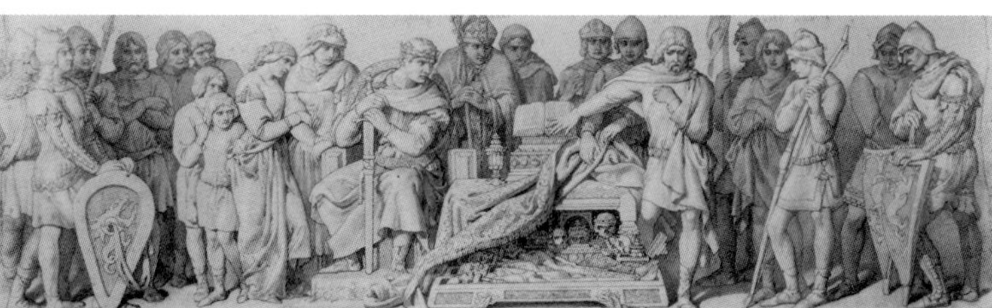

D.1904.40

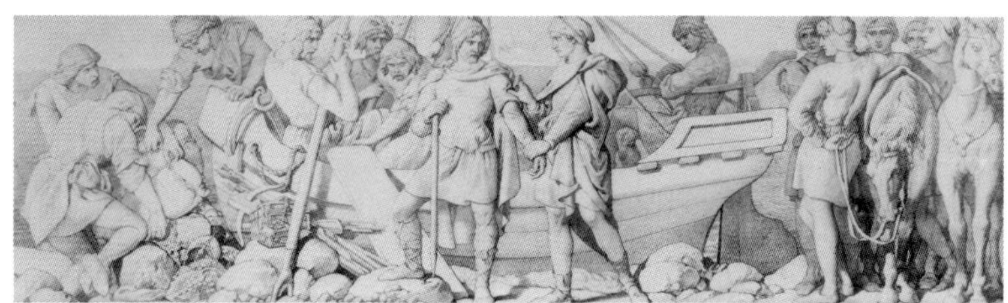

D.1904.41

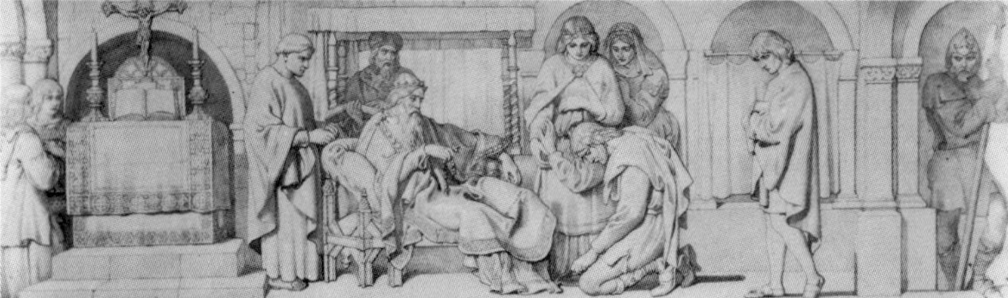

D.1904.42

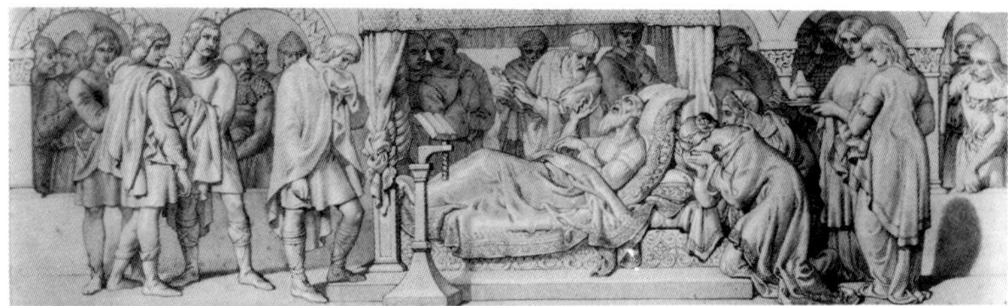

D.1904.43

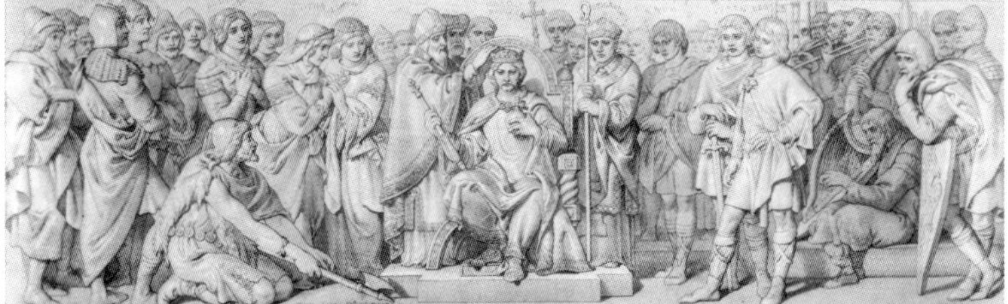

D.1904.44

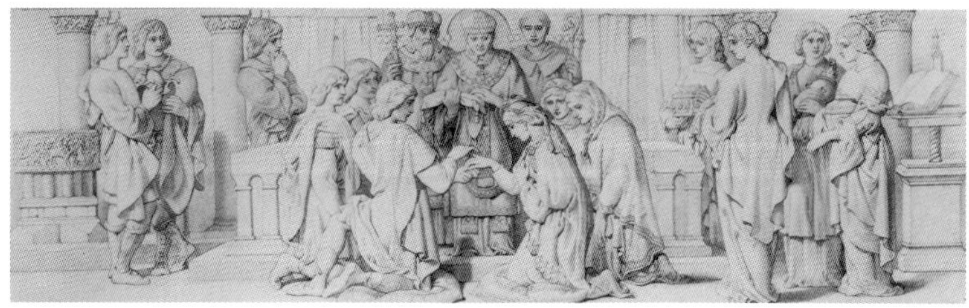

D.1904.45

Guy of Ponthieu gives further Audience to Harold
pencil, bodycolour (heightened with white); buff paper
182 × 578 mm
Worthington, Mary (bequest, 1904) (D.1904.36)

Harold and Duke William meet
pencil, bodycolour (heightened with white); buff paper
182 × 574 mm
Worthington, Mary (bequest, 1904) (D.1904.37)

Harold receives the Submission of Conan, Earl of Bretagne
pencil, bodycolour (heightened with white); buff paper
177 × 574 mm
Worthington, Mary (bequest, 1904) (D.1904.38)

William confers upon Harold the Dignity of a Norman Knight
pencil, bodycolour (heightened with white); buff paper
181 × 570 mm
Worthington, Mary (bequest, 1904) (D.1904.39)

Harold's Oath of Fidelity to William
pencil, bodycolour (heightened with white); buff paper
175 × 585 mm
Worthington, Mary (bequest, 1904) (D.1904.40)

Harold bids Adieu to William
pencil, bodycolour (heightened with white); buff paper
171 × 586 mm
Worthington, Mary (bequest, 1904) (D.1904.41)

Harold presents himself to Edward the Confessor
pencil, bodycolour (heightened with white); buff paper
177 × 580 mm
Worthington, Mary (bequest, 1904) (D.1904.42)

The Death of Edward the Confessor
pencil, bodycolour (heightened with white); buff paper
170 × 571 mm
Worthington, Mary (bequest, 1904) (D.1904.43)

The Coronation of Harold as King of England
pencil, bodycolour (heightened with white); buff paper
175 × 573 mm
Worthington, Mary (bequest, 1904) (D.1904.44)

The Marriage of Harold with Aldyth, Sister to Edwin and Morcar
pencil, bodycolour (heightened with white); buff paper
178 × 575 mm
Worthington, Mary (bequest, 1904) (D.1904.45)

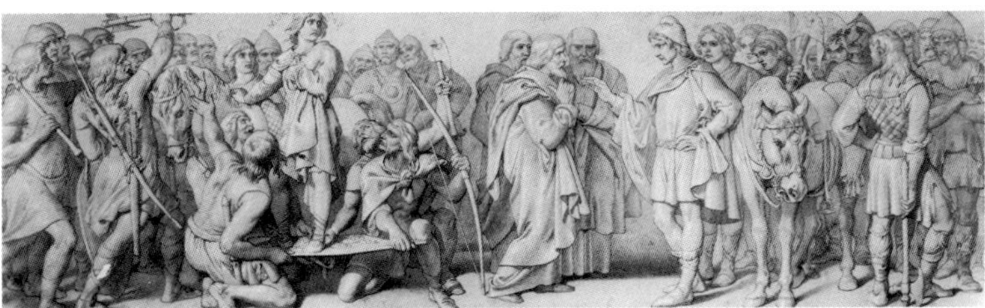

D.1904.46

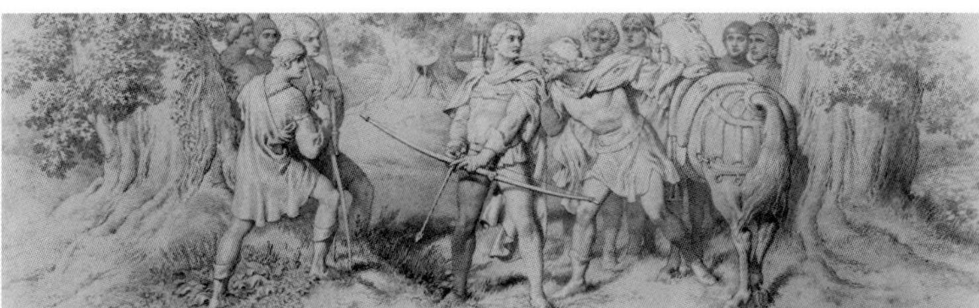

D.1904.47

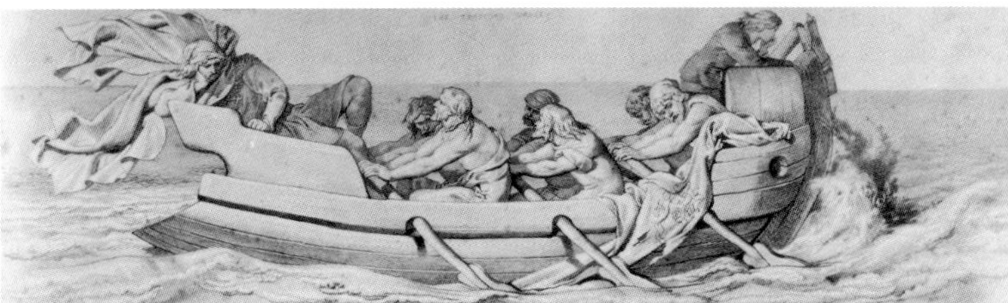

D.1904.48

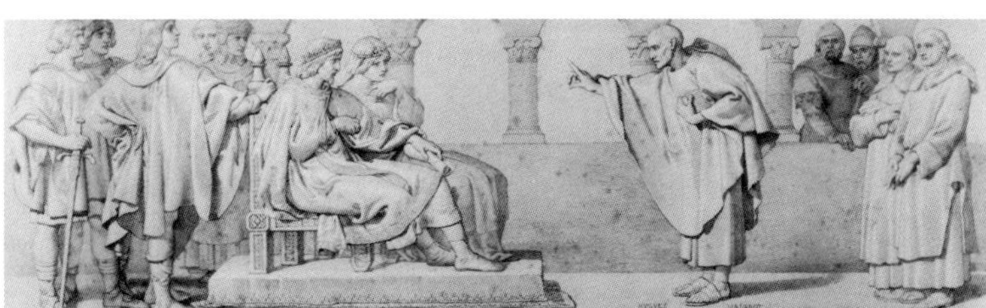

D.1904.49

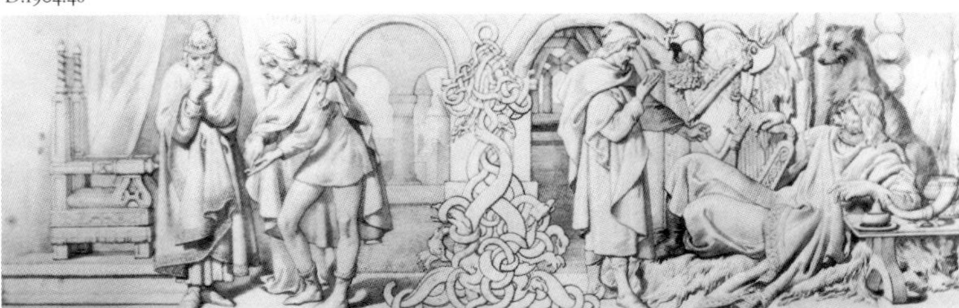

D.1904.50

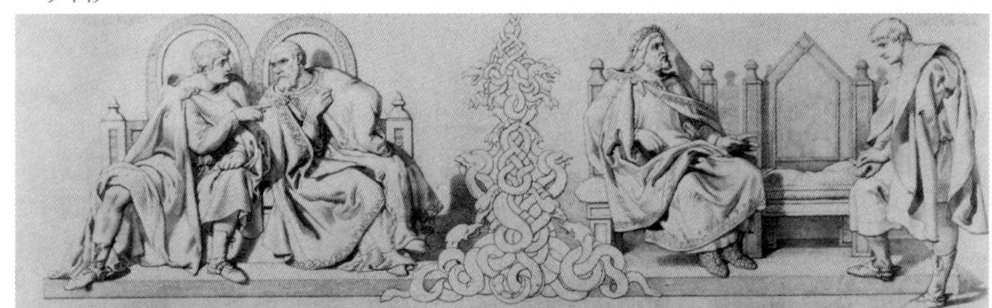

D.1904.51

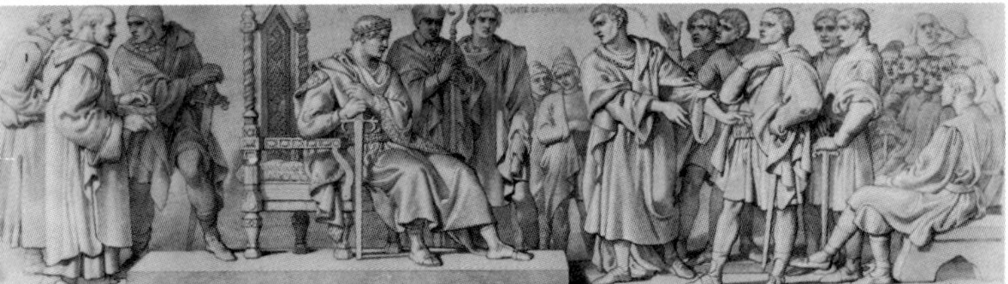

D.1904.52

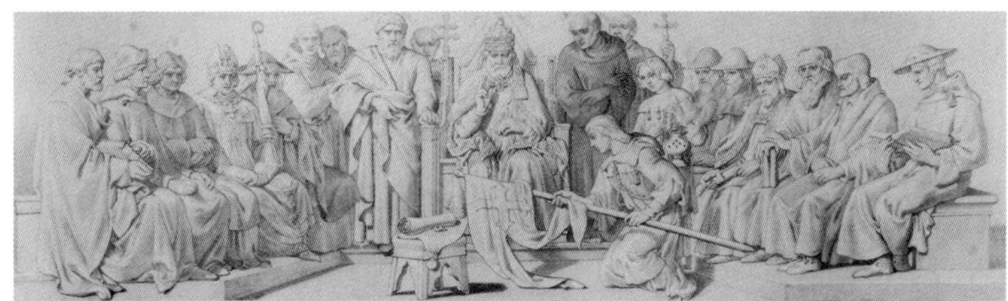

D.1904.53

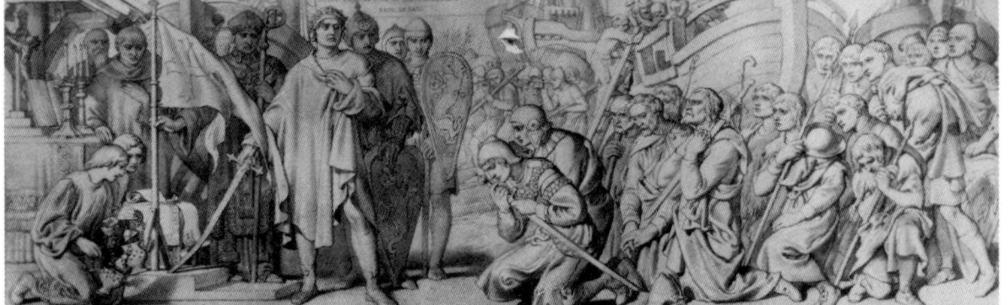

D.1904.54

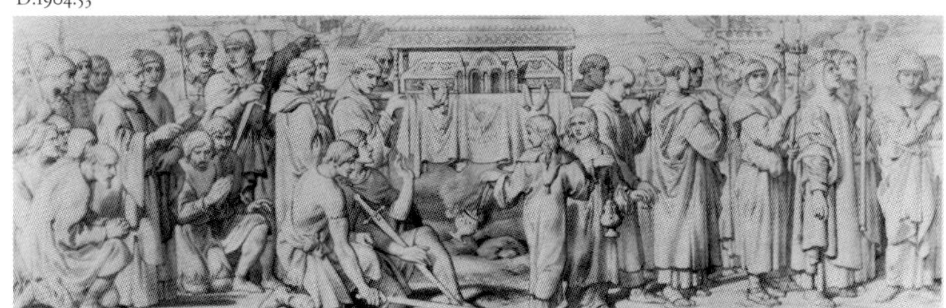

D.1904.55

Morcar elected Earl of Northumbria
pencil, bodycolour (heightened with white); buff paper
173 × 574 mm
Worthington, Mary (bequest, 1904) (D.1904.46)

William receives Intelligence from Tostig of Harold's Coronation
pencil, bodycolour (heightened with white); buff paper
173 × 574 mm
Worthington, Mary (bequest, 1904) (D.1904.47)

Tostig, defeated by Harold, flies in his Galley from the English Coast
pencil, bodycolour (heightened with white); buff paper
164 × 571 mm
Worthington, Mary (bequest, 1904) (D.1904.48)

Hughes Maigrot proposes to King Harold Conditions from Duke William
pencil, bodycolour (heightened with white); buff paper
166 × 574 mm
Worthington, Mary (bequest, 1904) (D.1904.49)

Tostig solicits the Aid of Sweyn, King of Denmark, and Harold Hardrada, King of Norway
pencil, bodycolour (heightened with white); buff paper
177 × 575 mm
Worthington, Mary (bequest, 1904) (D.1904.50)

William begs for Assistance from Philip I of France and Baldwin the Earl of Flanders
pencil, bodycolour (heightened with white); buff paper
175 × 575 mm
Worthington, Mary (bequest, 1904) (D.1904.51)

William consults the Nobles and Merchants of his Dukedom
pencil, bodycolour (heightened with white); buff paper
173 × 584 mm
Worthington, Mary (bequest, 1904) (D.1904.52)

Pope Alexander consecrates a Banner for William's Service
pencil, bodycolour (heightened with white); buff paper
174 × 584 mm
Worthington, Mary (bequest, 1904) (D.1904.53)

Homage rendered to the consecrated Banner
pencil, bodycolour (heightened with white); buff paper
188 × 586 mm
Worthington, Mary (bequest, 1904) (D.1904.54)

William displays the Relics of St Valery
pencil, bodycolour (heightened with white); buff paper
188 × 590 mm
Worthington, Mary (bequest, 1904) (D.1904.55)

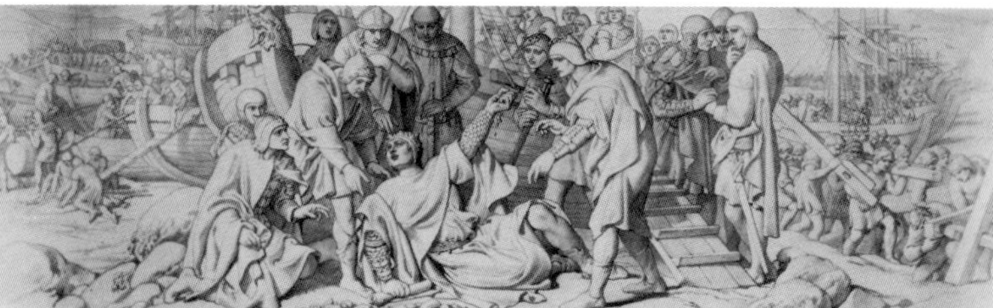

D.1904.56

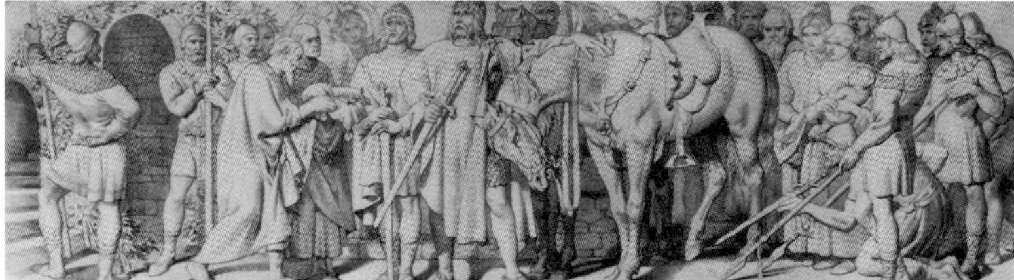

D.1904.57

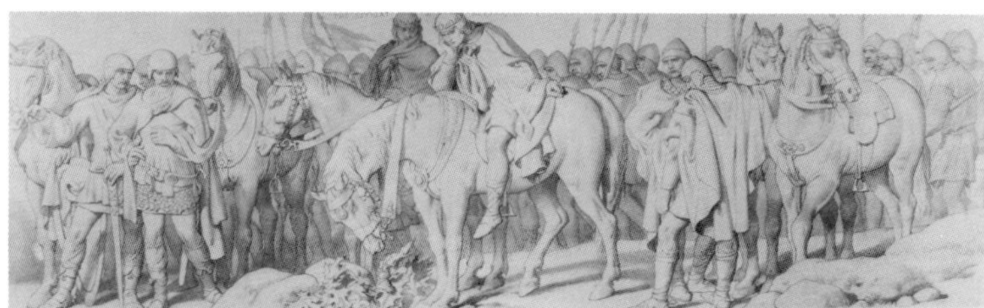

D.1904.58

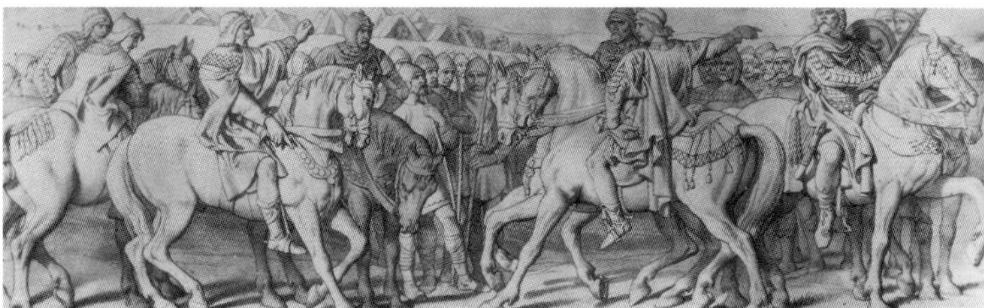

D.1904.59

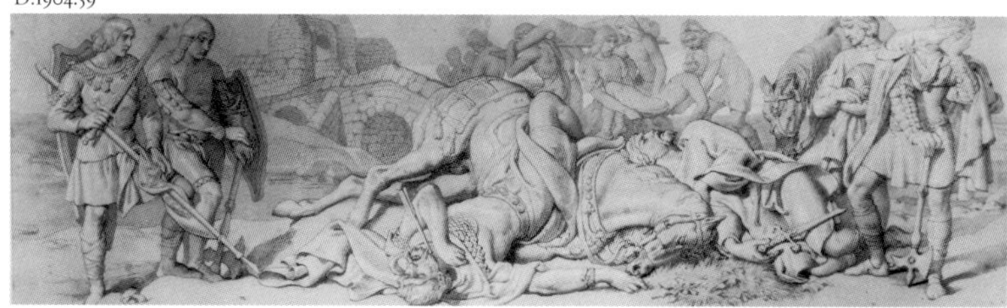

D.1904.60

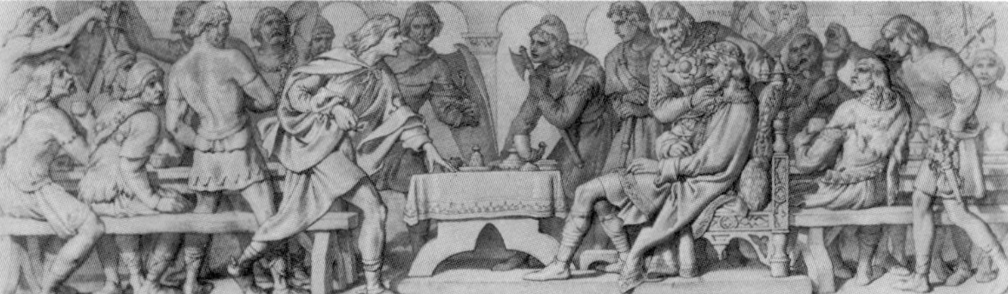

D.1904.61

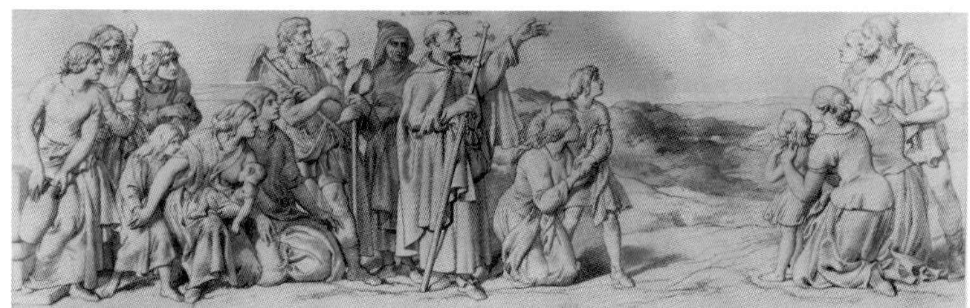

D.1904.62

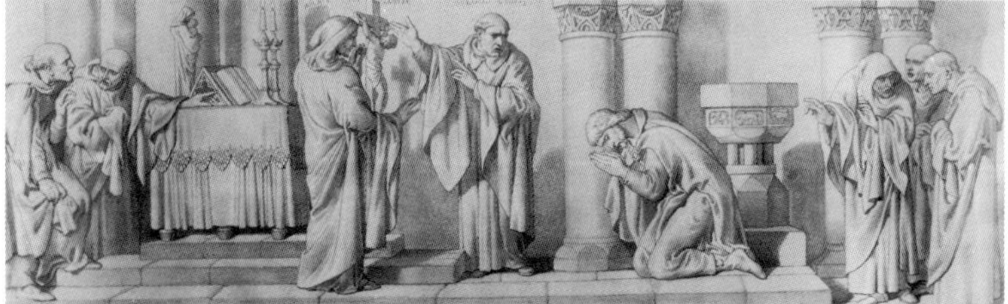

D.1904.63

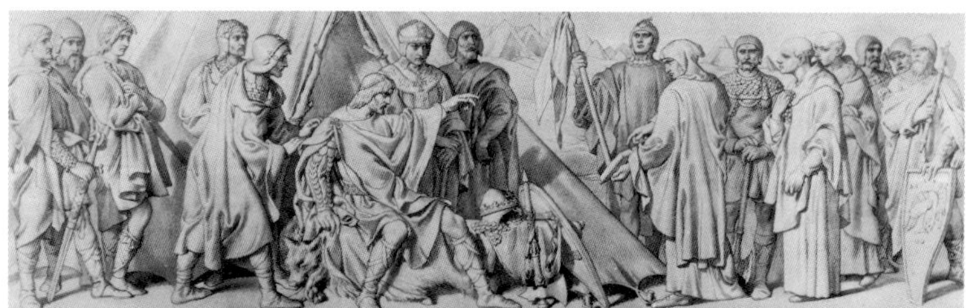

D.1904.64

D.1904.65

Duke William crosses the English Channel
pencil, bodycolour (heightened with white); buff paper
180 × 581 mm
Worthington, Mary (bequest, 1904) (D.1904.56)

**William stumbles and falls as he lands
in England**
pencil, bodycolour (heightened with white); buff paper
181 × 581 mm
Worthington, Mary (bequest, 1904) (D.1904.57)

**Tostig and Harold Hardrada receive the
Submission of the City of York**
pencil, bodycolour (heightened with white); buff paper
163 × 577 mm
Worthington, Mary (bequest, 1904) (D.1904.58)

The Retreat of Edwin and Morcar from York
pencil, bodycolour (heightened with white); buff paper
181 × 586 mm
Worthington, Mary (bequest, 1904) (D.1904.59)

**Harold's Interview with Tostig and Hardrada
before the Battle of Stamford**
pencil, bodycolour (heightened with white); buff paper
183 × 586 mm
Worthington, Mary (bequest, 1904) (D.1904.60)

**The Deaths of Tostig and Harold Hardrada after
the Battle of Stamford**
pencil, bodycolour (heightened with white); buff paper
167 × 571 mm
Worthington, Mary (bequest, 1904) (D.1904.61)

**Harold sits at a Banquet in York, a Herald
announces the Landing of Duke William**
pencil, bodycolour (heightened with white); buff paper
168 × 572 mm
Worthington, Mary (bequest, 1904) (D.1904.62)

**A fiery Star appears in England, portentous
of Disaster, and is apostrophised by the Monk
of Malmesbury**
pencil, bodycolour (heightened with white); buff paper
185 × 585 mm
Worthington, Mary (bequest, 1904) (D.1904.63)

**Harold offers Prayer and Adoration at the Abbey
Church of Waltham**
pencil, bodycolour (heightened with white); buff paper
187 × 589 mm
Worthington, Mary (bequest, 1904) (D.1904.64)

**The Day before the Battle: William's Knight and
Monks negotiate with Harold**
pencil, bodycolour (heightened with white); buff paper
186 × 587 mm
Worthington, Mary (bequest, 1904) (D.1904.65)

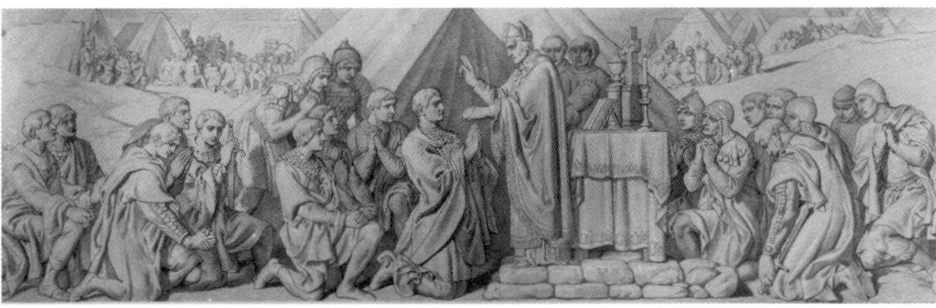

D.1904.66

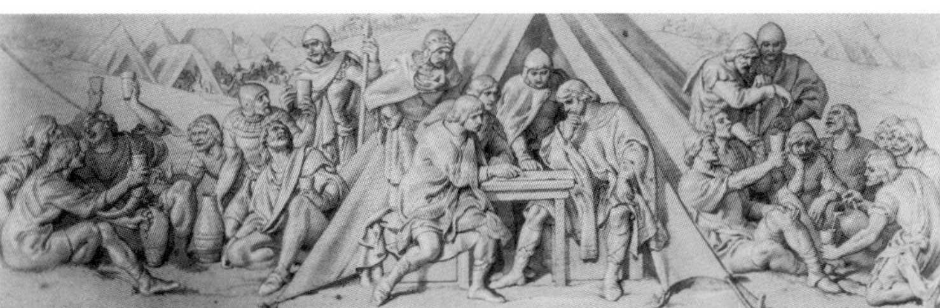

D.1904.67

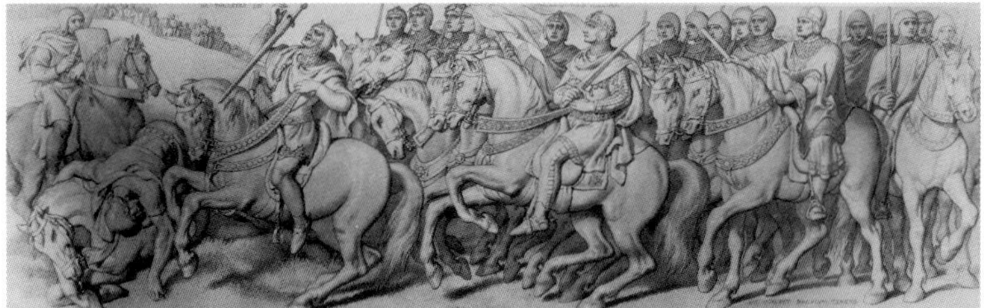

D.1904.68

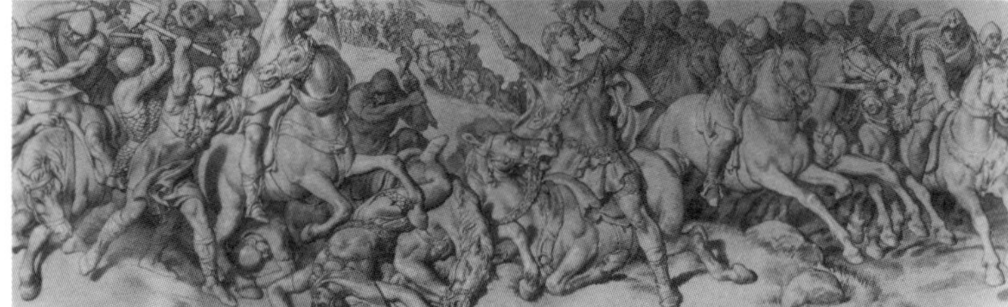

D.1904.69

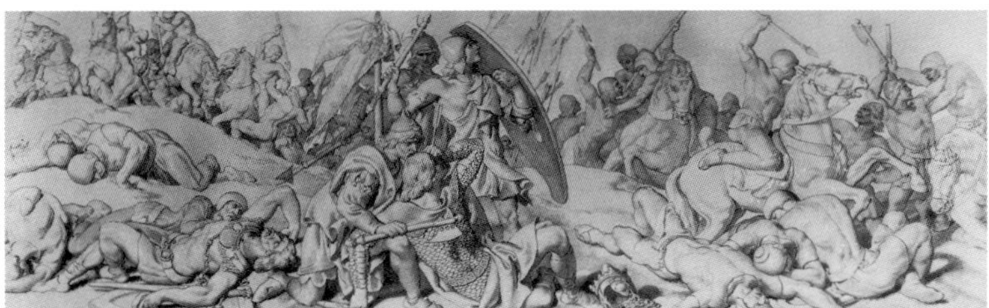

D.1904.70

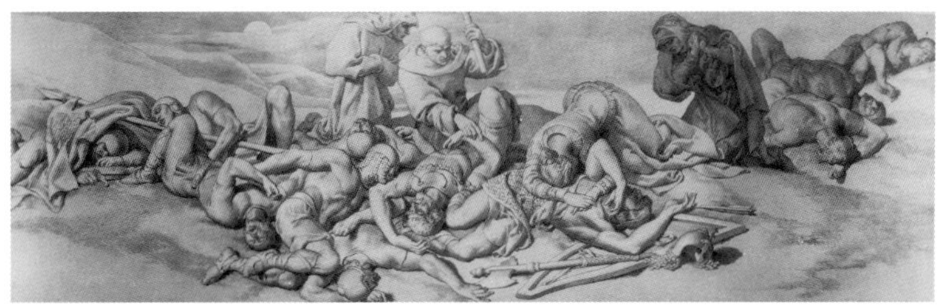

D.1904.71

The Eve before the Battle: pious Observance of the Normans
pencil, bodycolour (heightened with white); buff paper
187 × 585 mm
Worthington, Mary (bequest, 1904) (D.1904.66)

The Eve before the Battle: Riot and Wassail of the Saxons
pencil, bodycolour (heightened with white); buff paper
186 × 584 mm
Worthington, Mary (bequest, 1904) (D.1904.67)

Morning of the Battle: the Norman Minstrel Taillifer leads Duke William's Van
pencil, bodycolour (heightened with white); buff paper
186 × 587 mm
Worthington, Mary (bequest, 1904) (D.1904.68)

The retreating Normans are stayed and turned by William
pencil, bodycolour (heightened with white); buff paper
186 × 586 mm
Worthington, Mary (bequest, 1904) (D.1904.69)

Harold is pierced by a falling Arrow
pencil, bodycolour (heightened with white); buff paper
190 × 593 mm
Worthington, Mary (bequest, 1904) (D.1904.70)

The Night after the Battle: Edith discovers the Body of Harold
pencil, bodycolour (heightened with white); buff paper
188 × 587 mm
Worthington, Mary (bequest, 1904) (D.1904.71)

■ **MALCHAIR, JOHN BAPTISTE (1731–1812)**
Born in Cologne, Malchair came to England in 1754. He taught music and drawing in Sussex and Bristol before being appointed leader of the Music Room Band in Oxford in 1759. Malchair held this post until his retirement in 1792 and supplemented it by teaching drawing to undergraduates; his pupils were very numerous and include Sir George Beaumont. Malchair was the first artist working in England to inscribe the time of day on his drawings.

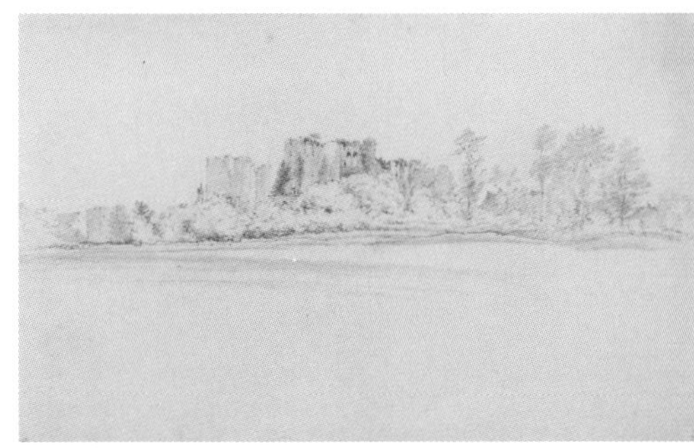

D.1926.302

Kenilworth Castle, Warwickshire, from the North
18.5.1785
pencil, black chalk, grey watercolour
dated & inscribed lower left verso: *Kennilworth Castle from the North – May 18 – 1785 –/8*; numbered lower left: *13*
290 × 454 mm
Ogden, William Sharp (bequest, 1926) (D.1926.302)

Kenilworth Castle, Warwickshire, from the North
17.5.1785
pencil, black chalk, grey watercolour
dated & inscribed lower edge verso: *Kennilworth Castle Warwickshire, taken from the North Side – May 17 – 1785–/* [final digit cut]
299 × 376 mm
Ogden, William Sharp (bequest, 1926) (D.1926.303)

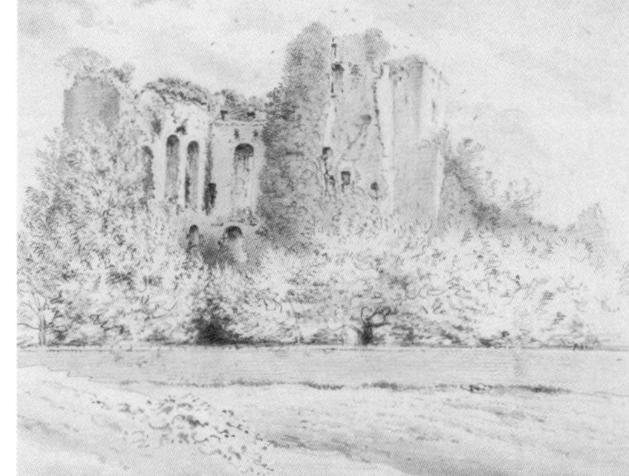

D.1926.303

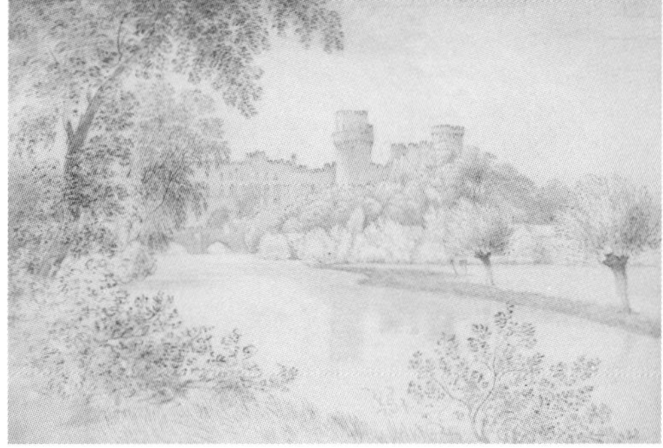

D.1926.304

Warwick Castle, from the East
6.6.1787
pencil, black chalk, grey watercolour
inscribed & dated lower left verso: *June 6 – 1787 – Warwick Castle*
376 × 541 mm
Ogden, William Sharp (bequest, 1926) (D.1926.304)

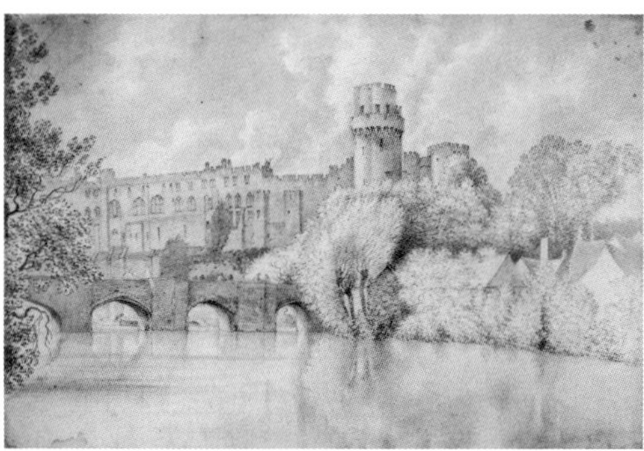

D.1926.305

Warwick Castle, from the River Avon
28.5.1785
pencil, black chalk, grey watercolour
inscribed & dated lower edge verso: *A View of
W[ar]wick Castle, from an Orchard belonging to Mr.
Brooks – May 28 – 1787 – /1 / again May* [blank] *With
the Revd Mr* [blank] *Willes of Newbold Comyn*
372 × 540 mm
Ogden, William Sharp (bequest, 1926) (D.1926.305)

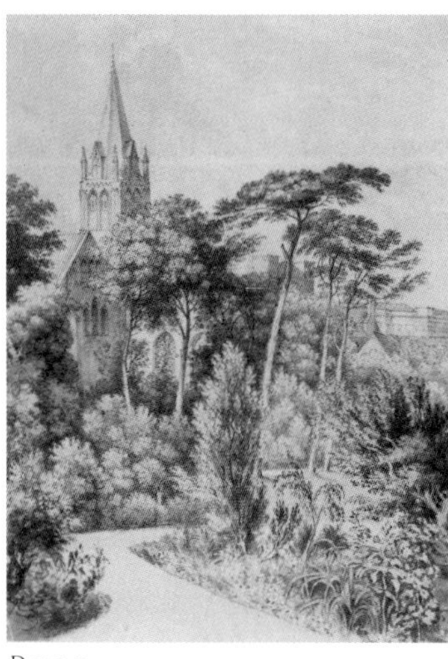

D.1947.51

The Canon's Garden, Christ Church, Oxford
1775 & 2.2.1784
pencil, watercolour
inscribed upper left verso; not a signature: *Malchair*;
inscribed & dated lower edge verso: *from the Canon's
gearden* (sic) *in the Cloisters / Ch.Ch.Oxon: 1775.
Retuched* (sic) *on the Spote* (sic) *Feb: 2d. 1784 / verry
heard* (sic) *frost*
283 × 204 mm
Friends of the Whitworth (gift, 1947) (D.1947.51)

**A Capriccio Landscape with a Castle
above a Lake**
pencil, watercolour
342 × 480 mm
Towlson, Hector J. (gift, 1952) (D.1952.9)

**Part of Kenilworth Castle from the
North Side, Warwickshire**
17.5.1785
pencil, black chalk, grey watercolour
inscribed and dated lower edge verso: *Part of
Kenilworth Castle from the North Side – May 17 – 1785
/7; numbered lower left:* 12; *numbered lower right:* 2
456 × 306 mm
Agnew's (purchase, 10.5.1996) (D.1996.7)

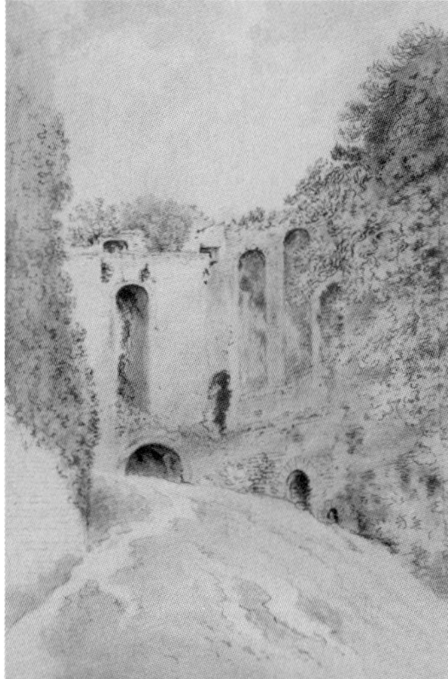

D.1996.7

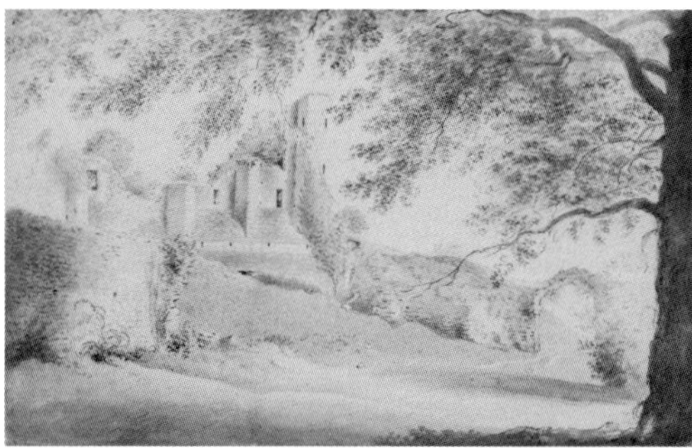

D.1996.8

**Part of Kenilworth Castle from within the
Walls, Warwickshire**
19.5.1785
pencil, black chalk, grey watercolour
watermark Strasbourg lily
inscribed and dated lower edge verso: *Part of
Kenilworth Castle from within the Walls. May 19 – 1785
–/8; numbered lower left:* 10
351 × 546 mm
Agnew's (purchase, 10.5.1996) (D.1996.8)

Kenilworth Castle from the Abby's, Warwickshire
20.5.1785
pencil, black chalk, grey watercolour; paper
watermark Pz
inscribed and dated lower edge verso: *Kenilworth Castle
from the Abby's – May 20 – 1785 –/7*
370 × 541 mm
Agnew's (purchase, 10.5.1996) (D.1996.9)

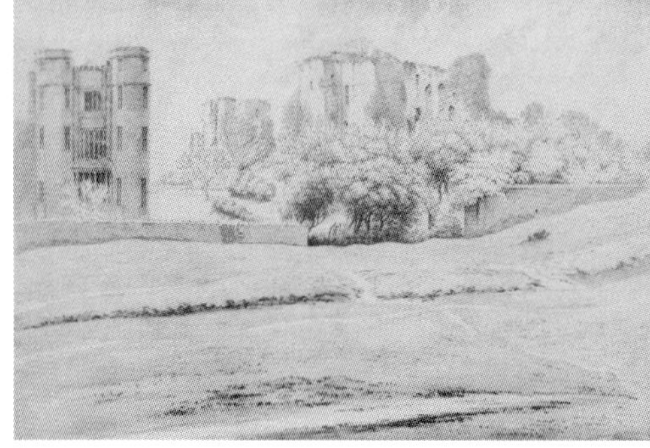

D.1996.10

Kenilworth Castle from the North, Warwickshire
20.5.1785
pencil, black chalk, grey watercolour
inscribed and dated in grey watercolour lower edge
verso: *Kenilworth Castle from the North – May 20 – 1785
– 8/ / From Drury's the WoolComber*
370 × 542 mm
Agnew's (purchase, 10.5.1996) (D.1996.10)

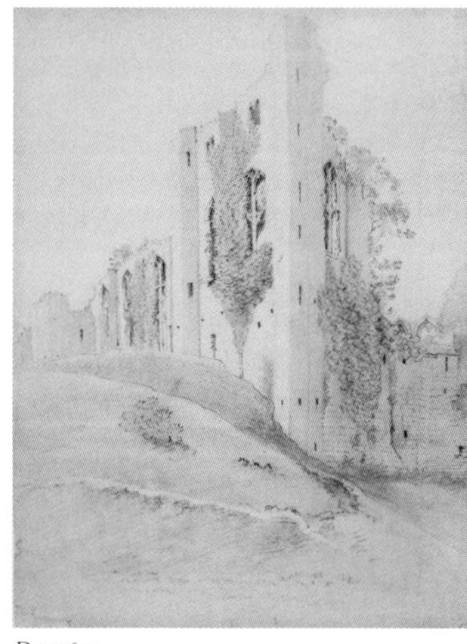

D.1996.11

Kenilworth Castle, Warwickshire
29.5.1787
pencil, black chalk, grey watercolour; watermark
Strasbourg lily
inscribed and dated lower edge verso: *Kenilworth May
29 – 1787 – /8 / again May* [illegible] *– between twelve
and one o'clock*
377 × 533 mm
Agnew's (purchase, 10.5.1996) (D.1996.11)

D.1996.12

Kenilworth Castle, Warwickshire
2.6.1787
pencil, black chalk, grey watercolour; watermark
Strasbourg lily
inscribed and dated lower edge verso: *Kenilworth June
2/ – 1787 – /8*
522 × 380 mm
Agnew's (purchase, 10.5.1996) (D.1996.12)

**South End of the Great Hall at Kenilworth
Castle, Warwickshire**
4.6.1787
pencil, black chalk, grey watercolour; watermark
Strasbourg lily
inscribed and dated lower edge verso: *South end of the
Great Hall at Kenilworth – Monday June 4 – 1787 – /1*
375 × 544 mm
Agnew's (purchase, 10.5.1996) (D.1996.13)

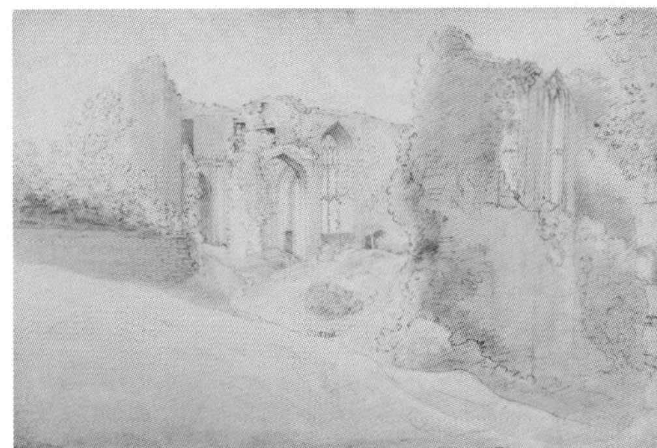

D.1996.13

■ Malton, James (1766–1803)

An architectural draughtsman, James Malton accompanied his father Thomas Malton Sen. to Dublin, where he worked for the architect James Gandon. Malton exhibited at the Royal Academy from 1792 until his death, producing architectural views of Dublin and London.

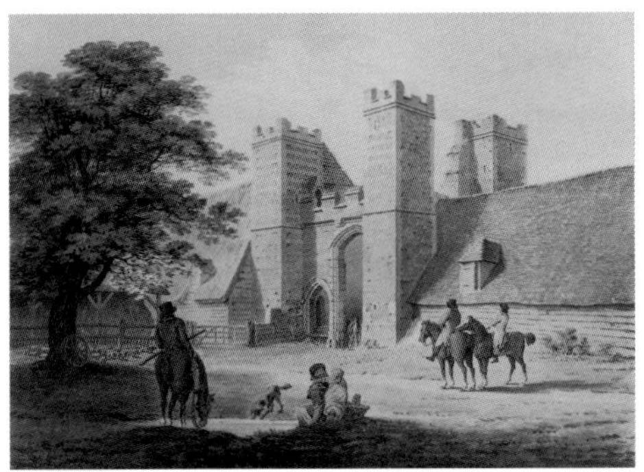

D.1921.10

Dent-de-Lion Gatehouse, Garlinge, Kent
1799
watercolour
signed & dated lower left: *James Malton 1799–*
282 × 381 mm
Anderson, A. E. (gift, 1921) (D.1921.10)

■ Malton, Sen.,Thomas (1726–1801)

Malton was an architectural draughtsman and lecturer on perspective who exhibited in London from 1772. He moved to Dublin in 1785 where he produced topographical views and continued to teach.

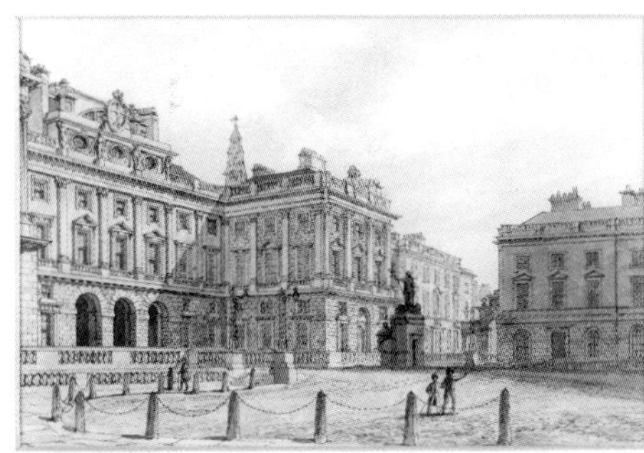

D.1898.1

Somerset House, London, the north Side of the Great Court
pen and brown ink, watercolour
165 × 241 mm
Worthington, Mary (gift, 1898) (D.1898.1)

■ Malton, Jun.,Thomas (1748–1804)

Thomas Malton Jun., son of Thomas Malton and brother of James, accompanied his father to Dublin in 1785. He then settled in London and produced architectural views as well as holding evening classes in perspective, which were attended by the young Turner. Between 1792 and 1801, Malton published a series of aquatints of London buildings entitled *A Picturesque Tour through the Cities of London and Westminster*.

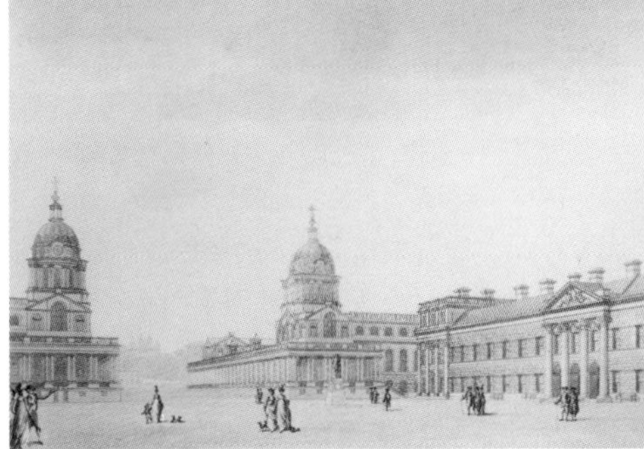

D.1892.16

The Queen Mary and King William Blocks, Greenwich Hospital, London, seen from the Courtyard
pen and ink, watercolour (over etched outline)
211 × 303 mm
Taylor, John Edward (gift, 1892) (D.1892.16)

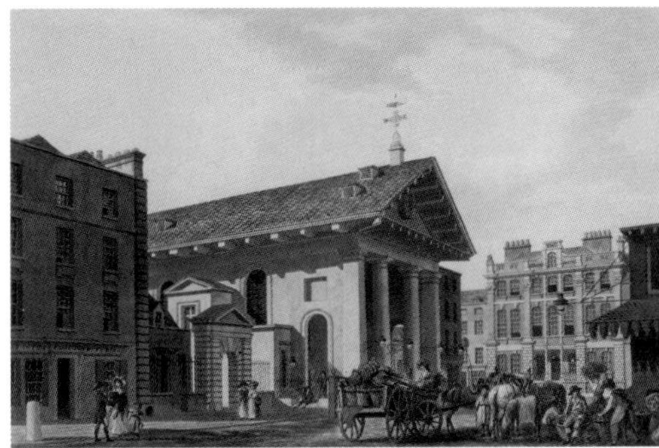

D.1951.14

St Paul's Church, Covent Garden, London, from the Piazza
watercolour
318 × 472 mm
Friends of the Whitworth (gift, 1951) (D.1951.14)

■ Manby, Thomas (1633 (?)–1695)

Manby is one of the earliest English artists known to have visited Italy. He is said to have been – but almost certainly was not – a pupil of Salvator Rosa (d. 1673). Manby was probably in Rome in the 1680s and produced a number of topographical views of Roman ruins which are now very rare. In England, he is known to have worked with the portrait painter Mary Beale and is mentioned in her correspondence. No known paintings by him survive and he may well have been an amateur.

Study of Trees by a Road
pencil, brown watercolour
signed & numbered upper left: *Manby 6*
395 × 260 mm
Sotheby's, London (purchase, 17.11.1992) (V. & A., F.O.W.) (D.1992.5)

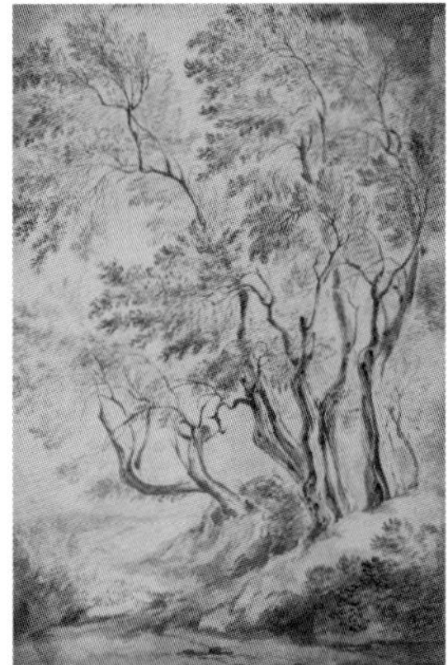

D.1992.5

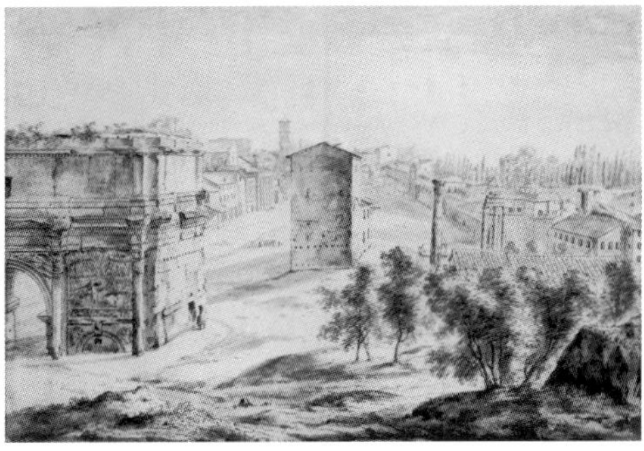

D.1999.12

The Roman Forum
pen and grey ink, grey watercolour; watermark a cross over a fleur-de-lys
signed upper left: *Manby*
inscribed on verso along upper edge; partially illegible: *Campo Vachino e* [illegible] *vespasiano*
330 × 488 mm
Boyd of Merton, Viscount (purchase, 1999) (V. & A., N.A.C.F., F.O.W.) (D.1999.12)

■ Marks, Henry Stacy (1829–98)

Now best known for his paintings of birds, Marks was a versatile talent who was elected a member of the Royal Academy in 1878 and the Royal Watercolour Society in 1883. As well as painting birds, he painted stage scenery and designed stained glass. Marks was a friend of Ruskin, who admired his work.

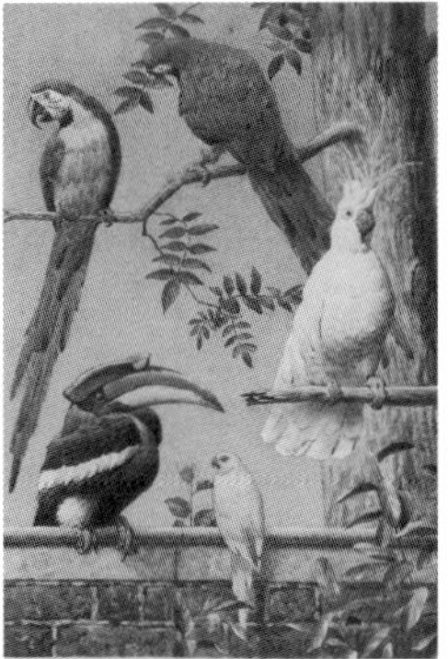

D.1902.5

Macaw, Cockatoo, Hornbill and Parakeet
pen and brown ink, watercolour
signed lower left with initials: *H S M*
306 × 206 mm
Agnew, Sir William (gift, 1902) (D.1902.5)

■ MARLOW, WILLIAM (1740–1813)

Apparently a pupil of Samuel Scott, Marlow began exhibiting at the Society of Artists in 1762. In 1765–66 he travelled through France and Italy; this provided him with material for the rest of his life. Marlow exhibited at the Royal Academy between 1788 and 1807. In common with Samuel Scott, he had a preference for marine or river subjects and can be classed as one of the English followers of Canaletto.

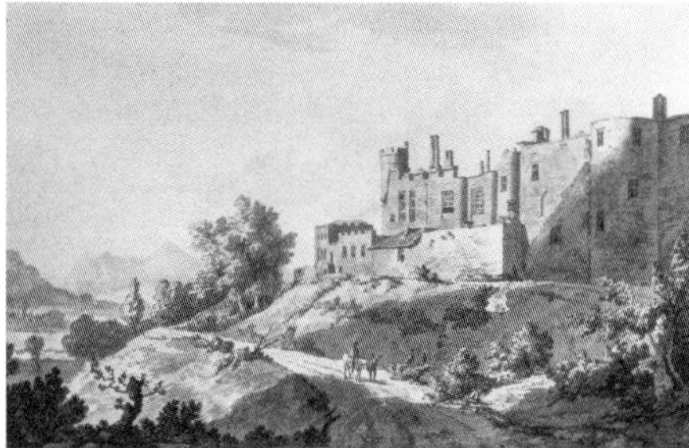
D.1893.1

Powis Castle, Montgomeryshire, Wales, from the North
watercolour
243 × 372 mm
Agnew's (purchase, 18.12.1893) (D.1893.1)

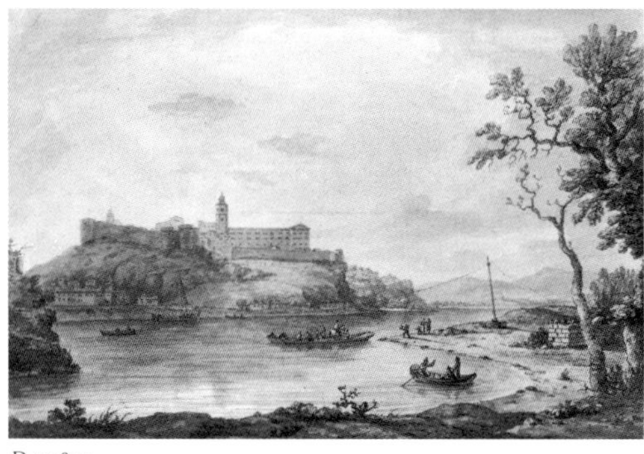
D.1908.22

The Papal Palace, Avignon
pencil, pen and brown ink, watercolour
signed lower right with initials: *W M*; inscribed on mount lower centre: *View at Avignon*
371 × 638 mm
Darbishire, Robert Dukinfield (gift, 1908) (D.1908.22)

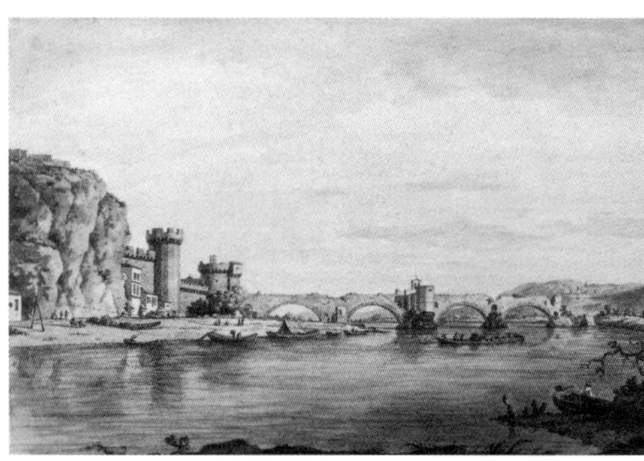
D.1908.23

The Bridge of St Bénézet, Avignon
pencil, pen and brown ink, watercolour
signed lower right with initials: *W M*; inscribed on mount lower centre: *View at Avignon*
367 × 541 mm
Darbishire, Robert Dukinfield (gift, 1908) (D.1908.23)

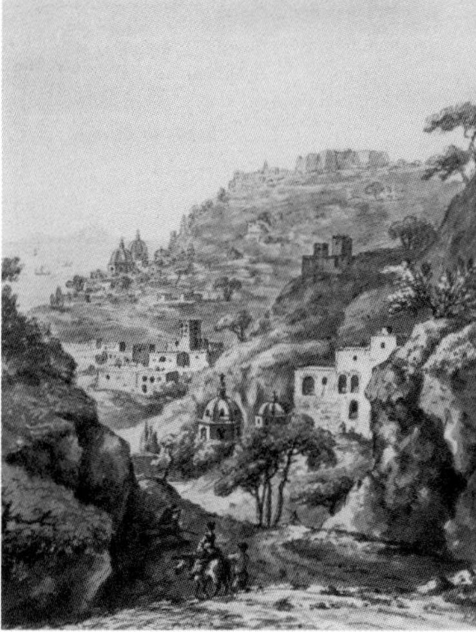
D.1987.52

View of Naples from the Hills near Capodimonte, with the Island of Capri in the Distance
pencil, watercolour
signed lower right with initials: *W M*
283 × 223 mm
Leger Galleries, London (purchase, 1987) (N.A.C.F., F.O.W.) (D.1987.52)

Study for 'View of Naples from the Hills near Capodimonte, with the Island of Capri in the Distance'
pencil
139 × 142 mm
Leger Galleries, London (gift, 1988) (D.1988.2)

■ MARSHALL, CHARLES (1806–90)

A theatrical scene painter, Marshall worked at Covent Garden and Drury Lane. He also painted landscapes and exhibited at various London venues between 1828 and 1884.

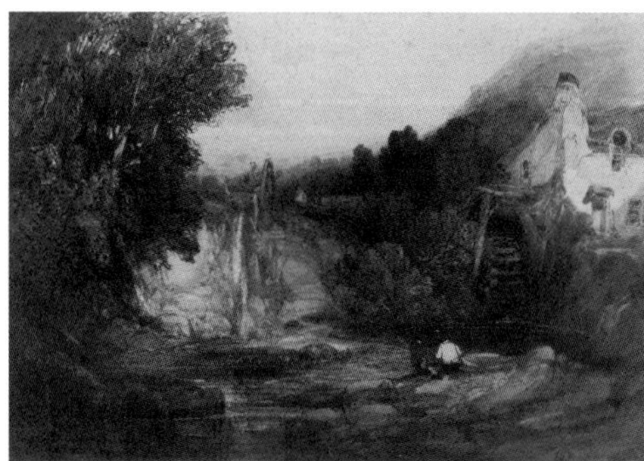
D.1919.4

Pandy Mill, Caernarvonshire, Wales
watercolour, bodycolour (heightened with white)
signed lower left: *C Marshall*
219 × 312 mm
Philips, Mrs Herbert (bequest, 1919) (D.1919.4)

■ MARTIN, ELIAS (1739–1818)

Born in Stockholm, Martin came to England in 1768 and entered the Royal Academy Schools. In 1780 he returned to Sweden and became Court Painter to the King. He exhibited at the Royal Academy between 1769 and 1790 and specialised in figure subjects.

A Woman at a Table with two Girls blowing Bubbles
watercolour, varnish
signed centre right: *E.Martin*
169 × 141 mm
Ogden, William Sharp (bequest, 1926) (D.1926.179)

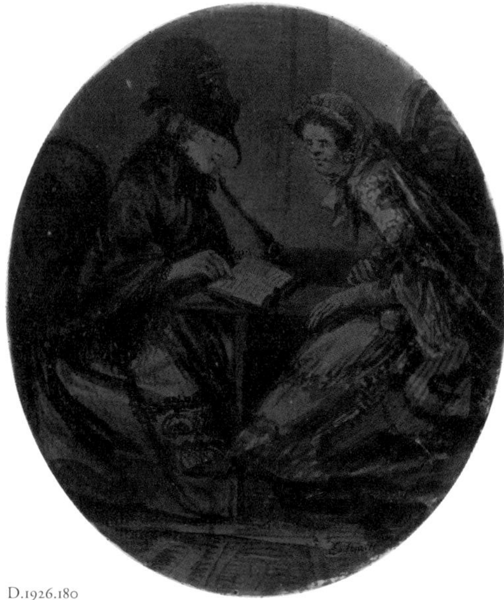
D.1926.180

Two Women at a Table reading
watercolour, varnish
signed lower right: *E.Martin*
166 × 138 mm
Ogden, William Sharp (bequest, 1926) (D.1926.180)

■ MARTIN, JOHN (1789–1854)

One of the most remarkable figures in British Romantic art, Martin first exhibited at the Royal Academy in 1811. He specialised in large and melodramatic literary, Biblical and Miltonic subjects, highly coloured and with dramatic lighting effects, which were often conceived as the basis for ambitious printmaking projects. Martin also used watercolour for a more controlled treatment of landscape and for his projects to improve London's sewerage and water supply systems.

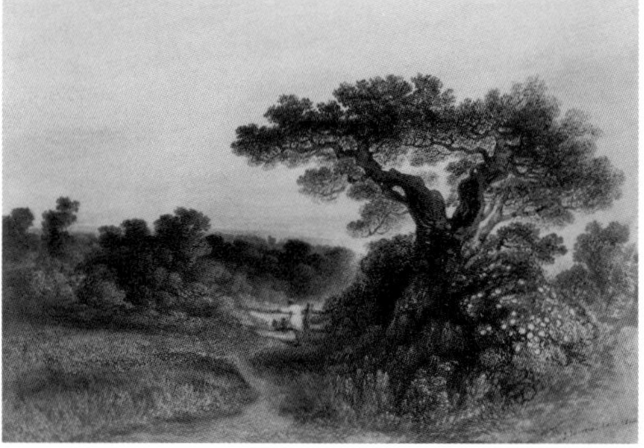
D.1892.68

Landscape, near St Albans, Hertfordshire
6.1840
watercolour
signed & dated lower right: *J.Martin.June 1840*
251 × 351 mm
Taylor, John Edward (gift, 1892) (D.1892.68)

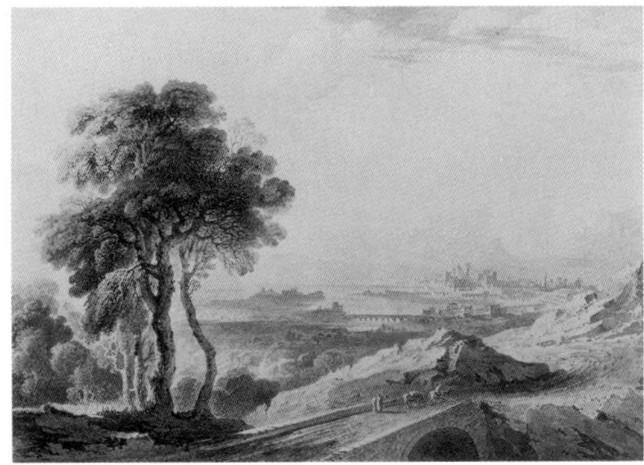

D.1900.7

An Egyptian Landscape
1817
pencil, brown watercolour
signed & dated lower left: *J.Martin 1817*
200 × 270 mm
Worthington, Mary (gift, 1900) (D.1900.7)

The Wye Valley, View from Wyndcliffe looking towards Chepstow
1844
pencil, watercolour
signed & dated lower right: *Martin 1844*
303 × 721 mm
untraced (gift, 1957) (D.1957.10)

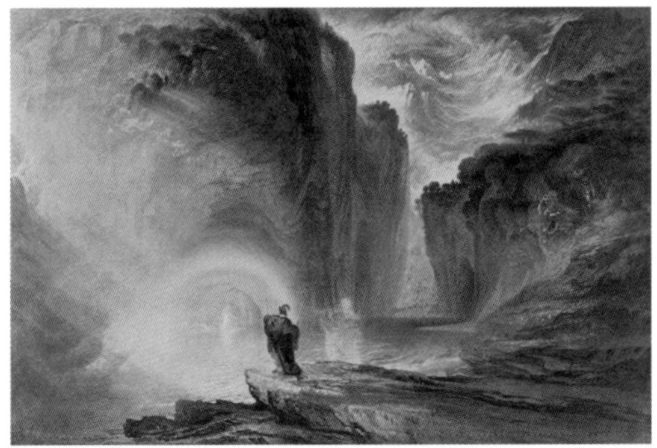

D.1974.6

Manfred and the Witch of the Alps
1837
watercolour, bodycolour
signed & dated lower centre: *J.Martin 1837*
388 × 558 mm
Hazlitt, Gooden and Fox Ltd (purchase, 1974) (V. & A., F.O.W) (D.1974.6)

■ Master of the Giants (fl. 1779)

The Master of the Giants was an unknown artist whose only known work derives from an album of drawings that was on the London art market in 1949. Clearly produced in Rome under the influence of John Henry Fuseli, the subjects of his drawings are often obscure and macabre and show elongated figures with exaggerated gestures.

Incantation Scene (recto); Study of central Scene (verso)
1779
pen and black ink
191 × 235 mm
Roland, Browse & Delbanco (purchase, 1949) (D.1949.3)

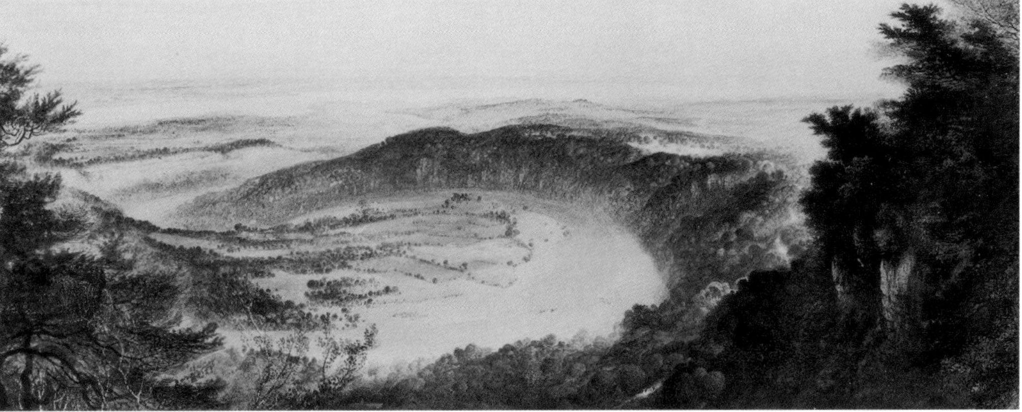

D.1957.10

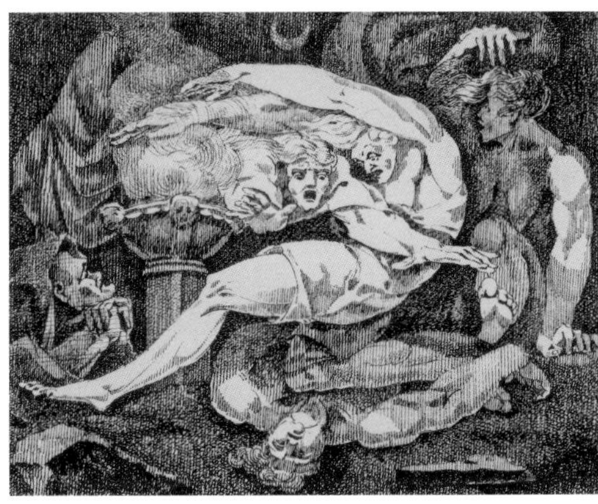

D.1949.3

■ Master of the Wire Line (late 18th century)

The Master of the Wire Line was an unknown and probably provincial drawing master, who is thus named because of his scratchy pen and ink outlines. His watercolours are common but often have grander names attached to them.

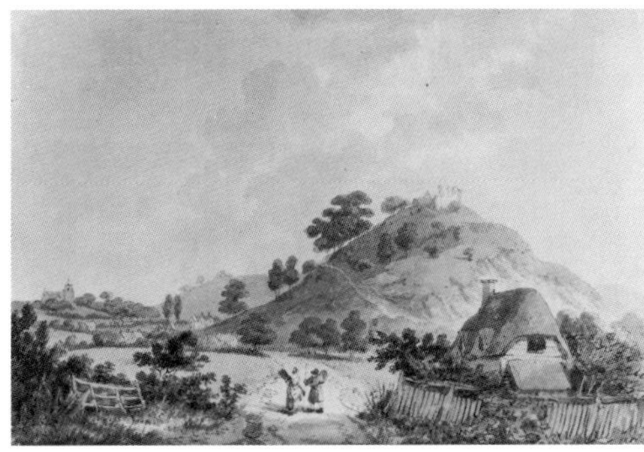

D.1934.31

Figures on a Country Road with a Town and a Castle on a Hill beyond
pen and grey ink, watercolour
256 × 367 mm
Peer Groves, Major W. (gift, 1934) (D.1934.31)

Washerwomen outside a Cottage
pen and grey ink, watercolour
inscribed lower right (false signature and date):
F.Wheatly.1801
196 × 152 mm
Towlson, Hector J. (bequest, 1969) (D.1970.81)

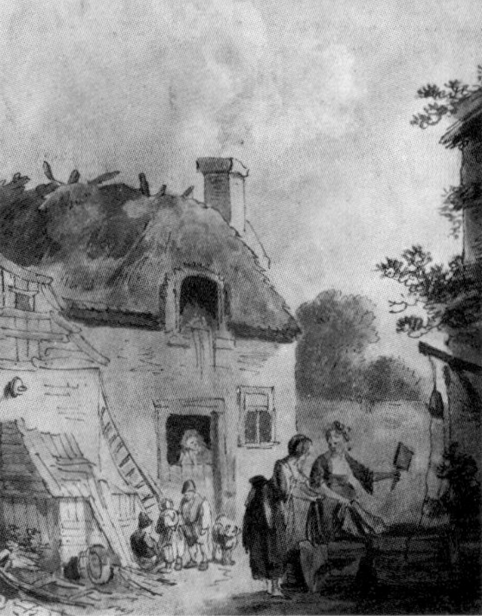

D.1970.81

■ Matley, Josiah (1851–1927)

A gas engineer who worked for the Manchester firm Mather and Platt, Matley supported and developed the Workers' Education Association in Ashton-under-Lyne. He lectured part time in Perspective Drawing at Owens College, Manchester.

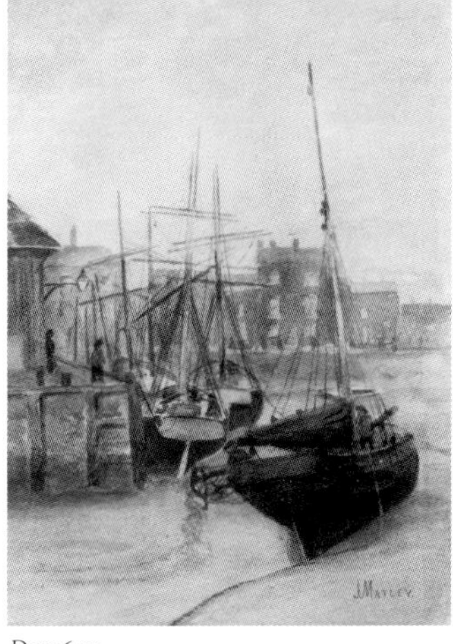

D.1996.20

Low Tide at Whitehaven
watercolour
signed lower right: *J.Matley.*; inscribed on verso of mount: *WHITEHAVEN / Cumberland*
217 × 153 mm
Warren, Jean (gift, 1996) (D.1996.20)

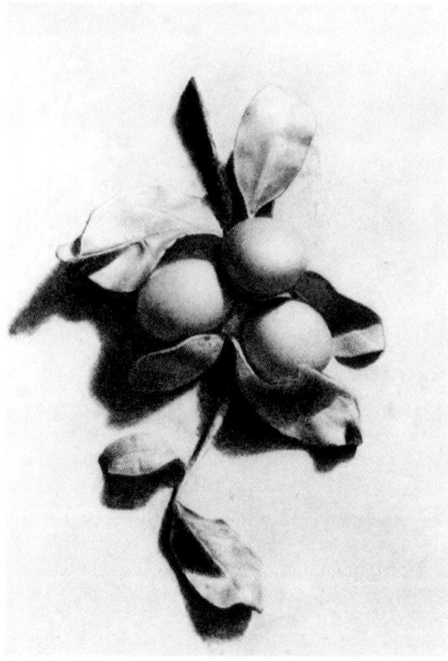

D.1996.21

Study of Fruit and Leaves
black chalk; grey paper, watermark JWHATMAN/1879
415 × 303 mm
Warren, Jean (gift, 1996) (D.1996.21)

Study of Fruit and Leaves
black chalk
inscribed upper right: *1 hour 40 minutes*
392 × 283 mm
Warren, Jean (gift, 1996) (D.1996.22)

■ MAY, PHILIP WILLIAM (1864–1903)

The greatest black-and-white illustrator and caricaturist
of the 1890s, May was born near Leeds and came to
London about 1883. He worked in Australia between
1885 and 1888 and returned to England to work for
various periodicals including *Punch*, which he joined in
1895. May was elected a member of the Royal Institute
in 1897. He led a very bohemian lifestyle and
eventually died of alcohol abuse.

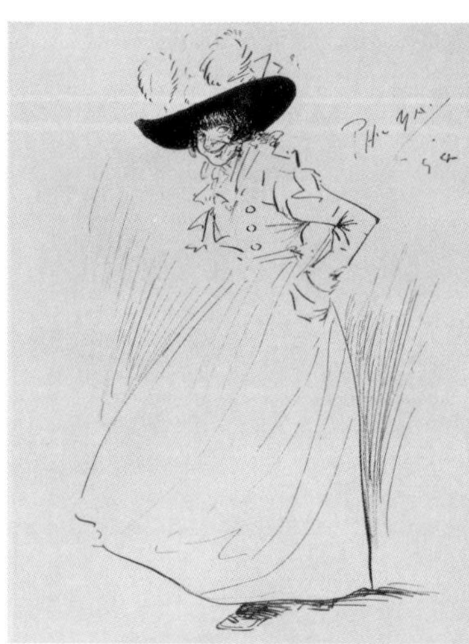

D.1960.108

'The Glad Eye'
1894
pen and black ink; card
signed & dated upper right: *PHIL MAY / 94*
239 × 191 mm
University of Manchester, History of Art Department
(transfer, 1960) (D.1960.108)

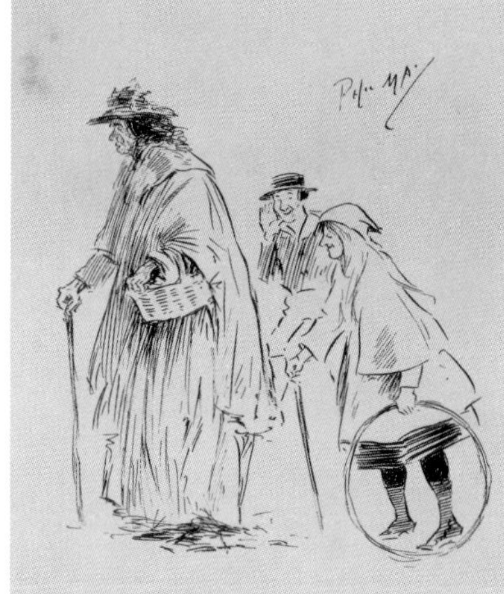

D.1960.109

'Never Mind. I was a Child Myself Once!'
pen and black ink; card
signed upper right: *PHIL MAY*
244 × 184 mm
University of Manchester, History of Art Department
(transfer, 1960) (D.1960.109)

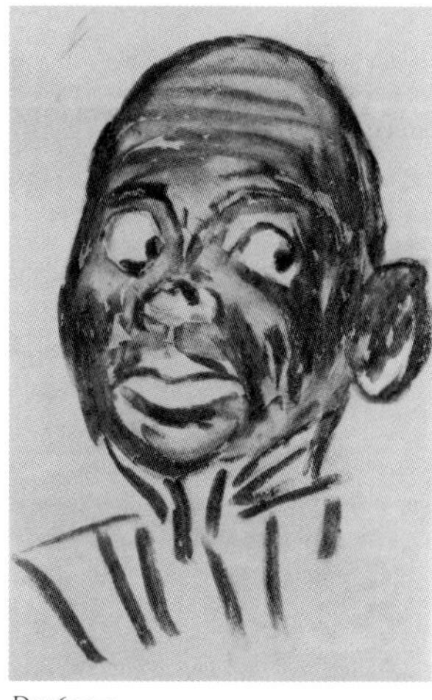

D.1960.170

'Don't You Call Me A Niggar'
4.6.1894
black chalk, black watercolour
signed, inscribed & dated on detached label stuck to
mount below image: *'Dont you call me a Niggar' /
Drawn by Phil May. June 4th.1894.*
474 × 307 mm
University of Manchester, History of Art Department
(transfer, 1960) (D.1960.170)

■ MAYER, LUIGI (1755–1803)

Mayer was an Italian artist who worked in Greece and
Turkey and later came to England.

View of a Farm, near Holbrook, Suffolk
25.9.1799
coloured chalk, watercolour
signed lower left on mount: *L.Mayer dipin* [rest of
word illegible]; inscribed & dated lower centre on
mount: *Veduta nelle vicinanzes di Holbrook / Dipinta
sopra Luogo Mercoledi 25 Settembre 1799 trale 5 e 6 di
Sera.*; numbered lower right on mount: *39*
240 × 355 mm
Anderson, A. E. (gift, 1934) (D.1934.10)

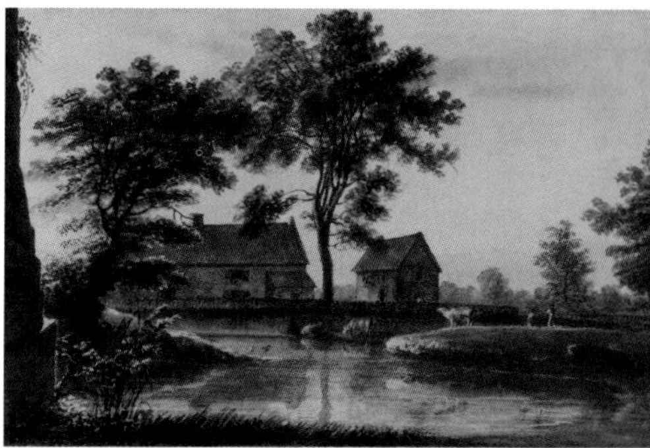

D.1934.10

■ MAYOR, WILLIAM FREDERICK (1868–1916)

Mayor studied at South Kensington and the Academie
Julien in Paris, and was a friend of Frank Brangwyn
and Edward Stott. He painted beach scenes in an
impressionist manner.

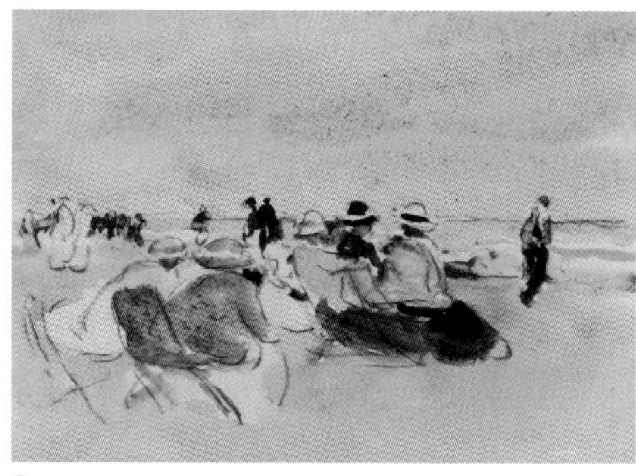

D.1921.43

The Beach, Montreuil, France
black chalk, watercolour
signed lower right: *FredMayor*
249 × 331 mm
Smith, Frank Hindley (gift, 1921) (D.1921.43)

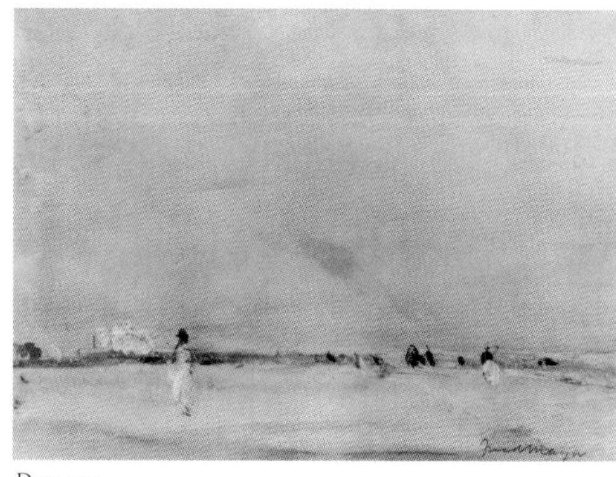

D.1924.27

The red Shore, Paris-Plage, Normandy, France
watercolour, bodycolour; brown paper
signed lower right: *FredMayor*
250 × 331 mm
Anderson, A. E., National Art Collections Fund (via)
(gift, 1924) (D.1924.27)

Shore Scene, Paris-Plage, Normandy, France
black chalk, watercolour, bodycolour; brown paper
293 × 388 mm
Anderson, A. E., National Art Collections Fund (via)
(gift, 1924) (D.1924.28)

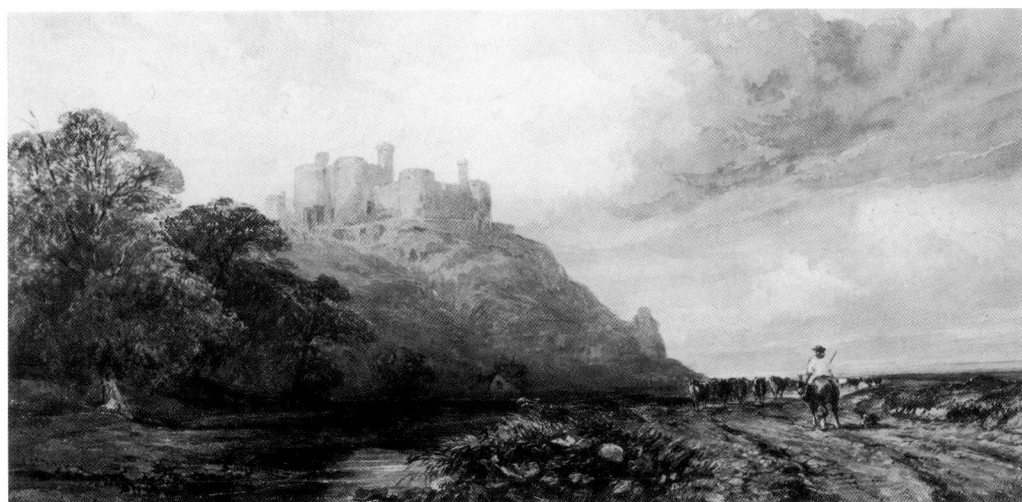

D.1970.56

■ McKewan, David Hall (1816–73)

McKewan, pupil and follower of David Cox, exhibited at the Royal Academy and elsewhere from 1836. He was elected a member of the New Watercolour Society in 1850.

Harlech Castle, Merioneth, Wales, from the North East
1852
pencil, watercolour
signed & dated lower right: *DHMcKewan / 1852*
297 × 594 mm
Towlson, Hector J. (bequest, 1969) (D.1970.56)

■ Melville, Arthur (1858–1904)

Born in Scotland, Melville studied at the Royal Scottish Academy Schools from 1875 and then in Paris from 1878. He made an extensive tour of the Middle East and returned to Scotland in 1884. Recognised as a leading member of the Glasgow School, Melville moved to London in 1889 and was elected a member of the Royal Watercolour Society in 1899. His style is indebted to Japanese art and to Whistler.

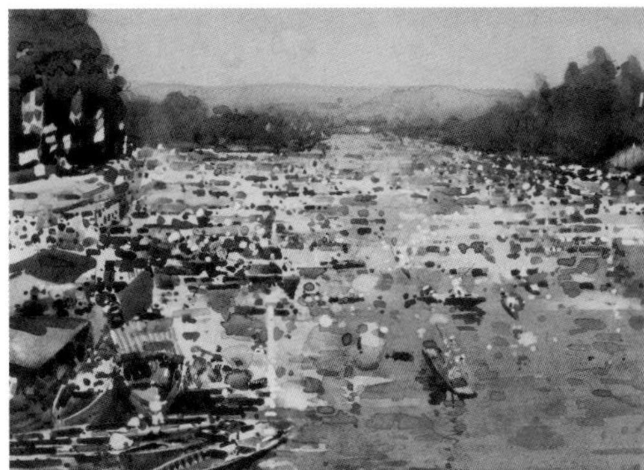

D.1928.37

Henley Regatta
watercolour, bodycolour; card
signed lower centre: *Arthur Melville.Henley*
267 × 363 mm
Anderson, A. E., National Art Collections Fund (via) (gift, 1928) (D.1928.37)

■ Menton, E. P. (fl. after 1807)

Unknown amateur marine painter.

The Spartan on the Morning after the Hurricane
watercolour; watermark JWHATMAN/1807
signed & inscribed lower centre verso: *The Spartan on the Morning after the Hurricane– / EPMenton deld.*
368 × 533 mm
Ogden, William Sharp (bequest, 1926) (D.1926.384)

■ Middleton, John (1827–59)

Middleton was a Norwich artist who came to London in 1847 but returned to Norwich two years later. He exhibited at the Royal Academy between 1847 and 1855 and specialised in woodland and farmyard scenes.

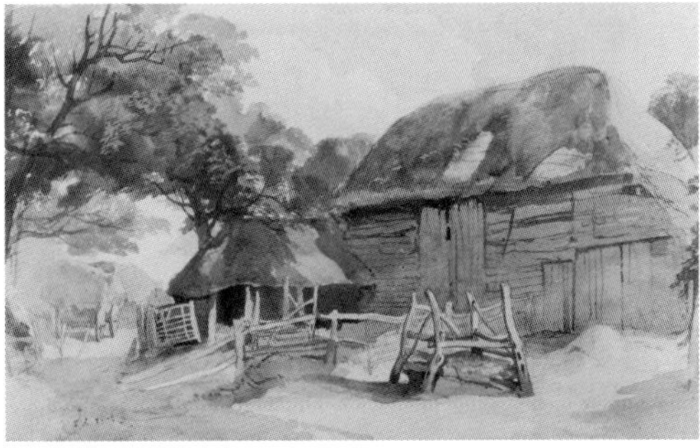

D.1920.3

The Farmyard
pencil, watercolour
280 × 439 mm
Meatyard, F. R. (purchase, 1920) (D.1920.3)

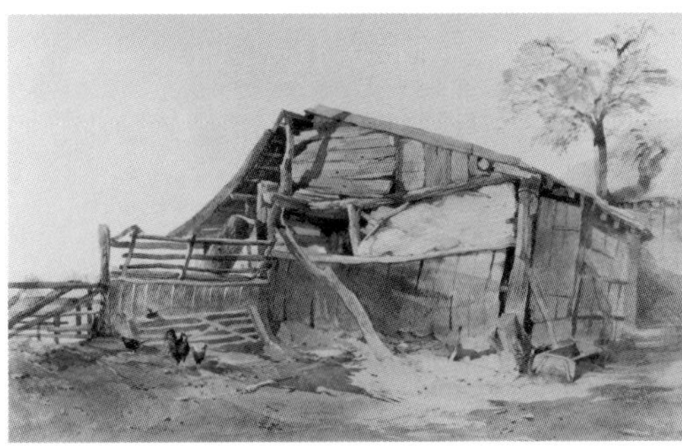

D.1921.36

Old Barn, Easton, Norfolk
pencil, watercolour
364 × 564 mm
Mase, J. A. (purchase, 1921) (D.1921.36)

■ Millais, Sir John Everett (1829–96)

Millais was one of the founder members of the Pre-Raphaelite Brotherhood and one of the most famous of all Victorian artists. Elected a member of the Royal Academy in 1863, Millais became its President in 1896 shortly before his death. Some of his paintings, such as *The Black Brunswicker*, *The Order of Release* and *Autumn Leaves*, are now regarded as icons of the Victorian era. He made a significant contribution to book illustration in the 1850s and 1860s.

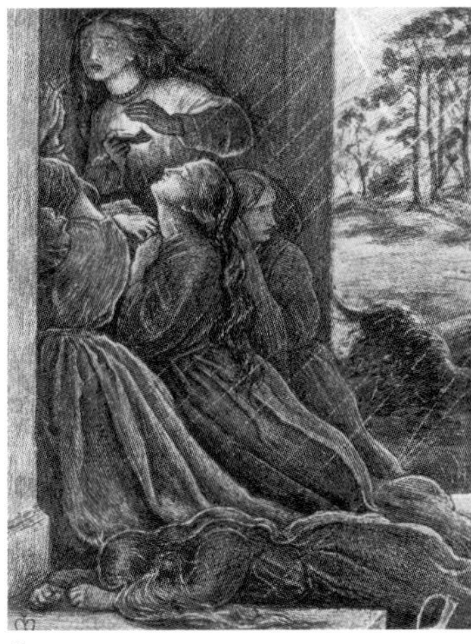

D.1913.9

The Foolish Virgins: Illustration for 'The Parables of Our Lord'
1864
pen and grey ink, grey watercolour
signed lower left with monogram: *JM*
143 × 109 mm
Agnew's (purchase, 1913) (D.1913.9)

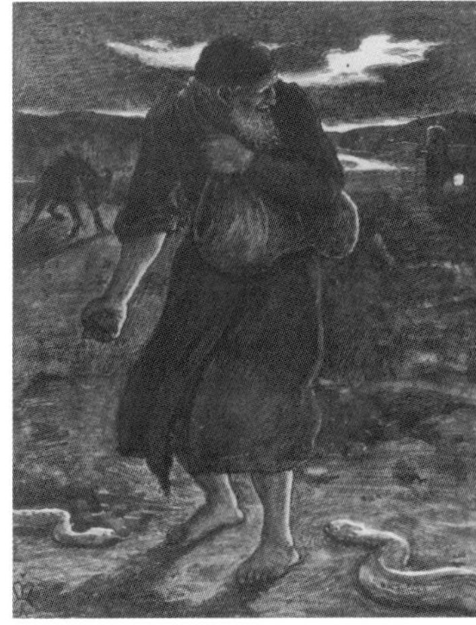

D.1920.11

An Enemy sowing Tares: Illustration for 'The Parables of Our Lord'
1864
watercolour
signed lower left with monogram: *JM*
143 × 109 mm
Leicester Galleries, London (purchase, 1920) (D.1920.11)

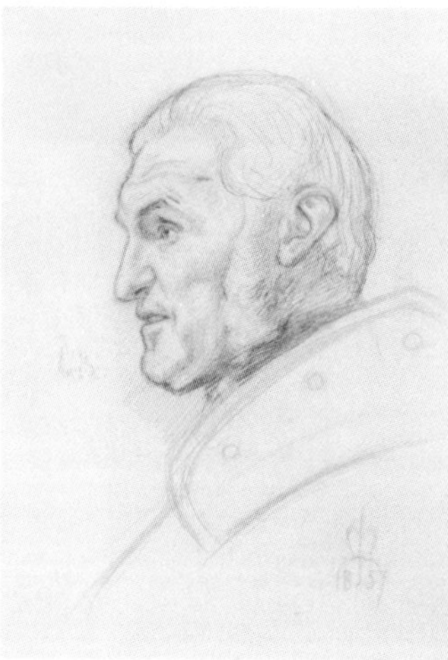

D.1927.145

Study for the Head of Sir Isumbras for 'Sir Isumbras at the Ford'
1857
pencil
signed & dated in pencil lower right with initials in monogram: *JM / 1857*
270 × 191 mm
Holliday, J. R. (bequest, 1927) (D.1927.145)

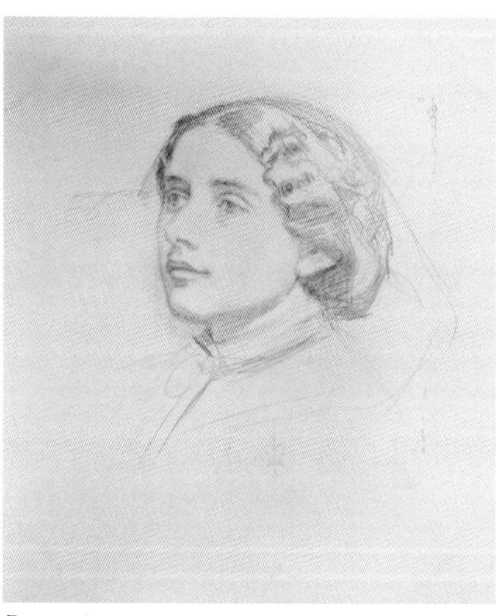

D.1927.146

Study for the Woman's Head in 'The Order of Release 1745' (recto); Study for the Dog in 'The Order of Release 1745' (verso)
1852
pencil
signed lower centre with monogram: *JM*
213 × 178 mm
Holliday, J. R. (bequest, 1927) (D.1927.146)

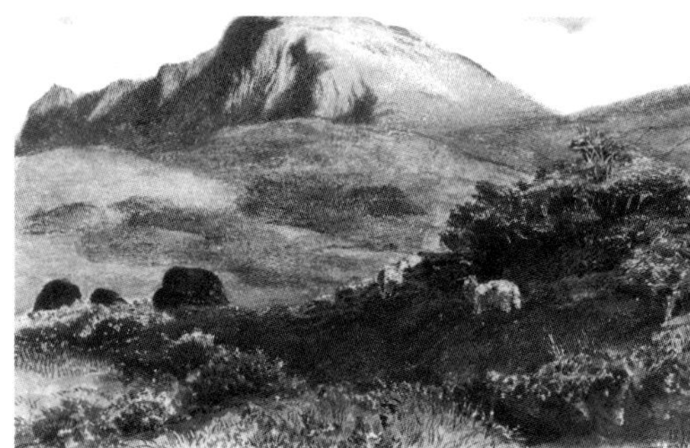

D.1928.38

Ben Nevis, Invernessshire, Scotland
4.9.1854
watercolour, bodycolour (heightened with white)
signed & dated lower right with monogram; added later over pencil inscription (date wrong): *18JM53*; inscribed & dated lower right; original and correct inscription: *Ben Nevis 4 Septr.*
121 × 195 mm
Anderson, A. E., National Art Collections Fund (via) (gift, 1928) (D.1928.38)

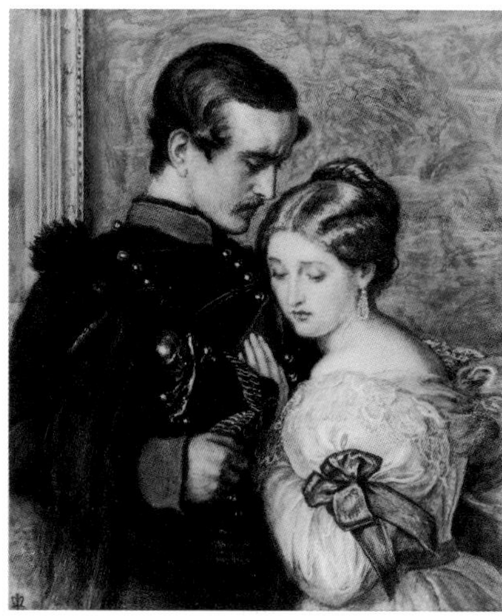

D.1937.16

The black Brunswicker
1867
watercolour, bodycolour
signed lower left with monogram: *JM*
294 × 241 mm
Haworth, Jesse (bequest, 1937) (D.1937.16)

■ MILLS AND MURGATROYD (office of)

A prolific firm of Manchester architects responsible for, amongst other buildings, the Manchester Royal Exchange (1869–74, remodelled in 1914–21, Bradshaw, Gass & Hope) and the Assembly Rooms (1857, demolished 1966).

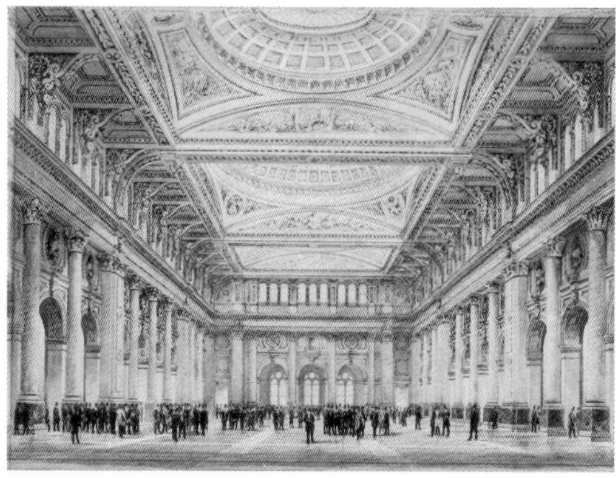

D.1998.27

Design for the Royal Exchange, Manchester: Perspective View of the Hall
1869–74
pencil, pen and brown ink, watercolour
523 × 694 mm
University of Manchester, Architecture Department (transfer, 1998) (D.1998.27)

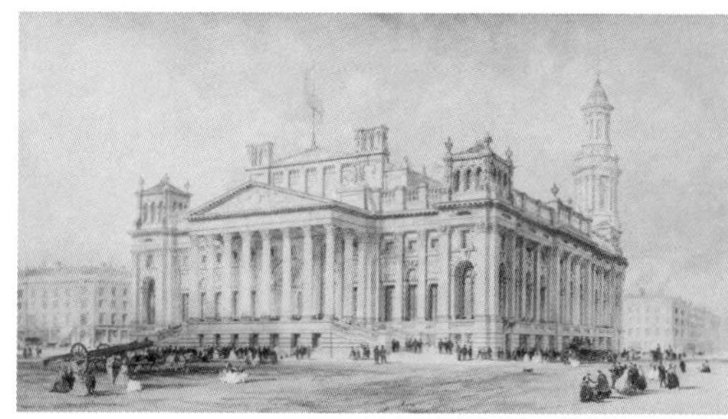

D.1998.28

Design for the Royal Exchange, Manchester: Perspective
1869–74
pencil, pen and brown ink, watercolour, bodycolour (heightened with white)
740 × 1401 mm
University of Manchester, Architecture Department (transfer, 1998) (D.1998.28)

■ MONAMY, PETER (attributed to) (1670–1749)

Monamy, a marine painter born in Jersey, may have been a pupil of the younger van de Velde and certainly painted much in his style.

A Squadron of Ships at Sea
pencil, pen and brown ink, grey watercolour; two joined sheets
200 × 620 mm
Ogden, William Sharp (bequest, 1926) (D.1926.151)

■ MONRO, ALEXANDER (1802–44)

The youngest son of the amateur artist and watercolour patron Dr Monro, Alexander Monro was a competent draughtsman working in Britain and the Channel Islands.

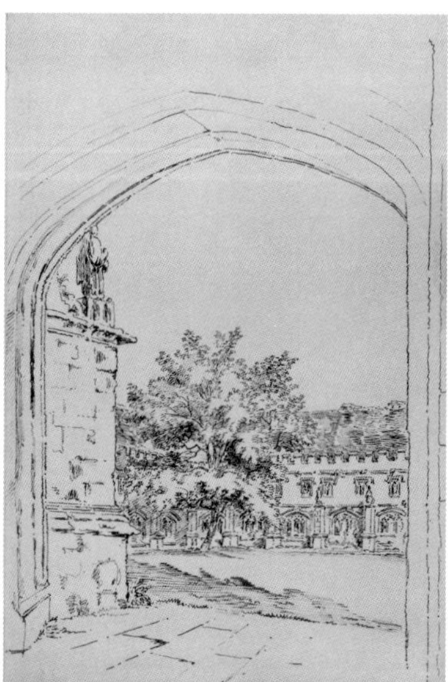

D.1928.15

The Cloister, Magdalen College, Oxford
pen and brown ink
inscribed lower right verso: *Magdalen Quadrangle Oxford –*
598 × 345 mm
Le Geyt, Miss (gift, 1928) (D.1928.15)

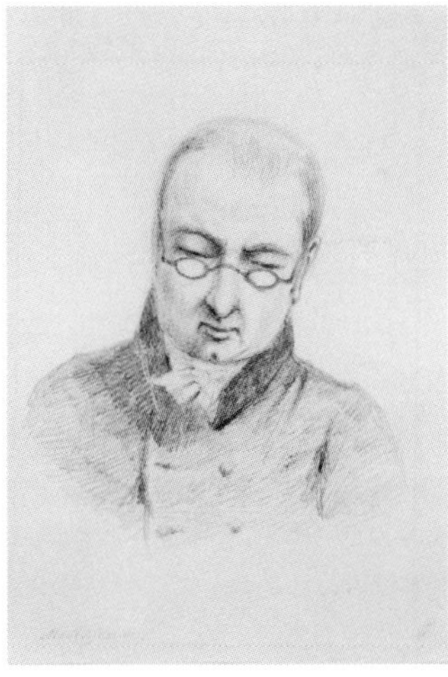

D.1995.12

**Portrait of Dr Thomas Monro,
bust length, looking downwards**
28.9.1821
pencil
initialled, inscribed & dated lower left with initials in
monogram: *AM fecit Sept 28 1821.*
182 × 122 mm
Girtin, Tom (bequest, 1995) (D.1995.12)

■ MONRO, HENRY (1791–1814)
The most accomplished of Dr Monro's artist sons,
Henry Monro's few landscapes are indebted in style to
William Henry Hunt. Monro exhibited portraits at the
Royal Academy between 1811 and 1813.

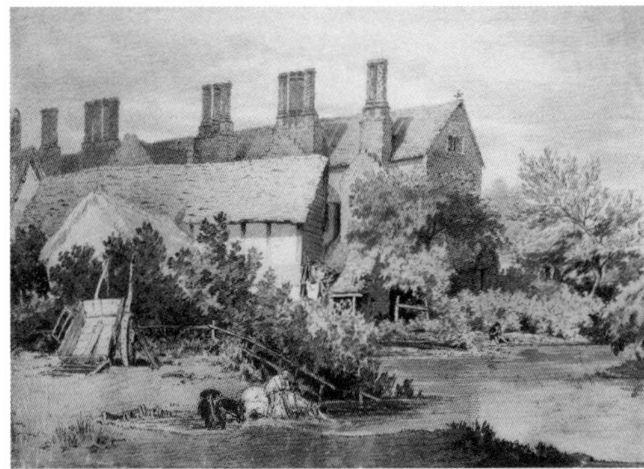

D.1970.49

Chenies Manor House, Buckinghamshire
27.8.1812
black chalk, white chalk, pen and brown ink, brown
watercolour, grey watercolour, bodycolour (heightened
with white); grey paper
inscribed & dated lower left verso: *Chenies– / Aug. 27.
1812*
366 × 497 mm
Towlson, Hector J. (bequest, 1969) (D.1970.49)

■ MONRO, JOHN (1801–80)
Another of Dr Monro's artist sons, John Monro's style
is indebted to Henry Edridge, one of the many artists
whom his father encouraged and patronised.

Landscape with Stream
pencil, watercolour
179 × 248 mm
Wilson, Sir Harry (gift, 1922) (D.1922.23)

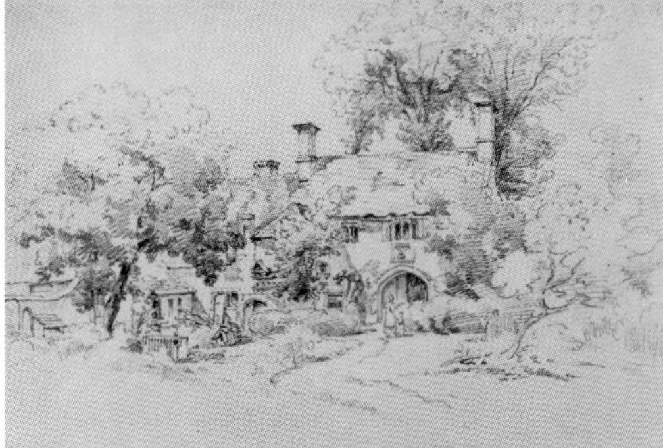

D.1928.14

Stanton Harcourt, Oxfordshire
1820
pencil
inscribed & dated lower left verso:
Stanton Harcourt nr Oxford – 1820
254 × 365 mm
Le Geyt, Miss (gift, 1928) (D.1928.14)

■ MONRO, DR THOMAS (1759–1833)
One of the most notable patrons and collectors in the
history of English watercolours, Dr Monro was a
doctor who specialised in insanity and numbered John
Robert Cozens and George III among his patients. At
his London house in Adelphi Terrace, Monro held an
informal 'academy' for young student artists who were
employed to copy works by Hearne, Canaletto and
others in his collection. His landscape drawings, which
are quite numerous, owe a strong stylistic debt to the
landscape drawings of Gainsborough.

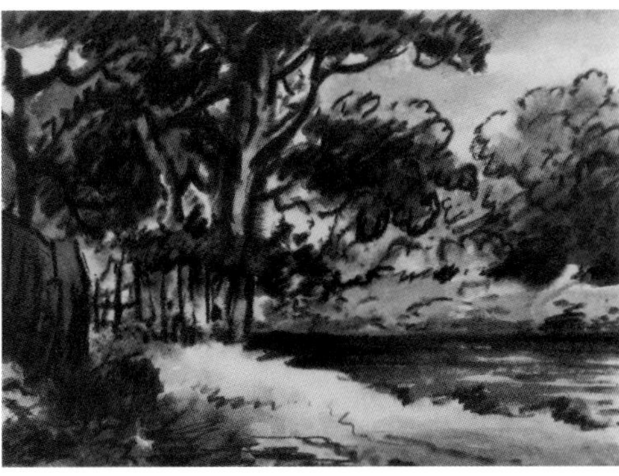

D.1917.28

Landscape with Trees on a River Bank
black chalk, grey watercolour
164 × 222 mm
Wilson, Sir Harry (gift, 1917) (D.1917.28)

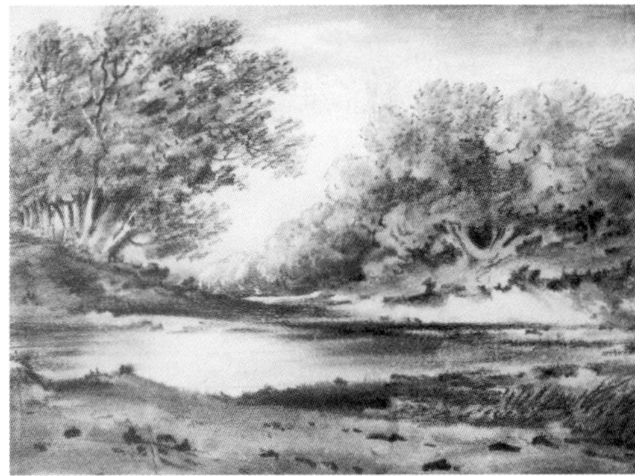

D.1922.24

Landscape with Trees near Water
black chalk, grey watercolour
151 × 202 mm
Wilson, Sir Harry (gift, 1922) (D.1922.24)

**Landscape with a Man and Dog walking
along a Road**
black chalk, grey watercolour
199 × 255 mm
Ogden, William Sharp (bequest, 1926) (D.1926.137)

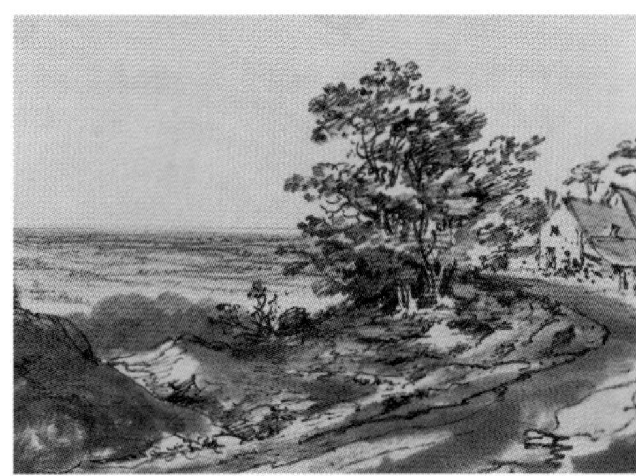

D.1926.138

Landscape with Trees and Cottages
black chalk, grey watercolour
314 × 436 mm
Ogden, William Sharp (bequest, 1926) (D.1926.138)

Coast Scene
coloured chalk; blue paper
298 × 448 mm
Le Geyt, Miss (gift, 1928) (D.1928.13)

View across a Lake
black chalk, grey watercolour
134 × 204 mm
Le Geyt, Miss (gift, 1928) (D.1928.16)

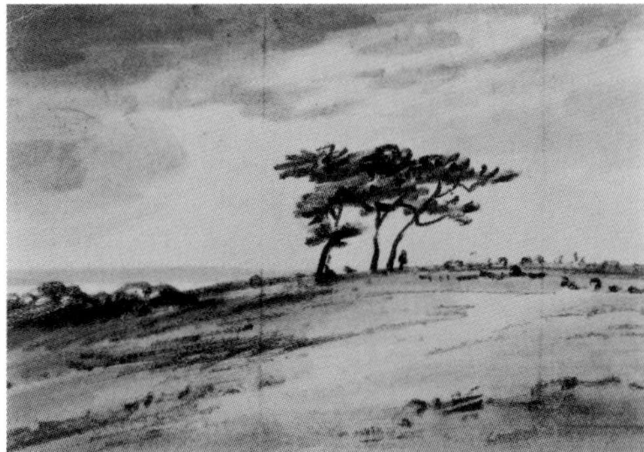

D.1928.17

Landscape with Trees
1829–33
black chalk, grey watercolour
inscribed & dated verso a letter of invitation:
*Mr.Rosden requests the / pleasure of Dr Monro's /
Company at Dinner, on / Saturday the 18th. at – / 6
oclock. / Bushey Rectory, / July 11, 1829*
121 × 170 mm
Le Geyt, Miss (gift, 1928) (D.1928.17)

Landscape with River
black chalk, grey watercolour
114 × 241 mm
Le Geyt, Miss (gift, 1928) (D.1928.18)

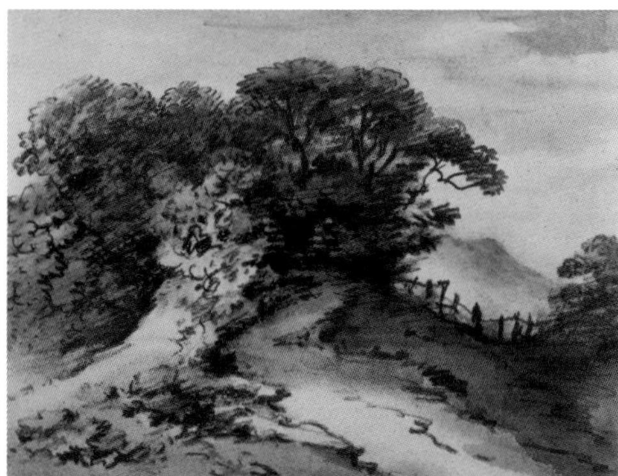

D.1947.61

Landscape with Trees on a Mound
black chalk, grey watercolour
190 × 245 mm
Beckett, R. B. (Justice) (gift, 1947) (D.1947.61)

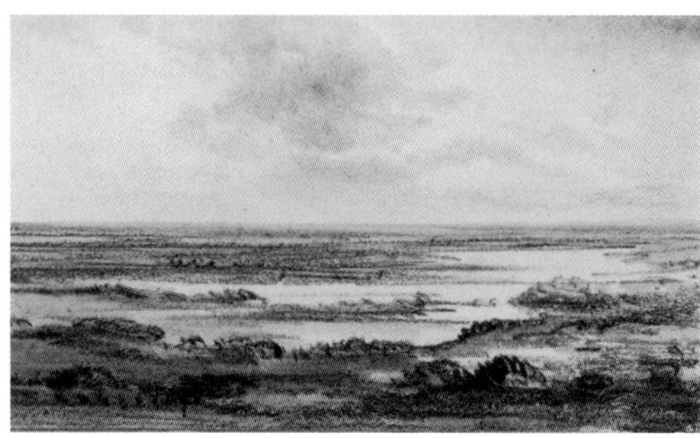

D.1999.20

A Moorland Landscape
black chalk
139 × 234 mm
Scott-Elliot, Miss Aydua, in memory of Paul Oppé
(gift, 4.11.1999) (D.1999.20)

■ MOORE, ALBERT JOSEPH (1841–92)

Born in York into a family of artists, Albert Joseph
Moore entered the Royal Academy Schools in 1858. He
began his career exhibiting natural history subjects but
turned to Biblical and later to Classical subjects. His
paintings of women in flowing classical robes anticipate
the work of Alma-Tadema and are an important part of
the Aesthetic Movement.

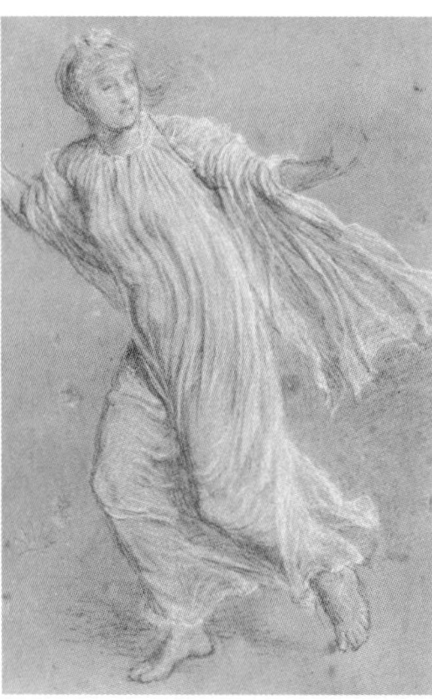

D.1954.4

**Study of a draped female Figure for
'Follow My Leader'**
1871–73
black chalk, white chalk; brown paper
signed lower left with anthemion
345 × 229 mm
untraced (gift, 1954) (D.1954.4)

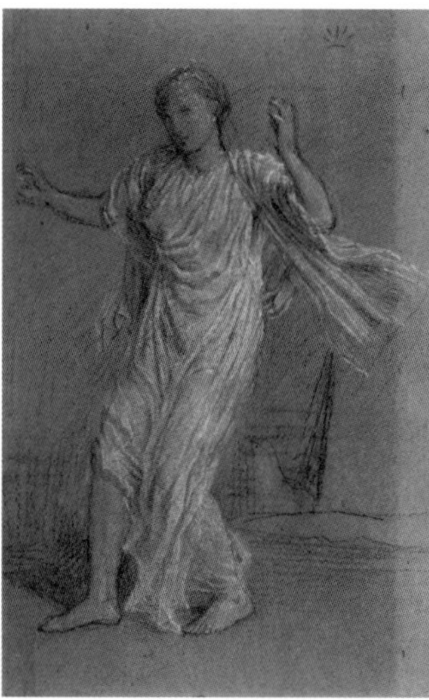

D.1960.111

**Study of a draped female Figure for
'Follow My Leader' (recto); Study of a
Woman for 'A Wardrobe' (verso)**
1871–73
black chalk, white chalk (recto); brown paper
signed upper right with anthemion; inscribed verso
with extensive colour notes
301 × 191 mm
University of Manchester, History of Art Department
(transfer, 1960) (D.1960.111)

■ MOORE, HENRY (1831–95)

The brother of Albert, Henry Moore was trained by his
father in York and at the Royal Academy Schools from
1853. He was elected a member of the Old Watercolour
Society in 1880 and of the Royal Academy in 1893.
Moore's work of the 1850s shows the influence of the
Pre-Raphaelites. Later he painted marine pictures.

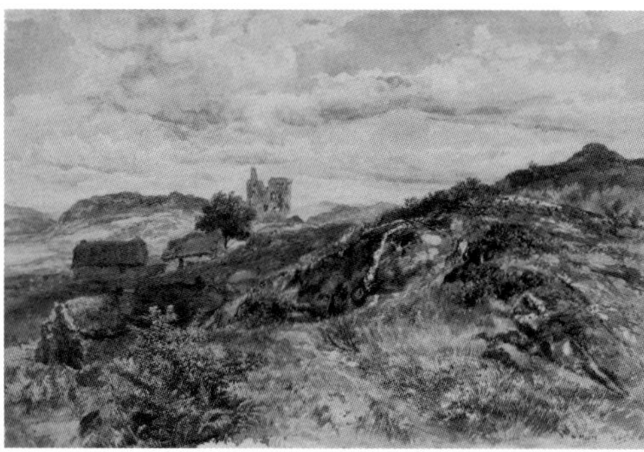

D.1947.7

A rocky Landscape with a ruined Castle
1865
pencil, watercolour; beige paper
signed lower right: *H. Moore.*; dated lower right: *1865*
[underlined]
373 × 551 mm
Barlow, Sir Thomas (gift, 1947) (D.1947.7)

■ MORLAND, GEORGE CHARLES (1763–1804)

Morland specialised in scenes of rustic and rural life.
His brother-in-law William Ward turned his paintings
into engravings, which were widely disseminated and
made Morland into a household name. Although
Morland was a very prolific painter and draughtsman,
he led a very dissolute lifestyle.

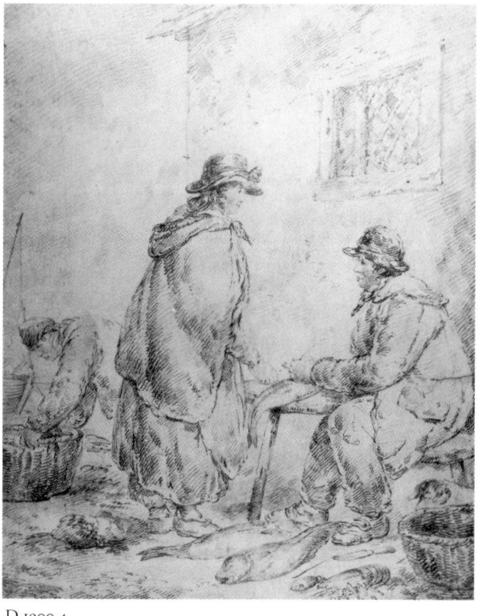

D.1900.4

Bargaining for Fish
red chalk
signed upper right on window frame with initials:
G.Md.
442 × 347 mm
Worthington, Mary (gift, 1900) (D.1900.4)

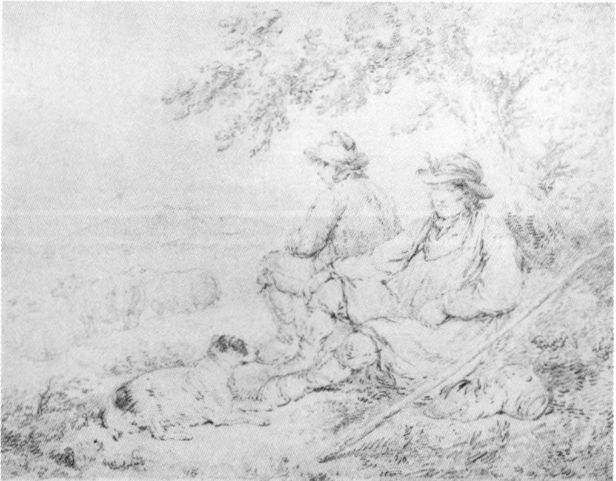

D.1954.24

Shepherds resting
pencil
316 × 408 mm
Laing, Dr A. W. (gift, 1954) (D.1954.24)

■ MORRIS, WILLIAM (1834–96)

Writer and poet, artist and designer, Morris began
a lifelong friendship with Burne-Jones in 1853.
In 1861 he founded the decorative arts firm by
which his name is chiefly known today. His work
in watercolour consists of designs for stained glass
and tracery. The most famous of all Victorian
designers, Morris can be regarded as the founder of
the Arts and Crafts movement.

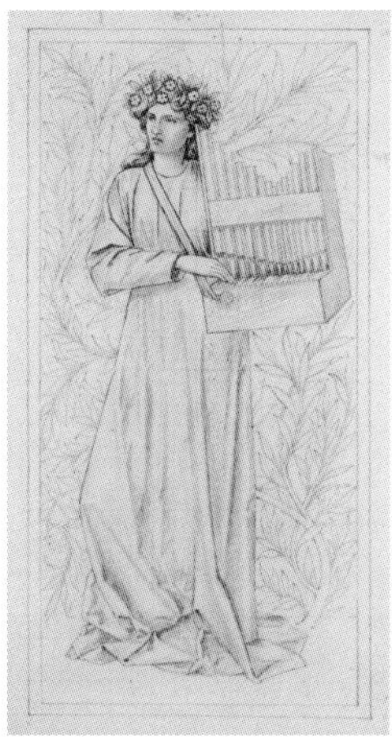

D.1940.9

The Organ Player
pencil, pen and blue ink, blue watercolour
327 × 172 mm
Wilson, R. E. A. (purchase, 1940) (D.1940.9)

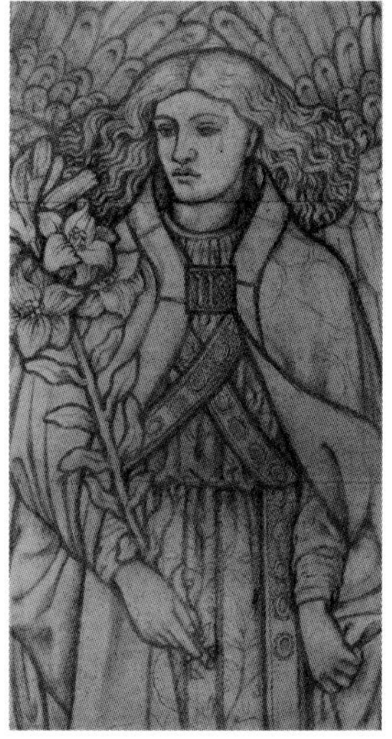

D.1960.35

**The Archangel Gabriel: Study for
the Cartoon of the West Window,
St. Michael and All Angels, Brighton**
1862
pencil, black chalk
547 × 282 mm
Friends of the Whitworth (gift, 1960) (D.1960.35)

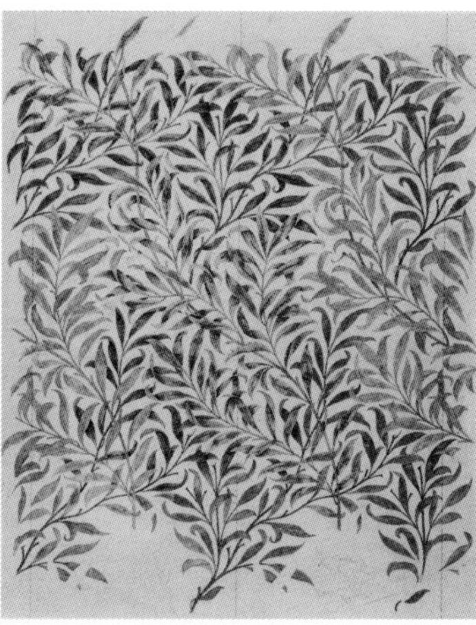

D.1981.15

Design for 'Willow Bough' Wallpaper
1887
pencil, watercolour
847 × 627 mm
Derek Lockett (gift, 1981) (V. & A.) (D.1981.15)

■ MORTIMER, JOHN HAMILTON (1741–79)

A skilled pen-and-ink draughtsman who studied
under Cipriani, Mortimer produced many book
illustrations as well as figure subjects and banditti.
He also painted a few large history pictures and
occasionally collaborated with Thomas Jones.
Mortimer was elected an associate member of the
Royal Academy in 1778 but died the following year.

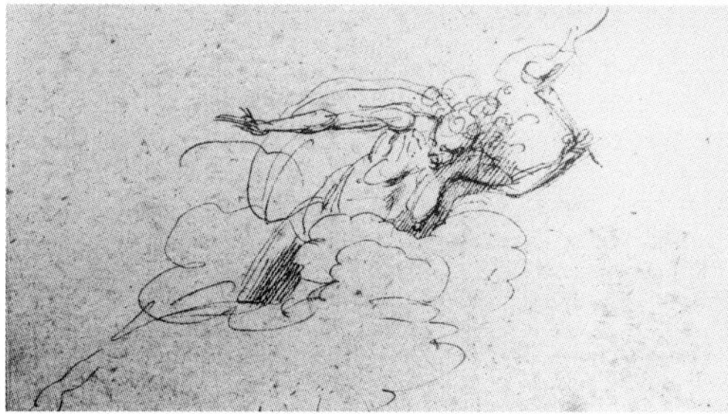

D.1960.112

A Witch with a Brand
pen and brown ink; buff paper
107 × 187 mm
University of Manchester, History of Art Department
(transfer, 1960) (D.1960.112)

■ MORTON, WILLIAM (fl. 1883–94)

Morton was an obscure Manchester-based artist.

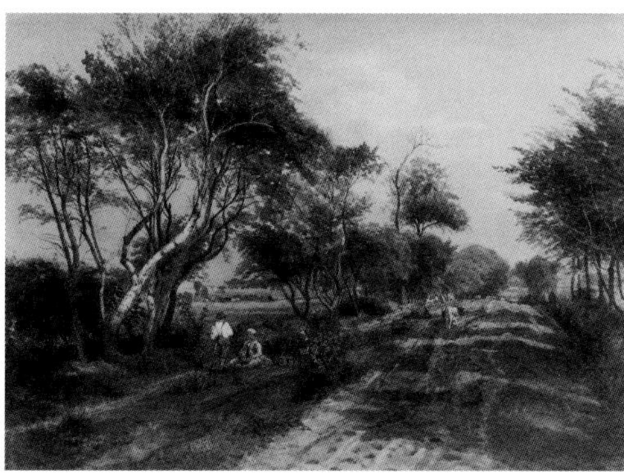

D.1892.149

Country Lane, Chat Moss, Lancashire
1889
watercolour
signed & dated lower left: *Wm Morton / 1889*
520 × 722 mm
untraced (purchase, 1892) (D.1892.149)

■ MUDD, JAMES (fl. 1882–93)

Mudd was a Cheshire-based illustrator who exhibited
in Liverpool and Manchester.

The Ancient Mariner
pencil, watercolour, bodycolour
470 × 648 mm
Sidebotham, J. W. (gift, 1923) (D.1923.27)

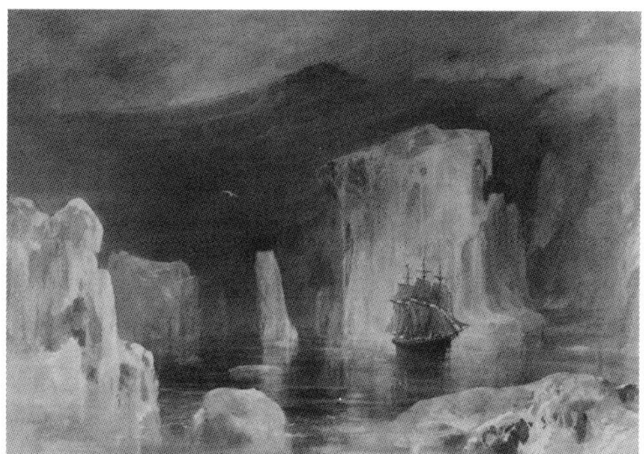

D.1923.27

■ MULLER, WILLIAM JAMES (1812–45)

Muller was a Bristol artist who travelled via the Rhine
to the Italian Lakes and Rome with G. A. Fripp in
1833–34. Muller visited Greece and Egypt in 1838–39
and went to France the following year in order to
gather material for the lithographs in *Muller's Sketches
of the Age of Francis Ist*, published in 1841. His final
foreign trip to Lycia in south-western Turkey was in
1843–44, when he joined Sir Charles Fellows'
archaeological expedition to Xanthus. Muller was
hugely prolific and had many imitators.

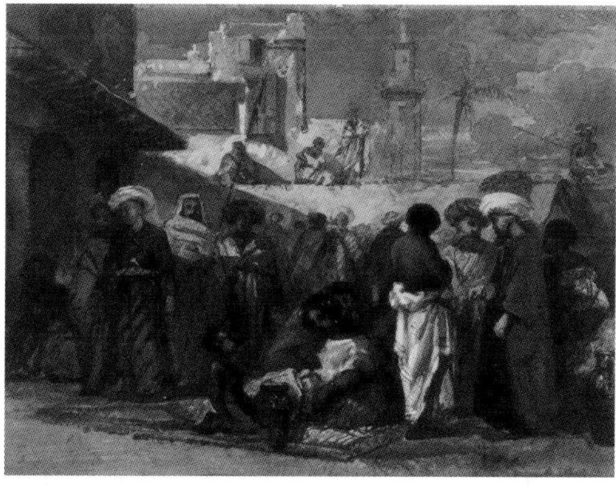

D.1892.120

The Slave Market, Cairo
pencil, watercolour, bodycolour
255 × 330 mm
Taylor, John Edward (gift, 1892) (D.1892.120)

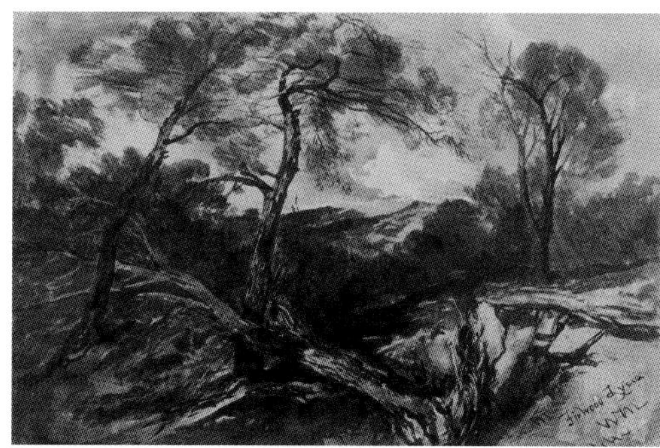

D.1892.138

Fir Wood, Lycia, Turkey
1844
pencil, watercolour
signed, inscribed & dated lower right with initials:
Fir Wood Lycia / W M / 44
374 × 552 mm
Taylor, John Edward (gift, 1892) (D.1892.138)

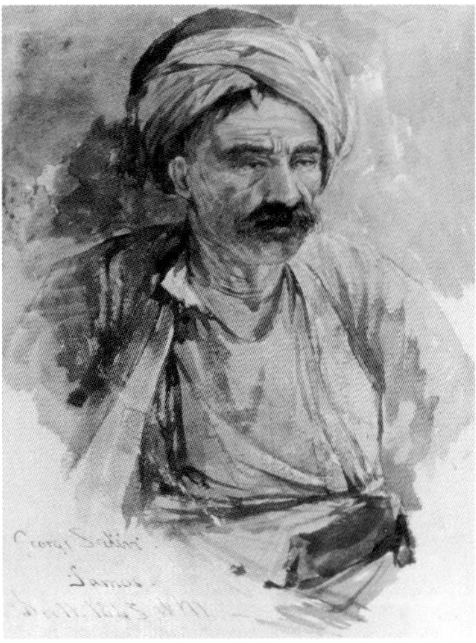

D.1892.139

Portrait Study of George Sativi, Lycia, Turkey
11.12.1843
watercolour, bodycolour (heightened with white)
signed, inscribed & dated lower left with initials:
George Sativi / Samos. / Dec 11.1843 WM
267 × 201 mm
Taylor, John Edward (gift, 1892) (D.1892.139)

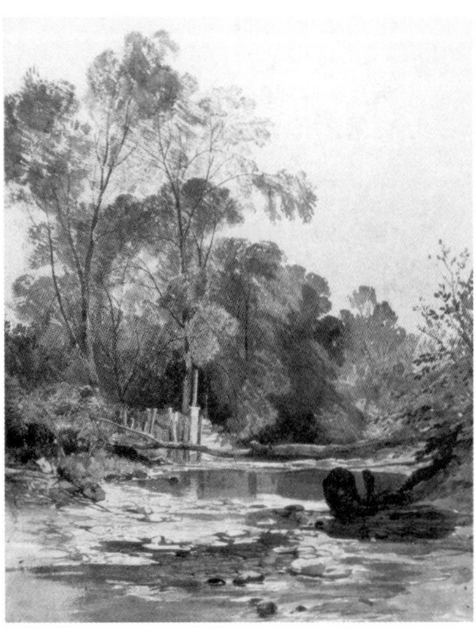

D.1892.140

Study of Birch Trees by a Stream
watercolour
462 × 359 mm
Taylor, John Edward (gift, 1892) (D.1892.140)

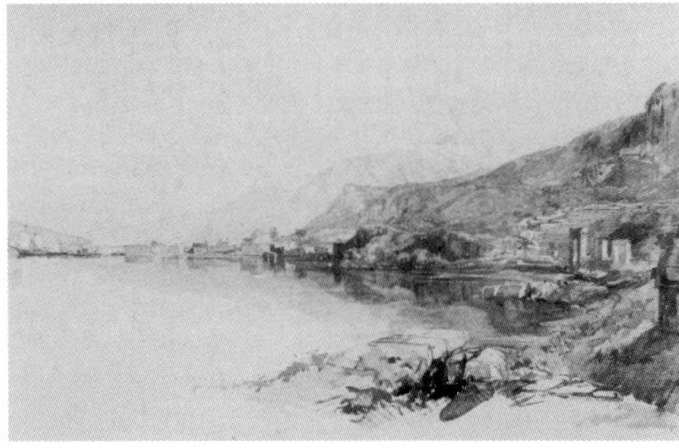

D.1905.5

Theatre at Macry or Ancient Telmessus, Lycia, Turkey
5.2.1844
pencil, watercolour
signed, inscribed & dated lower left with initials:
Theatre at Macry or Telmessus / Feby 5th.1844 WM Lycia
357 × 551 mm
Agnew's (purchase, 29.11.1905) (D.1905.5)

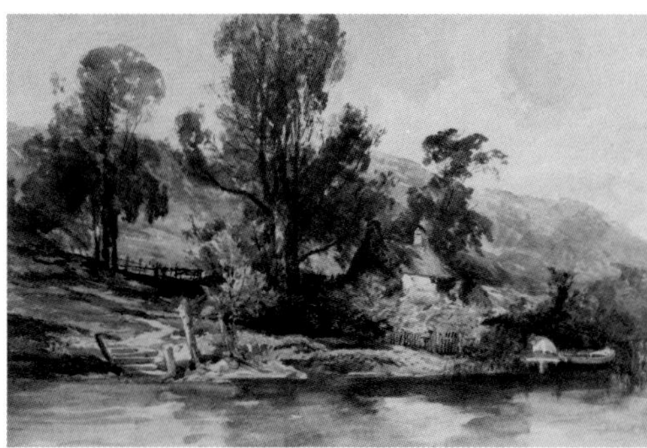

D.1924.86

The Ferry Boat
black chalk, watercolour
371 × 536 mm
Broadhurst, Sir Edward Tootal, Broadhurst, Lady
(bequest, 1924) (D.1924.86)

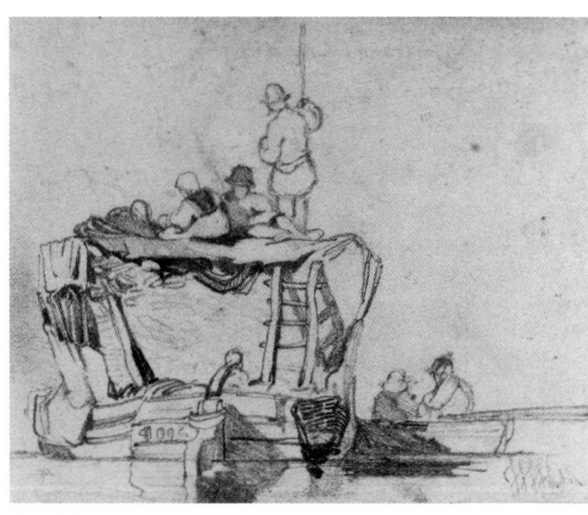

D.1927.148

**Study of Boats and Figures (recto);
Study of Figures (verso)**
pencil
signed lower right with monogram: *WM*
116 × 135 mm
Holliday, J. R. (bequest, 1927) (D.1927.148)

Study of Trees near Water
pencil
signed lower right with monogram: *WM*
208 × 151 mm
Holliday, J. R. (bequest, 1927) (D.1927.149)

Study of wooded Landscape
pencil, watercolour
311 × 233 mm
Holliday, J. R. (bequest, 1927) (D.1927.150)

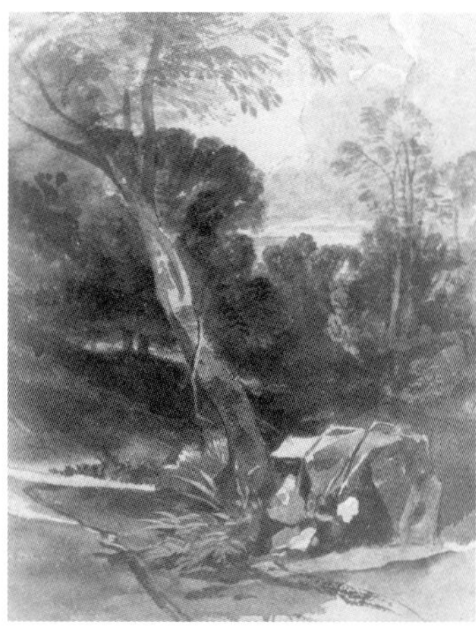

D.1927.150

■ **MULREADY, WILLIAM (1786–1863)**
Mulready, brother-in-law of John Varley, entered the
Royal Academy Schools in 1800 and exhibited at the
Royal Academy between 1804 and 1862. He painted in
watercolour and oil and produced portraits, landscapes
and figure subjects, which became increasingly
humorous. He was also a careful and meticulous pen
and ink draughtsman. Mulready was elected a member
of the Royal Academy in 1816.

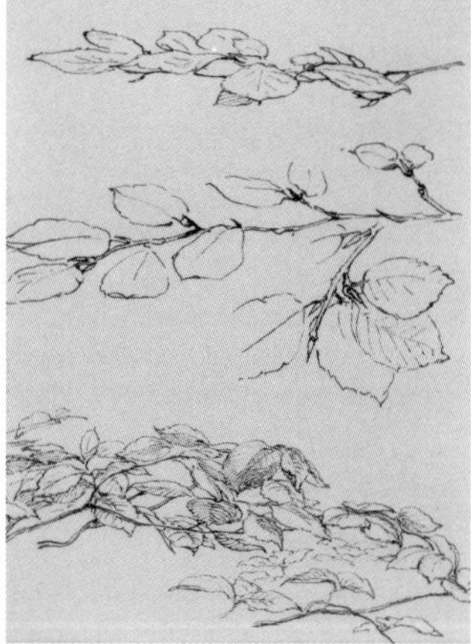

D.1895.30

Studies of Branches and Leaves
pen and brown ink
170 × 121 mm
Taylor, John Edward (gift, 1895) (D.1895.30)

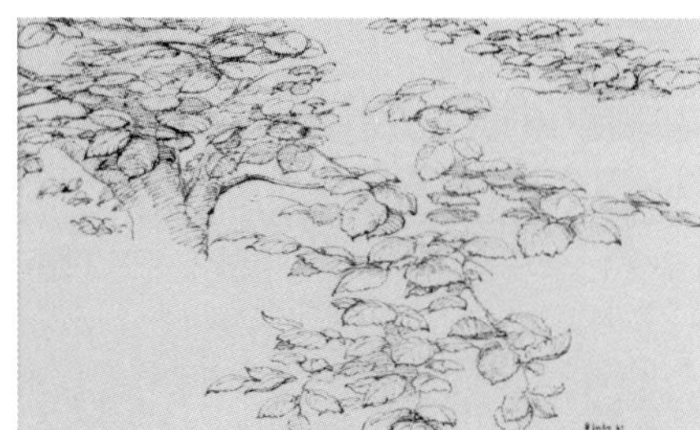

D.1895.31

Studies of Branches and Leaves
19.5.1861
pen and brown ink
dated upper left: *19 May 61*
121 × 200 mm
Taylor, John Edward (gift, 1895) (D.1895.31)

Studies of Branches and Leaves
8.7.1861
pen and brown ink
dated lower right: *8 July 61*
96 × 196 mm
Taylor, John Edward (gift, 1895) (D.1895.32)

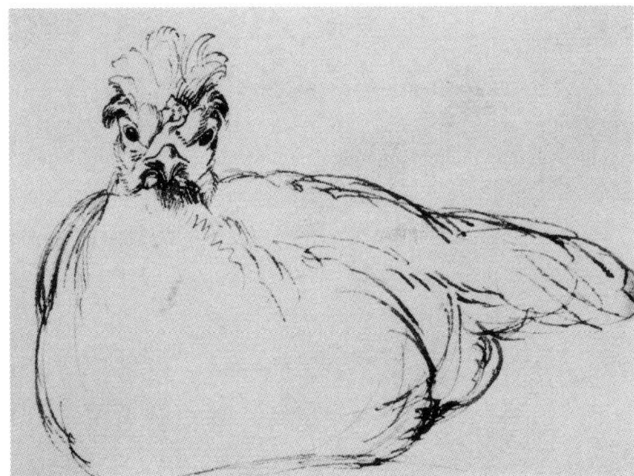

D.1895.33

Study of a sitting Hen
pen and brown ink
86 × 112 mm
Taylor, John Edward (gift, 1895) (D.1895.33)

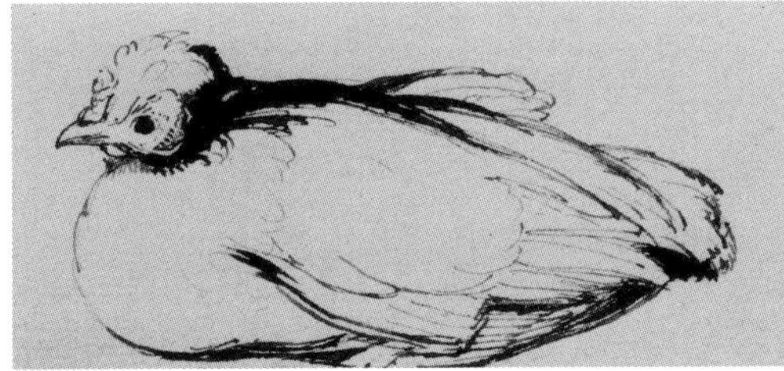

D.1895.34

Study of a sitting Hen
pen and brown ink
48 × 105 mm
Taylor, John Edward (gift, 1895) (D.1895.34)

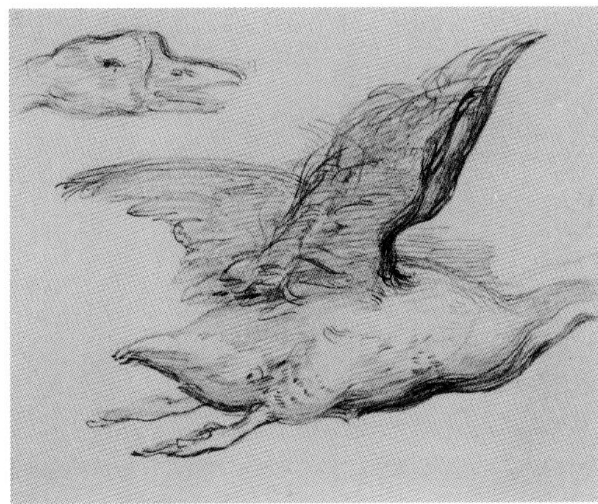

D.1895.35

Study of a flying Goose
pencil; blue paper
133 × 161 mm
Taylor, John Edward (gift, 1895) (D.1895.35)

Studies of swimming Ducks
pencil
89 × 85 mm
Taylor, John Edward (gift, 1895) (D.1895.36)

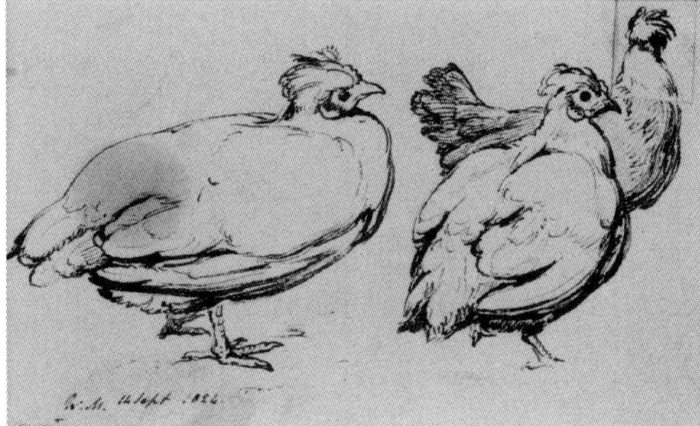

D.1895.37

Studies of Hens
14.9.1824
pen and brown ink
signed & dated lower left with initials: *W.M.14 Sept 1824*
80 × 132 mm
Taylor, John Edward (gift, 1895) (D.1895.37)

Study of a Wing
pen and brown ink
inscribed upper centre: *Cross of Linnet and Goldfinch*
75 × 71 mm
Taylor, John Edward (gift, 1895) (D.1895.38)

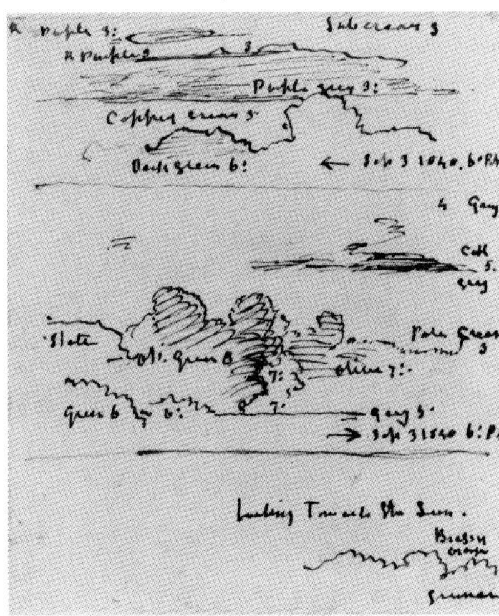

D.1895.39.1

Study of Clouds
3.9.1840
pen and brown ink; grey paper
extensively inscribed with colour notes & dated:
Sep 3 1840 6.PM (twice)
98 × 81 mm
Taylor, John Edward (gift, 1895) (D.1895.39.1)

Study of Clouds, Kensington
3.9.1840
pen and brown ink; grey paper
extensively inscribed with colour notes & dated: *Sep 3 1840 3 PM & 5 PM*
98 × 82 mm
Taylor, John Edward (gift, 1895) (D.1895.39.2)

Study of Clouds, Kensington
3.9.1840
pen and brown ink; grey paper
extensively inscribed with colour notes & dated:
Sept.3.1840 1 PM & 2 PM
102 × 82 mm
Taylor, John Edward (gift, 1895) (D.1895.39.3)

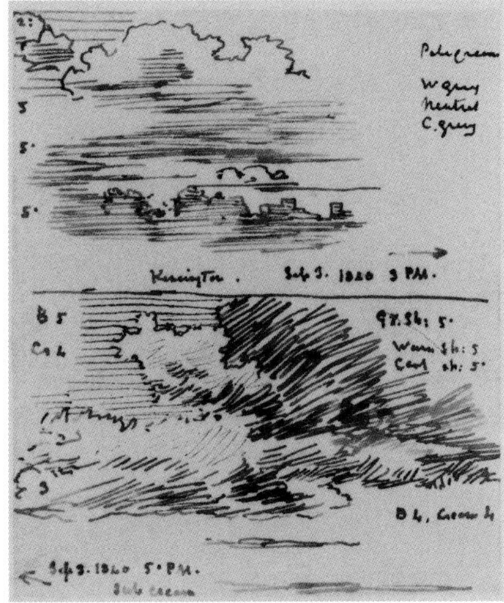

D.1895.39.2

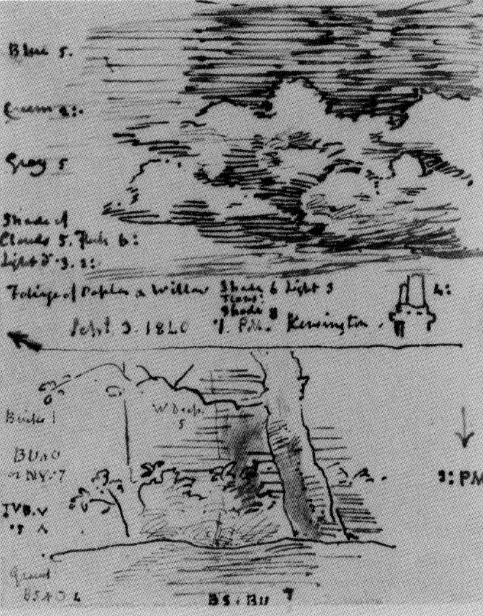

D.1895.39.3

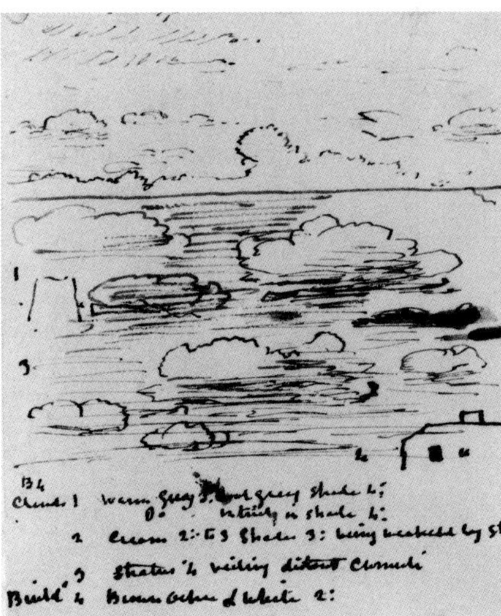

D.1895.39.4

Study of Clouds
1840
pen and brown ink; grey paper
extensively inscribed with colour notes
98 × 82 mm
Taylor, John Edward (gift, 1895) (D.1895.39.4)

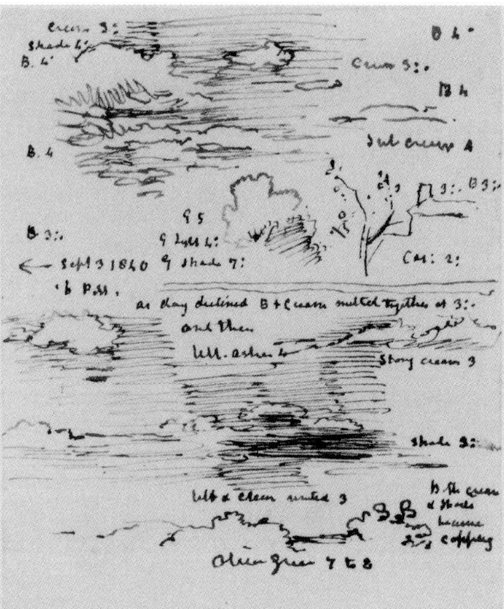

D.1895.39.5

Study of Clouds
3.9.1840
pen and brown ink; grey paper
extensively inscribed with colour notes & dated:
Sept 3 1840/6 PM
98 × 82 mm
Taylor, John Edward (gift, 1895) (D.1895.39.5)

Study of Clouds, Barnes Common
6.9.1840
pen and brown ink; grey paper
extensively inscribed with colour notes & dated:
Sep 6 1840. 3.PM
85 × 80 mm
Taylor, John Edward (gift, 1895) (D.1895.39.6)

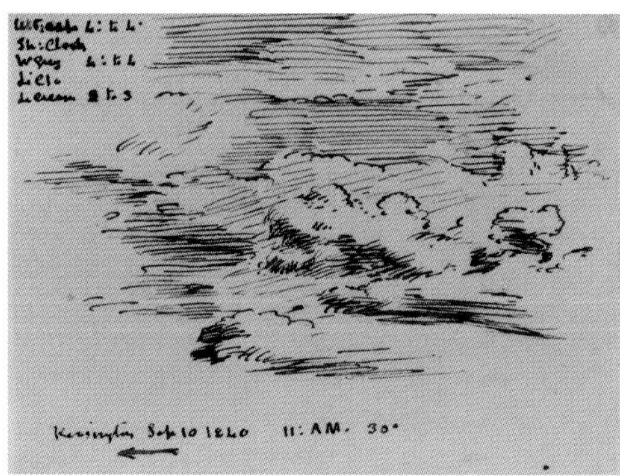

D.1895.39.7

Study of Clouds, Kensington
10.9.1840
pen and brown ink; grey paper
inscribed with colour notes & dated: *Kensington Sep 10
1840 11 AM.*
75 × 82 mm
Taylor, John Edward (gift, 1895) (D.1895.39.7)

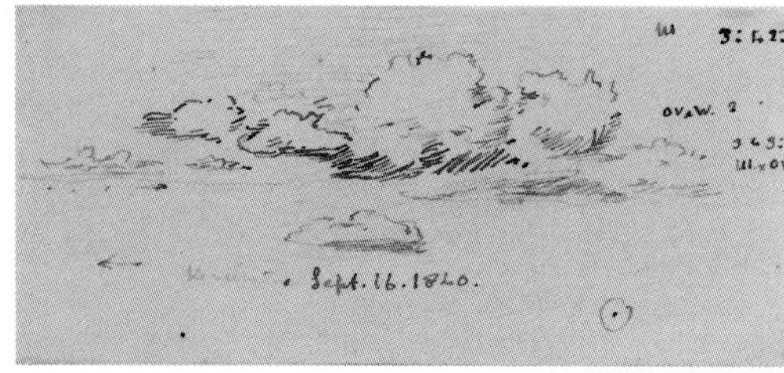

D.1895.39.8

Study of Clouds, Kensington
16.9.1840
pen and brown ink; grey paper
inscribed & dated lower edge: *Kensington Sept.16.1840*
45 × 82 mm
Taylor, John Edward (gift, 1895) (D.1895.39.8)

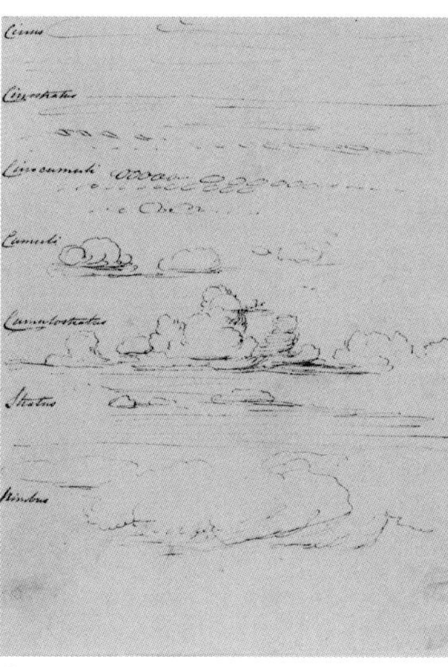

D.1895.39.9

**Diagrammatic Illustration of Luke Howard's
Classification of Clouds**
27.9.1840
pen and brown ink
inscribed left edge (cloud names): *Cirrus / Cirrostratus /
Cirrocumuli / Cumuli / Cumulostratus / Stratus /
Nimbus*; extensively inscribed & dated on verso
(compositional notes): *Sep 27.6 PM.*
149 × 108 mm
Taylor, John Edward (gift, 1895) (D.1895.39.9)

Written Notes
pen and brown ink
112 × 540 mm
Taylor, John Edward (gift, 1895) (D.1895.39.10)

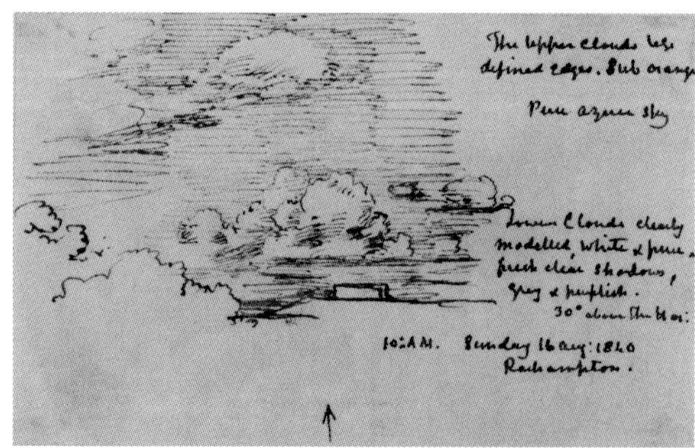

D.1895.39.11

Study of Clouds, Roehampton
16.8.1840
pen and brown ink
extensively inscribed with colour notes & dated right
edge: *10 AM. Sunday 16 Aug 1840 / Roehampton.*
65 × 100 mm
Taylor, John Edward (gift, 1895) (D.1895.39.11)

Study of Clouds
pen and brown ink
inscribed with colour notes left edge
49 × 103 mm
Taylor, John Edward (gift, 1895) (D.1895.39.12)

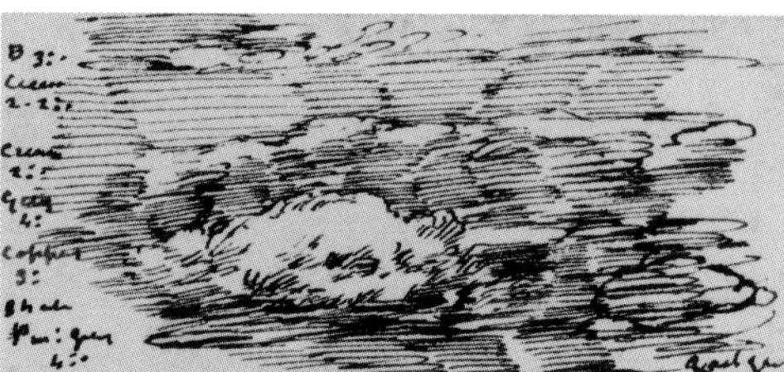

D.1895.39.12

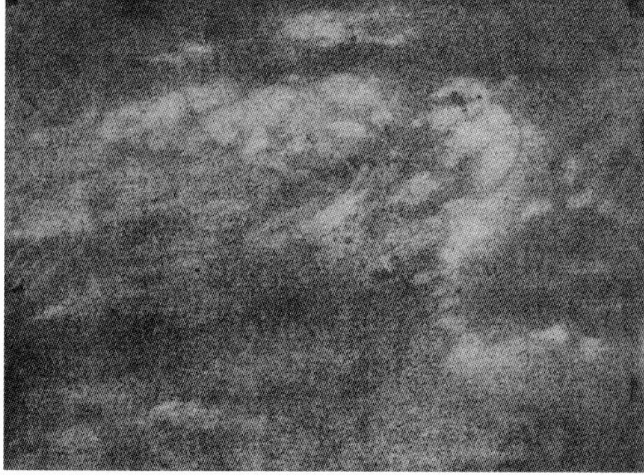

D.1895.39.13

Study of Clouds
white chalk; blue paper
70 × 92 mm
Taylor, John Edward (gift, 1895) (D.1895.39.13)

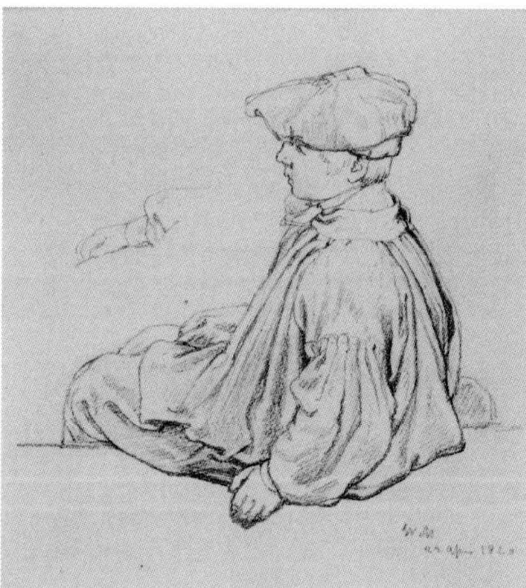

D.1895.40

Study of a seated Boy: left Profile
22.4.1840
pencil
signed & dated lower right with initials: *W M / 22
April 1840*
200 × 179 mm
Taylor, John Edward (gift, 1895) (D.1895.40)

Study of a seated Boy: right Profile
22.4.1840
pencil
signed & dated lower right with initials: *W.M. / 22
April 1840*
200 × 178 mm
Taylor, John Edward (gift, 1895) (D.1895.41)

Study of Branches and Leaves
pencil
126 × 159 mm
Taylor, John Edward (gift, 1895) (D.1895.42)

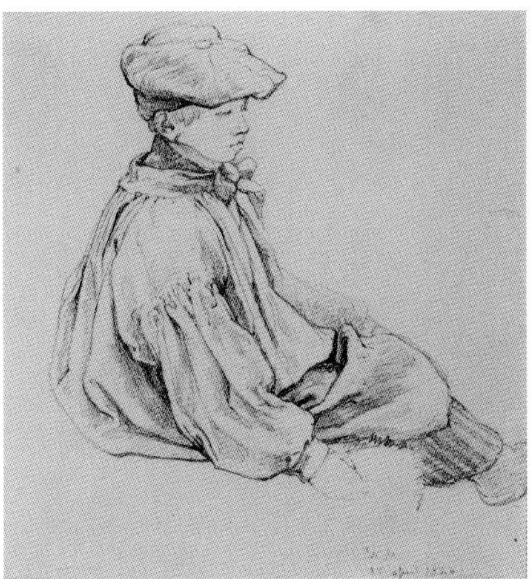

D.1895.41

Study of Branches and Leaves
pencil
117 × 115 mm
Taylor, John Edward (gift, 1895) (D.1895.43)

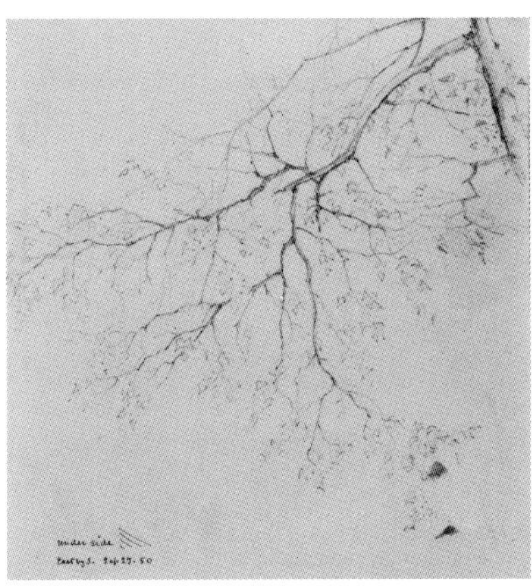

D.1895.44

Study of Branches and Leaves
27.9.1850
pencil
inscribed & dated lower left: *underside /*
East by 3.Sep 27.50
137 × 126 mm
Taylor, John Edward (gift, 1895) (D.1895.44)

Study of Foliage
pencil
175 × 155 mm
Taylor, John Edward (gift, 1895) (D.1895.45)

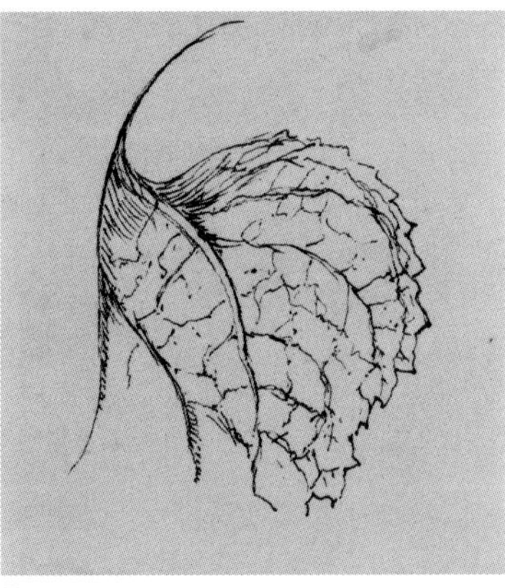

D.1895.46

Study of a Leaf
pen and brown ink
72 × 63 mm
Taylor, John Edward (gift, 1895) (D.1895.46)

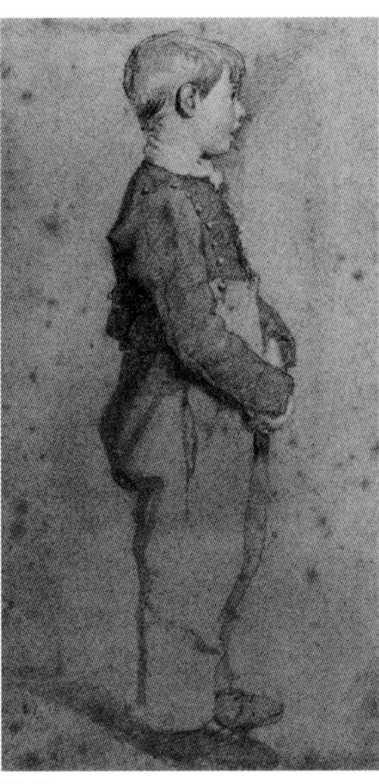

D.1895.47

Study for 'Idle Boys'
1815
pencil, white chalk; grey paper
222 × 115 mm
Taylor, John Edward (gift, 1895) (D.1895.47)

Study for 'Idle Boys'
1815
pencil, white chalk; grey paper
241 × 135 mm
Taylor, John Edward (gift, 1895) (D.1895.48)

Figure Studies
pen and brown ink
extensively inscribed on lower half of sheet
114 × 182 mm
Taylor, John Edward (gift, 1895) (D.1895.49)

Study of Hawkers
pen and brown ink
extensively inscribed with colour notes
94 × 207 mm
Taylor, John Edward (gift, 1895) (D.1895.50)

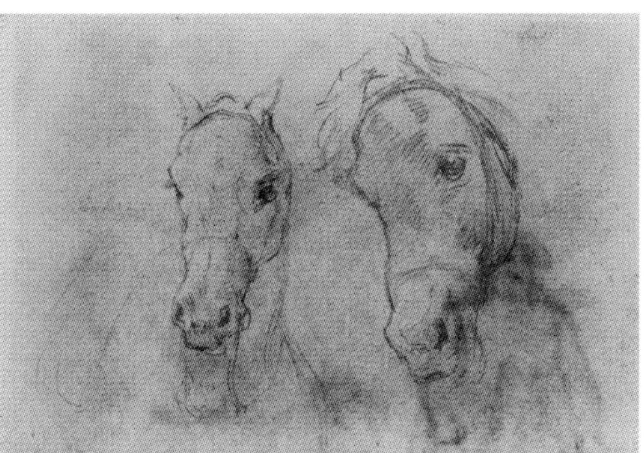

D.1895.51

Studies of Horses' Heads
pencil
68 × 102 mm
Taylor, John Edward (gift, 1895) (D.1895.51)

Studies of Hands for 'Lending a Bite'
1819
pen and brown ink
99 × 111 mm
Taylor, John Edward (gift, 1895) (D.1895.52)

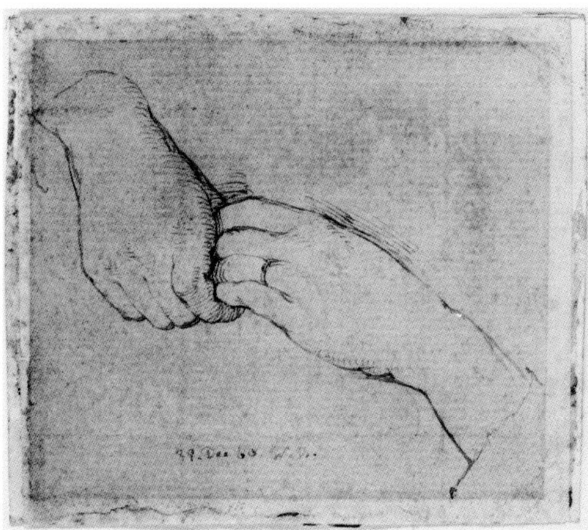

D.1895.53

Study of Hands
29.12.1860
pen and brown ink
signed & dated lower centre with initials:
29 Dec 60 W.M.
101 × 109 mm
Taylor, John Edward (gift, 1895) (D.1895.53)

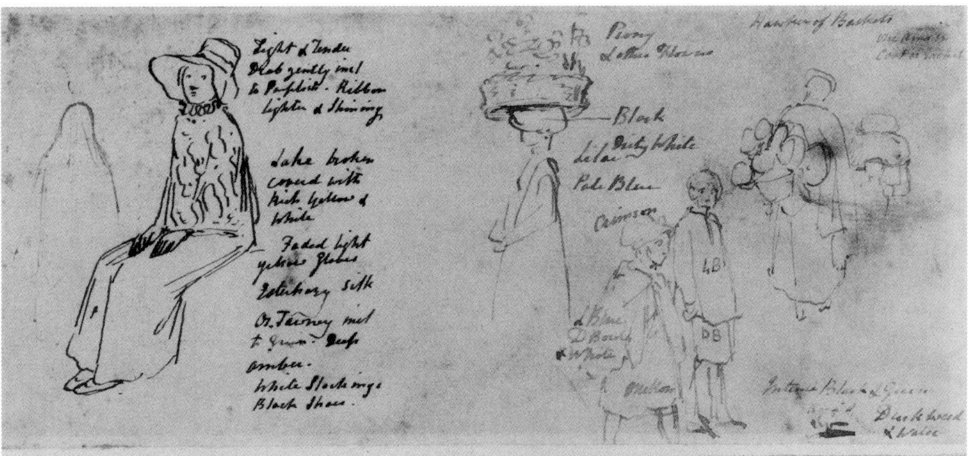

D.1895.50

Study of a Hand
pen and brown ink
70 × 46 mm
Taylor, John Edward (gift, 1895) (D.1895.54)

Study of Hands
9.10.1861
pen and brown ink
signed & dated centre of sheet with initials:
9 Oct 61 / WM.
115 × 113 mm
Taylor, John Edward (gift, 1895) (D.1895.55)

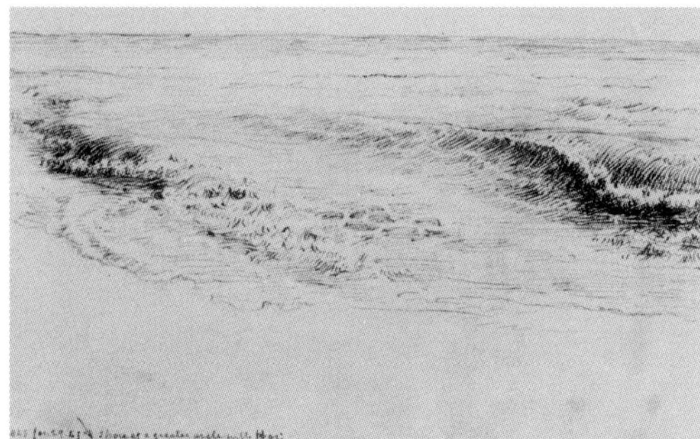
D.1895.56

Study of Waves
29.1.1845
pen and brown ink
inscribed & dated lower left: *1845 Jan 29 4* [arrow]
shore at a greater angle with [illegible]
114 × 180 mm
Taylor, John Edward (gift, 1895) (D.1895.56)

Study of Waves
30.1.1845
pen and brown ink
inscribed & dated along lower edge: *1845 Jan 30.11
A M* [arrow] *greatest equality just at the break of the
principal wave. Breaking generally from center to flank /
but sometimes in the points in succession*
114 × 180 mm
Taylor, John Edward (gift, 1895) (D.1895.57)

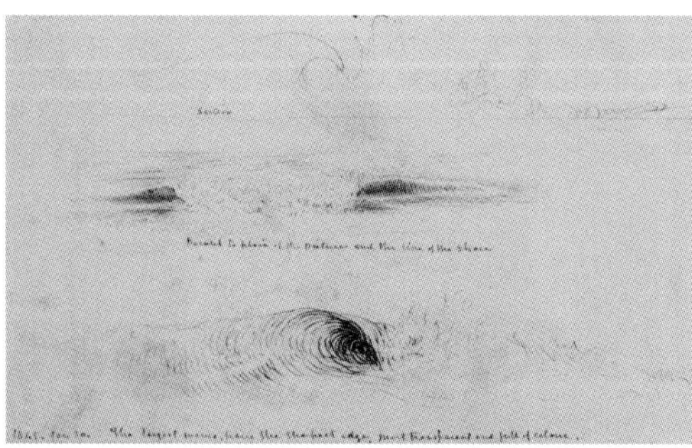
D.1895.58

Three Studies of Waves
30.1.1845
pen and brown ink
inscribed upper left describing top study: *section*,
inscribed on centre of sheet describing central study:
Painted to plain (sic) *of the picture and the line of the
shore*; inscribed & dated lower edge: *1845. Jan 30.
The largest waves have the sharpest edge, most
transparent and full of colour.*
114 × 179 mm
Taylor, John Edward (gift, 1895) (D.1895.58)

**Study of the Heads of a Boy and an
old Woman for 'Punch'**
1814
pencil, white chalk; beige paper
127 × 145 mm
Taylor, John Edward (gift, 1895) (D.1895.59)

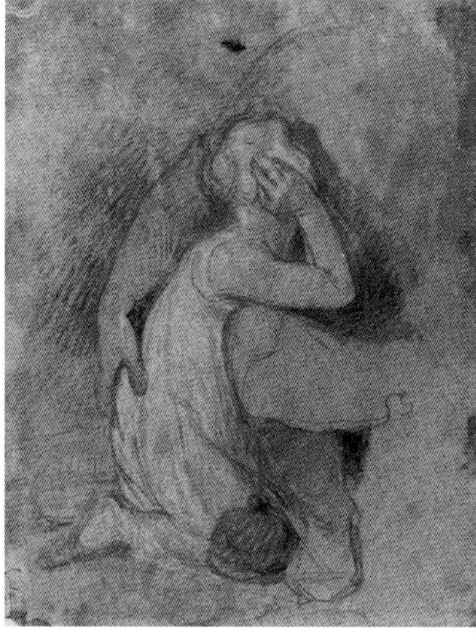
D.1895.60

**Study of a kneeling Child for 'Interior
of an English Cottage'**
1828
pencil; blue paper
145 × 114 mm
Taylor, John Edward (gift, 1895) (D.1895.60)

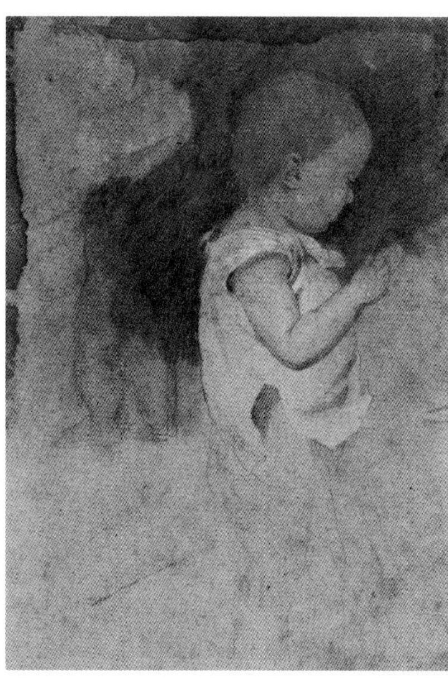
D.1895.61

Two Studies of a Baby
pencil, white chalk; blue paper
212 × 146 mm
Taylor, John Edward (gift, 1895) (D.1895.61)

Study of a Group of Figures
pencil
148 × 157 mm
Taylor, John Edward (gift, 1895) (D.1895.62)

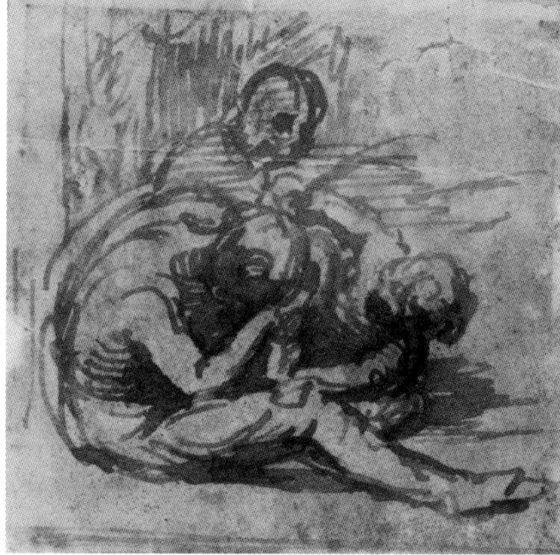
D.1895.63

Study of Figures for a Seal
29.7.1835
pen and brown ink, brown watercolour
inscribed & dated lower right verso: *Beating Father 29
July 1835*
59 × 60 mm
Taylor, John Edward (gift, 1895) (D.1895.63)

**Study of a kneeling Figure with Vultures
on a Cliff**
pen and brown ink, brown watercolour
117 × 59 mm
Taylor, John Edward (gift, 1895) (D.1895.64)

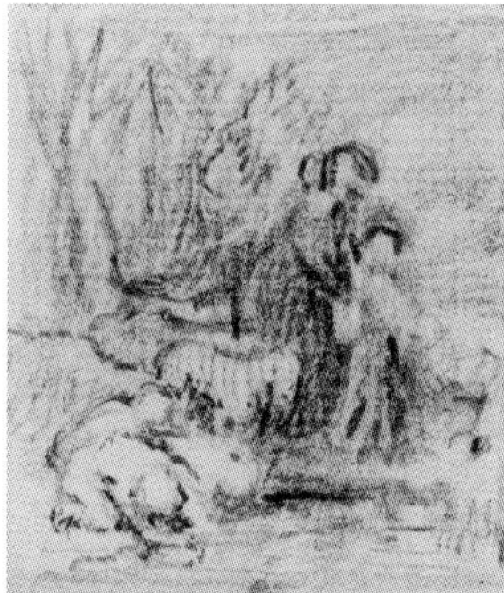
D.1895.65

Study for 'A Sailing Match'
1831
pencil, black chalk
46 × 38 mm
Taylor, John Edward (gift, 1895) (D.1895.65)

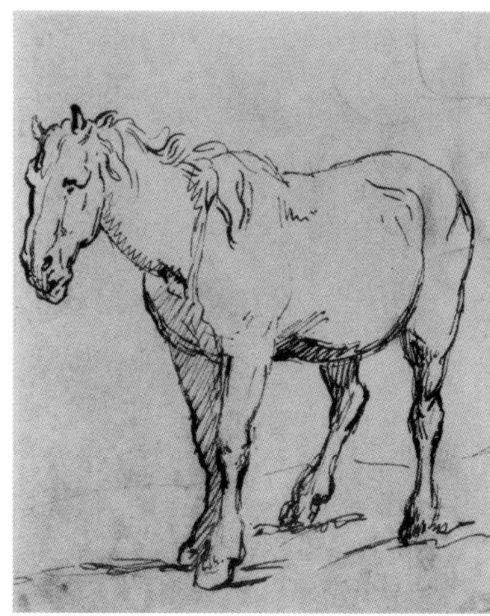
D.1895.66

Study of a Horse
pen and brown ink
175 × 115 mm
Taylor, John Edward (gift, 1895) (D.1895.66)

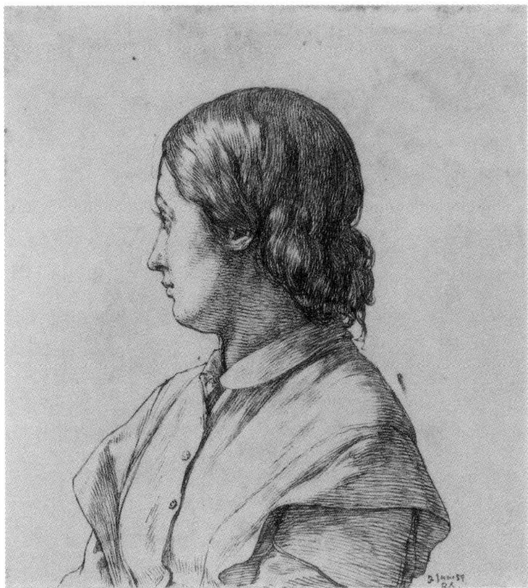

D.1895.67

Head and Shoulders of a Woman in left Profile
3.6.1859
pen and brown ink
inscribed & dated lower right: *3 June 59 / RA*
 numbered lower left: *155*
188 × 175 mm
Taylor, John Edward (gift, 1895) (D.1895.67)

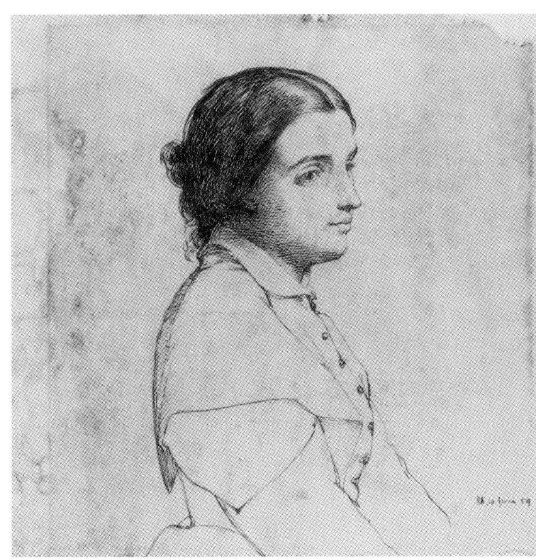

D.1895.68

Head and Shoulders of a Woman in right Profile
10.6.1859
pen and brown ink
inscribed & dated lower right: *RA.10 June 59*
 numbered lower left: *155*
202 × 186 mm
Taylor, John Edward (gift, 1895) (D.1895.68)

Studies of a Mouse
13.2.1849
pen and brown ink
signed, inscribed & dated lower right with initials:
Killed by Cold / Wm. / Feb.13.1849
106 × 153 mm
Taylor, John Edward (gift, 1895) (D.1895.69)

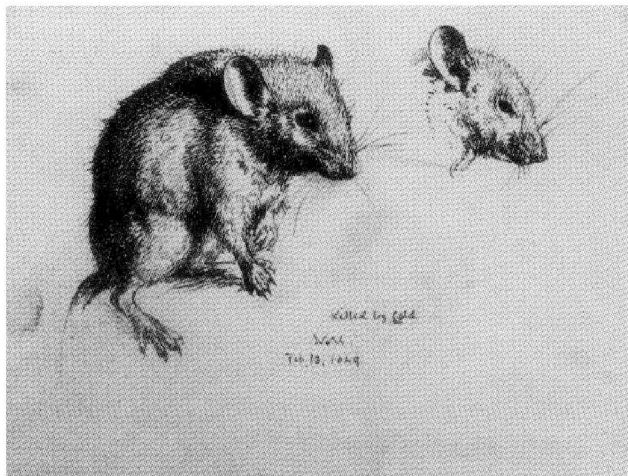

D.1895.69

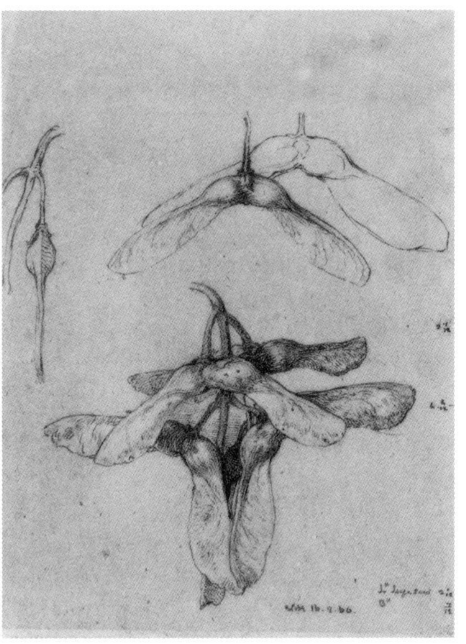

D.1895.70

Studies of Sycamore Keys
16.8.1860
pen and brown ink, watercolour; tracing paper
signed & dated lower right with initials: *WM 16.8.60*
178 × 129 mm
Taylor, John Edward (gift, 1895) (D.1895.70)

Study of Dogs for 'First Love'
1837–40
pen and brown ink
65 × 49 mm
Taylor, John Edward (gift, 1895) (D.1895.71)

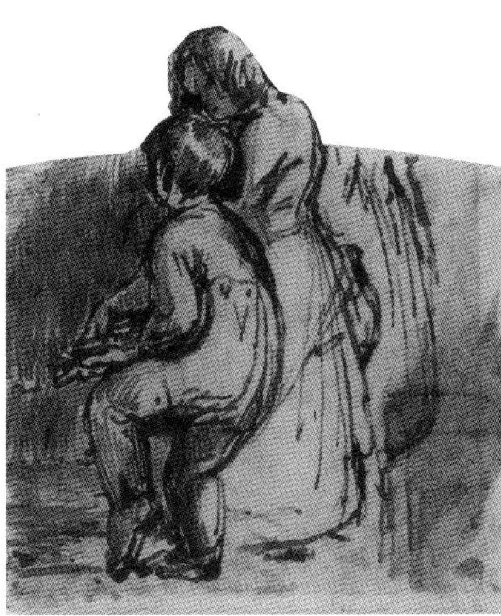

D.1895.72

Study of two Children for 'The Last In'
1835
pen and brown ink
61 × 54 mm
Taylor, John Edward (gift, 1895) (D.1895.72)

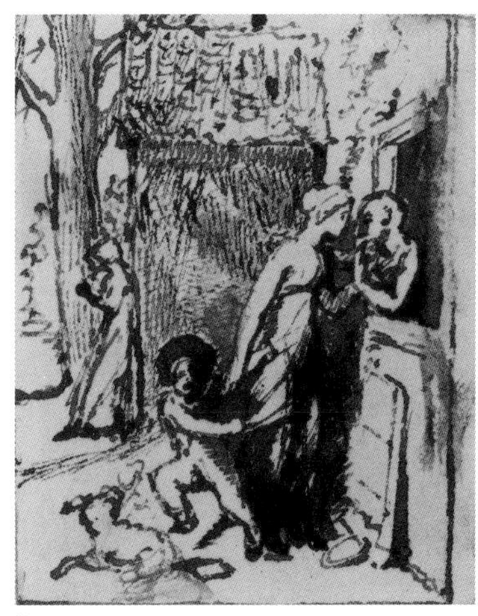

D.1895.73

Man, Woman and Child with Dog at a Stable Door
1837–40
pen and brown ink
73 × 57 mm
Taylor, John Edward (gift, 1895) (D.1895.73)

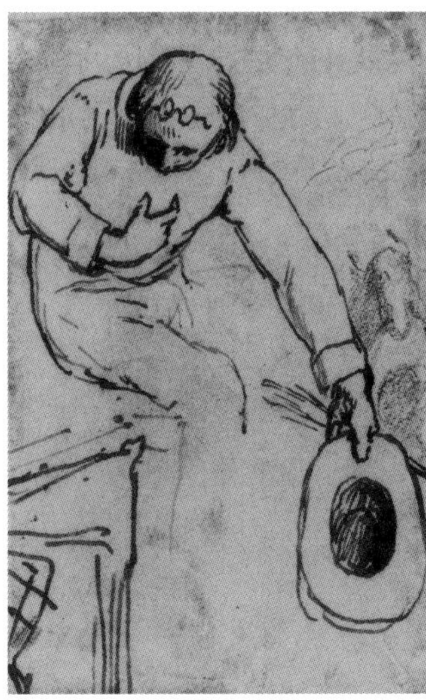

D.1895.74

Man with a Hat, Study for 'The Last In'
1835
pen and brown ink
86 × 53 mm
Taylor, John Edward (gift, 1895) (D.1895.74)

Studies of a Cat for 'Interior of an English Cottage'
1828
pen and brown ink, brown watercolour
102 × 95 mm
Taylor, John Edward (gift, 1895) (D.1895.75)

A kneeling Man with a Dog
pen and brown ink
101 × 97 mm
Taylor, John Edward (gift, 1895) (D.1895.76)

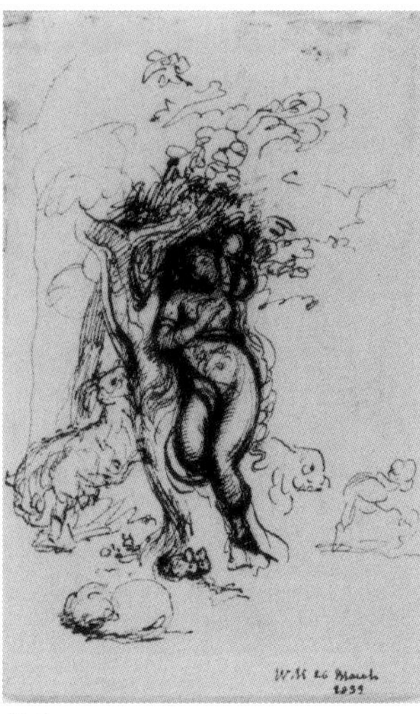

D.1895.77

A Woman with a Serpent by a Tree
26.3.1839
pen and brown ink
signed & dated lower right with initials:
WM 26 March / 1839
121 × 74 mm
Taylor, John Edward (gift, 1895) (D.1895.77)

A Dog barking at a Mountain Goat
pen and brown ink
39 × 37 mm
Taylor, John Edward (gift, 1895) (D.1895.78)

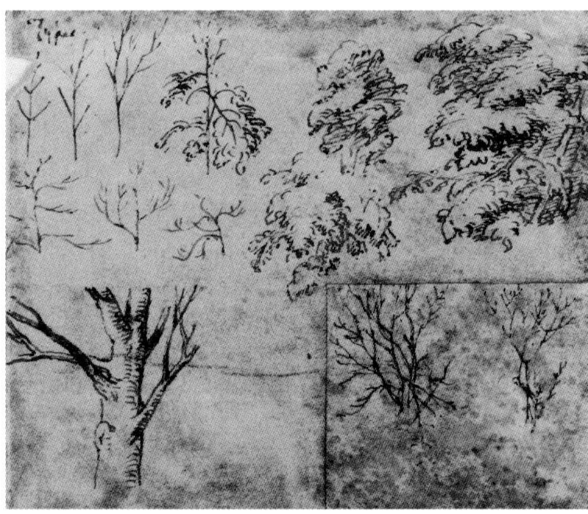

D.1895.79

Studies of Branches and Trees
pen and brown ink
104 × 114 mm
Taylor, John Edward (gift, 1895) (D.1895.79)

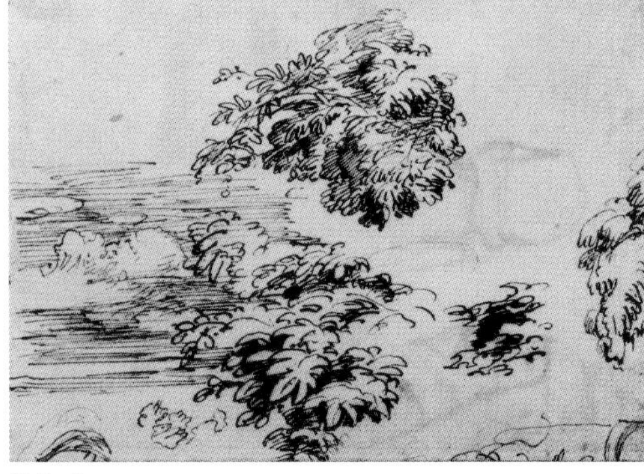

D.1895.80

Studies of Foliage (recto); Study of a Child (verso)
pen and brown ink
79 × 118 mm
Taylor, John Edward (gift, 1895) (D.1895.80)

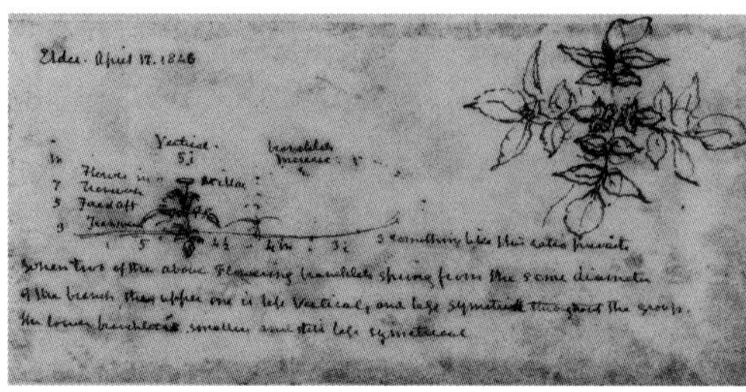

D.1895.81

Studies of Elder
17.4.1846
pen and brown ink
inscribed & dated upper left: *Elder.April 17.1846*;
extensively inscribed on lower half of sheet
57 × 115 mm
Taylor, John Edward (gift, 1895) (D.1895.81)

Studies of Branches
pen and brown ink
60 × 115 mm
Taylor, John Edward (gift, 1895) (D.1895.82)

Botanical Studies of a Flower, with Notes
pencil, pen and brown ink
extensively inscribed
93 × 129 mm
Taylor, John Edward (gift, 1895) (D.1895.83)

Study of a Sheep's Head
pen and brown ink
94 × 99 mm
Taylor, John Edward (gift, 1895) (D.1895.84)

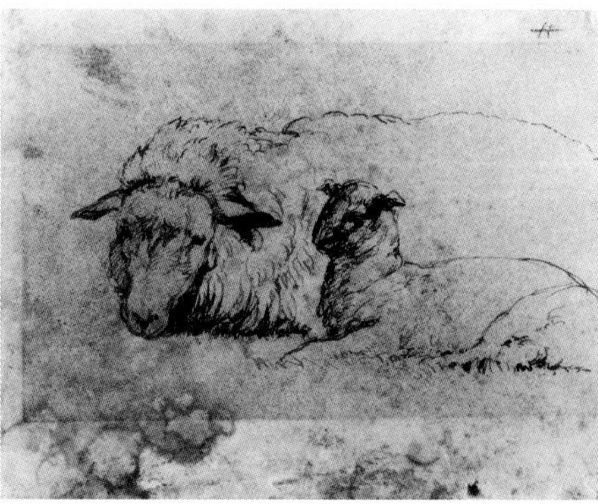

D.1895.85

Study of a Sheep with a Lamb
pen and brown ink
90 × 110 mm
Taylor, John Edward (gift, 1895) (D.1895.85)

Study of a Sheep with a Lamb
pen and brown ink, brown watercolour
69 × 62 mm
Taylor, John Edward (gift, 1895) (D.1895.86)

Study of a Sheep
pen and brown ink
110 × 149 mm
Taylor, John Edward (gift, 1895) (D.1895.87)

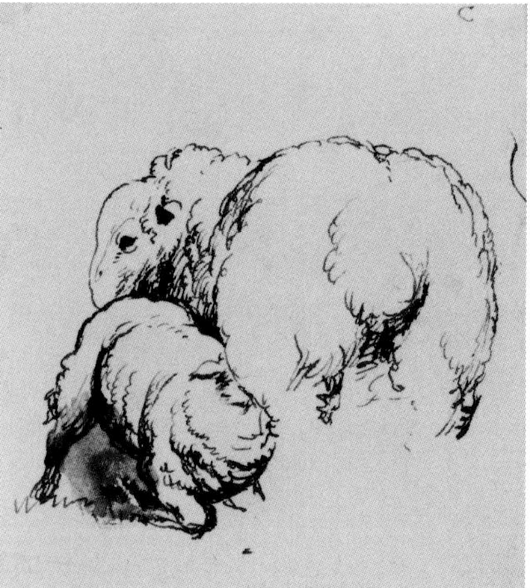

D.1895.86

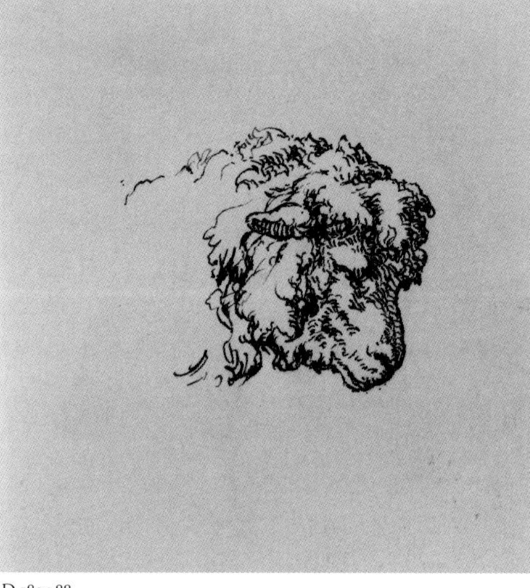

D.1895.88

Study of a Sheep's Head
pen and brown ink
93 × 100 mm
Taylor, John Edward (gift, 1895) (D.1895.88)

Study of a Sheep with a Lamb
pen and brown ink
68 × 112 mm
Taylor, John Edward (gift, 1895) (D.1895.89)

Study of an Ass's Ears
pencil; grey paper
54 × 84 mm
Taylor, John Edward (gift, 1895) (D.1895.90.1)

Study of a Cat for 'Interior of an English Cottage'
1828
pen and brown ink
96 × 80 mm
Taylor, John Edward (gift, 1895) (D.1895.90.2)

Study of the Hind Quarters of a Horse
pencil; buff paper
130 × 93 mm
Taylor, John Edward (gift, 1895) (D.1895.91)

Study of a Horse's Head
pen and brown ink
133 × 108 mm
Taylor, John Edward (gift, 1895) (D.1895.92)

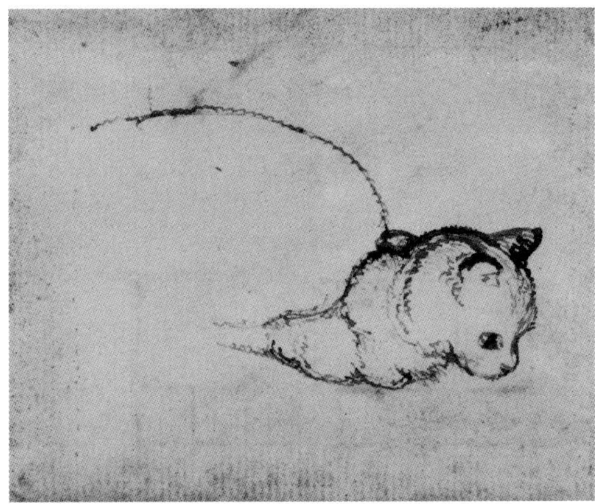

D.1895.90.2

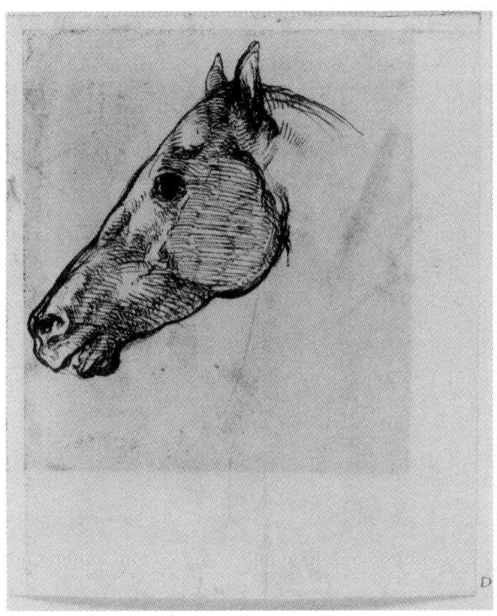

D.1895.92

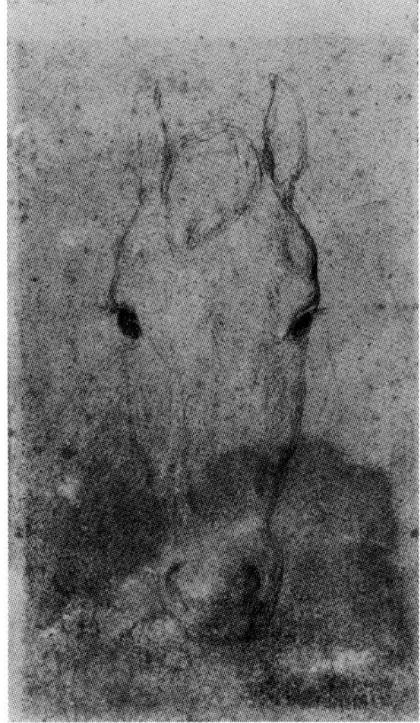

D.1895.93

Study of a Horse's Head
pencil; buff paper
177 × 100 mm
Taylor, John Edward (gift, 1895) (D.1895.93)

Study of a skinned Robin
9.12.1849
pen and brown ink
signed, inscribed & dated lower right: *A Hen Robin Hatched in May* / [illegible] *Dec / WM.9 Dec 1849*
211 × 195 mm
Taylor, John Edward (gift, 1895) (D.1895.94)

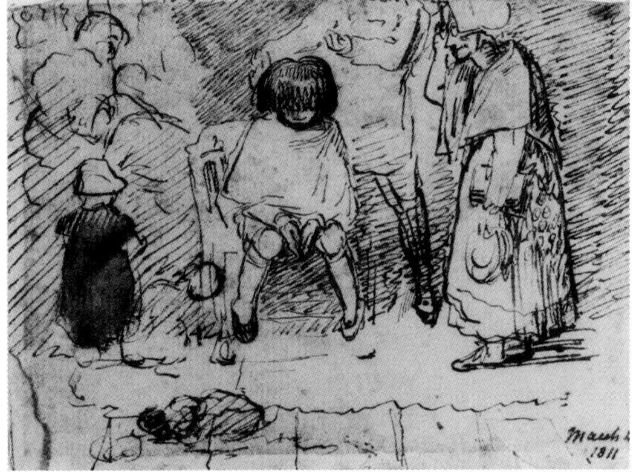

D.1895.95

Study for 'The Barber's Shop'
4.3.1811
pen and brown ink
dated lower right: *March 4 / 1811*
92 × 119 mm
Taylor, John Edward (gift, 1895) (D.1895.95)

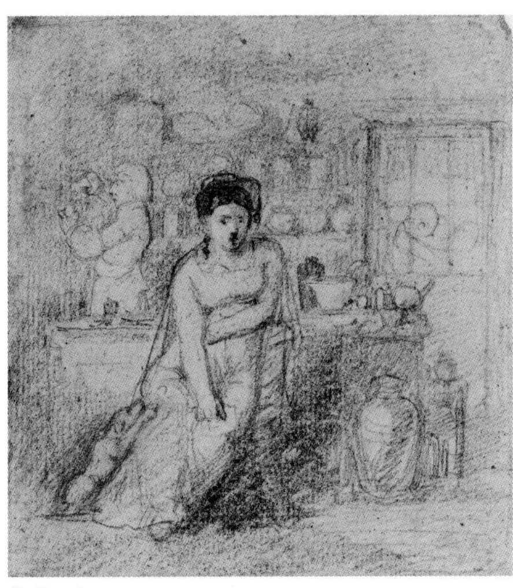

D.1895.96

A Woman in a Chemist's Shop
pencil, black chalk; beige paper
160 × 143 mm
Taylor, John Edward (gift, 1895) (D.1895.96)

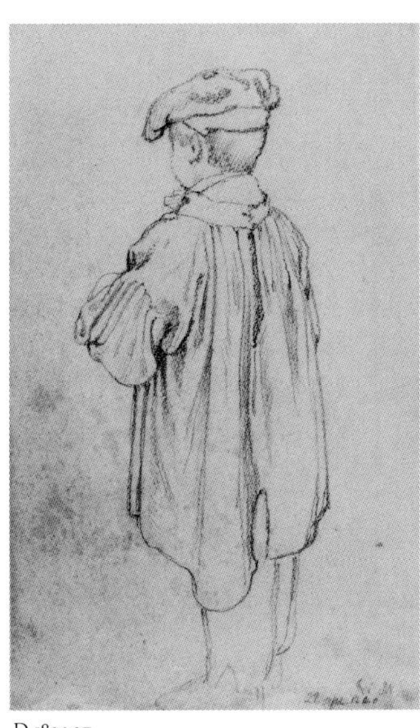

D.1895.97

Study of a small Boy
22.4.1840
pencil
signed & dated with initials: *WM / 22 Apl 1840*
254 × 185 mm
Taylor, John Edward (gift, 1895) (D.1895.97)

**Study for 'The Wolf and the Lamb' (recto);
Figure Studies (verso)**
1816–20
pencil, blue chalk, black chalk (recto)
104 × 83 mm
Taylor, John Edward (gift, 1895) (D.1895.98)

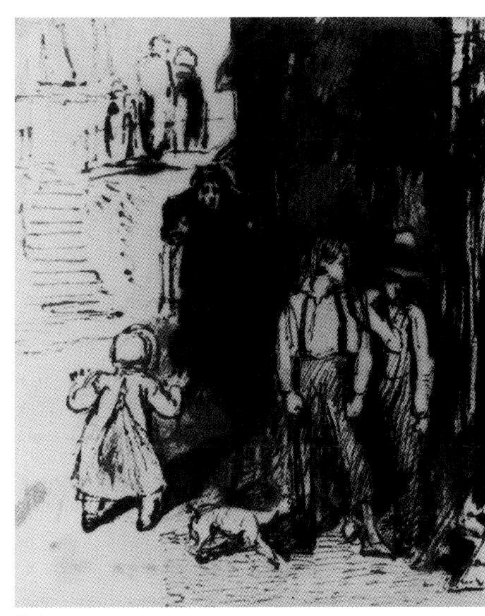

D.1895.99

Study for 'The Wolf and the Lamb'
1816–20
pen and brown ink, brown watercolour
116 × 92 mm
Taylor, John Edward (gift, 1895) (D.1895.99)

D.1895.100

A Chimney Sweep accosting four Boys
pen and brown ink, brown watercolour
72 × 66 mm
Taylor, John Edward (gift, 1895) (D.1895.100)

A Chimney Sweep accosting five Boys
pencil; tracing paper
103 × 87 mm
Taylor, John Edward (gift, 1895) (D.1895.101)

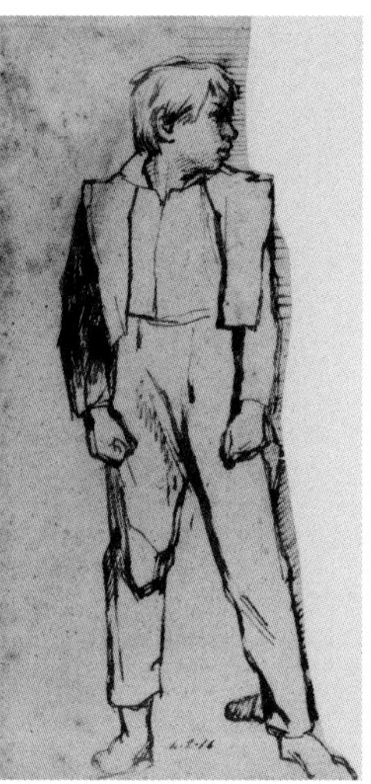

D.1895.102

**Full-length Study of a Boy for
'The Wolf and the Lamb'**
4.2.1816
pen and brown ink, brown watercolour
dated lower centre: *4.2.16*
288 × 134 mm
Taylor, John Edward (gift, 1895) (D.1895.102)

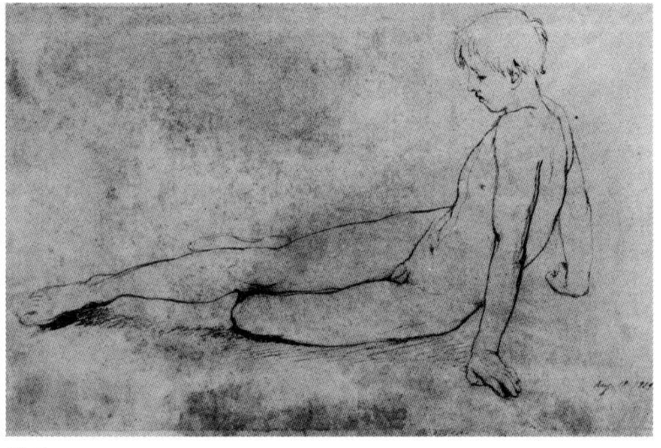

D.1895.103

A nude Boy reclining
18.8.1829
pen and brown ink
dated lower right: *Aug 18 1829.*
198 × 294 mm
Taylor, John Edward (gift, 1895) (D.1895.103)

Miscellaneous Studies, Compositions and Clouds
9.1824 & 10.1824
pen and brown ink
dated upper right centre, right and lower right: *Sep 24
1824 Sep 28 1824 Oct 18 1824*; extensively inscribed all
over sheet with colour and other notes
331 × 207 mm
Taylor, John Edward (gift, 1895) (D.1895.104)

Study of a seated nude Woman
pen and brown ink
405 × 248 mm
Taylor, John Edward (gift, 1895) (D.1895.105)

Study of a standing nude Woman
18.12.1858
pen and brown ink
signed, inscribed & dated lower right with initials: *RA.
Dec 18.58 / C W Cope Visitor WM.*
377 × 250 mm
Taylor, John Edward (gift, 1895) (D.1895.106)

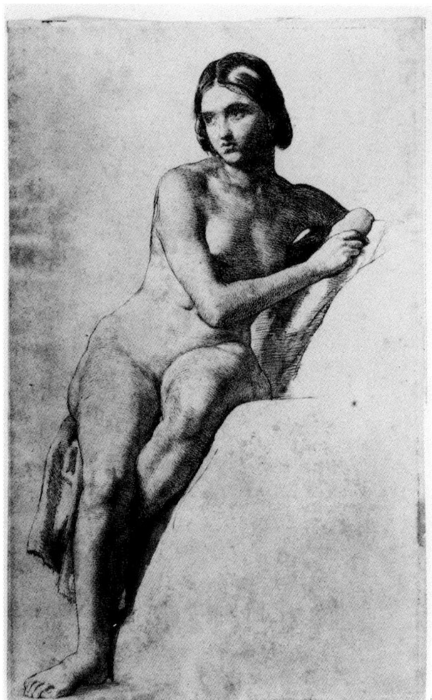

D.1895.105

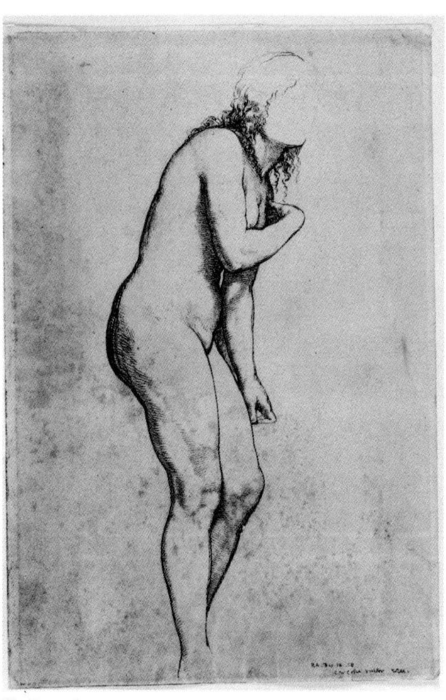

D.1895.106

Study of Foliage
10.6.1844–11.6.1844
pen and brown ink, watermark: [WHA] TMAN [18]34
dated upper right: *June 11.44*; dated lower right:
10.6.44; inscribed all over sheet with a descriptive scale
and colour notes
128 × 317 mm
Taylor, John Edward (gift, 1895) (D.1895.107)

Study of Foliage
8.6.1844–9.6.1844
pen and brown ink
dated lower right: *8.9.6–44*; extensively inscribed all
over sheet with compositional notes
128 × 203 mm
Taylor, John Edward (gift, 1895) (D.1895.108)

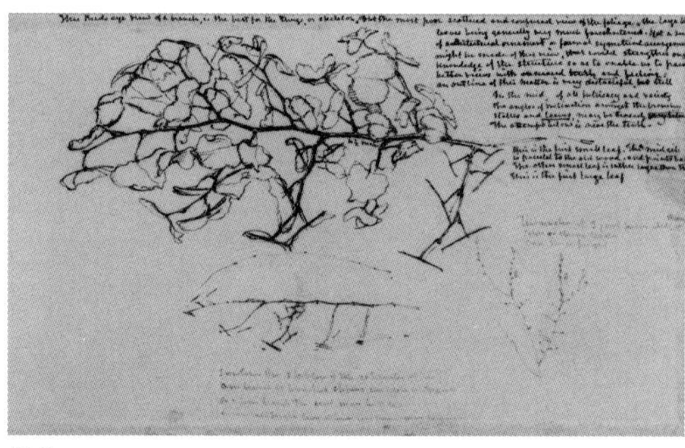

D.1895.109

Study of Foliage
pen and brown ink
extensively inscribed with descriptive notes
128 × 203 mm
Taylor, John Edward (gift, 1895) (D.1895.109)

Study of a seated Nude Woman
pen and brown ink; watermark WILMOT / 1829
369 × 242 mm
Taylor, John Edward (gift, 1895) (D.1895.110)

Study of a dead Dog
1814
pencil; beige paper
inscribed & dated lower right: *Bustle died Sunday
[illegible word] 19.1814*
153 × 195 mm
Taylor, John Edward (gift, 1895) (D.1895.111)

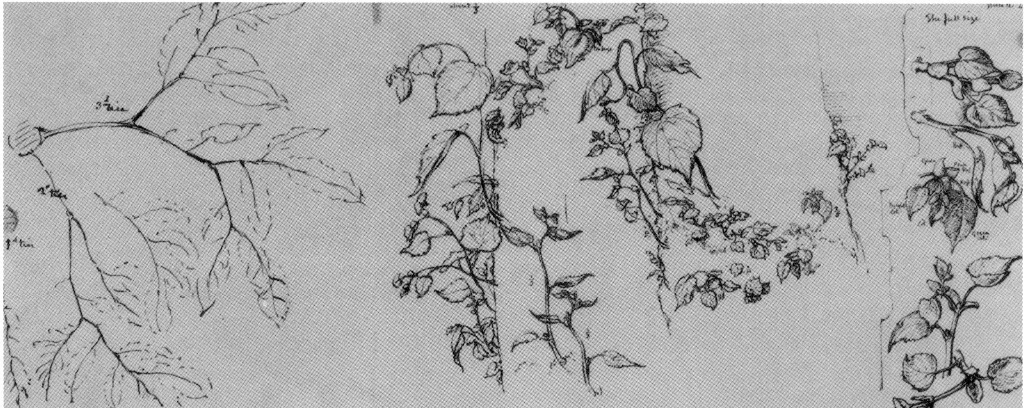

D.1895.107

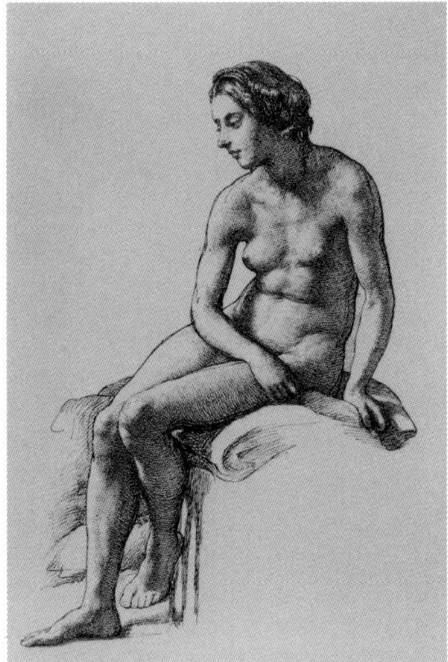

D.1895.110

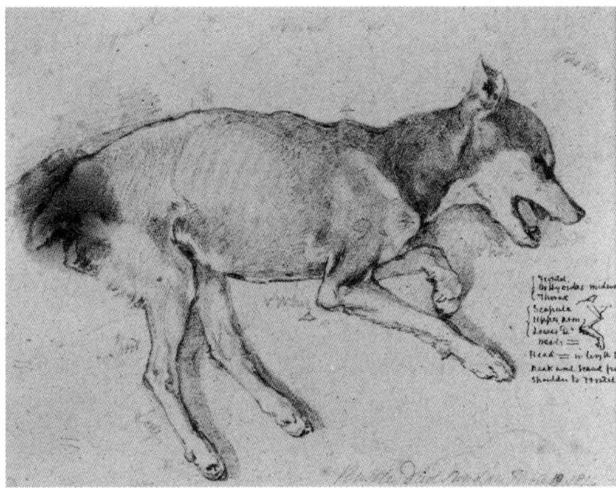

D.1895.111

Study of a Body of a dead Dog
pencil; beige paper
107 × 140 mm
Taylor, John Edward (gift, 1895) (D.1895.112)

Study of two Dogs
pencil; brown paper
84 × 93 mm
Taylor, John Edward (gift, 1895) (D.1895.113)

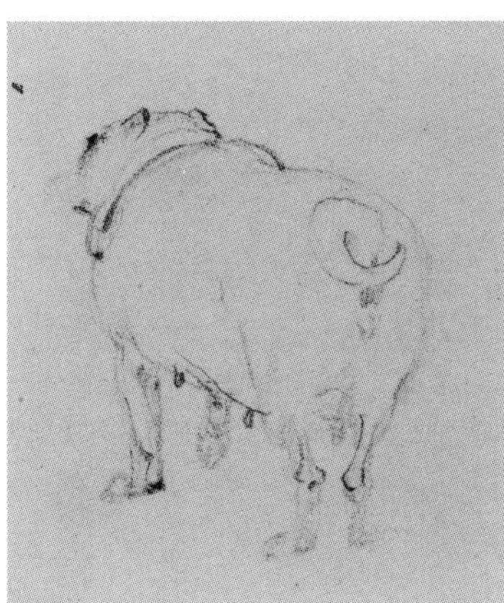

D.1895.114

Back View of a Bull Terrier Bitch
pencil
61 × 55 mm
Taylor, John Edward (gift, 1895) (D.1895.114)

Back View of a Spaniel
pencil
44 × 37 mm
Taylor, John Edward (gift, 1895) (D.1895.115)

Study of a Dog's Ear
pen and brown ink
53 × 53 mm
Taylor, John Edward (gift, 1895) (D.1895.116)

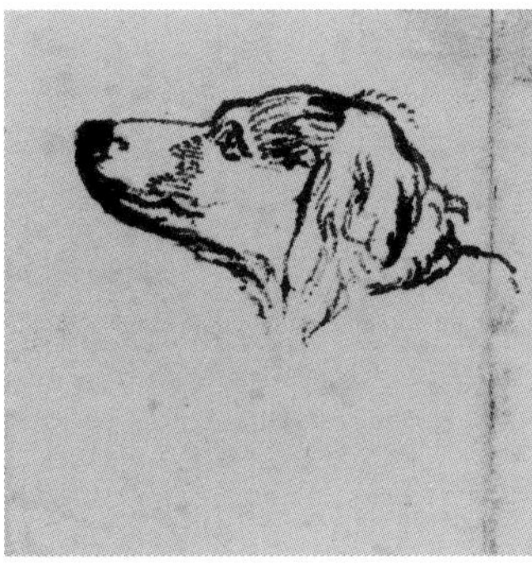

D.1895.117

Study of a left Profile of a Dog's Head
pen and brown ink
53 × 53 mm
Taylor, John Edward (gift, 1895) (D.1895.117)

Study of a Body of a Dog
pen and brown ink
65 × 43 mm
Taylor, John Edward (gift, 1895) (D.1895.118)

Study of a Dog's hind Leg
pen and brown ink
70 × 52 mm
Taylor, John Edward (gift, 1895) (D.1895.119)

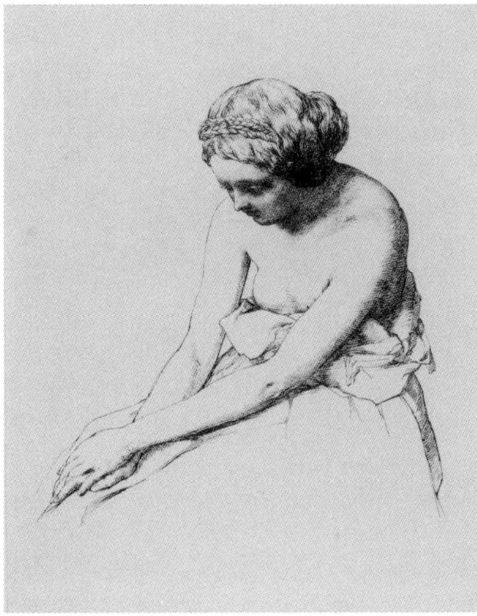

D.1895.120

Study of a seated draped Woman
pen and brown ink
344 × 267 mm
Taylor, John Edward (gift, 1895) (D.1895.120)

Two Studies of Men, with written Notes
pen and brown ink
extensively inscribed on recto and verso
154 × 96 mm
Taylor, John Edward (gift, 1895) (D.1895.121.1)

Written Notes
pen and brown ink
extensively inscribed on recto and verso
155 × 96 mm
Taylor, John Edward (gift, 1895) (D.1895.121.2)

Two Studies of Butchers, a Study of a Leather Gaiter, with written Notes
2.2.1822
pen and brown ink
extensively inscribed & dated on recto and verso
with notes on composition and mixing colours
128 × 96 mm
Taylor, John Edward (gift, 1895) (D.1895.121.3)

Four Studies of Brewers and Bakers, with written Notes
pen and brown ink
extensively inscribed on recto and verso
with colour notes
155 × 96 mm
Taylor, John Edward (gift, 1895) (D.1895.121.4)

Four Studies of Children with written Notes
pen and brown ink
extensively inscribed recto and verso
155 × 96 mm
Taylor, John Edward (gift, 1895) (D.1895.121.5)

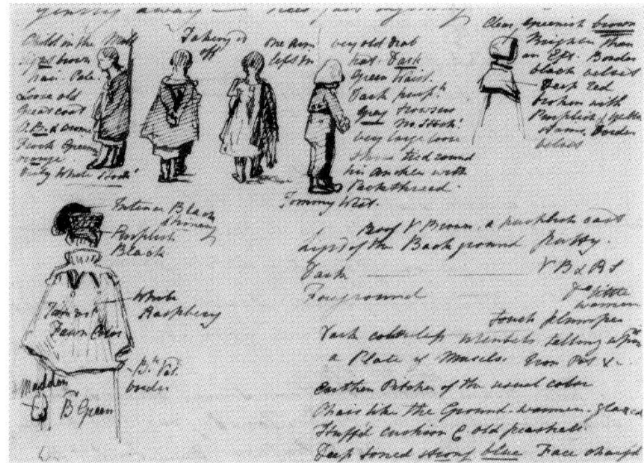

D.1895.121.6

Various Studies of Children with written Notes
pen and brown ink
extensively inscribed on recto and verso
144 × 200 mm
Taylor, John Edward (gift, 1895) (D.1895.121.6)

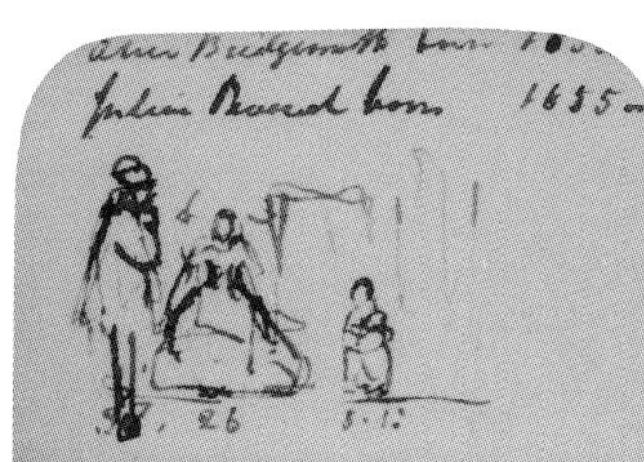

D.1895.121.7

Studies of three Figures with written Notes
pen and brown ink
31 × 45 mm
Taylor, John Edward (gift, 1895) (D.1895.121.7)

Written Notes in Greek and English
pencil, pen and brown ink
extensively annotated
212 × 41 mm
Taylor, John Edward (gift, 1895) (D.1895.121.8)

**Study of a Figure by a Fire and four
Figure and Face Studies with written
Notes in Greek and English**
pencil, pen and brown ink
extensively annotated
212 × 42 mm
Taylor, John Edward (gift, 1895) (D.1895.121.9)

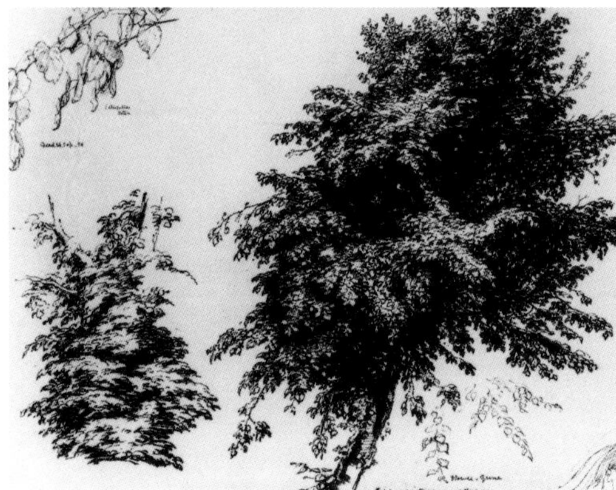

D.1895.122

Studies of Trees and Foliage
26.9.1856
pen and brown ink, brown watercolour; watermark R
TA [remainder unreadable] / 183 [last digit unreadable]
inscribed & dated upper left: *Caterpillar / eaten / Dead
26 Sep–56*; inscribed lower right: *Flower– June / Seldom
picturesque at this age*
185 × 228 mm
Taylor, John Edward (gift, 1895) (D.1895.122)

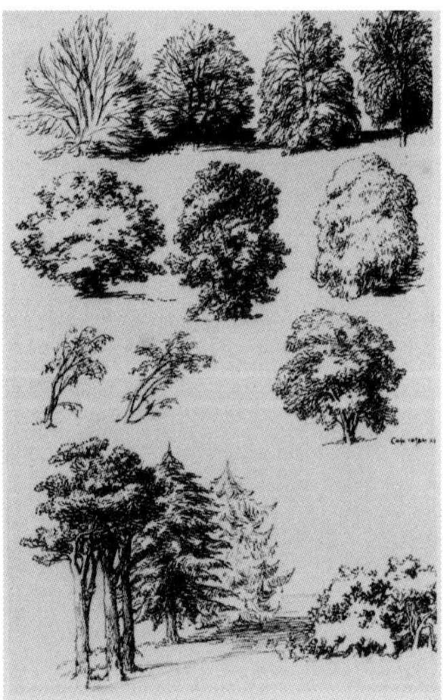

D.1895.123

**Studies of Trees, Capheaton
Hall, Northumberland**
10.1.1846
pen and brown ink
inscribed & dated centre right: *Cap 10 Jan 46*
177 × 111 mm
Taylor, John Edward (gift, 1895) (D.1895.123)

Study of a sleeping Mother and Children
2.11.1826
pen and brown ink, brown watercolour
dated lower centre: *Nov.2.1826*
105 × 108 mm
Richardson, Edward H. (gift, 1931) (D.1931.39.1)

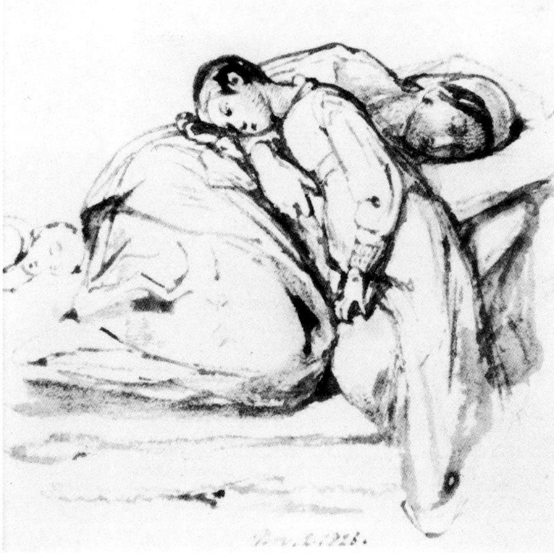

D.1931.39.1

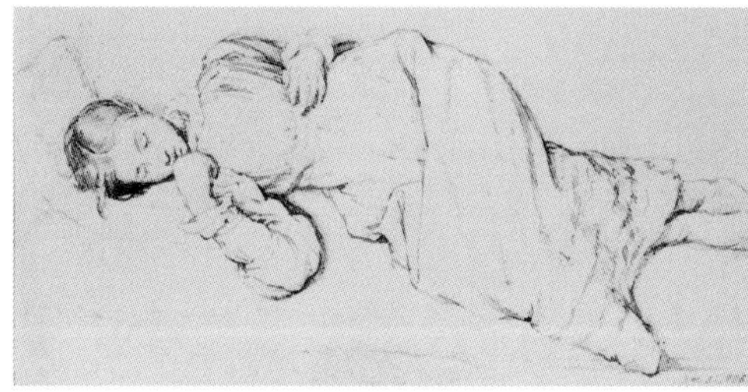

D.1931.39.2

Study of a sleeping Woman
5.11.1826
pen and brown ink, brown watercolour
dated lower right: *Nov 5. 1826*
84 × 165 mm
Richardson, Edward H. (gift, 1931) (D.1931.39.2)

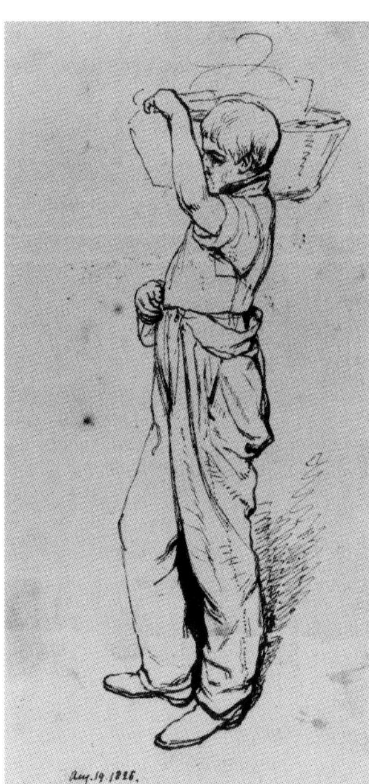

D.1931.40

Study of a Boy carrying a Basket on his Shoulder
19.8.1826
pen and brown ink; two joined sheets
dated lower left: *Aug.19.1826.*
202 × 100 mm
Richardson, Edward H. (gift, 1931) (D.1931.40)

■ **MUNN, PAUL SANDBY (1773–1845)**
Apparently the godson of Paul Sandby, Munn
visited Wales in 1802 and Yorkshire in 1803, on both
occasions accompanied by Cotman. Munn exhibited
landscapes at the Royal Academy between 1799 and
1805 and at the Old Watercolour Society from its
foundation until 1815.

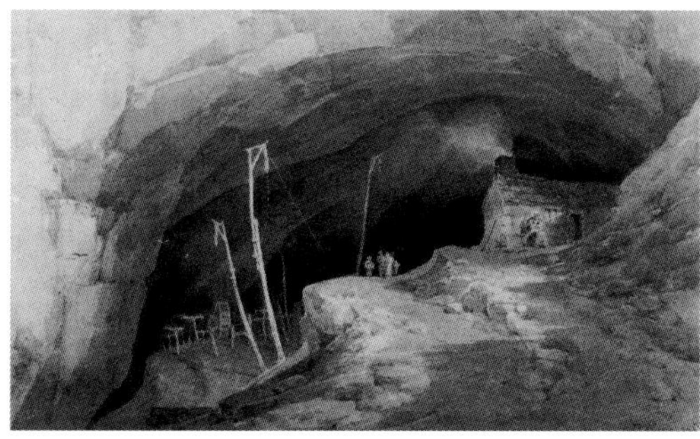

D.1892.56

The Peak Cavern, Derbyshire
1807
pencil, watercolour, bodycolour
(heightened with white)
signed & dated lower right: *P S Munn 1807.*
226 × 362 mm
Taylor, John Edward (gift, 1892) (D.1892.56)

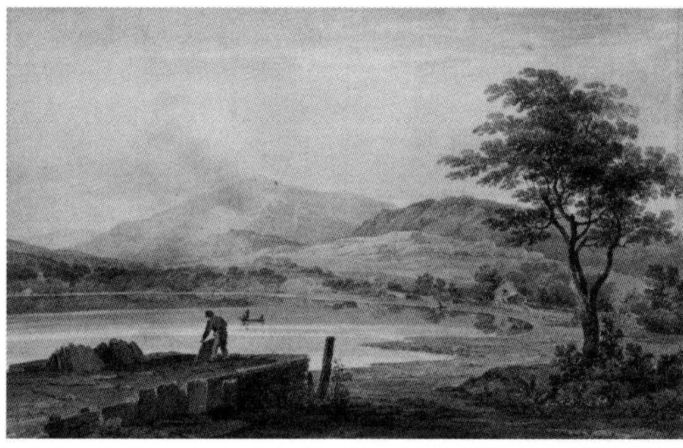

D.1948.1

Coniston Lake, Waterhead, Lancashire
1813
pencil, watercolour
signed & dated lower right: *P.S.Munn 1813*
238 × 358 mm
Friends of the Whitworth (gift, 1948) (D.1948.1)

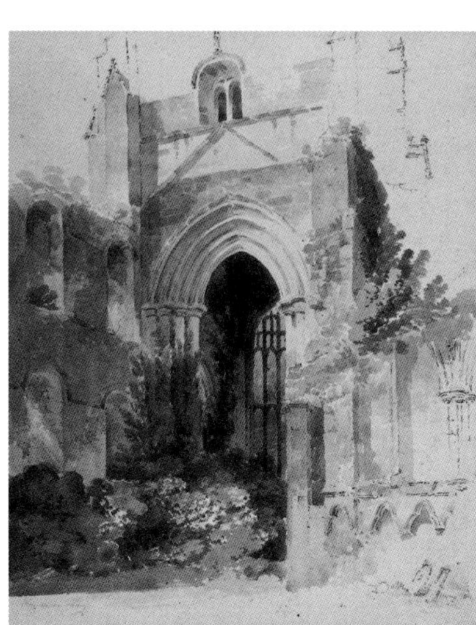

D.1954.18

The Base of Huberts Tower, Fountains Abbey, seen from within the North Transept, Yorkshire
1803
pencil, watercolour
inscribed & dated lower left: *Fountains Abbey / 1803*
343 × 270 mm
Friends of the Whitworth (gift, 1954) (D.1954.18)

■ MURRAY, CHARLES FAIRFAX (1849–1919)
Murray became Burne-Jones's first studio assistant in 1866. He also assisted Rossetti and George Frederick Watts and later worked as a copyist for Ruskin in Italy. His later career was as a collector and dealer and he had close associations with Agnew's. He had two families, the legitimate one in Italy, where he spent much of his time, and the illegitimate one in England. Neither was aware of the other's existence.

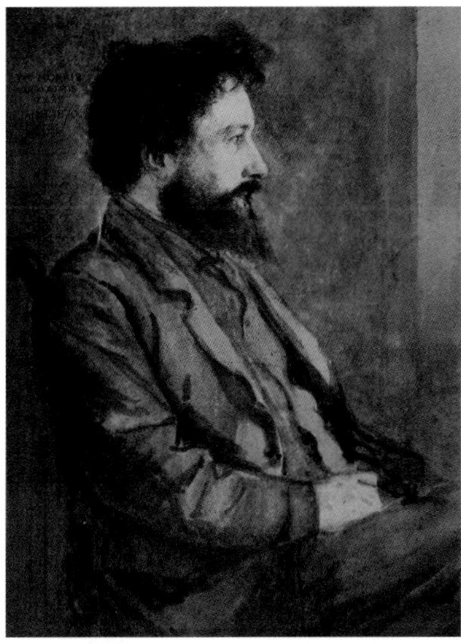
D.1921.31

Portrait of William Morris
1.1.1870
pencil, brown watercolour
signed, inscribed & dated upper left with initials:
WM.MORRIS / ANNO AETATIS / XXXV / JAN.1.1870. / CFM
356 × 255 mm
Corbould-Ellis, C. F. (purchase, 1921) (D.1921.31)

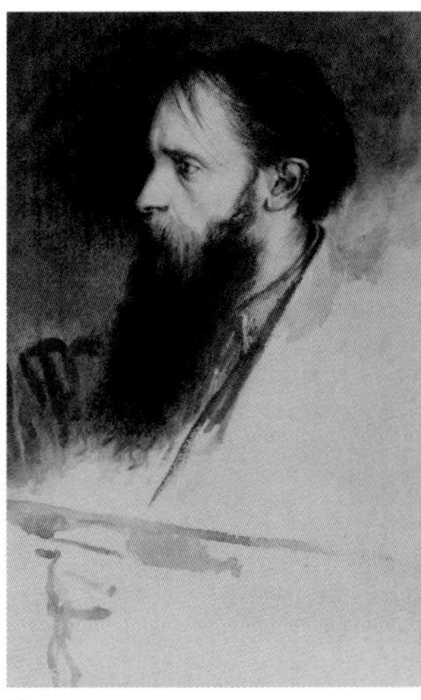
D.1921.33

Portrait of Sir Edward Burne-Jones
1868–69
pencil, brown watercolour
signed & inscribed upper left with initials:
EDWD.B.JONES / ANNO AETATIS / XXXV / C.F.M.
328 × 217 mm
Corbould-Ellis, C. F. (purchase, 1921) (D.1921.33)

■ NASH, FREDERICK (1782–1856)
Born in London, Frederick Nash studied architectural drawing under Thomas Malton Jun. and attended the Royal Academy Schools. He began his career as an architectural draughtsman and worked for the Society of Antiquaries in that capacity. His drawings of Paris of 1819 were bought by Sir Thomas Lawrence and he was elected a member of the Old Watercolour Society in 1824. He exhibited at the Royal Academy between 1799 and 1847. Nash travelled in England and on the Continent and lived in Brighton from 1834.

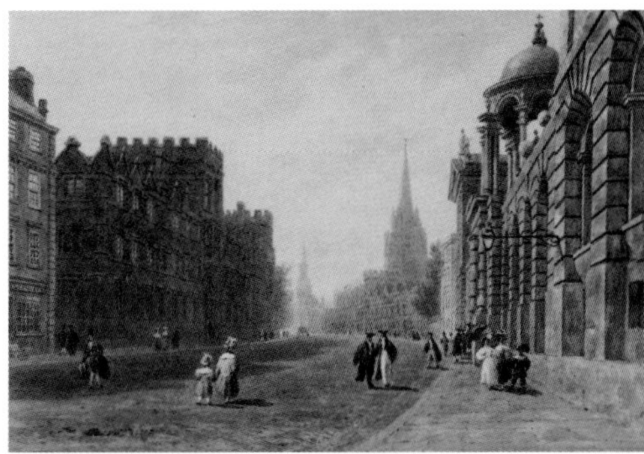
D.1892.128

High Street, Oxford
pencil, watercolour, bodycolour (heightened with white)
199 × 287 mm
Taylor, John Edward (gift, 1892) (D.1892.128)

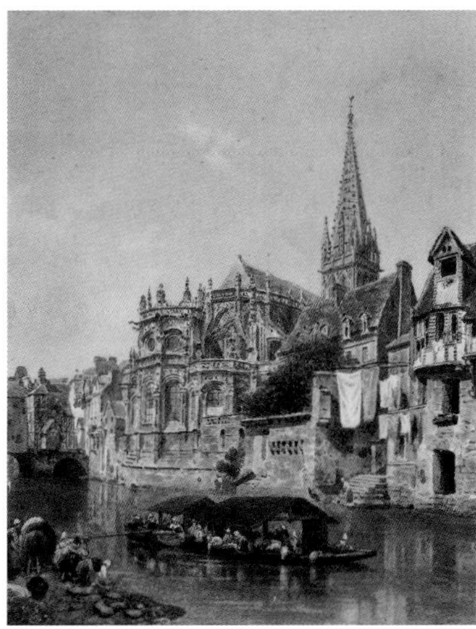
D.1892.129

The Apse of the Church of St Pierre, Caen, Normandy
watercolour
301 × 227 mm
Taylor, John Edward (gift, 1892) (D.1892.129)

■ NASH, JOSEPH (1808–78)
Joseph Nash studied with Augustus Charles Pugin and became an architectural draughtsman. A skilled lithographer, Nash was elected a member of the Old Watercolour Society in 1842. He specialised in Tudor and Elizabethan architectural interiors with figures in costume. Nash's most famous book of lithographs, *Mansions of England in the Olden Time*, was published in four volumes between 1839 and 1849 and contained 106 lithographs.

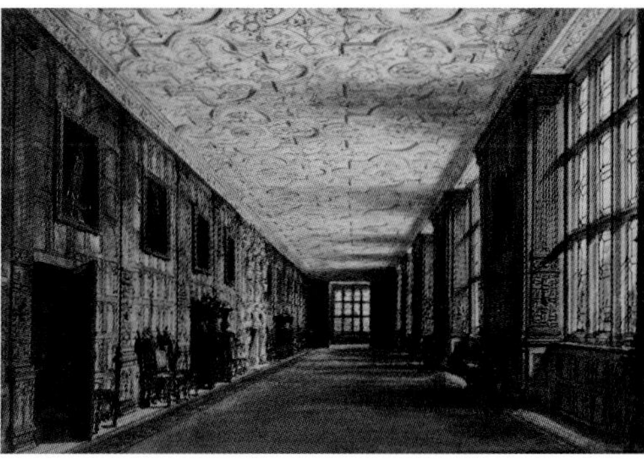
D.1887.48

The Long Gallery, Aston Hall, Birmingham
watercolour, bodycolour (heightened with white)
inscribed lower right in later hand (?): *Gallery Aston Warwick Joseph Nash*
335 × 486 mm
Agnew's (purchase, 27.6.1891) (D.1887.48)

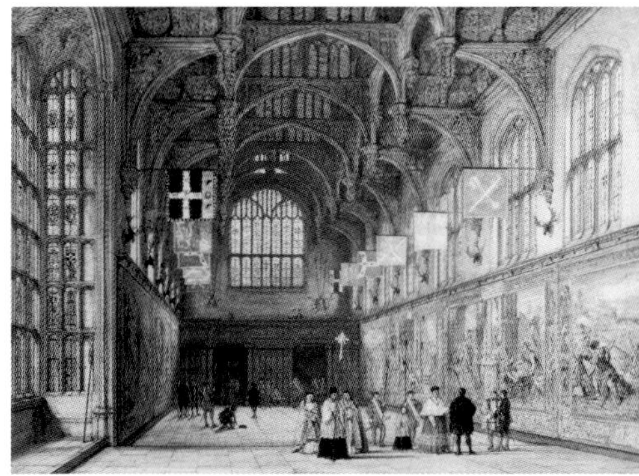
D.1913.7

The Great Hall, Hampton Court, with Cardinal Wolsey greeting the French Ambassadors
pencil, pen and brown ink, watercolour, bodycolour
475 × 652 mm
Palser, J. and Son, London (purchase, 1913) (D.1913.7)

■ NASMYTH, PATRICK (1787–1831)
Patrick Nasmyth, eldest son of the Scottish painter Alexander, exhibited in Edinburgh from 1808 to 1814 and at the Royal Academy between 1811 and 1830. He was much influenced by Dutch seventeenth-century painting.

View across Fields
1812 or 1817
pen and brown ink, watercolour
signed & dated lower left with initials: *P.N / 1812* [or7]
147 × 187 mm
untraced (purchase, 1916) (D.1916.6)

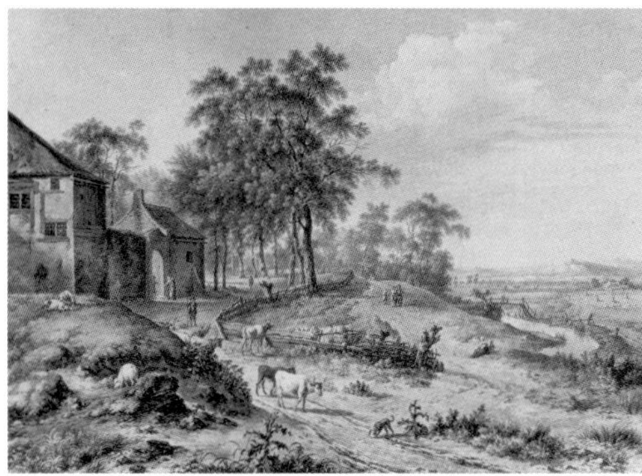

D.1935.1

A Dutch Farm
pen and grey ink, watercolour
signed lower right: *Patk.Nasmyth*
255 × 349 mm
Goldschmidt, R. F. (gift, 1935) (D.1935.1)

■ NATTES, JOHN CLAUDE (ca. 1765–1822)
Nattes, a draughtsman and drawing master, exhibited
European and British views at the Royal Academy
between 1781 and 1814. He was a founder member of
the Old Watercolour Society in 1804 but was expelled
after two years for trying to take a larger share of the
profits by exhibiting other people's drawings under
his own name.

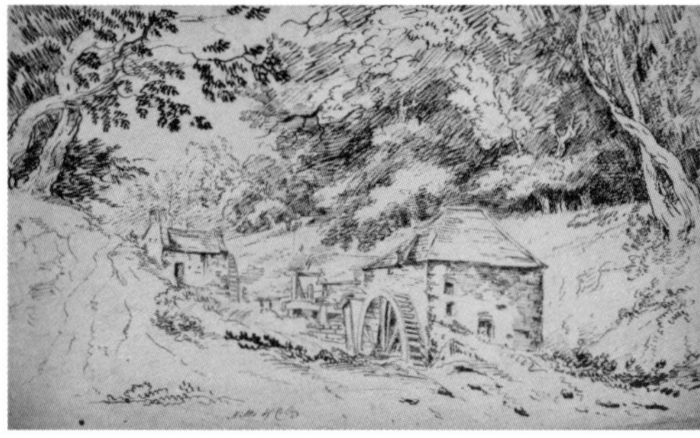

D.1926.135

Two undershot Mills in a wooded Landscape (recto); Landscape Study (verso)
pencil, pen and brown ink
signed on roof of nearer mill: *Nate*; inscribed lower
centre: *Mills of Colvy* (?) [last word hard to read]
292 × 474 mm
Ogden, William Sharp (bequest, 1926) (D.1926.135)

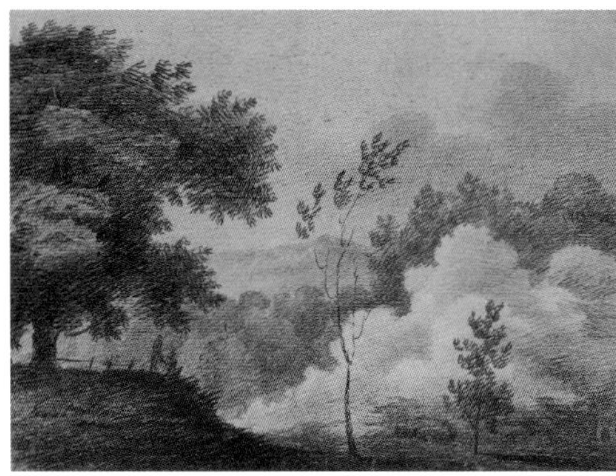

D.1926.136

Burning Furze in Devon
1788
pencil
signed & dated lower right on inner decorative mount:
Nattes delt.1788; dated lower right on outer mount:
incorrect(?): *1785*; inscribed lower centre on inner
decorative mount: *View in Devonshire, with the
Burning of the Furze*
187 × 247 mm
Ogden, William Sharp (bequest, 1926) (D.1926.136)

■ NICHOLL, ANDREW (1804–86)
Born in Belfast, Nicholl was a self-taught artist who
began his career painting solid but slightly naive views
of the Antrim coast. He later turned to Irish coastal
views seen through a bank of wild flowers, a daring
combination of landscape and still life. Nicholl
exhibited intermittently at the Royal Academy between
1832 and 1854. He spent some years in Ceylon as
drawing master at the Colombo Academy from 1846
and was elected a member of the Royal Hibernian
Academy in 1860.

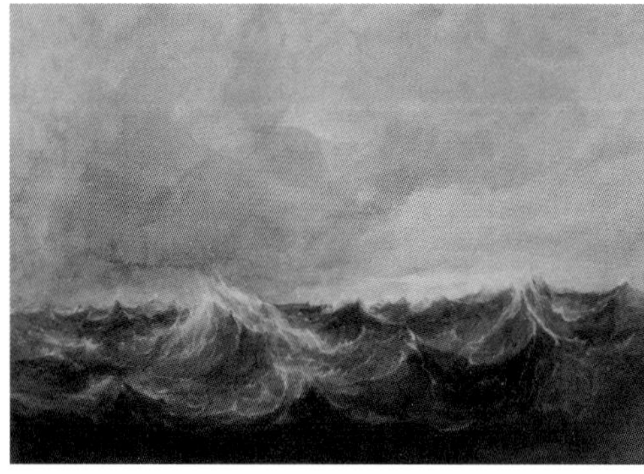

D.1987.7

A Squall in the Indian Ocean
24.7.1849
watercolour
dated lower centre verso: *July 24, 1849*
258 × 361 mm
Spink and Son Ltd (purchase, 1987) (D.1987.7)

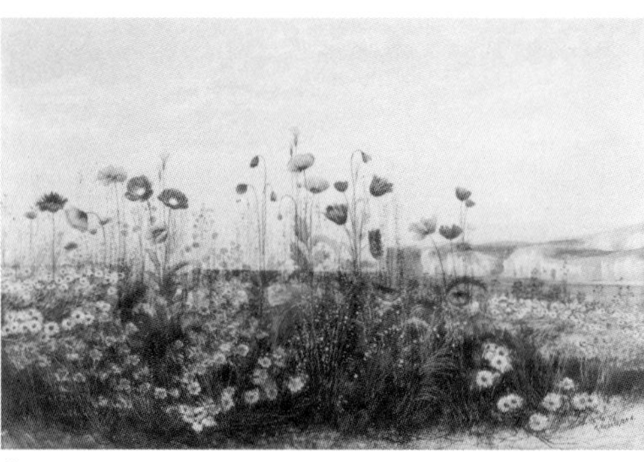

D.1995.19

Poppies and wild Flowers on the Northern Irish Coastline, with Dunluce Castle beyond
pencil, pen and brown ink, watercolour
signed lower right: *A.Nicholl, RHA.*
360 × 535 mm
Christie's (purchase, 7.11.1995) (F.O.W.) (D.1995.19)

■ NICHOLSON, FRANCIS (1753–1844)
Nicholson based himself in various Yorkshire towns,
painting portraits and local views until he moved
permanently to London in 1803. He exhibited
Yorkshire views intermittently at the Royal Academy
between 1789 and 1803 and was the oldest founder
member of the Old Watercolour Society in 1804.
Nicholson had a flourishing practice as a drawing
master and at least two of his daughters painted,
in a style similar to his own.

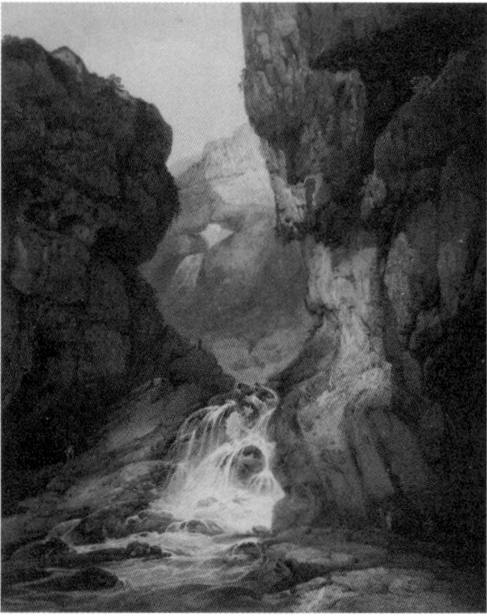

D.1892.23

The Falls, Gordale Scar, Yorkshire
pencil, watercolour
signed & dated verso: *Gordale, Yorkshire / F Nicholson*
601 × 477 mm
Taylor, John Edward (gift, 1892) (D.1892.23)

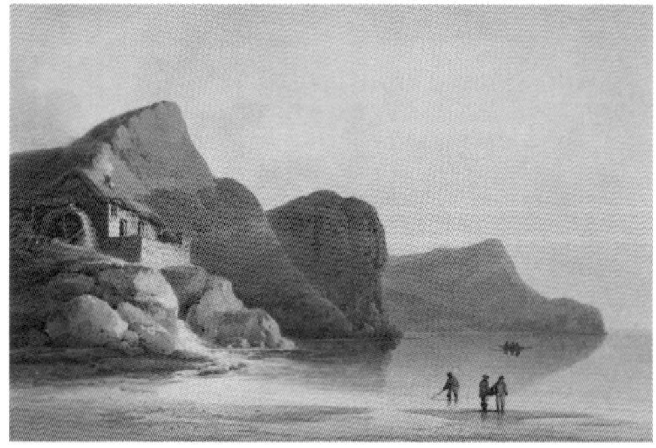

D.1893.4

Mill on the Coast, near Scarborough, Yorkshire
watercolour
294 × 428 mm
Agnew's (purchase, 18.12.1893) (D.1893.4)

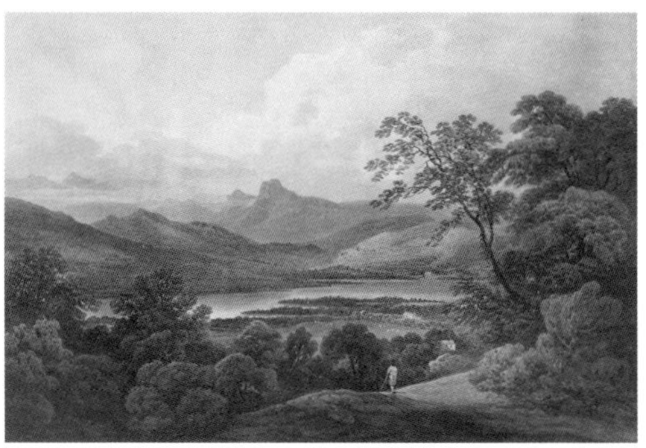

D.1908.2

**Windermere and the Langdale
Pikes, Westmorland**
pencil, watercolour
385 × 535 mm
Palser, J. and Son, London (purchase, 1908) (D.1908.2)

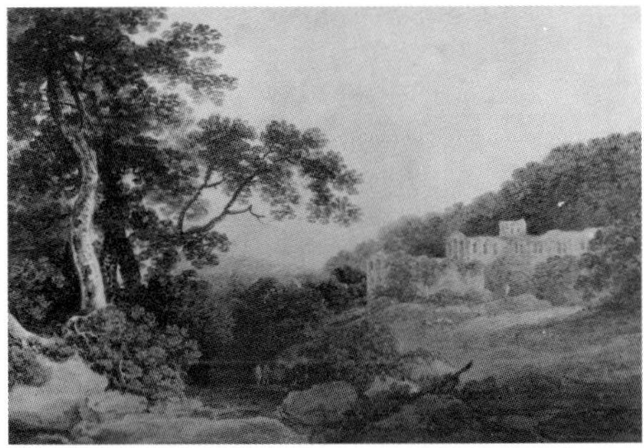

D.1970.58

Rievaulx Abbey, Yorkshire, seen from the River
pencil, watercolour
290 × 248 mm
Towlson, Hector J. (bequest, 1969) (D.1970.58)

■ NICHOLSON, FRANCIS (circle of)

View on the Avon, Clifton, Bristol
watercolour
245 × 347 mm
Towlson, Hector J. (bequest, 1969) (D.1970.12)

■ NIEMANN, EDMUND JOHN (1813–76)
A landscape painter in oil and watercolour,
Niemann moved from London to High Wycombe
in 1839. He exhibited at the Royal Academy between
1844 and 1872.

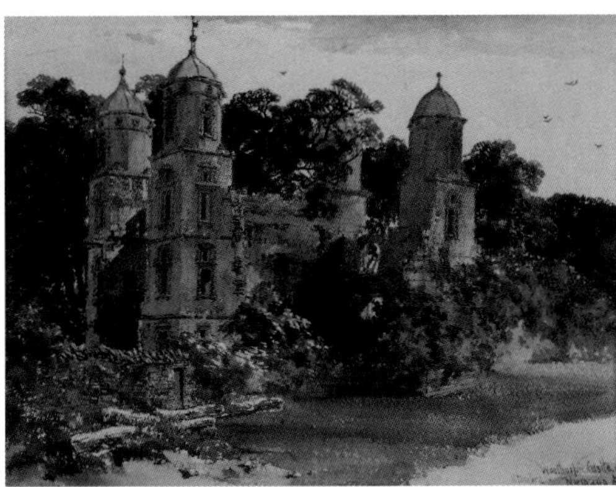

D.1894.5

Wothorpe Castle, Northamptonshire
1851
pencil, watercolour, bodycolour
(heightened with white)
signed, inscribed & dated lower right: *Woothorpe
Castle.nr Burleigh / Stamford Niemann 51*
362 × 478 mm
Lees, Charles E. (gift, 1894) (D.1894.5)

Streatley Mill, Goring, Berkshire
1850
watercolour, bodycolour; oatmeal paper
signed & dated lower right: *Niemann / 50*
300 × 477 mm
Towlson, Hector J. (bequest, 1969) (D.1970.59)

■ NINHAM, HENRY (1793–1874)
Born in Norwich, the son of a heraldic painter and
engraver, Ninham exhibited at the Norwich Society
between 1816 and 1831, specialising in architectural
views of the city in watercolour. He was a friend of
John Sell Cotman.

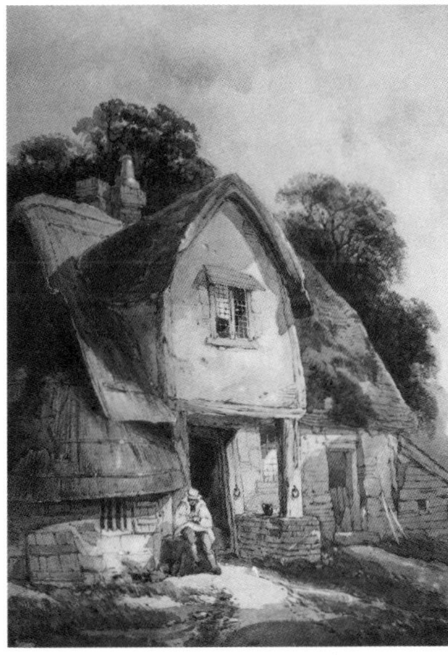

D.1970.60

Old Thatched Cottage
pencil, watercolour, bodycolour (heightened
with white)
419 × 292 mm
Towlson, Hector J. (bequest, 1969) (D.1970.60)

■ NOBLE, RICHARD PRATCHETT
(fl. 1836–60)
Noble was a landscape watercolourist who exhibited at
the Royal Academy between 1836 and 1860 from
various London addresses. He painted views of North
Wales, Sussex, Surrey and Kent. Noble's watercolours
are often misattributed to other artists.

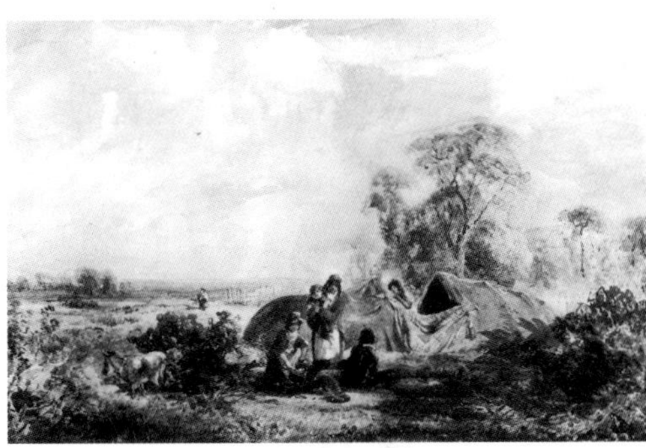

D.1970.42

Gypsy Encampment, Hindhead Common, Surrey
watercolour, bodycolour (heightened with white), gum
arabic, varnish
inscribed lower left: *Hindhead Common Surrey*
263 × 374 mm
Towlson, Hector J. (bequest, 1970) (D.1970.42)

■ NORTH, JOHN WILLIAM (1842–1924)
North began his career as an apprentice in Josiah Wood
Whymper's engraving business, where he worked with
Fred Walker, Charles Green and George Pinwell.
From 1862 to 1866 North worked for the Dalziel
brothers and is one of the most important of the
illustrators of the 1860s. From 1868, he lived in
Somerset. He visited Algiers with Fred Walker in the
winter of 1873–74. North was elected a member of
the Royal Watercolour Society in 1883 and an associate
of the Royal Academy in 1893.

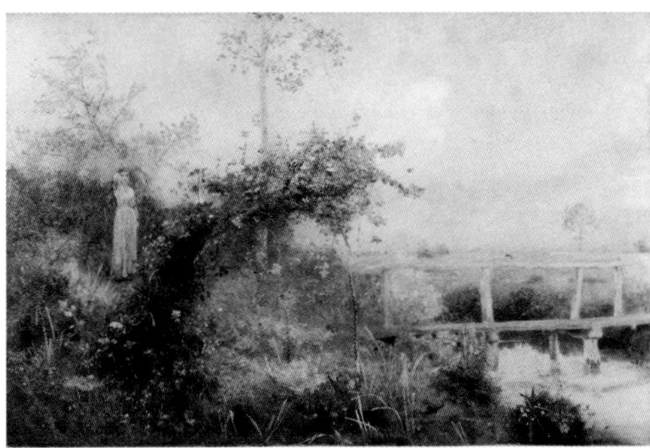

D.1995.13

The Return from the Harvest Field
1880
pencil, watercolour, bodycolour
signed and dated lower left: *J.W.North / 1880*
301 × 447 mm
Kaye Michie Fine Art (purchase, 1995) (V. & A., F.O.W.)
(D.1995.13)

■ OGDEN, WILLIAM SHARP (1844–1926)
A Manchester-based architect, Ogden is said to have
been a descendant of the eighteenth-century engraver
William Sharp. In 1926 he bequeathed to the
Whitworth a large quantity of prints and mostly
unattributed drawings and watercolours.

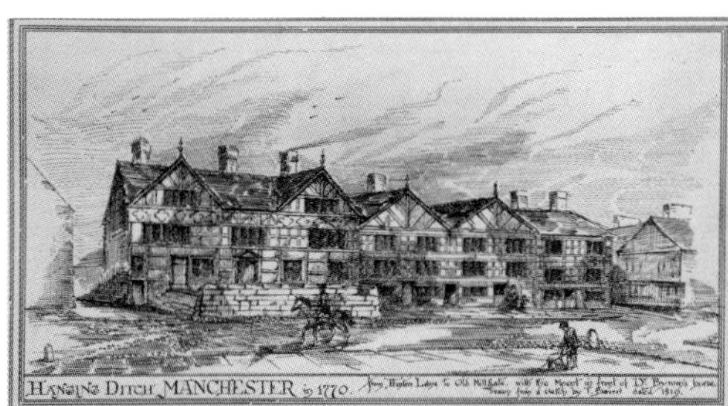

D.1926.279

Hanging Ditch, Manchester, in 1770
pen and black ink
inscribed along lower edge: *HANGING DITCH
MANCHESTER in 1770. from Hunters Lane to Old
Millgate. with the Mount in front of Dr.Byrom's house. /
drawn from a sketch by T.Barret* (sic) *dated 1819.*
306 × 508 mm
Ogden, William Sharp (bequest, 1926) (D.1926.279)

■ OLIVER, WILLIAM (1805–53)
Oliver, a landscape watercolourist, was a founder
member of the New Watercolour Society in 1834. He
painted in France, Italy and the Pyrenees and exhibited
English and Continental landscapes at the Royal
Academy between 1835 and 1853.

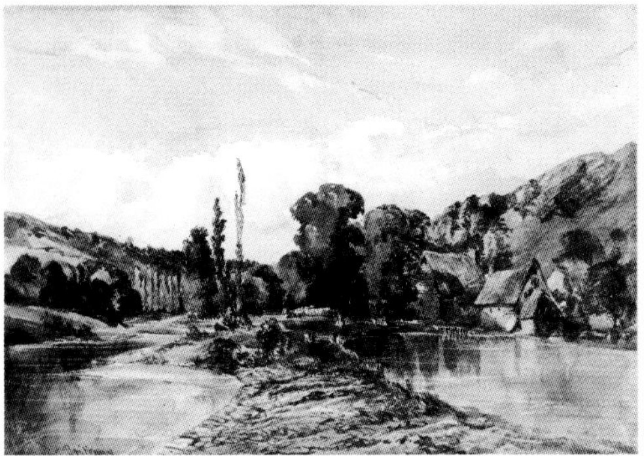

D.1917.18

Mill Stream, Brittany, France
pencil, watercolour
signed lower right: *William Oliver*, inscribed
lower left: *Brittany*
246 × 345 mm
untraced (purchase, 1917) (D.1917.18)

■ O'Neale, Jeffrey Hamet (1734–1801)

O'Neale decorated Chelsea porcelain in the 1750s
before working for Wedgwood.

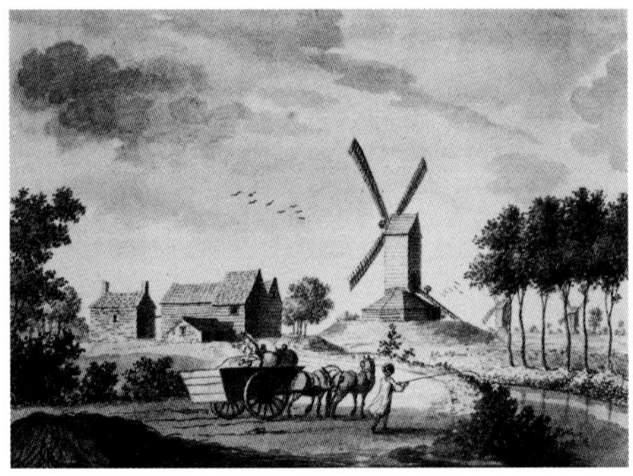

D.1926.287

Windmills at Bow, London
pen and brown ink, brown watercolour
inscribed lower centre in border below image: *taken
from behind ye China House at Bow*
190 × 250 mm
Ogden, William Sharp (bequest, 1926) (D.1926.287)

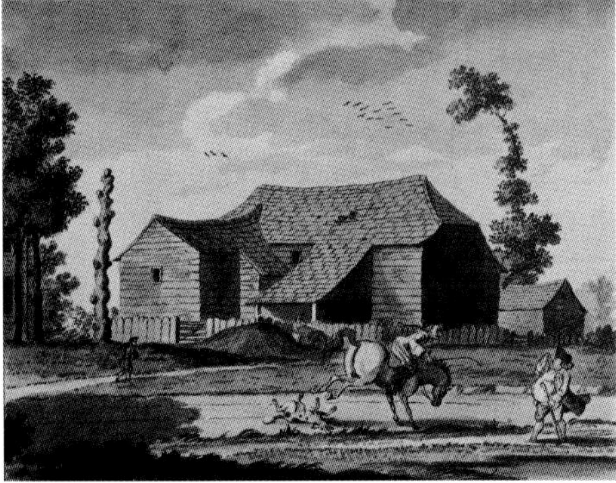

D.1926.288

View on Brixton Causeway, London
pencil, pen and brown ink, brown watercolour
signed lower left in border below image with initials:
O N delin; inscribed lower centre in border below
image: *View on Brixton Causeway*
188 × 224 mm
Ogden, William Sharp (bequest, 1926) (D.1926.288)

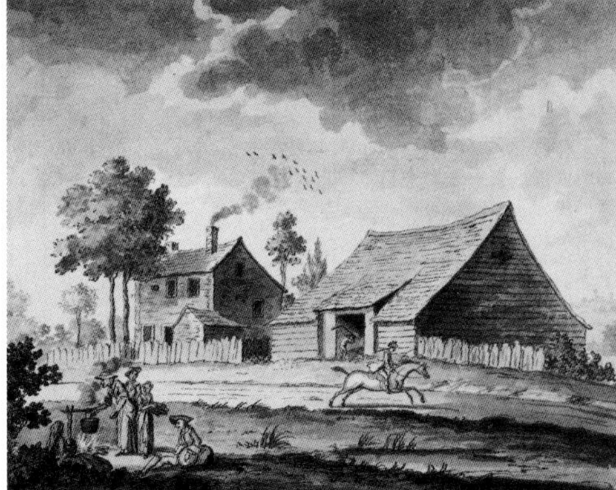

D.1926.289

On the Road to Streatham, London
pencil, pen and brown ink, brown watercolour
signed lower left in border below image: *O Neale delin.*
inscribed lower centre in border below image: *View on
the Hill near the 5 Mile Stone. road to Streatham.*
193 × 240 mm
Ogden, William Sharp (bequest, 1926) (D.1926.289)

■ O'Neill, Hugh (1784–1824)

The son of an architect, O'Neill was an architectural
and topographical draughtsman, specialising in
architectural drawing. He worked as a drawing master
in Oxford, Edinburgh and Bath from 1813 to 1821 and
in Bristol from 1821 to 1824.

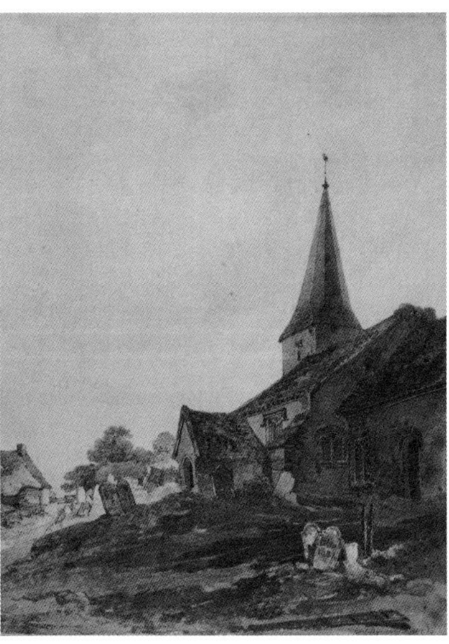

D.1900.6

Mottistone Church, Isle of Wight
1804
pencil, watercolour
signed & dated on tombstone lower right: *H.Neil* (?) /
1804; dated lower right: *1804*
224 × 163 mm
Worthington, Mary (gift, 1900) (D.1900.6)

Carisbrooke Church, Isle of Wight
pencil, watercolour
267 × 198 mm
Ogden, William Sharp (bequest, 1926) (D.1926.134)

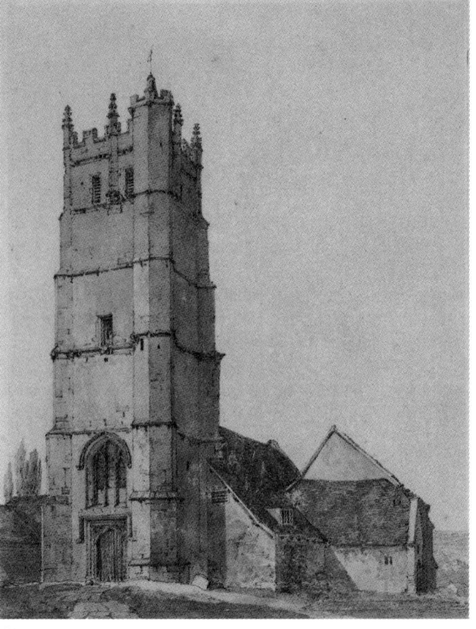

D.1926.134

■ Ospovat, Henry (1877–1909)

Ospovat, an illustrator and caricaturist, was born into a
Jewish family in Russia. He emigrated with his family
to Manchester and studied at Manchester School of
Art. His illustrative style was influenced by the Pre-
Raphaelites and the Birmingham School. Ospovat
illustrated the 1900 edition of Matthew Arnold's *Poems*,
as well as *Shakespeare's Sonnets* in 1899 and *Shakespeare's
Songs* in 1901.

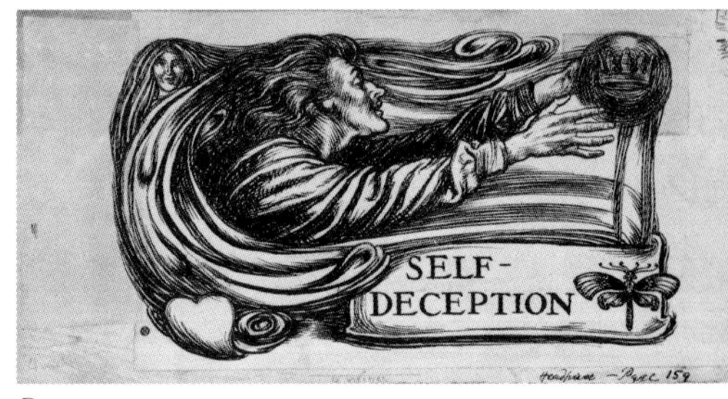

D.1909.1

**Design for the Headpiece to 'Self Deception' for
'Poems by Matthew Arnold'**
1900
pen and black ink
signed lower left with monogram: *H* within an *O*
inscribed lower right within cartouche: *SELF– /
DECEPTION*; inscribed lower right margin: *Headpiece
– Page 159*
116 × 229 mm
Anderson, A. E. (gift, 1909) (D.1909.1)

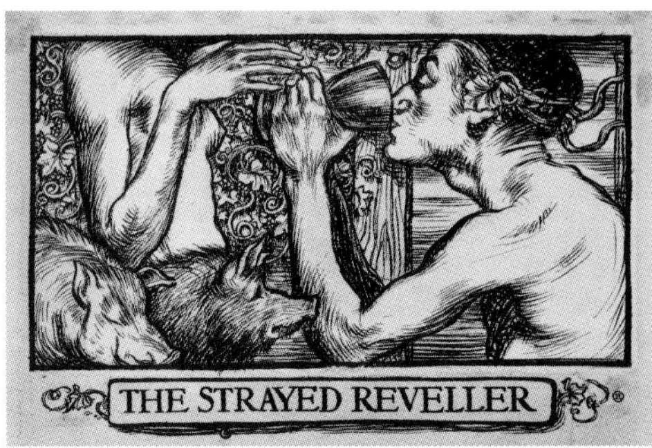

D.1909.2

Design for the Headpiece to 'The strayed Reveller' for 'Poems by Matthew Arnold' (recto); Study of a seated Woman (verso)
1900
pen and black ink
signed lower right with monogram: *H* within an *O*; inscribed lower centre within cartouche: *THE STRAYED REVELLER*
116 × 170 mm
Anderson, A. E. (gift, 1909) (D.1909.2)

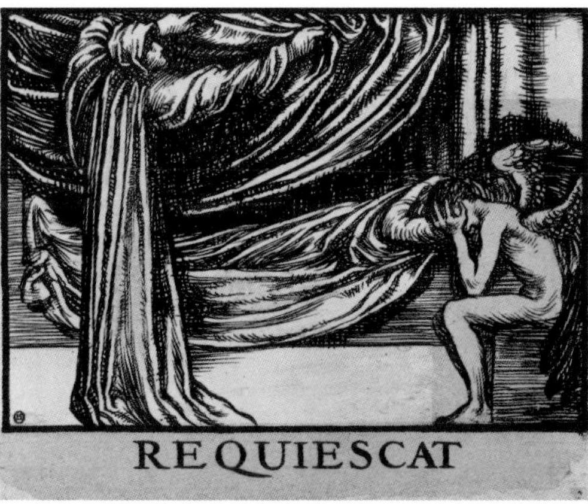

D.1909.3

Design for the Headpiece to 'Requiescat' for 'Poems by Matthew Arnold' (recto); Study of a Pig's Head (verso)
1900
pen and black ink
signed lower left with monogram: *H* within an *O*; inscribed lower centre: *REQUIESCAT*
sheet: 193 × 166 mm
Anderson, A. E. (gift, 1909) (D.1909.3)

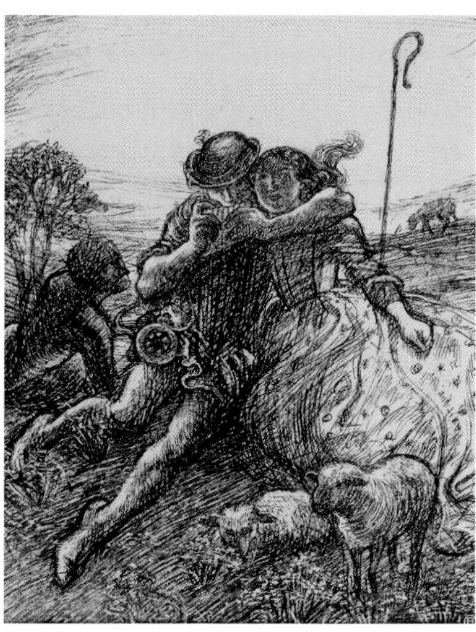

D.1909.4

'Spring' from 'Love's Labours Lost': Illustration to 'Shakespeare's Songs'
1901
pen and black ink, bodycolour (heightened with white)
signed lower right with monogram: *H* within an *O*
208 × 163 mm
Anderson, A. E. (gift, 1909) (D.1909.4)

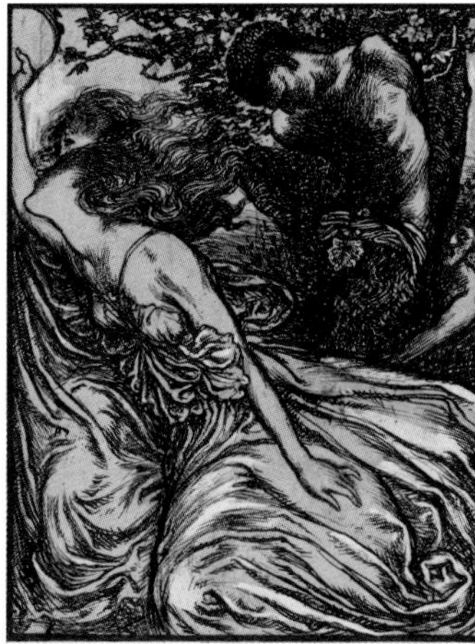

D.1909.5

"Then Apollo's minister hang'd upon a branching fir Marsyas, that unhappy faun": Illustration to 'Empedocles on Etna' for 'Poems by Matthew Arnold'
1900
pen and black ink, bodycolour (heightened with white)
186 × 138 mm
Anderson, A. E. (gift, 1909) (D.1909.5)

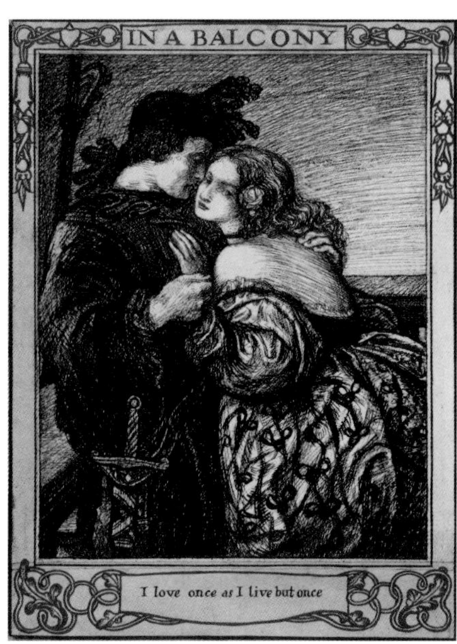

D.1909.6

"I love once as I live but once": Illustration to 'In a Balcony' for Robert Browning's 'Men and Women'
pen and black ink, pen and red ink
inscribed upper centre in decorative border within cartouche: *IN A BALCONY*; inscribed lower centre in decorative border within cartouche: *I love once as I live but once*
362 × 264 mm
Anderson, A. E. (gift, 1909) (D.1909.6)

Design for the Headpiece to 'The Scholar Gipsy' for 'Poems by Matthew Arnold'
1900
pen and ink, bodycolour (heightened with white); card
signed lower right with monogram: *H* within an *O*; inscribed along lower edge: *THE SCHOLAR GIPSY*
sheet: 118 × 152 mm
Anderson, A. E. (gift, 1913) (D.1913.1)

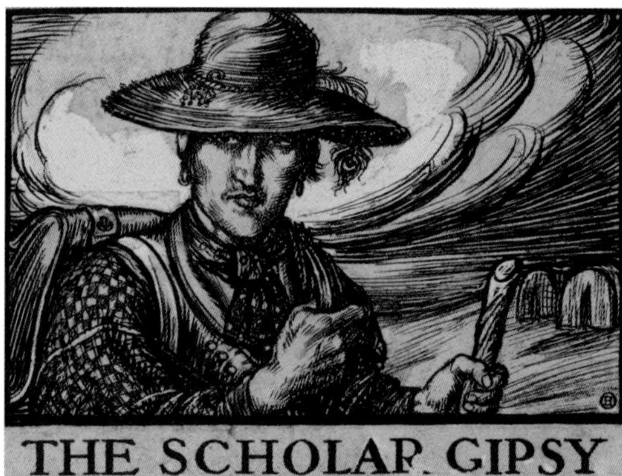

D.1913.1

Alternative Design for the Headpiece to 'The Scholar Gipsy' for 'Poems by Matthew Arnold' (recto); Caricature Studies (verso)
1900
pen and black ink; card
inscribed along lower edge: *THE SCHOLAR GIPSY*; inscribed lower right margin: *Headpiece / page 278*
sheet: 112 × 204 mm
Anderson, A. E. (gift, 1913) (D.1913.2)

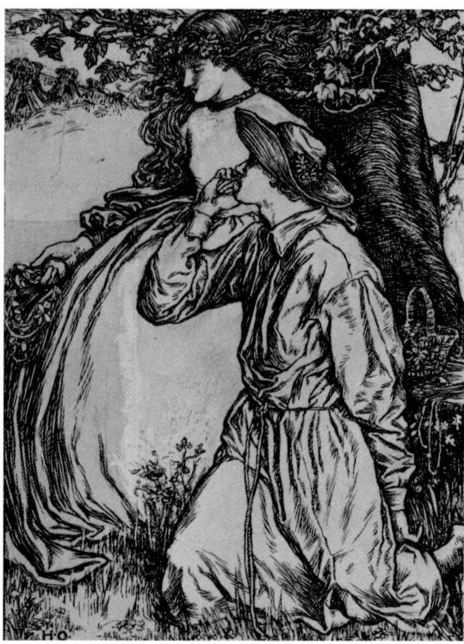

D.1913.3

An Illustration to Shakespeare's 'Sonnet XCI', for 'Shakespeare's Sonnets'
1899
pen and black ink, bodycolour (heightened with white); card
signed lower left with initials: *H.O.*; inscribed upper centre verso: *Illustration to / Sonnet XCI* [underlined] / *(All these I better in one general / best.) / Some glory in their birth, &c.*
sheet: 184 × 137 mm
Anderson, A. E. (gift, 1913) (D.1913.3)

Design for the Headpiece to 'Tristram and Iseult' for 'Poems by Matthew Arnold'
1900
pen and black ink, bodycolour (heightened with white)
signed lower centre with monogram: *H* within an *O*
inscribed across centre of image: *TRISTRAM / and ISEULT*
sheet: 162 × 201 mm
Anderson, A. E. (gift, 1913) (D.1913.4)

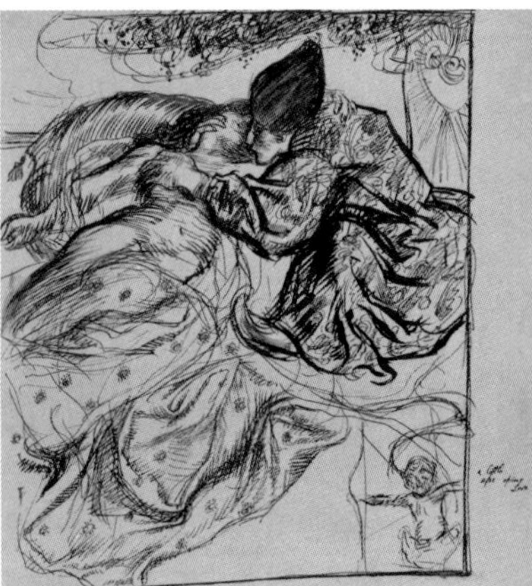

D.1913.5

**Study for 'An Eastern Tale' (recto);
Study of a Figure (verso)**
1900
pencil, pen and black ink
inscribed lower right margin: *a little / ape aping / Love*
sheet: 290 × 199 mm
Baillie Gallery, London (purchase, 1913) (D.1913.5)

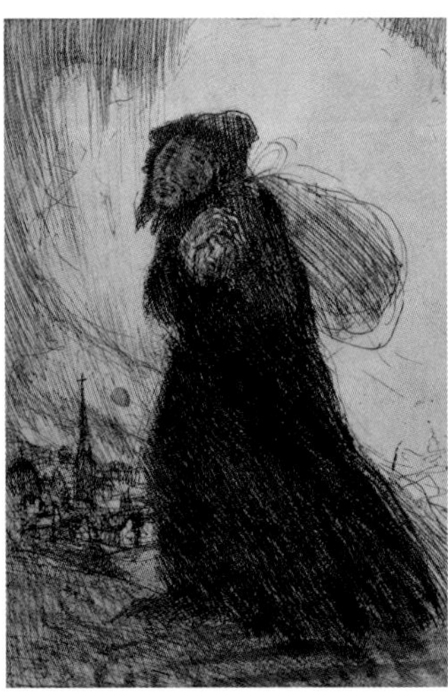

D.1913.6

**The Wandering Jew (recto);
Study of a Man's Head (verso)**
pen and black ink, grey watercolour
253 × 176 mm
Baillie Gallery, London (purchase, 1913) (D.1913.6)

**"One day the lady saw her youth depart":
Illustration to 'The Statue and the Bust' for
Robert Browning's 'Men and Women'**
pen and black ink
inscribed upper centre in decorative border: *THE
STATUE AND THE BUST*; inscribed lower centre
within decorative border: *one day the lady saw / her
youth depart*
sheet: 362 × 266 mm
Anderson, A. E. (gift, 1918) (D.1918.1)

Self Caricature
pen and black ink, black chalk, brush and black ink
signed lower right with monogram: *HO*; inscribed
lower right after monogram: *goes to the R.A. / to see the
old Masters & takes his dinner with him / to keep his
courage up*
354 × 253 mm
Anderson, A. E. (gift, 1921) (D.1921.5)

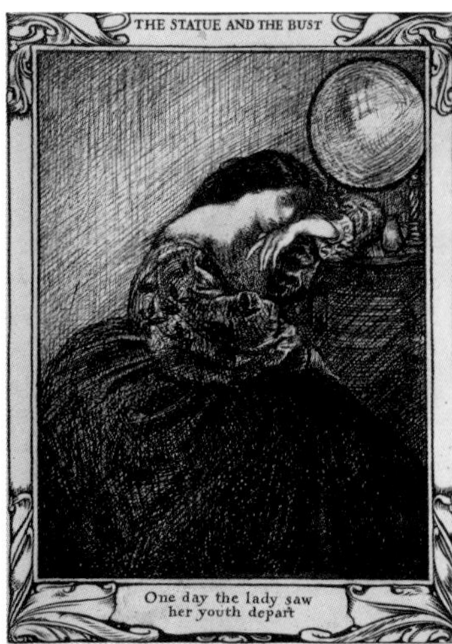

D.1918.1

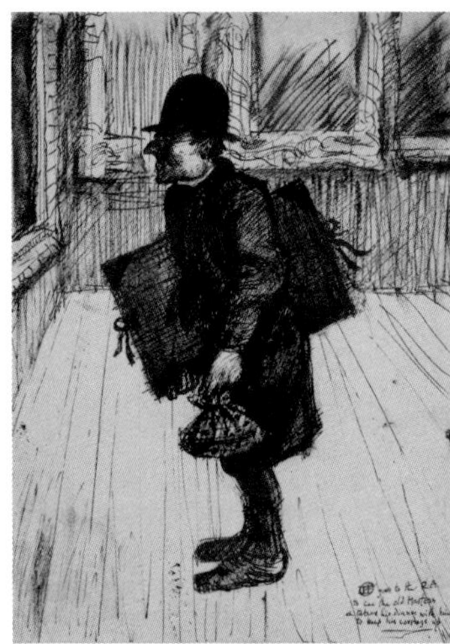

D.1921.5

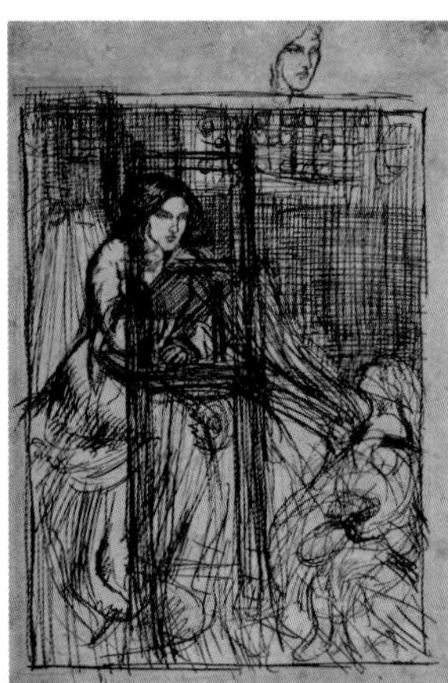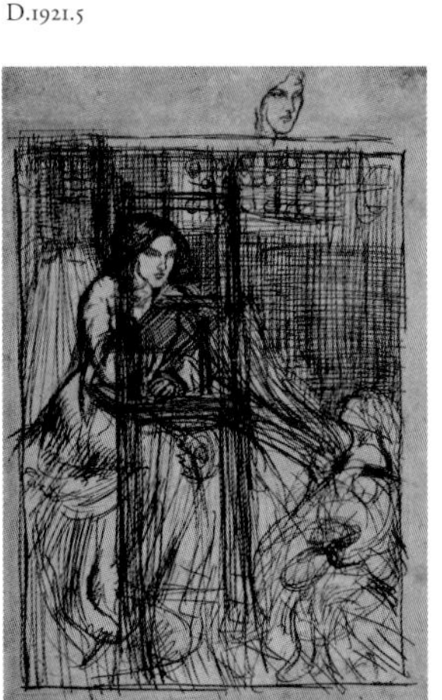

D.1921.8

**"There she weaves by night and day a magic web
with colours gay": Sketch for an Illustration to
Tennyson's 'The Lady of Shallott'**
pencil, pen and black ink
304 × 236 mm
Anderson, A. E. (gift, 1921) (D.1921.8)

**A seated Man and Woman kissing: Study for an
Illustration (recto); Study of Heads (verso)**
pencil, pen and black ink; card
225 × 171 mm
Anderson, A. E. (gift, 1921) (D.1921.9)

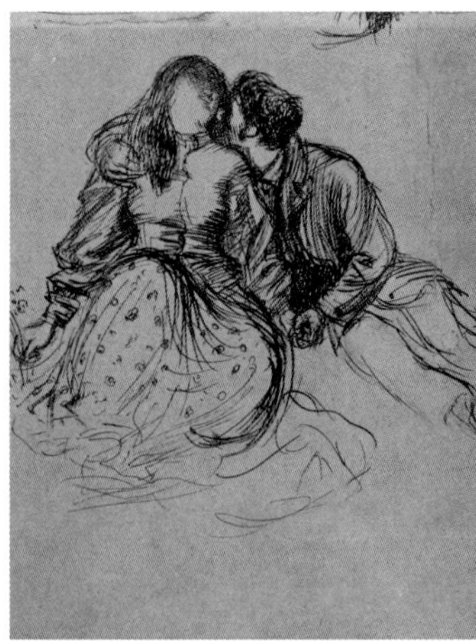

D.1921.9

■ **OWEN, SAMUEL (1768–1857)**
Samuel Owen, a prolific marine and coastal
painter, exhibited at the Royal Academy between
1794 and 1807.

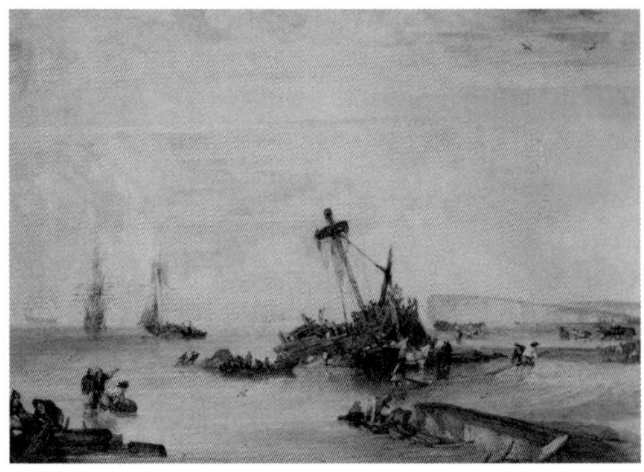

D.1892.50

Wreck off Seaford, Sussex
1829
watercolour
signed & dated on piece of wood lower right:
S.OWEN.29; inscribed lower right verso: *Near Beachy
Head / Sussex.*
194 × 264 mm
Taylor, John Edward (gift, 1892) (D.1892.50)

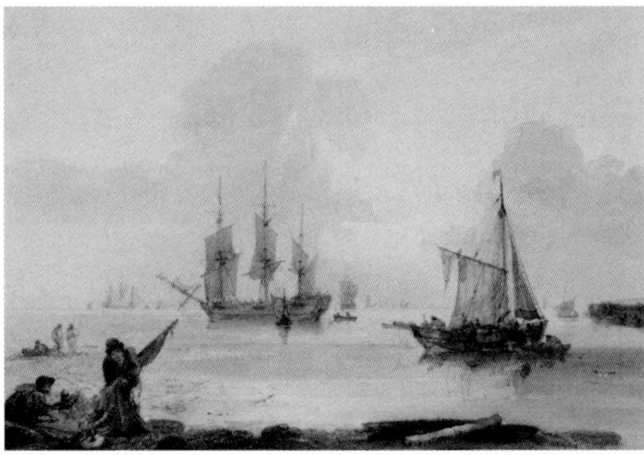

D.1892.51

Shipping at the Mouth of a River
1809
pencil, watercolour
signed & dated on a piece of wood lower right:
S.OWEN 1809.
231 × 331 mm
Taylor, John Edward (gift, 1892) (D.1892.51)

■ Owen, William (1769–1825)

William Owen, a painter of portraits and sentimental rustic subjects, exhibited at the Royal Academy between 1792 and 1824. He was elected a member of the Royal Academy in 1806 and became Principal Painter to the Prince Regent in 1813.

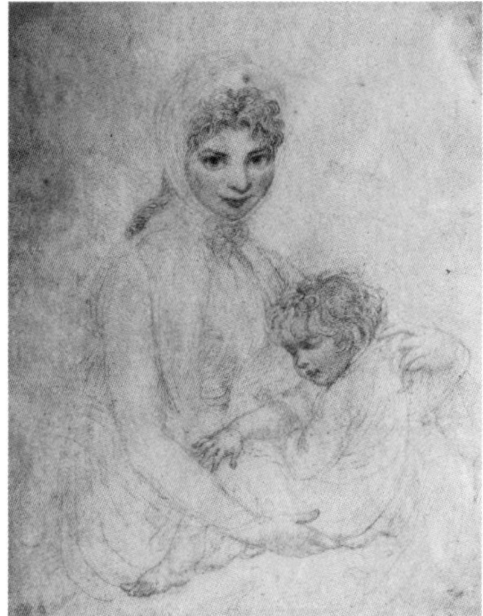

D.1931.9

Mother and Child
pencil, coloured chalk; watermark JWHATMAN
248 × 190 mm
Anderson, A. E. (gift, 1931) (D.1931.9)

■ Palmer, Harry Sutton (1854–1933)

Harry Sutton Palmer was a landscape painter who worked in a traditional style and exhibited intermittently at the Royal Academy between 1870 and 1904. He worked extensively for the colour plate book publishers A. & C. Black and between 1904 and 1922 painted well over 300 watercolours for their various publications. He was elected a member of the Royal Institute in 1920.

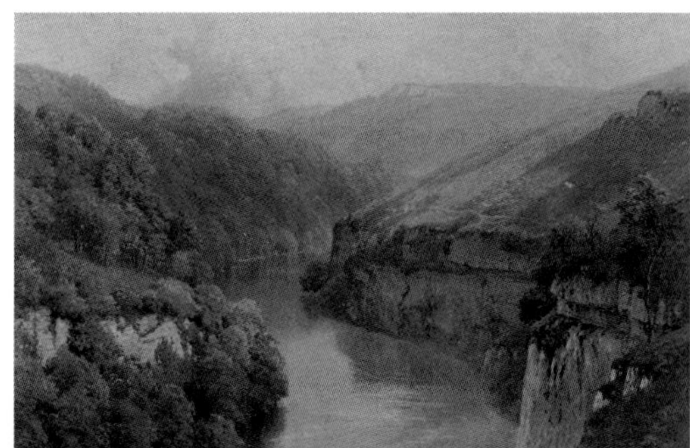

D.1892.150

Between Monsall and Miller's Dales, Derbyshire
watercolour
signed lower left: *Sutton Palmer*
355 × 530 mm
untraced (purchase, 1892) (D.1892.150)

Chee Tor, Cheedale, Derbyshire
watercolour, bodycolour (heightened with white)
signed lower left: *Sutton Palmer*
358 × 531 mm
untraced (purchase, 1892) (D.1892.151)

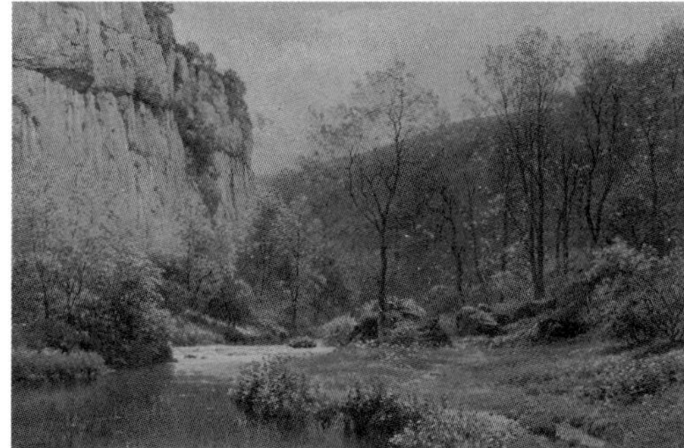

D.1892.151

■ Palmer, Samuel (1805–81)

Samuel Palmer first exhibited at the Royal Academy in 1819 and in 1824 was introduced by John Linnell to William Blake, who exercised a strong influence over the young artist. Between 1827 and 1835, Palmer lived at Shoreham and painted highly intense rural subjects, which have exercised a huge influence on twentieth-century landscape. In 1837, he married Linnell's daughter Hannah and spent 1837–39 in Italy. His early work from the Shoreham period contrasts strongly with his highly worked later exhibition pieces. Palmer was elected a member of the Old Watercolour Society in 1854.

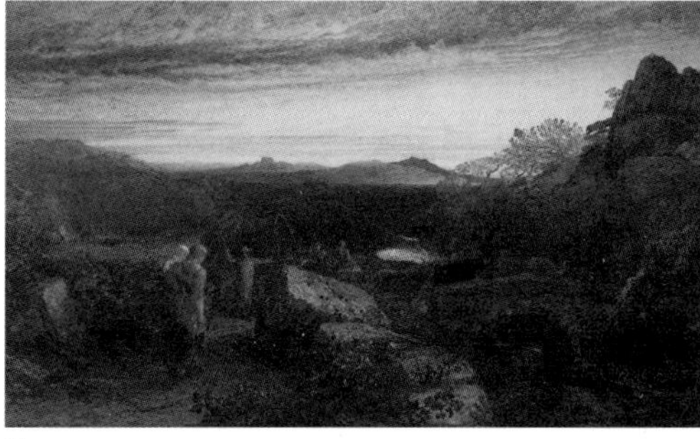

D.1905.2

The Travellers
1875
pencil, pen and brown ink, watercolour, bodycolour, gum arabic
signed lower left: *S.PALMER*
268 × 444 mm
Ward, William (purchase, 1905 (reported to the Picture Purchase Sub Committee on 28.11.1905) (D.1905.2)

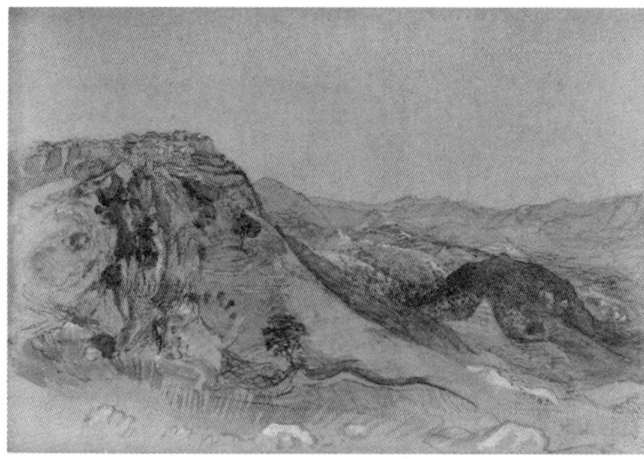

D.1929.1

Civitella, near Subiaco, Italy (recto); Two Figures in a Landscape (verso)
6.1839
pencil, black chalk, watercolour, bodycolour (heightened with white) (recto); buff paper
294 × 425 mm
Christie's, London (purchase, 4.3.1929) (D.1929.1)

The Sailor's Return
1859
pencil, watercolour, bodycolour (heightened with white)
205 × 441 mm
Anderson, A. E. (gift, 1931) (D.1931.10)

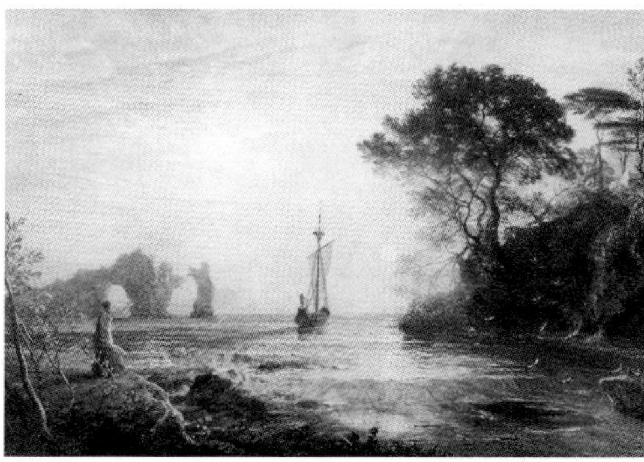

D.1937.17

Calypso's Island, Departure of Ulysses, or Farewell to Calypso
1848-49
watercolour, bodycolour
528 × 744 mm
Haworth, Jesse (bequest, 1937) (D.1937.17)

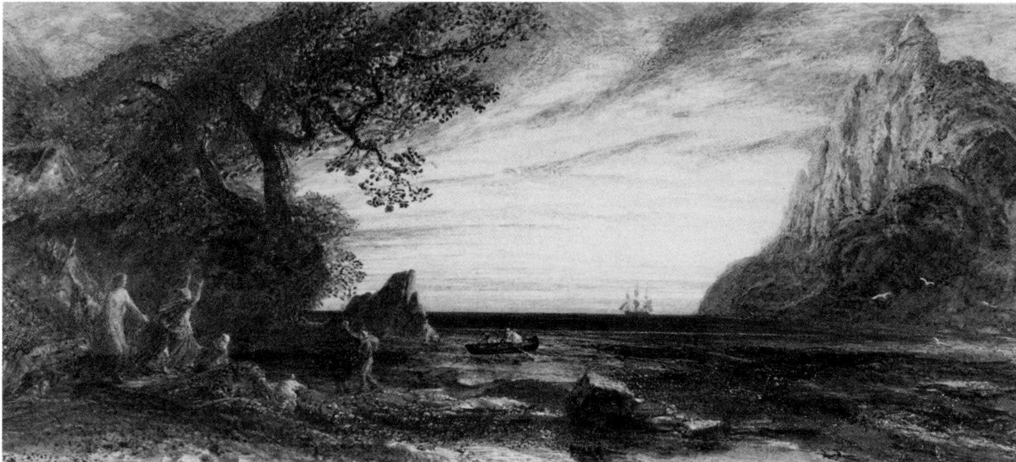

D.1931.10

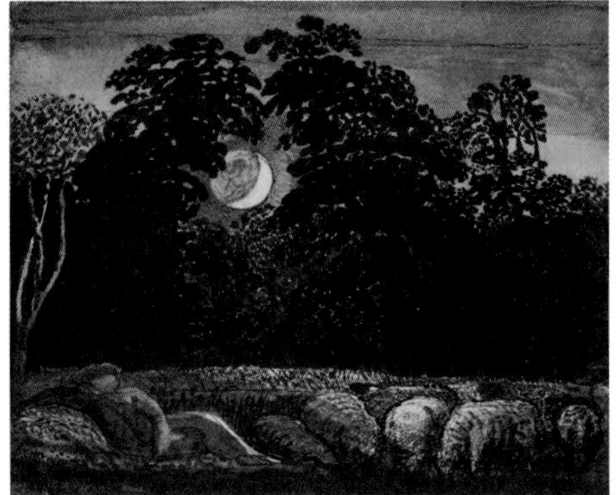

D.1954.2

The sleeping Shepherd
1826–32
pen and brown ink, brown watercolour
157 × 188 mm
Friends of the Whitworth (gift, 1954) (N.A.C.F.) (D.1954.2)

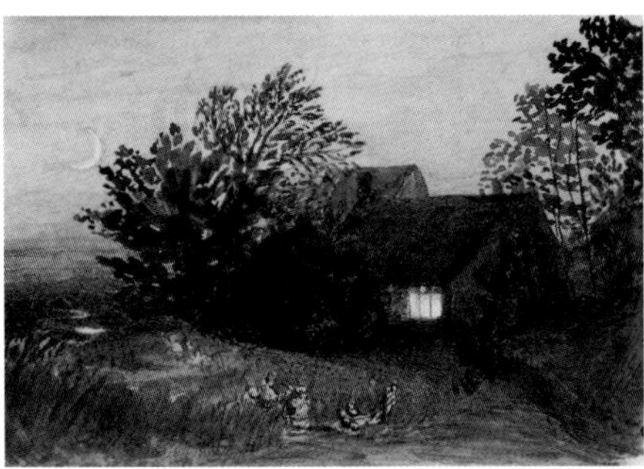

D.1984.3

The Cottager's Return
pencil, watercolour; card
inscribed centre verso in Carl Winter's hand: *S.Palmer*
"The Cottager's Return". / This watercolour was given by
Sir Thomas Barlow, Bt., / to his sister Annie, c.1930–36,
and after her / death at "Greenings", Edgworth, Bolton,
Lancs, in / June 1941, was given by her nephew, Sir T.D.
Barlow, / to his daughter Theodora and her husband Carl
/ Winter, The Vicarage, Wendover, Bucks. C.W.
161 × 209 mm
Winter, Theodora (in memory of her father, Sir Thomas
Barlow) (gift, 1984) (D.1984.3)

■ **Pars, William** (1742–82)
Pars studied at Shipley's drawing school and at the
St Martin's Lane Academy. He was selected by the
Society of Dilletanti to accompany Sir Richard
Chandler and Nicholas Revett to Greece and Asia
Minor, a journey from which he returned in 1766.
He visited Switzerland in 1770. Pars visited Italy in
1775, again funded by the Society of Dilletanti.
He became a close friend of Thomas Jones (he is
frequently mentioned in Jones's *Memoirs*).

The Campo Vaccino, Rome
pencil, watercolour
373 × 552 mm
Taylor, John Edward (gift, 1892) (D.1892.12)

Roman Monument at Igel, Luxemburg
1770–71
pencil, pen and brown ink, watercolour, bodycolour
(heightened with white)
338 × 493 mm
Taylor, John Edward (gift, 1892) (D.1892.13)

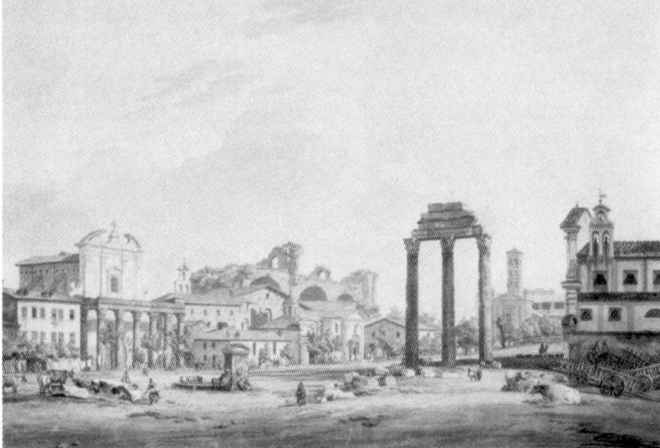

D.1892.12

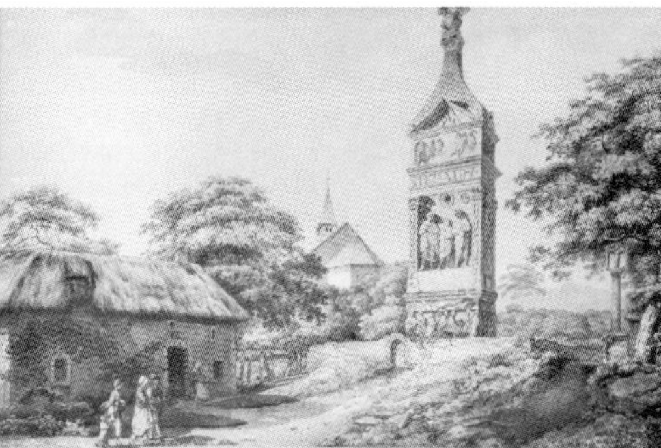

D.1892.13

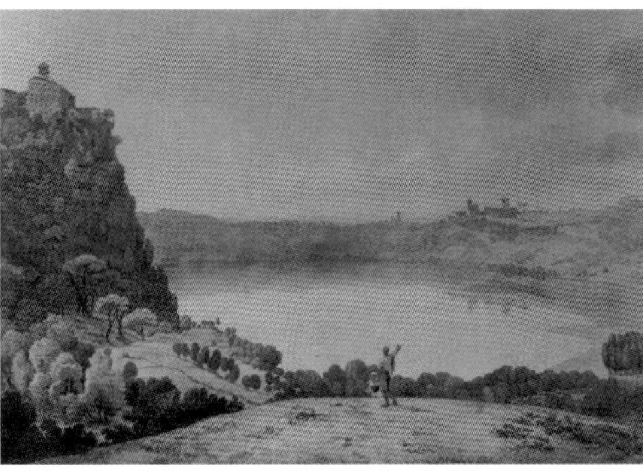

D.1892.142

Lake Nemi, Italy
pencil, watercolour
396 × 570 mm
Taylor, John Edward (gift, 1892) (D.1892.142)

■ **Parsons, Alfred William**
(1847–1920)
Parsons began his career as a Post Office Clerk
before studying at the South Kensington Schools.
He was a member of the Institute of Painters in
Watercolours from 1882 to 1898 but defected to the
Royal Watercolour Society, of which he was elected a
member in 1905 and President in 1913. He visited Japan
in 1892, where his work was exhibited at the Tokyo
School of Fine Arts and exercised an influence on a
receptive Japanese audience. Parsons was elected a
member of the Royal Academy in 1911.

Bickleigh on the Exe, Devon
pen and brown ink, watercolour, bodycolour
buff paper
signed lower right: *ALFRED PARSONS.*
246 × 350 mm
Coleman, H. C. (bequest, 1949) (D.1949.25)

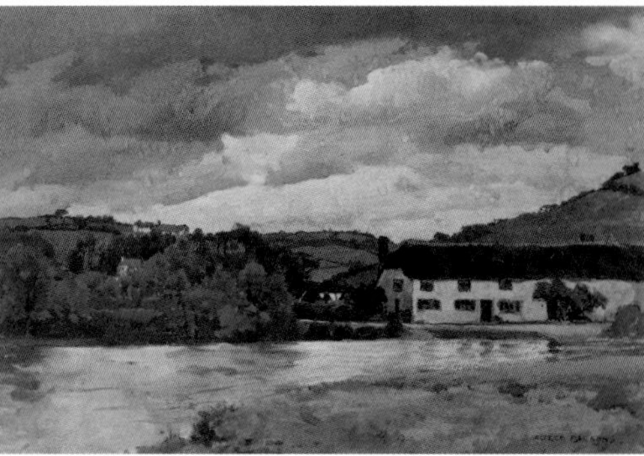

D.1949.25

■ **Pasquier, James Abbott** (fl. 1851–68)
A genre painter, watercolourist and illustrator, Pasquier
worked for various London-based periodicals and
magazines in the 1850s and 1860s.

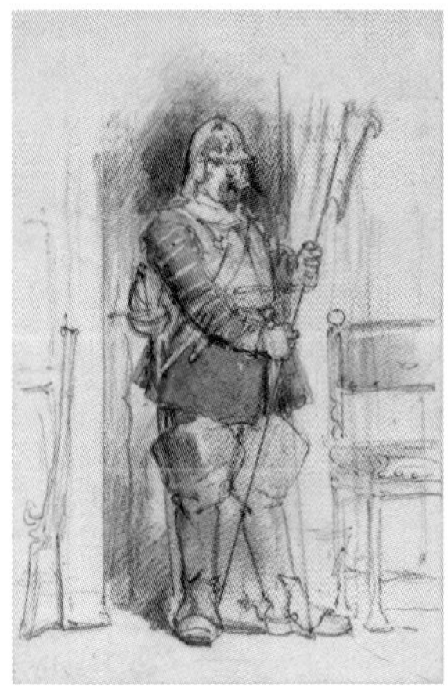

D.1967.4

A Man at Arms in an Interior
pencil, watercolour
166 × 105 mm
Sewter, Albert Charles (gift, 1967) (D.1967.4)

Alpine Scene with Man and Shepherdess
pencil, watercolour
127 × 90 mm
Sewter, Albert Charles (gift, 1967) (D.1967.5)

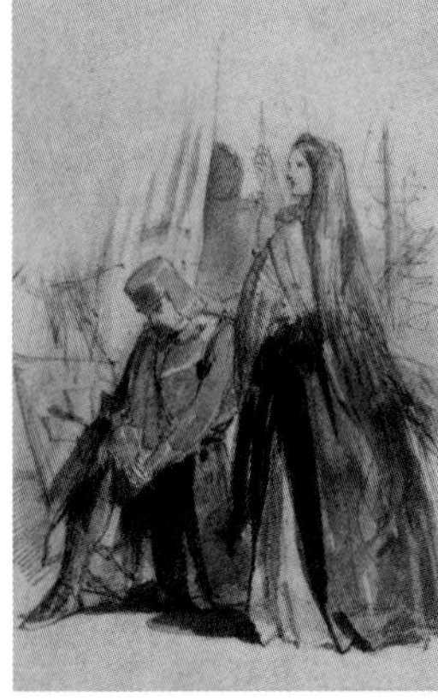

D.1967.6

Soldier and Lady
pencil, watercolour
166 × 105 mm
Sewter, Albert Charles (gift, 1967) (D.1967.6)

Study of a Continental Gatehouse
pencil, watercolour
86 × 22 mm
Sewter, Albert Charles (gift, 1967) (D.1967.7)

■ PATERSON, EMILY MURRAY (1858–1934)

Paterson studied in Edinburgh, where she was born, as well as in London and Paris. She painted landscape and coastal watercolours all over Europe and exhibited Venetian, Swiss and Dutch subjects and flower pieces at the Royal Academy between 1909 and 1934.

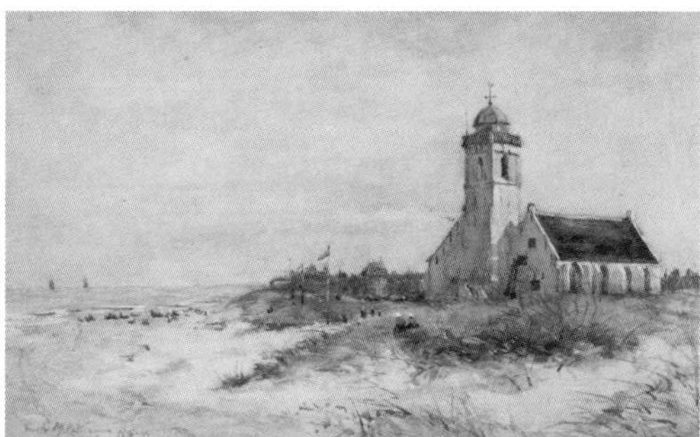

D.1936.6

The Church on the Coast, Katwijk, Holland
1918–20
watercolour, bodycolour (heightened with white)
signed lower left: *Emily M.Paterson R.S.W*
234 × 374 mm
Paterson, Emily Murray (executors and relatives of) (gift, 1936) (D.1936.6)

■ PAYNE, WILLIAM (1760–1830)

Born in London, Payne was appointed in 1778 as a draughtsman on the Board of Ordnance; he worked in the Tower of London, Sheerness and Plymouth. He returned to London in 1790 and became one of the most successful drawing masters of the day, advertising himself as the teacher of a 'system' which bypassed first principles and enabled pupils to produce finished landscapes by a method that was easily taught. Payne invented a pigment which became known as 'Payne's grey'.

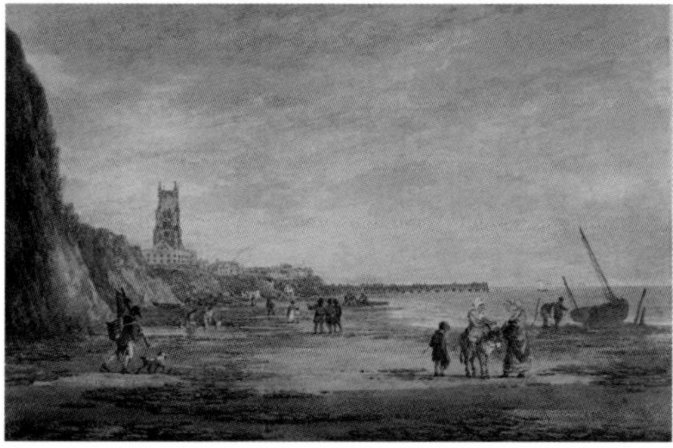

D.1892.55

The Beach at Cromer, Norfolk
1824
pencil, pen and grey ink, watercolour
signed lower left: *W.Payne*; inscribed & dated on verso: *–Cromer– / 1824*
231 × 343 mm
Taylor, John Edward (gift, 1892) (D.1892.55)

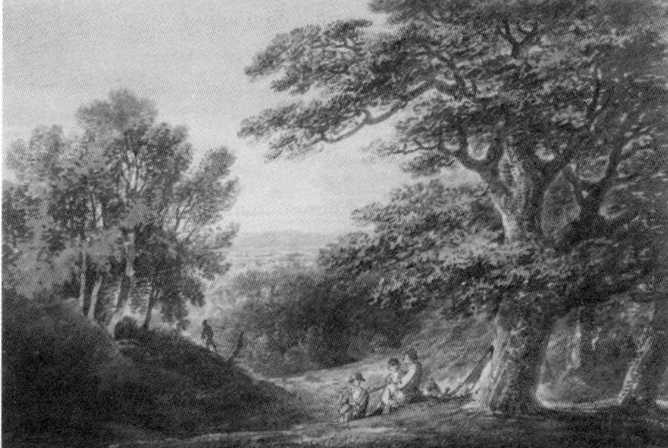

D.1900.16

Landscape in Devon
pen and grey ink, watercolour
signed lower right: *W.Payne*
210 × 305 mm
Worthington, Mary (gift, 1900) (D.1900.16)

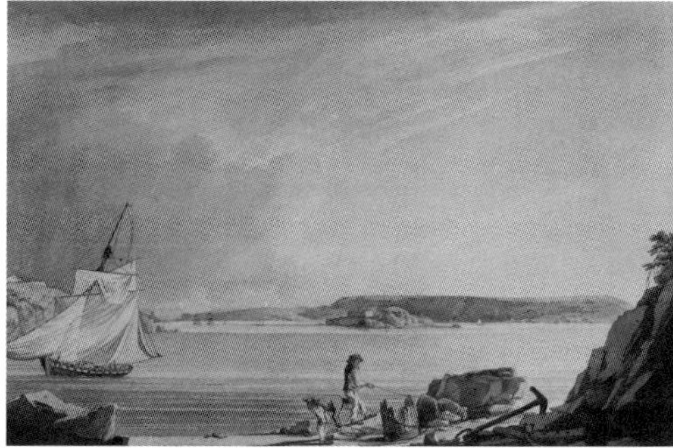

D.1949.6

View from the Battery, Mount Edgecumbe, Devon, looking towards Plymouth
pen and grey ink, watercolour
inscribed lower left (false signature): *J.T.Serres*; inscribed on reverse of backing: *Vie*[w ta] [torn] *ken under the Battery, Mount Edgecumbe, looking into Plymouth Sound – The Ba*[ttery upon] / [Shadon] [cut] *Hill is i* [n t] [torn] *he right hand corner, St. Nicholas or Drakes Island in the center, and to the left ar*[e Mount][cut] [Dalton] [cut] *and the Redout upon Western-King.——J.T. Serres*
268 × 392 mm
Barlow, Sir Thomas (gift, 1949) (D.1949.6)

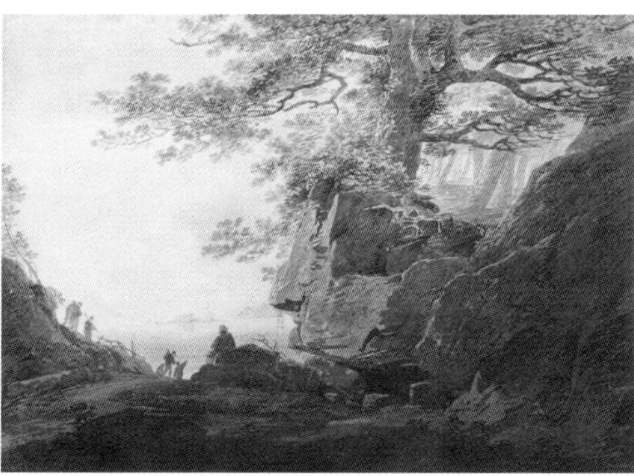

D.1970.61

Coastal View with Rocks and Trees
pen and brown ink, watercolour
signed lower left: *W.Payne*
273 × 381 mm
Towlson, Hector J. (bequest, 1969) (D.1970.61)

■ PEARCE, CHARLES MARESCO (1874–1964)

Educated at Christ Church, Oxford, Pearce was apprenticed to the architect Sir Ernest George. He then studied at Chelsea Art School, in Paris under J. E. Blanche and then with Sickert. He was elected a member of the New English Art Club in 1912.

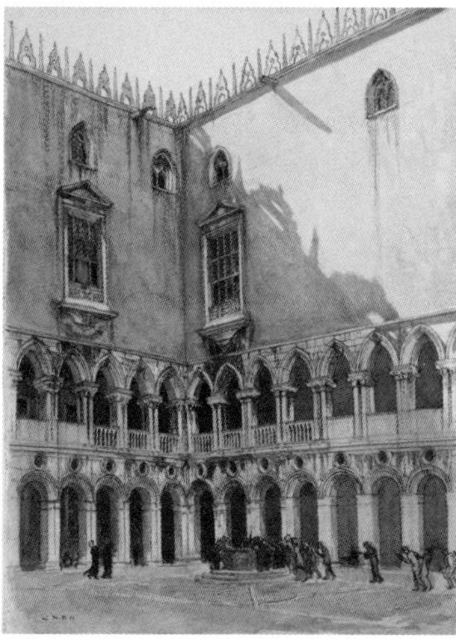

D.1916.8

The Well of Nicolo de Conti, the Courtyard, the Doge's Palace, Venice
1911
pencil, pen and black ink, watercolour, bodycolour (heightened with white)
signed and dated lower left with initials: *C.M.P.11*
426 × 311 mm
untraced (purchase, 1916) (D.1916.8)

■ PEARSON, CORNELIUS (1809–91)

Pearson was a landscape watercolourist who worked all over the British Isles and was an unsuccessful candidate for the New Watercolour Society on several occasions between 1845 and 1865. Pearson sometimes collaborated with Thomas Francis Wainewright, who provided the sheep and cattle in his landscapes.

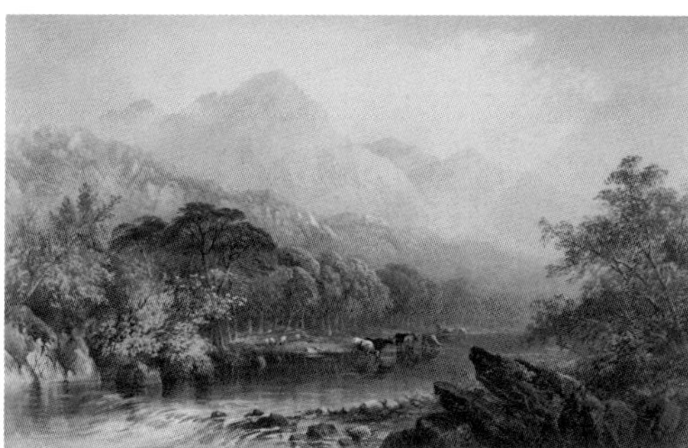

D.1910.7

Loch Katrine, Perthshire/Stirlingshire, Scotland
1859
watercolour
signed & dated on a rock lower left: *C.Pearson / 1859*
606 × 965 mm
Cox, G. F. (bequest, 1910) (D.1910.7)

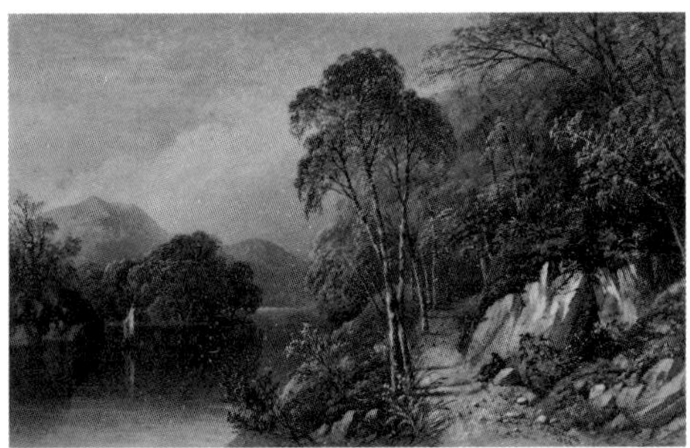

D.1910.15

The Trossachs, Perthshire, Scotland
1858
watercolour, bodycolour
signed & dated lower right: *C.Pearson / 1858.*
329 × 508 mm
Cox, G. F. (bequest, 1910) (D.1910.15)

■ **PEARSON, WILLIAM (1772–1849)**
Pearson was a watercolourist who exhibited landscapes
at the Royal Academy between 1799 and 1804 and was
a close imitator of Girtin.

Church of St Giles, Cripplegate, London
1.3.1810
pen and grey ink, grey watercolour
inscribed centre verso: *Cripplegate Church / London*;
inscribed lower right verso: *Drawn by W.Pearson March
1 1810 / The View in Booth's series of London / Churches
was engraved from this drawing*
169 × 204 mm
Ogden, William Sharp (bequest, 1926) (D.1926.133)

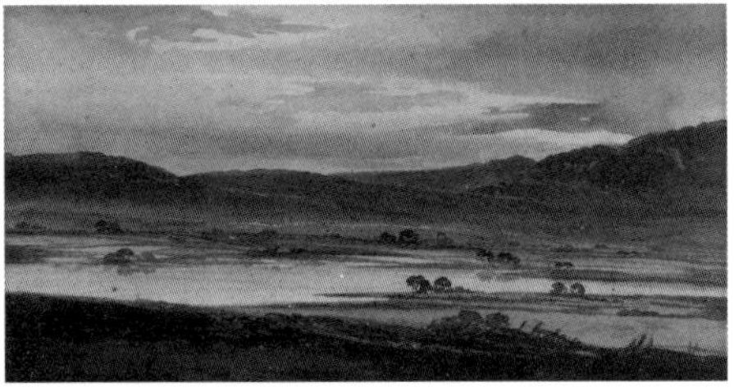

D.1947.56

Landscape with stormy Sky
watercolour
184 × 347 mm
anonymous, Friends of the Whitworth (via) (gift, 1947)
(D.1947.56)

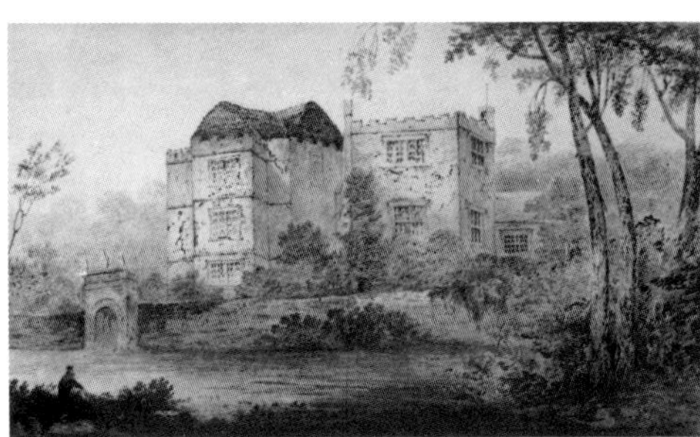

D.1970.62

Heythrop House, Oxfordshire
1803
pencil, watercolour
signed & dated lower left: *W.Pearson.1803*
340 × 579 mm
Towlson, Hector J. (bequest, 1969) (D.1970.62)

■ **PENLEY, AARON EDWIN (1807–70)**
Penley began his career in Manchester and exhibited at
the Royal Academy from 1835. In 1851, he became
Senior Professor of Landscape Drawing at the Royal
Military College at Addiscombe, subsequently moving
to the Royal Military Academy at Woolwich. Penley
published a number of books on the theory and
practice of watercolour painting, which were illustrated
with chromolithographs. These include *A System of
Painting in Watercolours* (1850), *Elements of Perspective*
(1851) and *The English School of Painting in
Watercolours: Its Theory and Practice* (1861).

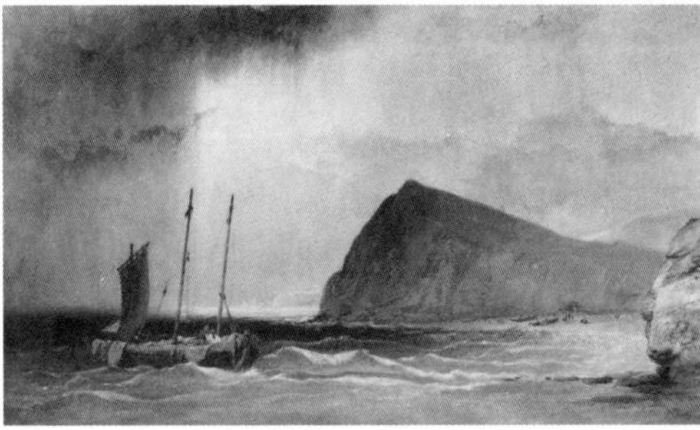

D.1970.63

Shakespeare's Cliff, Dover
1848
pencil, watercolour, bodycolour
(heightened with white)
signed & dated lower right: *APenley 1848.*
310 × 531 mm
Towlson, Hector J. (bequest, 1969) (D.1970.63)

■ **PENN, STEPHEN (fl. 1732–33)**
There is no information on Penn beyond the fact that
four bird's eye landscape watercolours by him appeared
at Colnaghi's in 1941. Three of these were of Coniston
Water and the fourth showed Peel Castle looking south
over Morecambe Bay.

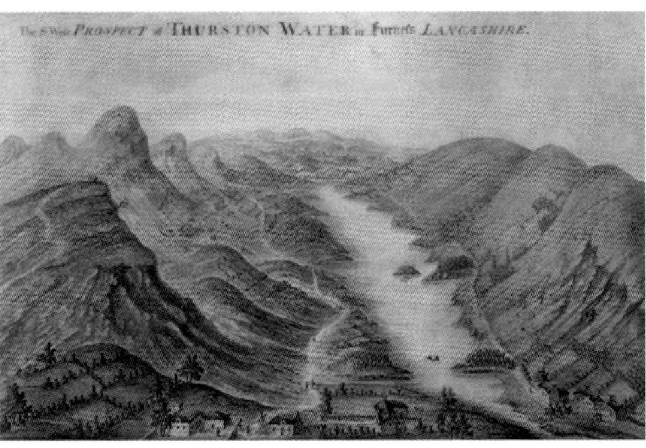

D.1941.9

**South West Prospect of Coniston
Lake, Lancashire**
1732
pen and brown ink, watercolour
signed & dated upper right: *for Stephen Penn 1732*;
inscribed along upper edge: *The S.West PROSPECT of
THURSTON WATER in Furness LANCASHIRE.*
inscribed along lower edge (partially illegible key): *2
Whitepike 3 Dowcraigs.4 Torver Church 5 Snaebe Harvey
hill. 6 Coniston Hall. 7. Water head 8.Peel Island 9
Peelness…..12 Selsed hill. 13. Brookborough hill.14…..*
339 × 496 mm
Friends of the Whitworth (gift, 1941) (D.1941.9)

■ **PEPPERCORN, ARTHUR DOUGLAS
(1847–1926)**
Peppercorn, a landscape painter in oil and watercolour,
studied at the Ecole des Beaux Arts in Paris. He was
strongly influenced by Corot and the Barbizon School.
Peppercorn exhibited at the Royal Academy from 1883.

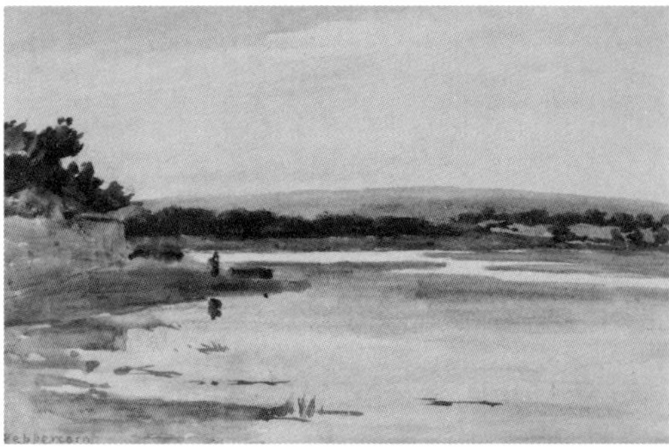

D.1933.27

Yarmouth, Isle of Wight
pencil, watercolour
signed lower left: *Peppercorn*
165 × 248 mm
Anderson, A. E. (gift, 1933) (D.1933.27)

■ **PETERS, REV. MATTHEW WILLIAM
(1741/42–1814)**
Peters studied in Dublin under Robert West and in
London under Thomas Hudson. He visited Italy from
1762 to 1765 and again from 1772 to 1776. He painted
portraits and slightly titillating female figure subjects,
which were popularised through engravings. Peters was
elected a member of the Royal Academy in 1777. He
was ordained in 1781 but continued to paint,
contributing to Boydell's Shakespeare Gallery.

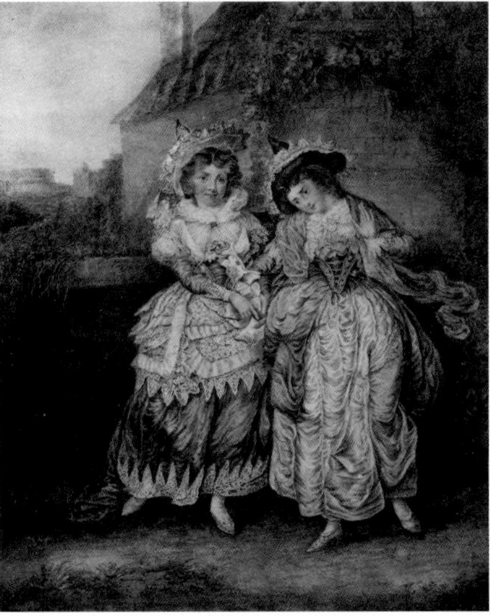

D.1930.55

'The Merry Wives of Windsor', Act II, Scene I
1800
watercolour
248 × 202 mm
Brockbank, Victor (purchase, 1930) (D.1930.55)

■ **PETTY, LUTHER (ca. 1860–ca. 1930)**
Petty was a Manchester-based artist.

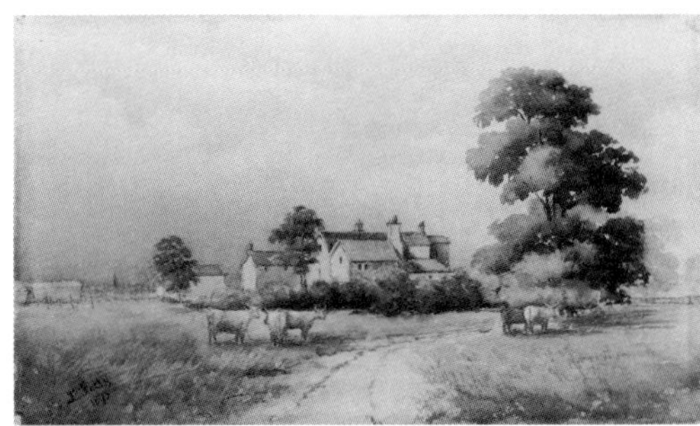

D.1998.12

Pepper Hill Farm, Moss Side, Manchester
1893
pencil, watercolour, bodycolour
(heightened with white)
signed & dated lower left: *LPetty / 1893*; signed,
inscribed & dated centre verso of backing: *Pepper Hill
Farm. / Moss Side. Manchester / by / Luther Petty.1893.*
198 × 331 mm
Crann, Mrs Sarah (gift, 1.10.1998) (D.1998.12)

■ PHILIPS, HERBERT (1834–1905)
An amateur artist of whom little is known.
He was the son-in-law of William Langton

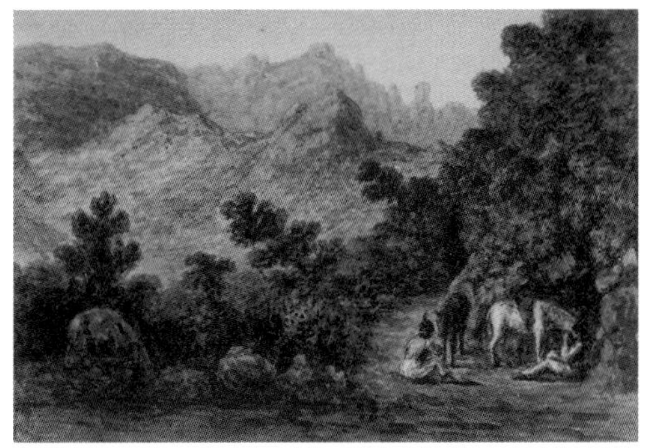

D.1913.12

Between Rebiera Fria and Rio di Metado, Brazil
pencil, watercolour
inscibed lower left verso: *between Ribiera fria & R.di
Metado*
171 × 242 mm
Philips, Mrs Herbert (gift, 1913) (D.1913.12)

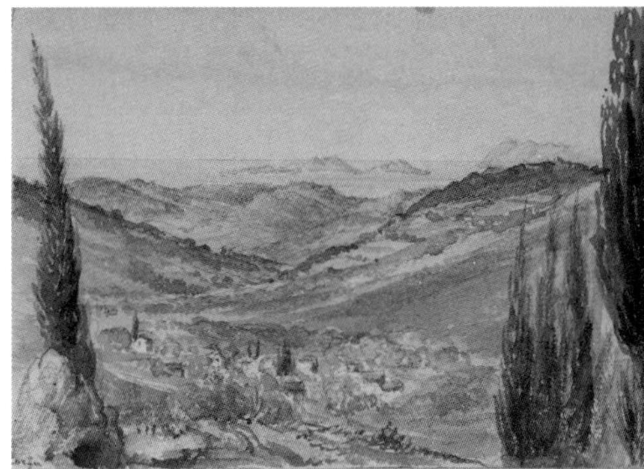

D.1913.13

**Corfu: Landscape with a Village looking
out to Sea**
pencil, watercolour
inscribed lower left: *Corfu*
126 × 175 mm
Philips, Mrs Herbert (gift, 1913) (D.1913.13)

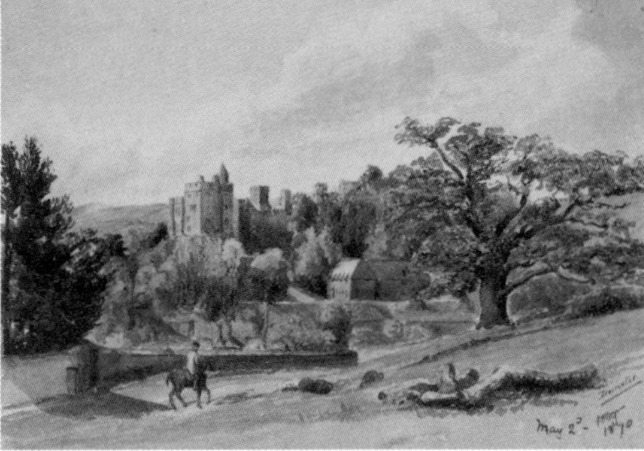

D.1913.14

Dunster Castle, Somerset
2.5.1870
pencil, watercolour
dated lower right: *May 2d – 1870*; dated
lower right above ink date: *1869* [erased]
inscribed lower right: *Dunster.* [underlined]
203 × 289 mm
Philips, Mrs Herbert (gift, 1913) (D.1913.14)

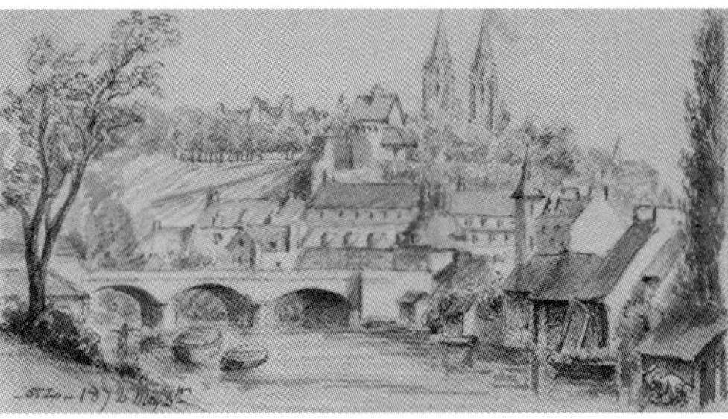

D.1913.15

View of St Lo, France, from the River
6.5.1872
pencil, pen and brown ink, watercolour
inscribed & dated lower left: *– St.Lo – 1872 May 6th*
95 × 170 mm
Philips, Mrs Herbert (gift, 1913) (D.1913.15)

View across a Lake
pencil, watercolour
148 × 229 mm
Philips, Mrs Herbert (gift, 1913) (D.1913.16)

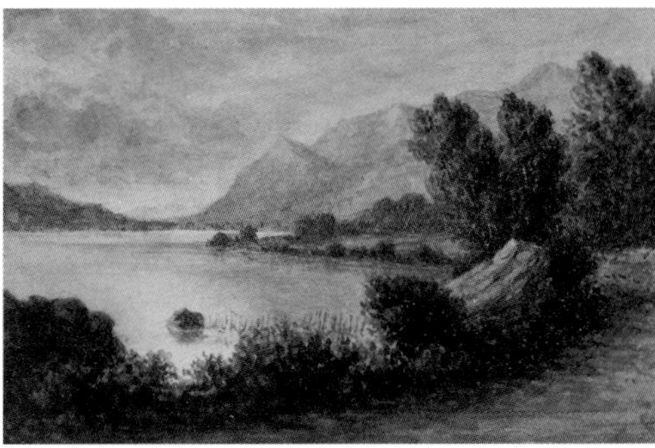

D.1913.17

Skiddaw, Cumberland
pencil, watercolour
115 × 172 mm
Philips, Mrs Herbert (gift, 1913) (D.1913.17)

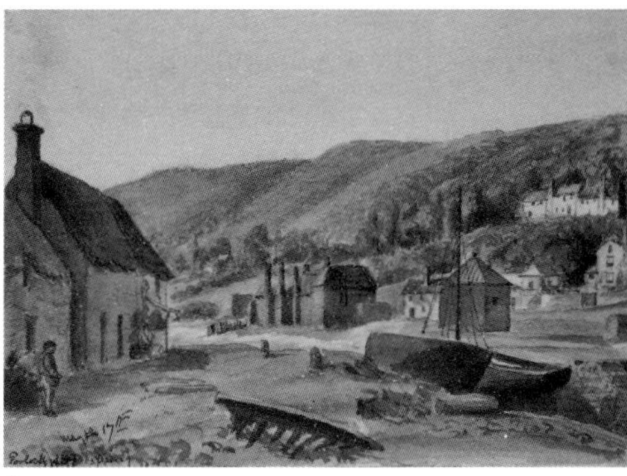

D.1913.19

Cottages at Porlock, Somerset
17.5.1869
pencil, watercolour
inscribed & dated lower left: *May 12* [erased] *17th /
Porlock 1869 Spring*
165 × 229 mm
Philips, Mrs Herbert (gift, 1913) (D.1913.19)

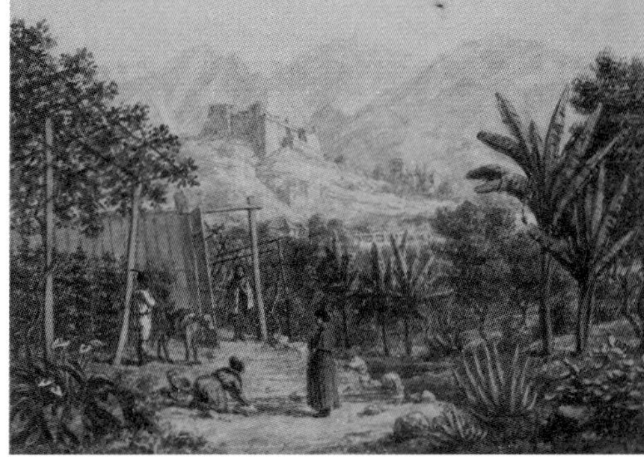

D.1913.20

**Figures in a mountainous Landscape with a
Castle on a Hill**
pencil, watercolour
146 × 201 mm
Philips, Mrs Herbert (gift, 1913) (D.1913.20)

Landscape with Mountains
pencil, watercolour
178 × 266 mm
Philips, Mrs Herbert (gift, 1913) (D.1913.21)

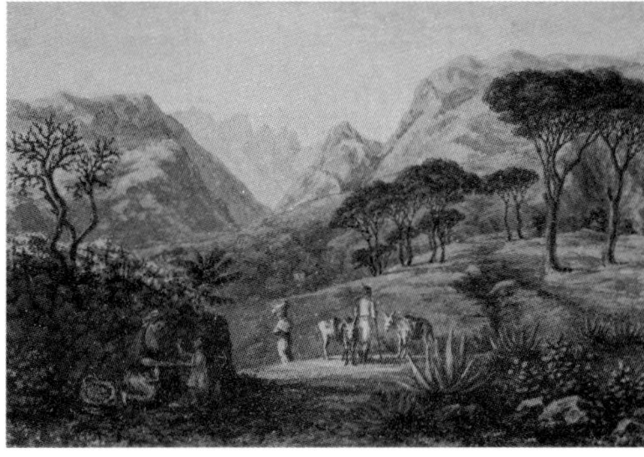

D.1913.22

Mountainous Landscape with Figures
watercolour
178 × 255 mm
Philips, Mrs Herbert (gift, 1913) (D.1913.22)

View of a Mountain Range (recto);
Lake Scene (verso)
pencil, watercolour
144 × 225 mm
Philips, Mrs Herbert (gift, 1913) (D.1913.23)

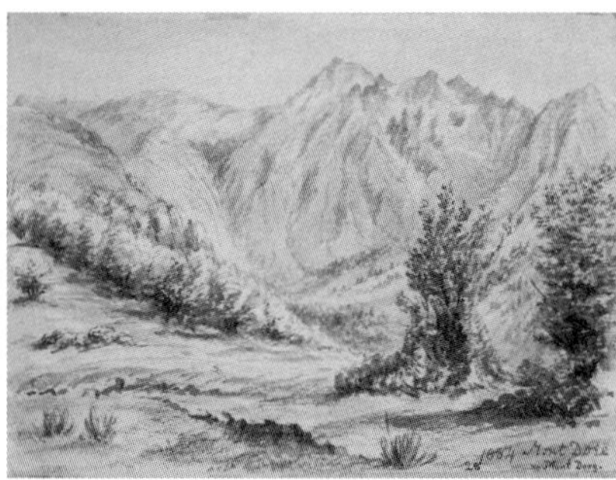

D.1913.24

Mont Dore, France
1884
black chalk, watercolour
inscribed & dated lower right: *1884 Mont Dore*;
inscribed lower right below ink inscription: *Mont Dore.*; numbered lower right: *28*
134 × 173 mm
Philips, Mrs Herbert (gift, 1913) (D.1913.24)

Distant View of Lyndhurst, Hampshire
15.5.1873
watercolour; blue paper
dated lower right: *May 15th 1873*; inscribed lower right: *Lyndhurst.*
126 × 182 mm
Philips, Mrs Herbert (gift, 1913) (D.1913.25)

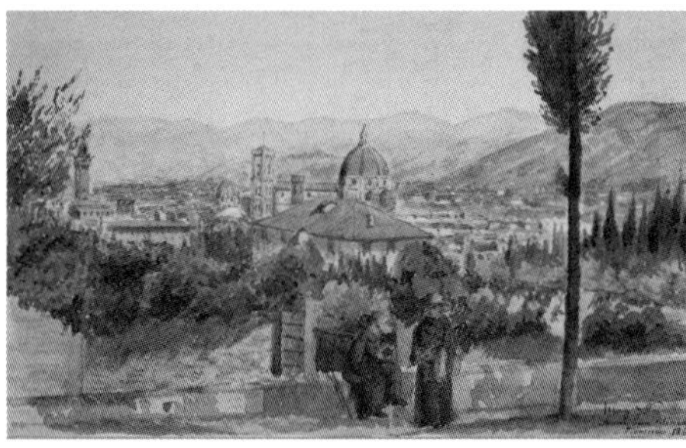

D.1913.26

View of Florence from San Miniato
7.5.1867
pencil, watercolour
dated lower right: *May 7th*; inscribed & dated lower right; added later: *from San Miniato / – Florence.1867*
140 × 225 mm
Philips, Mrs Herbert (gift, 1913) (D.1913.26)

Lake Annecy, France
1890
pencil, watercolour
dated lower left; added later after inscription: *1890*
inscribed lower left: *Lake of Annecy –*
127 × 176 mm
Philips, Mrs Herbert (gift, 1913) (D.1913.27)

On the Coast, Banff, Banffshire, Scotland (recto); Lake Scene and Mountains (verso)
pencil, watercolour
inscribed lower right verso: *"on the coast Banff"*
138 × 224 mm
Philips, Mrs Herbert (gift, 1913) (D.1913.28)

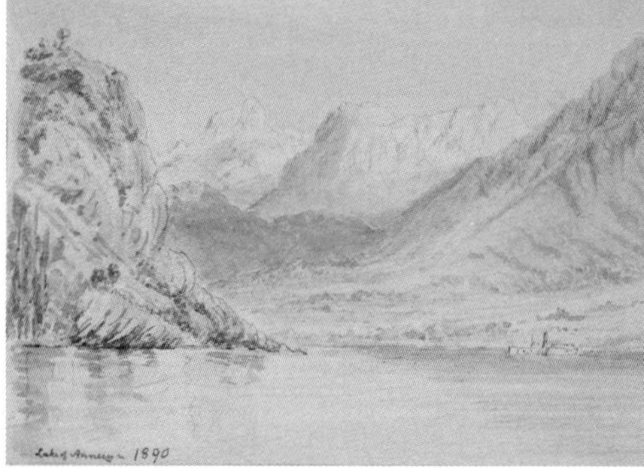

D.1913.27

Women gathering Shellfish
pen and brown ink, watercolour
185 × 227 mm
Philips, Mrs Herbert (gift, 1913) (D.1913.29)

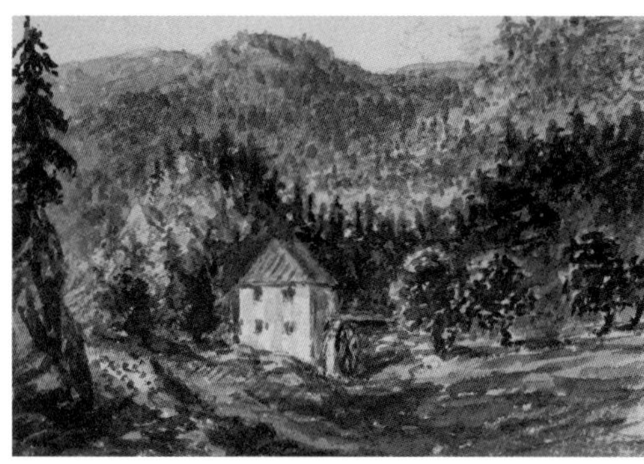

D.1913.30

A Watermill in a wooded Landscape
pencil, watercolour
96 × 137 mm
Philips, Mrs Herbert (gift, 1913) (D.1913.30)

Landscape with Donkeys
pencil, watercolour
134 × 215 mm
Philips, Mrs Herbert (gift, 1913) (D.1913.32)

■ PILKINGTON, SIR WILLIAM (1775–1850)
An amateur English artist, Pilkington visited Italy.

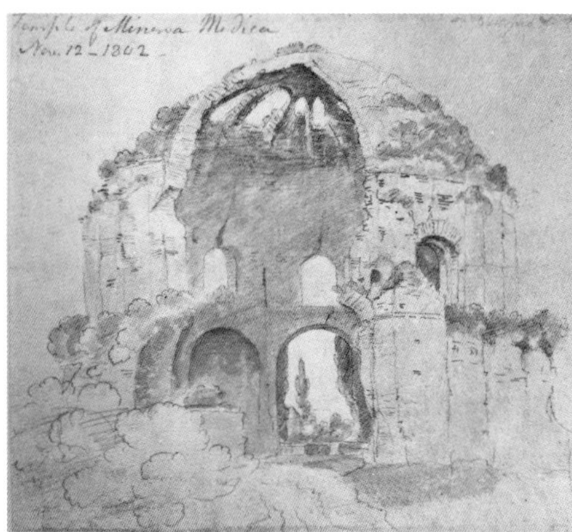

D.1969.7

The Temple of Minerva Medica, Rome
12.11.1802
pencil, watercolour
inscribed & dated upper left: *Temple of Minerva Medica / Nov.12–1802–*
205 × 228 mm
Lockett, Richard, Friends of the Whitworth (via) (gift, 1969) (D.1969.7)

■ PINWELL, GEORGE JOHN (1842–75)
After studying at the St Martin's Lane Academy and at Heatherley's, Pinwell began to work for the Dalziel brothers in 1864. He also sometimes worked in collaboration with Fred Walker for various magazines and periodicals in the 1860s. Pinwell was elected a member of the Old Watercolour Society in 1870.

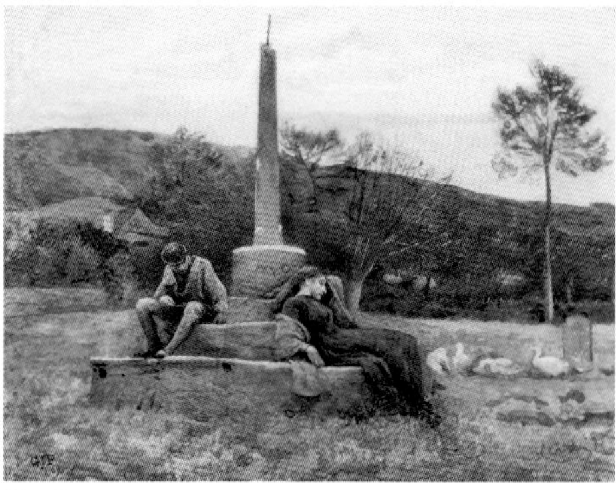

D.1938.1

The Old Cross
1869
pencil, watercolour, bodycolour
(heightened with white)
signed & dated lower left with initials: *GJP / 69*
146 × 185 mm
Webster, T. B. L. (Professor) (via Friends of the Whitworth in memory of his mother Lady Webster) (gift, 1938) (D.1938.1)

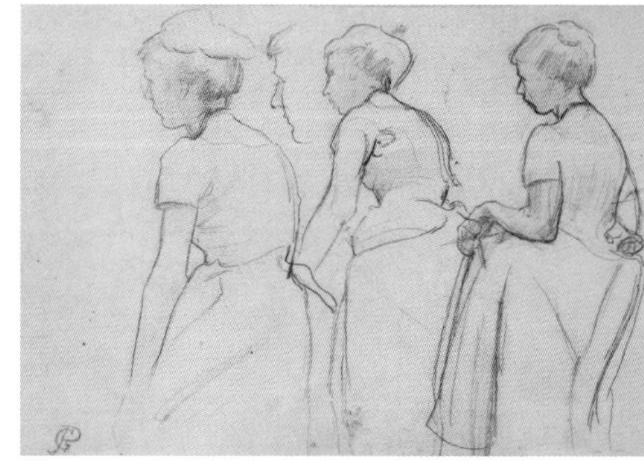

D.1960.116

Studies of a Girl (recto); Study of a Girl (verso)
pencil
signed lower left with monogram: *GJP*
259 × 359 mm
University of Manchester, History of Art Department (transfer, 1960) (D.1960.116)

Study for 'The Captive'
black chalk
signed lower right with initials: *GJP*
347 × 251 mm
University of Manchester, History of Art Department (transfer, 1960) (D.1960.117)

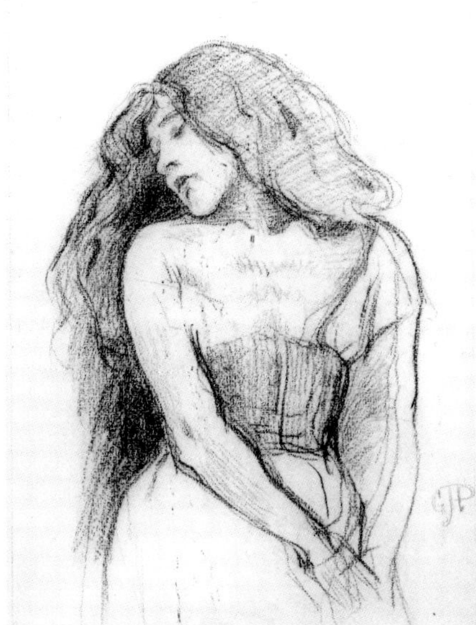

D.1960.117

■ PLACE, FRANCIS (1647–1728)

Born in County Durham, Place is one of the earliest English draughtsmen. He studied law in London but left on the outbreak of plague in 1665. For many years he was part of a group of antiquarians and amateur artists based in York; many of his views are of the North of England, although he did travel elsewhere in the British Isles. Although perhaps not a pupil in the formal sense, Place was certainly a friend and disciple of the great Bohemian draughtsman and printmaker Wenceslaus Hollar.

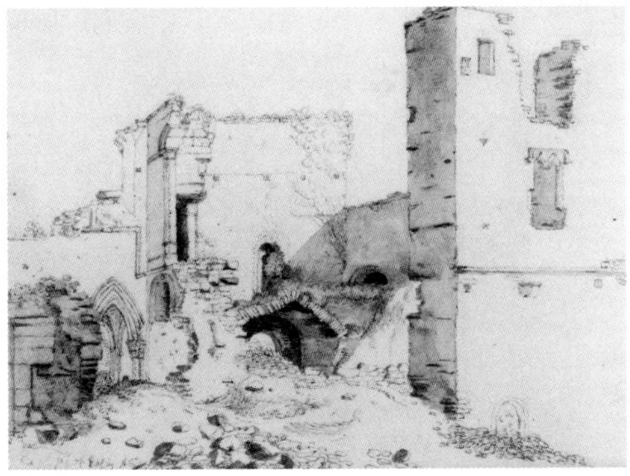

D.1932.3

Easby Abbey, near Richmond, Yorkshire
pencil, pen and brown ink, grey watercolour, brown watercolour
inscribed lower left: *pt of Easby Abbey*
150 × 200 mm
Anderson, A. E. (gift, 1932) (D.1932.3)

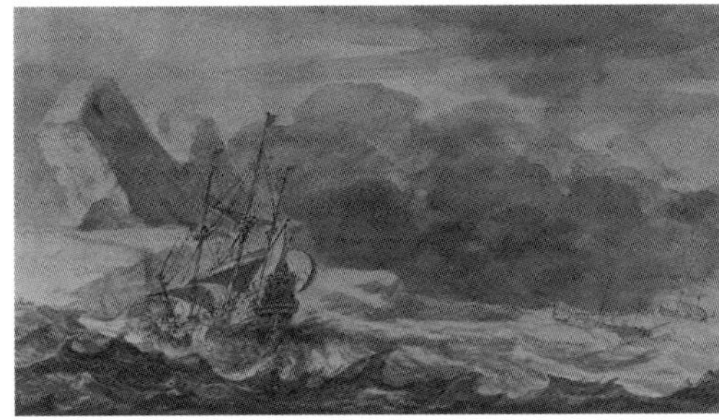

D.1965.9

Men of War in a Storm (recto); Studies of Poppies and Geraniums (verso)
1716–18
pen and brown ink, brown watercolour
180 × 315 mm
Friends of the Whitworth (gift, 1965) (D.1965.9)

■ PLIMER, ANDREW (attributed to) (1763–1837)

Plimer was a prolific painter of miniatures.

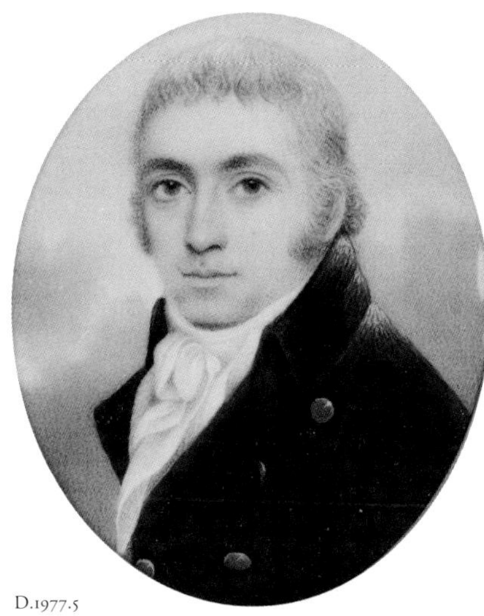

D.1977.5

Portrait of Israel Hess
1795
watercolour, bodycolour
69 × 54 mm
Langdon, Margaret (gift, 1977) (D.1977.5)

■ POCOCK, NICHOLAS (1740–1821)

Pocock began his career as a sailor but turned to marine painting. He began to exhibit at the Royal Academy in 1782 and continued to show mostly marine paintings there until 1815. Pocock also painted landscapes and was a founder member of the Old Watercolour Society in 1804.

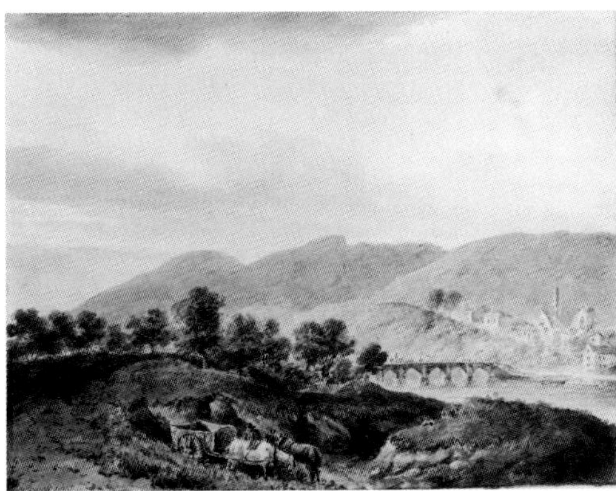

D.1893.3

Carrick on Suir, Co Tipperary, Ireland
1805
pencil, watercolour
signed & dated lower right: *N Pocock 1805*
249 × 317 mm
Agnew's (purchase, 18.12.1893) (D.1893.3)

■ POLLITT, ALBERT (1856–ca. 1920)

Pollitt was a landscape watercolourist who worked in the Midlands and North Wales from the late 1880s to about 1920.

River View with wooded Banks
1872
watercolour
signed & dated lower left: *APollitt / 1872*
252 × 354 mm
Bolwell, Harry (bequest, 1985) (D.1985.3)

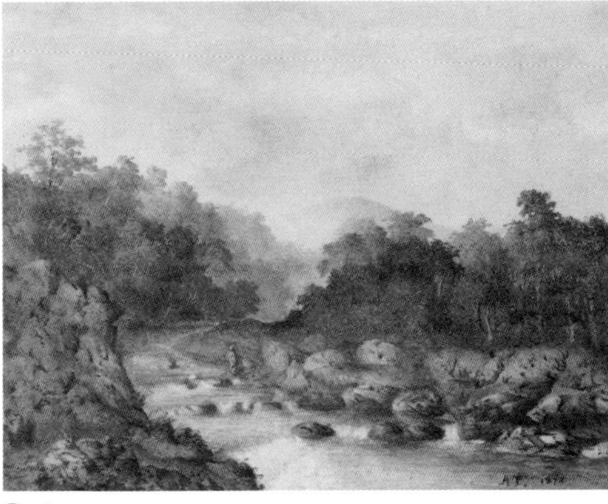

D.1985.4

An Angler beside a River with Trees beyond
1872
watercolour
signed & dated lower right with initials: *AP.1872*
255 × 325 mm
Bolwell, Harry (bequest, 1985) (D.1985.4)

■ POUNCEY, BENJAMIN THOMAS (ca. 1750–99)

A landscape watercolourist and engraver, Pouncey was the pupil and brother-in-law of the engraver William Woollett. Pouncey engraved the work of others, and exhibited watercolours, between 1772 and 1789. Very little is known of his life and the rarity of his drawings suggests that many have been erroneously ascribed to other artists.

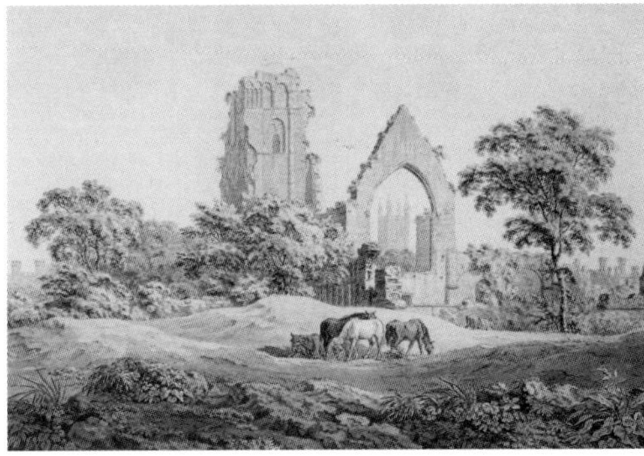

D.1893.2

St Ethelbert's Tower and St Augustine's Gate, Canterbury, with the Cathedral Tower
1780
pen and grey ink, watercolour
signed & dated lower centre: *Pouncy delin / 1780*
320 × 460 mm
untraced (purchase, 1893) (D.1893.2)

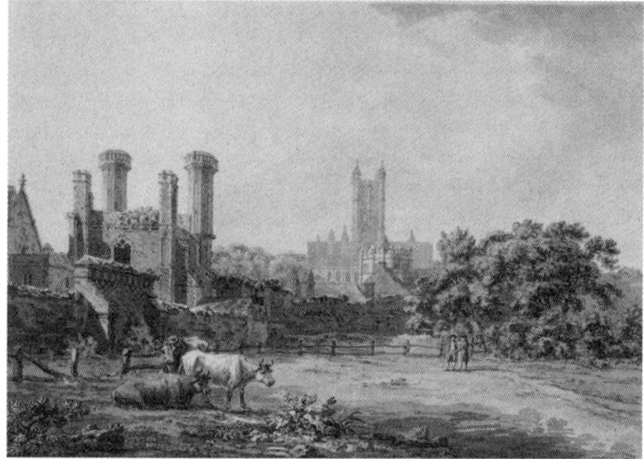

D.1921.19

**Canterbury Cathedral and
St Augustine's Gateway**
1782
pen and grey ink, watercolour
signed & dated lower right with monogram; *BTP 1782*;
signed, inscribed & dated lower centre on mount: *B.T.
Pouncey delin.1782. / VIEW OF CANTERBURY
CATHEDRAL from ST. AUSTIN'S.*
345 × 486 mm
Barlow, Sir Thomas, National Art Collections Fund (via) (gift,
1921) (D.1921.19)

■ Powell, J. (fl. 1861–63)
J. Powell was a Kent-based, presumably amateur, artist.

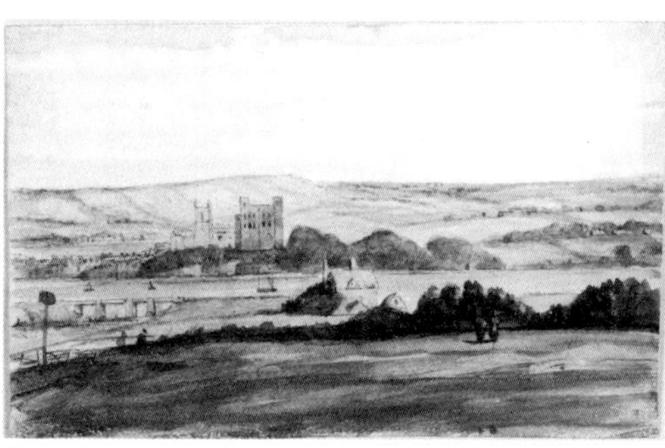

D.1926.131

**View of Rochester, Kent, from across the
River Medway**
9.1863
pencil, watercolour
signed lower right verso with initials: *JAP*; inscribed &
dated lower left verso: *Rochester Sep 1863*
177 × 281 mm
Ogden, William Sharp (bequest, 1926) (D.1926.131)

View of Ramsgate, Kent
1861
pencil, watercolour
signed lower right verso with initials: *JAP*; inscribed &
dated lower left verso: *[R]amsgate – 1861 –*
139 × 230 mm
Ogden, William Sharp (bequest, 1926) (D.1926.132)

■ Powell, Joseph (1780–1834)
A pupil of Benjamin Thomas Pouncey, Powell
exhibited at the Royal Academy between 1796
and 1833. He was the first President of the New
Watercolour Society in 1832 and painted in Wales,
Shropshire, the Lake District and the southern
counties. He was also a drawing master and
produced etchings and lithographs.

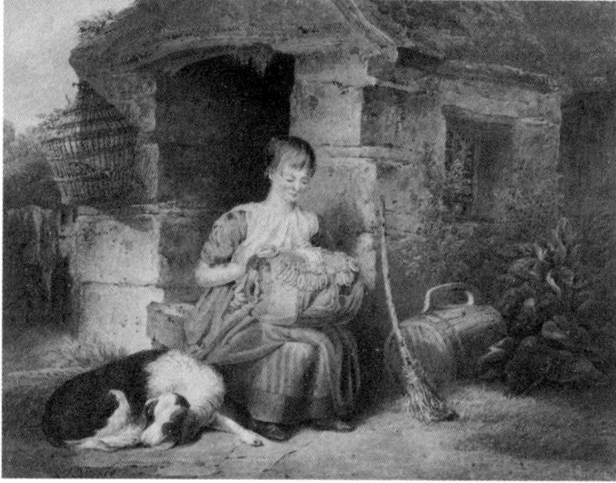

D.1900.15

The Lace Maker
pencil, watercolour
signed lower left: *J.POWELL*
267 × 341 mm
Worthington, Mary (gift, 1900) (D.1900.15)

Landscape, near Ramsgate, Kent
watercolour
signed lower right: *J.Powell*; inscribed
centre verso: *Ramsgate*
106 × 189 mm
Friends of the Whitworth (gift, 1934) (D.1934.14)

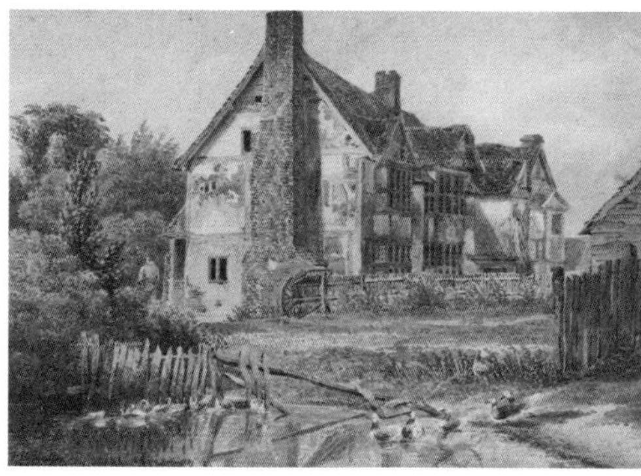

D.1934.15

Farmhouse, Mill Hill, London
1822
watercolour
signed & dated lower left: *J.Powell / 1822*; inscribed
centre verso: *Mill Hill Hendon*
143 × 199 mm
Friends of the Whitworth (gift, 1934) (D.1934.15)

■ Poynter, Sir Edward John (1836–1919)
Poynter studied at the Royal Academy Schools and in
Gleyre's studio in Paris from 1856 to 1859. He exhibited
at the Royal Academy from 1861, was elected a member
in 1876 and was President from 1896 to 1918. He
produced many drawings as figure studies for his large
Biblical or Classical pictures, but he also painted
landscape watercolours for his own pleasure. One of
the greatest of the Victorian neo-classical painters,
Poynter was elected a member of the Royal
Watercolour Society in 1883. He was Director of the
National Gallery from 1894 to 1905.

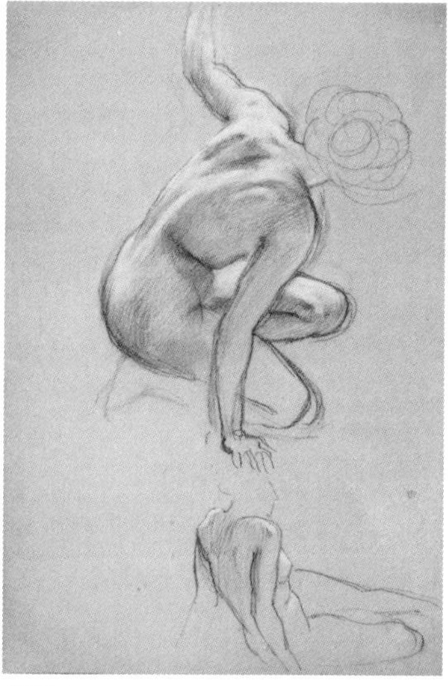

D.1921.1

**Two Studies of a nude female Figure crouching
and reclining for 'Water Babies'**
1900
black chalk, white chalk; brown paper
stamped with initials lower right (studio stamp)
(L.874): *EJP*
381 × 255 mm
Agnew, Gerald (gift, 1921) (D.1921.1)

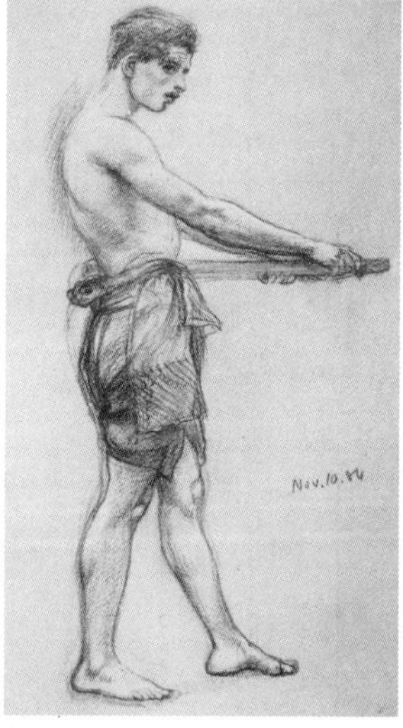

D.1921.2

**Study of a male Slave for 'The Queen of Sheba's
Visit to King Solomon'**
10.11.1884
black chalk, white chalk; brown paper
dated lower centre right margin: *Nov.10.84*; stamped
with initials lower right (studio stamp) (L.874): *EJP*
370 × 216 mm
Agnew, Gerald (gift, 1921) (D.1921.2)

**Study for the Figure of Milarion for
'Atalanta's Race' (recto); Two Studies for
the same Figure (verso)**
27.12.1873
pencil, black chalk; grey paper
dated centre left: *Dec 27 / 73*; stamped with initials
centre right (studio stamp) (L.874): *EJP*
511 x 360 mm
Agnew, Gerald (gift, 1921) (D.1921.3)

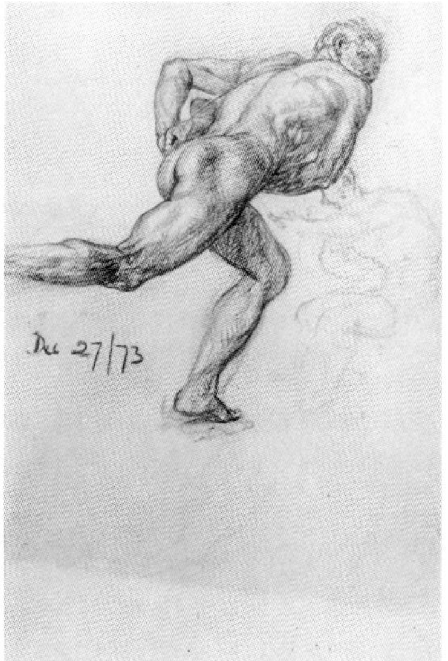

D.1921.3

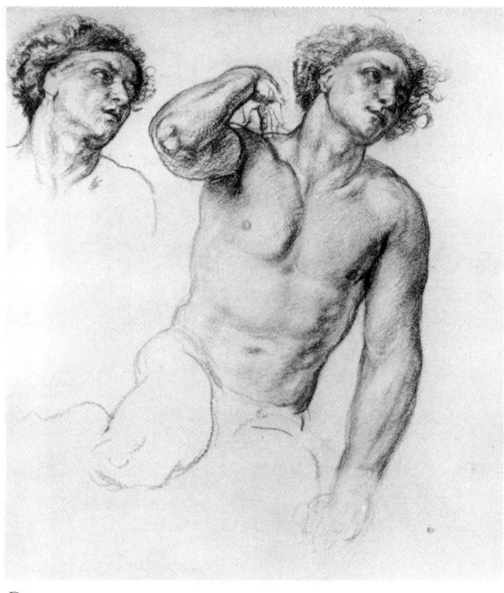

D.1921.4

Study of a seated male Nude and Head, for 'Atalanta's Race'
1873–76
black chalk
stamped with initials lower right (studio stamp)
(L.874): *EJP*
450 × 353 mm
Agnew, Gerald (gift, 1921) (D.1921.4)

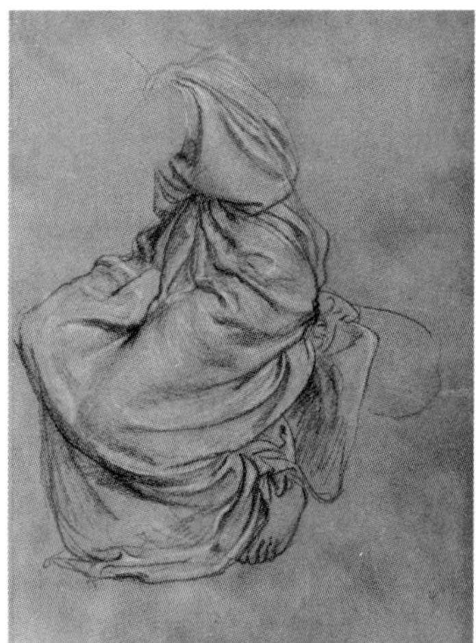

D.1960.118

Female Drapery Study
black chalk, white chalk; grey paper
stamped with initials lower right (studio stamp)
(L.874): *EJP*
354 × 253 mm
University of Manchester, History of Art Department
(transfer, 1960) (D.1960.118)

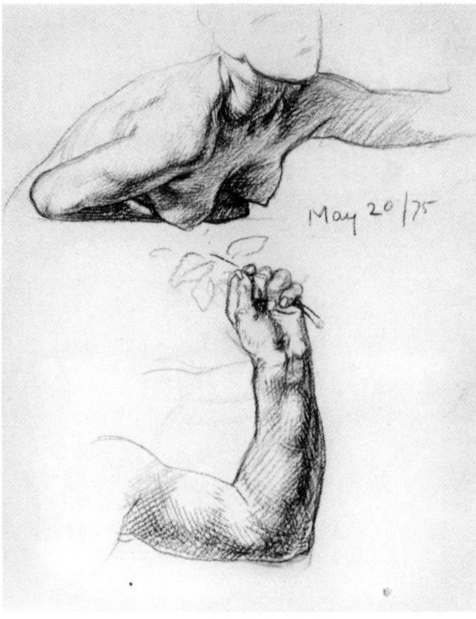

D.1960.119

Two Figure Studies for 'Atalanta's Race'
20.5.1875
black chalk
dated upper right: *May 20 / 75*; stamped with initials
lower right (studio stamp) (L.874): *EJP*
456 × 303 mm
University of Manchester, History of Art Department
(transfer, 1960) (D.1960.119)

■ **PRIESTMAN, BERTRAM (1868–1951)**
Priestman was born in Yorkshire and came to
London in 1888 where he studied at the Slade. He
exhibited at the Royal Academy from 1890 to 1961
and was elected a member in 1923. Priestman also
exhibited in Europe and the United States. From
1915 he lived at Walberswick in Suffolk.

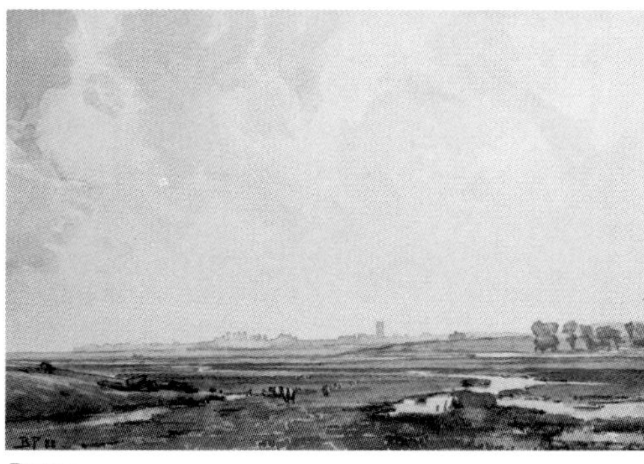

D.1923.3

Walberswick Marshes, Suffolk
1922
pencil, watercolour
signed & dated lower left with initials: *B P 22*
245 × 362 mm
Anderson, A. E., National Art Collections Fund (via)
(gift, 1923) (D.1923.3)

■ **PRINSEP, WILLIAM (1794–1874)**
Prinsep, son of an East India Company merchant,
arrived in Calcutta in 1817 and lived there until his
retirement in 1842. From 1830, together with his
brother George, he ran a prosperous mercantile,
banking and agency house. In the 1820s Prinsep was
one of a group of amateur pupils of George Chinnery,
who lived in Calcutta from 1807 to 1825. Prinsep's
drawings came to light in a Spink exhibition in 1982.

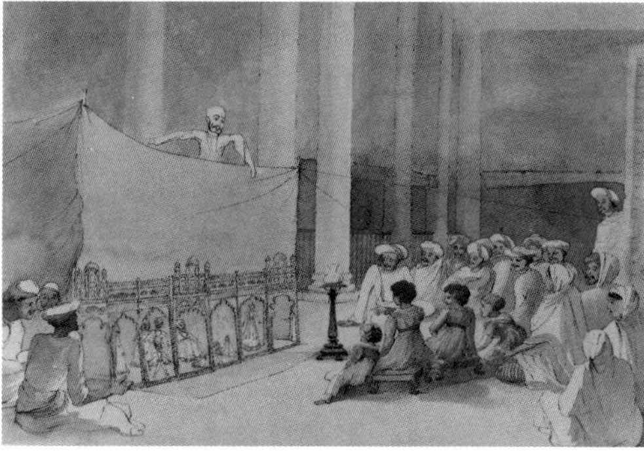

D.1982.6

Puppet Show on the Artist's Verandah
pencil, pen and brown ink, watercolour
231 × 333 mm
Spink and Son Ltd, London (purchase, 1982) (V. & A.)
(D.1982.6)

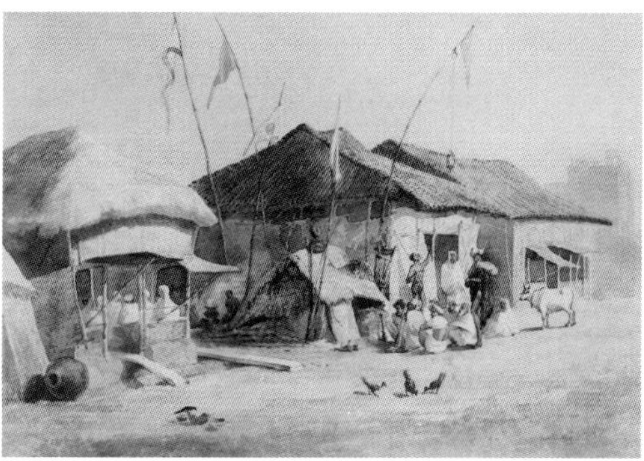

D.1982.7

Pilgrim's Hut, near the New Mint, Calcutta
pencil, watercolour; watermark RUSE &
TURNERS/1825
229 × 328 mm
Spink and Son Ltd, London (purchase, 1982) (V. & A.)
(D.1982.7)

■ **PRIOR, MELTON (1845–1910)**
An illustrator, Prior was war correspondent of the
Illustrated London News from 1873, covering the
Ashanti war, the Carlist Rising, the Zulu war, the
Sudanese campaign and both Boer wars, as well as
many other military campaigns around the world.
Prior also went on a number of Royal tours,
accompanying the Prince of Wales to India in 1875–76.
Prior was one of the last great artist reporters, and his
rapidly executed pencil drawings were reproduced in
the *ILN* by Direct Photo-Engraving Process.

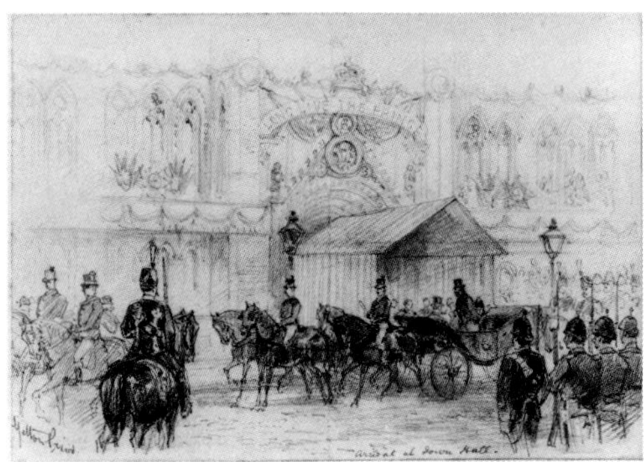

D.1990.1

Royal Jubilee Exhibition, Manchester: The Arrival of the Royal Party at the Town Hall
1887
pencil
signed lower left: *Melton Prior*; inscribed lower right:
Arrival at Town Hall
176 × 246 mm
Christie's, London (purchase, 1989) (D.1990.1)

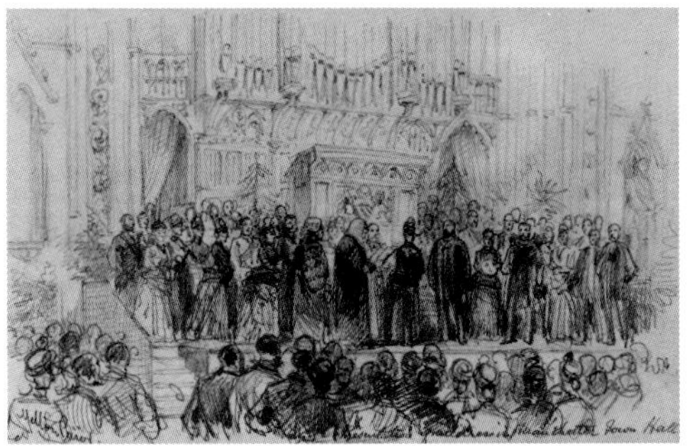

D.1990.2

**Royal Jubilee Exhibition, Manchester:
The Presentation of the Address to the
Prince and Princess of Wales**
1887
pencil
signed lower left: *Melton Prior*; inscribed lower right:
Presentation of Address in Manchester Town Hall
140 × 214 mm
Christie's, London (purchase, 1989) (D.1990.2)

**Royal Jubilee Exhibition, Manchester: The Royal
Procession through the Streets of Manchester**
1887
pencil
signed lower left: *Melton Prior*
184 × 140 mm
Christie's, London (purchase, 1989) (D.1990.3)

**Royal Jubilee Exhibition, Manchester: The Royal
Procession passes under Street Decorations**
1887
pencil
signed lower left: *Melton Prior*
140 × 186 mm
Christie's, London (purchase, 1989) (D.1990.4)

**Royal Jubilee Exhibition, Manchester: The Royal
Procession passing along Market Street**
1887
pencil
signed lower left: *Melton Prior*; inscribed lower right:
Procession passing up Market Street
256 × 358 mm
Christie's, London (purchase, 1989) (D.1990.5)

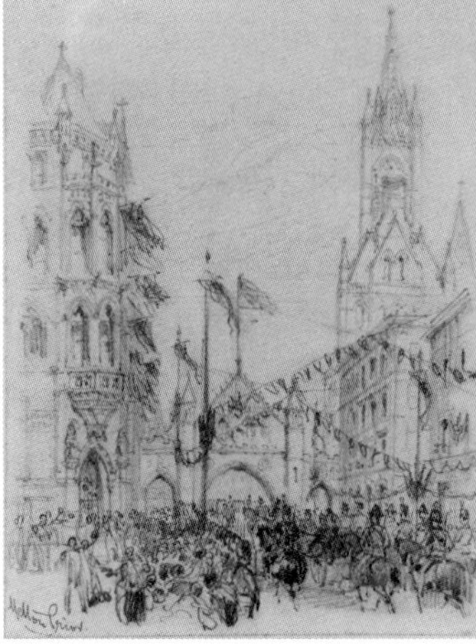

D.1990.3

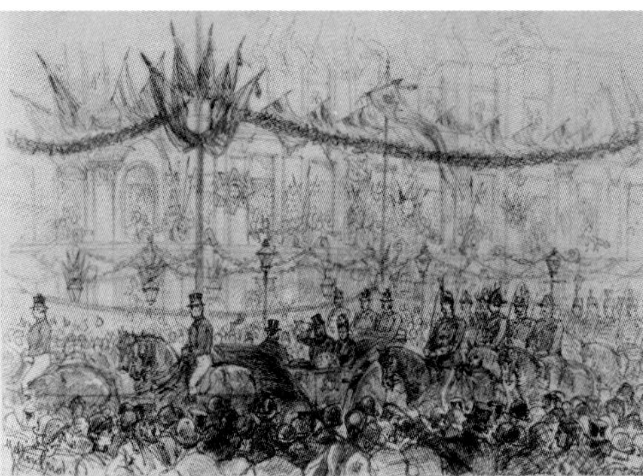

D.1990.5

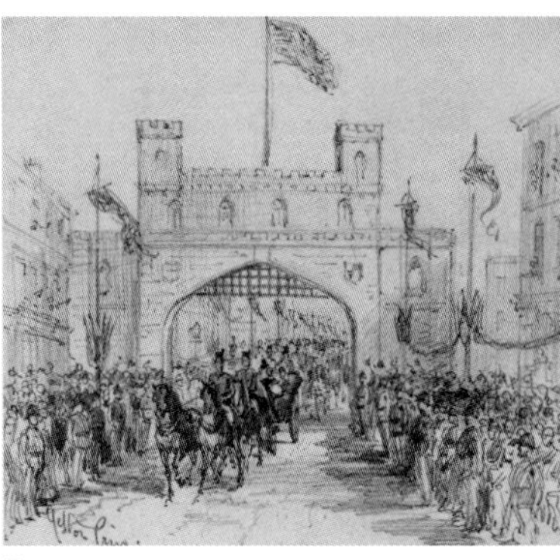

D.1990.6

**Royal Jubilee Exhibition, Manchester:
The Royal Procession to the Exhibition Site**
1887
pencil
signed lower left: *Melton Prior*
140 × 148 mm
Christie's, London (purchase, 1989) (D.1990.6)

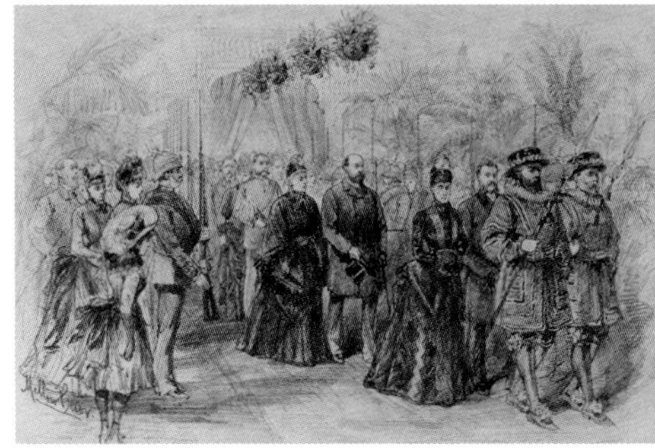

D.1990.7

**Royal Jubilee Exhibition, Manchester:
The Royal Couple arrive at the Exhibition**
1887
pencil
signed lower left: *Melton Prior*
266 × 390 mm
Christie's, London (purchase, 1989) (D.1990.7)

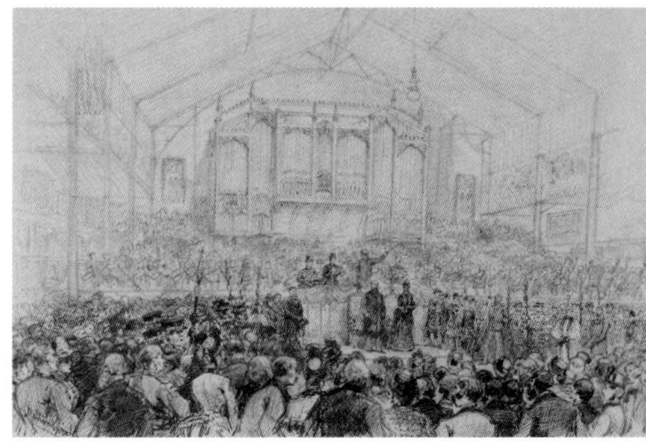

D.1990.8

**Royal Jubilee Exhibition, Manchester:
The Opening Ceremony**
1887
pencil
signed lower left: *Melton Prior*
349 × 517 mm
Christie's, London (purchase, 1989) (D.1990.8)

**Royal Jubilee Exhibition, Manchester:
The Royal Couple are welcomed at Doulton's
Indian Pavilion**
1887
pencil
signed lower left: *Melton Prior*
140 × 155 mm
Christie's, London (purchase, 1989) (D.1990.9)

**Royal Jubilee Exhibition, Manchester:
The Fairy Fountains**
1887
pencil
signed lower left: *Melton Prior*
139 × 430 mm
Christie's, London (purchase, 1989) (D.1990.10)

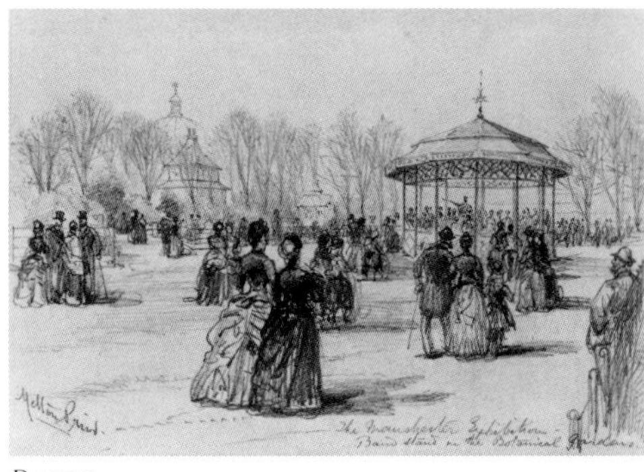

D.1990.11

**Royal Jubilee Exhibition, Manchester: The
Western Band Stand in the Botanical Gardens**
1887
pencil
signed lower left: *Melton Prior*; inscribed lower right:
*The Manchester Exhibition – / Band stand in the
Botanical Gardens.*
169 × 250 mm
Christie's, London (purchase, 1989) (D.1990.11)

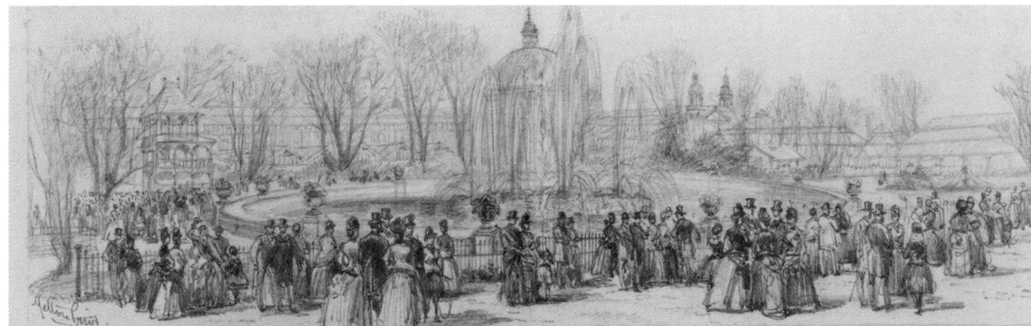

D.1990.10

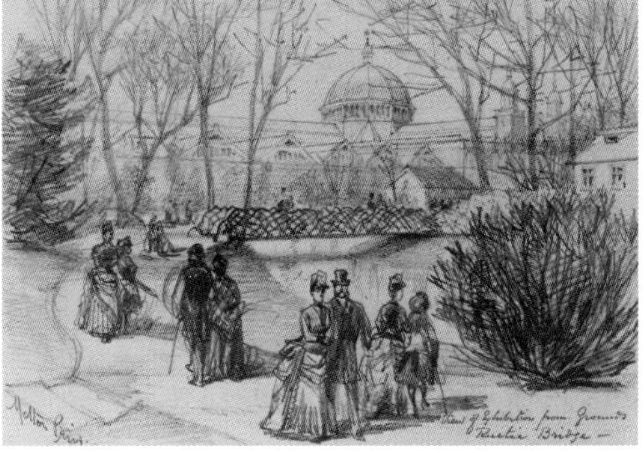

D.1990.12

**Royal Jubilee Exhibition, Manchester:
View of the Exhibition Buildings from the
Grounds with the Rustic Bridge**
1887
pencil
signed lower left: *Melton Prior*; inscribed lower right:
View of Exhibition from Grounds. / Rustic Bridge –
180 × 234 mm
Christie's, London (purchase, 1989) (D.1990.12)

**Royal Jubilee Exhibition, Manchester:
Portion of Terracotta Arcading in the
Industrial Design Section**
1887
pencil
signed lower left: *Melton Prior*; inscribed lower right:
Portion of / Terra Cotta Arcading
136 × 212 mm
Christie's, London (purchase, 1989) (D.1990.13)

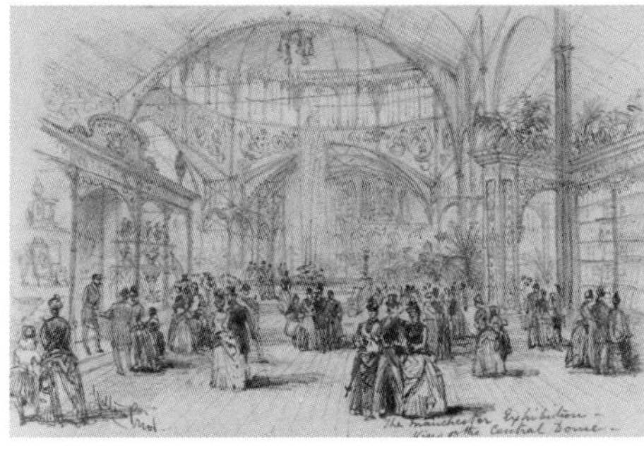

D.1990.14

**Royal Jubilee Exhibition, Manchester: View of
the Central Dome Looking West**
1887
pencil
signed lower left: *Melton Prior*; inscribed lower left: *The
Manchester Exhibition – View of the Central Dome –*
137 × 199 mm
Christie's, London (purchase, 1989) (D.1990.14)

■ Pritchett, Edward (fl. 1828–64)

Pritchett was a painter of mainly Venetian scenes in oil
and watercolour. His works have sometimes been
mistaken for those of Bonington.

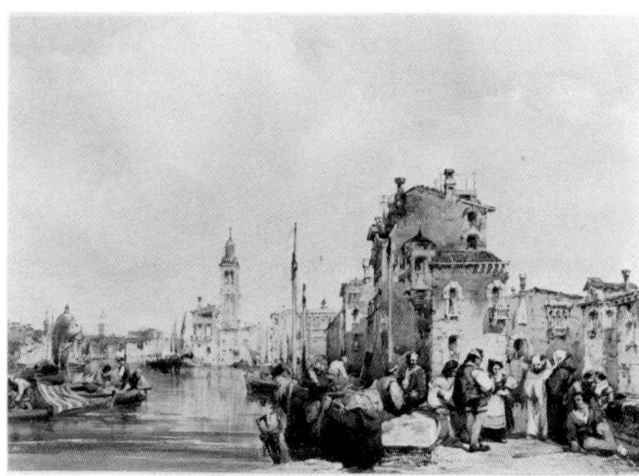

D.1921.30

Canal Scene, Venice
pen and brown ink, watercolour
246 × 339 mm
Palser, J. and Son, London (purchase, 1921) (D.1921.30)

■ Prout, John Skinner (1805–76)

John Skinner Prout, son of Samuel, was largely self-
taught. He was elected a member of the New
Watercolour Society in 1838, losing his membership
when he visited Australia. He was re-elected in 1862.
Prout lived in Bristol and was a friend of William
James Muller with whom he was a founder member of
the Bristol Sketching Club.

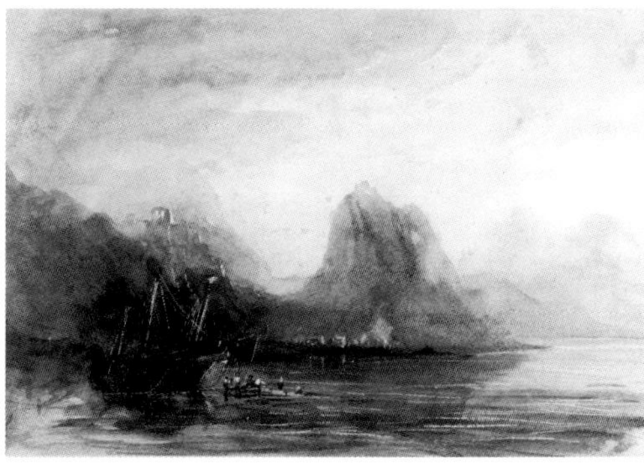

D.1900.22

Morning after the Wreck
pencil, watercolour
192 × 279 mm
untraced (purchase, 1900) (D.1900.22)

■ Prout, Samuel (1783–1852)

Samuel Prout began his career working for the
antiquarian John Britton and exhibited at the Royal
Academy from 1803. In 1813 he published *Rudiments
of Landscape in Perspective Studies*, the first of his
drawing books for beginners. He went on to publish
seventeen more, many of them illustrated with
lithographs after his own drawings, which were hugely
influential on a whole generation of amateurs. Prout
was elected a member of the Old Watercolour Society
in 1819 when he made his first trip abroad. His
speciality was crowded urban continental street
scenes with Gothic architecture.

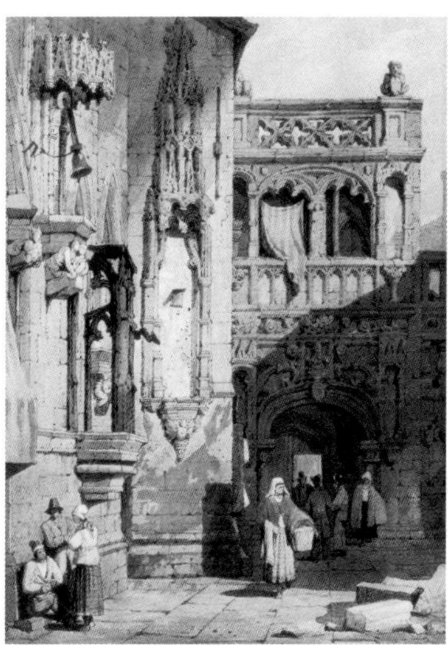

D.1887.21

Church Porch, Normandy
pen and brown ink, watercolour, bodycolour
(heightened with white)
signed lower right with initial in monogram: *SProut*
335 × 231 mm
Agnew's (purchase, 19.5.1891) (D.1887.21)

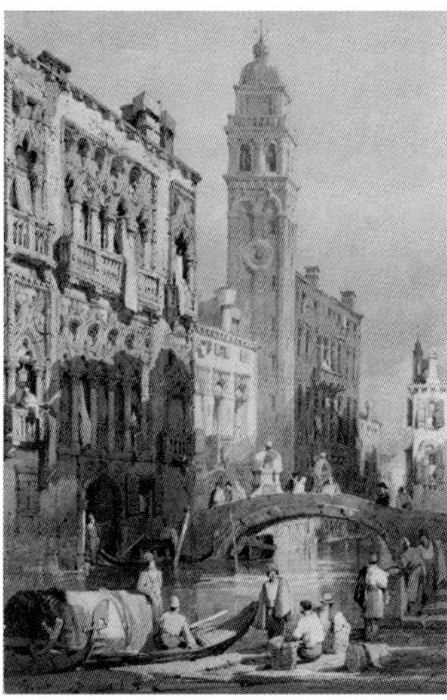

D.1887.22

**A Capriccio Canal Scene in Venice with a Palace
and the Campanile of San Giorgio dei Greci**
pen and brown ink, watercolour, bodycolour
(heightened with white)
signed lower left with initial in monogram: *SProut*
421 × 275 mm
Wright, Thomas W. (purchase, 1887) (D.1887.22)

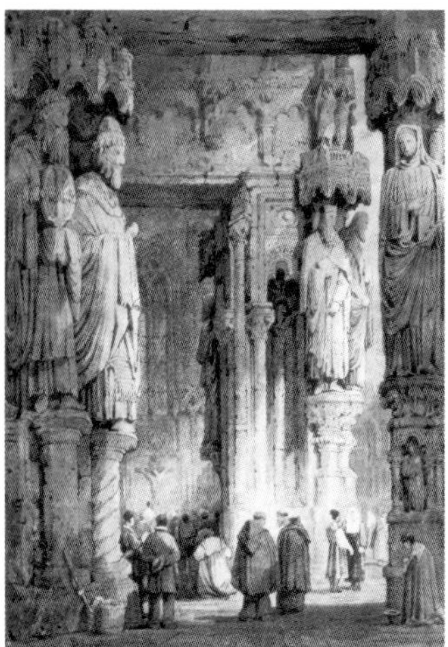

D.1887.23

North Porch of Chartres Cathedral, France
pen and brown ink, watercolour, bodycolour
(heightened with white)
signed lower left with initial in monogram: *SProut*
335 × 231 mm
Agnew's (purchase, 19.5.1891) (D.1887.23)

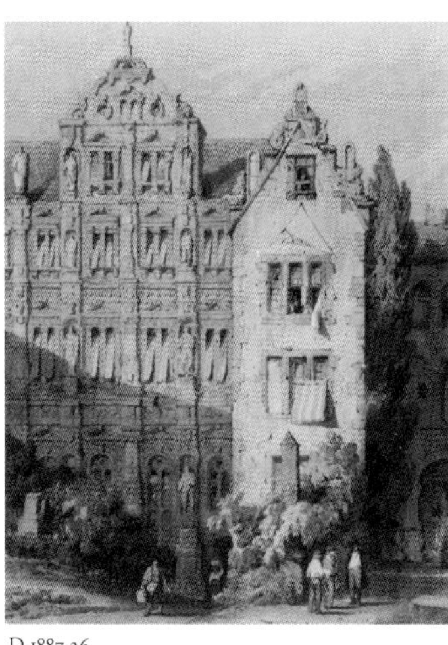

D.1887.26

**Heidelberg Castle, Germany, showing the Wing
built by Elector Otto Heinrich**
pen and brown ink, watercolour, bodycolour
(heightened with white)
signed lower right with initial in monogram: *SProut*
400 × 290 mm
Agnew's (purchase, 13.11.1893) (D.1887.26)

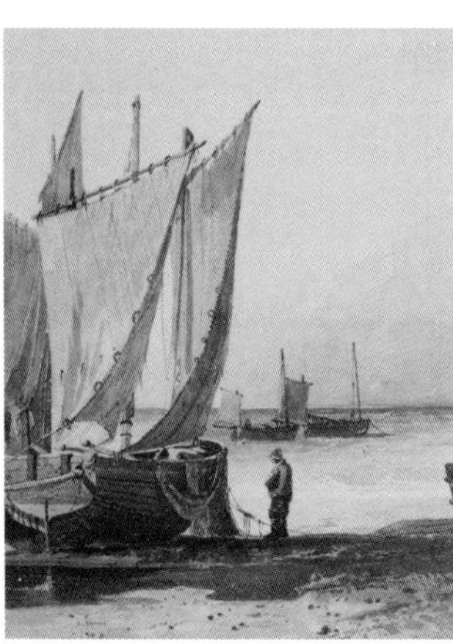

D.1893.7

Coast Scene with Luggers
pencil, watercolour
signed lower left: *S.Prout*
295 × 224 mm
Agnew's (purchase, 18.12.1893) (D.1893.7)

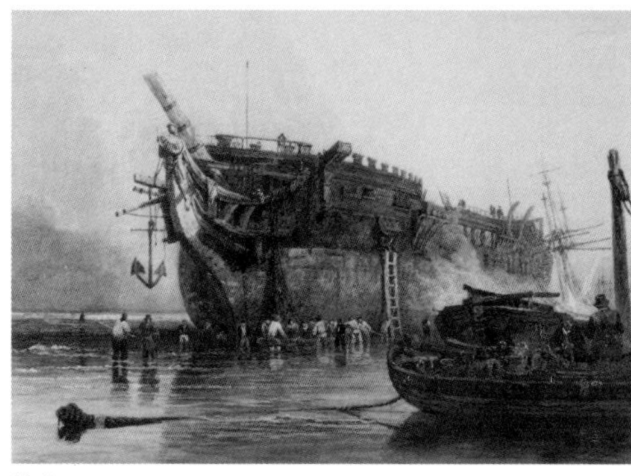

D.1899.5

An East Indiaman ashore
watercolour
495 × 680 mm
Agnew's (purchase, 21.11.1899) (D.1899.5)

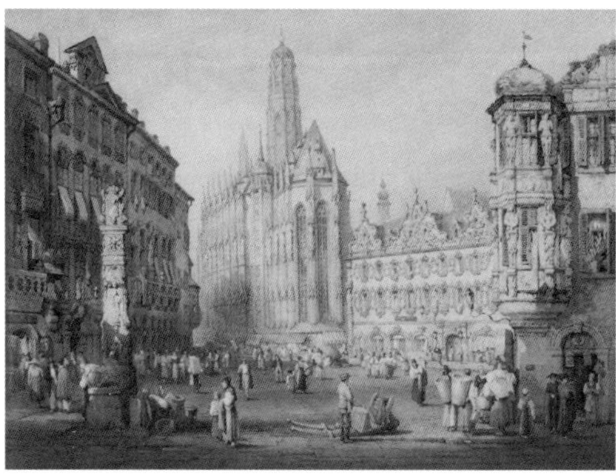

D.1904.21

**The Market Place, Würzburg, Germany, with the
Marienkapelle and Falkenhaus**
pen and brown ink, watercolour
signed lower left with initial in monogram: *SProut*
540 × 718 mm
Worthington, Mary (bequest, 1904) (D.1904.21)

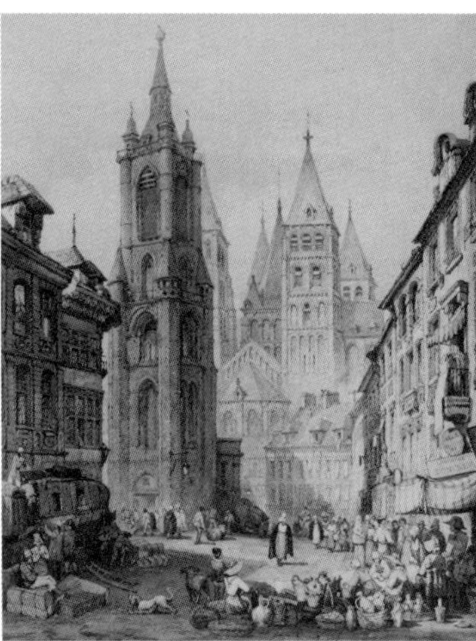

D.1904.22

**Tournai Cathedral, Belgium, with the Belfry,
seen from Rue Saint Martin**
pen and brown ink, watercolour
630 × 478 mm
Worthington, Mary (bequest, 1904) (D.1904.22)

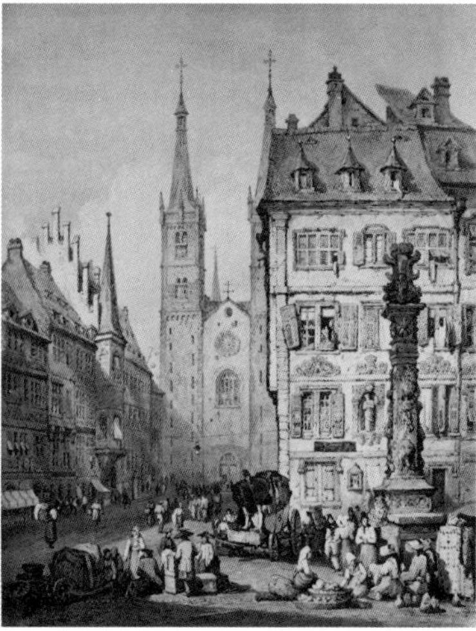

D.1904.23

Street Scene, Würzburg, Germany
pen and brown ink, watercolour
630 × 478 mm
Worthington, Mary (bequest, 1904) (D.1904.23)

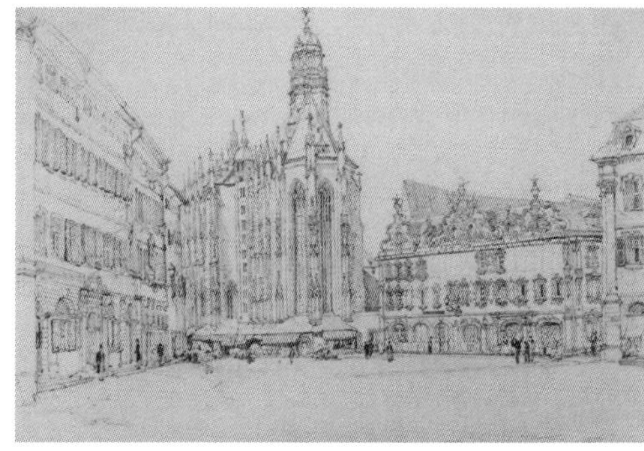

D.1905.6

Study for 'The Market Place, Würzburg'
pencil
extensively inscribed with mostly illegible colour notes
286 × 418 mm
Worthington, Hubert, Worthington, Lady Joan (gift, 1905)
(D.1905.6)

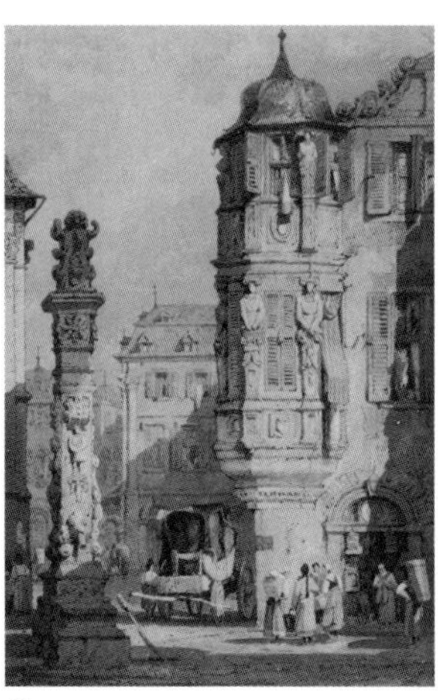

D.1910.12

Street Scene, Würzburg, Germany, looking towards the Cathedral
pen and brown ink, watercolour, bodycolour (heightened with white)
signed lower right with initial in monogram: *SProut*
420 × 270 mm
Cox, G. F. (bequest, 1910) (D.1910.12)

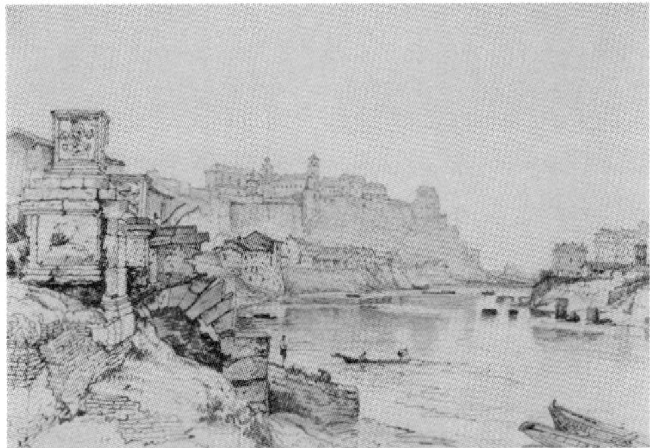
D.1922.26

Mount Aventine, with a View along the Tiber, Rome
pencil
inscribed lower left (identifying ruined bridge in left foreground): *Ponte Rotto*; inscribed lower centre (identifying hill in distance): *Monte Aventino*; inscribed lower right (identifying remains of bridge on far bank of the river): *remains Ponte Sublicio*
260 × 370 mm
Wilson, Sir Harry (gift, 1922) (D.1922.26)

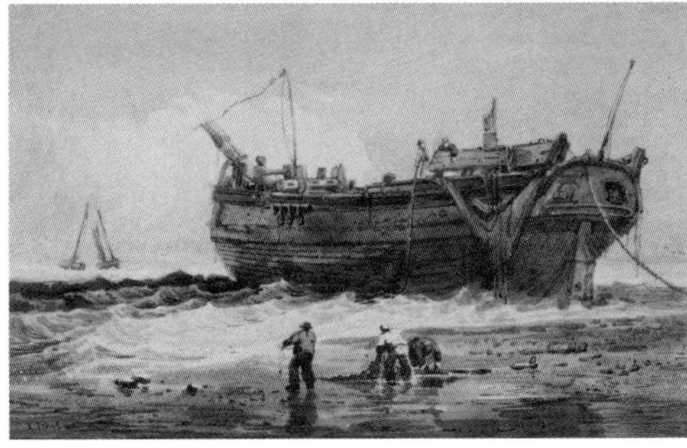
D.1924.46

The Wreck
pencil, pen and brown ink, brown watercolour
signed lower left: *S.Prout*
220 × 334 mm
Broadhurst, Sir Edward Tootal, Broadhurst, Lady (bequest, 1924) (D.1924.46)

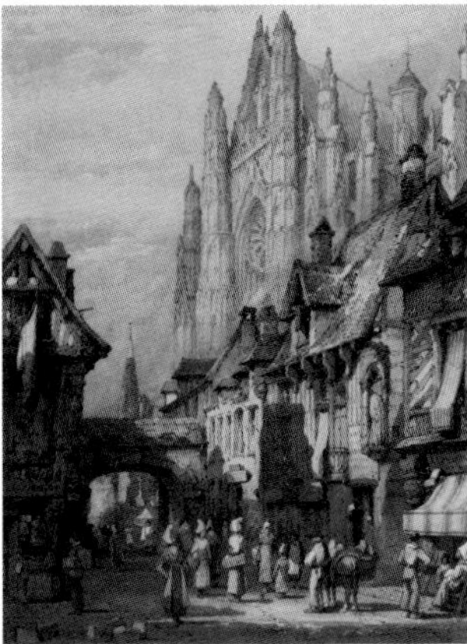
D.1924.49

Street Scene, Beauvais, France, with the South Transept of the Cathedral
pen and brown ink, watercolour, bodycolour (heightened with white)
454 × 375 mm
Broadhurst, Sir Edward Tootal, Broadhurst, Lady (bequest, 1924) (D.1924.49)

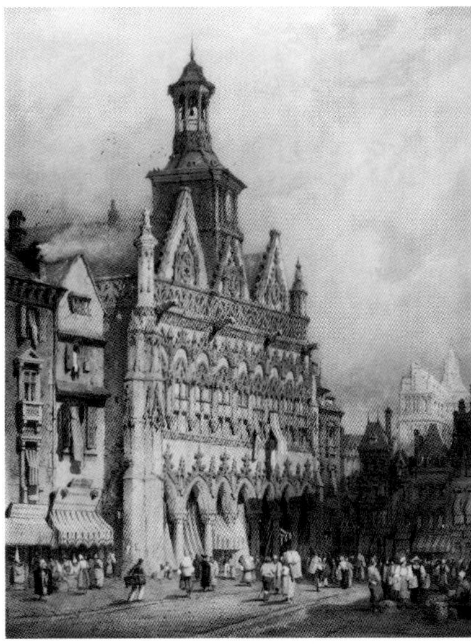
D.1924.60

The Town Hall, St Quentin, France
1845
pen and brown ink, watercolour, bodycolour (heightened with white)
signed, inscribed & numbered on artist's label: *No.2*[erased] *1 / Hotel de Ville St.Quentin / France / From a Sketch by J.Ruskin Junr.Esqr. / [long underline] / SProut*
734 × 552 mm
Broadhurst, Sir Edward Tootal, Broadhurst, Lady (bequest, 1924) (D.1924.60)

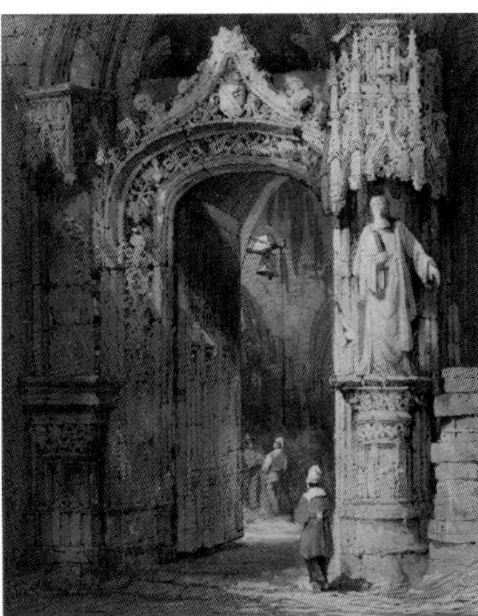
D.1924.61

The Corn Hall, Tours, France, formerly a Church
pen and brown ink, watercolour, bodycolour (heightened with white)
signed lower right with initial in monogram: *SProut*
318 × 244 mm
Broadhurst, Sir Edward Tootal, Broadhurst, Lady (bequest, 1924) (D.1924.61)

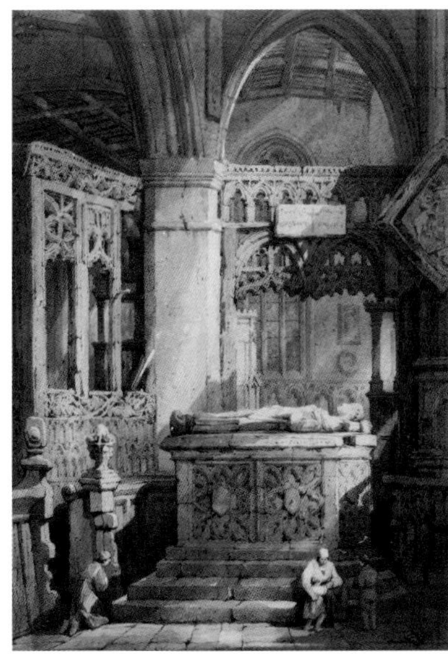
D.1924.62

Harbour Scene, Exmouth, Devon
watercolour
signed lower centre: *S.Prout*
278 × 211 mm
Broadhurst, Sir Edward Tootal, Broadhurst, Lady (bequest, 1924) (D.1924.62)

Interior of a Church, Caen, Normandy, with a Tomb
pen and brown ink, watercolour
signed lower right with initial in monogram: *SProut*
434 × 302 mm
Haworth, Jesse (bequest, 1937) (D.1937.18)

D.1937.18

Palais de Justice, Rouen, Normandy
27.9.1817
pencil
inscribed & dated along lower edge starting left hand side: *Palais de Justice – Rouen – Sepr.27.1817.*
410 × 264 mm
Withers, Monica (gift, 1978) (D.1978.2)

■ PUGIN, AUGUSTUS CHARLES (1762–1832)

An architectural draughtsman and father of the celebrated architect A. W. N. Pugin, Augustus Charles Pugin came to England from France in the 1790s and began to work for the architect John Nash. Pugin first exhibited architectural designs at the Royal Academy in 1799 and began to exhibit at the Old Watercolour Society in 1807, being elected a member in 1812. He did much work for the print publisher Rudolph Ackermann, contributing to the *Repository of Arts* and the *Microcosm of London*. In the 1820s, with Nash's encouragement, Pugin set up an unofficial school of architectural drawing.

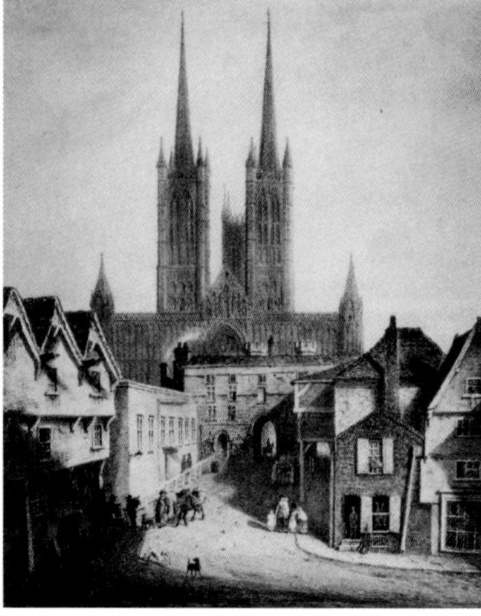

D.1892.36

Lincoln Cathedral, from the West
pencil, watercolour
350 × 275 mm
Taylor, John Edward (gift, 1892) (D.1892.36)

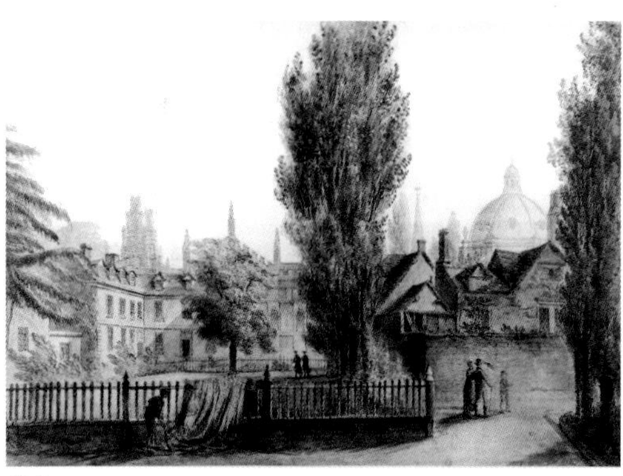

D.1892.37

Hertford College, Oxford, from the Grove
pencil, pen and brown ink, watercolour
278 × 381 mm
Taylor, John Edward (gift, 1892) (D.1892.37)

■ PYNE, JAMES BAKER (1800–1870)

Pyne initally exhibited at the Royal Academy between 1836 and 1839 but then turned to the Society of British Artists, where he exhibited every year from 1842 until his death. He was well travelled on the Continent and produced paintings on commission from Agnew's. His paintings, many of which are numbered (corresponding to his sales ledgers in the Victoria & Albert Museum), are reminiscent of Turner's later style.

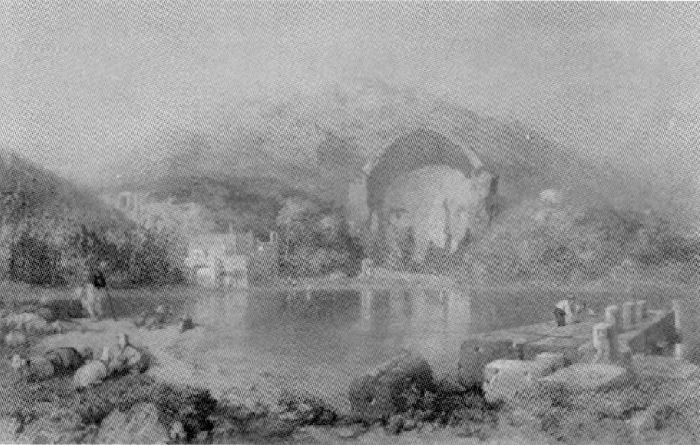

D.1887.37

Temple of Diana, Bay of Baia, Italy
1852
pencil, watercolour, bodycolour
(heightened with white)
signed & dated lower right: *JBPYNE1852*; numbered lower right above and to right of signature and date: *No.455*.
312 × 500 mm
Agnew's (purchase, 13.11.1893) (D.1887.37)

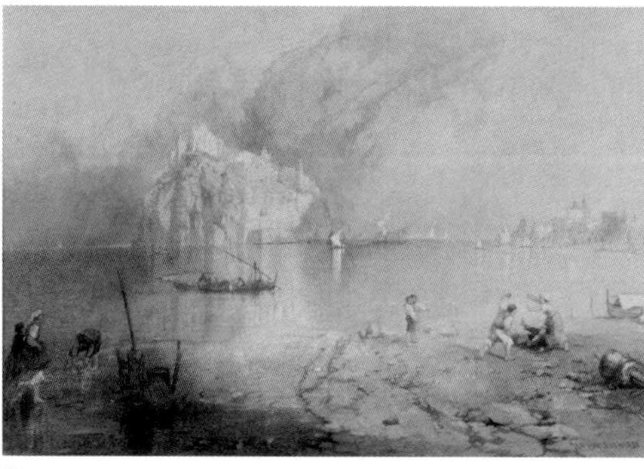

D.1937.19

Castle of Ischia, Italy
1852
pencil, watercolour, bodycolour
(heightened with white)
signed, numbered & dated lower right:
JBPYNE1852No.451.
332 × 487 mm
Haworth, Jesse (bequest, 1937) (D.1937.19)

■ PYNE, WILLIAM HENRY (1769–1843)

Pyne first exhibited at the Royal Academy in 1790 and was one of the founder members of the Old Watercolour Society in 1804. Between 1802 and 1807 he was working on his *Microcosm*, which contained more than a thousand figure groups and details published as soft-ground etchings for the use of landscape watercolourists. Pyne's later career was more concerned with publishing ventures and critical writing; his essays in the *Literary Gazette*, republished in 1823 as *Wine and Walnuts*, are an important contemporary source for historians of the English watercolour school.

Gossip by the Cottage Door
1794
pencil, pen and grey ink, watercolour
signed & dated lower right: *W.H.Pyne.1794*
227 × 170 mm
Taylor, John Edward (gift, 1892) (D.1892.60)

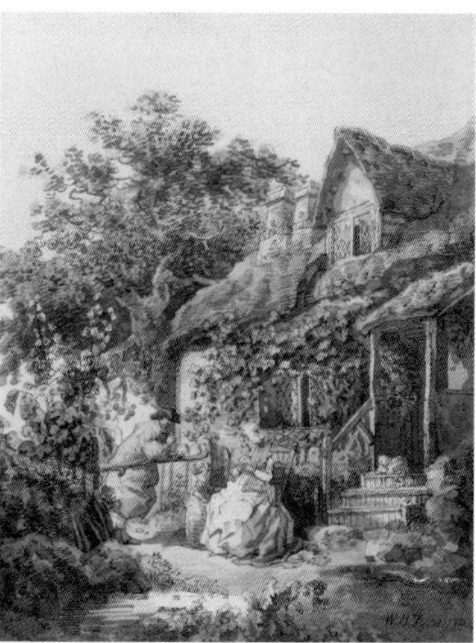

D.1892.60

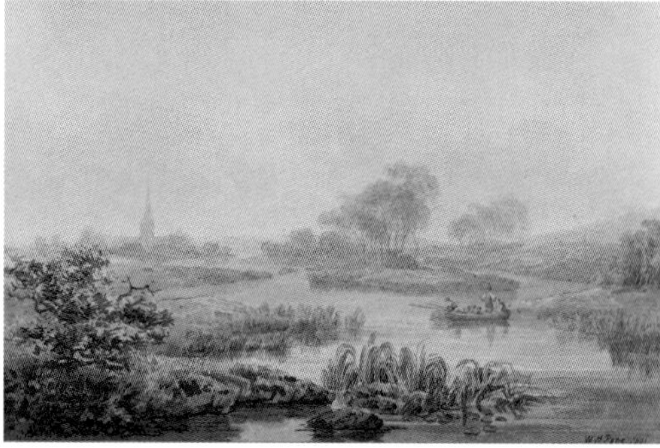

D.1892.61

View near Salisbury, the Cathedral in the Distance
1801
pencil, watercolour
signed & dated lower right: *W.H.Pyne.1801*
169 × 253 mm
Taylor, John Edward (gift, 1892) (D.1892.61)

Part of Old Lombard Street, London
watercolour
inscribed centre verso: *View of Part of Lombard St as now pulled down for / the New St King William St / £2.2*
168 × 262 mm
Westmacott, Lt Col F. H. (bequest, 1936) (D.1936.3)

Rochester Castle, Kent
watercolour, bodycolour (heightened with white)
190 × 268 mm
Towlson, Hector J. (bequest, 1969) (D.1970.65)

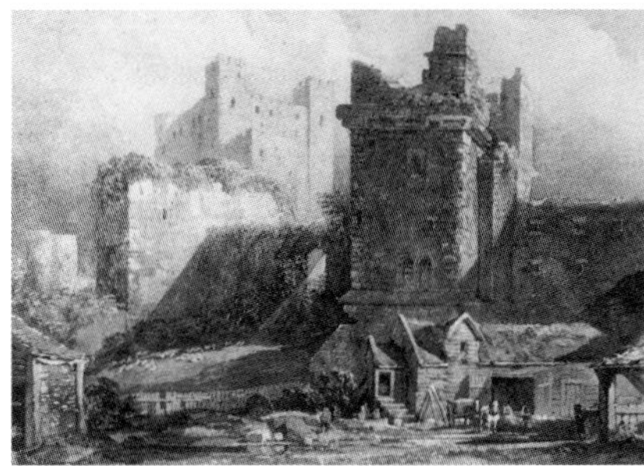

D.1970.65

■ **RATHBONE, JOHN (ca. 1750–1807)**

Rathbone was born in Cheshire and worked in Liverpool and Manchester before exhibiting at the Royal Academy between 1785 and 1806. Described by Ellis Waterhouse as a 'prolific painter of nondescript landscapes in oil and watercolour', Rathbone sometimes collaborated with George Morland and Julius Caesar Ibbetson, who painted the figures in his landscapes.

Country Courtship
pen and brown ink, watercolour
signed lower left: *J Rathbone*
203 × 279 mm
Towlson, Hector J. (bequest, 1969) (D.1970.66)

■ **RAVEN-HILL, LEONARD (1867–1942)**

Raven-Hill was born in Bath and studied at Lambeth School of Art – where he met Ricketts and Shannon – and in Paris. Raven-Hill, a black-and-white cartoonist and illustrator, worked for *Punch* from 1896. An admirer of Ricketts and Charles Keene, Raven-Hill illustrated Kipling's *Stalky & Co.* in 1899 and worked for other periodicals and magazines. He was one of the most versatile of the Edwardian illustrators.

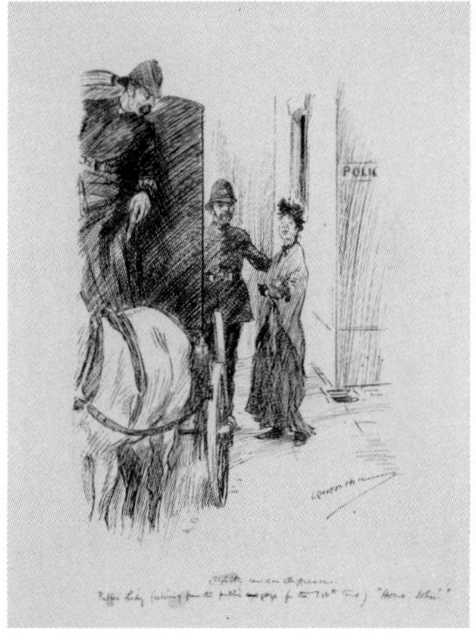

D.1927.143

Dignity under Difficulties: '"Puffec" Lady retiring from the Public Gaze for the 150th Time', Illustration for 'Punch' Magazine
1904
pen and brown ink
signed lower right: *LRAVENHILL*; inscribed along lower edge: *Dignity under Difficulties. / Puffec' Lady (retiring from the public eye* [erased] *gaze for the 150th time) "Home, John!"*
375 × 273 mm
Holliday, J. R. (bequest, 1927) (D.1927.143)

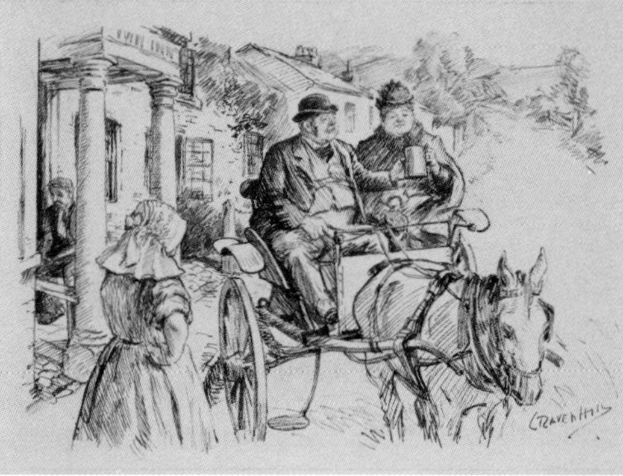

D.1927.144

His Bitter Half: 'John, Drink, earty Maria, Drink werry nigh "arf"': Illustration for 'Punch' Magazine
1904
pen and brown ink, brown watercolour
signed lower right: *LRAVENHILL*
234 × 314 mm
Holliday, J. R. (bequest, 1927) (D.1927.144)

■ **RAWLE, SAMUEL (1771–1860)**

A painter in oil and watercolour, Rawle contributed illustrations to *The Gentleman's Magazine* and to a number of the antiquarian John Britton's publications.

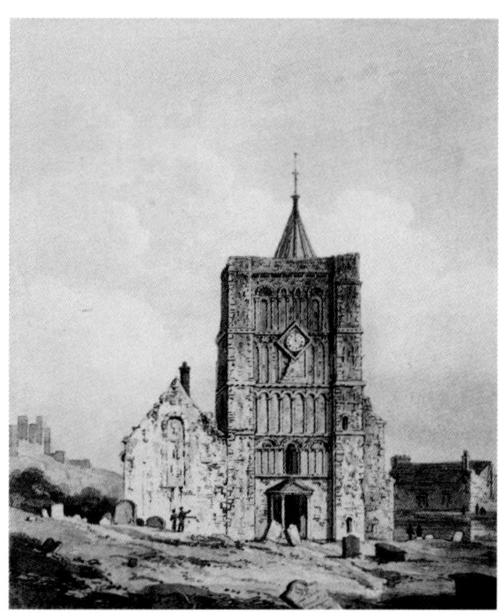

D.1970.67

St Mary's Church, Dover
pencil, watercolour
169 × 137 mm
Towlson, Hector J. (bequest, 1969) (D.1970.67)

■ **REID, SIR GEORGE (1841–1913)**

Sir George Reid was a Scottish portrait painter and illustrator who studied in Edinburgh, Utrecht and Paris. From the 1870s, Reid was Scotland's leading portrait painter; he was elected a member of the Royal Scottish Academy in 1877 and its President in 1891, in which year he was knighted. Reid also painted landscapes.

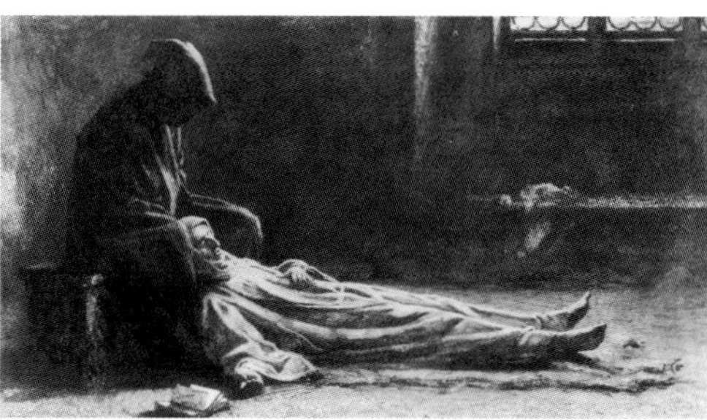

D.1920.25

The last Sleep of Savonarola
grisaille; card
184 × 287 mm
Thomson, D. Croal (purchase, 1920) (D.1920.25)

■ **REID, JOHN ROBERTSON (1851–1926)**

John Robertson Reid, a Scottish painter in oil and watercolour of genre scenes and landscape and coastal subjects, studied at the Royal Scottish Academy Schools under William Mactaggart and George Paul Chalmers. He painted slightly sentimental scenes of rural life and exhibited at the Royal Academy from 1877 to 1925.

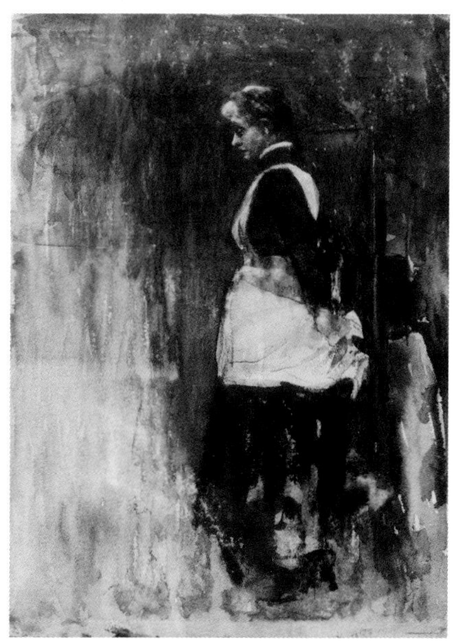

D.1954.28

Female domestic Servant
watercolour
352 × 252 mm
untraced (purchase, 1954) (D.1954.28)

■ **REINAGLE, RAMSAY RICHARD (1775–1862)**

Ramsay Richard Reinagle, son of the painter Philip, first exhibited at the Royal Academy in 1788. He was elected a member of the Old Watercolour Society in 1806 and served as President from 1809 to 1812. Thereafter he concentrated more on oil painting and was elected a member of the Royal Academy in 1823. Reinagle was a skilful copyist and restorer and was forced to resign from the Royal Academy for having exhibited a picture by another artist under his own name.

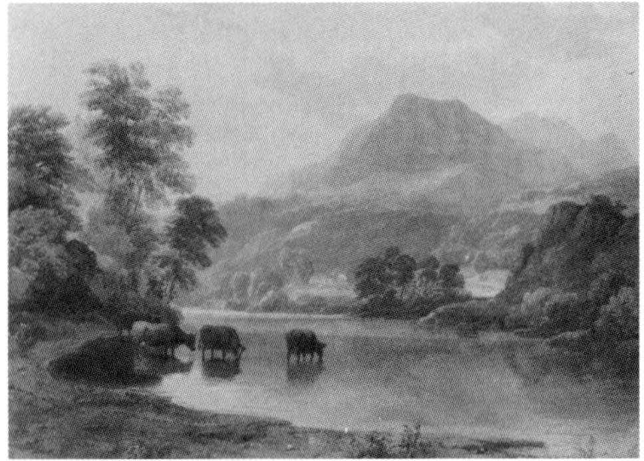

D.1892.71

Loughrigg Fell and River Brathay, Head of Windermere, Westmorland
pencil, watercolour
signed & inscribed on upper centre verso: *Loughrigg Mountain and River Brathy, above Clappersgate bridge / Near the head of Windermere Westmoreland / SunSet – / R R Reinagle*
285 × 392 mm
Taylor, John Edward (gift, 1892) (D.1892.71)

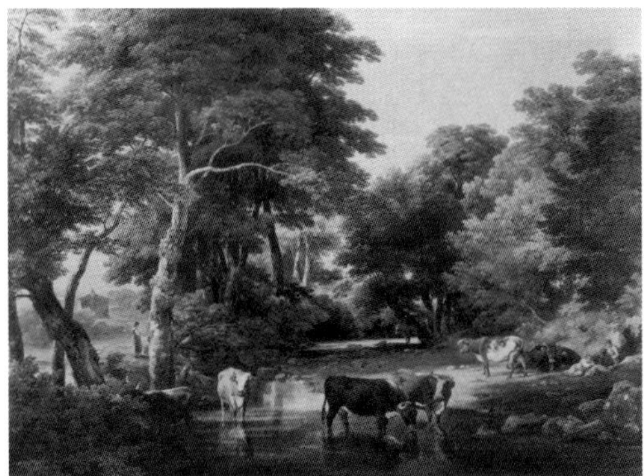

D.1924.42

Cattle watering at Evening
1809
watercolour
signed & dated lower right with initials: *R R R 1809*
597 × 797 mm
Broadhurst, Sir Edward Tootal, Broadhurst, Lady
(bequest, 1924) (D.1924.42)

■ RICH, ALFRED WILLIAM (1856–1921)
A landscape watercolourist and follower of Peter de Wint, Rich studied at Westminster School of Art and at the Slade under Legros. He lived and worked in Sussex and exhibited at the New English Art Club from 1896. In 1918 he published *Water Colour Painters*, which was profusely illustrated with his own works and those by earlier watercolourists he admired.

The Inner Bailey, Ludlow Castle, Shropshire
watercolour
signed lower left: *Alfred W.Rich*
284 × 393 mm
Anderson, A. E. (gift, 1921) (D.1921.17)

The Lock, Tewkesbury, Gloucestershire
watercolour; buff paper
numbered lower left: *20*
280 × 391 mm
Anderson, A. E., National Art Collections Fund (via)
(gift, 1923) (D.1923.15)

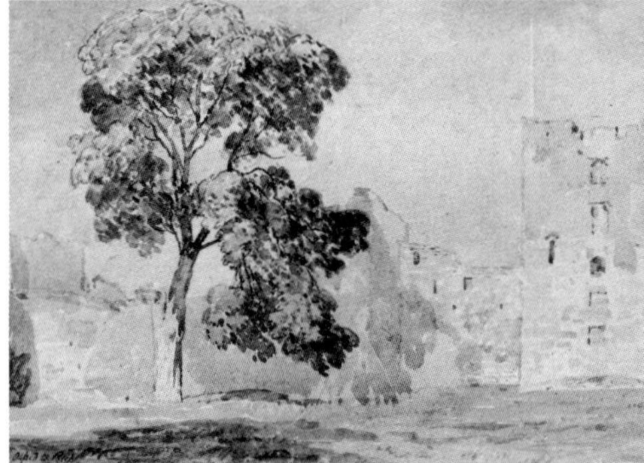

D.1921.17

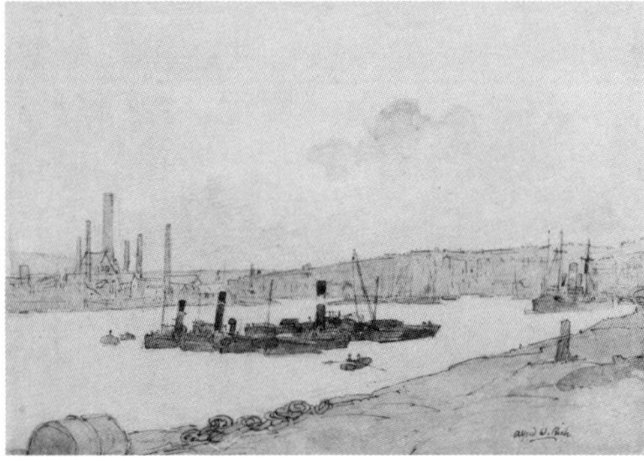

D.1923.16

View of Chatham, Kent, from across the River Medway
pencil, pen and brown ink, watercolour
signed lower right: *Alfred W.Rich*
293 × 406 mm
Anderson, A. E., National Art Collections Fund (via)
(gift, 1923) (D.1923.16)

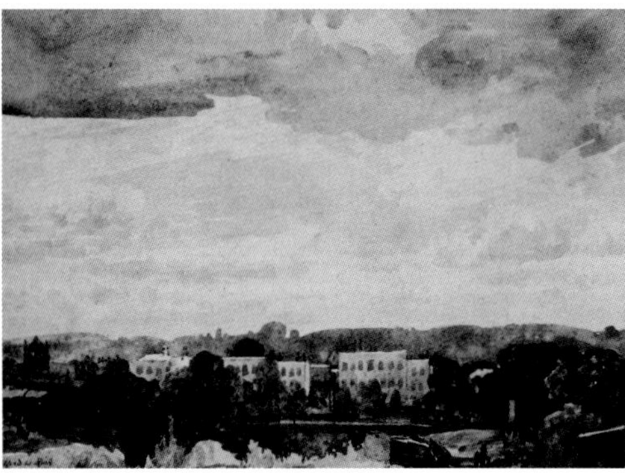

D.1946.13

Houses along the River, near Durham
watercolour
signed lower left: *Alfred WRich*
310 × 422 mm
Pilkington, Margaret (gift, 1946) (D.1946.13)

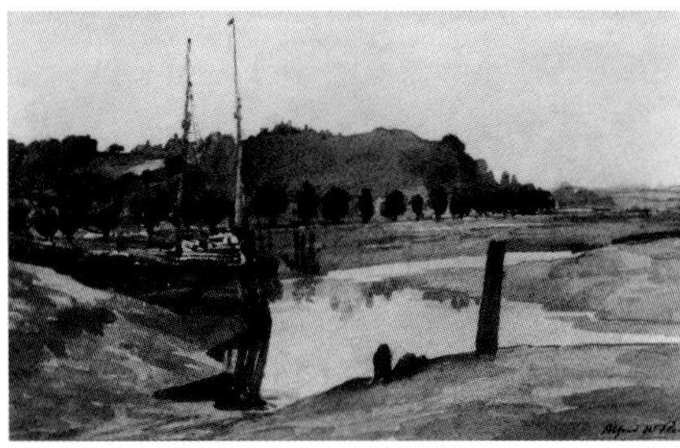

D.1949.26

River View near Rye, Sussex
pencil, watercolour
signed lower right: *Alfred W.Rich*
174 × 279 mm
Coleman, H. C. (bequest, 1949) (D.1949.26)

■ RICHARDSON, J. M.
(fl. late 18th century)
Unknown amateur artist.

Landscape, possibly in the South Seas
pen and brown ink, watercolour
signed lower left: *JMRichardson*
269 × 419 mm
Peer Groves, Major W. (gift, 1934) (D.1934.29)

■ RICHARDSON, JONATHAN (1665–1745)
Jonathan Richardson was the leading British portrait painter of the first 40 years of the eighteenth century. Along with Charles Jervas, Richardson was the busiest of the native-born portrait painters and was the rival of Sir Godfrey Kneller and Michael Dahl. Richardson wrote on artistic and literary topics and published *The Theory of Painting* in 1715; he was also an assiduous collector of drawings.

Portrait of John Gay
black chalk, red chalk, white chalk; blue paper
416 × 297 mm
Meatyard, F. R. (purchase, 1922) (D.1922.16)

■ RICHARDSON, Jun., THOMAS MILES
(1813–90)
Thomas Miles Richardson Jun. was the son of a Newcastle painter of the same name, from whom he received his training. He moved to London in 1846 and was elected a member of the Old Watercolour Society in 1851. Richardson travelled in Scotland and the North of England and also made extensive tours on the Continent; his large exhibition pieces were often highly coloured scenes in the Swiss, French and Italian Alps.

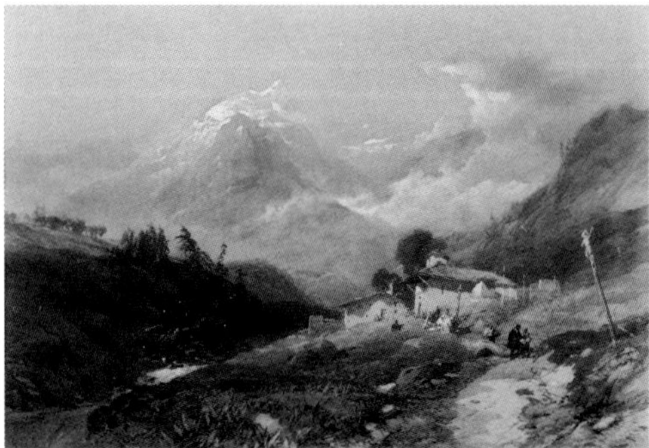

D.1937.20

Near Chamonix, France
1856
watercolour, bodycolour (heightened with white)
signed & dated lower right: *TMRichardson / ——— / 1856*
431 × 618 mm
Haworth, Jesse (bequest, 1937) (D.1937.20)

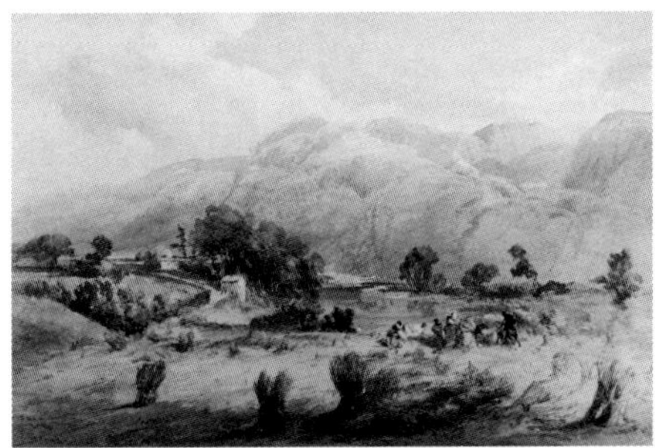

D.1970.68

Grange-in-Borrowdale, Cumberland
1849
pencil, watercolour, bodycolour
(heightened with white)
signed & dated lower right with initials: *TMR 1849*;
inscribed lower left: *Grange / Borrowdale / Cumbld*
321 × 474 mm
Towlson, Hector J. (bequest, 1969) (D.1970.68)

■ **RICHMOND, GEORGE (1809–96)**
Born in London into a family of painters, Richmond
entered the Royal Academy Schools in 1824. He was
part of a group of artists who met and were influenced
by William Blake in the mid-to-late 1820s. He then
turned to portraiture and was elected a member of the
Royal Academy in 1866. Richmond's characteristic
works are either small full-length portraits in
watercolour or life-size head and shoulders portraits in
chalk on brown paper. He also continued to paint
landscapes and was a friend of John Ruskin.

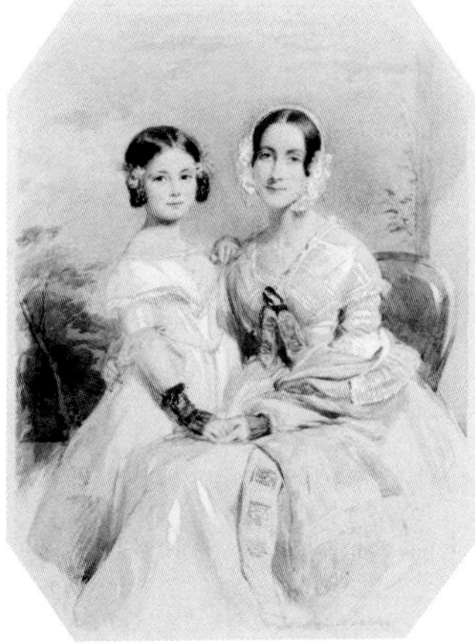

D.1939.15

**Portrait of Mrs Thomas Holroyd and her
Daughter, Sarah Morgan**
1842
pencil, watercolour, bodycolour (heightened with
white); corners cut
signed & dated lower right: *Geo Richmond delnt.1842*
480 × 347 mm
National Art Collections Fund (gift, 1939) (D.1939.15)

■ **RICHMOND, SIR WILLIAM BLAKE
(1842–1921)**
Sir William Blake Richmond, son of George
Richmond, entered the Royal Academy Schools in 1857
and exhibited there from 1861. He established a
successful portrait painting practice and went to Italy
in 1864, where he met Leighton and Giovanni Costa,
both of whom were a huge influence on his art. He

was elected a member of the Royal Academy in 1895
and was created a baronet in 1897. In addition to his
portrait painting practice, Richmond painted large
neo-classical pictures in the manner of Leighton; he
also designed mosaics for St Paul's Cathedral.

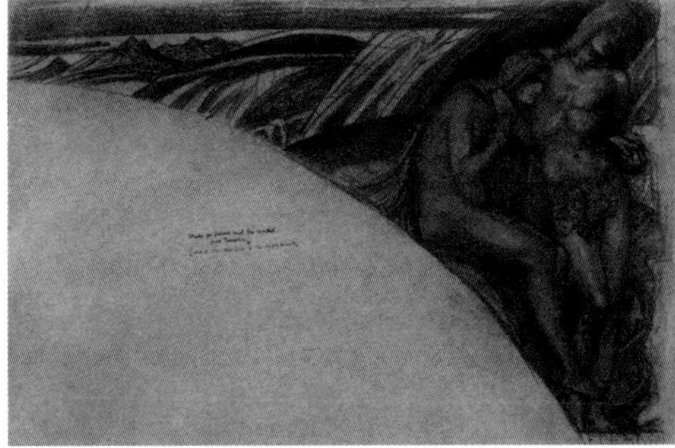

D.1960.33

**Study for 'Adam and Eve Expelled from
Paradise', for a Spandrel in the Choir Arcade,
St Paul's Cathedral, London**
black chalk; brown paper
inscribed centre left: *Study for Adam and Eve expelled /
from Paradise. / [one of the spandrels of the choir arcade]*
478 × 720 mm
Friends of the Whitworth (gift, 1960) (D.1960.33)

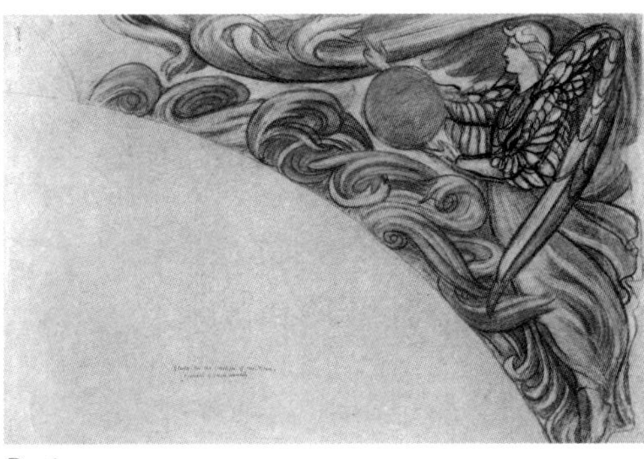

D.1960.34

**Study for the 'Creation of the Moon', for a
Spandrel in the Choir Arcade, St Paul's
Cathedral, London**
black chalk, watercolour; brown paper
inscribed lower left: *Study for the Creation of the Moon
– / [Spandrel of choir arcade] –*
478 × 720 mm
Friends of the Whitworth (gift, 1960) (D.1960.34)

■ **RIPPINGILLE, EDWARD VILLIERS
(1798–1859)**
Rippingille was self-taught and began his career in
Bristol, exhibiting at the Royal Academy and elsewhere
from 1813 to 1857. He painted subjects from English
rural life and, after a visit to Italy in 1837, Italian
peasant subjects.

Figures at a Cottage Door
pencil, brown watercolour
136 × 114 mm
Wallis, Miss J. K. Wallis, Miss R. (gift, 1926) (D.1926.12)

A Man seated on a Bank
black chalk
125 × 166 mm
Wallis, Miss J. K., Wallis, Miss R. (gift, 1926) (D.1926.13)

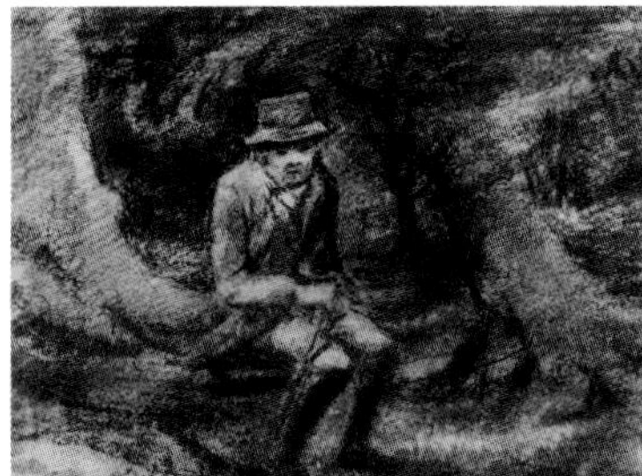

D.1926.13

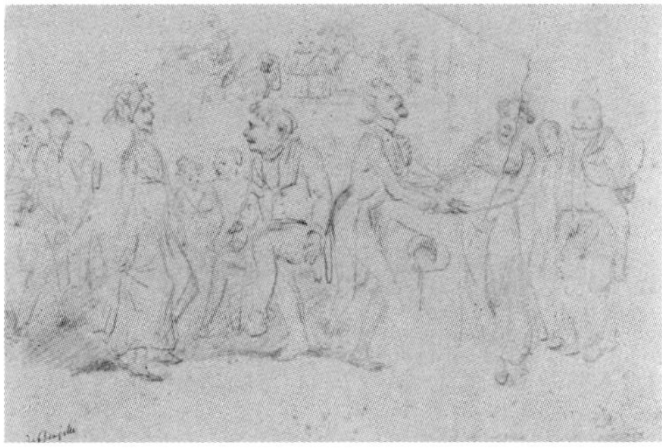

D.1926.14

Figures dancing
pencil; buff paper
signed lower left: *Rippingille*
181 × 267 mm
Wallis, Miss J. K., Wallis, Miss R. (gift, 1926) (D.1926.14)

■ **ROBERTS, DAVID (1796–1864)**
Roberts began his career as a theatrical scene painter in
Edinburgh and Glasgow before moving to London to
work at Drury Lane in 1822. He turned to easel
painting and travelled in Spain in 1832–33; he is best
known for his work deriving from his visits to Egypt
and Palestine in 1838–39. Roberts's lithographs in
Views in the Holy Land and Egypt, published in parts
between 1842 and 1849, brought him considerable
fame and fortune; he was elected a member of the
Royal Academy in 1841. Roberts was one of the
greatest Victorian artist-travellers and also visited
Italy and Germany.

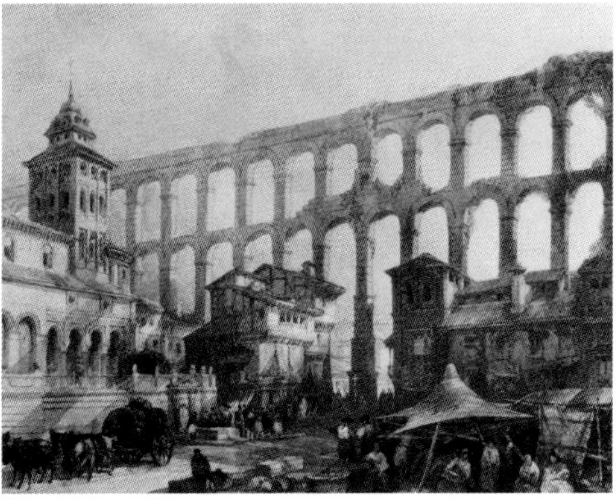

D.1887.20

The Roman Aqueduct, Segovia, Spain
1836
pencil, watercolour, bodycolour
(heightened with white)
signed & dated lower centre: *D Roberts 1836*
290 × 351 mm
Wright, Thomas W. (purchase, 1891) (D.1887.20)

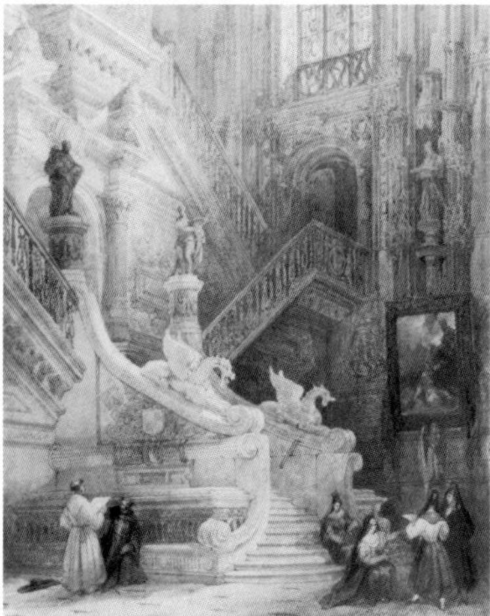

D.1887.40

Staircase in the North Transept, Burgos Cathedral, Spain
1836
watercolour, bodycolour (heightened with white)
signed & dated lower right: *David Roberts 1836*
346 × 272 mm
Agnew's (purchase, 12.5.1891) (D.1887.40)

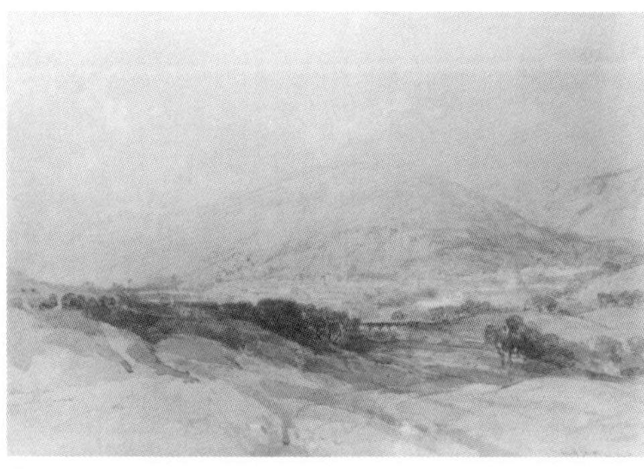

D.1887.41

View of Nablus, ancient Capital of Samaria
17.4.1839
pencil, watercolour, bodycolour (heightened with white); buff paper
signed lower right: *David Roberts.R.A.*; inscribed & dated lower left: *Nablous – or Shecem / ancient capital of Samaria /* [A]*pril 17.1839;* inscribed upper centre: *Mount Gerizin*
244 × 347 mm
Agnew's (purchase, 12.5.1891) (D.1887.41)

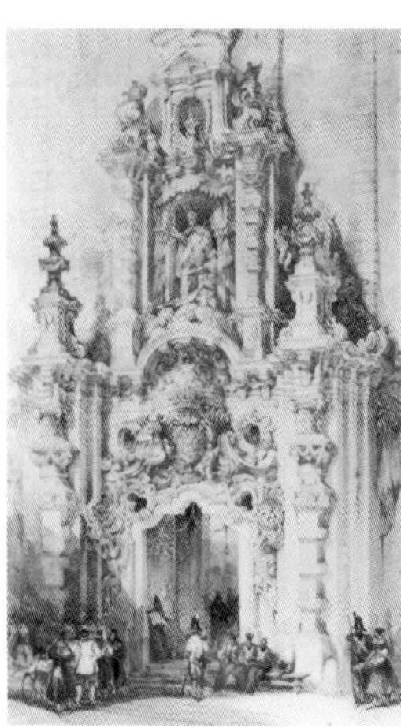

D.1887.42

The Gate of the Hospice, Madrid
1837
pencil, watercolour, bodycolour (heightened with white)
signed & dated lower left: *DRoberts / 1837*
408 × 235 mm
Agnew's (purchase, 14.5.1891) (D.1887.42)

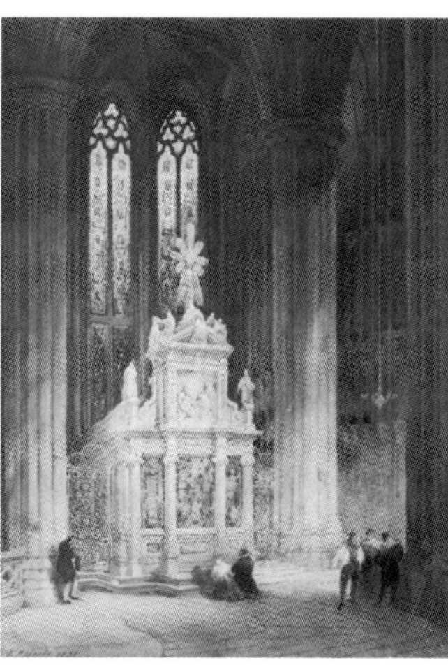

D.1910.8

The Shrine of the Three Kings, Cologne Cathedral
1831
watercolour, bodycolour (heightened with white)
signed & dated lower left: *D.Roberts 1831.*
313 × 228 mm
Cox, G. F. (bequest, 1910) (D.1910.8)

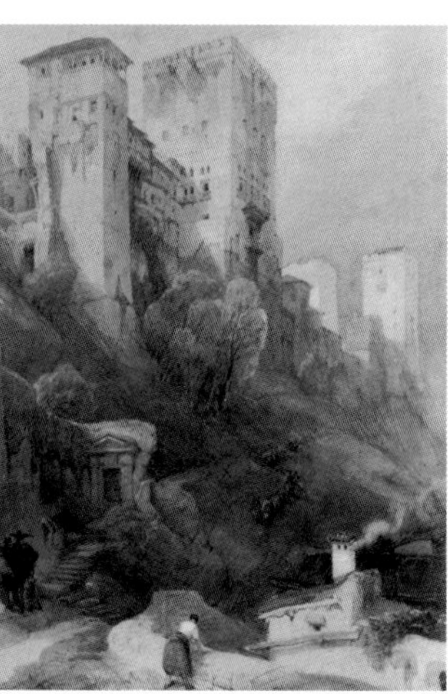

D.1914.7

The Tower of Comares, in the Alhambra Palace, Granada, Spain
1834
pencil, watercolour, bodycolour (heightened with white); buff paper
405 × 282 mm
untraced (purchase, 1914) (D.1914.7)

The Alcazar, or the Palace of the Moorish Kings, Cordoba, Spain
1835
watercolour, bodycolour (heightened with white)
signed & dated lower left: *D.Roberts 1835*
230 × 326 mm
Broadhurst, Sir Edward Tootal, Broadhurst, Lady (bequest, 1924) (D.1924.80)

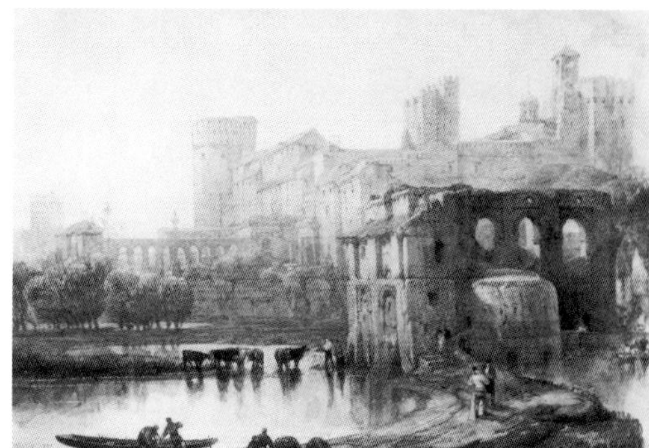

D.1924.80

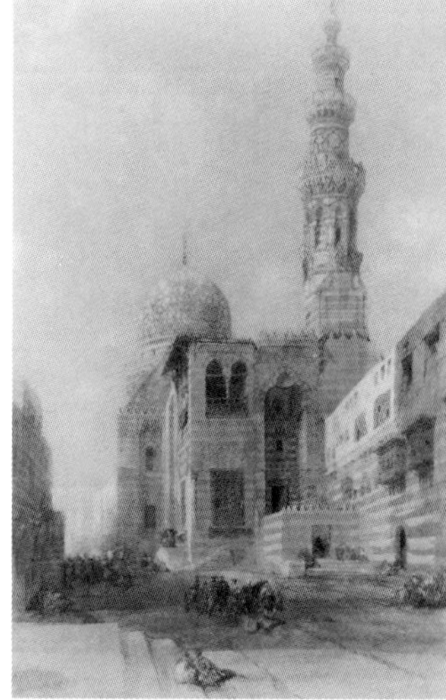

D.1927.21

The Tombs of the Caliphs, Cairo
16.1.1839
pencil, watercolour, bodycolour (heightened with white)
signed lower left: *David Roberts*; inscribed & dated lower left above the signature: *Tombs of the Caliphs / Cairo Jany.16th 1839*
532 × 331 mm
Newman and Co., London (purchase, 1927) (D.1927.21)

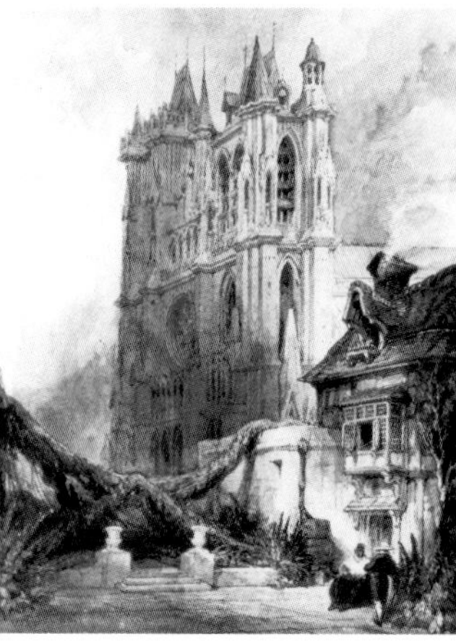

D.1937.21

The West Front, Amiens Cathedral, France
1830
watercolour, bodycolour (heightened with white)
signed & dated lower left: *D.Roberts 1830*
313 × 226 mm
Haworth, Jesse (bequest, 1937) (D.1937.21)

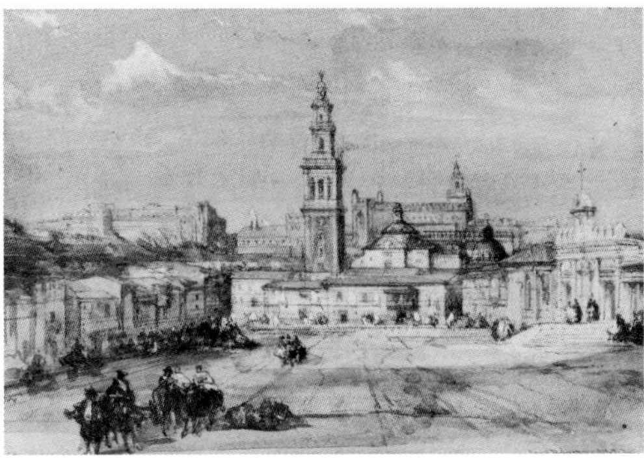

D.1960.14

The Great Square and Market Place, Carmona, near Seville, Spain (recto); Studies of the Tower and Facade (verso)
1833
black chalk, watercolour, bodycolour (heightened with white); grey paper
signed & dated lower right: *David Roberts.1833*;
inscribed lower left: *Carmona*
245 × 350 mm
Angus-Butterworth, L. M. (in memory of his father Walter Butterworth), National Art Collections Fund (via) (gift, 1960) (D.1960.14)

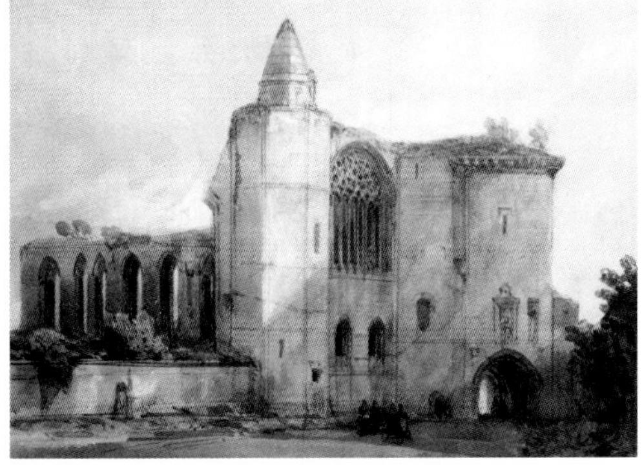

D.1968.6

Dunfermline Abbey, Fife, Scotland
pencil, watercolour, bodycolour (heightened with white); grey paper
251 × 342 mm
Fairhurst, P. Garland (gift, 1968) (D.1968.6)

■ **ROBERTS, HENRY BENJAMIN (1832–1915)**
Roberts, a Liverpool-born genre painter and follower of William Henry Hunt, exhibited at the Royal Academy intermittently between 1859 and 1875. He was a member of the Liverpool Academy from 1859.

An old Woman and Child in an Interior
watercolour
signed lower left with initial in monogram: *HRoberts*
118 × 86 mm
Faulkner Hill, Mrs (gift, 1947) (D.1947.55)

■ **ROBERTSON, GEORGE (1748–1788)**
Robertson studied at Shipley's Drawing School and then accompanied William Beckford of Somerley Hall to Rome, and to Jamaica in 1774; some of his Jamaican views were engraved. Robertson practised as a drawing master in London and provided drawings for the print market.

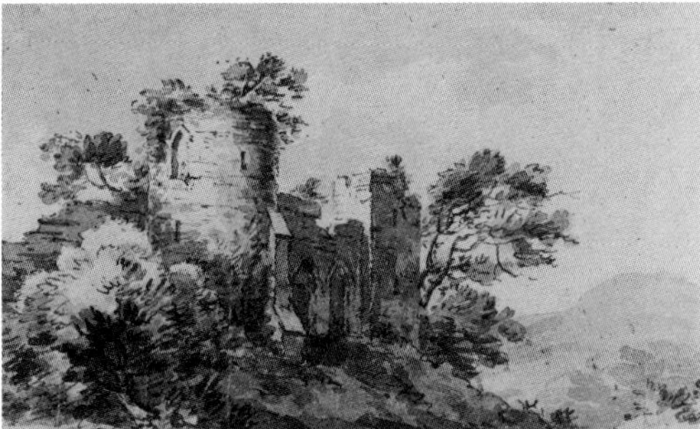

D.1954.11

A Castle on a Hill
pen and brown ink, brown watercolour
147 × 237 mm
untraced (gift, 1954) (D.1954.11)

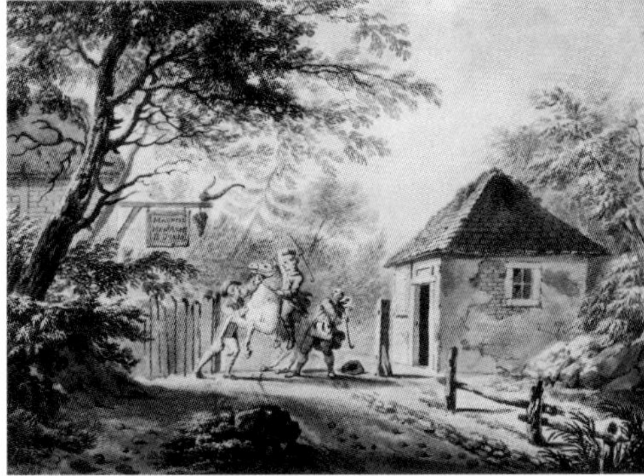

D.1971.5

An Attack by Robbers outside the married Men's Arms
pencil, pen and brown ink, watercolour
262 × 348 mm
Friends of the Whitworth (gift, 1971) (D.1971.5)

■ **ROBINSON, WILLIAM (1835–95)**
A Manchester-based landscape watercolourist, Robinson exhibited British and Continental views in London and Manchester.

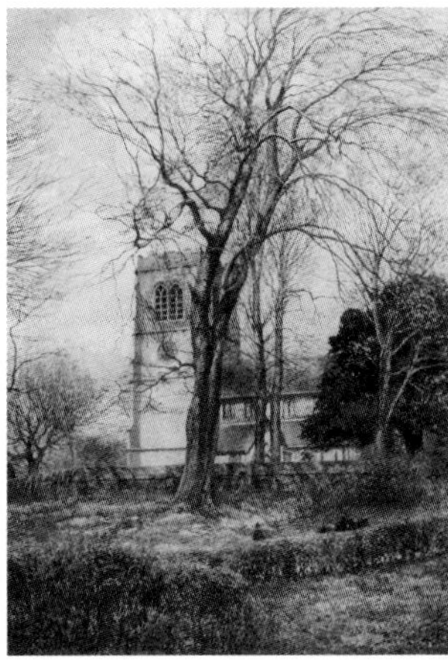

D.1892.157

St Wilfrid's Church, Mobberley, Cheshire
1891
pencil, watercolour
signed & dated lower left: *WRobinson / 1891*
554 × 385 mm
untraced (purchase, 1892) (D.1892.157)

■ **ROBSON, GEORGE FENNEL (1788–1833)**
Born in Durham, Robson moved to London in about 1804 and first exhibited at the Royal Academy in 1804. He exhibited at the Old Watercolour Society from 1813 until his death, showing views all over the British Isles, in particular Scottish and Irish scenes. Robson sometimes collaborated with Robert Hills, who provided the sheep and cattle in his landscapes.

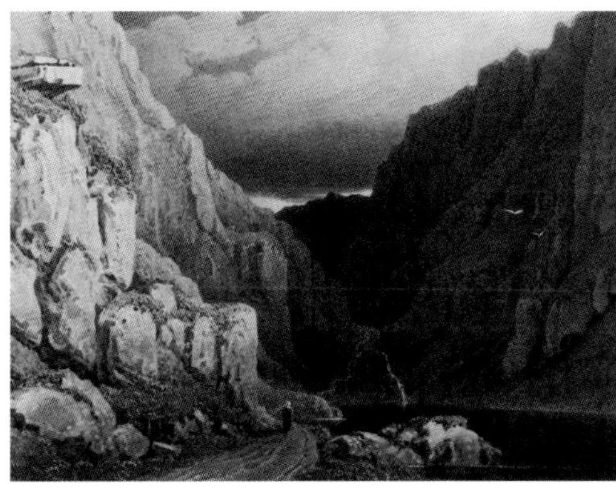

D.1892.126

Gap of Dunloe, near Killarney, Co. Kerry, Ireland
watercolour
213 × 280 mm
Taylor, John Edward (gift, 1892) (D.1892.126)

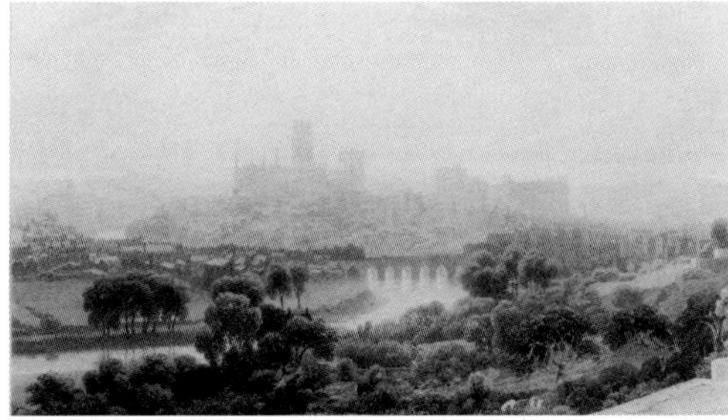

D.1934.24

Durham from the North East
pencil, watercolour
217 × 378 mm
Anderson, A. E. (gift, 1934) (D.1934.24)

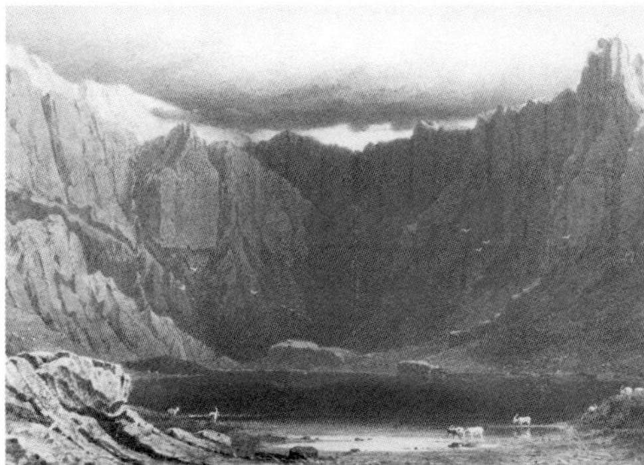

D.1946.14

The Devil's Kitchen, Llyn Idwal, Caernarvonshire, Wales
watercolour
199 × 272 mm
Pilkington, Margaret (gift, 1946) (D.1946.14)

■ ROMNEY, GEORGE (1734–1802)

Romney was apprenticed to Christopher Steele in
Kendal from 1755 to 1757. From 1757 to 1762 he
practised on his own before coming to London.
Romney studied in Italy from 1773 to 1775 and on his
return became, alongside Reynolds and Gainsborough,
the third of the fashionable portrait painters, with a
very extensive clientele. In the 1780s he painted
numerous portraits of Emma Hart (later to be Lady
Hamilton), many with her impersonating mythological
or allegorical characters. Romney was a frustrated
history painter and many of his drawings relate to
unexecuted history pictures.

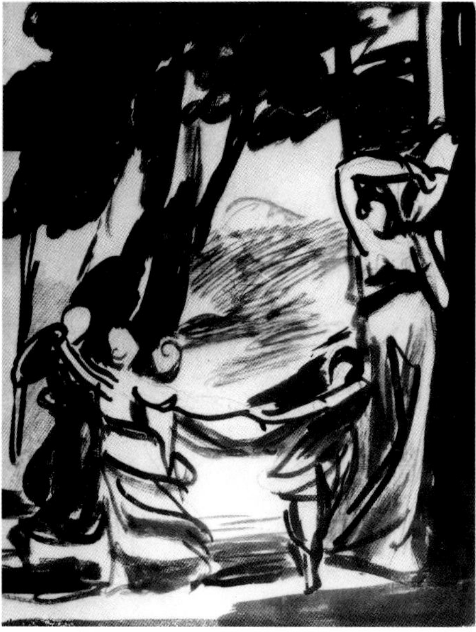

D.1933.30

Study for 'The Gower Children'
1777
pencil, brown watercolour
418 × 264 mm
Anderson, A. E. (gift, 1933) (D.1933.30)

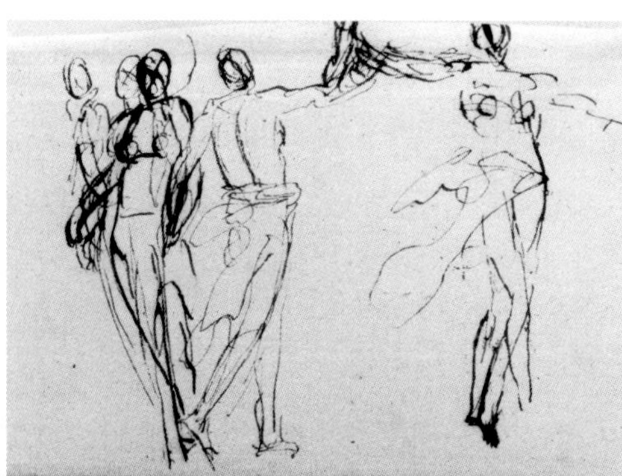

D.1960.120

Group of three dancing Figures
pen and brown ink
98 × 137 mm
University of Manchester, History of Art Department
(transfer, 1960) (D.1960.120)

A dancing Figure seen from behind
pen and brown ink
97 × 114 mm
University of Manchester, History of Art Department
(transfer, 1960) (D.1960.121)

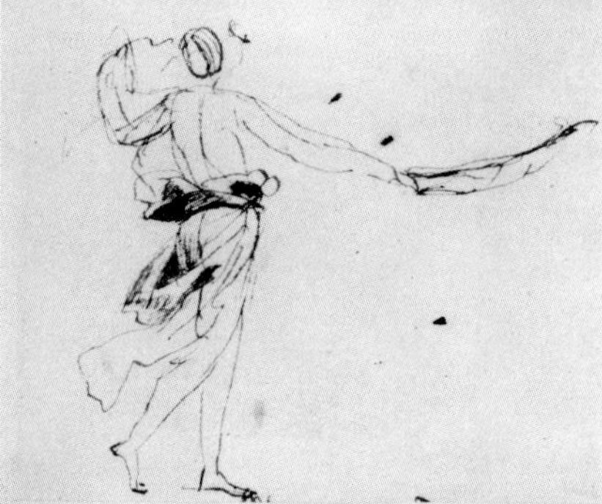

D.1960.121

**A reclining female Nude, probably a Study for
'Titania's Attendants chasing Bats'**
pen and brown ink
104 × 152 mm
University of Manchester, History of Art Department
(transfer, 1960) (D.1960.122)

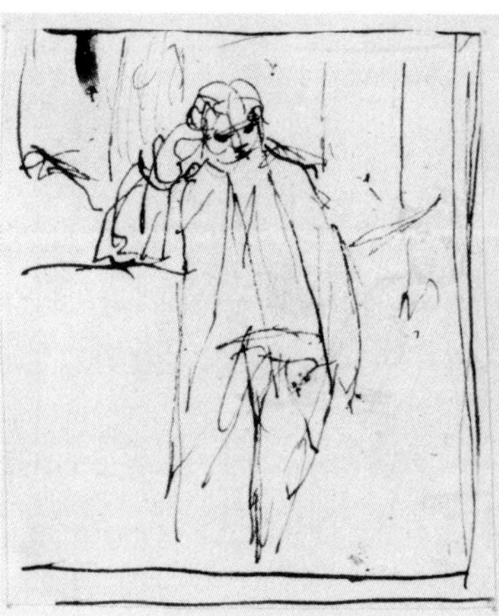

D.1960.123

**Study for a Portrait of a Man leaning on a Plinth
(recto); Study of a Man (verso)**
pen and brown ink
81 × 69 mm
University of Manchester, History of Art Department
(transfer, 1960) (D.1960.123)

Study for a Portrait of a Man holding a Book
pen and brown ink
108 × 84 mm
University of Manchester, History of Art Department
(transfer, 1960) (D.1960.124)

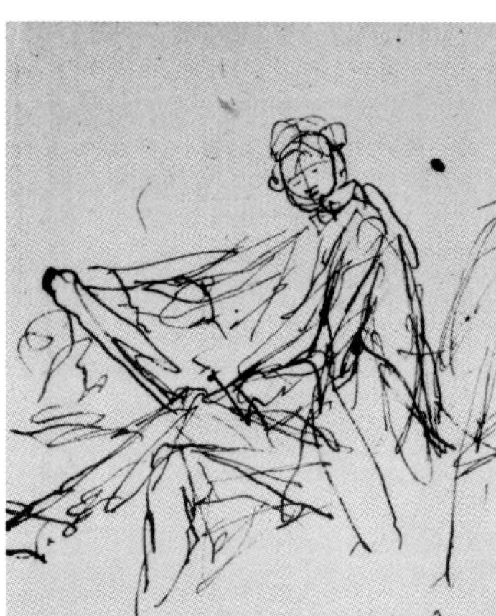

D.1960.125

Study for a Portrait of an Artist sketching
pen and brown ink
88 × 72 mm
University of Manchester, History of Art Department
(transfer, 1960) (D.1960.125)

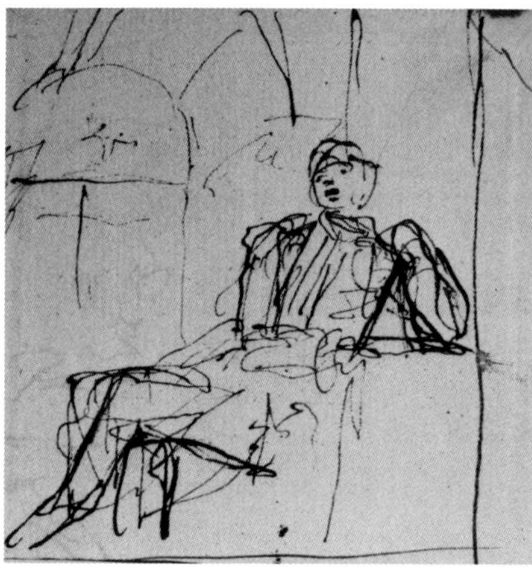

D.1960.126

Study for a Portrait of a Man seated by a Pillar
pen and brown ink
87 × 84 mm
University of Manchester, History of Art Department
(transfer, 1960) (D.1960.126)

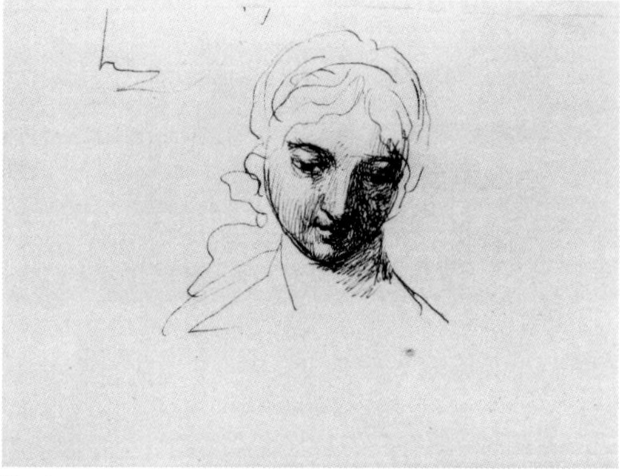

D.1960.127

Study of a female Head
pen and brown ink
118 × 143 mm
University of Manchester, History of Art Department
(transfer, 1960) (D.1960.127)

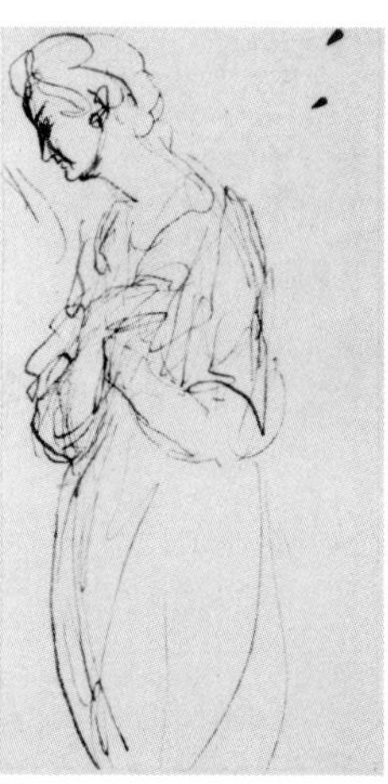

D.1960.128

Study for a Portrait of a Woman
pen and brown ink
159 × 79 mm
University of Manchester, History of Art Department
(transfer, 1960) (D.1960.128)

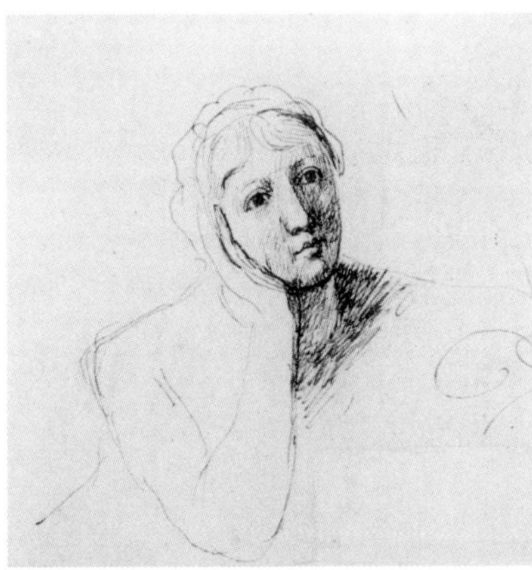
D.1960.129

Study of a female Figure
pen and brown ink
119 × 110 mm
University of Manchester, History of Art Department
(transfer, 1960) (D.1960.129)

Study for 'John Howard visiting a Lazaretto'
pen and brown ink
112 × 187 mm
Lockett, G. Derek (gift, 1962) (D.1962.13)

■ ROOKER, MICHAEL 'ANGELO'
(1746–1801)
Michael 'Angelo' was the son of the engraver Edward
Rooker, from whom he learnt the art of engraving.
Rooker was one of the few professional pupils of Paul
Sandby, who gave him the nickname 'Angelo'. He
entered the Royal Academy Schools in 1769 and was
elected an associate member the following year. He
produced engravings after his own drawings of ancient
buildings and castles. Alongside Thomas Hearne,
Rooker was one of the two eminent topographical
draughtsmen of the generation that followed Sandby.

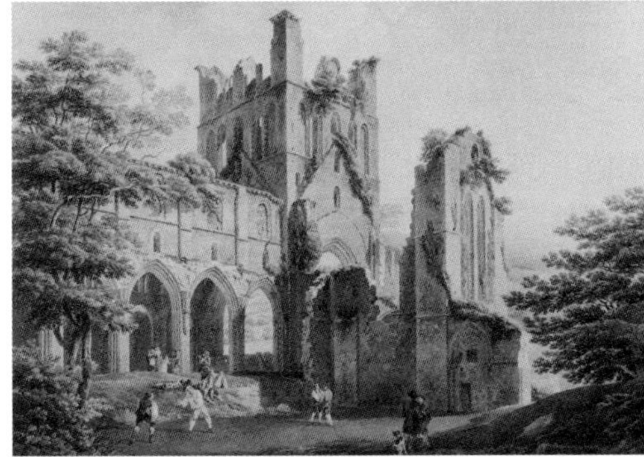
D.1892.14

Llanthony Abbey, Monmouthshire, Wales
1796
pencil, watercolour
signed & dated with initials in monogram:
MARooker 1796
388 × 542 mm
Taylor, John Edward (gift, 1892) (D.1892.14)

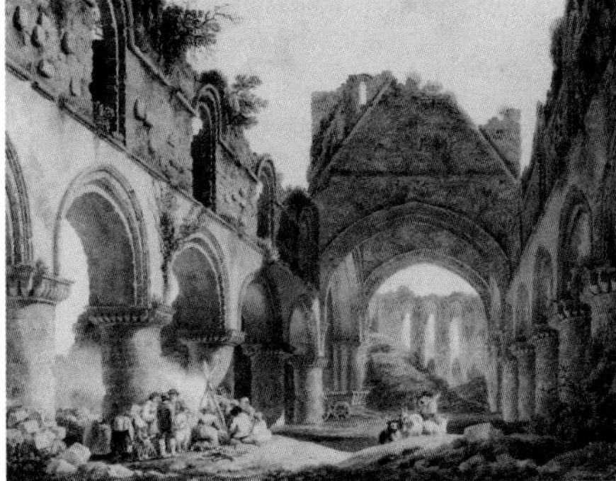
D.1892.15

Buildwas Abbey, Shropshire
pencil, watercolour
370 × 465 mm
Taylor, John Edward (gift, 1892) (D.1892.15)

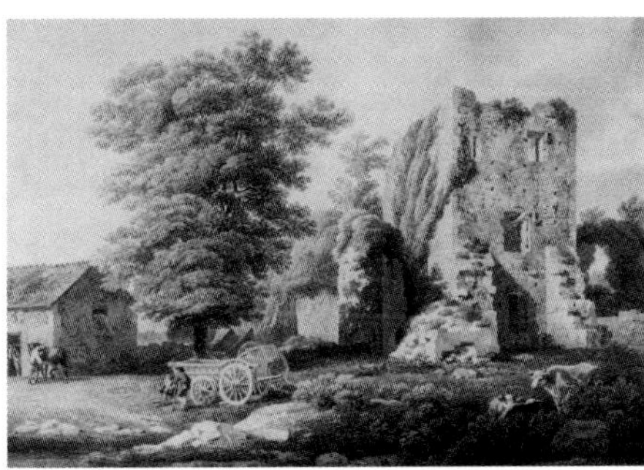
D.1900.13

Usk Castle, Monmouthshire, Wales
watercolour
signed lower right with initials in monogram:
MARooker
301 × 428 mm
Worthington, Mary (gift, 1900) (D.1900.13)

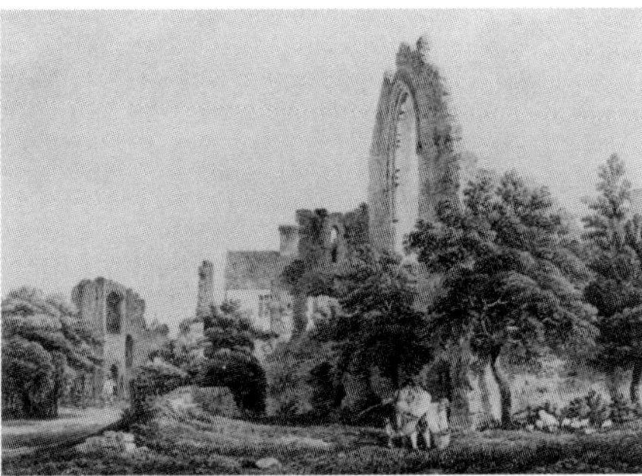
D.1924.87

Leiston Abbey, Suffolk
pencil, watercolour
signed lower left with initials in monogram: *MARooker*
inscribed centre verso: *Leiston Abbey Suffolk*
263 × 364 mm
Broadhurst, Sir Edward Tootal, Broadhurst, Lady
(bequest, 1924) (D.1924.87)

**Study for 'Llanthony Abbey,
Monmouthshire, Wales'**
1794–96
pencil, grey watercolour; watermark 1794 /
J WHATMAN
inscribed centre verso: *Lantony* (sic) *Abbey,
Monmouthshire.*
286 × 265 mm
Friends of the Whitworth (gift, 1999) (D.1999.11)

■ ROSSETTI, DANTE GABRIEL (1828–82)
Rossetti, son of an Italian political refugee who was
Professor of Italian at King's College, London, was one
of the three main founder members of the Pre-
Raphaelite Brotherhood in 1848. During the 1850s he
painted mainly watercolours, some of which were
commissioned by John Ruskin, whom he met in 1854.
Later he turned to mythological and literary subjects in
oil, some derived from the writings of Dante; he also
wrote poetry.

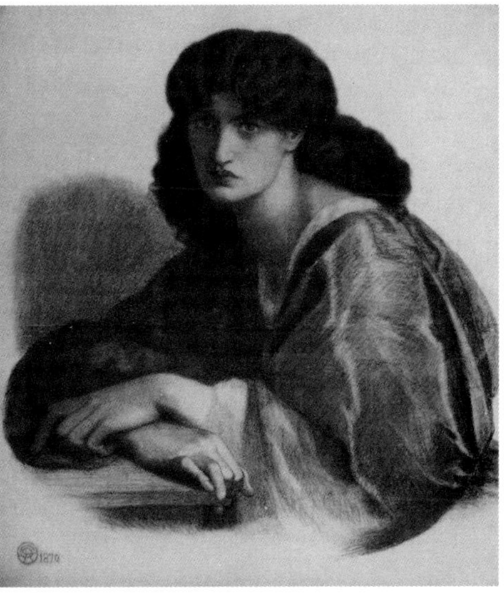
D.1921.35

La Donna della Finestra
1870
pastel; green paper
signed & dated lower left with monogram: *DGR 1870*
848 × 720 mm
Thomson, D. Croal (purchase, 1921) (D.1921.35)

**Portrait Study of Ruth Herbert (recto);
Studies of Heads (verso)**
1858–59
pencil; brown paper
signed lower right with monogram: *GR*; inscribed
lower right: *Miss Herbert / her gown*
265 × 207 mm
Thomson, D. Croal (purchase, 1922) (D.1922.10)

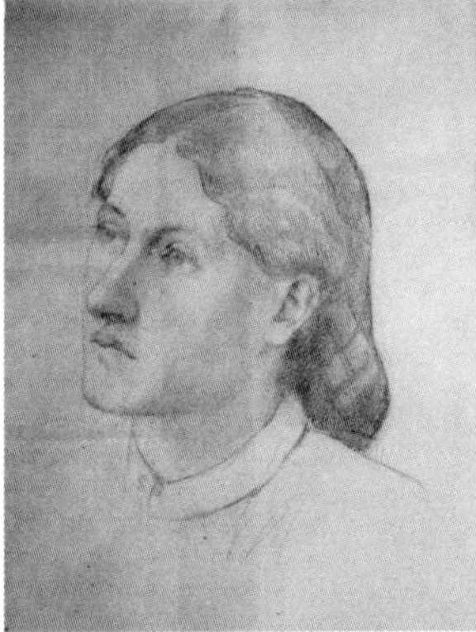
D.1922.11

Portrait Study of Ruth Herbert
1858–59
pencil
264 × 207 mm
Thomson, D. Croal (purchase, 1922) (D.1922.11)

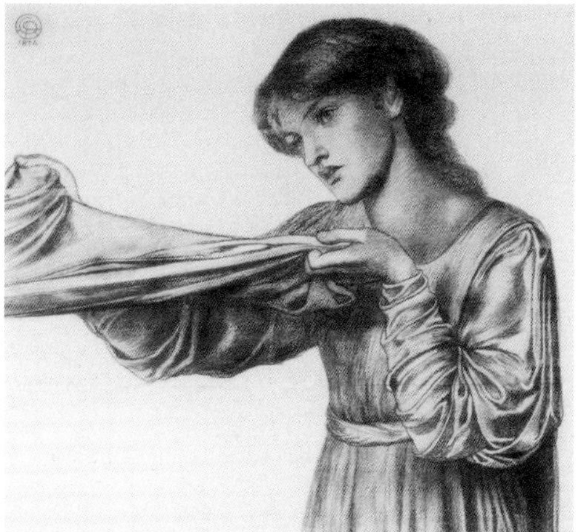

D.1923.14

Study of a Pallbearer for 'Dante's Dream'
1874
black chalk, red chalk, white chalk; green paper
signed & dated upper left with monogram: *DGR / 1874*
683 × 745 mm
Anderson, A. E., National Art Collections Fund (via)
(gift, 1923) (D.1923.14)

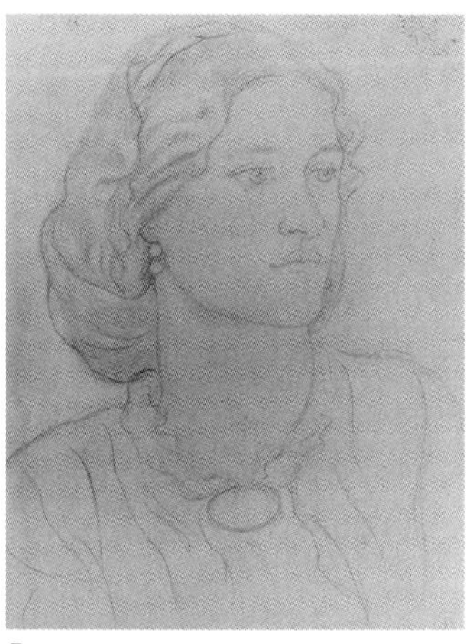

D.1923.17

Portrait Study of Ruth Herbert
1858–59
pencil
signed lower right with monogram: *DGR*
265 × 208 mm
Anderson, A. E., National Art Collections Fund (via)
(gift, 1923) (D.1923.17)

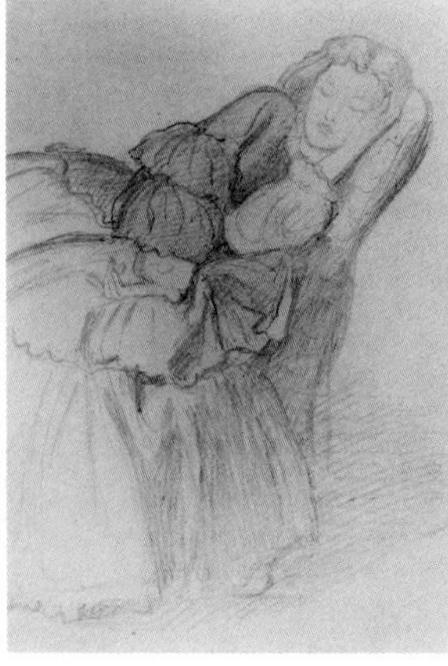

D.1923.23

Study of Ruth Herbert asleep
1858–59
pencil
264 × 199 mm
Thomson, D. Croal (purchase, 1923) (D.1923.23)

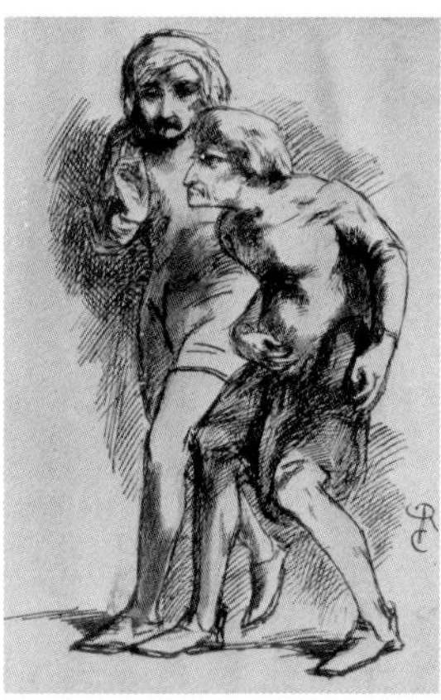

D.1927.152

Francesca's deformed Husband being told of her Infidelity with Paolo: Illustration to Dante's 'Inferno' (The Story of Paolo and Francesca)
1846
pencil, pen and brown ink, brown watercolour
signed lower right with monogram: *DGR*
228 × 154 mm
Holliday, J. R. (bequest, 1927) (D.1927.152)

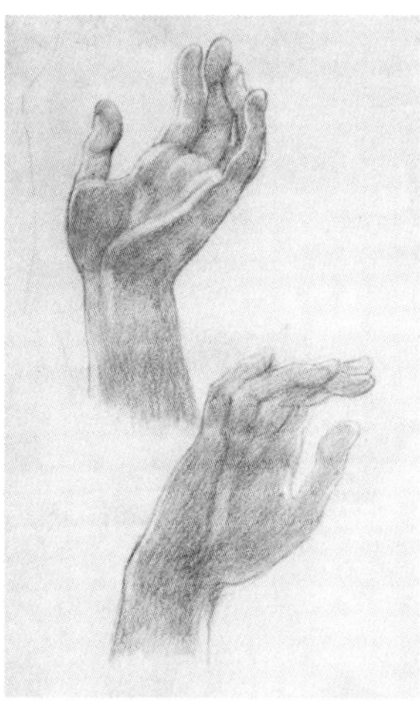

D.1934.34

Study of Hands for the Attendant Spirits in 'Astarte Syriaca'
1875–77
black chalk, red chalk
424 × 262 mm
Matthews, J. Hilditch (gift, 1934) (D.1934.34)

Jane Morris reclining on a Sofa
1869–71
pencil
246 × 347 mm
Barningham, W. (gift, 1948) (D.1948.6)

St Jude: Cartoon for a Window in the Nave, West Wall, Christ Church, Southgate, London
1862–63
pencil, brown watercolour
873 × 344 mm
Friends of the Whitworth (gift, 1959) (D.1959.9)

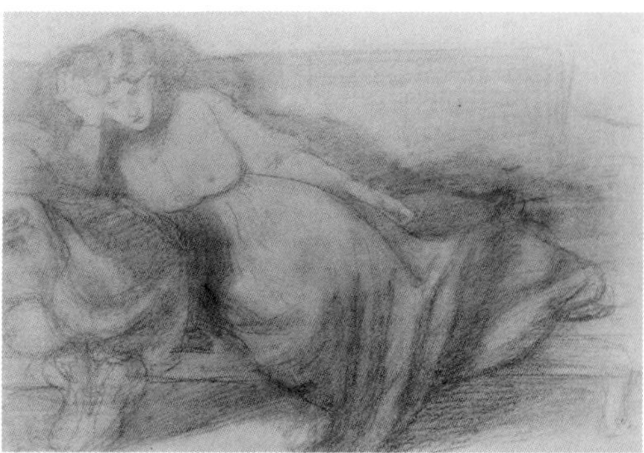

D.1948.6

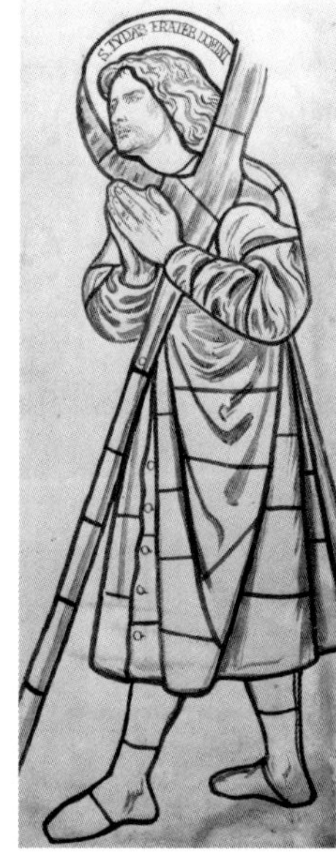

D.1959.9

■ Rowbotham, Thomas Charles Leeson (1823–75)
Born in Dublin and from a family of artists, Rowbotham was elected a member of the New Watercolour Society in 1851. He was taught by his father, whom he succeeded as drawing master at the Royal Naval College at Greenwich.

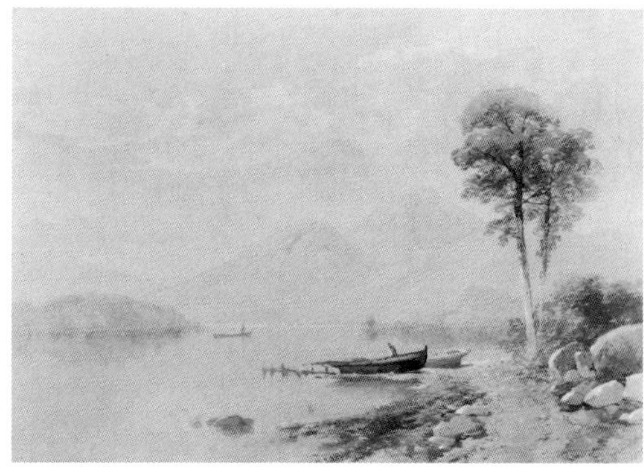

D.1970.69

Skiddaw from Derwentwater, Cumberland
1857
watercolour, bodycolour (heightened with white)
buff paper
signed & dated lower right: *TLRowbotham / 1857*
233 × 323 mm
Towlson, Hector J. (bequest, 1969) (D.1970.69)

ROWLANDSON, THOMAS (1756–1827)

Rowlandson, one of the most prolific and
accomplished caricaturists of his age, entered the
Royal Academy Schools in 1772 and exhibited
there between 1775 and 1787. He was also a book
illustrator, providing illustrations to *Tour of Dr Syntax
in Search of the Picturesque*, published between 1809
and 1811. Although sometimes dismissed as a mere
caricaturist, Rowlandson was also a sensitive and
original landscape draughtsman and was a tireless
sketcher on all his trips round London and further
afield. His works were widely faked.

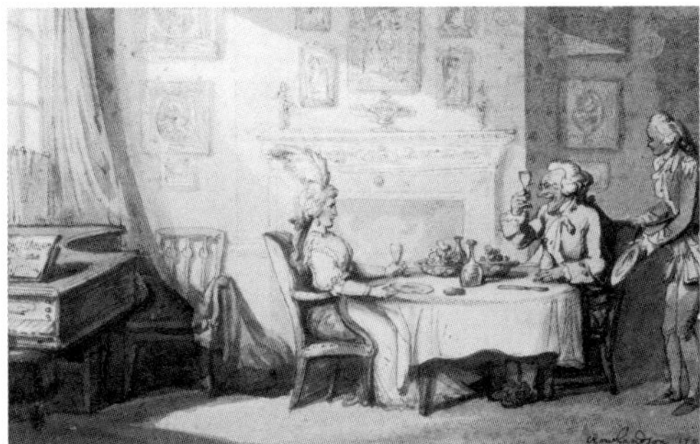

D.1892.33

High Life

1794
pen and brown ink, watercolour
signed & dated lower right: *Rowlandson 1794*
100 × 160 mm
Taylor, John Edward (gift, 1892) (D.1892.33)

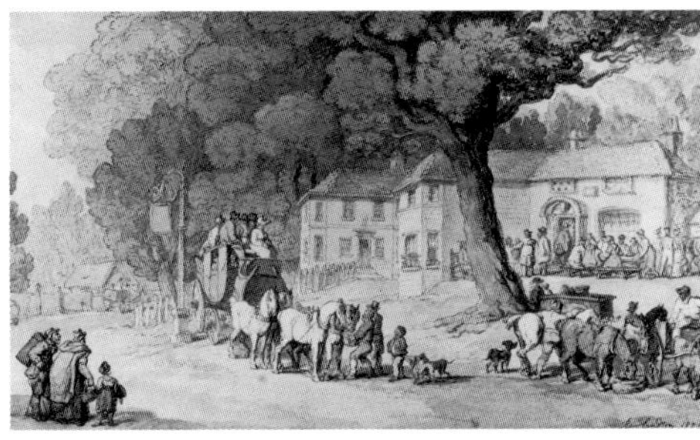

D.1892.34

The Roadside Inn

1824
pencil, pen and brown ink, watercolour
signed & dated lower right: *Rowlandson 1824*
238 × 386 mm
Taylor, John Edward (gift, 1892) (D.1892.34)

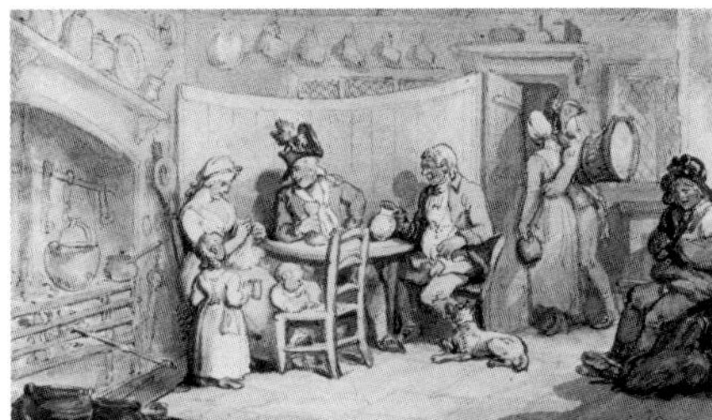

D.1892.35

Low Life

1794
pen and brown ink, watercolour
signed & dated lower right: *Rowlandson.1794*
97 × 159 mm
Taylor, John Edward (gift, 1892) (D.1892.35)

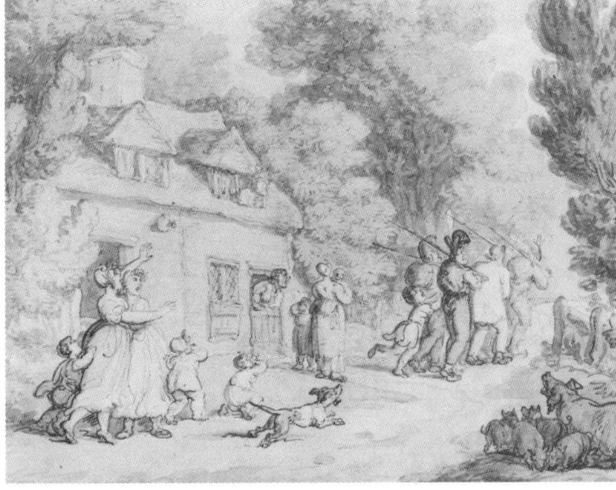

D.1915.10

The Press Gang

pen and brown ink, watercolour
227 × 294 mm
Hughes, C. E. (gift, 1915) (D.1915.10)

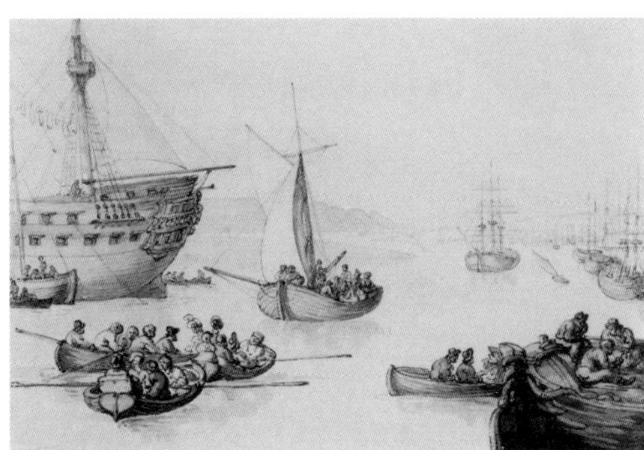

D.1915.11

The Estuary

pencil, pen and brown ink, watercolour
191 × 280 mm
Hughes, C. E. (gift, 1915) (D.1915.11)

Studies of Shipping in a Harbour, and a Village Church and Street

pencil, pen and brown ink
270 × 430 mm
Wilson, Sir Harry (gift, 1922) (D.1922.25)

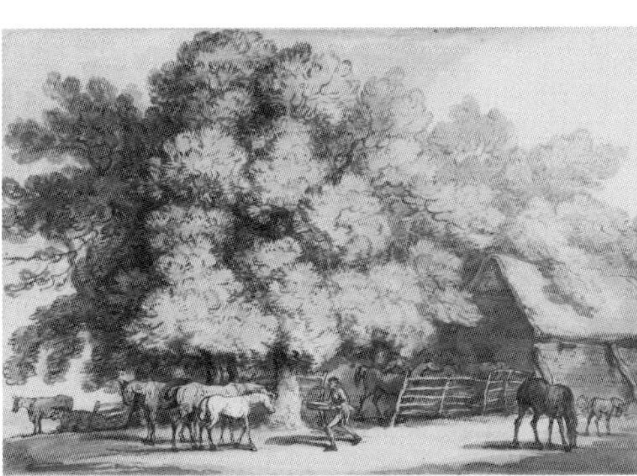

D.1926.48

Mares and Foals beside a Barn and Trees

pen and brown ink, watercolour
inscribed lower centre on wash line mount: *Brood
Mares*; inscribed lower right on wash line mount:
Drawing by Howitt; inscribed lower right corner of
wash line mount: *Howitt*
257 × 370 mm
Ogden, William Sharp (bequest, 1926) (D.1926.48)

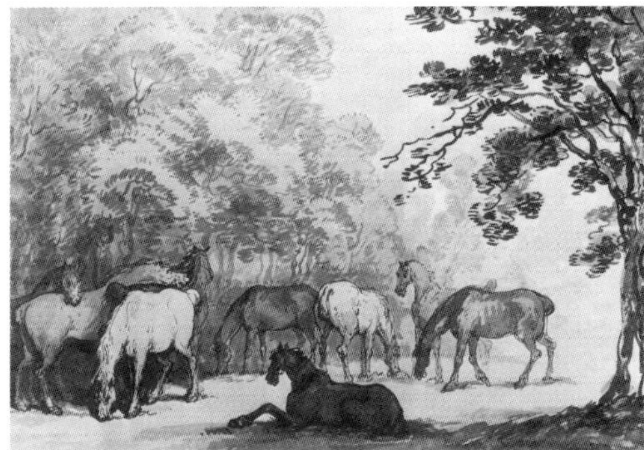

D.1934.25

The Stud Farm (recto); Study of a Man and a Lady (verso)

pencil, pen and brown ink, watercolour (recto)
275 × 388 mm
Anderson, A. E. (gift, 1934) (D.1934.25)

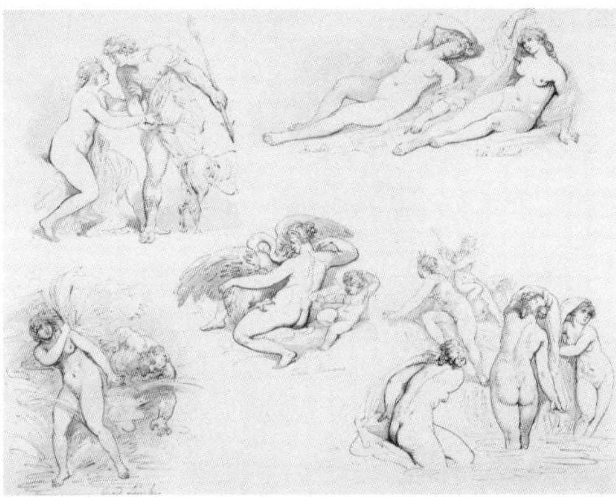

D.1961.16

Figure Studies after the Old Masters: Gerard de Lairesse, Carlo Maratta, Boucher and Giulio Romano

pencil, pen and brown ink, brown watercolour
inscribed all over drawing (the names of the artists
copied): *Boucher Carlo Marratt Julio Romano Gerard
Lairesse*
369 × 463 mm
Colnaghi's (purchase, 1961) (D.1961.16)

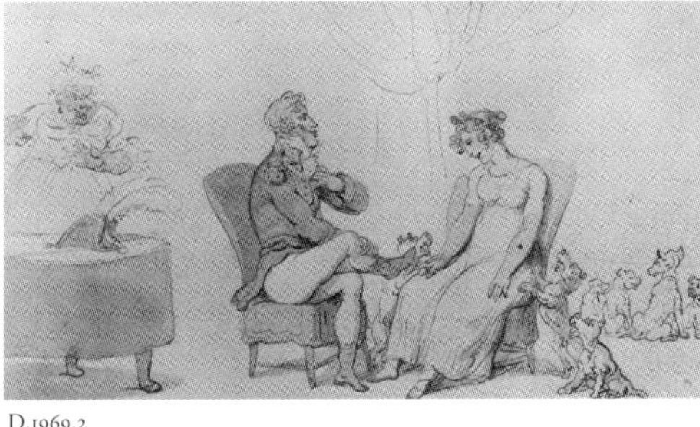

D.1969.2

An Officer's Declaration to an Admirer of Puppies

pencil, pen and brown ink, watercolour
108 × 182 mm
Pilkington, Margaret (gift, 1969) (D.1969.2)

Study of an antique Vase

pencil, pen and brown ink
320 × 238 mm
John Baskett Ltd, London (purchase, 1981) (V. & A.,
N.A.C.F., F.O.W.) (D.1981.7)

Study of an antique Vase
pencil, pen and brown ink
320 × 238 mm
John Baskett Ltd, London (purchase, 1981)
(V. & A., N.A.C.F., F.O.W.) (D.1981.8)

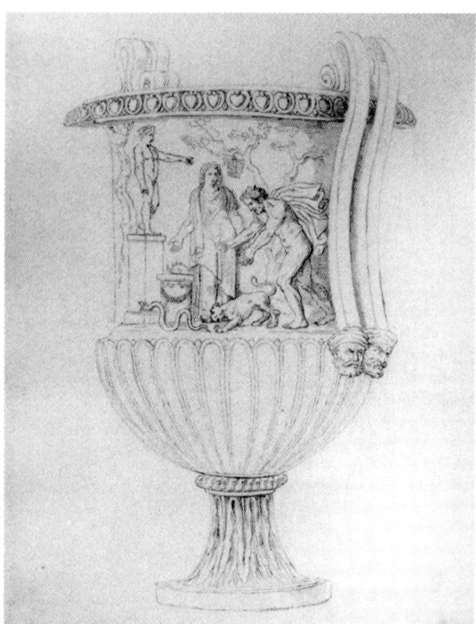

D.1981.9

Study of an antique Vase
pencil, pen and brown ink
320 × 238 mm
John Baskett Ltd, London (purchase, 1981)
(V. & A., N.A.C.F., F.O.W.) (D.1981.9)

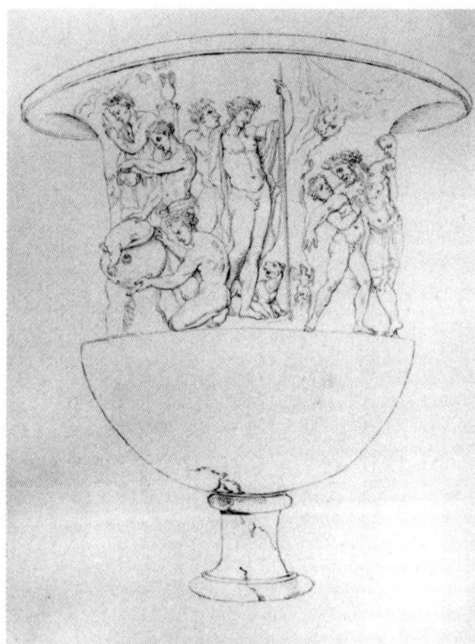

D.1981.10

Study of an antique Vase
pencil, pen and brown ink
320 × 238 mm
John Baskett Ltd, London (purchase, 1981)
(V. & A., N.A.C.F., F.O.W.) (D.1981.10)

Study of the Medici Krater, in reverse
pencil, pen and brown ink
320 × 238 mm
John Baskett Ltd, London (purchase, 1981)
(V. & A., N.A.C.F., F.O.W.) (D.1981.11)

Figure Studies after the Old Masters: Guercino and Domenichino
pen and brown ink, brown watercolour
inscribed centre left and lower right (the names of the artists copied): *Dominichino Guercino*
371 × 461 mm
Hawcroft, Francis Wilson (bequest, 1988) (D.1988.5)

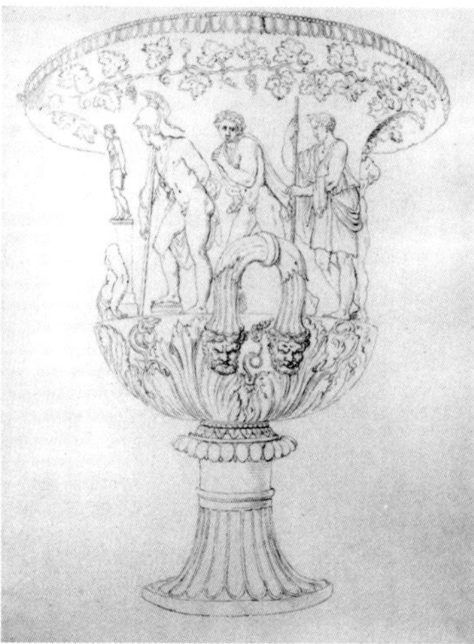

D.1981.11

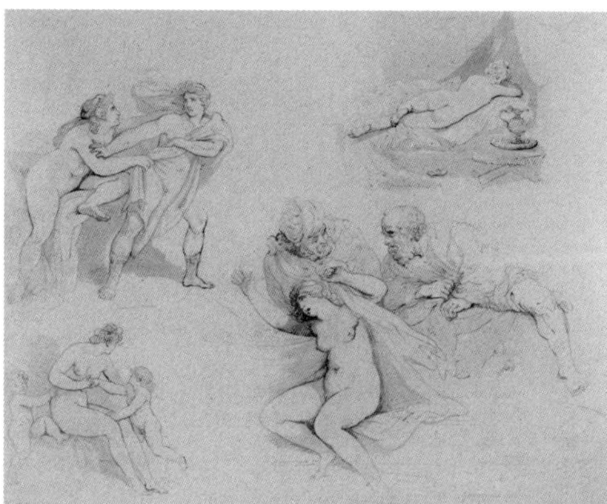

D.1988.5

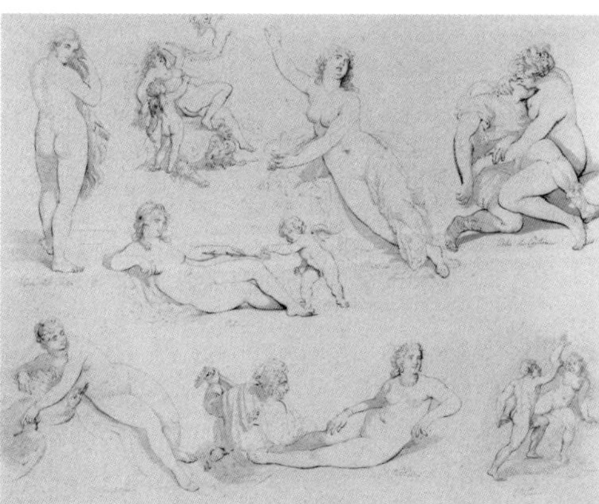

D.1988.6

Figure Studies after the Old Masters: Andrea del Sarto, Palma Vecchio, Pietro da Cortona, Polidoro, Carracci and Titian
pen and brown ink, brown watercolour
inscribed all over drawing (the names of the artists copied): *Andre del Sarto Palma Andre del Sarto Petro de Cortona Carrache Titian Polidore*
371 × 460 mm
Hawcroft, Francis Wilson (bequest, 1988) (D.1988.6)

Tintern Abbey, Monmouthshire, Wales
pencil, pen and brown ink, watercolour
inscribed lower right: *Tintern Abby S Wales*
283 × 435 mm
Ainscow, George (in memory of his wife, Ainscow, Margaret) (gift, 16.8.1996) (D.1996.23)

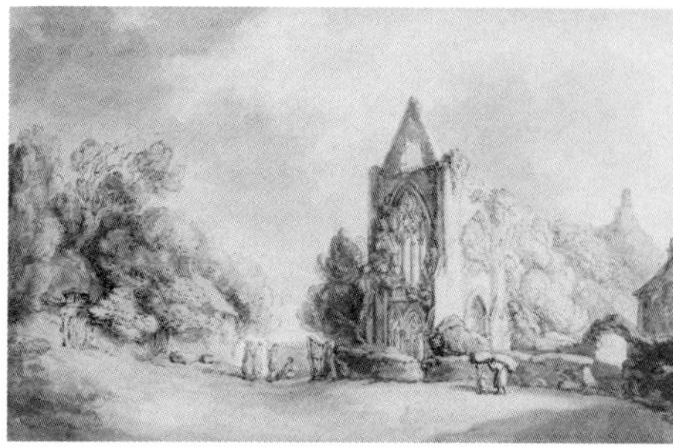

D.1996.23

■ Runciman, Alexander (1736–85)

Born in Edinburgh, Runciman was apprenticed to the decorating firm of Robert Norie. In 1766 he was working for Sir James Clerk at Penicuik, and the following year he left for Rome where he was largely supported by Sir James. He met John Henry Fuseli, who was a strong influence on his art. Runciman returned to Scotland in 1771 and exhibited history pictures at the Royal Academy from 1772 to 1774 and again in 1780 and 1781.

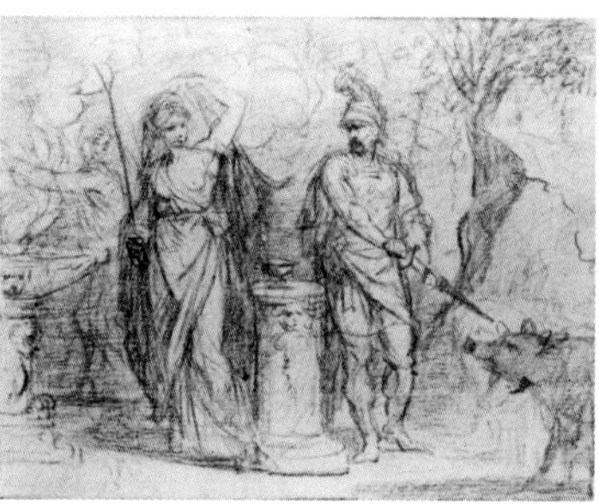

D.1960.130

Ulysees and Circe (recto); Figure and other Studies (verso)
black chalk
142 × 165 mm
University of Manchester, History of Art Department (transfer, 1960) (D.1960.130)

■ Ruskin, John (1819–1900)

The greatest art critic and writer of the nineteenth century, Ruskin was a highly accomplished draughtsman whose drawings were used as teaching tools or to illustrate his numerous publications. His most famous book *Modern Painters*, initially instigated as a defence of Turner, moved on to embrace earlier periods and a wider range of subjects; it was published in five volumes between 1843 and 1860. Ruskin is also known for having championed the Pre-Raphaelites in 1851. His writings, which cover subjects as diverse as art to social criticism and the environment, were hugely influential.

The Tower of Strasbourg Cathedral
1842
pencil, watercolour, bodycolour (heightened with white); grey-blue paper
signed & inscribed on a separate sheet of paper attached to the mount lower right below window mount (extract from a letter): *I can see you now / any evening you like to come. / most truly yours. / JRuskin*; inscribed lower left: *Strasburg*; inscribed lower right: *Strasbourg*.
499 × 336 mm
Walker's Galleries, London (purchase, 1921) (D.1921.27)

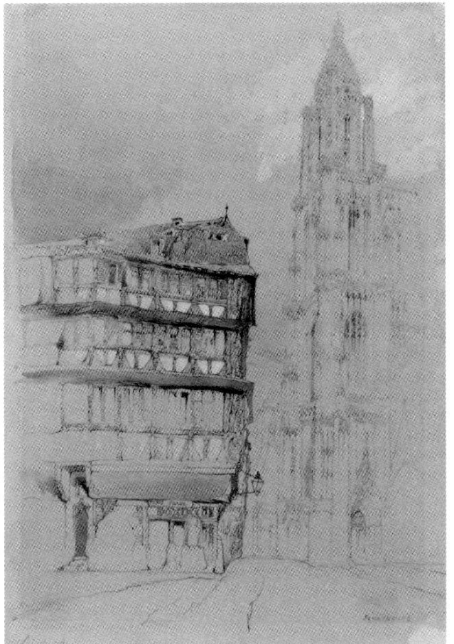

D.1921.27

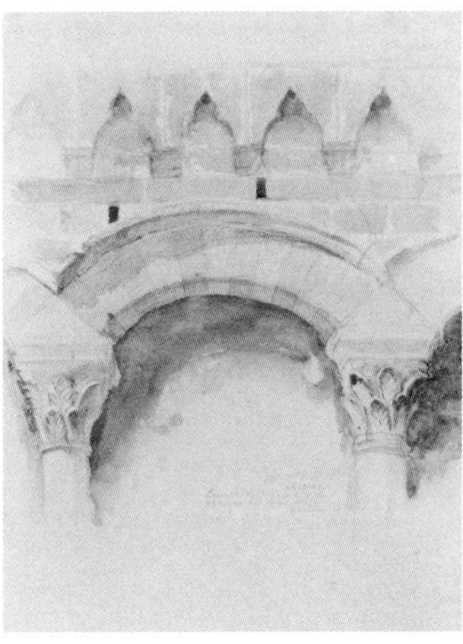

D.1946.4

An Archway in Assisi, Italy
1874
pencil, watercolour, bodycolour; grey paper
signed, inscribed & dated lower right: *In main Street, / Assisi / Leaves of capitals are / oblique set – as drifting / JRuskin 1874*
241 × 176 mm
Blunt, Anthony, National Art Collections Fund (via) (gift, 1946) (D.1946.4)

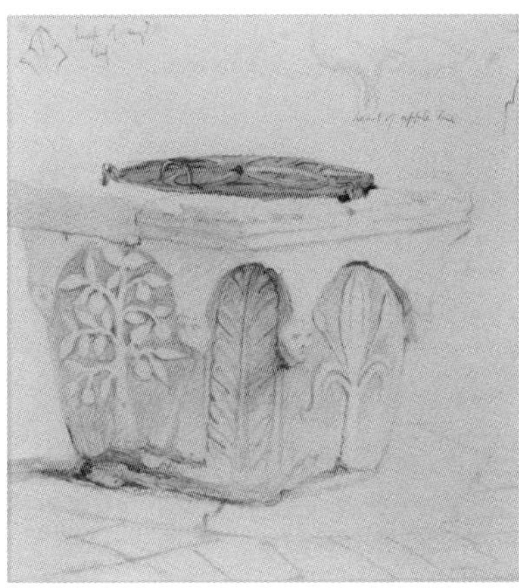

D.1949.1

Venetian Well-head (recto); Architectural Studies (verso)
1850–53
pencil, pen and brown ink, watercolour, bodycolour (heightened with white) (recto)
inscribed upper left describing the decoration on the well-head: *Head of angle / leaf*; inscribed upper right: *head of apple tree*
196 × 174 mm
Sidebotham, Dr E. J. (gift, 1949) (D.1949.1)

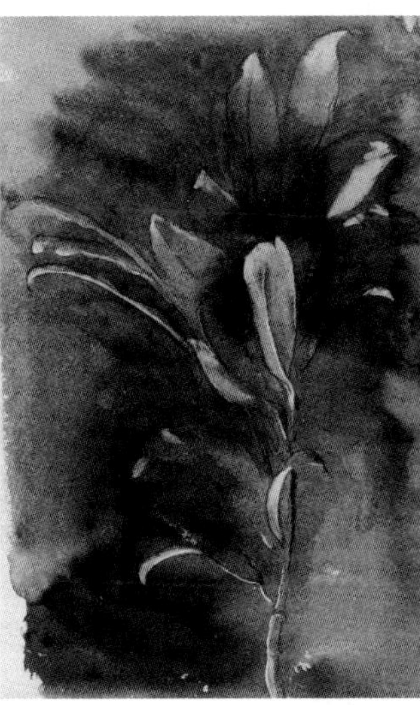

D.1953.3

Study of a Laurel Branch
pen and brown ink, watercolour, bodycolour (heightened with white); light blue paper
243 × 150 mm
Waterhouse, Miss (gift, 1953) (D.1953.3)

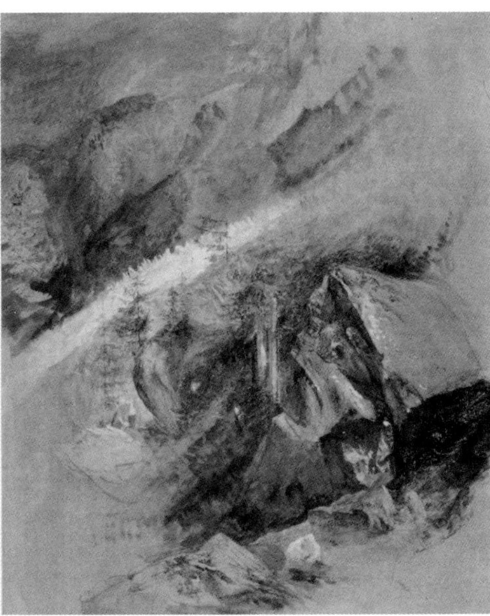

D.1968.3

Mer de Glace, Chamonix, France
1860
pencil, watercolour, bodycolour, pen and ink
grey paper
signed, inscribed & dated: *J.Ruskin.Chamonix.1860.*
421 × 331 mm
Pilkington, Dorothy L., Pilkington, Margaret (gift, 2.1968) (D.1968.3)

Ponte Pietra, Verona, Italy
1869
pencil, watercolour, bodycolour; buff paper
signed lower right: *JRuskin*
257 × 177 mm
Brocklehurst, Lt Col C. P. (bequest, 1977) (D.1977.13)

■ RUSSELL, JOHN (1745–1806)

Although predominantly a painter of portraits in pastel, Russell also worked in oil. He was elected a member of the Royal Academy in 1788. Russell published *Elements of Painting with Crayons* in 1772 and was appointed Crayon Painter to the King and the Prince of Wales in 1790.

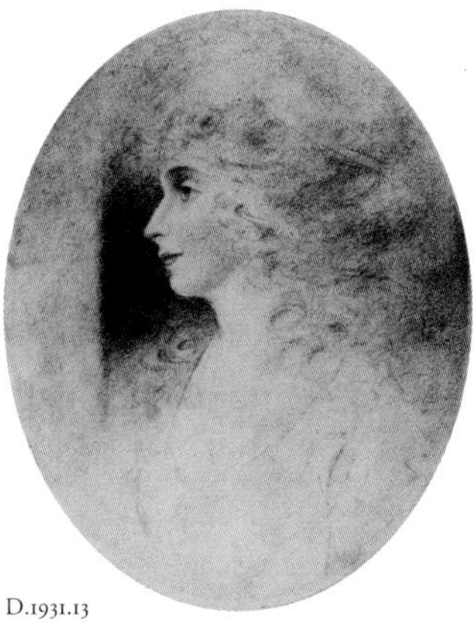

D.1931.13

Portrait of Isabella Turnour
coloured chalk
228 × 180 mm
Anderson, A. E. (gift, 1931) (D.1931.13)

■ SALOMONS, EDWARD (1827–1906)

Salomons, a leading Manchester-based architect, was responsible for the building of the Art Treasures Palace for the Manchester Art Treasures Exhibition in 1857 and was an unsuccessful entrant in the Manchester Town Hall competition in 1867. He also built the Manchester Reform Club (1870–71) in a Ruskinian Veneto-Gothic style.

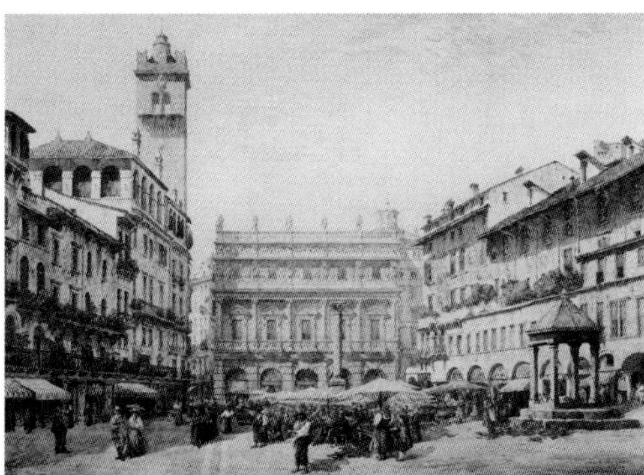

D.1905.8

Piazza Erbe, Verona
1899
pencil, watercolour, bodycolour (heightened with white)
signed, inscribed & dated lower right: *PIAZZA DEL'ERBE / VERONA / E.Salomons / 1899*
538 × 736 mm
Salomons, Edward (purchase, 1905) (D.1905.8)

■ SAMUEL, GEORGE (attributed to) (ca. 1760–1823)

Samuel was a landscape watercolourist who exhibited at the Royal Academy from 1786 to 1823. He was a member of Girtin and Francia's Sketching Society in 1799.

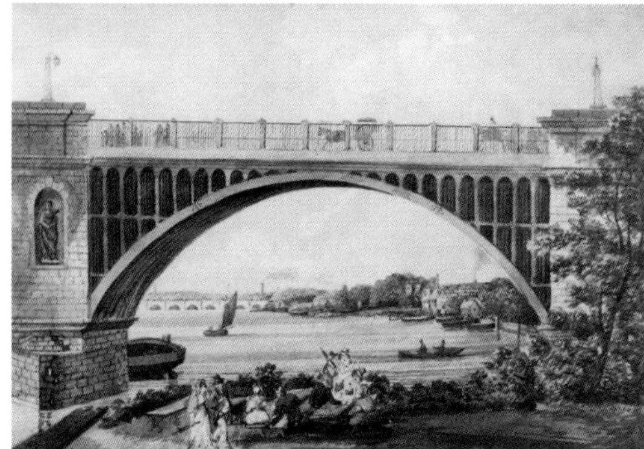

D.1932.8

Span of Vauxhall Bridge, London
1816 (after)
pen and brown ink, watercolour
inscribed lower right (false signature and date):
E.Dayes.1784.
291 × 405 mm
Anderson, A. E. (gift, 1932) (D.1932.8)

■ SANDBY, PAUL (1725–1809)

Paul Sandby, born in Nottingham, has been called 'the father of English watercolour'. He began his career as a draughtsman to the Military Survey of Scotland in 1747. With his architect brother Thomas, he was a founder member of the Royal Academy in 1768 and did much to raise the status of watercolour painting. From 1768 to 1796 he was Chief Drawing Master at the Royal Military Academy at Woolwich. Sandby introduced the technique of aquatint into England and was a highly influential teacher.

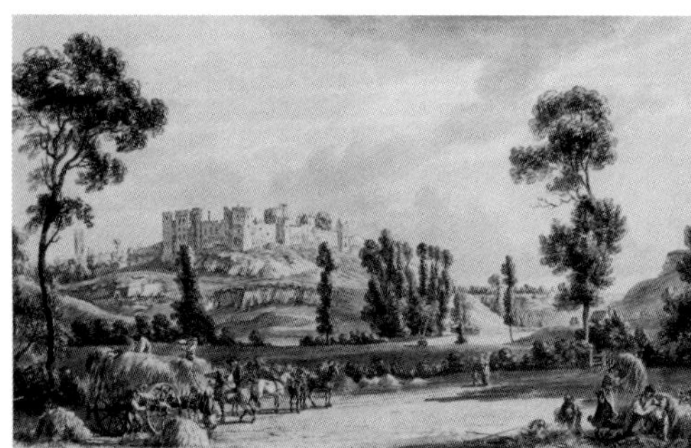

D.1892.145

Ludlow Castle, Shropshire, from the South
pencil, pen and grey ink, watercolour
327 × 509 mm
Taylor, John Edward (gift, 1892) (D.1892.145)

Conway Castle, Caernarvonshire, Wales, from the South West
1802
pencil, watercolour, bodycolour
signed, inscribed & dated: *P Sandby RA / 1802 / CONWAY / 1802*; signed, inscribed & dated verso of backing: *South West View of Conway / P Sandby 1802*
328 × 478 mm
Lees, Charles E. (gift, 1894) (D.1894.1)

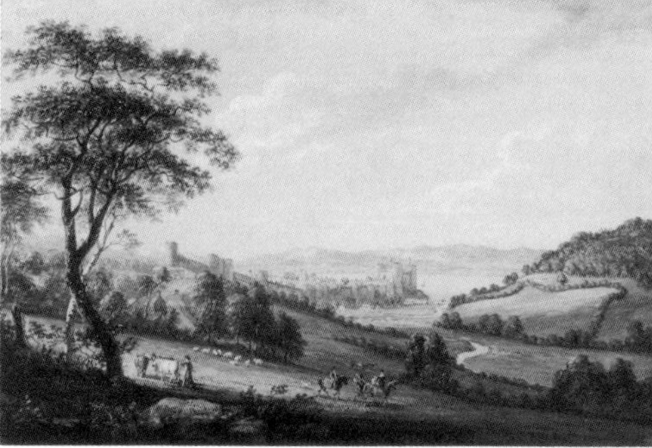

D.1894.1

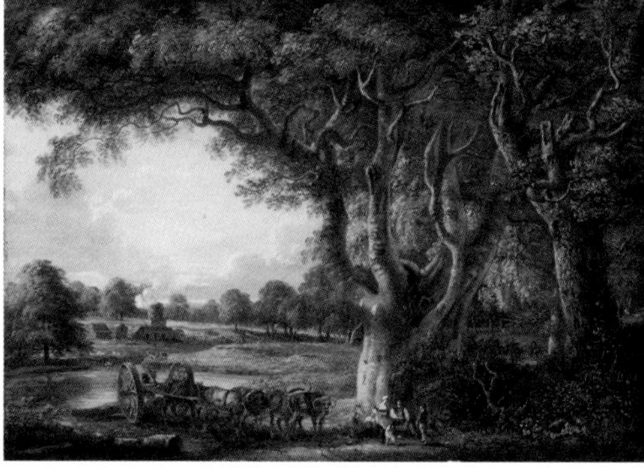

D.1901.1

The Timber Waggon, Windsor Great Park, Berkshire
bodycolour
661 × 908 mm
Agnew's (purchase, 29.1.1901) (D.1901.1)

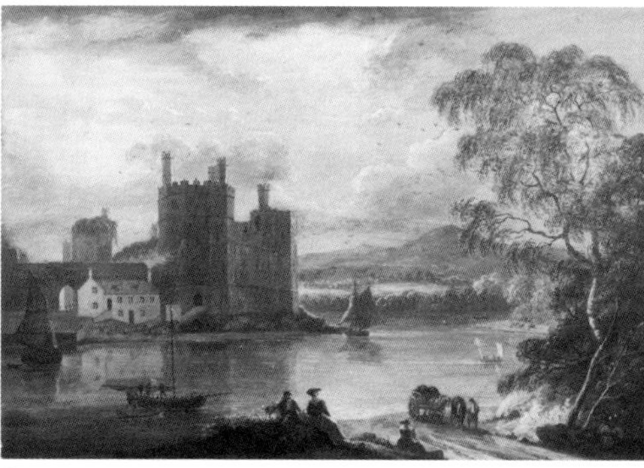

D.1901.2

The Eagle Tower, Caernarvon Castle, Caernarvonshire, Wales, from across the River
bodycolour
signed lower right with initials: *P.S.*
430 × 620 mm
Agnew's (purchase, 29.1.1901) (D.1901.2)

A Highland Loch with a ruined Castle
bodycolour
signed lower right: *P.Sandby R.A.*
445 × 625 mm
Agnew's (purchase, 29.1.1901) (D.1901.3)

Rochester Castle, Kent, from across the Medway
bodycolour
320 × 477 mm
Broadhurst, Sir Edward Tootal, Broadhurst, Lady
(bequest, 1924) (D.1924.85)

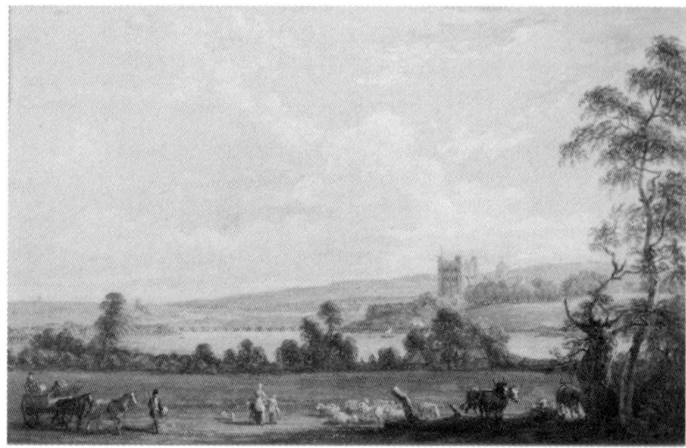

D.1924.85

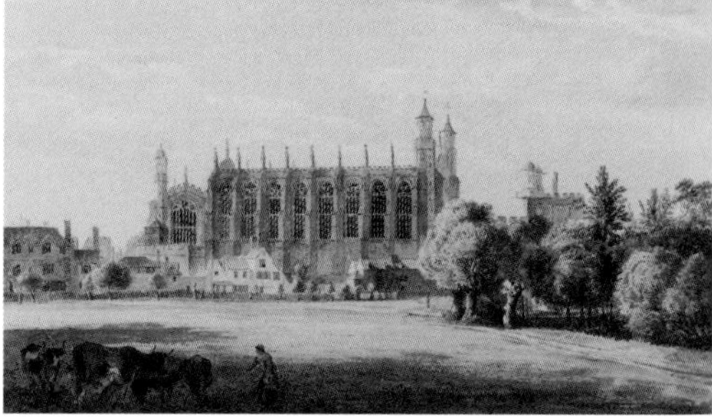

D.1948.17

Eton College Chapel, Buckinghamshire, from the South
pencil, pen and ink, watercolour, bodycolour (heightened with white)
279 × 454 mm
Kessler, P. W. (Mrs) (the daughters of) (gift, 1948) (D.1948.17)

The Timber Cart
pencil, brown watercolour
93 × 238 mm
University of Manchester, Picture Loan Scheme (transfer, 1994) (D.1994.5)

■ SANDBY, THOMAS PAUL (ca. 1768–1832)

The second son and biographer of his father Paul, Thomas Paul Sandby took over from his father the teaching post at the Royal Military Academy at Woolwich.

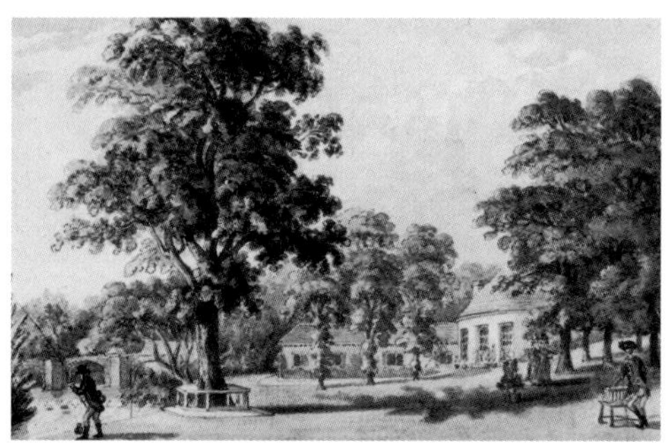

D.1892.7

Cottage, Gresford, Denbighshire, Wales
pencil, pen and grey ink, watercolour
102 × 157 mm
Taylor, John Edward (gift, 1892) (D.1892.7)

■ SANDERS, JOHN (1750–1825)

Sanders entered the Royal Academy Schools in 1769 where he exhibited portraits, topographical views, and biblical and literary subjects between 1771 and 1788.

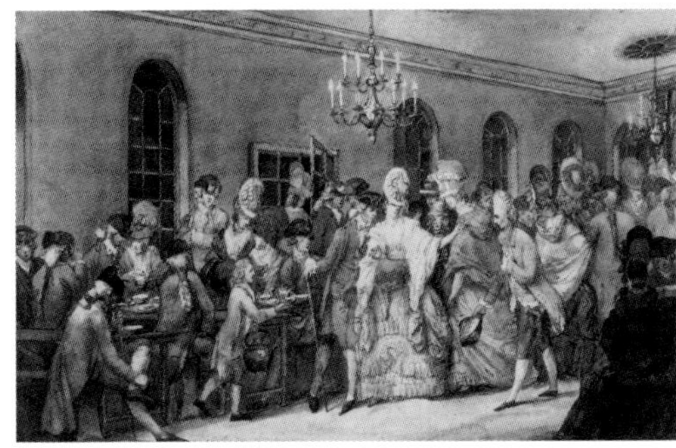

D.1892.9

Bagnigge Wells, Finsbury, London, on a Sunday Evening
4.1779
pencil, black chalk, watercolour, bodycolour
(heightened with white)
signed & dated lower centre: *J.Sanders Invt April 1779*
325 × 503 mm
Taylor, John Edward (gift, 1892) (D.1892.9)

■ **SANDYS, ANTHONY FREDERICK AUGUSTUS (1829–1904)**
Sandys, son of a Norwich portrait painter, exhibited
at the Royal Academy from 1851. He was influenced
by the Pre-Raphaelites, particularly Rossetti, and in
the 1860s contributed illustrations to periodical
magazines such as the *Cornhill Magazine, Once a Week*
and *Good Words*. Later he painted striking portraits
in coloured chalks.

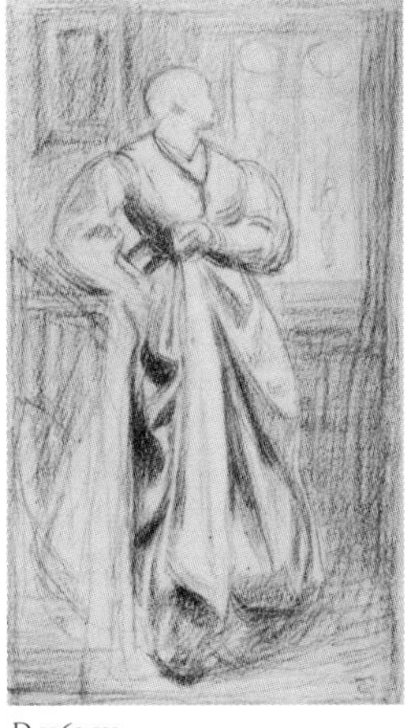

D.1960.131

A Woman in medieval Dress by a Window
black chalk
signed lower right with monogram: *FS*
220 × 127 mm
University of Manchester, History of Art Department
(transfer, 1960) (D.1960.131)

■ **SASSE, RICHARD (1774–1849)**
Sasse, a landscape watercolourist and drawing
master, exhibited at the Royal Academy from 1791
to 1813. He taught drawing to Princess Charlotte
and became Landscape Painter to the Prince Regent.
He eventually settled in Paris.

Village on the Banks of a Mere
pencil, watercolour
210 × 297 mm
Barlow, Sir Thomas (gift, 1951) (D.1951.13)

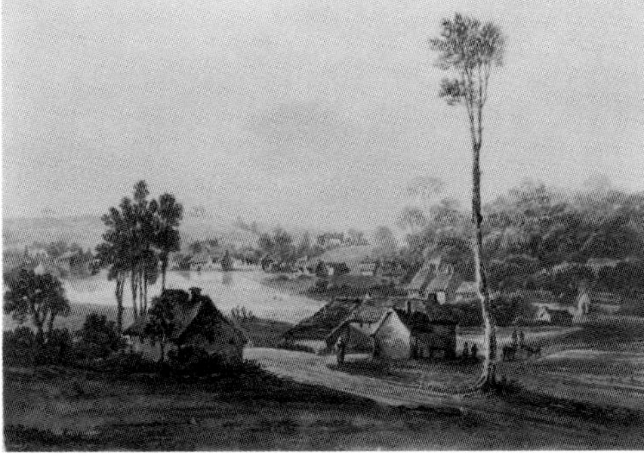

D.1951.13

■ **SCHNEBBELIE, JACOB CHRISTOPHER (1760–92)**
Schnebbelie, a pupil of Paul Sandby, was a drawing
master at Westminster and other London schools, until
he became Draughtsman to the Society of Antiquaries.
He worked with James Moore and George Isham
Parkyns on *Monastic Remains and Ancient Castles in
England and Wales* (1791–92).

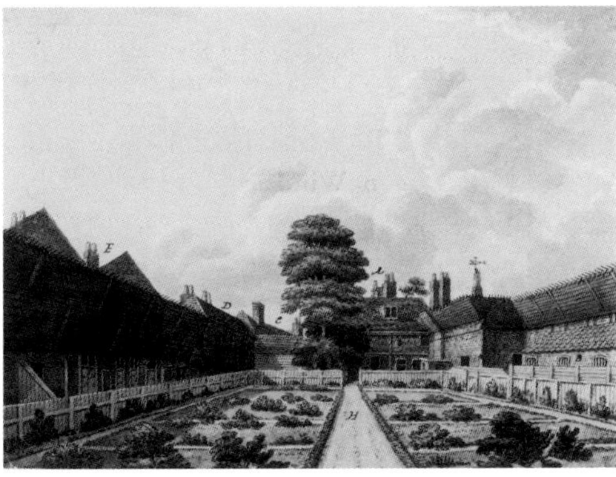

D.1947.16

The Courtyard, the House of Correction
1790
pen and brown ink, watercolour
inscribed & dated along upper edge of verso: *Interior of
House of Correction* [illegible word] *1790*
154 × 205 mm
Friends of the Whitworth (gift, 1947) (D.1947.16)

■ **SCOTT, JOHN HENDERSON (1829–86)**
John Henderson Scott, a member of the Scott
family of painters from Brighton, exhibited
intermittently in London from 1849 and worked
in England and on the Continent.

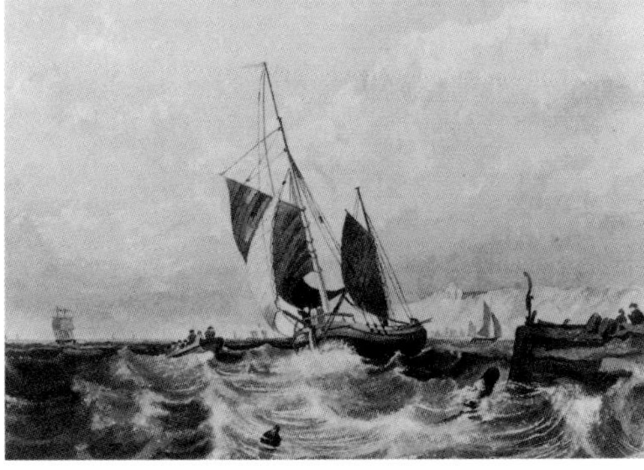

D.1951.12

Coast Scene with Shipping
watercolour
204 × 284 mm
Pilkington, Margaret (gift, 1951) (D.1951.12)

■ **SCOTT, SAMUEL (ca. 1702–72)**
Samuel Scott was a painter of marine subjects and
topographical river landscapes. He painted in the
manner of Willem van de Velde and became the
leading native-born specialist in London river views
before the arrival of Canaletto. He exhibited at the
Society of Artists between 1761 and 1765 and at the
Royal Academy from 1771. Scott taught Sawrey Gilpin
and William Marlow.

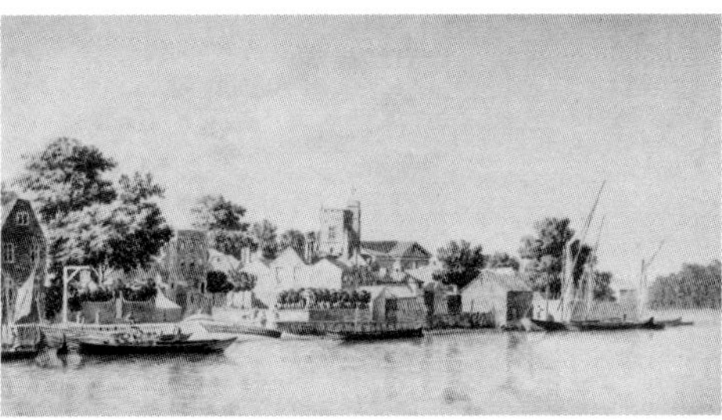

D.1892.3

Twickenham on the Thames, London
pencil, pen and brown ink, watercolour
263 × 468 mm
Taylor, John Edward (gift, 1892) (D.1892.3)

■ **SCOTT, SAMUEL (1756–1825)**
Scott was the founder of the Scott family of
painters from Brighton.

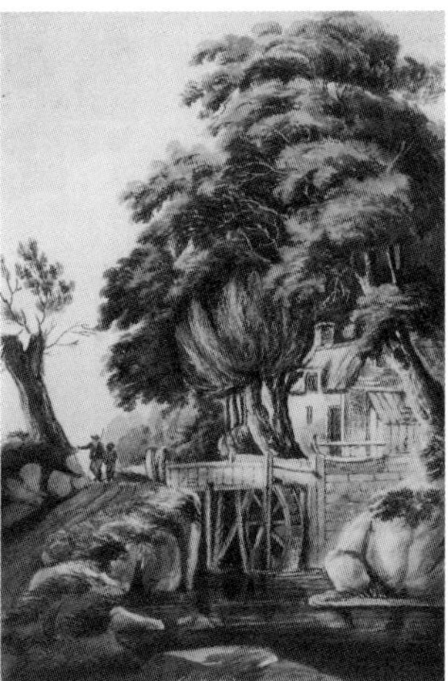

D.1934.30

Sussex Watermill
1817
pencil, watercolour
signed & dated lower centre: *S.Scott 1817*
486 × 326 mm
Peer Groves, Major W. (gift, 1934) (D.1934.30)

■ **SCOTT, WILLIAM HENRY STOTHARD (1783–1850)**
Known as 'Scott of Brighton', Scott exhibited British
and Continental views at the Old Watercolour Society
between 1811 and 1850. He is one of the few English
watercolourists to have visited the Pyrenees.

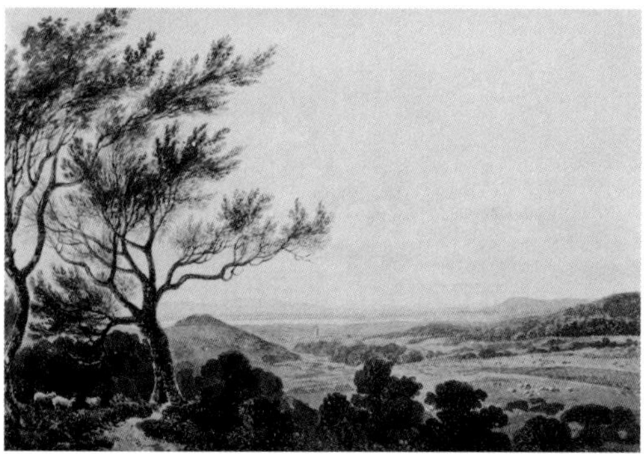

D.1892.123

**Meeting of the River Wye and the Severn,
Welsh Hills in the Distance**
pencil, watercolour
229 × 330 mm
Taylor, John Edward (gift, 1892) (D.1892.123)

■ SERRES, DOMINIC (1719–93)

Born in Gascony in south-western France, Dominic
Serres ran away to sea as a young man, serving on ships
in the Mediterranean and the West Indies. He came to
England as a prisoner of war, captured during the War
of the Austrian Succession with Spain, probably in
about 1745. Serres became one of the leading marine
painters of the day and a founder member of the Royal
Academy in 1768, exhibiting coastal landscapes, marine
battle subjects and sea pieces there continuously until
his death. He was appointed Marine Painter to the
king in 1780.

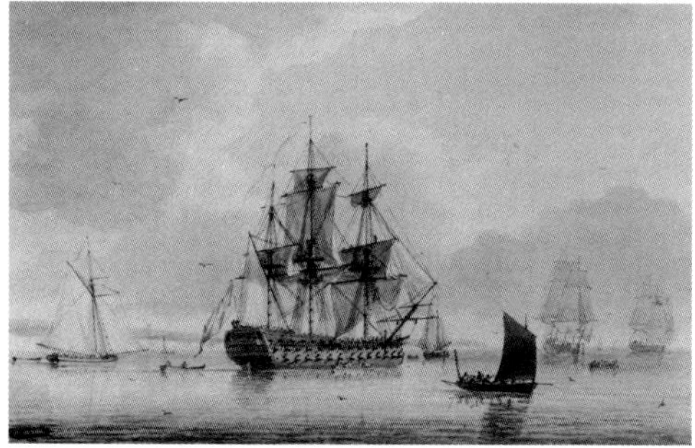

D.1892.21

Shipping off the east Coast of Kent
pen and grey ink, watercolour
signed lower left on a spar floating in the water with
initials: *D.S.*
185 × 292 mm
Taylor, John Edward (gift, 1892) (D.1892.21)

**Study for 'Gibraltar relieved by Sir George
Rodney, January 1780'**
1780–82
pencil, pen and grey ink, grey watercolour
inscribed lower left (false signature or identification):
Van de Velde
228 × 522 mm
Ogden, William Sharp (bequest, 1926) (D.1926.194)

■ SERRES, JOHN THOMAS (1759–1825)

John Thomas Serres, son of Dominic, succeeded his
father as Marine Painter to the King in 1793. He
exhibited at the Royal Academy between 1776 and
1820. In 1790–91 he made a tour of France and Italy,
returning to England in order to marry Olivia Wilmot.

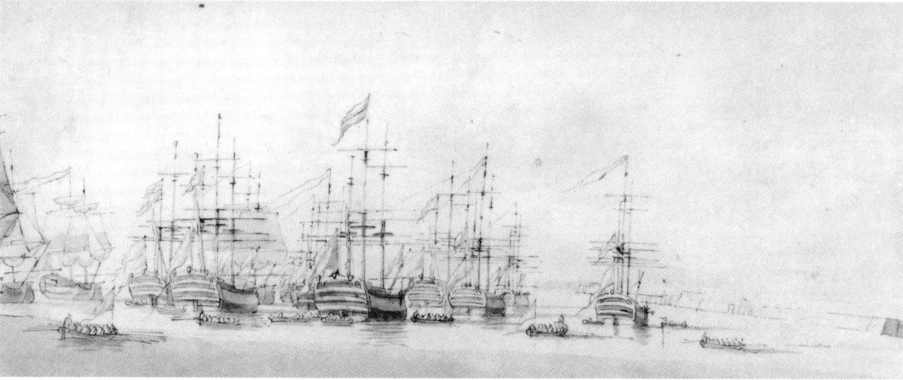

D.1926.194

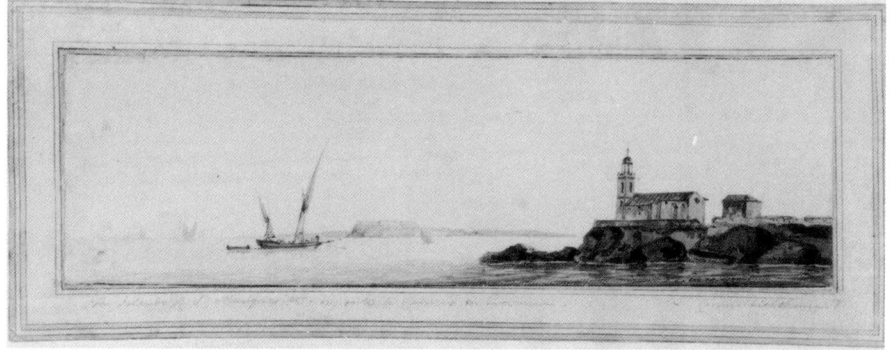

D.1900.18

Her eccentricities, which included claiming to be the
daughter of the Duke of Cumberland, ruined Serres's
career. Although he obtained a separation from her in
1804, she continued to run up debts in his name and
Serres fled to Edinburgh in 1818. As well as marine and
coastal views, he also painted landscapes.

Lighthouse, Cannes, South of France
1790
pencil, pen and brown ink, watercolour
signed & dated lower right: *J T Serres.1790*;
inscribed lower left on artist's mount: *The Islands
of St. Marguerite opposite to Cannes in Provance*
(sic); inscribed lower right on artist's mount:
Cannes Lighthouse
110 × 363 mm
Worthington, Mary (gift, 1900) (D.1900.18)

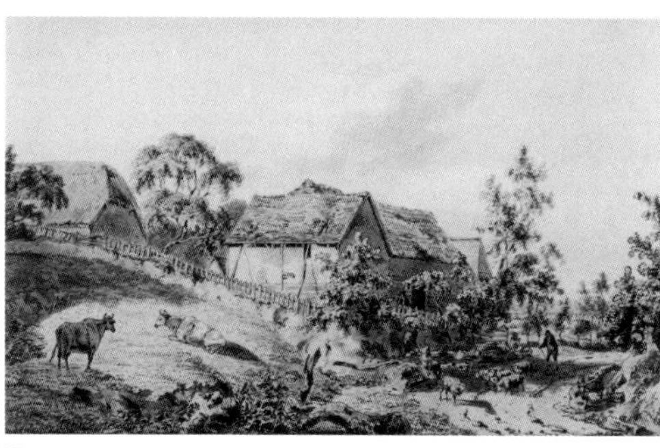

D.1947.59

A Farm Scene
pen and brown ink, watercolour; watermark
JWHATMAN
inscribed on a separate label attached to secondary
support: *John Serries*
212 × 338 mm
Friends of the Whitworth (gift, 1947) (D.1947.59)

■ SEVERN, JOSEPH (1793–1879)

Now best known for having accompanied the dying
poet John Keats to Rome in 1820 and for having been
present at his deathbed, Severn exhibited at the Royal
Academy and elsewhere from 1817 to 1868. He was
British Consul in Rome from 1861 until his retirement
in 1872 but remained in Rome until his death.

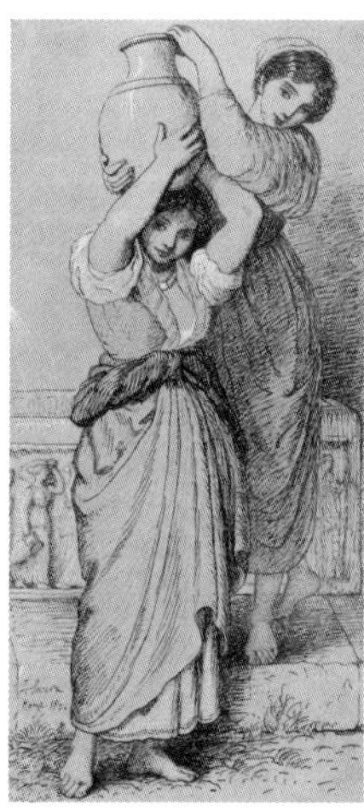

D.1943.4

**Study of Peasant Girls holding a Pitcher for
'Italian Fountain'**
1824
pencil, pen and brown ink, bodycolour (heightened
with white); grey paper
signed, inscribed & dated lower left: *J.Severn / Rome
1824*; inscribed on verso reading down lower edge from
top : *group from the "Italian Fountain" the picture in the
possession of His / Majesty the King of the Belgians*
355 × 164 mm
Buckley, Francis (gift, 1943) (D.1943.4)

■ SHARPE, CHARLES KIRKPATRICK (1781–1851)

Sharpe, a portrait painter, antiquarian and caricaturist, also published a number of etchings.

Louis XIV in his Bedchamber
pen and brown ink, brown watercolour
310 × 235 mm
Ogden, William Sharp (bequest, 1926) (D.1926.129)

■ SHEFFIELD, GEORGE (1839–92)

Born in Cumberland, Sheffield studied at Warrington Art School and moved to Manchester. He later settled in Bettws-y-Coed, becoming a member of the Manchester Academy in 1871. Sheffield exhibited six pictures at the Royal Academy betwen 1873 and 1878.

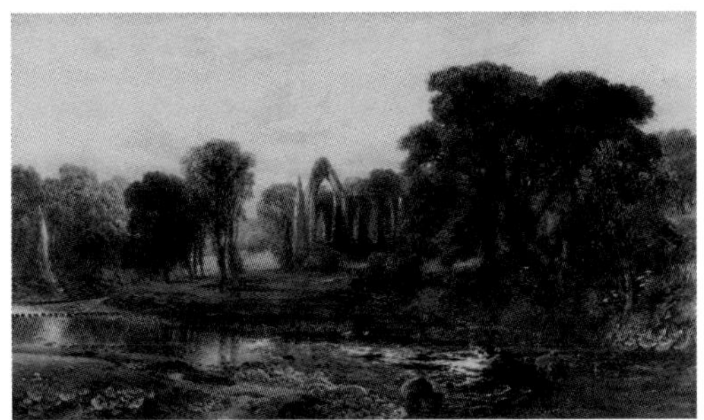

D.1918.6

Bolton Abbey, Yorkshire
1873
watercolour, bodycolour (heightened with white)
signed & dated lower right: *G.Sheffield / 1873*
745 × 1250 mm
Grantham, William (bequest, 1918) (D.1918.6)

■ SHELLEY, SAMUEL (1750–1808)

Shelley, a miniaturist and figure painter, was a founder member of the Old Watercolour Society and exhibited portraits and literary subjects there from 1805 to 1808.

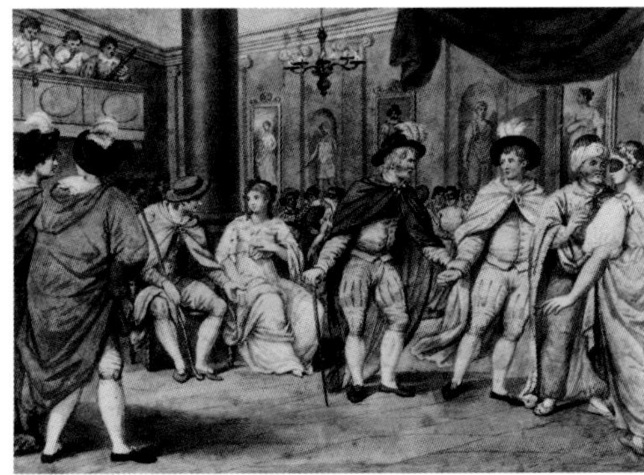

D.1947.52

The Ball: Illustration for Shakespeare's 'Romeo and Juliet', Act I, Scene IV
pencil, watercolour
302 × 409 mm
Friends of the Whitworth (gift, 1947) (D.1947.52)

Hamlet and the Gravedigger: Illustration for Shakespeare's 'Hamlet', Act V, Scene I
pencil, watercolour
302 × 408 mm
J. Davey and Son (gift, 1948) (D.1948.5)

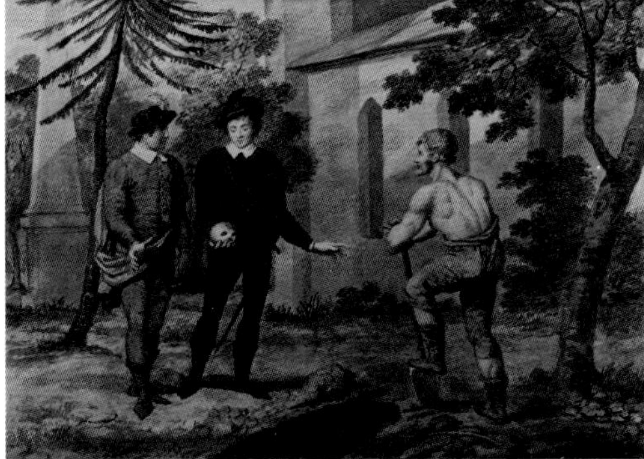

D.1948.5

■ SHEPHERD, GEORGE (ca. 1782–1830)

Known for his topographical and architectural views, mainly of London, George Shepherd exhibited at the Royal Academy between 1800 and 1829.

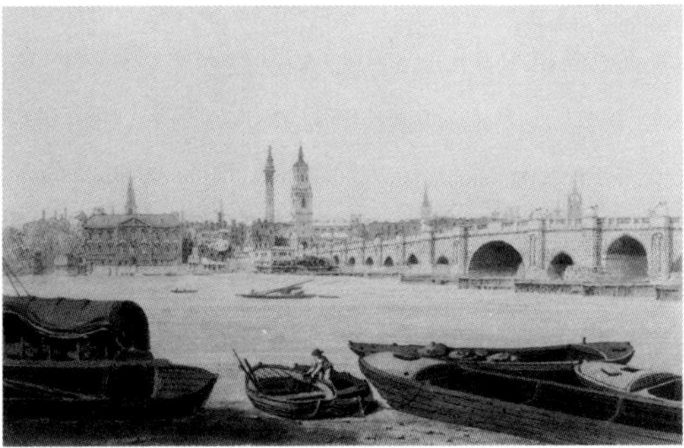

D.1892.106

Old London Bridge
1808
pencil, watercolour
signed lower left on the back of a moored boat and in centre on the bows of a beached boat (christian name and surname separated): *GEORGE SHEPHERD*; dated lower right on the bows of a beached boat: *1808*
201 × 308 mm
Taylor, John Edward (gift, 1892) (D.1892.106)

■ SHEPHERD, J. N. (fl. 19th century)

J. N. Shepherd was a copyist, presumably amateur, of whom nothing is known.

The New Hall, Christ's Hospital, London
pencil, brown watercolour (vignette)
signed lower left: *J N Shepherd*
141 × 192 mm
Ogden, William Sharp (bequest, 1926) (D.1926.310)

■ SHERRIN, JOHN (1819–96)

Sherrin, still-life painter and pupil of William Henry Hunt, was elected a member of the New Watercolour Society in 1879.

The Bedtime Story ended
1869
watercolour, bodycolour (heightened with white); card
signed & dated lower right with initial in monogram: *JSherrin 1869*
197 × 243 mm
Barnes, Peter C. (purchase, 1974) (D.1974.1)

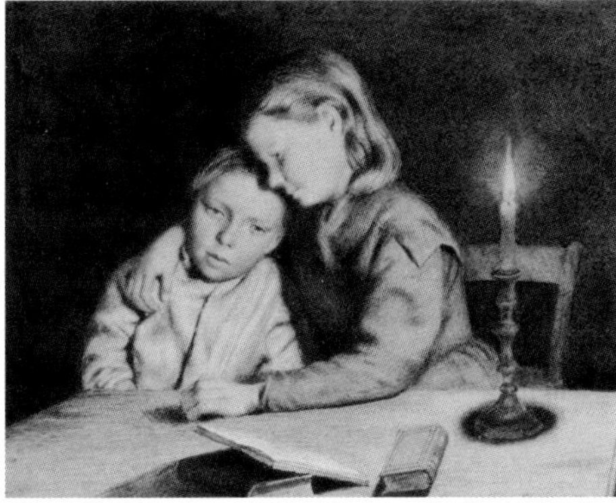

D.1974.1

■ SHIELDS, FREDERIC JAMES (1833–1911)

Shields was a landscape painter, illustrator and stained-glass designer. A very versatile artist and follower of the Pre-Raphaelites, he also painted murals, religious pictures, easel paintings and portraits.

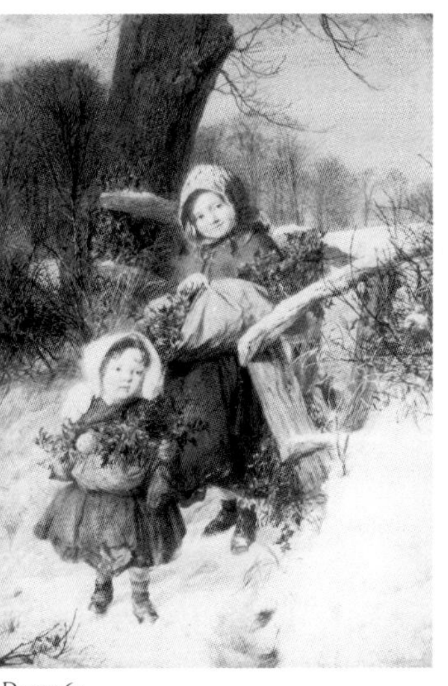

D.1930.60

The Holly Gatherers
1858
watercolour, bodycolour (heightened with white)
signed & dated lower left: *F.Shields.1858.*
480 × 336 mm
Falkner, Frank (bequest, 1930) (D.1930.60)

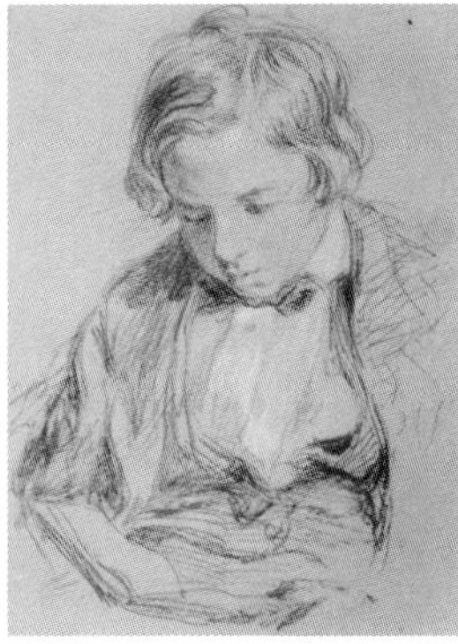

D.1939.5

Study of a Boy reading
black chalk, white chalk; grey paper
190 × 139 mm
Mills, Ernestine, Davies, Randall (via) (gift, 1939) (D.1939.5)

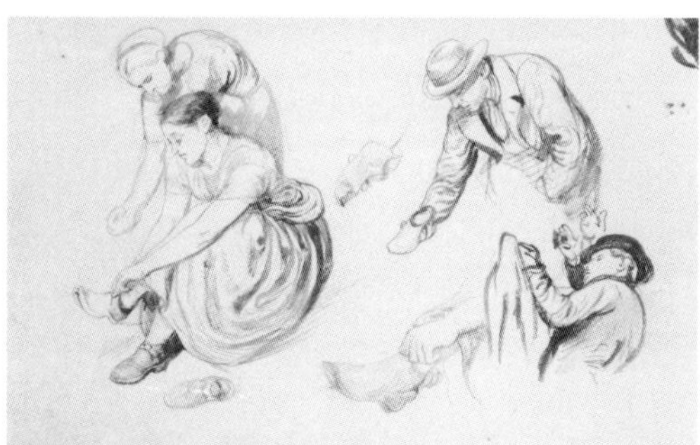

D.1939.6

Figure Studies for 'Knott Mill Fair'
1875
pencil, pen and brown ink, brown watercolour
208 × 331 mm
Mills, Ernestine, Davies, Randall (via) (gift, 1939) (D.1939.6)

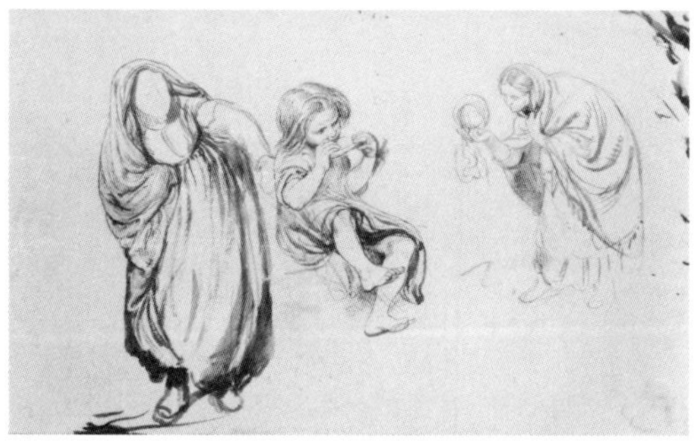

D.1939.7

**Figure Studies for 'Knott Mill Fair' (recto);
Studies of a standing Girl (verso)**
1875
pencil, pen and brown ink, brown watercolour
206 × 333 mm
Mills, Ernestine, Davies, Randall (via) (gift, 1939) (D.1939.7)

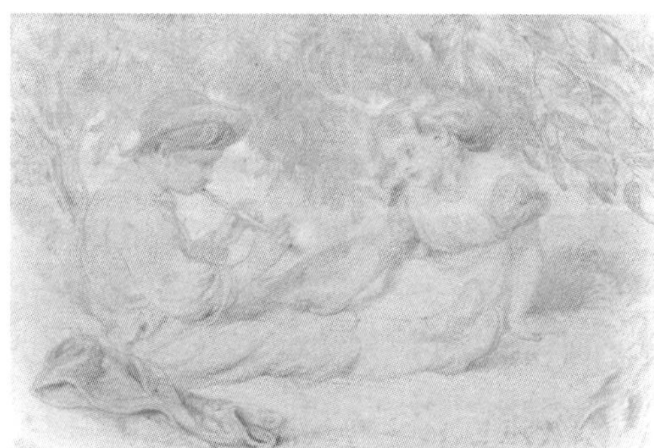

D.1945.4

Pastoral Scene
red chalk
signed lower left on shield with monogram: *FS*
144 × 208 mm
Knight, Joseph (gift, 23/03/1945) (D.1945.4)

Landscape with Reapers
5.9.1898
watercolour
dated lower right: *Sep 5 1898*
144 × 245 mm
Brockbank, J. E. (bequest, 1987) (D.1987.46)

■ **SHORT, SIR FRANK (1857–1945)**
Short, a painter, etcher and aquatint engraver, was
Head of the Engraving School at the Royal College of
Art from 1891 to 1924. He reissued and added to
Turner's *Liber Studiorum*. He was elected a member of
the Royal Academy in 1911.

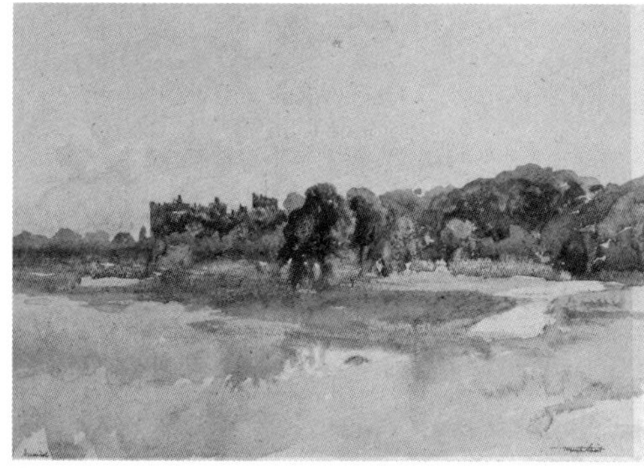

D.1924.10

Arundel Castle, Sussex
watercolour, pencil; beige paper
278 × 392 mm
Watson, A. (gift, 1924) (D.1924.10)

Dutch River Barges
watercolour
171 × 246 mm
Jackson, F. W. (gift, 1926) (D.1926.7)

■ **SIBERECHTS, JAN (1627–1703)**
Born in Antwerp, Siberechts was living in England by
1674 and became the leading topographical painter of
the period. His country-house portraits and his view
paintings were in much demand. His few landscape
watercolours are amongst the earliest to have been
painted in this medium in England.

View in Derbyshire with Figures hunting
pencil, pen and brown ink, watercolour
inscribed lower right: *Wooton / & Sybrecht*
147 × 396 mm
Friends of the Whitworth (gift, 1951) (D.1951.10)

■ **SIDNEY, HERBERT (fl. 1876–1923)**
Sidney was a caricaturist of whom little is known.

The Masquerade
1878
pen and brown ink
signed & dated lower right: *HERBERT SIDNEY– /
PARIS 1878* [second line underlined]
98 × 227 mm
Wallis, Miss J. K., Wallis, Miss R. (gift, 1926) (D.1926.11)

■ **SKELTON, JONATHAN (ca. 1735–59)**
Skelton's life and work are only known from a group
of drawings and watercolours that were sold at auction
in 1909, and a series of letters written by him from
Italy to his patron in England in 1758. He is known to
have painted in oil while in Italy, but these paintings
are now lost.

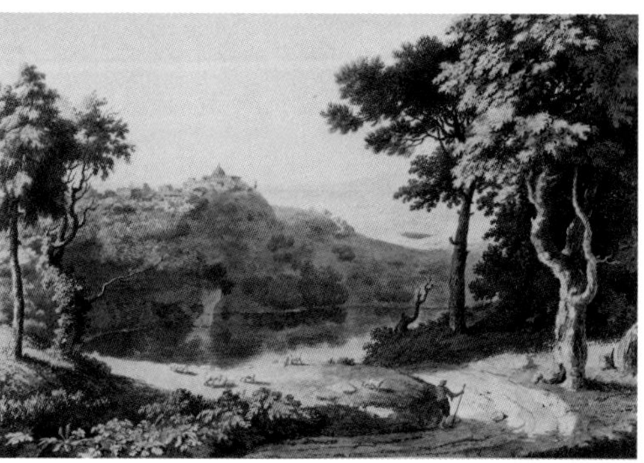

D.1925.28

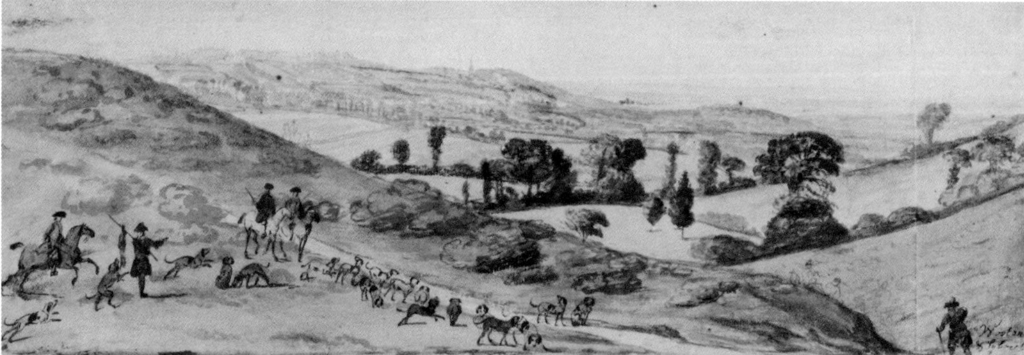

D.1951.10

D.1926.11

Lake Albano and Castel Gandolfo, Italy
6.1758
pen and ink, watercolour; watermark VI
signed, inscribed & dated on verso: *A View of Castello Gondolfo with the Lake of Albano / & the Campagna of Rome J Skelton 1758*
370 × 531 mm
Walker's Galleries, London (purchase, 1925) (D.1925.28)

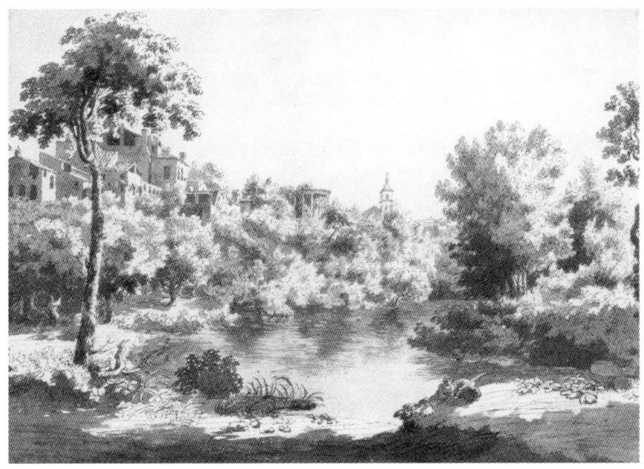
D.1930.30

The Temple of the Sibyl, Tivoli, Italy (recto); Landscape Study with Waterfall (verso)
1758
pen and brown ink, brown watercolour
267 × 370 mm
Anderson, A. E. (gift, 1930) (D.1930.30)

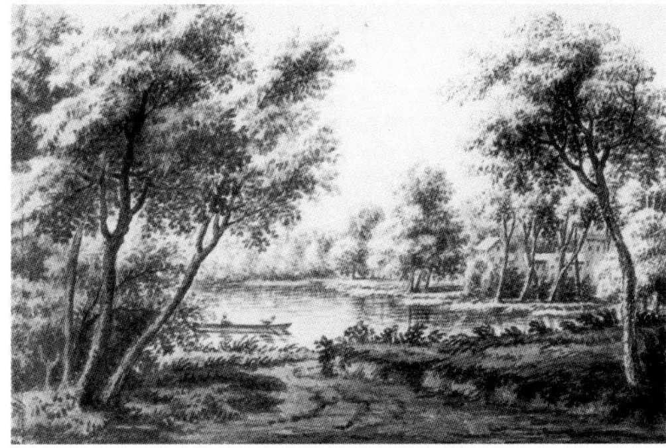
D.1933.14

A Lake among Trees with Houses beyond
pencil, watercolour
142 × 216 mm
Anderson, A. E. (gift, 1933) (D.1933.14)

Canterbury Castle, near the Postern Gate of St Mildred's Churchyard
1757
pen and grey ink, watercolour
250 × 450 mm
National Art Collections Fund (to commemorate the Directorship of Professor John White) (gift, 1966) (D.1966.20)

■ **Skippe, John (1741–1811)**
Skippe, an amateur draughtsman, connoisseur and collector, was a pupil of John Baptiste Malchair in Oxford in the early 1760s. Skippe made his first trip to Italy in 1766–67 and again from 1772 to 1778, when he also visited Egypt. From 1781 to 1783 he made a series of chiaroscuro woodcuts after old master drawings in his collection.

Sketchbook
1805
pencil, pen and ink, watercolour
223 × 151 mm
Christie's, London (purchase, 1980) (V. & A.)(D.1980.18)

Landscape with Trees
1805
pencil, pen and brown ink, brown watercolour
193 × 143 mm
Christie's, London (purchase, 1980) (D.1980.18.1)

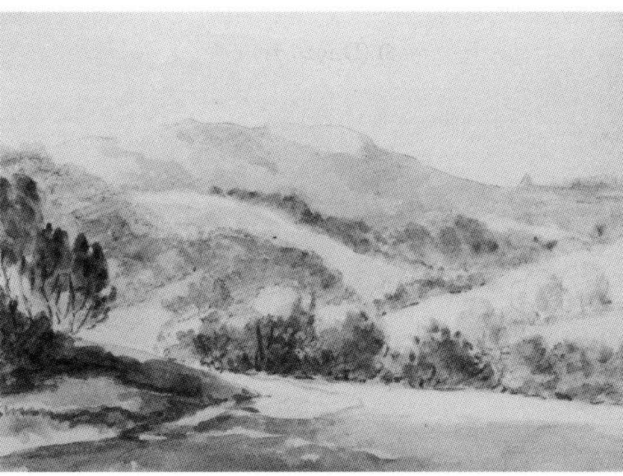
D.1980.18.2

Study of a wooded Valley
1805
pencil, brown watercolour
193 × 143 mm
Christie's, London (purchase, 1980) (D.1980.18.2)

Study of a Group of Figures, probably an Adoration of the Shepherds
1805
pencil
193 × 143 mm
Christie's, London (purchase, 1980) (D.1980.18.4)

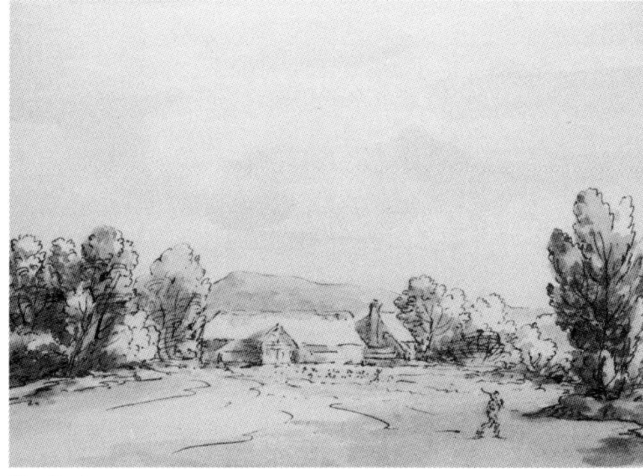
D.1980.18.5

Landscape with Cottage and Barn
1805
pencil, pen and brown ink, brown watercolour
193 × 143 mm
Christie's, London (purchase, 1980) (D.1980.18.5)

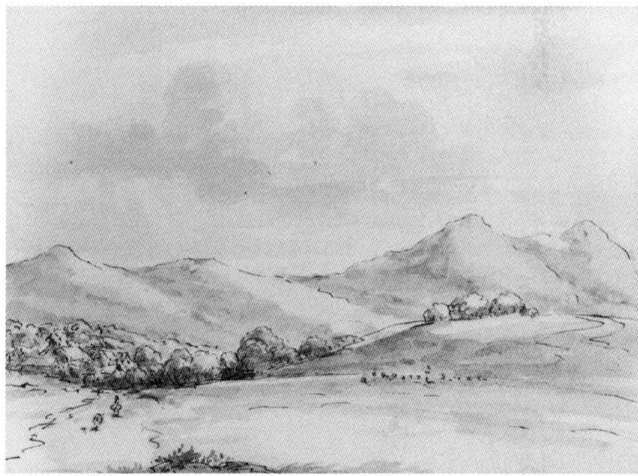
D.1980.18.6

A hilly Landscape with a Village among Trees
1805
pencil, pen and brown ink, brown watercolour
193 × 143 mm
Christie's, London (purchase, 1980) (D.1980.18.6)

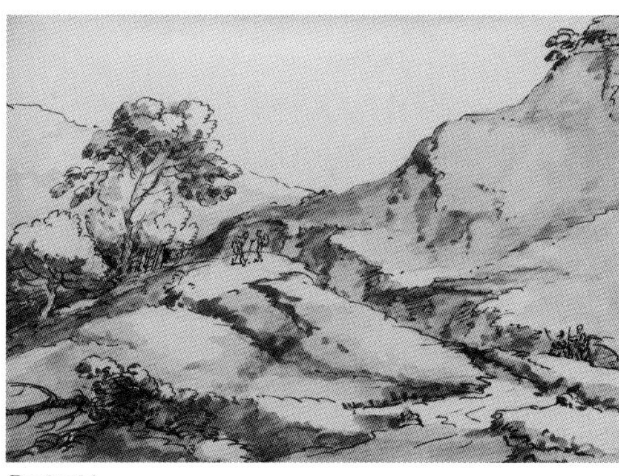
D.1980.18.8

Landscape with Travellers
1805
pencil, pen and brown ink, brown watercolour
193 × 143 mm
Christie's, London (purchase, 1980) (D.1980.18.8)

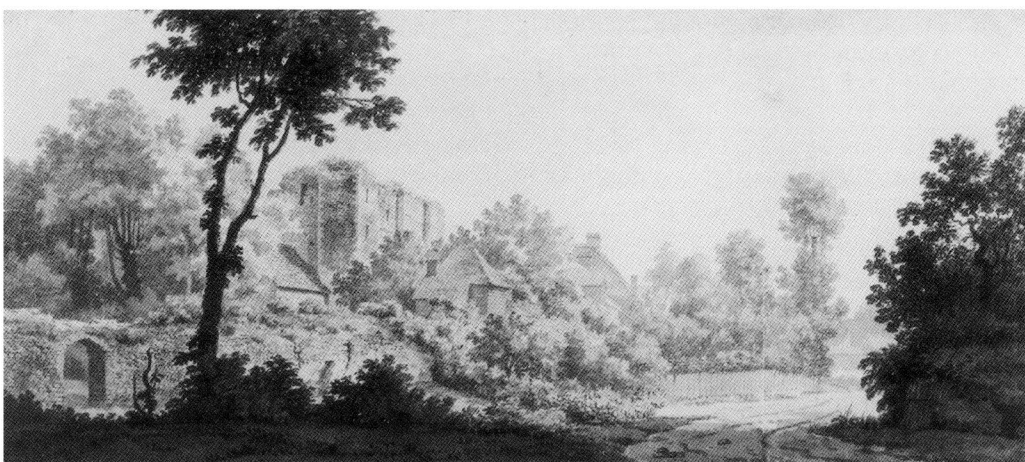
D.1966.20

Study of a Cottage
1805
pencil, pen and brown ink, brown watercolour
193 × 143 mm
Christie's, London (purchase, 1980) (D.1980.18.9)

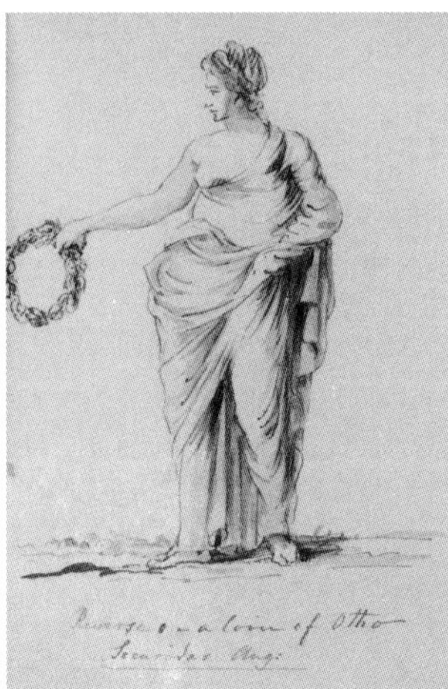

D.1980.18.12

Study of the Figure of 'Security' holding a Wreath, from a Roman Coin
1805
pencil, pen and brown ink, brown watercolour
inscribed on page of sketchbook below drawing:
Reverse on a Coin of Otho / Securitas Aug [last two words underlined]
193 × 143 mm
Christie's, London (purchase, 1980) (D.1980.18.12)

Study of the Figure of 'Liberty of the People', from a Roman Coin
1805
pencil, pen and brown ink, brown watercolour
inscribed on page of sketchbook below drawing:
Reverse on a Coin of Galba / Libertas Publica
193 × 143 mm
Christie's, London (purchase, 1980) (D.1980.18.13)

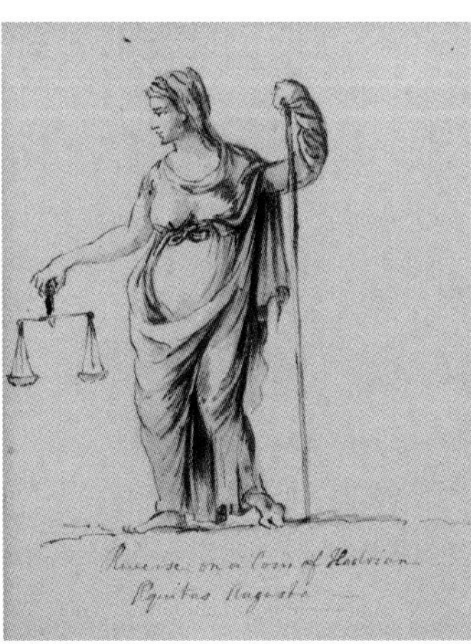

D.1980.18.14

Study of the Figure of 'Equity' holding the Scales of Justice, from a Roman Coin
1805
pencil, pen and brown ink, brown watercolour
inscribed on page of sketchbook below drawing:
Reverse on a Coin of Hadrian / Aequitas Augusta
193 × 143 mm
Christie's, London (purchase, 1980) (D.1980.18.14)

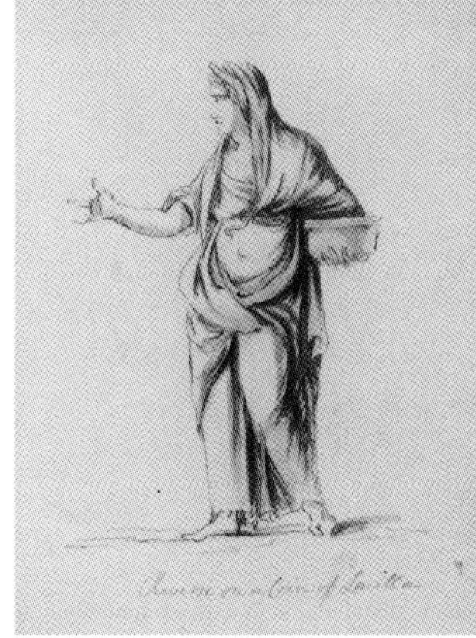

D.1980.18.15

Study of the Figure of 'Modesty/Chastity' holding a Patera, from a Roman Coin
1805
pencil, pen and brown ink, brown watercolour
inscribed on page of sketchbook below drawing:
Reverse on a Coin of Lucilla
193 × 143 mm
Christie's, London (purchase, 1980) (D.1980.18.15)

Study of the Figure of 'Hope' holding a Dove, from a Roman Coin
1805
pencil, pen and brown ink, brown watercolour
inscribed on page of sketchbook below drawing:
Reverse on a Coin of Claudius / Spes Augusta
193 × 143 mm
Christie's, London (purchase, 1980) (D.1980.18.16)

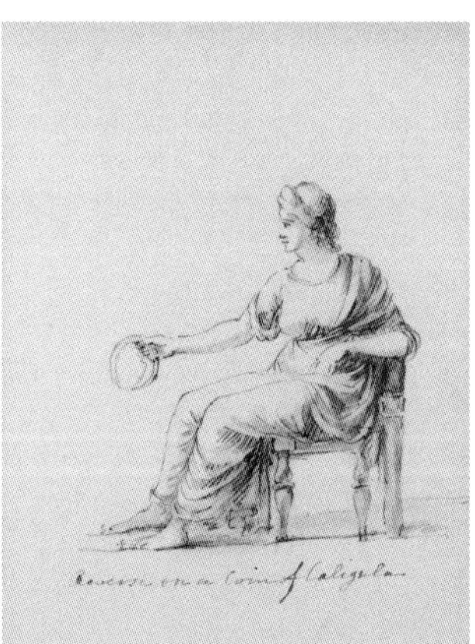

D.1980.18.17

Study of a seated female Roman Figure holding a Patera, from a Roman Coin
1805
pencil, pen and brown ink, brown watercolour
inscribed on page of sketchbook below drawing:
Reverse on a Coin of Caligula
193 × 143 mm
Christie's, London (purchase, 1980) (D.1980.18.17)

Study of the Figure of 'Liberty of the People' holding the Pileus (the Cap of Liberty) and a Staff, from a Roman Coin
1805
pencil, pen and brown ink, brown watercolour
inscribed on page of sketchbook below drawing:
Reverse on a Coin of Galba / Libertas Aug
193 × 143 mm
Christie's, London (purchase, 1980) (D.1980.18.18)

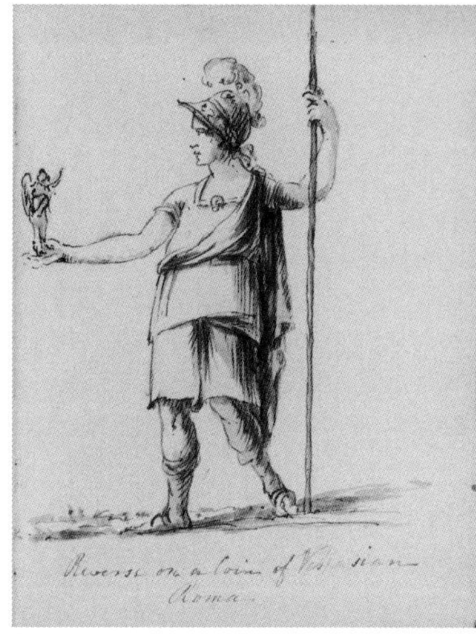

D.1980.18.19

Study of the Personification of Rome holding a Staff, and a Figure of ' Victory', from a Roman Coin
1805
pencil, pen and brown ink, brown watercolour
inscribed on page of sketchbook below drawing:
Reverse on a Coin of Vespasian / Roma
193 × 143 mm
Christie's, London (purchase, 1980) (D.1980.18.19)

Study of the Figure of 'Prosperity' holding a Staff and a Cornucopia, from a Roman Coin
1805
pencil, pen and brown ink, brown watercolour
inscribed on page of sketchbook below drawing:
Reverse on a Coin of Titus / Felicitas Aug
193 × 143 mm
Christie's, London (purchase, 1980) (D.1980.18.20)

Study of the Figure of 'Health' feeding a Snake rising from an Altar, from a Roman Coin
1805
pencil, pen and brown ink, brown watercolour
inscribed on page of sketchbook below drawing:
Reverse on a Coin of Antoninus / Salus Aug
193 × 143 mm
Christie's, London (purchase, 1980) (D.1980.18.21)

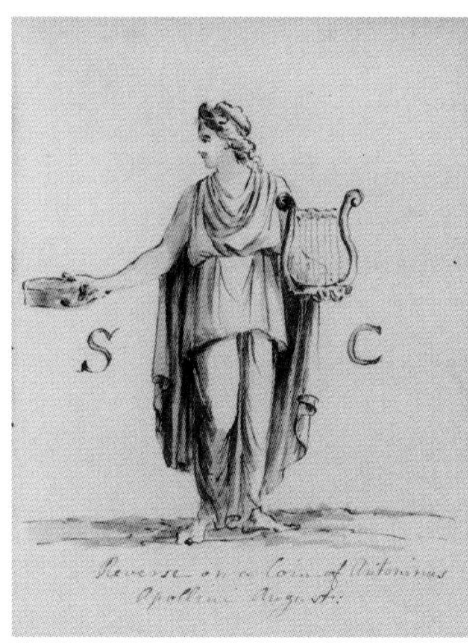

D.1980.18.22

Study of the Figure of 'Apollo', holding a Lyre and Patera, from a Roman Coin
1805
pencil, pen and brown ink, brown watercolour
inscribed on page of sketchbook below drawing:
Reverse on a Coin of Antoninus / Apollini August
193 × 143 mm
Christie's, London (purchase, 1980) (D.1980.18.22)

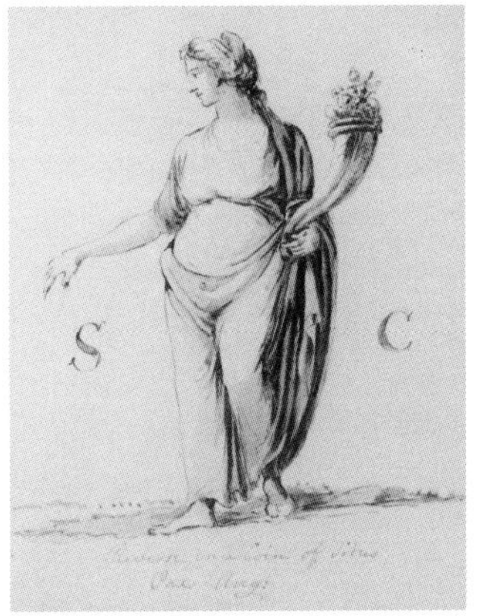
D.1980.18.23

Study of the Figure of 'Peace' holding a Cornucopia and Olive Branch, from a Roman coin
1805
pencil, pen and brown ink, brown watercolour
inscribed on page of sketchbook below drawing:
Reverse on a Coin of Titus / Pax Aug
193 × 143 mm
Christie's, London (purchase, 1980) (D.1980.18.23)

Study of the 'Genius of the Emperor' holding a Torch in each Hand, from a Roman Coin
1805
pencil, pen and brown ink, brown watercolour
inscribed on page of sketchbook below drawing:
Reverse on a Coin of Antoninus / Genio Aug
193 × 143 mm
Christie's, London (purchase, 1980) (D.1980.18.24)

Study of a Corn Goddess holding Corn Ears and a long Torch, from a Roman Coin
1805
pencil, pen and brown ink, brown watercolour
inscribed on page of sketchbook below drawing:
Reverse on a Coin of Faustina / Augusta
193 × 143 mm
Christie's, London (purchase, 1980) (D.1980.18.25)

Study of the Figure of 'Venus' holding an Apple and Sceptre, from a Roman Coin
1805
pencil, pen and brown ink, brown watercolour
inscribed on page of sketchbook below drawing:
Reverse on a Coin of Faustina / Venus
193 × 143 mm
Christie's, London (purchase, 1980) (D.1980.18.26)

Study of the Figure of 'Eternity' holding a Globe, Phoenix and Sceptre, from a Roman Coin
1805
pencil, pen and brown ink, brown watercolour
inscribed on page of sketchbook below drawing:
Reverse on a Coin of Faustina / Aeternitas
193 × 143 mm
Christie's, London (purchase, 1980) (D.1980.18.27)

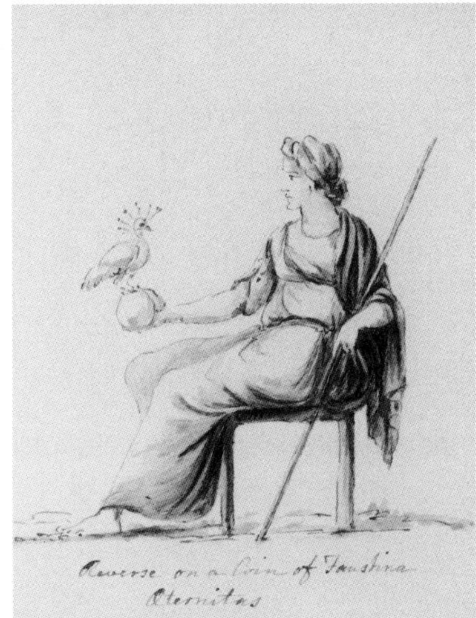
D.1980.18.27

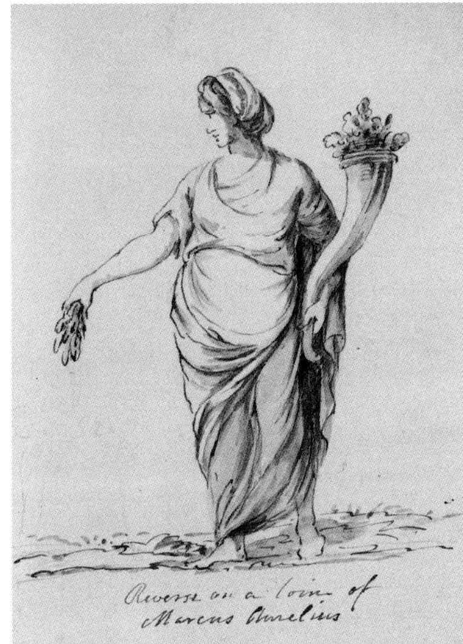
D.1980.18.28

Study of the Figure of 'Plenty' holding a Cornucopia and pouring a Libation onto an Altar, from a Roman Coin
1805
pencil, pen and brown ink, brown watercolour
inscribed on page of sketchbook below drawing:
Reverse on a Coin of / Marcus Aurelius
193 × 143 mm
Christie's, London (purchase, 1980) (D.1980.18.28)

Study of the Figures of 'Mars' holding a Sword and Shield with 'Venus' grasping his Arm, from a Roman Coin
1805
pencil, pen and brown ink, brown watercolour
inscribed on page of sketchbook below drawing:
Reverse on a Coin of Faustina
193 × 143 mm
Christie's, London (purchase, 1980) (D.1980.18.29)

Study of the Figure of 'Health' holding a Snake and a Staff, from a Roman Coin
1805
pencil, pen and brown ink, brown watercolour
inscribed on page of sketchbook below drawing:
Reverse on a Coin of Hadrian
193 × 143 mm
Christie's, London (purchase, 1980) (D.1980.18.30)

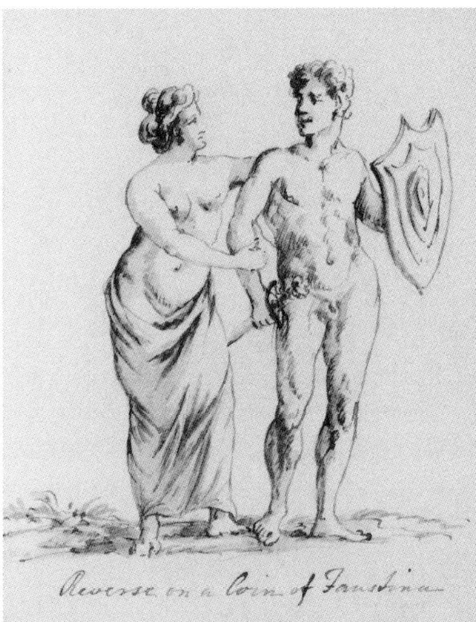
D.1980.18.29

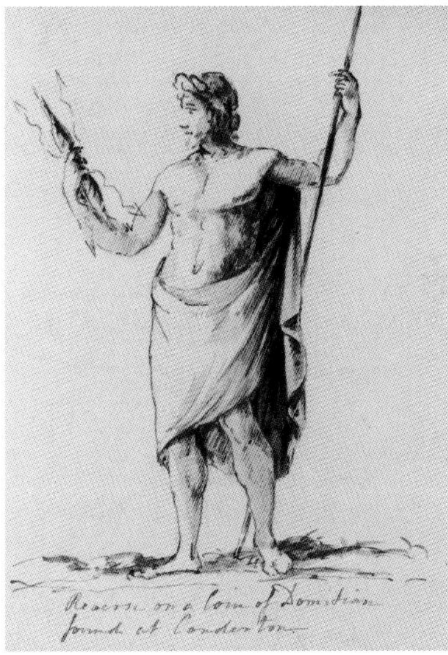
D.1980.18.31

Study of the Figure of 'Zeus' holding a Thunderbolt and a Staff, from a Roman Coin
1805
pencil, pen and brown ink, brown watercolour
inscribed on page of sketchbook below drawing:
Reverse on a Coin of Domitian / found at Conderton.
193 × 143 mm
Christie's, London (purchase, 1980) (D.1980.18.31)

Study of the Figure of 'Peace' holding a Patera over a lighted Altar, from a Roman Coin
1805
pencil, pen and brown ink, brown watercolour
inscribed on page of sketchbook below drawing:
Pax Aug / Reverse on a Coin of Vespasian
193 × 143 mm
Christie's, London (purchase, 1980) (D.1980.18.32)

Study of the Figure of 'Providence' or 'Forethought' raising a Globe, from a Roman Coin
1805
pencil, pen and brown ink, brown watercolour
inscribed on page of sketchbook below drawing:
Providentia Deorum / Reverse on a Coin of Pertinax
193 × 143 mm
Christie's, London (purchase, 1980) (D.1980.18.33)

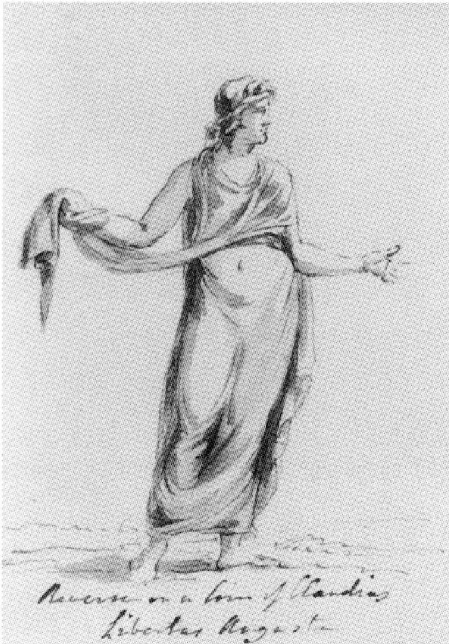

D.1980.18.34

**Study of the Figure of 'Liberty',
from a Roman Coin**
1805
pencil, pen and brown ink, brown watercolour
inscribed on page of sketchbook below drawing:
Reverse on a Coin of Claudius / Libertas Augusta
193 × 143 mm
Christie's, London (purchase, 1980) (D.1980.18.34)

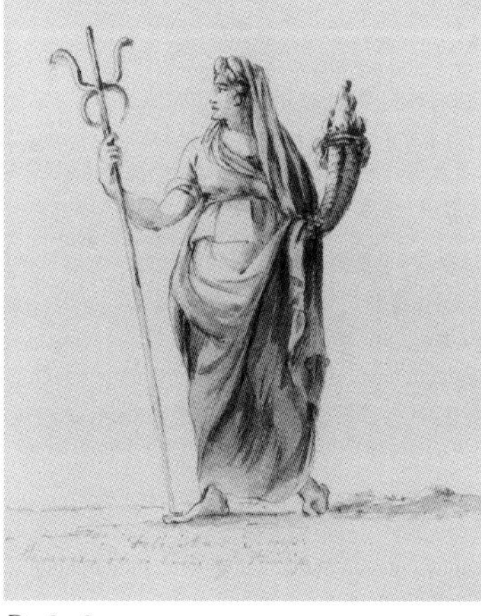

D.1980.18.35

**Study of the Figure of 'Happiness/Prosperity'
holding a Cornucopia and Caduceus, from a
Roman Coin**
1805
pencil, pen and brown ink, brown watercolour
inscribed on page of sketchbook below drawing:
Felicitas Temp / Reverse on a Coin of Philip
193 × 143 mm
Christie's, London (purchase, 1980) (D.1980.18.35)

**Study of the Figure of 'Venus' holding a
Cupid, from a Roman Coin**
1805
pencil, pen and brown ink, brown watercolour
inscribed on page of sketchbook below drawing:
Reverse on a Coin of Julia Mamaea
193 × 143 mm
Christie's, London (purchase, 1980) (D.1980.18.36)

Study of two Children
1805
red chalk
193 × 143 mm
Christie's, London (purchase, 1980) (D.1980.18.105)

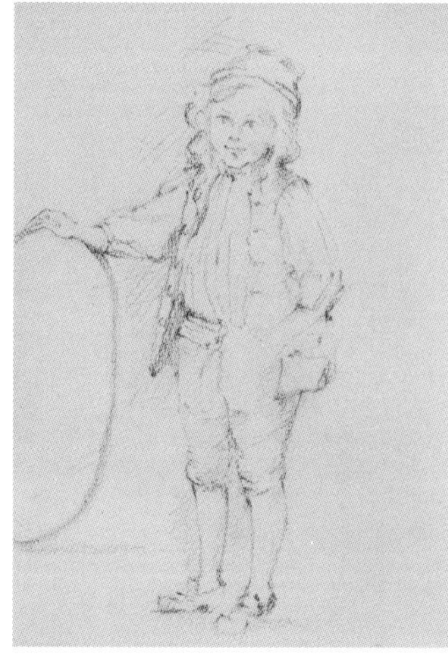

D.1980.18.121

Study of a young Boy holding a Hoop
1805
pencil, red chalk
193 × 143 mm
Christie's, London (purchase, 1980) (D.1980.18.121)

■ SMITH, JOHN RAPHAEL (1752–1812)

John Raphael Smith, one of the leading pastel
portrait painters of the late eighteenth century, also
worked as a mezzotint engraver. Smith exhibited his
works – mostly portraits – at the Royal Academy
between 1779 and 1805.

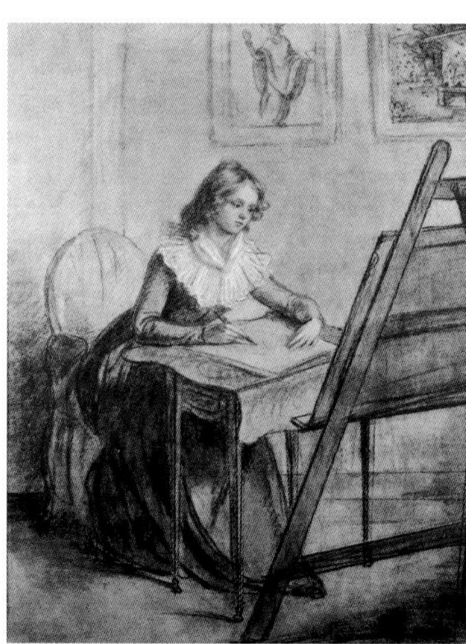

D.1971.7

A young Girl seated at a Desk copying a Painting
coloured chalk; grey paper
654 × 422 mm
Christie's, London (purchase, 1971) (D.1971.7)

■ SMITH, JOHN 'WARWICK' (1749–1831)

Born in Cumberland, John 'Warwick' Smith was
introduced to the young Earl of Warwick in about
1775. Warwick financed Smith's stay in Italy from 1776
until 1781, after which time Smith travelled back to
England via the Swiss and Italian Alps with Francis
Towne. On his return Smith was based in Warwick but
made tours of Derbyshire, Devon and North Wales.
He was elected a member of the Old Watercolour
Society in 1806. Smith's later work is highly repetitive
and often exists in many versions.

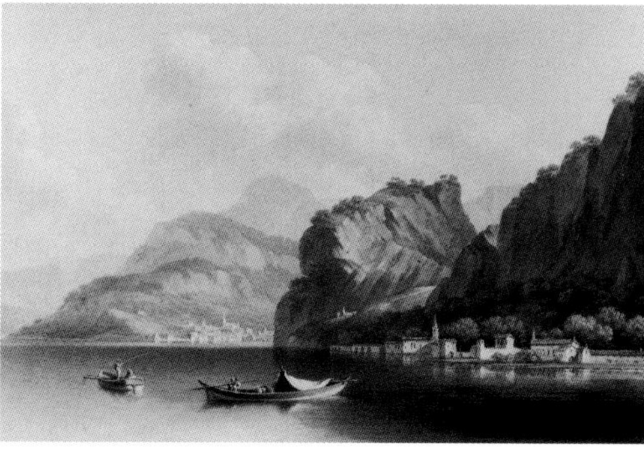

D.1908.1

Lake Lugano, Switzerland
pencil, watercolour
302 × 440 mm
Palser, J. and Son, London (purchase, 1908) (D.1908.1)

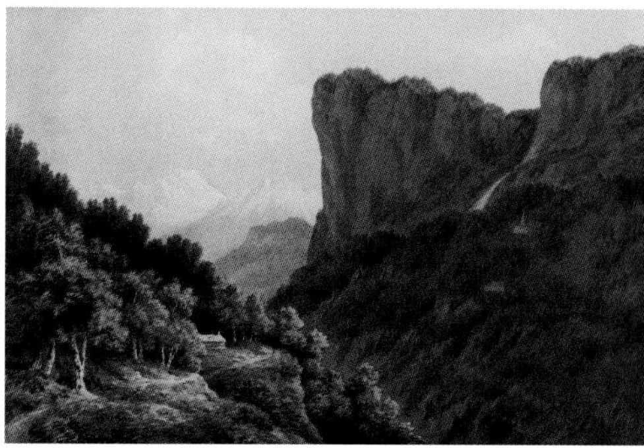

D.1938.9

Valley of the Pissevache, Pays de Valais, France
pencil, watercolour
344 × 506 mm
Reekie, W. Maxwell (gift, 1938) (D.1938.9)

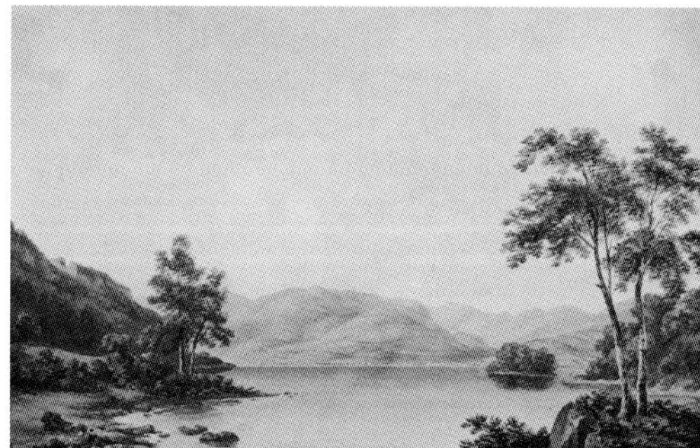

D.1972.13

**Lake Windermere looking North with
Part of Belle Isle**
1791
pencil, watercolour
signed & dated: *J.Smith 1791*; inscribed & numbered in
centre on mount (overmounted): *on the Lancashire side,
opposite the great Island No.19*
349 × 515 mm
Agnew's (purchase, 1972) (D.1972.13)

■ SMITH, JOSEPH CLARENDON (1778–1810)

Joseph Clarendon Smith was a landscape and
topographical draughtsman who worked mostly in
London and exhibited at the Royal Academy between
1806 and 1808.

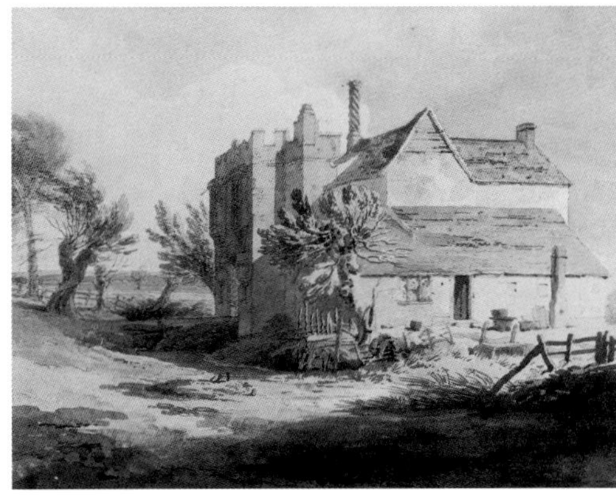

D.1892.58

Rye House, Hertfordshire
pencil, watercolour
234 × 295 mm
Taylor, John Edward (gift, 1892) (D.1892.58)

■ SMITH, MARY (fl. 1790–1810)
Mary Smith, an amateur artist who was possibly an illegitimate daughter of the Prince Regent, lived at Ince Castle, Cornwall. Her only significant known work is at the Whitworth.

Ince Castle, Cornwall, the Front Entrance
pencil, blue watercolour, grey watercolour
178 × 483 mm
Ogden, William Sharp (bequest, 1926) (D.1926.245)

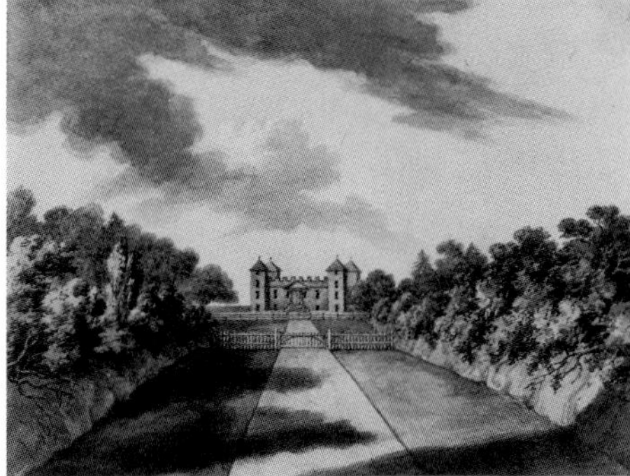

D.1926.246

Ince Castle, Cornwall, the front Entrance
pencil, blue watercolour, grey watercolour
178 × 231 mm
Ogden, William Sharp (bequest, 1926) (D.1926.246)

Ince Castle, Cornwall, View from the Plantation
pencil, blue watercolour, grey watercolour
178 × 483 mm
Ogden, William Sharp (bequest, 1926) (D.1926.247)

The Bowling Green, Ince Castle, Cornwall
pencil, blue watercolour, grey watercolour
178 × 241 mm
Ogden, William Sharp (bequest, 1926) (D.1926.248)

The Bowling Green, Ince Castle, Cornwall
pencil, blue watercolour, grey watercolour
178 × 483 mm
Ogden, William Sharp (bequest, 1926) (D.1926.249)

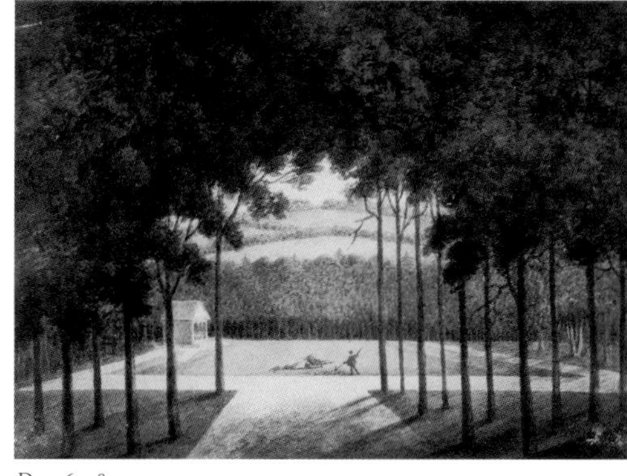

D.1926.248

Ince Castle, Cornwall, View from the Hall Door
pencil, blue watercolour, grey watercolour
181 × 483 mm
Ogden, William Sharp (bequest, 1926) (D.1926.250)

Ince Castle, Cornwall, View from the Breakfast Parlour
pencil, blue watercolour, grey watercolour
182 × 485 mm
Ogden, William Sharp (bequest, 1926) (D.1926.251)

Ince Castle, Cornwall, from Greeps Hill
pencil, blue watercolour, grey watercolour
175 × 478 mm
Ogden, William Sharp (bequest, 1926) (D.1926.252)

Ince Castle, Cornwall, from Antony Ferry
pencil, blue watercolour, grey watercolour
180 × 482 mm
Ogden, William Sharp (bequest, 1926) (D.1926.253)

Ince Castle, Cornwall, the lower Boat-House
pencil, blue watercolour, grey watercolour
180 × 241 mm
Ogden, William Sharp (bequest, 1926) (D.1926.254)

Ince Castle, Cornwall, the upper Boat-House
pencil, blue watercolour, grey watercolour
182 × 485 mm
Ogden, William Sharp (bequest, 1926) (D.1926.255)

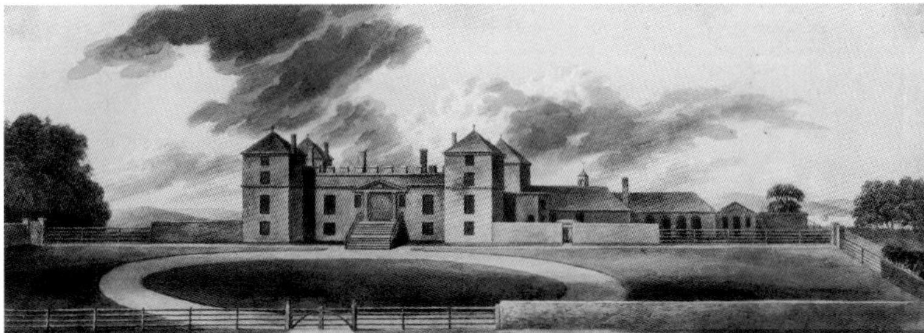

D.1926.245

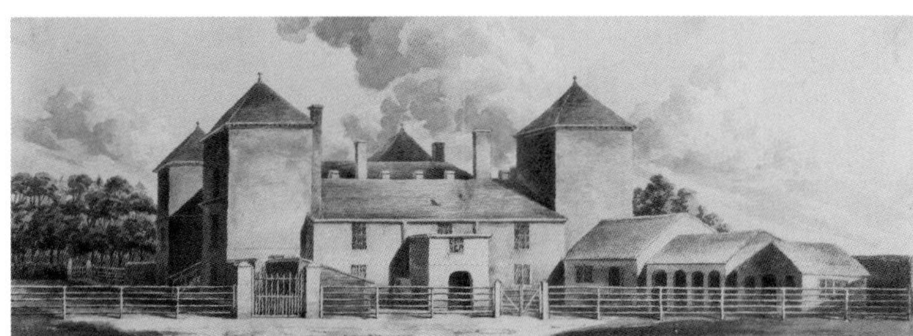

D.1926.247

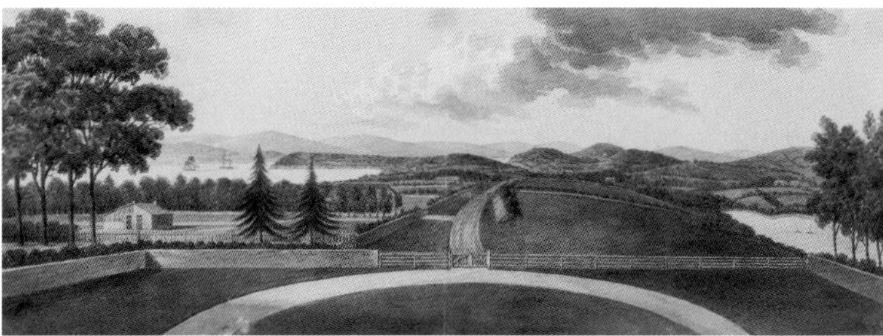

D.1926.250

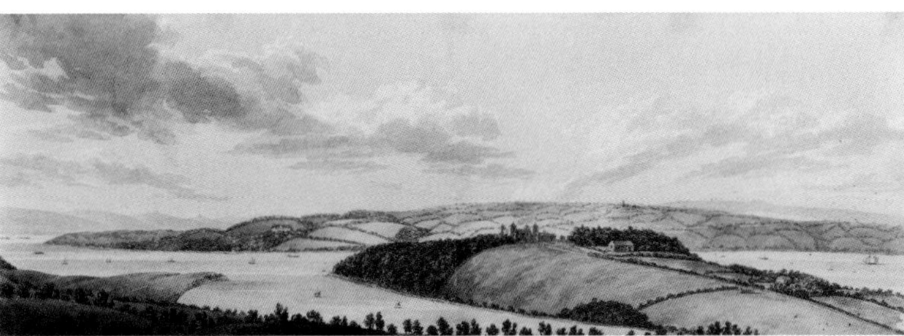

D.1926.252

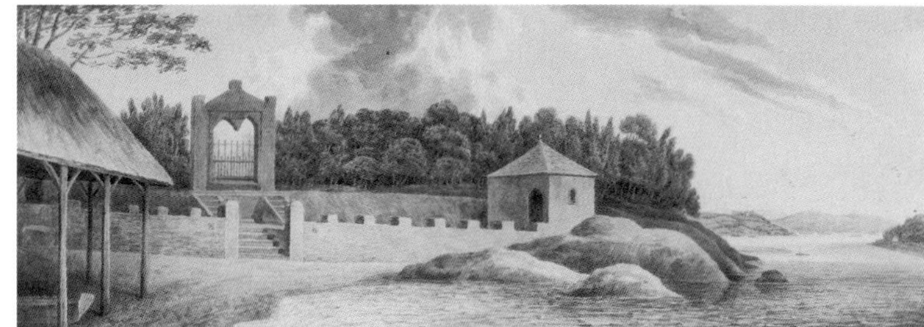

D.1926.255

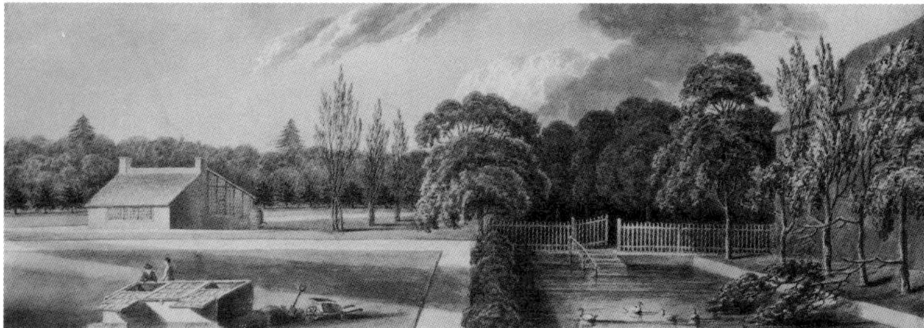

D.1926.257

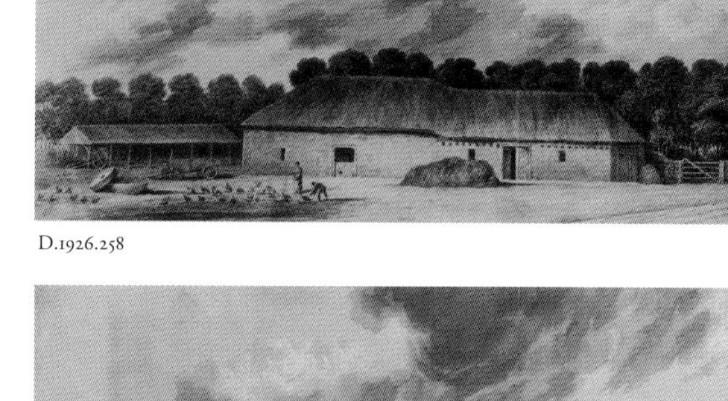

D.1926.258

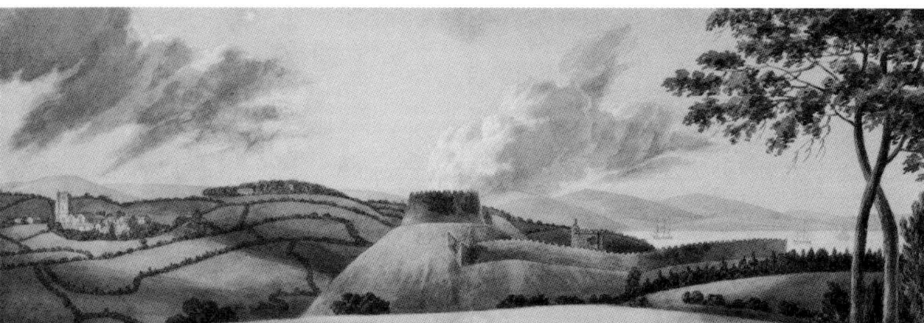

D.1926.260

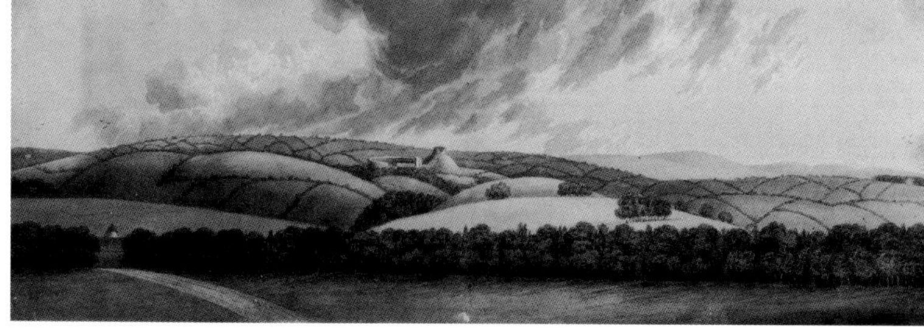

D.1926.262

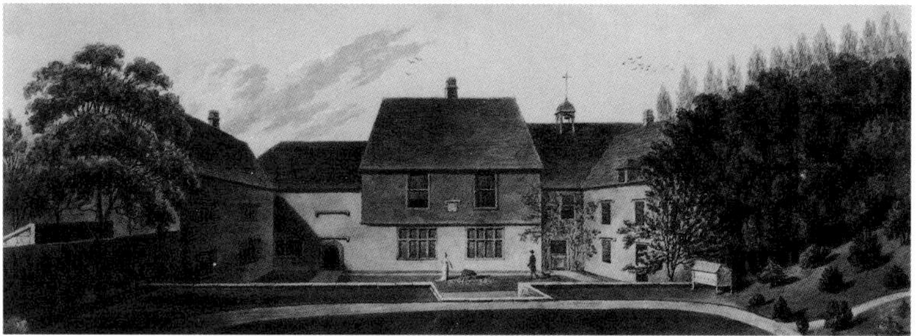

D.1926.264

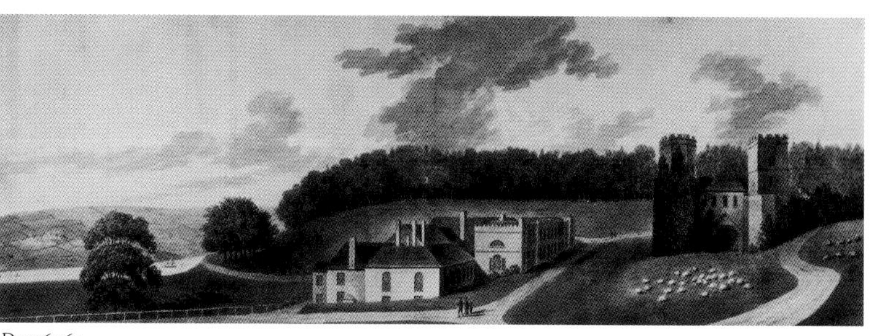

D.1926.265

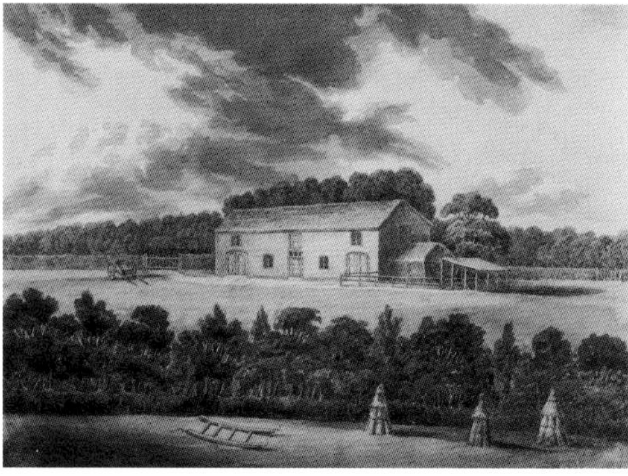

D.1926.256

Ince Castle, Cornwall, the Coach Houses
pencil, blue watercolour, grey watercolour
180 × 241 mm
Ogden, William Sharp (bequest, 1926) (D.1926.256)

Ince Castle, Cornwall, the Garden and Pond
pencil, blue watercolour, grey watercolour
182 × 482 mm
Ogden, William Sharp (bequest, 1926) (D.1926.257)

Ince Castle, Cornwall, the Barn and Farmyard
pencil, blue watercolour, grey watercolour
178 × 483 mm
Ogden, William Sharp (bequest, 1926) (D.1926.258)

Ince Castle, Cornwall, the back of the Barn
pencil, blue watercolour, grey watercolour
178 × 483 mm
Ogden, William Sharp (bequest, 1926) (D.1926.259)

**Trematon Castle, Cornwall, with
St Stephen's Church**
pencil, blue watercolour, grey watercolour
watermark 1794
178 × 483 mm
Ogden, William Sharp (bequest, 1926) (D.1926.260)

**Trematon Castle, Cornwall, from
St Stephen's Church**
pencil, blue watercolour, grey watercolour
watermark 1794
180 × 483 mm
Ogden, William Sharp (bequest, 1926) (D.1926.261)

**Trematon Castle, Cornwall, from the
Hill at Antony**
pencil, blue watercolour, grey watercolour
178 × 483 mm
Ogden, William Sharp (bequest, 1926) (D.1926.262)

Trematon Castle, Cornwall, from the Ferry
pencil, blue watercolour, grey watercolour
182 × 488 mm
Ogden, William Sharp (bequest, 1926) (D.1926.263)

View of the back of Burrell House, Cornwall
pencil, blue watercolour, grey watercolour
178 × 480 mm
Ogden, William Sharp (bequest, 1926) (D.1926.264)

Port Eliot, Cornwall
pencil, blue watercolour, grey watercolour
182 × 482 mm
Ogden, William Sharp (bequest, 1926) (D.1926.265)

**View of a rocky Cave, with Figures
seated at a Picnic**
pencil, blue watercolour, grey watercolour
187 × 446 mm
Ogden, William Sharp (bequest, 1926) (D.1926.266)

Distant View of Lands End, Cornwall
pencil, blue watercolour, grey watercolour
178 × 483 mm
Ogden, William Sharp (bequest, 1926) (D.1926.267)

Portwrinkle and Lands End, Cornwall
pencil, blue watercolour, grey watercolour
178 × 483 mm
Ogden, William Sharp (bequest, 1926) (D.1926.268)

**Looking toward Hamoaze from
Crafthole, Cornwall**
pencil, blue watercolour, grey watercolour
178 × 485 mm
Ogden, William Sharp (bequest, 1926) (D.1926.269)

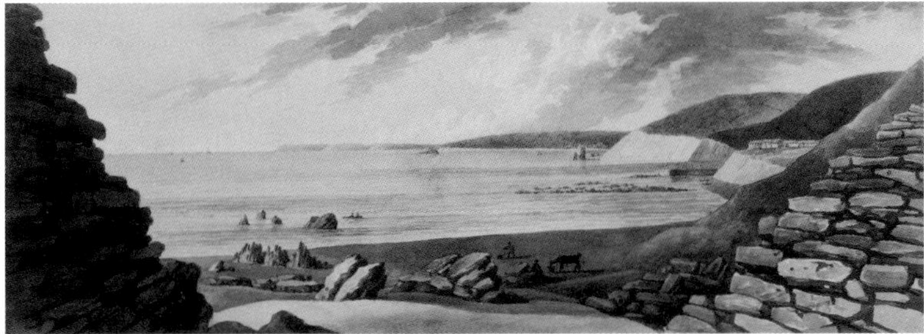

D.1926.267

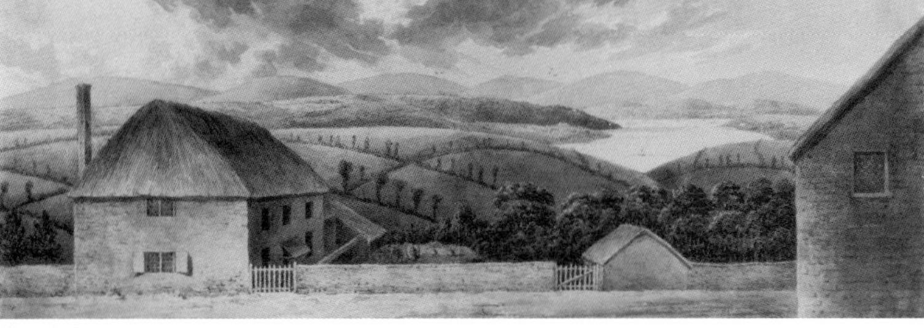

D.1926.269

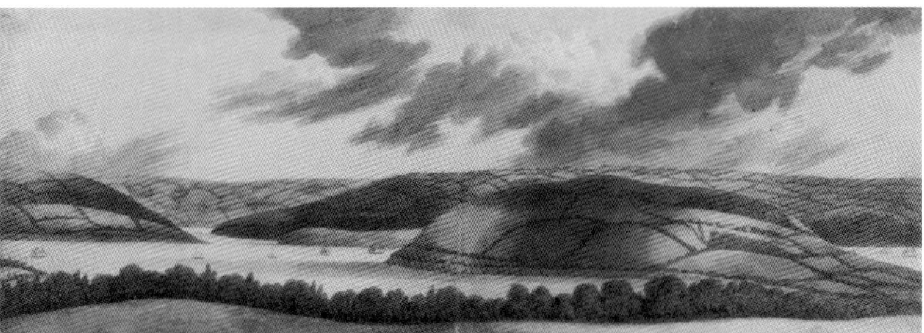

D.1926.270

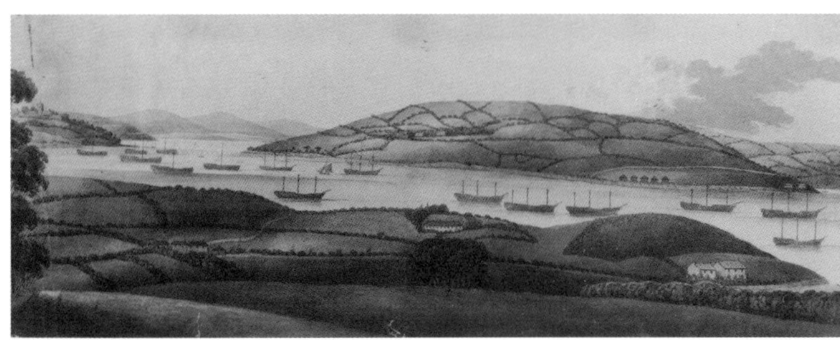

D.1926.271

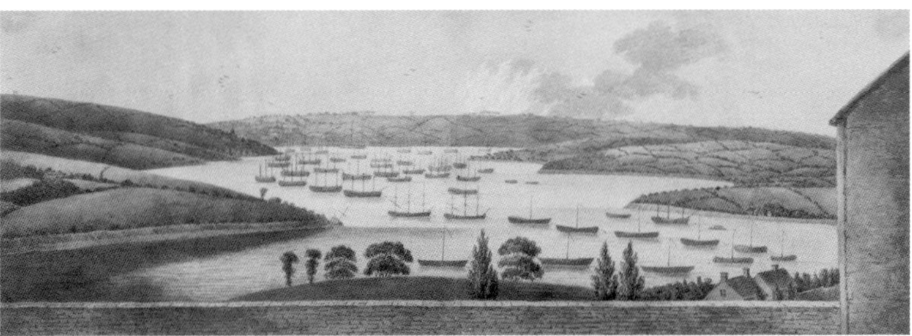

D.1926.272

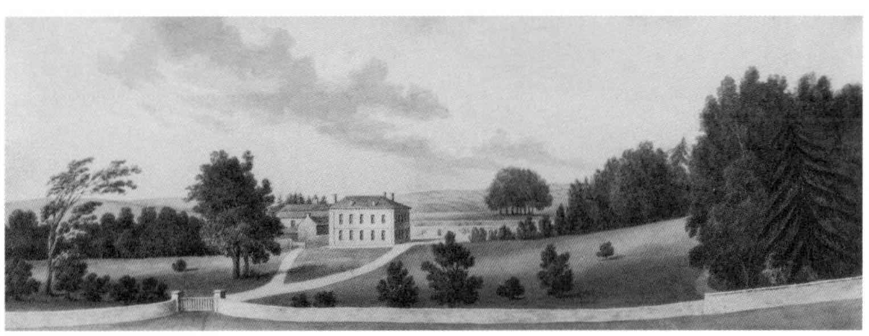

D.1926.274

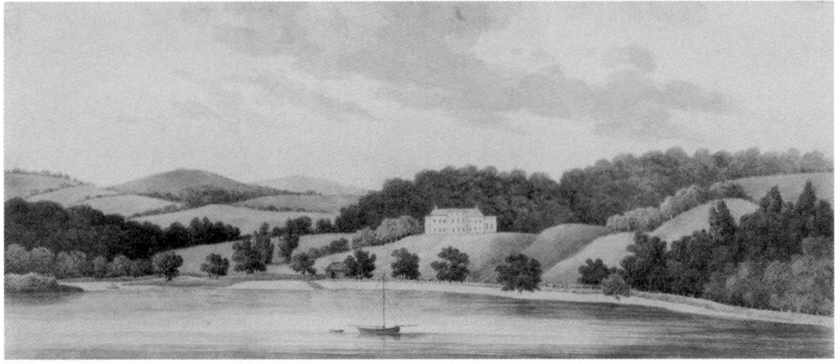

D.1926.275

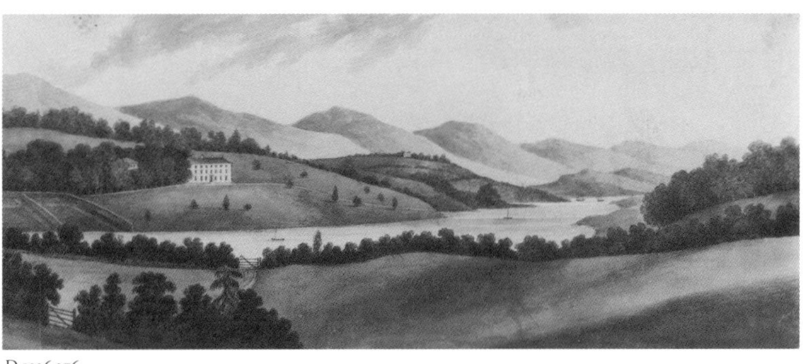

D.1926.276

View from Greeps Hill, Cornwall
pencil, blue watercolour, grey watercolour
175 × 480 mm
Ogden, William Sharp (bequest, 1926) (D.1926.270)

Looking toward the River Tamar from Antony House, Cornwall
pencil, blue watercolour, grey watercolour
180 × 461 mm
Ogden, William Sharp (bequest, 1926) (D.1926.271)

View across Plymouth Sound, Cornwall
pencil, blue watercolour, grey watercolour
182 × 482 mm
Ogden, William Sharp (bequest, 1926) (D.1926.272)

View over an Estuary with Ships
pencil, blue watercolour, grey watercolour
185 × 477 mm
Ogden, William Sharp (bequest, 1926) (D.1926.273)

View of a Country House
pencil, blue watercolour, grey watercolour
181 × 485 mm
Ogden, William Sharp (bequest, 1926) (D.1926.274)

View across an Estuary with a Country House
pencil, blue watercolour, grey watercolour
185 × 410 mm
Ogden, William Sharp (bequest, 1926) (D.1926.275)

View of a Country House across a River
pencil, blue watercolour, grey watercolour
185 × 432 mm
Ogden, William Sharp (bequest, 1926) (D.1926.276)

■ SMITH, THOMAS (ca. 1750–ca. 1822)

The only records pertaining to the life of Thomas Smith come from an album of his Swiss and Italian views that was on the London art market in 1973. He seems to have been working on the Continent between 1780 and 1795, and probably knew John 'Warwick' Smith, Francis Towne and Thomas Jones, although there is no mention of him in Jones's *Memoirs*.

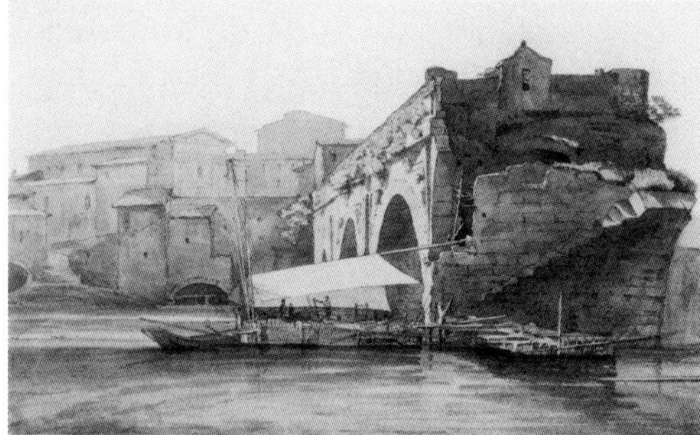

D.1973.14

The Ponte Rotto, Rome

1780–95
pencil, pen and ink, watercolour
inscribed: *Ponte Rotto, Rome*; inscribed verso: *My drawings want finish – or in light chiefly / shadow eno'. – not to wash general washes / of yellow or ochre – give rotten look. / nor wash* [deleted] *work one colour over another. / This wants strength of shadow. Distance right and not to confound colours one over the other as in / water, yellow or blue over it*
213 × 333 mm
Albany Gallery, London (purchase, 1973) (D.1973.14)

■ SMITH, WILLIAM COLLINGWOOD (1815–87)

William Collingwood Smith, a prolific landscape and marine watercolourist, was an influential drawing master and was elected a member of the Old Watercolour Society in 1849, exhibiting there from 1843.

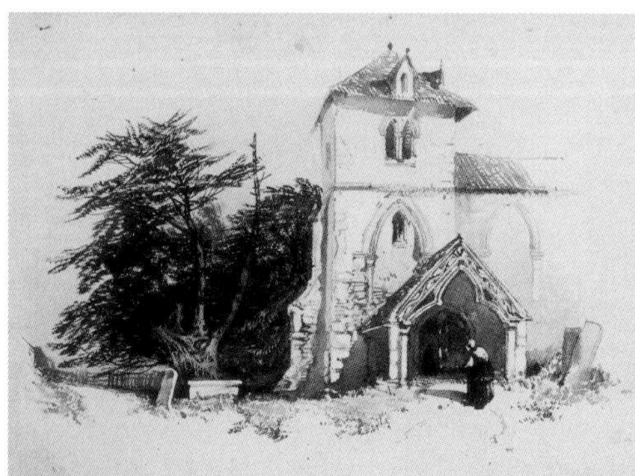

D.1926.124

A Church with a Yew Tree

watercolour, bodycolour (heightened with white)
brown paper
275 × 370 mm
Ogden, William Sharp (bequest, 1926) (D.1926.124)

The Bank of a River with Buildings and Boats

black chalk, bodycolour (heightened with white)
grey paper
243 × 334 mm
Ogden, William Sharp (bequest, 1926) (D.1926.125)

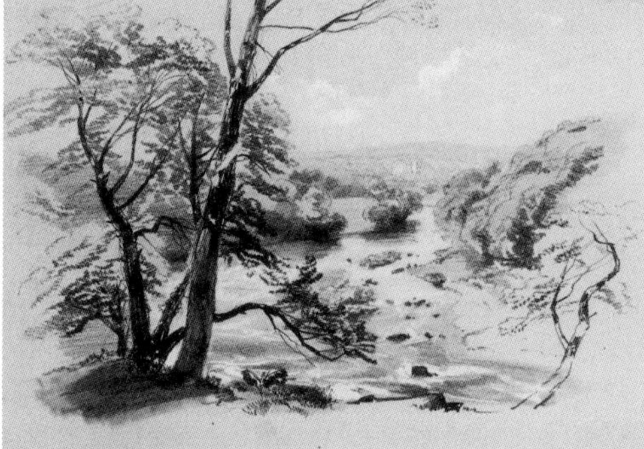

D.1926.126

A Landscape with a River and distant Castle

black chalk, bodycolour (heightened with white)
grey paper
239 × 335 mm
Ogden, William Sharp (bequest, 1926) (D.1926.126)

Shipping Scene with the Hulk of a Man O'War

black chalk, white chalk, bodycolour (heightened with white); brown paper
246 × 351 mm
Ogden, William Sharp (bequest, 1926) (D.1926.127)

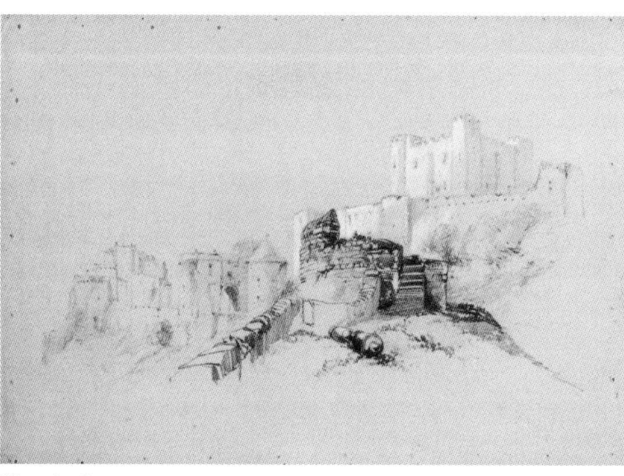

D.1926.128

Dover Castle: Say's Tower with Constable's Tower, Peverell's Tower and the Keep beyond

pencil, black chalk, bodycolour (heightened with white); brown paper
274 × 388 mm
Ogden, William Sharp (bequest, 1926) (D.1926.128)

Villas on the Shore of a Lake (recto); Landscape Studies (verso)

pencil, brown watercolour, bodycolour (heightened with white); brown paper
Ogden, William Sharp (bequest, 1926) (D.1926.228)

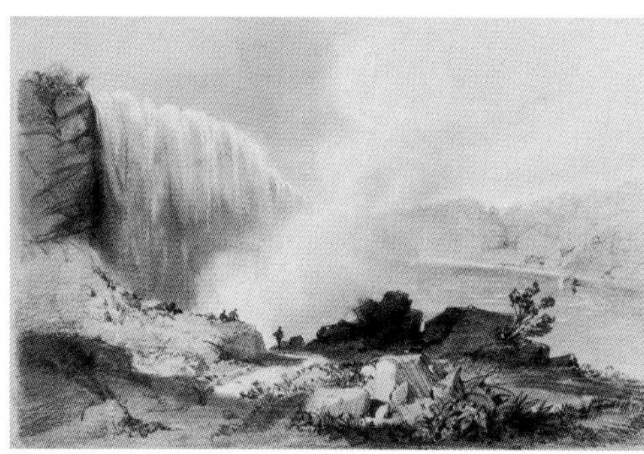

D.1926.229

The Niagara Falls from the American Side

black chalk, bodycolour (heightened with white)
grey paper
280 × 382 mm
Ogden, William Sharp (bequest, 1926) (D.1926.229)

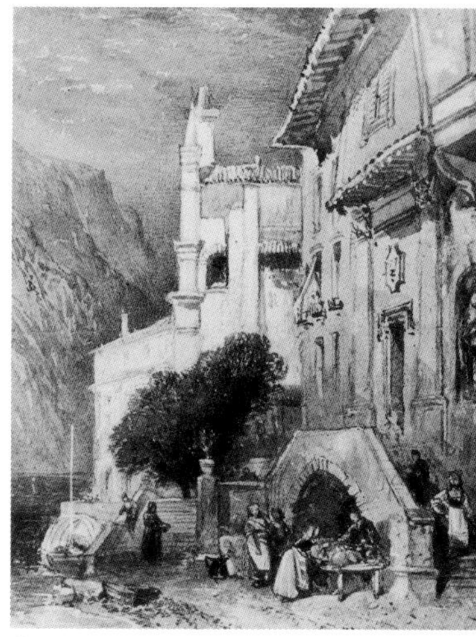

D.1970.71

Buildings by an Italian Lake

pencil, watercolour, bodycolour (heightened with white)
252 × 187 mm
Towlson, Hector J. (bequest, 1969) (D.1970.71)

■ SOLOMON, ABRAHAM (1824–62)

A portrait painter and illustrator, Abraham Solomon entered the Royal Academy Schools in 1839, and exhibited at the Royal Academy between 1841 and 1862. He is now best known for his railway compartment pictures of 1854.

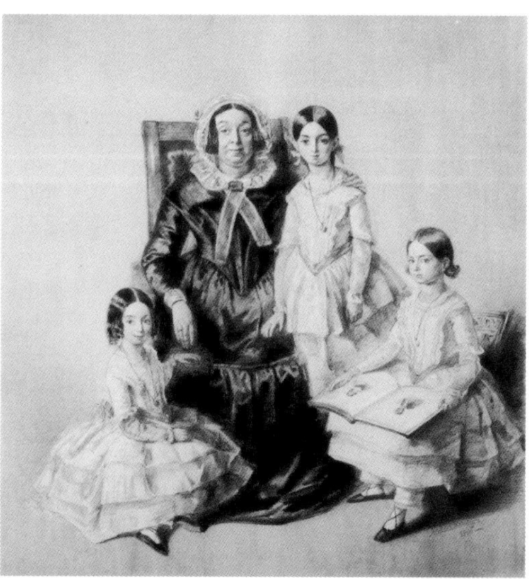

D.1977.1

Mrs Rosa Samuel and her three Daughters

1845
pencil, black chalk, white chalk, red chalk; grey paper
signed & dated lower right: *Abraham Solomon / 1845–*
584 × 527 mm
Langdon, Margaret (gift, 1977) (D.1977.1)

■ SOLOMON, SIMEON (1840–1905)

The younger brother of Abraham and Rebecca, Simeon Solomon was intimate with the Pre-Raphaelites and friend of Rossetti and Burne-Jones. His earlier watercolours often show Jewish ritual or biblical subject matter. After a conviction for homosexual offences in 1873, Solomon dropped out of society but continued to paint, concentrating on single figure allegorical and symbolist subjects.

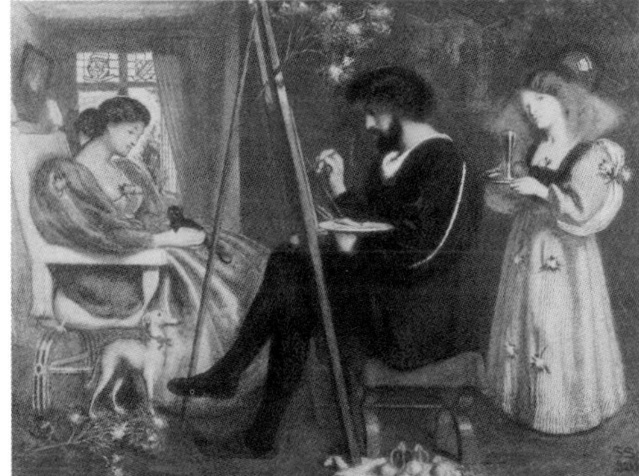

D.1911.4

The Painter's Pleasaunce
1861
watercolour, bodycolour, varnish
signed & dated with initials: *S S. / 12/61*
256 × 331 mm
Agnew, C. Morland (gift, 1911) (D.1911.4)

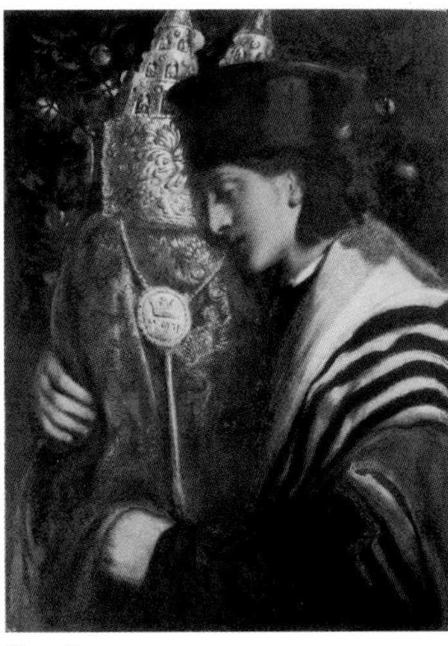

D.1919.8

Carrying the Scrolls of the Law
1867
watercolour, bodycolour, varnish; paper laid on canvas
signed, inscribed & dated upper right date and location written one above the other and together of the same size as the initials: *S S 1867 / ROME*
357 × 255 mm
untraced (purchase, 1919) (D.1919.8)

■ STANFIELD, CLARKSON (1793–1867)

Stanfield was born in Sunderland and began his career as a sailor before working as a scene painter in London from 1816. He first exhibited at the Royal Academy in 1827 and was elected a member in 1835. Stanfield was a prolific watercolourist, providing illustrations for publishers such as Charles Heath in the 1830s.

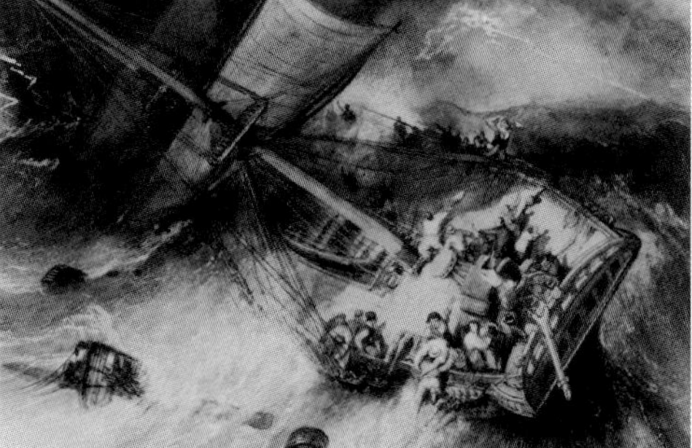

D.1887.38

Cutting away the Masts: Illustration to Marryatt's Novel, 'The Pirate'
1836
pencil, watercolour, bodycolour
261 × 388 mm
Christie's, London (purchase, 2.5.1891) (D.1887.38)

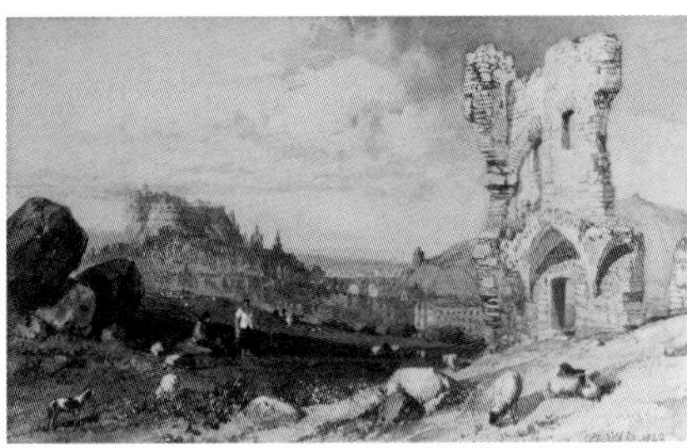

D.1887.39

Edinburgh from St Anthony's Chapel
1842
pencil, watercolour, bodycolour
(heightened with white)
signed & dated lower right with initial in monogram:
CStanfield RA.1842
179 × 278 mm
Agnew's (purchase, 13.11.1893) (D.1887.39)

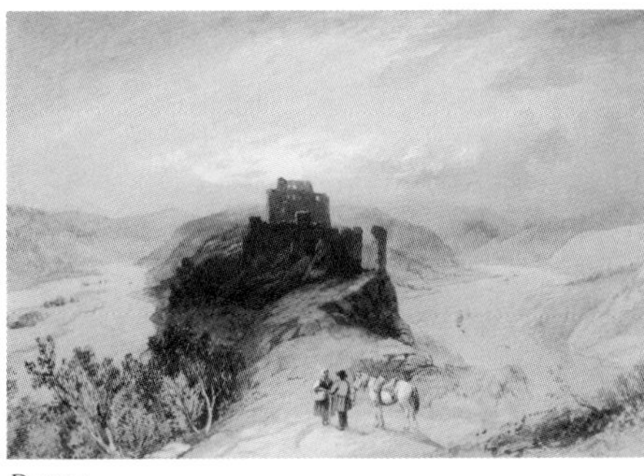

D.1910.9

The Castle of Marienburg, Germany
1838
pencil, watercolour, bodycolour (heightened with white); buff paper
275 × 392 mm
Cox, G. F. (bequest, 1910) (D.1910.9)

The Belem Tower, Lisbon
1833
pen and brown ink, watercolour, bodycolour (heightened with white)
signed lower right with initial in monogram:
CStanfield.RA.
241 × 334 mm
Broadhurst, Sir Edward Tootal, Broadhurst, Lady (bequest, 1924) (D.1924.53)

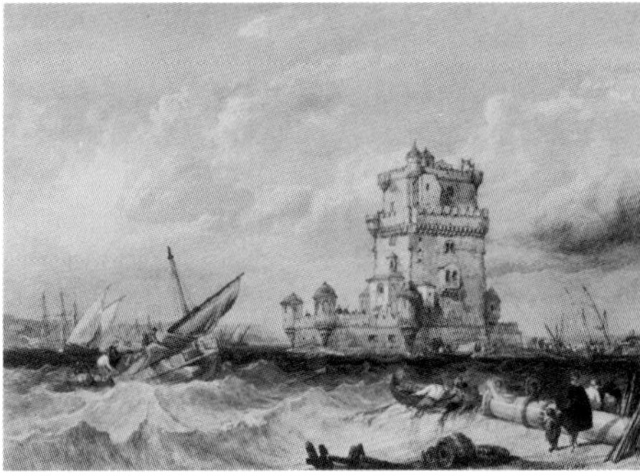

D.1924.53

Two Sailing Boats and a Ship in a rough Sea
pencil, brown watercolour, bodycolour (heightened with white); grey paper
signed lower right: *C.Stanfield*
275 × 387 mm
Ogden, William Sharp (bequest, 1926) (D.1926.237)

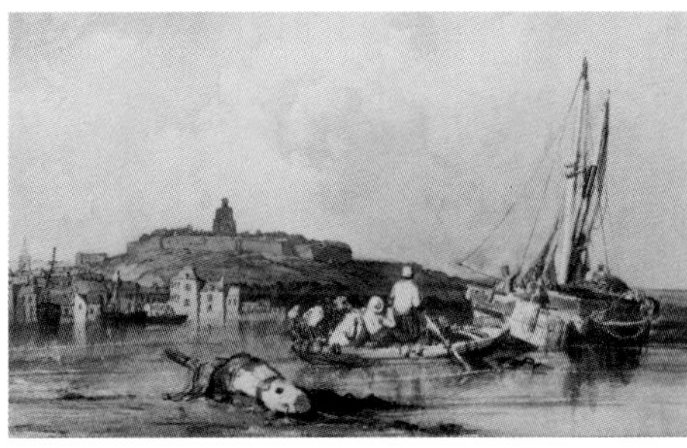

D.1970.72

Upper Harbour, Boulogne, France
1836
watercolour, bodycolour (heightened with white)
signed & dated lower centre on a piece of wreckage with initials: *C.S.1836*
164 × 273 mm
Towlson, Hector J. (bequest, 1969) (D.1970.72)

■ STARK, JAMES (1794–1859)

Born in Norwich, Stark was elected a member of the Norwich Society of Artists in 1812. He moved to Windsor in 1840 and painted landscapes in oil and watercolour of mainly southern subjects.

Landscape and Ricks
pencil, watercolour
150 × 440 mm
Meatyard, F. R. (purchase, 1920) (D.1920.2)

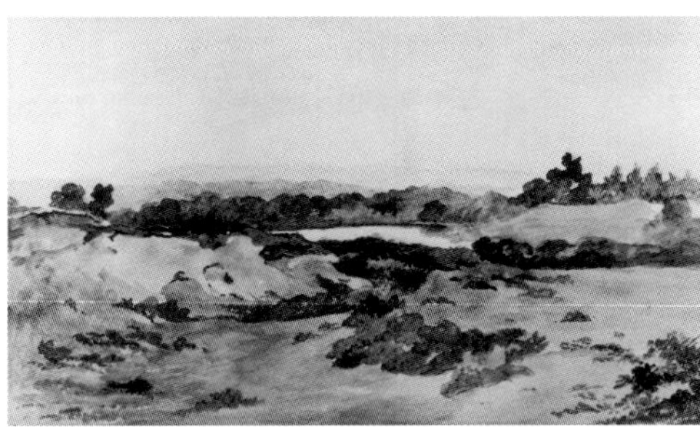

D.1920.4

Moorland Pool
pencil, watercolour
235 × 411 mm
Meatyard, F. R. (purchase, 1920) (D.1920.4)

■ STEADMAN, CHARLES (dates unknown)

Unknown amateur artist.

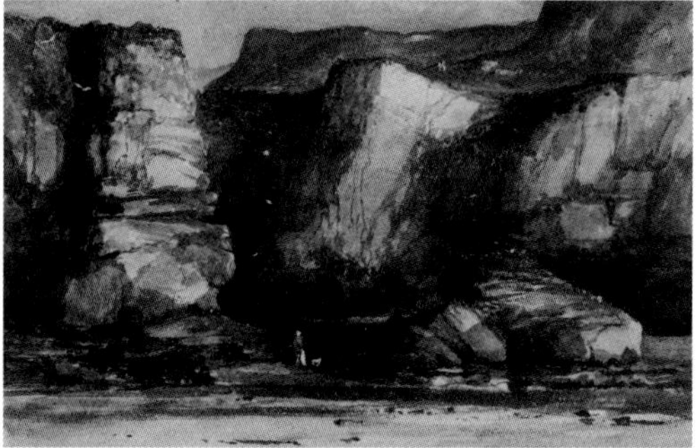

D.1926.324

A Figure on a Beach below Cliffs
1840
watercolour, bodycolour (heightened with white)
signed & dated centre verso: *Charles Steadman / 1840*
154 × 236 mm
Ogden, William Sharp (bequest, 1926) (D.1926.324)

■ STEEPLE, JOHN (ca. 1820–87)

Steeple, a landscape watercolourist who lived in
Birmingham and London, painted in North Wales,
the Home Counties and Sussex.

Hollington Valley, near St Leonards, Sussex
1875
watercolour
signed & dated lower left: *John Steeple 1875*
350 × 500 mm
Claye, Misses (gift, 1955) (D.1955.8)

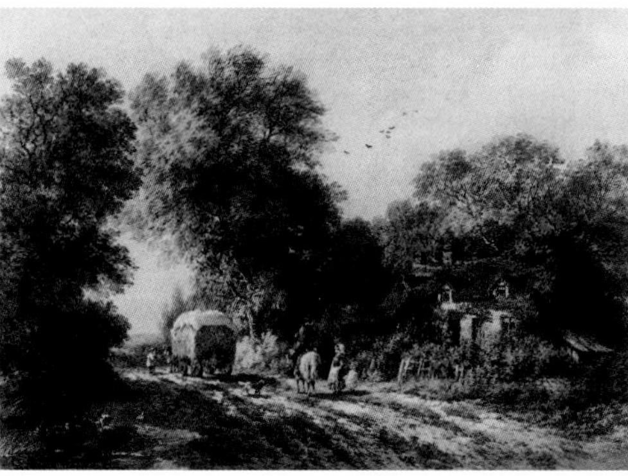

D.1970.73

The Outskirts of a Warwickshire Village
1862
pencil, watercolour, bodycolour (heightened
with white)
signed & dated lower left: *John Steeple 1862*
199 × 274 mm
Towlson, Hector J. (bequest, 1969) (D.1970.73)

■ STEVENS, ALFRED GEORGE (1817–75)

A sculptor and designer, Stevens worked in
Thorvaldsen's studio in Rome before returning to
England in 1842. He is known for his chalk drawings
which often relate to his grandiose decorative schemes.
Stevens's magnum opus is the Wellington monument
in St Paul's Cathedral, which he began in 1857 and
worked on till his death.

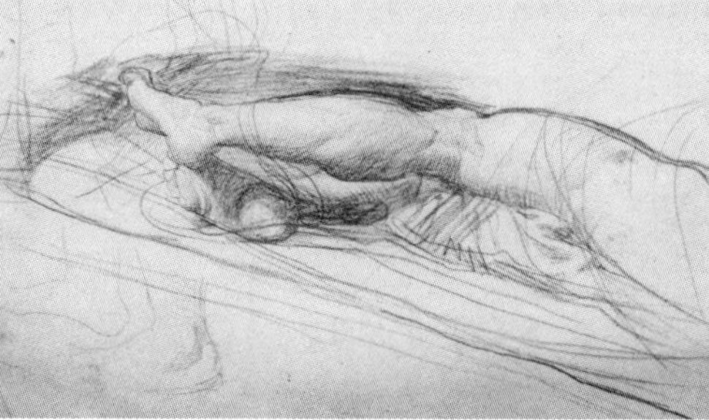

D.1915.13

Study of a Man's Legs in a reclining Position
red chalk
190 × 325 mm
Messrs E. Parsons and Sons (purchase, 1915) (D.1915.13)

Three-Quarter Length Study of a standing female Figure (recto); Study of a Woman (verso)
pencil
262 × 164 mm
Messrs E. Parsons and Sons (purchase, 1915) (D.1915.14)

Half-length Study of a seated Woman (recto); Study of Hands (verso)
red chalk
376 × 281 mm
Messrs E. Parsons and Sons (purchase, 1915) (D.1915.15)

Study of the Arms and Hands of an Angel, for the proposed Decoration of the Dome of St Paul's Cathedral, London (recto); Study of a draped Arm (verso)
1862–69
pencil, red chalk (recto)
264 × 180 mm
Messrs E. Parsons and Sons (purchase, 1915) (D.1915.17)

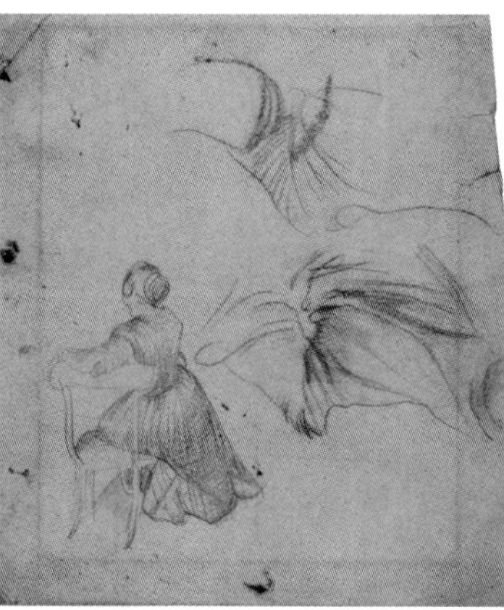

D.1915.18

Full-length back View of a seated Woman, with two Drapery Studies (recto); Two further Studies of a Woman, one seated, one standing by a Chair
pencil, red chalk (recto)
268 × 244 mm
Messrs E. Parsons and Sons (purchase, 1915) (D.1915.18)

Designs for an illuminated Bible, including Saints, a Putto and ornamental Lettering (recto); Further Study (verso)
1846
pencil, pen and brown ink, bodycolour
(heightened with white)
285 × 135 mm
Messrs E. Parsons and Sons (purchase, 1915) (D.1915.19)

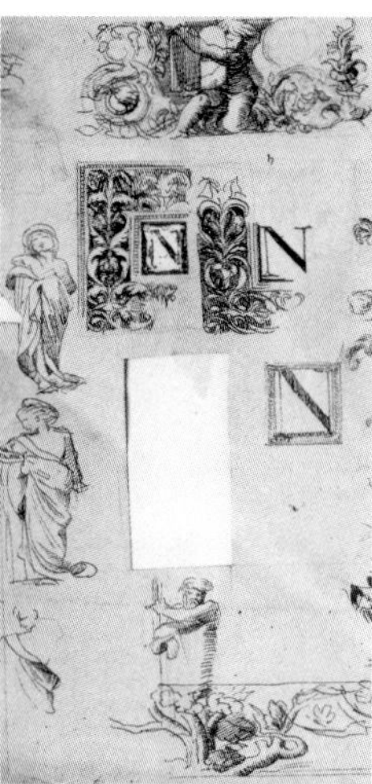

D.1915.19

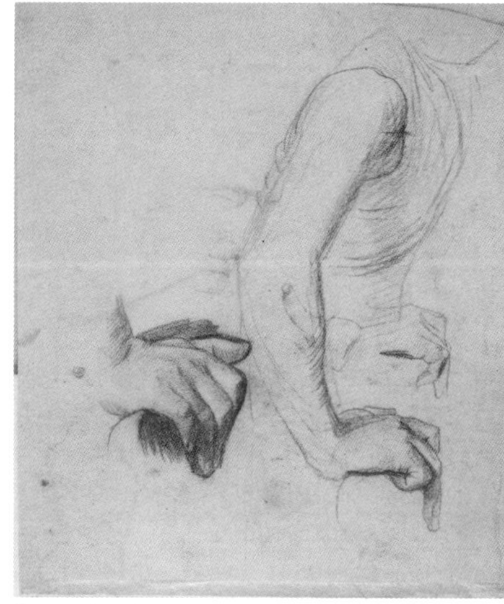

D.1915.20 (verso)

Studies of a cross-legged Figure for the proposed Decoration of the Dome of St Paul's Cathedral, London (recto); Studies of an Arm, Hands and a Face (verso)
1862–69
red chalk
316 × 263 mm
Messrs E. Parsons and Sons (purchase, 1915) (D.1915.20)

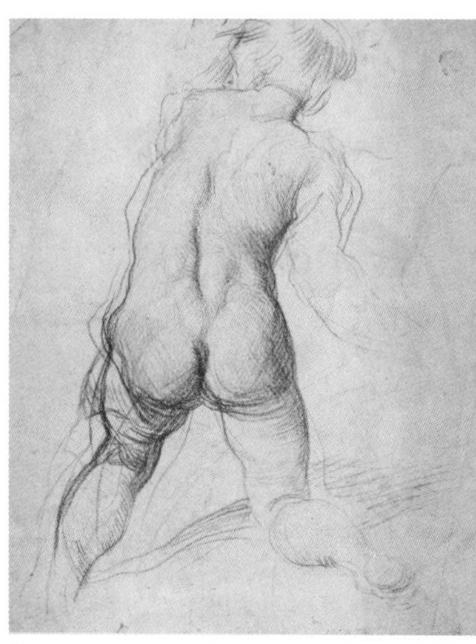

D.1926.6

**Full-length Study of a male Figure from behind
(recto); Study of two female Figures (verso)**
red chalk
inscribed lower right: *by / Alfred Stevens*; inscribed
lower right verso: *by / Alfred Stevens*
328 × 252 mm
Birch, H. (purchase, 1926) (D.1926.6)

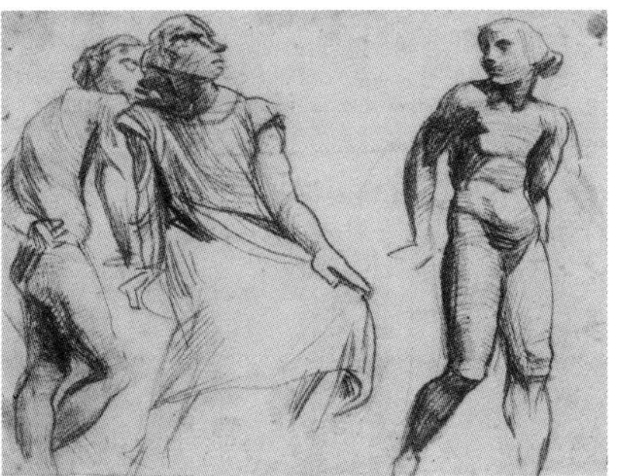

D.1938.2

**Figure Studies for 'The Judgement of Paris'
(recto); Studies of a seated Figure (verso)**
1858–65
red chalk
241 × 312 mm
Friends of the Whitworth (gift, 1938) (D.1938.2)

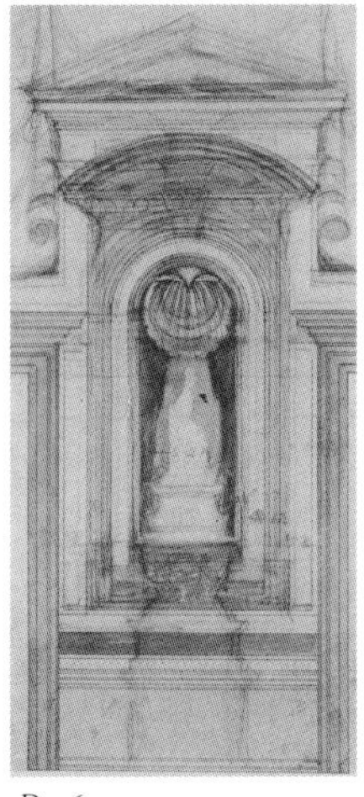

D.1960.135

**Study for a Monument with Architectural
Framework (recto); Architectural Studies (verso)**
pencil, pen and brown ink, watercolour (recto)
443 × 202 mm
University of Manchester, History of Art Department
(transfer, 1960) (D.1960.135)

■ **STEVENS, FRANCIS (1781–1823)**
Stevens first exhibited at the Royal Academy in
1804, and was one of the nine associates elected to
join the sixteen original members of the Old
Watercolour Society in December 1805; he became
a full member in 1809. Stevens taught at the Royal
Military College at Sandhurst.

Classical Landscape with Figures
1812
pencil, watercolour, bodycolour
(heightened with white)
signed & dated lower right: *F Stevens / 1812*
650 × 474 mm
Taylor, John Edward (gift, 1892) (D.1892.104)

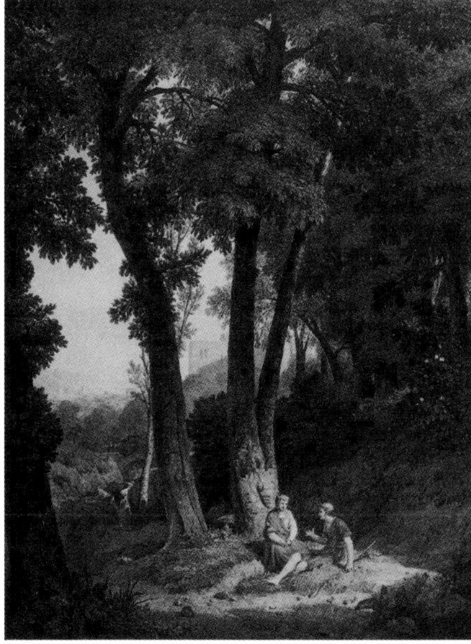

D.1892.104

■ **STEWART, SIR JOHN JAMES (1779–1849)**
Stewart was an amateur painter of equestrian and
battle subjects.

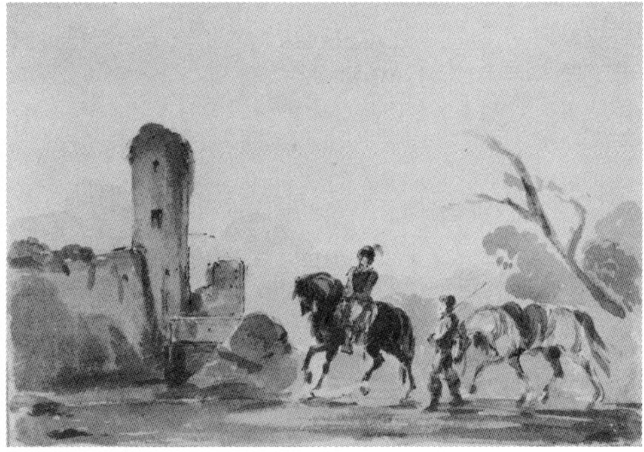

D.1926.122

Landscape with two Horsemen by a Tower
pencil, pen and brown ink, watercolour
152 × 219 mm
Ogden, William Sharp (bequest, 1926) (D.1926.122)

■ **STONE, SARAH (ca. 1760–1844)**
Stone was a painter of museum and natural history
objects who exhibited intermittently at the Royal
Academy and the Society of Artists.

Study of Shells and Coral
pencil, watercolour, bodycolour
(heightened with white)
395 × 543 mm
Sally, Duchess of Westminster (gift, 1987) (D.1987.5)

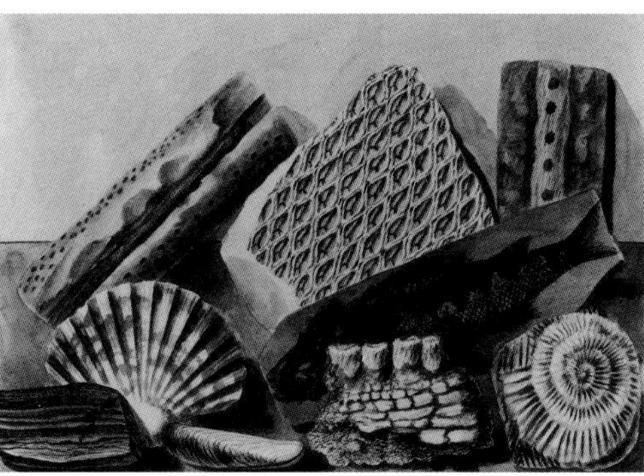

D.1987.6

Study of Fossils and Shells
pencil, watercolour
395 × 547 mm
Sally, Duchess of Westminster (gift, 1987) (D.1987.6)

■ **STOTHARD, THOMAS (1775–1834)**
The most prolific and distinguished illustrator of his
day, Stothard was elected a member of the Royal
Academy in 1794. He became Librarian to the Royal
Academy in 1812 and was very active in Academy
affairs. Stothard exhibited literary and poetic subjects
in oil and painted some landscape watercolours; he also
designed silver.

Frieze of Shakespearean Characters
pen and brown ink, watercolour
128 × 466 mm
Taylor, John Edward (gift, 1892) (D.1892.38)

Phillis and Brunetta: Scene from 'The Spectator'
pen and grey ink, watercolour
140 × 111 mm
Taylor, John Edward (gift, 1892) (D.1892.39)

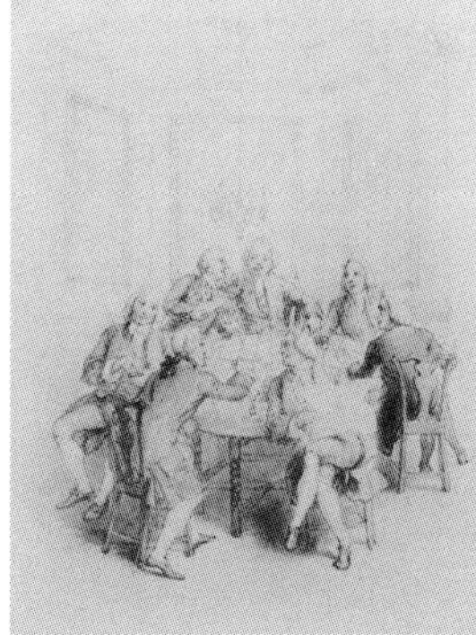

D.1892.40

The Club: Scene from 'The Spectator'
pen and grey ink, watercolour
141 × 105 mm
Taylor, John Edward (gift, 1892) (D.1892.40)

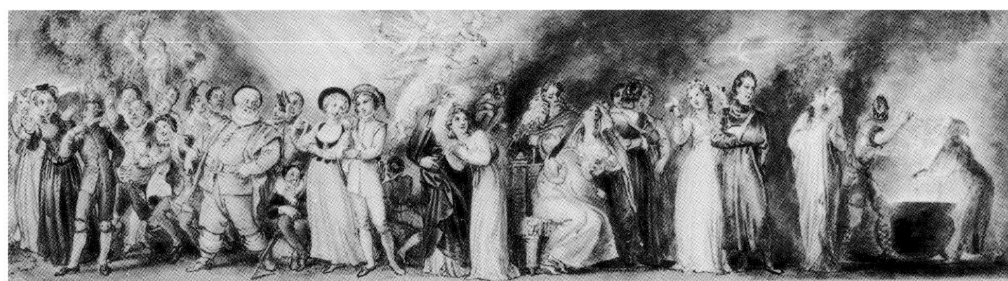

D.1892.38

Young Fellow's first discovering his Passion to his Mistress: Scene from 'The Spectator'
pen and grey ink, watercolour
140 × 112 mm
Taylor, John Edward (gift, 1892) (D.1892.41)

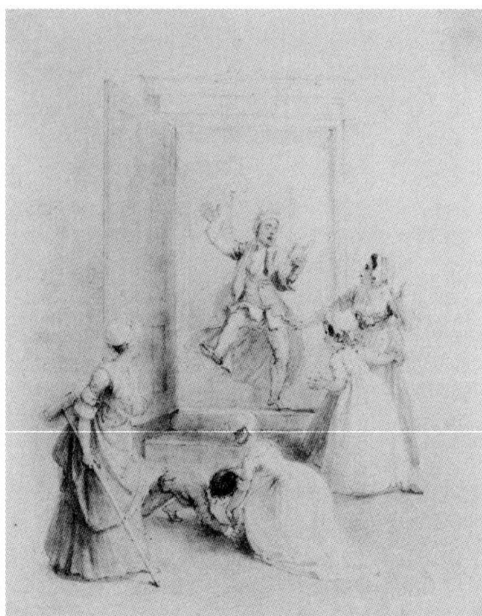

D.1892.42

The Effect of reading Milton out loud: Scene from 'The Spectator'
pen and grey ink, watercolour
138 × 108 mm
Taylor, John Edward (gift, 1892) (D.1892.42)

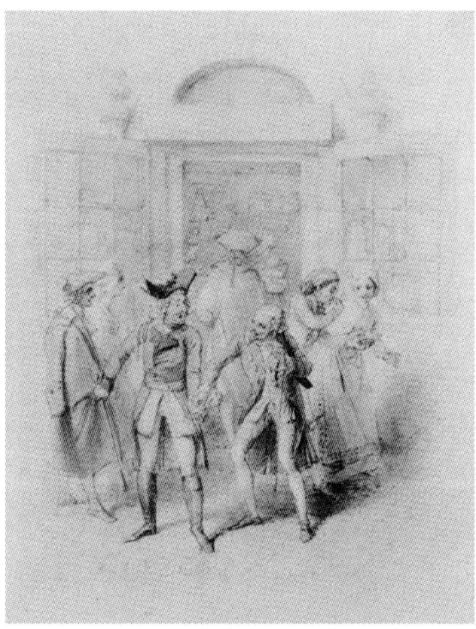

D.1892.43

The Ceremony of the Snuff-Box: Scene from 'The Spectator'
pen and grey ink, watercolour
142 × 109 mm
Taylor, John Edward (gift, 1892) (D.1892.43)

Tom Meggot's Letter: Scene from 'The Spectator'
pen and grey ink, watercolour
138 × 106 mm
Taylor, John Edward (gift, 1892) (D.1892.44)

Chepstow Castle, Monmouthshire, Wales, from across the River Wye
13.10.1813
pen and brown ink, watercolour
dated lower left: *Octr 13 1813*; dated lower centre: *October Wednesday 13.1813*
196 × 348 mm
Anderson, A. E. (gift, 1921) (D.1921.6)

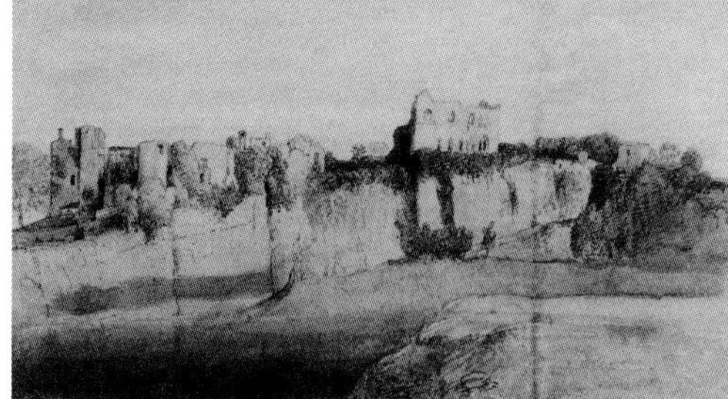

D.1921.6

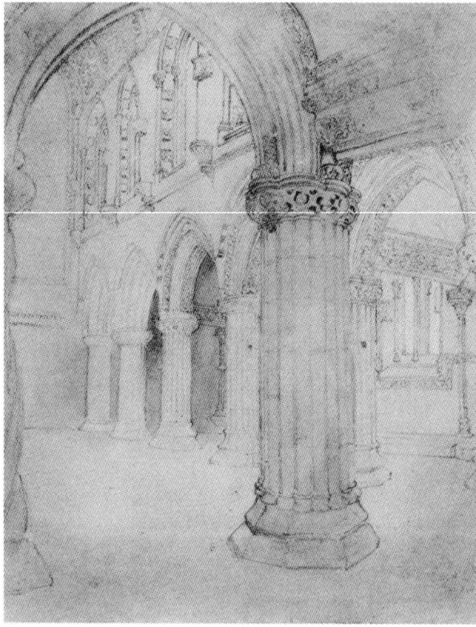

D.1921.13

Interior of St Matthew's Chapel, Rosslyn, Midlothian, Scotland
pencil, grey watercolour
inscribed lower centre margin: *Interior of Roslin Chapel*
254 × 198 mm
Anderson, A. E. (gift, 1921) (D.1921.13)

Study for 'Murder of the Duke of Orleans by Order of the Duke of Burgundy': a Panel for the Library at Hafod House, Cardiganshire, Wales
pencil, pen and brown ink; watermark [BALSTO]N & WH[ATMAN] / 1807
74 × 220 mm
Ogden, William Sharp (bequest, 1926) (D.1926.123)

The Shepherds
pen and brown ink, watercolour
signed lower right: *T.Stothard*
70 × 110 mm
Scott-Elliot, Miss Aydua, in memory of Paul Oppé (gift, 4.11.1999) (D.1999.21)

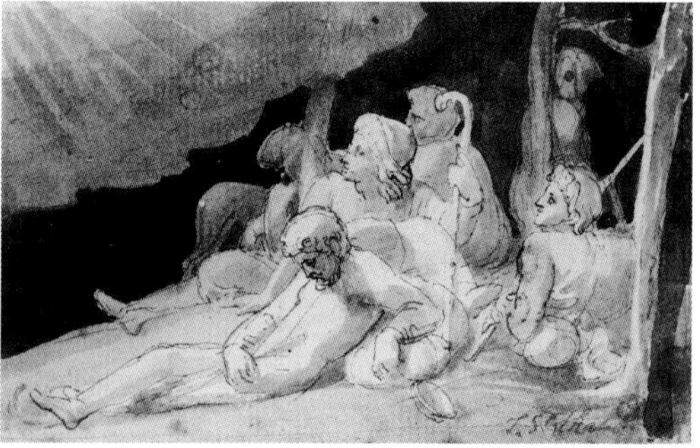

D.1999.21

■ **STOTT, EDWARD (1859–1918)**
Born in Rochdale, Edward Stott studied in Paris in the studio of Carolus-Duran. He was influenced by Bastien-Lepage and Corot. Stott exhibited at the Royal Academy from 1883 and was a founder member of the New English Art Club.

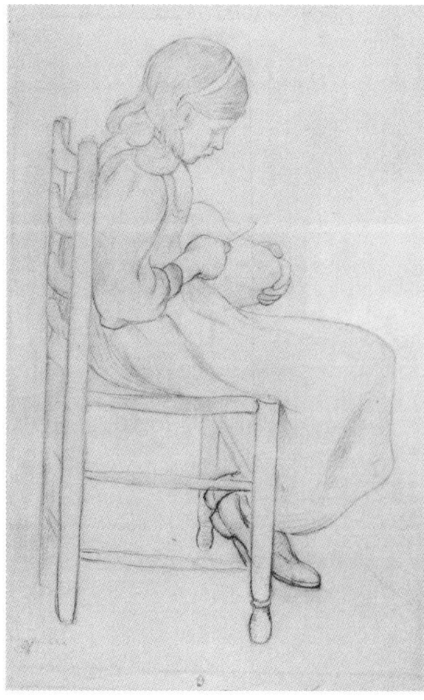

D.1924.18

Cutting Bread
pencil, bodycolour (heightened with white)
stamped lower left (studio stamp): *Edward Stott, A.R.A.*
458 × 280 mm
Coleman, H. (gift, 1924) (D.1924.18)

The Gateway
pencil, watercolour, bodycolour; beige paper
283 × 380 mm
Messrs E. Jackson and Sons (purchase, 1926) (D.1926.2)

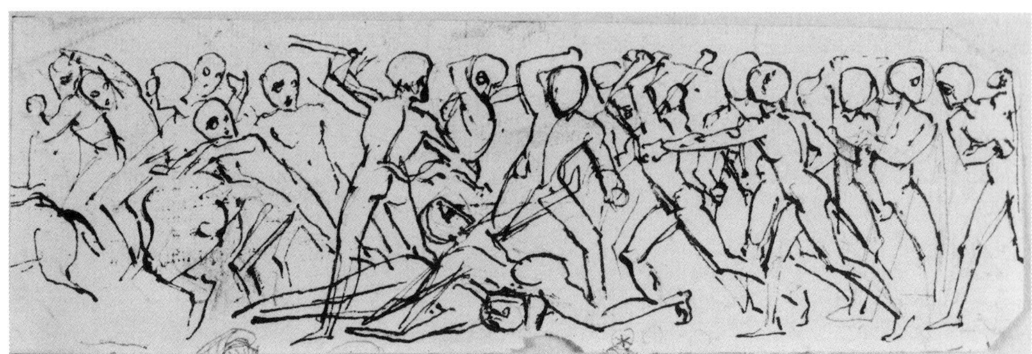

D.1926.123

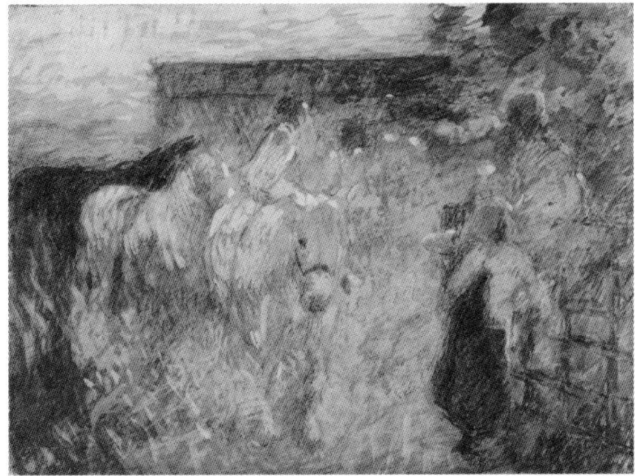

D.1926.2

Study of a Child's Head
pastel; brown paper
signed lower right with initials: *ES*
127 × 277 mm
Anderson, A. E. (in memory of his brother Frank Anderson)
(gift, 1927) (D.1927.40)

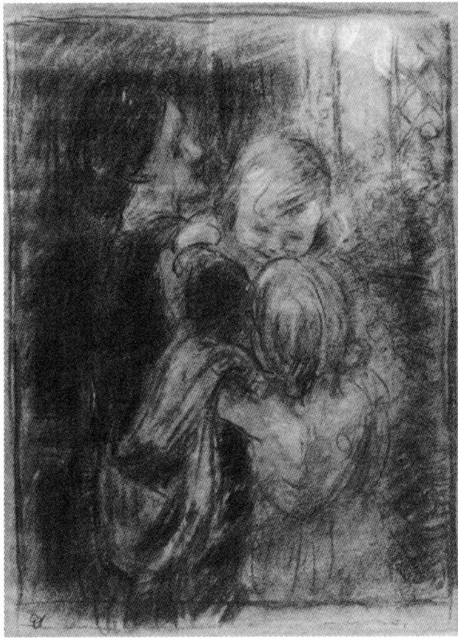

D.1927.41

Study for 'The Kiss'
chalk; brown tracing paper
297 × 222 mm
Anderson, A. E. (in memory of his brother Frank Anderson)
(gift, 1927) (D.1927.41)

Hagar and Ishmael
pastel; brown paper
stamped lower left (studio stamp): *Edward Stott, A.R.A*
322 × 348 mm
Anderson, A. E. (gift, 1933) (D.1933.4)

■ **STOTT, WILLIAM (1857–1900)**
Born in Oldham and known as Stott of Oldham,
William Stott went to study in Paris in the studio of
Gérôme in 1879. He then returned to England and
exhibited at the Royal Academy from 1882. Stott
painted landscapes, portraits and allegorical and
literary figure compositions.

Ice River
pastel
signed lower right: *WILLIAM-STOTT-OLDHAM*
230 × 310 mm
anonymous (gift, 1950) (D.1950.15)

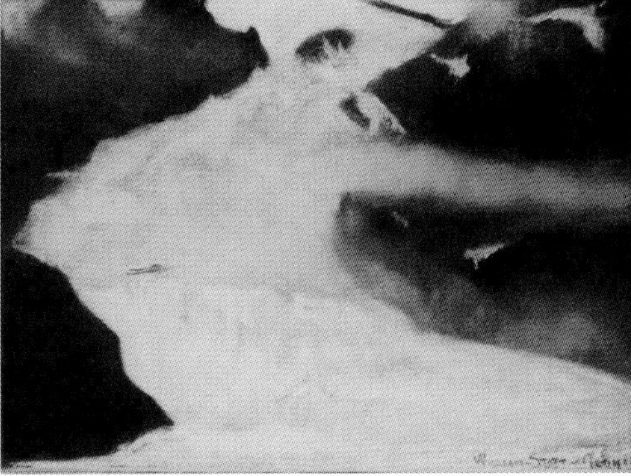

D.1950.15

■ **STRUDWICK, JOHN MELHUISH
(1849–1935)**
Having studied at South Kensington and the Royal
Academy Schools, Strudwick became studio assistant in
the early 1870s, firstly to Spencer Stanhope and then to
Burne-Jones, whose artistic follower he was. Like his
mentor, he exhibited at the Grosvenor Gallery from
1877, transferring to the New Gallery in 1888.
Strudwick was still exhibiting at the last exhibition of
the New Gallery in 1909, but seems to have ceased
painting about this time.

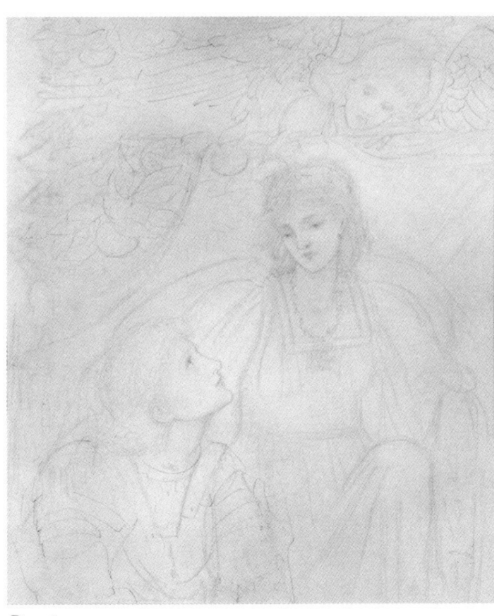

D.1946.21

**Sir Galahad with a Woman and an Angel (recto);
A standing female Nude (verso)**
pencil
356 × 256 mm
Schwabe, H. E. (gift, 1946) (D.1946.21)

■ **STUART, LOUISA ANN, LADY
WATERFORD (1818–91)**
Louisa, daughter of Lord Stuart de Rothesay and sister
of Lady Canning, married the Marquis of Waterford in
1841. After the Marquis was killed while hunting in
1859, she inherited Ford Castle in Northumberland.
Lady Waterford knew Ruskin and was a very
competent amateur artist, concentrating, unusually, on
figures and with a good sense of colour. Her main
artistic achievement was the decoration of the village
school at Ford with large watercolour murals of biblical
childhood scenes.

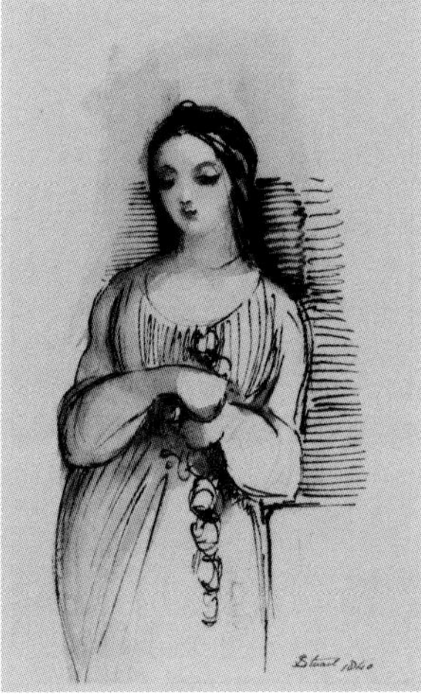

D.1993.12

Study of a Woman holding a Garland
1840
pencil, pen and brown ink, brown watercolour
signed & dated lower right with initial in monogram:
L Stuart 1840
220 × 130 mm
Berwick Fine Art, Shrewsbury (Christopher Powney)
(purchase, 1993) (D.1993.12)

■ **STUMP, SAMUEL JOHN (ca. 1783–1863)**
Stump, a miniaturist, landscape painter and member
of the Sketching Society, Stump exhibited landscapes
and portrait miniatures at the Royal Academy between
1802 and 1849.

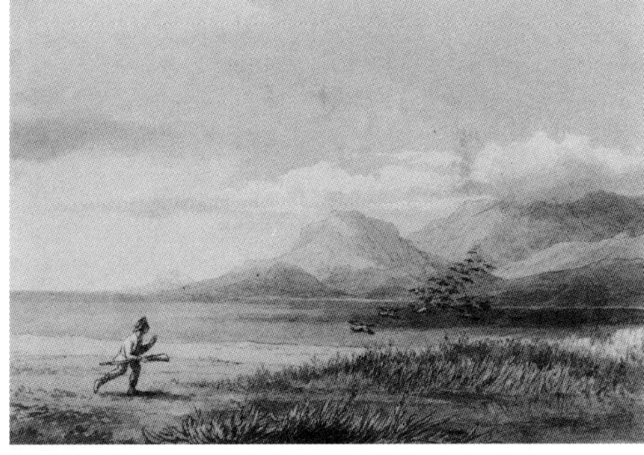

D.1926.313

A Wild Goose Chase
pencil, brown watercolour, grey watercolour
inscribed lower left on mount: *S.J.Stump*; inscribed
lower centre on mount: *A Wild Goose Chase.*
317 × 446 mm
Ogden, William Sharp (bequest, 1926) (D.1926.313)

■ **SUNDERLAND, THOMAS (1744–1828)**
Born near Kirkby Lonsdale, Sunderland moved to
Ulverston and became a pioneer of the iron ore
industry in Furness. He was an immensely prolific
amateur, producing landscape drawings, some drawn
from life, but the majority copied from prints or other
artists' drawings; he placed these in albums to record
real or imaginary picturesque tours. Sunderland's views
of the Lake District, an area he knew well, show a
real understanding of the principles of landscape
composition. He is mentioned in the Farington *Diary*
and may have known John Robert Cozens.

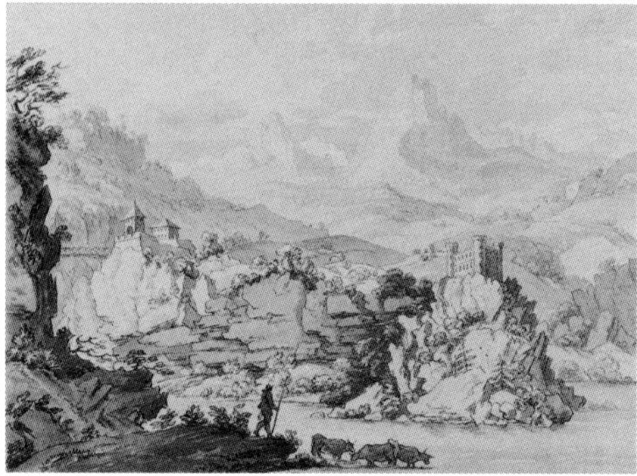

D.1925.53

Barrier of the Tyrol at Vernstein Castle, Switzerland

1795
pencil, pen and grey ink, pen and
brown ink, watercolour
signed, inscribed & dated lower centre of mount with
initials: *Barriere* (sic) *of Tyrol at Vernstein Castle. TS.
1795*; inscribed centre verso of mount: *Castle of
Vernstein/One of the Barriers of Tyrol, built on the edge of
a steep Rock, at the foot of which runs the/Torrent Klans.
The Mountain at the back of the Bridge is called Lovea; it
is Calcareous & / covered with Trees. Mount Vanech the
highest Peak – at the foot of which are the Mines of /
Fengenstein in the environs of Nassereit. The base of this
Mountain is a species of Camellated / Horn-Stone.
Sigmundsberg, an ancient Castle, flanked with four round
Towers is seated on a / Rock nearly in the center of the
Lake. This Rock appears like large stones heaped one upon
/ another. The Mountains in the background covered with
Snow, are part of the Chain called / Mundi. / From
Albanis Beaumont's Travels through the Rhoetian Alps in
1786 / from Italy to Germany, through Tyrol*
335 × 449 mm
Messrs W. M. Sabin (purchase, 1925) (D.1925.53)

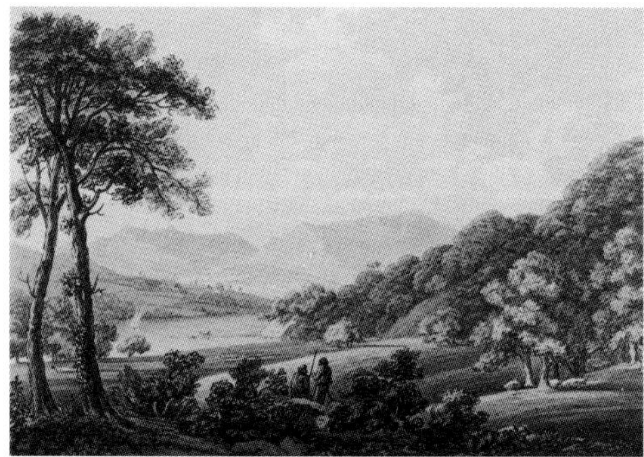

D.1925.55

View over Lake Windermere from Ecclerigg, Westmorland

pencil, pen and ink, watercolour
327 × 454 mm
Agnew's (purchase, 1925) (D.1925.55)

View of Ross-on-Wye, Herefordshire

1794
pencil, blue watercolour, grey watercolour
inscribed & dated lower left verso: *View of Ross, from a
Field / of Mr.Mund's at Ash; copied / from a tinted
Drawing by Turner, Artist. / from a Sketch of Mr.Wathen's
of Hereford. / 1794.*; inscribed on mount below image:
View near Ross – Herefordshire. / River Wye.
236 × 350 mm
University of Manchester, History of Art Department
(transfer, 1960) (D.1960.284)

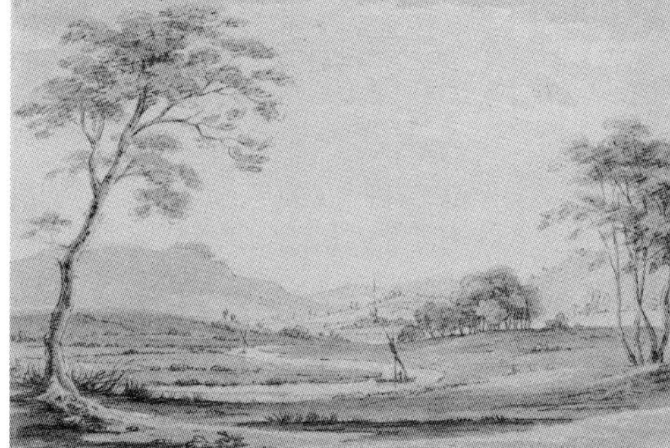

D.1960.284

Chepstow Castle, Monmouthshire, Wales

pencil, black chalk, blue watercolour, grey watercolour
grey paper
inscribed upper left verso: *Chepstow Castle / from Varley*;
inscribed on page of album below image: *Chepstow
Castle Monmouths.*
237 × 345 mm
University of Manchester, History of Art Department
(transfer, 1960) (D.1960.285)

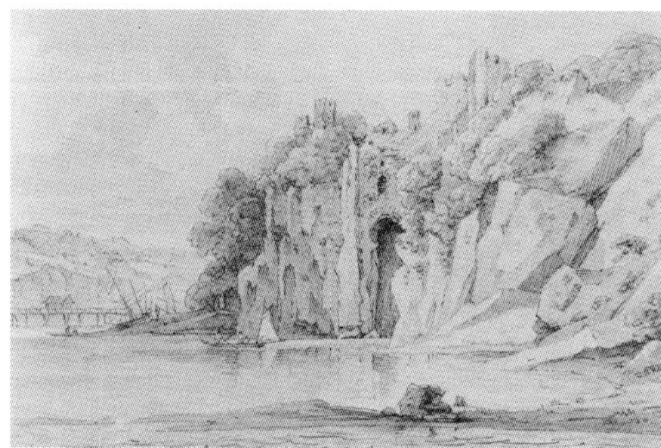

D.1960.286

Chepstow Castle, Monmouthshire, Wales, from across the Wye

1807
pencil, black chalk, blue watercolour, grey watercolour
grey paper
inscribed & dated upper left verso: *Chepstow Castle /
from the Wye / after J.Wathen's Sketch / 1807*; inscribed
on page of album below image: *Chepstow Castle, on the
Wye side.*
235 × 346 mm
University of Manchester, History of Art Department
(transfer, 1960) (D.1960.286)

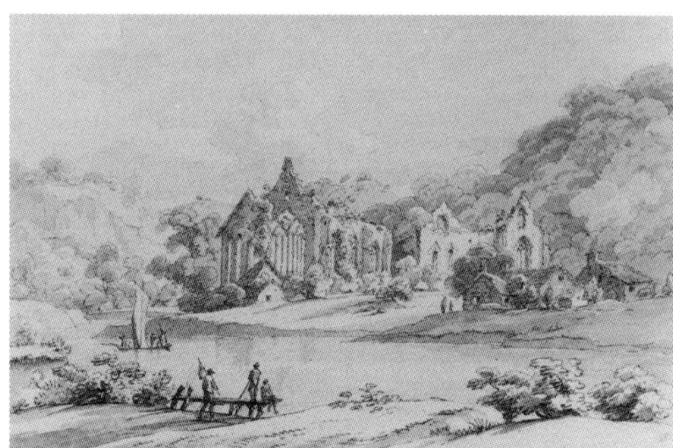

D.1960.287

Tintern Abbey, Monmouthshire, Wales, from across the Wye

1792
pencil, black chalk, blue watercolour, grey watercolour
grey paper
inscribed & dated lower left verso: *Tintern Abbey / after
T Gerton* (sic) *1792 –* ; inscribed on mount below
image: *Tintern Abbey – on the Wye,side.*
245 × 352 mm
University of Manchester, History of Art Department
(transfer, 1960) (D.1960.287)

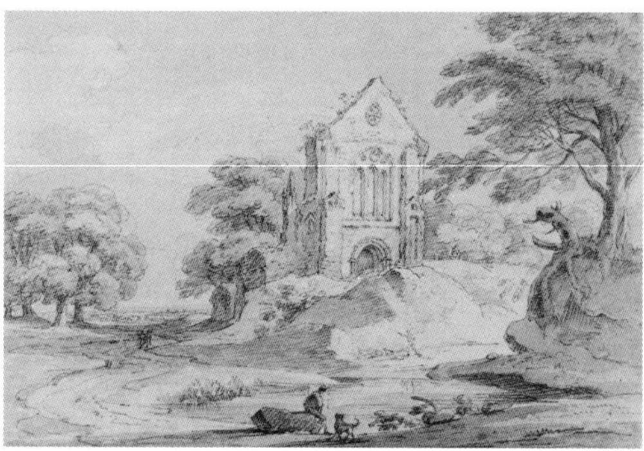

D.1960.288

Valle Crucis Abbey, Denbighshire, Wales

pencil, blue watercolour, grey watercolour; grey paper
inscribed upper left verso: *Valle Crusis* (sic) */ Varley*;
inscribed on mount below image: *Abbey Crusis* (sic).
Denbighsh.
248 × 349 mm
University of Manchester, History of Art Department
(transfer, 1960) (D.1960.288)

Monnow Bridge, Monmouth, Monmouthshire, Wales

pencil, black chalk, blue watercolour, brown
watercolour; grey paper
inscribed on page of album below image:
Monmouth Bridge.
245 × 347 mm
University of Manchester, History of Art Department
(transfer, 1960) (D.1960.289)

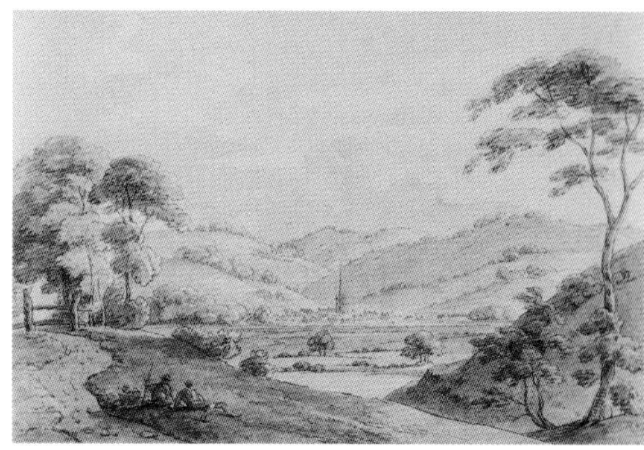

D.1960.290

View of Monmouth, Monmouthshire, Wales

pencil, black chalk, blue watercolour, grey watercolour;
grey paper
inscribed on page of album below image: *Monmouth –
Taken from* [illegible word] *Wynnistow* [overwritten in
pencil] *Hill Hill* [overwritten in pencil]
245 × 352 mm
University of Manchester, History of Art Department
(transfer, 1960) (D.1960.290)

View from a Hill in the Forest of Dean, looking over the Severn to Westbury
pencil, black chalk, blue watercolour, grey watercolour
grey paper
inscribed lower centre verso: *From a Hill in Dean Forrest above Newnham Gloucestershire – / and looking over the Severn to the Village / of Westbury –*; inscribed on mount below image: *From a Hill in Dean Forrest near Newnham, / and looking over the Severn to the Village of Westbury. Gloucesters.*
243 × 345 mm
University of Manchester, History of Art Department (transfer, 1960) (D.1960.291)

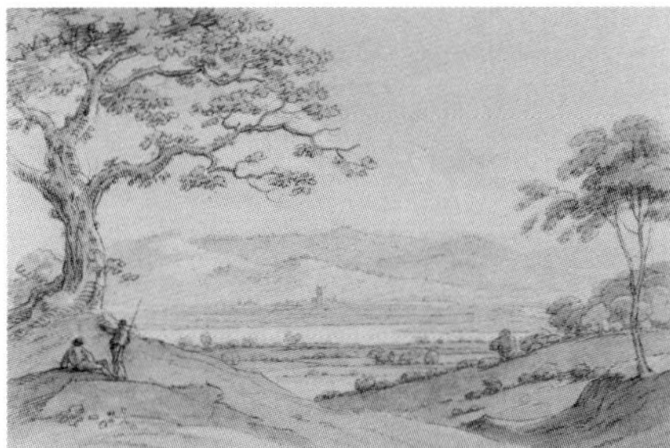
D.1960.292

View across the Severn from the Village of Westbury, Somerset
pencil, black chalk, white chalk, blue watercolour, brown watercolour; grey paper
inscribed on page of album below image: *From the Village of Westbury looking across / the Severn to Dean Forest. Glocesters.*
237 × 339 mm
University of Manchester, History of Art Department (transfer, 1960) (D.1960.292)

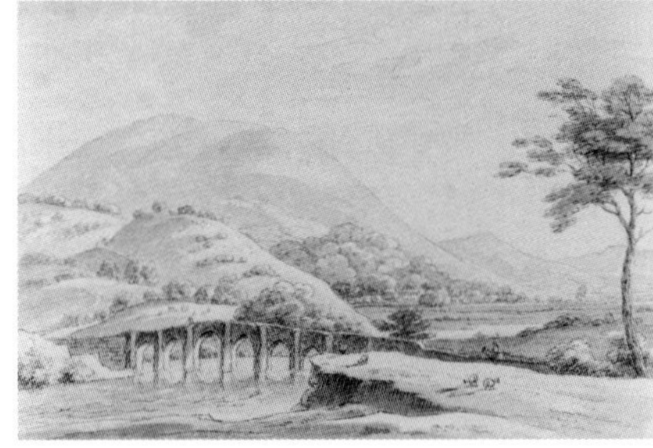
D.1960.293

Bridge over the Usk, Abergavenny, Monmouthshire, Wales
pencil, black chalk, blue watercolour, grey watercolour; grey paper
inscribed on page of album below image: *Abergavenny Bridge over the Taark Usk* [written above in pencil] / *with the Blorrinsh Mountain & Lanfoist House*
245 × 351 mm
University of Manchester, History of Art Department (transfer, 1960) (D.1960.293)

Lane near Abergavenny, Monmouthshire, Wales
1799
pencil, black chalk, blue watercolour, grey watercolour; grey paper
inscribed & dated upper left verso: *Near Abergavenny in Monmouthshire / Copy fm. Pocok – 1799.*; inscribed on mount below image: *Near Abergavenny. Monmouths.*
325 × 251 mm
University of Manchester, History of Art Department (transfer, 1960) (D.1960.294)

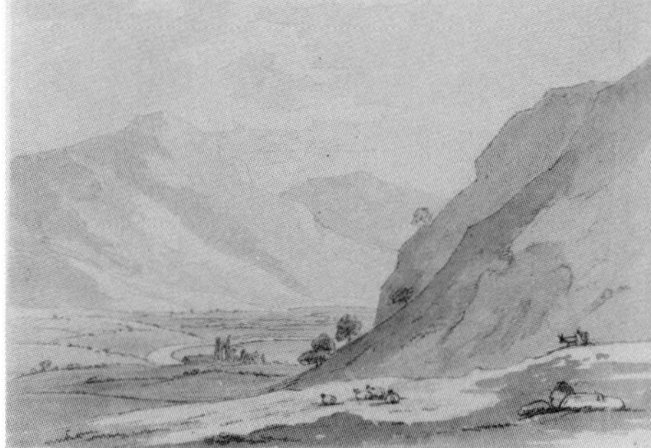
D.1960.295

Distant View of Llanthony Priory, Monmouthshire, Wales
pencil, black chalk, blue watercolour, grey watercolour; grey paper
inscribed lower left verso: *Lantony Abbey– / In the Vale of Euras in Monmouthshire / On the Westside the Hatterill Mountains / 22m. from Hereford / After a Sketch of J. Wathen Esqr.*; inscribed on page of album below image: *Lanthony Abbey. / In the Vale of Ewras – Monmouths. Hatterill Mountn. on the left.*
237 × 335 mm
University of Manchester, History of Art Department (transfer, 1960) (D.1960.295)

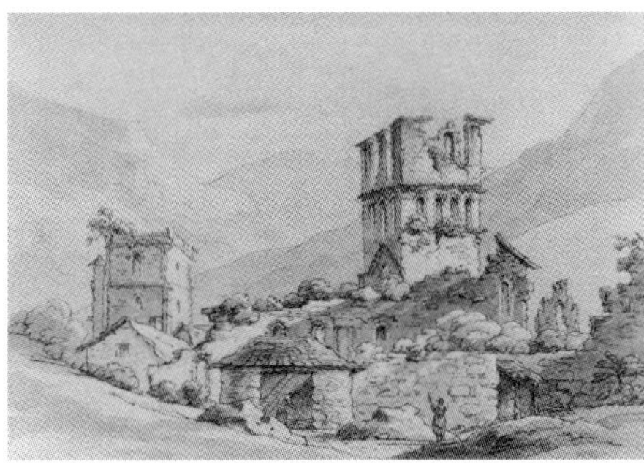
D.1960.296

Near View of Llanthony Priory, Monmouthshire, Wales
pencil, black chalk, grey watercolour; grey paper
inscribed lower centre verso: *Llanthony Abbey / Monmouthshire*; inscribed on page of album below image: *Near View of Llanthony Abbey*
253 × 362 mm
University of Manchester, History of Art Department (transfer, 1960) (D.1960.296)

On the Dee, Road to Corwen, Merioneth, Wales
pencil, black chalk, watercolour, grey watercolour; grey paper
inscribed on page of album below image: *On the Dee. Road to Corwen*
237 × 348 mm
University of Manchester, History of Art Department (transfer, 1960) (D.1960.297)

View of a Town on the River Wye, Monmouthshire, Wales
1800
pencil, black chalk, blue watercolour, grey watercolour; grey paper
inscribed & dated upper left verso: *On the Wye / from the Wye Meadows / after JWathen 1800*; inscribed on page of album below image: *On the Wye.*
233 × 342 mm
University of Manchester, History of Art Department (transfer, 1960) (D.1960.298)

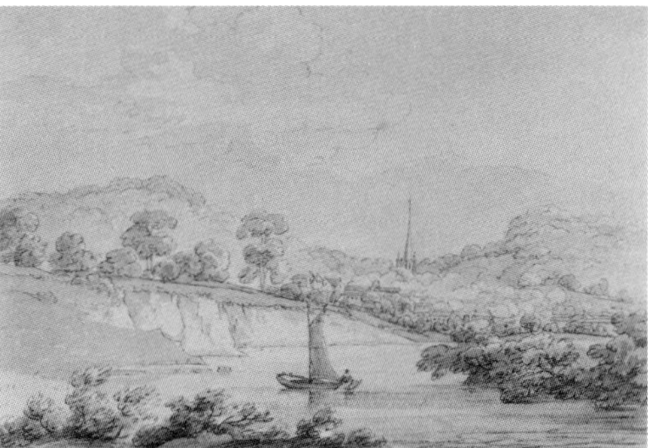
D.1960.298

View of Goodrich Castle overlooking the River Wye, Monmouthshire, Wales
pencil, black chalk, blue watercolour, grey watercolour; grey paper
inscribed upper left verso: *Looking up the Wye / Holworthy*; inscribed on page of album below image: *On the Wye.*
239 × 337 mm
University of Manchester, History of Art Department (transfer, 1960) (D.1960.299)

Symonds Yat on the River Wye, Herefordshire
1806
pencil, black chalk, blue watercolour, grey watercolour; grey paper
inscribed & dated upper left verso: *Wye Scene / Symonds Rock / from JW 1806*; inscribed on page of album below image: *Symonds Rock. on the Wye.*
237 × 343 mm
University of Manchester, History of Art Department (transfer, 1960) (D.1960.300)

Scene on the River Wye, Monmouthshire, Wales
black chalk, white chalk, grey watercolour; grey paper
inscribed on mount below image: *Scene – On the Wye*
261 × 357 mm
University of Manchester, History of Art Department (transfer, 1960) (D.1960.301)

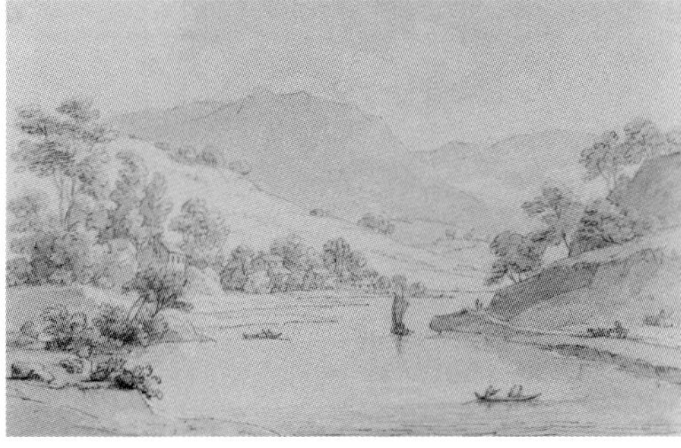
D.1960.302

Village of Brockweir on the River Wye, Gloucestershire
pencil, black chalk, blue watercolour, grey watercolour; grey paper
inscribed upper left verso: *Part of Brackwies Village / looking down the Wye / Holworthy after J. Wathens Sketch*; inscribed on page of album below image: *Village of Brackwring, Brookweir* [written above in pencil] *on the Wye*
219 × 341 mm
University of Manchester, History of Art Department (transfer, 1960) (D.1960.302)

View across the River Wye to the Severn, Monmouthshire, Wales
pencil, black chalk, blue watercolour, grey watercolour; grey paper
inscribed upper left verso: *Wye & Severn / fm JW.*; inscribed on page of album below image: *Scene looking over the Wye / to the Severn.*
239 × 345 mm
University of Manchester, History of Art Department (transfer, 1960) (D.1960.303)

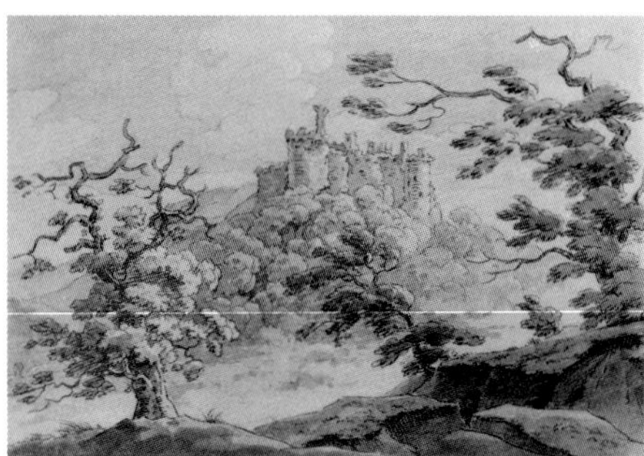
D.1960.304

Powis Castle from the Road to Welshpool, Montgomeryshire, Wales
pencil, black chalk, white chalk, blue watercolour, grey watercolour; grey paper
inscribed lower left verso: *Powis Castle – / from the Welch–Pool Road – / copied from Holdsworthys drawing / after a sketch of Mr.Wathen's.*; inscribed on mount below image: *Powis Castle – from the road to WelchPool*
242 × 342 mm
University of Manchester, History of Art Department (transfer, 1960) (D.1960.304)

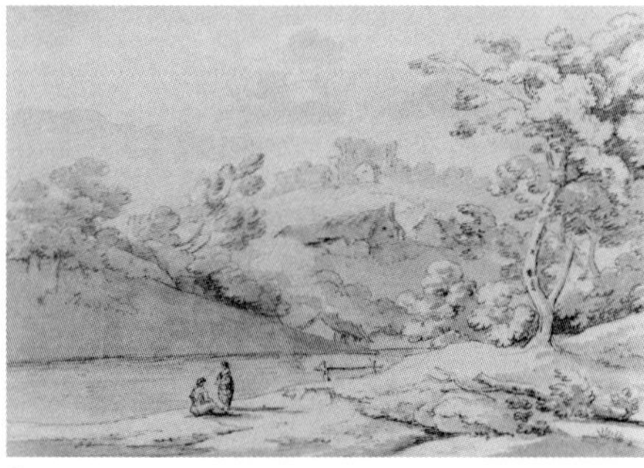
D.1960.305

Denbigh Castle, Denbighshire, Wales
1802
pencil, black chalk, blue watercolour, grey watercolour grey paper
inscribed & dated upper left verso: *Denbigh Castle / from Nicholson / 1802*; inscribed on mount below image: *Denbigh Castle.*
247 × 353 mm
University of Manchester, History of Art Department (transfer, 1960) (D.1960.305)

The Gatehouse, Beaumaris Castle, Anglesey, Wales
pencil, grey watercolour, brown watercolour grey paper
inscribed upper left verso: *Beaumarais Castle in the Isle of Anglesey*; inscribed on page of album below image: *Beaumaris Castle. Anglesey.*
224 × 297 mm
University of Manchester, History of Art Department (transfer, 1960) (D.1960.306)

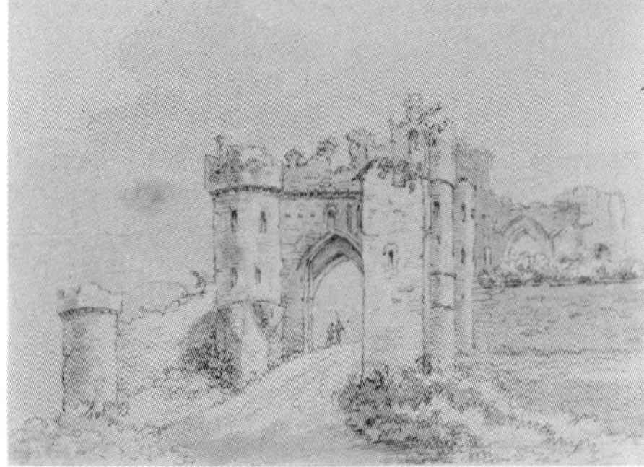
D.1960.306

Harlech Castle, Merioneth, Wales, from the South
pencil, blue watercolour, grey watercolour; grey paper
inscribed upper left verso: *Harleck Castle. Merionethshire*; inscribed on page of album below image: *Haerleck Haerleok* [written above in pencil] *Castle. Merionethsre.*
236 × 347 mm
University of Manchester, History of Art Department (transfer, 1960) (D.1960.307)

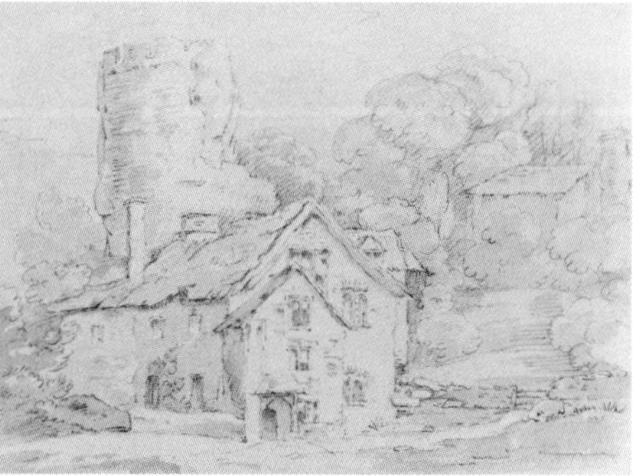
D.1960.308

Cottage with Part of Usk Castle, Monmouthshire, Wales
pencil, black chalk, blue watercolour, grey watercolour; grey paper
inscribed upper left verso: *Cottage with part of Usk Castle / JScott*; inscribed on mount below image: *Cottage with part of Usk Castle. / Monmouthshire.*
230 × 303 mm
University of Manchester, History of Art Department (transfer, 1960) (D.1960.308)

Near the Village of Llanelli, Glamorgan, Wales
pencil, black chalk, blue watercolour, grey watercolour; grey paper
inscribed lower left verso: *View near the Village of Llanelthy / looking over Swansea Bay*; inscribed on page of album below image: *Near the Village of Llanenthy / looking over Swansea Bay.*
242 × 351 mm
University of Manchester, History of Art Department (transfer, 1960) (D.1960.309)

Briton Ferry, Glamorgan, Wales
pencil, black chalk, blue watercolour, grey watercolour; grey paper
inscribed lower centre verso: *Cottages at Brittan Ferry – Swansea Bay.*; inscribed on mount below image: *Brittan ferry – Swansea Bay. / Glamorganshire.*
236 × 345 mm
University of Manchester, History of Art Department (transfer, 1960) (D.1960.310)

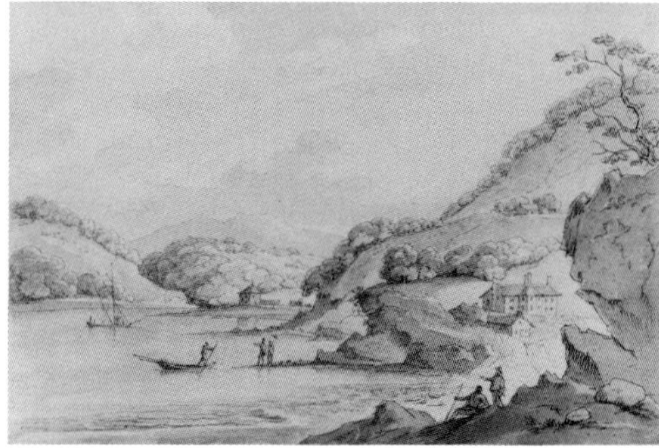
D.1960.310

Near Briton Ferry, Glamorgan, Wales
pencil, black chalk, blue watercolour, grey watercolour; grey paper
inscribed upper left verso: *Near Britton Ferry– / J.Barden*; inscribed on page of album below image: *Near Britton Ferry – Glamorganshire.*
237 × 342 mm
University of Manchester, History of Art Department (transfer, 1960) (D.1960.311)

The Vale of Neath, Glamorgan, Wales
pencil, black chalk, blue watercolour, grey watercolour; grey paper
inscribed on page of album below image: *In the Vale of Carn Coom* [written above in pencil] *Neath / The cross road to Brittan Ferry and Swansea.*
240 × 348 mm
University of Manchester, History of Art Department (transfer, 1960) (D.1960.312)

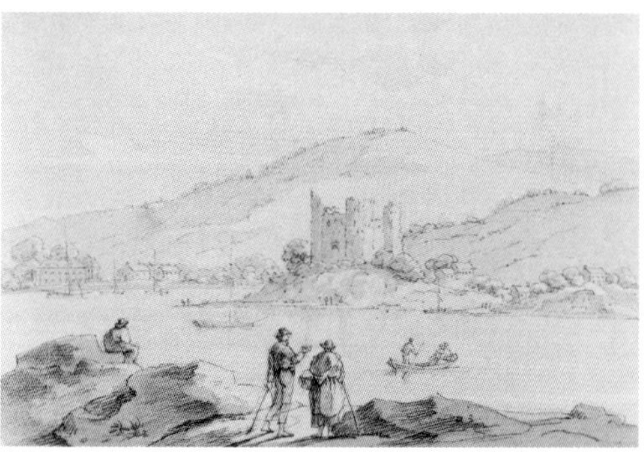
D.1960.313

Laugharne Castle, Carmarthenshire, Wales, from across the Taff Estuary
pencil, black chalk, blue watercolour, grey watercolour; grey paper
inscribed lower centre verso: *Langharne Castle. Caermarthenshire.*; inscribed on page of album below image: *Langharne Castle / Carmarthenshire.*
235 × 340 mm
University of Manchester, History of Art Department (transfer, 1960) (D.1960.313)

Caerphilly Castle, Glamorgan, Wales, with Part of the Town
pencil, black chalk, blue watercolour, grey watercolour; grey paper
inscribed lower left verso: *Caerphilly Town & Castle / from the Turnpike Road*; inscribed on page of album below image: *Caerphilly Castle, with part of the Town / Glamorganshire.*
237 × 345 mm
University of Manchester, History of Art Department (transfer, 1960) (D.1960.314)

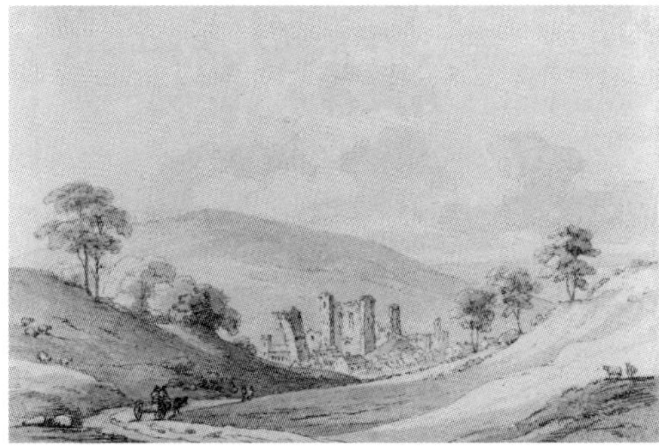

D.1960.314

View looking towards the Coast, near Swansea, Glamorgan, Wales

1802
pencil, black chalk, blue watercolour,
grey watercolour; grey paper
inscribed & dated upper left verso: *Near Swansea / after Raudan (?) [name difficult to read] 1802*; inscribed on mount below image: *Near Swansey (sic). Glamorganshire.*
231 × 345 mm
University of Manchester, History of Art Department (transfer, 1960) (D.1960.315)

On the Neath River, near Briton Ferry, Glamorgan, Wales

pencil, black chalk, blue watercolour,
grey watercolour; grey paper
inscribed on page of album below image: *On the Neath River / Glamorganshire / near Brittan Ferry*
236 × 346 mm
University of Manchester, History of Art Department (transfer, 1960) (D.1960.316)

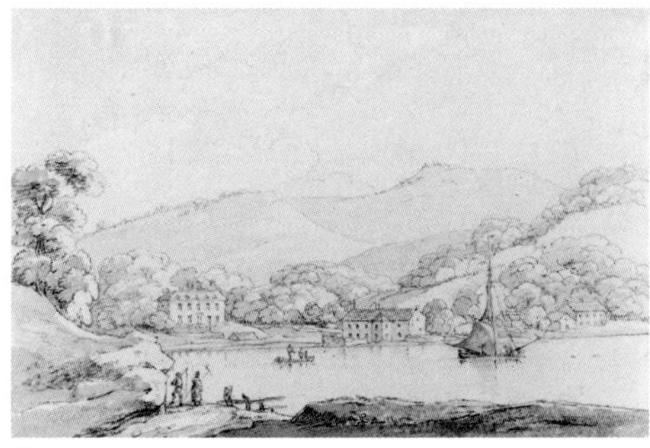

D.1960.317

On the Neath River, Glamorgan, Wales

pencil, black chalk, blue watercolour,
grey watercolour; grey paper
inscribed lower centre verso: *On Neath River*; inscribed on page of album below image: *On Neath River / Glamorganshire.*
237 × 343 mm
University of Manchester, History of Art Department (transfer, 1960) (D.1960.317)

Cilgerran Castle, Pembrokeshire, Wales

pencil, black chalk, grey watercolour; grey paper
inscribed lower centre verso: *On the Tivey / with the remains of Skilgaroon Castle / Glamorganshire*; inscribed on page of album below image: *Skilgaroon Killgarron [written above in pencil] Castle on the Tivy / Glamorganshire*
237 × 344 mm
University of Manchester, History of Art Department (transfer, 1960) (D.1960.318)

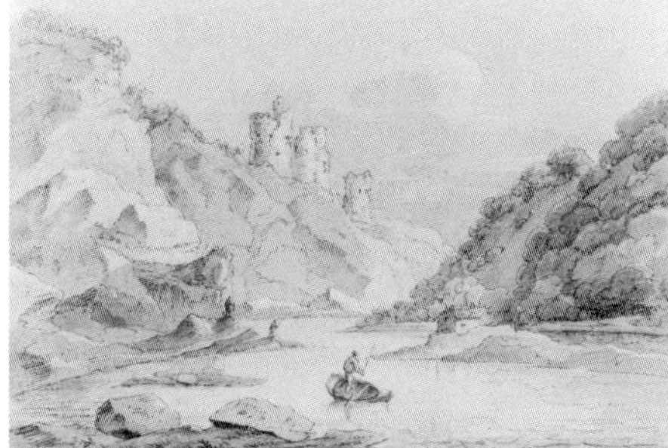

D.1960.318

Part of Caerphilly Castle, Glamorgan, Wales

pencil, black chalk, grey watercolour; grey paper
inscribed lower left verso: *Part of Caerphilly castle / Glamorganshire.*; inscribed on page of album below image: *Part of Caerphilly Castle, Glamorganshire.*
236 × 318 mm
University of Manchester, History of Art Department (transfer, 1960) (D.1960.319)

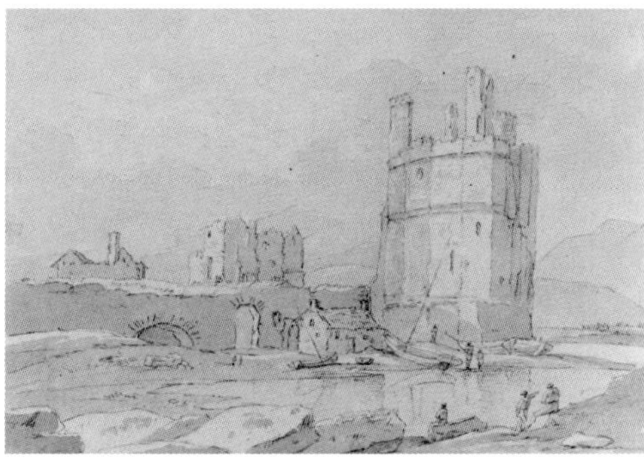

D.1960.320

The Eagle Tower, Caernarvon Castle, Caernarvonshire, Wales

pencil, black chalk, grey watercolour; grey paper
inscribed upper left verso: *Eagle Tower, / Caernarvon Castle / after J.Eagles*; inscribed on mount below image: *Eagle Tower, Carnarvon Castle.*
240 × 342 mm
University of Manchester, History of Art Department (transfer, 1960) (D.1960.320)

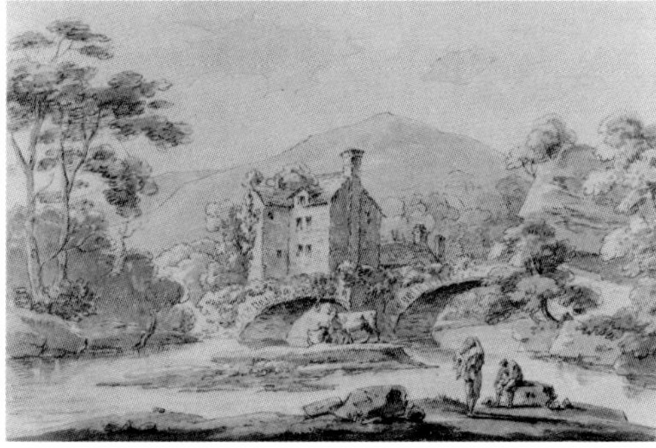

D.1960.321

Penylyn Bridge, North Wales

pencil, black chalk, blue watercolour, grey watercolour grey paper
inscribed upper left verso: *Pinyllyn Bridge / Wales – / after Arnold – f.*; inscribed on page of album below image: *Penylyn Bridge. No.Wales*
242 × 348 mm
University of Manchester, History of Art Department (transfer, 1960) (D.1960.321)

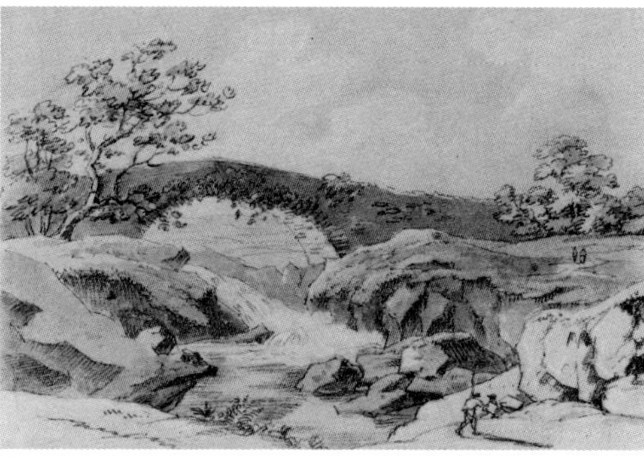

D.1960.322

Pont Cannal, North Wales

pencil, black chalk, blue watercolour, grey watercolour grey paper
inscribed on mount below image: *Pont Cannal. N.W.*
234 × 340 mm
University of Manchester, History of Art Department (transfer, 1960) (D.1960.322)

Pont Adu near Ffestiniog, Merioneth, Wales

pencil, black chalk, blue watercolour,
grey watercolour; grey paper
inscribed lower left verso: *Pont Adu / near Festiniog*; inscribed on page of album below image: *Pont Adu, near Festionag (sic) / N.W.*
247 × 339 mm
University of Manchester, History of Art Department (transfer, 1960) (D.1960.323)

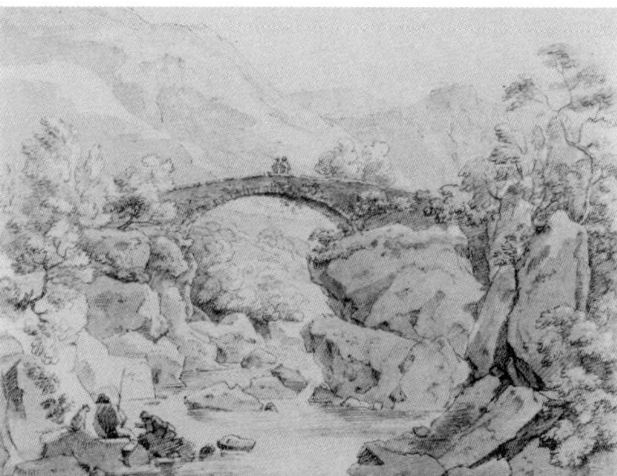

D.1960.324

Bridge over the River Dyfi, near Mallwyd, Merioneth, Wales

pencil, blue watercolour, grey watercolour; grey paper
inscribed upper left verso: *Pont y Mallyd –*; inscribed on mount below image: *Pont y Mallid Mallnyd [written above in pencil] N.W.*
242 × 317 mm
University of Manchester, History of Art Department (transfer, 1960) (D.1960.324)

Landscape with River and Mountains, near Holywell, Flintshire, Wales

pencil, black chalk, blue watercolour,
grey watercolour; grey paper
inscribed upper left verso: *Holywell*; inscribed on page of album below image: *Near Holywell. Flintshire.*
240 × 348 mm
University of Manchester, History of Art Department (transfer, 1960) (D.1960.325)

Coast View, North Wales
pencil, blue watercolour, grey watercolour; grey paper
inscribed upper left verso: *Hollsworthy* (sic); inscribed on page of album below image: *In North Wales*
211 × 300 mm
University of Manchester, History of Art Department
(transfer, 1960) (D.1960.326)

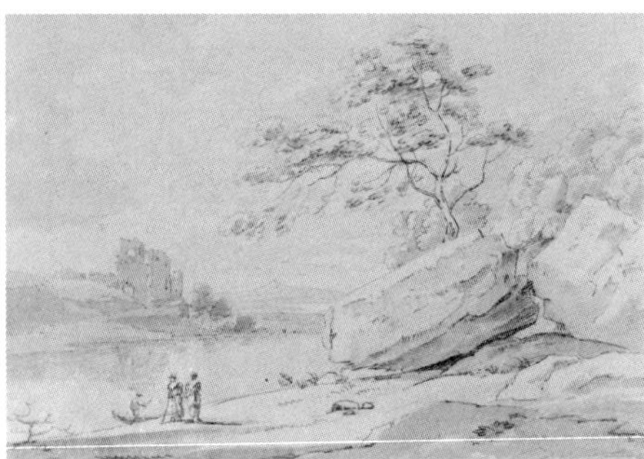

D.1960.327

**Castle by a River, North Wales (recto);
Study of Buildings on a Crag (verso)**
pencil, black chalk, blue watercolour, grey watercolour
(recto); grey paper
inscribed upper left verso: *No. Wales / R.S.Booth*;
inscribed on mount below image: *In North Wales.*
243 × 342 mm
University of Manchester, History of Art Department
(transfer, 1960) (D.1960.327)

Mountain Scene with Waterfall, North Wales
pencil, black chalk, blue watercolour,
grey watercolour; grey paper
inscribed on page of album below image:
In North Wales.
242 × 347 mm
University of Manchester, History of Art Department
(transfer, 1960) (D.1960.328)

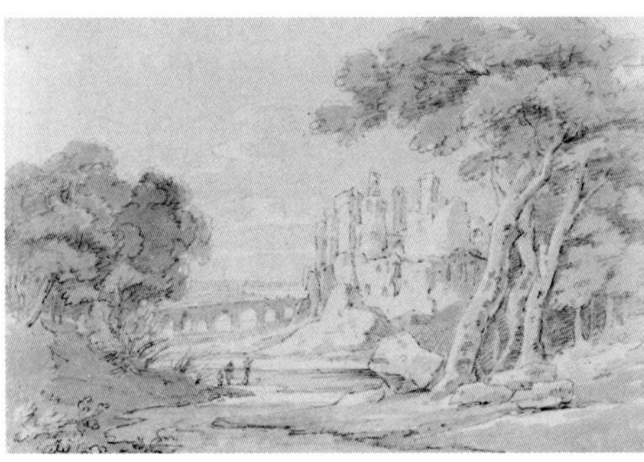

D.1960.329

Landscape with Bridge and Castle, North Wales
pencil, black chalk, blue watercolour,
grey watercolour; grey paper
inscribed upper left verso: *No. Wales / JVarley*; inscribed
on page of album below image: *In North Wales*
242 × 350 mm
University of Manchester, History of Art Department
(transfer, 1960) (D.1960.329)

House near a Waterfall, North Wales
pencil, black chalk, blue watercolour,
grey watercolour; grey paper
inscribed upper left verso: *No. Wales / from Varley*;
inscribed on mount below image: *In North Wales*
242 × 342 mm
University of Manchester, History of Art Department
(transfer, 1960) (D.1960.330)

**River Scene, near the Vale of Pont Nedd Fechan,
Breconshire, Wales**
pencil, black chalk, white chalk, blue watercolour,
grey watercolour; grey paper
inscribed lower left verso: *Near the Vale of Pont Neath
Vechan / after R.S.Booth*; inscribed on mount below
image: *Near the Vale of Pont Ned Neath* [written above
in pencil] *Vychan. / No.W.*
245 × 352 mm
University of Manchester, History of Art Department
(transfer, 1960) (D.1960.331)

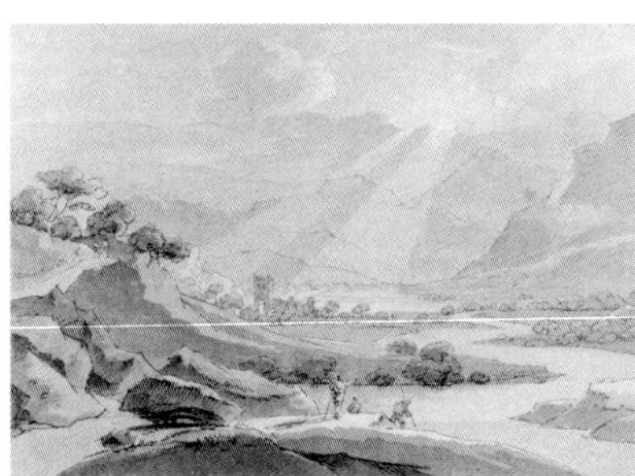

D.1960.332

**A River Valley with a ruined Church,
North Wales**
pencil, black chalk, white chalk,
grey watercolour; grey paper
inscribed on page of album below image:
In North Wales
238 × 325 mm
University of Manchester, History of Art Department
(transfer, 1960) (D.1960.332)

Honister, North Wales
1802
pencil, black chalk, blue watercolour,
grey watercolour; grey paper
inscribed & dated lower left verso: *Honister – No.Wales
1802 / after Holsworthy* (sic) / *from a Sketch of JWathen's.*;
inscribed on page of album below image: *Honister.
No.Wales.*
243 × 346 mm
University of Manchester, History of Art Department
(transfer, 1960) (D.1960.333)

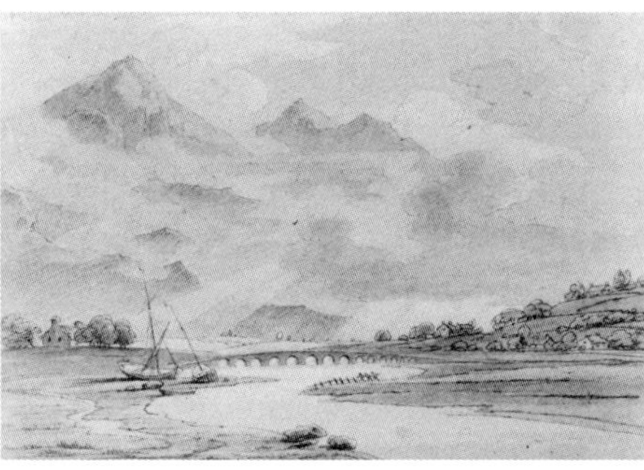

D.1960.334

**Bridge over the Mawddach at Llanelltyd,
Merioneth, Wales**
pencil, black chalk, white chalk,
grey watercolour; grey paper
inscribed lower left verso: *Llanelted* (sic) – *near Dolgelly
No.Wales / from J.Varley Artist*; inscribed on page of
album below image: *Llannyllid* (sic) *near Dolgelly.
Merionethshire.*
255 × 361 mm
University of Manchester, History of Art Department
(transfer, 1960) (D.1960.334)

View over Nantlle Lake, Caernarvonshire, Wales
pencil, black chalk, blue watercolour,
grey watercolour; grey paper
inscribed lower left verso: *Lywyin* (sic) *Nantle Lake / 4
m. fm Snowdon*; inscribed on page of album below
image: *On Nuntle* (sic) *Lake, near Llywyn, Carnarvonsh.
/ 4m. from Snowdon.*
248 × 345 mm
University of Manchester, History of Art Department
(transfer, 1960) (D.1960.335)

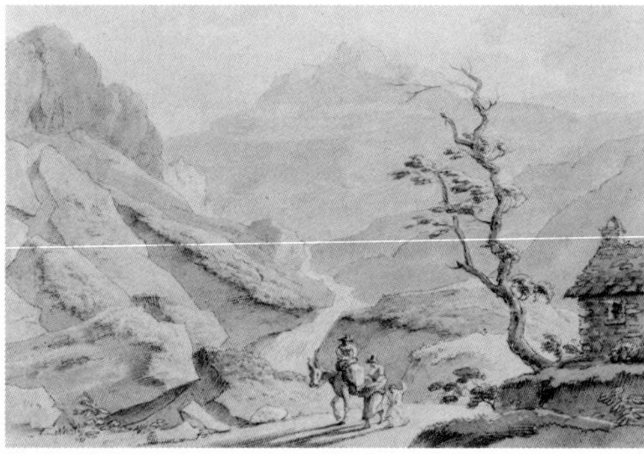

D.1960.336

**View looking towards Snowdon,
Caernarvonshire, Wales**
pencil, black chalk, blue watercolour,
grey watercolour; grey paper
inscribed on page of album below image: *near Snowden*
(sic) / *Carnarvonshire.*
240 × 345 mm
University of Manchester, History of Art Department
(transfer, 1960) (D.1960.336)

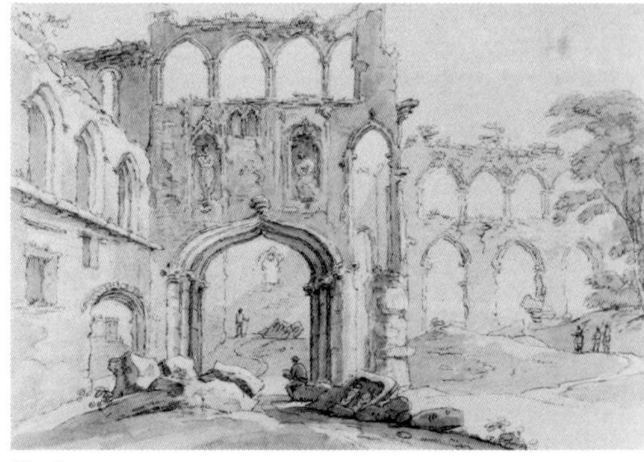

D.1960.337

**Gate of St John's Hall, St Davids,
Pembrokeshire, Wales**
1803
pencil, black chalk, white chalk, blue watercolour,
grey watercolour; grey paper
inscribed & dated lower centre verso: *Gate of King
Johns Hall / near the Cathedral of St.Davids, So.Wales
Pembrokes – / 1803 JW –* ; inscribed on page of album
below image: *Gate of St. John's Hall, / near the Cathedral
of St. David's. Pembrokeshire.*
245 × 338 mm
University of Manchester, History of Art Department
(transfer, 1960) (D.1960.337)

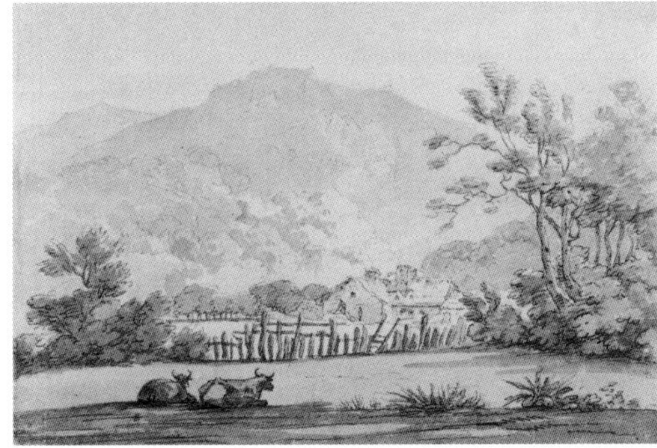

D.1960.338

Craig-y-foel, Pembrokeshire, Wales
1792
pencil, black chalk, blue watercolour,
grey watercolour; grey paper
inscribed & dated upper left verso: *Craggy Vale* (sic) *in
Pembrokeshire / near the River Ellen / after Turner 1792*
234 × 332 mm
University of Manchester, History of Art Department
(transfer, 1960) (D.1960.338)

**View from Pembroke looking towards Milford
Haven, Pembrokeshire, Wales**
pencil, black chalk, blue watercolour,
grey watercolour; grey paper
inscribed lower centre verso: *from Pembroke – looking to
Milford Haven.*; inscribed on page of album below
image: *From Pembroke – looking to Milford Haven.*
244 × 344 mm
University of Manchester, History of Art Department
(transfer, 1960) (D.1960.339)

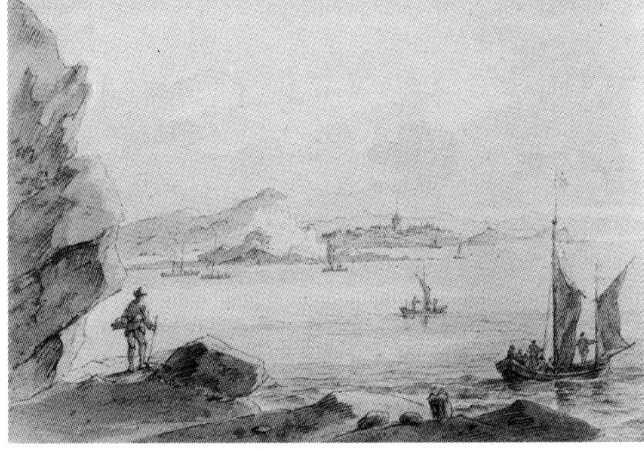

D.1960.340

**View of Tenby, Pembrokeshire, Wales, from
St Margaret's Isle**
pencil, black chalk, blue watercolour,
grey watercolour; grey paper
inscribed lower centre verso: *Town of Tenby, with the
Gilshene Rock & c – / taken from St. Maynett's* (sic)
Island.; inscribed on mount below image: *Tenby –
Pembrokeshire – taken from St. Maynell's* (sic) *Island.*
251 × 351 mm
University of Manchester, History of Art Department
(transfer, 1960) (D.1960.340)

**The Bristol Channel from near Kings Weston,
Gloucestershire**
pencil, black chalk, blue watercolour,
grey watercolour; grey paper
inscribed upper left verso: *Severn / after Pocock*;
inscribed on page of album below image: *On the Severn*
245 × 350 mm
University of Manchester, History of Art Department
(transfer, 1960) (D.1960.341)

**A wooded Landscape with a Stream and a
distant Church**
pencil, black chalk, white chalk, blue watercolour,
grey watercolour; grey paper
242 × 338 mm
University of Manchester, History of Art Department
(transfer, 1960) (D.1960.342)

A Village near Bristol with beached Boats
pencil, black chalk, blue watercolour,
grey watercolour; grey paper
inscribed upper left verso: *Near Bristol / after JEagle*
(sic); inscribed on mount below image: *Near Bristol*;
inscribed below pencil inscription: *Near Bristol.*
239 × 348 mm
University of Manchester, History of Art Department
(transfer, 1960) (D.1960.343)

**On the River Wye between New Weir and
Monmouth, Monmouthshire, Wales**
pencil, black chalk, white chalk, blue watercolour,
grey watercolour; grey paper
inscribed on page of album below image: *On Bristol
River*; inscribed below inscription: *On the Wye between
New Weir & Monmouth*
239 × 325 mm
University of Manchester, History of Art Department
(transfer, 1960) (D.1960.344)

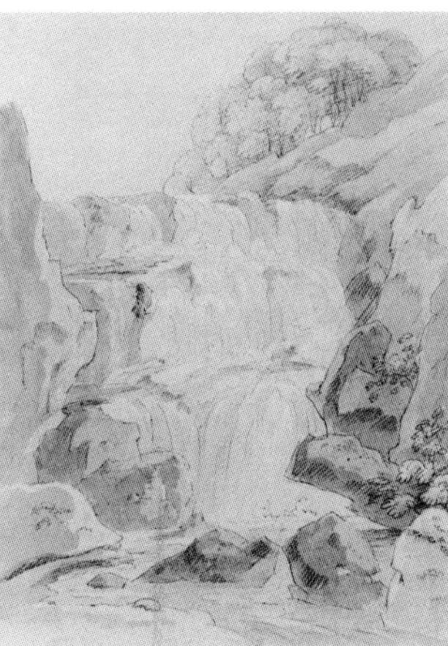

D.1960.345

Cilycwm Falls, Carmarthenshire, Wales
pencil, black chalk, white chalk, blue watercolour,
grey watercolour; grey paper
inscribed upper right verso: *Cilgwym Fall over / the
Velk*; inscribed on page of album below image:
Cilgwym Fall, over the Velk; inscribed below inscription
identifying the source of the drawing: *J.W.*
339 × 245 mm
University of Manchester, History of Art Department
(transfer, 1960) (D.1960.345)

■ **SUSSUM** (fl. 1895)
Unknown amateur artist.

**Grove House, Whitworth Park, Manchester,
from the South**
1895
pencil, watercolour
inscribed & dated on verso of mount: *Grove House /
originally on the site of the / Whitworth Art Gallery / by
Mr Sussum / 1895*
300 × 243 mm
Banfield, B. W. (gift, 1931) (D.1931.34)

■ **SWAINE, FRANCIS** (ca. 1740–82)
Swaine, a marine painter in oil and monochrome wash,
was exhibiting in London from 1762. His numerous
pictures and small wash drawings are in the manner of
the younger van de Velde.

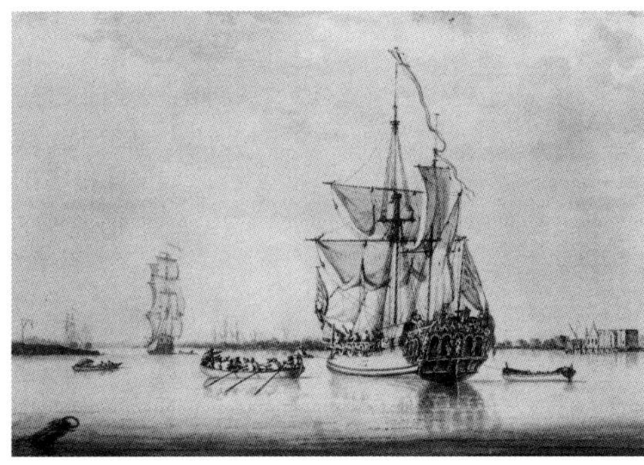

D.1892.141

On the River Maas, Holland
1772
grey watercolour
signed & dated lower left on a buoy: *FSwaine / 1772*
357 × 537 mm
Taylor, John Edward (gift, 1892) (D.1892.141)

Shipping off the Dutch Coast
pen and brown ink, watercolour
signed lower left: *FSwaine*
183 × 229 mm
Rienaecker, Victor, National Art Collections Fund (via)
(gift, 1928) (D.1928.9)

■ **SWINBURNE, EDWARD** (1788–1844)
Edward Swinburne, son of Sir John Swinburne of
Capheaton Hall, Northumberland, the long-lived
patron of many artists, including Turner, was a
competent amateur. He should not be confused
with his uncle of the same name, who was also an
accomplished amateur and visited Italy in 1792–23
and in 1797.

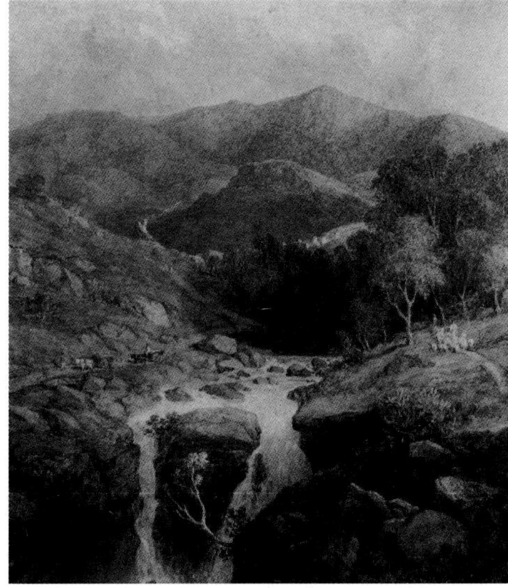

D.1968.10

Church Beck and Coniston Old Man, Lancashire
pencil, watercolour
335 × 302 mm
Bonham-Carter, Lady (gift, 1968) (D.1968.10)

■ Syer, John (1815–85)

A landscape painter in oil and watercolour, Syer settled in Bristol – and in Bath during the social season – until he moved to London in 1872. He was elected a member of the New Watercolour Society in 1875.

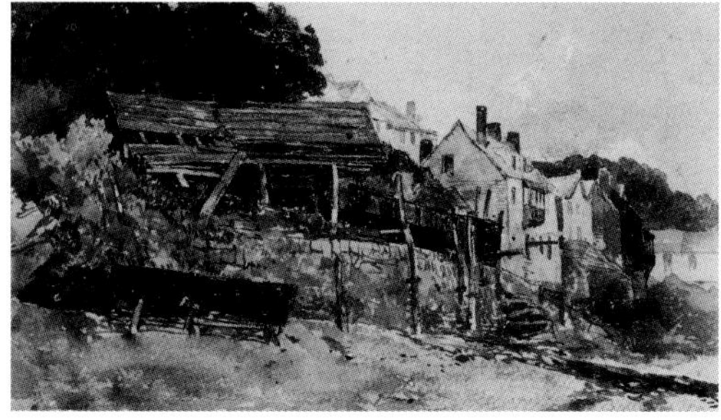

D.1917.19

Pitt Hill, Bristol
watercolour
194 × 333 mm
untraced (purchase, 1917) (D.1917.19)

■ Tavare, Frederick L. (1846–after 1892)

Unknown amateur artist.

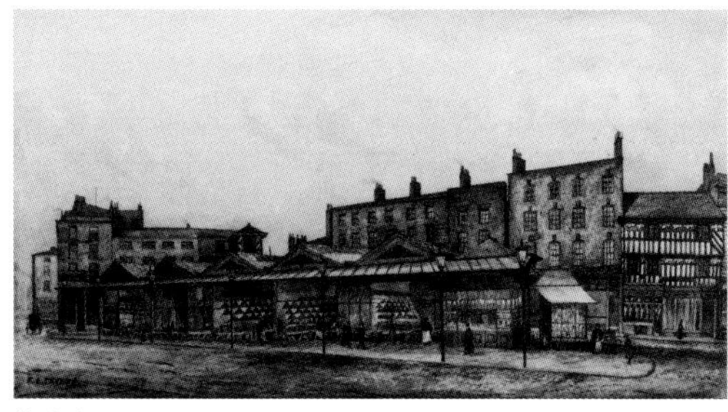

D.1896.2

Market Stalls, Smithy Door, Manchester
watercolour
signed lower left: *F.L. TAVARE*
380 × 688 mm
untraced (purchase, 1896) (D.1896.2)

Grove House, Whitworth Park, Manchester
1892
pencil, pen and brown ink
172 × 257 mm
Banfield, B. W. (gift, 1931) (D.1931.35)

■ Taverner, William (1703–72)

Although by profession a lawyer in the Court of Arches, Taverner enjoyed a considerable reputation among his contemporaries as a landscape artist. His work was admired and collected by professional artists and he can be regarded as the first major English landscape watercolour painter. As well as painting topographical landscapes, he also painted classical subjects and ideal compositions.

The Thames at Richmond, Surrey
pencil, watercolour; two joined sheets
stamped lower left with the collector's mark of Paul Sandby (L.2112): P.S.
221 × 541 mm
Taylor, John Edward (gift, 1892) (D.1892.2)

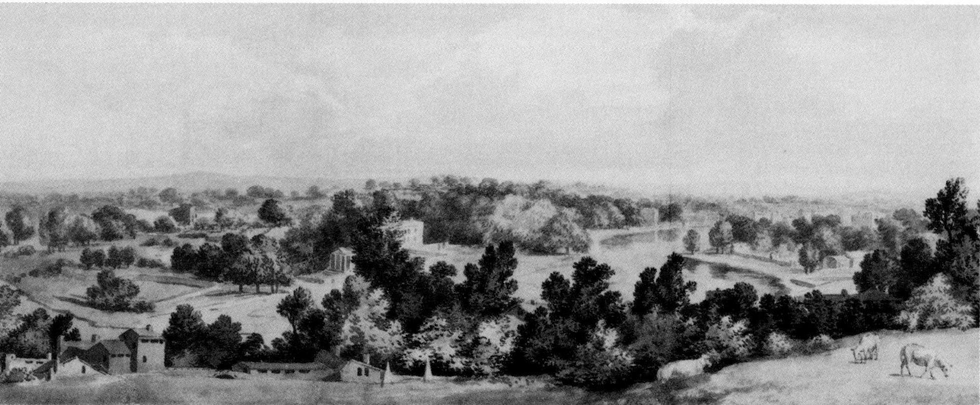

D.1892.2

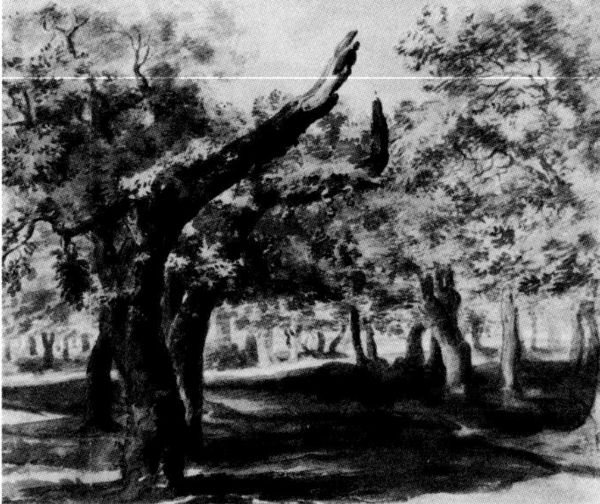

D.1933.32

Trees at Windsor
pencil, watercolour
310 × 370 mm
Anderson, A. E. (gift, 1933) (D.1933.32)

■ Tayler, John Frederick (1802–89)

Educated at both Eton and Harrow, Tayler was destined for the Church but opted for a career as painter, studying at Sasse's and the Royal Academy Schools as well as under Vernet in Paris. He first exhibited at the Royal Academy in 1830 and became a member of the Old Watercolour Society in 1834. Tayler specialised in Scottish and sporting subjects and was President of the Old Watercolour Society from 1858 to 1871.

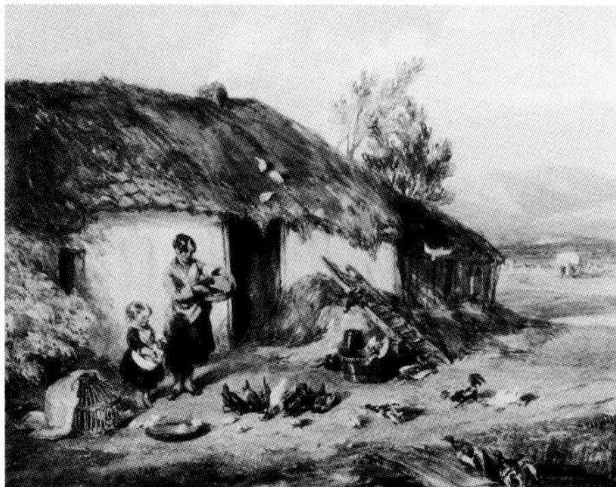

D.1887.43

Feeding Chickens
pencil, watercolour, bodycolour (heightened with white)
312 × 399 mm
Agnew's (purchase, 22.6.1891) (D.1887.43)

■ Tenniel, Sir John (1820–1914)

One of the best-known Victorian cartoonists and illustrators, Tenniel joined *Punch* in 1851 and became principal cartoonist in 1864. He also illustrated *Alice in Wonderland* in 1865 and *Alice Through the Looking Glass* in 1872. Tenniel was elected a member of the New Watercolour Society in 1874. He was knighted in 1893.

'Who said "Dead?"': Illustration for 'Punch' Magazine
1900
pencil
signed & dated lower right with monogram: *JT / 1900*
inscribed & dated on a separate label attached to the mount: *John Tenniel / Who Said "Dead"?* [underlined] / *Punch.march 7.1900.*
158 × 205 mm
University of Manchester, History of Art Department (transfer, 1960) (D.1960.136)

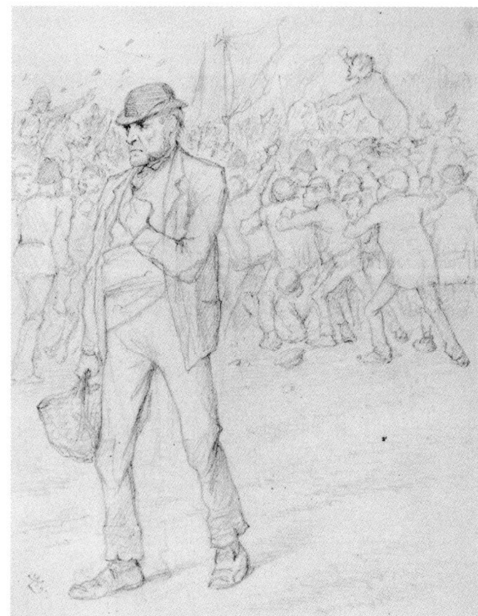

D.1960.137

'The Two Voices': Illustration for 'Punch' Magazine
1887
pencil
signed lower left with monogram: *JT*
sheet: 286 × 195 mm
University of Manchester, History of Art Department (transfer, 1960) (D.1960.137)

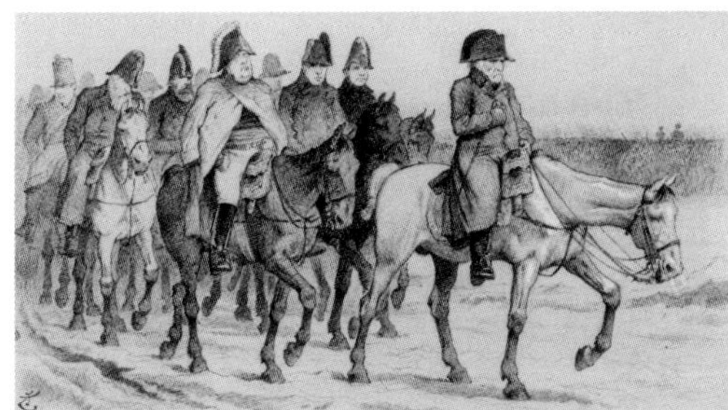

D.1961.14

1886: A playful Adaptation of Meissonier's Famous Picture '1814': Illustration for 'Punch' Magazine
4.3.1886
pencil, bodycolour (heightened with white)
signed & dated lower left with monogram *JT / 1886*;
dated lower right margin: *4th Mar*; inscribed & dated on a label attached to front of mount : *"1886"* [underlined] / *(a playful adaptation of Meissonier's famous picture, "1814".)*
sheet 224 × 372 mm
untraced (untraced, 1961) (D.1961.14)

■ **THIRTLE, JOHN (1777–1839)**
Thirtle trained as a frame maker before turning to painting, and was founder member of the Norwich Society in 1803. He was second only to Cotman (his brother-in-law) as a watercolourist in the Norwich School. Thirtle painted landscapes and portraits and also had a practice as a drawing master.

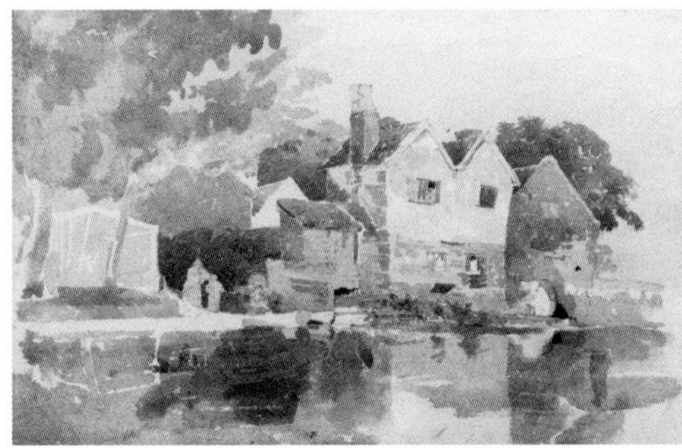

D.1915.4

Old Waterside Cottage, Norwich
pencil, watercolour
210 × 303 mm
Anderson, A. E. (gift, 1915) (D.1915.4)

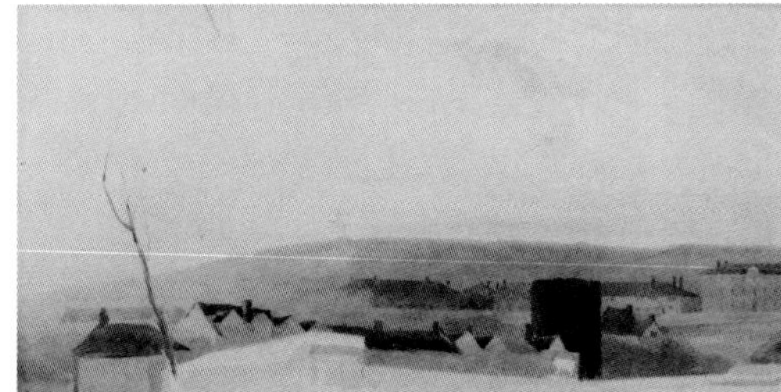

D.1923.13

Bishopgate Bridge and Cow Tower, Norwich
pencil, watercolour
276 × 652 mm
Anderson, A. E., National Art Collections Fund (via) (gift, 1923) (D.1923.13)

■ **THOMAS, JAMES HAVARD (1854–1921)**
Thomas was a draughtsman and sculptor who was born in Bristol and studied there, at the Royal College of Art and in Paris. He spent some years in Italy from 1889 and exhibited portrait and mythological busts at the Royal Academy between 1872 and 1914. He was elected Professor of Sculpture at the Slade in 1915.

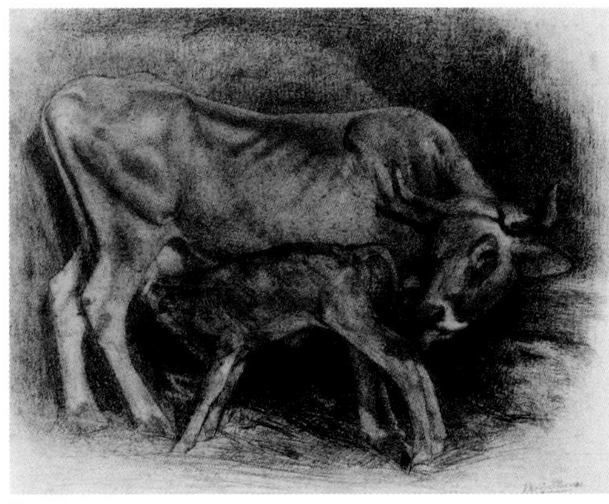

D.1922.18

Study of a Cow and Calf for a Relief Sculpture
1897
pencil
signed lower right: *JHavard Thomas*
273 × 357 mm
Leicester Galleries, London (purchase, 1922) (D.1922.18)

Study of a young Shepherdess
black chalk, white chalk; brown paper
318 × 202 mm
Anderson, A. E., National Art Collections Fund (via) (gift, 1923) (D.1923.1)

■ **THOMAS, MATTHEW EVAN (fl. 1799–1822)**
Thomas studied at the Royal Academy Schools, gaining a gold medal in 1815. The following year he travelled to Florence and Rome: he exhibited four works at the Royal Academy between 1820 and 1822.

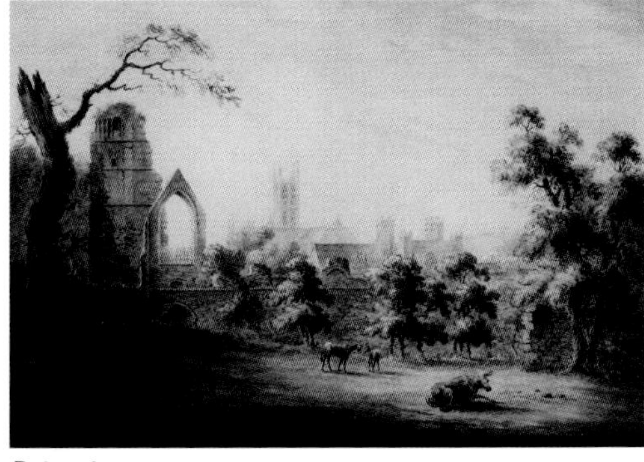

D.1892.118

St Ethelbert's Tower with Canterbury Cathedral in the Distance
1799
pencil, watercolour, bodycolour
signed & dated lower left initial in monogram: *MThomas / 1799*
535 × 754 mm
Taylor, John Edward (gift, 1892) (D.1892.118)

■ **THOMPSON, JACOB (1806–79)**
Thompson was a landscape and portrait painter known as Thompson of Penrith from the town of his birth in Cumberland. He exhibited at the Royal Academy between 1831 and 1866. Thompson lived at Hackthorpe near Penrith from the mid-1840s until his death.

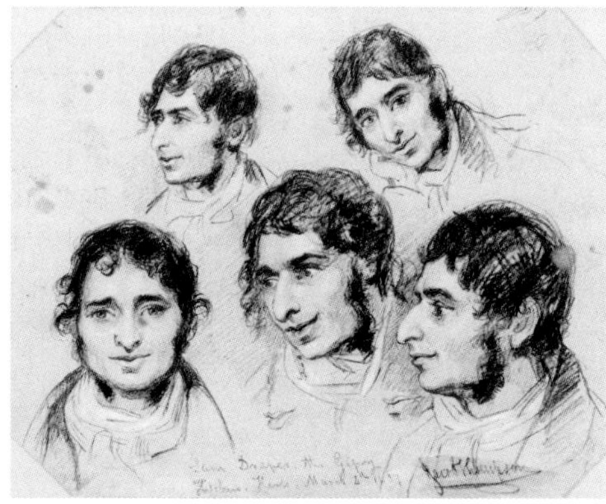

D.1926.231

Five Studies of the Head of Sam Draper the Gypsy
4.3.1839
black chalk, white chalk; brown paper
signed lower right: *Jacob Thompson*; inscribed & dated lower centre: *Sam Draper, the Gipsy / Hitchin, Herts.March 4th 1839*
217 × 262 mm
Ogden, William Sharp (bequest, 1926) (D.1926.231)

■ **THORNHILL, SIR JAMES (1675–1734)**
Born in Dorset, Thornhill became the leading decorative history painter in the baroque tradition. He was the only British painter who was able to compete successfully with the many foreigners working in England. His most successful extant work is at St Paul's Cathedral and Greenwich Hospital; he also worked at Blenheim Palace. Thornhill succeeded Joseph Highmore as Serjeant-Painter to the King. His daughter married William Hogarth.

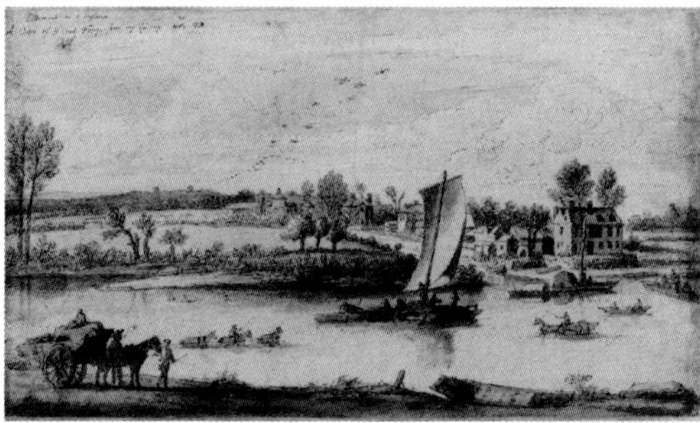

D.1935.4

View of Hampton Court Ferry from the Artist's Lodgings
20.4.1731
pen and brown ink, grey watercolour
signed, inscribed & dated upper left with initials: *Clermont at a Distance / A View of H.Court Ferry. from my Lodgings Apr.20 1731 / JTh*; inscribed lower centre on mount: *Sr JamesThorhhill.*; inscribed lower right on mount with the initials of the collector William Esdaile (L.2617): *WE*
278 × 476 mm
Anderson, A. E. (gift, 1935) (D.1935.4)

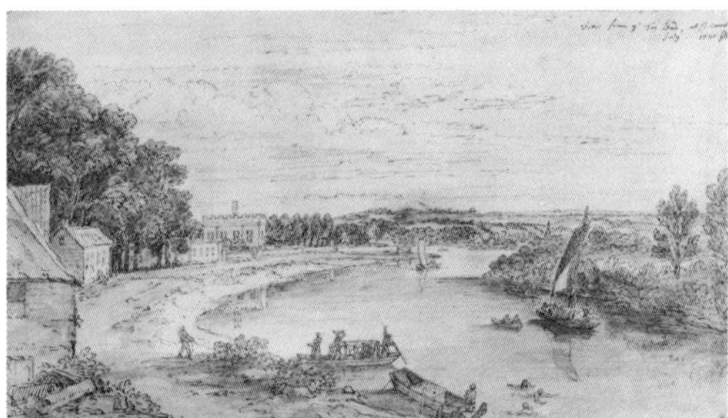

D.1935.5

View of Hampton Court Ferry

7.1730
pencil, pen and brown ink, brown watercolour
signed, inscribed & dated upper right with initials:
View from ye Toy Leads, at H.Court / July – 1730 / JTh ;
inscribed lower centre on mount: *Sr James Thornhill.*;
inscribed lower right on mount with the initials of the
collector William Esdaile (L.2617): *WE*
275 × 471 mm
Anderson, A. E. (gift, 1935) (D.1935.5)

Mythological Figures among Clouds: Study for a Ceiling (recto); Further Study (verso)

pencil, black chalk, brown watercolour
289 × 207 mm
University of Manchester, History of Art Department
(transfer, 1960) (D.1960.138)

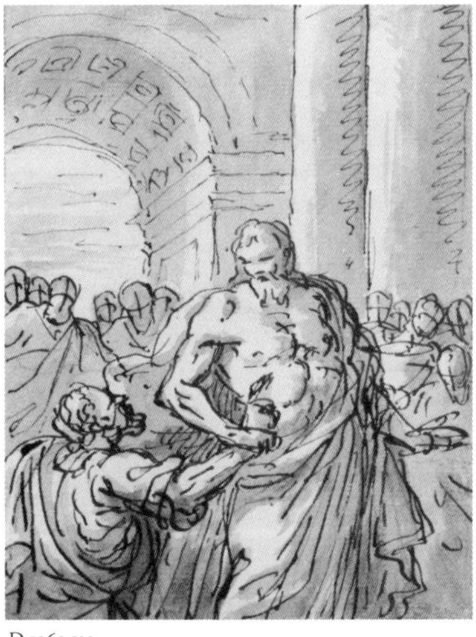

D.1960.139

Christ and St Thomas

pencil, pen and brown ink, brown watercolour
145 × 110 mm
University of Manchester, History of Art Department
(transfer, 1960) (D.1960.139)

The Marriage of Hercules and Hebe: Ceiling Design for Blenheim Palace

1716
pen and brown ink, grey watercolour
326 × 143 mm
Friends of the Whitworth (gift, 1962) (D.1962.25)

St Paul before Agrippa: Study for the Dome of St Paul's Cathedral, London

1714–17
pencil, black chalk, grey watercolour
186 × 140 mm
Friends of the Whitworth (gift, 1964) (D.1964.5)

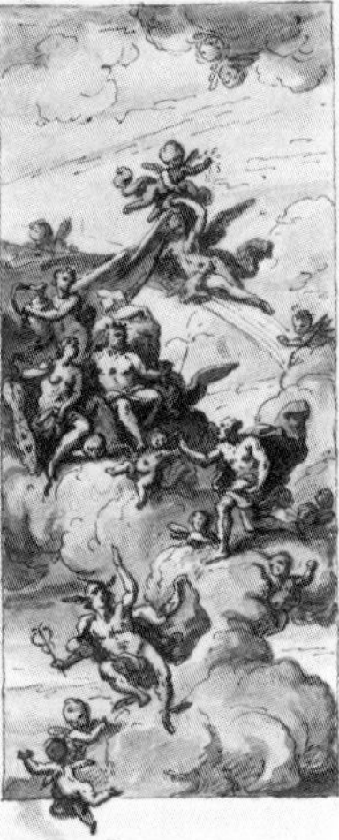

D.1962.25

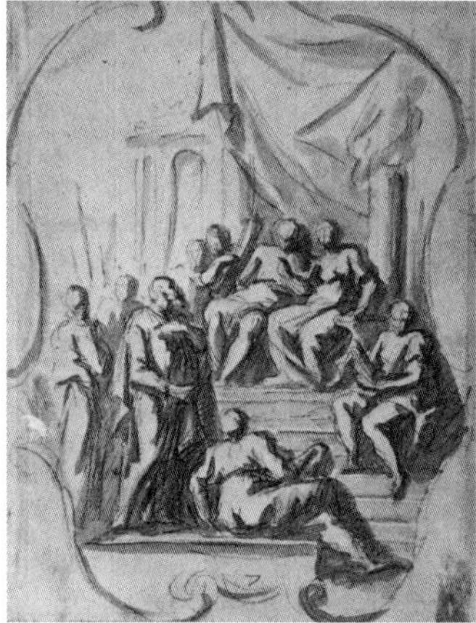

D.1964.5

The Angel appearing to the Shepherds

pencil, pen and brown ink, brown watercolour
191 × 111 mm
Powney Gallery, London (purchase, 1965) (D.1965.10)

■ TOMKINS, PELTRO WILLIAM (1760–1840)

Tomkins, who came from a family of painters and
engravers, was an engraver and portrait painter who
trained under Bartolozzi. He worked as an etcher and
stipple and aquatint engraver of portraits and
decorative and military subjects after his own designs,
Old Master painters and his contemporaries.

Children feeding Chickens, after a John Russell design

1792
coloured chalk
271 × 335 mm
Anderson, A. E. (gift, 1932) (D.1932.11)

■ TOPHAM, FRANCIS WILLIAM (1808–77)

Born in Leeds, Topham trained as an engraver and
came to London in about 1830. He turned to
watercolour painting and was elected a member of the
New Watercolour Society in 1843. Topham seceded
from this in 1847 and joined the Old Watercolour
Society in 1848. He visited Ireland in 1844, 1860 and
1862 and was in Spain in 1852–53. His most popular
subjects were Irish or Spanish peasants.

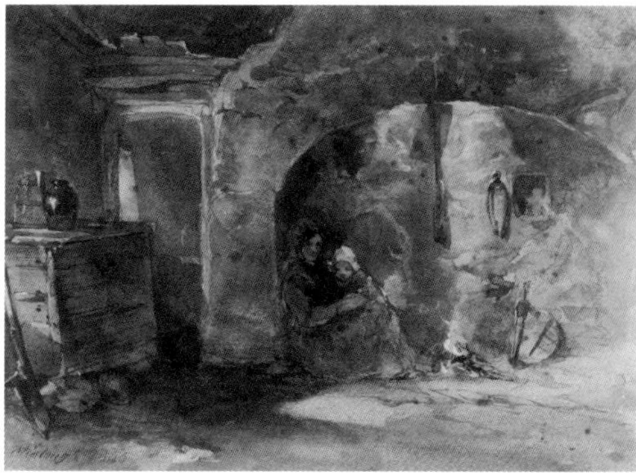

D.1897.7

Interior of a Peasant's Cottage, Minlough, Co. Galway, Ireland

1845
pencil, watercolour, bodycolour
(heightened with white)
inscribed & dated lower left: *Minlough 1845*
191 × 258 mm
Phillips, H. (gift, 1897) (D.1897.7)

■ TOWNE, FRANCIS (1739–1816)

Born in London, Towne later practised as a
drawing master in Exeter. He was a pupil at
Shipley's drawing school in the Strand in the 1750s
and exhibited landscapes at the Society of Artists
between 1762 and 1773. He toured Wales in 1777
and visited Italy and Switzerland in 1780–81, the high
point of his artistic career. He also made a tour of the
Lake District in 1786. He made his living mostly by
teaching and painting in oils. After his death Towne
was almost forgotten until he was rediscovered in the
twentieth century.

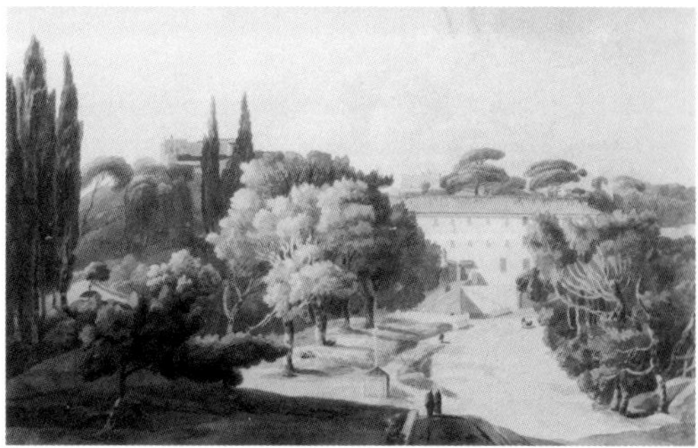

D.1922.28

The Convent of St Efremo, near Naples

1783
pen and brown ink, watercolour
signed & dated lower left: *Francis Towne / delt 1783*
323 × 496 mm
Duxbury, Percival (purchase, 1922) (D.1922.28)

Ambleside, Lake Windermere, Westmorland

7.8.1786
pen and brown ink, watercolour; two joined sheets
signed, dated & numbered lower left: *No.1.F.Towne /
delt 1786*; inscribed, numbered & dated verso of
mount: *No.1. A View at Ambleside, at the head of the
Lake of Windermere / drawn on the Spot / by / Francis
Towne / August 7th.1786 / Light from the right hand*
159 × 352 mm
Agnew, Gerald, National Art Collections Fund (via)
(gift, 1922) (D.1922.29)

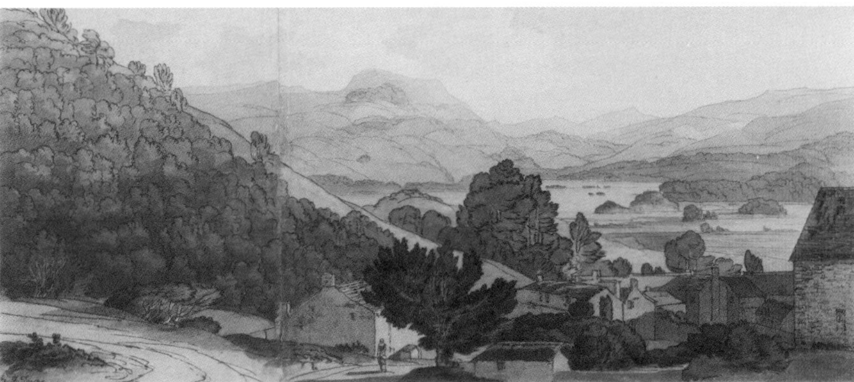

D.1922.29

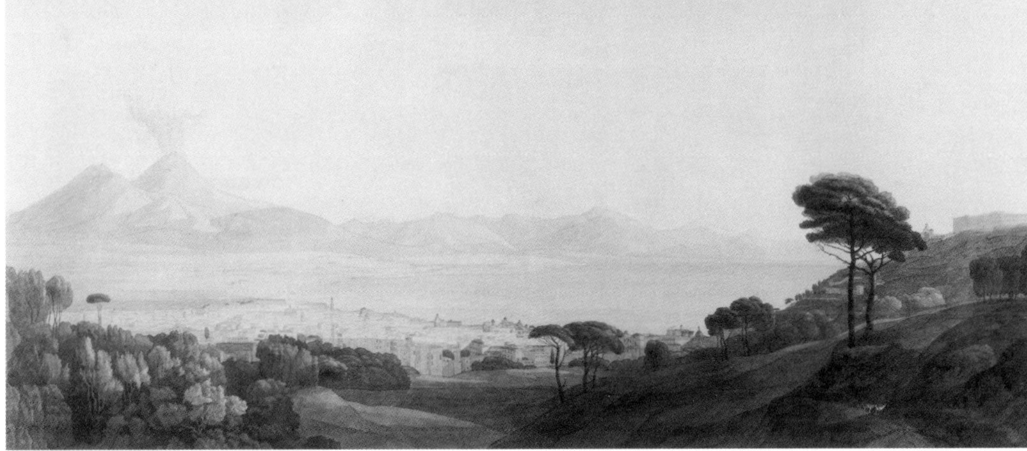

D.1927.15

The Bay of Naples
1785
pencil, pen and grey ink, watercolour
signed & dated: *F Towne delt 1785*
404 × 885 mm
Abbott, E. S. (purchase, 1927) (D.1927.15)

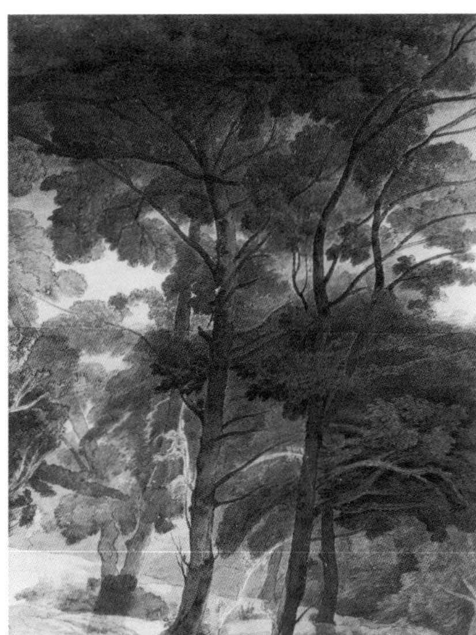

D.1938.4

Trees in Peamore Park, near Exeter, Devon
1804
pen and brown ink, watercolour; three joined sheets
signed, inscribed & dated verso of mount: *A Study after Nature in Peamore Park near Exeter / drawn on the Spot by Francis Towne / 1804*; inscribed lower left: *Sunshine*
369 × 268 mm
Pilkington, Margaret, Friends of the Whitworth (via) (gift, 1938) (D.1938.4)

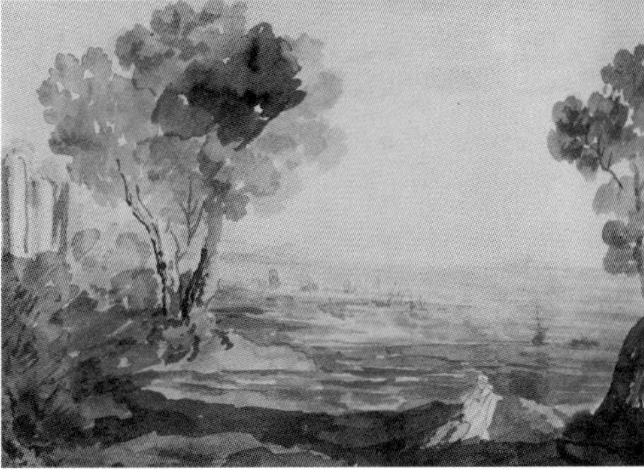

D.1950.2

Coast View of Naxos with Ariadne and Bacchus
brown watercolour, grey watercolour
inscribed lower left verso: *From memory of a Claude / which Lord Ashburnham has*; inscribed & numbered upper centre verso (Barton Place number in Paul Oppé's hand): *259* [within a circle] *B.P.*
208 × 267 mm
Pilkington, Margaret (gift, 1950) (D.1950.2)

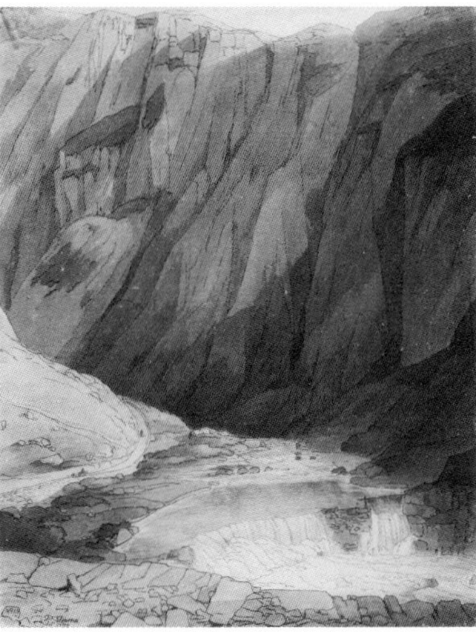

D.1999.22

The Salmon Leap, Pont Aberglasllyn
7.1777
pen and brown ink, watercolour
signed, dated & numbered lower left: *No23 / F. Towne / delt.1777*; signed, inscribed & dated verso of mount upper centre: *A View of the Salmon Leap / from Pont Aberglasllyn / Drawn on the Spot / by / Francis Towne / 1777* ; inscribed verso of mount upper right: *morning light from the right hand*; numbered verso of mount upper left: *No.23*; inscribed verso of mount centre right: *Leicester Square / London*; inscribed & numbered centre verso (Barton Place number in Paul Oppé's hand): *112* [within a circle] *B.P.*; inscribed lower right verso: *Miss Merivale / 4 Park Town. Oxford*
279 × 215 mm
Scott-Elliot, Miss Aydua, in memory of Paul Oppé (gift, 4.11.1999) (D.1999.22)

■ **TUCKER, ARTHUR (1864–1929)**
Born in Bristol, Tucker moved to the Lake District and was a founder member of the Lake Artists' Society in 1904. He exhibited intermittently at the Royal Academy between 1887 and 1902 and annually from 1904 to 1919. Tucker specialised in landscapes, mainly of the Lake District, although he also painted Welsh and Yorkshire views.

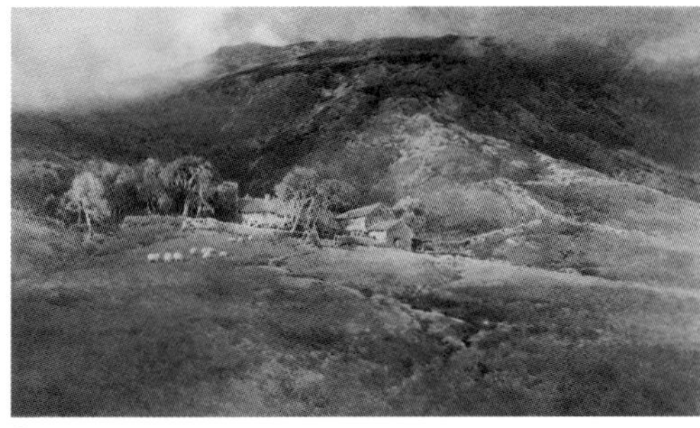

D.1901.4

Kentmere Hall, Westmorland
watercolour
signed lower left: *Arthur Tucker*; inscribed on artist's label attached to backboard: *2* [erased] *1 / Kentmere Hall – Westmorland / by Arthur Tucker.R.B.A. / Windermere / Westmorland*
616 × 1026 mm
untraced (purchase, 1901) (D.1901.4)

Sketchbook
1898–1903
pencil
126 × 182 mm
MacAlister, Donald, Victoria and Albert Museum (via)
(gift, 1956) (D.1956.6)

Cramond, near Edinburgh
7.1898
pencil
inscribed & dated lower right: *Cramond– / Edinburgh– / July.1898.*
126 × 182 mm
MacAlister, Donald, Victoria and Albert Museum (via)
(gift, 1956) (D.1956.6.1)

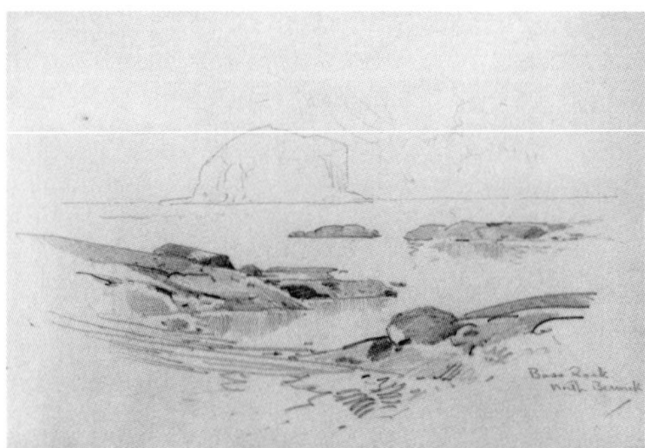
D.1956.6.2

Bass Rock, North Berwick, East Lothian, Scotland
pencil
inscribed lower right: *Bass Rock / North Berwick*
126 × 182 mm
MacAlister, Donald, Victoria and Albert Museum (via)
(gift, 1956) (D.1956.6.2)

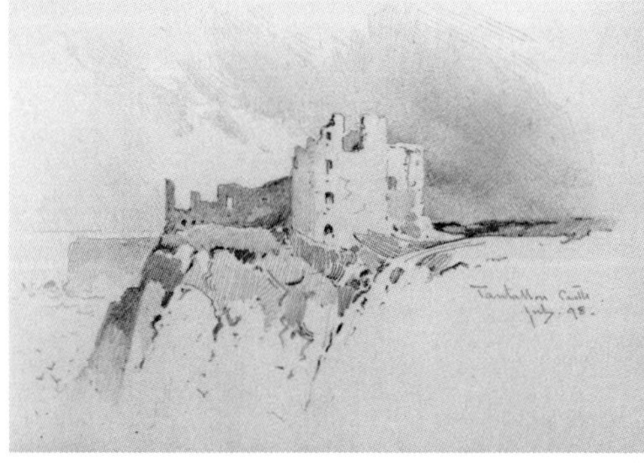
D.1956.6.3

Tantallon Castle, East Lothian, Scotland
7.1898
pencil
inscribed & dated lower right: *Tantallon Castle. / July.98.*
126 × 182 mm
MacAlister, Donald, Victoria and Albert Museum (via)
(gift, 1956) (D.1956.6.3)

Borwick Hall, Lancashire
3.1899
pencil
inscribed & dated lower right: *Borwick Hall– / March.99–*
126 × 182 mm
MacAlister, Donald, Victoria and Albert Museum (via)
(gift, 1956) (D.1956.6.4)

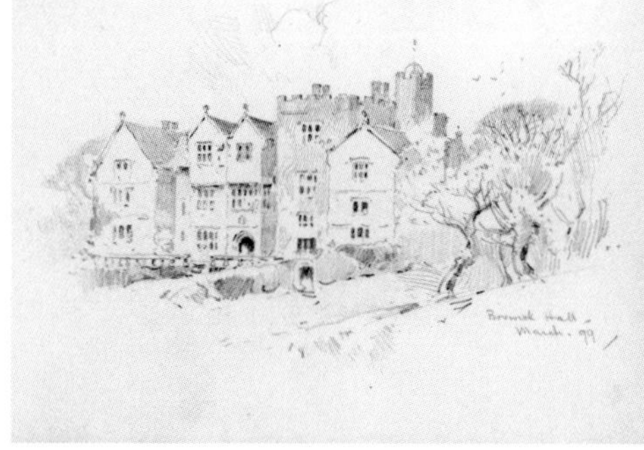
D.1956.6.4

Jenny Lind's House, near Malvern, Worcestershire
pencil
inscribed lower right: *Wind's point. / Jenny Lind's house / near Malvern*
126 × 182 mm
MacAlister, Donald, Victoria and Albert Museum (via)
(gift, 1956) (D.1956.6.5)

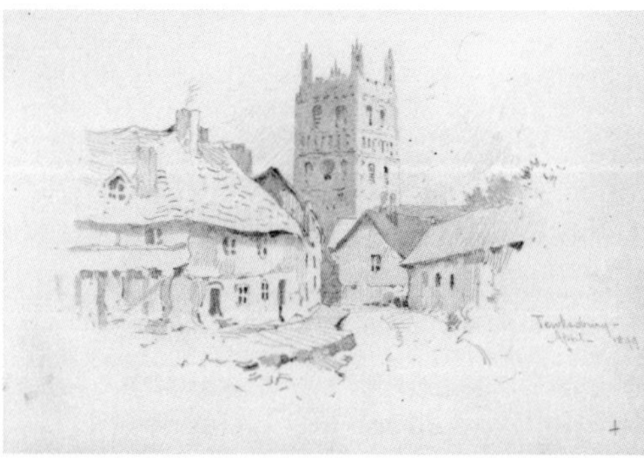
D.1956.6.6

Tewkesbury, Gloucestershire
4.1899
pencil
inscribed & dated lower right: *Tewkesbury– / April– 1899*
126 × 182 mm
MacAlister, Donald, Victoria and Albert Museum (via)
(gift, 1956) (D.1956.6.6)

Houses and a ruined Castle
pencil
126 × 182 mm
MacAlister, Donald, Victoria and Albert Museum (via)
(gift, 1956) (D.1956.6.7)

High Tide, Laugharne, Carmarthenshire, Wales
1899
pencil
inscribed & dated lower right: *High Tide / Laugharne / 1899.*
126 × 182 mm
MacAlister, Donald, Victoria and Albert Museum (via)
(gift, 1956) (D.1956.6.8)

Llanstephan Castle, Carmarthenshire, Wales
4.1899
pencil
inscribed & dated lower right: *Llanstephan / April 1899.*
126 × 182 mm
MacAlister, Donald, Victoria and Albert Museum (via)
(gift, 1956) (D.1956.6.9)

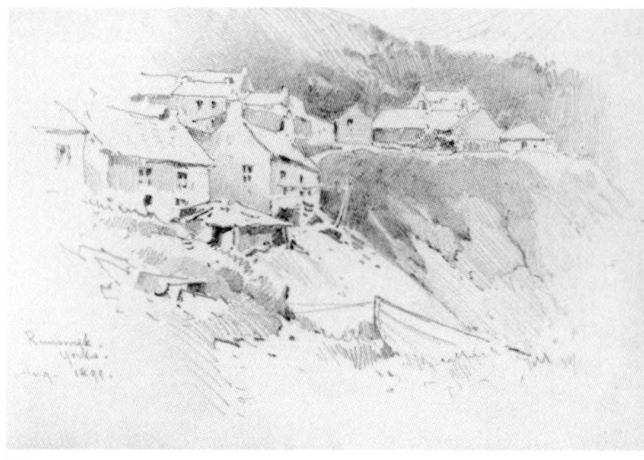
D.1956.6.10

Runswick Bay, Yorkshire
8.1899
pencil
inscribed & dated lower left: *Runswick. / Yorks. / Aug.1899.*
126 × 182 mm
MacAlister, Donald, Victoria and Albert Museum (via)
(gift, 1956) (D.1956.6.10)

Hinderwell, Yorkshire
pencil
inscribed lower left: *Hinderwell*
126 × 182 mm
MacAlister, Donald, Victoria and Albert Museum (via)
(gift, 1956) (D.1956.6.11)

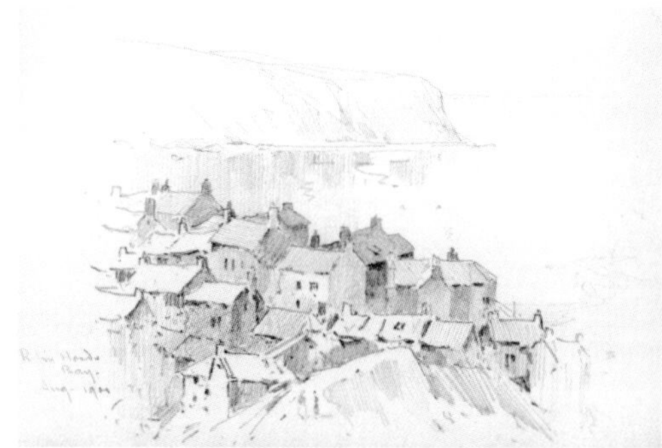
D.1956.6.12

Robin Hood's Bay, Yorkshire
8.1900
pencil
inscribed & dated lower left: *Robin Hood's / Bay. / Aug.1900*
126 × 182 mm
MacAlister, Donald, Victoria and Albert Museum (via)
(gift, 1956) (D.1956.6.12)

Thorpe, Yorkshire
pencil
inscribed lower left: *Thorpe*
126 × 182 mm
MacAlister, Donald, Victoria and Albert Museum (via)
(gift, 1956) (D.1956.6.13)

A Street Scene
pencil
126 × 182 mm
MacAlister, Donald, Victoria and Albert Museum (via)
(gift, 1956) (D.1956.6.14)

View of a Bridge
pencil
126 × 182 mm
MacAlister, Donald, Victoria and Albert Museum (via)
(gift, 1956) (D.1956.6.15)

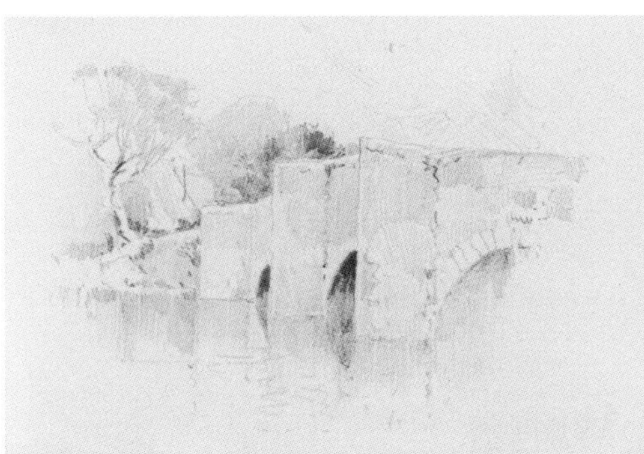

D.1956.6.15

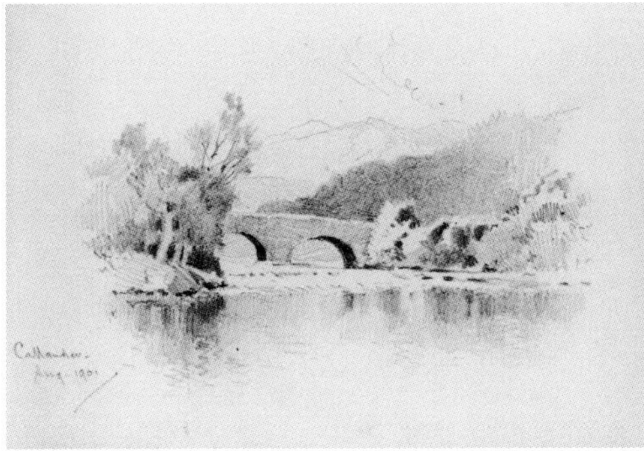

D.1956.6.16

A Bridge over a River near Callander, Perthshire, Scotland
8.1901
pencil
inscribed & dated lower left: *Callander– / Aug.1901*
126 × 182 mm
MacAlister, Donald, Victoria and Albert Museum (via)
(gift, 1956) (D.1956.6.16)

Study of Water and Trees
pencil
126 × 182 mm
MacAlister, Donald, Victoria and Albert Museum (via)
(gift, 1956) (D.1956.6.17)

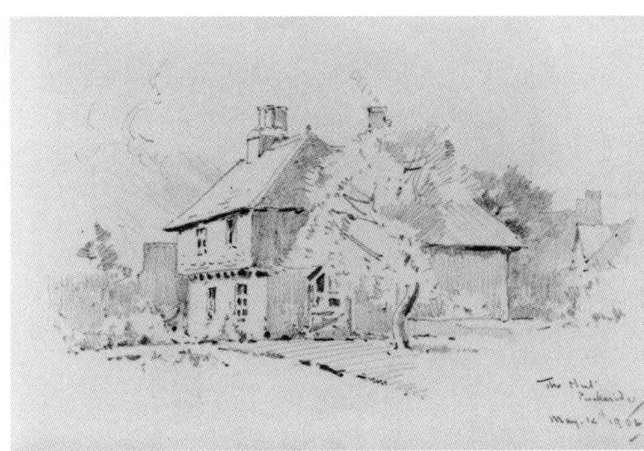

D.1956.6.18

The Hut, Puckeridge, Hertfordshire
14.5.1902
pencil
inscribed & dated lower right: *The Hut / Puckeridge / May.14th.1902*
126 × 182 mm
MacAlister, Donald, Victoria and Albert Museum (via)
(gift, 1956) (D.1956.6.18)

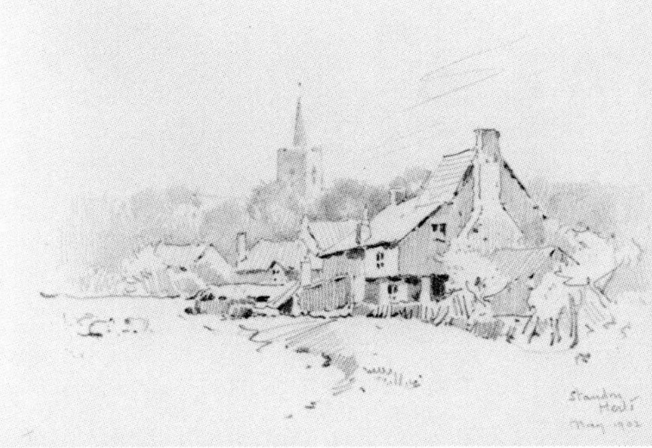

D.1956.6.19

Standon, Hertfordshire
5.1902
pencil
inscribed & dated lower right: *Standon / Herts / May.1902*
126 × 182 mm
MacAlister, Donald, Victoria and Albert Museum (via)
(gift, 1956) (D.1956.6.19)

Braughing, Hertfordshire
16.5.1902
pencil
inscribed & dated lower left: *Braughing. / May. 16th.* [1902]
126 × 182 mm
MacAlister, Donald, Victoria and Albert Museum (via)
(gift, 1956) (D.1956.6.20)

Braughing, Hertfordshire
5.1902
pencil
inscribed lower right: *Braughing.*
126 × 182 mm
MacAlister, Donald, Victoria and Albert Museum (via)
(gift, 1956) (D.1956.6.21)

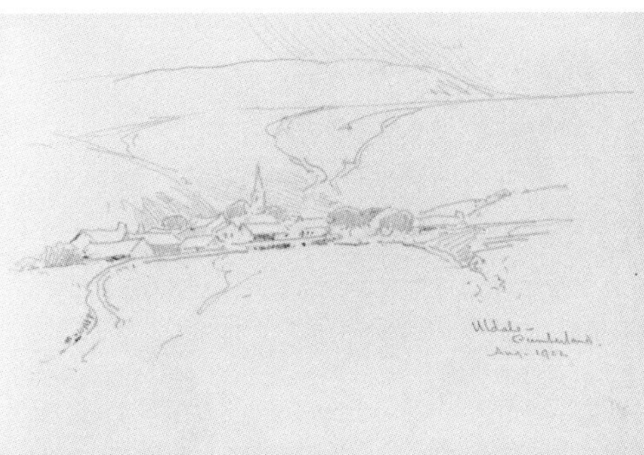

D.1956.6.22

Uldale, Cumberland
8.1902
pencil
inscribed & dated lower right: *Uldale– / Cumberland. / Aug.1902*
126 × 182 mm
MacAlister, Donald, Victoria and Albert Museum (via)
(gift, 1956) (D.1956.6.22)

Bassenthwaite, Cumberland
8.1902
pencil
inscribed & dated lower left: *Bassenthwaite– / Aug.1902*
126 × 182 mm
MacAlister, Donald, Victoria and Albert Museum (via)
(gift, 1956) (D.1956.6.23)

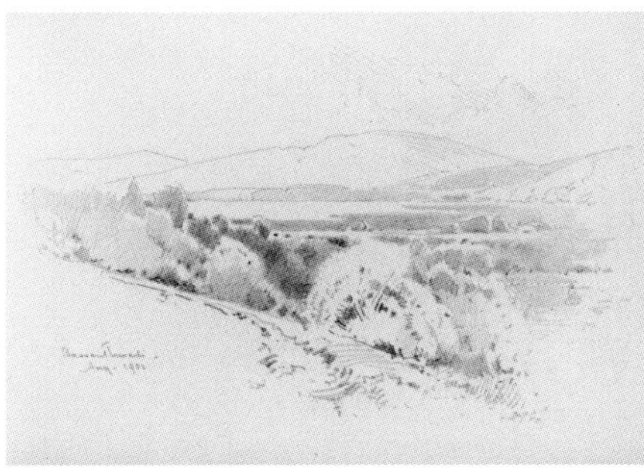

D.1956.6.23

View through Hills down to a Lake
pencil
126 × 182 mm
MacAlister, Donald, Victoria and Albert Museum (via)
(gift, 1956) (D.1956.6.24)

View along a Road
pencil
126 × 182 mm
MacAlister, Donald, Victoria and Albert Museum (via)
(gift, 1956) (D.1956.6.25)

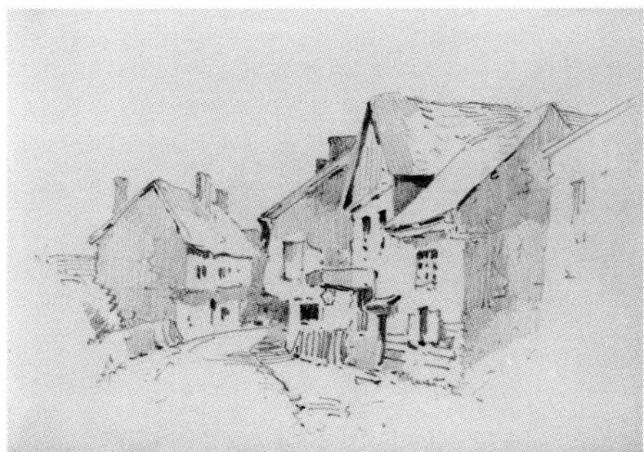

D.1956.6.26

Street Scene
pencil
126 × 182 mm
MacAlister, Donald, Victoria and Albert Museum (via)
(gift, 1956) (D.1956.6.26)

View of a Bridge
pencil
126 × 182 mm
MacAlister, Donald, Victoria and Albert Museum (via)
(gift, 1956) (D.1956.6.27)

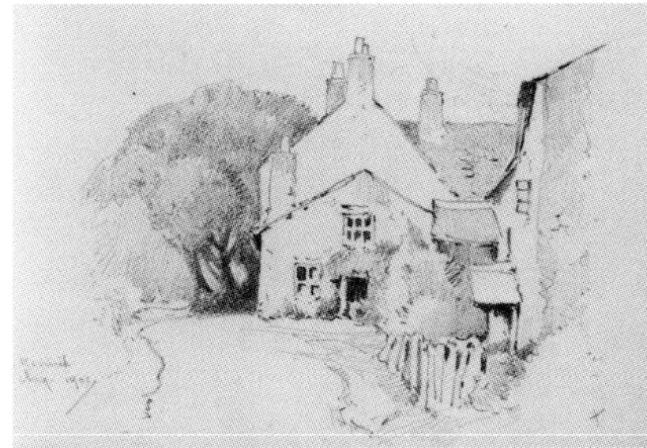

D.1956.6.28

Houses by a Road, Keswick, Cumberland
8.1903
pencil
inscribed & dated lower left: *Keswick / Aug.1903*
126 × 182 mm
MacAlister, Donald, Victoria and Albert Museum (via)
(gift, 1956) (D.1956.6.28)

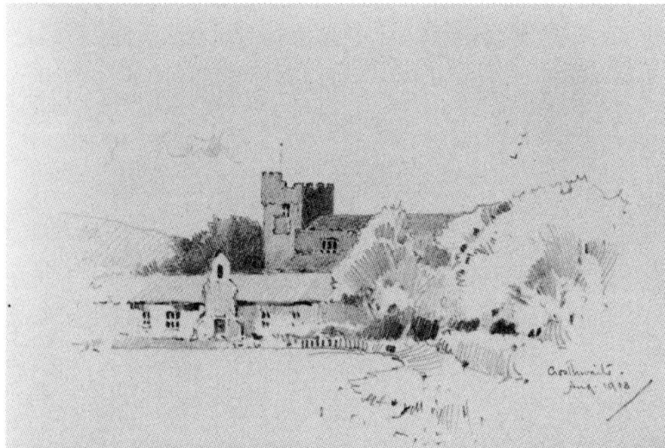

D.1956.6.29

Crosthwaite, Cumberland
8.1903
pencil
inscribed & dated lower right: *Crosthwaite. / Aug.1903*
126 × 182 mm
MacAlister, Donald, Victoria and Albert Museum (via)
(gift, 1956) (D.1956.6.29)

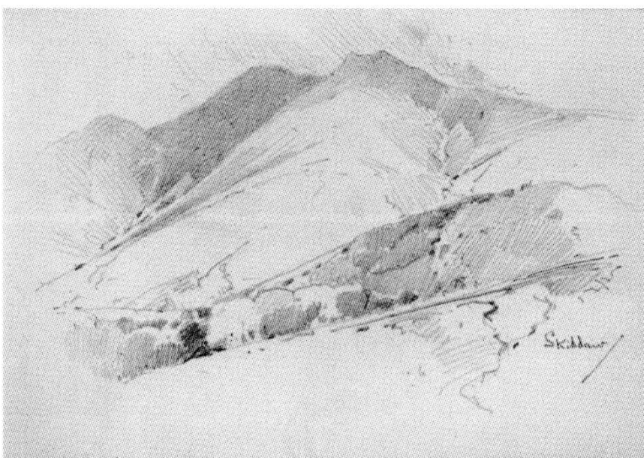

D.1956.6.30

Skiddaw, Cumberland
pencil
inscribed lower right: *Skiddaw*
126 × 182 mm
MacAlister, Donald, Victoria and Albert Museum (via)
(gift, 1956) (D.1956.6.30)

A distant View of Keswick Church with Latrigg beyond
pencil
126 × 182 mm
MacAlister, Donald, Victoria and Albert Museum (via) (gift, 1956) (D.1956.6.31)

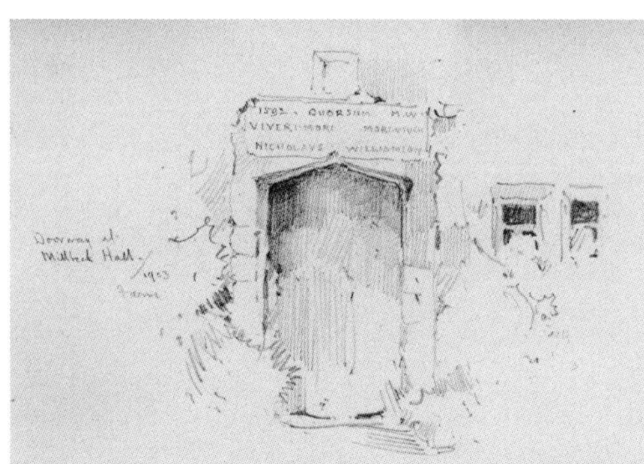

D.1956.6.32

Doorway at Millbeck Hall Farm, Cumberland
1903
pencil
inscribed & dated lower left: *Doorway at / Millbeck Hall. / 1903 / Farm*
126 × 182 mm
MacAlister, Donald, Victoria and Albert Museum (via)
(gift, 1956) (D.1956.6.32)

View of Blencathra from the East, Cumberland
pencil
126 × 182 mm
MacAlister, Donald, Victoria and Albert Museum (via)
(gift, 1956) (D.1956.6.33)

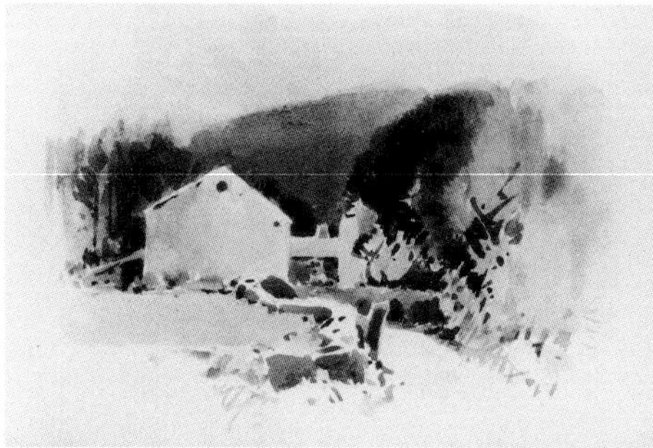

D.1956.6.34

A Lane at Rosthwaite, Cumberland
8.9.1903
pencil, grey watercolour
inscribed & dated lower right verso of previous drawing in the book: *Rosthwaite– / Sep 8th / 1903*
126 × 182 mm
MacAlister, Donald, Victoria and Albert Museum (via)
(gift, 1956) (D.1956.6.34)

View of a Cottage and Trees
pencil
126 × 182 mm
MacAlister, Donald, Victoria and Albert Museum (via)
(gift, 1956) (D.1956.6.35)

View from the Top of a Hill
pencil
126 × 182 mm
MacAlister, Donald, Victoria and Albert Museum (via)
(gift, 1956) (D.1956.6.36)

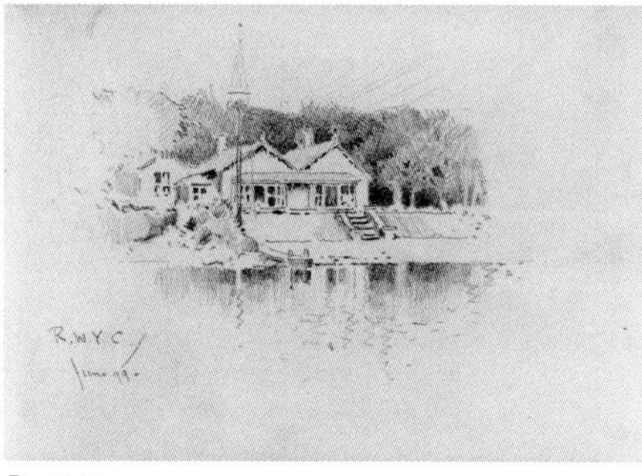

D.1956.6.37

Royal Windermere Yacht Club (recto); Miscellaneous Notes (verso)
6.1899
pencil
inscribed & dated lower left: *R.W.Y.C. / June 99*
126 × 182 mm
MacAlister, Donald, Victoria and Albert Museum (via)
(gift, 1956) (D.1956.6.37)

Three Studies of Children
pencil
126 × 182 mm
MacAlister, Donald, Victoria and Albert Museum (via)
(gift, 1956) (D.1956.6.38)

View of a Coastline
pencil
126 × 182 mm
MacAlister, Donald, Victoria and Albert Museum (via)
(gift, 1956) (D.1956.6.39)

Road through Trees
pencil
126 × 182 mm
MacAlister, Donald, Victoria and Albert Museum (via)
(gift, 1956) (D.1956.6.40)

■ TUDOR, THOMAS (1785–1855)
Tudor, a prolific draughtsman, may be the T. Tudor who exhibited portraits and Welsh views at the Royal Academy between 1809 and 1819.

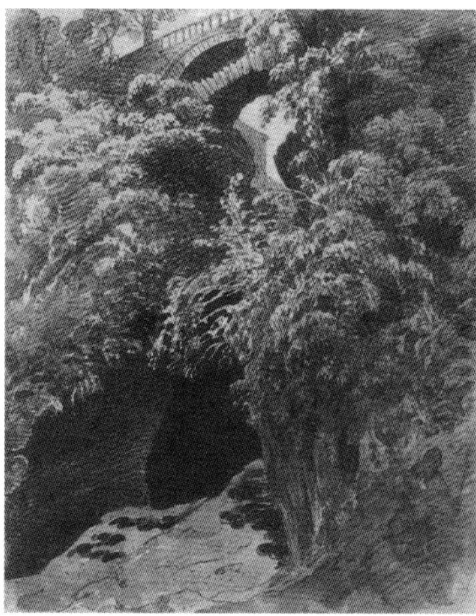

D.1963.7

The Devil's Bridge, Cardiganshire, Wales
pencil, black chalk, grey watercolour
310 × 246 mm
Pilkington, Margaret (gift, 1963) (D.1963.7)

■ TURNER, JOSEPH MALLORD WILLIAM (1775–1851)
Probably the greatest English watercolourist, Turner was born in London and entered the Royal Academy Schools in 1789. During the 1790s he travelled extensively throughout Britain and was elected a member of the Royal Academy in 1802, the same year in which he first visited the Continent. Turner's influential series of mezzotint engravings, the *Liber Studiorum*, was published between 1807 and 1819. He visited Italy for the first time in 1819 and returned to the Continent nearly every year until 1845. Turner was hugely prolific and worked on a number of large engraving projects, the biggest being the *Picturesque Views in England and Wales* series (1825–38).

Magdalen Tower and Bridge, Oxford
1794
pencil, watercolour
signed & dated lower left: *1794 Turner*
286 × 222 mm
Agnew's (purchase, 12.5.1891) (D.1887.6)

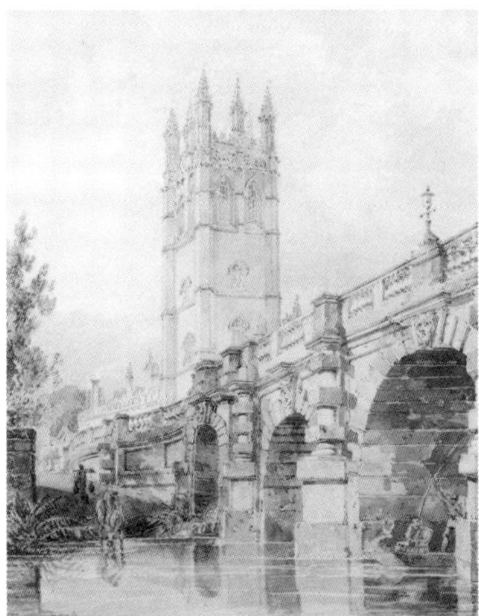

D.1887.6

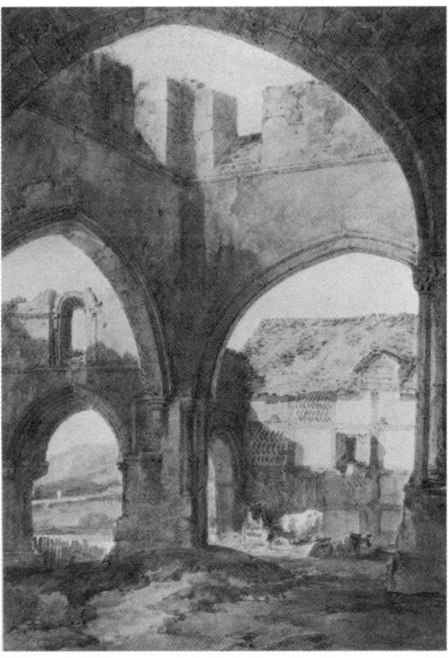

D.1887.10

Buildwas Abbey, Shropshire
1797
pencil, watercolour
inscribed verso written over previous inscription:
Buildwas Abbey – near Shrewsbury
481 × 328 mm
Agnew's (purchase, 6.6.1891) (D.1887.10)

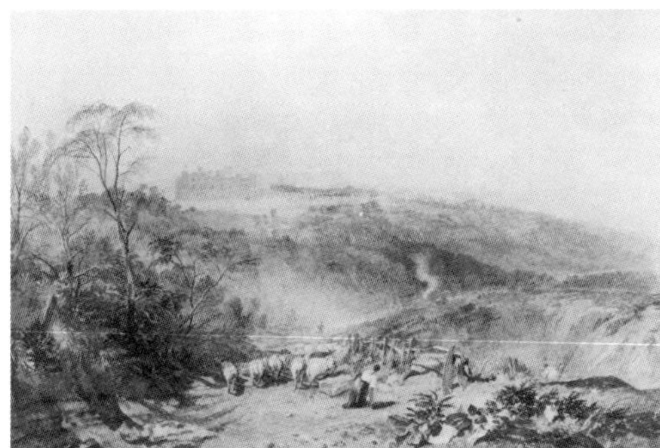

D.1887.12

Eridge Castle, Sussex
1816
pencil, watercolour, bodycolour
369 × 543 mm
Agnew's (purchase, 5.5.1891) (D.1887.12)

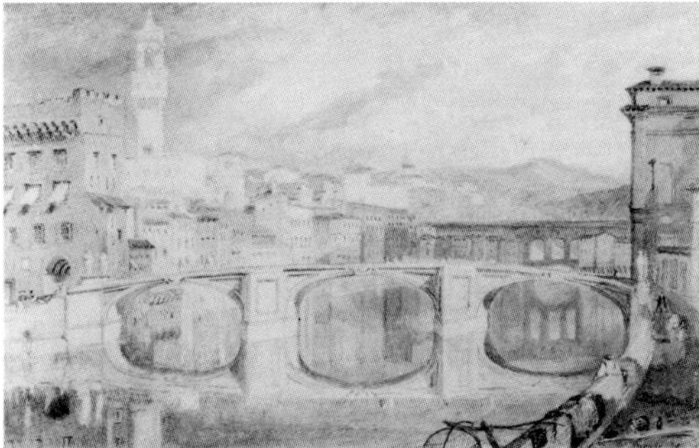

D.1887.13

Florence from the Ponte alla Carraia
1818
pencil, watercolour, bodycolour
signed lower right: *J M W Turner RA*
216 × 400 mm
Agnew's (purchase, 12.5.1891) (D.1887.13)

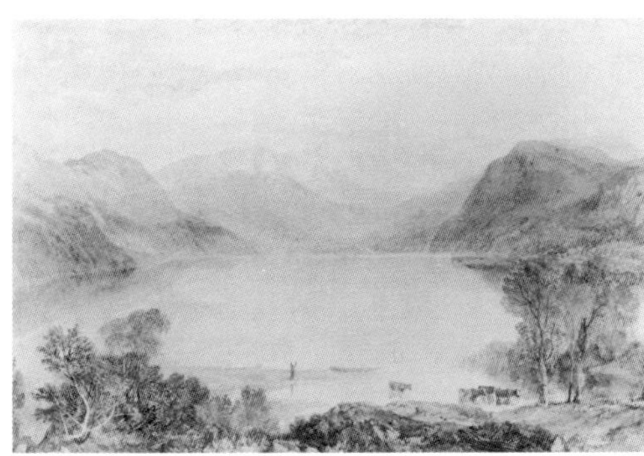

D.1887.14

**Ullswater Lake from Gowbarrow Park,
Cumberland**
1815
watercolour; watermark J WHATMAN / 1814
280 × 413 mm
Agnew's (purchase, 6.6.1891) (D.1887.14)

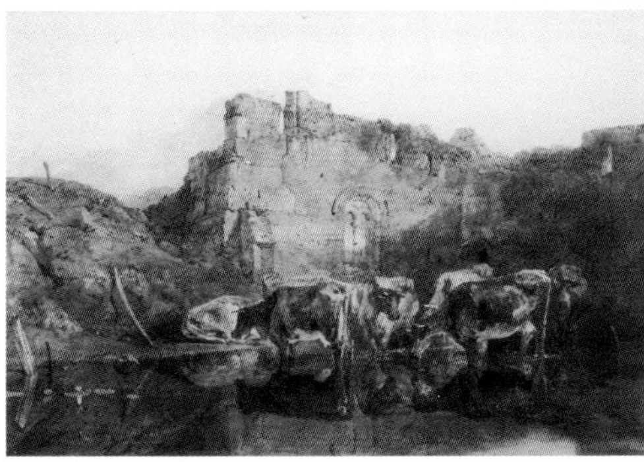

D.1887.15

The Abbey Pool
1800–1801
pencil, watercolour
signed: *WTurner*
514 × 762 mm
Agnew's (purchase, 5.5.1891) (D.1887.15)

**Moonlight on Lake Lucerne with the
Righi in the Distance, Switzerland**
1841
watercolour, bodycolour
230 × 307 mm
Wright, Thomas W. (purchase, 1891) (D.1887.16)

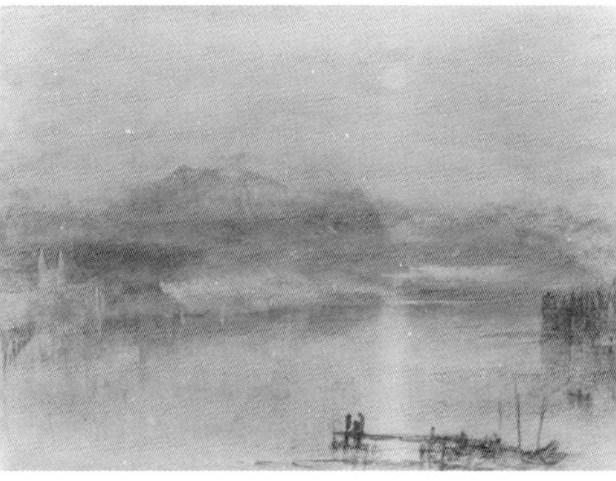

D.1887.16

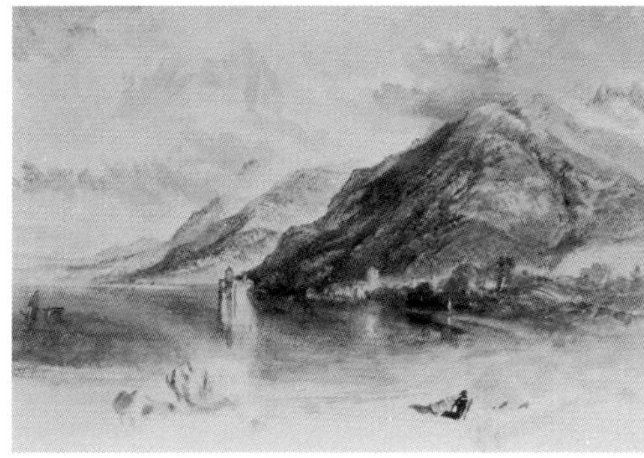

D.1887.17

**Chillon Castle, Lac Leman, Switzerland,
from Villeneuve**
1836
pencil, watercolour
236 × 325 mm
Agnew's (purchase, 12.5.1891) (D.1887.17)

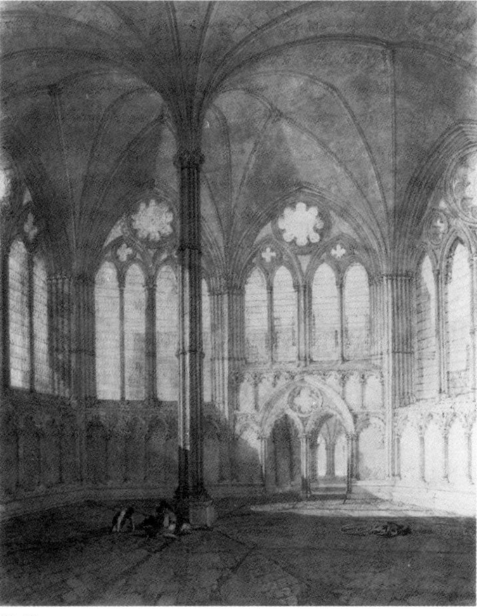

D.1889.3

**The Chapter House, Salisbury Cathedral,
Hampshire**
1799
pencil, pen and brown ink, watercolour
645 × 512 mm
Agnew, Sir William (gift, 1889) (D.1889.3)

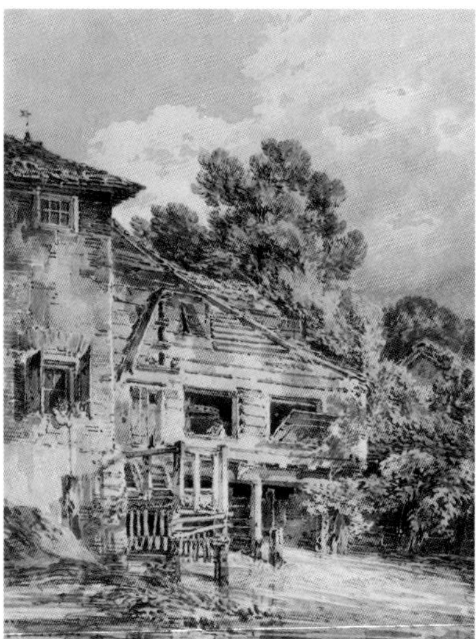

D.1892.87

The old Water Mill
1794
pencil, watercolour
signed lower right: *Turner*
252 × 189 mm
Taylor, John Edward (gift, 1892) (D.1892.87)

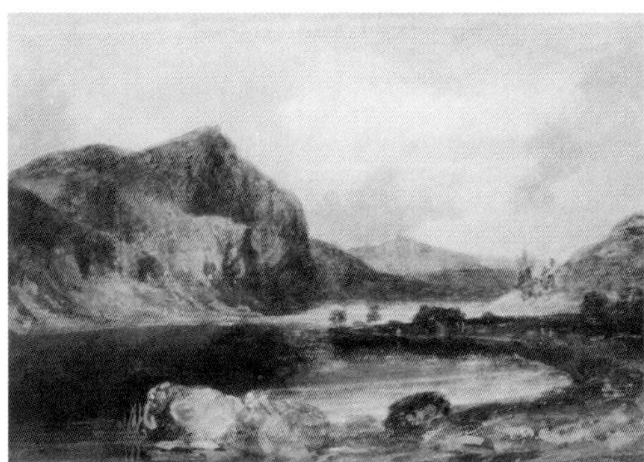

D.1892.88

Llyn Cwellyn, Caernarvonshire, Wales
1798
pencil, watercolour
255 × 362 mm
Taylor, John Edward (gift, 1892) (D.1892.88)

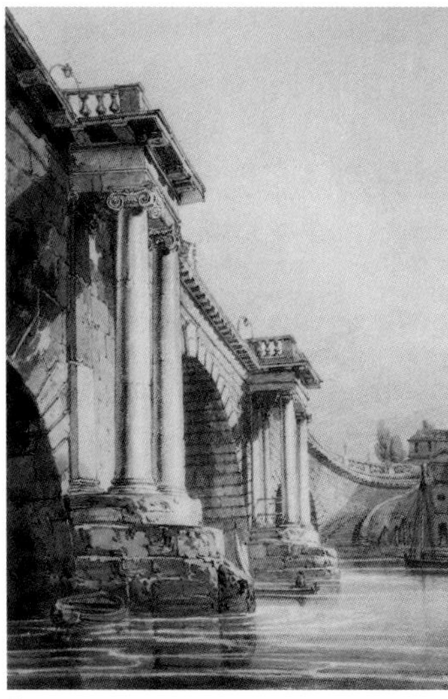

D.1892.89

Old Blackfriars Bridge, London
1795
pencil, watercolour
262 × 171 mm
Taylor, John Edward (gift, 1892) (D.1892.89)

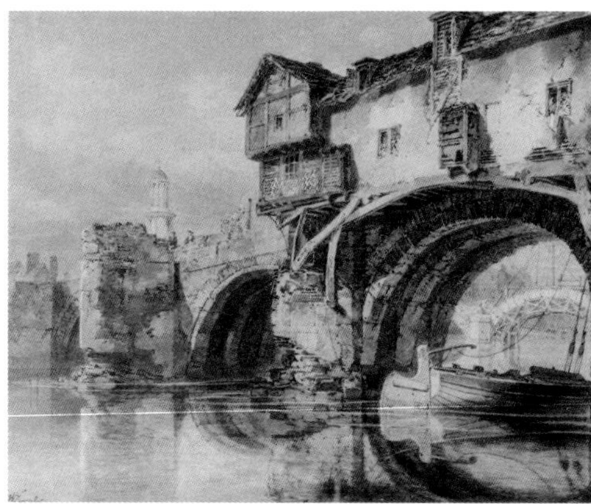

D.1892.90

Old Welsh Bridge, Shrewsbury, Shropshire
1794
pencil, watercolour
signed & dated lower left: *WTurner / 1794*
224 × 274 mm
Taylor, John Edward (gift, 1892) (D.1892.90)

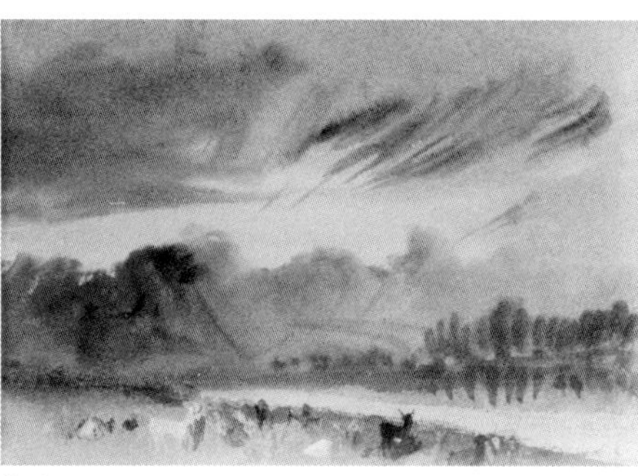

D.1892.91

Deer in Petworth Park, Sussex
1827
watercolour, bodycolour; blue paper
140 × 194 mm
Taylor, John Edward (gift, 1892) (D.1892.91)

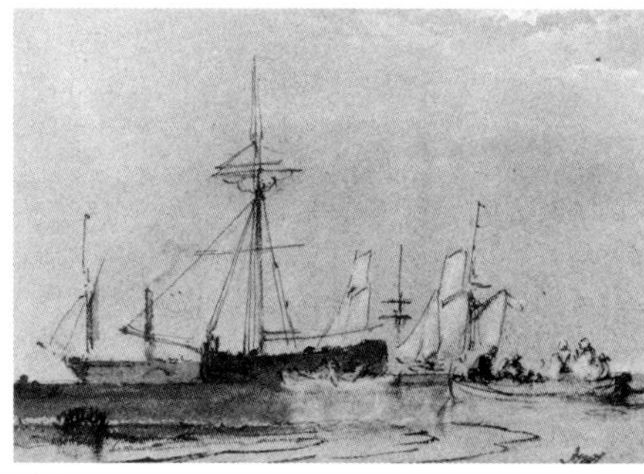

D.1892.92

Study of Boats
1828–30
pen and brown ink, brown watercolour, bodycolour
(heightened with white); blue paper
signed lower right with initials: *JMWT*
130 × 182 mm
Taylor, John Edward (gift, 1892) (D.1892.92)

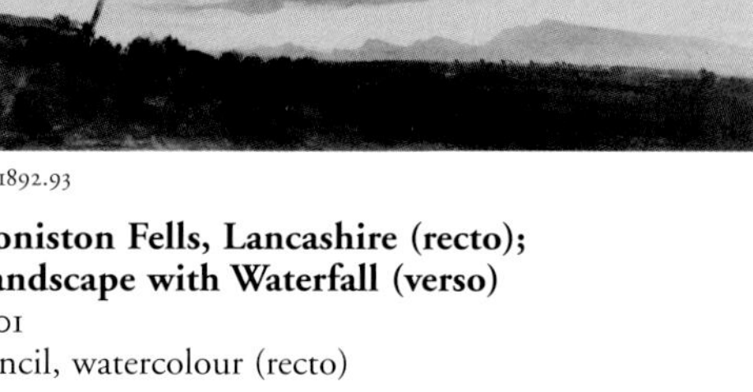

D.1892.93

**Coniston Fells, Lancashire (recto);
Landscape with Waterfall (verso)**
1801
pencil, watercolour (recto)
251 × 412 mm
Taylor, John Edward (gift, 1892) (D.1892.93)

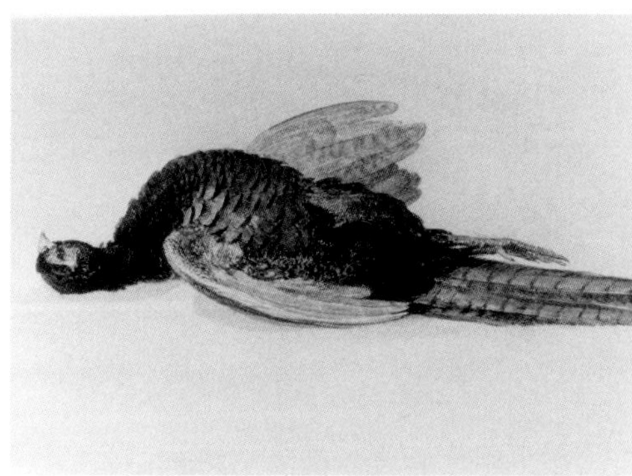

D.1892.94

Dead Pheasant
1815–18
pencil, watercolour
282 × 377 mm
Taylor, John Edward (gift, 1892) (D.1892.94)

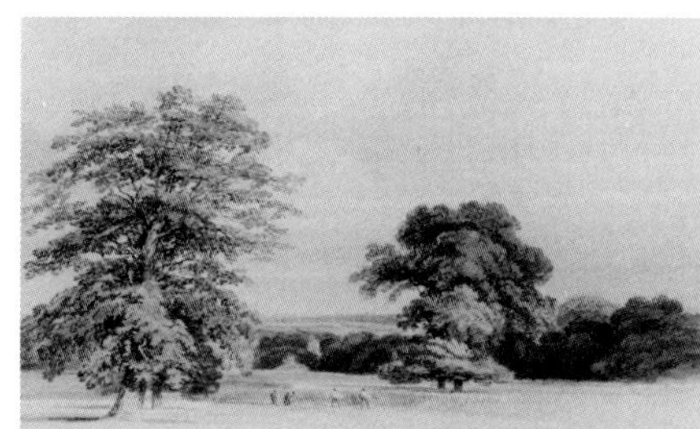

D.1892.95

A View in Kent
1795–96
pencil, watercolour
222 × 359 mm
Taylor, John Edward (gift, 1892) (D.1892.95)

**View of Hampton Court, Herefordshire,
from the North West**
1795–96
pencil, watercolour
320 × 425 mm
Taylor, John Edward (gift, 1892) (D.1892.96)

Autumn Morning near Fonthill, Wiltshire
1799
pencil, watercolour
321 × 462 mm
Taylor, John Edward (gift, 1892) (D.1892.97)

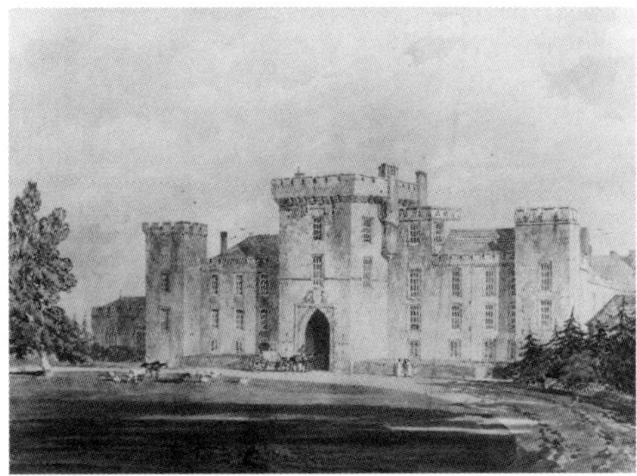

D.1892.96

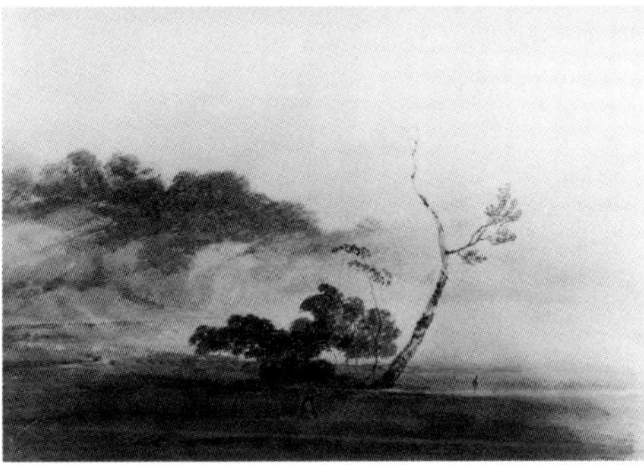

D.1892.97

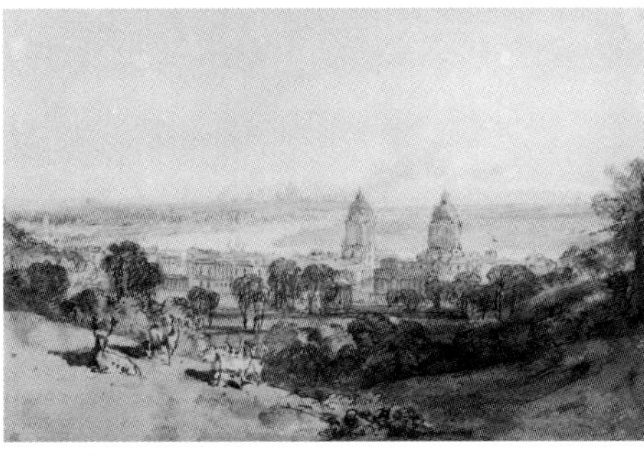

D.1892.98

**View of London from behind
Greenwich Hospital**
pencil, pen and brown ink, brown watercolour;
watermark [JWHA]TMAN / [18]01
181 × 263 mm
Taylor, John Edward (gift, 1892) (D.1892.98)

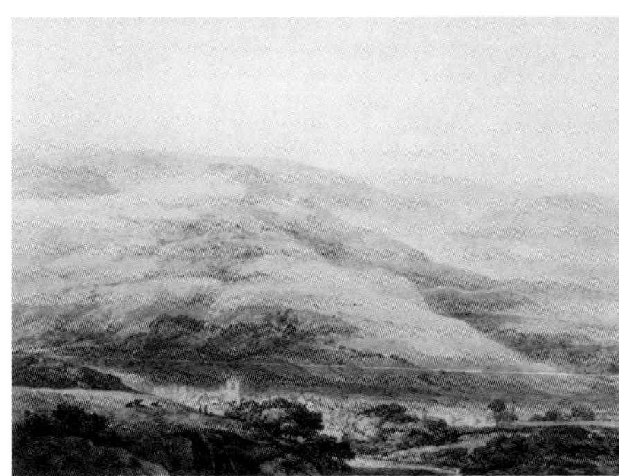

D.1892.99

Llangollen, Denbighshire, Wales
1794
pencil, watercolour
signed lower left: *W Turner*
202 × 263 mm
Taylor, John Edward (gift, 1892) (D.1892.99)

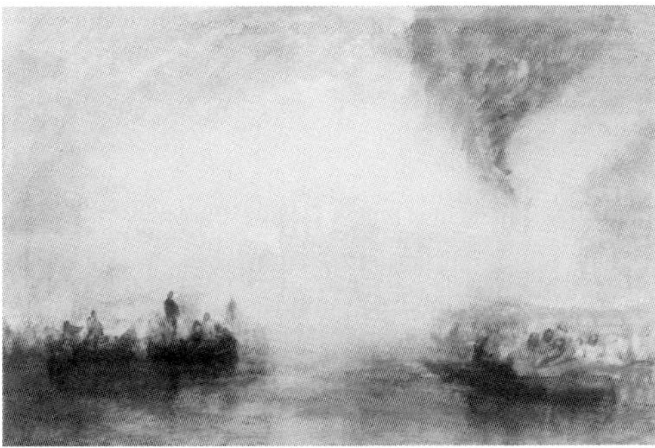

D.1892.100

**Fire at Fennings Wharf, on the Thames
at Bermondsey**
1836
pencil, watercolour
294 × 441 mm
Taylor, John Edward (gift, 1892) (D.1892.100)

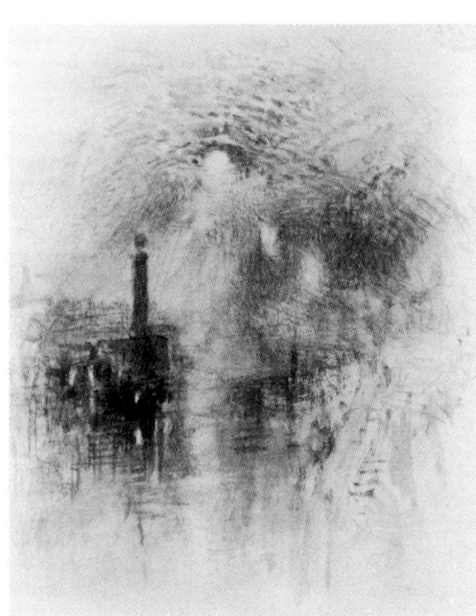

D.1892.101

Vignette Study of a Lighthouse
1833–35
pencil, watercolour; card (embossed with a crown) and
EXTRA / SUPERFINE / DRAWING / BOARD
198 × 155 mm
Taylor, John Edward (gift, 1892) (D.1892.101)

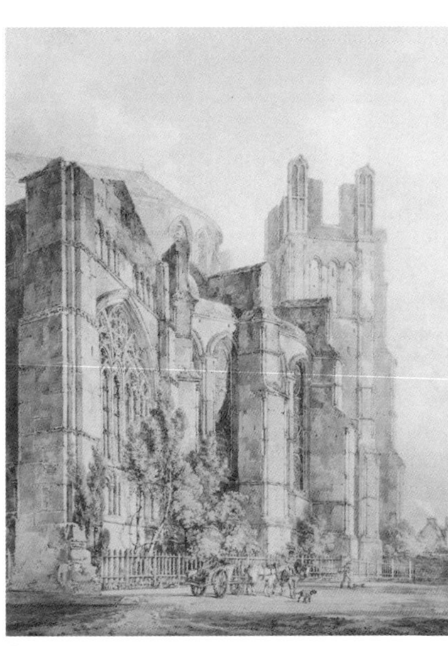

D.1892.113

**St Anselm's Chapel, Canterbury Cathedral,
with Part of Thomas-a-Becket's Crown**
1794
pencil, watercolour
signed & dated lower right; last digit
trimmed: *Turner 179-*
517 × 374 mm
Taylor, John Edward (gift, 1892) (D.1892.113)

D.1892.114

**Venice: San Giorgio Maggiore from the
Entrance to the Grand Canal**
watercolour
inscribed on verso: artist's illegible handwriting
195 × 276 mm
Taylor, John Edward (gift, 1892) (D.1892.114)

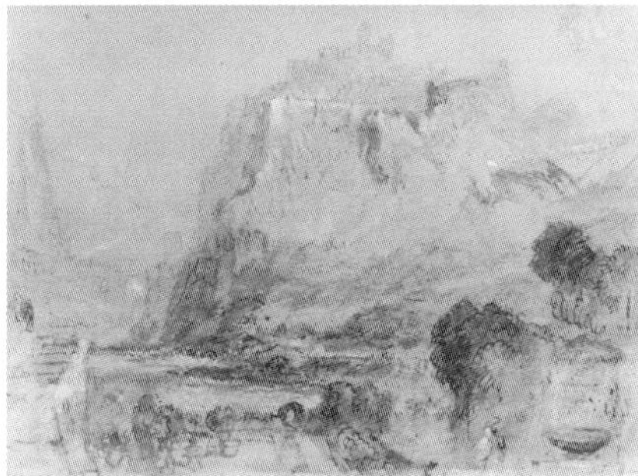

D.1892.115

Sisteron, France
1836
pen and brown ink, watercolour, bodycolour
(heightened with white); buff paper
138 × 185 mm
Taylor, John Edward (gift, 1892) (D.1892.115)

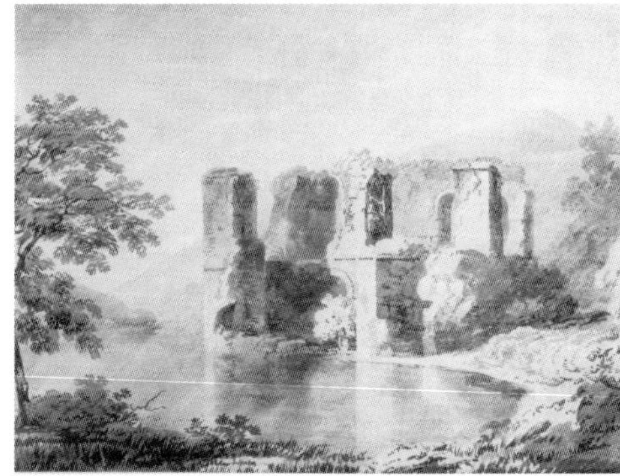

D.1892.132

The Temple of Apollo, Lake Avernus
1794–97
pencil, blue watercolour, grey watercolour
382 × 492 mm
Taylor, John Edward (gift, 1892) (D.1892.132)

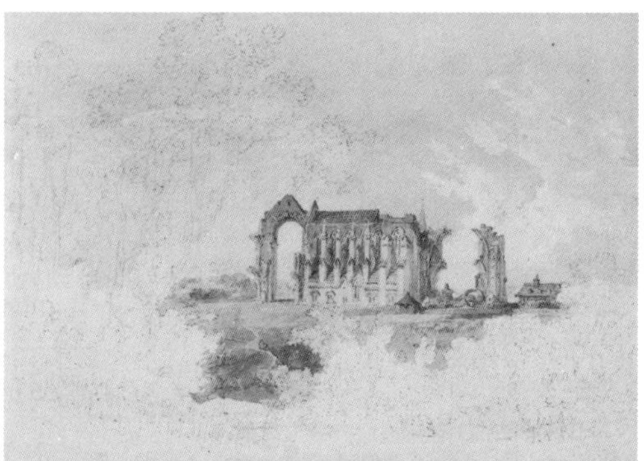

D.1894.2

North East View of Malmesbury Abbey, Wiltshire
1792
pencil, watercolour
inscribed lower right: *Malmsbury Abby* (sic)
186 × 257 mm
Lees, Charles E. (gift, 1894) (D.1894.2)

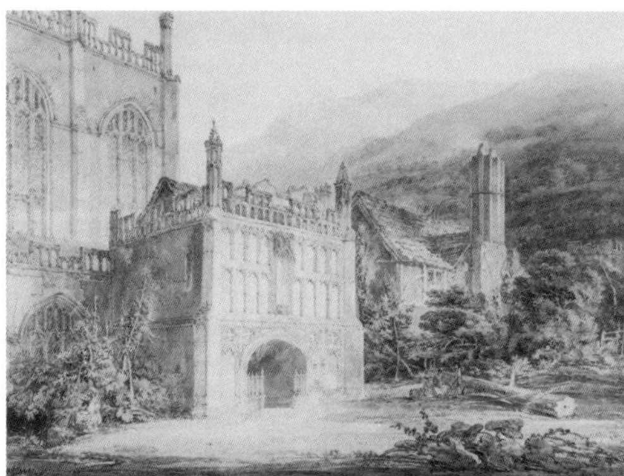

D.1904.10

The Porch of Great Malvern Priory, Worcestershire
1794
pencil, watercolour
signed lower right: *WTurner*
231 × 429 mm
Worthington, Mary (bequest, 1904) (D.1904.10)

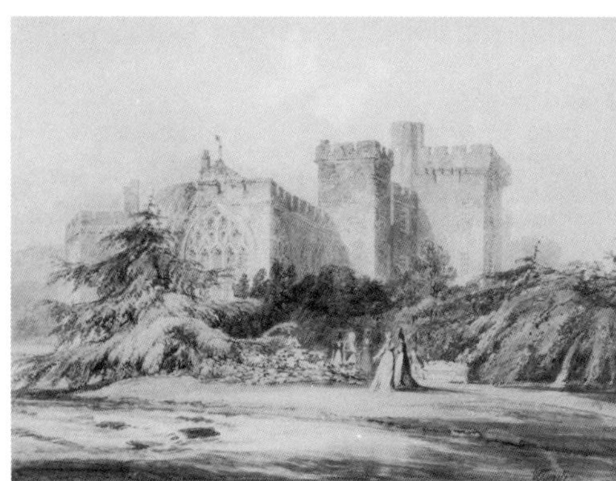

D.1904.11

The Chapel, Hampton Court, Herefordshire
1795–96
pencil, watercolour
signed: *WTurner*
318 × 424 mm
Worthington, Mary (bequest, 1904) (D.1904.11)

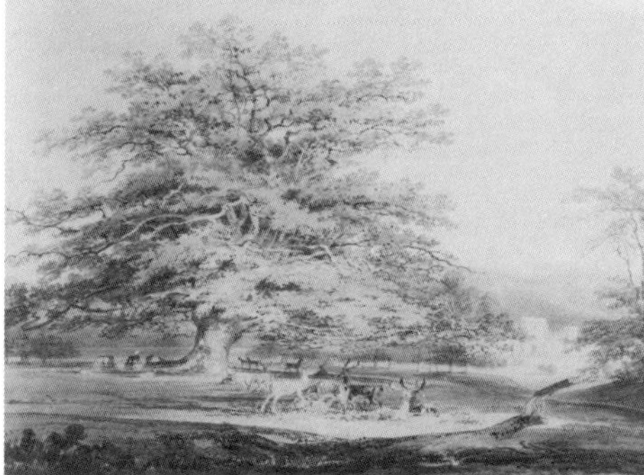

D.1904.12

Oak Tree, Hampton Court, Herefordshire
1795
watercolour
309 × 419 mm
Worthington, Mary (bequest, 1904) (D.1904.12)

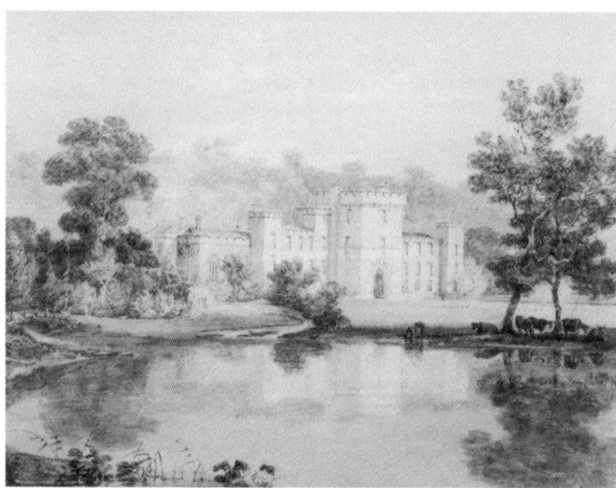

D.1904.13

View of Hampton Court, Herefordshire, from the North East
1798–99
pencil, watercolour
356 × 470 mm
Worthington, Mary (bequest, 1904) (D.1904.13)

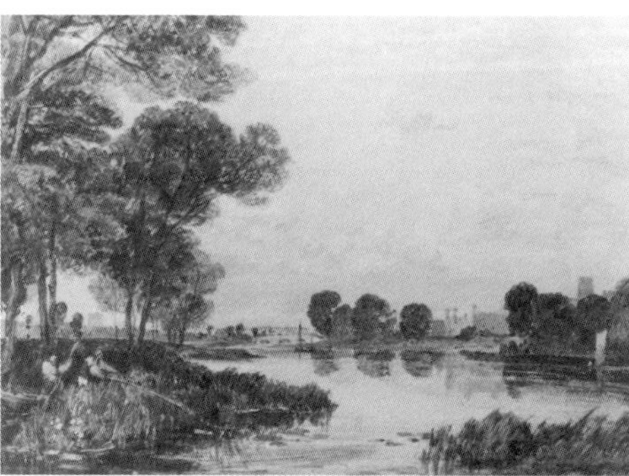

D.1904.14

Kew Palace from the Thames
1804–05
pencil, watercolour
252 × 350 mm
Worthington, Mary (bequest, 1904) (D.1904.14)

St Agatha's Abbey, Easby, Yorkshire, from the River Swale
1798–99
pencil, watercolour
630 × 890 mm
Worthington, Mary (bequest, 1904) (D.1904.18)

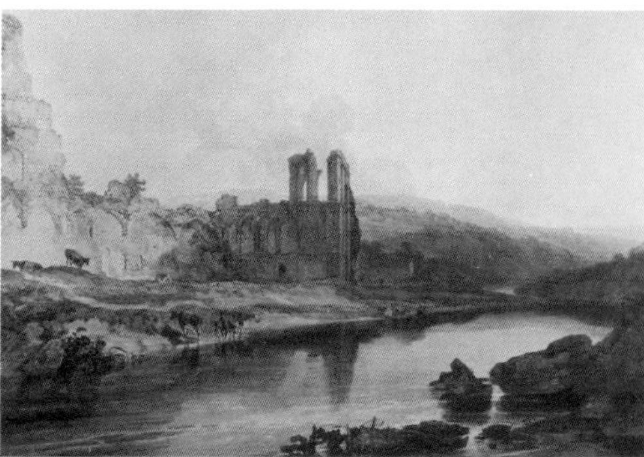

D.1904.18

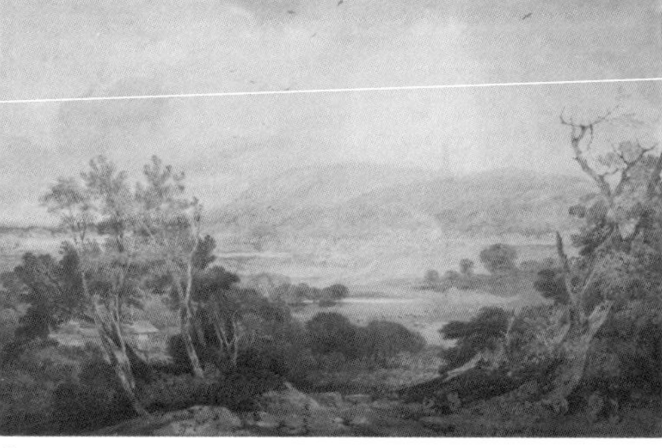

D.1904.19

North East View of Fonthill Abbey, Wiltshire: Sunset
1800
pencil, watercolour
696 × 1035 mm
Worthington, Mary (bequest, 1904) (D.1904.19)

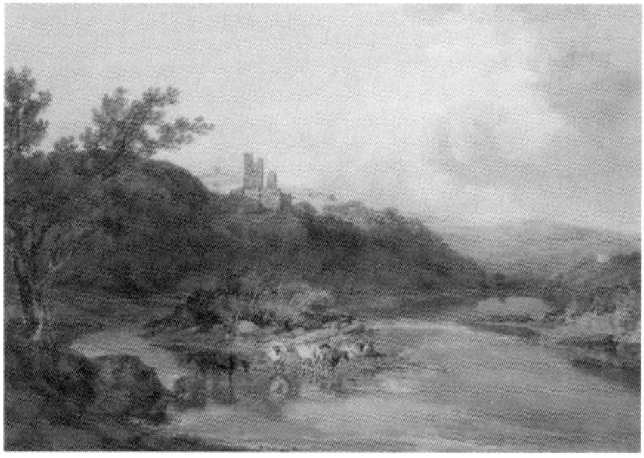

D.1904.20

A River Landscape with a Castle on a Hill
1798–99
pencil, watercolour
432 × 610 mm
Worthington, Mary (bequest, 1904) (D.1904.20)

The Neupfarrkirche, Regensburg, Germany
watercolour, bodycolour
240 × 305 mm
Allen, Arthur A. & Allen, C. P. & Allen, J. E. Taylor & Allen, Russell E. T. (in memory of John Edward Taylor) (gift, 1912) (D.1912.6)

Sunset on wet Sand
1845
pencil, watercolour
229 × 292 mm
Allen, Arthur A. & Allen, C. P. & Allen, J. E. Taylor & Allen, Russell E. T. (in memory of John Edward Taylor) (gift, 1912) (D.1912.7)

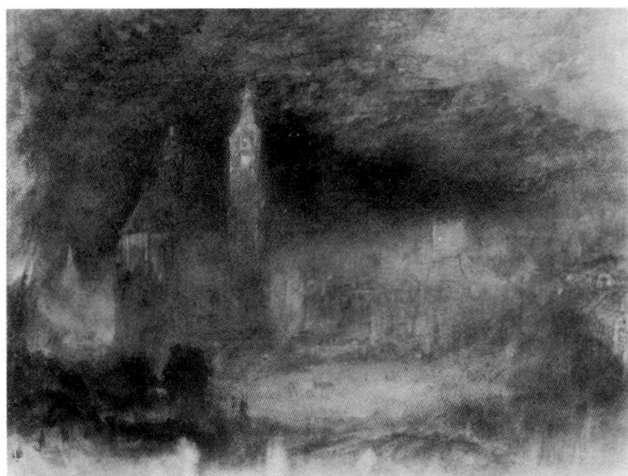

D.1912.6

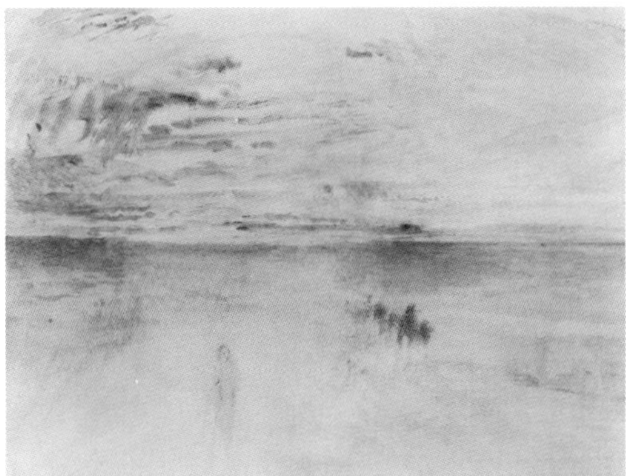

D.1912.7

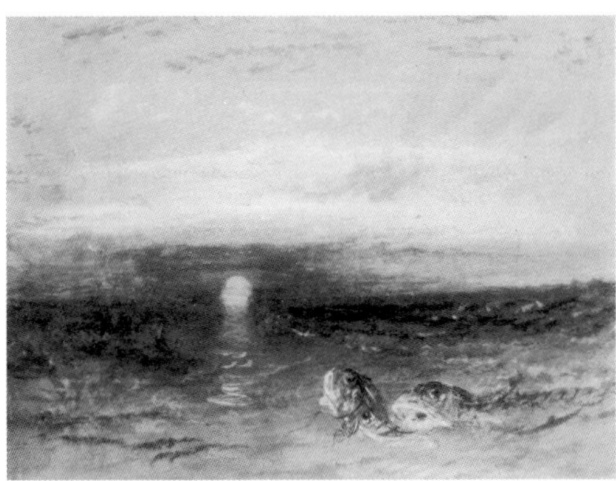

D.1912.8

Sunset at Sea with Gurnets

black chalk, watercolour, bodycolour; buff-grey paper
218 × 284 mm
Allen, Arthur A. & Allen, C. P. & Allen, J. E.Taylor & Allen,
Russell E. T. (in memory of John Edward Taylor) (gift, 1912)
(D.1912.8)

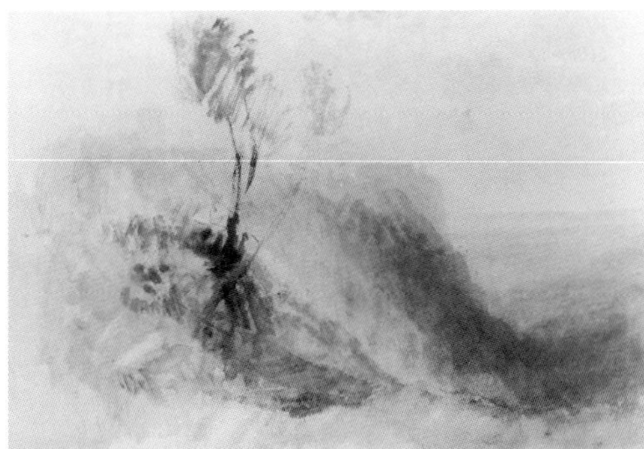

D.1922.31

'Tivoli': A Colour Beginning

1827–29
watercolour
303 × 436 mm
Cotswold Gallery, London (purchase, 1922) (D.1922.31)

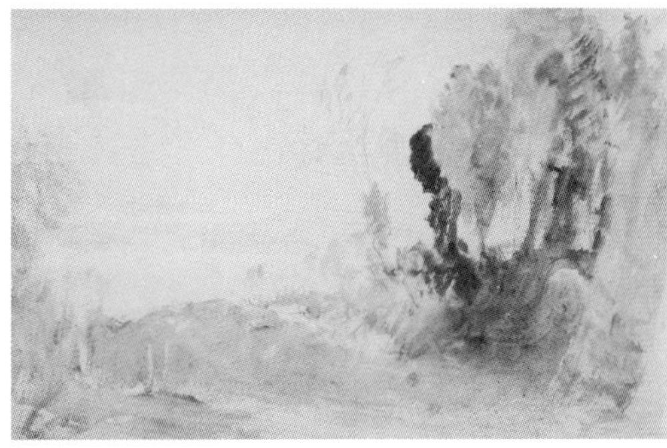

D.1922.45

'Loch Katrine': A Colour Beginning

1827–29
pencil, watercolour
303 × 457 mm
Anderson, A. E., National Art Collections Fund (via)
(gift, 1922) (D.1922.45)

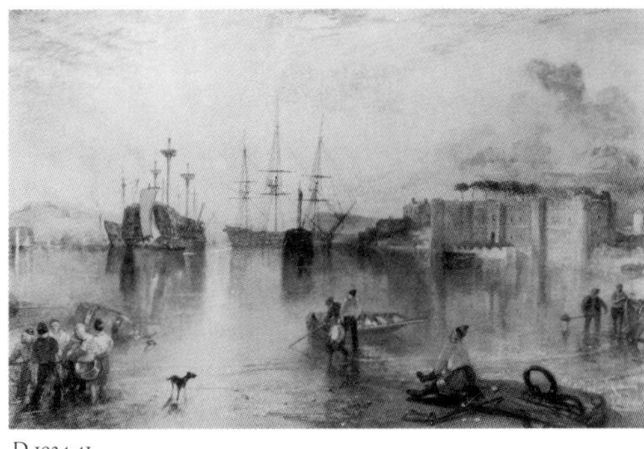

D.1924.41

Upnor Castle, Kent

1831–32
watercolour, bodycolour
290 × 437 mm
Broadhurst, Sir Edward Tootal, Broadhurst, Lady
(bequest, 1924) (D.1924.41)

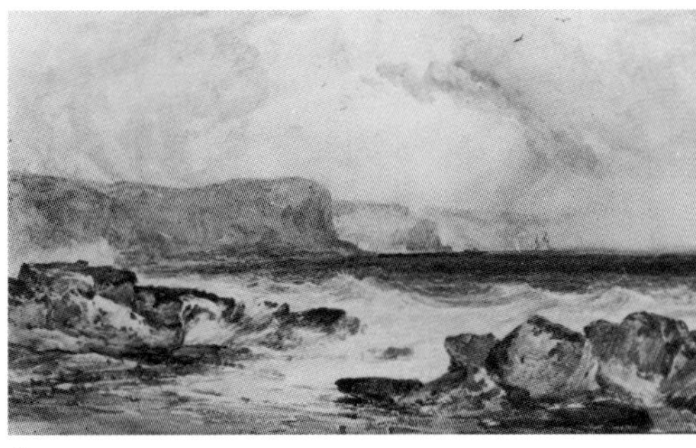

D.1924.52

Whitehaven from Parton, Cumberland

1810–15
pencil, watercolour; watermark JWHATMAN 1808
inscribed on verso: *Whitehaven from* [P]*arton / small*
[?*ships*]
218 × 353 mm
Broadhurst, Sir Edward Tootal, Broadhurst, Lady
(bequest, 1924) (D.1924.52)

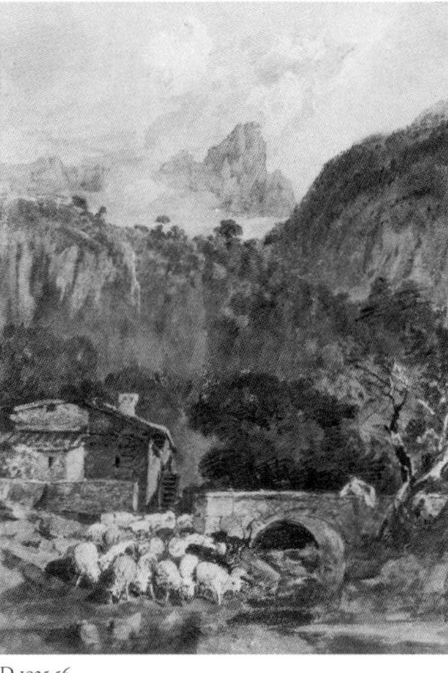

D.1925.56

The Aiguillette, Valley of Cluses, France

1802
pencil, black chalk, watercolour; paper (prepared grey)
477 × 322 mm
Agnew's (purchase, 1925) (D.1925.56)

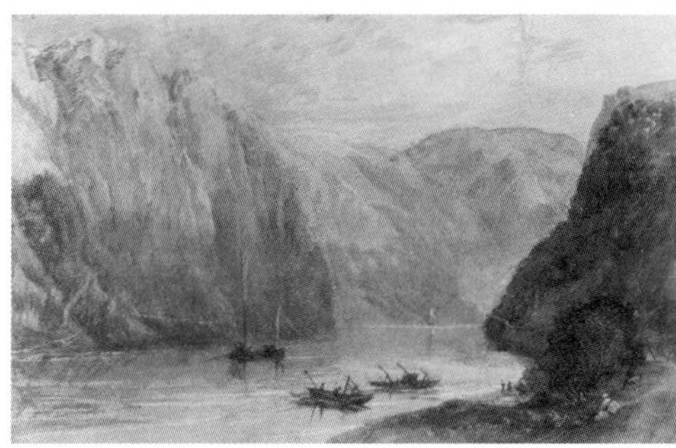

D.1925.57

The Lorelei, Germany (recto); Study of the Lorelei (verso)

1817
watercolour, bodycolour (recto)
197 × 305 mm
Agnew's (purchase, 1925) (D.1925.57)

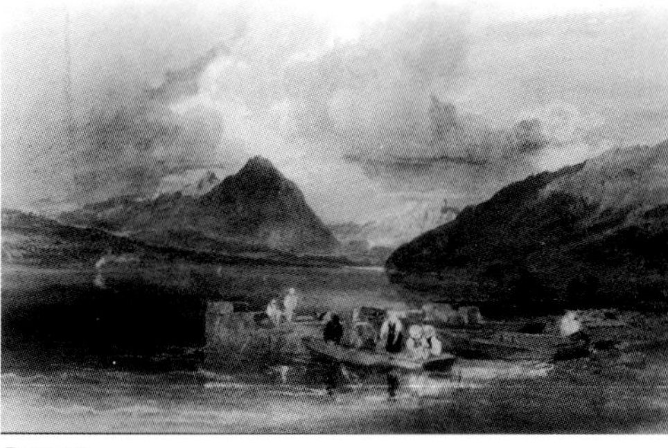

D.1925.58

Lake of Thun from the Landing-place at Neuhaus, Switzerland

1802
pencil, black chalk, watercolour; paper (prepared grey)
325 × 478 mm
Agnew's (purchase, 1925) (D.1925.58)

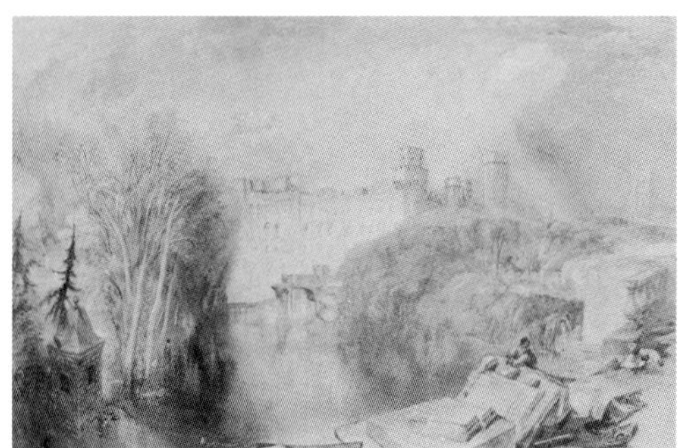

D.1937.22

Warwick Castle, Warwickshire
1830–31
watercolour, bodycolour
297 × 451 mm
Haworth, Jesse (bequest, 1937) (D.1937.22)

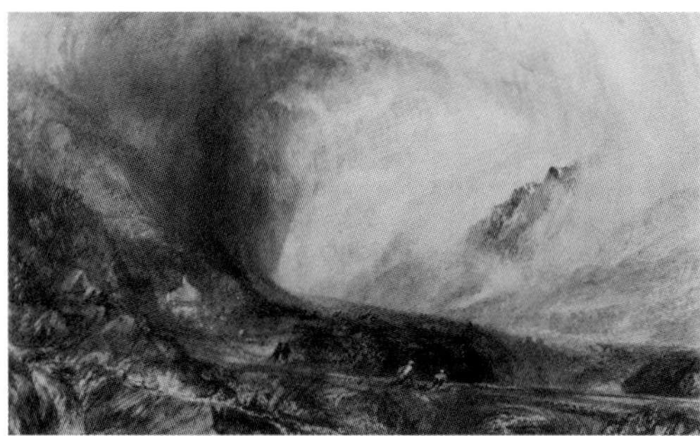

D.1937.23

Storm in the Pass of St Gotthard, Switzerland
1845
watercolour
290 × 470 mm
Haworth, Jesse (bequest, 1937) (D.1937.23)

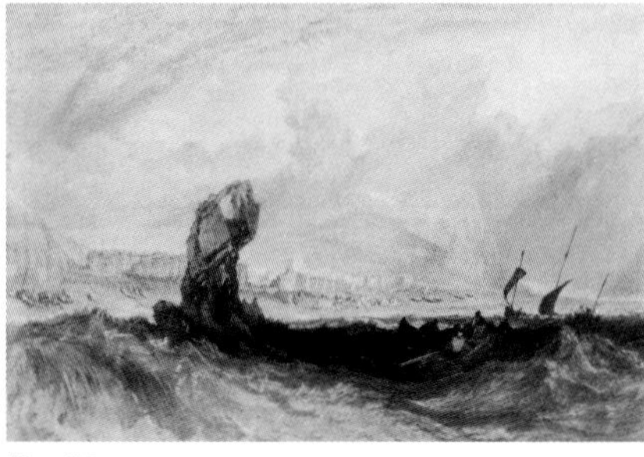

D.1948.8

Sidmouth, Devon
1825–27
watercolour
184 × 263 mm
Nettlefold, F. J. (gift, 1948) (D.1948.8)

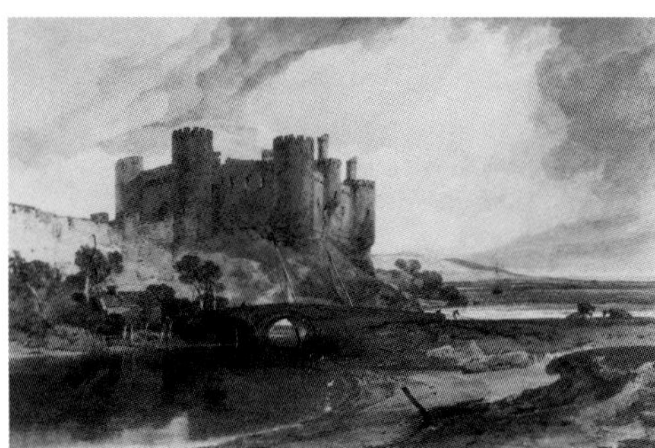

D.1948.18

Conway Castle, Caernarvonshire, Wales
1801–02
pencil, watercolour
signed lower right with initials: *JMWT RA*
427 × 629 mm
Kessler, P. W. (Mrs) (the daughters of) (gift, 1948) (D.1948.18)

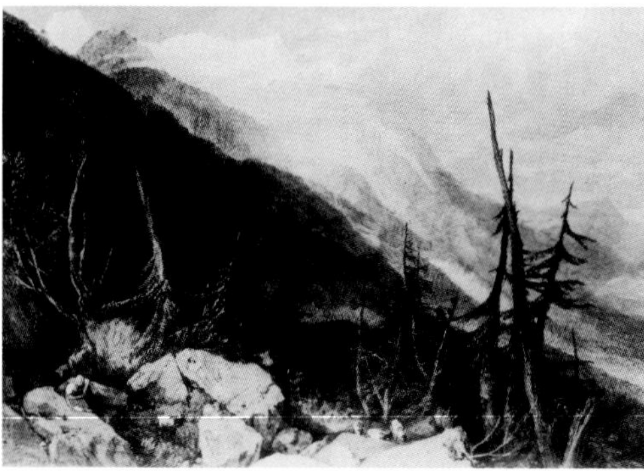

D.1955.18

Valley of Chamonix, Switzerland, Mont Blanc in the Distance
1809
watercolour, bodycolour
signed & dated lower left: *JMWTurner RA pp*
279 × 395 mm
Cook, E. E. (executors of), National Art Collections Fund (via) (gift, 1955) (D.1955.18)

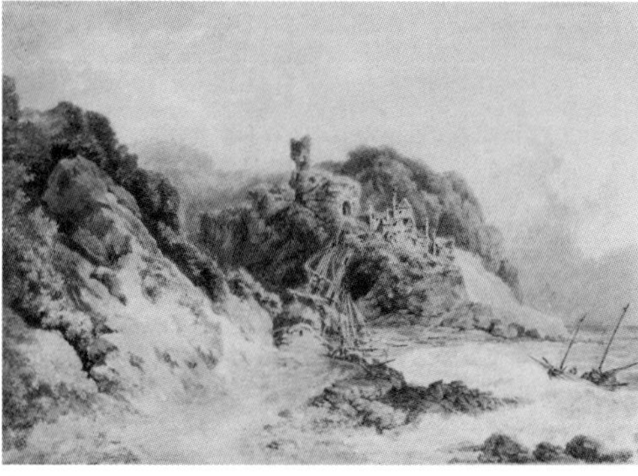

D.1970.54

A Shipwreck on a rocky Coastline with a ruined Castle
1792–93
pencil, watercolour
169 × 236 mm
Towlson, Hector J. (bequest, 1969) (D.1970.54)

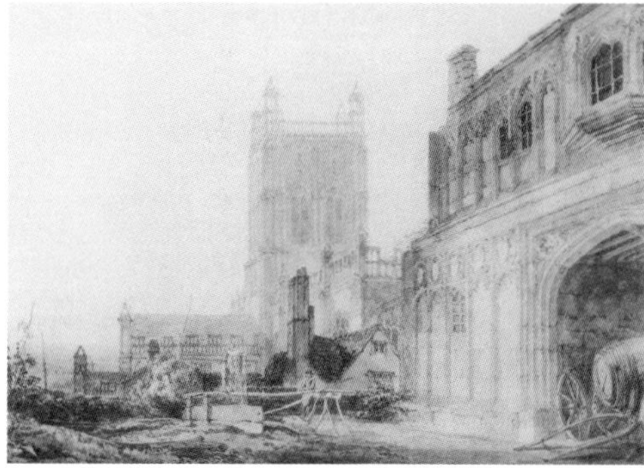

D.1984.2

Great Malvern Abbey and Gatehouse, Worcestershire, from the North West
1794
pencil, watercolour
305 × 414 mm
Winter, Theodora (in memory of her father, Sir Thomas Barlow) (gift, 1984) (D.1984.2)

■ **TURNER, JOSEPH MALLORD WILLIAM and GIRTIN, THOMAS**

Convents, near Capo di Monte, Naples
1794–97
pencil, blue watercolour, grey watercolour
177 × 417 mm
Langton, Miss F. M., National Art Collections Fund (via) (bequest, 1963) (D.1963.1)

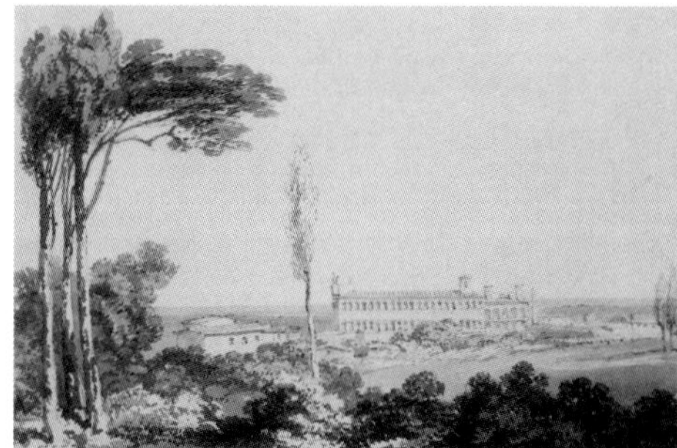

D.1963.2

Villa Negroni, Rome
1794–97
pencil, blue watercolour, grey watercolour
271 × 384 mm
Langton, Miss F. M., National Art Collections Fund (via) (bequest, 1963) (D.1963.2)

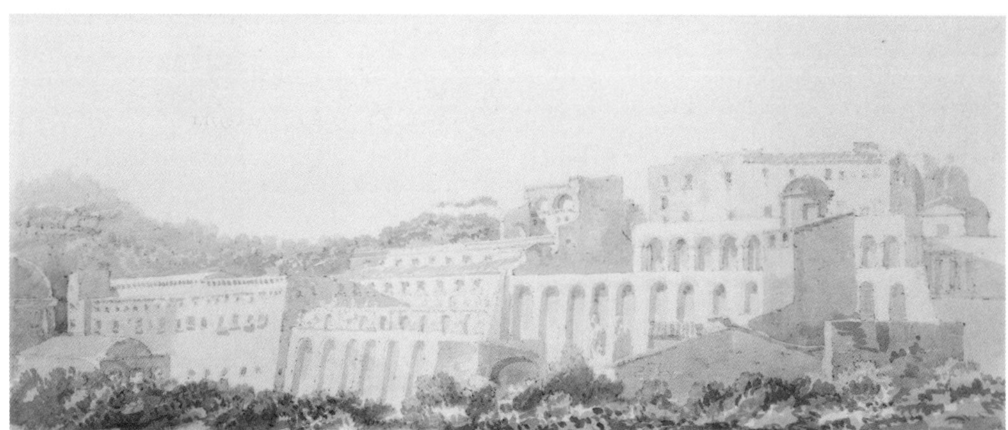

D.1963.1

■ TURNER, WILLIAM (1789–1862)

William Turner became a pupil of John Varley in
about 1804 and was elected a member of the Old
Watercolour Society in 1808. In about 1812 Turner
decided to base himself in Oxford, where he remained
for the rest of his life and where he had a teaching
practice. He made many sketching tours round Britain,
visiting the Lake District in 1814, Wales in 1817 and
the Peak District in 1818; he made an extensive tour
of Soctland in 1838. Turner was a regular exhibitor at
the Old Watercolour Society.

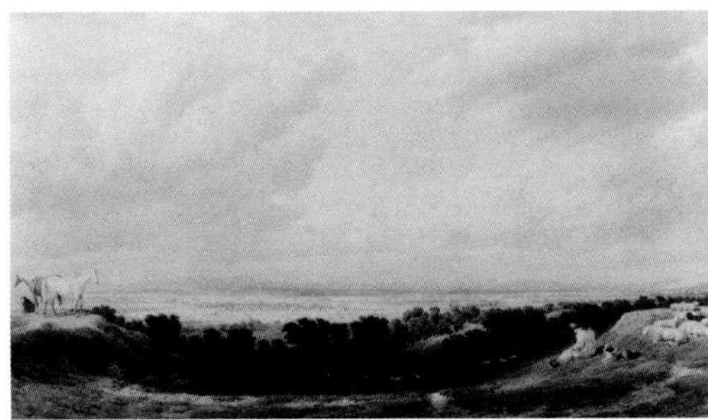

D.1894.4

The Vale of Gloucester, from Robin Hood's Hill
1846
watercolour
signed, inscribed & dated verso: *The Vale of Gloucester
from Robin Hood's Hill / W Turner / Oxford 1846*
608 × 1103 mm
Lees, Charles E. (gift, 1894) (D.1894.4)

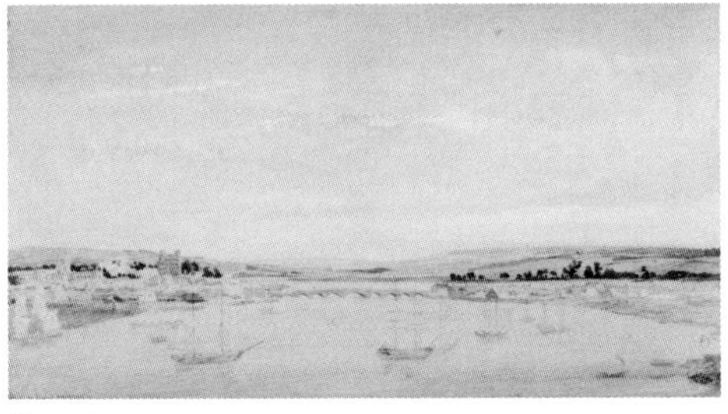

D.1947.9

Rochester, Kent, from the River Medway
17.7.1835
pencil, watercolour, bodycolour
(heightened with white)
signed & dated lower left with initials: *W T 17 July/35*
211 × 370 mm
Barlow, Sir Thomas (gift, 1947) (D.1947.9)

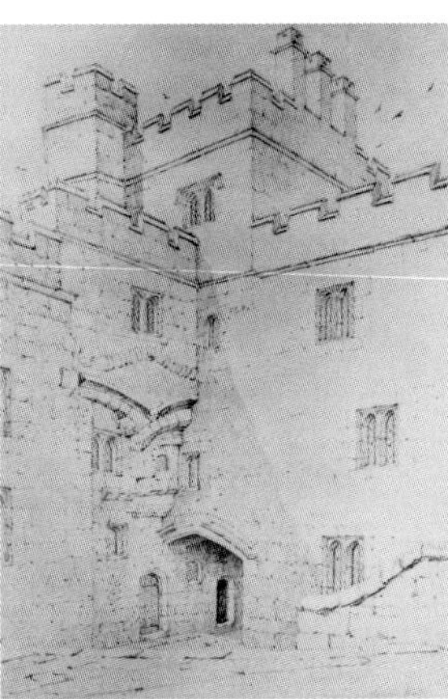

D.1969.12

Upper Courtyard, Haddon Hall, Derbyshire
pencil
371 × 243 mm
Lockett, G. Derek (gift, 1969) (D.1969.12)

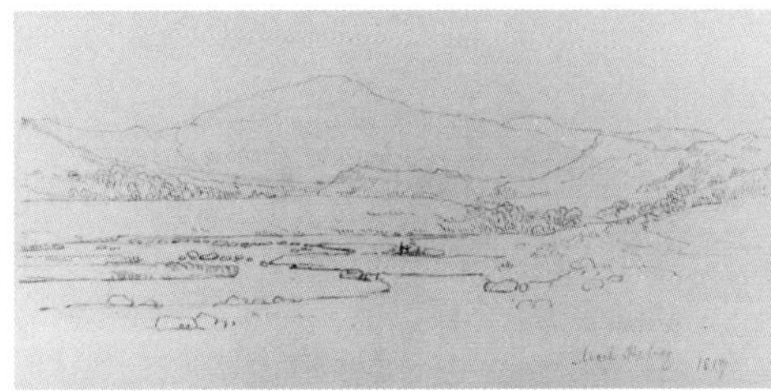

D.1971.8

Moel Hebog, Caernarvonshire, Wales
1817
pencil, pen and brown ink
inscribed & dated lower right: *Moel Hebog / 1817*
113 × 229 mm
Lockett, G. Derek (gift, 1971) (D.1971.8)

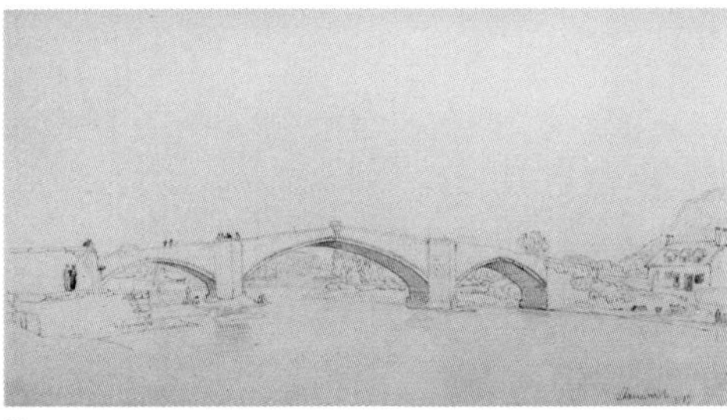

D.1971.9

The Bridge at Llanrwst, Denbighshire, Wales
1817
pencil, brown watercolour
inscribed & dated lower right: *Llanwirt* (sic) / *1817*
198 × 359 mm
Lockett, G. Derek (gift, 1971) (D.1971.9)

Stream with Cottage, near Beddgelert, Caernarvonshire, Wales
1817
pencil, pen and brown ink
inscribed lower left: *Near Beddgelart* (sic) / *N W*
214 × 355 mm
Lockett, G. Derek (gift, 1971) (D.1971.10)

Rhayadr Du, near Tan-y-Bwlch, Merioneth, Wales
1817
pencil, bodycolour (heightened with white)
brown paper
signed & inscribed lower left with initials: *Rhaidyr Du /
nr. Tan y Bwlch. N.Wales / W.T. / Oxfd.*; inscribed lower
right on verso: *Rhaydy Du, near Tan y Bwlch*
227 × 317 mm
Lockett, G. Derek (gift, 1971) (D.1971.11)

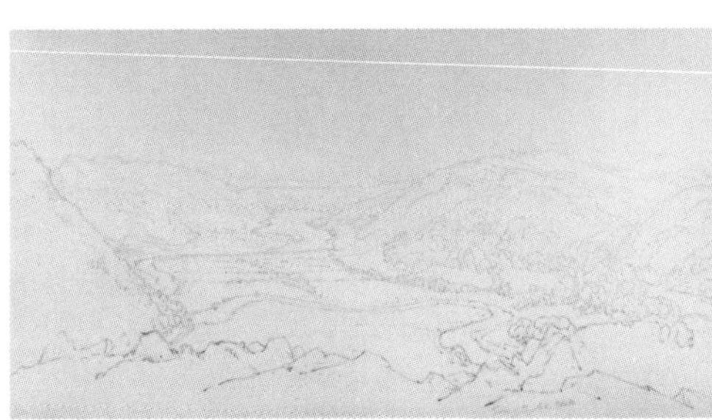

D.1971.12

View near Tan-y-Bwlch, Merioneth, Wales
1817
pencil
inscribed lower right: *Tan y Bwlch Vall*
[last word erased]
212 × 377 mm
Lockett, G. Derek (gift, 1971) (D.1971.12)

Pont-y-Pair, Bettws-y-Coed, Caernarvonshire, Wales
1817
pencil
inscribed lower left: *PontyParr*
223 × 326 mm
Lockett, G. Derek (gift, 1971) (D.1971.13)

Gorge near Castleton, Derbyshire
1818
pencil, pen and brown ink
inscribed & dated lower right: *Castleton / 1818*
289 × 228 mm
Lockett, G. Derek (gift, 1971) (D.1971.14)

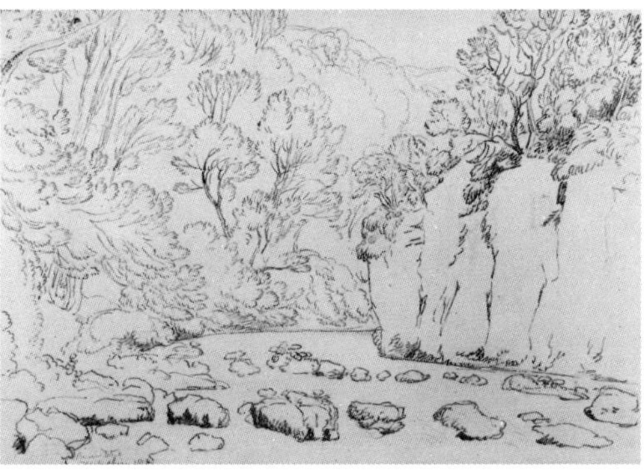

D.1971.15

The River Wye, Derbyshire
1818
black chalk, pen and brown ink; buff paper
inscribed & dated lower left: *River Wye /
Derbyshire 1818*
191 × 272 mm
Lockett, G. Derek (gift, 1971) (D.1971.15)

Dove Dale, Derbyshire
1818
pencil, pen and brown ink
inscribed & dated lower right: *Dove Dale / 1818*
326 × 264 mm
Lockett, G. Derek (gift, 1971) (D.1971.16)

■ UNDERWOOD, THOMAS RICHARD (1772–1835)

Underwood was a draughtsman who was part of the
Monro Academy in the 1790s and one of the founder
members of Girtin's sketching club The Brothers.
Apparently of private means, Underwood spent the
latter part of his life in France. His work is sometimes
mistaken for Thomas Malton, Jnr.

The Great Hall, Eltham Palace, Greenwich, London
pencil, grey watercolour
213 × 167 mm
Ogden, William Sharp (bequest, 1926) (D.1926.232)

■ UNDERWOOD, THOMAS RICHARD (attributed to) (1772–1835)

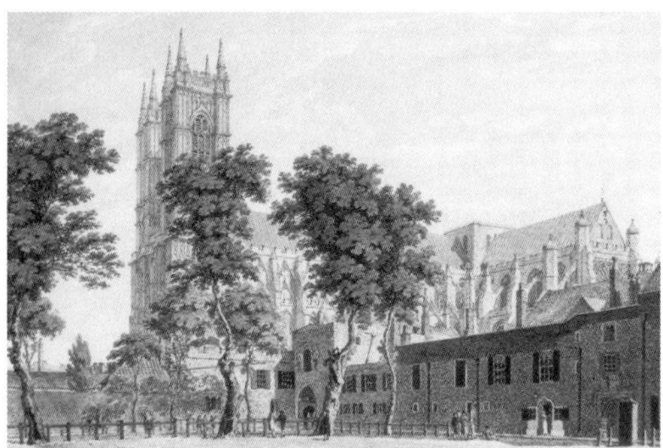

D.1900.17

Westminster Abbey, London, from the Dean's Yard
pen and grey ink, pen and brown ink, watercolour
253 × 353 mm
Worthington, Mary (gift, 1900) (D.1900.17)

■ UWINS, THOMAS (1782–1857)
Uwins studied at the Royal Academy Schools and began to exhibit at the Old Watercolour Society in 1809, becoming a member in 1810. Having resigned his membership in 1818, Uwins went to Italy in 1824, remaining there until 1831. Much of his later work is in oil and he was elected a member of the Royal Academy in 1838.

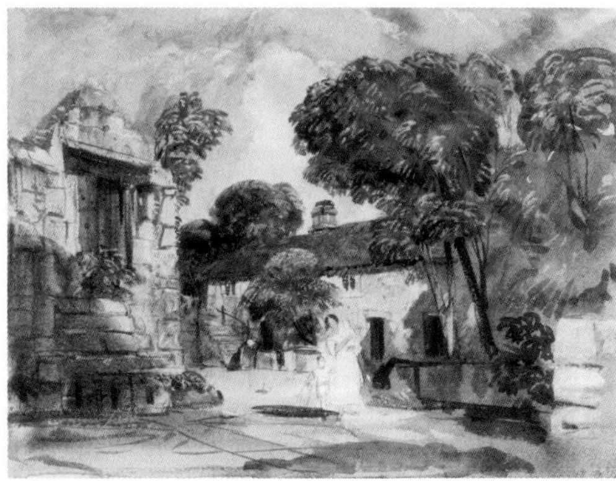

D.1943.8

Landscape with Buildings and Figures
pencil, watercolour
228 × 288 mm
Colnaghi's (purchase, 1943) (D.1943.8)

■ VAN ASSEN, BENEDICTUS ANTONIO (fl. 1788–1817)
An engraver and draughtsman who exhibited portraits and literary subjects at the Royal Academy from London addresses between 1788 and 1804.

Nude Man holding a Stick
pencil, pen and grey ink, brown watercolour
signed lower left: *A. Van Assen delt.*
160 × 130 mm
University of Manchester, History of Art Department
(transfer, 1960) (D.1960.165)

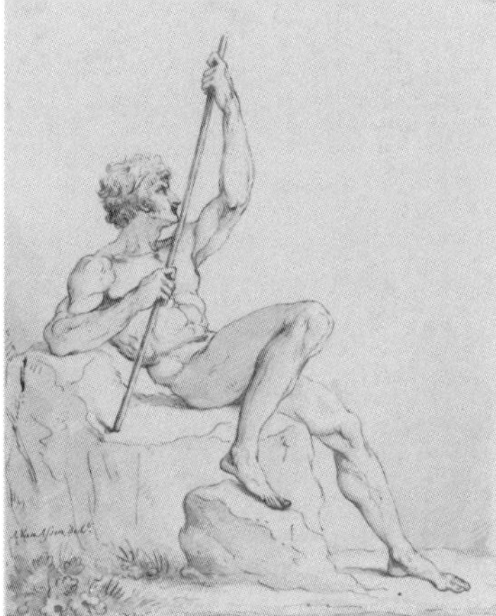

D.1960.165

■ VANDERBANK, JOHN (1694–1739)
A history and portrait painter and book illustrator, Vanderbank studied at Kneller's Academy in 1711. He founded his own Academy in St Martin's Lane in 1720 with Louis Chéron and had a busy portrait-painting practice.

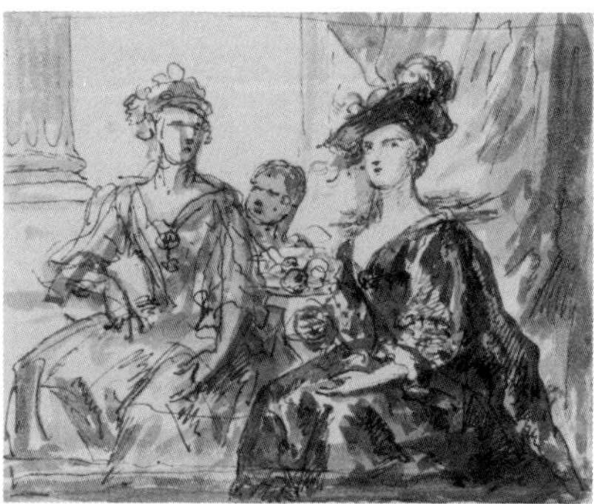

D.1957.12

Two seated Women
pen and brown ink, grey watercolour
110 × 139 mm
Friends of the Whitworth (gift, 1957) (D.1957.12)

Study for a full-length Portrait of a Girl
pen and brown ink, brown watercolour, bodycolour (heightened with white)
119 × 79 mm
University of Manchester, History of Art Department
(transfer, 1960) (D.1960.67)

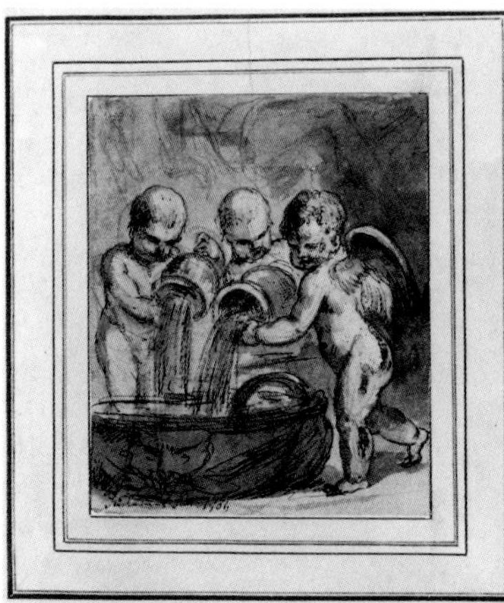

D.1960.141

Three Putti filling a Basin
1731
pencil, pen and brown ink, brown watercolour, bodycolour (heightened with white)
signed & dated lower left; surname illegible:
Jno. Vanderbank Fecit. 1731.
135 × 111 mm
University of Manchester, History of Art Department
(transfer, 1960) (D.1960.141)

■ VARLEY, CORNELIUS (1781–1873)
Cornelius Varley, the younger brother of John, was brought up by his uncle Samuel, an instrument and watchmaker. Varley combined the practice of watercolour painting with an interest in science and instruments. He visited Wales in 1802 and 1803 and the following year was a founder member of the Old Watercolour Society. In 1809 he invented the drawing device the Graphic Telescope, which he patented in 1811. Having resigned from the Old Watercolour Society in 1820, Varley devoted his time to scientific interests but exhibited intermittently at the Royal Academy until 1859.

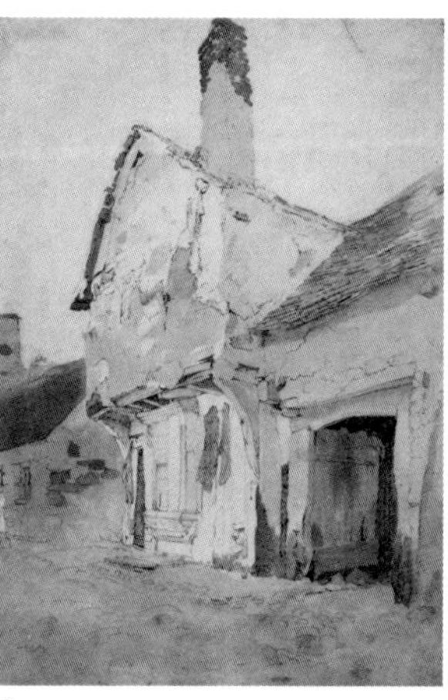

D.1927.154

A derelict House, Caernarvon, Caernarvonshire, Wales
1802
pencil, watercolour
signed, inscribed & numbered lower right verso:
Carnarvon C Varley 20 / 1802
347 × 236 mm
Holliday, J. R. (bequest, 1927) (D.1927.154)

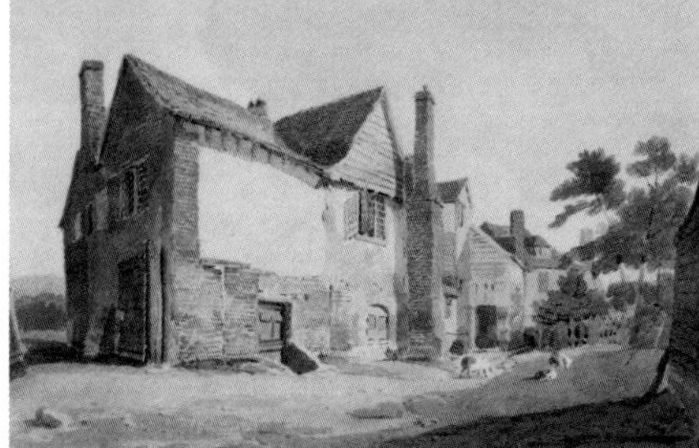

D.1954.21

Farmhouse with Pigs
1803
watercolour
dated centre upper edge verso upside down: *1803*
230 × 348 mm
Friends of the Whitworth (gift, 1954) (D.1954.21)

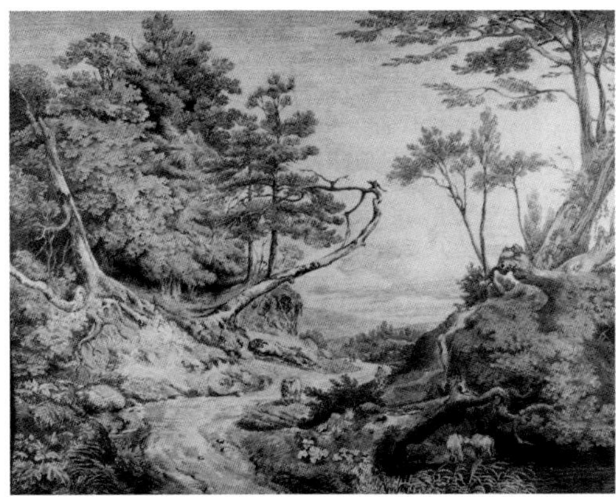

D.1970.76

A wooded Road with Cattle

1803
pencil, grey watercolour
signed & dated lower centre: *Corn Varley 1803*
282 × 357 mm
Towlson, Hector J. (bequest, 1969) (D.1970.76)

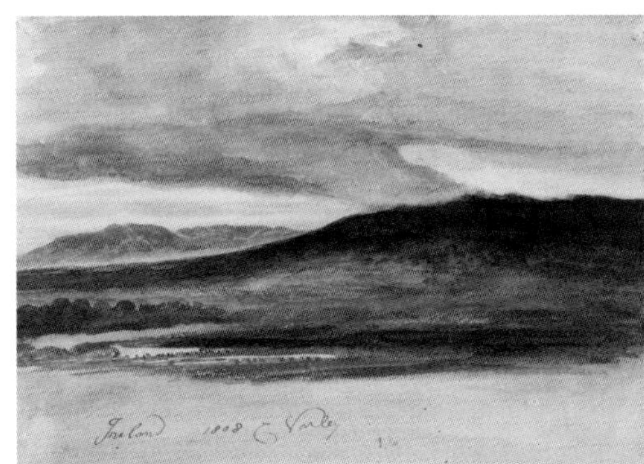

D.1973.4

Mountain Landscape, Ireland (recto); Study of Clouds (verso)

1808
watercolour
signed, inscribed & dated lower left:
Ireland 1808 C Varley
193 × 269 mm
Colnaghi's (purchase, 1973) (D.1973.4)

■ VARLEY, JOHN (1778–1842)

One of the sixteen founder members of the Old
Watercolour Society in 1804 (where he exhibited over
700 works) John Varley was the most important and
prolific of his generation of artist teachers. His visits to
Wales in 1799 and 1802 provided him with sketches
that formed the basis of much of his exhibited work for
the rest of his life. Varley's earlier watercolours appear
to be influenced by Girtin but his later work is
repetitive and slack, relying on standard compositional
formulae. A popular teacher, Varley also published
drawing manuals.

Lake Bala, Merioneth, Wales

pencil, watercolour
signed lower right: *J. Varley*
259 × 353 mm
Agnew's (purchase, 3.6.1891) (D.1887.5)

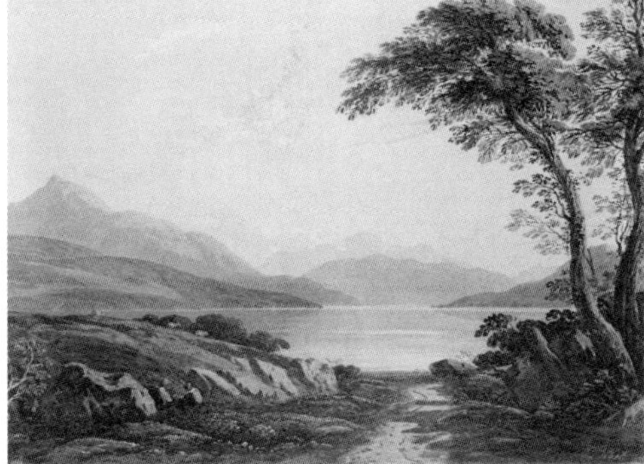

D.1887.5

Carisbrooke Castle from the Mill Dam, Isle of Wight

1839
pencil, watercolour, bodycolour (heightened with
white), gum arabic
signed lower right: *J. Varley*; signed, inscribed & dated
centre verso: *Carisbrooke Castle / Isle of Wight / J Varley /
1839*
231 × 428 mm
Taylor, John Edward (gift, 1892) (D.1892.65)

Harlech Castle, Merioneth, Wales, from the South

watercolour, bodycolour (heightened with
white); varnished
318 × 484 mm
Anderson, A. E. (gift, 1906) (D.1906.1)

Figures on a Road beside a Cottage (recto); Coast Scene with Boats (verso)

pencil, blue watercolour, grey watercolour (recto)
inscribed lower right (false signature): *J.S Cotman*
196 × 260 mm
Anderson, A. E. (gift, 1912) (D.1912.1)

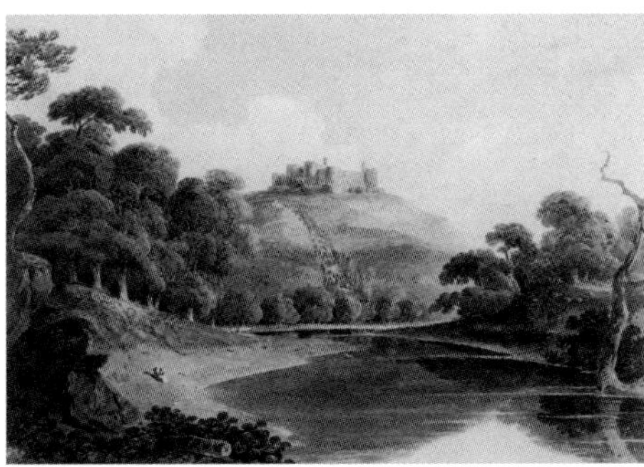

D.1924.43

Harlech Castle, Merioneth, Wales, from the North-East

pencil, watercolour
signed lower left: *J. VARLEY*
349 × 497 mm
Broadhurst, Sir Edward Tootal, Broadhurst, Lady
(bequest, 1924) (D.1924.43)

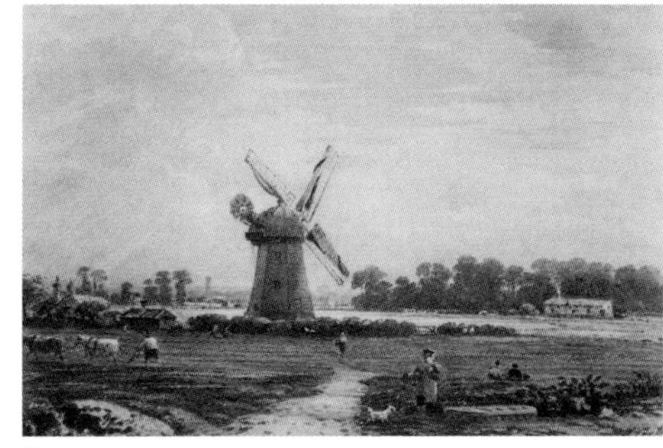

D.1924.44

The Windmill, Acton, London

18.5.1833
pencil, watercolour
signed & dated lower right: *J. Varley / 1833*; signed,
inscribed & dated centre verso: *View in the fields
looking towards / Acton Middlesex. the Pagoda / at Kew
being seen in the distance on / the Right*
183 × 271 mm
Broadhurst, Sir Edward Tootal, Broadhurst, Lady
(bequest, 1924) (D.1924.44)

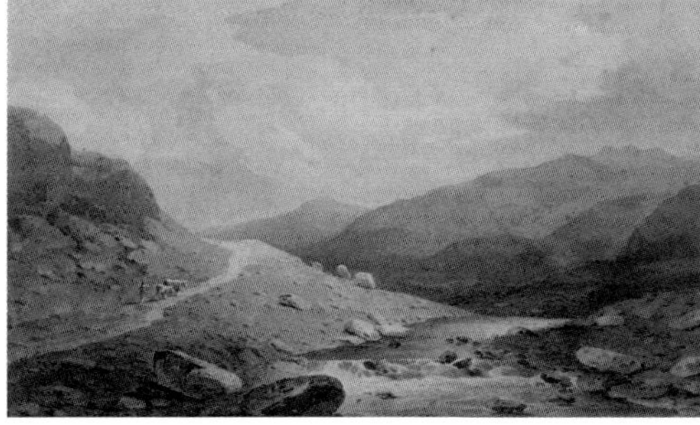

D.1924.45

The Pass of Llanberis, Caernarvonshire, Wales

1803
pencil, watercolour
signed & dated lower left: *VARLEY.1803.*
251 × 411 mm
Broadhurst, Sir Edward Tootal, Broadhurst, Lady
(bequest, 1924) (D.1924.45)

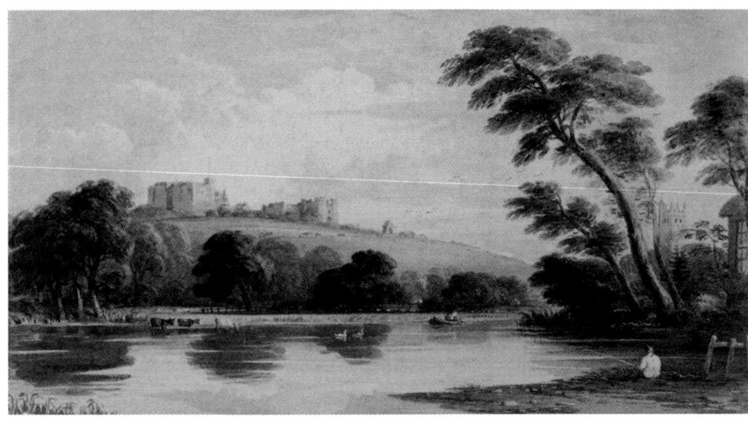

D.1892.65

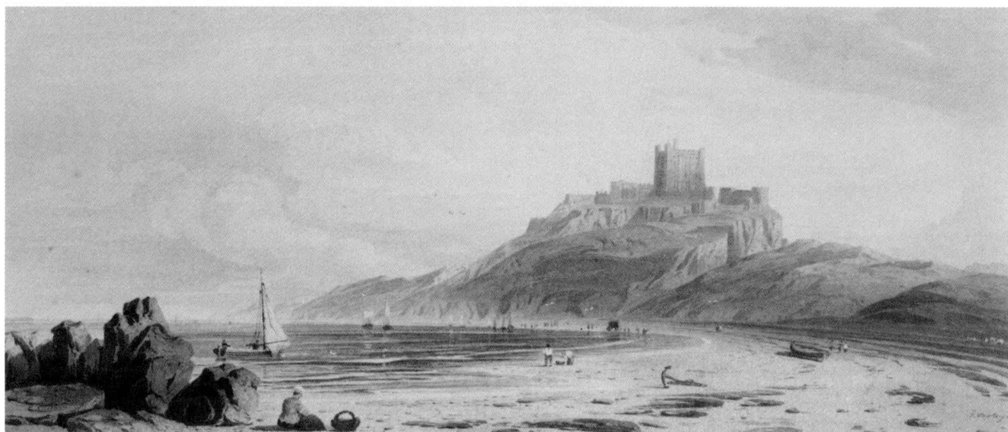

D.1924.76

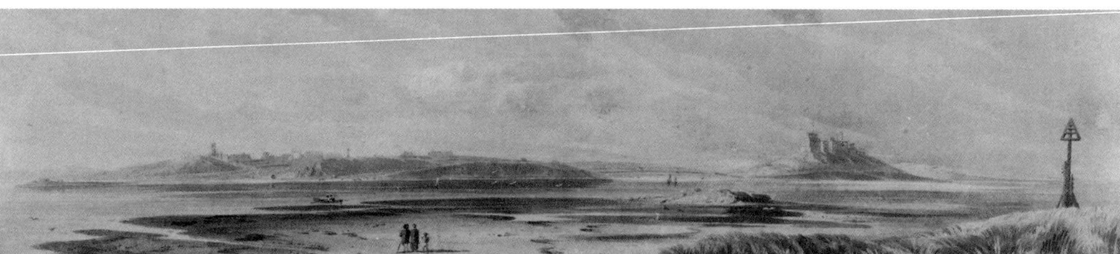

D.1924.77

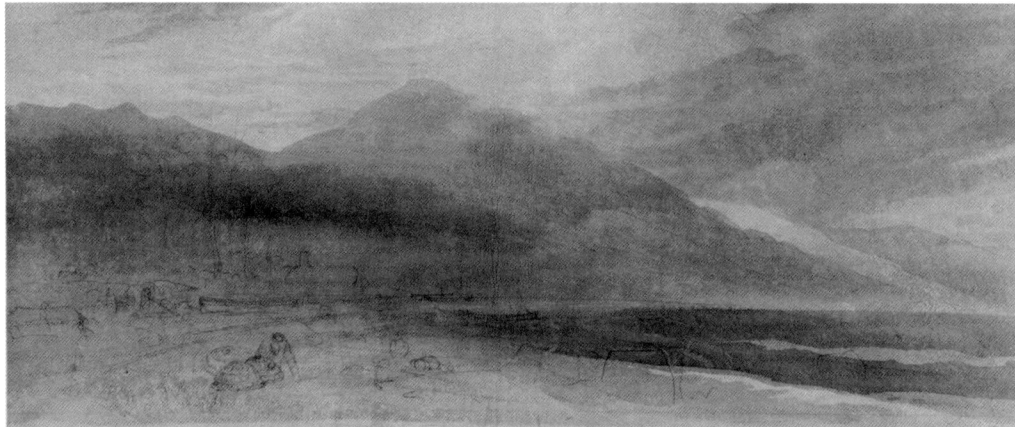

D.1924.90

Bamburgh Castle, Northumberland, from the North-West
1811
pencil, watercolour
signed & dated (twice) lower right (second signature erased): *J. Varley 1811*
285 × 667 mm
Broadhurst, Sir Edward Tootal, Broadhurst, Lady (bequest, 1924) (D.1924.76)

Holy Island, Northumberland
1809
pencil, watercolour
signed & dated lower left: *J. VARLEY.1809.*
174 × 764 mm
Broadhurst, Sir Edward Tootal, Broadhurst, Lady (bequest, 1924) (D.1924.77)

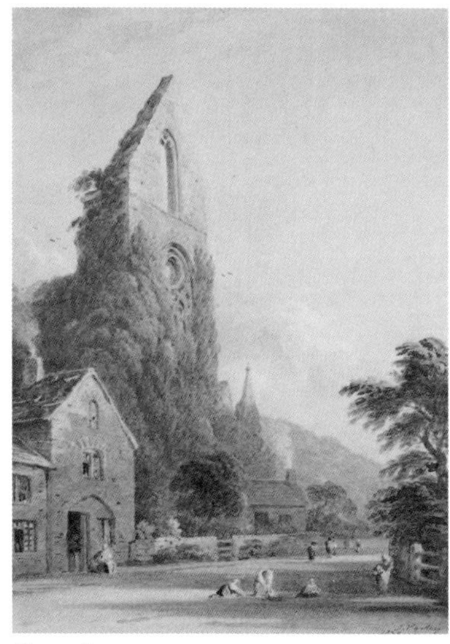

D.1924.78

The West Front, Tintern Abbey, Monmouthshire, Wales
1839
pencil, watercolour
signed & dated lower right: *J. Varley / 1839*
268 × 189 mm
Broadhurst, Sir Edward Tootal, Broadhurst, Lady (bequest, 1924) (D.1924.78)

A mountainous coastal Scene, possibly in North Wales
1801–03
pencil, watercolour
287 × 666 mm
Broadhurst, Sir Edward Tootal, Broadhurst, Lady (bequest, 1924) (D.1924.90)

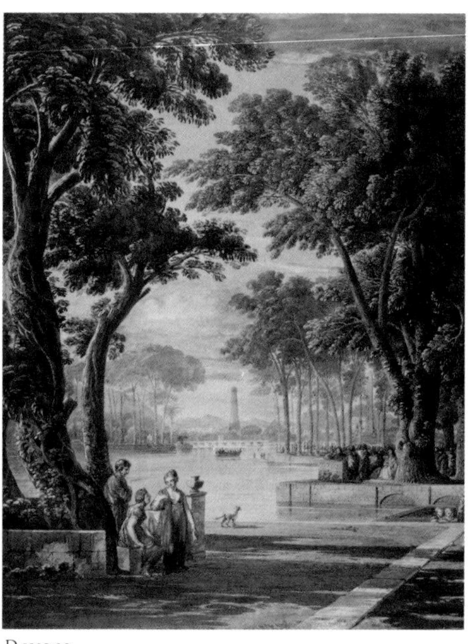

D.1930.20

Classical Composition
1824
watercolour, bodycolour (heightened with white) gum arabic
signed & dated lower right: *J. VARLEY.1824.*
772 × 577 mm
Meatyard, F. R. (purchase, 1930) (D.1930.20)

Composition with Italianate Buildings
pencil, watercolour
inscribed lower right verso (later hand ?): *Glen with*(?) *Castle*
246 × 338 mm
Friends of the Whitworth (gift, 1947) (D.1947.24)

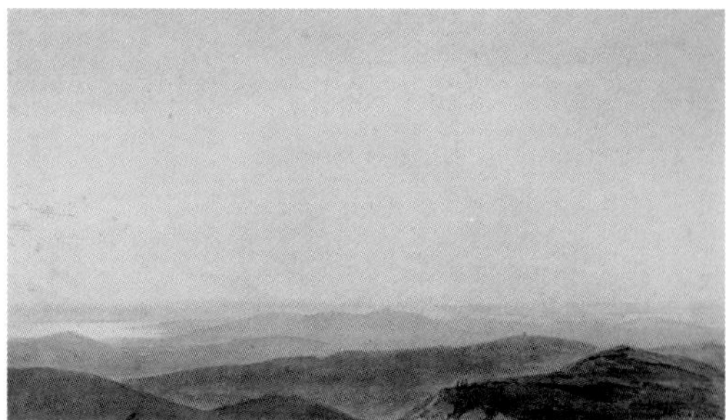

D.1999.23

Sunrise from the Top of Cader Idris
1804
watercolour
signed & dated lower right: *J.VARLEY.1804*; signed, inscribed & dated centre of verso of mount: *View of Sunrise from the Top of Cader Idris N.Wales / with Bala Lake in the Distance, at Half Past 3 in the Morning / by J. Varley. 1804*
289 × 490 mm
Scott-Elliot, Miss Aydua, in memory of Paul Oppé (gift, 4.11.1999) (D.1999.23)

■ VARLEY, Jun., JOHN (1850–1933)
The grandson of John Varley and a specialist in foreign topographical views, John Varley Jun. exhibited mainly Egyptian views at the Royal Academy between 1876 and 1895. He visited Japan in 1890.

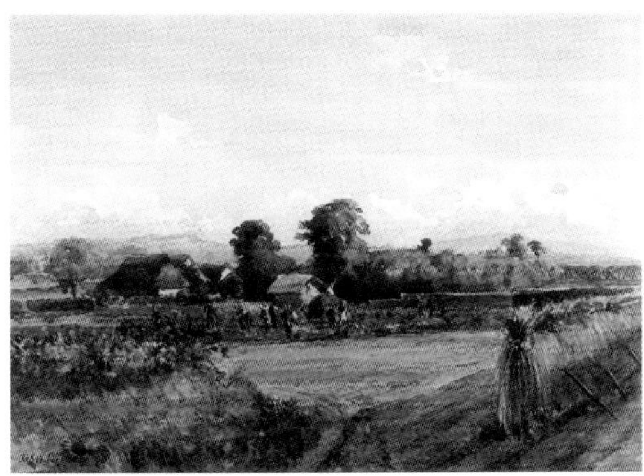

D.1919.3

Rice Harvest in Japan
1890
pencil, watercolour
signed & dated lower left: *John.Varley 90*; numbered upper left verso: *49*; inscribed upper edge verso: *Gathering in the rice harvest on the road to Mino*
268 × 365 mm
Philips, Mrs Herbert (bequest, 1919) (D.1919.3)

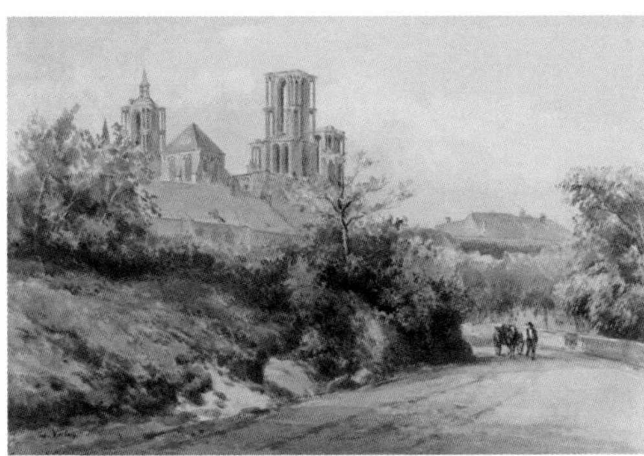

D.1919.5

Laon Cathedral, France
pencil, watercolour
signed lower left: *John.Varley.*; inscribed & numbered along upper edge on verso of backboard (later hand ?): *97 Laon Cathedral 12th & 13th Centy* (sic) *celebrated for its fine group of lofty towers & spires / the façade a masterpiece of pure Gothic –*
368 × 533 mm
Philips, Mrs Herbert (bequest, 1919) (D.1919.5)

■ VICKERS, ALFRED GOMERSAL (1810–37)
Alfred Gomersal Vickers, son of the artist Alfred Vickers and a follower of Francia and Bonington, exhibited at the Royal Academy between 1827 and 1836. In 1833 he was commissioned to visit Russia by Charles Heath and his drawings were engraved in *Heath's Landscape Annual* for 1836.

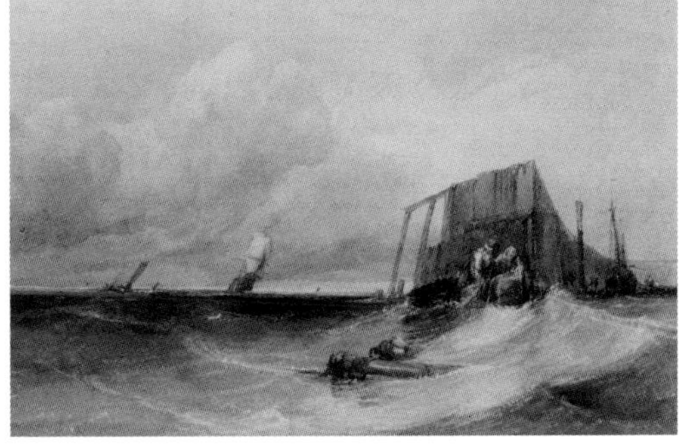

D.1892.137

Ships and fishing Boats off the South Coast
watercolour
244 × 347 mm
Taylor, John Edward (gift, 1892) (D.1892.137)

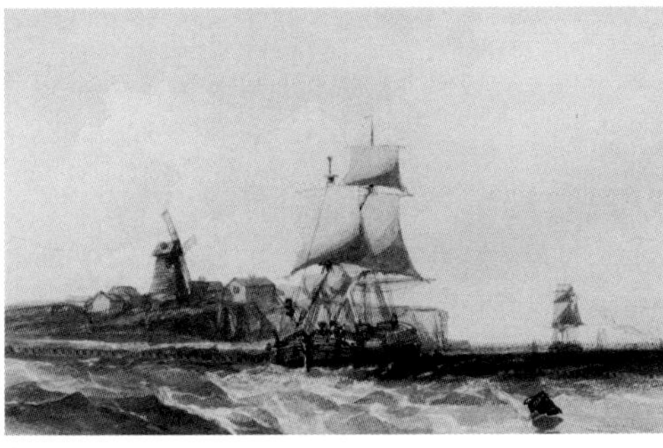

D.1893.11

In the English Channel
watercolour
164 × 249 mm
Agnew's (purchase, 18.12.1893) (D.1893.11)

■ VYSE, WILLIAM (fl. late 18th century)
Vyse was a copyist.

Copy of Hogarth's Etching 'A Chorus of Singers'
1760
pen and brown ink
signed lower left margin: *W Vyse*; dated lower right margin: *1760.*
212 × 193 mm
Ogden, William Sharp (bequest, 1926) (D.1926.80)

■ WAGEMAN, THOMAS CHARLES (1787–1863)
A portrait and landscape painter, Wageman was a founder member of the New Watercolour Society in 1831. Many of his sitters were famous actors and actresses and he was much involved in theatrical portraiture.

Portrait of Robert William Elliston
pencil
sheet 163 × 100 mm
untraced (purchase, 1916) (D.1916.11)

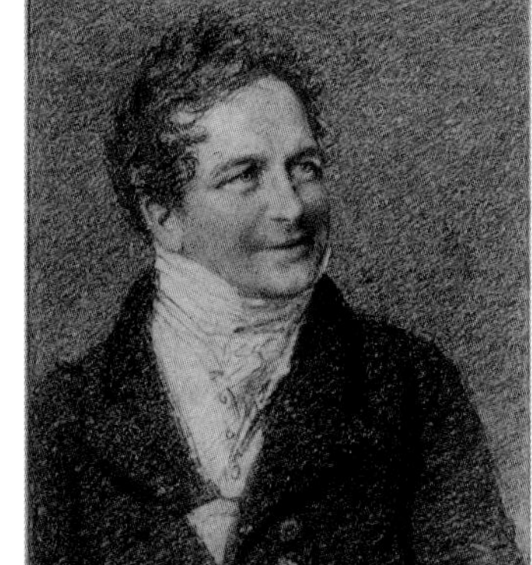

D.1916.11

■ WALKER, FREDERICK (1840–75)
Trained as a wood engraver under Josiah Wood Whymper and established a reputation as a black and white illustrator for periodicals such as *Good Words*, *Once a Week* and the *Cornhill Magazine*. Walker began to exhibit at the Royal Academy in 1863 and was elected an associate member in 1871. Elected a member of the Old Watercolour Society in 1866, Walker is one of the most significant artists of the generation that followed the Pre-Raphaelites; he died young of consumption.

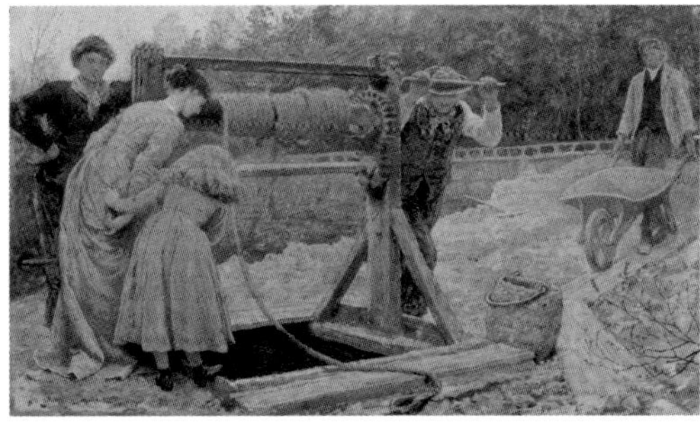

D.1906.2

The Well Sinkers
1868
pencil, watercolour, bodycolour (heightened with white)
signed lower left with initials: *F.W*
260 × 429 mm
Agnew, Sir William (gift, 1906) (D.1906.2)

Reading in the Park
1870
watercolour, bodycolour; card
signed & dated lower right: *Fd.W. / 1870*
121 × 194 mm
Barlow, Sir Thomas (gift, 1948) (D.1948.15)

■ WALKER, WILLIAM EYRE (1847–1930)
Born in Manchester, the son of a drawing master, Walker exhibited three pictures at the Royal Academy beween 1885 and 1898 and was a more frequent exhibitor at the Royal Watercolour Society, of which he was elected a member in 1896. Walker painted all over the British Isles.

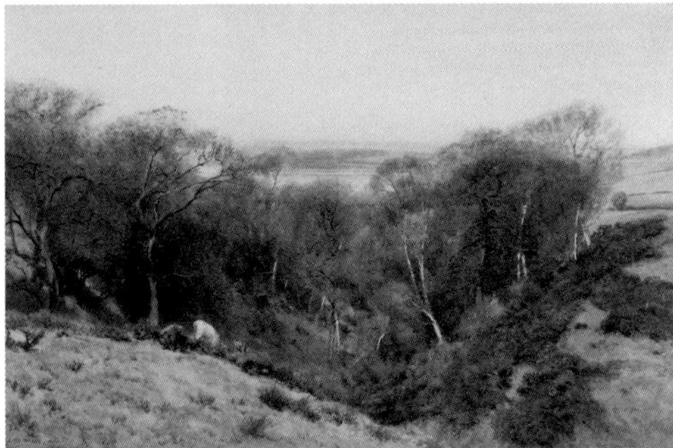

D.1892.148

Stockport Waterworks Reservoir, Disley, Cheshire
1892
watercolour
signed & dated lower left: *W.EYRE WALKER.1892.*
472 × 699 mm
Walker, William Eyre (purchase, 11.7.1892) (D.1892.148)

Summer Day at Prestbury, Cheshire
1892
watercolour
signed & dated lower left: *W.EYRE WALKER.1892.*
487 × 674 mm
Walker, William Eyre (purchase, 2.3.1893) (D.1893.14)

Still Day on Dartmoor, Devon
1901
watercolour
signed & dated lower left: *W.EYRE WALKER / 1901*
465 × 696 mm
untraced (purchase, 1902) (D.1902.6)

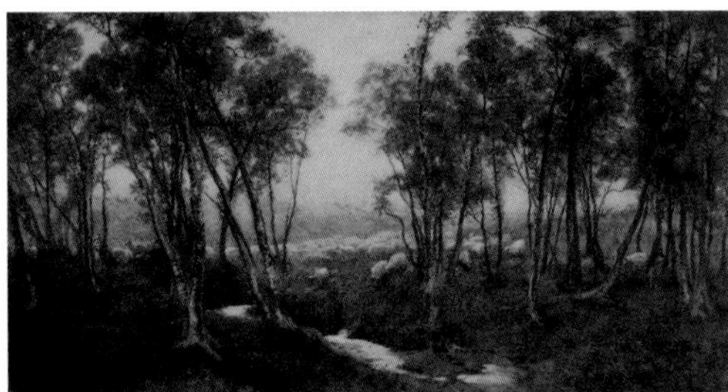

D.1904.4

Land of Showers, a Westmorland Pastoral
watercolour
signed lower left: *W.EYRE WALKER*
345 × 659 mm
untraced (purchase, 1904) (D.1904.4)

■ **WALLIS, GEORGE (1811–91)**
Wallis, an art teacher who taught in London, Manchester and Birmingham, was Keeper of Art at the South Kensington Museum from 1863 to 1891.

The Chasm on Sir Joseph Whitworth's Estate, Stancliffe, Darley Dale, Derbyshire
9.1881
pencil, watercolour
signed & dated lower right: *George Wallis.1881.*;
inscribed & dated centre verso: *The Chasm. 3rd Level*[underlined] / *At.Stancliffe / Darley Dale / Sir Jos.Whitworth Bart / Grounds. / Sepr.20.26.&27. 1881*
279 × 387 mm
Wallis, Sir Whitworth (gift, 1918) (D.1918.12)

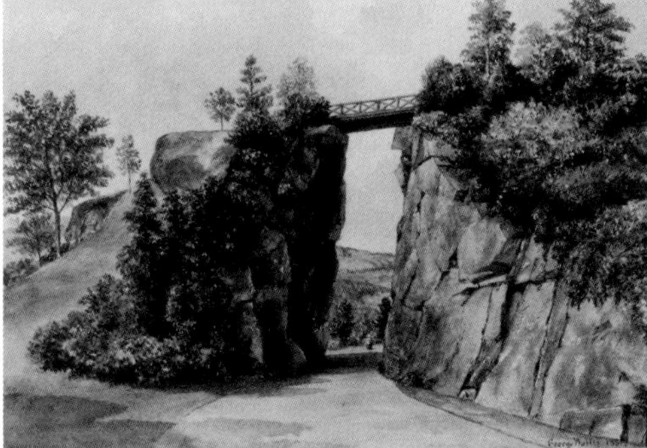

D.1918.12

The Chasm and Cavern Walk, Stancliffe, Darley Dale, Derbyshire
9.1881
pencil, watercolour
signed & dated lower right with initials: *G W / 1881*;
inscribed & dated centre verso: *From the Cavern Walk. Sir Joseph Whitworth's / Grounds. / 2nd Level / Stancliffe / Darley Dale / Derbyshire / Sepr.26.27 and 28. 1881*
280 × 386 mm
Wallis, Sir Whitworth (gift, 1918) (D.1918.13)

■ **WALTERS, EDWARD (1808–72)**
Walters was a Manchester architect who built a number of warehouses for cotton merchants on Charlotte Street as well as the Free Trade Hall (1853–56), Peter Street, described by Pevsner as 'perhaps the noblest monument in the Cinquecento style in England'. Walters also built The Firs (1851), the Manchester residence of Sir Joseph Whitworth.

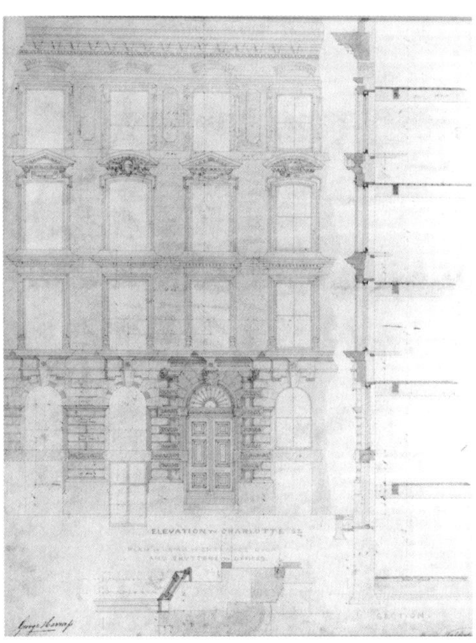

D.1998.18

Design for a Warehouse: Partial Section and Elevation to Charlotte Street
pencil, pen and grey ink, watercolour
569 × 434 mm
University of Manchester, Architecture Department (transfer, 1998) (D.1998.18)

■ **WALTON, ELIJAH (1832–80)**
Born in Birmingham, Walton exhibited at the Royal Academy between 1851 and 1865. During the 1860s he spent much time in Egypt and wrote a book on the camel, published in 1865. He also visited the Alps and produced many watercolours of mountain scenery.

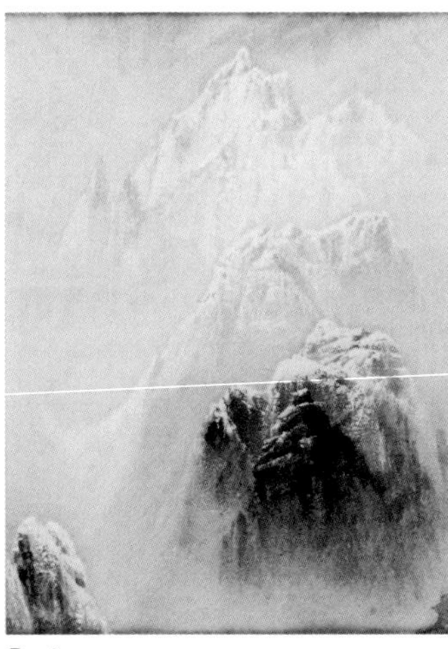

D.1987.59

Val Tournanche, Italy
1866
watercolour, bodycolour (heightened with white)
signed, inscribed & dated upper centre on reverse of backing: *Val Tournanche / Italy.1866– / Elijah Walton*
176 × 126 mm
Hitchon, Brian (Dr) (in appreciation of his student years at Manchester University, 1949-1955) (gift, 1987) (D.1987.59)

■ **WALTON, JAMES (attributed to) (fl. mid-1790s)**
Walton was a landscape watercolourist who painted views of the Lake District. He may be the J. Walton who collaborated with T. H. Fielding on *A Tour of the English Lakes*, published in 1821.

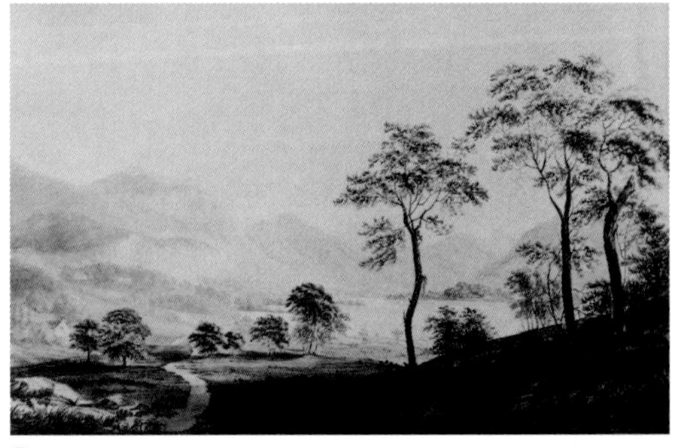

D.1922.33

Loweswater, Cumberland
pencil, watercolour
inscribed lower right (false signature): *P Sandby.1793*;
inscribed upper centre verso of mount: *Lowes Water / Cumberland / 1793.–*
363 × 547 mm
Anderson, A. E., National Art Collections Fund (via) (gift, 1922) (D.1922.33)

St Kentigern's Church, Crosthwaite, and the Vale of Keswick, Cumberland
pencil, watercolour
inscribed lower right (false signature): *P Sandby.1793*;
inscribed lower centre on mount: *Crosthwaite Church – Vale of Keswick*
340 × 508 mm
Anderson, A. E., National Art Collections Fund (via) (gift, 1922) (D.1922.34)

■ WARD, EDWARD MATTHEW (1816–79)

Ward visited Rome between 1836 and 1839 and exhibited at the Royal Academy between 1834 and 1879. He specialised in literary subjects and scenes from French and English history. Ward was elected a member of the Royal Academy in 1855.

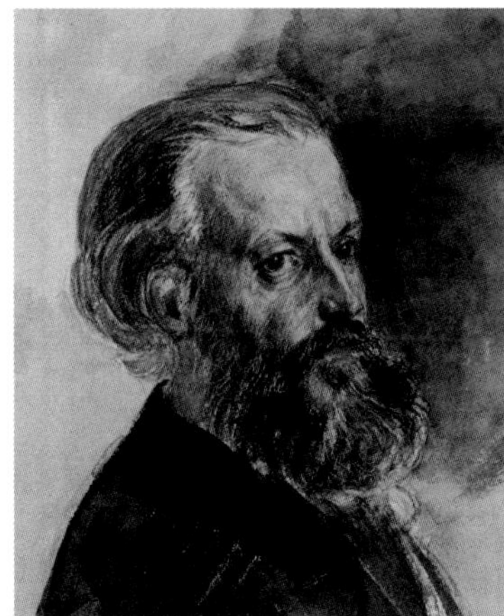

D.1922.6

Portrait of Charles Gounod
pencil, watercolour, bodycolour (heightened with white)
250 × 197 mm
untraced (gift, 1922) (D.1922.6)

■ WARD, J. (fl. mid-19th century)

Unknown amateur artist.

The River Thames at Greenwich
9.1852
watercolour
signed & dated lower right: *JWard / Sep 1852*
101 × 155 mm
Ogden, William Sharp (bequest, 1926) (D.1926.78)

■ WARD, JAMES (1769–1859)

Born in London, Ward's early career was as an engraver after being apprenticed to J. R. Smith and his brother William Ward. He only turned to painting in the 1790s, probably influenced by his brother-in-law George Morland. Ward made his name as a painter of animals, principally cattle, horses and pigs. He was an inveterate sketcher and virtually all his works, even the slightest of sketches, carry his characterisitic monogram.

Study of a Pony
pencil, watercolour
signed lower left letters of surname in monogram: *JWD.RA*
141 × 199 mm
Anderson, A. E. (gift, 1908) (D.1908.4)

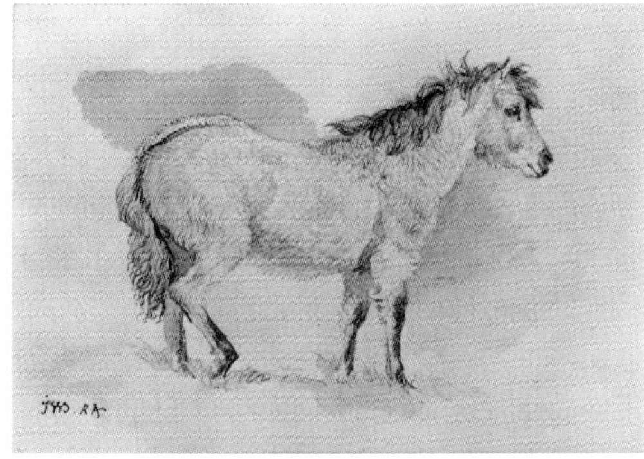

D.1908.4

Study of a Boy
pencil
signed lower left letters of surname in monogram: *JWD.RA*
182 × 122 mm
Anderson, A. E. (gift, 1908) (D.1908.5)

Study of a Pig's Head
pencil, watercolour
signed lower right with initials: *J. W.*
53 × 65 mm
Anderson, A. E. (gift, 1908) (D.1908.6)

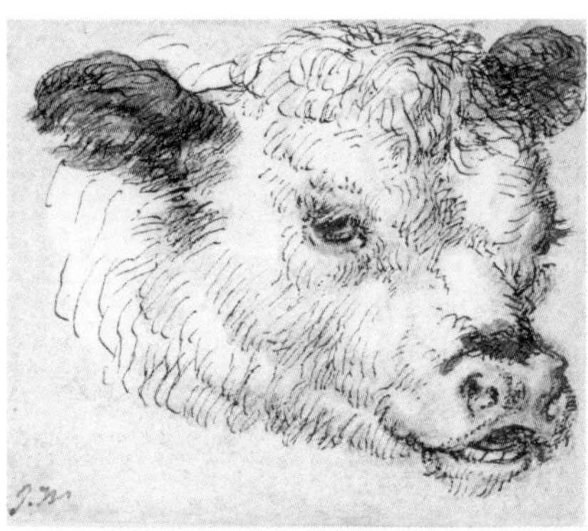

D.1908.7

Study of a Calf's Head
pencil, pen and brown ink, watercolour
signed lower left with initials: *J. W*
66 × 76 mm
Anderson, A. E. (gift, 1908) (D.1908.7)

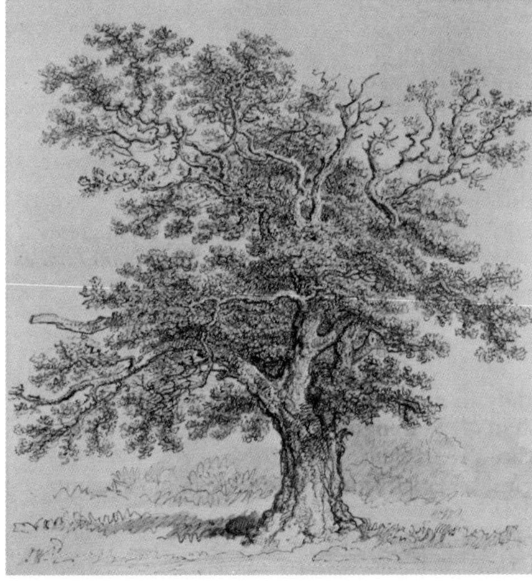

D.1908.8

Oak Tree (recto); Landscape Study (verso)
pencil, pen and brown ink, brown watercolour (recto)
signed lower left recto with initials: *JWd–* ; signed lower right recto with initials: *J.W*; inscribed lower left verso colour notes: *right Building red / with Slate / [illegible] tile & Brick*
272 × 255 mm
Anderson, A. E. (gift, 1908) (D.1908.8)

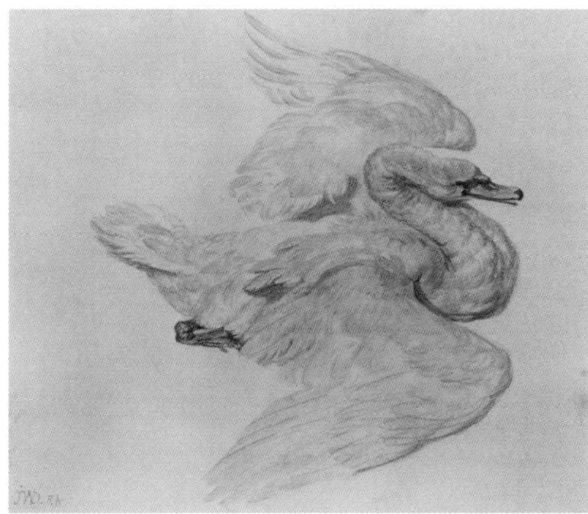

D.1908.9

Study for 'The Descent of the Swan'
1817
signed lower left letters of surname in monogram: *JWD.RA*
pencil, watercolour, bodycolour
250 × 290 mm
Anderson, A. E. (gift, 1908) (D.1908.9)

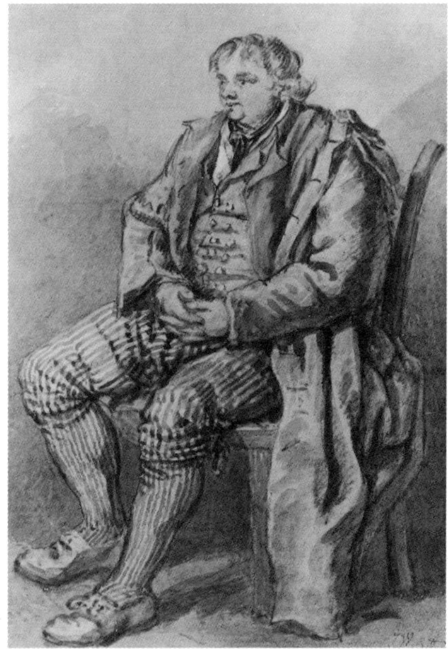

D.1908.10

Portrait of William Crane, seated on a Chair
1791
pencil, watercolour
signed lower right with initials: *JW.RA.*; inscribed across verso of mount in centre: *Willm Crane / Camden Town / who removed my goods to / Hendon when I left my mother*
284 × 193 mm
Anderson, A. E. (gift, 1908) (D.1908.10)

Study of Sir Charles Forbes' Arabian Horse
pencil, watercolour
inscribed lower left: *Sir Charles Forbes Arabian*
278 × 381 mm
Anderson, A. E. (gift, 1908) (D.1908.11)

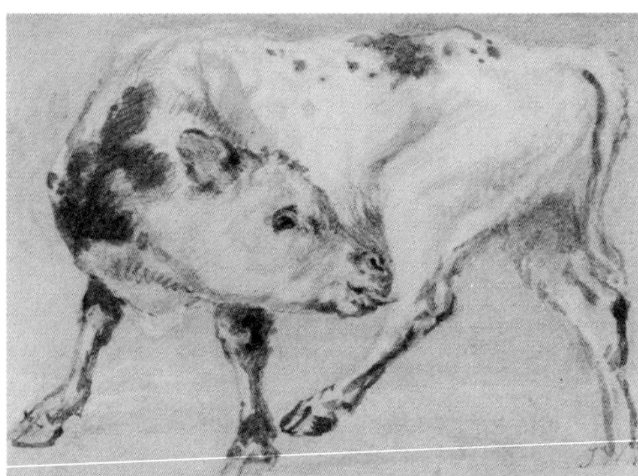

D.1908.12

Study of a Calf
pencil, watercolour
signed lower right with initials: *JW*
141 × 192 mm
Anderson, A. E. (gift, 1908) (D.1908.12)

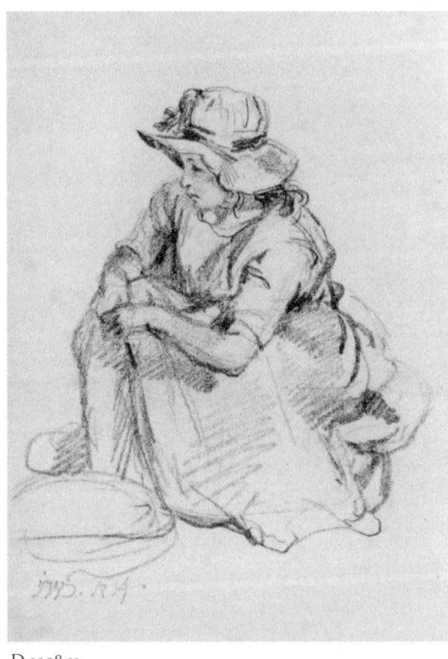

D.1908.13

Study of the Artist's Daughter, Matilda
pencil
signed lower left letters of surname in monogram:
JWD.RA
182 × 130 mm
Anderson, A. E. (gift, 1908) (D.1908.13)

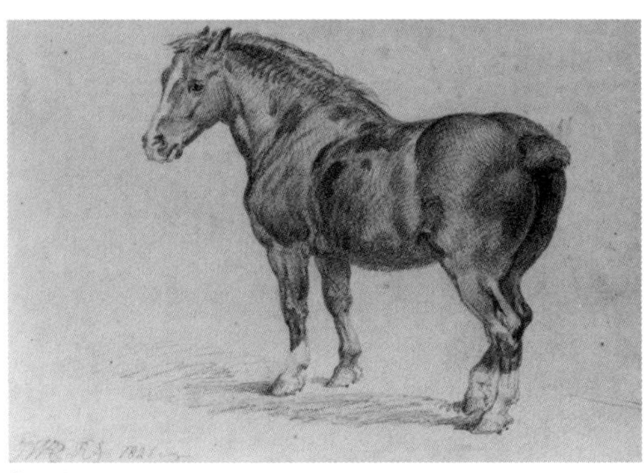

D.1908.14

Study of a Shire Horse
1821
pencil, red chalk, black chalk
signed & dated lower left letters of surname in
monogram: *JWARD RA 1821–*
230 × 317 mm
Anderson, A. E. (gift, 1908) (D.1908.14)

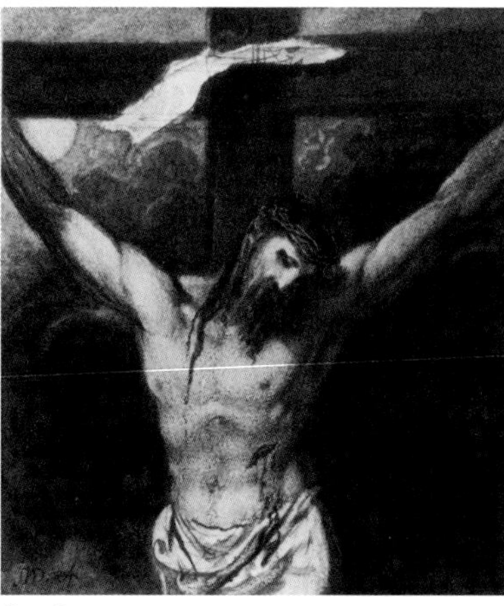

D.1908.15

Christ on the Cross: Study for 'The Triumph over Sin, Death and Hell'
pencil, pen and brown ink, brown watercolour
signed lower left initials of surname in monogram:
JWD RA
183 × 160 mm
Anderson, A. E. (gift, 1908) (D.1908.15)

Study of a Sheep lying down
pencil, black chalk, brown chalk, white chalk
buff paper
signed lower left with initials: *JW.RA.*
187 × 282 mm
Anderson, A. E. (gift, 1908) (D.1908.16)

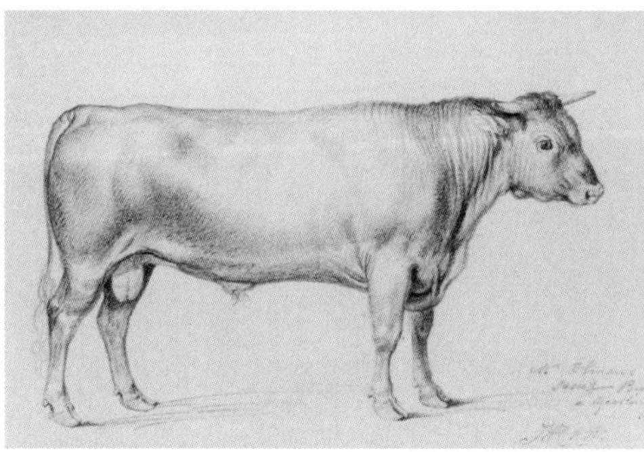

D.1908.17

Study of Mr Elman's Sussex Bull
pencil, black chalk
signed lower right letters of surname in monogram:
JWARD RA.; inscribed lower right: *Mr Elmans / Sussex Bull / a yearling*
186 × 275 mm
Anderson, A. E. (gift, 1908) (D.1908.17)

Study of a Horse, possibly Napoleon's Charger, Marengo
pencil, watercolour
signed lower left letters of surname in monogram:
JWARD RA
179 × 242 mm
Anderson, A. E. (gift, 1908) (D.1908.18)

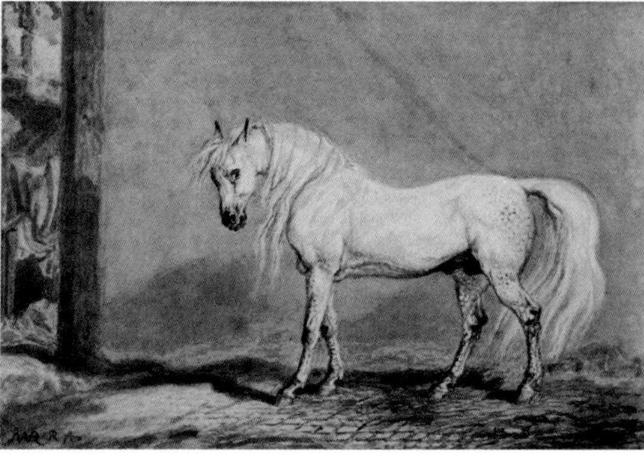

D.1908.18

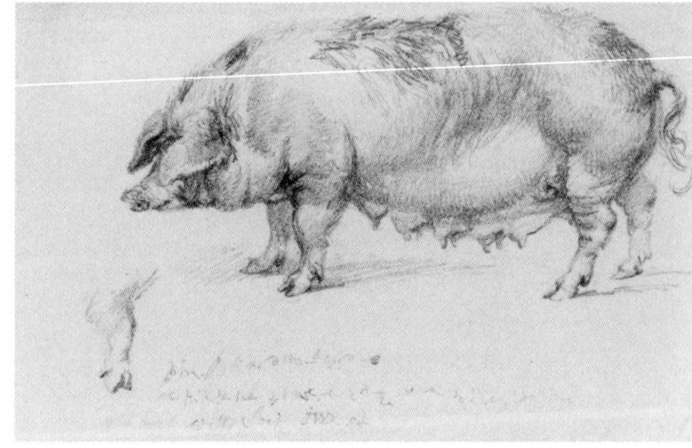

D.1908.19

A Wiltshire Sow
pencil
signed & inscribed lower centre in longhand and the
artist's shorthand initials of surname in monogram:
[illegible] / [illegible] / *old breed Wilts Sow JWD. RA*
174 × 260 mm
Anderson, A. E. (gift, 1908) (D.1908.19)

Study of the Torso of an Old Man, and Studies of Hands
black chalk, red chalk, white chalk; buff paper
signed centre right letters of surname in monogram:
JWARD.; inscribed with six lines of illegible shorthand
310 × 512 mm
Anderson, A. E. (gift, 1908) (D.1908.20)

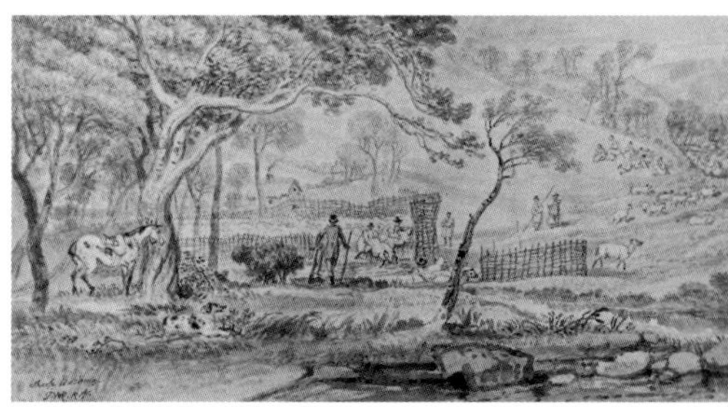

D.1908.21

Sheep-washing
black chalk, grey watercolour
signed lower left with monogram: *JWD RA*; signed &
inscribed lower left with monogram: *JWD.RA.*
325 × 577 mm
Anderson, A. E. (gift, 1908) (D.1908.21)

Study of a Cow lying down, for 'Bull, Cow and Calf'
pencil, watercolour
signed lower right with initials: *JW.RA.*
165 × 238 mm
Anderson, A. E. (gift, 1910) (D.1910.1)

The obstinate Cart Horse
pencil, grey watercolour
signed lower left: *J. WARD*; numbered lower left: *513*
140 × 206 mm
Anderson, A. E. (gift, 1911) (D.1911.3)

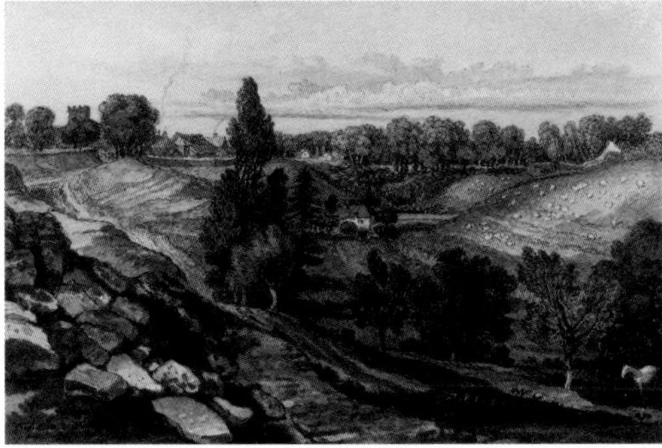
D.1925.27

Chisledon, near Marlborough, Wiltshire
17.8.1822
pen and brown ink, watercolour
signed, inscribed & dated lower left with monogram:
Chisseldon – Wilts – / Augt.17th 1822 JWD RA
263 × 381 mm
Walker's Galleries, London (purchase, 1925) (D.1925.27)

Saxmundham Mill, Suffolk
1833
pencil, pen and brown ink, watercolour
signed lower right with monogram: *JWD.RA*
210 × 430 mm
Anderson, A. E. (gift, 1931) (D.1931.14)

Clump of Holly Trees at Hanbury
20.8.1820
pencil; watermark crown over J&M / 1819
signed lower right with initials of surname in
monogram: *JWD.RA*; inscribed & dated lower left in
longhand and the artist's shorthand: [illegible] /
Hanbury / Augt. 10.1820 / Holly. [illegible] / [illegible] /
[illegible]; stamped upper right: collector's mark of
Thomas E. Lowinsky (1892-1947) (L.2420a): *TEL*
191 × 227 mm
University of Manchester, History of Art Department
(transfer, 1960) (D.1960.143)

Highland Landscape
1803
pencil, black chalk
signed lower right letters of surname in monogram:
JWARD.RA; stamped lower left: collector's mark of
Thomas E. Lowinsky (1892–1947) (L.2420a): *TEL*
98 × 202 mm
University of Manchester, History of Art Department
(transfer, 1960) (D.1960.144)

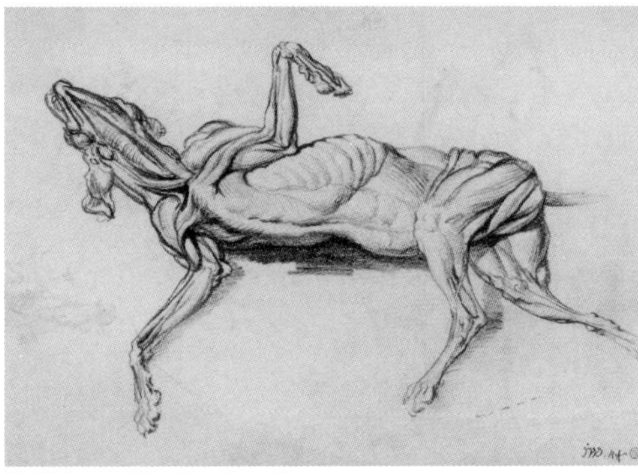
D.1960.145

Anatomical Study of a flayed Dog
pencil
signed lower right letters of surname in monogram:
JWD.RA; stamped lower right collector's mark of
Thomas E. Lowinsky (1892–1947) (L.2420a): *TEL*
268 × 372 mm
University of Manchester, History of Art Department
(transfer, 1960) (D.1960.145)

*N.B. The rectos of the two following drawings are genuine
James Ward drawings but the versos are forgeries.*

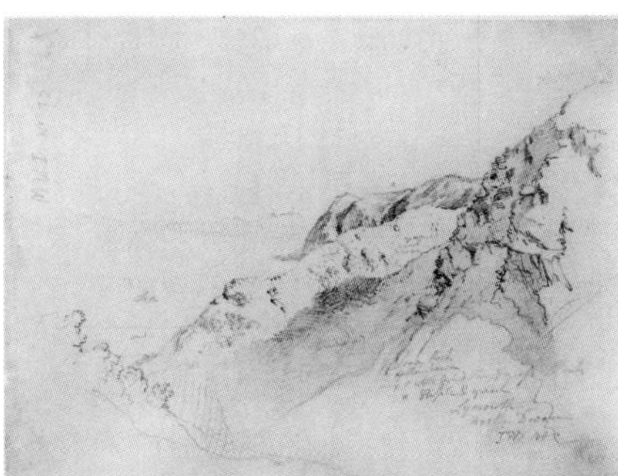
D.1911.1

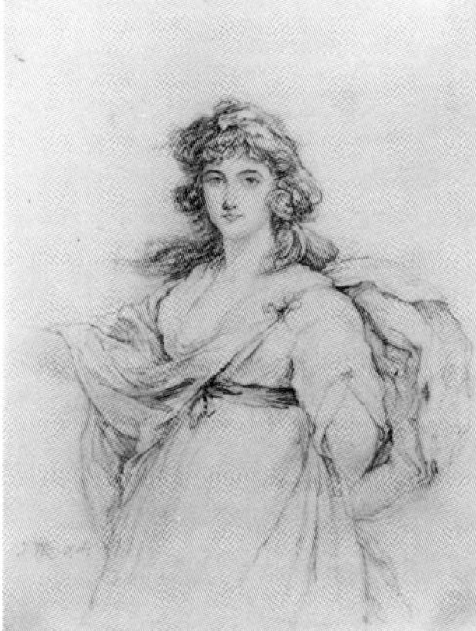
D.1911.1 (verso)

Lynmouth, Devon (recto); Copy after James Ward's Engraving of Hoppner's Portrait of Mrs Michael Angelo Taylor as Miranda (verso)
pencil
signed & inscribed lower right recto colour notes and
monogram: *loose Rocks / falling down / next with dried
Fern & grey Rock / a Couple & green / Lynmouth / North
Devon / JWD.RA*; signed lower left verso fake
monogram: *J WRD.RA.*
recto 248 × 330 mm
Anderson, A. E. (gift, 1911) (D.1911.1)

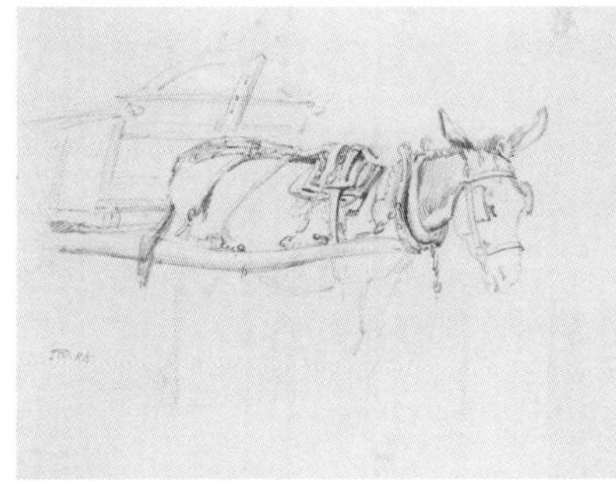
D.1911.2

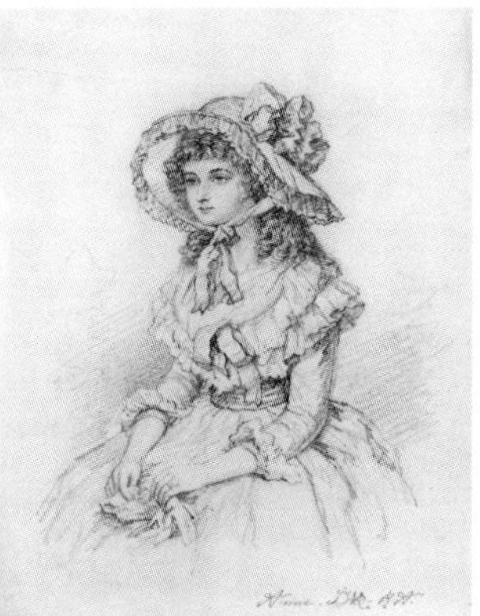
D.1911.2 (verso)

A Donkey between the Shafts of a Cart (recto); Copy after William Ward's Engraving of his Painting Portrait of Anne Ward (Mrs George Morland) (verso)
pencil
signed lower left recto artist's monogram: *JWD.RA*;
signed & inscribed lower right verso fake inscription
and monogram: *Anne.JWRD.RA.*
recto 248 × 336 mm
Anderson, A. E. (gift, 1911) (D.1911.2)

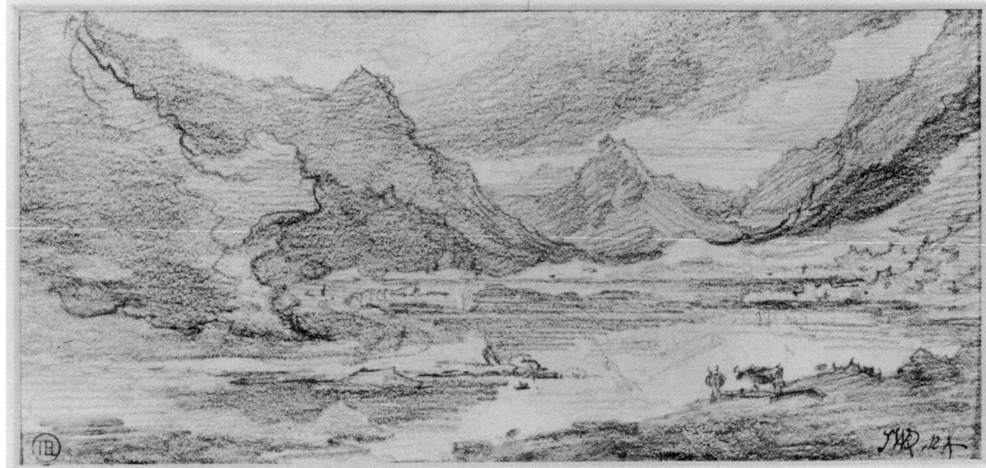
D.1960.144

■ WARD, SIR LESLIE MATTHEW (1851–1922)

Ward was the son of E. M. Ward and studied architecture at the Royal Academy Schools. He is chiefly remembered today for the caricatures that he produced for *Vanity Fair* between 1873 and 1909, which made him the most celebrated caricaturist of the day. He was knighted in 1918.

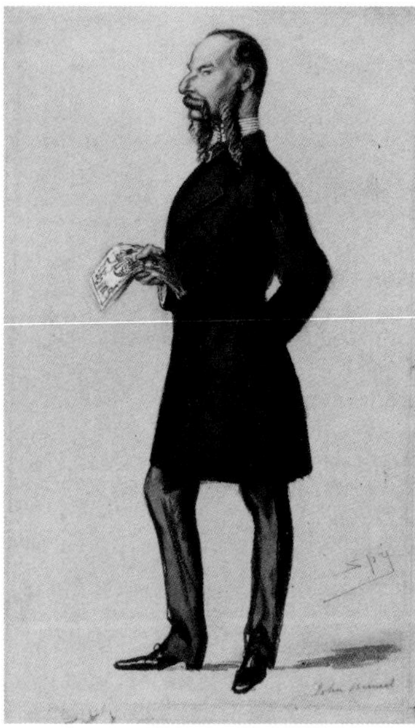

D.1952.4

Caricature of Sir John Tenniel, holding a Copy of 'Punch': Illustration for 'Vanity Fair' Magazine (recto); Similar Study (verso)
1878
watercolour, bodycolour (heightened with white) blue paper
signed lower right (artist's pseudonym): *Spy*; inscribed lower right (name of sitter): *John Tenniel*
324 × 191 mm
Pilkington, Margaret (gift, 1952) (D.1952.4)

■ WARREN, HAROLD BROADFIELD (fl. late 19th century)

Unknown artist.

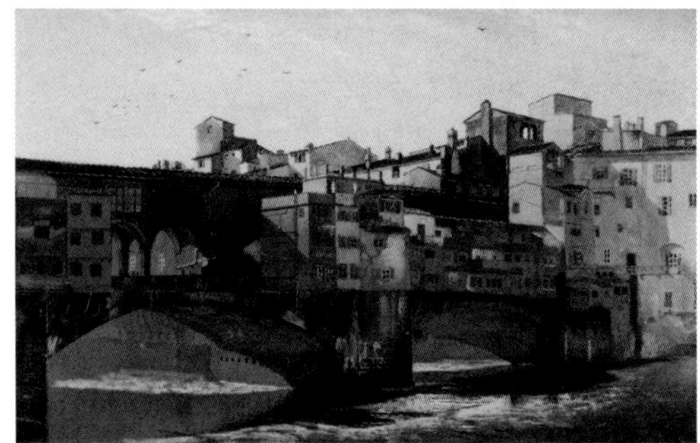

D.1917.21

Ponte Vecchio, Florence
pencil, pen and brown ink, watercolour, bodycolour
signed lower left with initials: *H B W*
169 × 267 mm
Hughes, Mrs C. (gift, 1917) (D.1917.21)

■ WATERHOUSE, ALFRED (1830–1905) and OFFICE

The greatest Victorian architect connected with Manchester, Waterhouse came from a Liverpool family and set up a practice in Manchester. After winning the national competition for the Manchester Assize Courts in 1864, he moved to London, from where he designed his masterpiece Manchester Town Hall (1867-80) and the main Manchester University building (1870-88). His most important London building is the Natural History Museum.

Design for the Church of St John, Brooklands, near Manchester: Perspective
1865
pencil, pen and brown ink, brown watercolour
inscribed on mount below image: *CHURCH OF ST. JOHN AT BROOKLANDS NR MANCHESTER*
332 × 228 mm
Martin, Sir Leslie (gift, 1996) (D.1996.28)

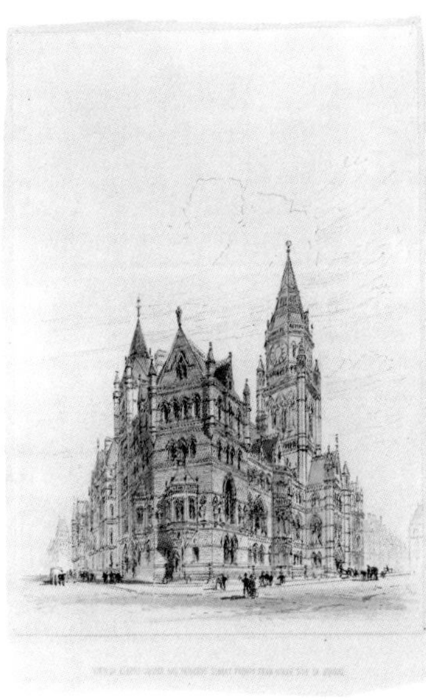

D.1996.29

Design for Manchester Town Hall: Perspective View of the Albert Square and Princess Street Fronts from the North Side of the Square
1868
pencil, pen and brown ink, brown watercolour
inscribed on mount below image: *VIEW OF ALBERT SQUARE AND PRINCESS STREET FRONTS FROM NORTH SIDE OF SQUARE*
366 × 228 mm
Martin, Sir Leslie (gift, 1996) (D.1996.29)

Design for Manchester Town Hall: Elevation of the Cooper Street Front
1868
pencil, pen and brown ink, brown watercolour
361 × 247 mm
Martin, Sir Leslie (gift, 1996) (D.1996.30)

Design for Manchester Town Hall: Bird's Eye Perspective View from Albert Square
2.11.1869
pen and brown ink, watercolour, bodycolour (heightened with white)
signed & dated lower right: *AWaterhouse / 2 Nov 1869*
688 × 509 mm
University of Manchester, Architecture Department (transfer, 1998) (D.1998.19)

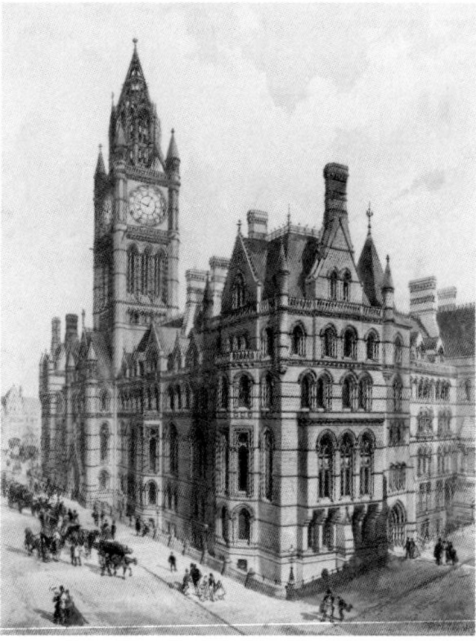

D.1998.19

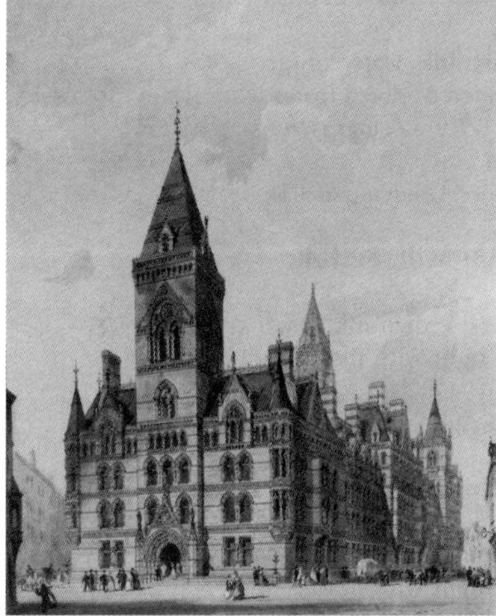

D.1998.20

Design for Manchester Town Hall: Perspective View from Princess Street showing the Cooper Street Entrance
pen and brown ink, watercolour, bodycolour (heightened with white)
737 × 570 mm
University of Manchester, Architecture Department (transfer, 1998) (D.1998.20)

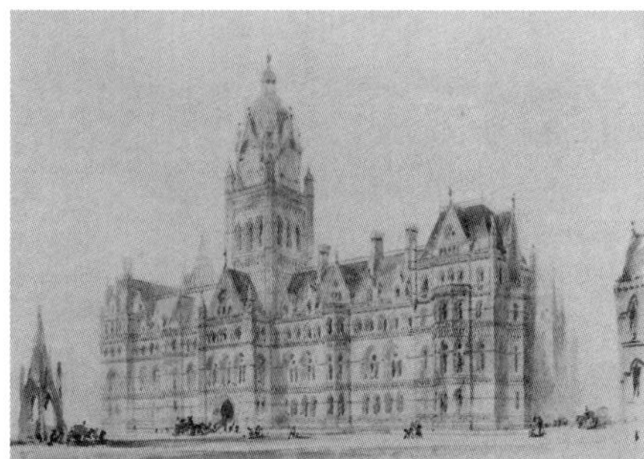

D.1998.21

Design for Manchester Town Hall: Perspective View from Albert Square
pencil, pen and brown ink, watercolour
signed lower right with initials: *AW.*
315 × 433 mm
University of Manchester, Architecture Department (transfer, 1998) (D.1998.21)

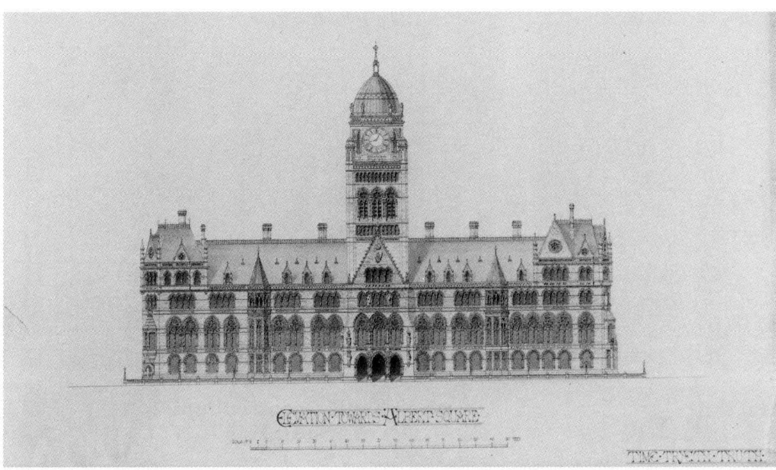

D.1998.22

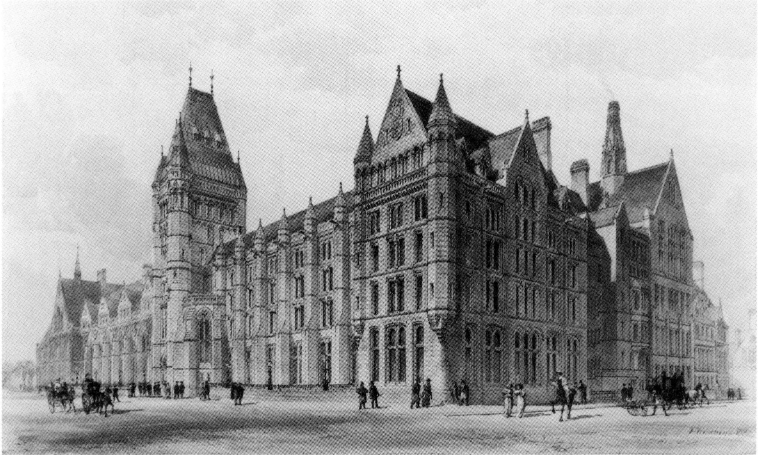

D.1998.25

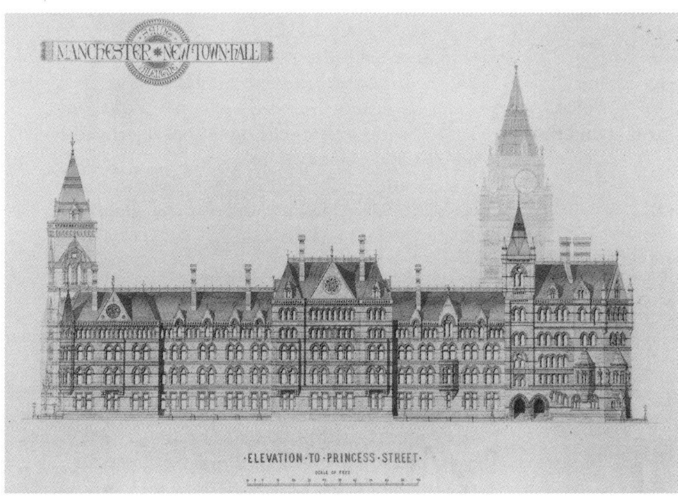

D.1998.23

Design for Manchester Town Hall: Elevation towards Albert Square
pen and brown ink, watercolour
inscribed in centre along upper edge: *NEW. TOWN HALL. MANCHESTER.*; inscribed in centre along lower edge: *ELEVATION. TOWARDS. ALBERT. SQUARE. and with scale*; inscribed lower right: *TIME. TRYETH. TRUTH.*
558 × 832 mm
University of Manchester, Architecture Department (transfer, 1998) (D.1998.22)

Design for Manchester Town Hall: Elevation to Princess Street
pen and brown ink, watercolour
inscribed upper left inscription within a cartouche imposed on a round medallion reading: *SAINT VALENTINE MANCHESTER. NEW. TOWN. HALL.*; inscribed lower centre: *ELEVATION. TO. PRINCESS. STREET. and with scale*
510 × 713 mm
University of Manchester, Architecture Department (transfer, 1998) (D.1998.23)

Design for Manchester Town Hall: Elevation towards Princess Street
pen and brown ink, watercolour
inscribed in centre along upper edge: *NEW. TOWN HALL. MANCHESTER*; inscribed in centre along lower edge: *ELEVATION. TOWARDS. PRINCESS. ST. and with scale*; inscribed lower right: *TIME. TRYETH. TRUTH*
508 × 778 mm
University of Manchester, Architecture Department (transfer, 1998) (D.1998.24)

Design for Owens College, Manchester: Perspective View from Oxford Road
1882
pen and brown ink, watercolour, bodycolour (heightened with white)
signed & dated lower right: *AWaterhouse 1882*
524 × 755 mm
University of Manchester, Architecture Department (transfer, 1998) (D.1998.25)

Design for the Congregational Chapel, Great Ancoats Street, Manchester: Perspective and Ground Plan
1864
pen and brown ink, watercolour
signed lower left: *AWaterhouse*
518 × 364 mm
University of Manchester, Architecture Department (transfer, 1998) (D.1998.26)

■ WATTS, GEORGE FREDERICK (1817–1904)

Historical and portrait painter, Watts won prizes in the Westminster Hall competition of 1843 and the House of Lords competition of 1847. Although elected a member of the Royal Academy in 1867, he did not achieve fame until the 1880s with exhibitions at the Grosvenor Gallery in 1882 and New York in 1884. Watts painted large and grand historical and allegorical subjects as well as penetrating portraits of many of his contemporaries.

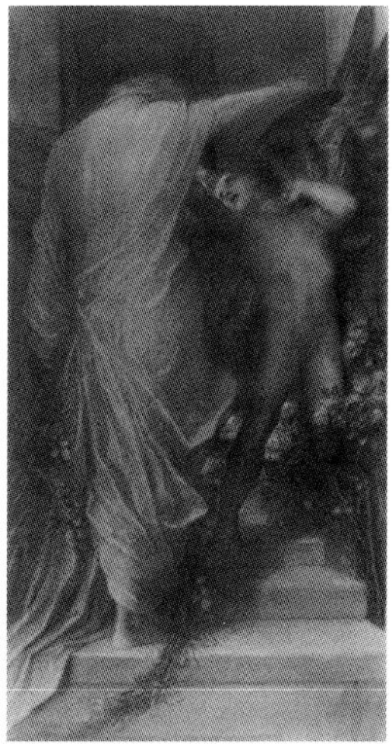

D.1887.2

Love and Death
1890
black chalk, red chalk
signed & dated lower left: *G F Watts / 1890*
645 × 330 mm
Watts, George Frederick (purchase, 1891) (D.1887.2)

■ WATTS, JAMES THOMAS (1853–1930)

Born in Birmingham and educated at King Edward's
School and then at Birmingham School of Art, Watts
was influenced by the writings of Ruskin and the work
of the Pre-Raphaelites. His watercolours are generally
seasonal and show wooded landscapes. Watts exhibited
in Birmingham, Liverpool, the city to which he moved
in 1874, at the Royal Academy between 1878 and 1922
and at the Royal Cambrian Academy in Wales.

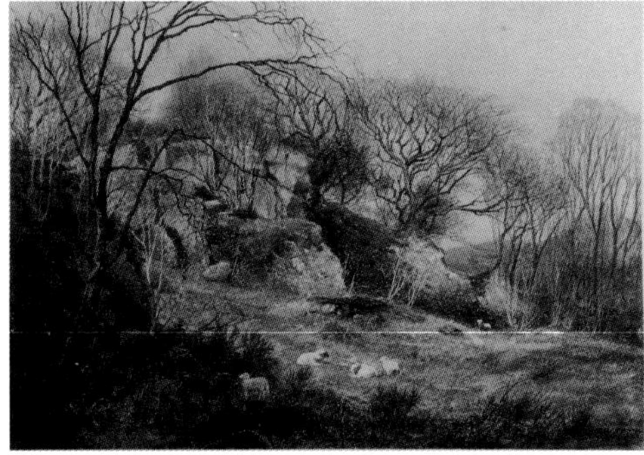

D.2000.2

A wooded Landscape with Sheep in the Foreground near Bettws-y-Coed
pencil, watercolour, bodycolour
(heightened with white)
signed lower right: *J Watts*
263 × 367 mm
Christie's, Hazlitt, Gooden & Fox (via) (purchase, 7.4.2000)
(V. & A./N.A.C.F./F.O.W.) (D.2000.2)

■ WEBBER, JOHN (1750–93)

Born in London, the son of a Swiss sculptor, Webber
(originally Wäber) trained in Berne under Aberli and
in Paris under Wille before entering the Royal
Academy Schools in 1775. From 1776 to 1780 he was
the official artist on Captain Cook's last expedition to
the Pacific. During the following years he worked on
the official publication of the voyage. Webber made
sketching tours on the Continent (1787), the Wye
valley (1788), Derbyshire (1789) and North Wales (1790
and 1791). He was elected a member of the Royal
Academy in 1791.

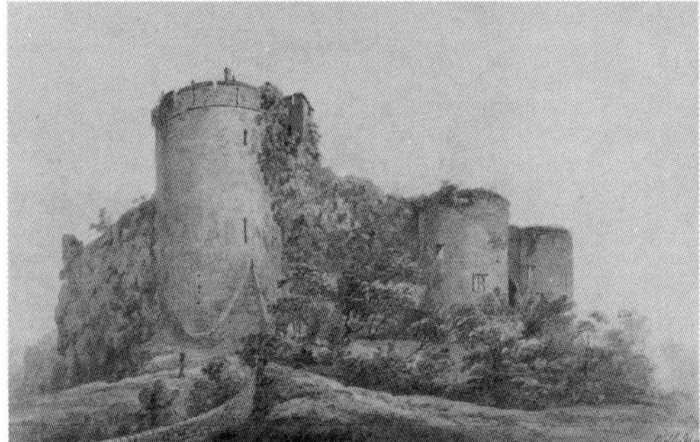

D.1900.12

Chepstow Castle, Monmouthshire, Wales from the South East
1788
pencil, watercolour
signed & dated lower right on narrow paper strip
added along lower edge: *J Webber. / del 1788*; inscribed
on mount lower centre: *Chepstow Castle*
299 × 468 mm
Worthington, Mary (gift, 1900) (D.1900.12)

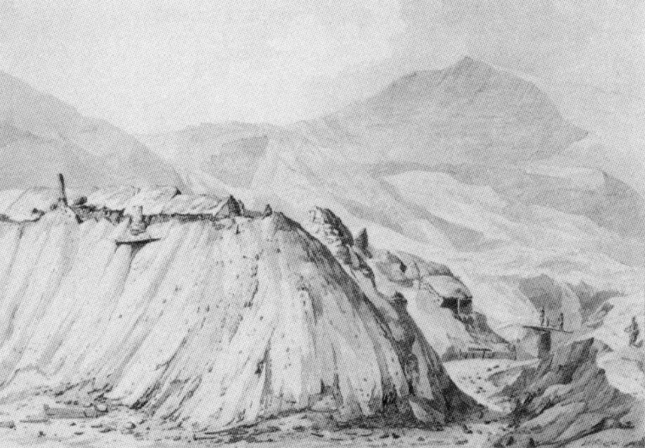

D.1934.7

Oden Mine, Mam Tor, Derbyshire
1789
pencil, watercolour
signed & dated lower right: *J Webber del 1789*; inscribed
on mount lower centre: *Oden Mine, near Mam Tor*
332 × 479 mm
Friends of the Whitworth (gift, 1934) (D.1934.7)

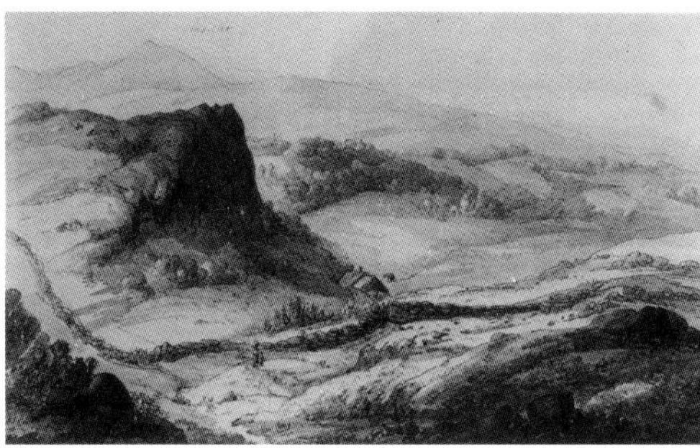

D.1962.5

View at Maillio near Bangor, Caernarvonshire, Wales
pencil, pen and brown ink, brown watercolour
grey watercolour
signed on mount lower centre: *John Webber delt.*;
inscribed within cartouche on mount lower centre:
A View at Maillio near Bangor / Ferry. North Wales.;
inscribed on mount lower right in later hand giving the
price: *J Webber R.A 7/6*
213 × 342 mm
Friends of the Whitworth (gift, 1962) (D.1962.5)

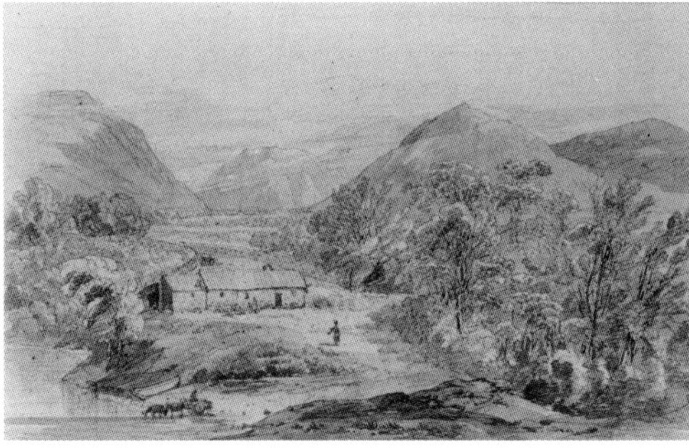

D.1962.6

The Nant Ffrancon Valley looking south from near Bethesda, Caernarvonshire, Wales
pencil, pen and brown ink, brown watercolour
grey watercolour
inscribed within cartouche on mount lower centre:
Scene in North Wales; inscribed on mount lower right
in later hand giving the price: *J.Webber.R.A / 6/*
220 × 345 mm
Friends of the Whitworth (gift, 1962) (D.1962.6)

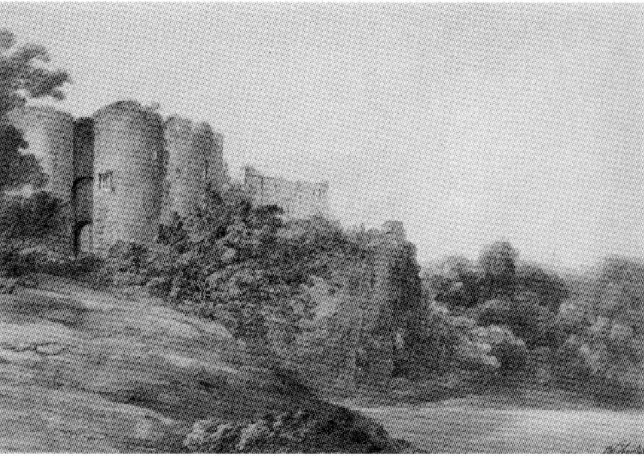

D.1970.77

Chepstow Castle, Monmouthshire, Wales from the North East
1788
pencil, watercolour
signed & dated lower right: *J Webber.del 1788*
287 × 417 mm
Towlson, Hector J. (bequest, 1970) (D.1970.77)

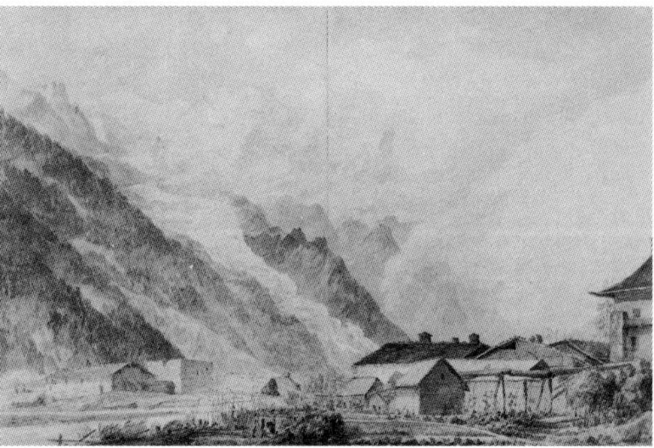

D.1999.24

Mont Blanc and Chamonix
1787
pencil, watercolour; two joined sheets
signed & dated lower right: J *Webber.del 1787.*;
inscribed lower left: *River Arve*; inscribed upper right:
laiguille du Gaute; inscribed upper left: *Mont Blanc*;
inscribed within cartouche on mount lower centre:
Mont Blanc. / Chamouni.
305 × 454 mm
Scott-Elliot, Miss Aydua, in memory of Paul Oppé
(gift, 4.11.1999) (D.1999.24)

■ WEST, RAPHAEL LAMAR (1766–1850)

There is little information on the life of Raphael Lamar
West, elder son of Benjamin. He was his father's
assistant and although he had talent he never made a
name for himself. West was brought up improvidently
and soon exhausted his share of his father's fortune so
that he had to appeal to the Royal Academy for
financial help. C. R. Leslie described him as possessing
'more talent than industry'.

Cadmus slaying the Dragon
pencil, pen and brown ink, brown watercolour
552 × 432 mm
Colnaghi's (purchase, 1964) (D.1964.3)

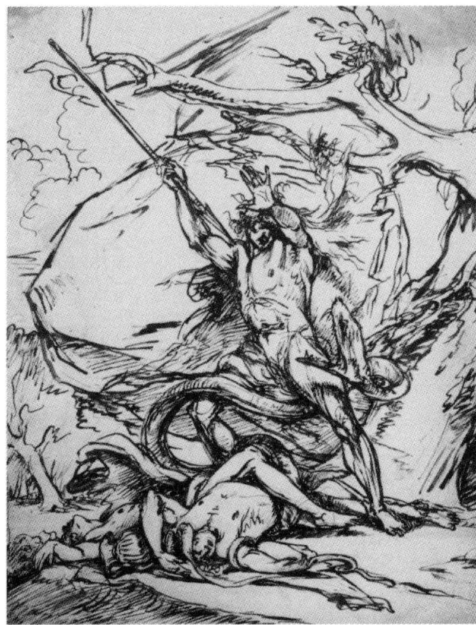
D.1964.3

■ WESTALL, RICHARD (1765–1836)

Richard Westall was a figure and historical painter who entered the Royal Academy schools in 1785. He was elected a member of the Royal Academy in 1794 and was an extremely prolific book illustrator, illustrating virtually all the standard works of poetry of the day.

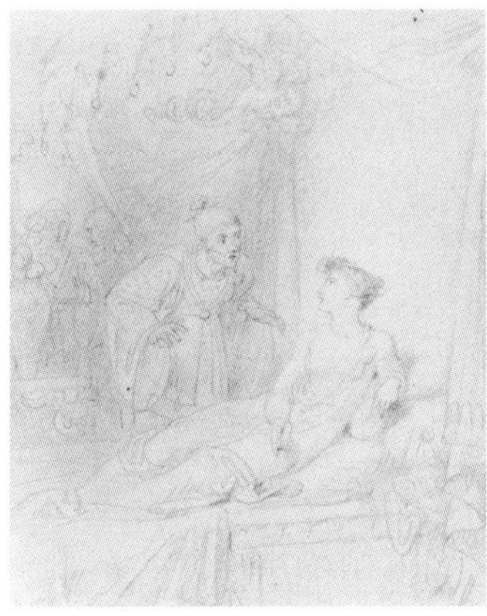
D.1926.72

A Woman reclining: an Illustration to an Oriental Tale
pencil
signed lower left with initials: *R. W*
125 × 101 mm
Ogden, William Sharp (bequest, 1926) (D.1926.72)

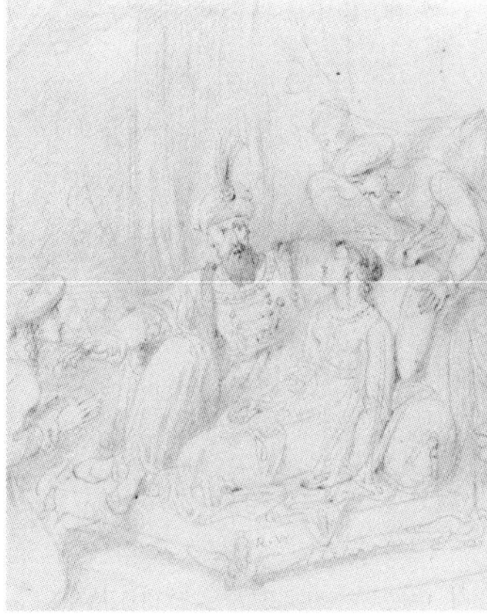
D.1926.73

A young Woman swooning: an Illustration to an Oriental Tale
pencil
signed lower centre with initals: *R. W*
126 × 100 mm
Ogden, William Sharp (bequest, 1926) (D.1926.73)

A Man kneeling by a reclining Woman: an Illustration to an Oriental Tale
pencil
124 × 100 mm
Ogden, William Sharp (bequest, 1926) (D.1926.74)

Two Serpents fighting: an Illustration to an Oriental Tale
pencil
signed lower right with initials: *R. W*
124 × 99 mm
Ogden, William Sharp (bequest, 1926) (D.1926.75)

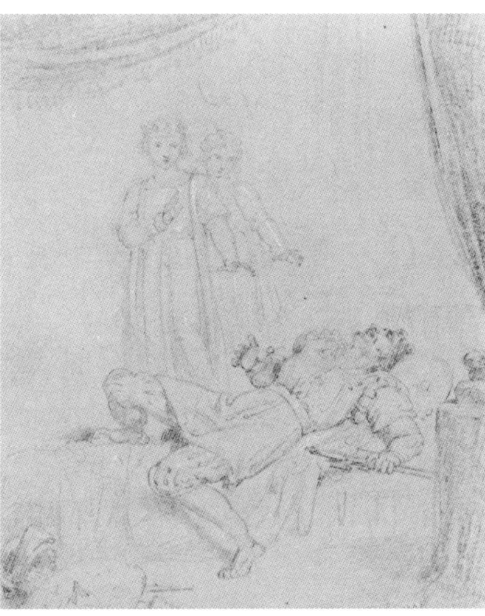
D.1960.62

Richard's Vision of the two Princes: Illustration to Shakespeare's 'Richard III'
pencil, bodycolour (heightened with white); buff paper
signed lower right with initials: *R W*
124 × 101 mm
Abbott and Holder, London (purchase, 1960) (D.1960.62)

A Girl and a Rider by a Mill
pencil, brown watercolour
69 × 53 mm
University of Manchester, History of Art Department (transfer, 1960) (D.1960.146)

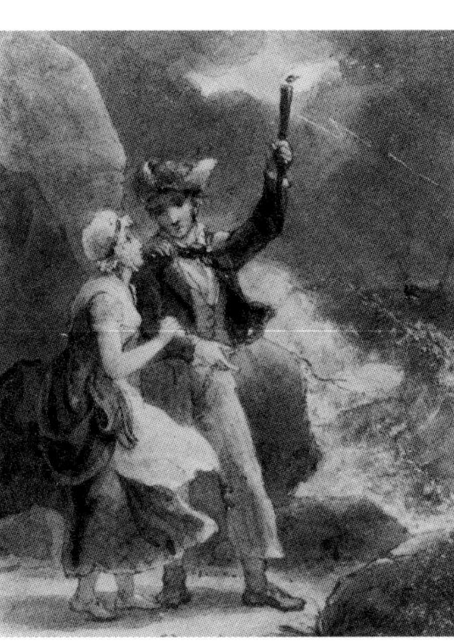
D.1960.147

A Couple on a stormy Seashore at Night
pencil, brown watercolour, bodycolour (heightened with white)
69 × 52 mm
University of Manchester, History of Art Department (transfer, 1960) (D.1960.147)

A Couple under a Tree
pencil, grey watercolour, brown watercolour
69 × 53 mm
University of Manchester, History of Art Department (transfer, 1960) (D.1960.148)

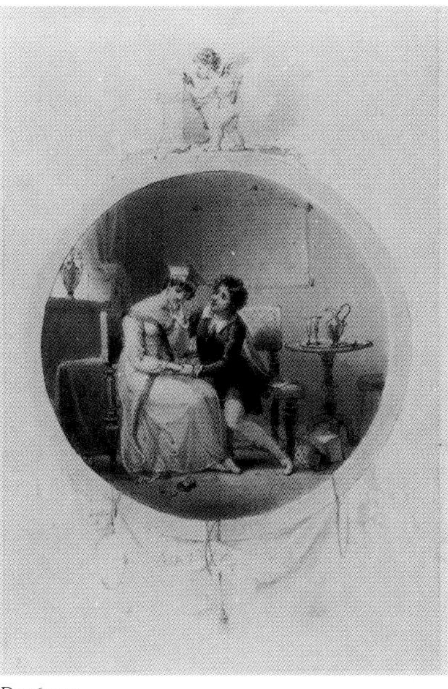
D.1960.149

Illustration to Byron's 'Mazeppa', Stanza VI
pencil, grey watercolour, brown watercolour
inscribed lower centre below image: *MAZEPPA*; inscribed lower centre below image after inscription: *Stanza VI*
121 × 80 mm
University of Manchester, History of Art Department (transfer, 1960) (D.1960.149)

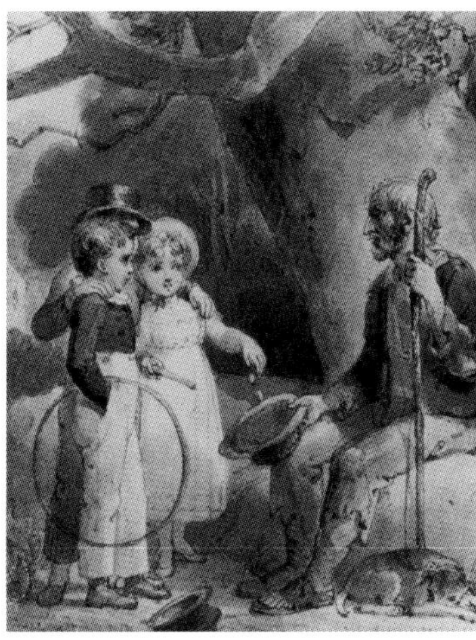
D.1960.150

A Group of Children with a Beggar
pencil, grey watercolour, brown watercolour
68 × 52 mm
University of Manchester, History of Art Department (transfer, 1960) (D.1960.150)

Illustration to Byron's 'Parisina'
pencil, brown watercolour, bodycolour
(heightened with white)
inscribed lower centre below image: *PARISINA*
120 × 80 mm
University of Manchester, History of Art Department
(transfer, 1960) (D.1960.151)

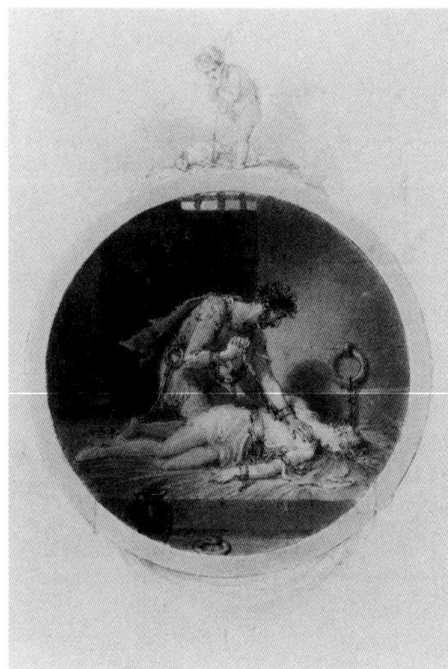

D.1960.152

Illustration to Byron's 'The Prisoner of Chillon', Stanza VIII
pencil, grey watercolour
120 × 82 mm
University of Manchester, History of Art Department
(transfer, 1960) (D.1960.152)

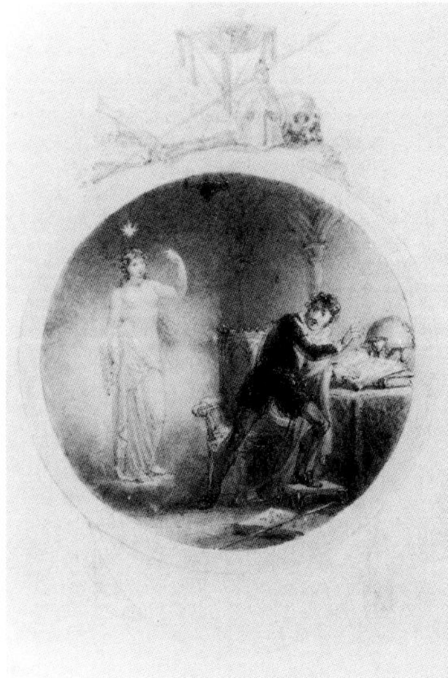

D.1960.153

A Woman appearing to a Man in a Vision, Illustration to (?) Byron's 'Manfred'
pencil, brown watercolour
121 × 80 mm
University of Manchester, History of Art Department
(transfer, 1960) (D.1960.153)

Peace(?) appearing to a Man in Oriental Dress
pencil, brown watercolour
120 × 80 mm
University of Manchester, History of Art Department
(transfer, 1960) (D.1960.154)

■ WESTALL, WILLIAM (1781–1850)
The younger brother and pupil of Richard, William
Westall was principally a topographer. In 1801 he was
draughtsman to Matthew Flinders's expedition to
Australia, during which time he was shipwrecked. He
returned by way of China in 1803 and India in 1804.
Westall first visited the Lake District in 1811 and
published *Views of the Lake and Vale of Keswick* in 1820.
He produced many small topographical views which
were engraved in numerous publications, including
Views on the Thames (1824) and *Landscape Illustrations
of the Waverley Novels* (1834).

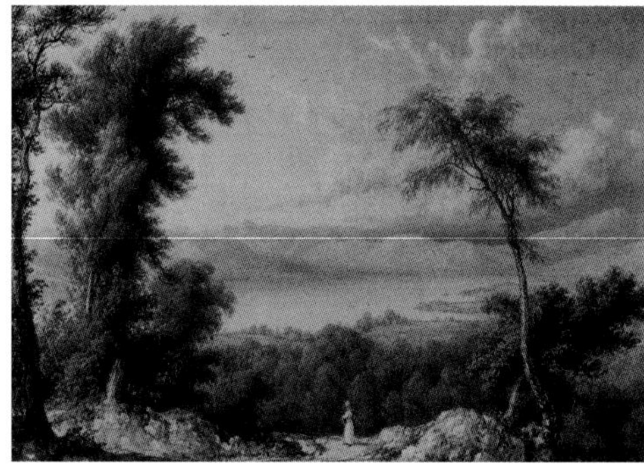

D.1892.63

Lake Windermere: an Illustration to Sir Walter Scott's 'Guy Mannering'
1832
pencil, watercolour
127 × 174 mm
Taylor, John Edward (gift, 1892) (D.1892.63)

■ WESTCOTT, PHILIP (1815–78)
Born in Liverpool, Westcott, a painter of portraits,
landscapes and historical subjects, became a member
of the Liverpool Academy in 1844. He exhibited
portraits at the Royal Academy from 1848 to 1861 and
in 1855 moved to London. Westcott's move to London
was not a success and the latter part of his career was
spent in Manchester.

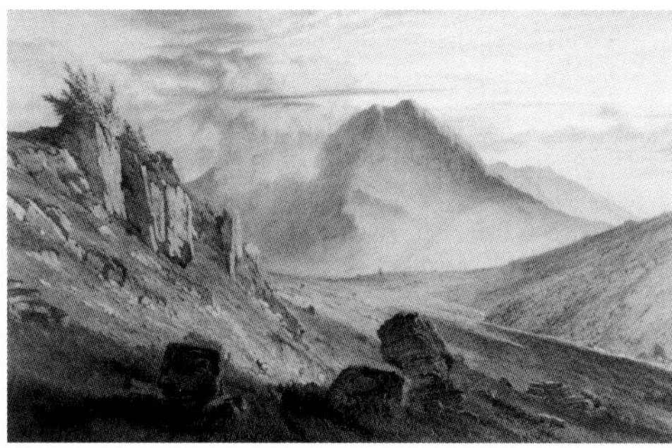

D.1924.26

Cader Idris, Merioneth, Wales
1868
watercolour
signed & dated lower centre: *Philip Westcott.1868*
550 × 856 mm
Allen, C. P. (gift, 1924) (D.1924.26)

■ WHAITE, HENRY CLARENCE (1828–1912)
Born in Manchester, Whaite exhibited landscapes at
the Old Watercolour Society, of which he was elected a
member in 1882. He was President of the Manchester
Academy and exhibited at the Royal Academy
intermittently between 1851 and 1904. Whaite
was an enthusiastic supporter of the artists' colony at
Bettws-y-Coed and the first President of the Royal
Cambrian Academy.

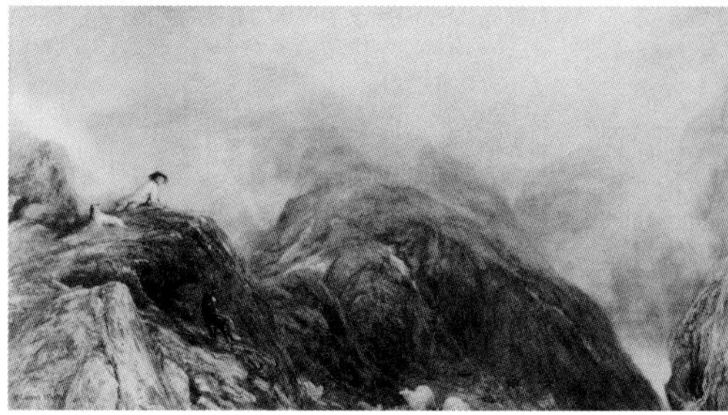

D.1913.10

The Snowdonian Shepherd
watercolour, bodycolour (heightened with white)
signed lower left: *H Clarence Whaite*
765 × 1340 mm
untraced (purchase, 1913) (D.1913.10)

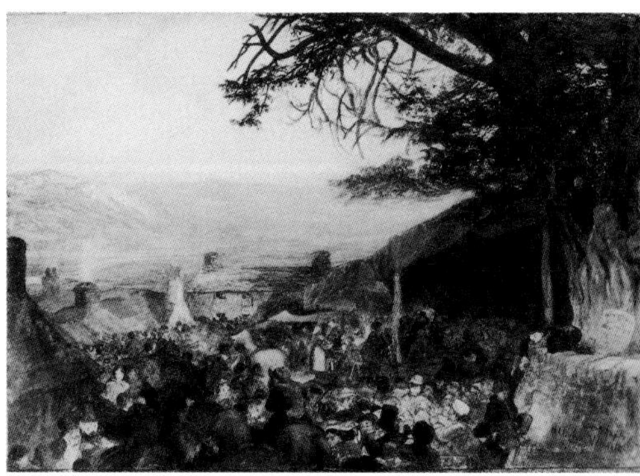

D.1922.30

Fair at Llanbedrog, Caernarvonshire, Wales
watercolour, bodycolour (heightened with white)
signed & inscribed lower right: *Llandbedof /
H Clarence Whaite*
280 × 397 mm
untraced (purchase, 1922) (D.1922.30)

■ WHEATLEY, FRANCIS (1747–1801)
Wheatley, a figure, portrait and landscape painter,
studied at Shipley's before entering the Royal
Academy Schools in 1769. In 1779 he eloped to
Dublin with the wife of fellow artist J. A. Gresse
but was forced to return in 1783 or 1784. He exhibited
at the Royal Academy from 1784 until his death and
was elected a member in 1791. Now best known for
his series of prints of London street sellers, *The Cries
of London*, Wheatley led an improvident life and by
1793 was bankrupt.

Going to School
pencil, pen and grey ink, watercolour
348 × 447 mm
Taylor, John Edward (gift, 1892) (D.1892.8)

Coniston Lake, Lancashire
1785
pen and grey ink, watercolour
280 × 400 mm
Anderson, A. E., National Art Collections Fund (via)
(gift, 1925) (D.1925.41)

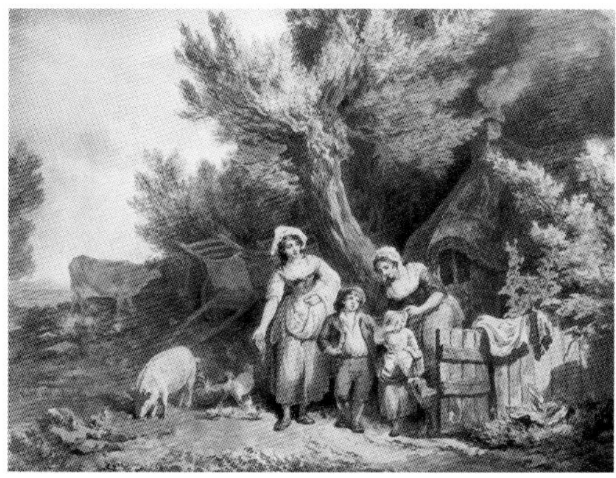

D.1892.8

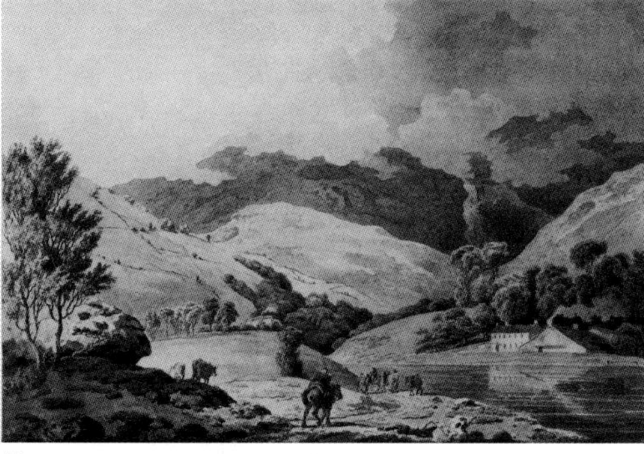

D.1925.41

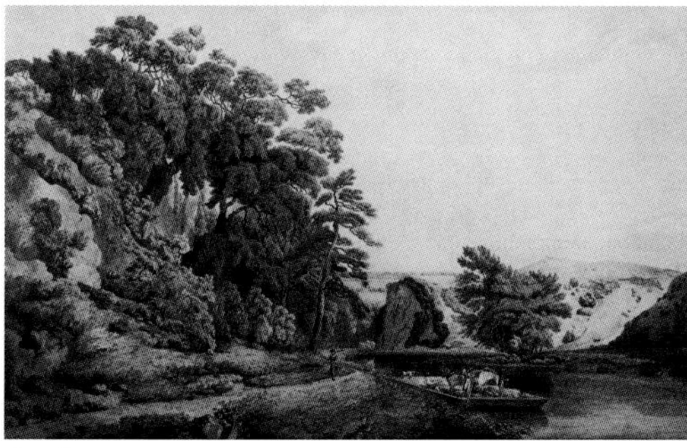

D.1948.14

The Ferry
pencil, pen and ink, watercolour
427 × 664 mm
Pilkington, Margaret (gift, 1948) (D.1948.14)

Gypsy Encampment
pencil, pen and brown ink, watercolour
198 × 251 mm
Towlson, Hector J. (bequest, 1969) (D.1970.78)

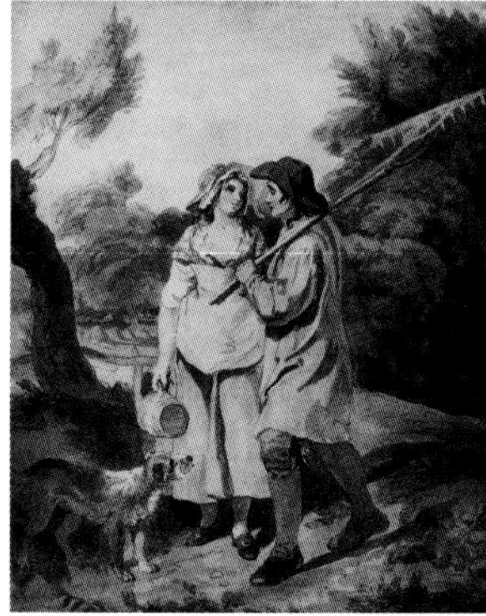

D.1970.80

Rustic Courtship
pen and grey ink, watercolour
260 × 205 mm
Towlson, Hector J. (bequest, 1969) (D.1970.80)

■ **WHITE, ROBERT (1645–1703)**
White was a pupil of David Loggan, and like his
master specialised in miniature portrait drawings.
He was also a prolific portrait engraver and over
400 plates are known to be by him, dating between
1666 and 1702.

Portrait of Lord Chief Baron Ward
pencil
inscribed along lower edge: *Ld Chief Baron Ward*
129 × 99 mm
Ogden, William Sharp (bequest, 1926) (D.1926.70)

■ **WHITTLE, Jun., THOMAS (fl. 1865–85)**
A landscape painter and son of an artist of the same
name, Whittle exhibited mainly at Suffolk Street but
intermittently at the Royal Academy between 1865 and
1885. Little is known of his life.

Gypsies on Dartford Heath, Kent
5.6.1869
pencil, watercolour, bodycolour (heightened with
white); buff paper
signed lower right: *Thos. Whittle–*; inscribed & dated
on verso upper left: *Dartford Heath / 5 June 1869*
277 × 383 mm
Ogden, William Sharp (bequest, 1926) (D.1926.71)

Snodland-on-the-Medway, Kent
1870
pencil, watercolour
inscribed & dated lower left: *Snodland on the Medway. /
1870.*
192 × 362 mm
Ogden, William Sharp (bequest, 1926) (D.1926.76)

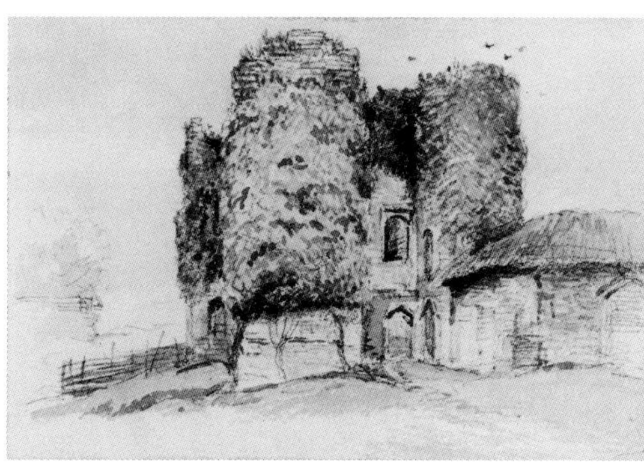

D.1926.77.1

Archbishop's Palace, Otford, Kent
5.9.1878
pencil, watercolour
inscribed & dated on mount lower right in later hand:
Otford Castle Kent 5 Sept 1878 / T Whittle
126 × 182 mm
Ogden, William Sharp (bequest, 1926) (D.1926.77.1)

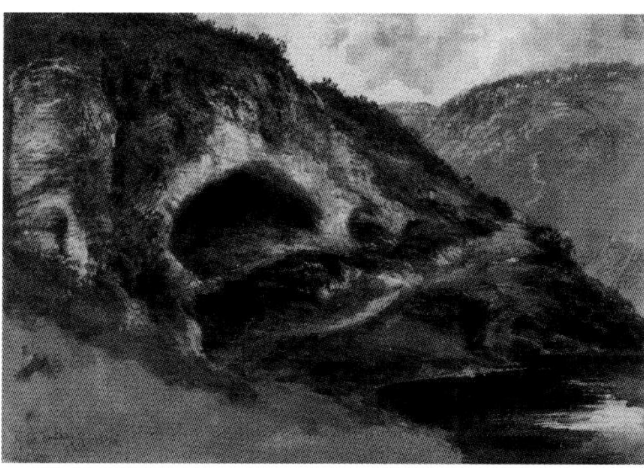

D.1926.77.2

Dove Holes, Dovedale, Derbyshire
7.9.1870
pencil, watercolour, bodycolour (heightened
with white); buff paper
signed, inscribed & dated lower left: *Dove Holes / 7 Sept
1870 / Thos Whittle*
177 × 252 mm
Ogden, William Sharp (bequest, 1926) (D.1926.77.2)

■ **WILD, CHARLES (1781–1855)**
Wild was an architectural draughtsman who trained
under Thomas Malton Jun. He was elected a member
of the Old Watercolour Society in 1812. Wild
specialised in the depiction of the interiors and
exteriors of cathedrals and colleges, most of which were
intended for the engraving market. His drawings are
frequently mistaken for those of more significant artists
such as Turner and Girtin.

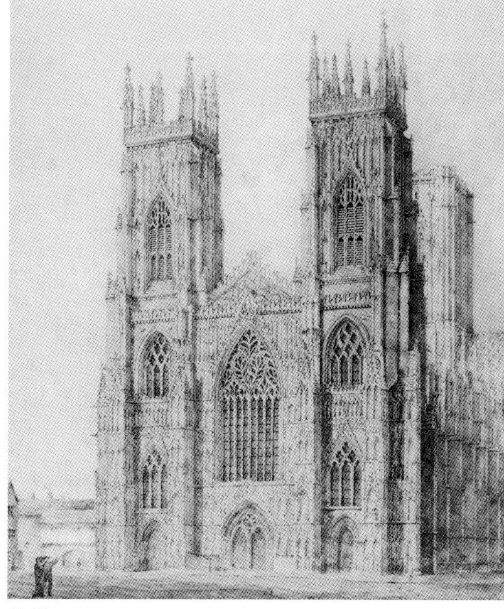

D.1887.9

The West Front, York Minster
1808
pencil, watercolour
304 × 254 mm
Agnew's (purchase, 12.5.1891) (D.1887.9)

Trinity Chapel, Canterbury Cathedral
watercolour
signed lower left: *CWild*
282 × 208 mm
Worthington, Mary (gift, 1899) (D.1899.1)

■ WILKIE, SIR DAVID (1785–1841)

One of the most important Scottish historical and genre painters, Wilkie trained firstly in Scotland and then at the Royal Academy Schools. He exhibited at the Royal Academy – of which he was elected a member in 1811 – from 1806 to 1842. Wilkie was an accomplished draughtsman and produced many drawings preparatory to his paintings. He visited Turkey and the Middle East in 1840 but died on the return voyage. His funeral was recorded by his friend Turner in the painting *Burial at Sea*.

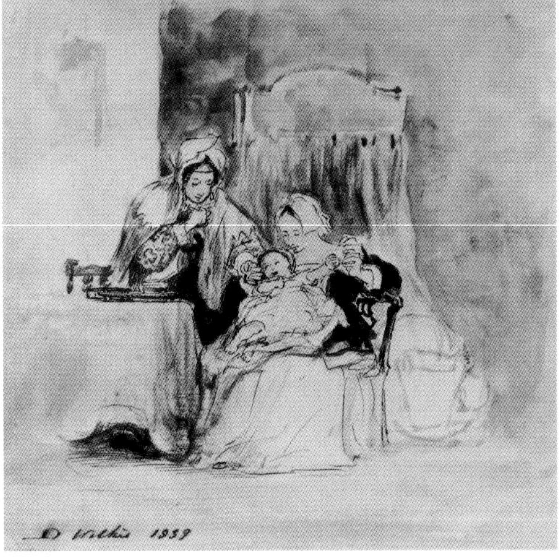
D.1920.5

The Grandmother's Visit

1839
pencil, pen and brown ink, watercolour
signed & dated lower left: *D Wilkie 1839*
180 × 180 mm
Leicester Galleries, London (purchase, 1920) (D.1920.5)

■ WILKINSON, REV. JOSEPH (1764–1831)

Born in Carlisle and educated at Cambridge, Wilkinson was an enthusiastic amateur artist who lived at Ormathwaite in Cumberland until he was appointed Rector of East and West Wretham in Norfolk in 1804. He is now chiefly known for the 48 illustrations he produced for *Select Views in Cumberland, Westmorland and Lancashire* (1810), for which Wordsworth anonymously supplied the text.

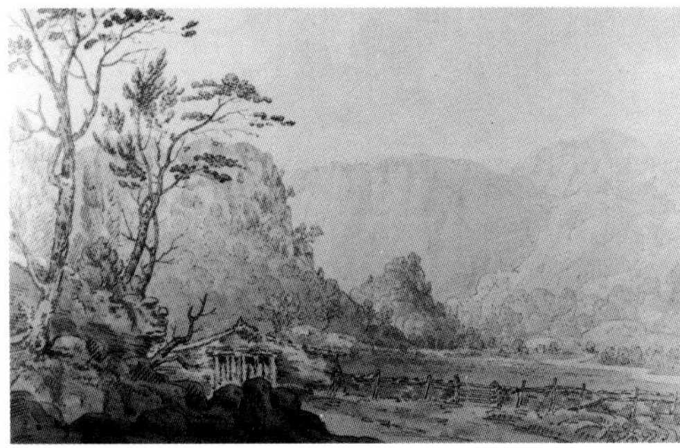
D.1970.82

Borrowdale from High Lodore, Cumberland

pencil, watercolour
inscribed lower centre below image: *Borrowdale from High Lowdore.*
sheet 282 × 413 mm
Towlson, Hector J. (bequest, 1969) (D.1970.82)

■ WILLIAMS, CHARLES (fl. 1797–1830) (attributed to)

Charles Williams was a caricaturist and engraver of his own work and the work of others, in particular G. M. Woodward.

The Right Time: Honi Soit Qui Mal y Pense

pencil; watermark JWHATMAN / 1808
inscribed upper left (the man's speech): *Come tell me Nan! when is it best / At morning, Noon, or time of rest*; inscribed upper right (the woman's speech): *Why faith dear Ned! to tell you right / I like it morning, Noon, and Night!*; inscribed along lower edge: *The right Time – Honi Soit Qui Mal y Pense*
249 × 337 mm
Ogden, William Sharp (bequest, 1926) (D.1926.107)

■ WILLIAMS, CHARLES FREDERICK (1810–94)

Charles Frederick Williams was a painter and drawing master who worked in Exeter from the 1830s to the 1850s and provided illustrations for a number of local topographical publications, including *A Perambulation of The Antient and Royal Forest of Dartmoor* (1848). Williams later lived and worked in Southampton.

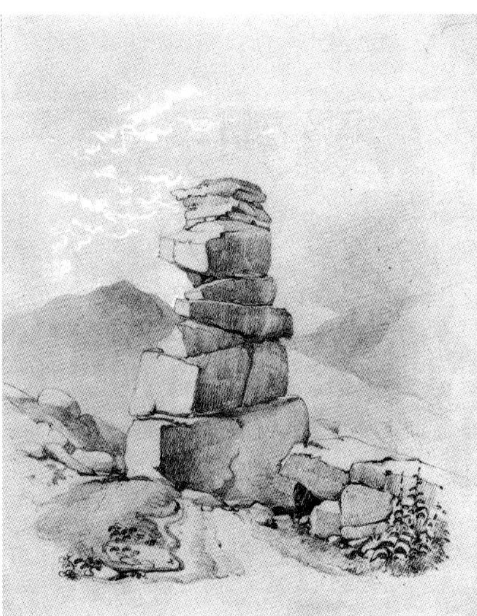
D.1926.235

Rock Idol (Bowerman's Nose), near Manaton, Dartmoor, Devon

1848
pencil, white chalk; grey paper
inscribed in centre verso: *ROCK IDOL (BOWERMAN'S NOSE) NEAR MANATON*; inscribed lower left verso (William Sharp Ogden's hand ?): *by C F Williams* [name underlined]; inscribed in pencil lower right verso: *nr Dartmoor / Devon*
204 × 160 mm
Ogden, William Sharp (bequest, 1926) (D.1926.235)

The Logan Stone, near Rippon Tor, Dartmoor, Devon

1848
pencil, white chalk; grey paper
inscribed on verso in centre: *LOGAN STONE NEAR RIPPON TOR*; inscribed verso in centre below capital letters (William Sharp Ogden's hand ?): *nr Dartmoor Devon*; inscribed in pencil lower left verso: *by CFWilliams*
207 × 159 mm
Ogden, William Sharp (bequest, 1926) (D.1926.236)

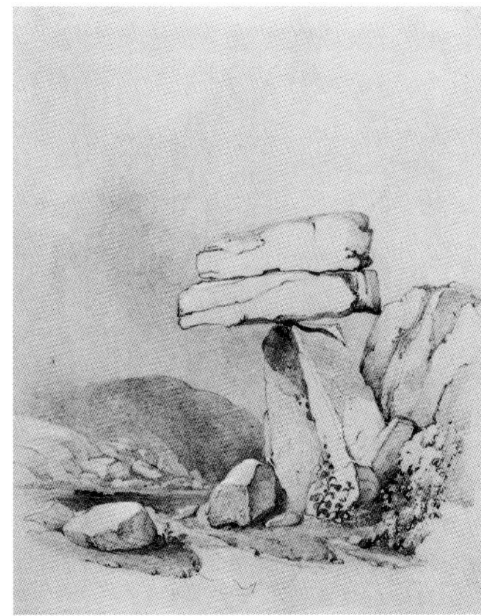
D.1926.236

Kistvaen, near Houndtor, Dartmoor, Devon

1848
pencil, white chalk; grey paper
inscribed lower right margin: *Take Miss Robinsons* [pound sign]*8. a drawing* [all erased]; inscribed verso in centre the lithographer's address: *P.Gauci Esqr. / 9 North Cresct / Tottenham Court Road / London.*; inscribed verso lower right (William Sharp Ogden's hand?): *Pgauci was the artist who lithographed these / drawings by C F Williams*
Sheet: 191 × 272 mm
Ogden, William Sharp (bequest, 1926) (D.1926.277)

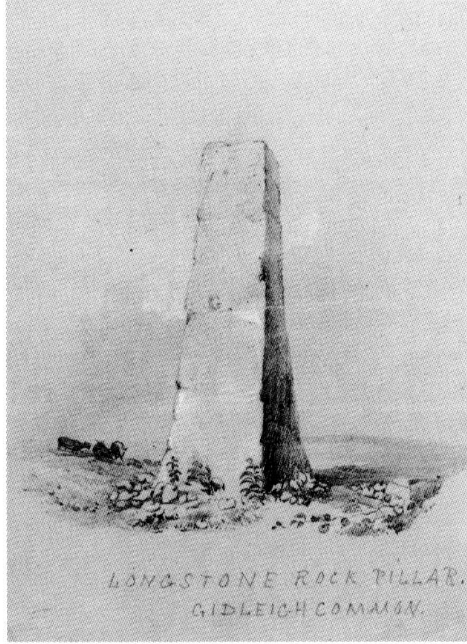
D.1926.278

Longstone Rock Pillar, Gidleigh Common, Dartmoor, Devon

1848
pencil, white chalk; grey paper
inscribed along lower edge: *LONGSTONE ROCK PILLAR. / GIDLEIGH COMMON*; inscribed along upper edge verso instructions to the lithographer: *The words Gidleigh Common / had better be in the line / under as written*; inscribed verso lower left (William Sharp Ogden's hand?): *by CFWilliams / the original drawing / lithod by PGauci*; inscribed verso lower right (William Sharp Ogden's hand?): *Gidleigh is near Moreton Hampstead Dartmoor / Devon*
203 × 146 mm
Ogden, William Sharp (bequest, 1926) (D.1926.278)

Stone Avenue on the North Teign, Dartmoor, Devon
1848
pencil, white chalk; grey paper
inscribed on mount lower left (William Sharp Ogden's hand ?): *by CFWilliams–*
123 × 192 mm
Ogden, William Sharp (bequest, 1926) (D.1926.326)

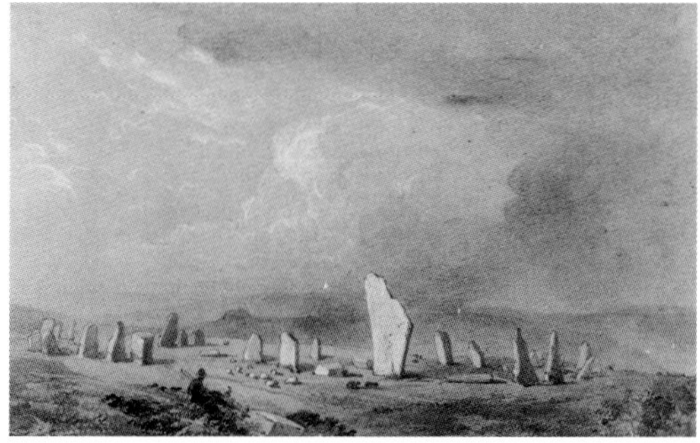

D.1926.327

Sacred Circle, Gidleigh Common, Dartmoor, Devon
1848
pencil, white chalk; grey paper
inscribed lower left on mount (William Sharp Ogden's hand ?): *by CFWilliams*; inscribed lower right on mount (William Sharp Ogden's hand ?): *DrewStanton* [second part of word erased] *Steighton* [written above] *– Dartmoor Devon*
122 × 190 mm
Ogden, William Sharp (bequest, 1926) (D.1926.327)

Grimspound Fortified Aboriginal Village, Dartmoor, Devon
1848
pencil, white chalk; grey paper
inscribed lower left on mount (William Sharp Ogden's hand ?): *Ancient fortification – Dartmoor / By an unknown artist* [illegible] *CFWilliams*
123 × 194 mm
Ogden, William Sharp (bequest, 1926) (D.1926.328)

■ WILLIAMS, HUGH WILLIAM (1773–1829)

Born at sea, the orphaned son of a sea captain, Hugh William Williams was brought up in Edinburgh but moved to London and was elected to the short-lived Associated Artists in 1808. He visited Italy and Greece in 1818 and the finished watercolours deriving from this trip were exhibited to universal acclaim in 1822. His illustrated volumes *Travels in Italy, Greece and the Ionian Islands* (1820) and *Select Views in Greece* (1827–29) earned him the nickname 'Grecian', by which he is now best known.

A Ravine with a Waterfall
pencil, watercolour
505 × 358 mm
Taylor, John Edward (gift, 1892) (D.1892.5)

Welsh Landscape
pen and brown ink, watercolour
signed lower left: *HWWilliams*
275 × 385 mm
Worthington, Mary (gift, 1900) (D.1900.14)

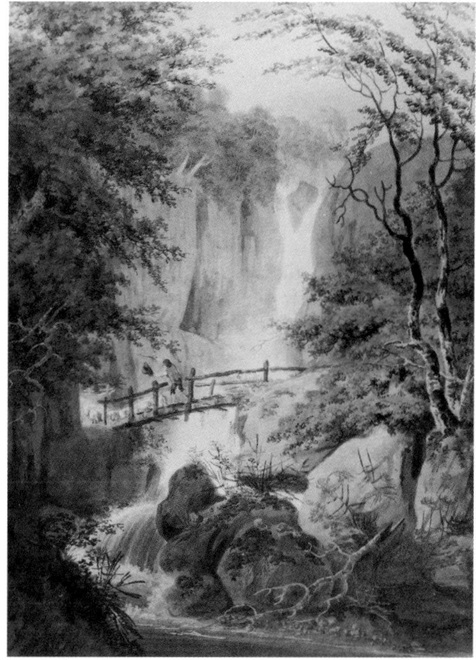

D.1892.5

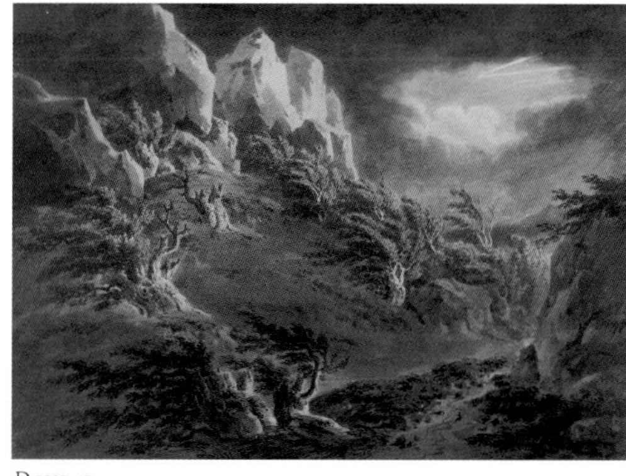

D.1937.41

Birnam Wood in a Storm
1801
pencil, watercolour
signed & dated lower left: *Williams 1801*; inscribed lower centre: *Birnam Woods*
362 × 491 mm
Weymouth, Mrs C. (gift, 1937) (D.1937.41)

Head of Loch Katrine, Perthshire/Stirlingshire, Scotland, Evening
1801
pencil, watercolour
signed lower right: *Williams Delint.*
357 × 507 mm
Weymouth, Mrs C. (gift, 1937) (D.1937.42)

The Temple of the Sybil, Tivoli
pen and brown ink; blue paper
inscribed lower left: *Tivoli / Temple of Vesta & the Cybil* (sic)
438 × 283 mm
Somerville, Stephen Ltd, London (purchase, 1988) (D.1988.9)

The Forum, Rome
pencil, pen and brown ink
inscribed lower centre: *Forum.*
281 × 463 mm
Somerville, Stephen Ltd, London (purchase, 1988) (D.1988.10)

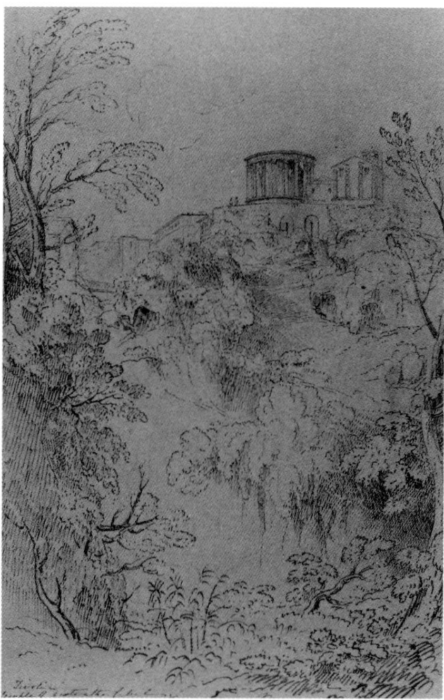

D.1988.9

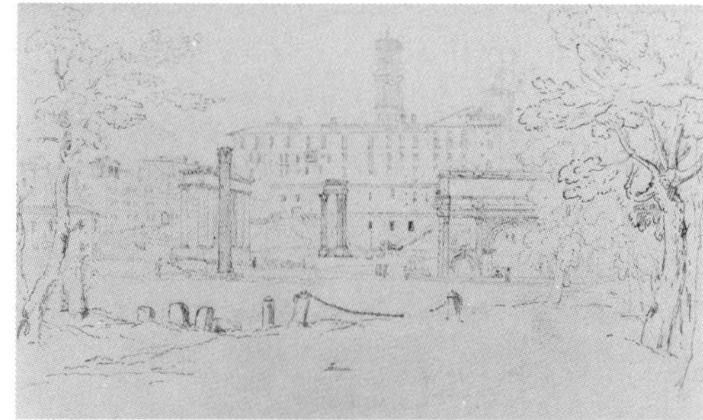

D.1988.10

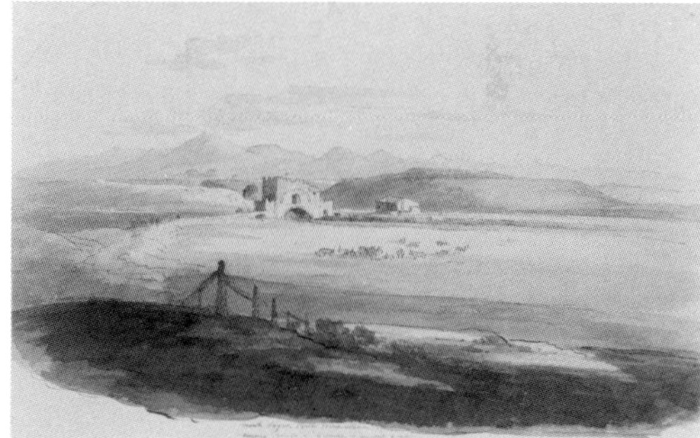

D.1988.11

The Ponte Nomentano, Rome
30.1.1818
pencil, pen and brown ink, brown watercolour
signed with initials, inscribed & dated lower centre: *Monte Sagro.Ponta Nomentana.10th. / Annio. Monte So.Ginaro.30 Jany 1818. H.W.W.*
224 × 346 mm
Somerville, Stephen Ltd, London (purchase, 1988) (D.1988.11)

■ WILLIAMS, M. E. (fl. 1846)

Unknown amateur artist.

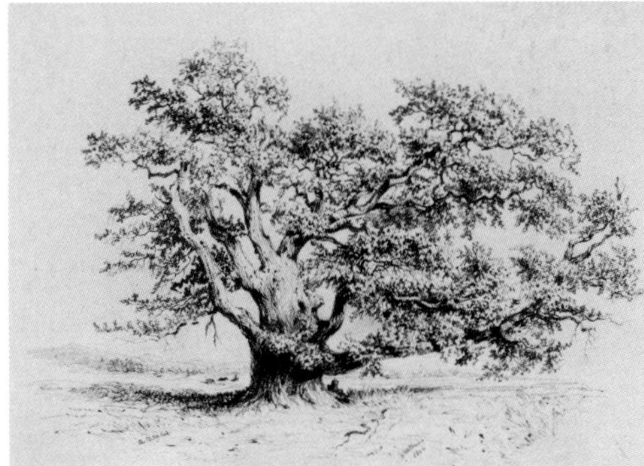

D.1926.317

The Shelly Oak
1846
pencil
signed & dated lower right: *MEWilliams / 1846*;
inscribed lower left: *The Shelly Oak*
183 × 255 mm
Ogden, William Sharp (bequest, 1926) (D.1926.317)

■ WILLIAMSON, DANIEL (1783–1843)

A Liverpool artist, Williamson is recorded as having
copied works by Wright of Derby.

**Cavern in the Gulf of Salerno, after Joseph
Wright of Derby**
pencil, pen and brown ink, watercolour
115 × 165 mm
Ogden, William Sharp (bequest, 1926) (D.1926.69)

■ WILSON, ANDREW (1780–1848)

Wilson was a Scottish painter who studied under
Alexander Nasmyth and at the Royal Academy
Schools. He visited Rome and Naples in about 1802
and again in 1803–05. Wilson was Professor of Drawing
at the Royal Military Academy at Sandhurst until 1818.
He returned to Italy in 1826 and lived for twenty years
in Rome, Florence and Genoa.

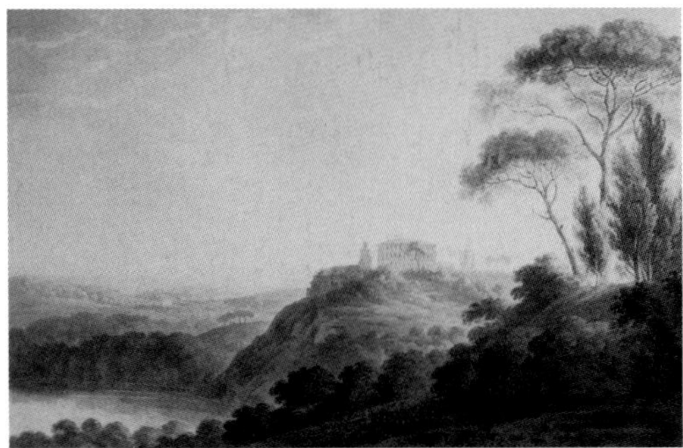

D.1892.122

The Lake of Nemi, Italy, Evening
pencil, watercolour
348 × 518 mm
Taylor, John Edward (gift, 1892) (D.1892.122)

■ WILSON, RICHARD (1713/14–1782)

Born in Wales, Wilson moved to London in 1729 as an
apprentice to a portrait painter. He went to Italy in
1750 visiting Venice before proceeding to Rome, where
he spent most of the rest of his stay, returning in 1756
or 1757. He exhibited at the Society of Artists from
1760 to 1768, and in 1768 was a founder member of the
Royal Academy, where he exhibited until 1780.
Primarily a painter in oils, Wilson was the first British
artist of note to visit Italy.

Lake Avernus, Italy
black chalk, white chalk; grey paper
278 × 414 mm
Anderson, A. E., National Art Collections Fund (via)
(gift, 1923) (D.1923.10)

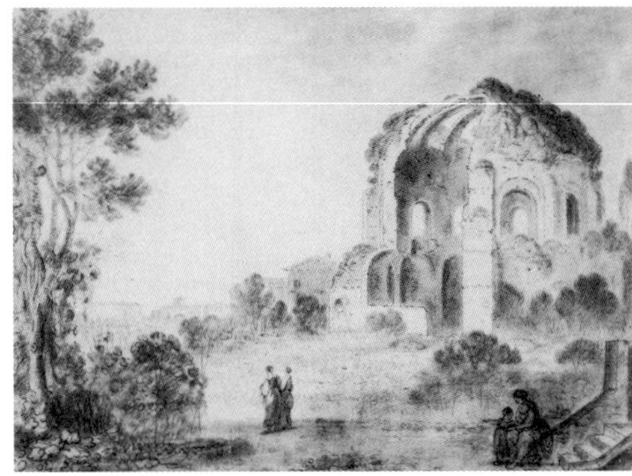

D.1935.19

The Temple of Minerva Medica, Rome
black chalk; blue-grey paper
inscribed lower right margin: *temple di Minerva Medica*
306 × 410 mm
Anderson, A. E. (gift, 1935) (D.1935.19)

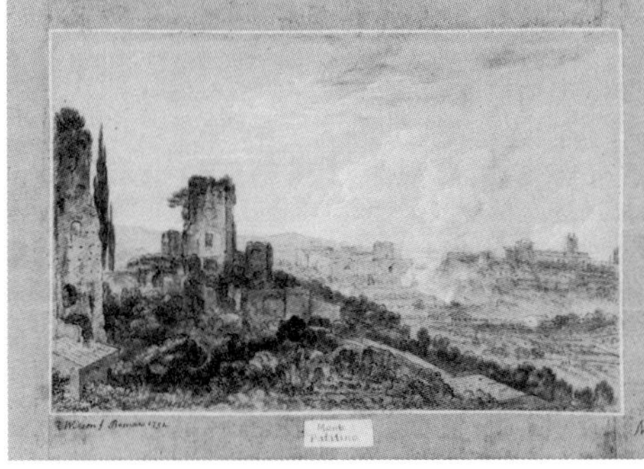

D.1954.3

The Palatine Hill, Rome
1754
black chalk, white chalk; blue-grey paper
signed, inscribed & dated lower left on artist's original
lilac mount: *R Wilson f Romae 1754*; numbered lower
right on artist's original lilac mount: *No.11*; inscribed
lower centre on a white piece of paper attached to lilac
mount: *Monte / Palatino.*
283 × 424 mm
Friends of the Whitworth (gift, 1954) (D.1954.3)

**View in the Galleria di Sopra, above Lake
Albano, Italy**
black chalk, white chalk, blue chalk; grey paper
signed lower left with initials with the R inverted: *RW*
321 × 462 mm
Pilkington, Margaret (in memory of H. B. Milling) (gift, 1954)
(D.1954.14)

■ WILTON, JOSEPH (1722–1803)

One of the most important sculptors of the eighteenth
century, Wilton trained in France and Italy, where he
remained until 1755. He then returned to England and
was appointed Sculptor to His Majesty by George III
in 1764. Wilton was a founder member of the Royal
Academy in 1768 and exhibited there until 1783.

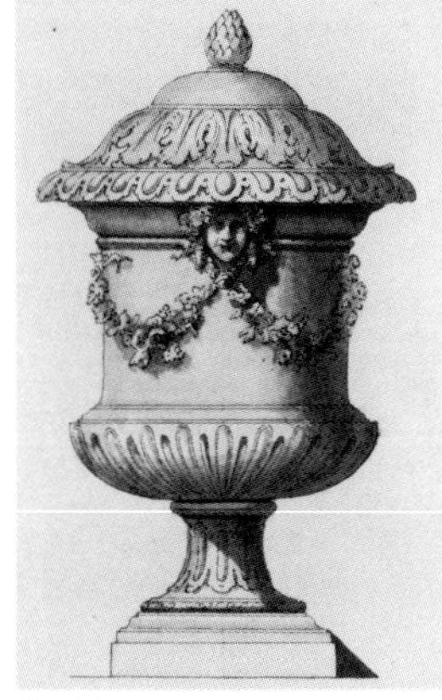

D.1966.1

Study of an Urn, from an antique Model
pen and brown ink, brown watercolour
grey watercolour
279 × 199 mm
Friends of the Whitworth (gift, 1966) (D.1966.1)

■ WIMPERIS, EDMUND MORISON (1835–1900)

Wimperis began his career as a wood-engraver
and worked for the *Illustrated London News*.
Later he turned to landscape watercolour painting
and was elected a member of the New Watercolour
Society in 1875. His moorland landscapes are similar
to those of Thomas Collier and are very much in
the de Wint tradition.

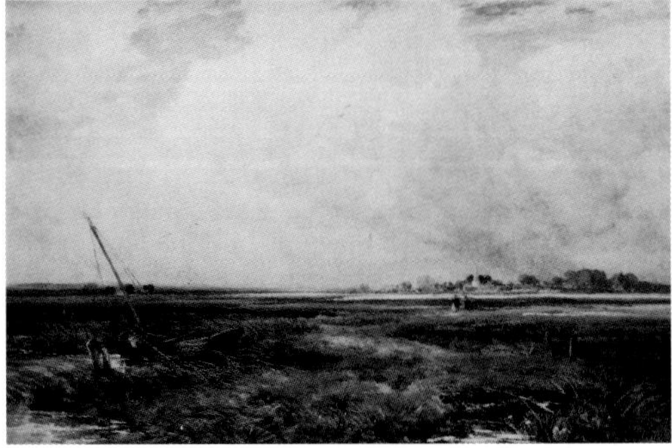

D.1975.3

On the River Arun, Sussex
watercolour
signed lower right: *EMWIMPERIS*
656 × 955 mm
Pilkington, Margaret (executors of) (purchase, 1.1975)
(F.O.W.) (D.1975.3)

Landscape with Village and Cows
1898
pencil, watercolour
signed with initials & dated lower left: *EMW.1898*;
inscribed on verso upper centre: *The Village*
243 × 349 mm
Brockbank, J. E. (bequest, 1987) (D.1987.47)

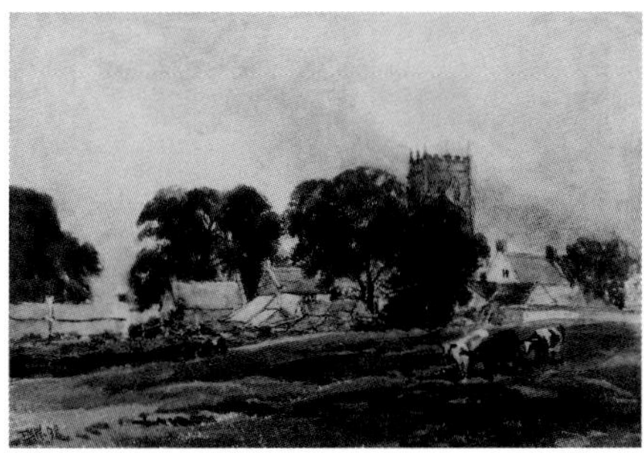

D.1987.47

■ WOLLASTON, GEORGE B. (fl. 1860)

Unknown amateur artist.

Stone Formation, near Frensham, Surrey

22.5.1860
pencil, pen and brown ink, watercolour
signed lower left with initials: *G B W*; signed, inscribed
& dated verso lower left: *Curious Iron–stone formation /
near Frensham Surrey / 22 May 1860 / Geo.BWollaston*
222 × 288 mm
Ogden, William Sharp (bequest, 1926) (D.1926.323)

■ WOOD, ELEANOR STUART (ca. 1856–after 1922)

Unknown amateur artist.

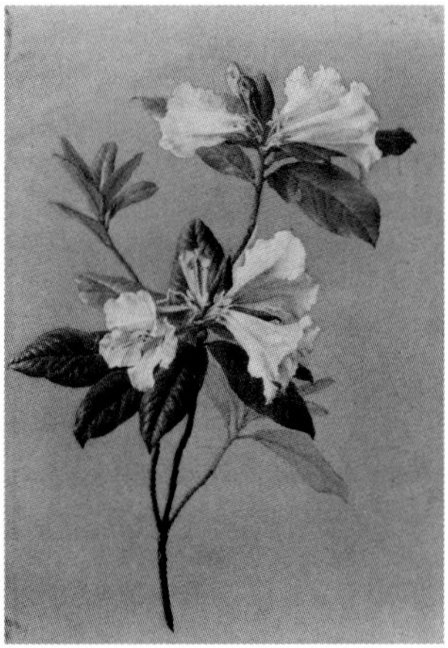

D.1898.7

Sprig of Rhododendron

3.1872
pencil, watercolour, bodycolour (heightened with
white); grey-green paper (drystamped ESK)
signed, inscribed & dated lower right verso: *Eleanor
S.Wood / Art Student / Aged 15 years / March 1872.*
536 × 367 mm
Barrett, Mrs S. A. (gift, 1898) (D.1898.7)

■ WOODHOUSE, WILLIAM (1857–1934)

Woodhouse was an animal painter who lived at
Heysham in Lancashire and studied at Lancaster
School of Art.

The Mussel Cart

pencil, watercolour
210 × 332 mm
Hitchon, Brian (Dr) (in appreciation of his student years at
Manchester University, 1949-1955) (gift, 1987) (D.1987.60)

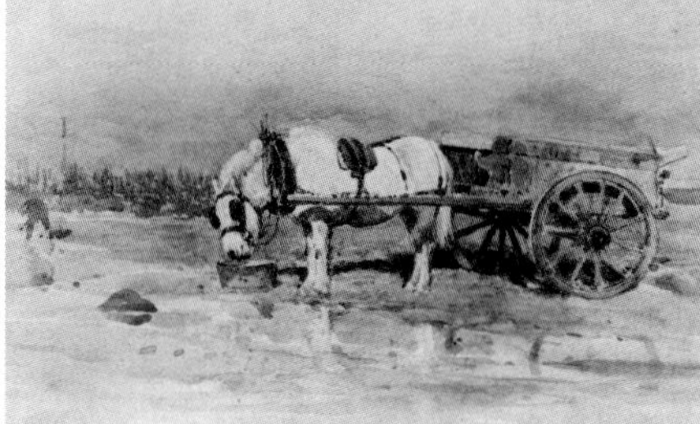

D.1987.60

■ WORLIDGE, THOMAS (1700–1766)

Worlidge was a miniaturist, portrait painter and
printmaker. Known in his time as the English
Rembrandt, he was one of the first English printmakers
to make extensive use of the drypoint technique.
Worlidge moved from Bath to London in 1740. He
excelled as an etcher and copied many of Rembrandt's
etched portraits.

Head of a Man

black chalk; brown paper
198 × 173 mm
Ogden, William Sharp (bequest, 1926) (D.1926.234)

■ WREN, SIR CHRISTOPHER (1632–1723) (office of)

The son of a clergyman and educated at Westminster
and Oxford, Wren began his career as a scientist and
astronomer. He turned to architecture and is
responsible for the majority of the churches of the City
of London rebuilt after the Great Fire of 1666. His
major architectural achievement was the rebuilding of
St Paul's Cathedral, a project which lasted most of his
life. Wren was the most important and influential of
the English baroque architects.

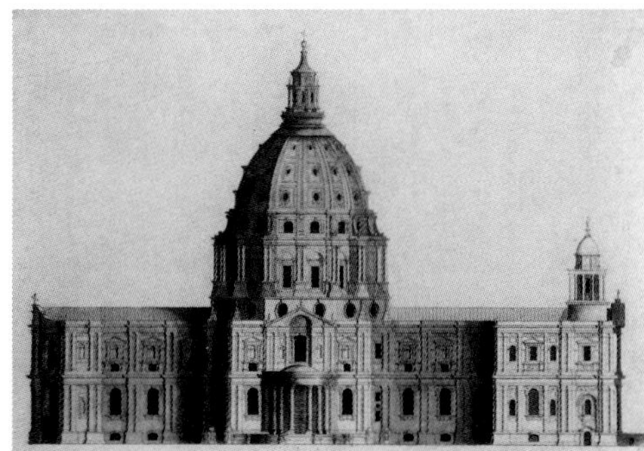

D.1926.363

Design for the North Elevation, St Paul's Cathedral, London

pencil, pen and brown ink, watercolour
inscribed lower left verso: *St Pauls as Intended
to be Built*
334 × 478 mm
Ogden, William Sharp (bequest, 1926) (D.1926.363)

■ WRIGHT, JOHN MASEY (1777–1866)

John Masey Wright was an illustrator who originally
trained with Stothard and exhibited a few works at the
Royal Academy between 1808 and 1820. He also
worked as a scene painter. His watercolours focused on
literary and particularly Shakesperean subjects.
Wright exhibited at the Old Watercolour Society
between 1827 and 1855.

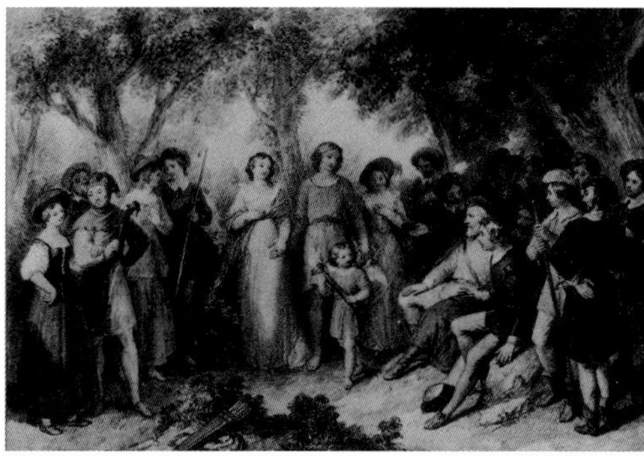

D.1892.103

Scene from 'As You Like It', Act V, Scene IV

pencil, watercolour, bodycolour
(heightened with white)
302 × 435 mm
Taylor, John Edward (gift, 1892) (D.1892.103)

Julian Peveril and Alice Bridgenorth, from Sir Walter Scott's 'Peveril of the Peak'

pencil, watercolour, bodycolour
(heightened with white)
291 × 228 mm
Neville, Constance (gift, 1983) (D.1983.3)

■ WRIGHT (OF DERBY), JOSEPH (1734–97)

Principally known as an oil painter of portraits and
figure subjects, Wright of Derby trained in Thomas
Hudson's studio from 1751 to 1753 and again in
1756–57, where he learnt from copying prints and
drawings in Hudson's collection. Wright, known as 'of
Derby' to distinguish him from a Liverpool artist with
the same surname, made his name with candlelit
subjects, such as *The Air Pump* (1768), by which he is
still best known. He spent most of his life in Derby
and his only trip abroad was to France and Italy from
1773 to 1775, from which the majority of his landscape
drawings derive.

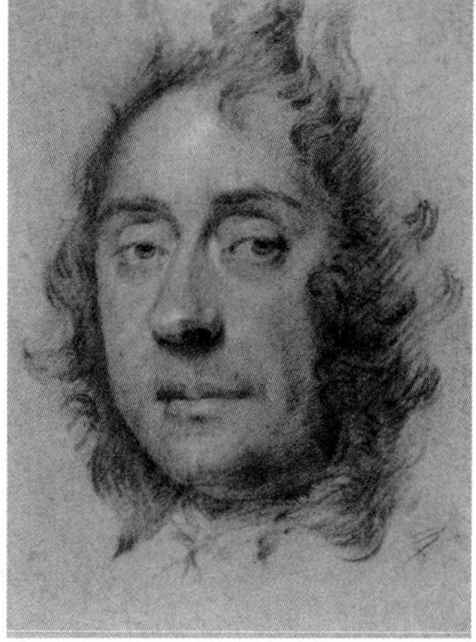

D.1926.210

Portrait Head of a Man

1751–57
black chalk, white chalk; blue paper
339 × 246 mm
Ogden, William Sharp (bequest, 1926) (D.1926.210)

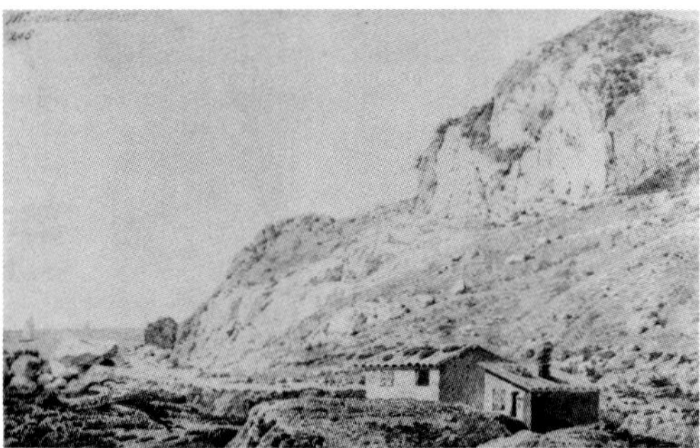

D.1926.308

Coast Scene, near Nice
22.12.1773
pencil, grey watercolour
signed with initials, inscribed, dated & numbered
upper left : *JW.22d.Decr.1773 / 206*
283 × 445 mm
Ogden, William Sharp (bequest, 1926) (D.1926.308)

■ WYATT, JAMES (1746–1813) and OFFICE

One of the principal architects of the eighteenth
century, Wyatt came from a family of architects and
trained in Italy, returning to Britain in about 1768.
Described as 'a brilliant but facile designer', Wyatt
worked equally well in the classical and gothic style.
Elected a member of the Royal Academy in 1785, Wyatt
had a controversial reputation both in his time and up
to the present day as an over-zealous restorer of
medieval gothic buildings, which gave him the
nickname 'Wyatt the Destroyer'.

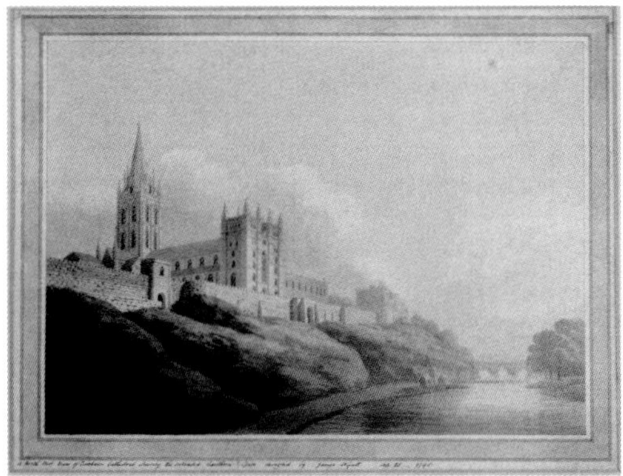

D.1998.13

**Design for Durham Cathedral: View from the
River showing intended Alterations**
25.9.1795
grey watercolour
inscribed & dated along lower edge outside wash line
border: *West View of Durham Cathedral shewing the
intended Lanthorn & Spire design'd by James Wyatt Sep
25 1795*
321 × 420 mm
University of Manchester, Architecture Department (transfer,
1998) (D.1998.13)

**Design Drawing: Elevation and Top Plan
of an open Tower with a Pedestal**
1795
pen and brown ink, watercolour
494 × 288 mm
University of Manchester, Architecture Department
(transfer, 1998) (D.1998.14)

**Design for Durham Cathedral: Elevation and
Section of an intended Altar Screen**
1795
pen and grey ink, watercolour
inscribed centre left in between the two drawings and
outside the wash line borders: *Elevation and Section of
the intended Altar Screen Durham Cathedral*
524 × 317 mm
University of Manchester, Architecture Department
(transfer, 1998) (D.1998.15)

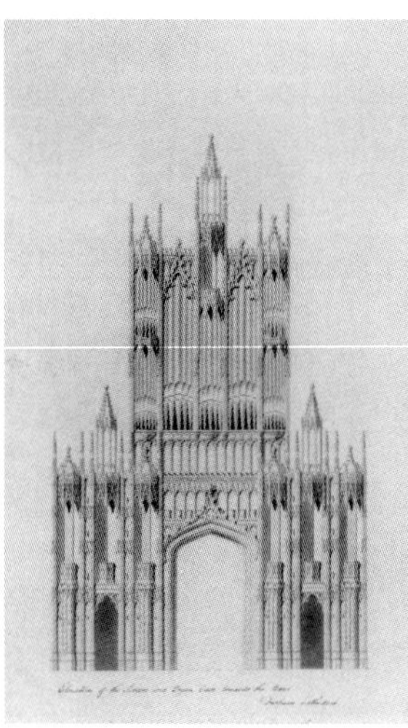

D.1998.16

**Design for Durham Cathedral:
Elevation of the Screen and Organ Case**
1795
pen and grey ink, watercolour
inscribed along lower edge: *Elevation of the Screen and
Organ Case towards the Nave / Durham Cathedral*
495 × 290 mm
University of Manchester, Architecture Department
(transfer, 1998) (D.1998.16)

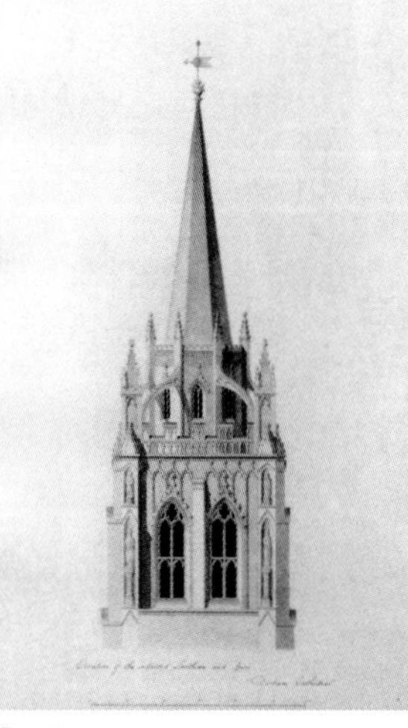

D.1998.17

**Design for Durham Cathedral: Elevation of
the intended Lanthorn and Spire**
1795
pen and grey ink, watercolour
inscribed along lower edge: *Elevation of the intended
Lanthorn and Spire / Durham Cathedral*
495 × 290 mm
University of Manchester, Architecture Department
(transfer, 1998) (D.1998.17)

■ WYLD, WILLIAM (1806–89)

A diplomat and later a wine-merchant who spent most
of his life in France, Wyld began his career in 1826 as
Secretary to the British Consul in Calais, where he was
a pupil of Francia. Strongly influenced by Bonington
whose work he knew, he visited Algeria in 1833. Wyld
travelled throughout Europe, and exhibited views of
European towns and cities at the Paris Salon and the
Royal Academy.

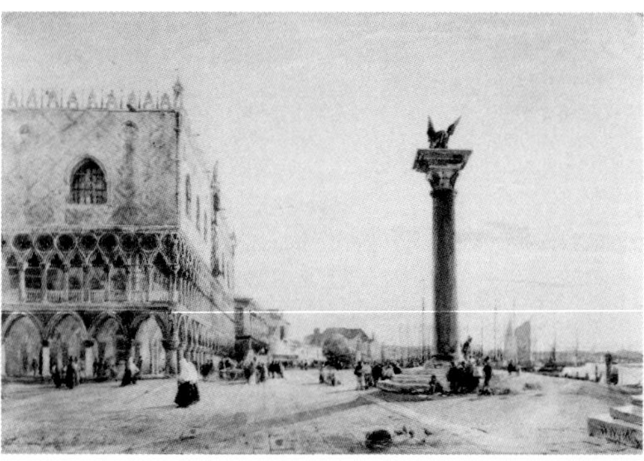

D.1920.9

**The Piazzetta, Venice, with a Corner of the
Doge's Palace**
9.1833
watercolour
signed lower right: W *Wyld*; numbered lower left: *49.*;
inscribed & dated lower left: *Venice Septr.1833*
294 × 426 mm
Bles, Marcus S. (gift, 1920) (D.1920.9)

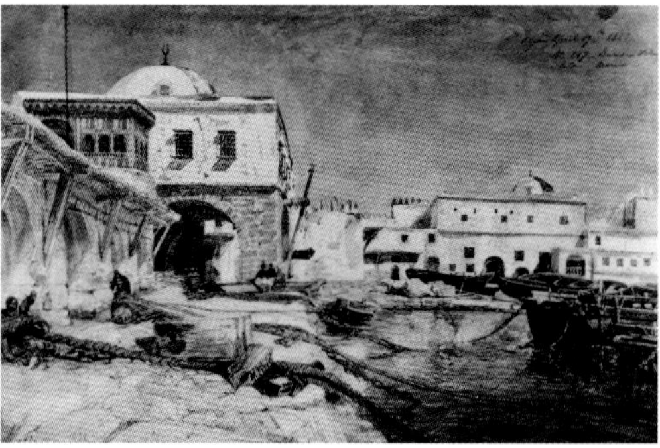

D.1920.10

Bureaux des Magasins de la Marine, Algiers
19.4.1833
watercolour, bodycolour (heightened with white);
corners cut
signed on a wooden block lower centre: *W Wyld*;
inscribed & dated upper right: *Algiers April 19th 1833 /
No 217 Bureaux de Maga* [cut] */ de la Marine*;
numbered lower left: *62*
277 × 414 mm
James Connell and Sons (purchase, 1920) (D.1920.10)

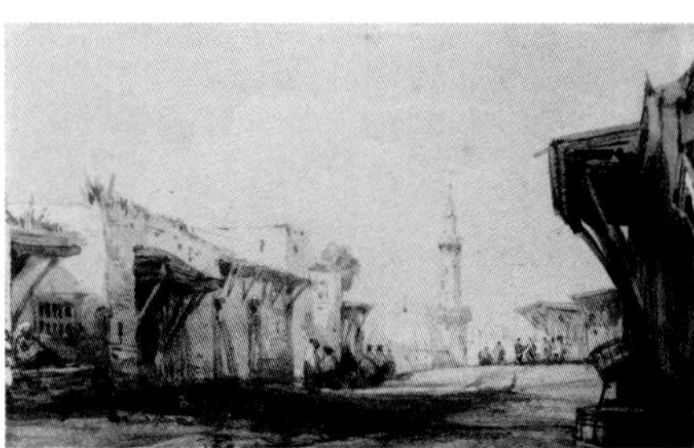

D.1926.55

North African Street Scene
pencil, watercolour
100 × 161 mm
Ogden, William Sharp (bequest, 1926) (D.1926.55)

Castle Uovo, Naples, with Vesuvius in the Distance
pen and brown ink, brown watercolour, bodycolour
(heightened with white)
signed lower right with initials: *W W*
87 × 222 mm
Ogden, William Sharp (bequest, 1926) (D.1926.57)

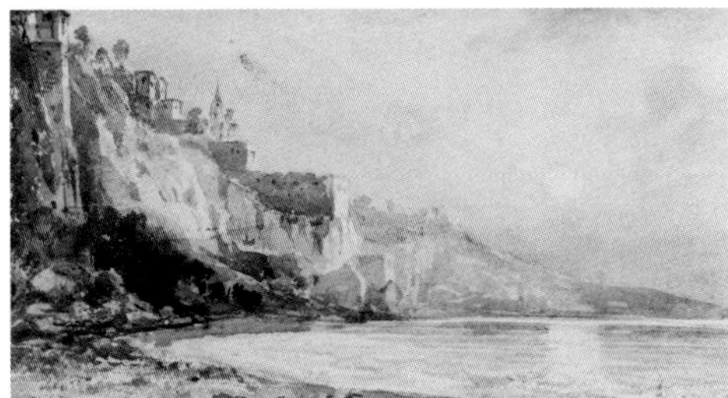
D.1926.58

Coast Scene at Sunset
pencil, pen and ink, watercolour
93 × 168 mm
Ogden, William Sharp (bequest, 1926) (D.1926.58)

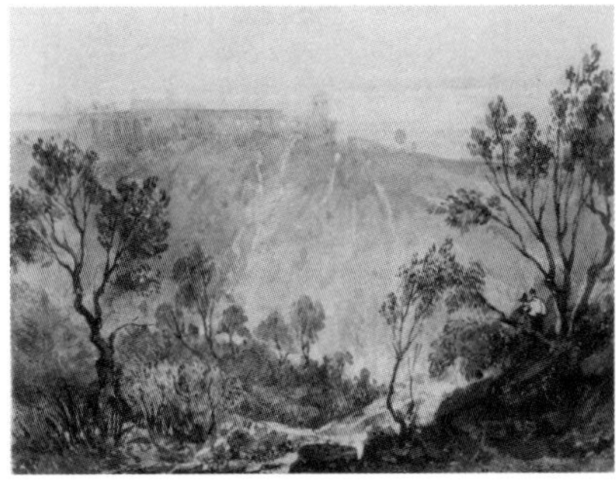
D.1926.52

Distant View of Tivoli, Italy
brown watercolour
109 × 141 mm
Ogden, William Sharp (bequest, 1926) (D.1926.52)
The following works were executed by Wyld in collaboration with an unknown artist signed 'HMD'

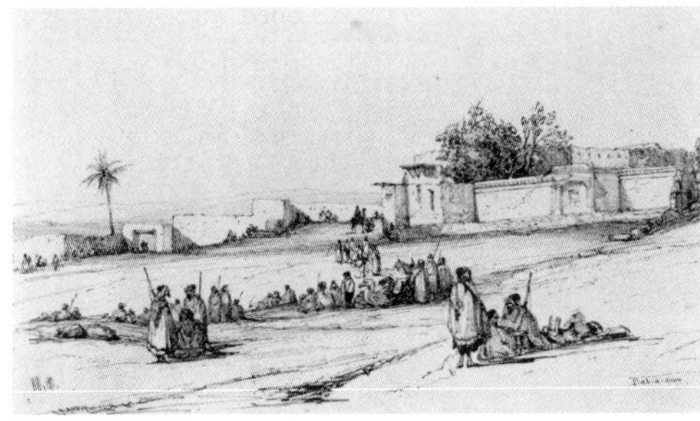
D.1926.68

Rue Bab-a-Zoun, Algiers
1833
pen and ink
signed lower left with initials of both artists: *WW & HMD (collaboration)*
139 × 233 mm
Ogden, William Sharp (bequest, 1926) (D.1926.68)

Lake Scene
pen and ink, watercolour, bodycolour
signed lower right with initials of both artists: *WW & HMD (collaboration)*
127 × 225 mm
Ogden, William Sharp (bequest, 1926) (D.1926.54)

North African Bazaar
pen and ink, watercolour, bodycolour
signed lower left with initials of both artists: *WW & HMD (collaboration)*
129 × 117 mm
Ogden, William Sharp (bequest, 1926) (D.1926.60)

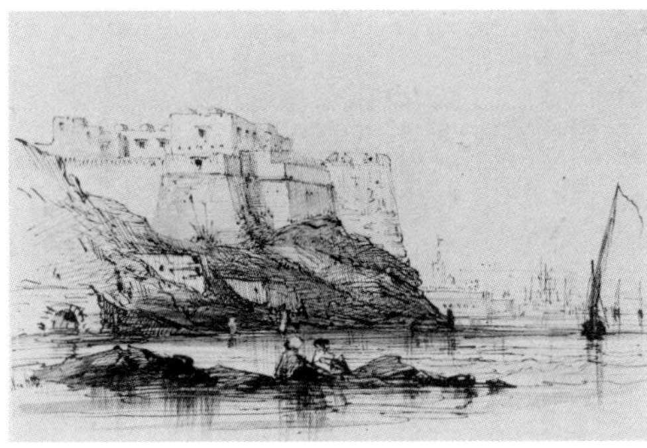
D.1926.61

Coastal Fortress, Algiers
1833
pen and ink, watercolour
signed lower left with initials of both artists (first letter cut): *WW & HMD (collaboration)*
91 × 139 mm
Ogden, William Sharp (bequest, 1926) (D.1926.61)

Bridge over a Canal, Amsterdam
pen and ink, watercolour, bodycolour
signed lower right with initials of both artists: *WW & HMD (collaboration)*
169 × 117 mm
Ogden, William Sharp (bequest, 1926) (D.1926.62)

Mosque Towers, North Africa
pencil
signed lower left with initals of both artists: *WW & HMD (collaboration)*
168 × 117 mm
Ogden, William Sharp (bequest, 1926) (D.1926.63)

■ YATES, GIDEON (fl. 1830s)
A little-known artist, whose only recorded works are London subjects, particularly views of bridges over the Thames.

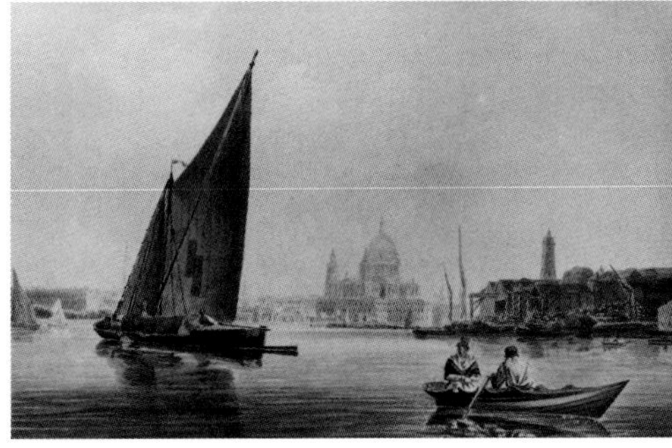
D.1892.6

The Thames with St Paul's Cathedral, London
pencil, watercolour, bodycolour
(heightened with white)
275 × 426 mm
Taylor, John Edward (gift, 1892) (D.1892.6)

■ YOUNG, W. (fl. 1839)
Unknown artist.

The Cross House, Church Street, Tewkesbury, Gloucestershire
19.10.1839
pencil
signed & dated lower right: *WYoung 19th Oct 1839–*;
inscribed lower right: *Tewkesbury / & Jacob Allis*;
numbered lower right: *no2*
175 × 219 mm
Ogden, William Sharp (bequest, 1926) (D.1926.297)

Old Cottages, Barton Street, Tewkesbury, Gloucestershire
1839
pencil
inscribed lower right: *Tewkesbury*; numbered lower right: *no3*
164 × 196 mm
Ogden, William Sharp (bequest, 1926) (D.1926.298)

The Old Coach Office, High Street, Tewkesbury, Gloucestershire
17.10.1839
pencil
signed & dated lower right: *WYoung 17th. Oct. / 1839*;
inscribed lower right: *Tewkesbury*; numbered lower right: *no5*
255 × 202 mm
Ogden, William Sharp (bequest, 1926) (D.1926.299)

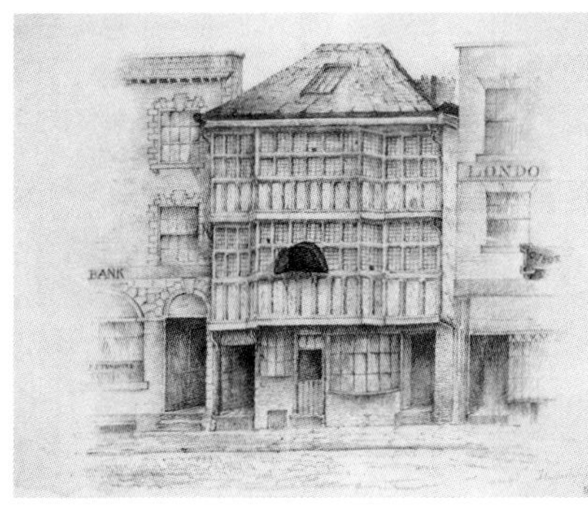

D.1926.300

Thomas Osborne's Hat Shop, Church Street, Tewkesbury, Gloucestershire
1839
pencil
dated lower right: *1839*
inscribed lower right: *Tewkesbury*; numbered lower right: *no6*
205 × 252 mm
Ogden, William Sharp (bequest, 1926) (D.1926.300)

The Wheatsheaf Inn, High Street, Tewkesbury, Gloucestershire
1839
pencil
inscribed & dated lower right: *Tewkesbury 1839*;
numbered lower right: *no7*
235 × 175 mm
Ogden, William Sharp (bequest, 1926) (D.1926.301)

Bibliography

Colvin, H., *A Biographical Dictionary of British Architects 1600–1840*, 2nd. ed., John Murray, 1978

Croft-Murray E. & Hulton, P., *Catalogue of British Drawings*, Volume One: XVI & XVII Centuries, British Museum, 1960

Ford, B. ed., 'The Letters of Jonathan Skelton written from Rome and Tivoli in 1758', in Walpole Society, XXXVI, 1960

Garlick, K., Mackintyre A. & Cave, K. eds., *The Diary of Joseph Farington*, Vols. I–XVI, Yale, 1978–84

Graves, A., The Royal Academy of Arts, *A Complete Dictionary of Contributors and their Work from its Foundation in 1769 to 1904*, Vols. I–VIII, Henry Graves & George Bell and Sons, 1905–6

Gunnis, R., *Dictionary of British Sculptors 1660–1851*, rev. ed., Abbey Library, 1964`

Hardie, M., *Watercolour Painting in Britain*, 3 Vols., Batsford, 1966–68

Ingamells, J. ed., compiled from the Brinsley Ford Archive, *A Dictionary of British and Irish Travellers in Italy, 1701–1800*, Yale, 1997

Lambourne L. & Hamilton, J., *British Watercolours in the Victoria and Albert Museum, An Illustrated Summary Catalogue of the National Collection*, Sotheby Parke Bernet, 1980

Lugt, F., *Les Marques de Collections de Dessins et d'Estampes* Vereenigde Drukkerijen, 1921, & *Supplement*, Martinus Nijhaff, 1956 (collectors mark noted as L. followed by number in catalogue text)

Mallalieu, H. L., *The Dictionary of British Watercolour Artists up to 1920*, Antique Collectors Club, 1976

'Memoirs of Thomas Jones', Walpole Society, XXXII, 1951

Millar, D., *The Victorian Watercolours and Drawings in the Collection of her Majesty the Queen*, 2 Vols., Philip Wilson, 1995

Newall C. & Wilcox, S., *Victorian Landscape Watercolours*, Hudson Hill Press, 1992

Newby, E., *The Diary of Joseph Farington – Index*, Yale, 1998

Pevsner, Sir N. et al., *The Buildings of England Series, 1951– the present* (now *The Pevsner Architectural Guides*)

The Pre-Raphaelites, Tate exhibition catalogue, 1984

Roget, J. L., *History of the 'Old Watercolour Society'*, 2 Vols., Longmans, 1891

Royal Academy Exhibitors 1905-1970, A dictionary of artists and their work in the Summer Exhibitions of the Royal Academy of Arts, Vols. I–VI, E P Publishing Ltd, 1977–82

Scenery of Great Britain and Ireland in Aquatint and Lithography 1770–1860 from the Library of J.R. Abbey, Curwen Press, 1952

Sewter, A. C., *The Stained Glass of William Morris and his Circle*, Yale, 1974

Sloan, K., *'A Noble Art', Amateur Artists and Drawing Masters c. 1600–1800*, British Museum Press, 2000

The Royal Watercolour Society, The First Fifty Years, 1805–1855, Antique Collectors Club, 1992

Travel in Aquatint and Lithography 1770–1860 from the Library of J.R. Abbey, 2 Vols., Curwen Press, 1956–57

Waterhouse, E., *The Dictionary of British 18th Century Painters*, Antique Collectors Club, 1981

Waters, G. M., Dictionary of British Artists working 1900–1950, Eastbourne Fine Art, 1975

Williams, I. A., *Early English Watercolours and some cognate Drawings by Artists born not later than 1785*, London, *The Connoisseur*, 1952

Wood, J., *Hidden Talents, A Dictionary of Neglected Artists working 1880–1950*, Jeremy Wood, 1994

Index of Donors and Provenances

Index of Places